THE
COMPLETE
ENCYCLOPEDIA OF
POPULAR MUSIC
AND JAZZ
1900-1950

THE COMPLETE ENCYCLOPEDIA OF POPULAR MUSIC AND JAZZ 1900-1950

VOLUME 2

BIOGRAPHIES

A THROUGH K

ROGER D. KINKLE

ARLINGTON HOUSE·PUBLISHERS

NEW ROCHELLE, N.Y.

Library of Congress Cataloging in Publication Data

Kinkle, Roger D   1916-
   The complete encyclopedia of popular music and jazz,
1900-1950.

   Includes discographies.
   1. Music, Popular (Songs, etc.)--Dictionaries.
2. Jazz music--Dictionaries. 3. Musicians, American--
Biography. 4. Jazz musicans--Biography. I. Title.
ML102.P66K55   780'.42'0973   74-7109
ISBN 0-87000-229-5

1. AARONSON, IRVING   p cm lyr B

Born February 7, 1895, New York, N.Y.
Died May 10, 1963, Hollywood, Calif.

Bandleader of late 20s and 30s. Band called Irving Aaronson and His Commanders. Formal musical training. At 11 played movie houses. Led early group known as the Versatile Sextette. Formed large dance band; by late 20s some popularity. The Commanders played vaudeville, night clubs and dance spots in U.S. and Europe. Good stage band. Lengthy engagements in Hollywood area. 1928 band in Broadway musical PARIS. Recorded and played radio to minor extent. Future bandleaders played in band early in careers—Artie Shaw and Tony Pastor in 1929, Gene Krupa in 1932, later Bob Chester, also vocalist Harmon Nelson in early 30s. Band reached musical peak 1933-4, good sweet-styled group. By late 30s career as bandleader waned. Later musical supervisor for MGM in Hollywood. Aided in adapting to classical themes two popular songs for Mario Lanza movies, *The Loveliest Night of the Year* (1951 movie THE GREAT CARUSO) and *The Song Angels Sing* (1952 movie BECAUSE YOU'RE MINE).

RECORDS

IRVING AARONSON

Vi 20002 Wimmin'—Aaah!/Poor Papa
Vi 20059 Ya Gotta Know How to Love
Vi 20063 What Good Is Good Morning?/Hi-Ho the Merrio
Vi 20094 Waffles/I'm Just Wild About Animal Crackers
Vi 20473 I Never See Maggie Alone/Crazy Words—Crazy Tune
Vi 21260 Let's Misbehave/An' Furthermore
Vi 21451 Evening Star
Vi 21745 Let's Do It/Land of Going to Be
Vi 21786 I'll Get By
Vi 21867 All by Yourself in the Moonlight/If I Had You
Vo 2536 Thanks/The Day You Came Along
Vo 25004 Lazybones/Shadows on the Swanee
Vo 25005 Ah, But Is It Love?/I've Gotta Get Up and Go to Work
Co 2980-D Flirtation Walk/Me Without You
Co 2981-D Let's Be Thankful/In an Old Log Cabin
Co 3037-D 'Way Back Home/An Evening in June
Co 3043-D Commanderism/Jazzeroo

1A. ABARBANELL, LINA   VO

Born February 3, 1880, Berlin, Germany
Died January 6, 1963, New York, N.Y.

German singer-actress of early Broadway musicals. Earlier career abroad in light opera. Played Hansel in premier of HANSEL AND GRETEL at Metropolitan Opera House in New York late 1905. In short-run 1907 Broadway show THE STUDENT

KING. Joined THE MERRY WIDOW show during long 1907-8 run. Most famous role in MADAME SHERRY (1910). Later active as stage production assistant.

BROADWAY MUSICALS

1907—THE STUDENT KING; THE MERRY WIDOW (joined later)
1909—THE LOVE CURE
1910—MADAME SHERRY
1912—MISS PRINCESS
1913—THE GEISHA (operetta; revival)
1916—FLORA BELLA
1921—THE GRAND DUKE (non-musical)
1926—HAPPY GO LUCKY
1929—THE SILVER SWAN (unsuccessful)

2. ACUFF, ROY   vo g v cm lyr B

Born September 15, 1903, Maynardsville, Tenn.

All-time great country entertainer, called The King of Country Music. Known for *The Precious Jewel, Wabash Cannon Ball, Night Train to Memphis, Freight Train Blues, Great Speckle Bird, Wreck on the Highway*. Records sold in the multimillions. Late start in music due to early aspirations for career as major league baseball player. In 1932-3 toured with medicine show. Performed on Knoxville radio in 1933, on Nashville radio in later 30s. Began appearing on Nashville's Grand Ole Opry in 1940. Worked on various network radio shows, had own series. By 1942 top star in country field, billed as Roy Acuff & The Smoky Mountain Boys. Many records big sellers. 1943 teamed with songwriter Fred Rose to form publishing company. Appeared in country and western movies in middle and late 40s. Several trips abroad in 40s, partly to entertain U.S. troops. Made unsuccessful attempt as Republican candidate to win governorship of Tennessee in 1948. Continued active in 50s and 60s and did some TV work. Devoted time to publishing company; also had record company. Recovered from injuries received in auto accident in 1965. Only semiactive as performer in later years. Composer of *The Precious Jewel, Great Speckle Bird*, others.

RECORDS

ROY ACUFF

Cq 9434 Weary River (1 & 2)
Cq 9741 The Precious Jewel/Broken Heart
Cq 9889 Be Honest with Me/A Worried Mind
Vo 04505 You're the Only Star/She No Longer Belongs to Me
Vo 04730 Singing My Way to Glory/Lonesome Valley
Vo 04795 Bonnie Blue Eyes/An Old Three Room Shack
Vo 05359 Ida Red/Old-Fashioned Love
Vo 05512 What Good Will It Do? (1 & 2)
OK 04252 Great Speckle Bird/My Mountain Home Sweet Home
OK 04374 Great Speckle Bird No. 2/-Tell Mother I'll Be There
OK 05638 Streamlined Cannon Ball/Mule Skinner Blues
OK 05956 The Precious Jewel/Come Back Little Pal
OK 06585 No Letter in the Mail/Things That Might Have Been
OK 06685 Fire Ball Mail/Wreck on the Highway
OK 06693 Night Train to Memphis/Low and Lonely
OK 6735 Blues in My Mind/I Heard a Silver Trumpet
OK 6745 Wait for the Light to Shine/It's Too Late Now to Worry Anymore
Co 36856 We Live in Two Different Worlds/Pins and Needles
Co 20559 Smoky Mountain Rag/Pretty Little Widow
Co 20684 If I Could Hear My Mother Pray Again/Jesus Died for Me
Cap 2739 Whoa, Mule/Rushin' Around

LPs

Co CS-1034 Roy Acuff's Greatest Hits
Co HL-7080 Great Speckled Bird and Other Favorites
Co(10″)HL-9004 Songs of the Smoky Mountains
Co(10″)HL-9013 Songs of the Saddle
Cap T-1870 Best of Roy Acuff
Hilltop 6028 (religious songs)
Hickory H-101 Presenting Roy Acuff

3. ADAIR, TOM   lyr
Born June 15, 1913, Newton, Kan.

Lyricist who first came into prominence in 1941 collaborating with composer Matt Dennis on several songs featured by Tommy Dorsey band. Sophisticated lyricist, as evidenced on Dorsey's hit record of *Will You Still Be Mine?* Most hits written in early 40s. Military service, World War II. In 40s wrote special material for radio shows including Duffy's Tavern, Bing Crosby, Tommy Dorsey, Dinah Shore. Wrote lyrics for 1949 Broadway musical ALONG FIFTH AVENUE, collaborating with composer Gordon Jenkins. In 50s and 60s wrote for TV shows including This Is Your Life, Ann Sothern, Tennessee Ernie Ford, Hazel, Disneyland, Mickey Mouse Club. Wrote for movies, also special material for acts, revues and night club presentations.

SONGS
1941—Everything Happens to Me; Let's Get Away from It All; Violets for Your Furs; Nine Old Men; Will you Still Be Mine?; Free for All
1942—In the Blue of Evening; The Night We Called It a Day
1944—There's No You
1946—Walkin' Away with My Heart
1949—ALONG FIFTH AVENUE stage score (Skyscraper Blues; Fifth Avenue; The Best Time of the Day; I Love Love in New York; Weep No More)
1956—Julie (movie title song); Paul Bunyan (movie title song)

Other songs: *Everybody Ev'ry Payday*; *A Home Sweet Home in the Army*; *March for the New Infantry*; *How Will I Know My Love?*; *Sing a Smiling Song*; *Manhattan Tower Suite*

4. ADAMS, STANLEY   lyr
Born August 14, 1907, New York, N.Y.

Lyricist of popular songs in 30s and 40s. Served on board of directors of ASCAP, also as president. Most noteworthy songs: *What a Difference a Day Made, Little Old Lady, Yesterthoughts* (adapted old Victor Herbert tune), *There Are Such Things.* Attended NYU, also NYU Law School.

Had first professional songwriting assignment for Connie's Inn revue. Wrote songs for Broadway musicals SHADY LADY (1933) and THE SHOW IS ON (1937), collaborated on book for A LADY SAYS YES (1945). Wrote songs for movies. Collaborators included Fats Waller, Louis Alter, Hoagy Carmichael, Xavier Cugat, Maria Grever, Milton Ager.

SONGS
(with related shows)
1930—Rollin' Down the River
1931—Take It from Me
1933—SHADY LADY stage show (songs unimportant)
1934—I Couldn't Be Mean to You; La Cucaracha; My Shawl; What a Difference a Day Made; Dust on the Moon; Extra! (All About That Gal of Mine)
1935—I Threw a Bean Bag at the Moon; Heartstrings; Seein' Is Believin'
1936—Papa Tree-Top Tall; Sing Me a Swing Song; Sing a Song of Nonsense
1937—THE SHOW IS ON stage show (The Show Is On; Little Old Lady)
1938—EVERY DAY'S A HOLIDAY movie (Jubilee); Wacky Dust
1940—Yesterthoughts; My Silent Mood; Shadows on the Sand
1942—There Are Such Things; There Are Rivers to Cross
1948—On the Little Village Green; In the Market Place of Old Monterey
1955—While You're Away

5. ADAMSON, HAROLD   lyr
Born December 10, 1906, Greenville, N.J.

Lyricist with long and prolific career. Most famous songs: *Time on My Hands, You, You're a Sweetheart, Manhattan Serenade, It's a Most Unusual Day, Around the World.* Educated at Kansas and Harvard universities; active in songwriting at both schools. Left Harvard to work at songwriting in New York in late 20s. Wrote songs for Broadway musicals SMILES (1930), THE THIRD LITTLE SHOW and EARL CARROLL'S VANITIES (1931), KEEP OFF THE GRASS (1940), BANJO EYES (1942), AS THE GIRLS GO (1948). To Holly-

wood in 1933 to become important songwriter for movies; wrote many scores, title
songs, miscellaneous songs. Chief collaborator many years was Jimmy McHugh.
Others included Hoagy Carmichael,
Louis Alter, Peter DeRose, Walter
Donaldson, Vernon Duke, Duke Ellington, Burton Lane, Vincent Youmans, Victor Young.

SONGS
(with related shows)

1930—SMILES stage show (Time on My
Hands)

1931—EARL CARROLL'S VANITIES OF 1931
stage show (Love Came into My
Heart; Heigh Ho, the Gang's All
Here; Have a Heart); THE THIRD
LITTLE SHOW stage show (Say the
Word)

1932—Here's Hoping

1933—DANCING LADY movie (Everything
I Have Is Yours; Let's Go Bavar-
ian); Tony's Wife

1934—BOTTOMS UP movie (Little Did I
Dream; Turn on the Moon; I'm
Throwin' My Love Away)

1935—RECKLESS movie (Everything's
Been Done Before); Tender Is the
Night

1936—SUZY movie (Did I Remember?);
THE GREAT ZIEGFELD movie (You;
You Never Looked So Beautiful;
You Gotta Pull Strings); BANJO ON
MY KNEE movie (There's Some-
thing in the Air; Where the Lazy
River Goes By; With a Banjo on
My Knee); It's Been So Long

1937—TOP OF THE TOWN movie (Top of
the Town; Where Are You?; That
Foolish Feeling; Jamboree; Blame
It on the Rhumba; There's No
Two Ways About It; Fireman,
Save My Child); HITTING A NEW
HIGH movie (This Never Happen-
ed Before; Let's Give Love An-
other Chance; I Hit a New High);
YOU'RE A SWEETHEART movie
(You're a Sweetheart; My Fine
Feathered Friend; Broadway Jam-
boree; So It's Love; Scrapin' the
Toast); MERRY-GO-ROUND OF 1938
movie (More Power to You;
You're My Dish); WHEN LOVE IS

YOUNG movie (When Love Is
Young; Did Anyone Ever Tell
You?)

1938—MAD ABOUT MUSIC movie (A Ser-
enade to the Stars; Chapel Bells; I
Love to Whistle); THAT CERTAIN
AGE movie (My Own; You're as
Pretty as a Picture; Be a Good
Scout; That Certain Age)

1939—The Little Man Who Wasn't There

1940—Ferryboat Serenade; The Wood-
pecker Song; It's a Wonderful
World; 720 in the Books; This
Changing World

1941—HOLD THAT GHOST movie (Aurora)

1942—BANJO EYES stage show (songs unimportant); Daybreak; Manhattan
Serenade; Moonlight Mood; Sentimental Rhapsody (lyrics added
to Alfred Newman's classic melody, Street Scene)

1943—HIT PARADE OF 1943 movie
(Change of Heart; Do These Old
Eyes Deceive Me?; Who Took Me
Home Last Night?; Harlem Sand-
man); Comin' In on a Wing and a
Prayer; You Send Me

1944—FOUR JILLS IN A JEEP movie (How
Blue the Night; How Many Times
Do I Have to Tell You?); HIGHER
AND HIGHER movie score (The
Music Stopped; A Lovely Way to
Spend an Evening; I Couldn't
Sleep a Wink Last Night; I Saw
You First; You're on Your Own;
Minuet in Boogie); SOMETHING
FOR THE BOYS movie (In the Mid-
dle of Nowhere; Wouldn't It Be
Nice?); AROUND THE WORLD movie
(Candlelight and Wine; Don't Be-
lieve Everything You Dream;
Great News Is in the Making;
They Just Chopped Down the Old
Apple Tree; He's Got a Secret
Weapon); HOLLYWOOD CANTEEN
movie (We're Having a Baby); THE
PRINCESS AND THE PIRATE movie
(How Would You Like to Kiss Me
in the Moonlight?)

1945—NOB HILL movie (I Walked In; I
Don't Care Who Knows It; Tour-
ing San Francisco); BRING ON THE
GIRLS movie (You Moved Right
In)

1946—DOLL FACE movie (Here Comes Heaven Again; Somebody's Walkin' in My Dreams; Red Hot and Beautiful; Dig You Later; Chico-Chico); SMASH-UP movie (Life Can Be Beautiful; I Miss That Feeling; Hush-a-Bye Island); DO YOU LOVE ME? movie (I Didn't Mean a Word I Said)

1947—CALENDAR GIRL movie (I'm Telling You Now; Lovely Night to Go Dancing)

1948—AS THE GIRLS GO stage score (As the Girls Go; I Got Lucky in the Rain; You Say the Nicest Things, Baby; It's More Fun Than a Picnic; Father's Day); A DATE WITH JUDY movie (It's a Most Unusual Day); IF YOU KNEW SUSIE movie (My, How the Time Goes By; My Brooklyn Love Song; We're Living the Life We Love; What Do I Want with Money?)

1951—HIS KIND OF WOMAN movie (You'll Know)

1953—GENTLEMEN PREFER BLONDES movie (two songs with Hoagy Carmichael added to Jule Styne's original score—Anyone Here for Love?; When Love Goes Wrong)

1955—Too Young to Go Steady

1956—AROUND THE WORLD IN EIGHTY DAYS movie (Around the World)

1957—AN AFFAIR TO REMEMBER movie (An Affair to Remember)

1958—SEPARATE TABLES movie (Separate Tables); THE SEVEN HILLS OF ROME movie (The Seven Hills of Rome)

1962—SATAN NEVER SLEEPS movie (Satan Never Sleeps)

6. ADDISON, BERNARD   g bn B

Born April 15, 1905, Annapolis, Md.

Guitarist, sometime bandleader, active from early 20s through 60s. Moved to Washington, D.C., as teenager. Played banjo in early 20s in various groups, including stint as co-leader of combo with pianist Claude Hopkins. In mid-20s moved to New York, led own combo awhile. Switched to guitar in 1928 while with Louis Armstrong. In early 30s Addison played with Jelly Roll Morton, Fats Waller and Bubber Miley, also with Art Tatum accompanying singer Adelaide Hall. With Fletcher Henderson 1933-4. Led own combo in New York clubs in 1935. In 1936-8 accompanied Mills Brothers. In 1938-9 played in Stuff Smith combo. Continued to lead own groups at intervals. Military service, World War II. Recorded at intervals with various groups. Later worked in Canada several years, then accompanied Ink Spots in late 50s. Also appeared in concerts and accompanied various singers through the years. Still jobbed in the 60s but worked mostly as guitar teacher.

RECORDS

JELLY ROLL MORTON
Vi 38125 Pontchartrain Blues/Fussy Mabel
Vi 38135 Little Lawrence/Harmony Blues

BUBBER MILEY
Vi 38138 I Lost My Gal from Memphis/Without You, Emaline
Vi 38146 Black Maria/Chinnin' and Chattin' with May

COLEMAN HAWKINS
OK 41566 Jamaica Shout/Heart Break Blues
CMS 533 Dedication

FREDDY JENKINS
Bb 6129 Old Fashioned Love/Nothin' but Rhythm
Bb 6193 Swingin' 'Em Down

BILLIE HOLIDAY
Vo 5021 Some Other Spring/Them There Eyes

MEZZ MEZZROW
Vi 25612 Hot Club Stomp/The Swing Session's Called to Order
Vi 25636 Blues in Disguise/That's How I Feel Today

CHOCOLATE DANDIES
CMS(12")1506 I Surrender Dear/I Can't Believe That You're in Love with Me

SIDNEY BECHET
Vi 26640 Shake It and Break It/Wild Man Blues
Vi 26663 Old Man Blues/Nobody Knows the Way I Feel This Mornin'

BERNARD ADDISON
  Bb 6144 Lovely Liza Lee
  Bb 6174 I Can't Dance/Toledo Shuffle
       LPs
SIDNEY BECHET
  "X"(10")LVA-3024 (Bb, Vi RIs)
MEZZ MEZZROW
  "X"(10")LVA-3015 Mezz Mezzrow's
    Swing Session (Vi RIs)

7. AGER, MILTON   cm p ar
Born October 6, 1893, Chicago, Ill.

Important composer of 20s and 30s. Most famous songs: *I'm Nobody's Baby*; *Ain't She Sweet*; *A Young Man's Fancy*; *I Wonder What's Become of Sally*; *Happy Days Are Here Again*; *Auf Wiedersehen, My Dear*; *Trust in Me*. Early in career worked as pianist for film-vaudeville theatres. Accompanied vaudeville singers and song-pluggers. Went to New York in 1913. Arranged for Waterson, Berlin & Snyder. Military service, World War I. Arranged for George M. Cohan in 1918. Began career as composer; first hit in 1918, *Everything Is Peaches Down in Georgia*. Wrote score for Broadway musicals WHAT'S IN A NAME? (1920) and RAIN OR SHINE (1928), contributed music for JOHN MURRAY ANDERSON'S ALMANAC (1929). Wrote most of score for early important movie musical, KING OF JAZZ (1930). His original score used for movie RAIN OR SHINE (1930) when that show adapted from stage. Wrote for several lesser movies. In 1922 organized publishing firm of Ager, Yellen & Bornstein. Remained active as songwriter through the 30s. Chief collaborator was lyricist Jack Yellen; others included Grant Clarke, Benny Davis, Joe Young, Stanley Adams.

SONGS
(with related shows)

1918—Everything Is Peaches Down in Georgia
1919—Freckles
1920—WHAT'S IN A NAME? stage score (hit song: A Young Man's Fancy)
1921—I'm Nobody's Baby (revived 1940); BOMBO stage show (one song: Who Cares?)
1922—Lovin' Sam
1923—Louisville Lou; Mama Goes Where Papa Goes
1924—Bagdad; Hard Hearted Hannah; Big Boy; I Wonder What's Become of Sally
1925—Are You Sorry?; No One
1926—I Wish I Had My Old Gal Back Again; Have You Forgotten?
1927—Ain't She Sweet; Vo-Do-Do-De-O Blues; Ain't That a Grand and Glorious Feeling?; Crazy Words —Crazy Tune; Forgive Me; Is She My Girl Friend?
1928—RAIN OR SHINE stage show (Rain or Shine; Falling Star; Forever and Ever; So Would I); My Pet; I Still Love You; If You Don't Love Me; In My Bouquet of Memories
1929—JOHN MURRAY ANDERSON'S ALMA-NAC stage show (songs unimportant); HONKY TONK movie (He's a Good Man to Have Around; I'm the Last of the Red Hot Mamas; I'm Doing What I'm Doing for Love); Glad Rag Doll; Wait for the Happy Ending
1930—KING OF JAZZ movie (A Bench in the Park; Song of the Dawn; Happy Feet; I Like to Do Things for You); RAIN OR SHINE movie (original stage score); CHASING RAIN-BOWS movie (Happy Days Are Here Again; Lucky Me, Lovable You)
1931—If I Didn't Have You; What Good Am I Without You?
1932—Auf Wiedersehen, My Dear; Sing a New Song; So Ashamed
1933—Trouble in Paradise; If I Didn't Care; I Envy the Moon
1934—I Hate Myself; In a Little Red Barn; Wish Me Good Luck, Kiss Me Goodbye
1935—I Threw a Bean Bag at the Moon; Seein' Is Believin'
1936—It's No Fun; West Wind; You're Giving Me a Song and a Dance; You Can't Pull the Wool Over My Eyes
1937—Trust in Me; You Can Tell She Comes from Dixie
1938—LISTEN, DARLING movie (Ten Pins in the Sky); Sweet Stranger; There's Rain in My Eyes

1939—Sweet Dreams, Sweetheart

8. AGNEW, CHARLIE   t vb reeds B

Bandleader, well known in Chicago area in 30s. Sideman with Dell Lampe band in late 20s. Formed own dance band and played leading hotels and ballrooms in Chicago and midwest in 30s. Had Chicago radio coverage on many engagements; also had own commercial radio series. In late 30s and 40s played spots in Kansas City, Pittsburgh and Las Vegas, returning to Chicago at frequent intervals. In late 40s led combo doing radio staff work in Chicago. Still active into 50s. Never attained national renown but important on midwest musical scene. Sparse recording.

RECORDS

CHARLIE AGNEW

Co 2793-D Don't Blame Me/Trouble in Paradise
Co 2797-D To Be or Not to Be in Love/My Last Year's Girl

9. AHLERT, FRED E.   cm ar p

Born September 19, 1892, New York, N.Y.
Died October 20, 1953, New York, N.Y.

Composer of 20s and 30s. Very popular hits: *I Don't Know Why*; *Mean to Me*; *I'll Get By*; *Walkin' My Baby Back Home*; *Where the Blue of the Night* (Bing Crosby's theme song); *Love, You Funny Thing*; *The Moon Was Yellow*; *I'm Gonna Sit Right Down and Write Myself a Letter*. Educated at CCNY and Fordham Law School. Arranged for Waterson, Berlin & Snyder. Wrote special material for vaudeville performers. Arranged for Fred Waring Glee Club's early efforts. First song published in 1914; began composing seriously in 1920. On board of directors for ASCAP 1933-53, president 1948-50. Most of his songs were written independently of stage or movies. Chief collaborator lyricist Roy Turk; others included Sam M. Lewis, Joe Young, Harry Richman, Edgar Leslie.

SONGS
(with related shows)

1920—You Oughta See My Baby; I'd Love to Fall Asleep and Wake up in My Mammy's Arms
1922—I Gave You Up Just Before You Threw Me Down
1924—Put Away a Little Ray of Golden Sunshine
1927—There's a Cradle in Caroline
1928—I'll Get By; Evening Star
1929—I'll Never Ask for More; To Be in Love; Mean to Me; The One That I Love Loves Me
1930—FREE AND EASY movie (The "Free and Easy"; It Must Be You); CHILDREN OF PLEASURE movie (The Whole Darned Thing's for You); IN GAY MADRID movie (Into My Heart); We're Friends Again
1931—Can't You See?; I Don't Know Why; Walkin' My Baby Back Home; Where the Blue of the Night
1932—How Can You Say You Love Me?; I'll Follow You; Just a Little Home for the Old Folks; Love, You Funny Thing
1933—I Wake Up Smiling; Lovely
1934—And I Still Do; The Moon Was Yellow; Were You Foolin'?
1935—I'm Keeping Those Keepsakes You Gave Me; Sweet Thing; Life Is a Song; Two Hearts Carved on a Lonesome Pine
1936—I'm Gonna Sit Right Down and Write Myself a Letter; Sing an Old Fashioned Song; Take My Heart; There's Two Sides to Ev'ry Story; You Dropped Me Like a Red Hot Penny
1937—The Goona Goo; The Image of You; I've Got a New Lease on Love; There's Frost on the Moon; I'm Happy, Darling, Dancing with You; To a Sweet Pretty Thing
1939—Many Dreams Ago
1940—IT HAPPENS ON ICE stage show (songs unimportant); Where Do You Keep Your Heart?
1945—In the Middle of May

10. AKST, HARRY   cm p B

Born August 15, 1894, New York, N.Y.
Died March 31, 1963, Hollywood, Calif.

Composer of 20s and 30s. Most famous

songs: *Dinah, Baby Face, Am I Blue?, Guilty.* Became professional pianist as teenager. Organized orchestral bureau. Accompanist four years for star performer Nora Bayes. Military service, World War I, at Camp Upton, N.Y., where associated with Irving Berlin. Later worked for Berlin. Led dance band in night clubs. Wrote music for Broadway musicals ARTISTS AND MODELS (1927) and CALLING ALL STARS (1934), also for movies in late 20s and 30s. During World War II toured military bases in U. S. and abroad with Al Jolson. Chief collaborators were lyricists Grant Clarke, Benny Davis, Sam M. Lewis, Joe Young, Bert Kalmar, Al Jolson, Gus Kahn. As late as 1954 had beautiful hit song, *Anema E Core.*

SONGS
(with related shows)

1921—Home Again Blues
1923—First, Last and Always; South Sea Eyes; A Smile Will Go a Long Long Way; Dearest, You're the Dearest to My Heart
1925—Dinah
1926—Baby Face; Everything's Gonna Be All Right; If I'd Only Believed in You
1927—ARTISTS AND MODELS stage show (songs unimportant); Gorgeous; No Wonder I'm Happy; It's a Million to One You're in Love
1929—IS EVERYBODY HAPPY? movie (I'm the Medicine Man for the Blues; Wouldn't It Be Wonderful?); ON WITH THE SHOW movie (Am I Blue?; Let Me Have My Dreams; Birmingham Bertha; other lesser songs); BROADWAY BABIES movie (Wishing and Waiting for Love; Broadway Baby Dolls); BULLDOG DRUMMOND movie (There's the One for Me); This Is Heaven
1930—NO, NO, NANETTE movie (songs unimportant); Nobody Cares If I'm Blue
1931—Guilty; I Can't Get Mississippi Off My Mind; Nothing's Too Good for My Baby
1932—THE KID FROM SPAIN movie (Look What You've Done; What a Perfect Combination; In the Moonlight)

1934—CALLING ALL STARS stage show (I'd Like to Dunk You in My Coffee; If It's Love; Just Mention Joe; Stepping Out of the Picture; I Don't Want to Be President); STAND UP AND CHEER movie (Stand Up and Cheer)
1936—THE MUSIC GOES 'ROUND movie (Taking Care of You; Suzannah; Rolling Along; There'll Be No South)
1937—SING AND BE HAPPY movie (Sing and Be Happy; What a Beautiful Beginning)
1938—RASCALS movie (songs unimportant)
1940—Where Were You Last Night?
1947—The Egg and I; All My Love
1954—Anema E Core

11. ALAMO, TONY   VO

Baritone singer along Perry Como lines, active in 40s and 50s. In late 40s Alamo won attention as smooth-voiced featured singer with popular Sammy Kaye band. Probably best known for vocal on *Wanderin'* with Kaye band. Left Kaye in early 50s, worked with Art Mooney band, then tried career as a single but faded from musical scene.

RECORDS

SAMMY KAYE
   Vi 20-3366 The Right Girl for Me
   Vi 20-3459 The Four Winds and the Seven Seas/Out of Love
   Vi 20-3680 Wanderin'
   Co 38963 Harbor Lights/Sugar Sweet
   Co 39013 Guilty
   Co 39015 Music, Maestro, Please/You've Got Me Crying Again
   Co 39325 I'm Yours to Command
   Co 39421 Del Rio
   Co 39499 Mary Rose/Longing for You
ART MOONEY
   MGM 11115 Slow Poke
TONY ALAMO
   MGM 11353 If I Had Wings/After Your Love
   MGM 11380 Merry Christmas, Darling/It's Merry Christmas Time
   MGM 11415 Is It Love You're After?/The Clown

Majar 131 Love, You Didn't Do Right
By Me/Just Like a Fairy Tale
Majar 136 Idle Gossip/You're the
Sweetest Sweetheart in the World

LPs

SAMMY KAYE
Co CL-668 Music, Maestro, Please
Co(10″)CL-6155 Sunday Serenade

12. ALBAM, MANNY bs ts cl ar cm B

Born June 24, 1922, Samana, Domini-can Republic, while mother visiting there

Talented arranger and composer, very active in 50s and 60s. Grew up in New York. Played reeds with Bob Chester and George Auld in early 40s. Acquired arranging technique, furnished arrangements for Charlie Spivak band several years. Military service, 1945-6. Later worked with Charlie Barnet and Charlie Ventura, developed writing. Arranged for Jerry Wald in 1949. In 1951 turned entirely to arranging, furnishing charts for such top bands as Woody Herman, Count Basie, Stan Kenton, Charlie Barnet, Charlie Ventura, and for top singers. Also composed lengthy jazz works. Later 50s and 60s prominent arranging and conducting for numerous sessions of leading jazzmen.

RECORDS
(all LPs)

MANNY ALBAM
Cor CRL-57142 Jazz Greats of Our Time, Vol. 2
Cor CRL-57173 The Jazz Charts of Our Time, Vol. 1
Cor CRL-59101 The Blues Is Everybody's Business
De DL-4517 West Side Story
Vi LPM-1211 The Jazz Workshop
Dot DLP-9004 Jazz New York
Top Rank RM-313 Double Exposures
Solid State 18000 Brass on Fire
Solid State 18009 Soul of the City
(as conductor or arranger)
THE FIRST MODERN PIANO QUARTET
Cor CRL-59102 A Gallery of Gershwin
BILLY BUTTERFIELD
Vi LPM-1212 New York Land Dixie

MOREY FELD
Kapp KL-1007 Jazz Goes to Broadway
HAL MCKUSICK
Vi LPM-1164 In a 20th-Century Drawing Room
TERRY GIBBS
EmArcy MG-36064 Vibes on Velvet
Mer MG-36148 More Vibes on Velvet

13. ALBERT, DON   t B
(ALBERT DOMINIQUE)

Born c. 1909, New Orleans, La.

Leader of hard-swinging Texas band in 30s. As youngster worked in bands in New Orleans area. With Troy Floyd in Texas in 1926; remained several years. Late 1929 back in New Orleans, formed band, toured, became based in Texas. Continued to tour at intervals. Recorded little. Band broke up 1939. In 40s to New York as booker and organizer. Later in 50s and 60s lived in San Antonio, occasionally played jobs.

RECORDS

TROY FLOYD
OK 8571 Shadowland Blues (1 & 2)
OK 8719 Dreamland Blues (1 & 2)
DON ALBERT
Vo 3401 Rockin' and Swingin'/True Blue Lou
Vo 3411 The Sheik of Araby/You Don't Love Me
Vo 3423 Deep Blue Melody/On the Sunny Side of the Street
Vo 3491 Liza/Tomorrow

LPs

DON ALBERT
(one side) IAJRC 3 (Vo RIs)

14. ALBERT, EDDIE   vo
(EDWARD ALBERT HEIMBERGER)

Born April 22, 1908, Rock Island, Ill.

Talented actor-singer, known primarily for excellent acting in many movies. On mid-30s radio show in New York, The Honeymooners, starring Grace and Eddie Albert. Actor-singer on various radio shows. Gained fame in Broadway play BROTHER RAT (1936), followed by ROOM SERVICE (1937). Appeared in Broadway musicals THE BOYS FROM SYRACUSE (1938),

MISS LIBERTY (1949). Began successful movie career in 1938 in BROTHER RAT. Many movies followed, with Albert usually secondary male lead, friend of leading man. During movie career, Albert's singing forgotten. In later 40s had own radio show for a time. In mid-50s he and wife Margo played night clubs with highly professional act that included singing. Albert starred in 1955 TV production of A CONNECTICUT YANKEE. Made frequent appearances on TV variety shows in later 50s and 60s, displaying competent singing voice and professional manner. Also busy in many TV dramas. In 60s co-starred with Eva Gabor on long-running TV series, Green Acres.

MOVIES
1938—BROTHER RAT
1939—FOUR WIVES; ON YOUR TOES
1940—AN ANGEL FROM TEXAS; MY LOVE CAME BACK; BROTHER RAT AND THE BABY; A DISPATCH FROM REUTER'S
1941—FOUR MOTHERS; THE GREAT MR. NOBODY; OUT OF THE FOG; WAGONS ROLL AT NIGHT; THIEVES FALL OUT
1942—EAGLE SQUADRON; TREAT 'EM ROUGH
1943—LADY BODYGUARD; LADIES' DAY; BOMBARDIER
1945—STRANGE VOYAGE
1946—RENDEZVOUS WITH ANNIE; THE PERFECT MARRIAGE; SMASH-UP
1947—FUN ON A WEEKEND; TIME OUT OF MIND; HIT PARADE OF 1947; HIGH AND HAPPY
1948—THE DUDE GOES WEST; YOU GOTTA STAY HAPPY
1950—THE FULLER BRUSH GIRL
1951—YOU'RE IN THE NAVY NOW; MEET ME AFTER THE SHOW
1952—CARRIE; ACTORS AND SIN
1953—ROMAN HOLIDAY
1955—GIRL RUSH; OKLAHOMA!; I'LL CRY TOMORROW
1956—ATTACK!; THE TEAHOUSE OF THE AUGUST MOON
1957—THE JOKER IS WILD; THE SUN ALSO RISES
1958—THE ROOTS OF HEAVEN; THE GUN RUNNERS; ORDERS TO KILL
1959—BELOVED INFIDEL; INTENT TO KILL

1961—THE YOUNG DOCTORS; THE TWO LITTLE BEARS
1962—MADISON AVENUE; THE LONGEST DAY; WHO'S GOT THE ACTION?
1963—MIRACLE OF THE WHITE STALLIONS; CAPTAIN NEWMAN, M. D.
1965—THE FOOL KILLER
1966—SEVEN WOMEN
1968—THE PARTY'S OVER

RECORDS
(all LPs)
EDDIE ALBERT
　Co CS-9399(S)
EDDIE ALBERT & MARGO
　Kapp KL-1017
(original Broadway cast)
　Co ML-4220 MISS LIBERTY

15. ALBERTINE, CHARLES
　　　　　　　　　　　　　　ts ar cm
Born c. 1929

Noted as arranger for Les & Larry Elgart band in 50s and 60s. Created new, distinctive sound for dance band. From Passaic, N.J. Sideman with Jimmy Palmer six months in 1946 and Johnny Dee 1947-8. With Bobby Byrne about a year, doubling as arranger, then Sammy Kaye six months. In pit band of Broadway show TOP BANANA, 1951-2. Prominence in 1953 with arrangements for new Les Elgart band. Brother Larry Elgart's lead alto sax, combined with Albertine's arrangements, gave band unique sound and style: modern, mellow, haunting, with a subtle swing. In following years continued to arrange for band under name of both Elgarts. Also arranged, in more orthodox style, for singers Nat Cole, Frankie Avalon, Neil Sedaka, Conway Twitty, Adam Wade, Dion, The Four Lads. Mid-60s arranged for Sammy Kaye, giving band Elgart sound although at intervals retaining well-known Kaye sax section style and trombone glisses. Some composing for movies, e.g. title song of 1964 movie THE LONG SHIPS.

RECORDS
(all LPs)
(as arranger)
LES ELGART
　Co CL-536 Sophisticated Swing
　Co CL-875 The Elgart Touch

Co CL-904 The Most Happy Fella
Co CL-1008 For Dancers Only
Co CL-1052 Les & Larry Elgart & Their Orchestra

THE THREE SUNS
Vi LPM-1669 Love in the Afternoon

AL NEVINS
Vi LPM-1654 Dancing with the Blues

HARRY JAMES
(1 side, cm-arr) MGM E-3897 The Spectacular Sound of Harry James

SAMMY KAYE
De DL-4357 Come Dance with Me
De DL-4590 Come Dance with Me, Vol. 2
De DL-74754(S) Shall We Dance?

16. ALDA, ROBERT   vo
(ALPHONSO D'ABRUZZO)
Born Feb. 26, 1914, New York, N.Y.

Stage and screen star, best known for 1945 movie RHAPSODY IN BLUE in which he portrayed composer George Gershwin. Despite excellent performance, movie career did not flourish. Ensuing roles and movies mostly minor, nonsinging. Sang and starred in highly successful 1950 Broadway musical GUYS AND DOLLS. Good role in stage show WHAT MAKES SAMMY RUN? (1964). In 50s and 60s made occasional appearances on TV, in early 70s TV commercials.

MOVIES
1945—RHAPSODY IN BLUE
1946—CINDERELLA JONES; CLOAK AND DAGGER
1947—THE BEAST WITH FIVE FINGERS; NORA PRENTISS; THE MAN I LOVE
1948—APRIL SHOWERS
1949—HOMICIDE
1950—HOLLYWOOD VARIETIES; TARZAN AND THE SLAVE GIRL
1951—MR. UNIVERSE; TWO GALS AND A GUY
1958—BEAUTIFUL BUT DANGEROUS
1959—IMITATION OF LIFE; UN MILITAIRE E MEZZO
1960—CLEOPATRA'S DAUGHTER; SEPULCHRE DEI REI
1961—FORCE OF IMPULSE
1962—REVENGE OF THE BARBARIANS; THE DEVIL'S HAND; MOSSCHETTIERE DEI MARE; TOTTO E PEPPINO

1968—THE GIRL WHO KNEW TOO MUCH

RECORDS
(all LPs)
(original Broadway cast)
De DL-9023 GUYS AND DOLLS
Co KOL-6040 WHAT MAKES SAMMY RUN?

17. ALEXANDER, VAN   p ar cm B
Born May 2, 1915, New York, N.Y.

Well-known swing arranger of 30s and sometime bandleader. Attended Columbia University. Led bands at times but swing arranging brought renown. Arranged for Chick Webb band beginning 1936. Arrangement of *A-Tisket A-Tasket* for Webb and vocalist Ella Fitzgerald big 1938 novelty hit. Important stock arranger in late 30s. Late 1938 formed band featuring own swing arrangements. Theme: *Alexander's Ragtime Band*. Band musically sound, recorded, no great popularity. Alexander bandleader into early 40s. Defense work, 1944-5. After bandleader Abe Lyman came out of military service in 1944, Alexander helped set up new band and arranged for him. Arranged for Tommy Tucker band in mid-40s. In later 40s arranged and conducted for top singers on records. Some compositions of swing-novelty type. In 50s settled in Hollywood, scored movie and TV backgrounds. Among movie credits: BABY-FACE NELSON, STRAIGHT-JACKET, BIG OPERATOR, ANDY HARDY COMES HOME. Also worked as arranger-conductor for Gordon and Sheila MacRae.

RECORDS
CHICK WEBB (as arranger)
De 1840 A-Tisket A-Tasket

VAN ALEXANDER
Bb 10049 I Cried for You/No Star Is Lost
Bb 10073 Night and Day/On the Road to Mandalay
Bb 10118 Heaven Can Wait/The Masquerade Is Over
Bb 10130 This Night/Honolulu
Bb 10158 I'm Happy About the Whole Thing/Hooray for Spinach
Bb 10164 Don't Look Now/Dancing in the Dark

Bb 10181 East Side of Heaven/Hang Your Heart on a Hickory Limb
Bb 10189 How Strange/Ya Had It Comin' to Ya
Bb 10197 Moon of Manakoora/Another Night Alone
Bb 10231 If I Didn't Care/For No Reason at All
Bb 10271 Tony's Wife/Thou Swell
Bb 10297 Let There Be Love/In the Middle of a Dream
Bb 10301 Begone/You Are My Dream
Bb 10330 Ragtime Cowboy Joe/The Jumpin' Jive
Bb 10338 Stumbling/La Rosita
Vs 8102 The Little Red Fox/Yodelin' Jive
Vs 8126 I Wanna Wrap You Up/Oh, What a Lovely Dream
Vs 8133 Pinch Me/Prelude to the Bughouse
Vs 8172 My My!/Say It

(as conductor or arranger)
GORDON MACRAE
Cap 1941 Baby Doll/Green Acres and Purple Mountains
Cap 2010 Gentle Hands/These Things Shall Pass
Cap 2114 Mansion over the Hilltop/Peace in the Valley
Cap 2196 Blame It on My Youth/There's a Lull in My Life
ART LUND
MGM 10878 Velvet Lips/Nothin' Like You
BUTCH STONE
Cap 15301 Etiquette Blues/My Feet's Too Big
JERRY DUANE
Trend 59 Will You Still Be Mine?/London in July

LPs

VAN ALEXANDER
Cap T-1243 The Home of Happy Feet (The Savoy)
Cap T-1635 Swing! Staged for Sound
(as conductor or arranger)
GORDON AND SHEILA MACRAE
Cap T-1353 Our Love Story
SAMMY FAIN
MGM(10″)E-241 I'll Be Seeing You
GLEN GRAY
Cap T-1938 Today's Best

18. ALLEN, BOB   vo B

Born c. 1913, Cincinnati, Ohio, suburb

Capable vocalist with Hal Kemp band in middle and late 30s. Had early training at conservatory in Cincinnati. Joined Kemp 1934; big baritone contrasted with featured vocals of Skinnay Ennis. When Ennis left Kemp in 1938, Allen became star vocalist. Heard on Kemp's radio show in late 30s. Remained with band until Kemp's death in auto crash, December 1940. After Kemp's death, Allen led unsuccessful band featuring young Randy Brooks as lead trumpet and musical director. Formed more successful band 1942-3 (again with Brooks). With Tommy Dorsey as vocalist 1944. Military service, 1945-6. After service freelance vocalist for a time.

RECORDS

HAL KEMP
Br 6947 For All We Know
Br 6974 It's All Forgotten Now
Br 7745 Easy to Love
Br 7783 Goodnight My Love
Br 7830 Sweet Is the Word for You/What Will I Tell My Heart?
Vi 25722 Goodnight Angel
Vi 25893 Meet the Beat of My Heart/What Do You Know About Love?
Vi 26194 I Never Knew Heaven Could Speak/Have a Heart
Vi 26247 Blue Evening
Vi 26368 I Didn't Know What Time It Was
Vi 26576 Where Do I Go from You?
Vi 27255 It All Comes Back to Me Now
Vi 27261 I Can't Remember to Forget
CARMEN CAVALLARO
De 24154 I Have but One Heart/Ain'tcha Ever Comin' Back?
ISHAM JONES
Bantam 9001 How Many Tears Must Fall?/She Picked It Up in Mexico
HOAGY CARMICHAEL ORCHESTRA
ARA 141 Somewhere in Via Roma

LPs

HAL KEMP
Vi(10″)LPT-3016 This Is Hal Kemp (Vi RIs)

19. ALLEN, HENRY "RED"

t vo cm B

Born January 7, 1908, Algiers, La.
Died April 17, 1967, New York, N.Y.

Noted jazz trumpet star and combo leader. Long career from late 20s to late 60s. Played spirited Harlem jazz rather than New Orleans style. As youngster Allen played in father's brass band. In New Orleans jazz groups including George Lewis. In 1927 joined famous King Oliver in St. Louis, then went to New York with him. Late 1927-9 back in New Orleans with Fate Marable on riverboats.

Important period with Luis Russell 1929-33. Solos attracted attention; name sometimes used as leader. Three important band jobs established him as jazz star: Fletcher Henderson 1933-4, Mills Blue Rhythm Band 1934-6, Louis Armstrong 1937-40. (Armstrong band actually old Luis Russell band.) In 1933-7 Allen recorded frequently as leader of small jazz groups, small-band jazz at its best. On most, handled vocals in fine jazz style.

Late 1940 Allen formed small band with trombonist J. C. Higginbotham, who remained till 1947. In 40s and early 50s Allen had long runs in New York, Boston, Chicago, California. Good front man and entertainer. In early 1954 Allen opened at Metropole in New York, a fabulous run lasting till mid-1965, interrupted occasionally by tours or special jobs (including European jaunt with Kid Ory late 1959). Later in 60s Allen toured Europe several times leading groups. Last big job at Jimmy Ryan's in New York 1966. European trip early 1967. Died of cancer several weeks after return to New York. Recording prolific. Composed several jazz pieces: *Siesta at the Fiesta*; *Red Jump*; *Pleasing Paul*; *Angiers Stomp*; *Get the Mop*; *Biffly Blues*; and his famous *Ride, Red, Ride*.

RECORDS

COLEMAN HAWKINS
    OK 41566 Heart Break Blues/Jamaica Shout

J. C. HIGGINBOTHAM
    OK 8772 Give Me Your Telephone Number/Higginbotham Blues

JELLY ROLL MORTON
    Vi 23402 Sweet Peter/Jersey Joe
    Vi 23424 Mississippi Mildred
    Gen 1704 Good Old New York/Big Lip Blues

KING OLIVER
    Vi 23009 Stingaree Blues/Shake It and Break It

FLETCHER HENDERSON
    Co 2825-D It's the Talk of the Town/ Nagasaki
    De 157 Wrappin' It Up/Limehouse Blues
    De 214 Happy as the Day Is Long/Big John Special
    De 18254 Night Life/I've Got to Sing a Torch Song

MILLS BLUE RHYTHM BAND
    Co 3087-D Ride, Red, Ride/Congo Caravan
    Br 7534 Tallahassee

BUSTER BAILEY
    Vo 2887 Call of the Delta/Shanghai Shuffle

HENRY ALLEN (with Luis Russell band)
    Vi 38073 It Should Be You/Biffly Blues
    Vi 38080 Feeling Drowsy/Swing Out

ALLEN-HAWKINS ORCHESTRA (Allen and Coleman Hawkins)
    Pe 15802 Swingin' Along on a Shoe String/Shadows on the Swanee
    Pe 15851 You're Gonna Lose Your Gal/My Galveston Gal

RED ALLEN
    Pe 15933 Don't Let Your Love Go Wrong/Why Don't You Practice What You Preach?
    Pe 15948 I Wish I Were Twins/I Never Slept a Wink Last Night
    Pe 15994 Rug Cutter's Swing/There's a House in Harlem
    Vo 2965 Body and Soul/Rosetta
    Vo 3302 Algiers Stomp/When Did You Leave Heaven?
    OK 6281 Ol' Man River/K.K. Boogie
    OK 6357 Indiana/A Sheridan "Square"
    Vi 20-1808 Get the Mop/Buzz Me

LPs

RED ALLEN
    Vi LPV-556 (Vi RIs, various bands)
    Vi LPM-1509 Ride, Red, Ride in Hi-Fi

"X"(10")LVA-3033 Ridin' with Red Allen (Vi RIs)

RED ALLEN-CHARLIE SHAVERS COMBOS
Beth BCP-21 Jazz at the Metropole

RED ALLEN-PEE WEE RUSSELL
Impulse A-9137 The College Concert of Pee Wee Russell and Red Allen

FLETCHER HENDERSON
Co C4L19 (4-LP set) A Study in Frustration (RIs)

LUIS RUSSELL
Parlo(E) PMC-7025 (OK RIs)

JELLY ROLL MORTON
CMS(10")FL-20018 (Gen RIs)

19A. ALLEN, LESTER   vo

Born c. 1891, England
Died November 6, 1949, North Hollywood, Calif.

Singer-actor in Broadway musicals of 20s. In GEORGE WHITE'S SCANDALS 1919 through 1924, important musical THE THREE MUSKETEERS (1928).

BROADWAY MUSICALS

1919—GEORGE WHITE'S SCANDALS OF 1919
1920—GEORGE WHITE'S SCANDALS OF 1920
1921—GEORGE WHITE'S SCANDALS OF 1921
1922—GEORGE WHITE'S SCANDALS OF 1922
1923—GEORGE WHITE'S SCANDALS OF 1923
1924—GEORGE WHITE'S SCANDALS OF 1924
1925—FLORIDA GIRL
1927—RUFUS LEMAIRE'S AFFAIRS
1928—THE THREE MUSKETEERS
1930—TOP SPEED
1933—SHADY LADY

20. ALLEN, REX   vo g v cm lyr
Born December 31, 1924, Wilcox, Ariz.

One of best western singers. Excellent baritone voice. Best known as star of westerns. In early life cowboy and rodeo performer. Worked into important radio career. In mid-40s on radio in East. Later 40s popular singing on WLS National Barn Dance from Chicago. Own CBS radio show in Hollywood several years beginning 1949. Signed by Republic to

star in westerns, made 32 from 1950-7. Known as The Arizona Cowboy. Also recorded, with popular hit in 1953, *Crying in the Chapel*. Composed some songs he featured. Performed on TV in 50s and 60s as guest star. Own film series, FRONTIER DOCTOR. Film and record work for Walt Disney early 60s. Narrated Disney TV series, TV commercials early 70s, announced country music shows.

RECORDS

REX ALLEN
Mer 5573 The Roving Kind/Wreck of the John B.
Mer 5597 Sparrow in the Tree Top/Always You
Mer 5619 Sentimental Fool/Ten More Miles to Go
Mer 5647 Mr. and Mississippi/Lonely LIttle Robin
Mer 6140 Happy Mary Polka/Who Shot Hole in Sombrero?
Mer 6252 Dixie Boogie/Put Your Arms Around Me
De 27876 Tuck Me to Sleep in My Old 'Tucky Home/Ragtime Melody
De 28341 Jambalaya/Two-Faced Clock
De 28758 Crying in the Chapel/I Thank the Lord
De 28897 To Be Alone/If God Can Forgive You
De 28933 Why, Daddy?/Where Did My Snowman Go?

REX ALLEN-PATTI PAGE
Mer 6231 Broken Down Merry-Go-Round/Tag Along

LPs

REX ALLEN
De DL-8776 Mister Cowboy
De DL-75011 The Smooth Country Sound of Rex Allen
Mer 12324 Sings and Tells Tales
Hilltop 6009
Buena 3307 Sixteen Favorite Songs

21. ALLEN, STEVE   p vo cm lyr B
Born December 26, 1921, New York, N.Y.

Well-known, multitalented TV personality and entertainer of 50s and 60s. Parents vaudeville performers, Belle Montrose & Billy Allen; Steve traveled widely with them. Attended Arizona State Teachers

College. Radio work in Phoenix as announcer-pianist-writer, later in Los Angeles. 1947 disc jockey on CBS radio, Hollywood. Other radio shows late 40s. To New York 1950 for radio and early TV. Founded Tonight Show, top late-night TV attraction mid-50s. Introduced singers Steve Lawrence, Eydie Gorme, Andy Williams. Easy-going format of this and similar shows later showed Allen at his best. Great flair for comedy and foolishness, adept at adlibbing. Played capable piano, also sang. Popularity and jazz rapport led to title role in important 1956 movie THE BENNY GOODMAN STORY. Allen took clarinet lessons from Sol Yaged to help him play the role realistically. After completing film, landed Sunday evening TV show opposite Ed Sullivan. Show lasted several years, brought fame to comedians Louis Nye, Don Knotts, Tom Poston, Bill Dana, Dayton Allen.

In 60s Allen ran several TV shows of varying formats, some late-night syndicated shows. He and wife Jayne Meadows appeared on many shows as guest stars. Allen also served as moderator on popular show I've Got a Secret. Always had excellent bands on TV shows: Bobby Byrne 1953-4, Skitch Henderson 1954-6, Les Brown on Sunday show in late 50s, Donn Trenner all-star combo on syndicated show in 60s. Recorded frequently, featuring his piano in small groups or large orchestras. Author of several books, mostly comedy. Songs include: *This Could Be the Start of Something Big, Let's Go to Church Next Sunday, Cotton Candy and a Toy Balloon, An Old Piano Plays the Blues, Gravy Waltz, Tonight* (theme), *Impossible* (theme) and film title songs *Picnic, Houseboat, On the Beach, Sleeping Beauty* and *Bell, Book and Candle*. Scored soundtrack of movie A MAN CALLED DAGGER. Remains active in 70s.

RECORDS
(all LPs)

STEVE ALLEN
Cor CRL-57004 Music for Tonight
Cor CRL-57015 Tonight at Midnight
Cor CRL-57018 Jazz for Tonight
Cor CRL-57019 Steve Sings

Cor CRL-57028 Let's Dance
Cor CRL-57047 Allen Plays Allen
Cor CRL-57070 The Steve Allen Show
Cor CRL-57138 Romantic Rendez-vous
Cor CRL-57211 Plays Neal Hefti
Si SS-1021(S) Steve Allen Monday Nights
Dot DLP-3150 Around the World
Dot DLP-3473 Presents 12 Golden Hits
Dot DLP-3519 Plays the Piano Greats
Mer MG-20304 Music for Swingers

22. ALLEN, STUART   vo
Born June 16, 1907

Singer with the Richard Himber band in middle and late 30s. Baritone contrasted with soft tenor of Joey Nash, whom he replaced. Performed excellently with band from early 1935 to 1939 on records and radio. On other radio shows such as Your Hit Parade at intervals 1936-7, Hobby Lobby 1937-8, and with Eddy Duchin show 1937.

RECORDS
RICHARD HIMBER
Vi 25037 Footloose and Fancyfree/ Give a Broken Heart a Break
Vi 25077 I Never Saw a Better Night
Vi 25119 Without a Word of Warning
Vi 25161 I'm Painting the Town Red
Vi 25189 You Hit the Spot/I Feel Like a Feather in the Breeze
Vi 25239 Suzannah/Life Begins When You're in Love
Vi 25298 Would You?/I've Got a Heavy Date
Vi 25392 Picture Me without You/The World Is Mine
Vi 25443 Thru the Courtesy of Love/ Wintertime Dreams
Vi 25742 Thrill of a Lifetime/I Live the Life I Love
Vi 26142 You Call It Madness

23. ALLEN, TERRY   vo
Excellent baritone with big bands, 1939-42: Red Norvo 1939, Larry Clinton August 1939 through 1940, Will Bradley 1941-2, Claude Thornhill mid-1942. Military service, World War II. After release

491

in late 1944, Allen appeared for a time on CBS radio.

RECORDS

RED NORVO
Vo 4648 I Get Along without You Very Well/Kiss Me with Your Eyes
Vo 4785 You're So Desirable
Vo 4953 My Love for You/In the Middle of a Dream

LARRY CLINTON
Vi 26341 The Moon Is Low/'S Wonderful
Vi 26374 At Least You Could Say Hello
Vi 26392 A Table in a Corner/Can I Help It
Vi 26435 This Is My Song
Vi 26468 I Dream of Jeanie
Vi 26521 How High the Moon
Vi 26534 From Another World/It Never Entered My Mind
Vi 26626 How Can I Ever Be Alone
Bb 10801 Love Lies
Bb 10850 A Brown Bird Singing
Bb 10984 You Forgot About Me

WILL BRADLEY
Co 36052 Talking to the Wind
Co 36101 (Bradley theme) Think of Me
Co 36147 Flamingo
Co 36248 Get Thee Behind Me, Satan
Co 36444 I Think of You
Co 36470 Who Can I Turn To?/Sleepy Time Gal
Co 36547 I Guess I'll Be on My Way/ Seeing You Again Did Me No Good

24. ALLYSON, JUNE vo
(ELLA GEISMAN)

Born October 7, 1917 or 1923, Bronx, N.Y.

Husky-voiced singer who came into prominence in movie musicals of 40s, later developed into excellent dramatic actress and comedienne. Early training as singer-dancer. Small roles in Broadway musicals SING OUT THE NEWS (1938), VERY WARM FOR MAY (1939), HIGHER AND HIGHER (1940). In 1940 played bit part in PANAMA HATTIE and understudied Betty Hutton. Starring role in BEST FOOT FORWARD (1941). Went to Hollywood, played

supporting roles in three 1943 musicals, including screen version of BEST FOOT FORWARD. Lead part in 1944 movie TWO GIRLS AND A SAILOR established her as star. Reached peak mid-50s. Portrayed Miller's wife in 1954 THE GLENN MILLER STORY. She and husband Dick Powell important on TV in 50s and early 60s with guest appearances and each one's own series. Mostly inactive later 60s. Came back early 70s in TV dramas and stage productions.

MOVIES

1943—BEST FOOT FORWARD; GIRL CRAZY; THOUSANDS CHEER
1944—MEET THE PEOPLE; TWO GIRLS AND A SAILOR
1945—MUSIC FOR MILLIONS; HER HIGHNESS AND THE BELLBOY
1946—TWO SISTERS FROM BOSTON; THE SAILOR TAKES A WIFE; SECRET HEART
1947—TILL THE CLOUDS ROLL BY; GOOD NEWS; HIGH BARBAREE
1948—THE BRIDE GOES WILD; WORDS AND MUSIC; LOVE BITES MAN; THE THREE MUSKETEERS
1949—LITTLE WOMEN; THE STRATTON STORY
1950—RIGHT CROSS; THE REFORMER AND THE REDHEAD
1951—TOO YOUNG TO KISS; CALLAWAY WENT THATAWAY (cameo)
1952—GIRL IN WHITE; SO BRIGHT THE FLAME
1953—BATTLE CIRCUS; REMAINS TO BE SEEN
1954—THE GLENN MILLER STORY; EXECUTIVE SUITE; A WOMAN'S WORLD
1955—STRATEGIC AIR COMMAND; THE SHRIKE; THE MCCONNELL STORY
1956—YOU CAN'T RUN AWAY FROM IT; THE OPPOSITE SEX
1957—INTERLUDE; MY MAN GODFREY
1959—STRANGER IN MY ARMS

RECORDS

JUNE ALLYSON
MGM 30004 Leave It to Jane/Cleopatterer
MGM 30081 Just Imagine/The French Lesson (with PETER LAWFORD)
MGM 30170 Thou Swell

JUNE ALLYSON-PETER LAWFORD
MGM 30082 The Best Things in Life Are Free
MGM 30083 The Varsity Drag
JUNE ALLYSON-PETER LAWFORD-PAT MARSHALL
MGM 30080 Lucky in Love

LPs
(movie soundtrack)
Metro M-580 WORDS AND MUSIC

25. ALMEIDA, LAURINDO   g ar cm

Born September 2, 1917, Sao Paulo, Brazil

Talented guitarist active in U.S. late 40s into 70s. Adept at both jazz and classical music. Staff guitarist on Rio de Janeiro radio. Led club orchestra there. Bandleader Stan Kenton heard Almeida in Brazil. Impressed, he persuaded Almeida to come to U.S. (1947). In Kenton's band late 40s. Later settled in California to play club jobs and do composing and scoring for movies. Among movie credits: MARACAIBO, CRY TOUGH, THE NAKED SEA. Chief collaborators Sally Terri and Nestor Amaral. Made U.S. concert tour with Sally Terri as co-star. Among his compositions: *Naked Sea, Gold Brazilian Sun, Pancho's Guitar, Johnny Peddler, Sighs, The Gypsy with Fire in His Shoes, Sunset in Copacabana, Guitar Tristesse.* Guitar style of taste, beauty, excellent technique. He was playing bossa nova long before it had that name and became a popular style, and he became one of its premier stylists when it reached immense popularity in U.S. in 60s. Active into 70s; appeared on educational TV.

RECORDS
LAURINDO ALMEIDA
Cor 60547 Adios/Brazilian Ukulele
Cor 60883 Veradero/Samba Sud

LPs
LAURINDO ALMEIDA
Cap ST-1759 (S) Viva Bossa Nova
Cap ST-1872 (S) Ole! Bossa Nova
Cap ST-2866 (S) The Look of Love and the Sounds of Laurindo Almeida
World Pac T-90078 Brazilliance

Pac Jazz(10″)PJLP-7 Laurindo Almeida Quintet
Pac Jazz(10″)PJLP-13 Laurindo Almeida Quintet, Vol. 2
LAURINDO ALMEIDA-RAFAEL MENDEZ
De DL-4921 Together
STAN GETZ
Verve V-8665 With Guest Artist Laurindo Almeida
BUD SHANK (as arranger)
World Pac WP-1259 Holiday in Brazil
STAN KENTON
Cap(10″)H-172

26. ALPERT, TRIGGER   b
(HERMAN ALPERT)

Born September 3, 1916, Indianapolis, Ind.

Outstanding bassist from early 40s. Attended Indiana University. After early period with Alvino Rey, worked with Frankie Trumbauer in 1940. Joined Glenn Miller band in September 1940, remained till June 1941. Left for military service, later playing in Miller's service band. In later 40s worked briefly with Woody Herman and Tex Beneke, then settled into career as freelance recording artist and staff musician on radio, later TV (including several years on Garry Moore show). Active through 60s. Retired from music to become successful portrait photographer in Connecticut.

RECORDS
FRANKIE TRUMBAUER
Vs 8223 Jimtown Blues/Laziest Gal in Town
Vs 8236 Little Rock Getaway/Honky Tonk Train Blues
GLENN MILLER
Bb 10906 You've Got Me This Way/ I'd Know You Anywhere
Bb 10936 Isn't That Just Like Love?/ Do You Know Why?
Bb 10982 Anvil Chorus (1 & 2)
Bb 11029 Song of the Volga Boatmen/Chapel in the Valley
Bb 11230 Chattanooga Choo Choo/I Know Why
MUGGSY SPANIER
VD(12″)588 Tin Roof Blues/Cherry
VD(12″)611 China Boy

ELLA FITZGERALD
VD(12″)569 I'll Always Be in Love with You
ROY ELDRIDGE
VD(12″)605 Old Rob Roy
VD(12″)612 Roy Meets Horn
TED NASH
Key 628 I've Got a Pocketful of Dreams/The Girl in My Dreams Tries to Look Like You
BERNIE LEIGHTON
Key 643 Beyond the Moon/Things Are Looking Up
Key 644 Have You Met Miss Jones?/Moten Swing
TONY MOTTOLA
Maj 1106 Trigger Fantasy/Guilty
Maj 1125 Coquette/Tony's Touch
BUDDY WEED
MGM 10087 Sugar/Fun and Fancy Free

LPs

TRIGGER ALPERT
Riv 12-225 Trigger Happy
RAY MCKINLEY (one side)
GA 33-333 The Swinging 30s
WILL BRADLEY (one side)
GA 33-310 Dixieland Jazz
BOBBY BYRNE
GA 207-SD (S) Great Song Hits of the Glenn Miller Orchestra
MUNDELL LOWE
Riv 12-208 Guitar Moods by Mundell Lowe
Offbeat 3010 The Music of Alec Wilder
AL KLINK (one side)
GA 33-325 Progressive Jazz
SAUTER-FINEGAN
Vi LPM-1240 Adventures in Time
JACK HASKELL
Jub 1036 Let's Fall in Love

27. ALTER, LOUIS   cm ar p
Born June 18, 1902, Haverhill, Mass.

Important composer of 30s and 40s. Most famous songs: *Manhattan Serenade, A Melody from the Sky, Dolores*. Educated at New England Conservatory of Music. At 13 worked as pianist in movie theatre. Accompanist for Nora Bayes 1924-8; toured with her in U.S. and abroad. Also accompanied Irene Bordoni, Helen Morgan, Beatrice Lillie. Did arranging for publishing companies. First song hit, *Hugs and Kisses*, in 1926. Composed most important song *Manhattan Serenade* in 1928, (later revived in 1942 with lyrics by Harold Adamson). Public became acquainted with tune in early and mid-30s as theme song of Easy Aces radio show. Contributed music for several Broadway musicals, including score for BALLYHOO (1931). Wrote for several early Hollywood movie musicals. In military service, World War II, coordinated entertainment for numerous air bases on west coast. Collaborators included Raymond Klages, Jo Trent, Oscar Hammerstein II, Charlotte Kent, Sidney D. Mitchell.

SONGS
(with related shows)

1926—Hugs and Kisses
1927—A LA CARTE stage show (Give Trouble the Air)
1928—EARL CARROLL'S VANITIES OF 1928 stage show (Blue Shadows); PARIS stage show (title song); Manhattan Serenade (revived 1942)
1929—HOLLYWOOD REVUE OF 1929 movie (Gotta Feelin' for You); UNTAMED movie (That Wonderful Something); Love Ain't Nothin' but the Blues
1930—SWEET AND LOW stage show (Overnight)
1931—BALLYHOO stage show (I'm One of God's Children Who Hasn't Got Wings; No Wonder I'm Blue)
1932—What a Life
1933—HOLD YOUR HORSES stage show (songs unimportant); TAKE A CHANCE movie (Come Up and See Me Sometime); Morning, Noon and Night; What Have We Got to Lose?
1934—I've Got Sand in My Shoes
1936—TRAIL OF THE LONESOME PINE movie (A Melody from the Sky; Twilight on the Trail); RAINBOW ON THE RIVER movie (Rainbow on the River; A Thousand Dreams of You; You Only Live Once); SING, BABY, SING movie (You Turned the Tables on Me)
1937—MAKE A WISH movie (Make a Wish; Music in My Heart)

1940—The Sky Fell Down
1941—LAS VEGAS NIGHTS movie (Dolores;
I Gotta Ride; Moments Like This;
Mary, Mary, Quite Contrary);
CAUGHT IN THE DRAFT movie (Love
Me As I Am)
1942—Fun to Be Free
1946—BREAKFAST IN HOLLYWOOD movie
(If I Had a Wishing Ring)
1947—NEW ORLEANS movie (Do You
Know What It Means to Miss
New Orleans?; Endie; Blues Are
Brewin'); Strange What a Song
Can Do; Arizona Sundown
1949—Circus
1952—Nina Never Knew

Serious works: *Manhattan Moonlight,
Metropolitan Nocturne, Side Street in
Gotham, Manhattan Masquerade, Ameri-
can Serenade, Jewels from Cartier suite*

28. ALTMAN, ARTHUR   cm lyr v
Born in Brooklyn, N.Y.

Songwriter with comparatively sparse
output but several popular songs. Best-
known: *Play, Fiddle, Play* and *All or
Nothing At All*. Composed former in 1932.
Years elapsed without further songs. Attended St. John's School of Law. Played
violin in dance orchestras early in career.
Wrote for radio and later TV. Chief
collaborators Jack Lawrence, Hal David.

SONGS

1932—Play, Fiddle, Play
1938—I Fall in Love with You Every
Day
1942—I'll Pray for You; Be Brave, Beloved; WHAT'S COOKIN'? movie
(You Can't Hold a Memory in
Your Arms); Romance a la Mode
1943—All or Nothing at All (revival from
1940)
1949—Single Saddle; Blue for a Boy,
Pink for a Girl
1950—American Beauty Rose
1951—Music by the Angels
1952—And So I Waited Around; Love,
Where Are You Now?; I Am a
Heart
1953—With All My Tears for You
1954—Changeable; When I Plunk on My
Guitar; I'm Blessed
1963—I Will Follow Him

*Other songs: Green years; Hello Loser;
So It Always Will Be; Theme from
"Sudden Fear"; You're Breaking My
Heart All Over Again; Harbor of Dream-
boats: I Wish I Had a Record*

29. ALVIN, DANNY   d B
(DANNY VINIELLO)
*Born November 29, 1902, New York,
N.Y.*
Died December 5, 1958, Chicago, Ill.

Drummer associated with many dixieland
groups of 30s and 40s. Own combo in 50s.
Became professional drummer in teens.
Early jobs backing singers Aunt Jemima
and Sophie Tucker. Went to Chicago in
early 20s. Band jobs with Frankie Quartell and Charley Straight. With Arnold
Johnson 1926-7 in Florida. Back to Chicago in late 20s with Wayne King and
others. Early 30s to 1934 mostly led
combo in Chicago. 1934-6 mostly with
pianist Art Hodes combo. Later 1936 to
New York to play jazz clubs. Jobs included 1937-8 with Wingy Manone. Played with George Brunis, Joe Marsala, Art
Hodes, Mezz Mezzrow 1940-5. Back in
Chicago with Doc Evans and George
Zack bands 1947-8. From late 1949 led
combo in Chicago and in last few years
owned club.

RECORDS

ART HODES
BN 34 Sugar Foot Stomp/Sweet Geor-
gia Brown
Sess 10-007 Feather's Lament/Mezzin'
Around
Sess 10-008 Really the Blues/Milk for
Mezz
JOE MARSALA
Va 565 Wolverine Blues/Jazz Me
Blues
WINGY MANONE
Bb 6806 Boo-Hoo/Oh Say, Can You
Swing?
Bb 6816 Formal Night in Harlem/
Sweet Lorraine
Bb 7198 Jazz Me Blues/I Ain't Got
Nobody
Bb 7389 Annie Laurie/Loch Lomond
Bb 7621 Martha/Flat Foot Floogee
BUD FREEMAN
Bb 10370 I've Found a New Baby/
Easy to Get

Bb 10386 China Boy/The Eel
GEORG BRUNIS
  CMS 608 Sweet Lovin' Man/Wang
    Wang Blues
BECHET-NICHOLAS BLUE FIVE
  BN 517 Quincy Street Stomp/Weary
    Way Blues
WILD BILL DAVISON
  CMS 563 Confessin'/Big Butter and
    Egg Man
BUCK CLAYTON
  Melrose 1201 Diga Diga Doo/Love
    Me or Leave Me
  Melrose 1202 We're in the Money/B.
    C. Blues

LPs

ART HODES
  BN(10")7004 Art Hodes & His Chi-
    cagoans (BN RIs)
MEZZ MEZZROW
  BN(10")7023
WILD BILL DAVISON
  CMS(10")FL-20011
GEORGE ZACK
  CMS(10")FL-20001
TEDDY WILSON
  Dial(10")213

30. ALVIS, HAYES   b tu d ar

Born May 1, 1907, Chicago, Ill.
Died December 30, 1972, New York,
N.Y.

Bass man with jazz groups from late 20s
to 60s. Played drums as youngster but
concentrated on bass as professional, first
on tuba then on string bass. Early important job touring with Jelly Roll Morton
1927-8. Jobbed in Chicago much of 1928.
Late 1928-30 with great Earl Hines band
in Chicago. Went with Jimmie Noone to
New York in 1931, switched to string
bass. With Mills Blue Rhythm Band
1931-5, including interval as manager,
and with Duke Ellington 1935-8. Formed
band with Freddy Jenkins briefly, then
jobbed in New York. Periods with Benny
Carter 1939, Joe Sullivan 1940, Louis
Armstrong 1940-1. New York radio work
1942. Military service several years,
World War II. In later 40s with various
bands in New York, including long run at
Cafe Society as house musician. Continued to job in New York in 50s. In late 50s

worked with Wilbur DeParis. Continued
active in 60s, also working as interior
decorator.

RECORDS

EARL HINES
  Vi 38042 Chicago Rhythm/Everybody
    Loves My Baby
  Vi 38043 Beau Koo Jack/Good Little
    Bad Little You
  Vi 38096 Blue Nights/Grand Piano
    Blues
DUKE ELLINGTON
  Br 7989 I've Got to Be a Rug Cutter/
    The New East St. Louis Toodle-oo
  Br 7994 The New Birmingham Break-
    down/Scattin' at the Kit Kat
  Br 8063 Steppin' into Swing Society/
    New Black and Tan Fantasy
MILLS BLUE RHYTHM BAND
  Co 3156-D Balloonacy/Barrelhouse
  Co 3157-D Showboat Shuffle/The
    Moon Is Grinning at Me
BARON LEE & THE BLUE RHYTHM BAND
  Me 12366 The Scat Song/Heat Waves
  Pe 15629 Rhythm Spasm/White Light-
    ning
REX STEWART
  Va 618 Back Room Romp/Tea and
    Trumpets
  Va 664 Sugar Hill Shim Sham/Love in
    My Heart
COOTIE WILLIAMS
  Va 555 I Can't Believe That You're in
    Love with Me/Diga Diga Doo
BENNY CARTER
  Vo 5112 Scandal in A Flat/Savoy
    Stampede
  Vo 5458 Among My Souvenirs/Fish
    Fry
LIONEL HAMPTON
  Vi 26739 Charlie Was a Sailor/Martin
    on Every Block
  Vi 26793 Pigfoot Sonata/Just for Laffs
JOE MARSALA
  De 18111 Twelve Bar Stampede/
    Feather Bed Blues
PETE BROWN
  De 18118 Tempo di Jump/Ocean Mo-
    tion

LPs
(misc. bands)
De(10")5133 Gems of Jazz (De RIs)

WILBUR DEPARIS
Atl 1363 On the Riviera

31. AMBROSE, BERT   v B

Born 1897, London, England
Died 1973

Leader of one of England's top bands of 30s and 40s, billed as Ambrose & His Orchestra. Studied in New York after World War I, playing violin in theatre and symphony orchestras. In U. S. till late 1922, except for one return to England in 1920. Back in England in late 1921, organized dance band and opened at Luigi's Embassy Club in London for six years. Six-year run at London's New Mayfair Hotel established band as one of England's most popular, 1927-33. Returned to Embassy Club 1933-5, then toured. By 1932 most popular band on English radio.

Band had rich, full ensemble sound with solid beat. Arrangements featured top British jazzmen. By mid-30s band tightly knit, could swing mightily. Featured compositions and arrangement of Sid Phillips; best known probably *The Night Ride*. Recorded extensively through 30s and 40s. Early 30s mostly sweet hotel-band style with occasional semi-hot numbers. When band entered swing phase in mid-30s, records popular on Decca in U.S. Featured in British movie musical SOFT LIGHTS AND SWEET MUSIC. Band active through 40s in clubs and theatres, on radio and records. During war, band achieved melodious sound, at times using Glenn Miller reed style and boasting notable arrangements.

Through the years Ambrose featured outstanding musicians. Future bandleaders Ted Heath and Lew Stone worked for him late 20s. Sidemen of 30s included Danny Polo (cl), Tommy McQuater (t), Bill Amstell (ts), Bert Barnes (p), Max Bacon (d), Lew Davis (tb). Future bandleaders Stanley Black, George Melachrino, Kenny Baker, Eddie Calvert and George Shearing also worked for him, as well as vocalist Vera Lynn. Ronnie Munro was another of his arrangers. By early 50s Ambrose was out of limelight but still touring England with smaller band, playing smaller spots. Enjoyed brief upsurge in mid-50s. Later years turned to talent management.

RECORDS

AMBROSE & HIS ORCHESTRA
HMV (E)6110 Love Letters in the Sand/I Don't Know Why
HMV (E)6125 You're Blasé/Mona Lisa
HMV (E)6260 Moon
Zono (E)6163 My Silent Love/If You Were Only Mine
De (E)5245 Then I'll Be Tired of You/Tina
De (E)5375 Hors d'Oeuvres/Embassy Stomp
De (E)7909 Learn to Croon/I Cover the Waterfront
De (E)8313 Darling/Taking a Chance on Love
De (E)8441 Going My Way/Time Alone Will Tell
De (E)8564 China Moon/I'd Rather Be Me
De (E)41000 The Night Ride/Wood and Ivory
Lon (E)120 Rose of Washington Square/Dardanella
Lon (E)174 Pony Express/Stage Coach
Br 6755 Love Locked Out/Without That Certain Thing
Br 6890 No More Heartaches, No More Tears/Because It's Love
Vi 22893 I Found You
Vi 22953 Close Your Eyes
De 500 Hors d'Oeuvres/Streamline Strut
De 726 Copenhagen/B'wanga
De 971 Crazy with Love/I'm in a Dancing Mood
De 972 My Red Letter Day/Wood and Ivory
De 992 The Night Ride/Cafe Continental
De 1526 Deep Henderson/Cotton Picker's Congregation
De 2513 There's a New World/I Heard a Song in a Taxi
De 2667 Plain Jane
De 3469 A Nightingale Sang in Berkeley Square/If I Should Fall in Love Again

LPs
AMBROSE & HIS ORCHESTRA
   Mon-Ever 7032 (1928-32 RIs)
   Lon(E)(10")LB-706 Hors d'Oeuvres

32. AMECHE, DON   vo
   (DOMINIC FELIX AMICI)
   Born May 31, 1908, Kenosha, Wis.

Important movie star late 30s to early 40s. Excellent dramatic actor with distinctive speaking voice. Sang in some movies, also on Broadway stage in pleasant though not outstanding voice. Received education at several colleges. Played with stock company in Madison, Wis. Began working on New York radio late 1930. Big break spring 1931 on First Nighter network show, on which he appeared into mid-30s. On other shows. Brother Jim also on radio, with voice almost identical to Don's.

Starring role in 1936 movie SINS OF MAN launched Don's Hollywood career. Stardom after great portrayal of young Indian in RAMONA, late 1936. First singing role in early 1937 movie ONE IN A MILLION (skating star Sonja Henie's first movie). Co-star in big 1938 musical ALEXANDER'S RAGTIME BAND. Appeared in important films in late 30s, portraying famous inventor in THE STORY OF ALEXANDER GRAHAM BELL (1939) and composer Stephen Foster in SWANEE RIVER (1940). Starred with Alice Faye and Betty Grable in several movie musicals of early 40s. Also continued on radio. On 1937 summer show with Dorothy Lamour. Nelson Eddy joined late 1937-8 as show became popular for Chase & Sanborn. Ameche stayed as M. C. through 30s, had own variety show 1940 and Kraft Music Hall summer show 1941. Also appeared on radio dramatic shows. Late 40s to early 50s co-starred with Frances Langford on shows which included their skits as The Bickersons. Appeared with Miss Langford on TV in 1951. Surprisingly, Ameche's movie career waned after mid-40s. Starred in Broadway musicals SILK STOCKINGS (1955), GOLDILOCKS (1958), HENRY, SWEET HENRY (1967). Appeared on TV occasionally in 50s, had run in early 60s as ringmaster on popular circus series. In later years did some TV commercials.

MOVIES
1936—SINS OF MAN; LADIES IN LOVE; RAMONA
1937—ONE IN A MILLION; YOU CAN'T HAVE EVERYTHING; LOVE UNDER FIRE; LOVE IS NEWS; FIFTY ROADS TO TOWN
1938—IN OLD CHICAGO; ALEXANDER'S RAGTIME BAND; HAPPY LANDING; JOSETTE; GATEWAY
1939—THE THREE MUSKETEERS; THE STORY OF ALEXANDER GRAHAM BELL; HOLLYWOOD CAVALCADE, LITTLE OLD NEW YORK; MIDNIGHT
1940—SWANEE RIVER; LILLIAN RUSSELL; FOUR SONS; DOWN ARGENTINE WAY
1941—THAT NIGHT IN RIO; MOON OVER MIAMI; KISS THE BOYS GOODBYE; CONFIRM OR DENY; THE FEMININE TOUCH
1942—THE MAGNIFICENT DOPE; GIRL TROUBLE
1943—SOMETHING TO SHOUT ABOUT; HEAVEN CAN WAIT; GUEST WIFE; HAPPY LAND
1944—GREENWICH VILLAGE; A WING AND A PRAYER
1945—IT'S IN THE BAG; A GENIUS IN THE FAMILY
1946—SO GOES MY LOVE
1947—THAT'S MY MAN; WILL TOMORROW EVER COME?
1948—SLEEP, MY LOVE
1949—SLIGHTLY FRENCH
1954—PHANTOM CARAVAN
1955—FIRE ONE
1957—THE STORY OF MANKIND
1961—A FEVER IN THE BLOOD
1966—RINGS AROUND THE WORLD (narration); PICTURE MOMMY DEAD
1968—SHADOW OVER ELVERON (for TV)
1969—SUPPOSE THEY GAVE A WAR AND NOBODY CAME

RECORDS
DON AMECHE-FRANCES LANGFORD
   Co CL-1692 The Bickersons
   Co CL-1883 The Bickersons Fight Back
(original Broadway cast)
   Vi LSO-1102 SILK STOCKINGS

33. AMES BROTHERS   vo

(brothers Ed, Gene, Joe, Vic; real name URICK)

Popular singing quartet, late 40s to late 50s. Home town Malden, Mass. First sang professionally in Boston. Later played theatres, clubs in New York, Chicago, Hollywood. Popular early 50s via recordings, personal and TV appearances. Own TV series 1955. Quartet boasted excellent musicianship, handling ballads in tasteful, straightforward style with good blend. Put on excellent stage show, mixing ample comedy with music. Quartet broke up in late 50s, Ed Ames continuing as single with good role in Broadway musical CARNIVAL and long run on Daniel Boone TV series, playing an Indian. Career received big boost from appearances on Johnny Carson show. Especially popular was his rendition of hit record *Try to Remember*, Ed's popular LP big seller. Frequent TV guest shots into 70s.

RECORDS

AMES BROTHERS

Cor 60036 It Only Happens Once/You Can't Buy Happiness
Cor 60153 Music! Music! Music!/I Love Her Oh Oh Oh!
Cor 60209 Stars Are the Windows of Heaven/Hoop-Dee-Doo
Cor 60253 Can Anyone Explain?/Sittin' and Starin' and Rockin'
Cor 60300 Thirsty for Your Kisses/I Don't Mind Being All Alone
Cor 60352 Music by the Angels/Loving Is Believing
Cor 60404 My Love Serenade/I Love You Much Too Much
Cor 60566 Sentimental Journey/Undecided
Cor 60617 I'll Still Love You/I Wanna Love You
Cor 60680 And So I Waited Around/The Sheik of Araby
Cor 60773 Auf Wiedersehen, Sweetheart/Break the Bands That Bind Me
Cor 60804 Absence Makes the Heart Grow Fonder/String Along
Cor 60870 No Moon at All/Do Nothin' Till You Hear from Me

Cor 61005 This Is Fiesta/Always in My Dreams
De 24411 On the Street of Regret
Vi 20-5325 You, You, You/Once Upon a Tune
Vi 20-5530 Boogie Woogie Maxixe/I Can't Believe That You're in Love with Me

LPs

AMES BROTHERS

Cam CAL-571 Sweet and Swing
Vi LPM-1142 Exactly Like You
Vi LPM-1487 Sweet Seventeen
Vi LPM-1680 Destination Moon
Vi LPM-1859 The Best of the Ames
Vi LPM-1998 Sing the Best in the Country

ED AMES

Vi LSP-3774 (S) My Cup Runneth Over
Vi LSP-3834 (S) Time, Time
Vi LSP-3961 (S) Who Will Answer?
Vi LSP-4079 (S) Hits of Broadway and Hollywood
Vi LSP-4172 (S) Windmills of Your Mind

34. AMMONS, ALBERT   p B

Born 1907, Chicago, Ill.
Died December 5, 1949, Chicago, Ill.

A leading boogie woogie pianist, instrumental in popularizing that style in late 30s and 40s. Father of tenor sax star Gene Ammons. Played in Chicago in 20s as piano soloist or with small jazz groups. In Louis Banks band several years in early 30s. In 1934 formed combo and played Chicago clubs till 1938. To New York 1938; important in surge of boogie woogie, often teaming with pianists Meade Lux Lewis and Pete Johnson. In 1942-6 he and Johnson worked as duo and played New York spots, including long run at Cafe Society Downtown. Also toured. In later 40s worked as soloist, also recording with combo he called His Rhythm Kings. (Some records included son Gene on tenor sax.) Illness curtailed activities in last year.

RECORDS

ALBERT AMMONS' RHYTHM KINGS

De 749 Nagasaki/Boogie Woogie Stomp

De 975 Early Mornin' Blues/Mile-or-
Mo' Bird Rag
CMS(12")1516 Jammin' the Boogie/
Bottom Blues
ALBERT AMMONS
Vo 4608 Shout for Joy
BN(12")2 Boogie Woogie Stomp/
Boogie Woogie Blues
BN(12")21 Suitcase Blues/Bass Goin'
Crazy
ALBERT AMMONS-PETE JOHNSON
Vi 27504 Cuttin' the Boogie/Barrel-
house Boogie
Vi 27505 Boogie Woogie Man/Walkin'
the Boogie
SIPPIE WALLACE
Mer 2010 Buzz Me/Bedroom Blues
ALBERT AMMONS & HIS RHYTHM KINGS
Mer 8070 The Sheik of Araby/You
Are My Sunshine
Mer 8075 The   Clipper/Ammons
Stomp
Mer 8100 Baltimore Breakdown/In a
Little Spanish Town
Mer 8140 Roses of Picardy/Why I'm
Leavin' You
Mer 8242 Rhythm Boogie/When You
and I Were Young, Maggie
HARRY JAMES
BR 8318 Woo-Woo
J. C. HIGGINBOTHAM
BN 501 Weary Land Blues
MEADE LUX LEWIS-PETE JOHNSON-ALBERT
AMMONS
Vo 4606 Boogie Woogie Prayer (1 & 2)
Vo 5186 Cafe Society Rag
PORT OF HARLEM JAZZ MEN
BN(12")3 Mighty Blues/Rocking the
Blues
BN(12")14 Port of Harlem Blues

LPs

ALBERT AMMONS
BN(10")PLP-7017 Boogie Woogie
Classics
Mer(10")MG-25012 Boogie Woogie
Piano
(miscellaneous artists)
Riv 12-106 Giants of Boogie Woogie

35. AMMONS, GENE   ts cm B
(nicknamed Jug)
Born April 14, 1925, Chicago, Ill.
Big-toned, hard-swinging tenor sax star in

early bop era of 40s. Son of famed boogie
woogie pianist Albert Ammons. First important job with Billy Eckstine's progressive band in mid-40s, where featured in
tenor sax duels with Dexter Gordon.
Early 1947 with Jimmy Dale band, then
led own group 1947-8 in Chicago area.
Early 1949 with Woody Herman band. In
1949 and early 50s Ammons teamed with
sax star Sonny Stitt and again featured
sax duels. Since then mostly led own
groups, in later years turning more commercial and doing honking rhythm and
blues numbers. 1962-9 jailed on narcotics
charge, resuming career upon release.
Active into 70s. Composer of some jazz
numbers, best-known *Red Top*.

RECORDS

BILLY ECKSTINE
Del 2001 Blowing the Blues Away
Nat 9018 Second Balcony Jump
Nat 9049 Jitney Man
Nat 9052 Cool Breeze
ALBERT AMMONS & HIS RHYTHM KINGS
Mer 8053 St. Louis Blues/Shufflin' the
Boogie
Mer 8063 Hiroshima/S.P. Blues
WOODY HERMAN
Cap 57-682 More Moon
GENE AMMONS
Mer 8048 Red Top/Idaho
Mer 8123 "Harold" the Fox/Jeet Jet
Mer 8125 Brother Jug's Sermon/Ab-
dullah's Fiesta
Mer 8185 Little Slam/When You're
Gone
Pres 734 When the Saints Go March-
ing In/Hot Stuff
Pres 805 Wow!/When I Dream of You
Pres 916 Charmaine/Undecided
Pres 921 Undecided/Until the Real
Thing Comes Along
Bird 6006 Bye Bye/Let It Be
Alad 3012 Blowing Red's Bop/Con-
centration
GENE AMMONS-SONNY STITT
Pres 709 Blues Up and Down/You
Can Depend on Me
Pres 748 Stringin' the Jug (1 & 2)

LPs

GENE AMMONS
Pres 7039 The Happy Blues
Pres 7083 Funky

Pres 7146 Blue Gene
Pres 7192 "Jug"
Pres 7445 Boss Soul!
Pres 7708 The Best of Gene Ammons
Pres 7739 The Boss Is Back!
Cadet 783 Gene Ammons Makes It Happen
GENE AMMONS-SONNY STITT
Pres 7234 Soul Summit
Verve V-8426 Boss Tenors
BENNY GREEN
VJ 1005 The Swingin'est
(miscellaneous artists)
VJ 3024 Juggin' Around

36. ANDERSON, CAT   t cm B
(WILLIAM ALONZO ANDERSON)

Born September 12, 1916, Greenville, S.C.

High-note trumpet star noted for power and wild style, mainly with Duke Ellington. Studied music in orphanage in Charleston, S.C., where received nickname Cat. Played with band formed from orphanage musicians, the Carolina Cotton Pickers, in early and mid-30s. Toured south to east and back again. In 1937 joined Hartley Toots band in Florida, then to New York. Soon joined Claude Hopkins, then in 1938-41 the Sunset Royal Orchestra (under direction of Doc Wheeler). Wrote *How 'Bout That Mess* and was featured on band's recording of it. In 1942 spent brief periods with Lucky Millinder, Erskine Hawkins, Stan Kenton, Lionel Hampton. Joined Sabby Lewis, 1943. Rejoined Hampton 1944. Late 1944-7 played with Ellington, where frantic trumpet work won attention. For rest of 40s, mostly led own band. Rejoined Ellington for long association, 1950-9. Left to lead own band awhile and play with Count Basie, then played with Ellington off and on during 60s. Freelanced in 70s on west coast, especially with Hampton and Bill Berry. Composed several jazz numbers.

RECORDS
DUKE ELLINGTON
Mus 461 Happy Go Lucky Local (1 & 2)
Mus 484 Trumpet No End (Blue Skies)

Co 39496 The Eighth Veil
Co 39670 Jam with Sam
Vi 47-4281 A Gathering in a Clearing
LIONEL HAMPTON
De 18613 Chop-Chop/Hamp's Boogie Woogie
De 23639 Flying Home No. 2
DOC WHEELER
Bb 11314 How 'Bout That Mess
THE CORONETS
Mercer 1969 Night Walk/The Happening
CAT ANDERSON
Apo 771 Swingin' the Cat/I Gotta Go, Baby
Apo 774 For Jumpers Only/Cat's Boogie
Go 174 Cat's in the Alley/Caruba
Go 177 Black Eyed Blues/Home Town Stomp

LPs
DUKE ELLINGTON
Vi LPM-3782 Far East Suite
Co CS-8072 (S) Newport 1958
Beth BCP-60 Historically Speaking —The Duke
DUKE ELLINGTON-COUNT BASIE
Co CL-1715 First Time! The Count Meets the Duke
MERCER ELLINGTON
Cor CRL-57293 Colors in Rhythm
CAT ANDERSON
EmArcy MG-36142 Cat on a Hot Tin Horn
LaBrea L-8026 In the Elegant Ellington Manner

37. ANDERSON, IVY   vo

Born 1904, Gilroy, Calif.
Died December 28, 1949, Los Angeles, Calif.

Featured vocalist with Duke Ellington 1931-42, blending with band's style in excellent fashion. Had formal voice training, did early work in small clubs in Los Angeles. Toured as dancer in a Fanchon & Marco revue, later singing with the show. Through 20s continued to tour in clubs and stage revues. At intervals sang briefly with bands of Paul Howard and Earl Hines. Toured Australia with Sonny Clay revue. In early 1931 joined Ellington for long, successful association. Featured with Ellington through 30s until mid-1942. Consistently superior; elegant stylist. Appeared with Ellington in 1937 Marx Brothers movie, A DAY AT THE RACES. Left Ellington to settle in California and play clubs there as a single. Also had her own club in Los Angeles several years, the Chicken Shack. Late 1946 enjoyed good run at a Hollywood spot. Generally inactive musically in last years.

RECORDS

DUKE ELLINGTON
  Br 6265 It Don't Mean a Thing
  Br 6571 Happy as the Day Is Long/ Raisin' the Rent
  Br 6607 Get Yourself a New Broom
  Br 7514 Truckin'
  Br 7526 Cotton
  Br 7625 Isn't Love the Strangest Thing?
  Br 7627 Love Is Like a Cigarette
  Br 8099 Carnival in Caroline
  Vi 24651 My Old Flame/Troubled Waters
  Vi 26719 At a Dixie Roadside Diner
  Vi 26748 Five O'Clock Whistle
  Vi 27531 I Got It Bad/Chocolate Shake
  Vi 20-1505 Hayfoot, Strawfoot
  Co 35427 Mood Indigo/Solitude
  Ma 117 There's a Lull in My Life/It's Swell of You
IVY ANDERSON
  Va 591 Old Plantation/All God's Chillun Got Rhythm
  Excl 3113-4 Play Me the Blues/Mexico Joe
  B&W 771 I've Got It Bad/On the Sunny Side of the Street
  B&W 772 I Thought You Ought to Know/The Voot Is Here to Stay
  B&W 823 Twice Too Many/Tall, Dark and Handsome

LPs

PEARL BAILEY-ROSE MURPHY-IVY ANDERSON
  Design 238
DUKE ELLINGTON
  Co KG-32064 (2-LP set) Presents Ivy Anderson (1932-40 RIs)

38. ANDERSON, JOHN MURRAY

lyr

Born September 20, 1886, St. John's, Newfoundland
Died January 30, 1954, New York, N.Y.

Director of GREENWICH VILLAGE FOLLIES shows on Broadway, 1919-24. Also wrote book and lyrics. Educated at Edinburgh Academy in Scotland and Lausanne University in Switzerland. During World War I with American Bureau of Information. In 1919 began Broadway career by staging first of the GREENWICH VILLAGE FOLLIES, very successful series in ensuing years. Noted for stagecraft. Productions rivaled Flo Ziegfeld's in beauty and pageantry, presented talented performers. During career Anderson directed, wrote or produced 29 revues on Broadway and five in London, as well as many circus extravaganzas, theatre presentations and night club shows. Directed important early movie musical, KING OF JAZZ, in 1930. Director of New York's Radio City Music Hall in 1933 and Cleveland's Great Lakes Exposition in 1937. Director of Billy Rose's Diamond Horseshoe 1938-50; Ringling Brothers Circus 1942-51. Wrote autobiography, *Out Without My Rubbers.* Wrote lyrics to many songs for his productions, best known *A Young Man's Fancy* in 1920 show WHAT'S IN A NAME?. Chief collaborators were composers A. Baldwin Sloane and Carey Morgan. Songs from various productions included *Eileen Avourneen, The Girl in the Moon, The Valley of Dreams, That Reminiscent Melody, The Last Waltz, Come to Vienna, At the Krazy Kat's Ball, Some Day When Dreams Come True, In the Year of Fifty-Fifty, My Bridal Veil, Marimba.*

BROADWAY SHOWS
(as lyricist-director; *also wrote book)

1919—GREENWICH VILLAGE FOLLIES
1920—GREENWICH VILLAGE FOLLIES OF 1920; WHAT'S IN A NAME? (*)
1921—GREENWICH VILLAGE FOLLIES OF 1921 (*)
1922—GREENWICH VILLAGE FOLLIES OF 1922 (*)
1923—GREENWICH VILLAGE FOLLIES OF 1923 (*)

1924—GREENWICH VILLAGE FOLLIES OF 1924 (book only)

Director or producer of other shows including THE LEAGUE OF NOTIONS (London); MUSIC BOX REVUE OF 1924; DEAREST ENEMY; JOHN MURRAY ANDERSON'S ALMANAC (1929 and 1953); BOW BELLS (London); FANFARE (London); ZIEGFELD FOLLIES (1934, 1936, 1943); LIFE BEGINS AT 8:40; THUMBS UP!; JUMBO; ONE FOR THE MONEY; TWO FOR THE SHOW; LAFFING ROOM ONLY; THREE TO MAKE READY; NEW FACES OF 1952; TWO'S COMPANY

39. ANDERSON, LEROY

cm ar p o B

Born June 29, 1908, Cambridge, Mass.

Noted composer of tuneful descriptive pieces. Best known: *Blue Tango, Fiddle Faddle, Belle of the Ball, Sleigh Ride, A Trumpeter's Lullaby.* Studied piano at New England Conservatory, attended Harvard. Church organist and choirmaster. Orchestra director at Harvard 1929-30 and 1932-5. Later 30s freelanced as arranger-composer-conductor with various concert bands and orchestras, including arranging stint with Boston Pops Orchestra. Military service, World War II and Korean War. In later 40s concentrated on composing. First big hit: *Fiddle Faddle* in late 40s. In early 50s had series of hit pieces widely recorded; *Blue Tango* probably most popular. His works were especially adaptable to large studio or classical-type orchestras featuring strings. Led large orchestra on recordings of many of his compositions. Wrote score for 1958 Broadway show GOLDILOCKS that abounded in tuneful melodies (*Lazy Moon; Give the Little Lady; Save a Kiss; No One'll Ever Love You; The Pussy Foot; Who's Been Sitting in My Chair?; There Never Was a Woman; The Beast in You; Shall I Take My Heart and Go?; I Can't Be in Love; Bad Companions; I Never Know When; Two Years in the Making*). Lyrics were by Joan Ford, Walter & Jean Kerr. Anderson's best compositions include *Fiddle Faddle; Sleigh Ride; The Syncopated Clock; Blue Tango; Belle of the Ball; The Typewriter; Serenata; Jazz Le-* gato; *Jazz Pizzicato; The Girl in Satin; The Penny-Whistle Song; China Doll; Forgotten Dreams; Plink, Plank, Plunk; A Trumpeter's Lullaby; The Bugler's Holiday; Sandpaper Ballet; Promenade; The Phantom Regiment; Saraband; Ticonderoga; Irish Suite; Song of Jupiter; A Christmas Festival; Horse and Buggy; The Waltzing Cat; Summer Skies; Song of the Bells; The First Day of Spring; The Blue Bells of Scotland; Turn Ye to Me; The Minstrel Boy.* Mitchell Parrish wrote lyrics for several of his songs.

RECORDS

LEROY ANDERSON
De 27875 Blue Tango/Belle of the Ball
De 28168 Plink, Plank, Plunk/Serenata
De 28300 Fiddle Faddle/A Trumpeter's Lullaby
De 28429 Sleigh Ride/Saraband

LPs

LEROY ANDERSON
De DL-8121 Leroy Anderson Conducts
De DL-9749 A Leroy Anderson "Pops" Concert
De(10″)DL-7509 Conducts His Own Songs
De(10″)DL-7519 Conducts His Own Compositions, Vol. 2
(other artists performing his compositions)
FREDERICK FENNELL & THE EASTMAN-ROCHESTER "POPS" ORCHESTRA
Mer SR-90009 (S) Music of Leroy Anderson, Vol. 1
Mer SR-90043 (S) Music of Leroy Anderson, Vol. 2
STRADAVARI STRINGS
Spinorama S-32 Ping Pong Percussion Sound of Leroy Anderson
(original Broadway cast)
Co OL-5340 GOLDILOCKS

40. ANDERSON, MAXWELL

lyr

Born December 15, 1888, Atlantic, Pa.
Died February 28, 1959, Stamford, Conn.

Playright and lyricist. Best-known song *September Song,* from Broadway show KNICKERBOCKER HOLIDAY, Educated at

North Dakota and Stanford universities. Taught school in North Dakota and California. Reporter on newspapers in Grand Forks, N. D., and San Francisco (latter 1914-8). Editorial writer on New York newspapers 1918-24. As playright, productions on Broadway included WHAT PRICE GLORY?, SATURDAY'S CHILDREN, ELIZABETH THE QUEEN, BOTH YOUR HOUSES (Pulitzer Prize for drama 1933), MARY OF SCOTLAND, VALLEY FORGE, WINTERSET, THE MASQUE OF KINGS, THE WINGLESS VICTORY, HIGH TOR (also TV score), KEY LARGO, THE BAD SEED, WHITE DESERT, OUTSIDE LOOKING IN, GODS OF THE LIGHTNING, THE STAR-WAGON, THE EVE OF ST. MARK. Wrote book and lyrics for Broadway shows KNICKERBOCKER HOLIDAY (1938) and LOST IN THE STARS (1949). Collaborated with composer Kurt Weill on both scores.

SONGS
(with related shows)

1938—KNICKERBOCKER HOLIDAY stage show (September Song; It Never Was You; The Scars; There's Nowhere to Go but Up; How Can You Tell an American?)

1944—KNICKERBOCKER HOLIDAY movie (adapted from original stage play)

1949—LOST IN THE STARS stage show (Lost in the Stars; The Little Grey House; Who'll Buy?; Stay Well)

1959—NEVER STEAL ANYTHING SMALL movie (Never Steal Anything Small; It Takes Love to Make a Home)

1960—MIDNIGHT LACE movie (What Does a Woman Do?)

41. ANDREWS SISTERS   vo

All born in Minneapolis, Minn.
Patti born February 16, 1920
Maxene born January 3, 1918
LaVerne born July 6, 1915 (died 1967)

Popular singing trio of late 30s and 40s. Brash style and showmanship effective on novelty and jazz numbers. Achieved tasteful blend on ballads. Patti sang lead and solo, served as personable leader and spokesman. In 1932, while teenagers, sisters toured with Larry Rich band in vaudeville. In ensuing years played clubs and theatres. In 1937 with Leon Belasco. Began making radio appearances later in 1937, which increased with their big record hit, *Bei Mir Bist du Schon*. Featured in mid-1938 on Just Entertainment radio show with Jack Fulton, in 1939 on Honolulu Bound with Phil Baker. In 40s starred on several radio shows of varying formats, did many guest spots, poured out steady record output. Big sellers: *Rum and Coca Cola*; *I Can Dream, Can't I?*; *Hold Tight—Hold Tight*; *Boogie Woogie Bugle Boy*; *In Apple Blossom Time*; *Pennsylvania Polka*. Joined Bing Crosby for other big sellers: *Pistol Packin' Mama*, *Don't Fence Me In*, *Jingle Bells*. Scored with Guy Lombardo orchestra on *Christmas Island*. Trio reached peak during World War II. Frequent movie appearances. Featured in several Abbott & Costello films and wartime B musicals. Team continued into 50s. Retirement in later 50s and part of 60s, though Patti worked at times as single. Later in 60s, well-received TV appearances and occasional location jobs till death of LaVerne in 1967. Later, some appearances with substitute for La Verne, but not for long. Patti continued to work occasionally; in 1969 film THE PHYNX. Bette Midler 1973 record hit *Boogie Woogie Bugle Boy* aped Andrews Sisters version, led to revival of latter's records. Patti and Maxene starred in 1974 40s-style Broadway musical OVER HERE.

MOVIES

1940—ARGENTINE NIGHTS
1941—IN THE NAVY; BUCK   ATES; HOLD THAT GHOST
1942—WHAT'S COOKIN'?;
AROO; GIVE OUT, SISTERS
1943—HOW'S ABOUT IT?; ALWAYS A BRIDESMAID
1944—FOLLOW THE BOYS; HOLLYWOOD CANTEEN; MOONLIGHT AND CACTUS; SWING TIME JOHNNY
1945—HER LUCKY NIGHT
1946—MAKE MINE MUSIC (on soundtrack only)
1947—ROAD TO RIO
1948—MELODY TIME

RECORDS

LEON BELASCO
Br 7863 Jammin'

Br 7872 Wake Up and Live/There's a Lull in My Life (PATTI ANDREWS solo vocal, 2nd side)

ANDREWS SISTERS

De 1562 Bei Mir Bist du Schon/Nice Work If You Can Get It

De 1691 Joseph Joseph/It's Easier Said Than Done

De 2214 Hold Tight-Hold Tight/Billy Boy

De 2462 Beer Barrel Polka/Well, All Right

De 2840 Oh Johnny, Oh Johnny, Oh!/South American Way

De 3097 Rhumboogie/Tuxedo Junction

De 3328 Ferryboat Serenade/Hit the Road

De 3598 Boogie Woogie Bugle Boy/Bounce Me, Brother

De 3622 In Apple Blossom Time/I, Yi, Yi, Yi, Yi

De 3960 The Booglie Wooglie Piggy/The Nickel Serenade

De 4008 Elmer's Tune/Honey

De 4094 Chattanooga Choo Choo/For All We Know

De 4097 Shrine of St. Cecilia/Jack of All Trades

De 18398 Pennsylvania Polka/That's the Moon, My Son

De 18470 Strip Polka/Mr. Five by Five

De 18636 Rum and Coca Cola/One Meat Ball

De 24705 I Can Dream, Can't I?/Wedding of Lili Marlene

De 28929 This Little Piggie/Love Sends a Little Gift of Roses

ANDREWS SISTERS-BING CROSBY

De 23277 Pistol Packin' Mama/Victory Polka

De 23281 Jingle Bells/Santa Claus Is Comin' to Town

De 23364 Don't Fence Me In/The Three Caballeros

ANDREWS SISTERS-DICK HAYMES

De 23412 Great Day/Smile, Smile, Smile!

ANDREWS SISTERS with GUY LOMBARDO ORCHESTRA

De 23722 Christmas Island/Winter Wonderland

De 27652 Night on the Water/Dimples and Cherry Cheeks

LPs

ANDREWS SISTERS

De(10″)DL-5065 Tropical Songs

Vo VL-3611 Near You (De RIs)

Dot DLP-3406 The Andrews Sisters' Greatest Hits

Dot DLP-3452 Great Golden Hits

Dot DLP-3529 The Andrews Sisters Present

42. ANTHONY, RAY   t vo ar B
(RAYMOND ANTONINI)

Born January 20, 1922, Bentleyville, Pa.

Trumpet-playing leader of one of most popular dance bands of 50s. Grew up in Cleveland, playing with area bands as teenager. At 17 landed first important job with Al Donahue band. Then Glenn Miller band, late 1940 to mid-1941. With Jimmy Dorsey about six months. In early 1942 led band briefly in Cleveland. Led service band in World War II. In early 1946 Anthony organized band, gained first recognition in midwest. In 1949 played important engagement in New York. By early 50s Anthony had a top band, continued on top through much of 50s. Band had crisp ensemble sound with full modern arrangements (many by George Williams), featured Glenn Miller reed sound. Anthony did not build up sidemen as jazz soloists. Featured own rich-toned, sweet trumpet on ballads. Fast-tempo numbers on clean-swinging ensemble lines spotted only occasional solos. Several singers and vocal groups worked with band, with Tommy Mercer most prominent. Ray's brother Leo played sax most of this time.

Recording output prolific. Leading hit probably *Dragnet*. Band popular with young people especially; played proms, made extensive college tour 1953. Anthony co-composer of popular novelty song and dance, *The Bunny Hop*. Band had good spot in 1955 movie DADDY LONG LEGS. Anthony played small roles in several minor movies in late 50s. In 1953 band joined singers Bob Eberly and Helen O'Connell on TV series. In 1956 appeared with Frank Leahy and sports guests in another series. Featured in its own series in late 50s. In 1954 Anthony bought Billy May band, turned it over to

Sam Donahue to lead for several years. Anthony disbanded in 60s, later formed combo to play clubs.

RECORDS

RAY ANTHONY
Son 3034 Margie/I'll Close My Eyes
Cap 721 Slider/My Baby Missed the Train
Cap 923 Sentimental Me/Spaghetti Rag
Cap 968 Tenderly/Autumn Nocturne
Cap 979 Count Every Star/Darktown Strutters' Ball
Cap 1040 Scattered Toys/Skip to My Lou
Cap 1190 Harbor Lights/Nevertheless
Cap 1502 Mr. Anthony's Blues/Cook's Tour
Cap 1758 The Fox/Rollin' Home
Cap 1912 At Last/I'll See You in My Dreams
Cap 2104 As Time Goes By/Scatterbrain
Cap 2293 People in Love/Idaho
Cap 2393 True Blue Lou/They Didn't Believe Me
Cap 2427 The Bunny Hop/The Hokey Pokey
Cap 2532 Jersey Bounce/I Guess It Was You All the Time
Cap 2562 Dragnet/Dancing in the Dark

LPs

RAY ANTHONY
Cap T-678 Big Band Dixieland
Cap T-786 Dancers in Love
Cap T-831 Star Dancing
Cap T-969 The Dream Girl
Cap T-1252 More Dream Dancing
Cap T-1608 Dream Dancing Medley
Cap(10″)T-373 The Young Man with the Horn
Cap(10″)H-362 Campus Rumpus!
Cap(10″)H-476 I Remember Glenn Miller

43. ARBELLO, FERNANDO
tb ar cm B

Born May 30, 1907, Puerto Rico
Trombonist-arranger with numerous important hot bands of 20s, 30s and 40s. After earlier musical experience in native Puerto Rico, Arbello came to New York

in mid-20s. Jobs in later 20s and early 30s included periods with Earle Howard, Wilbur DeParis, June Clark, Bingie Madison. With Claude Hopins 1931-4, Chick Webb briefly late 1934-5, Fletcher Henderson 1936-7 (except for interval with Mills Blue Rhythm Band). In late 30s rejoined Mills Blue Rhythm Band; later played with Edgar Hayes, Fats Waller, Claude Hopkins, Benny Carter. In 1940 with Zutty Singleton; also led own band. In 1941 with Fletcher Henderson and Joe Marsala; 1942-6 with Jimmie Lunceford. In 50s Arbello worked mostly as leader of own band, mainly in New York area. In 60s played with Machito's band. In late 60s returned to Puerto Rico, remaining active as bandleader. Co-composer of 1936 swing number, *Big Chief De Sota.*

RECORDS

BILLY HICKS
Va 601 Fade Out/Joe the Bomber
MIDGE WILLIAMS
Va 620 I Know Now/That Old Feeling
Va 639 I Was Born to Swing/Oh Miss Hannah

LPs

REX STEWART
Jazztone J-1202 Dixieland Free-for-all
FLETCHER HENDERSON
Co C4L19 (4-LP set) A Study in Frustration (RIs)

44. ARCHER, HARRY   cm t tb tu B
(HARRY AURACHER)

Born February 21, 1888, Creston, Iowa
Died April 23, 1960, New York, N.Y.
Bandleader and composer of 20s and 30s. Wrote all-time song hit, *I Love You*, for 1923 Broadway musical LITTLE JESSIE JAMES. Attended Michigan Military Academy, Princeton University and Knox College. Mastered all brass instruments except French horn. Led dance orchestra in Chicago. Worked with Paul Whiteman. Wrote scores for Broadway musicals THE PEARL MAIDEN (1912), LITTLE JESSIE JAMES (1923), MY GIRL and PARADISE ALLEY (1924), TWINKLE, TWINKLE and MERRY, MERRY (1925), JUST A MINUTE (1928). Chief collaborators were lyricists Harlan Thompson and Howard Johnson.

SONGS
(with related shows)

1912—THE PEARL MAIDEN stage show (songs unimportant)

1923—LITTLE JESSIE JAMES stage show (I Love You; Little Jessie James; My Home Town in Kansas; From Broadway to Main Street)

1924—MY GIRL stage show (You and I; A Girl Like You; Before the Dawn; Desert Isle); PARADISE ALLEY stage show (included title song)

1925—MERRY, MERRY stage show (It Must Be Love; I Was Blue); TWINKLE, TWINKLE stage show (Twinkle, Twinkle; Find a Girl; Get a Load of This; You Know, I Know)

1926—I'd Rather Be the Girl in Your Arms

1928—JUST A MINUTE stage show (Anything Your Heart Desires; The Break-Me-Down; Heigh-Ho Cheerio; Pretty, Petite and Sweet)

1930—Where the Golden Daffodils Grow

1939—White Sails

Other songs; *Suppose I Had Never Met You*; *I'm Goin' to Dance with the Guy What Brung Me*; *Rainbow*; *Alone in My Dreams*; *The Sweetest Girl This Side of Heaven*; *Ev'ry Little Note*; *My Own*

RECORDS
HARRY ARCHER

Vo 15155 It Must Be Love/I Was Blue

Br 2997 Sunny/Who?

Br 3155 My Own/Ev'ry Little Note

Br 3399 There Ain't No Maybe in My Baby's Eyes/When Day Is Done

Br 3491 Lily/I'll Always Remember You

Br 3659 Rain/'Way Back When

Br 3704 Thinking of You/Up in the Clouds

Br 3720 My Heart Stood Still/I Feel at Home with You

45. ARCHEY, JAMES   tb B

Born October 12, 1902, Norfolk, Va. Died November 16, 1967, New Jersey

Good hot trombonist in New Orleans style. Played locally as teenager. Attended Hampton Institute. In 1923 settled in New York, worked there with various groups, did some touring. 1926-7 in Edgar Hayes pit band at Alhambra Theatre. Played two years at Bamboo Inn with several bands. Late 1929 joined King Oliver, toured with him in 1930. With Luis Russell briefly in 1930 and with Bingie Madison early 1931. Long association with Russell band 1931-7 (under leadership of Louis Armstrong 1935-7). With Willie Bryant 1937-9, then Benny Carter 1939-40. Later 1940 intervals with Ella Fitzgerald and Coleman Hawkins. In early 40s Archey worked with Carter again, Claude Hopkins, Noble Sissle, others. With Bob Wilber dixieland combo 1948-50, became leader when Wilber left. Successful runs in Boston and New York, European tour 1952. After group broke up, Archey toured Europe again 1954-5 with Mezz Mezzrow. Mostly with Earl Hines Sextet in 1955-62, main base in San Francisco; also some work there with Muggsy Spanier. Tours overseas with all-star groups. Active until shortly before death.

RECORDS
KING OLIVER

Vi 38124 You're Just My Type/I Must Have It

Vi 38134 Mule Face Blues/Boogie Woogie

Vi 22298 St. James Infirmary/When You're Smiling

Vi 23001 Don't You Think I Love You/Struggle Buggy

Vi 23009 Stingaree Blues/Shake It and Break It

JIMMY JOHNSON

Vi 38099 You've Got to Be Modernistic/You Don't Understand

HENRY ALLEN, JR. (LUIS RUSSELL)

Vi 23006 Roamin'/Patrol Wagon Blues

Vi 23338 Singing Pretty Songs/I Fell in Love with You

BOB WILBER

Ci 1062 Sweet Georgia Brown/Coal Black Shine

Ci 1063 When the Saints Go Marching In/The Mooche

Ci 1064 Zig Zag/Limehouse Blues

ALL-STAR STOMPERS

Ci 1023 Eccentric/Tishomingo Blues

Ci 1024 Baby, Won't You Please Come Home?/Big Butter and Egg Man

507

TONY PARENTI
Ci 1029 Hysterics Rag/Sunflower Slow Drag
Ci 1030 Grace and Beauty/Praline
Ci 1031 Swipesy Cake Walk/Hiawatha
Jazzology 1 When the Saints Go Marching In/Chinatown, My Chinatown
Jazzology 2 Blues for Faz/Bugle Call Rag

GEORGE WETTLING
Co 39497 Collier's Clambake/Collier's Climb

MUTT CAREY
Cen 4007 Joplin's Sensation/The Entertainer
Cen 4013 Indiana/Ostrich Walk
Cen 4017 Shim-Me-Sha-Wabble/Cake Walkin' Babies
Cen 4018 Slow Drivin' (1 & 2)

LPs

LOUIS ARMSTRONG
De DL-9225 Rare Items 1935-44 (De RIs)

GEORGE WETTLING
Co(10")CL-6189

TONY PARENTI
Jazzology(10")1

SIDNEY BECHET
Riv(10")2516

ALBERTA HUNTER with LOVIE AUSTIN & HER BLUES SERENADERS
Riv RLP-418 (recorded in 1961)

46. ARDEN, TONI   vo

Popular recording artist of 50s. Strong voice with plaintive quality. Sang with Al Trace in 1945 and Joe Reichman in 1946. Some recording with Shep Fields and Ray Bloch. Appeared on early TV at same time her records were popular. Important Columbia record star of 50s. Infrequent appearances on TV, late 50s and early 60s. Club dates into 1974.

RECORDS

TONI ARDEN
Co 38612 I Can Dream, Can't I?/A Little Love, a Little Kiss
Co 38739 Rain/Mother, Mother, Mother
Co 38905 Don't Ever Leave Me/It's Love

Co 38930 Can't We Talk It Over?/ Only a Moment Ago
Co 39003 And You'll Be Home/My Tears Won't Dry
Co 39117 My Man/They're Playing Our Song
Co 39271 Too Late Now/Too Young
Co 39348 Come Back to Sorrento/Little Child
Co 39427 Wonder Why/Dark Is the Night
Co 39440 If You Turn Me Down/Invitation to a Broken Heart
Co 39737 I'm Yours/Kiss of Fire
Co 39768 Tell Your Tale, Nightingale/Take My Heart
Co 39878 Take a Chance/Sweet Forgiveness
Co 40125 I Wish I Knew/Take Me Now

TONI ARDEN-THE FOUR LADS
Co 40019 All I Desire/The Lover's Waltz

LPs

TONI ARDEN
De DL-74375 (S) Italian Gold
De DL-8651 Miss Toni Arden
De DL-8765 Sing a Song of Italy
De DL-8875 Besame!
Ha HL-7212 The Exciting Toni Arden (Co RIs)

47. ARDEN, VICTOR   p B

Born c. 1903, Winona, Ill.

Co-leader, with Phil Ohman, of Arden-Ohman Orchestra in 20s and 30s. Later led orchestra alone. Attended American Conservatory of Music. After World War I Arden went to New York, made piano rolls. Teamed with Phil Ohman to form piano duo on records and appeared in Broadway musicals: LADY BE GOOD (1924), TIP TOES and OH, KAY! (1926), FUNNY FACE (1927), SPRING IS HERE (1929). As piano duo they appeared on radio from late 20s to mid-30s as guests, also regulars on such series as American Album of Familiar Music 1934-5 and Bayer Musical Review 1935. Recorded with large orchestra featuring good arrangements, good musicianship. Used various vocalists (Frank Luther frequently). Mainly recorded show tunes.

In mid-30s duo split up, each leading own orchestra. Arden soon dropped dance band, turning to conducting studio orchestras on network radio. In 1934-7 shows included Rings of Melody, Broadway Varieties, Outdoor Girl Beauty Parade, Harv & Esther Show, Sunday Musical Matinee, and Sweetest Love Songs Ever Sung (starring Frank Munn). Conductor for Abe Lyman's orchestra on many shows in popular Waltz Time series. Most important radio job in early and mid-40s as conductor on highly-rated Manhattan Merry-Go-Round on Sunday evening. Also on American Melody Hour in 1947.

RECORDS

ARDEN-OHMAN (piano duo)
  Vi 19041 Dance of the Demon/Salut a' Pesth
  Vi 21929 Ragamuffin/Dance of the Paper Dolls
  Vi 22608 Maple Leaf Rag/Canadian Capers
(with REGENT CLUB ORCHESTRA)
  Br 2984 Sentimental Me/Manhattan
(with BENNIE KRUEGER ORCHESTRA)
  Br 2667 Charley, My Boy
ARDEN-OHMAN ORCHESTRA
  Br 3035 Looking for a Boy/That Certain Feeling
  Br 3197 The Girl Friend/The Blue Room
  Br 3457 Mine/There's Everything Nice About You
  Br 3527 Sometimes I'm Happy/Hallelujah
  Vi 1114 Funny Face/'S Wonderful
  Vi 21776 Marianne/Lover, Come Back to Me
  Vi 22111 How Am I to Know?
  Vi 22255 Should I?
  Vi 22275 Nina Rosa/My First Love, My Last Love
  Vi 22308 Soon/Strike Up the Band
  Vi 22383 I Love You So Much/Dancing the Devil Away
  Vi 22552 Fine and Dandy/Can This Be Love?
  Vi 22558 I Got Rhythm/Embraceable You
  Vi 22627 I've Got Five Dollars/We'll Be the Same

  Vi 22818 Ooh! That Kiss/You're My Everything
  Vi 22892 I Love a Parade/Music in My Fingers
  Vi 22893 Who's Your Little Who-zis?
  Vi 22910 When We're Alone
  Vi 22911 Of Thee I Sing/Who Cares?
  Vi 24170 Strike Me Pink/Let's Call It a Day
DICK POWELL (with Victor Arden Orchestra)
  Br 7468 Lonely Gondolier/Outside of You

48. ARLEN, HAROLD   cm ar p vo
(HYMAN ARLUCK)

Born February 15, 1905, Buffalo, N.Y.

Top composer with prolific career from 1929 through the 50s, his many excellent songs particular favorites of leading vocalists. Most famous: *Stormy Weather*, *I've Got the World on a String*, *It's Only a Paper Moon*, *Let's Fall in Love*, *Over the Rainbow*, *Blues in the Night*, *That Old Black Magic*, *Come Rain or Come Shine*, *The Man That Got Away*. At 15 was professional pianist, played clubs and excursion boats in Buffalo area. Went to New York in mid-20s, worked as pianist-singer-arranger. In Arnold Johnson's pit band for Broadway show GEORGE WHITE'S SCANDALS OF 1928. Rehearsal pianist for 1929 show GREAT DAY. Played theatre circuits as pianist-singer. Began composing in 1929. First hit *Get Happy* in 1930. Attracted attention in early 30s writing for Harlem's Cotton Club revues. Wrote great 1933 hit *Stormy Weather*. Scores for Broadway musicals YOU SAID IT (1931), LIFE BEGINS AT 8:40 (1934), HOORAY FOR WHAT? (1937), BLOOMER GIRL (1944), ST. LOUIS WOMAN (1946), HOUSE OF FLOWERS (1955), JAMAICA (1957), SARATOGA (1959). Contributed songs to other shows: EARL CARROLL'S VANITIES OF 1930 AND 1932, AMERICANA (1932), GEORGE WHITE'S MUSIC HALL VARIETIES (1932), THE SHOW IS ON (1937). Wrote songs for many movies, most memorable the excellent score (including *Over the Rainbow*) for THE WIZARD OF OZ, 1939. Chief collaborator in early years was lyricist Ted Koehler. Later collaborators included lyricists E. Y. Harburg, Ira Gershwin, Johnny Mercer, Lew Brown, Dorothy Fields, Leo Robin, Jack Yellen. Arlen became less active in 60s, occasionally appeared on TV. Several TV specials honored his music.

SONGS
(with related shows)

1929—RIO RITA movie (Long Before You Came Along); The Album of My Dreams

1930—EARL CARROLL'S VANITIES OF 1930 stage show (Hittin' the Bottle); Get Happy

1931—YOU SAID IT stage show (Sweet and Hot; Learn to Croon); Between the Devil and the Deep Blue Sea; Kickin' the Gong Around; Tell Me with a Love Song; Linda

1932—GEORGE WHITE'S MUSIC HALL VARIETIES stage show (I Love a Parade); EARL CARROLL'S VANITIES OF 1932 stage show (I Gotta Right to Sing the Blues); AMERICANA stage show (Satan's Little Lamb); Stepping into Love; Minnie the Moocher's Weddin' Day; Music, Music, Everywhere; That's What I Hate About Love

1933—TAKE A CHANCE movie (It's Only a Paper Moon); Stormy Weather; Happy as the Day Is Long; I've Got the World on a String

1934—LIFE BEGINS AT 8:40 stage show (You're a Builder Upper; Let's Take a Walk Around the Block; Fun to Be Fooled; What Can You Say in a Love Song?); LET'S FALL IN LOVE movie (Let's Fall in Love; Love Is Love Anywhere); Ill Wind; As Long as I Live; Here Goes

1936—THE SINGING KID movie (You're the Cure for What Ails Me; I Love to Sing-a); STAGE STRUCK movie (Fancy Meeting You); STRIKE ME PINK movie (songs unimportant); Last Night When We Were Very Young

1937—HOORAY FOR WHAT? stage show (Moanin' in the Mornin'; Down with Love; God's Country; In the Shade of the New Apple Tree; I've

Gone Romantic on You); THE SHOW IS ON stage show (Song of the Woodman); ARTISTS AND MODELS movie (Public Melody #1); GOLD DIGGERS OF 1937 movie (Let's Put Our Heads Together; Speaking of the Weather)

1939—THE WIZARD OF OZ movie (Over the Rainbow; Ding Dong, the Witch Is Dead; We're Off to See the Wizard; others); THE MARX BROTHERS AT THE CIRCUS movie (Two Blind Loves; Lydia, the Tattooed Lady); LOVE AFFAIR movie (Sing, My Heart)

1940—ANDY HARDY MEETS DEBUTANTE movie (Buds Won't Bud)

1941—BLUES IN THE NIGHT movie (Blues in the Night; This Time the Dream's on Me); When the Sun Comes Out

1942—STAR SPANGLED RHYTHM movie (That Old Black Magic; Hit the Road to Dreamland; others); CAPTAINS OF THE CLOUDS movie (Captains of the Clouds, which became official song of Royal Canadian Air Force)

1943—THE SKY'S THE LIMIT movie (My Shining Hour; One for My Baby); RIDING HIGH movie (He Loved Me Till the All-Clear Came); CABIN IN THE SKY movie (Happiness Is Just a Thing Called Joe)

1944—BLOOMER GIRL stage show (I Got a Song; Evelina; Right as the Rain; Pretty as a Picture; When the Boys Come Home; The Eagle and Me); HERE COME THE WAVES movie (Accent-tchu-ate the Positive; I Promise You; Let's Take the Long Way Home); KISMET movie (Willow in the Wind; Tell Me, Tell Me, Evening Star); UP IN ARMS movie (Now I Know; Tess's Torch Song)

1945—OUT OF THIS WORLD movie (Out of This World; I'd Rather Be Me; June Comes Around Every Year)

1946—ST. LOUIS WOMAN stage show (Come Rain or Come Shine; Any Place I Hang My Hat Is Home; others)

1948—CASBAH movie (What's Good About Goodbye?; It Was Written in the Stars; Hooray for Love; For Every Man There's a Woman)

1950—MY BLUE HEAVEN movie (The Friendly Islands; Don't Rock the Boat, Dear; Hallowe'en; I Love a New Yorker)

1951—MR. IMPERIUM movie (Andiamo; Let Me Look at You; My Love an' My Mule)

1953—THE FARMER TAKES A WIFE movie (Today I Love Everybody)

1954—A STAR IS BORN movie; Ira Gershwin-lyr (The Man That Got Away; Here's What I'm Here For; Gotta Have Me Go with You; Born in a Trunk; It's a New World; Someone at Last; Lose That Long Face); THE COUNTRY GIRL movie (Live and Learn; The Search Is Through; The Pitchman)

1955—HOUSE OF FLOWERS stage show; Truman Capote-lyr (Two Ladies in de Shade of de Banana Tree; A Sleepin' Bee; House of Flowers; One Man Ain't Enough; Has I Let You Down?; I Never Has Seen Snow; Gladiola)

1957—JAMAICA stage show; E. Y. Harburg-lyr (Cocoanut Sweet; Take It Slow, Joe; Ain't It the Truth?; Push the Button; Leave the Atom Alone; Napoleon; Savannah; Little Biscuit; Incompatibility)

1959—SARATOGA stage show; Johnny Mercer-lyr (Dog Eat Dog; A Game of Poker; Goose Never Be a Peacock; Love Held Lightly; The Man in My Life; The Parks of Paris; Petticoat High; You for Me; Saratoga)

1962—GAY PURR-EE movie cartoon score, E. Y. Harburg-lyr (Little Drops of Rain; Mewsette; Paris Is a Lonely Town; Roses Red—Violets Blue)

RECORDS
(as vocalist)

LEO REISMAN
  Vi 22913 Stepping into Love
  Vi 24262 Stormy Weather
HAROLD ARLEN
  Vi 24467 Let's Fall in Love/This Is Only the Beginning
  Vi 24569 As Long as I Live/Ill Wind

LPs
HAROLD ARLEN and COLE PORTER (Composers at Play)
  "X" LVA-1003 (singing their own compositions)

49. ARMEN, KAY   VO

Excellent singer, very professional in presentation. Voice somewhat along Kate Smith lines. Early career in Chicago clubs and on Nashville radio. Mid-40s singing series on radio at intervals, always excellent. 1948-51 on Stop the Music. Late 1948-9 became regular on former Buddy Clark show after Clark's death. Role in 1955 movie musical HIT THE DECK. Recorded occasionally. Some TV appearances in 50s and 60s, including late-night talk shows. Never attained the popularity she deserved.

RECORDS
KAY ARMEN
  Fed 14001 Just in Case/Come on-a My House
  Maj 1020 Give My Regards to Broadway
  MGM 12078 Suddenly There's a Valley/He
  Vi 20-5160 It's a Sin to Cry Over You/Smoky Mountain Lullaby
  Lon 677 St. Louis Blues/I've Got Misery
  Lon 760 Where Do I Go from You?/I'm in the Middle of a Riddle
  Lon 764 Don't Play with Fire/Just Say I Love Him
  King 15168 Love Me a Little Bit Less/I Can't Afford Another Broken Heart
  King 15169 Mean to Me/Jealous
KAY ARMEN with GUY LOMBARDO ORCHESTRA
  De 18672 All at Once/Back Home for Keeps
KAY ARMEN with GLENN OSSER ORCHESTRA
  Sil(12″)29 The Song Is You

LPs
KAY ARMEN
  De DL-8835 The Golden Songs of Tin Pan Alley
(movie soundtrack)
  MGM E-3163 HIT THE DECK

50. ARMSTRONG, LIL p ar cm vo B
(maiden name LILLIAN HARD-IN)

Born February 3, 1902, Memphis, Tenn.
Died August 27, 1971, Chicago, Ill.

Jazz pianist with early bands, later led small band. Long career from pre-1920 till death. Studied music at Fisk University. Family moved to Chicago in 1917. Began playing sheet music at music store, jobbed with several bands. Worked briefly with Freddie Keppard. Led first group in 1920. With famed King Oliver at intervals 1921-4. Lil married trumpet jazz great Louis Armstrong in 1924 (separated several years later, divorced 1938). Continued to lead own band; Louis worked with it at intervals. In 1927 Lil recorded classic jazz works with Louis. Toured with Freddie Keppard. In late 20s Lil took more formal musical training in Chicago and New York. In 1930-32 led all-girl orchestra, played theatres and clubs. Then formed all-male orchestra, did radio work. Also worked as pianist in several stage revues. In mid-30s toured with all-male orchestra, finally settled in New York. In late 1936 began recording for Decca. Using all-star jazzmen, produced excellent small-band jazz. Featured vocalist on some of these records. In late 1940 returned to Chicago, worked there through 40s and early 50s, mostly as piano soloist. Long runs at several clubs. Played in Europe in 1952. Remained active through 50s and 60s, mostly in Chicago area. Jobs included long runs at club in Stickney, Ill. Composed several jazz numbers, including *Just for a Thrill*, *Brown Gal*, *Perdido Street Blues*, and her most famous (with Louis Armstrong), *Struttin' with Some Barbecue*. Lil suffered fatal heart attack August 27, 1971, while playing concert at Chicago's Civic Center Plaza to honor Louis, who had died July 6.

RECORDS

KING OLIVER
Para 12088 Southern Stomp
Para 20292 Mabel's Dream/Riverside Blues

Ge 5132 Dipper Mouth Blues/Weather Bird Blues
Ge 5133 Just Gone/Canal Street Blues
Ge 5274 Krooked Blues/Alligator Hop

NEW ORLEANS WANDERERS
Co 698-D Perdido Street Blues/Gatemouth
Co 735-D Too Tight/Papa Dip

LOUIS ARMSTRONG
OK 8299 Oriental Strut/You're Next
OK 8343 Don't Forget to Mess Around/I'm Gonna Gitcha
OK 8503 Potato Head Blues/Put 'Em Down Blues
OK 8566 Struttin' with Some Barbecue/Once in a While

LONNIE JOHNSON
Bb 8749 Lazy Woman Blues/In Love Again
Bb 8779 I Did All I Could/Chicago Blues

ZUTTY SINGLETON
De 18093 King Porter Stomp/Shim-Me-Sha-Wabble

LIL'S HOT SHOTS
Vo 1037 Drop That Sack/Georgia Bo Bo

LIL ARMSTRONG
De 1059 My Hi-De-Ho Man/Doin' the Susy Q
De 1092 Brown Gal/Or Leave Me Alone
De 1299 Bluer Than Blue/Born to Swing
De 7803 Riffin' the Blues/Why Is a Good Man So Hard to Find?
B&W(12")1210 Confessin'/East Town Boogie
B&W(12")1211 Lady Be Good/Little Daddy Blues

LPs

KING OLIVER
Epic LN-3208 (RIs)
LOUIS ARMSTRONG with KING OLIVER'S CREOLE JAZZ BAND
Riv(10")RLP-1029 (Ge RIs)
LOUIS ARMSTRONG
Co CL-851-4(4-LP set) The Louis Armstrong Story (OK RIs)
LIL HARDIN ARMSTRONG
Riv 401

51. ARMSTRONG, LOUIS t vo cm B
(nicknamed Satchelmouth and Satchmo)

Born July 4, 1900, New Orleans, La.
Died July 6, 1971, New York, N.Y.

All-time great trumpet star. Fabulous career pre-1920 till death. Achieved jazz fame as well as commercial success. Also celebrated for rough jazz-styled vocals. Much beloved figure in music. Grew up in rough neighborhood and as youngster sang, danced, clowned in streets for money. Put in waifs' home, learned trumpet. After release worked at odd nonmusical jobs several years. Occasionally played band jobs, finally had own group. First big job in 1918, replacing famous King Oliver in Kid Ory band. Riverboat jobs with Fate Marable for three years. In late 1921-2 worked with various bands in New Orleans, including those of Zutty Singleton and Papa Celestin. Joined King Oliver in mid-1922, toured, remained till mid-1924. Married Oliver's pianist, Lil Hardin. Later 1924-5 with Fletcher Henderson, became toast of New York jazz circles. Then worked at intervals with wife's band in Chicago. During 1926-8 led own groups and worked with Erskine Tate and Carroll Dickerson. In late 20s recorded a body of classic jazz with his Hot Five and Hot Seven. Through the years his recording output was prolific and rich. Jazzmen in early groups included Johnny and Baby Dodds, Earl Hines, Albert Nicholas, J. C. Higginbotham, Kid Ory. By late 20s Louis was acclaimed by most musicians and jazz fans as the greatest trumpeter. Style simple, tasteful and swinging, with purity of tone and effective use of high and middle register. Playing ahead of its time; stood out, all by itself; brought jazz of age, raised it to status of a sophisticated art. His jazz vocals important part of that art.

In 1929 Louis took a band to New York. Later freelanced, played jobs across the country, reached California mid-1930. Toured more, conquered Europe in 1932 and again in 1933-4. From late 1935 till mid-40s fronted Luis Russell big band. He and Lil Armstrong divorced 1938 after long separation. Formed new big band in 1944-5. In mid-1947 formed small jazz combo, Louis Armstrong & His All-Stars. Maintained truly all-star group for years, featuring at various times Jack Teagarden, Barney Bigard, Billy Kyle, Earl Hines, Trummy Young, Peanuts Hucko. Regular concert tours in U.S. and abroad from late 40s through 60s. Also on TV and in movies. Louis made many concert and TV appearances as single, later years featuring singing more than playing (which remained close to early style). Several hit records in early 50s with Gordon Jenkins orchestra backing. Great early 60s hit in *Hello, Dolly*, which remained associated with him ever after. Became great showman and entertainer, widely acclaimed wherever he appeared. Late 60s declining health slowed him down. Appeared infrequently 1971. When he died everyone felt a great loss. Tributes poured in from all over the world.

Louis composed such classic jazz numbers as *Heah Me Talkin' to Ya*; *Satchel Mouth Swing*; *Sugar Foot Stomp*; *Wild Man Blues*; *Ol' Man Mose*; *Struttin' with Some Barbecue*; *No Variety Blues*; *Hobo, You Can't Ride This Train*; *I Want a Big Butter and Egg Man, Someday You'll Be Sorry*. Made numerous movies: PENNIES FROM HEAVEN (1936), ARTISTS AND MODELS (1937), EVERY DAY'S A HOLIDAY (1938), CABIN IN THE SKY (1943), ATLANTIC CITY (1944), PILLOW TO POST (1945), NEW ORLEANS and CARNEGIE HALL (1947), A SONG IS BORN (1948), THE STRIP and HERE COMES THE GROOM (1951), GLORY ALLEY (1952), THE GLENN MILLER STORY (1954), HIGH SOCIETY (1956), SATCHMO THE GREAT (1957), THE FIVE PENNIES (1959), PARIS BLUES (1961), WHERE THE BOYS MEET THE GIRLS (1965), A MAN CALLED ADAM (1966), HELLO, DOLLY (1969).

RECORDS

KING OLIVER
Ge 5132 Dipper Mouth Blues
Ge 5135 Chimes Blues/Froggie Moore
OK 8235 Mabel's Dream
OK 40034 Riverside Blues

ERSKINE TATE
Vo 1027 Stomp Off, Let's Go/Static Strut

FLETCHER HENDERSON
Co 395-D Sugar Foot Stomp
Co 35669 Money Blues
Re 9753 One of These Days

CLARENCE WILLIAMS
OK 8181 Everybody Loves My Baby/ Of All the Wrongs You've Done to Me
OK 40260 Mandy, Make Up Your Mind/I'm a Little Blackbird

BESSIE SMITH
Co 14056-D Reckless Blues/Sobbin' Hearted Blues
Co 14064-D St. Louis Blues/Cold in Hand Blues

CLARA SMITH
Co 14077-D Shipwrecked Blues/My John Blues

BERTHA "CHIPPIE" HILL
OK 8453 Lonesome Weary Blues/ Lovesick Blues

LIL'S HOT SHOTS
Vo 1037 Drop That Sack/Georgia Bo Bo

LOUIS ARMSTRONG
OK 8299 Oriental Strut/You're Next
OK 8300 Heebie Jeebies/Muskrat Ramble
OK 8318 Georgia Grind/Come Back Sweet Papa
OK 8320 Cornet Chop Suey/My Heart
OK 8566 Struttin' with Some Barbecue/Once in a While
OK 8609 A Monday Date/Sugar Foot Strut
OK 8714 Ain't Misbehavin'/Black and Blue
OK 41448 Confessin'/If I Could Be with You
OK 41463 Memories of You/You're Lucky to Me
OK 41530 Star Dust/Wrap Your Troubles in Dreams
Vi 24233 I Gotta Right to Sing the Blues/Hustlin' and Bustlin' for Baby
Vi 24245 I've Got the World on a String/Sittin' in the Dark
De 648 On Treasure Island/Red Sails in the Sunset

De 685 The Music Goes 'Round and Around/Rhythm Saved the World
De 866 Swing That Music/Thankful
De 1661 Struttin' with Some Barbecue/Let That Be a Lesson to You
De 4327 Coquette/Among My Souvenirs
De 24752 Blueberry Hill/That Lucky Old Sun
Vi 20-2088 Where the Blues Were Born in New Orleans/Mahogany Hall Stomp

LOUIS ARMSTRONG & HIS ALL-STARS
Vi 20-2348 Rockin' Chair/Jack-Armstrong Blues
De 29102 Basin Street Blues (1 & 2)
(with GORDON JENKINS)
De 27899 It's All in the Game/When It's Sleepytime Down South
De 28076 Indian Love Call/Jeannine, I Dream of Lilac Time

LPs

FLETCHER HENDERSON
Co C4L19 (4-LP set) A Study in Frustration (Co, Ha, Vo RIs)

BESSIE SMITH
Co CL-855 The Bessie Smith Story, Vol. 1 (Co RIs)

KING OLIVER
Epic LN-3208 ((OK RIs)
Riv(10″)RLP-1029 Louis Armstrong with King Oliver's Creole Jazz Band (Ge RIs)

LOUIS ARMSTRONG
Co CL-851-2-3-4 (4-LP set) The Louis Armstrong Story (OK, Co RIs)
Riv 12-101 The Young Louis Armstrong (RIs)
De DL-8284 Jazz Classics (De RIs of 30s)
Vi LPM-1443 Town Hall Concert Plus
De DL-8329 New Orleans Nights (His All-Stars)
Kapp KS-3364 (S) Hello, Dolly!

LOUIS ARMSTRONG-ELLA FITZGERALD
Verve MGV-4011-1&2 (2-LP set) Porgy and Bess

52. ARNAZ, DESI   d vo B
Born c. 1917, Santiago, Cuba

Cuban singer and bongo-player, achieved prominence in TV in 50s co-starring with wife Lucille Ball in long-running series, I

Love Lucy. Educated in Miami. At 17 sang in local band, later sang with Xavier Cugat in mid-30s. In late 30s became bandleader, sang and played bongo drums. Good showman. Had role in 1939 Broadway musical TOO MANY GIRLS, minor roles in some movies, including movie version of TOO MANY GIRLS (1940) and FOUR JACKS AND A JILL (1941). Lucille Ball was one of the stars in the 1940 film and Arnaz married her that year. Continued as bandleader into late 40s. Band featured Latin-American music but could play smooth, sweet music as well. Featured Jane Harvey as vocalist for a time. Late 1946-7 Arnaz and band appeared on Bob Hope's radio show. Arnaz retired from music for a period but in 1950 reorganized band on west coast.

In 1951 Arnaz and Lucille began now-famous TV series, I Love Lucy. It caught on quickly and ran into late 50s, then continued as reruns. They established Desilu Productions, branched out producing other comedy shows and dramatic series that brought them tremendous TV success. Divorced in 1960. In 60s Arnaz continued producing, appeared infrequently on TV, sometimes with son Desi (also in show business).

RECORDS
DESI ARNAZ
    Co 35216 South American Way/La Conga en Nueva York
    Co 35400-1-2-3 (Conga Album)
    Co 39937 (TV theme) I Love Lucy/Brand New Baby
    Vi 20-2020 Tia Juana/I'll Never Love Again
    Vi 20-2052 Another Night Like This/Mi Vida
    Vi 20-2094 A Rainy Night in Rio/Through a Thousand Dreams
    Vi 20-2279 Tabu/La Cumparsita
    Vi 20-2281 Tico Tico/The Peanut Vendor
    Vi 25-1058 Cuban Pete/Without You

53. ARNELL, AMY   vo
Born c. 1919, Portsmouth, Va.
Vocalist with Tommy Tucker band in 30s and 40s. Attended William & Mary College. Performed on local radio, landed job with Tommy Tucker in 1937 when he was in Portsmouth. Remained with Tucker until late 1943. In 1938 they appeared on George Jessel's radio show, 30 Minutes in Hollywood. Greatest recognition came in late 1941 with Tucker hit record, *I Don't Want to Set the World on Fire*. Miss Arnell launched career as single in 1944. Tried dramatic roles, played summer stock. In 1946 on Abbott & Costello radio show. By late 40s, career had waned.

RECORDS
TOMMY TUCKER
    Pe 70522 There's a Lull in My Life
    Vo 3680 Ebb Tide/I Still Love to Kiss You Goodnight
    Vo 4399 Is That the Way to Treat a Sweetheart?
    Vo 5254 So Many Times/How Long Has This Been Going On?
    Vo 5543 Ain't You Ashamed!
    OK 5789 There I Go
    OK 5815 How Come, Baby, How Come?
    OK 6060 You're Dangerous
    OK 6177 Time and Time Again/Minnie from Trinidad
    OK 6211 New Worried Mind
    OK 6268 Kiss the Boys Goodbye
    OK 6320 I Don't Want to Set the World on Fire/This Love of Mine
    OK 6353 Jim
    OK 6592 How Do I Know It's Real?

54. ARNHEIM, GUS   p cm B
Born September 11, 1897, Philadelphia, Pa.
Died January 19, 1955, Los Angeles, Calif.
Bandleader of 20s and 30s, based on west coast. Early job as pianist in Abe Lyman band 1921-3 at Cocoanut Grove in Los Angeles. Played other jobs, composed several popular songs. Most famous: *I Cried for You* (1923), followed by *Mandalay* and *In the Land of Shady Palm Trees* (1924). Popular songs of early 30s were *It Must Be True* (1930), *Sweet and Lovely* and *I'm Gonna Get You* (1931). Formed own band in late 20s, toured U.S. and Europe, played theatres, clubs, ballrooms, appeared in 1929 film THE STREET GIRL.

Long runs at Cocoanut Grove, popular spot with film celebrities. Future singing star Russ Columbo in Arnheim band 1929-31. In early 1931 Bing Crosby's career as single received first boost when Bing and Rhythm Boys sang and recorded with band. Singer Donald Novis worked with band and future bandleader Jimmie Grier was saxman-arranger. At this time Arnheim band had tightly-knit sound and light-swinging, distinctive arrangements. Received nationwide attention late 1931 on Lucky Strike radio show, which featured "magic carpet" remotes of bands from dance spots across U.S. Band scored with popular 1931 record, *Sweet and Lovely*. By mid-30s developed into typical hotel-style group. Toured, appeared on Bing Crosby radio show 1934. Clarinet stars Woody Herman, Joe Dixon, Irving Fazola worked with Arnheim at different times. In 1936 Arnheim developed excellent swing-styled band with smooth, fluid sax section, biting brass. Budd Johnson of Earl Hines band did most of arranging. In 1937 pianist Stan Kenton joined, did some arranging. Good vocalist Jimmy Farrell featured during this period. Arnheim led band into mid-40s in various spots on west coast. Retired from band business several years but came back in 1954 to lead small band on west coast TV show for a time.

RECORDS

GUS ARNHEIM
(*Bing Crosby vocal; **Russ Columbo vocal)
OK 41037 Back in Your Own Backyard**/If I Can't Have You
OK 41174 I'll Get By/Avalon Town
Vi 22012 Singin' in the Rain
Vi 22054 Lovable and Sweet
Vi 22384 All I Want Is Just One/Dancing to Save Your Sole
Vi 22505 I'm Doin' That Thing/Go Home and Tell Your Mother
Vi 22546 A Peach of a Pair**
Vi 22561 It Must Be True*/Fool Me Some More*
Vi 22618 I Surrender Dear*/La Rosita
Vi 22691 Ho Hum*/I'm Gonna Get You*

Vi 22700 One More Time*/Thanks to You*
Vi 22758 Just One More Chance/At Your Command
Vi 22770 Sweet and Lovely/Red Red Roses
Vi 24054 You're Blasé/It Might Have Been You
Br 6729 Let's Fall in Love/Like Me a Little Bit Less
Br 6734 Coffee in the Morning, Kisses at Night
Br 6751 Don't Say Goodnight/Goin' to Heaven on a Mule
Br 7900 The Image of You/I'm Happy, Darling, Dancing with You
Br 7922 The Folks Who Live on the Hill/High, Wide and Handsome
Br 7931 My Cabin of Dreams/All You Want to Do Is Dance

55. ARNOLD, EDDY   vo g cm lyr B
Born May 15, 1918, near Henderson, Tenn.

Top artist in country and western music. After long career rose to great prominence in 60s. During career sometimes billed as The Tennessee Ploughboy. Grew up on farm, took early interest in music. Played for square dances in area. Early in career played on radio in Jackson, Tenn., in 1936. Later played radio, minor clubs, "joints" in Memphis, St. Louis, Louisville, many other locales. With Pee Wee King 1940-3. Attracted attention when featured with King group on Grand Ole Opry in Nashville. Became popular enough by 1943 to work as single. Landed own radio show in Nashville. Many appearances on Grand Ole Opry during 40s. First big year 1946 with hit record, *That's How Much I Love You*. Following years brought more hits: *Bouquet of Roses, Anytime, I'll Hold You in My Heart, Just a Little Lovin', Texarkana Baby, I Really Don't Want to Know, That Do Make It Nice*. Daily show in 1947 on Mutual radio used theme *The Cattle Call*.

Active on TV in early 50s with guest spots and syndicated series, Eddy Arnold Time. Made land deals and other investments which brought great wealth. With music scene in turmoil due to rock & roll and popular trends, career waned during 1955-63 and Arnold worked only occasionally. Decided to try comeback, changed to middle-of-road music style with good arrangements and attractive backing. Astutely selected good material to record. In later 60s had two great hit records, *What's He Doing in My World?* and *Make the World Go Away*. Latter became all-time favorite with Arnold fans, launched comeback. Appeared on top TV shows in later 60s and early 70s, also hosted many shows. Consistent crowd-pleaser, popular wherever he played in later years. Resumed busy recording schedule. Co-composer of many songs. Best known: *Just a Little Lovin', I'll Hold You in My Heart, C-H-R-I-S-T-M-A-S, I'm Throwing Rice at the Girl I Love, Easy on the Eyes, One Kiss Too Many, Will Santy Come to Shanty Town?, You Don't Know Me, Then I Turned and Slowly Walked Away.*

RECORDS

EDDY ARNOLD

Vi 20-1948 That's How Much I Love You/Chained to a Memory

Vi 20-2128 The Cattle Call/I Walk Alone

Vi 20-2332 I'll Hold You in My Heart/Don't Bother to Cry

Vi 20-2489 It Makes No Difference Now/Molly Darling

Vi 20-2700 Anytime/What a Fool I Was

Vi 20-2806 Bouquet of Roses/Texarkana Baby

Vi 20-3013 Just a Little Lovin'/My Daddy Is Only a Picture

Vi 20-3174 A Heart Filled with Love/Then I Turned and Slowly Walked Away

Vi 20-4413 Bundle of Southern Sunshine/Call Her Your Sweetheart

Vi 20-5415 If I Never Get to Heaven/Mama, Come Get Your Baby Boy

Vi 20-5525 I Really Don't Want to Know/I'll Never Get Over You

Vi 20-6139 The Kentuckian Song/The Cattle Call

Vi 21-0135 I'm Throwin' Rice at the Girl I Love/Just a Little Lovin'

Vi 21-0342 Cuddle Buggin' Baby/Enclosed, One Broken Heart

Vi 21-0390 White Christmas/Santa Claus Is Comin' to Town

Vi 21-0476 I Wanna Play House with You/Something Old, Something New

LPs

EDDY ARNOLD

Vi LPM-1223 All-Time Favorites

Vi LPM-1224 Any Time

Vi LPM-1293 A Dozen Hits

Vi LPM-1928 Have Guitar, Will Travel

Vi LPM-2337 Let's Make Memories Tonight

Vi LPM-2951 Pop Hits from the Country Side

Vi LPM-3466 My World

Vi LPM-3565 Best of Eddy Arnold

Vi LPM-3869 Turn the World Around

56. ASH, MARVIN   p o B
(MARVIN ASHBAUGH)

Born October 4, 1914, Lamar, Colo.

Barrelhouse-style pianist. Grew up in Kansas, played locally in early 30s. Band jobs with Connie Conrad, Herman Waldman, Jack Crawford in various areas. In mid-30s did staff work on Tulsa radio, played clubs, remained in area through 30s. In 1942 went to Los Angeles to play clubs. Military service, World War II. In 1945 worked with Wingy Manone in Los Angeles. Soloist in west coast clubs in later 40s. In 1950 played on radio and TV in Chicago. In 1951 back working on west coast. Late 1951 joined Jack Teagarden combo, remained till early 1953. Continued to work solo, lead small dixieland group or work in similar groups.

RECORDS

NAPPY LAMARE

Cap 884 Washington & Lee Swing/How Come You Do Me Like You Do?

MARVIN ASH

Cap 855 Sweethearts on Parade/Pearl House Rag

Cap 15435 Cannon Ball Rag/Maple Leaf Rag

Mirror 48 Sugar/I Left My Sugar Standing in the Rain

Mirror 49 Sugar, I'm Leaving/Sugar Bowl Boogie

Mirror 50 Sugar Blues/When My Sugar Walks Down the Street

Veltone 208 Cannon Ball/Peg o' My Heart

Veltone 209 Hangover Square/You Took Advantage of Me

LPs

MARVIN ASH

De DL-8346 New Orleans at Midnight JM(10″)335

GEORGE BRUNIS

Maximus 2584 Have a Good Time with Big George Brunis

(miscellaneous artists)

Cap(10″)H-188 Honky Tonk Piano

Blue Angel BAJC-505 (S) Jazz Party at Pasadena 1969, Vol. I

Blue Angel BAJC-506 (S) Jazz Party at Padadena 1969, Vol. II

57. ASH, PAUL   p cm lyr B

Born February 11, 1891, Saxony, Germany
Died July 13, 1958, New York, N.Y.

Leader of good dance band in 20s and early 30s. Came to U.S. in 1892, his family settling in Milwaukee. Received formal musical training. As youngster worked in band at burlesque house. In 1910 led first band in Springfield, Ill. Military service, World War I. In early 20s did some acting in silent movies, resumed leading band, began recording. In mid-20s composed several songs that enjoyed some popularity: *I'm Knee Deep in Daisies* and *What Do We Care If It's One O'clock?* (1925), *That's Why I Love You* and *Thinking of You* (1926; latter became Kay Kyser's theme song in 30s), *Hoosier Sweetheart* and *Just Once Again* (1927). By mid-20s Ash's band was playing sweet and semi-hot arrangements in fine style. Clarinetist Danny Polo played with band for a time. By late 20s Ash began to specialize as theatre conductor, led band at Chicago's Oriental Theatre for long run. Gave unknown singer Helen Kane first big break with his band at New York's Paramount Theatre, where she

became big hit. Led featured band at Chicago World's Fair in 1933. In mid-30s was musical director of Paramount Theatres in Brooklyn and New York. Led band at New York's Roxy Theatre from 1936 into mid-40s. Many famous jazzmen worked with Ash in various theatre bands.

RECORDS

MILTON WATSON (as pianist)

Co 712-D The Journey's End/I Can't Get Over a Girl Like You

PAUL ASH

Br 2428 Rememb'ring/Betty

Br 2964 Look Who's Here/Bam Bam Bamy Shore

Co 574-D Lantern of Love/After I Say I'm Sorry

Co 586-D Let's Talk About My Sweetie/Thanks for the Buggy Ride

Co 694-D Looking at the World Through Rose Colored Glasses/Her Beaus Are Only Rainbows

Co 839-D When I'm in Your Arms/There Ain't No Maybe in My Baby's Eyes

Co 944-D Shanghai Dream Man/Beedle Um Bo

Co 1066-D Ain't That a Grand and Glorious Feeling/I Ain't That Kind of a Baby

Co 1090-D Love and Kisses/Just Once Again

Co 1243-D Everywhere You Go/Looking for a Girl Like You

Co 1349-D My Pet/Dolores

Co 1531-D Ten Little Miles from Town/Out of the Dawn

Co 2796-D Blue Roses/Shadows on the Swanee

Co 2798-D Free/Louisville Lady

Va 505 Jamboree/Tiger Rag

Va 649 Raggin' the Scale/Yaaka Hula Hickey Dula

Ha 1234 I Got Rhythm

58. ASHBY, IRVING   g

Born December 29, 1920, Somerville, Mass.

Good rhythm guitarist, capable soloist. Active with several key groups in 40s and 50s. Attended New England Conservatory. Early important job with Lionel

Hampton late 1940-2. Military service, World War II. After discharge worked in Los Angeles area. With Jazz at the Philharmonic unit in 1946. Joined King Cole Trio late 1947, replacing Oscar Moore. Remained till 1951. With Oscar Peterson Trio 1951-2, including tour with Jazz at the Philharmonic. In mid-50s played rhythm and blues jobs on west coast with Ernie Freeman.

RECORDS

LIONEL HAMPTON
Vi 27278 Lost Love/Smart Alec
Vi 27316 Altitude/I Nearly Lost My Mind
Vi 27364 Fiddle Dee Dee/Bouncing at the Beacon

JAZZ AT THE PHILHARMONIC
Clef 101-2 J.A.T.P. Blues (1 & 2)
Clef 103-4 J.A.T.P. Blues (3 & 4)

FATS WALLER
Vi(12″)40-4003 Moppin' and Boppin'/Ain't Misbehavin'

HOLLYWOOD HUCKSTERS
Cap 40022 Them There Eyes/Happy Blues

HOWARD MCGHEE
B&W 150 Oodie Coo Bop (1 & 2)

ILLINOIS JACQUET
Clef 89164 Learnin' the Blues/Honeysuckle Rose

LESTER YOUNG
Alad 137 You're Driving Me Crazy/New Lester Leaps In
Alad 138 She's Funny That Way/Lester's Be-Bop Boogie

ANDRE PREVIN
Sun 7363 Take the "A" Train/I Got It Bad
Sun 7365 Warm Valley/Subtle Slough

KING COLE TRIO
Cap 813 When I Take My Sugar to Tea/If I Had You
Cap 15036 The Geek/I've Only Myself to Blame
Cap 15165 Little Girl

IRVING ASHBY
Imp 5426 Loco-Motion/Night Winds

LPs

LIONEL HAMPTON
Jazztone J-1246 Lionel Hampton's All-Star Groups (Vi RIs)

JAZZ AT THE PHILHARMONIC
Clef(10″)MG-6 J.A.T.P. Blues
Clef(10″)MG-14 I Got Rhythm/I Surrender Dear

KING COLE TRIO
Cap(10″)H-177

OSCAR PETERSON
Clef(10″)119 Oscar Peterson Plays Pretty

JACKIE DAVIS
Cap T-815 Chasing Shadows

WARDELL GRAY
Cr 5004 Way Out Wardell

DICK MARX
Omega OSL-2 (S) Marx Makes Broadway

(miscellaneous artists)
Tops(10″)L-928-69 Junior Jazz at the Auditorium

59. ASMUSSEN, SVEND   v p vo B

Born February 28, 1916, Copenhagen, Denmark

Jazz violinist with tasteful, inventive style. Although began career during swing period of mid-30s, he adapted well to progressive jazz. Began professionally in 1933. Next year led own combo, playing violin along Joe Venuti lines and doubling on piano. Spent entire career in Denmark except for occasional tours. In addition to jazz talents, excellent entertainer. With singing and comedy, his combo provided versatile floor show. Came to U.S. in 1955 as part of a cafe act but played no jazz clubs. Had prolific recording career in Denmark. Still active playing clubs during 60s.

RECORDS

SVEND ASMUSSEN
Hit 8057 Tea for Two/Ring Dem Bells
Hit 8058 June Night/Miss Annabelle Lee
Od(Fr) 5535 C'est Si Bon/Your Voice
Od(Den) 398 Star Dust/Honeysuckle Rose
Od(Den) 408 Night and Day/Some of These Days
Od(Den) 412 An Old Curiosity Shop/I've Got My Eyes on You
Od(Den) 429 Yodel Swing/Choo-Bang
Od(Den) 448 Sweet Sue/Limehouse Blues

Od(Den) 449 Japanese Sandman/Lady
  Be Good
Od(Den) 471 Den Lille Melodi/When
  You Wish Upon a Star
Tono(Swed) 4283 Gershwin Medley (1
  & 2)
Tono(Swed) 4352 Cherokee/My Rev-
  erie
Tono(Swed) 18019 Three   Little
  Words/Sonny Boy
Od(Swed) 5234 Believe It, Beloved/
  Just a Gigolo
Od(Swed) 5243 St. Louis Blues/Lone-
  some Road
Od(Swed) 5369 They Didn't Believe
  Me/Nature Boy

LPs

SVEND ASMUSSEN
  Angel(10")60000 And His Unmelan-
    choly Danes
  Angel(10")60010 Rhythm Is Our Busi-
    ness
SVEND ASMUSSEN-JOHN LEWIS
  Atl 1392 European Encounter

60. ASTAIRE, ADELE   vo
  (ADELE AUSTERLITZ)

Born in Omaha, Nebr.

Dancing-singing star of Broadway shows
in dance team with brother Fred. Performed in show business 1906-32. Ended
career for marriage, became Lady Charles
Cavendish in 1932.
(See FRED ASTAIRE biography for details
of career.)

RECORDS

FRED & ADELE ASTAIRE
  Co (E)3970 "Oh, Lady Be Good"
    Medley (1 & 2)
  Vi L-24003 "The Band Wagon" Med-
    ley

LPs

FRED & ADELE ASTAIRE
  Mon-Ever MES-7036 Lady Be Good!
    (RIs)

61. ASTAIRE, FRED   vo cm
  (FREDERICK AUSTERLITZ)

Born May 10, 1899, Omaha, Nebr.

Dancing giant, singing and acting star of
stage and screen over 50 years. Generally
considered most talented of dancers. Performed in smooth, elegant style, developed many intricate and innovative routines. Sang in light and sophisticated
manner, adept in delivery of lyrics. A
favorite of many composers for performing their songs. Co-starred with Ginger
Rogers in distinguished series of popular
movie musicals in middle and late 30s.
Later worked with other dancing partners. Top movie star for four decades.
First professional appearance at 5 in
Paterson, N. J. Performed in vaudeville
with sister Adele in dancing act until
1916. They began Broadway career with
supporting roles in OVER THE TOP (1917).
Other shows followed: THE PASSING SHOW
OF 1918, APPLE BLOSSOMS (1919), THE
LOVE LETTER (1921). By this time, Astaire
were headliners. Starred in FOR GOODNESS
SAKE and THE BUNCH AND JUDY (1922),
LADY BE GOOD (1924), FUNNY FACE (1927),
SMILES (1930), THE BAND WAGON (1931).
Also appeared in London in STOP FLIRT-
ING (1923; actually THE BUNCH AND JUDY
retitled) and LADY BE GOOD (1926). Team
broke up in 1932 when Adele married and
became Lady Charles Cavendish.
Fred's first solo stage role in GAY
DIVORCE (1932), later played same show
in London. This led to movie test and
contract. Played small, uneventful dancing role in movie DANCING LADY (1933).
But in late 1933 movie FLYING DOWN TO
RIO joined with Ginger Rogers as dance
team in secondary leads, was instant hit.
Personality, charm, dancing and singing,
made Astaire a natural for films. Co-
starred with Miss Rogers during 30s in
eight other popular musicals which introduced many great songs. Team then
broke up (reunited once in 1949 movie)
and Astaire danced in 40s and 50s movies
with Rita Hayworth, Vera-Ellen, Cyd
Charisse, Audrey Hepburn, others. Also
appeared in dramatic roles. Starred on
own radio series in mid-30s, made appearances on others over the years. Appearances on TV in 50s, 60s and 70s including two series, It Takes a Thief and
The Over-the-Hill Gang. Two widely
acclaimed specials of his own in 1958
and 1960.
Leading songs associated with Astaire
include: *Oh, Lady Be Good*; *Fascinating*

Rhythm; *'S Wonderful*; *Dancing in the Dark*; *I Love Louisa*; *Night and Day*; *Carioca*; *The Continental*; *I Won't Dance*; *Cheek to Cheek*; *Top Hat, White Tie and Tails*; *Let's Face the Music and Dance*; *The Way You Look Tonight*; *A Fine Romance*; *Bojangles of Harlem*; *They Can't Take That Away from Me*; *A Foggy Day*; *Change Partners*; *Dearly Beloved*; *One for My Baby*; *Steppin' Out with My Baby*. In 1953 Astaire made outstanding LP record set, The Fred Astaire Story, featuring songs associated with him. Done in impeccable taste, it featured excellent jazz backing by small combo of leading modern musicians. Astaire composed popular song of 1936, *I'm Building Up to an Awful Letdown*. Other compositions: *I'll Never Let You Go*; *Blue without You*; *Sweet Sorrow*; *Just One More Dance, Madame*; *If Swing Goes, I Go Too*; *Just Like Taking Candy from a Baby*; *Oh, My Achin' Back*. By late 60s Astaire became less active in show business.

MOVIES
(*with Ginger Rogers*)
1933—DANCING LADY; FLYING DOWN TO RIO*
1934—THE GAY DIVORCEE*
1935—ROBERTA*; TOP HAT*
1936—FOLLOW THE FLEET*; SWING TIME*
1937—SHALL WE DANCE?*; A DAMSEL IN DISTRESS
1938—CAREFREE*
1939—THE STORY OF VERNON AND IRENE CASTLE*
1940—BROADWAY MELODY OF 1940
1941—SECOND CHORUS; YOU'LL NEVER GET RICH
1942—HOLIDAY INN; YOU WERE NEVER LOVELIER
1943—THE SKY'S THE LIMIT
1945—YOLANDA AND THE THIEF
1946—ZIEGFELD FOLLIES; BLUE SKIES
1948—EASTER PARADE
1949—THE BARKLEYS OF BROADWAY*
1950—THREE LITTLE WORDS; LET'S DANCE
1951—ROYAL WEDDING
1952—BELLE OF NEW YORK
1953—THE BAND WAGON
1955—DADDY LONG LEGS
1956—FUNNY FACE
1957—SILK STOCKINGS
1959—ON THE BEACH

1961—THE PLEASURE OF HIS COMPANY
1962—NOTORIOUS LANDLADY
1968—FINIAN'S RAINBOW
1969—THE MIDAS RUN

RECORDS
LEO REISMAN
Vi 22755 I Love Louisa/New Sun in the Sky
Vi 24193 Night and Day/I've Got You on My Mind
Vi 24262 Maybe I Love You Too Much
Vi 24315 The Gold Digger's Song
FRED & ADELE ASTAIRE
Co (E)3970 "Oh, Lady Be Good" Medley (1 & 2)
Vi L-24003 "The Band Wagon" Medley
FRED ASTAIRE with BENNY GOODMAN ORCHESTRA
Co 35517 Who Cares?/Just Like Taking Candy from a Baby
FRED ASTAIRE
Co 2912-D Flying Down to Rio/Music Makes Me
Br 7486 Cheek to Cheek/No Strings
Br 7487 Top Hat, White Tie and Tails/Isn't This a Lovely Day?
Br 7608 Let's Face the Music and Dance/Let Yourself Go
Br 7610 I'm Building Up to an Awful Letdown/I'd Rather Lead a Band
Br 7717 The Way You Look Tonight/Pick Yourself Up
Br 7718 Bojangles of Harlem/Never Gonna Dance
Br 7855 They Can't Take That Away from Me/Beginner's Luck
Br 7856 They All Laughed/Slap That Bass
Br 7982 A Foggy Day/Can't Be Bothered Now
Br 7983 Nice Work If You Can Get It/Things Are Looking Up
Br 8189 Change Partners/I Used to Be Color Blind
Co 35815 Love of My Life/Me and the Ghost Upstairs
De 18187 So Near and Yet So Far/Since I Kissed My Baby Goodbye
De 18489 You Were Never Lovelier/On the Beam
De 23650 Puttin' on the Ritz/A Cou-

ple of Song and Dance Men (with BING CROSBY)

MGM 30517 Baby Doll/When I'm Out with the Belle of New York

MGM 30520 I Wanna Be a Dancin' Man/Bachelor Dinner Song

FRED ASTAIRE-JANE POWELL

MGM 30316 How Could You Believe Me?

FRED ASTAIRE-JACK BUCHANAN

MGM 30795 I Guess I'll Have to Change My Plan

LPs

FRED ASTAIRE

Epic LN-3137 The Best of Fred Astaire (Br RIs)

"X" LVA-1001 (with LEO REISMAN ORCHESTRA) (Vi RIs)

Mer 1001-2-3-4 (4-LP set) The Fred Astaire Story

MGM PR-1 Sings and Swings Irving Berlin

FRED & ADELE ASTAIRE

Mon-Ever MES-7036 Lady Be Good! (RIs)

(movie soundtracks)

MGM E-3051 THE BAND WAGON

MGM(10″)E-502 EASTER PARADE

MGM(10″)E-516 THREE LITTLE WORDS

MGM(10″)E-543 ROYAL WEDDING

Metro M-615 THREE LITTLE WORDS

62. ATTERIDGE, HAROLD   lyr

Born July 9, 1886, Lake Forest, Ill.
Died January 15, 1938, Lynbrook, N.Y.

Important writer for Broadway shows 1911-29. Prolific career writing book and lyrics. Songs mostly effective in context of shows. Best known: *By the Beautiful Sea* (1914), *Fascination* (1915), *Bagdad* (1918). Specialized in extravaganzas and shows of revue type, particularly THE PASSING SHOW series. Connected with Al Jolson hit shows ROBINSON CRUSOE, JR., SINBAD, BOMBO, BIG BOY, others. Educated at University of Chicago. In addition to work on Broadway shows, in later years wrote for radio and helped adapt stage productions to movies. Chief collaborators were composers Harry Carroll, Louis Hirsch, Al Jolson, Otto Motzan, Sigmund Romberg, Jean Schwartz, Al Goodman.

BROADWAY MUSICALS
(wrote book and/or lyrics)

1911—REVUE OF REVUES; VERA VIOLETTA

1912—BROADWAY TO PARIS; TWO LITTLE BRIDES; THE PASSING SHOW OF 1912; THE WHIRL OF SOCIETY

1913—THE HONEYMOON EXPRESS; THE MAN WITH THREE WIVES; THE PASSING SHOW OF 1913

1914—THE BELLE OF BOND STREET; DANCING AROUND; THE PASSING SHOW OF 1914; THE WHIRL OF THE WORLD

1915—MAID IN AMERICA; THE PASSING SHOW OF 1915; THE PEASANT GIRL; A WORLD OF PLEASURE

1916—RUGGLES OF RED GAP; ROBINSON CRUSOE, JR.; THE SHOW OF WONDERS; THE PASSING SHOW OF 1916

1917—DOING OUR BIT; OVER THE TOP; THE PASSING SHOW OF 1917

1918—FOLLOW THE GIRL; THE PASSING SHOW OF 1918; SINBAD

1919—THE LITTLE BLUE DEVIL; MONTE CRISTO, JR.; THE PASSING SHOW OF 1919

1920—CINDERELLA ON BROADWAY

1921—BOMBO; THE LAST WALTZ; MIDNIGHT ROUNDERS OF 1921; THE PASSING SHOW OF 1921

1922—MAKE IT SNAPPY; THE PASSING SHOW OF 1922; THE ROSE OF STAMBOUL

1923—ARTISTS AND MODELS OF 1923; THE DANCING GIRL; TOPICS OF 1923; THE PASSING SHOW OF 1923

1924—THE DREAM GIRL; INNOCENT EYES; MARJORIE; THE PASSING SHOW OF 1924

1925—ARTISTS AND MODELS OF 1925; BIG BOY; GAY PAREE; SKY HIGH

1926—GREAT TEMPTATIONS; A NIGHT IN PARIS

1927—A NIGHT IN SPAIN; ZIEGFELD FOLLIES OF 1927

1928—GREENWICH VILLAGE FOLLIES OF 1928

1929—PLEASURE BOUND

63. ATWELL, ROY   vo cm

Born May 2, 1878, Syracuse, N.Y.
Died February 6, 1962, New York, N.Y.

Comedian, sometime singer who played

supporting and starring roles in Broadway shows. Composed *Some Little Bug Is Going to Find You* featured in show ALONE AT LAST (1915). Member of Fortune Gallo Opera Company. Active in radio in 30s. Appeared several years on Fred Allen show as tongue-twisted comic.

BROADWAY MUSICALS

1905—MOONSHINE
1906—MARRYING MARY
1908—THE MIMIC WORLD
1912—THE FIREFLY
1914—THE LAUGHING HUSBAND
1915—ALONE AT LAST
1918—OH, MY DEAR!
1919—APPLE BLOSSOMS
1923—HELEN OF TROY, NEW YORK
1926—AMERICANA
1929—JOHN MURRAY ANDERSON'S ALMA-
NAC
1933—STRIKE ME PINK

64. AUGUST, JAN   p xyl B
(JAN AUGUSTOFF)

Born c. 1912, New York, N.Y.

Popular recording artist of 40s and 50s with "society" piano style. Specialized in Latin-American music. Self-taught musician, played in Greenwich Village clubs as youngster. Later studied with prominent teachers. Early important job as pianist with Paul Specht band several years. Hand injury forced temporary retirement from music. Later led own band, took up xylophone. Played xylophone with Paul Whiteman, Ferde Grofe and Joe Moss on radio in early and mid-30s. Then as piano soloist played clubs and hotels in New York and Brooklyn. Attained prominence by mid-40s through records. Scored in 1946 with *Misirlou*. Continued recording and playing clubs in 50s. Gradually faded.

RECORDS

JAN AUGUST

Mer 1056 Dancing in the Dark/Oye
Negra
Mer 5112 Misirlou/Zigeuner
Mer 5175 Yours Is My Heart Alone/
Dark Eyes
Mer 5288 Nola/Cumbanchero
Diam 2032 My Shawl/Without You
Diam 2069 Malaguena/Ay Ay Ay
Diam 2078 Tango of Roses/Jan's
Boogie
(with THE HARMONICATS)
Mer 5399 Bewitched/Blue Prelude
Mer 70056 Finesse/Ti-Pi-Tin
(with ROBERTA QUINLAN and THE HAR-
MONICATS)
Mer 5420 I Never Had a Worry in the
World/Buffalo Billy
(with RICHARD HAYMAN)
Mer 7078 Moritat/In Apple Blossom
Time

LPs

JAN AUGUST

Mer MG-20078 Music for the Quiet
Hour
Mer MG-20408 Cha-Cha Charm
Mer MG-20513 Plays Great Piano
Hits
Mer(10")MG-25003

65. AULD, GEORGE ts as cm B
(JOHN ALTWERGER)

Born May 19, 1919, Toronto, Canada

Tenor sax star of swing era who bridged gap to progressive jazz. Played gutty, forceful jazz solos in excellent taste. Child prodigy on alto sax, won scholarship and studied with sax virtuoso Rudy Wiedoeft in U.S. Became interested in jazz, switched to tenor sax. Led own combo at intervals, jobbed in New York. Won prominence as featured soloist with Bunny Berigan band early 1937 to late 1938; work shone with Artie Shaw in 1939. When Shaw quit abruptly in late 1939, Auld led band briefly. With Jan Savitt during early 1940, then with Benny Goodman late 1940 to mid-1941. Again with Shaw to early 1942. Led own band in 1942. Brief military service in 1943. During 1943-6 led own groups, small and large. As bop emerged in mid-40s, Auld adapted easily. With Billy Eckstine in 1948. Led several outstanding groups in late 40s and early 50s. With Count Basie briefly in 1950. Played role in Broadway play THE RAT RACE. Early 50s some commercial recordings, sometimes with chorus in background. Settled in California, ran own night club mid-50s. Studio work on west coast and New York late 50s. Composed several jazz numbers. Settled in Las Vegas and continued semiactive through 60s mostly in that area, freelancing or leading band.

RECORDS

BUNNY BERIGAN

Vi 25609 All God's Chillun Got Rhythm/The Lady from Fifth Avenue

Vi 25811 Down Stream/Sophisticated Swing

Vi 26001 Russian Lullaby

Vi 26086 Simple and Sweet/I Won't Tell a Soul

Vi 26138 Black Bottom/Trees

ARTIE SHAW

Bb 10202 One Night Stand/One Foot in the Groove

Bb 10307 When Winter Comes

Bb 10319 All I Remember Is You/Octoroon

Bb 10324 I Can't Afford to Dream/Comes Love

Bb 10430 Oh, Lady Be Good

Bb 10468 A Table in a Corner

Bb 10502 I Didn't Know What Time It Was

Vi 27705 Make Love to Me/Solid Sam

BENNY GOODMAN ORCHESTRA

Co 35863 Hard to Get/Frenesi

Co 35916 I'm Always Chasing Rainbows/Somebody Stole My Gal

Co 35977 Birds of a Feather/You're Dangerous

Co 36180 Scarecrow/Time on My Hands

Co(12")55002 Superman

BENNY GOODMAN SEXTET

Co 35810 Wholly Cats/Royal Garden Blues

Co 35901 As Long as I Live/Benny's Bugle

Co 35938 On the Alamo/Gone with What Draft

Co 36039 Breakfast Feud/I Found a New Baby

Co 36099 Good Enough to Keep/A Smo-o-o-ooth One

Co 36755 I Can't Give You Anything but Love, Baby

BARNEY BIGARD

B&W(12")1206 Poon Tang/Blues Before Dawn

CHUBBY JACKSON

NJ 830 Sax Appeal

AULD-HAWKINS-WEBSTER SAXTET

Apo 754 Pick-up Boys/Porgy

GEORGE AULD

Vs 8159 This Is Romance/The Juke Box Jump

Vs 8212 Sweet Sue/With the Wind and the Rain in Your Hair

Mus 374 Co-Pilot/Stormy Weather

Mus 394 Mo-Mo/You're Blasé

Mus 15059 Blue Moon/Seems Like Old Times

Dis 109 Darn That Dream/Vox Bop

Dis 117 Settin' the Pace/Mild and Mellow

Roost 523 New Air Mail Special/Out of Nowhere

Roost 527 Taps Miller/What's New?

Apo 359 Taps Miller/Concerto for Tenor

Mer 70797 Tippin' In/Love Is Just Around the Corner

LPs

GEORGE AULD

Br BL-54034 That's Auld

GA 33-316 Jazz Concert (1 side, Apo RIs)

EmArcy MG-36090 Dancing in the Land of Hi-Fi

Dis(10")DL-3007 That's Auld!

Cap 1045 Sax Gone Latin

ARTIE SHAW

Vi LPM-1244 Moonglow (Bb, Vi RIs)

CHARLIE CHRISTIAN with BENNY GOODMAN SEXTET & ORCHESTRA

Co CL-652 (Co RIs)

BUDDY DEFRANCO

Verve MGV-2089 Plays Benny Goodman

MAYNARD FERGUSON

EmArcy MG-36076 Around the Horn

BUNNY BERIGAN

Vi LPV-581 His Trumpet and Orchestra, Original 1937-9 Recordings (Vi RIs)

Cam CAL-550 Bunny (Vi RIs)

66. AUSTIN, GENE   p vo cm

Born June 24, 1900, Gainesville, Texas
Died January 24, 1972, Palm Springs, Calif.

Well-known entertainer, top recording artist of 20s. Had soft voice and effortless manner, played piano in same easy style to complement voice perfectly. Grew up in Yellow Pine, La., and Minden, La. At 15 ran off with circus, there learned to play calliope. Military service, World War I. Later teamed with Roy Bergere in vaudeville. They composed hit song of 1924, *How Come You Do Me Like You Do?*, which became standard, as did two other Austin songs: *When My Sugar Walks Down the Street* (1924) and *The Lonesome Road* (1929). *Ridin' Around in the Rain* enjoyed popularity in 1934.

Austin began recording career in mid-20s, established himself as star with 1927 hit record of *My Blue Heaven*. Multimillion seller, remained top all-time seller until supplanted by Bing Crosby's *White Christmas* fifteen years later. By early 30s Austin's name had faded. He remained active, working clubs as soloist or with small group. Good M.C., entertainer and showman, sometimes worked with Candy & Coco. In 1934 appeared in movie GIFT OF GAB, singing *Blue Sky Avenue* (probably an attempt at a sequel to his great hit of 1927). Brief roles in SADIE MCKEE (1934) and KLONDIKE ANNIE (1935; wrote song for film's star, Mae West, *I'm an Occidental Woman in an Oriental Mood for Love*). In mid-30s dropped out of show business for a time but came back as featured vocalist on Joe Penner radio show late 1936-8. In early 40s Austin ran own club in California, titled Blue Heaven. In later years largely inactive in entertainment world, save for occasional club jobs and rare TV appearances. Probably last public appearance early 1971 on Merv Griffin late-night TV show that spotlighted various composers.

RECORDS

GENE AUSTIN
Vi 19625 Yearning/No Wonder
Vi 19857 Save Your Sorrow
Vi 20411 Sunday/Thinking of You
Vi 20964 My Blue Heaven/Are You Thinking of Me Tonight?
Vi 21015 My Melancholy Baby/There's a Cradle in Caroline
Vi 21098 The Lonesome Road
Vi 21779 Sonny Boy/She's Funny That Way

Vi 21798 I Can't Give You Anything but Love/If You Miss Me Tonight
Vi 21856 Weary River/The Song I Love
Vi 22223 My Fate Is in Your Hands/All I'm Asking Is Sympathy
Vi 22341 Let Me Sing and I'm Happy/To My Mammy
Vi 22416 Under a Texas Moon/Telling It to the Daisies
Vi 22451 Absence Makes the Heart Grow Fonder/Rollin' Down the River
Vi 24663 All I Do Is Dream of You/Ridin' Around in the Rain
Vi 24725 Blue Sky Avenue/When the Roll Is Called Up Yonder
Pe 15513 What Is It?/Who Am I?
Pe 15526 Guilty/Blue Kentucky Moon
De 926 If I Had My Way/I Cried for You
De 1656 (with CANDY & COCO) China Boy/Dear Old Southland
De 3939 Carolina Moon/Tonight You Belong to Me
Universal 131 I'm Coming Home/Give Me a Home in Oklahoma

LPs

GENE AUSTIN
Vik LX-998 Sings All-Time Favorites (Vi RIs)
De DL-8433 My Blue Heaven
Dot DLP-3300 Gene Austin's Great Hits
(miscellaneous artists)
De DEA-7-2 (2-LP set) Those Wonderful Thirties

67. AUSTIN, JOHNNY   t d B

Best known for hot trumpet with Jan Savitt band in late 30s and early 40s. Solo work became distinctive part of band, an intense and steady flow of notes, dirty-toned and hard-swinging. With young Glenn Miller band from early 1938 to early 1939, just before it soared to the heights. With Savitt 1939 to early 1941. Joined Larry Clinton in mid-1941. In 1943 played in Abe Lyman band. Jobbed about during following years and in late 40s led own group. Based in Philadelphia, led band in 50s, sometimes on tours which included college dates. Through

60s Austin was still fronting bands occasionally in Philadelphia area.

RECORDS

JAN SAVITT

De 2540 That's a-Plenty/When Buddha Smiles

De 2583 I'll Always Be in Love with You

De 2771 El Rancho Grande

De 3019 Rose of the Rio Grande/ Blues in the Groove

LPs

JAN SAVITT

De DL-79243 The Top Hatters, 1939-41 (De RIs)

68. AUSTIN, LOVIE   p B
(CORA CALHOUN)

Born September 19, 1897, Chattanooga, Tenn.
Died July 10, 1972, Chicago, Ill.

Jazz pianist of 20s. College training in Nashville and Knoxville. Toured in vaudeville and with revues. Played widely before settling in Chicago, where during 20s and 30s she worked mostly as musical director at theatres. Long run at Monogram Theatre. Recorded extensively in 20s, leading own jazz groups and accompanying blues singers. Combo billed as Lovie Austin & Her Blues Serenaders, used outstanding jazzmen. Defense work, World War II. Returned to theatre work, later served as dancing school pianist. Remained active through 50s.

RECORDS

LOVIE AUSTIN

Para 12255 Steppin' on the Blues/ Travelin' Blues

Para 12277 Peepin' Blues

Para 12283 Heebie Jeebies/Mojo Blues

Para 12300 Don't Shake It No More/ Rampart Street Blues

Para 12313 Too Sweet for Words

Para 12361 Jackass Blues/Frog Tongue Stomp

Para 12380 Chicago Mess Around/ Galion Stomp

Para 12391 Merry Makers' Twine/In the Alley Blues

IDA COX

Para 12044 Graveyard Dream Blues/ Weary Way Blues

Para 12053 Any Woman's Blues/Blue Monday Blues

Para 12291 Black Crepe Blues/Fare Thee Well Poor Gal

Para 12298 Mistreatin' Daddy Blues/ Southern Woman's Blues

Para 12307 Long Distance Blues/ Lonesome Blues

MA RAINEY

Para 12080 Boweavil Blues/Last Minute Blues

Para 12081 Bad Luck Blues/Those All Night Long Blues

Para 12215 Those Dogs of Mine/ Lucky Rock Blues

EDMONIA HENDERSON

Para 12084 Black Man Blues/Worried 'Bout Him Blues

Para 12095 Brownskin Man/Traveling Blues

VIOLA BARTLETTE

Para 12322 Go Back Where You Stayed Last Night/Tennessee Blues

Para 12363 You Don't Mean Me No Good/Out Bound Train Blues

OZIE MCPHERSON

Para 12327 Outside of That/You Gotta Know How

Para 12350 Standing on the Corner Blues/He's My Man

ETHEL WATERS

Para 12214 Tell 'Em 'Bout Me/You'll Need Me When I'm Long Gone

Para 12230 Black Spatch Blues/I Want Somebody All My Own

LPs

TOMMY LADNIER with LOVIE AUSTIN'S BLUES SERENADERS

Riv(10″)1026 (Para RIs)

MA RAINEY

Riv(10″)1016 (Para RIs)

ALBERTA HUNTER with LOVIE AUSTIN & HER BLUES SERENADERS

Riv RLP-418 (recorded in 1961)

69. AUTREY, HERMAN   t B

Born December 4, 1904, Evergreen, Ala.

Trumpet jazzman in Fats Waller combo of 30s. Distinctive style and fresh ideas in solo work as well as accompaniment. Went to Pittsburgh in 1923, played locally and toured. Jobbed in Washington, D.C., in late 20s, also did pit band work.

Jobbed in Philadelphia 1929-32, did much theatre band work. In 1933 joined Charlie Johnson band in New York. In 1934-9 with popular Fats Waller combo, Autrey enjoyed his greatest period. On group's recordings, Autrey's happy and inventive trumpet sparked many a session, especially those on which he teamed with Eugene Sedric (cl, ts). Two combined to produce fine free-wheeling jazz behind Waller. Autrey wrote good swing number, *Yacht Club Swing*. In 1940 joined Claude Hopkins (also briefly with him in 1938). In early 40s with Stuff Smith and Una Mae Carlisle. Freelanced in late 40s and 50s, led own band at times. Jobs with Sol Yaged in New York in mid-50s. Continued active into 70s, mostly with The Saints and Sinners group, touring abroad and freelancing.

RECORDS

FATS WALLER
    Vi 24641 I Wish I Were Twins/Armful of Sweetness
    Vi 24737 Sweetie Pie
    Vi 24742 Let's Pretend There's a Moon/Serenade for a Wealthy Widow
    Vi 24889 What's the Reason?/Pardon My Love
    Vi 24892 Whose Honey Are You?
    Vi 25087 12th Street Rag/Sweet Sue
    Vi 25116 Truckin'/The Girl I Left Behind Me
    Vi 25120 You're So Darn Charming
    Vi 25342 It's a Sin to Tell a Lie/Big Chief DeSota
    Vi 25348 Let's Sing Again/The More I Know You
    Vi 25530 I Can't Break the Habit of You
    Bb 10008 You Look Good to Me
    Bb 10035 Yacht Club Swing
    Bb 10369 Anita
MABEL ROBINSON
    De 8601 Me and My Chauffeur/I've Got Too Many Blues
SAM PRICE
    De 8624 Blow Katy Blow
    De 8649 It's All Right Jack
SEDRIC & HIS HONEY BEARS
    Vo 4552 Choo-Choo/The Wail of the Scromph

    Vo 4576 The Joint Is Jumpin'/Off Time

LPs

FATS WALLER
    Jazztone J-1247 Plays and Sings (Bb RIs)
    Vi LPV-537 Fractious Fingering (Vi RIs)
    Vi LPT-1001 Plays and Sings (Vi RIs)
    Vi LPM-1502 Handful of Keys (Vi RIs)
THE SAINTS & SINNERS
    MPS 15174 In Europe

70. AUTRY, GENE   vo g cm lyr B
Born September 29, 1907, Tioga Springs, Texas

First cowboy singing star of movies. Fabulous career in films, radio, records, TV. All-time great in country and western music. Grew up in Oklahoma and Texas. Worked as cowboy in early days, also as telegrapher in Sapulpa, Okla. Sang on radio in Oklahoma in late 20s, including period on Tulsa station 1929-30. During 1930-4 appeared on WLS National Barn Dance from Chicago. Also played vaudeville and recorded. Went to Hollywood in 1934. First movie role in Ken Maynard movie IN OLD SANTA FE. Then 13-chapter serial, THE PHANTOM EMPIRE. First starring feature film TUMBLING TUMBLEWEEDS.

During movie career lasting into early 50s, Autry made about 100 movies. Also became star on radio. Had own show, Melody Ranch, beginning early 1940 and running into early 50s, interrupted by military service, World War II. In later 40s and 50s maintained heavy work schedule. Made hit records for children: *Rudolph the Red-Nosed Reindeer*, *Peter Cottontail*, *Frosty the Snowman*—all perennial big sellers.

Prolific recording output. Made about 100 half-hour films for early TV, adding further to his popularity with younger fans in early 50s. By late 50s had grown less active in show business, concentrating on various business enterprises. Developed into astute, highly respected businessman. Investor in radio and TV stations, record and publishing companies, movie studios, California Angels baseball

527

team. Composer or co-composer of note-worthy country and western songs: *Ridin' Down the Canyon*; *That Silver-Haired Daddy of Mine*; *Dust*; *Be Honest with Me*; *Tears on My Pillow*; *Tweedle O'Twill*; *Yesterday's Roses*; *I Wish I Had Never Met Sunshine*; *Back in the Saddle Again*; *Lonely River*; *Have I Told You Lately That I Love You?*; *Rainbow on the Rio Colorado*; *You're the Only Star (in My Blue Heaven)*; *You Waited Too Long*; *Goodbye, Little Darlin', Goodbye*; *That Little Kid Sister of Mine*; *Here Comes Santa Claus*.

RECORDS

GENE AUTRY

Me 12430 Missouri, I'm Calling/My Alabama Home
Me 13354 Ole Faithful/Some Day in Wyomin' (with JIMMY LONG)
Me 70151 Guns and Guitars/Red River Valley (with JIMMY LONG)
Pe 13113 Tumbling Tumbleweeds/Old Missouri Moon (with JIMMY LONG)
Pe 80458 Dust/When the Tumble Weeds Come Tumbling Down Again
MW 4067 Jail House Blues
Cq 7831 Cowboy's Yodel/Blue Days
Cq 8191 There's an Empty Cot in the Bunkhouse Tonight/The Last Round-up
Cq 9098 You're the Only Star/Goodbye, Pinto
Cq 9388 The Singing Hills/El Rancho Grande
Vo 02991 Mississippi Valley Blues/That Silver-Haired Daddy of Mine
Vo 03138 I'll Go Riding Down That Texas Trail/My Old Saddle Pal
Vo 03358 Gold Mine in the Sky/Sail Along, Silv'ry Moon
Vo 04172 Dust/Boots and Saddle
Vo 04485 Way Out West in Texas/The Last Round-up
OK 05080 Back in the Saddle Again/Little Old Band of Gold
OK 05122 South of the Border/Gold Mine in Your Heart
OK 05780 Sierra Sue/When the Swallows Come Back to Capistrano
OK 05980 Be Honest with Me/What's Gonna Happen to Me?
OK 06274 You Are My Sunshine/It Makes No Difference Now
OK 6690 Jingle Jangle Jingle/I'm a Cow Poke Pokin' Along
Co 38610 Rudolph the Red-Nosed Reindeer/If It Doesn't Snow on Christmas
Co 38750 Peter Cottontail/The Funny Little Bunny
Co 38907 Frosty the Snowman/When Santa Claus Gets Your Letter
Co 20020 I Wish I Had Never Met Sunshine/You Only Want Me When You're Lonely
Co 20037 Goodbye, Little Darlin', Goodbye/When I'm Gone You'll Soon Forget
Co 20087 Ridin' Down the Canyon/Twilight on the Trail
Co 20129 Don't Fence Me In/Gonna Build a Big Fence Around Texas

LPs

GENE AUTRY

Vi LPM-2623 Gene Autry's Golden Hits
Co CL-1575 Gene Autry's Greatest Hits
Ha HL-7332 Gene Autry's Great Hits
Ha HL-7399 You Are My Sunshine and Other Great Hits
Ha HL-11276 Back in the Saddle Again

71. AVON COMEDY FOUR vocal quartet

Entertaining comedy and singing group that featured dialects and song specialties. After several years in vaudeville, quartet appeared on Broadway in THE PASSING SHOW OF 1919. Original members: Joe Smith, Charlie Dale, John Coleman, Will Lester. Smith and Dale remained; other members later included Eddie Rash, Charles Adams, Irving Kaufman, Harry Goodwin, Jack Goodwin, Eddie Miller. Group later dissolved into comedy team of Smith & Dale, which had long and successful career.

RECORDS

AVON COMEDY FOUR

Vi 18081 My Mother's Rosary/Yaaka Hula Hickey Dula

Vi 18088 I'm Going Way Back Home/You're a Dangerous Girl

Vi 18125 Gila, Galah, Galoo

Vi 18126 Songs of Yesterday/When the Black Sheep Returns to the Fold

Vi 18129 On a Summer Night

Vi 18133 Way Out Yonder in the Golden West

Vi(12″)35602 Cohen's Wedding/Hungarian Restaurant Scene

Vi(12″)35606 Ginsberg's Stump Speech/The Professor's Birthday

Vi(12″)35750 Clancy's Minstrels/New School Teacher

72. AYRES, MITCHELL   v ar cm B
(MITCHELL AGRESS)

Born December 24, 1910, Milwaukee, Wis.

Died September 5, 1969, Las Vegas, Nev., struck by car

Bandleader who rose to prominence backing popular singer Perry Como on radio in late 40s and on TV in 50s and 60s. Attended Columbia University. In early 30s first important job with Little Jack Little band. In late 1936 musicians left Little to form co-op band, with Agress fronting (later took name Ayres). Ayres led good, solid sweet band in the late 30s and early 40s. Good arrangements generously spotlighted beautifully toned, fluid alto sax of Harry Terrell. Theme song: *You Go to My Head.* Vocalists were Mary Ann Mercer and Tommy Taylor. The band appeared in a few minor movies like LADY, LET'S DANCE and MOONLIGHT AND CACTUS in 1944. Frequently featured novelty numbers on jobs and records, but made many good dance records as well. Played some radio too, including Jack Pepper and Andy Russell shows in 1944. Ayres disbanded, then in late 40s radio regular as musical director for Perry Como many years during Como's reign. They entered TV in early 50s, also continuing on radio for a time. In 1955 Como on full-hour highly rated weekly show into mid-60s. Ayres and band of top musicians provided excellent backing. When show folded Ayres moved

to The Hollywood Palace on TV during middle and later 60s until death. Recording director for Columbia late 40s and early 50s, accompanying singers. Composed a few minor songs.

RECORDS

MITCHELL AYRES

Vo 4664 I Want My Share of Love/ Could Be

Vo 4665 Gotta Get Some Shut-Eye/ We've Come a Long Way Together

Vo 4699 Heaven Can Wait/Blame It on My Last Affair

Bb 10550 Angel/Dingbat the Acrobat

Bb 10585 Playmates/Between You and Me

Bb 10609 How High the Moon/House with a Little Red Barn

Bb 10650 This Is the Beginning of the End/Your Kiss

Bb 10653 Where Do I Go from You?/I Can't Love You Any More

Bb 10687 Make-Believe Island/Poor Ballerina

Bb 10738 Blue Lovebird/Down by the Ohio

Bb 10814 You Go to My Head (theme)/Deep in My Heart, Dear

Bb 10877 Two Dreams Met/Goodnight, Mother

Bb 10960 Walkin' by the River/I Look at You

Bb 11046 Boogie Woogie Bugle Boy/ You're a Lucky Fellow, Mr. Smith

(as conductor)

BUDDY CLARK

Co 37920 The Little Old Mill/Don't You Love Me Anymore?

CURT MASSEY

Co 36885 Don't Lie to Me/The Gang That Sang "Heart of My Heart"

DINAH SHORE

Co 37140 Who'll Buy My Violets?

BEATRICE KAY

Co 38232 At the Rodeo/I Wanna Be a Cowboy in the Movies

PEARL BAILEY

Co 37068 I Ain't Talkin'/He Didn't Ask Me

THE MODERNAIRES

Co 36800 You Belong to My Heart/ There, I've Said It Again

Co 37569 Something in the Wind/The Turntable Song

PERRY COMO

Vi 20-3747 On the Outgoing Tide/Hoop-Dee-Doo

Vi 20-4033 More than You Know/Without a Song

Vi 20-4112 We Kiss in a Shadow/Hello, Young Lovers

LPs

MITCHELL AYRES

Cam CAL-266 Dance Time (Bb RIs)

Vi LPM-1603 Have a Wonderful Weekend

Comm RS902SD (S) Hollywood Palace

(as conductor)

PERRY COMO

Vi LOP-1004 Saturday Night with Mr. C

Vi LPM-1463 We Get Letters

PEARL BAILEY

Co(10″)CL-6099 Pearl Bailey Entertains

BUDDY CLARK

Co(10″)CL-6007 For You Alone

73. BABASIN, HARRY   b cel B

Born March 19, 1921, Dallas, Texas

Bass player with various bands from 40s to 60s. Pioneer in use of cello as jazz instrument. Attended North Texas State College. First musical work with bands in midwest, then worked in New York and California. Played in bands of Gene Krupa, Boyd Raeburn and Charlie Barnet in mid-40s. Late 1946-7 with Benny Goodman, 1948 with Woody Herman. Freelanced in Hollywood in 50s, doing radio and TV work. Head of Nocturne record company in middle and late 50s. Worked with Harry James in 1959. Led own combo at intervals. In early 60s studied composing at San Fernando Valley State College. Continued active in music in 60s.

RECORDS

BOYD RAEBURN
  Je 10002 Boyd Meets Stravinsky/I Only Have Eyes for You
  DL-1-5 Dalvatore Sally/Temptation
JULIA LEE
  Cap 40028 Snatch and Grab It
DODO MARMAROSA
  Dial 752 Bopmatism/Trade Winds
BENNY GOODMAN (combos)
  Cap 394 The Lonesome Road/Fine and Dandy
  Cap 439 Tattle Tale/Dizzy Fingers (both ORCHESTRA)
  Cap 15186 Cherokee/Love Is Just Around the Corner
  Cap 20126 Benny's Boogie/How High the Moon
  Cap 20127 Music, Maestro, Please/The Bannister Slide
HARRY BABASIN
  Dis 163 Night and Day/Where or When
  PJ 603 How About You?/Sanders Meanders

LPs

HARRY BABASIN
  Noc(10″)NLP-3
HERBIE HARPER
  Noc(10″)NLP-1
BARNEY KESSEL
  Contemp(10″)C-2508
BUD SHANK
  PJ 1205 Bud Shank Quintet
LAURINDO ALMEIDA
  PJ(10″)7
  PJ(10″)13 (Vol. 2)
BENNY GOODMAN
  Cap(10″)H-202 Session for Six
BUDDY CHILDERS
  Lib LJH-6013
WARDELL GRAY
  Cr 5004 Way Out Wardell

74. BABBITT, HARRY   vo d

Born November 2, 1913, St.Louis, Mo.

A featured vocalist with popular Kay Kyser band late 30s and 40s. High baritone voice with smooth, silken quality. Had formal voice training, also played drums. Performed on St. Louis radio in

531

early 30s. Joined Kyser in 1937 and soon became well known through band's records and long-running radio series. Often teamed with band's female vocalist Ginny Simms on duets. Also heard in singing song titles gimmick used by Kyser in early years. Sang on hit record, *Who Wouldn't Love You?*. Featured in movies built around Kyser's band and vocalists: THAT'S RIGHT—YOU'RE WRONG (1939), YOU'LL FIND OUT (1940), PLAYMATES (1942), SWING FEVER (1943), AROUND THE WORLD and CAROLINA BLUES (1944). Left band in mid-40s for period as a single, rejoined 1947 and remained through 40s. Again worked as single in 50s, played clubs and recorded, then retired.

RECORDS

KAY KYSER

Br 7891 The You and Me That Used to Be
Br 8120 Lost and Found
Br 8193 Love Is Where You Find It
Br 8215 When I Go a-Dreamin'/When a Prince of a Fella Meets a Cinderella
Br 8317 Heaven Can Wait/I Promise You
Co 35946 You Stepped Out of a Dream
Co 35993 Everything Happens to Me
Co 36433 Humpty Dumpty Heart
Co 36517 When the Roses Bloom Again
Co 36526 Who Wouldn't Love You?
Co 36551 Somewhere, Sometime
Co 36604 He Wears a Pair of Silver Wings/Jingle Jangle Jingle
Co 38202 Little Girl/Takin' Miss Mary to the Ball
Co 38262 Ring, Telephone, Ring
Co 38301 On a Slow Boat to China/In the Market Place of Old Monterey
Co 38374 It Only Happens Once

HARRY BABBITT

Cor 60301 Timeless/What Can You Do?
Cor 60332 I'll Get By/One-Finger Melody
Cor 60367 Between Two Trees/My Dear One
Mer 3026 Sunny Weather/Derry Dum

Mer 3056 How Are Things in Glocca Morra?/Oshkosh, Wisconsin
Seeco 4115 Portrait of Jenny/Baby, I Need You
Popular 3028 You Were Meant for Me/Who Do You Love, I Hope?

HARRY BABBITT-THE MODERNAIRES

Cor 60521 Never Again/Shanghai

HARRY BABBITT-MARTHA TILTON

Cor 60335 You're Just in Love/It's a Lovely Day Today
Cor 60468 Music in My Heart/Powder Blue

LPs

KAY KYSER

Ha HL-7041 (Co RIs)
Ha HL-7136 Campus Rally (college songs)

75. BAER, ABEL   cm lyr p ar B

Born March 16, 1893, Baltimore, Md.

Songwriter mostly active in 20s. Most famous songs: *June Night*; *I Miss My Swiss*; *My Mother's Eyes*; *Gee, But You're Swell*; *There Are Such Things*. Attended College of Physicians and Surgeons in Boston, left to join AAF during World War I. Then began career in music leading dance band in Boston. To New York in 1920 to work in music publishing house. Began composing in 1921. Worked as accompanist to Nora Bayes. To Hollywood in 1929 to write music for early sound movies. During 30s wrote songs infrequently. Entertained at army camps and hospitals during World War II. In mid-50s was manager of show sponsored by ASCAP and USO that entertained armed forces in Germany. Baer's chief collaborators were L. Wolfe Gilbert, Stanley Adams, Cliff Friend, Sam M. Lewis, Mabel Wayne.

SONGS
(with related shows)

1921—All That I Need Is You
1923—Mama Loves Papa; I'm Sitting Pretty in a Pretty Little City
1924—June Night; Let Me Linger Longer in Your Arms; When the One You Love Loves You; Where the Dreamy Wabash Flows

1925—Don't Wake Me Up, Let Me Dream; I Miss My Swiss
1926—Hello, Aloha, How Are You?
1927—Collette; Lucky Lindy; LADY DO stage show (songs unimportant)
1928—High Upon a Hill Top; Lonesome in the Moonlight; When You're with Somebody Else
1929—If You Believed in Me; My Mother's Eyes
1930—HAPPY DAYS movie (I'm on a Diet of Love); PARAMOUNT ON PARADE movie (Dancing to Save Your Sole; I'm in Training for You; Drink to the Girl of My Dreams)
1931—I'll Love You in My Dreams (Horace Heidt theme song); It's the Girl; I'm Happy When You're Happy
1932—Me Minus You
1935—Sweet Thing
1937—Gee, But You're Swell
1939—The Last Two Weeks in July
1942—There Are Such Things
1951—Chapel of the Roses

Other songs: *It's Mating Time*; *A Garden in Granada*; *Don't Wait 'Til the Night Before Christmas*; *The Night When Love Was Born*; *Harriet*; *Piggy Wiggy Woo*; *On a Snowy Blowy Day*

76. BAILEY, BUSTER   cl as ss B
(WILLIAM C. BAILEY)
Born July 19, 1902, Memphis, Tenn.
Died April 12, 1967, Brooklyn, N.Y.

A top jazz clarinetist known chiefly for his work with Fletcher Henderson and John Kirby. Had thin-toned sound with constant, fluent flow of notes, distinctive style. Early job with W. C. Handy 1917-19. With Erskine Tate 1919-23, King Oliver late 1923-4. Then began important association with Henderson in late 1924 which was to last, off and on, to 1937. With Henderson until late 1928 (except for brief interval). In 1929 toured U.S. and Europe with Noble Sissle. During 20s Bailey appeared on many records accompanying blues singers, recorded widely through the years.

Upon return to U.S., played with Edgar Hayes and others, rejoined Sissle 1931-3.

With Henderson again for most of 1934. Joined Mills Blue Rhythm Band late 1934-5. Rejoined Henderson late 1935 till early 1937. In this period Henderson's great swing records brought Bailey acclaim as never before. Next important period 1937-44 as star with Kirby combo. This group's tightly knit sound and intricate arrangements caught fancy of jazz fans. Bailey's great technique fit in perfectly. Freelanced in mid-40s, at times led own combo, returned to Kirby at intervals. With Wilbur DeParis 1947-9 and Red Allen 1950-1. Versatile musician, did pit band and symphonic work. Many jobs with Allen later 50s. Early 60s long periods with Wild Bill Davison, also with The Saints and Sinners. In mid-1965 joined Louis Armstrong All-Stars, remaining until death.

RECORDS
MA RAINEY
    Para 12238 Jelly Bean Blues/Countin' the Blues
    Para 12242 Blues and Booze/Toad Frog Blues
BESSIE SMITH
    Co 14133-D Jazzbo Brown from Memphis Town
    Co 14179-D Young Woman's Blues
CLARENCE WILLIAMS
    OK 8181 Everybody Loves My Baby/ Of All the Wrongs You've Done to Me
    OK 8525 Yama Yama Blues/Church Street Sobbin' Blues
FLETCHER HENDERSON
    Co 654-D Jackass Blues/The Stampede
    Co 1059-D Whiteman Stomp/I'm Coming Virginia
    Co 1543-D King Porter Stomp/D Natural Blues
    Vo 1092 Fidgety Feet/Sensation
    Vo 3213 Stealin' Apples/Big Chief De Sota
    De 157 Limehouse Blues/Wrappin' It Up
    De 555 Hotter Than 'Ell
    Vi 24699 Harlem Madness
    Vi 25375 Sing, Sing, Sing/Shoe Shine Boy

RED ALLEN

Pe 15970 Pardon My Southern Accent/How's About Tomorrow Night?

Pe 15994 Rug Cutter's Swing/There's a House in Harlem

LIL ARMSTRONG

De 1059 My Hi-De-Ho Man/Doin' the Susy Q

De 1092 Or Leave Me Alone/Brown Gal

De 1502 Let's Call It Love/You Mean So Much to Me

CHU BERRY

Va 532 Too Marvelous for Words/Now You're Talking My Language

Va 587 Limehouse Blues/Indiana

JOHN KIRBY

De 2216 Undecided/From A Flat to C

De 2367 Rehearsin' for a Nervous Breakdown/Pastel Blue

Vo 4653 Dawn on the Desert/The Turf

Vo 5187 Blue Skies/Royal Garden Blues

LIONEL HAMPTON

Vi 25592 I Know That You Know

TEDDY WILSON

Br 7903 I'll Get By/Mean to Me

Br 7911 Foolin' Myself/Easy Living

BUSTER BAILEY

Vo 2887 Call of the Delta/Shanghai Shuffle

Vo 4089 Planter's Punch/Sloe Jam Fizz

Vo 4564 Light Up/Man with a Horn Goes Berserk

Vs 8333 The Blue Room/Am I Blue?

Vs 8337 Should I?/April in Paris

LPs

BUSTER BAILEY

Felsted FAJ-7003 All About Memphis

WILLIE (THE LION) SMITH

Ace of Hearts (E) AH-162 The Swinging Cub Men (De RIs)

FLETCHER HENDERSON

De(10″)DL-6025 Fletcher Henderson Memorial (De RIs)

Co C4L19 (4-LP set) A Study in Frustration (Co, Ha, Vo Ris)

Jazztone J-1285 The Big Reunion

DON REDMAN

Roul 25070 Dixieland in High Society

BESSIE SMITH

Co CL-855-6-7-8 (4-LP set) (Co RIs)

JIMMY RUSHING

Co CL-1605 The Smith Girls

77. BAILEY, MILDRED vo p

Born February 27, 1907, Tekoa, Wash. Died December 12, 1951, Poughkeepsie, N.Y.

An all-time great vocalist, with jazz-styled interpretations of songs, warmth and feeling. Achieved most fame singing with bands of Paul Whiteman and husband Red Norvo in 30s. Educated in Spokane. At 16 played piano in movie house. Also worked in Seattle music shop demonstrating sheet music, where heard and hired by night club owner. Performed on Los Angeles radio and at various clubs on west coast. Via brother Al Rinker, member of Paul Whiteman's Rhythm Boys vocal trio, she landed plum job with Whiteman in 1929. Received good coverage with popular Whiteman band on records and radio, and by early 30s was called The Rockin' Chair Lady because of her association with song *Rockin' Chair*. Remained with Whiteman till 1933 except for interval in 1932. Seriously injured in auto accident, and prolonged inactivity caused her to take on plumpness which remained through the years.

Freelanced as soloist in mid-30s, cutting excellent records using outstanding jazzmen. In 1934-5 on radio shows of George Jessel and Willard Robison. In swing years husband Red Norvo formed great band featuring subtle swing arrangements of Eddie Sauter. Mildred featured, did best work 1936-9. Red and Mildred billed as Mr. & Mrs. Swing. Mildred joined Benny Goodman in fall of 1939 on radio and records. In 40s pursued career as soloist, though illness caused intervals of inactivity. From mid-1944 to early 1945 featured on musically outstanding radio show. Worked intermittently during late 40s and into 1951. Recorded heavily over the years under own name.

RECORDS

PAUL WHITEMAN

Vi 22828 Can't You See?/When It's Sleepy Time Down South

Vi 22876 My Goodbye to You

Vi 22879 All of Me

Vi 22883 'Leven Pounds of Heaven
Vi 24088 We Just Couldn't Say Good-
bye/I'll Never Be the Same
RED NORVO
Br 7732 Picture Me without You/It All
Begins and Ends with You
Br 7813 I've Got My Love to Keep Me
Warm/Slummin' on Park Avenue
Br 8068 I Was Doing All Right/Love
Is Here to Stay
Br 8069 It's Wonderful/Always and
Always
Br 8088 Please Be Kind/The Weekend
of a Private Secretary
BENNY GOODMAN
Co 2892-D Junk Man/Ol' Pappy
Co 2907-D Emaline
Co 35313 Make with the Kisses/I
Thought About You
Co 35331 Darn That Dream/Peace,
Brother
DORSEY BROTHERS ORCHESTRA
Br 7542 But I Can't Make a Man
EDDIE LANG
Pa (E)840 What Kind o' Man Is You?
GLEN GRAY
Br 6679 Heat Wave
MILDRED BAILEY
Vi 22874 Home/Too Late
Vi 22891 Georgia on My Mind
Vi 24117 Rockin' Chair/Love Me To-
night
Br 6587 Lazybones/There's a Cabin in
the Pines
Br 6680 Give Me Liberty or Give Me
Love/Doin' the Uptown Lowdown
Vo 3056 I'd Rather Listen to Your
Eyes/I'd Love to Take Orders from
You
Vo 3057 Someday Sweetheart/When
Day is Done
Vo 3378 'Long About Midnight/More
Than You Know
Vo 3456 Where Are You?/You're
Laughing at Me
Vo 3553 Rockin' Chair/Little Joe
Vo 4016 Don't Be That Way/I Can't
Face the Music
Vo 5268 Prisoner of Love/There'll Be
Some Changes Made
Co 35463 Fools Rush In/From Anoth-
er World
De 3888 All Too Soon/Everything De-
pends on You

Maj 1140 All of Me/Almost Like Being in Love

LPs

MILDRED BAILEY
Co C3L22 (3-LP set) Her Greatest Per-
formances (1929-46 RIs)
Mon-Ever MES-6814 All of Me
De(10")DL-5387 The Rockin' Chair
Lady
Regent 6032 (Maj RIs)

78. BAILEY, PEARL   VO

*Born March 29, 1918, Newport News,
Va.*

Singing comedienne prominent on records and TV in 50s and 60s. Excellent
entertainer. Educated in Philadelphia and
Washington, D.C. Toured Pennsylvania
mining towns as dancer, later sang in
vaudeville. In early 40s performed on
USO tour, in vaudeville and clubs. Also
worked with Cootie Williams band. Stage
debut in ST. LOUIS WOMAN in 1946, a hit
even though show unsuccessful. Attracted
attention with rendition of *Tired* in 1947
movie VARIETY GIRL. Appeared in other
movies in later years: ISN'T IT ROMANTIC?
(1948), CARMEN JONES (1954), THAT CER-
TAIN FEELING (1956), ST. LOUIS BLUES
(1958), PORGY AND BESS (1959), ALL THE
FINE YOUNG CANNIBALS (1960), THE LAND-
LORD (1969). In 1950 Pearl played in two
more Broadway musicals which enjoyed
only modest success, ARMS AND THE GIRL
and BLESS YOU ALL. In 1955 starred in
HOUSE OF FLOWERS, again only modest
success.

Performing style featured songs in comic,
novelty or philosophical vein, spiced with
wit, timing and showmanship. 50s records
enjoyed some popularity, especially *Takes
Two to Tango* in 1953. In great demand on
TV in late 50s and through 60s. Concert
tours with husband drummer Louis Bellson in U.S. and abroad. Acclaim from
critics and public for lead in all-Negro
stage version of HELLO, DOLLY, which
opened in November 1967 for long run.
Own TV show for season in 1971 with
husband Bellson leading excellent big
band.

RECORDS

PEARL BAILEY
Co 36837 Tired/Fifteen Years
Co 36930 Personality/Don't Like 'Em
Co 37068 I Ain't Talkin'/He Didn't Ask Me
Co 37280 Row, Row, Row/That's Good Enough for Me
Co 37570 St. Louis Blues/Get It Off Your Mind
Co 38113 Blue Grass/Protect Me
Co 38722 Nothin' for Nothin'/There Must Be Somethin' Better Than Love
Co 38928 Vagabond Shoes/Some Days There Just Ain't No Fish
Co 38969 Down in the Cellar/He Didn't Have the Know-How No How
Cor 60817 Takes Two to Tango/Let There Be Love
Cor 60877 Toot Toot Tootsie/My Ideal
Cor 60945 I Always Shake the Tree/Hug Me a Hug
Cor 61070 Me and My Shadow/I Love My Argentine
PEARL BAILEY-FRANK SINATRA
Co 38362 A Little Learnin' Is a Dangerous Thing (1 & 2)

LPs

PEARL BAILEY
Co CL-985 The Definitive Pearl Bailey
Co(10")CL-6099 Pearl Bailey Entertains
Cor CRL-57037 Pearl Bailey
Cor(10")CRL-56068 Say Si Si
Roul R-25063 Sings PORGY AND BESS and Other Gershwin Melodies
Roul R-25144 The Best of Pearl Bailey
Mer MG-20187 The One and Only Pearl Bailey Sings
(original stage cast)
Co ML-4969 HOUSE OF FLOWERS

79. BAIRD, EUGENIE vo
Good band singer of 40s. With Tony Pastor 1942-3, with Glen Gray 1943-4 where she attracted most attention. Sang on Bing Crosby radio show in 1945, and in 1946 with Paul Whiteman on radio. Freelanced in later 40s and early 50s, appearing on a few records.

RECORDS

TONY PASTOR
Bb 11168 Blues (My Naughty Sweetie Gave to Me)
Bb 11481 The Mem'ry of This Dance
Bb 30-0802 Soft-Hearted
GLEN GRAY
De 18567 My Shining Hour/My Heart Tells Me
De 18596 Sure Thing/Suddenly It's Spring
De 18615 Don't Take Your Love from Me/Forget-Me-Nots in Your Eyes
De 18639 This Heart of Mine
De 18695 All by Myself
EUGENIE BAIRD
Vinrob 1 Be Good to Yourself/Why Should I Want You?
Vinrob 2 Hootin' Holler/Say "Si Si"
Hi-Tone 119 Blue Room
(with MEL TORME & HIS MEL-TONES)
De 18707 Am I Blue?/I Fall in Love Too Easily

LPs

EUGENIE BAIRD
Design DLP-93 Sings Duke Ellington
Design DCF-1021 Eugenie Baird Sings—Duke's Boys Play "Duke Ellington"

80. BAKER, BELLE vo
Born c. 1895
Died 1957
Vaudeville entertainer, attractive and buxom, with deep throaty voice and strong theatrical presentation. Played New York's Palace Theatre early in career. Top vaudeville star many years. Minor role in 1911 Broadway show VERA VIOLETTA, starring role in short-lived BETSY in 1927. Appeared in movies THE SONG OF LOVE (1929), ATLANTIC CITY (1944).

RECORDS

BELLE BAKER with THE VIRGINIANS
Vi 19135 I've Got the Yes We Have No Bananas Blues/Jubilee Blues
BELLE BAKER
Vi 19436 Hard Hearted Hannah/Sweet Little You
Vi 19605 My Kid

536

Br 3706 Baby Your Mother/There Must Be Somebody Else
Br 4086 My Man/That's How I Feel About You
Br 4343 My Sin/Underneath the Russian Moon
Br 4550 Aren't We All?/If I Had a Talking Picture of You
Br 4558 Take Everything but You/I'm Walking with Moonbeams
Br 4624 Wanting You/Love
Br 4714 Crying for the Carolines/Can't Be Bothered with Me
Br 4765 You Brought a New Kind of Love to Me/Sing You Sinners
Br 4843 Cheer Up/I'm Needin' You
Br 4962 Sweetheart of My Student Days/Laughing at Life
Br 6051 Overnight/You're the One I Care For
Gala 1006 Mad About the Boy/Atlas
Gala 1007 Eli Eli/Yiddishe Momme
Gala 1008 Flying Tony/Ginsberg from Scotland Yard
HMV (E)233 Stay as Sweet as You Are/The Continental

RECORDS

ORRIN TUCKER
Vo 4241 Especially for You
Co 35228 Oh Johnny, Oh Johnny, Oh!
Co 35249 Stop! It's Wonderful
Co 35256 If I Knew Then
Co 35328 Pinch Me/Would Ja Mind?
Co 35344 You'd Be Surprised
Co 35452 Not Yet
Co 35468 My Resistance Is Low
Co 35546 Go Way—Can't You See I'm Dreaming?
Co 35576 Oh, Lady Be Good
Co 35639 I Wouldn't Take a Million
Co 35858 Strawberry Lane/I Could Kiss You for That
Co 35948 Aren't You Gonna Kiss Me Goodnight?
Co 36093 You Can Depend on Me
Co 36223 Will You Marry Me, Mr. Laramie?

LPs

ORRIN TUCKER
Ha HL-7146 Oh Johnny! (mostly Co RIs)
Tops L-1684 I Remember Orrin Tucker—Bonnie Baker

81. BAKER, BONNIE   vo
(EVELYN NELSON)

Born c. 1918

Small-voiced singer with Orrin Tucker band who rose to prominence in 1939 with hit record of old song, *Oh Johnny, Oh Johnny, Oh!*. Called Wee Bonnie Baker. Early experience singing at proms and parties while attending school in Macon, Ga. Embarked on professional career as vocalist, played clubs in various cities. In 1936 bandleader Orrin Tucker heard her performing at Claridge Hotel in St. Louis, hired her as band singer, changed her name to Bonnie Baker. With Tucker till 1942. Tucker's was successful ballroom band with modest recording output. 1939 hit record boosted their careers briefly, brought better bookings, more records, radio appearances (including spots on Your Hit Parade). They were featured in 1941 movie YOU'RE THE ONE. In 1942 Bonnie worked again as single, continuing into late 40s, but she gradually faded.

82. BAKER, HAROLD   t B
(nicknamed Shorty)

Born May 26, 1914, St. Louis, Mo.
Died November 8, 1966, New York, N.Y.

Capable lead trumpet, section man, jazz soloist. Active from 30s to 60s. Early experience in brother's band, Winfield Baker & His St. Louis Crackerjacks. In early 30s worked with Erskine Tate, Fate Marable and Eddie Johnson. Important period 1936-8 with Don Redman and with Duke Ellington briefly in 1938. In 1939-40 with Teddy Wilson's big band and 1940-2 with Andy Kirk. Also in 1942 he and wife Mary Lou Williams led combo for a spell. With Duke Ellington 1946-52. Freelanced in early and mid-50s, including stint with Johnny Hodges combo. During 1957-63 mostly with Duke Ellington, with intervals away freelancing and leading own band. Remained active till 1965 when throat cancer ended long career.

RECORDS

DUKE ELLINGTON
Mus 484 Trumpet No End (Blue Skies)
Vi 20-1718 Time's a-Wastin'
Vi 20-2326 Beale Street Blues
Co 38237 Three Cent Stomp
Co (E)2504 Stomp, Look and Listen
Co 39670 Jam with Sam

MARY LOU WILLIAMS
De 18122 Baby Dear/Harmony Blues

JOHNNY HODGES
Norg 124 Sweet as Bear Meat/Skokiaan

LPs

DUKE ELLINGTON
Co CL-1085 Ellington Indigos
Co CS-8072 (S) Newport 1958

MERCER ELLINGTON
Cor CRL-57293 Colors in Rhythm

JOHNNY HODGES
Norg MGN-1009
Norg MGN-1060 Used to Be Duke

GEORGE WEIN & STORYVILLE SEXTET
Beth 6050 Jazz at the Modern

TYREE GLENN
Forum SF-9068(S) At the Embers

HAROLD "SHORTY" BAKER
King 608(S) The Broadway Beat

83. BAKER, KENNY   vo

Born September 30, 1912, Monrovia, Calif.

Tenor known for work in movies, on radio and records. Studied music at Long Beach Junior College. Won Texaco Radio Open singing contest, awarded engagement at famed Cocoanut Grove in Los Angeles, where contract extended several months. This led to coveted spot on popular Jack Benny radio show late 1935 through 30s. Late 1939-40 on Texaco Star Theatre radio show, then on Fred Allen show during early 40s. Own radio show beginning 1944. Daily daytime show later in 40s. Singing roles in several movies. In 1943 starred in Broadway musical ONE TOUCH OF VENUS. Later in 50s became less active in show business, retired in California.

MOVIES

1936—KING OF BURLESQUE
1937—52ND STREET; MR. DODD TAKES THE AIR; TURN OFF THE MOON; THE KING AND THE CHORUS GIRL
1938—RADIO CITY REVELS; GOLDWYN FOLLIES
1939—THE MARX BROTHERS AT THE CIRCUS; THE MIKADO
1940—HIT PARADE OF 1941
1943—SILVER SKATES; STAGE DOOR CANTEEN; DOUGHBOYS IN IRELAND
1946—THE HARVEY GIRLS
1947—THE CALENDAR GIRL

RECORDS

KENNY BAKER
De 1795 Love Walked In/Lost and Found
De 2190 Hark! The Herald Angels Sing/It Came Upon the Midnight Clear
De 18262 Always in My Heart/Blue Tahitian Moon
De 24117 An Apple Blossom Wedding/Love and the Weather
Vi 26252 The Moon and I/A Wandering Minstrel, I
Vi 26268 Melancholy Mood/Ain'tcha Comin' Out?
Vi 26280 White Sails/Stairway to the Stars
Vi 26297 Cinderella, Stay in My Arms/Let's Make Memories Tonight
Vi 26373 South of the Border/Stop Kicking My Heart Around
Vi 26413 Two Blind Loves/Last Night
Vi 26456 Faithful Forever/On a Little Street in Singapore
Vi 26504 The Starlit Hour/When You Wish Upon a Star
Vi 26520 On the Isle of May/Make Love with a Guitar
Vi 26768 Yesterthoughts/Two Dreams Met
Vi 27207 There I Go/You and Your Kiss
Vi 27250 You Walk By/Chapel in the Valley

LPs

KENNY BAKER
Cam CAL-131 Sings Song Hits Through the Years
De(10″)DL-7004 Babes in Toyland

84. BAKER, KENNY   t ar B

Born March 1, 1921, Withersnea, Yorks, England

A top trumpet star in England from early 40s to 70s. Brilliant tone and powerful style, adept at high notes. Began career in 1939 with Lew Stone. Also worked with Maurice Winnick, Jack Hylton, Ambrose. Outstanding records in 1944-5 with swinging Harry Hayes and Buddy Featherstonhaugh combos. With Ted Heath 1946-8 as featured trumpet star and arranger. In 1949-51 did studio work. In 1951 formed own group, continued popular and successful through 50s and 60s. At times in later years played more commercial style of trumpet.

RECORDS

BUDDY FEATHERSTONHAUGH
HMV (E)9361 King Porter Stomp
HMV (E)9367 Ain't Misbehavin'/One O'clock Jump
HMV 9372 Stevedore Stomp/Ain'tcha Got Music?
HMV 9384 How Am I to Know?/I Wish I Were Twins

HARRY HAYES
HMV (E)9397 My Love/Sequence
HMV 9404 Needlenose
HMV 9409 Drop Me Off in Harlem/First Edition
HMV 9413 Merely a Minor/Two, Three, Four Jump
HMV 9422 Up/No Script

TED HEATH
Lon (E)259 Dark Eyes

GEORGE SHEARING
De (E)8454 Riff Up Them Stairs/Five Flat Flurry

MELODY MAKER ALL-STARS
Esq (E)10-353 For Victors Only/Gallop Poll

KENNY BAKER
Pa (E)3452 I Only Have Eyes for You/I Can't Get Started
Pa (E)3490 Lullaby of Broadway/Exploitation
Pa (E)3646 Afternoon in Paris/'Round About Midnight
Pa (E)3905 Peg o' My Heart/The Other Side

Nixa (E)2010 I'm a Ding Dong Daddy/Blues in Thirds
Melodisc (E)1216 The Night Is Young and You're So Beautiful/The Very Thought of You

LPs

KENNY BAKER
Lon(E) SP-44114(S) The Spectacular Trumpet of Kenny Baker
LANSDOWNE JAZZ GROUP
Ha HS-11025(S) The Songs of Percy Faith
BENNY GOODMAN
Philips 6308023 London Date

85. BAKER, PHIL   acc cm lyr

Born August 24, 1896, Philadelphia, Pa.
Died November 30, 1963, Copenhagen, Denmark

Comedian active in Broadway musicals and on radio shows. Played simple style on accordion. Grew up in Boston, first played amateur shows there. Played vaudeville many years, teaming with violinist Ed Janis, then with violinist Ben Bernie. Military service, World War I. Resumed vaudeville career. One of first to use stooge in act. Temporary replacement in Broadway show GREENWICH VILLAGE FOLLIES OF 1920. Later, important roles in shows MUSIC BOX REVUE OF 1923, THE PASSING SHOW OF 1923, ARTISTS AND MODELS OF 1925, A NIGHT IN SPAIN (1927), PLEASURE BOUND (1929), ARTISTS AND MODELS OF 1930, BILLY ROSE'S CRAZY QUILT (1931), AMERICANA (1932; joined after show opened), CALLING ALL STARS (1934), PRIORITIES OF 1942. Began on radio in 1933-4 with own show, late 1934-5 with Irene Beasley on Armour show, 1935-6 own show with Hal Kemp band. New show 1937 with Charles Dornberger band. Continued on radio in late 30s with stooges Beetle and Bottle. In early 40s appeared on Take It or Leave It quiz show, stayed many years. Composed several popular songs, notably *Strange Interlude* (1932). Other songs: *Did You Mean It?, Love and Kisses, Look at Those Eyes, Park Avenue Strut, Just Suppose, Antoinette, Humming a Love Song, Rainy Day Pal, Pretty Little Baby, My Heaven on*

Earth, Invitation to a Broken Heart. Appeared in movies GIFT OF GAB (1934), THANKS A MILLION (1935), GOLDWYN FOLLIES (1938), THE GANG'S ALL HERE (1943). By 50s career had waned.

RECORDS

BERNIE & BAKER (Ben Bernie & Phil Baker, v-acc)
  Vi 18499 Waters of Venice/Goodbye Alexander
MORTON DOWNEY (with Phil Baker-acc)
  Pe 12874 Strange Interlude
PHIL BAKER
  Co 521-D Big Butter and Egg Man/ Ann and Her Little Sedan
  Ed 51634 Big Butter and Egg Man/ Ann and Her Little Sedan
  Vi 20970 (with SID SILVERS) At the Theatre (1 & 2)
  Vi 22350 Happy Days Are Here Again/Humming a Love Song

86. BALL, ERNEST R.   cm p
Born July 22, 1878, Cleveland, Ohio
Died May 3, 1927, Santa Ana, Calif.

Composer of many popular songs 1904-27. Specialized in sentimental and Irish songs. Most famous: *Mother Machree, When Irish Eyes Are Smiling, A Little Bit of Heaven, Dear Little Boy of Mine, Let the Rest of the World Go By, I'll Forget You.* Studied music at Cleveland Conservatory. First New York job as relief pianist in vaudeville theatre. Later played vaudeville houses throughout U. S. Worked many years as staff composer for music publishing company in New York. Wrote musical scores for Broadway musicals starring Irish-style tenor Chauncey Olcott: BARRY OF BALLYMORE (1910), THE ISLE O' DREAMS (1913), HEART OF PADDY WHACK (1914). Chief collaborators were Olcott, J. Keirn Brennan, George Graff, Jr. Brilliant career ended by death in 1927 at 48. Good movie musical, IRISH EYES ARE SMILING (1944), featured his songs and starred Dick Haymes as Ball.

SONGS
(with related shows)

1904—In the Shade of the Pyramids; My Honey Moon
1905—Will You Love Me in December as You Do in May?
1906—Love Me and the World Is Mine
1907—As Long as the World Rolls On; My Dear; When Sweet Marie Was Sweet Sixteen; When the Birds in Georgia Sing of Tennessee
1908—All for Love of You; In the Garden of My Heart; To the End of the World with You
1910—BARRY OF BALLYMORE stage show (Mother Machree; I Love the Name of Mary); Your Love Means the World to Me
1911—Till the Sands of the Desert Grow Cold
1913—THE ISLE O' DREAMS stage show (The Isle o' Dreams; When Irish Eyes Are Smiling); To Have, to Hold, to Love
1914—HEART OF PADDY WHACK stage show (A Little Bit of Heaven)
1915—Ireland Is Ireland to Me; She's the Daughter of Mother Machree; That's How the Shannon Flows
1916—For Dixie and Uncle Sam; Goodbye, Good Luck, God Bless You; Turn Back the Universe and Give Me Yesterday
1917—All the World Will Be Jealous of Me; My Sunshine Jane
1918—Dear Little Boy of Mine; One More Day; Who Knows?; With All My Heart and Soul
1919—Let the Rest of the World Go By
1921—I'll Forget You
1922—Down the Winding Road of Dreams
1923—Out There in the Sunshine with You; Ten Thousand Years from Now
1924—West of the Great Divide
1927—Rose of Killarney

87. BALL, LUCILLE   vo
Born August 6, 1910, Butte, Montana

Primarily a major TV actress and comedienne, later in career displayed talent in song and dance. Appeared in many movies, including important musicals in which she occasionally sang. Vivacious redhead with winning personality. Did not achieve stardom in movies. Often played the heavy or second lead. Entered early TV, co-starred with husband Desi Arnaz in series, I Love Lucy, beginning 1951. This series showcased Miss Ball's talent as comedienne, put her into TV orbit. Show ran long, was hugely successful. Miss Ball followed with specials, tried other formats after divorcing Arnaz. Top TV star from 50s into 70s. Starred in 1960 Broadway musical WILDCAT. In late 60s began working occasional musical sequences into TV shows with top guest stars, proved herself excellent entertainer.

MOVIES
(bit parts in many movies 1933-6)

1937—LOVE FROM A STRANGER; STAGE DOOR; DON'T TELL THE WIFE
1938—JOY OF LIVING; GO CHASE YOURSELF; HAVING A WONDERFUL TIME; AFFAIRS OF ANNABEL; ROOM SERVICE; ANNABEL TAKES A TOUR; THE NEXT TIME I MARRY
1939—BEAUTY FOR THE ASKING; TWELVE CROWDED HOURS; PANAMA LADY; FIVE CAME BACK; THAT'S RIGHT —YOU'RE WRONG
1940—THE MARINES FLY HIGH; DANCE GIRL DANCE; YOU CAN'T FOOL YOUR WIFE; TOO MANY GIRLS
1941—A GIRL, A GUY AND A GOB; LOOK WHO'S LAUGHING
1942—VALLEY OF THE SUN; THE BIG STREET
1943—SEVEN DAYS LEAVE; DUBARRY WAS A LADY; THOUSANDS CHEER; BEST FOOT FORWARD
1944—MEET THE PEOPLE
1945—WITHOUT LOVE; ABBOTT AND COSTELLO IN HOLLYWOOD
1946—EASY TO WED; ZIEGFELD FOLLIES; THE DARK CORNER; LOVER COME BACK; TWO SMART PEOPLE; WHEN LOVERS MEET
1947—PERSONAL COLUMN; LURED; HER HUSBAND'S AFFAIR
1949—SORROWFUL JONES; INTERFERENCE; EASY LIVING; MISS GRANT TAKES RICHMOND
1950—THE FULLER BRUSH GIRL; FANCY PANTS
1951—THE MAGIC CARPET
1954—THE LONG LONG TRAILER
1956—FOREVER DARLING
1960—THE FACTS OF LIFE
1963—CRITIC'S CHOICE

1964—BIG PARADE OF COMEDY
1967—A GUIDE FOR THE MARRIED MAN (cameo)
1968—YOURS, MINE AND OURS
1969—DIAMOND JIM BRADY

88. BALLEW, SMITH   vo bn g B
Born January 21, 1902, Palestine, Texas

Prolific freelance recording artist of 1929-36 period, on hundreds of records as vocalist with every type of band. Had high baritone voice, silken smooth. Consistently good singer on all types of lyrics. In great demand in record studios because of wide voice range and ability to sing songs in original key, requiring no special arrangements. Attended University of Texas. After college led band in Dallas-Fort Worth area several years, including long engagement at exclusive Fort Worth Club around 1923-4. Toured with band in years following. Ended up in Chicago in early 1927, disbanded. Briefly with Ben Pollack, Ted Fio Rito. To New York, freelanced. In late 20s with Meyer Davis, George Olsen, Hal Kemp, Sam Lanin as sideman-vocalist. Played in pit band awhile for Broadway musical GOOD NEWS. Became known to leading New York musicians, worked into recording scene, soon in demand as vocalist. Recorded under own name and fronted bands of varying sizes. Led band on key job at Whyte's Restaurant in New York early 1929. Band small semi-hot at times.

Several years later led smooth, larger hotel band. Early personnel at times included Dorseys, Joe Venuti, Eddie Lang, Babe Russin, Pete Pumiglio, Mickey Bloom, Mannie Klein, Jack Teagarden, Bunny Berigan. Glenn Miller served as chief aide and arranger 1932-4, when band included at times Chummy MacGregor, Jimmy McPartland, Ray McKinley, Harry Goodman, Stew Pletcher, Skeets Herfurt. Toured, often played Blue Room of Roosevelt Hotel in New Orleans. In mid-1936 Ballew replaced Al Jolson as singing host of radio show The Shell Chateau, with Victor Young Orchestra. At end of 1936 replaced by Joe Cook and new format. In 1936 effective role in movie PALM SPRINGS co-starring Frances Langford. In late 30s starred in low-budget westerns. After 1936 seldom recorded. World War II defense work on west coast. In 1946 resumed movies with a few minor roles, including spot in 15-chapter western serial. Left show business for good in 1950, eventually settled in Fort Worth and worked for General Dynamics.

RECORDS

BEN POLLACK
    Vi 21941 Louise/Wait Till You See Ma Cherie
    Vi 22158 From Now On/You've Made Me Happy Today
JOE VENUTI
    OK 41192 Weary River/That's the Good Old Sunny South
    OK 41320 Chant of the Jungle/That Wonderful Something
FRANKIE TRUMBAUER
    OK 41231 Louise/Wait Till You See Ma Cherie
    OK 41301 Love Ain't Nothin' but the Blues/How Am I to Know?
    OK 41313 Turn on the Heat/Sunny Side Up
RED NICHOLS
    Br 6118 Love Is Like That
    Br 6138 Little Girl/Slow but Sure
DORSEY BROTHERS ORCHESTRA
    OK 41210 Mean to Me/Button Up Your Overcoat
    OK 41220 I'll Never Ask for More/Deep Night (GOOFUS FIVE)
HOTSY TOTSY GANG
    Br 4200 Futuristic Rhythm/Out Where the Blues Begin
IPANA TROUBADOURS
    Co 2147-D I Never Dreamt/Hangin' on the Garden Gate
BENNY GOODMAN
    Co 2542-D Help Yourself to Happiness/Not That I Care
FRED RICH
    Co 2536-D If I Didn't Have You/As Time Goes By (THE COLUMBIANS
BEN SELVIN
    Co 2024-D Don't Ever Leave Me/Here Am I

Co 2150-D Let Me Sing and I'm Happy/Across the Breakfast Table
ED LLOYD
    OK 41367 Singing a Vagabond Song/There's Danger in Your Eyes, Cherie
DUKE ELLINGTON
    Vi 22586 Nine Little Miles from Ten-Ten-Tennessee
LLOYD KEATING
    Ha 1246 I'm Tickled Pink with a Blue-Eyed Baby
THE KNICKERBOCKERS
    Co 2129-D Thank Your Father/Good for You, Bad for Me
EMIL COLEMAN
    Br 6006 Where Have You Been?/Getting Myself Ready for You
GLENN MILLER
    Co 3051-D A Blues Serenade/Moonlight on the Ganges
SMITH BALLEW
    OK 41282 Blondy/Just You, Just Me
    OK 41299 Tiptoe Through the Tulips with Me/Painting the Clouds with Sunshine
    OK 41352 Charming/Shepherd's Serenade
    OK 41464 (BOB BLUE pseudonym) My Baby Just Cares for Me/I'll Be Blue, Just Thinking of You
    Co 2320-D You're Simply Delish/Passing Time with Me
    Co 2503-D I Love Louisa/What Is It?
    Co 2544-D Time on My Hands/You Call It Madness
    Cr 3227 I'm for You a Hundred Per Cent/You Try Somebody Else
    Pe 15600 Happy-Go-Lucky You/That's What Heaven Means to Me
    Pe 15626 Sleep, Come On and Take Me/If You Were Only Mine
    Pe 15636 The Lady I Love/Who's to Blame?
    Me 13343 Lovely to Look At/I Won't Dance

LPs

BEN SELVIN
    Tom 17 (Co RIs)
JOE VENUTI
    Tom 7 (OK RIs)

BEN POLLACK
TOM 22 (Vi RIs)

89. BARBARIN, PAUL   d B

Born May 5, 1901, New Orleans, La.
Died February 10, 1969, New Orleans,
La.

Drummer in dixieland groups, mainly in New Orleans. 50-year musical career. Began playing locally at early age. Later played in various cities but came back to New Orleans many times, spending most of career there. With King Oliver 1925-8, with Luis Russell 1928-31 and again 1934-8. (Most of latter period Louis Armstrong fronted band.) Led own band in New Orleans late 1939-40. In Chicago 1942-3 with Red Allen, led own band awhile, then with Sidney Bechet in 1944. In later 40s, 50s and 60s Barbarin based mostly in New Orleans. Played with traditional groups there and led own band. Became ill while marching in New Orleans parade, died shortly after of heart attack. Recorded extensively during long career.

RECORDS

KING OLIVER
Vo 1059 Someday Sweetheart/Dead Man Blues
Vo 1112 Black Snake Blues/Willie the Weeper
Vo 1225 Aunt Hagar's Blues/Speakeasy Blues
Br 4028 Got Everything/Four or Five Times

JELLY ROLL MORTON
Vi 23402 Sweet Peter/Jersey Joe
Vi 23424 Mississippi Mildred

LOUIS ARMSTRONG
OK 8669 I Can't Give You Anything but Love
OK 8680 Mahogany Hall Stomp
OK 8756 I Ain't Got Nobody/Rockin' Chair
De 579 I'm in the Mood for Love/Got a Bran' New Suit
De 623 I'm Shooting High/I've Got My Fingers Crossed
De 1661 Struttin' with Some Barbecue/Let That Be a Lesson to You

RED ALLEN
Vi 38073 It Should Be You/Biffly Blues
Pe 16071 Believe It, Beloved/It's Written All Over Your Face
Pe 16080 Smooth Sailing/Whose Honey Are You?
Vo 3564 A Love Song of Long Ago/ Sticks and Stones

J. C. HIGGINBOTHAM
OK 8772 Give Me Your Telephone Number/Higginbotham Blues

PAUL BARBARIN
Ci 1065 Panama/Just a Little While to Stay Here
Ci 1066 Clarinet Marmalade/Fidgety Feet
Ci 1077 Eh La Bas/Lily of the Valley
Ci 1078 A Closer Walk with Thee/ Walk Through the Streets of the City

LPs

PAUL BARBARIN
Atl 1215 New Orleans Jazz
GTJ 12019 Recorded in New Orleans, Vol. 1
Riv 12-217 New Orleans Contrasts
Jazztone J-1205 New Orleans Jamboree
GHB 2 Paul Barbarin & His New Orleans Jazz Band

PAUL BARBARIN & PUNCH MILLER
Atl 1410

JOHNNY WIGGS
Southland(10″)SLP-204 Johnny Wiggs & His New Orleans Kings

RED ALLEN
"X"(10″)LVA-3033 Ridin' with Red Allen (Vi RIs)

LUIS RUSSELL
Pa(E) PMC-7025 (OK RIs)

90. BARBOUR, DAVE   g cm ar B

Born May 28, 1912, Flushing, N.Y.
Died December 11, 1965, Malibu, Calif.

Guitarist with many jazz combos and bands in 30s and 40s. Good rhythm guitarist and capable soloist. Began professionally with name bands Wingy Manone 1934, Red Norvo combo 1935-6, Lennie Hayton 1936-7, Hal Kemp 1938,

Artie Shaw 1939. In early 40s with Raymond Scott big band and Lou Holden. Also worked accompanying singers and on radio shows. With Benny Goodman 1942-3. Married Goodman's vocalist, Peggy Lee. They teamed up in later 40s to compose successful songs including *I Don't Know Enough About You* (1946), *It's a Good Day* and *Don't Be So Mean to Baby* (1947), and their biggest hit *Manana* (1947). Musical conductor for Curt Massey radio show in 1945. Did little jobbing in following years. In late 40s and early 50s settled on west coast, did some writing, led bands behind various singers in record sessions. Substantial recording. Role in 1950 movie THE SECRET FURY. Divorced from Peggy Lee and after early 50s mostly inactive in music.

RECORDS

LIL ARMSTRONG
De 1904 Oriental Swing/Let's Get Happy Together
BUNNY BERIGAN
Vo 3178 I'd Rather Lead a Band/Let Yourself Go
Vo 3179 It's Been So Long/Swing, Mister Charlie
BENNY GOODMAN
Co 36641 Dearly Beloved
CAPITOL JAZZMEN
Cap 10009 Clambake in B-Flat/I'm Sorry I Made You Cry
HERBIE HAYMER
Key 640 I Saw Stars/Sweet and Lovely
RED MCKENZIE
Vo 3898 You're Out of This World/Georgianna
RED NORVO
De 691 Gramercy Square/Decca Stomp
De 779 Lady Be Good
Br 7732 Picture Me without You/It All Begins and Ends with You
ANDRE PREVIN
Sun 10057 Blue Skies/Good Enough to Keep
CHARLIE VENTURA
Sun 10051 Tea for Two/Ghost of a Chance
Sun 10054 "C.V." Jump/I Surrender Dear

MAHLON CLARK
Je 5000 I'm a Dreamer (Aren't We All?)/Atomic Did It
PEGGY LEE
Cap 197 What More Can a Woman Do?/You Was Right, Baby
Cap 48014 Baby
DAVE BARBOUR
Cap 358 Forever Paganini/Forever Nicki
Cap 973 Dave's Boogie/The Mambo
(as conductor)
PEGGY LEE
Cap 302 It's a Good Day/He's Just My Kind
Cap 375 Speaking of Angels/Swing Low, Sweet Chariot
Cap 961 Once Around the Moon/Cry, Cry, Cry
Cap 10118 Why Don't You Do Right?/I Can't Give You Anything but Love
Cap 15298 Hold Me/Then I'll Be Happy
GLORIA DEHAVEN
De 27781 The Closer You Are/Let the Worry Bird Worry for You
KAY STARR
Cap 1492 Come Back My Darling

LPs

PEGGY LEE
Cap(10")H-151 Rendezvous (as conductor)
JERI SOUTHERN
De DL-8761 Southern Hospitality (with his trio)
De(10")DL-5531 Warm, Intimate Songs (with his trio)

91. BAREFIELD, EDDIE   cl as ar B
Born December 12, 1909, Scandia, Iowa
Competent performer on clarinet and alto sax. With many name bands from 1930 into 70s. Began playing professionally in mid-20s, touring with various bands. Studied music in Chicago 1930. In early 30s worked with Teddy Wilson, Art Tatum, Bennie Moten and McKinney's Cotton Pickers. Joined Cab Calloway in mid-1932, remained till 1934, went with

him on European tour in 1934. In 1935-7 did studio work on west coast, led own band, worked with Les Hite. Joined Fletcher Henderson in 1938, later that year Don Redman. In 1939 rejoined Calloway. With Ella Fitzgerald several months in 1940. Then freelanced in New York, also led own band. In 1941 with Benny Carter several months. In late 1941-2 served as musical director for Ella Fitzgerald. From late 1942 till 1946, radio staff musician. With Sy Oliver late 1946-7; with Duke Ellington awhile in 1947. Late 1947-9 musical director for stage play A STREETCAR NAMED DESIRE. In 1950 with Sy Oliver and Fletcher Henderson. Another foreign tour with Calloway in 1951. Freelanced in New York in the 50s, did some theatre work. Toured with Don Redman in 1953. European tour with Sam Price in 1958. Continued active through 60s and into 70s, including jobs with Paul Lavalle and Wilbur DeParis. Led revival of Chick Webb band at 1973 Newport-New York Jazz Festival.

RECORDS

CAB CALLOWAY
    Vi 24690 Moonglow
DON REDMAN
    Bb 10071 Milenberg Joys
ELLA FITZGERALD
    De 3026 Sing Song Swing/If It Weren't for You
    De 3236 Jubilee Swing/Take It from the Top
    De 3441 Tea Dance
BILLIE HOLIDAY
    OK 6134 Let's Do It/Georgia on My Mind
    OK 6214 All of Me/Romance in the Dark
COZY COLE
    Sav 519 Jersey Jump Off/On the Sunny Side of the Street
PETE JOHNSON
    De 18121 627 Stomp/Piney Brown Blues (JOE TURNER)
HOT LIPS PAGE
    De 18124 Lafayette/South
EDDIE BAREFIELD
    Son 102 That Ain't Right/After Hours
    Son 104 What's Mine Is Mine/Three Buckets o' Jive
    Son 112 Clarinet Blues/'F 'Tain't One Thing It's Another
    Son 114 Clara 'n' Eddie/Right Off the Ice

LPs

ROY ELDRIDGE
    Verve V-1010 Swing Goes Dixie
BOBBY SHORT
    Atl 1302 The Mad Twenties
RED ALLEN-CHARLIE SHAVERS COMBOS
    Beth BCP-21 Jazz at the Metropole
LIONEL HAMPTON
    Vi LJM-1000

92. BARGY, ROY   p ar cm B
Died January 15, 1974, Vista, Calif.

Early pianist and musical director, best known for association with Paul Whiteman in 20s and 30s as pianist-arranger. Played strong piano, pit-band type. Early 20s musical director of Benson Orchestra of Chicago on some Victor records. As pianist he played theatres, hotels and ballrooms. Composed rags for piano, including *Knice and Knifty* and *Pianoflage*. Recorded piano solos. Joined Whiteman band late 20s, remained to late 30s. In mid-30s often featured with band's vocalist Ramona. Provided many arrangements for band, appeared on many of band's records, as well as a few with jazz greats. By 1936 he was getting billing on Whiteman's Musical Varieties radio show. In 1940 began career in radio as conductor. Led bands for shows of Lanny Ross, Xavier Cugat, Jimmy Durante, Garry Moore, Rexall Theatre. Also worked on record sessions, backing singers. Continued active into 50s.

RECORDS

BENSON ORCHESTRA (as musical director)
    Vi 18757 Scandinavia/Ain't We Got Fun
    Vi 18819 Ma!/My Sunny Tennessee
    Vi 18871 Ten Little Fingers and Ten Little Toes/In Bluebird Land
    Vi 18980 The World Is Waiting for the Sunrise/Tomorrow Morning
RAMONA with ROY BARGY
    Vi 24260 A Penny for Your Thoughts/My Cousin in Milwaukee

Vi 24304 I've Got to Sing a Torch Song
Vi 24310 Was My Face Red?
Vi 24440 I'm No Angel/I've Found a New Way to Go to Town
Vi 24445 Not for All the Rice in China

ADRIAN'S RAMBLERS
Br 6877 I've Got a Warm Spot in My Heart for You/Why Don't You Practice What You Preach?
Br 6889 I Wish I Were Twins/The Better to Love You, My Dear

THE THREE T'S (TRUMBAUER & TEAGARDENS)
Vi 25273 I'se a-Muggin' (1 & 2)

FRANKIE TRUMBAUER
Br 6763 Break It Down/Juba Dance
Br 6788 Emaline/'Long About Midnight
Br 7629 Announcer's Blues/Flight of a Haybag
Br 7665 Ain't Misbehavin'/Somebody Loves Me
Vi 24812 Blue Moon/Down t' Uncle Bill's
Vi 24834 Plantation Moods/Troubled

PAUL WHITEMAN PRESENTS PEGGY HEALY
Vi 24452 When You Were the Girl on the Scooter/That's How Rhythm Was Born

PAUL WHITEMAN
Co 2277-D Nola/New Tiger Rag
Co(12")50140-D Concerto in F
Vi 21453 It Was the Dawn of Love
Vi 24574 Sun Spots/The Bouncing Ball

JIMMY DURANTE-HELEN TRAUBEL
Vi(12")12-3229 The Song's Gotta Come from the Heart/A Real Piano Player

ROY BARGY (piano solos)
Vi 18969 Knice and Knifty/Pianoflage
Vi 19320 Sunshine Capers/Ruffenreddy
Vi 19537 Jim Jams/Justin-Tyme

LPs

ROY BARGY
Tops(10")L-949 Music for Young Lovers

JIMMY DURANTE (as conductor)
De DL-9049 Club Durant
MGM E-4207 The Very Best of Jimmy Durante

93. BARKER, DANNY   g bn B

Born January 13, 1909, New Orleans, La.

Good rhythm guitarist. With many bands from late 20s through 60s. Early in career played clarinet, drums and ukulele, then switched to banjo and guitar. Played in various groups locally, including Lee Collins' in late 20s. In early and mid-30s jobbed around New York with Fess Williams, Buddy Harris, Albert Nicholas and James P. Johnson. With Lucky Millinder 1937-8 and late 1938 with Benny Carter. Also worked with wife Blue Lu Barker on records. In 1939 began long period with Cab Calloway lasting to 1946. In late 40s and 50s at intervals Barker led groups accompanying his wife, also worked with Lucky Millinder, Bunk Johnson, Albert Nicholas. In 50s with Conrad Janis, Paul Barbarin and Albert Nicholas. Active through 60s, in New Orleans since 1965. Recorded with many jazz greats during long career.

RECORDS

RED ALLEN
Pe 16071 Believe It, Beloved/It's Written All Over Your Face
Pe 16080 Smooth Sailing/Whose Honey Are You?
Vo 3339 Midnight Blue/Whatcha Gonna Do When There Ain't No Swing?
Vo 3340 Lost in My Dreams/Sitting on the Moon

BUSTER BAILEY
Vo 2887 Call of the Delta/Shanghai Shuffle
Vo 4564 Light Up/Man with a Horn Goes Berserk

CHU BERRY
Va 657 My Secret Love Affair/Ebb Tide
Co 37571 Chuberry Jam/Maelstrom
CMS 516 Forty-Six West Fifty-Two/Sittin' In

CAB CALLOWAY
Vo 5444 Boog It/Chop Chop, Charlie Chan
OK 5687 A Ghost of a Chance/Come On with the "Come On"
OK 6084 Bye Bye Blues/Run, Little Rabbit

LIONEL HAMPTON
Vi 26296 Stand By for Further Announcements/Big Wig in the Wigwam

JONAH JONES
CMS 602 Rose of the Rio Grande/Stomping at the Savoy

BILLY KYLE
Va 531 Margie/Big Boy Blues
Va 574 Havin' a Ball/Sundays Are Reserved

LITTLE RAMBLERS
Bb 6130 I'm on a See-Saw/I'm Painting the Town Red
Bb 6131 Red Sails in the Sunset/Tender Is the Night

TEDDY WILSON
Br 8319 Sugar/More Than You Know

MEZZROW-BECHET SEPTET
KJ 143 House Party/Blood on the Moon
KJ 144 Levee Blues/Saw Mill Man Blues

BLUE LU BARKER
De 7506 He Caught the B & O/Don't You Make Me High
De 7560 I Got Ways Like the Devil/You're Going to Leave the Old Home, Jim
De 7588 Georgia Grind/Nix on Those Lush Heads
De 7709 Handy Andy/Blue Deep Sea Blues
Cap 57-70007 Now You're Down in the Alley

TONY PARENTI
Ci 1030 Grace and Beauty/Praline
Ci 1031 Swipesy Cake Walk/Hiawatha

LPs

CHU BERRY
Epic LN-3124 "Chu" (Va, Vo RIs)

MUGGSY SPANIER
Ci(10")L-423 This Is Jazz

PAUL BARBARIN
Jazztone J-1205 New Orleans Jamboree

WILD BILL DAVISON
Riv 12-211 Sweet and Hot

CONRAD JANIS
Ci(10")L-404 Conrad Janis' Tailgate Jazz Band

MUTT CAREY (1 side)
Sav MG-12038 Jazz—New Orleans, Vol. 1

94. BARKSDALE, EVERETT   g B
Born April 28, 1910, Detroit, Mich.

Excellent guitarist for small combo, adept at feeding chords to soloists, very tasteful style. As youngster also played alto sax, violin, bass and piano but early concentrated on guitar. Played locally, then moved to Chicago about 1930. Early jobs there included period with Erskine Tate. Joined violinist Eddie South's combo in 1932 and remained till 1939, except for intervals. Settled in New York in 1939. Jobbed about and in early 40s worked with Benny Carter, Leon Abbey, Herman Chittison, Cliff Jackson and Lester Boone. In mid-40s led own combo, also did studio work. In 1949-55 with Art Tatum off and on, his guitar complementing perfectly the work of the great pianist. In 1956 with Ink Spots, then rejoined Tatum and remained until Art's last job in October. In late 50s worked with Buddy Tate, also freelanced. Studio work in radio and TV, late 50s into 60s.

RECORDS

EDDIE SOUTH
Vi 24324 Old Man Harlem/No More Blues
Vi 24343 Gotta Go/My Oh My
Vi 24383 Nagasaki/Mamma Mocking Bird

BENNY CARTER
Bb 10962 All of Me/The Very Thought of You
Bb 10998 Cocktails for Two/Takin' My Time

ED HALL
BN 511 It's Been So Long/I Can't Believe That You're in Love with Me
BN(12")36 Big City Blues/Steamin' and Beamin'

SIDNEY BECHET
Vi 27600 I'm Coming Virginia/Georgia Cabin
Vi 27707 Rose Room/Lady Be Good
Vi 27904 Limehouse Blues/Texas Moaner
Vi 20-3120 12th Street Rag

UNA MAE CARLISLE
Bb 11033 Walkin' by the River/I Met You Then, I Know You Now
CLIFF JACKSON
B&W(12")1204 Quiet Please/Walking and Talking to Myself
B&W(12")1205 Cliff's Boogie Blues/ Jeepers Creepers
BOB HOWARD
Atl 852 Button Up Your Overcoat/ Mo'lasses

LPs

HERMAN CHITTISON
Co(10")CL-6182 Herman Chittison Trio
ART TATUM
Cap(10")H-408
RED ALLEN
Vi LPM-1509 Ride, Red, Ride in Hi-Fi
LOCKJAW DAVIS-PAUL GONSALVES
Vi LSP-3882 Love Calls
CHRIS CONNER
Beth(10")BCP-1001

95. BARLOW, HOWARD   cm B
Born May 1, 1892, Plain City, Ohio
Died January 31, 1972

Conductor on radio many years. Noted particularly for long tenure on popular Voice of Firestone show 1943-59. Educated at Reed College and Columbia University. Conductor of CBS Symphony Orchestra 1927-43, Baltimore Symphony Orchestra 1939-42. Guest conductor with New York Philharmonic Orchestra 1943-4. Compositions include *Margaret*; *Mother, I Can Not Mind My Wheel*; *Lament*; *Garden*.

96. BARNES, GEORGE   g ar cm B
Born July 17, 1921, Chicago Heights, Ill.

Talented solo guitarist. Swing style, great technique. As youngster led own combo 1935-9 in midwest, did some touring. Staff musician on Chicago radio 1939-42, where gained prominence on popular Plantation Party show. His outstanding guitar work ahead of its time. In 1942 had own radio show on NBC, played clubs in midwest. Military service, World War II. In 1946 resumed radio staff work in Chicago till late 1951. Led excellent com-

bo in 1950-1 on radio. Then to New York for radio-TV-recording work. In early 60s he formed guitar duo with veteran Carl Kress until death of Kress in mid-1965. Barnes later teamed with guitarist Bucky Pizzarelli, then Art Ryerson. Also did some teaching. Active into 70s. Formed quartet with cornetist Ruby Braff 1973. Group played Newport—New York Jazz Festival and backed Tony Bennett in concerts.

RECORDS

GEORGE BARNES
OK 5798 I Can't Believe That You're in Love with Me/I'm Forever Blowing Bubbles
Key 646 Blue Lou/Quiet—Two Gibsons at Work
Key 651 Barnes at Dublin's/Laughing at Life
Key 652 Pink Elephants/Lover, Come Back to Me
Key 653 Windy City Flash/What's the Use?
De 27706 Clarinet Polka/Hot Guitar Polka
De 28083 Plink, Plank, Plunk/Tin Whistle Blues
De 28688 It Must Be True/Flibberty Gibbet
DOROTHY COLLINS
Audivox 107 Crazy Rhythm
ALAN DALE
De 27961 Broken Hearted/Silver and Gold

LPs

GEORGE BARNES
GA 33-358 Guitar in Velvet
Mer-Wing SRW-16392 Guitar Galaxy
Mer-Wing SRW-16393 Guitars Galore
Colortone 33-4915 Country Jazz
GEORGE BARNES-CARL KRESS
UA 6335 Town Hall Concert
GEORGE BARNES-BUCKY PIZZARELLI
A&R ARL-7100/007 Guitars: Pure and Honest
KAY STARR
Prem K-584 Kay Starr Sings (Cry RIs)
BUD FREEMAN
Cap(10")H-625 Classics in Jazz
UA 15033 Something Tender
LOU MCGARITY
Jub 1108 Some Like It Hot

LAWSON-HAGGART JAZZ BAND
De(10″)DL-5439 Blues on the River
De(10″)DL-5529 South of the Mason-
Dixon Line
TOMMY REYNOLDS
King 395-510 Jazz for Happy Feet
GARRY MOORE PRESENTS
Co CL-717 My Kind of Music
JAZZ RENAISSANCE QUINTET
Mer MG-20605 Movin' Easy

97. BARNES, WALTER   ts cl B

Born c.1907, Vicksburg, Miss.
Died April 23, 1940, Natchez, Miss., in
night club fire

Leader of good big hot band that played
mostly in south. Came to public attention
in 1940 through tragedy: disastrous fire
that destroyed club in Natchez, Miss.,
where Barnes band playing. Holocaust
took many lives, including those of
Barnes and most of band. Studied music
in Chicago and through middle and late
20s played in that area and in Detroit.
Became bandleader, his band billed as
Walter Barnes & His Royal Creolians.
Played in Detroit, Chicago and New
York, through 30s toured south, sometimes north. Reorganized band in 1939,
played in Chicago, toured. Unfortunately,
band recorded little.

RECORDS

WALTER BARNES & HIS ROYAL CREOLIANS
Br 4187 My Kinda Love/How Long
How Long
Br 4244 It's Tight Like That
Br 4480 Birmingham Bertha/If You're
Thinking of Me
Br 7072 Buffalo Rhythm/Third Rail

LPs

WALTER BARNES
OFC(10″)47 (Br RIs)

98. BARNET, CHARLIE

ts ss as vo cm B
(CHARLES DALY BARNET,
nicknamed Mad Mab)

Born October 26, 1913, New York, N.Y.

Tenor sax jazzman, leader of a top swing
band from mid-30s into 60s. Ardent ad-
mirer of Duke Ellington, his bands usually bore Ellington stamp. Colorful leader

noted for his many marriages, several to
his band vocalists. Barnet had wealthy
parents, received good education including musical training. In 1929 at 16 led
combo aboard ship on many trans-At-
lantic, Mediterranean and South American trips. Played also in bands in New
York, then went south with Beasley
Smith, working his way to Texas and
California. Upon his return to New York
in early 1933, formed big hotel-style
band. Played New York's Paramount Hotel Grill, Park Central Hotel, other top
hotels in and out of New York. By 1935
band also featured hot style. Disbanded
and tried a movie career briefly, playing
small roles. Organized new band in 1936-
7, did some vocals in this period, also
used pioneer modern-harmony singing
group, The Modernaires. This band
boasted clean-cut swing arrangements.

In late 1938 Barnet formed outstanding
big swing band. Scored at 52nd Street's
Famous Door, moved on to other top
spots including Palomar Ballroom in Los
Angeles. Extensive recordings 1939-41.
Solid band with outstanding arrangements, many Ellington-influenced. Barnet
featured prominently on tenor sax, at
times led sax section on soprano sax to
achieve distinctive, beautiful sound. Judy
Ellington was female vocalist, followed by
Mary Ann McCall. Larry Taylor was
male vocalist, followed by Bob Carroll.
Billy May played trumpet and furnished
arrangements, notably that of Barnet's
all-time hit *Cherokee*. Skip Martin also
did arrangements. The band had capable
jazz soloists, although none of renown.
Theme song was first *Make Believe Ballroom*, then *Cherokee*, then *Redskin Rhumba*, later *Skyliner*. In 40s Barnet's vocalists
included Lena Horne and Kay Starr for
brief periods. Big instrumental hit records
in *Pompton Turnpike* (1940) and *Skyliner*
(1945). In 1949 he brought to fame Maynard Ferguson, fantastic high-note trumpet star. Barnet and band appeared in
movies, notably SYNCOPATION (1942),
IDEA GIRL (1946), THE FABULOUS DORSEYS
(1947), A SONG IS BORN (1948), MAKE
BELIEVE BALLROOM(1949). Composer or
co-composer of swing numbers featured

by his band, including *Leapin' at the Lincoln*, *The Duke's Idea*, *The Count's Idea*, *Dark Avenue*, *Murder at Peyton Hall*, *Mother Fuzzy*, *The Heart You Stole from Me*, *Lament for May*. As band business became unstable in late 40s and 50s, Barnet changed band sizes and personnel, with inactive periods in between. Settled on west coast late 50s. Occasionally fronted combo or big band on special jobs, including Las Vegas and New York spots. In later years switched to soprano sax almost exclusively. Infrequent TV appearances. Rather inactive by late 60s.

RECORDS

RED NORVO
    Co 2977-D Tomboy/I Surrender Dear
    Co 3059-D Old Fashioned Love
ADRIAN'S RAMBLERS (Adrian Rollini)
    Br 6786 Get Goin'/Keep On Doin' What You're Doin'
METRONOME ALL-STAR BAND
    Co 35389 King Porter Stomp
    Co 36499 I Got Rhythm
CALIFORNIA RAMBLERS (Charlie Barnet)
    Va 577 Down South Camp Meeting/Take My Word
    Va 603 Chris and His Gang/Swingin' Down to Rio
CHARLIE BARNET
    Me 12817 I'm No Angel/I Want You —I Need You
    Me 12992 Emaline/I Lost Another Sweetheart
    Bb 5814 I'm Keeping Those Keepsakes You Gave Me/Don't Be Afraid to Tell Your Mother
    Bb 6432 Long Ago and Far Away/Where Is My Heart?
    Bb 6488 A Star Fell Out of Heaven/When Did You Leave Heaven?
    Bb 6504 Make Believe Ballroom/Bye Bye, Baby
    Bb 6594 You Do the Darndest Things, Baby/It's Love I'm After
    Bb 6973 The First Time I Saw You/Love Is a Merry-Go-Round
    Bb 10131 Tin Roof Blues/Knockin' at the Famous Door
    Bb 10373 (theme) Cherokee/The All Night Record Man
    Bb 10453 The Duke's Idea/The Count's Idea

    Bb 10610 It's a Wonderful World/Busy as a Bee
    Bb 10774 Leapin' at the Lincoln/Dark Avenue
    Bb 10825 Pompton Turnpike/I Don't Want to Cry Any More
    Bb 10944 (theme) Redskin Rhumba/Southern Fried
    Bb 11194 Little Dip/Ponce de Leon
    De 18547 Oh Miss Jaxon/Washington Whirligig
    De 18659 (theme) Skyliner/West End Blues
    Cap 843 All the Things You Are/Ill Wind
    Cap 1404 Spain/Over the Rainbow
    Cap 15417 Lonely Street/Cu-ba
    Cap 60010 Portrait of Edward Kennedy Ellington (1 & 2)

LPs

CHARLIE BARNET
    Vi LPM-2081 The Great Dance Bands of the 30s & 40s (Bb RIs)
    Vi LPV-551 Charlie Barnet, Vol. 1 (Bb RIs)
    Vi LPV-567 Charlie Barnet, Vol. 2 (Bb RIs)
    De DL-8098 Hop on the Skyliner (De RIs)
    Cap T-624 Classics in Jazz (Cap RIs)
    Everest 5008 Cherokee
    Verve MGV-2040 Lonely Street

99. BARRIE, GRACIE   vo B
Born c. 1917

Singer with beauty, poise and talent. At 16 had minor role in Broadway show STRIKE ME PINK. Sang on radio with Leon Belasco orchestra in 1935. Had roles in Broadway shows GEORGE WHITE'S SCANDALS OF 1936 and THE SHOW IS ON (1937). Sang with Abe Lyman in later 30s. Vocalist with husband Dick Stabile's band in early 40s. Fronted band while Stabile was in military service. Soon after Stabile discharged in 1945, they separated. Miss Barrie continued career for a time as single.

RECORDS

DICK STABILE
    De 4301 You Know
    De 4351 You're Easy to Dance With

De 4352 At Last/He's My Guy

100. BARRIS, HARRY p vo ar cm lyr B

Born November 24, 1905, New York, N.Y.
Died December 13, 1962, Burbank, Calif.

Composer of several all-time pop standards. Bit parts in numerous movies. Chief composition: *I Surrender Dear* (1931). Others of note: *From Monday On* and *Mississippi Mud* (1928), *It Must Be True* (1930), *At Your Command, Lies, What Is It?* and *Wrap Your Troubles in Dreams* (1931), *It Was So Beautiful* (1932), *Little Dutch Mill* and *Let's Spend an Evening at Home* (1934), *Thrilled* (1935), *How Little I Knew* and *Naturally* (1938). Grew up in Denver. Professional pianist at 14, took own band on Oriental tour at 17. In late 1926 joined Bing Crosby and Al Rinker to form Rhythm Boys vocal trio featured by Paul Whiteman. Wrote most of trio's special material. Trio became top attraction with Whiteman, appeared in 1930 movie KING OF JAZZ. After movie, Rhythm Boys left Whiteman, later in year worked with Gus Arnheim band at famed Cocoanut Grove in Los Angeles. Group broke up when Crosby began career as single. Barris led a band briefly, managed by Richard Himber. In late 1936-7 fronted Bob Kinney band, also performed on radio show Jack Oakie's College. During 30s and 40s often seen in bit parts in movies, particularly those of old pal Crosby. Barris played small, slick, jive-talking personality, fit perfectly Hollywood's idea of typical band musician. Usually played role of rehearsal pianist, bandsman or bandleader. Better roles in HOLLYWOOD PARTY (1934), DOUBLE OR NOTHING and SOMETHING TO SING ABOUT (1937), SOME LIKE IT HOT (1939). In late 1943-4 accompanied comedian Joe E. Brown overseas to entertain troops. In early 1945 led big band on series of one-nighters, featured wife Loyce Whiteman on vocals. Made Alaskan USO tour in 1957.

RECORDS

PAUL WHITEMAN'S RHYTHM BOYS
Vi 20783 Sweet Li'l/Ain't She Sweet?/ /Mississippi Mud/I Left My Sugar Standing in the Rain
Vi 21104 Miss Annabelle Lee
Vi 21302 From Monday On/What Price Lyrics?
Vi 27688 That's Grandma
Co 1455-D That's Grandma/Wa Da Da
Co 1629-D Rhythm King/My Suppressed Desire
Co 1819-D Louise/So the Bluebirds and Blackbirds Got Together
Co 2223-D A Bench in the Park
PAUL WHITEMAN (vocals by The Rhythm Boys)
Vi 20627 Side by Side/Pretty Lips
Vi 21103 Changes
Vi 21274 Mississippi Mud
Vi 21464 There Ain't No Sweet Man
Co 1845-D Your Mother and Mine

LPs

PAUL WHITEMAN
"X"(10")LVA-3040 Featuring Bix Beiderbecke (Vi RIs)

100A. BARRISON, MABEL vo

Born 1882
Died 1912

Singer and leading actress on Broadway beginning at turn of century. Important role in long-running FLORODORA (1900). Starring role in important show BABES IN TOYLAND (1903).

BROADWAY MUSICALS

1900—FLORODORA
1901—THE PRIMA DONNA
1902—TWIRLY WHIRLY (joined after opening)
1903—BABES IN TOYLAND
1906—THE DISTRICT LEADER (unsuccessful)
1907—THE LAND OF NOD
1908—THE FLOWER OF THE RANCH; THE BLUE MOUSE (non-musical)
1910—LULU'S HUSBAND (non-musical)

101. BARRON, BLUE B

Born March 22, 1911, Cleveland, Ohio

Leader of stylized sweet band from mid-30s into 60s. Popular hotel band. Attended college in Ohio. Began musical career booking hotel bands in Cleveland area. In 1935 formed own band along same lines. Style similar to Kay Kyser's and Sammy Kaye's, featuring glissing trombone and mellow sax section. Theme song: *Sometimes I'm Happy*. Particularly popular in midwest. By late 30s recording regularly. Russ Carlyle first featured vocalist, followed by Clyde Burke and Don Brown. Barron entered military service in 1944 and singer Tommy Ryan took over band. Upon return to civilian life, Barron resumed career as bandleader but failed to attain former popularity. Did some recording, was active through the 50s and into 60s, mostly in Chicago area.

RECORDS

BLUE BARRON

Va 582 And Then They Called It Love/Don't Ever Change

Vo 3772 Yours and Mine/I'm Feelin' Like a Million

Bb 7419 At a Perfume Counter/Did an Angel Kiss You?

Bb 7608 I Hadn't Anyone 'Til You/In a Little Dutch Kindergarten

Bb 7736 The Yam/I Used to Be Color Blind

Bb 7856 Angels with Dirty Faces/It's a Lonely Trail

Bb 7872 Heart and Soul/Love Doesn't Grow on Trees

Bb 10221 Night Must Fall/Then Came the Rain

Bb 10230 Grateful/Down Linger Longer Lane

Bb 10277 I'll Never Fail You/Roller Skating on a Rainbow

Bb 10380 It's Funny to Everyone but Me/Up-sy Down-sy

Bb 10525 Darn That Dream/Peace, Brother

Bb 10537 Pinch Me/Wouldja Mind?

Bb 10594 On the Isle of May/Gotta Get Home

Bb 10808 Trade Winds/In a Moonboat

Bb 10826 (theme) Sometimes I'm Happy/Get the Moon Out of Your Eyes

Bb 10894 You Walk By/It's Eight O'clock

El 5001 Elmer's Tune/Shepherd Serenade

MGM 10121 Mary Lou/Let's Be Sweethearts Again

MGM 10766 Beyond the Reef/Bubbles

MGM 11136 Tears/I Wish I Had a Girl

LPs

BLUE BARRON

Roy(10″)1863 (Elite RIs)

102. BARTON, EILEEN   VO

Born c. 1928

Singer known for hit record of *If I Knew You Were Comin' I'd've Baked a Cake*. Parents were vaudevillians and as child Eileen played vaudeville. Performed on children's radio programs, also had spots on Rudy Vallee and Eddie Cantor shows. At 9 appeared on Milton Berle's radio show and toured with him. Out of show business from 11 to 15. Then dramatic work on radio, understudy role in Broadway musical BEST FOOT FORWARD. In 1944 appeared in theatres and on radio with singing idol Frank Sinatra. In 1945 with Milton Berle on radio. In later 40s kept singing in clubs, having her ups and downs, until 1950 brought her big hit record. This boosted her career for several years, leading to better bookings, more records, frequent TV appearances. In later 50s career waned. Though associated with hit novelty song, also a capable performer with other material.

RECORDS

SKITCH HENDERSON

Cap 402 Would You Believe Me?

EILEEN BARTON

Nat 9103 If I Knew You Were Comin' I'd've Baked a Cake/Popo, Loco in the Coco

Nat 9109 Dixieland Ball/Honey, Won't You Honeymoon with Me?

Mer 5410 You Brought a New Kind of Love to Me/They Say It's Wonderful

Cor 60592 Cry/Hold Me Just a Little Longer, Daddy

Cor 60691 To Be Loved by You/Wrong

Cor 60805 You Intrigue Me/You Like

Cor 60833 Easy Easy Baby/Some Folks Do and Some Folks Don't

Cor 60880 The Night Before Christmas Song/The Little Match Girl
Cor 60882 Don't Let the Stars Get in Your Eyes/Tennessee Tango
Cor 60927 Pretend/Too Proud to Cry
Cor 61057 Toys/Anytime, Anywhere
Cor 61185 Sway/When Mama Calls

EILEEN BARTON-JOHNNY DESMOND-MCGUIRE SISTERS
Cor 61126 Cling to Me/Pine Tree, Pine Over Me

EILEEN BARTON-BUDDY GRECO
Cor 60753 Red Rose Waltz/You Belong to Me

103. BARTON, JAMES vo

Born 1890
Died 1962

Great clog dancer, also singer and actor famed for stage roles in TOBACCO ROAD and PAINT YOUR WAGON. Played many years in burlesque and vaudeville, became known for drunk imitation. Sang in rough theatrical voice. Appeared in Broadway shows THE PASSING SHOW OF 1919, THE LAST WALTZ (1921), THE ROSE OF STAMBOUL (1922), DEW DROP INN (1923), THE PASSING SHOW OF 1924, NO FOOLIN' (1926; later titled ZIEGFELD'S AMERICAN REVUE OF 1926), SWEET AND LOW (1930), PAINT YOUR WAGON (1951). Star of long-running drama TOBACCO ROAD (1937-9), also starred in play THE ICEMAN COMETH (1946). Also appeared in movies, proved a competent actor and comedian.

MOVIES

1935—CAPTAIN HURRICANE; HIS FAMILY TREE
1941—THE SHEPHERD OF THE HILLS
1944—LIFEBOAT
1948—TIME OF YOUR LIFE; YELLOW SKY
1950—DAUGHTER OF ROSIE O'GRADY; WABASH AVENUE
1951—HERE COMES THE GROOM; THE SCARF; GOLDEN GIRL
1956—THE NAKED HILIS
1957—QUANTEZ
1961—THE MISFITS

RECORDS

JAMES BARTON
OK 40136 Fabricatin' Phil/Going Where the Climate Fits My Clothes

OK 40215 I'se Got to Be Sweet to Mah Feet/Don't Take My Breath Away
OK 40276 Voodoo/Railroad Man's Goodbye
Vi 19-0025 I Still See Elisa

LPs
(original Broadway cast)
Vi LSO-1006 PAINT YOUR WAGON

104. BASCOMB, DUD t B
(WILBER ODELL BASCOMB)

Born May 16, 1916, Birmingham, Ala.
Died December 25, 1972

Trumpeter best known for work with Erskine Hawkins and particularly for solo on band's all-time hit record, *Tuxedo Junction*. Younger brother of tenor sax star Paul Bascomb, also with Hawkins. Brothers with Bama State Collegians band in 1932, later led by Hawkins, went to New York with band in 1934. Dud remained with Hawkins till 1944. Popularity of band soared with *Tuxedo Junction* in 1939. Public thought trumpet solo was by Hawkins, since he was always featured prominently, but it was actually by Dud. In mid-40s Dud and Paul were co-leaders of combo, then led big band. Dud worked two stints with Duke Ellington. In late 40s led own band, continued in 50s and 60s off and on. Also recorded, played in 60s with tenor sax stars Sam Taylor and Buddy Tate. Led bands backing singers. Still active into 70s.

RECORDS

ERSKINE HAWKINS
Bb 7839 Weary Blues
Bb 10029 Easy Rider (2nd trumpet solo)
Bb 10224 Swing Out/Raid the Joint
Bb 10292 Swingin' on Lenox Avenue
Bb 10364 Hot Platter (2nd trumpet solo)/Weddin' Blues
Bb 10409 Tuxedo Junction (2nd trumpet solo)/Gin Mill Special
Bb 10504 Uptown Shuffle
Bb 10709 Midnight Stroll
Bb 11547 Bicycle Bounce

DUD BASCOMB
Son 103 Not Bad, Bascomb/Just One More Chance
Son 105 Late Hour Rock/That's My Home

553

DeL 2004 Victory Bells/Time and Time Again
DeL 2005 Let's Jump/Somebody's Knockin'
Alert 200 Walkin' Blues
Alert 201 Sweet Georgia Brown/Indiana

105. BASCOMB, PAUL   ts B

Born February 12, 1910, Birmingham, Ala.

Tenor sax star featured with Erskine Hawkins band. Older brother of trumpet star Dud Bascomb, also with Hawkins. Brothers with Bama State Collegians band in 1932, later led by Hawkins, went to New York with band in 1934. Paul remained with Hawkins till 1944, was band's star jazzman along with leader and pianist Avery Parish. In mid-40s Paul and Dud were co-leaders of combo, then led big band. In later 40s Paul led own band and freelanced. Remained active into 70s.

RECORDS

ERSKINE HAWKINS
Vo 3280 I Can't Escape from You
Bb 10854 Sweet Georgia Brown
Bb 11049 No Use Squawkin'
PAUL BASCOMB
Alert 205 Tell It to Me/Nora
Alert 206 Leap Frog Blues/Lady Ginger Snap
Hub 3027 Behind Closed Doors/I Know Who Threw the Whiskey in the Well
Manor 1106 There Ain't None Bad/It's My Nerves, Baby
Manor 1108 Dextrose/Robbins Bop
Manor 1117 Doin' Your Tricks/Jumpin' at Small's
Manor 1118 Bad Weather Blues/Boppin' the Blues
Manor 1137 Rock and Roll/Two Ton Tessie
Mer 8299 Nona/Mumbles Blues

106. BASIE, COUNT   p o cm B
(WILLIAM BASIE)

Born August 21, 1904, Red Bank, N.J.

Pianist-leader of a top big swing band from late 30s into 70s. Worked constantly during latter lean years for big bands. Piano style simple blues with light swing riffs, emphasis on beat. In early 20s began playing locally, then in New York. Toured several years with vaudeville shows. Stranded in Kansas City in 1927, began working there as theatre organist. Joined Walter Page's Blue Devils there 1928-9, then Bennie Moten 1929. Remained with latter until Moten's death in April 1935, then he and Bus Moten led band several months to fulfill bookings. Worked as single, later led small combo. By early 1936 group evolved into nucleus for his future big band, with Lester Young (ts), Walter Page (b), Jo Jones (d), singer Jimmy Rushing. Band played Reno Club in Kansas City, its jobs there broadcast over local radio. Jazz critic John Hammond heard band, helped bring it to Chicago and New York in late 1936. Rough going and personnel changes for a year. Attained first success early 1938 at New York's Savoy Ballroom, later in year at Famous Door. Good stints followed in Chicago, again in New York and on west coast. By 1940 band established, recording extensively and playing top spots throughout U.S. Jazz public came to admire outstanding jazzmen in band. Top star Lester Young, his cool and swinging sax style far ahead of its time. Also on tenor sax was Herschel Evans, till unfortunate early death in 1939. Featured trumpet soloist Buck Clayton. Other important sideman through next few years: Harry Edison (t), Shad Collins (t), Al Killian (t), Joe Newman (t), Dicky Wells (tb), Earl Warren (as), Tab Smith (as), Don Byas (ts), Buddy Tate (ts). All-time great rhythm section remained constant through early 40s: Walter Page (b), Freddy Green(g), Jo Jones (d) and Basie (p). Helen Humes was good female vocalist.

Basie's swing tune *One O'clock Jump*, introduced in 1937, became top jazz standard, also served as band theme song. Basie composer or co-composer of numerous blues and swing numbers: *Every Tub, Good Morning Blues, John's Idea, Jumpin' at the Woodside, Basie Boogie, Blue and Sentimental, Swingin' the Blues, Miss Thing, Don't You Miss Your Baby?,*

Riff Interlude, Panassié Stomp, Shorty George, Out the Window, Hollywood Jump, Nobody Knows, Sent for You Yesterday, Swinging at the Daisy Chain, Platterbrains, Red Bank Boogie, Tune Town Shuffle, The King, Mutton-Leg, Feather Merchant.

Band often on west coast in 40s. Appeared in several movies, 1943 a particularly busy year with CRAZY HOUSE, HIT PARADE OF 1943, TOP MAN, REVEILLE WITH BEVERLY, STAGE DOOR CANTEEN. In 1950 Basie disbanded, then organized small combo including star soloists Wardell Gray (ts), Buddy DeFranco (cl), Clark Terry (t). Continued with combo in 1951, then in 1952 formed another big band. This band achieved modern sound, featured swinging blues and jazz originals predominately. Became a top band, had regular bookings, recorded extensively on LPs. Stars in early and mid-50s: Paul Quinichette (ts), Eddie "Lockjaw" Davis (ts), Joe Newman (t), Henry Coker (tb), Marshall Royal (as, cl). Latter remained with Basie many years as chief aide and lead sax. In later 50s stars included: Frank Foster (ts), Thad Jones (t), Frank Wess(ts, f), Bennie Powell (tb), Joe Wilder (t). Blues singer Joe Williams featured several years. Arrangements by Ernie Wilkins, Neal Hefti, Johnny Mandel, Foster and Wess. Guitarist Freddy Green remained with Basie almost continually into 70s. Record hit in late 50s was unique jazz-styled arrangement of *April in Paris*. Band appeared in several movies in this later period, including CINDERFELLA (1960) and SEX AND THE SINGLE GIRL (1964). Also featured on TV occasionally during 60s. Basie and band remained popular into 70s, toured here and abroad.

RECORDS

BENNIE MOTEN
  Vi 24216 Lafayette/New Orleans
  Vi 24381 Milenberg Joys/The Blue Room
JONES-SMITH, INC.
  Vo 3441 Shoe Shine Swing/Evenin'
BENNY GOODMAN SEXTET
  Co 35810 Wholly Cats/Royal Garden Blues

Co 35901 As Long as I Live/Benny's Bugle
PAUL QUINICHETTE
  Mer 8272 I'll Always Be in Love with You/Sequel
COUNT BASIE
  De 1121 Pennies from Heaven/Swinging at the Daisy Chain
  De 1363 (theme) One O'clock Jump/John's Idea
  De 1728 Every Tub/Now Will You Be Good?
  De 1880 Sent for You Yesterday/Swingin' the Blues
  De 1965 Blue and Sentimental/Doggin' Around
  De 2355 Basie Boogie/How Long Blues
  Vo 4860 Miss Thing (1 & 2)
  Vo 5036 Moonlight Serenade/I Can't Believe That You're in Love with Me
  Vo 5118 Lester Leaps In/Dickie's Dream
  OK 5732 Moten Swing/Evenin'
  OK 5987 Who Am I?/Stampede in G Minor
  OK 6365 H and J/Diggin' for Dex
  Co 35338 Hollywood Jump/Someday Sweetheart
  Co 35521 I Never Knew/Tickle Toe
  Co 36766 I Didn't Know About You/Red Bank Boogie
  Co 37070 The King/Blue Skies
  Co 38888 The Golden Bullet/Bluebeard Blues
  Co 39406 Little Pony/Beaver Junction
  Clef 89120 Cherry Point/Right On
  Clef 89162 April in Paris/Roll 'Em Pete

LPs

COUNT BASIE
  De DL-8049 Count Basie & His Orchestra (De RIs)
  Epic LG-3107 Lester Leaps In (Vo RIs)
  Epic LN-3169 Basie's Back in Town (Vo, OK RIs)
  Co CL-754 Count Basie Classics (Co RIs)
  Clef MGC-647 Count Basie Dance Session Album #2

Roul R-52024 Basie One More Time
Roul R-52089 The Best of Basie, Vol. 2
Verve V-8687 Basie's Beat

JO JONES
Jazztone J-1242 The Jo Jones Special

CHARLIE CHRISTIAN
Co CL-652 With Benny Goodman Sextet and Orchestra (Co RIs)

107. BAUDUC, RAY   d cm B

Born June 18, 1909, New Orleans, La.

Famed dixieland drummer of 30s through 60s, notably with Bob Crosby band. At 14 Bauduc played drums in local combos, toured later (including jobs with Dorsey Brothers early band). In 1926 went to New York with Scranton Sirens, played with Joe Venuti and Fred Rich. Late 1928 joined Ben Pollack band, remained till break-up in 1934. Original member of Bob Crosby band, formed as corporation in early 1935 from nucleus of Pollack band. Also with Wingy Manone band on many record sessions 1935-6. As Crosby band rose to fame in later 30s, so did Bauduc. Considered a leading exponent of dixieland drumming. He and bassist Bob Haggart had hit duet with *Big Noise from Winnetka*, featuring Bob whistling between his teeth. *Noise* was a Bauduc jazz composition. Others, all featured with band or Bobcats (combo with band): *South Rampart Street Parade, Smokey Mary, Big Crash from China, I Hear You Talking, Big Tom, March of the Bob Cats, Big Foot Stomp*. Remained with Crosby till 1942, then in military service two years. In early 1945 Bauduc formed big band with Gil Rodin as partner-manager-saxman. Following year formed small combo with Nappy Lamare. With Jimmy Dorsey 1947-50, Jack Teagarden 1952-5. In later 50s and 60s freelanced with various dixieland groups, based mostly on west coast. Led own band at times, sometimes with Nappy Lamare.

RECORDS

VENUTI-LANG ALL-STARS
Me 12277 Farewell Blues/Someday Sweetheart
Me 12294 Beale Street Blues/After You've Gone

BEN POLLACK
Vi 21944 My Kinda Love/On with the Dance
Vi 22158 From Now On/You've Made Me Happy Today
Vi 22267 Keep Your Undershirt On
Vi 24284 Two Tickets to Georgia/Linger a Little Longer in the Twilight
Co 2905-D Here Goes/The Beat o' My Heart

GENE GIFFORD
Vi 25041 Nothin' but the Blues/New Orleans Twist
Vi 25065 Squareface/Dizzy Glide

MOUND CITY BLUE BLOWERS
Ch 40059 Thanks a Million/I'm Sittin' High on a Hilltop

GLENN MILLER
Co 3058-D In a Little Spanish Town/Solo Hop

WINGY MANONE
Bb 6375 Dallas Blues/Swinging at the Hickory House

BOB CROSBY
De 1196 The Old Spinning Wheel/Between the Devil and the Deep Blue Sea
De 1756 Coquette/Big Crash from China (both BOBCATS)
De 1865 Who's Sorry Now?/March of the Bob Cats (both BOBCATS)
De 2207 I Hear You Talking/Call Me a Taxi (both FOUR OF THE BOBCATS)
De 2208 Big Noise from Winnetka/Honky Tonk Train Blues
De 2209 Loopin' the Loop (BOBCATS)/My Inspiration
De 2282 Skater's Waltz/Eye Opener
De 2464 Rose of Washington Square/I Never Knew Heaven Could Speak
De 2569 South Rampart Street Parade/Smokey Mary
De 3248 Spain/All by Myself (both BOBCATS)

JIMMY DORSEY
Co 38649 Charley My Boy/Johnson Rag
Co 38654 Jazz Me Blues/Panama

RAY BAUDUC
Cap 919 Susie/Down in Honky Tonky Town
Cap 15131 Li'l Liza Jane/When My Sugar Walks Down the Street

RAY BAUDUC-ARMAND HUG
OK 6950 Tea for Two/Fascinatin' Rag

LPs

RAY BAUDUC-NAPPY LAMARE
Cap T-877 Riverboat Dandies
Cap T-1198 Two-Beat Generation

BOB CROSBY
Cor(10″)56000
Cor(10″)56003

JIMMY DORSEY
Co(10″)CL-6095

WINGY MANONE
"X"(10″)LVA-3014 Vol. 1 (Bb RIs)

108. BAUER, BILLY   g cm

*Born November 14, 1915, New York,
N.Y.*

Good rhythm guitarist as well as soloist.
Active in development period of progressive jazz. First important job with Jerry
Wald in 1939. In early 40s worked with
Carl Hoff, Dick Stabile and Abe Lyman.
With Woody Herman's progressive band
1944-6. With avant-garde groups of
Chubby Jackson 1947, Lennie Tristano
1949. Worked with Benny Goodman at
brief intervals in 1948, 1958, 1961. In
Bobby Byrne's band regularly on Steve
Allen TV show 1953-4. Late 1956 with
Lee Konitz. During 50s and 60s freelanced on radio, TV and records. Composer of jazz numbers *Skyscraper, Blue
Boy, Jonquil, Pam, Purple Haze, Blue
Mist, Burma Bombers.* Opened teaching
studio on Long Island. Remained active
into 70s.

RECORDS

WOODY HERMAN
Co 37059 Fan It/Blowin' Up a Storm
Co 37228 Igor/Nero's Conception

CHUBBY JACKSON
Key 625 Head Quarters/Sam's Caravan
Queen 4101 I Gotcha Covered/Popsie
Queen 4103 Bass Face/Don't Get Too
Wild, Child

LENNIE TRISTANO
Cap 7-1224 Intuition/Yesterdays
Key 647 Out on a Limb/I Can't Get
Started

BILL HARRIS
Key 618 Mean to Me/Cross Country

Key 626 Characteristically B.H./She's
Funny That Way

NEAL HEFTI
Key 669 I Woke Up Dizzy/Sloppy
Joe's

FLIP PHILLIPS
Si 28106 Pappiloma/Skyscraper

CHARLIE VENTURA
Nat 7015 Please Be Kind/How High
the Moon
Nat 9020 Moon Nocturne (1 & 2)

LEE KONITZ
NJ 834 Rebecca/Ice Cream Konitz

LEE KONITZ-BILLY BAUER
Pres 755 Duet for Sax and Guitar

METRONOME ALL-STARS
Cap 1550 Early Spring/Local 802
Blues
Cap 15039 Leap Here/Metronome
Riff
Co 38734 No Figs/Double Date

LPs

BILLY BAUER
Norg MGN-1079

WOODY HERMAN
Ha HL-7013 Bijou (Co RIs)
Everest 1003 The Herd Rides Again
... In Stereo

LEE KONITZ
Atl 1258 Lee Konitz Inside Hi-Fi
Verve MGV-8281 Tranquility

BOBBY HACKETT-JACK TEAGARDEN
Cap T-933 Jazz Ultimate

CHUBBY JACKSON-BILL HARRIS ALL-STARS
Mer(10″)MG-25076 Jazz Journey

LEE KONITZ-MILES DAVIS
Pres(10″)116

JAZZ RENAISSANCE QUINTET
Mer MG-20605 Movin' Easy

109. BAUR, FRANKLYN   vo

*Died February 24, 1950, New York,
N.Y.*

Freelance singer of 20s and early 30s.
Active career on radio and records. Appeared in ZIEGFELD FOLLIES OF 1927. In
1929 was original Voice of Firestone on
radio.

RECORDS

ROGER WOLFE KAHN
Vi 20717 Calling

THE KNICKERBOCKERS
Co 1187-D Thou Swell/My Heart Stood Still

IPANA TROUBADOURS
Co 662-D When the Red Red Robin Comes Bob, Bob, Bobbin' Along

NAT SHILKRET
Vi 20899 Are You Happy?
Vi 21082 Humpty Dumpty

CASS HAGAN
Co 966-D Hallelujah/Sometimes I'm Happy

ALL-STAR ORCHESTRA
Vi 21149 Chloe

HARRY RESER
Co 1109-D Shaking the Blues Away

FRANKLYN BAUR
Vi 19806 Pal of My Cradle Days/ Brown Eyes, Why Are You Blue?
Vi 20504 At Sundown/I'll Take Care of Your Cares
Vi 20758 Just Like a Butterfly
Vi 21220 Together/Four Walls
Vi 21734 Sally of My Dreams/I Loved You Then as Now
Vi 21904 When Summer Is Gone/ Where Is the Song of Songs for Me?
Vi 21989 When My Dreams Come True/Just Another Kiss
Vi 22050 My Sin/Junior
Vi 22281 With a Song in My Heart/ Through
Br 3318 Moonlight on the Ganges/ Your Heart Looked into Mine
Br 3319 Tonight You Belong to Me/ Cheritza
Br 3590 Just a Memory/My Heart Is Calling
Co 499-D Just a Cottage Small/Sleepy Time Gal
Co 888-D If You See Sally/What Does It Matter?

FRANKLYN BAUR-VAUGHN DELEATH
Co 1236-D Up in the Clouds/Thinking of You

FRANKLYN BAUR-GLADYS RICE
Co 998-D Sometimes I'm Happy
Vi 21854 You're the Cream in My Coffee/Red Rose
Vi 22226 Just You, Just Me/I May Be Wrong

110. BAXTER, LES   p vo ar cm B

Born March 14, 1922, Mexia, Texas

Orchestra leader of 50s and 60s, active in recording work. Concert pianist as teenager. Attended Detroit Conservatory of Music and Pepperdine College in Los Angeles. Member of vocal group, Mel Torme & the Mel-Tones, in mid-40s. Developed as arranger and conductor. By late 40s was musical director on radio shows (Bob Hope, Abbott & Costello, Halls of Ivy). Arranged for Nat Cole, Margaret Whiting, Frank DeVol. In 50s signed by Capitol Records as producer and recording artist. Records with large orchestra featured Latin-American and jungle drum themes, as well as standard popular music. Hits: *The Poor People of Paris, The High and the Mighty, Unchained Melody.* Composer of descriptive themes: *A Day in Rome, Coffee Bean, Sunshine at Kowloon, Brandy, Ceremony, Fiesta Brava, Congale, Asheville Junction, Shooting Star, La Sacre du Sauvage.*

RECORDS

FRANK DEVOL (in vocal quartet)
Cap 1178 Love Letters in the Sand

NAT COLE (conductor)
Cap 1010 Mona Lisa/The Greatest Inventor

BOB EBERLY (conductor)
Cap 1887 I Can't Help It/Somebody's Been Beatin' My Time
Cap 2525 You Are Too Beautiful/ Cryin' My Heart to Sleep

LES BAXTER
Cap 1299 Tambarina / Somewhere, Somehow, Someday
Cap 1493 Unless/Because of You
Cap 1584 Vanity/The World Is Mine Tonight
Cap 1773 You'll Know/Stay Awhile
Cap 1785 California Moon/Be Mine Tonight
Cap 1966 Blue Tango/Please, Mr. Sun
Cap 2225 Quiet Village/Indian Summer
Cap 2274 Yours/Flute Salad
Cap 2374 April in Portugal/Suddenly
Cap 2405 Dance of the Flutes/No More Goodbyes
Cap 2479 I Love Paris/Gigi

Cap 2845 The High and the Mighty/
More Love Than Your Love
Cap 3120 I'll Never Stop Loving You/
Wake the Town and Tell the People
Cap 3336 Poor People of Paris/"Helen
of Troy" Theme
Vi 20-3691 Jet/Struttin' with Clayton

LPs

LES BAXTER
Cap T-263 Arthur Murray Favorites
(Tangos)
Cap T-655 Tamboo!
Cap T-733 Caribbean Moonlight
Cap T-1388 Baxter's Best
Cap(10")H-474 Thinking of You

111. BAXTER, PHIL   p vo cm lyr B

Born September 5, 1896, Navarro Coun-
ty, Texas
Died November 21, 1972, Dallas, Texas

Composer of 1929 novelty hit *Piccolo Pete*
and several hit songs of 30s. Educated at
Daniel Baker College. Military service,
World War I; member of band at Mare
Island Navy Yard. Led small band in 20s
called Phil Baxter's Texas Tommies, toured country. Led large band in Kansas
City about three years. After 1932 led
bands occasionally. Composer: *Piccolo
Pete* (1929), *I'm a Ding Dong Daddy* and
Harmonica Harry (1930), *A Faded Summer Love* and *One Man Band* (1931), *Let's
Have a Party* (1932), *Going! Going!!
Gone!!!* and *Uncle Joe's Music Store*
(1933), *Have a Little Dream on Me*
(1934). After 30s became inactive in
music, settled in Dallas.

RECORDS

PHIL BAXTER
OK 40522 Waiting/Something Tells
Me
OK 40637 If I Had You
Vi 40160 I Ain't Got No Gal Now/
Down Where the Blue Bonnets
Grow
Vi 40204 Honey Child/I Don't Love
Nobody but You

112. BAYES, NORA   vo cm lyr

(DORA GOLDBERG)

Born 1880
Died March 19, 1928, Brooklyn, N.Y.

Leading early entertainer, contralto voice,
featured witty songs with great presentation. Flamboyant style on and off stage.
Married five times, co-starred with husband Jack Norworth in shows and in
writing songs. As teenager was chorus girl
at Chicago Opera House. Began featuring
song *Down Where the Wurzburger Flows*
early in career, made it a hit in 1902,
became known for years as "The Wurzburger Girl." First Broadway appearance
in 1901 show ROGERS BROTHERS IN WASH-
INGTON. Joined ZIEGFELD FOLLIES OF 1907
after it opened. Starred in other Broadway shows ZIEGFELD FOLLIES OF 1908 and
ZIEGFELD FOLLIES OF 1909, THE JOLLY
BACHELORS (1910), LITTLE MISS FIX-IT
(1911), ROLY-POLY (1912), MAID IN AMER-
ICA (1915), THE COHAN REVUE OF 1918,
LADIES FIRST (1918), HER FAMILY TREE
(1921), SNAPSHOTS OF 1921, QUEEN O'
HEARTS (1922). Most famous song written
by Bayes and Norworth *Shine On Harvest
Moon*, introduced by them in ZIEGFELD
FOLLIES OF 1908. They wrote songs for
several stage shows in which they ap-
peared, including *Turn Off Your Light,
Mr. Moon Man* in LITTLE MISS FIX-IT
(1911). Other songs included *I'm Sorry*;
Young America; *Come Along, My Mandy*;
Fancy You Fancying Me; *Way Down in
Cuba*. Miss Bayes also co-composer with
Seymour Simons of *Just Like a Gypsy* in
LADIES FIRST (1918). Between shows team
of Bayes and Norworth in vaudeville, a
high-priced, top act. Shortly before death,
Nora's last job at Fox's Academy of
Music. Good 1944 movie on lives of Nora
and Norworth, SHINE ON HARVEST MOON,
starring Ann Sheridan and Dennis Mor-
gan in Bayes-Norworth roles.

RECORDS

NORA BAYES-JACK NORWORTH
Vi(12")70016 Come Along, My Mandy
Vi(12")70019 Rosa Rosetta
Vi(12")70038 Turn Off Your Light,
Mr. Moon Man
NORA BAYES
Co A-2687 How Ya Gonna Keep 'Em
Down on the Farm?/When Yankee
Doodle Sails
Co A-2785 Jerry/In Miami
Co A-2816 Freckles/Everybody Calls
Me Honey

Co A-2823 Taxation Blues/Prohibition Blues
Co A-2997 The Japanese Sandman/ You're Just as Beautiful at Sixty
Co A-3311 Singin' the Blues/Broadway Blues
Co A-3360 Just Snap Your Fingers at Care/Why Worry?
Co A-3397 Broken Moon/In a Little Front Parlor
Co A-3416 Wyoming/Tea Leaves
Co A-3592 Sing Song Man/Oh Sing-A-Loo
Co A-3757 Lovin' Sam/Daddy's Goin' Huntin' Tonight
Co A-3826 Keep Off My Shoes/Runnin' Wild
Co A-3862 Dearest/You Know You Belong to Somebody Else
Vi 45099 When Old Bill Bailey Plays the Ukulele/Hello, Hawaii, How Are You?
Vi 45100 Homesickness Blues/For Dixie and Uncle Sam
Vi 45130 Over There/Laddy Boy
Vi 60013 Has Anybody Here Seen Kelly?
Vi 60019 Daffydils
Vi 60023 That Lovin' Rag
Vi 60041 Strawberries
Vi(12″)70015 Young America
Vi(12″)70020 What Good Is Water When You're Dry?

LPs

(miscellaneous artists; one song on each)
Audio Rarities LPA-2290 They Stopped the Show (RIs)
Vi LCT-1112 Old Curiosity Shop (RIs)

113. BEASLEY, IRENE   vo cm
Born c. 1900-5, Whitehaven, Tenn.

Popular singer on radio in 30s. Attended Sweetbriar College, showed early interest in singing and composing poems and music. Early professional job singing with Francis Craig band in 1925. Radio and theatre work in Chicago. Went to New York and after hard going broke in radio. By early 30s had own show. Popularity peaked when voted Radio Queen of 1934. Appeared on other shows such as those of Phil Baker and The Rendezvous. In late 30s and 40s mostly had daytime show. Career continued into late 40s.

560

RECORDS
JOE VENUTI
Vi 23015 My Man from Caroline
Vi 23018 Wasting My Love on You
IRENE BEASLEY
Vi 21266 Good Mornin'/Go 'Long, Lasses
Vi 21467 St. Louis Blues/Choo Choo Train
Vi 21639 If I Could Just Stop Dreaming/Missin' My Pal
Vi 40125 Moon Song/Sometimes I Wonder

114. BEAU, HEINIE   cl as ts ar cm
Born March 8, 1911, Calvary, Wis.

Good clarinet jazzman of 40s, later developed into talented arranger. Born into musical family, gained early experience writing arrangements for their orchestra. Early job with Nick Harper in Milwaukee, later with Scat Davis. With Red Nichols early 1940, then Tommy Dorsey mid-1940 to 1943. Left Dorsey late 1943 for defense work on west coast. In early 1944 worked with Benny Goodman in movie SWEET AND LOWDOWN, in late 1944-5 with Red Nichols. With Benny Goodman late 1946 to mid-1947. Stints with Ray Noble, John Scott Trotter and Paul Weston. Settled in Hollywood and freelanced, concentrating on arranging for radio-movies-records. Arranged for singers Peggy Lee, Frank Sinatra, Gisele MacKenzie, Frankie Laine, Doris Day, Dinah Shore. In later years his work extended to TV and he remained active into 70s. Arrangements excellent on all types of music, particularly on swing numbers with modern influence. Kept pace with changing trends. Composed instrumentals: *Forever Paganini, Forever Nicki, Harlem Mambo, Blue Iris, Blues at Midnight, Delta Roll, Guitar Mambo, Jasmine Jade*, and more extensive works, *Moviesville Jazz*.

RECORDS
(Clarinetist)
TOMMY DORSEY
Vi 27962 Blue Blazes
DAVE BARBOUR
Cap 358 Forever Nicki/Forever Paganini

JACK TEAGARDEN
Cap 10027 'Deed I Do/Stars Fell on Alabama
HERBIE HAYMER
Key 640 I Saw Stars/Sweet and Lovely
ART LUND
MGM 10648 Sugarfoot Rag
RED NICHOLS
OK 5648 Overnight Hop/Meet Miss Eight Ball
OK 5676 Lowland Blues/Beat Me, Daddy
Cap 15150 If I Had You/Love Is the Sweetest Thing
Cap 40062 Little by Little/When You Wish Upon a Star
Cap 48012 You're My Everything
CHARLES LIND (conductor)
Excl 115 I Love You Just the Same/Rose of Broken Heart Lane

LPs

HEINIE BEAU
Cor CRL-57247 Heinie Beau and Hollywood Jazz Stars
RED NICHOLS
Cap T-775 Hot Pennies
MORTY CORB
Tops L-1581 Strictly from Dixie
(miscellaneous artists)
Cr CLP-5129 Kings of Dixieland, Vol. 2
Golden Tone C-4021 Dixieland
LAWRENCE WELK (arranger)
Dot DLP-3317 Lawrence in Dixieland
RAY ANTHONY (clarinetist & arranger)
Cap T-678 Big Band Dixieland

115. BECHET, SIDNEY   ss cl B

Born May 14, 1897, New Orleans, La.
Died May 14, 1959, Paris, France

Jazz virtuoso on soprano sax, also on clarinet. Long career pre-1920 until death in 1959. Soprano sax style distinguished by wide vibrato. As youngster in New Orleans, played clarinet in bands of Bunk Johnson, Clarence Williams, King Oliver and others, also worked parades and toured with road shows. Left New Orleans permanently in 1917 with a show, ended up in Chicago. There jobbed with King Oliver, Freddie Keppard, Tony Jackson. Toured to New York with Will Marion Cook and in 1919 in Europe. Remained abroad 1919-21, played in London and Paris, began to concentrate on soprano sax. Back in U.S. late 1921. Through early 20s worked with Ford Dabney, Mamie Smith, several shows, Duke Ellington, James P. Johnson. Abroad again, in 1926 played in Russia and Germany, toured Europe in 1927. In 1928 joined Noble Sissle in Paris, later with Benny Peyton toured Europe again. Rejoined Sissle in New York late 1930, remained over a year. Later with Sissle 1934-8, with intervals away freelancing and sometimes leading own group. In late 30s with Zutty Singleton, Willie "The Lion" Smith. Through the 40s Bechet mostly led own combo, made several trips abroad. In late 40s had young clarinetist Bob Wilber as pupil and protege, worked some with Wilber's Wildcats group. In 1951 settled in France, returning occasionally to U.S. for engagements. Continued career abroad, touring many countries. Active until shortly before death. Prolific recording career with many top jazzmen.

RECORDS

CLARENCE WILLIAMS
OK 8171 Texas Moaner/House Rent Blues
OK 40260 I'm a Little Blackbird/Mandy, Make Up Your Mind
NOBLE SISSLE
De 153 Polka Dot Rag/Under the Creole Moon
De 154 Loveless Love/The Old Ark Is Moverin'
De 2129 Blackstick/When the Sun Sets Down South
Va 552 Bandana Days/I'm Just Wild About Harry
Va 648 Okey Doke/Characteristic Blues
TOMMY LADNIER
Bb 10086 Weary Blues/Ja-da
JELLY ROLL MORTON
Bb 10429 Oh, Didn't He Ramble/Winin' Boy Blues
Bb 10434 High Society/I Thought I Heard Buddy Bolden Say
LOUIS ARMSTRONG
De 18090 Perdido Street Blues/2:19 Blues
ART HODES
BN 532 Memphis Blues/Shine

CLIFF JACKSON
B&W(12″)1205 Cliff's Boogie Blues/ Jeepers Creepers

BOB WILBER'S WILDCATS
Co 38319 Polka Dot Stomp/Kansas City Man Blues

CLAUDE LUTER
Vogue(Fr) 2027 Maryland, My Maryland/Lastic

HUMPHREY LYTTLETON
Melodisc(E) 1103 Black and Blue/ Some of These Days
Melodisc(E) 1105 Georgia/I Told You Once, I Told You Twice

BECHET-SPANIER BIG FOUR
HRS(12″)2000 Sweet Lorraine/Lazy River
HRS(12″)2001 China Boy/Four or Five Times

SIDNEY BECHET
Vo 4537 Hold Tight/Jungle Drums
Vo 4575 Chant in the Night/What a Dream
Bb 7614 Maple Leaf Rag/Sweetie Dear
Bb 10472 Lay Your Racket/I Want You Tonight
Bb 10623 Indian Summer/Preachin' Blues
Vi 27204 One O'clock Jump/Blues in Thirds
Vi 27447 When It's Sleepy Time Down South/I Ain't Gonna Give Nobody None of This Jelly Roll
Vi 27485 The Sheik of Araby/Blues of Bechet
BN 43 Blue Horizon/Muskrat Ramble
BN 49 Salty Dog/Weary Blues

LPs

SIDNEY BECHET
Co CL-836 Sidney Bechet (RIs)
Vi LPV-535 The Blue Bechet (Vi RIs)
Allegro 1638 All Star Jazz Concert (HRS RIs)
GTJ 12013 King of the Soprano Saxophone
"X"(10″)LVA-3024 (Bb, Vi RIs)

BOB WILBER
Riv 12-216 Creole Reeds
(miscellaneous artists)
Vi LPV-542 The Panassié Sessions (Vi RIs)

116. BEIDERBECKE, BIX c p ar cm B
(LEON BIX BEIDERBECKE)

Born March 10, 1903, Davenport, Iowa
Died August 6, 1931, Queens, N.Y.

Great jazz musician of 20s and early 30s, far ahead of his time. An all-time great on cornet; clean-cut and powerful solo style with pure, beautiful tone. Also a capable pianist with leaning to advanced, modernistic chord structures. Idol of many musicians. A few years after his tragic death, Bix became a legend that endured and grew through the years. Played piano early, then cornet at 14. Played locally in all types of jobs. In 1921 enrolled at Lake Forest Military Academy near Chicago, but music interfered. Soon entered jazz field. Early 20s work included important late 1923-4 period with The Wolverines in Ohio and Indiana, which brought him attention in jazz circles. With Charley Straight in Chicago a while in 1925, then jobbed there. Joined Frankie Trumbauer late 1925 in St. Louis; in 1926 they played summer job at Hudson Lake, Indiana. Both joined Jean Goldkette in late 1926, remained about a year, were featured on band's records. Joined Paul Whiteman band, where both gained greater fame. Whiteman's arrangements, many by Bill Challis, often spotted Bix's cornet to great effect. Numerous recordings with Whiteman. Beiderbecke and Trumbauer also recorded frequently with jazz combos under own names. These records had great impact on musicians of late 20s, are still considered jazz classics. Their recording of *Singin' the Blues* drew particular attention.

Bix drank heavily and his health began to deteriorate, necessitating periods away from Whiteman in late 1928 and late 1929, when he left band permanently and returned to Davenport to convalesce. Freelanced in New York much of 1930 and early 1931 (with another interval back in Davenport). In 1931 was able to play only at intervals. Played several college engagements during final months. Considerable uncertainty and myth exist pertaining to Bix's last days. Apparently stayed with bassist George Kreslow, was long inactive except for practicing, collapsed and died of lobar pneumonia and edema of the brain.

The public knew little of Bix; his death caused consternation only among jazz fans and musicians. By late 30s his devotion to jazz, his drinking and eccentricities and mysterious last days were legends. His records became treasures, reissued many times. Composed several modernistic pieces principally for piano: *In a Mist, Flashes, Candlelights*. Also composed gutty *Davenport Blues* for jazz bands. Subject of definitive 1974 biography *Bix: Man and Legend* by Richard M. Sudhalter and Philip R. Evans.

RECORDS

THE WOLVERINES
Ge 5408 Fidgety Feet/Jazz Me Blues
Ge 5565 Tia Juana/Big Boy
SIOUX CITY SIX
Ge 5569 I'm Glad/Flock o' Blues
JEAN GOLDKETTE
Vi 20469 I'm Proud of a Baby Like You
Vi 20588 My Pretty Girl
Vi 20926 Slow River
Vi 20994 Clementine
PAUL WHITEMAN
Vi 21103 Changes/Mary
Vi 21214 Lonely Melody
Vi 21274 From Monday On/Mississippi Mud
Vi 21398 You Took Advantage of Me
Vi 21438 Louisiana
Vi 25238 Dardanella
Vi 25675 Coquette
Vi 27689 Back in Your Own Backyard/When You're with Somebody Else
Co 1945-D China Boy/Oh, Miss Hannah
FRANKIE TRUMBAUER
OK 40772 Singin' the Blues/Clarinet Marmalade
OK 40822 Ostrich Walk/Riverboat Shuffle
OK 40843 I'm Coming Virginia/"Way Down Yonder in New Orleans
OK 40879 Blue River/There's a Cradle in Caroline
TRAM, BIX & LANG
OK 40871 For No Reason at All in

C/Trumbology (FRANKIE TRUMBAUER)
HOAGY CARMICHAEL
Vi 22864 Bessie Couldn't Help It
Vi 23013 Georgia on My Mind/One Night in Havana
Vi 38139 Rockin' Chair/Barnacle Bill the Sailor
BIX BEIDERBECKE
OK 40916 In a Mist (piano solo)/Wringin' and Twistin' (TRAM, BIX & LANG)
OK 40923 At the Jazz Band Ball/Jazz Me Blues
OK 41030 Thou Swell/Somebody Stole My Gal
OK 41173 Rhythm King/Louisiana
Vi 23008 I'll Be a Friend with Pleasure/I Don't Mind Walkin' in the Rain

LPs

BIX BEIDERBECKE
Vi LPM-2323 The Bix Beiderbecke Legend (RIs)
Co CL-844-6 (3-LP set) The Bix Beiderbecke Story (RIs)
Riv 12-123 Bix Beiderbecke & The Wolverines (RIs)
PAUL WHITEMAN
"X"(10")LVA-3040 (Vi RIs)
JEAN GOLDKETTE
"X"(10")LVA-3017 (Vi RIs)

117. BELAFONTE, HARRY vo cm
(HAROLD GEORGE BELAFONTE, JR.)
Born March 1, 1927, New York, N.Y.

Popular folk singer of 50s and 60s, specializing in calypso, West Indian material. Lived with parents several years in Jamaica. Back in New York, left high school to join navy in World War II. Later studied acting and singing, became ballad singer in clubs late 40s. Discouraged with pop field, in 1951 became part owner of restaurant in Greenwich Village. In late 1951 began to specialize in folk songs, drawing on early knowledge of West Indian music. Soon became success as folk singer, exciting and impressive stage performer. Stage shows: JOHN MURRAY ANDERSON'S ALMANAC (1953) and THREE FOR TONIGHT (1954). Starring roles in movies BRIGHT ROAD (1953), CARMEN JONES (1954), ISLAND IN THE SUN (1957), THE WORLD, THE FLESH AND THE DEVIL and ODDS AGAINST TOMORROW (1959), THE ANGEL LEVINE (1969), BUCK AND THE PREACHER (1972). Played top clubs throughout U.S. By later 50s appeared often on TV. Played important role in popularity surge of calypso songs during 1956-7. Record hits: *Jamaica Farewell, Day-O, Brown-Skin Girl, Matilda*. Composed *Shake That Little Foot, Turn Around, Glory Manger*, others. Became owner of publishing firm and film company. After early 60s activities as singer and TV performer dropped sharply.

RECORDS

HARRY BELAFONTE
    Cap 1018 I Still Get a Thrill/Farewell to Arms
    Vi 20-4676 Chimney Smoke/A-Roving
    Vi 20-4892 Jerry/Man Smart
    Vi 20-5051 Shenandoah/Scarlet Ribbons
    Vi 20-5210 Springfield Mountain/Gomen Nasai
    Vi 20-5311 Matilda/Suzanne
    Vi 20-5617 I'm Just a Country Boy/Hold 'Em, Joe
    Vi 20-6663 Jamaica Farewell/Once Was
    Jub 5158 Venezuela/Annabelle Lee

LPs

HARRY BELAFONTE
    Vi LPM-1150 Belafonte
    Vi LPM-1248 Calypso
    Vi LPM-1402 An Evening with Belafonte
    Vi LPM-2449 The Midnight Special
    Vi LPM-2695 Streets I Have Walked
    Vi LSO-6006 (S) (2-LP set) Belafonte at Carnegie Hall
HARRY BELAFONTE-LENA HORNE
    Vi LOP-1507 Porgy and Bess

118. BELL, GRAEME   p B
Born 1914, Australia

Leader of The Australian Jazz Band, dixieland group, from 40s into 60s. Band originated in Melbourne in 1943, featured veteran musicians of area. To London in 1947. Big hit at Leicester Square Jazz Club. Band played primarily for dancers,

with drive and enthusiasm. Enlivened British jazz scene. With dixieland revival in U.S. in late 40s and early 50s, recordings of Bell band well received here. Band continued to perform in Australia, on tour and in England. After dixieland revival subsided somewhat in later years, U.S. heard little of Bell.

RECORDS

GRAEME BELL
    Swaggie(Aus) 2 At a Georgia Camp Meeting/Irish Black Bottom
    Swaggie(Aus) 5 Ole Miss/Jumbuck Jamboree
    Pa(Aus) 7776 When the Saints Go Marching In/Black & White Rag
    Pa(Aus) 7786 Black & Tan Fantasy/Rocking Horse Rag
    Pa(Aus) 7790 Muskat Ramble/High Society
    Amp(Aus) 3 At the Jazz Band Ball/Alma Street Requiem
    Amp(Aus) 25 Strut Miss Lizzie/Singin' the Blues
    Wilco(Aus) 116 Fidgety Feet/I Wish I Could Shimmy Like My Sister Kate
    Tempo(E) 13 Alexander's Ragtime Band/I'm a Little Blackbird
    Tempo(E) 90 Daddy Do/Shake That Thing
    Pac(Fr) 90011 It's Right Here for You/Come Back Sweet Papa
    ReZono(Aus) 25115 That Woodburne Strut/The Lizard
    ReZono(Aus) 25116 Ugly Child/Smoky Mokes
    ReZono(Aus) 25117 South/Tessa's Blues
    Jump 22 Oh Peter/Free Man's Blues
    Summit 1008 Jazz Me Blues/Sobbin' Blues
    Ramp 9 I'm a Little Blackbird/The Aztec Princess
    Ramp 10 Big Bad Banksia Man/Jenny's Ball
    JC 1 South/Shim-Me-Sha-Wabble
    JC 2 Big Chief Battle Axe/Yama Yama Blues

LPs

GRAEME BELL
    Angel(10")60002 Inside Jazz Down Under
    Swaggie(Aus) S-1268 Classics of Australian Jazz

119. BELLSON, LOUIS   d ar cm B
(LOUIS BALASSONI)
Born July 26, 1924, Rock Falls, Ill.

A top jazz drummer, exciting soloist, good showman. Active from early 40s into 70s. As teenager Bellson played professionally, won Gene Krupa national drum contest for under-18s in 1940. First big job with Ted Fio Rito in 1942. Joined Benny Goodman in late 1942 for several months before entering military service. Upon release rejoined Goodman mid-1946 for most of year. With Tommy Dorsey 1947-9. With Terry Gibbs combo 1949-50. Periods later in 1950 with Tommy Dorsey and Harry James. With Duke Ellington early 1951 to early 1953, featured prominently. Since then has freelanced, somtimes leading own group. Married singer Pearl Bailey, made many club and concert appearances with her. Rejoined Ellington in 1965 for another period. Appeared as single on various TV shows, displaying great drum technique. In 1971 led excellent big band on wife's TV show. With Doc Severinson on Johnny Carson TV show since 1972. Composed several jazz numbers: *The Hawk Talks, Skin Deep, You Gotta Dance, Ting-a-Ling.*

RECORDS
BENNY GOODMAN
  Co(12″)55039 Oh, Baby! (1 & 2)
  Co 37091 My Blue Heaven/Put That Kiss Back Where You Found It
  Co 37187 Benjie's Bubble/A Gal in Calico
TOMMY DORSEY
  Vi 20-2419 Trombonology/Deep Valley
  Vi 20-2852 Mississippi Mud/On the Painted Desert
DUKE ELLINGTON
  Co 39428 The Hawk Talks/Fancy Dan
  Co 39670 VIP's Boogie/Jam with Sam
LOUIS BELLSON
  Clef 89083 Caxton Hall Swing/Phalanges

LPs
LOUIS BELLSON
  Norg MGN-1011 Louis Bellson Quintet

  Norg MGV-2123 The Brilliant Bellson Sound
  Norg MGV-2131 Louis Bellson Swings Jule Styne
  Norg MGV-8016 Concerto for Drums
  Norg MGV-8137 Skin Deep
  Impulse 9107 Thunderbird
  Project PR-5029SD(S) Break Through!
BENNY GOODMAN
  Cap(10″)H-202 Session for Six
DUKE ELLINGTON
  Co ML-4639 Ellington Uptown
  Vi LJM-1002 Seattle Concert
COUNT BASIE
  Roul R-52099 Basie in Sweden

120. BENEKE, TEX   ts vo B
(GORDON BENEKE)
Born February 12, 1914, Fort Worth, Texas

Well-known featured tenor sax soloist and sometime vocalist with Glenn Miller band in its most popular period 1939-42. Later a bandleader many years. Early musical experience locally, then with Ben Young band touring Texas 1935-8. Joined Miller, quickly attained prominence as a foremost asset of band. Tenor sax solos smooth and warm on ballads, very facile on fast-tempo Miller flag-wavers but not particularly exciting. Handled novelty and jazz-tinged vocals with band in distinctive, raspy voice. Career was enhanced by prominent roles in two movies built around Miller band, SUN VALLEY SERENADE (1941) and ORCHESTRA WIVES (1942). After Miller disbanded in late 1942 for military service, Beneke freelanced. Brief, publicized stay (five days!) with Horace Heidt band in early 1943, then entered military service.

In early 1946, by agreement with Miller's widow, Beneke formed band to perpetuate Miller sound and style. Billed as "The Glenn Miller Band with Tex Beneke," featured vocalist Garry Stevens. Band could also swing in modern fashion. Late 40s band recorded, played top spots, got good coverage via own radio series. By end of 1950, Beneke split with Miller estate, thereafter led band under own name. Good sweet band, still featuring Miller reed sound at times. Performed on TV in 50s, recorded, toured. Later in 60s

Beneke's activities dropped off, but still led band on special engagements, TV spots and concert tours into 70s.

RECORDS

GLENN MILLER
Bb 10214 Sunrise Serenade
Bb 10229 The Lady's in Love with You
Bb 10269 Runnin' Wild
Bb 10317 Guess I'll Go Back Home/ Slip Horn Jive
Bb 10665 Star Dust/My Melancholy Baby
Bb 10740 Bugle Call Rag
Bb 10754 Pennsylvania 6-5000
Bb 10900 Shadows on the Sand/Five O'clock Whistle
Bb 10982 Anvil Chorus (1 & 2)
Bb 11230 Chattanooga Choo Choo
THE GLENN MILLER BAND with TEX BENEKE
Vi 20-2016 Star Dust/Falling Leaves
Vi 20-2234 Sunrise Serenade/Through
Vi 20-2260 My Heart Is a Hobo/As Long as I'm Dreaming
Vi 20-2616 But Beautiful/You Don't Have to Know the Language
Vi 20-2722 St. Louis Blues March/ Cherokee Canyon
Vi 20-2924 Look for the Silver Lining/Whip-poor-will
Vi 20-3553 I Can Dream, Can't I?/ Over Three Hills
Vi 20-3703 Dream a Little Longer/ Sunshine Cake
TEX BENEKE
MGM 10079 'S Wonderful/Tennessee Central
MGM 11189 Singin' in the Rain/Wedding of the Painted Doll
MGM 11423 Dancer's Delight/Diga Diga Doo

LPs

TEX BENEKE
Cam CAL-316 Star Dust
FTR 1510 Tex Beneke & His Orchestra (1946)
GLENN MILLER
Vi LPM-2080 (Bb RIs)
BOBBY BYRNE
GA 207-SD (S) Great Song Hits of the Glenn Miller Orchestra
(miscellaneous artists)
Cam CAL-318 The Biggest Hits of 1956, Vol. 1

121. BENJAMIN, BENNIE cm lyr g bn
Born November 4, 1907, Christiansted, St. Croix, Virgin Islands

Songwriter of 40s and 50s, mostly in collaboration with George Weiss on music and lyrics. Biggest song hits: *I Don't Want to Set the World on Fire*; *When the Lights Go On Again*; *Oh, What It Seemed To Be*; *Rumors Are Flying*; *Wheel of Fortune*. Went to New York in 1927. Studied banjo and guitar with Hy Smith. Played guitar in dance bands, also worked for publishing companies. Began successful composing career in early 40s.

SONGS
(with related shows)

1941—I Don't Want to Set the World on Fire
1942—When the Lights Go On Again
1946—Oh, What It Seemed to Be; Rumors Are Flying; You'll See What a Kiss Can Do; Surrender; How Could I?
1947—FUN AND FANCY FREE movie cartoon (Fun and Fancy Free); I Can't Get Up the Nerve to Kiss You; I Want to Thank Your Folks; Dreamy Lullaby; Speaking of Angels
1948—MELODY TIME movie cartoon (Melody Time); Confess; Pianissimo; Win or Lose
1949—I Don't See Me in Your Eyes Anymore; I'll Keep the Lovelight Burning
1950—Can Anyone Explain?; I'll Never Be Free; Jet; How Near to My Heart
1951—Out of Breath; I Ran All the Way Home; To Think You've Chosen Me; These Things I Offer You
1952—Wheel of Fortune; Wedding Bells Will Soon Be Ringin'; I May Hate Myself in the Morning; A Shoulder to Weep On
1953—Dancin' With Someone
1954—Cross Over the Bridge; Don't Call My Name; A Girl, a Girl; Every Road Must Have a Turning
1955—I'll Step Aside; How Important Can It Be?
1965—Don't Let Me Be Misunderstood
Other songs: *Just for Tonight*; *Of This I'm*

Sure; *Lonely Man*; *I Wonder What My Shadow Thinks of Me*; *Jack Climbed a Beanstalk*; *The Menace of Venice*; *Cancel the Flowers*; *The Clock Is Fast*; *Echoes*; *When You Return*; *Virgin Islands*; *Christmas Time*; *Christmas Feeling*

122. BENNETT, LEE vo B
Born July 4, 1911, Lincoln, Neb.

Deep-voiced romantic singer featured with Jan Garber band in its greatest years. Early in career Bennett worked on radio and toured with stock company. In 1933 joined Garber band, then soaring to popularity through ballroom engagements, good radio coverage and records. Became well known as Garber's featured vocalist, remained with band into 1936. In late 1936-7 Bennett led own band, failed to make it. Rejoined Garber through late 30s and early 40s. In 1942 became staff announcer on WGN in Chicago. In later years his name faded from view.

RECORDS
JAN GARBER
   Vi 24498 Temptation/Boulevard of Broken Dreams
   Vi 24727 Isn't It a Shame?
   Vi 24730 Blue Sky Avenue
   Vi 24809 Blame It On My Youth/The Object of My Affection
   Vi 24878 When Love Knocks at Your Heart
   Vi 24880 It's Easy to Remember
   Vi 25025 In the Middle of a Kiss
   Vi 25110 Accent on Youth/Ridin' up the River Road
   De 646 Quicker Than You Can Say "Jack Robinson"
   De 647 I'm Shooting High/I Feel Like a Feather in the Breeze
   De 717 The Wheel of the Wagon Is Broken
   De 733 If You Love Me
   De 738 The Hills of Old Wyomin'
   Vo 4687 It's Never Too Late
   Vo 4873 Let's Disappear
   OK 6039 Come Down to Earth, My Angel

LPs
JAN GARBER
   Cam CAL-297 (Vi RIs)

123. BENNETT, MAX b B
Born May 24, 1928, Des Moines, Iowa

Bass man with modern combos and bands in 50s and 60s. Attended University of Iowa. First important job with Herbie Fields 1949-50. In 1950-1 with George Auld, Terry Gibbs and Charlie Ventura. Later 1951-3 in military service. Late 1953 resumed professional career, joined Stan Kenton in 1954. Settled in Hollywood, freelanced, led own combos. Accompanied Ella Fitzgerald in Jazz at the Philharmonic tour in 1958, went abroad. With Terry Gibbs in 1959. In 60s heavy work with Jimmy Rowles. Also worked with Shorty Rogers, Peggy Lee, Pete Jolly. Active into 70s.

RECORDS
(all LPs)

LAURINDO ALMEIDA
   Cap ST-1759(S) Viva Bossa Nova!
RUSS GARCIA-MARTY PAICH
   Beth 6039 Jazz Music for the Birds and the Hep Cats
CONTE CANDOLI
   Beth(10")BCP-1016
MAX BENNETT
   Beth BCP-48 Max Bennett
   Beth BCP-50 Max Bennett Plays
   Beth(10")BCP-1028

124. BENNETT, TONY vo
Born August 13, 1926, Queens, N.Y.

Popular singer of 50s and 60s, his jazz-styled vocals well regarded by musicians and jazz buffs. While still in high school Bennett had night club experience. In military service sang with army bands. Later enrolled in theatrical school, sang in small clubs occasionally. Heard by Bob Hope, who used him for New York stage engagement. Record of *Boulevard of Broken Dreams* won him good contract with Columbia Records in early 1950. Soon waxed hits *Because of You* and *Cold Cold Heart*, big hit in *Rags to Riches*. Appeared on TV in early and mid-50s. In late 50s Bennett's career faded a bit. Then did a succession of popular concerts, including one at Carnegie Hall. Pianist Ralph Sharon began long association with him as musical director for concerts and records. Career enjoyed great revival in

1962 with hit record of *I Left My Heart in San Francisco,* soon followed by *I Wanna Be Around (to Pick up the Pieces).* Busy round of TV and club appearances followed through 60s. Often performed with jazzmen or big swing bands like Count Basie's. Still active into early 70s.

RECORDS

TONY BENNETT

    Co 38825 Boulevard of Broken Dreams/I Wanna Be Loved

    Co 39060 Don't Cry, Baby/One Lie Leads to Another

    Co 39187 Once There Lived a Fool/I Can't Give You Anything but Love

    Co 39362 Because of You/I Won't Cry Anymore

    Co 39449 Cold Cold Heart/While We're Young

    Co 39555 Blue Velvet/Solitaire

    Co 39695 Somewhere Along the Way/Sleepless

    Co 39815 Roses of Yesterday/You Could Make Me Smile Again

    Co 39910 Take Me/Congratulations to Someone

    Co 40004 I'll Go/Someone Turned the Moon Upside Down

    Co 40048 Rags to Riches/Here Comes That Heartache Again

    Co 40121 Stranger in Paradise/Why Does It Have to Be Me?

    Co 40632 Sing You Sinners/Capri in May

LPs

TONY BENNETT

    Co C2L-23 (2-LP set) Tony Bennett at Carnegie Hall (6-9-62)

    Co CL-621 Cloud 7

    Co 938 Tony

    Co 1186 Long Ago ...

    Co 1658 My Heart Sings

    Co 1869 I Left My Heart in San Francisco

    Co 2285 Who Can I Turn To?

124A. BENNETT, WILDA   vo

Born 1894
Died December 20, 1967, Winnemucca, Nev.

Beautiful singer-actress of Broadway musicals. Debut 1913 with small roles in plays EVERYMAN (revival), THE GOOD LITTLE DEVIL. Starred mostly in important long-running shows.

BROADWAY MUSICALS

1914—THE ONLY GIRL
1917—THE RIVIERA GIRL
1918—THE GIRL BEHIND THE GUN
1919—APPLE BLOSSOMS
1921—MUSIC BOX REVUE
1922—LADY IN ERMINE
1924—MADAME POMPADOUR

125. BERIGAN, BUNNY   t vo B
(ROLAND BERNARD BERIGAN)

Born November 2, 1908, Hilbert, Wis.
Died June 2, 1942, New York, N.Y.

Outstanding trumpet star and bandleader of 30s swing era. Noted for treatment of famous theme song, *I Can't Get Started.* Trumpet style distinctive, with gutty and sometimes growling tone, wide range, sometimes a pause on a high note to use a lip trill. His always swinging, uninhibited style sometimes produced a fluff. As teenager played locally with various bands, including jobs with dance bands at University of Wisconsin (though not a student). In late 20s played in Philadelphia and New York. In early 1930 got first important job with Hal Kemp, made European trip with him. Upon return to U.S., freelanced in New York, did heavy studio and record work in early 30s with top jazzmen. Worked with Dorsey Brothers, Fred Rich, Benny Krueger, Smith Ballew. In late 1932-3 with Paul Whiteman, featured on trumpet solos. Resumed freelancing. With Abe Lyman 1934, Benny Goodman's early swing band in 1935. Busy in record work in 1936 as staff musician for ARC (American Record Corporation). Featured that year for a time on Saturday Night Swing Session radio show and with Richard Himber and Red Norvo. Led own groups at intervals in mid-30s and recorded with them. Two months with Tommy Dorsey at beginning of 1937 resulted in some famous Berigan solos, particularly on *Marie* and *Song of India,* which remain among most popular jazz classics.

In early 1937 formed first big band, powerful crew with excellent, swinging arrangements. Led band until early 1940 when financial difficulties forced him to disband. Outstanding jazz soloists were George Auld (ts) and Joe Dixon (cl). Berigan's trumpet featured on every number. Occasionally he "sang" in half-talking, uneven style. Band sported excellent personnel. Vocalists included Ruth Gaylor, Ford Leary, Dick Wharton, Gail Reese, Jayne Dover, Kathleen Lane. The band recorded extensively, got good radio coverage. Berigan rejoined Tommy Dorsey for about five months in 1940, then led own combo awhile. In late 1941 worked in Hollywood, recording much of trumpet work for movie SYNCOPATION (1942). Formed new big band with obscure musicians. Tough one-nighter schedule and heavy drinking contributed to Berigan's failing health. Finally collapsed, died in New York hospital several days later from severe hemorrhage. Music world stunned to lose this giant, whose reputation endures.

RECORDS

CHICK BULLOCK
Me 60310 I'm Gonna Sit Right Down and Write Myself a Letter/Sing an Old Fashioned Song
Me 60707 And Still No Luck with You
CAROLINA CLUB ORCHESTRA
Me 12110 Smile, Darn Ya, Smile
DORSEY BROTHERS ORCHESTRA
Br 6537 Mood Hollywood/Shim Sham Shimmy
Br 7542 She's Funny That Way
TOMMY DORSEY
Vi 25508 The Goona Goo
Vi 25509 Lookin' Around Corners for You/Mr. Ghost Goes to Town
Vi 25519 Melody in F
Vi 25523 Marie/Song of India
Vi 25539 Liebestraum/Mendelssohn's Spring Song
Bb 10726 East of the Sun
BUD FREEMAN
De 18112 The Buzzard/Tillie's Downtown Now
De 18113 What Is There to Say?/Keep Smilin' at Trouble

GENE GIFFORD
Vi 25041 New Orleans Twist/Nothin' but the Blues
Vi 25065 Squareface/Dizzy Glide
BENNY GOODMAN
Vi 25090 Sometimes I'm Happy/King Porter
Vi 25136 Blue Skies/Dear Old Southland
Vi 25145 Jingle Bells
RICHARD HIMBER
Vi 25293 Tormented/Every Once in Awhile
Vi 25298 I've Got a Heavy Date/Would You?
A JAM SESSION AT VICTOR
Vi 25569 Honeysuckle Rose/Blues
SAM LANIN
HoW K-2 Me!
ED LOYD
Me 12326 Too Many Tears
DICK MCDONOUGH
Me 60908 Dear Old Southland/'Way Down Yonder in New Orleans
Me 70204 Dardanella/Between the Devil and the Deep Blue Sea
RED MCKENZIE
De 667 Sing an Old Fashioned Song/I'm Building Up to an Awful Letdown
De 790 I Can't Get Started/I Can Pull a Rabbit Out of My Hat
GLENN MILLER
Co 3058-D In a Little Spanish Town/Solo Hop
FRED RICH
HoW J-4 Little Girl
Co 2484-D At Your Command/Pardon Me, Pretty Baby
ADRIAN ROLLINI
Me 12829 Sweet Madness/Savage Serenade
Me 12855 Sittin' on a Log/I Raised My Hat
Me 12893 Who Walks In When I Walk Out?/Got the Jitters
DICK STABILE
De 716 Just Because/Deep Elm Blues
De 977 Jada/If I Could Be with You
FRANKIE TRUMBAUER
Vi 24812 Blue Moon/Down t' Uncle Bill's
Vi 24834 Troubled/Plantation Moods

PAUL WHITEMAN
Vi 24285 Look What I've Got
Vi 24304 (RAMONA) I've Got To Sing a Torch Song/I'll Take an Option on You
Vi 24365 Are You Makin' Any Money?
Vi 24403 Sittin' on a Backyard Fence

BUNNY BERIGAN
Vo 3179 It's Been So Long/Swing, Mister Charlie
Vo 3225 I Can't Get Started/Rhythm Saved the World
Br 7832 The Goona Goo/Blue Lou
Br 7858 Dixieland Shuffle/Let's Do It
Vi(12")36208 (theme) I Can't Get Started/The Prisoner's Song
Vi 25588 Love Is a Merry-Go-Round/Swanee River
Vi 25609 All God's Chillun Got Rhythm/The Lady from Fifth Avenue
Vi 25811 Downstream/Sophisticated Swing
Vi 26001 Russian Lullaby
Vi 26113 Jelly Roll Blues/'Deed I Do
Vi 26138 Black Bottom/Trees
Vi 26244 There'll Be Some Changes Made/Jazz Me Blues
El 5005 'Tis Autumn/Two in Love
El 5020 Skylark/My Little Cousin

LPs

BUNNY BERIGAN
Vi LPV-581 His Trumpet and Orchestra, Original 1937-9 Recordings (Vi RIs)
Vi LPT-1003 Bunny Berigan Plays Again (Vi RIs)
Epic LN-3109 Take It, Bunny (Br, Vo RIs)
Cam CAL-550 Bunny (Vi RIs)

LEE WILEY
LMS(10")1003 Cole Porter Songs (LMS RIs)

RED NORVO
Epic LN-3128 Red Norvo & His All-Stars (Br, Co RIs)

BOSWELL SISTERS
Ace of Hearts (E)116 (Br RIs)

BILL DODGE
Melodeon MLP 7328-9 (2 LPs) (1934 ETs by Benny Goodman and pickup groups)

126. BERLE, MILTON   vo lyr cm
(MILTON BERLINGER)

Born July 12, 1908, New York, N.Y.

Popular comedian of stage, screen, radio and TV. First big star of TV beginning late 40s. Comic style featured fast patter and great delivery. Had running gag that he stole other comedians' jokes. Educated at New York Professional Children's School. Began performing at 5. Child actor in silent movies, played vaudeville billed as The Boy Wonder. Continued in vaudeville many years; 1931 job as M. C. at Palace Theatre led to top bookings in night clubs and theatres. Appeared in Broadway musicals EARL CARROLL'S VANITIES OF 1932, SALUTA (1934), ZIEGFELD FOLLIES OF 1943, also in play SEE MY LAWYER (1939). Guest spots in radio in mid-30s. Late 1936-7 took over as M. C. on Gillette's Community Sing variety show, rose to great popularity. Continued on radio with gag quiz show 1939-40, Three Ring Time show 1941-2, popular series mid-40s to early 50s. Began on TV fall 1948, soon had top-rated show, came to be known as Mr. Television. Used theme *Near You*, which he sang. Continued with own TV show into mid-50s, had other shows in ensuing years, did numerous guest spots. Also played dramatic roles. Appeared in many movies during career, mostly comedies and musicals. Creditable acting job in drama MARGIN FOR ERROR (1943). Composer or lyricist of songs: *I'd Give a Million Tomorrows*; *What Do I Have to Do to Make You Love Me?*; *Just Say the Word*; *Moon Magic*; *Here Comes the Girl*; *Gotta Darn Good Reason*; *We Incorporated*; *I'll Never Make the Same Mistake Again*; *Lucky Lucky Lucky Me*; *Stars Never Cry*; *Foolishly*; *Always Leave 'Em Laughing*; *I'll Kiwl You a Miwl-yun Times*; *Save Me a Dream*; *The Song of Long Ago*; *It Only Takes a Moment to Fall in Love*; *I'm So Happy I Could Cry*; *I Wuv a Wabbit*; *If I Knew You Were There*; *Summer Love*; *What's Gonna Be*; *Sam, You Made the Pants Too Long*; *I'm Living in the Past*; *For the First Time in My Life*; *Your Eyes Are Bigger Than Your Heart*; *Give Her My Love*; *Leave the Dishes in the Sink, Ma*; *Let's*

Keep It That Way; *Shave and a Haircut —Shampoo*; *There's Green Grass Under the Snow*; *It's Just a Mile from Treasure Isle*; others.

MOVIES
(excluding silent movie roles as child)

1937—NEW FACES OF 1937
1938—RADIO CITY REVELS
1941—SUN VALLEY SERENADE; RISE 'N' SHINE; A GENTLEMAN AT HEART; TALL, DARK AND HANDSOME
1942—OVER MY DEAD BODY; WHISPERING GHOSTS
1943—MARGIN FOR ERROR
1945—THE DOLLY SISTERS
1949—ALWAYS LEAVE THEM LAUGHING
1960—THE BELL BOY; LET'S MAKE LOVE
1963—IT'S A MAD MAD MAD MAD WORLD
1965—THE LOVED ONE
1966—THE OSCAR; DON'T WORRY, WE'LL THINK OF A TITLE
1967—THE HAPPENING; WHO'S MINDING THE MINT?; WHERE ANGELS GO TROUBLE FOLLOWS
1968—THE SILENT TREATMENT; THE APRIL FOOLS; FOR SINGLES ONLY; CAN HIERONYMUS MERKIN EVER FORGET MERCY HUMPPE AND FIND TRUE HAPPINESS?

RECORDS
MILTON BERLE-BETTY GARRETT
  Vi 45-0015 This Can't Be Love
MILTON BERLE
  Vi 20-3750 I'll Kiwl You a Miwl-yun Times/I Found My Mama
  Vi 20-3948 Lucky Lucky Lucky Me/ This Is the Chorus

127. BERLIN, IRVING   cm lyr p vo
(ISRAEL BALINE)

Born May 11, 1888, Temun, Russia

All-time great songwriter. Most prolific of all. First known as mostly Tin Pan Alley writer of popular songs for the common people. Later in career did considerable work for stage and movies. Early in career collaborated with other writers; soon began writing both music and lyrics himself. Most famous songs: *Alexander's Ragtime Band, Say It with Music, A Pretty Girl Is Like a Melody, All Alone, Always, What'll I Do?, Blue Skies, Marie, How Deep Is the Ocean?, Say It Isn't So, Cheek to Cheek, Easter Parade, God Bless America, White Christmas*. Came to U.S. as a youngster, family settled in New York. Father died early. Berlin left home at 14 to earn living singing and playing piano in saloons. Worked as singing waiter and song plugger. Changed name to Irving Berlin, began trying to compose songs. In 1909 hired as staff lyricist by Ted Snyder publishing company, became partner several years later. Collaborated with Snyder on early songs; they appeared together in 1910 Broadway musical UP AND DOWN BROADWAY. In 1911 first big hit, *Alexander's Ragtime Band*, a sensation, launched successful songwriting career. Wrote *When I Lost You* in 1912 when first wife died. Played vaudeville in U.S. and abroad. In military service at Camp Upton, N.Y., during World War I, wrote army show YIP, YIP, YAPHANK which featured *Oh, How I Hate to Get Up in the Morning*.

After discharge founded own publishing firm. In 1921 built Music Box Theatre with Sam Harris, wrote musical revues presented there. Wrote for many Broadway musicals. Most important: ZIEGFELD FOLLIES of 1919-1920-1927, WATCH YOUR STEP (1914), STOP! LOOK! LISTEN! (1916), MUSIC BOX REVUE of 1921-1922-1923-1924, THE COCOANUTS (1925), FACE THE MUSIC (1932), AS THOUSANDS CHEER (1933), LOUISIANA PURCHASE (1940), THIS IS THE ARMY (1942), ANNIE GET YOUR GUN (1946), MISS LIBERTY (1949), CALL ME MADAM (1950), MR. PRESIDENT (1962). Especially popular: his excellent scores for AS THOUSANDS CHEER and ANNIE GET YOUR GUN.

Wrote music for early sound movies, continued in 30s with popular scores for three Astaire-Rogers vehicles: TOP HAT (1935), FOLLOW THE FLEET (1936), CAREFREE (1938). Excellent score for 1937 movie ON THE AVENUE. Big movie musical of 1938, ALEXANDER'S RAGTIME BAND, featured many old Berlin favorites. Perennial hit, *White Christmas*, appeared in 1942 Bing Crosby movie HOLIDAY INN, for which he wrote long, outstanding score. Several of his stage successes converted to movies in later years. By late 50s and 60s Berlin largely inactive. Appeared on TV occasionally, sometimes honored in tribute specials.

SONGS
(with related shows; many minor songs omitted)

1908—THE BOYS AND BETTY stage show (She Was a Dear Little Girl)

1909—I Didn't Go Home at All; If I Thought You Wouldn't Tell; Next to Your Mother Who Do You Love?; That Mesmerizing Mendelssohn Tune; Wild Cherries

1910—THE JOLLY BACHELORS stage show (Stop That Rag; If the Managers Only Thought the Same as Mother; Sweet Marie, Make a Rag-a-Time Dance with Me); UP AND DOWN BROADWAY stage show (Oh, That Beautiful Rag; Sweet Italian Love); ZIEGFELD FOLLIES OF 1910 stage show (Goodbye Becky Cohen; Dance of the Grizzly Bear); Call Me Up Some Rainy Afternoon; Piano Man; Yiddle on Your Fiddle; Kiss Me, My Honey, Kiss Me

1911—TEMPTATIONS stage show (Answer Me; I Beg Your Pardon; Dear Old Broadway; Spanish Love; Keep a Taxi Waiting, Dear); ZIEGFELD FOLLIES OF 1911 stage show (Woodman, Woodman, Spare That Tree; Epraham); Alexander's Ragtime Band; Ragtime Violin; Everybody's Doing It Now

1912—HANKY-PANKY stage show (Million Dollar Ball); HOKEY-POKEY stage show (Alexander's Bagpipe Band); THE WHIRL OF SOCIETY stage show (That Society Bear; I Want to Be in Dixie); MY BEST GIRL stage show (Follow Me Around); THE PASSING SHOW OF 1912 stage show (Ragtime Jockey Man); ZIEGFELD FOLLIES OF 1912 stage show (Little Bit of Everything); Do It Again; When I Lost You; That Mysterious Rag; When the Midnight Choo-Choo Leaves for Alabam'; At the Devil's Ball

1913—Happy Little Country Girl; In My Harem; Snookey Ookums; Somebody's Coming to My House; That International Rag; We Have Much to Be Thankful For; You've Got Your Mother's Big Blue Eyes; Down in Chattanooga; Daddy Come Home

1914—WATCH YOUR STEP stage show (Play a Simple Melody; I Love to Have the Boys Around Me; Syncopated Walk; Minstrel Parade; When I Discovered You); QUEEN OF THE MOVIES stage show (Follow the Crowd); He's a Rag Picker; I Want to Go Back to Michigan; This Is the Life; When It's Night Time in Dixie Land; He's a Devil in His Own Home Town; Along Came Ruth; I Love to Quarrel with You; Stay Down Here Where You Belong

1915—Araby; My Bird of Paradise; When I Leave the World Behind; When You're Down in Louisville

1916—STOP! LOOK! LISTEN! stage show (I Love a Piano; The Girl on the Magazine; That Hula Hula; When I Get Back to the U.S.A.); THE CENTURY GIRL stage show (Alice in Wonderland; That Broadway Chicken Walk); In Florida Among the Palms; Someone Else May Be There While I'm Gone; When the Black Sheep Return to the Fold

1917—JACK O' LANTERN stage show (I'll Take You Back to Italy); Whose Little Heart Are You Breaking Now?; For Your Country and My Country; From Here to Shanghai; Let's All Be Americans Now; My Sweetie; There's Something Nice About the South

1918—THE COHAN REVUE OF 1918 stage show (King of Broadway; Down Where the Jack o' Lanterns Grow); THE CANARY stage show (It's the Little Bit of Irish); EVERYTHING stage show (The Circus Is Coming to Town; Come Along to Toy Town); ZIEGFELD FOLLIES OF 1918 stage show (I'm Gonna Pin a Medal on the Girl I Left Behind; Blue Devils of France); YIP, YIP,

YAPHANK stage show (Oh, How I Hate to Get Up in the Morning; Mandy); They Were All Out of Step but Jim; Goodbye France

1919—ZIEGFELD FOLLIES OF 1919 stage show (A Pretty Girl Is Like a Melody; Mandy; You'd Be Surprised; I Want to See a Minstrel Show); I've Got My Captain Working for Me Now; Nobody Knows (And Nobody Seems to Care); Sweeter Than Sugar; That Revolutionary Rag; The Hand That Rocked My Cradle Rules My Heart; Was There Ever a Pal Like You

1920—ZIEGFELD FOLLIES OF 1920 stage show (The Girls of My Dreams; Bells; Tell Me, Little Gypsy; The Leg of Nations; The Syncopated Vamp); ZIEGFELD GIRLS OF 1920 stage show (Metropolitan Ladies); ZIEGFELD MIDNIGHT FROLIC stage show (I'll See You in C-U-B-A); BROADWAY BREVITIES OF 1920 stage show (Beautiful Faces Need Beautiful Clothes); After You Get What You Want You Don't Want It

1921—MUSIC BOX REVUE stage show (Say It with Music; Everybody Step; They Call It Dancing; The Schoolhouse Blues); ZIEGFELD'S 9 O'CLOCK FROLIC stage show (I Like It); All by Myself; Home Again Blues

1922—MUSIC BOX REVUE OF 1922 stage show (Lady of the Evening; Pack Up Your Sins and Go to the Devil; Crinoline Days); Homesick; Some Sunny Day

1923—MUSIC BOX REVUE OF 1923 stage show (An Orange Grove in California; Learn to Do the Strut; Waltz of Long Ago; Tell Me a Bedtime Story); Tell All the Folks in Kentucky

1924—MUSIC BOX REVUE OF 1924 stage show (Tell Her in the Springtime; The Call of the South; Rock-a-bye Baby; Tokio Blues; In the Shade of a Sheltering Tree); Lazy; All Alone; What'll I Do?

1925—THE COCOANUTS stage show (Monkey Doodle Doo; Lucky Boy; Minstrel Days; A Little Bungalow; We Should Care; Why Do You Want to Know Why?); Always; Remember

1926—At Peace with the World; Because I Love You; How Many Times?; I'm on My Way Home; Just a Little Longer; That's a Good Girl

1927—ZIEGFELD FOLLIES OF 1927 stage show (Shaking the Blues Away; Ooh, Maybe It's You; It All Belongs to Me; It's Up to the Band; Jimmy; My New York); BETSY stage show (Blue Skies); Russian Lullaby; The Song Is Ended; Together, We Two; What Does It Matter?

1928—Coquette; How About Me?; Marie; I Can't Do without You; Roses of Yesterday; Sunshine; To Be Forgotten

1929—THE COCOANUTS movie (part of original stage score; new song: When My Dreams Come True); HALLELUJAH movie (Waiting at the End of the Road; Swanee Shuffle); LADY OF THE PAVEMENTS movie (theme: Where Is the Song of Songs for Me?)

1930—MAMMY movie (Let Me Sing and I'm Happy; Across the Breakfast Table, Looking at You; The Call of the South; Knights of the Road; To My Mammy; In the Morning); PUTTIN' ON THE RITZ movie (Puttin' on the Ritz; With You); Just a Little While; The Little Things in Life

1931—SHOOT THE WORKS stage show (Begging for Love); REACHING FOR THE MOON movie (Reaching for the Moon; When the Folks High-Up Do That Mean Low-Down); Me!

1932—FACE THE MUSIC stage show (Soft Lights and Sweet Music; Let's Have Another Cup o' Coffee; On a Roof in Manhattan; I Say It's Spinach; Manhattan Madness); Say It Isn't So; How Deep Is the Ocean?

1933—AS THOUSANDS CHEER stage show (Easter Parade; Supper Time; Harlem on My Mind; How's Chances?; Heat Wave; Not for All the Rice in China; Lonely Heart; To Be or Not to Be); I'm Playing with Fire; I Can't Remember; Maybe It's Because I Love You Too Much

1934—Butterfingers; I Never Had a Chance; So Help Me

1935—TOP HAT movie (Cheek to Cheek; Isn't This a Lovely Day?; Top Hat, White Tie and Tails; No Strings; The Piccolino)

1936—FOLLOW THE FLEET movie (I'm Putting All My Eggs in One Basket; But Where Are You?; We Saw the Sea; Let's Face the Music and Dance; Let Yourself Go; I'd Rather Lead a Band; Get Thee Behind Me, Satan)

1937—ON THE AVENUE movie (This Year's Kisses; He Ain't Got Rhythm; I've Got My Love to Keep Me Warm; The Girl on the Police Gazette; You're Laughing at Me; Slumming on Park Avenue)

1938—CAREFREE movie (Change Partners; I Used to Be Color Blind; The Night Is Filled with Music; The Yam); ALEXANDER'S RAGTIME BAND movie (many old Berlin songs; new songs: Now It Can Be Told; My Walking Stick)

1939—SECOND FIDDLE movie (I Poured My Heart into a Song; Back to Back; I'm Sorry for Myself; When Winter Comes; An Old Fashioned Tune Always Is New; Song of the Metronome); God Bless America; We'll Never Know

1940—LOUISIANA PURCHASE stage show (Louisiana Purchase; Outside of That, I Love You; You Can't Brush Me Off; You're Lonely and I'm Lonely; It's a Lovely Day Tomorrow; Fools Fall in Love; Latins Know How; It'll Come to You; The Lord Done Fixed Up My Soul)

1941—LOUISIANA PURCHASE movie (original stage score); A Little Old Church in England; Any Bonds Today?

1942—THIS IS THE ARMY stage show (This Is the Army, Mr. Jones; I Left My Heart at the Stage Door Canteen; I'm Getting Tired So I Can Sleep; That Russian Winter; What the Well-Dressed Man in Harlem Will Wear; How About a Cheer for the Navy; old song: Oh, How I Hate to Get Up in the Morning); HOLIDAY INN movie (White Christmas; Happy Holiday; Let's Start the New Year Right; I've Got Plenty to Be Thankful For; Abraham; Song of Freedom; Be Careful, It's My Heart; You're Easy to Dance With; I'll Capture Your Heart Singing; I Can't Tell a Lie; old songs: Lazy; Easter Parade); I Threw a Kiss in the Ocean; Angels of Mercy; Me and My Melinda; Arms for the Love of America; When That Man Is Dead and Gone; The President's Birthday Ball

1943—THIS IS THE ARMY movie (original stage score)

1945—All of My Life; Just a Blue Serge Suit

1946—ANNIE GET YOUR GUN stage show (They Say It's Wonderful; There's No Business Like Show Business; Doin' What Comes Natur'lly; The Girl That I Marry; You Can't Get a Man with a Gun; Anything You Can Do; I Got the Sun in the Morning; I Got Lost in His Arms; Who Do You Love, I Hope?; Let's Go West Again—withdrawn from the show, emerged later as 1950 song); BLUE SKIES movie (many old Berlin songs; new songs: You Keep Coming Back Like a Song; A Couple of Song and Dance Men; Getting Nowhere; A Serenade to an Old-Fashioned Girl); Everybody Knew but Me

1947—Kate; Love and the Weather

1948—EASTER PARADE movie (Steppin' Out with My Baby; Better Luck Next Time; A Fella with an Umbrella; It Only Happens When I Dance with You; Drum Crazy; Happy Easter; A Couple of

Swells; plus old Berlin songs); The Freedom Train

1949—MISS LIBERTY stage show (Miss Liberty; Let's Take an Old Fashioned Walk; A Little Fish in a Big Pond; Just One Way to Say "I Love You"; Give Me Your Tired, Your Poor; Homework; You Can Have Him; Paris Wakes Up and Smiles); I'm Beginning to Miss You; A Man Chases a Girl (Until She Catches Him)

1950—CALL ME MADAM stage show (You're Just in Love; The Best Thing for You; Marrying for Love; It's a Lovely Day Today); ANNIE GET YOUR GUN movie (original stage score); Let's Go West Again; Play a Simple Melody (revived)

1952—I Like Ike

1953—CALL ME MADAM movie (original stage score)

1954—WHITE CHRISTMAS movie (Count Your Blessings Instead of Sheep; Sisters; The Best Things Happen While You're Dancing; Love, You Didn't Do Right by Me; Choreography; Snow; What Can You Do with a General?; old song: White Christmas); THERE'S NO BUSINESS LIKE SHOW BUSINESS movie (many old Berlin songs; new song: A Sailor's Not a Sailor 'Til a Sailor's Been Tattooed)

1957—SAYONARA movie (title song); I Keep Running Away from You; Colors

1962—MR. PRESIDENT stage show (Is He the Only Man in the World?; Empty Pockets Filled with Love; Glad to Be Home; The First Lady; Don't Be Afraid of Romance; I'm Gonna Get Him; In Our Hideaway; Laugh It Up; I've Got to Be Around; Let's Go Back to the Waltz; This Is a Great Country)

128. BERMAN, SONNY   t
(SAUL BERMAN)

Born April 21, 1924, New Haven, Conn.
Died January 16, 1947, New York, N.Y.

Trumpet star with Woody Herman in mid-40s. Good modern style. Promising

career cut short by untimely death from heart attack. First important job with Louis Prima in 1940. Periods with Sonny Dunham, Tommy Dorsey, George Auld, Harry James, Boyd Raeburn in early 40s. Briefly with Benny Goodman in early 1945, then joined Woody Herman and remained almost two years until death. Important figure in Herman Herd. Death came as great shock.

RECORDS

WOODY HERMAN
  Co 36870 Your Father's Mustache
  Co 36909 Everybody Knew but Me
  Co 37197 Sidewalks of Cuba
GEORGE AULD
  Apo 359 Taps Miller
  Apo 763 I Can't Get Started (1 & 2)
BILL HARRIS
  Dial 1009 Woodchopper's Holiday
BENNY GOODMAN
  Co 36790 Ev'ry Time
METRONOME ALL-STARS
  Vi 40-4000 Look Out/Metronome All Out
SONNY BERMAN
  Dial 1006 Curbstone Scuffle
  Dial 1020 Nocturne

LPs

SONNY BERMAN
  Eso(12″)ES-532 (1946 home-recorded tapes, RIs)
WOODY HERMAN
  Co CL-592 The Three Herds (Co RIs)
  MGM E-3043 At Carnegie Hall
(miscellaneous artists)
  Dial(10″)210 The Woodchoppers

129. BERNARD, AL   vo

Comedian-singer of 20s, very active on stage and records. Specialized in novelty songs. Extensive record output.

RECORDS

THE DIXIE STARS (Al Bernard & Russel Robinson)
  Br 2689 Never Gettin' No Place Blues/Blue-Eyed Sally
  Br 2762 Keep On Going/My Poodle-oodle Dog
  Br 2813 Let My Home Be Your Home/Birmingham Papa
  Co 389-D New York Ain't New York Anymore/What Do I Care?

AL BERNARD
> Vo 14744 De Ducks Done Got Me/25 Years from Now
> Vo 15140 Old Uncle Bill/On a Slow Train Through Arkansas
> Vo 15262 Wal, I Swan/My Puppy Bud
> Sil 5004 I'm a Twelve O'clock Fellow in a Nine O'clock Town
> Emer 10296 St. Louis Blues
> OK 40840 Wal, I Swan/No, No, Positively No
> Br 2062 St. Louis Blues/Beale Street Blues
> Br 2107 Memphis Blues/Frankie and Johnnie
> Br 2187 Carolina Rolling Stone
> Br 4076 Read 'Em and Weep/Brother Pollasses' Sermon

ERNEST HARE-AL BERNARD
> Med 8203 See Old Man Moon Smile
> Med 8204 You're My Gal
> Ed 50558 I Want to Hold You in My Arms

AL BERNARD-BILLY BEARD
> OK 41388 Henry Jones/Cindy

AL BERNARD with THE GOOFUS FIVE
> OK 40962 St. Louis Blues/Hesitation Blues

AL BERNARD-FRANK KAMPLAIN
> Co 552-D Hokey Pokey/Yeedle-Deedle-Lena

130. BERNARD, SAM   vo

Short, pudgy comedy star, sometime singer. A top performer in vaudeville. Appeared in numerous Broadway productions.

BROADWAY MUSICALS

1896—THE ART OF MARYLAND; THE GEEZER
1897—THE GLAD HAND; POUSSE CAFE
1899—THE MAN IN THE MOON
1900—BELLE OF BOHEMIA; THE CASINO GIRL
1901—HOITY TOITY
1902—THE SILVER SLIPPER
1903—THE GIRL FROM KAY'S
1905—THE ROLLICKING GIRL
1906—THE RICH MR. HOGGENHEIMER
1908—NEARLY A HERO
1909—THE GIRL AND THE WIZARD
1910—HE CAME FROM MILWAUKEE

1913—A GLIMPSE OF THE GREAT WHITE WAY; ALL FOR THE LADIES
1914—THE BELLE OF BOND STREET
1916—THE CENTURY GIRL
1920—AS YOU WERE
1921—MUSIC BOX REVUE
1923—NIFTIES OF 1923
1927—PIGGY

131. BERNHART, MILT   tb

Born May 25, 1926, Valparaiso, Ind.

Superior modern trombonist from early 40s into 70s. Good technique, warm tone, exciting soloist. At 16 joined Boyd Raeburn band in Chicago. With Buddy Franklin and Jimmy James in 1943, later in year joined Teddy Powell and remained until military service in August 1944. After discharge joined Stan Kenton mid-1946, remained off and on till late 1951. During this period attained some prominence. Interval with Boyd Raeburn in 1947 and several months with Benny Goodman late 1948-9. In 50s settled in Hollywood, became studio musician, worked in movies and TV. Freelanced in club jobs and recording work, remained active into 70s.

RECORDS

STAN KENTON
> Cap 904 The Peanut Vendor
> Cap 1043 Evening in Pakistan
> Cap 10185 Somnambulism

HOWARD RUMSEY
> Light 351 Out of Somewhere/Viva Zapata
> Contemp 359 Witch Doctor

PETE RUGOLO
> Co 40195 Laura/Early Stan

LPs

STAN KENTON
> Cap W-724 Stan Kenton in Hi-Fi

PETE RUGOLO
> Co CL-604 Adventures in Rhythm

VIDO MUSSO
> Cr CLP-5007 The Swingin'st

ELMER BERNSTEIN
> Choreo A-11 Movie & TV Themes

HOWARD RUMSEY
> Contemp(10")C-2501 Lighthouse All-Stars, Vol. 2

Contemp(10″)C-2506 Lighthouse All-Stars, Vol. 3

VAN ALEXANDER

Cap T-1243 The Home of Happy Feet (The Savoy)

(miscellaneous artists)

WB WS-1272 (S) The Trombones, Inc.

MILT BERNHART

De DL-9214 The Sound of Bernhart

Vi LPM-1123 Modern Brass

132. BERNIE, BEN   v vo cm B
(BENJAMIN ANZELWITZ)

Born May 30, 1891, New York, N.Y. Died October 20, 1943, Beverly Hills, Calif.

Popular bandleader in late 20s and 30s. Excellent M.C. and entertainer with great sense of humor. Attended New York College of Music, City College of New York and Columbia School of Mines. Played vaudeville as monologist-violinist several years pre-1920. Performed in act with Phil Baker for a time. In 1922 Bernie formed dance band, beginning 20-year career as bandleader. By mid-20s band had achieved some popularity, was recording and playing on radio. Pianist-arranger Al Goering remained with Bernie through most of band's life, proved important asset. Also in early band: Jack Pettis (sax) and Bill "Jazz" Moore (t). In 1928 Bernie had role in Broadway musical HERE'S HOWE. By early 30s the band developed into excellent outfit, sweet-styled but sometimes semi-hot. Altoist Dick Stabile featured frequently. Bernie began heavy broadcasting, own series as well as dance spot remotes. Deep, soothing voice and humorous remarks became well known. Favorite expression: "Yowsah, Yowsah!" Two attractive theme songs: opened with moody *It's a Lonesome Old Town*, closed with *Au Revoir, Pleasant Dreams* on which he recited lyrics. He and columnist Walter Winchell kept up running "feud" through 30s which made good copy and formed basis for two movies in which they co-starred, WAKE UP AND LIVE (1937) and LOVE AND HISSES (1938). Dubbed himself The Old Maestro, referred to band as "Ben Bernie and All the Lads." Played Pabst Blue

Ribbon radio show 1933-7, appeared in Pabst pavillion at Chicago World's Fair in 1933. Featured vocalist Little Jackie Heller 1932-3. Bernie also did occasional vocals in sly, half-talking manner. Band appeared in movies SHOOT THE WORKS (1934) and STOLEN HARMONY (1935). Other radio shows in late 30s and early 40s, including at times a quiz format. In later 30s band had more substance, swung occasionally due to arrangements by Gray Rains. Bernie well-liked personality; public and music world saddened by death in 1943. Co-composer of four excellent songs: *Sweet Georgia Brown* (1925), *Who's Your Little Who-zis?* (1931), *I Can't Believe It's True* and *Strange Interlude* (1932). Lesser songs: *Holding My Honey's Hand, A Bowl of Chop Suey and Youey, After the Dance Was Over, Was Last Night the Last Night?, Ain't That Marvelous?, I Can't Forget That You Forgot About Me.*

RECORDS

BERNIE & BAKER (Ben Bernie & Phil Baker, v-acc)

Vi 18499 Waters of Venice/Goodbye Alexander

BEN BERNIE

Vo 14979 O Katharina/Titinia

Vo 15080 Collegiate/Yes, Sir, That's My Baby

Br(12″)20064 Ol' Man River/Soliloquy

Br 2992 Sleepy Time Gal/A Little Bit Bad

Br 3082 Bell Hoppin' Blues/Roses Brought Me You

Br 3631 Swanee Shore/Miss Annabelle Lee

Br 3771 The Man I Love/Dream Kisses

Br 3913 Crazy Rhythm/Imagination

Br 4132 How About Me?/She's Funny That Way

Br 4142 Makin' Whoopee/I'm Bringing a Red, Red Rose

Br 4943 (themes) It's a Lonesome Old Town/Au Revoir, Pleasant Dreams

Br 6008 To Whom It May Concern/Crying Myself to Sleep

Br 6024 The King's Horses/Sleepy Town Express

Br 6250 The Wooden Soldier and the China Doll/Can't We Talk It Over?
Br 6396 I'll Follow You/A Million Dreams
Br 6504 What Have We Got to Lose?/Let's All Sing Like the Birdies
Co 2804-D Marching Along Together/We Won't Have to Sell the Farm
Co 2820-D This Is Romance/You Gotta Be a Football Hero
Co 2824-D Shanghai Lil/Who's Afraid of the Big Bad Wolf?
De 874 San Francisco/Long Ago and Far Away
De 878 A Star Fell Out of Heaven/When Did You Leave Heaven?
Vo 4916 I'm Sorry for Myself/The Song of the Metronome
Vo 5492 My Wonderful One, Let's Dance/Where Was I?

LPs
(miscellaneous artists)
De(10")DL-7021 Curtain Call

133. BERNSTEIN, ARTIE   b cel

Born February 3, 1909, Brooklyn, N.Y. Died January 4, 1964, Los Angeles, Calif.

A top bassist of 30s with prolific recording career. Worked on many records considered jazz classics today. Bernstein talented youngster on cello, played classical jobs. Studied law but embarked on musical career, switched to bass and played in dance bands. Early freelance work in New York. Periods with Red Nichols and Dorsey Brothers early 30s, plus heavy studio work on radio and records through 30s. Joined Benny Goodman May 1939, remained till 1941—longest period with one band. Settled on west coast to do studio work. Military service, World War II. After discharge resumed studio work until early 60s.

RECORDS
RED NICHOLS
Br 6219 Get Cannibal/Junk Man Blues
Br 6266 Sweet Sue/Clarinet Marmalade

Br 6312 Goofus/Goin' to Town
MILDRED BAILEY
Vo 3056 I'd Love to Take Orders from You/I'd Rather Listen to Your Eyes
Vo 3057 When Day Is Done/Someday Sweetheart
EDDIE CONDON
Co 35680 The Eel/Home Cooking
Co 36009 Tennessee Twilight
DORSEY BROTHERS ORCHESTRA
Br 6722 Blue Room/Fidgety
Br 7542 She's Funny That Way/But I Can't Make a Man
BENNY GOODMAN
Co 2835-D I Gotta Right to Sing the Blues/Ain'tcha Glad
Co 2845-D Dr. Heckle and Mr. Jibe/Texas Tea Party
Co 2856-D Your Mother's Son-in-Law/Tappin' the Barrel
Co 2907-D Georgia Jubilee/Emaline
Co 35313 Make with the Kisses/I Thought About You
Co 35362 Opus Local 802/Stealin' Apples
Co 35410 Beyond the Moon/Night and Day
Co 35810 Wholly Cats/Royal Garden Blues (both SEXTET)
LIONEL HAMPTON
Vi 26447 I've Found a New Baby/Four or Five Times
Vi 26453 Munson Street Breakdown/I Can't Get Started
RED NORVO
Br 6562 Knockin' on Wood/Hole in the Wall
Br 6906 In a Mist/Dance of the Octopus
ADRIAN ROLLINI
De 265 Sugar/Riverboat Shuffle
De 359 Davenport Blues/Somebody Loves Me
JACK TEAGARDEN
Co 2558-D You Rascal You/That's What I Like About You
Br 6716 A Hundred Years from Today/I Just Couldn't Take It, Baby
Br 6741 Love Me/Blue River
FRANKIE TRUMBAUER
Vi 24812 Blue Moon/Down t' Uncle Bill's

Vi 24834 Troubled/Plantation Moods
COOTIE WILLIAMS
OK 6370 West End Blues/G-Men
TEDDY WILSON
Br 7917 Yours and Mine/Sun Showers
METRONOME ALL-STAR BAND
Vi 27314 Bugle Call Rag/One O'clock Jump
SONNY BERMAN
Dial 1006 Curbstone Scuffle
SERGE CHALOFF
Dial 1012 Blue Serge

LPs

RED NORVO
Epc LN-3128 Red Norvo & His All-Stars (Br, Co RIs)
JACK TEAGARDEN
Jolly Roger(10″)5026 (Br RIs)
BENNY GOODMAN
Co GL-500 Benny Goodman Combos (Co RIs)
CHARLIE CHRISTIAN
Co CL-652 (with Benny Goodman Sextet and Orchestra; Co RIs)
ARNOLD ROSS (one side)
EmArcy(10″)MG-26029 Holiday in Piano
ADRIAN ROLLINI (one side)
Br(10″)58039 Battle of Jazz (1934 De RIs)

133A. BERNSTEIN, ELMER

cm ar p B

Born April 4, 1922, New York, N. Y.

Composer-arranger of movie background music early 50s into 70s. Movie title songs *To Kill a Mockingbird, Walk on the Wild Side, The Man with the Golden Arm, The Magnificent Seven, The Sons of Katie Elder, Love with the Proper Stranger* and *Baby, the Rain Must Fall*. Serious works included *Serenade for Solo Violin, String Orchestra, Harp and Percussion*. Educated at Walden School, NYU, Juilliard. Career as concert pianist interrupted by military service, World War II. Many scores for Armed Forces Radio Service. Began Hollywood career 1950, scored minor films SATURDAY'S HERO and BOOTS MALONE (both 1951). Career established with excellent scoring on third film SUDDEN FEAR.

MOVIES
(as composer and probable arranger-conductor of background music; partial listing)
1951—SATURDAY'S HERO; BOOTS MALONE
1952—SUDDEN FEAR
1953—NEVER WAVE AT A WAC
1954—MAKE HASTE TO LIVE; SILENT RAIDERS
1955—THE VIEW FROM POMPEY'S HEAD; THE MAN WITH THE GOLDEN ARM
1956—THE TEN COMMANDMENTS
1957—FEAR STRIKES OUT; THE TIN STAR; SWEET SMELL OF SUCCESS
1958—DESIRE UNDER THE ELMS; KINGS GO FORTH; GOD'S LITTLE ACRE; THE BUCCANEER
1959—SOME CAME RUNNING; THE MIRACLE; ANNA LUCASTA
1960—THE RAT RACE; THE MAGNIFICENT SEVEN; FROM THE TERRACE; THE STORY ON PAGE ONE
1961—SUMMER AND SMOKE; BY LOVE POSSESSED; THE YOUNG DOCTORS; THE COMANCHEROS
1962—WALK ON THE WILD SIDE; BIRDMAN OF ALCATRAZ
1963—TO KILL A MOCKINGBIRD; THE GREAT ESCAPE; HUD; THE CARETAKERS; LOVE WITH THE PROPER STRANGER
1964—THE CARPETBAGGERS; THE WORLD OF HENRY ORIENT; FOUR DAYS IN NOVEMBER (documentary)
1965—BABY, THE RAIN MUST FALL; THE SONS OF KATIE ELDER; THE HALLELUJAH TRAIL
1966—HAWAII; SEVEN WOMEN; THE SILENCERS; CAST A GIANT SHADOW
1967—THOROUGHLY MODERN MILLIE
1968—THE SCALPHUNTERS; I LOVE YOU, ALICE B. TOKLAS!
1969—TRUE GRIT; THE GYPSY MOTHS
1970—A WALK IN THE SPRING RAIN
1971—BIG JAKE; SEE NO EVIL

RECORDS
(all LPs)
(movie soundtracks; as composer and probable arranger-conductor)
UA 5127 CAST A GIANT SHADOW
UA 6495 THE MAN WITH THE GOLDEN ARM
Co CL-1278 SWEET SMELL OF SUCCESS

Co OL-6420 BABY, THE RAIN MUST FALL
Ava 31 TO KILL A MOCKINGBIRD
Ava 53 HAWAII
Cap ST-263 TRUE GRIT
Cap W-1063 SOME CAME RUNNING
Cap W-1109 SUMMER AND SMOKE
Lib 3036 GOD'S LITTLE ACRE
Vi LOC-1067 THE CARPETBAGGERS
Vi LOC-1120 THE SONS OF KATIE ELDER
Choreo A-11 (themes from various movies)

134. BERNSTEIN, LEONARD
cm lyr ar p B

Born August 25, 1918, Lawrence, Mass.

Composer of classical music and several popular musicals on Broadway. Best known for show WEST SIDE STORY in 1957; popular score widely played in ensuing years. Grew up in Boston. Educated at Harvard and Curtis Institute in Philadelphia; also had extensive special musical training. Became assistant and protege of Serge Koussevitzky at Berkshire Music Centre. Assistant conductor of New York Philharmonic 1943-4, conductor of New York Symphony 1945-8. Wrote many serious works for classical orchestra. In 1945 penned good score in first Broadway show ON THE TOWN. Wrote scores for PETER PAN (1950), WONDERFUL TOWN (1953), CANDIDE (1956) and notably WEST SIDE STORY (1957). Chief popular-song collaborators Betty Comden, Adolph Green, John Latouche, Stephen Sondheim. Background music for 1954 movie ON THE WATERFRONT. Piano soloist and guest conductor with various symphony orchestras in U. S. and abroad. Taught at Berkshire Music Centre and Brandeis University. Conductor of New York Philharmonic late 50s and 60s. In 60s became well known on TV via his Young People's Concerts series explaining and popularizing classical music.

SONGS
(with related shows)

1945—ON THE TOWN stage show (New York, New York; Lonely Town; Lucky to Be Me; Some Other Time)
1949—ON THE TOWN movie (original stage score)

1950—PETER PAN stage show (Who Am I?; My House; Never Land, Peter, Peter)
1953—WONDERFUL TOWN stage show (Ohio; It's Love; A Quiet Girl; A Little Bit in Love; Wrong Note Rag)
1956—CANDIDE stage show (The Best of All Possible Worlds; Oh, Happy We; It Must Be So; Glitter and Be Gay; Eldorado; What's the Use?)
1957—WEST SIDE STORY stage show (Tonight; Maria; I Feel Pretty; Something's Coming; Somewhere; America)
1961—WEST SIDE STORY movie (original stage score)

Classical works include *Jeremiah Symphony*; *Serenade for Violin, String Orchestra with Percussion*; *Fancy Free ballet*; *Age of Anxiety (Symphony No. 2)*; *Kaddish (Symphony No. 3)*; *Chichester Psalms*; *Seven Anniversaries* (for piano); *Sonata for Clarinet and Piano*; *Facsimile* (ballet); *Four Anniversaries* (for piano); *Five Pieces for Brass*; *Bonne Cuisine*; *Prelude, Fugue and Riffs*; *Mass.*

RECORDS
(all LPs)

LEONARD BERNSTEIN
Co CL-919 What Is Jazz?
Co ML-5651 WEST SIDE STORY Ballet Music
Co MS-6091 (S) Gershwin
Co MS-6677 (S) Bernstein Conducts Bernstein
Comm 855 Music of Leonard Bernstein

135. BERRY, CHU   ts cm
(LEON BERRY)

Born September 13, 1910, Wheeling, W.Va.
Died October 31, 1941, Conneaut, Ohio, from injuries received in auto accident

Outstanding tenor sax star of 30s, especially known for work with Fletcher Henderson and Cab Calloway bands. Consistently excellent jazz soloist, warm tone and smooth-swinging style. Early dance work with Edwards' Collegians in West Virginia. 1929-30 with Sammy Stewart band on tour, ending up in New York. Freelanced there in early 30s, worked with Cecil Scott, Benny Carter and Charlie Johnson among others. With Teddy Hill 1933-5, attracted attention in jazz circles. Joined Henderson late 1935-7, became famous for solo work with band. Moved to Calloway band in mid-1937, where featured most prominently. Band had busy recording schedule, and many Berry solos with Calloway survive. Remained with band till death. Injured in auto crash while traveling between one-nighters, died four days later. Death at 31 tragic loss to jazz. In addition to many records with Henderson and Calloway, recorded widely with other groups. Composed Henderson's unusual theme song, *Christopher Columbus*, which in 1936 became popular number performed by many bands.

RECORDS

TEDDY HILL
Me 13351 Here Comes Cookie/Got Me Doin' Things
Me 13364 When the Robin Sings His Song Again/When Love Knocks at Your Heart

FLETCHER HENDERSON
Vo 3211 Blue Lou/Christopher Columbus
Vo 3213 Stealin' Apples/Grand Terrace Swing
Vo 3511 Rose Room/Back in Your Own Backyard
Vo 3641 Chris and His Gang
Vi 25297 Moonrise on the Lowlands
Vi 25317 I'll Always Be in Love with You/Jangled Nerves
Vi 25379 Jimtown Blues/You Can Depend on Me

CAB CALLOWAY
Vo 3896 Jubilee/Every Day's a Holiday
Vo 4511 Deep in a Dream/I'm Madly in Love with You
Vo 5005 Trylon Swing/The Jumpin' Jive
Vo 5566 Who's Yehoodi?/Hard Times
OK 5644 Rhapsody in Rhumba/Five Minute Intermission
OK 5687 A Ghost of a Chance/Come On with the "Come On"
OK 5754 Boo-Wah, Boo-Wah
OK 5950 Hot Air
OK 6084 Bye Bye Blues/Run Little Rabbit
OK 6305 Take the "A" Train/Chattanooga Choo Choo
Va 593 Congo/My Gal Mezzanine

RED ALLEN
Vo 2956 Get Rhythm in Your Feet/I'll Never Say "Never Again" Again
Vo 2965 Rosetta

LIL ARMSTRONG
De 1059 Doin' the Susy Q/My Hi-De-Ho Man
De 1092 Brown Gal/Or Leave Me Alone

PUTNEY DANDRIDGE
Vo 2982 Chasing Shadows/When I Grow Too Old to Dream

LIONEL HAMPTON
Vi 26209 Sweethearts on Parade/High Society
Vi 26233 Denison Swing/Wizzin' the Wizz
Vi 26254 Shufflin' at the Hollywood/It Don't Mean a Thing

GENE KRUPA
Vi 25263 Mutiny in the Parlor/I'm Gonna Clap My Hands
Vi 25276 Swing Is Here/I Hope Gabriel Likes My Music

WINGY MANONE
Bb 10296 Downright Disgusted Blues/Boogie Woogie
Bb 10331 Royal Garden Blues/In the Barrel

RED NORVO
Co 3059-D Honeysuckle Rose
Co 3079-D Bughouse/Blues in E Flat

TEDDY WILSON
Br 7550 Twenty-Four Hours a Day/Yankee Doodle Never Went to Town
Br 7684 Warmin' Up/Blues in C Sharp Minor

CHU BERRY
Va 532 Too Marvelous for Words/Now You're Talking My Language
Va 587 Limehouse Blues/Indiana
Co 37571 Chuberry Jam/Maelstrom
CMS(12")1502 Star Dust/Body and Soul

LPs

CHU BERRY
Epic LN-3124 "Chu" (Va, Vo RIs)
CMS(10″)20024 (CMS RIs)
Mainstream 56038 Sittin' In (CMS RIs)

LIONEL HAMPTON
Cam CAL-402 Jivin' the Vibes (Vi RIs)
Cam CAL-517 Open House (Vi RIs)

FLETCHER HENDERSON
Co CAL19 (4-LP set) A Study in Frustration (Co, Ha, Vo RIs)
(miscellaneous artists)
Vi LPV-578 Swing, Vol. 1 (Bb, Vi RIs)

136. BERRY, EMMETT   t B

Born July 23, 1916, Macon, Ga.

Good jazz trumpet man in mainstream style; played interesting Roy Eldridge-style solos. Grew up in Cleveland, played in Ohio on early jobs. Landed in Albany, N.Y., played in that area 1933-6. With Fletcher Henderson late 1936 to mid-1939, then joined Horace Henderson till late 1940. With Teddy Wilson combo about a year, 1941-2. With Raymond Scott big band on staff radio 1942-3. In 1943 spells with Lionel Hampton, Don Redman, Benny Carter. Rejoined Wilson late 1943-4, with John Kirby mid-1944 till end of year. Most of 1945 with Eddie Heywood. Late 1945 joined Count Basie and remained till 1950 for longest period with one band. Much of 1951 in band backing blues singer Jimmy Rushing. Good period with Johnny Hodges 1951-4. Freelanced in later 50s; stiuts with Earl Hines, Cootie Williams, Illinois Jacquet. European tours with Sam Price 1955-6 and Buck Clayton 1959 and 1961. Settled on west coast in early 60s to freelance. In later 60s moved to New York, again to freelance. Active into 70s, mostly with small jazz bands. Sometimes led own band. Though Berry played with many bands and on many of their recordings, he came to public notice mostly via combo records led by himself and others in mid-40s.

RECORDS

FLETCHER HENDERSON
Vo 3487 Rhythm of the Tambourine/It's Wearin' me Down
Vo 3534 Stampede/Great Caesar's Ghost

ED HALL
CMS 550 The Man I Love/Coquette
CMS(12″)1512 Downtown Cafe Boogie/Uptown Cafe Boogie

COLEMAN HAWKINS with COZY COLE'S ALL-STARS
Sav 583 Ridin' the Riff/Flat Rock

BILLIE HOLIDAY
OK 6369 Jim/Love Me or Leave Me
OK 6451 Gloomy Sunday
VD(12″)586 I Cover the Waterfront

ILLINOIS JACQUET
Sav 593 Jumpin' Jacquet/Blue Mood

JOHN KIRBY
Asch 357-1 9:20 Special/Maxixe Dengoza
Asch 357-3 K.C. Caboose/J.K. Special

SAM PRICE
De 8609 Why Don't You Love Me Anymore?/Harlem Gin Blues
De 8624 Match Box Blues

BILLY TAYLOR'S BIG EIGHT
Key 615 Night Wind/Carney-Val in Rhythm

WALTER THOMAS
JD 8125 Broke but Happy/Blues on the Delta
JD 8126 Jumpin' with Judy/Blues on the Bayou

TEDDY WILSON
Co 36737 Out of Nowhere/You're My Favorite Memory

COZY COLE
Sav 512 Ol' Man River/Wrap Your Troubles in Dreams

LEM DAVIS
Sun 7558 My Blue Heaven/Nothin' from Nothin'

HORACE HENDERSON
OK 5900 Ain't Misbehavin'/Smooth Sailing

COUNT BASIE
Vi 20-2148 Bill's Mill
Vi 20-2696 Sugar/Swingin' the Blues

JOHNNY HODGES
Norg 101 Good Queen Bess/The Jeep Is Jumping

Norg 113 Indiana/Easy Going Bounce
Clef 89086 Jappa/Sheik of Araby
Mer 89035 Latino/Through for the
   Night
EMMETT BERRY
   Nat 9001 Sweet and Lovely/White
      Rose Kick
   Nat 9002 Deep Blue Dreams/Byas'd
      Opinions
   Sav 594 Berry's Blues/Minor Romp
                    LPs
JO JONES
   Jazztone J-1242 The Jo Jones Special
COUNT BASIE
   Cam CAL-395 The Count (Vi RIs)
JOHNNY HODGES
   Mer(10")MGC-111 Johnny Hodges
      Collates
FLETCHER HENDERSON ALL-STARS
   Jazztone J-1285 The Big Reunion
JIMMY RUSHING
   Vang VRS-8508 Listen to the Blues
SAMMY PRICE
   Jazztone J-1236 In Concert
COLEMAN HAWKINS
   Jazztone J-1201 Timeless Jazz

137. BERT, EDDIE   tb B
Born May 16, 1922, Yonkers, N.Y.

Modern-style trombonist. Good tone, imaginative and gutty solos. First important
job in 1940 with Sam Donahue, then with
Red Norvo 1941-2. With Woody Herman
1943-4 and Cootie Williams 1945. Brief
military service. With Herbie Fields several months in late 1946, Stan Kenton
1947-8, Benny Goodman late 1948-9. In
early 50s with Woody Herman, Artie
Shaw, Bill Harris, Stan Kenton, Charlie
Barnet, Herbie Fields, Ray McKinley;
also did studio work in New York. In
1954 joined Les Elgart, then freelanced.
In late 50s worked with Benny Goodman,
Elliot Lawrence and Urbie Green among
others; also led own combo. In 60s
worked pit bands of Broadway shows,
TV, concerts, festivals. Active into 70s.

RECORDS
BENNY GOODMAN
   Cap 15409 Undercurrent Blues
RED NORVO
   Co 36557 Jersey Bounce

STAN KENTON
   Cap 906 Harlem Holiday
   Cap 907 Unison Riff
   Cap 911 How High the Moon
THE POLL CATS
   Atl 851 Sa-frantic
EDDIE BERT
   Dis 168 First Day of Spring/Mol-
      Shaja
   Dis 169 All the Things You Are/Ming
      Tree
                    LPs
EDDIE BERT
   Sav MG-12015 Musician of the Year
   Sav MG-12019 Encore
   Jazztone J-1223 Modern Moods
   Dis(10")DL-3020
   Somerset 5200
ELLIOT LAWRENCE
   Fan 3-206 Plays Gerry Mulligan Ar-
      rangements
   Fan 3-219 Plays Tiny Kahn and
      Johnny Mandel Arrangements
JOE HOLIDAY
   De DL-8487 Holiday in Jazz
FRANK SOCOLOW
   Beth BCP-70 Sounds by Socolow
COLEMAN HAWKINS
   Jazztone J-1201 Timeless Jazz
MACHITO
   Roul 52006 Kenya

138. BERTON, VIC   d B
Born May 7, 1896, Chicago, Ill.
Died December 26, 1951, Hollywood,
*   Calif.*

Drummer who worked with jazz greats in
20s and 30s; on many record sessions
with Red Nichols groups. At age 7, playing drums in pit band in Milwaukee! By
16 doing symphonic work. With John
Philip Sousa's navy band during World
War I. Then band jobs in Chicago in
early 20s with Art Kahn, Arnold Johnson,
others. In 1924 manager of Wolverines,
then featuring future great Bix Beiderbecke. In middle and late 20s extensive
recording output with combos of Red
Nichols, Miff Mole, others. Worked with
Roger Wolfe Kahn in 1925-7, also with
Don Voorhees, Paul Whiteman. Much
freelance work in New York. Co-com-

583

poser of *Sobbin' Blues* in 1922. Settled on west coast at beginning of 30s, worked at movie studios. Some symphonic work in area in later years. Still active in 40s in studios.

RECORDS

COTTON PICKERS
Br 2937 Milenberg Joys/If You Hadn't Gone Away
Br 2981 Carolina Stomp/Stomp Off, Let's Go
Br 3001 Fallin' Down/What Did I Tell Ya?

THE RED HEADS
Pe 14528 Nervous Charlie/Headin' for Louisville
Pe 14565 Fallen Arches
Pe 14600 'Tain't Cold/Hangover
Pe 14639 Hi Diddle Diddle/Dynamite
Pe 14708 Alabama Stomp/Brown Sugar
Pe 14738 Heebie Jeebies/Black Bottom

RED NICHOLS
Br 3407 Washboard Blues/That's No Bargain
Br 3477 Buddy's Habits/Boneyard Shuffle
Br 3550 Alabama Stomp/Hurricane
Br 3627 Riverboat Shuffle/Eccentric
Br 3854 Nobody's Sweetheart/Avalon
Br 4456 A Pretty Girl Is Like a Melody
Br 6198 Oh Peter/Honolulu Blues

CHARLESTON CHASERS
Co 446-D Red Hot Henry Brown/Loud Speakin' Papa
Co 861-D Someday Sweetheart/After You've Gone
Co 909-D Wabash Blues/Davenport Blues
Co 1229-D Five Pennies/Feelin' No Pain

MIFF MOLE
OK 40758 Alexander's Ragtime Band/Some Sweet Day
OK 40848 Hurricane
OK 40890 Imagination/Feelin' No Pain

VIC BERTON
Vo 2915 Jealous/Dardanella
Vo 2974 Blue/Taboo
Co 3074-D Devil's Kitchen/I've Been Waiting All Winter

Co 3092-D Imitations of You/Two Rivers Flow Through Harlem

LPs
CHARLESTON CHASERS
VJM(E)26 (1925-8 Co RIs)

139. BEST, DENZIL   d t p b cm
Born April 27, 1917, New York, N.Y.
Died May 24, 1965, New York, N.Y.,
from injury received in a fall

Good jazz drummer in subdued but swinging style. Master of brushes. Best known as member early years of popular George Shearing combo. Early in professional career Denzil played good trumpet, jobbing in New York in early 40s. Participated in jam sessions at Minton's. Forced to abandon trumpet because of health. Worked awhile on piano and bass, then switched to drums in 1943. In mid-40s played with Ben Webster, Illinois Jacquet, Coleman Hawkins. Late 1947 began tour of Sweden with Chubby Jackson. With George Shearing combo 1949-52. Serious auto accident necessitated retirement from music in 1952-3. Late 1953 joined Artie Shaw's Gramercy Five for brief period. Freelanced in late 50s, and lengthy stay with Errol Garner. Career curtailed by illness in 60s. Hard-luck drummer suffered fatal accident in 1965: fell down steps in subway, died following day from skull injury. Composer of several jazz numbers: *Move, Nothing but D. Best, Dee Dee's Dance, Geneva's Move, Wee, Bemsha Swing.*

RECORDS

COLEMAN HAWKINS
Cap 205 Stuffy/It's the Talk of the Town
Cap 10036 Hollywood Stampede/I'm Thru with Love

TEDDY WILSON
Mus 547 The Sheik of Araby

LENNIE TRISTANO
Cap 7-1224 Intuition/Yesterdays

JOE THOMAS
HRS 1016 Riff Street/A Touch of Blue

JIMMY JONES
Wax 103 Five O'clock Drag/New World a-Comin'

EDDIE DAVIS
  Sav 904 Hollerin' and Screaming/Maternity
GEORGE SHEARING
  Dis 105 Midnight on Cloud 69/Bebop's Fables
  Dis 106 Cotton Top/Sorry Wrong Rhumba
  Dis 107 Cherokee/Four Bars Short
  MGM 10530 East of the Sun/Conception
  MGM 10596 The Continental/Nothing but D. Best
  MGM 10687 I'll Remember April/Jumpin' with Symphony Sid
  MGM 10859 Roses of Picardy/Pick Yourself Up
  MGM 10956 Quintessence/I'll Be Around
  MGM 10986 I Remember You/The Breeze and I
  MGM 11199 Swedish Pastry/To a Wild Rose
  MGM 11282 Five O'clock Whistle/Simplicity
  MGM 30625 Over the Rainbow/Lonely Moments
  MGM 30627 Ghost of a Chance/How High the Moon
DENZIL BEST
  Wax 104 All Alone/As Long as I Live

LPs

JACK TEAGARDEN
  Urania US-41205 (S) Accent on Trombone
OSCAR PETTIFORD
  Pres 7813 Memorial Album (1949 & 1954 RIs)
(miscellaneous combos)
  Riv RLP-145 Giants of Small-Band Swing (HRS RIs)
GEORGE SHEARING
  MGM E-3265 Touch of Genius
  MGM E-3266 I Hear Music
COLEMAN HAWKINS
  Stin(10″)SLP-22 Originals with Hawkins (Asch RIs)

140. BEST, JOHNNY   t
Born October 20, 1913, Shelby, N.C.
Trumpet star from 30s to 70s with many bands. Capable soloist. Active in studio

work later in career. Played in college band at Duke, The Blue Devils, in 1932, also in University of North Carolina dance band. Late 1933-4 with Henry Biagini, later with Joe Haymes. 1935-6 again with Duke Blue Devils, under leadership of Les Brown. In early 1937 joined Charlie Barnet briefly, then with Artie Shaw mid-1937 to mid-1939. With Glenn Miller band during its great years, late 1939-42, as featured trumpet soloist. With Bob Crosby. Played in service bands of Artie Shaw and Sam Donahue. After discharge, joined Benny Goodman in late 1945 and remained till mid-1947 except for brief interval away. Rejoined Goodman briefly in late 1947. Then settled in Hollywood and became a studio musician in the late 40s. In 1950 played with Jerry Gray. In 1951 with Sonny Burke. Several years with Billy May in early 50s. In 1955 in studio band working on soundtrack for movie THE BENNY GOODMAN STORY, on subsequent LPs issued from soundtrack. Freelanced in late 50s and 60s, including periods with Bob Crosby. Had own club in San Diego. Continued active into 70s, often with Tex Beneke.

RECORDS

ARTIE SHAW
  Br 7895 It Goes to Your Feet
  Br 7914 Night and Day
  Br 8019 Free for All
  Bb 7759 Back Bay Shuffle
  Bb 7772 Comin' On
  Bb 10128 The Man I Love
GLENN MILLER
  Bb 10665 Star Dust
  Bb 10754 Pennsylvania 6-5000
  Bb 10832 What's Your Story, Morning Glory?
  Bb 11203 Peckaboo to You
  Bb 11299 The Man in the Moon
  Bb 11326 Orange Blossom Lane
  Vi 20-1509 Juke Box Saturday Night
BENNY GOODMAN
  Co 55039 Oh, Baby! (pt. 2)
SAM DONAHUE
  Encore 500 Hollywood Hop/Encore Essence
  Encore 502 Round the Block/Catch as Catch Can

VD(12″)583 Deep Night/I've Found a
New Baby
NAPPY LAMARE
Cap 15050 South Rampart Street Pa-
rade/Mama Inez

LPs

JOHNNY BEST ALL-STARS & DICK CATHCART
ALL-STARS
Mer PPS-2009 Dixieland Left and
Right
RAMPART STREET PARADERS
Co CL-1061 Texas! U.S.A.
MAXWELL DAVIS
Cr CLP-5050 A Tribute to Glenn Mil-
ler
ARTIE SHAW
Epic LN-3150 (Br, Vo RIs)
FTR 1502 Artie Shaw & His Orches-
tra, Vol. 2 (1937-8)
MORTY CORB
Tops L-1581 Strictly from Dixie
(miscellaneous bands)
Golden Tone C-4021 Dixieland
(miscellaneous artists)
Blue Angel BAJC-505(S) Jazz Party at
Pasadena, Vol. 1
Blue Angel BAJC-507/508(2-LP set)
The Complete 1970 Pasadena Jazz
Párty
BOB CROSBY
Dot DLP-3278 Bob Crosby's Great
Hits

141. BESTOR, DON   p vb cm B
*Born September 23, 1889, Langford,
S.D.*
Died January 13, 1970

Popular dance band leader, particularly
in 30s. Learned piano early and at 16
began extensive tours in vaudeville.
Worked as song plugger, tried composing
songs but was unsuccessful at first.
Formed dance band in early 20s, then
served as leader of Benson Orchestra for
awhile, recording for Victor Records. Resumed own band later. By early 30s it
developed into good sweet-styled band.
Attained some prominence via recordings
in 1933-5 and on radio. In 1934 on Walter
O'Keefe show, late 1934-5 on fast-rising
Jack Benny show. In later 30s popularity
waned, though still had band into late

40s. Composed beautiful song *Contented*
(1932), used for years as theme of popular
Carnation Milk radio show. Composed a
few other songs of minor importance:
Down by the Winegar Woiks; *Teach Me to
Smile* (sometime theme); *You're a Darling*; *I'm Not Forgetting* (used as his theme
at times); *Gee, But I Hate to Say Goodnight*; *The Whole World Is Dreaming of
Love*; and the J-E-L-L-O commercial for
Jack Benny's radio show.

RECORDS

BENSON ORCHESTRA (as director)
Vi 19022 Down in Maryland/Georgia
Cabin Door
Vi 19257 Oklahoma Indian Jazz
Vi 19470 Copenhagen/Keep On Danc-
ing

DON BESTOR
Vi 19751 Charleston   Baby   of
Mine/Summer Nights
Vi 21562 It Must Be Love
Vi 24135 Contented/Sweetheart Hour
Vi 24142 My Darling/Along Came
Love
Vi 24176 I'm Sure of Everything but
You/Speak to Me of Love
Vi 24253 42nd Street/Shuffle Off to
Buffalo
Vi 24344 Learn to Croon/Moonstruck
Vi 24345 Under a Blanket of Blue/
Hold Your Man
Vi 24585 Butterfingers/Love Me
Vi 24587 Little Dutch Mill/A Thou-
sand Goodnights
Vi 24658 Moonglow/Dancing on a
Rooftop
Br 6975 Wish Me Good Luck/Some-
where in Your Heart
Br 6981 Rain/Old Skipper
Br 7345 I'm 100 Percent for You/Like
a Bolt from the Blue
Br 7366 I Believe in Miracles/Tiny Lit-
tle Fingerprints
Br 7495 Simple Things in Life/Animal
Crackers in My Soup
Br 7516 You Are My Lucky Star/On a
Sunday Afternoon
Bb 7239 True Confession/Sailing
Home
Bb 7240 You're a Sweetheart/A
Strange Loneliness

142. BIGARD, BARNEY   cl ts cm B
(LEON ALBANY BIGARD)

Born March 3, 1906, New Orleans, La.

Outstanding jazz clarinetist. Long career
from early 20s into 70s. Noted for long
tenure as an ace soloist with Duke Ellington band. Clarinet work distinctive and
easily identifiable, with limpid tone and
flowing style full of notes and inflections.
Early in career played jobs on tenor sax,
first important one with Albert Nicholas
in 1922. After jobbing in local area, went
to Chicago in 1924. There worked with
King Oliver, began to concentrate on
clarinet instead of sax. With Oliver into
1927. Later that year played with Charlie
Elgar and Luis Russell. Late 1927 joined
Ellington for 15-year association. As
Ellington rose to prominence, so did Bigard and other key soloists. Enjoyed prc-
lific recording career with Ellington and
in ensuing years as freelance. Also recorded often with own groups.

After leaving Ellington in mid-1942, settled in California. Led own group awhile,
then worked with Freddie Slack late
1942-3. Freelanced, mostly on west coast,
led own band at intervals, did studio
work. In 1946 with Kid Ory. In mid-1947
became an original member of Louis
Armstrong All-Stars, small combo of outstanding jazzmen. Remained five years,
left, rejoined 1953-5. In late 50s with Ben
Pollack and Cozy Cole. Again with Armstrong All-Stars in 1960-1. After early 60s
his activities slowed though occasionally
played jobs into early 70s and toured with
Condon-Davison Group. Composer or
co-composer of several good jazz numbers: *Mood Indigo, Minnie the Moocher,
Rockin' in Rhythm, Clouds in My Heart,
Minuet in Blues, Stompy Jones, Step Steps
Up, Step Steps Down, Clarinet Lament,
Saturday Night Function, Lament to a Lost
Love* and *C-Jam Blues*, most of which
played by Ellington band. Appeared in
several movies, mostly with Ellington
band. Seen on TV occasionally with Armstrong All-Stars.

RECORDS

LUIS RUSSELL
  Vo 1010 29th and Dearborn/Sweet
    Mumtaz

JELLY ROLL MORTON
  Vi 38108 Smilin' the Blues Away/Tur-
    tle Twist
  Vi 38601 My Little Dixie Home/That's
    Like It Ought to Be
DUKE ELLINGTON
  Vi 22528 Ring Dem Bells/Three Little
    Words
  Vi 22587 Mood Indigo/When a Black
    Man's Blue
  Vi 22938 Dinah/Bugle Call Rag
  Vi 23022 Jungle Nights in Harlem
  Vi 23041 Shout 'Em Aunt Tillie
  Vi 24521 Stompy Jones/Blue Feeling
  Vi 24755 Delta Serenade/Solitude
  Vi 38036 Saturday Night Function
  Vi 38053 The Dicty Glide/Stevedore
    Stomp
  Br 6404 Lightnin'/Jazz Cocktail
  Br 6510 Tiger Rag (1 & 2)
  Br 7650 Clarinet Lament
  Br 8063 Steppin' into Swing Society
  Br 8099 Carnival in Caroline
  Co 35214 The Sergeant Was Shy
COOTIE WILLIAMS
  Vo 3960 Have a Heart
  Vo 4061 Swingtime in Honolulu/Car-
    nival in Caroline
  Vo 4425 Chasin' Chippies/Swing Pan
    Alley
REX STEWART
  HRS 1004 Finesse/I Know That You
    Know
  HRS 2004 Cherry/Digga Digga Doo
  HRS 2005 Solid Rock/Bugle Call Rag
CAPITOL JAZZMEN
  Cap 10011 Sugar/Ain't Goin' No
    Place
  Cap 10012 Someday Sweetheart
FREDDIE SLACK
  Cap 146 Furlough Fling
SONNY GREER
  Cap 10028 Mood Indigo/The Mooche
CHARLIE VENTURA
  Lamp 105 Stomping at the Savoy (1 &
    2)
JACK TEAGARDEN
  HRS 2006 Shine/St. James Infirmary
  HRS 2007 The World Is Waiting for
    the Sunrise/Big Eight Blues
ZUTTY SINGLETON
  Cap 10022 Barney's Bounce/Lulu's
    Mood

KID ORY
Co 37274 Tiger Rag/Bucket's Got a Hole in It

BENNY MORTON
Bn(12″)46 The Sheik of Araby/Conversing in Blue
BN(12″)47 Limehouse Blues/My Old Flame

BARNEY BIGARD
Va 525 Clouds in My Heart/Frolic Sam
Va 655 Demi-Tasse/Jazz a la Carte
Bb 10981 Charlie the Chulo/A Lull at Dawn
Bb 11098 Lament for Javanette/Ready Eddy
Bb 11581 Brown Suede/C-Jam Blues
Si 28114 Step Steps Up/Step Steps Down
B&W 14 Can't Help Lovin' Dat Man/Please Don't Talk About Me When I'm Gone

LPs

BARNEY BIGARD
Lib 3072 Barney Bigard
Delmark DS-211 Bucket's Got a Hole in It
(1 side) Vi LPV-566 (Bb RIs)

DUKE ELLINGTON
Vi LPV-517 Jumpin' Punkins (Vi RIs)
Vi LPM-1364 In a Mellotone (Vi RIs)
Co C3L27 (3-LP set) The Ellington Era (Vol. 1, 1927-40 RIs)

REX STEWART
CBS (E)52628 (Vo RIs)

JACK TEAGARDEN/Rex Stewart
Atl ALS-1209 Big Jazz (RIs)
(miscellaneous combos)
Epic 3108 The Duke's Men (Vo RIs)

LOUIS ARMSTRONG ALL-STARS
De DL-8329 New Orleans Nights

143. BISHOP, JOE   tu fl-h ar cm

Born November 27, 1907, Monticello, Ark.

Jazz composer of note and important figure with Isham Jones and Woody Herman bands of 30s because of arranging. Attended Hendrix College in Arkansas. Early dance band work, late 20's into 1930, including bands of Al Katz and Austin Wylie. With great Isham Jones band 1931-6. His arrangements, along with those of Gordon Jenkins, gave band its excellent ensemble sound and semiswing style. Bishop's tastefully played tuba added greatly to tone and beat of band. When Jones band broke up in 1936, saxman Woody Herman headed corporation that formed first Herman band from nucleus. Bishop with Herman band through 1940 on fluegelhorn. Chief arranger of band's blues-dominated style. Arranged Woody's all-time favorite, *Woodchopper's Ball*, which he and Herman wrote. Retired from music awhile due to serious illness. More arranging for Herman in 1942, also freelance arranging, but illness a few years later forced retirement from music. Composed *Blue Prelude* in 1933, which enjoyed considerable popularity, also 1939's *Blue Evening* and 1934's *Out of Space*. Other compositions and arrangements, mostly jazz numbers, were *Bishop's Blues, Bessie's Blues, Music by the Moon, Blue Lament, New Orleans Twist, Blues Upstairs, Blues Downstairs, Gotta Get to St. Joe, Blue Dawn, Midnight Echoes, Be Not Disencouraged, Ain't It Just Too Bad, Big Morning, Indian Boogie Woogie, Blue Flame.* Latter used by Herman as theme in the early 40s. Most Bishop compositions featured and recorded by Herman band.

RECORDS

ISHAM JONES (as arranger)
Vi 24298 Blue Prelude

WOODY HERMAN
De 2508 Blues Upstairs
De 2629 Riverbed Blues
De 3008 Peach Tree Street
De 3380 Bessie's Blues

COW COW DAVENPORT
De 7462 I Ain't No Ice Man/Railroad Blues
De 7486 That'll Get It/Don't You Loud Mouth Me
De 7813 The Mess Is Here

LPs

ISHAM JONES
Vi LPV-504 The Great Isham Jones and His Orchestra (Vi RIs)

WOODY HERMAN
De DL-8133 Woodchopper's Ball (De RIs)

Black Jack LP3002 (1937-44 transcriptions, airchecks, V-Discs)

144. BIVONA, GUS   cl as f B
Born November 25, 1915, New London, Conn.

Strong-toned, swinging clarinetist, adept at high-register work. Active from mid-30s into 70s. As teenager jobbed locally and toured. Jobs included period with Frank Dailey in Connecticut. Settled in New York in mid-30s; long period with Jimmy Monaco band. With Hudson-De Lange 1936-7. Joined Bunny Berigan mid-1938, remained almost a year. In late 1939 joined new Teddy Powell band, stayed several months. Led own band awhile, then joined Benny Goodman late 1940 for six months. Briefly with Jan Savitt and Les Brown, then entered military service during World War II and led service band. After discharge worked with Tommy Dorsey in 1945 and 1947, Bob Crosby 1946. In late 40s began studio work for MGM in Hollywood, continued in 60s. Freelanced, worked frequently with Steve Allen, sometimes led own band.

RECORDS
TEDDY POWELL
  De 3094 Ridin' the Subways/Am I Blue?
BUNNY BERIGAN
  Vi 26121 Flashes/Davenport Blues
WILL HUDSON
  Br 8147 China Clipper
JAN SAVITT
  Vi 27573 Chattanooga Choo Choo
  Vi 27809 Jersey Bounce

LPs
GUS BIVONA
  WB W-1219 Blast Off!
  WB WS-1264 Ballads, Bounce and Bivona
  Mer MG-20157 Hey! Dig That Crazy Band
  Mer 20304 Plays the Music of Steve Allen
JACK TEAGARDEN
  Cap T-721 This Is Teagarden!
GLEN GRAY
  Cap W-1022 Sounds of the Great Bands, Vol. 1

RAY ANTHONY
  Cap T-678 Big Band Dixieland

145. BLACK, FRANK   p ar cm B
Born November 28, 1896, Philadelphia, Pa.

A leading conductor on radio in 30s and 40s, specializing in classical and light-classical music but equally competent in popular. Studied piano very early, debuting at 10 as concert pianist. A few years later had job as pianist in Harrisburg hotel. Worked theatre jobs, served as assistant to musical director Erno Rapee at Philadelphia's Fox Theatre. Musical director at New York's Century Theatre. Active in radio by mid-20s, directed weekly broadcasts in Philadelphia. Pianist-arranger-coach for popular radio vocal quartet The Revelers for a time in early 30s. General musical director of NBC 1932-48.

In early 30s Black began directing NBC Symphony Orchestra programs. First bandleader on Jack Benny show, 1933-4. In mid-30s musical director on Radio City Party, The Contented Hour, Coca Cola show, String Symphony shows. In late 30s began long series with Cities Service running into early 40s. Shows in early and mid-40s were Music for the New World, On the Mall band show, Music America Loves Best, Harvest of Stars. By early 50s activities dropped off. During long broadcast career worked with almost every singing star of opera and light classics, Broadway and Hollywood musicals, and pop field. Highly respected by all. Composer of serious works: *Bells at Eventide* and *A Sea Tale*.

RECORDS
FRANK BLACK ORCHESTRA
  Br 3432 Where's That Rainbow?/A Tree in the Park
  Br 3600 It's a Million to One/Under the Moon
  Br 3619 Highways Are Happy Ways/I'd Walk a Million Miles
  Br 3657 The Varsity Drag/The Best Things in Life Are Free
  Br 3892 Heartaches and Dreams/Beside a Lazy Stream
  Co 240-M Estrellita/Songs My Mother Taught Me

Br(12″)20058 Rhapsody in Blue (1 &
2; with Oscar Levant-p)

146. BLACK, TED   B

Bandleader of 30s. At one time featured
arrangements somewhat in Lombardo
style. Good sweet band in its own right
with smooth style and big ensemble
sound. Minor work on radio. Late 1930-1
appeared in short-running Broadway musical BALLYHOO. Band's activities continued in 40s, but left its mark mainly with
excellent recordings in early 30s.

RECORDS
TED BLACK

Me 12188 On the Beach with You/Lit-
tle Girl
Pe 15499 Why Shouldn't I?
Vi 22762 Give Me Your Affection,
Honey/I Love You in the Same
Sweet Way
Vi 22799 Love Letters in the Sand/
Long Time Between Kisses
Vi 22807 If I Didn't Have You/Now
That You're Gone
Vi 22816 I'm with You/Sing Another
Chorus, Please
Vi 22854 You Try Somebody Else/I
Should Have Known Better
Vi 22857 Lucille
Vi 22872 An Evening in Caroline/Two
Loves Have I
Vi 22878 Pagan Moon/One More
Kiss, Then Goodnight
Vi 22996 I Can't Forget/I'll Get Along
Somehow
Vi 24046 Banking on the Weath-
er/Masquerade
Vi 24050 Rain, Rain, Go Away/In a
Shanty in Old Shanty Town
Vi 24051 We Were Only Walking in
the Moonlight
Bb 5370 I Knew You When/Without
That Certain Thing
Bb 5371 Hold My Hand/Sweet and
Simple
Bb 5375 True/Do You Miss Me To-
night?
Bb 5387 Ill Wind/As Long as I Live
Manor 1193 Lazy Summer/In My
Dreams You're Always Near Me
Dana 2040 I Kissed Her/She's a Good
Little Girl

147. BLAINE, VIVIAN   vo
(VIVIAN STAPLETON)
Born November 21, 1921, Newark, N.J.

Singing star of movies and Broadway,
best known for role in GUYS AND DOLLS in
both media. Good ballad singer, could
also belt out numbers. Early in career
with Art Kassel. Teamed with Pinky Lee
1951-3 on TV show The Two of Us. Other
Broadway shows SAY DARLING (1958),
ENTER LAUGHING (1963). Toured with various stage productions.

MOVIES
1942—GIRL TROUBLE; IT HAPPENED IN
FLATBUSH; THROUGH DIFFERENT
EYES
1943—HE HIRED THE BOSS; JITTERBUGS
1944—GREENWICH VILLAGE; SOMETHING
FOR THE BOYS
1945—NOB HILL; STATE FAIR
1946—DOLL FACE; IF I'M LUCKY; THREE
LITTLE GIRLS IN BLUE; COME BACK
TO ME
1952—SKIRTS AHOY!
1953—MAIN STREET TO BROADWAY
1955—GUYS AND DOLLS
1957—PUBLIC PIGEON NO. 1

RECORDS
(all LPs)

VIVIAN BLAINE

Mer MG-20321 Singing Selections
from PAL JOEY/ANNIE GET YOUR
GUN
Mer-Wing MGW-12166 Broadway's All
Time Hits
(original Broadway cast)
De DL-9023 GUYS AND DOLLS

148. BLAIR, JANET   vo
(MARTHA JANET LAFFERTY)
Born April 23, 1921, Altoona, Pa.

Vocalist with Hal Kemp, later successful
movie actress. Active from 1940 into 70s.
Joined Kemp band early 1940, replacing
Nan Wynn and remaining until leader's
death late in year. During this period had
taken successful screen test, so then embarked on movie career. Cute and talented, a natural for films from the start. A
hit in first movie in 1941, THREE GIRLS
ABOUT TOWN, next year landed important
lead in MY SISTER EILEEN. Several of her

subsequent movies were musicals. Movie career waned after 40s, left Hollywood to play clubs in 50s. Developed stronger singing voice to qualify for stage. In early 50s played road show lead in SOUTH PACIFIC about three years. Broadway debut in 1953 in unsuccessful play A GIRL CAN TELL. More road shows in middle and late 50s, also appeared frequently on TV. Beginning late 50s, more movies. TV activities continued in 60s on singing shows and Sid Caesar show. Still active in early 70s; in TV series The Smith Family in 1971-2 season.

RECORDS

HAL KEMP

    Vi 26576 I Can't Love You Any More
    Vi 26627 Meet the Sun Half-Way/The Girl Who Took a Second Look
    Vi 27222 Walkin' by the River/So You're the One
    Vi 27255 Talkin' to My Heart
    Vi 27261 You're the One

MOVIES

1941—THREE GIRLS ABOUT TOWN; BLONDIE GOES TO COLLEGE
1942—TWO YANKS IN TRINIDAD; BROADWAY; MY SISTER EILEEN
1943—SOMETHING TO SHOUT ABOUT
1944—ONCE UPON A TIME
1945—TONIGHT AND EVERY NIGHT
1946—TARS AND SPARS; GALLANT JOURNEY
1947—THE FABULOUS DORSEYS
1948—I LOVE TROUBLE; BLACK ARROW; THE FULLER BRUSH MAN
1957—PUBLIC PIGEON NO.1
1959—ISLAND OF LOST WOMEN; THE RABBIT TRAP; THE BEST OF EVERYTHING; THE LONE TEXAN
1962—NIGHT OF THE EAGLE; BOYS' NIGHT OUT; BURN, WITCH, BURN
1969—THE ONE AND ONLY GENUINE ORIGINAL FAMILY BAND

149. BLAKE, EUBIE   p o vo cm ar B

Born February 7, 1883, Baltimore, Md.

Ragtime pianist and composer active over 70 years. Best-known songs *I'm Just Wild About Harry* and *Memories of You*. As teenager played piano and organ in sporting houses and cafes, also for rent parties. Local jobs at Goldfield Hotel. Active in vaudeville and legitimate stage. First association 1915 with Noble Sissle in club work. After World War I they were with Jim Europe band on U.S. tour. Played vaudeville in U.S. and abroad as piano-vocal duo, composed score for long-running 1921 Broadway show SHUFFLE ALONG, separated 1928. Blake wrote for revues late 20s and 30s, scored two short-run Broadway shows BLACKBIRDS OF 1930 and SWING IT (1937). Teamed again with Sissle; active World War II entertaining for U.S.O. After mid-40s Blake semiactive at concerts and special events, occasional TV. Still performing in 1973 at 90, displaying keen mind and wit, skill at ragtime piano. Subject of elaborate 1973 picture biography, *Reminiscing with Sissle and Blake* by Robert Kimball and William Bolcom.

SONGS

(with related shows)

1921—SHUFFLE ALONG stage show (I'm Just Wild About Harry; Shuffle Along; Bandana Days; Love Will Find a Way)
1923—ELSIE stage show (songs unimportant)
1924—ANDRE CHARLOT REVUE OF 1924 stage show (I Was Meant for You); CHOCOLATE DANDIES stage show (songs unimportant)
1930—BLACKBIRDS OF 1930 stage show (Memories of You; You're Lucky to Me; That Lindy Hop; Baby Mine; Green Pastures)
1937—SWING IT stage show (songs unimportant)

RECORDS

NOBLE SISSLE-EUBIE BLAKE

    Emer 10296 Broadway Blues
    Emer 10396 Oriental Blues/Love Will Find a Way
    Ed 51572 Broken Busted Blues/You Ought to Know
    OK 40824 Slow River/Home, Cradle of Happiness
    Vi 19086 Waitin' for the Evenin' Mail/Down Hearted Blues
    Vi 19253 Old Fashioned Love/Sweet Henry

Vi 19494 Manda/Dixie Moon
Re 9180 Boo-Hoo-Hoo

EUBIE BLAKE ORCHESTRA
Vi 18791 Bandana Days/Baltimore Buzz
Vi 22735 Little Girl/My Blue Days Blew Over
Cr 3086 When Your Lover Has Gone
Cr 3090 Please Don't Talk About Me When I'm Gone/I'm No Account Anymore
Cr 3105 It Looks Like Love
Cr 3111 One More Time/Two Little Blue Little Eyes
Cr 3130 St. Louis Blues/Nobody's Sweetheart
Cr 3193 Life Is Just a Bowl of Cherries/River, Stay 'Way from My Door

LPs

EUBIE BLAKE
Co C2S847 (2-LP set) The 86 Years of Eubie Blake
20th Fox 3003 The Wizard of the Ragtime Piano

150. BLAKE, JERRY cl as bs vo ar
(JACINTO CHABANIA)
Born January 23, 1908, Gary, Ind.
Died c. 1961

Good jazz clarinetist featured with swing bands of 30s and 40s. Studied several musical instruments. Attended high school in Nashville, left 1924 to play in circus band. In Chicago in 1925 with Al Wynn. Jobbed in various spots in and out of Chicago. Toured Europe with Sam Wooding in late 20s, recorded in Spain. Back in U.S. in 1930 with Chick Webb and Zack Whyte. With Don Redman several months late 1933-4, then with Willie Lewis in Europe 1934-5. With Claude Hopkins later in 1935. Most important jobs with Fletcher Henderson 1936-8 and Cab Calloway 1938-42, with latter first as musical director. In 1942-3 worked with Count Basie, Earl Hines, Lionel Hampton, Don Redman. Suffered breakdown, in sanitarium many years before death.

RECORDS

SAM WOODING
Pa (Sp)25420 Carrie/Tiger Rag

Pa(Sp)25421 Sweet Black Blues/My Pal Called Sal
Pa(Sp)25424 Bull Foot Stomp/Indian Love

BENNY MORTON
Co 2902-D Get Goin'/Fare Thee Well to Harlem
Co 2924-D The Gold Digger's Song/Tailor Made

FLETCHER HENDERSON
Vo 3487 Rhythm of the Tambourine
Vo 3511 Rose Room/Back in Your Own Backyard
Vo 3641 All God's Chillun Got Rhythm/Chris and His Gang
Vo 3713 Let 'Er Go
Vo 3760 What's Your Story?
Vo 4125 Sing You Sinners

DON REDMAN
Br 6745 Got the Jitters

TEDDY WILSON
Br 7640 Christopher Columbus/All My Life
Br 7729 My Melancholy Baby

CAB CALLOWAY
OK 6720 A Smo-o-oth One

WILLIE LEWIS
Pat (Fr)591 Nagasaki/I Can't Dance

LPs

FLETCHER HENDERSON
Co C4L19 (4-LP set) A Study in Frustration (Co, Ha, Vo RIs)

151. BLAKEY, ART d B
Born October 11, 1919, Pittsburgh, Pa.

Jazz drummer and combo leader, active from 40s into 70s. A top drummer in modern idiom, his fiery style especially effective in combo work. Early jobs with Fletcher Henderson in 1939 and Mary Lou Williams in 1940. Led own group, freelanced. Important period with Billy Eckstine band, a proving ground for bop musicians. With Eckstine band all during its career, mid-1944 to early 1947. In late 40s jobbed in New York, led own group, worked with Lucky Millinder in 1949. With Buddy DeFranco combo 1951-3. Beginning in 1954 led own combo almost exclusively, titled it the Jazz Messengers. Personnel changed at intervals, included at times Horace Silver, Don Byrd, Kenny Dorham, Hank Mobley, Doug Watkins.

Also did much freelance recording, often teaming with Horace Silver and Percy Heath to form exciting rhythm section. Active career in 50s and 60s, into 70s.

RECORDS

BILLY ECKSTINE
DeL 2001 Blowin' the Blues Away/If That's the Way You Feel
DeL 2002 Opus X/The Real Thing Happened to Me
Nat 9014 I Love the Rhythm in a Riff/A Cottage for Sale
Nat 9015 Lonesome Lover Blues/Last Night
Nat 9018 Blue/Second Balcony Jump
Nat 9052 Cool Breeze/You're My Everything

MILES DAVIS
Pres 777 Dig? (1 & 2)

DIZZY GILLESPIE
DeeGee 3604 The Champ (1 & 2)

THELONIOUS MONK
BN 542 Thelonious/Suburban Eyes

LOU DONALDSON
BN 1609 The Best Things in Life Are Free/Sweet Juice

BUDDY DEFRANCO
Clef 89067 Show Eyes/Autumn in New York

ART BLAKEY
BN 545 Musa's Vision/The Thin Man
BN 546 Bop Alley/Groove Street
BN 1626 Nothing but the Soul/Message from Kenya
EmArcy 16007 In the Basement/Little Girl Blue

LPs

ART BLAKEY
BN 1521 A Night At Birdland, Vol. 1
BN 1522 A Night At Birdland, Vol. 2
Jazztone J-1281 Jazz Messages
Co CL-897 Jazz Messengers
PacJazz M-402 Ritual: The Jazz Messengers
Vik LX-1103 Selections of Lerner & Loewe

THELONIOUS MONK
BN 1510 Genius of Modern Music, Vol. 1
Riv 12-209 The Unique Thelonious Monk

DEXTER GORDON
Sav MG-12130 Dexter Rides Again

KENNY DORHAM
BN 1535

CLIFFORD BROWN
BN(10")5032

152. BLAND, JACK   bn g B
Born May 8, 1899, Sedalia, Mo.

Rhythm guitarist with several groups in 20s and early 30s that were important in development of jazz. After jobbing in St. Louis, Bland joined comb and paper and kazoo players Red McKenzie and Dick Slevin in St. Louis to form Mound City Blue Blowers. Novelty trio became instant hit on records in mid-20s, toured England in 1924. Bland remained with group most of later 20s. Then freelanced in New York, led own group at times. Worked with Billy Banks hot group (sometimes called The Rhythmakers) on some good hot recordings in 1932. In 1942-3 worked with Marty Marsala and Art Hodes. Led own group awhile in mid-40s. Later settled in California and became inactive in music.

RECORDS

MOUND CITY BLUE BLOWERS
Br 2581 Arkansas Blues/Blue Blues
Br 2602 San/Red Hot
Br 2648 Barb-Wire Blues/You Ain't Got Nothing I Want
Br 2804 Tiger Rag/Deep Second Street Blues
Br 2849 Gettin' Told/Play Me Slow
Br 2908 Wigwam Blues/Blues in F
Br 3484 Nervous Puppies/What Do I Care What Somebody Said?
Co 1946-D Indiana/Fire House Blues
Vi 38087 Tailspin Blues/Never Had a Reason to Believe in You
Vi 38100 Hello Lola/One Hour
OK 41515 Georgia on My Mind/I Can't Believe That You're in Love with Me
OK 41526 Darktown Strutters' Ball/You Rascal You

MCKENZIE'S CANDY KIDS
Vo 14977 Panama/When My Sugar Walks Down the Street
Vo 14978 Best Black/Stretch It, Boy

BILLY BANKS (The Rhythmakers)
Pe 15615 Spider Crawl/Bugle Call Rag
Pe 15620 Oh Peter/Margie

Pe 15642 Who's Sorry Now?/Bald-Headed Mama
Pe 15651 Anything for You/Yes Suh!
Pe 15669 Mean Old Bed Bug Blues/ Yellow Dog Blues
GEORGE WETTLING
De 18044 Bugle Call Rag/I Wish I Could Shimmy Like My Sister Kate
De 18045 Darktown Strutters' Ball/ I've Found a New Baby
ART HODES
BN 505 Maple Leaf Rag/Yellow Dog Blues
BN 506 She's Crying for Me/Slow 'Em Down Blues

LPs

THE RHYTHMAKERS (Billy Banks)
IAJRC 4 (1932 Pe-Me RIs)
GEORGE WETTLING (and miscellaneous artists)
De DL-8029 Chicago Jazz Album (De RIs)
EDDIE CONDON (plus Mound City Blue Blowers one side)
"X"(10″)LX-3005 (Bb, Vi RIs)

153. BLANE, RALPH lyr ar vo

Born July 26, 1914, Broken Arrow, Okla.

Lyricist who collaborated with composer Hugh Martin on successful scores for stage and movies. Best-known songs: *Buckle Down, Winsocki*; *The Trolley Song*; *The Boy Next Door*; *Have Yourself a Merry Little Christmas*. Attended Northwestern University. He and Martin were in cast of 1937 Broadway show HOORAY FOR WHAT?. Blane was vocal arranger for shows TOO MANY GIRLS, DUBARRY WAS A LADY, LOUISIANA PURCHASE, PAL JOEY, CABIN IN THE SKY, VERY WARM FOR MAY, STARS IN YOUR EYES. With Hugh Martin formed vocal quartet The Martins, sang on Fred Allen radio show. Began songwriting association with Martin, produced score for successful 1941 Broadway show BEST FOOT FORWARD. Team then wrote for movies in Hollywood. Blane later collaborated with other composers Harold Arlen, Roger Edens, Harry Warren. Remained active in songwriting during 50s.

SONGS

(with related shows; *—without Hugh Martin)

1941—BEST FOOT FORWARD stage show (Ev'ry Time; Shady Lady Bird; Buckle Down, Winsocki; Who Do You Think I Am?; That's How I Love the Blues)
1943—BEST FOOT FORWARD movie (original stage score); THOUSANDS CHEER movie (The Joint Is Really Jumping; Carnegie Hall)
1944—MEET ME IN ST. LOUIS movie (The Trolley Song; The Boy Next Door; Have Yourself a Merry Little Christmas)
1945—THRILL OF A ROMANCE movie* (Vive L'Amour)
1946—ZIEGFELD FOLLIES movie (Love); EASY TO WED movie* (Continental Polka; Gonna Fall in Love with You)
1947—GOOD NEWS movie (Pass That Peace Pipe); Connecticut
1948—SUMMER HOLIDAY movie* (The Stanley Steamer; Afraid to Fall in Love)
1949—MY DREAM IS YOURS movie* (My Dream Is Yours; Someone Like You; Love Finds a Way)
1950—MY BLUE HEAVEN movie* (The Friendly Islands; Don't Rock the Boat, Dear; Halloween; I Love a New Yorker)
1954—ATHENA movie (Love Can Change the Stars)

RECORDS

(LPs)

HUGH MARTIN-RALPH BLANE
Harlequin HQ-701 Sing Martin & Blane

154. BLANTON, JIMMY b

Born c. 1918, Chattanooga, Tenn.
Died July 30, 1942, Los Angeles, Calif.

Star bass man with Duke Ellington 1939-42. Pioneer in elevating bass to position as solo instrument. Exhibited excellent tone, knowledge of harmonics, facility, expert musicianship. Career cut short by early death. Played locally at early age, including jobs with mother's combo (she was pianist). Attended Tennessee State

College, worked in dance bands while there. Moved to St. Louis, worked with Jeter-Pillars and Fate Marable bands in late 30s, gained invaluable experience developing technique and style. Joined Duke Ellington in late 1939. Bass work with Ellington soon won acclaim. In 1941 health began to deteriorate. Another bass man hired to stand by and fill in as needed. Later diagnosis showed tuberculosis. Left Ellington in late 1941 to enter Los Angeles hospital, later transferred to sanitarium there. His death in 1942 cut short what promised to be great career. Became something of a legend in later years.

RECORDS

DUKE ELLINGTON
Vi 26536 Jack the Bear/Morning Glory
Vi 26537 So Far, So Good/You, You Darlin'
Vi 26577 Conga Brava/Ko-Ko
Vi 26598 Concerto for Cootie/Me and You
Vi 26644 Bojangles/A Portrait of Bert Williams
Vi 26677 Dusk/Blue Goose
Vi 26731 Sepia Panorama/Harlem Air-Shaft
Vi 26748 Five O'clock Whistle/There Shall Be No Night
Vi 26788 Rumpus in Richmond/In a Mellotone
Vi 26796 Warm Valley/The Flaming Sword

DUKE ELLINGTON and JIMMY BLANTON
Co 35322 Plucked Again/Blues
Vi 27221 Pitter Panther Patter/Sophisticated Lady
Vi 27406 Body and Soul/Mr. J. B. Blues

BARNEY BIGARD
OK 5422 Lost in Two Flats
OK 5663 Honey Hush
Bb 10981 Charlie the Chulo/A Lull at Dawn
Bb 11098 Ready Eddy/Lament for Javanette

JOHNNY HODGES
OK 5533 Skunk Hollow Blues/Tired Socks

Bb 11117 Good Queen Bess/That's the Blues, Old Man
Bb 11447 Squaty Roo/Things Ain't What They Used To Be

REX STEWART
Bb 10946 Without a Song/My Sunday Gal
Bb 11258 Subtle Slough/Some Saturday

COOTIE WILLIAMS
OK 5618 Black Butterfly
OK 6336 Toasted Pickle

LPs

DUKE ELLINGTON
Vi LPV-517 Jumpin' Punkins (Vi RIs)
Vi LPM-1715 At His Very Best (Vi RIs)

REX STEWART
"X"(10")LX-3001 (Bb RIS)

JOHNNY HODGES-REX STEWART
Vi LPV-533 Things Ain't What They Used to Be (Vi, Bb RIs)

155. BLEYER, ARCHIE   p cm ar B

Well-known arranger of 30s and 40s thanks to widely used stock arrangements for dance bands. Later musical director on TV and records. Also led dance band at times in early career. Composer of jazz number *Business in Q* performed by hot bands in 30s. Rose to prominence in TV in 50s as Arthur Godfrey's musical director. Then, as head of Cadence Records, produced some hits by singers, sometimes conducting orchestra behind them. Continued active in 60s.

RECORDS

ARCHIE BLEYER ORCHESTRA
Vo 2822 Stay as Sweet as You Are/The World Is Mine
Vo 2823 Wild Honey/Irresistible
Vo 2835 The Object of My Affection/I've Got an Invitation to a Dance
Vo 2836 Winter Wonderland/I'm Growing Fonder of You
Vo 2860 Sweet Music/A Little Angel Told Me So
Vo 2861 I Woke Up Too Soon/Throwin' Stones at the Sun
Me 350918 Cheek to Cheek/The Piccolino
Me 350919 Isn't This a Lovely Day?/Top Hat, White Tie and Tails

Me 351022 On a Sunday Afternoon/
I've Got a Feelin' You're Foolin'
Me 351023 Broadway Rhythm/You
Are My Lucky Star
Cad 1241 Si'l Vous Plait/Hernando's
Hideaway
Cad 1313 Jocko's Theme/The Strange
One
Cad 1320 Julie's Jump/Amber

(as conductor)

ARTHUR GODFREY

Co 38081 I'm Looking Over a Four-
Leaf Clover/The Thousand Islands
Song
Co 38246 The Trail of the Lonesome
Pine/Turkish Delight
Co 38721 Candy and Cake/Dear Old
Girl
Co 38785 Scattered Toys
Co 39632 Slow Poke/Dance Me Loose

JANETTE DAVIS

Co 38223 Put the Blame on Mame/
Just a Shade on the Blue Side
Co 39537 You

JANETTE DAVIS-BILL LAWRENCE

Co 39025 Longing/Li'l Ol' You

MARION MARLOWE

Cad 1266 The Man in the Raincoat/
Heartbeat

JULIUS LAROSA

Cad 1231 My Lady Loves to Dance/
Let's Make Up Before We Say
Goodnight

ALFRED DRAKE

Cad 1238 The Happy Wanderer/Des-
tiny's Darling

LPs

ARTHUR GODFREY

Co GL-521 Arthur Godfrey's TV Calendar Show

156. BLOCH, RAY p ar cm lyr vo B

Born August 3, 1902, Alsace-Lorraine

Best known as orchestra conductor on
many TV shows in 50s and 60s. Boy
soprano at 8, choir leader at 12. He and
family escaped to U.S. during World War
I, settled in New York. Studied piano,
early job as pianist with song publishing
company. Later played in ballroom
bands, also played vaudeville with own
band. In late 20s radio work as pianist. In

30s led choral groups and orchestras on
radio, also worked as a vocal coach. CBS
staff conductor. In middle and late 30s
radio shows included Musical Toast with
Jerry Cooper, Hollywood Observer,
Philip Morris show, What's My Name?,
Phil Cook's Almanac, Model Minstrels,
Gay Nineties Revue starring Beatrice
Kay and Joe Howard (ran into 1942),
Ray Bloch's Varieties. In 1940 had latter
two shows plus Take It or Leave It, Pipe
Smoking Time and another stint on Philip
Morris show. Busy radio schedule con-
tinued through 40s. Theme: *Music in My
Fingers*. Also became active in recording
work, mostly backing singers.

Gained fame as TV conductor for Jackie
Gleason show in early 50s and especially
for top-rated Ed Sullivan show all
through 50s and 60s. Bloch most capable
in exacting work of providing precision
accompaniment for variety singers and
acts. In 50s and 60s did many radio
transcriptions for U.S. military recruiting
shows. Composed 1938 pop song *In My
Little Red Book*, plus lesser songs *When
Love Has Gone*, *You're Everything That's
Lovely*, *In the Same Old Way*, *The Wide
Open Spaces*, *Sam the Vegetable Man*,
Let's Make Up a Little Party.

RECORDS

RAY BLOCH

Si 15017 All Through the Day/
Cinderella Sue
Si 15070 Lydia/When I Grow Too Old
to Dream
Si 15177 I'm Looking Over a Four-
Leaf Clover
Si 15265 Small Town
Si 15272 Till We Meet Again/Hi,
Neighbor!
Cor 60919 I Must Have Your Love/
Together
Cor 60963 Anna/Melancholy Sere-
nade

(as conductor)

MORDY BAUMAN

Co 36561 You're a Grand Old Flag/
Over There
Co 36562 Give My Regards to Broad-
way/Yankee Doodle Boy

CONNIE HAINES

Si 15235 Stormy Weather/My Man

ALAN DALE
Cor 60746 I'm Sorry/Here in My Heart
Cor 60809 My Thrill/You're My Destiny

TERESA BREWER
Cor 60676 Gonna Get Along without Ya Now/Roll Them Roly Boly Eyes

JUDY LYNN
Cor 60876 Baby Come Home/Lover Be Careful

LILY ANN CAROL
Cor 60874 Lazy River/Way Marie

LARRY DOUGLAS
Si 15107 The Egg and I/No Greater Love

MONICA LEWIS
Si 15028 Blue and Melancholy Mood/ I Got the Sun in the Morning

156A. BLOCK, MARTIN　　　　　lyr
Born 1903
Died September 19, 1967, New York, N.Y.

Most important disc jockey during big band era of 30s and 40s. Early career on west coast radio. Joined station WNEW in New York late 1934. Early break filling in gaps between news flashes on widely covered Bruno Richard Hauptmann kidnapping trial early 1935. Ad-libbed introducing records; persuasive personality. Used "Make Believe Ballroom" format pioneered by west coast disc jockey Al Jarvis. Powerful influence promoting records of singers and bands late 30s and 40s. Ran swing concerts late 30s. At height of career on 3-1/2 hours per day, six days per week. Excelled in selling products. Ran semi-annual band popularity contests late 30s and early 40s, attracted hundreds of thousands of votes. Occasional announcing on other radio shows including Kay Kyser show and Your Hit Parade. In Los Angeles 1947-8 on live radio from KFWB after Al Jarvis left station for KLAC. At same time furnished recorded shows for WNEW in New York. Announced for Chesterfield Supper Club radio show awhile. Mid-1948 returned to New York, continued with WNEW shows. With station WABC in

New York mid-50s, WNEW retaining rights to Make Believe Ballroom show title. Retired New York late 50s, returned 1961 with Hall of Fame show on station WOR in New York. Active mid-60s. Lyricist for songs *A New Moon and an Old Serenade* and *Faithful to You* (1939), *This Is No Laughing Matter* and *I Guess I'll Have to Dream the Rest* (1941), *Last Night I Said a Prayer* (1942).

157. BLOOM, RUBE　　　　p vo cm ar B
Born April 24, 1902, New York, N.Y.

Freelance pianist with many early recording groups, composer of popular songs. Won Victor Records song contest in late 1928 with descriptive piece *Song of the Bayou*, which received considerable play on radio 1929-30. Most popular songs: *The Man from the South, Truckin', Don't Worry 'Bout Me, Fools Rush In.* Also wrote descriptive pieces for piano or orchestra, notably *Soliloquy*. Early in career accompanied singers in vaudeville. Extensive recording career in late 20s as pianist with leading singers and jazz greats. Recorded piano solos, also six sides leading outstanding jazz combo called Rube Bloom & His Bayou Boys. Arranged for music publishers, wrote for night club revues in U. S. and London. Had success composing popular songs in 30s and 40s. Collaborators included lyricists Ted Koehler, Harry Ruby, Johnny Mercer, Harry Woods, Mitchell Parish, Sammy Gallop. Wrote several piano method books.

SONGS
1927—Soliloquy; Spring Fever
1929—Song of the Bayou; Where You Are
1930—The Man from the South
1933—Stay on the Right Side
1934—It Happens to the Best of Friends; Out in the Cold Again
1935—Truckin'; Cotton
1937—Love Is a Merry-Go-Round; Is This Gonna Be My Lucky Summer?
1938—Feelin' High and Happy; I Can't Face the Music; I'm in a Happy Frame of Mind
1939—Don't Worry 'Bout Me; What

Goes Up Must Come Down; Day In—Day Out; If I Were Sure of You; Floogie Walk; The Ghost of Smoky Joe

1940—Fools Rush In
1941—Good-for-Nothin' Joe
1942—Take Me
1945—WAKE UP AND DREAM movie (Give Me the Simple Life; I Wish I Could Tell You)
1947—Maybe You'll Be There
1949—Lost in a Dream
1952—Here's to My Lady

Other compositions: *Suite of Moods*; *Sapphire*; *Serenata*; *Silhouette*; *On the Green*; *Jumping Jack*; *Lady on a Late Evening*; *Got No Time*; *Fifth Avenue Bus*; *Savage in My Soul*

RECORDS

COTTON PICKERS
Br 2766 Prince of Wails/Jimtown Blues
SEGER ELLIS
Br 6022 It's a Lonesome Old Town/ My Love for You
Co 2362-D Cheerful Little Earful/I Miss a Little Miss
RUTH ETTING
Co 2307-D I'll Be Blue, Just Thinking of You
CHARLES KALEY
Co 910-D Alabama Stomp
ANNETTE HANSHAW
Co 1769-D Lover, Come Back to Me/ You Wouldn't Fool Me, Would You?
Ha 1047 He's So Unusual/I Think You'll Like It
Ha 1155 Telling It to the Daisies/I've Got "It"
LEE MORSE
Co 2417-D Walkin' My Baby Back Home/I've Got Five Dollars
RED NICHOLS
Br 4790 Nobody Knows/Smiles
THE RED HEADS (Red Nichols)
Pe 14568 Poor Papa
Pe 14600 'Tain't Cold/Hangover
SIOUX CITY SIX
Ge 5569 Flock O' Blues/I'm Glad
NOBLE SISSLE
OK 40964 Kentucky Babe/Lindy Lou

TENNESSEE TOOTERS
Vo 14952 Prince of Wails/I Ain't Got Nobody to Love
JOE VENUTI
OK 41025 Dinah/The Wild Dog
OK 41076 The Man from the South/ Pretty Trix
OK 41144 The Blue Room/Sensation
ETHEL WATERS
Co 2409-D When Your Lover Has Gone/Please Don't Talk About Me When I'm Gone
RUBE BLOOM (piano solos)
Ha 164 Soliloquy/Spring Fever
Co 1195-D Sapphire/Silhouette
Pe 15097 Sonny Boy/There's a Rainbow 'Round My Shoulder
OK 40842 Doll Dance/March of the Dolls
OK 40867 Soliloquy/Spring Fever
OK 40901 Dancing Tambourine/Silhouette
OK 41073 That Futuristic Rag/ Serenata
RUBE BLOOM & HIS BAYOU BOYS
Co 2103-D The Man from the South/ St. James Infirmary
Co 2186-D Mysterious Mose/Bessie Couldn't Help It
Co 2218-D On Revival Day/There's a Wah Wah Girl in Agua Caliente

158. BLOSSOM, HENRY   lyr
Born May 6, 1866, St. Louis, Mo.
Died March 23, 1919, New York, N.Y.

Important figure on Broadway scene during early years of century. Book and lyrics for many successful shows. Teamed with composer Victor Herbert for great shows MLLE. MODISTE and THE RED MILL (1906). Attended Stoddard School in St. Louis. Left insurance business with father to begin career as writer for stage. First play was dramatization of novel titled CHECKERS (1903), first musical show THE YANKEE CONSUL (1904). Most famous songs: *Kiss Me Again, In Old New York, Every Day Is Ladies' Day with Me, Thine Alone, When You're Away.* Many songs attained no popularity but were effective within context of shows. Active until death.

BROADWAY MUSICALS
(book and lyrics unless designated otherwise)

1904—THE YANKEE CONSUL (Ain't It Funny What a Difference Just a Few Hours Make?; My San Domingo Maid)

1906—MLLE. MODISTE (Kiss Me Again; I Want What I Want When I Want It; The Time, the Place and the Girl; When the Cat's Away; The Mascot of the Troop); THE RED MILL (Moonbeams; In Old New York; Every Day Is Ladies' Day with Me; Because You're You; I Want You to Marry Me; The Isle of Our Dreams; Whistle It)

1907—THE HOYDEN (lyrics only)

1908—THE PRIMA DONNA (I'll Be Married to the Music of a Military Band; If You Were I and I Were You; A Soldier's Love; Espagnola)

1911—THE SLIM PRINCESS

1912—BARON TRENCK (book only); THE MAN FROM COOK'S

1913—ALL FOR THE LADIES

1914—THE ONLY GIRL (When You're Away; Tell It All Over Again; You're the Only Girl for Me)

1915—PRINCESS PAT (Neapolitan Love Song; Two Laughing Irish Eyes; All for You; Love Is the Best of All)

1916—THE CENTURY GIRL (title song; several writers contributed material for show)

1917—EILEEN (Eileen Alanna Asthore; When Shall I Again See Ireland?; When Love Awakes; Thine Alone; The Irish Have a Great Day Tonight)

1918—FOLLOW THE GIRL (book only)

1919—THE VELVET LADY (Spooky Ookum; Life and Love; Fair Honeymoon)

159. BLYTH, ANN vo
Born August 16, 1928, Mt. Kisco, N.Y.
Singer-actress in movies from teenager to adult. Soprano voice most suited to classical and show music. Early show business experience at 13 on Broadway in play WATCH ON THE RHINE, then toured with it. Began movie career in 1944 in low-budget films. Effective heavy role in MILDRED PIERCE in 1945 led to other dramatic roles. Best musicals TOP O' THE MORNING (1949), THE GREAT CARUSO (1951), ROSE-MARIE and THE STUDENT PRINCE (1954), KISMET (1955). Title role in THE HELEN MORGAN STORY (1957), but Gogi Grant's singing voice was dubbed in because closer in style to Morgan voice.

MOVIES
1944—CHIP OFF THE OLD BLOCK; THE MERRY MONAHANS; BABES ON SWING STREET; BOWERY TO BROADWAY

1945—MILDRED PIERCE

1946—SWELL GUY

1947—BRUTE FORCE; KILLER MCCOY; A WOMAN'S VENGEANCE

1948—MR. PEABODY AND THE MERMAID; ANOTHER PART OF THE FOREST

1949—RED CANYON; FREE FOR ALL; TOP O' THE MORNING; ONCE MORE, MY DARLING

1950—OUR VERY OWN

1951—THE GREAT CARUSO; KATIE DID IT; THUNDER ON THE HILL; THE GOLDEN HORDE; I'LL NEVER FORGET YOU

1952—ONE MINUTE TO ZERO; THE WORLD IN HIS ARMS; SALLY AND ST. ANNE

1953—ALL THE BROTHERS WERE VALIANT

1954—ROSE-MARIE; THE STUDENT PRINCE

1955—KISMET; THE KING'S THIEF

1956—SLANDER

1957—THE BUSTER KEATON STORY; JAZZ AGE; THE HELEN MORGAN STORY

160. BLYTHE, JIMMY p vo B
Born c. 1899-1901, Louisville, Ky.
Died June 21, 1931, Chicago, Ill.
Jazz pianist of 20s known for extensive recording work. Based in Chicago. Many records under own name, some using clarinetist Johnny Dodds. Also accompanied singers on records: Ma Rainey, Trixie Smith, Viola Bartlette, Sodarisa Miller, Lottie Beaman, Ruth Coleman, Ed "Fats" Hudson, George Jefferson, Monette Moore, Teddy Moss, Bob Robinson, Priscilla Stewart, Hokum Boys. Career cut short by early death.

RECORDS

JIMMY BLYTHE
Para 12207 Chicago Stomp/Armour Avenue Struggle
Para 12304 Fat Meat and Greens/Jimmie Blues
Para 12368 Bohunkus Blues/Buddy Burton's Jazz
Para 12376 Messin' Around/Adam's Apple
Para 12428 Ape Man/Your Folks
Vo 1135 Weary Way Blues/Poutin' Papa
Bo 1180 My Baby/Oriental Man
Vo 1181 Alley Rat/Sweet Papa

JIMMY BLYTHE-W. E. BURTON (piano duet)
Ge 6502 Dustin' the Keys/Block and Tackle Blues

JIMMY BLYTHE-JAMES CLARK (piano duet)
Ch 16451 Bow to Your Papa/Don't Break Down

STATE STREET RAMBLERS
Ge 6232 Weary Way Blues/Cootie Stomp
Ge 6249 There'll Come a Day
Ge 6454 Pleasure Mad/My Baby
Ch 40007 Barrel House Stomp/Kentucky Blues

BLYTHE'S BLUE BOYS
Ch 40025 Endurance Stomp/Pleasure Mad
Ch 40062 Tack It Down/Some Do and Some Don't

THE CHICAGO STOMPERS
Ch 16297 Wild Man Stomp/Stomp Your Stuff

JIMMY BERTRAND
Vo 1099 I'm Goin' Huntin'/If You Want to Be My Sugar Papa
Vo 1100 Easy Come, Easy Go Blues/The Blues Stampede

MA RAINEY
Para 12352 Mountain Jack Blues

VIOLA BARTLETTE
Para 12345 Quit Knocking on My Door
Para 12351 Anna Mina Forty and St. Louis Shorty

SODARISA MILLER
Para 12231 Hot Springs Water Blues/Who'll Drive My Blues Away?
Para 12243 Don't Dog Me 'Round/Down by the River

Para 12306 Midnight Special/Reckless Don't Care Mama Blues

LOTTIE BEAMAN
Para 12254 Sugar Daddy Blues/Low Down Painful Blues

LPs

JIMMY BLYTHE
Riv(10")RLP-1031 (Para RIs)
Riv(10")RLP-1036 (Ge RIs)

JOHNNY DODDS
Riv(10")RLP-1002 Vol. 1 (Para and other RIs)

---

161. BOLAND, CLAY cm p
Born October 25, 1903, Olyphant, Pa.
Died July 23, 1963, Queens, N.Y.

Composer active in 30s. Best-known songs: *Gypsy in My Soul, Stop Beatin' 'Round the Mulberry Bush, When I Go a-Dreamin'*. Attended universities of Scranton and Pennsylvania. Studied and practiced dentistry. Self-taught pianist, worked in college playing in dance bands. Began writing and directing Mask & Wig shows at University of Pennsylvania in mid-30s, produced popular songs. Chief collaborator lyricist Bickley Reichner, others Moe Jaffe and Eddie DeLange. Officer in military service, World War II and Korean War. Active as publisher. Son Clay Boland, Jr., also began writing Mask & Wig shows in early 50s.

SONGS

1936—Too Good to Be True; Something Has Happened to Me; An Apple a Day
1937—The Morning After
1938—Gypsy in My Soul; Midnight on the Trail; I Live the Life I Love; Button, Button; Stop Beatin' 'Round the Mulberry Bush; There's No Place Like Your Arms; Ya Got Me; When I Go a-Dreamin'; Stompin' at the Stadium
1939—Stop! It's Wonderful; Delightful Delirium; When I Climb Down from My Saddle; How I'd Like to Be with You in Bermuda
1940—Tell Me at Midnight

162. BOLDEN, BUDDY   c B

Born c. 1868, New Orleans, La.
Died November 4, 1931, Jackson, La.

Jazz pioneer, strong and colorful personality, first "king" of cornet in New Orleans (later followed by King Oliver, Louis Armstrong). Played cornet with exceptional power. His band played New Orleans parades and dances, starting around 1895 or earlier, and Bolden became very popular. Health deteriorated in 1907, committed to East Louisiana State Hospital (mental home). Remained until death. Information sparse on Bolden's jazz activities in those ancient days, and no phonograph records. Yet as first important figure in birth of jazz, Bolden became legend.

163. BOLES, JOHN   vo

Born August 28, 1898, Greenville, Texas
Died February 27, 1969

Handsome leading man, popular baritone singing star of early sound films. Attended University of Texas. Military service, World War I. Studied singing in Paris. Minor roles in Broadway musicals LITTLE JESSIE JAMES (1923) and MOONLIGHT (1924). Starring role in KITTY'S KISSES (1926). Years later appeared in Broadway hit ONE TOUCH OF VENUS (1943). During 1927-9 active in silent movies. Attained considerable popularity 1929-30 singing in early movie musicals. Active movie career during 30s in several musicals but mostly dramatic roles. Occasional singing roles in stock musicals in Los Angeles area, such as SHOW BOAT in 1940, GENTLEMEN PREFER BLONDES in 1950. Inactive in show business after early 50s.

MOVIES

1929—THE DESERT SONG; RIO RITA
1930—KING OF JAZZ; SONG OF THE WEST; CAPTAIN OF THE GUARD; QUEEN OF SCANDAL
1931—ONE HEAVENLY NIGHT; RESURRECTION; FRANKENSTEIN; SEED; GOOD SPORT
1932—BACK STREET; CARELESS LADY; SIX HOURS TO LIVE
1933—CHILD OF MANHATTAN; MY LIPS BETRAY; ONLY YESTERDAY

1934—BELOVED; BOTTOMS UP; I BELIEVED IN YOU; STAND UP AND CHEER; WHITE GOLD; THE WHITE PARADE; THE LIFE OF VERGIE WINTERS; AGE OF INNOCENCE
1935—MUSIC IN THE AIR; CURLY TOP; REDHEADS ON PARADE; ORCHIDS TO YOU; THE LITTLEST REBEL
1936—ROSE OF THE RANCHO; A MESSAGE TO GARCIA; CRAIG'S WIFE
1937—AS GOOD AS MARRIED; STELLA DALLAS; FIGHT FOR YOUR LADY
1938—ROMANCE IN THE DARK; SINNERS IN PARADISE; SHE MARRIED AN ARTIST
1942—ROAD TO HAPPINESS; BETWEEN US GIRLS
1943—THOUSANDS CHEER
1952—BABES IN BAGDAD

RECORDS

JOHN BOLES
Vi 22229 West Wind/The One Girl
Vi 22230 Romance/After a Million Dreams
Vi 22372 It Happened in Monterey/Song of the Dawn
Vi 22373 You, You Alone/For You

164. BOLGER, RAY   vo

Born January 10, 1904, Dorchester, Mass.

Known primarily as talented dancer adept at comic routines, with occasional singing performances. Star of stage, movies, radio and TV. Most noted roles in movie THE WIZARD OF OZ and in Broadway hit WHERE'S CHARLEY? Supporting roles in Broadway musicals HEADS UP (1929) and GEORGE WHITE'S SCANDALS OF 1931. Starring roles in LIFE BEGINS AT 8:40 (1934), ON YOUR TOES (1936), KEEP OFF THE GRASS (1940), BY JUPITER (1942), THREE TO MAKE READY (1946). Greatest success as star of long-running WHERE'S CHARLIE? (1948), thereafter associated with its hit song *Once in Love with Amy.* Years later played in musical ALL AMERICAN (1962) and play COME SUMMER (1969). Supporting roles in movies beginning 1936. Better roles after playing scarecrow in popular THE WIZARD OF OZ in 1939, although movie work not extensive. Own radio show in mid-40s, own TV show in mid-50s. Occasional appearances on TV through the years. By early 60s less active in show business.

MOVIES

1936—THE GREAT ZIEGFELD
1937—ROSALIE
1938—GIRL OF THE GOLDEN WEST; SWEET-HEARTS
1939—THE WIZARD OF OZ
1941—SUNNY; FOUR JACKS AND A JILL
1943—STAGE DOOR CANTEEN
1946—THE HARVEY GIRLS
1949—LOOK FOR THE SILVER LINING; MAKE MINE LAUGHS
1952—WHERE'S CHARLEY?; APRIL IN PARIS
1961—BABES IN TOYLAND
1966—THE DAYDREAMER

RECORDS

RAY BOLGER-ETHEL MERMAN
  De 24873 Dearie/I Said My Pajamas
  De 27654 Don't Believe It
RAY BOLGER
  De 40065 Once in Love with Amy/ Make a Miracle

LPs

(movie soundtrack)
  MGM E-3464 THE WIZARD OF OZ

165. BOLTON, GUY   lyr

Born November 23, 1884, Broxbourne, Hertfordshire, England, of American parents

Important figure of Broadway stage as playwright and librettist, occasional lyricist. Prolific career associated with hit shows VERY GOOD, EDDIE and MISS SPRINGTIME (1916), OH, BOY! (1917), OH, LADY! LADY! (1918), SALLY and TANGERINE (1921), LADY BE GOOD (1924), OH, KAY! (1926), FIVE O'CLOCK GIRL and RIO RITA (1927), ROSALIE (1928), GIRL CRAZY (1930), ANYTHING GOES (1934). Collaborated on several shows with P. G. Wodehouse on books and lyrics, with Fred Thompson on books. Playwright for THE DRONE, THE SEA WOLF, POLLY WITH A PAST, ADAM AND EVA, ANASTASIA. Began writing for movies in 30s including RIO RITA, THE LOVE PARADE, DELICIOUS, ANYTHING GOES. Also wrote for London productions BLUE EYES, GIVE ME A RING, SEEING STARS, THIS'LL MAKE YOU WHISTLE, SWING ALONG, GOING GREEK.

BROADWAY MUSICALS
(wrote book)

1915—NOBODY HOME; 90 IN THE SHADE (also lyrics)
1916—VERY GOOD, EDDIE; MISS SPRING-TIME
1917—HAVE A HEART; LEAVE IT TO JANE; MISS 1917; OH, BOY!; THE RIVIERA GIRL (also lyrics)
1918—THE GIRL BEHIND THE GUN (also lyrics); OH, LADY! LADY!; OH, MY DEAR! (also lyrics)
1919—THE ROSE OF CHINA
1921—SALLY; TANGERINE
1922—DAFFY DILL; THE HOTEL MOUSE
1924—LADY, BE GOOD; SITTING PRETTY
1926—OH, KAY!; TIP TOES; THE RAMBLERS
1927—FIVE O'CLOCK GIRL; THE NIGHTIN-GALE; RIO RITA
1928—ROSALIE; SHE'S MY BABY
1929—POLLY
1930—GIRL CRAZY; SIMPLE SIMON
1934—ANYTHING GOES
1940—HOLD ON TO YOUR HATS; WALK WITH MUSIC
1944—FOLLOW THE GIRLS; JACK POT

166. BON BON   vo
(GEORGE TUNNELL)

Vocalist noted for work with Jan Savitt Band in late 30s and 40s. One of first Negroes to sing regularly with white band. Led vocal trio The Three Keys before joining Savitt. Smooth baritone voice which projected warm personality. Vocal work with Savitt consistently outstanding. Left Savitt in late 1941 to embark on career as single, played clubs and recorded. In act with Spirits of Rhythm awhile. Career continued into 50s. Worked awhile with Tommy Reynolds band in early 50s.

RECORDS

THE THREE KEYS
  Vo 2569 You Can Depend on Me/I've Found a New Baby
  Vo 2765 Oh by Jingo/Rasputin
JAN SAVITT
  Bb 7281 My Heaven on Earth/Am I in Another World?
  Bb 7283 A Kiss for Consolation/You Started Something

Bb 7295 The Gypsy in My Soul/I Live the Life I Love
Bb 7504 Moonshine Over Kentucky
Bb 7607 Dust/It's the Little Things That Count
Bb 7748 I Haven't Changed a Thing
Bb 7797 Ya Got Me/There's No Place Like Your Arms
Bb 10013 Just a Kid Named Joe
De 2390 Snug as a Bug in a Rug/And the Angels Sing
De 2391 Little Sir Echo
De 2738 The Paper Picker/It's a Hundred to One
De 2771 720 in the Books/Alla en el Rancho Grande
De 2805 Good Morning/Many Dreams Ago
De 2836 It's a Wonderful World/Honestly
De 2847 After All
De 2990 Imagination/Make Love with a Guitar
De 3019 Rose of the Rio Grande
De 3153 Secrets in the Moonlight
Vi 27699 Moonlight Masquerade

TOMMY REYNOLDS
Derby 820 It's a Wonderful World

BON BON
De 3980 I Don't Want to Set the World on Fire/Papa's Getting Mad
De 8567 Blow, Gabriel, Blow/All That Meat and No Potatoes
De 8603 Sleepy Old Town/Seeing You Again Did Me No Good
De 8622 Rickety Rocking Chair/I'm Not Much on Looks
Davis 7194 Most Emphatically Yes!/We Need Each Other

LPs

JAN SAVITT
De DL-79243 The Top Hatters (1934-41) (De RIs)

TOMMY REYNOLDS (one side)
Roy(10″)18117

167. BONANO, SHARKEY   t vo B
(JOSEPH BONANO)

Born April 9, 1904, New Orleans, La.
Died March 27, 1972, New Orleans, La.

New Orleans dixieland trumpet star noted for driving style and use of mutes. Jobbed mostly in New Orleans in early 20s. Worked with Brownlee's Orchestra late 1924-5 briefly and with Jimmy Durante band awhile. Also brief period with Jean Goldkette in 1927. He and Leon Prima had band in 1928. Also worked with Monk Hazel. Continued jobbing and leading bands to mid-30s. With Ben Pollack band briefly in 1936. Stayed in New York 1936-9, mostly led own band (usually billed as Sharkey & His Sharks of Rhythm). At times personnel included George Brunis, Irving Fazola, Santo Pecora, Joe Marsala, Clyde Hart, Joe Bushkin, George Wettling, Ben Pollack. Returned to New Orleans, later enlisted in service during World War II. Dixieland revival in late 40s brought Bonano to the fore for several years. For added novelty, Bonano featured himself playing old bugle. Continued into 50s, playing top spots in Chicago, New York, elsewhere. Active in 60s, mostly in New Orleans.

RECORDS

BROWNLEE'S ORCHESTRA
OK 40337 Peculiar/Dirty Rag
MONK HAZEL
Br 4181 Sizzling the Blues/High Society
Br 4182 Git-Wit-It/Ideas
JOHNNY MILLER
Co 1546-D Panama/Dippermouth Blues
SHARKEY BONANO
De 1014 Everybody Loves My Baby/Yes She Do—No She Don't
Vo 3353 Mudhole Blues/Swing In, Swing Out
Vo 3380 I'm Satisfied with My Gal/High Society
Vo 3450 Old Fashioned Swing/Big Boy Blue
Vo 3470 Swingin' on the Swanee Shore/Swing Like a Rusty Gate
Kappa 115 Tin Roof Blues/Farewell Blues
Kappa 120 That's a-Plenty/Bucket's Got a Hole in It
NOB 1 Muskat Ramble/Tailgate Ramble
Ci 3011 Missouri Waltz/Indiana
Ci 3012 Alice Blue Gown/The World Is Waiting for the Sunrise
Cap 951 In the Mood/Sole Mio Stomp
Cap 1332 Eyes of Texas/Corrine Corrina

603

Cap 1452 Sharkey Strut/I'm Goin' Home

Cap 2166 Auf Wiedersehen Sweetheart/How'm I Doin'?

Cap 2709 Have You Ever Been Lonely?/If I Had You

Dixieland Records 1000 Dippermouth Blues/When the Saints Go Marching In

Dixieland Records 1002 Milenberg Joys/I Like Bananas

LPs

SHARKEY BONANO

Cap T-266 Sharkey's Southern Comfort

Cap T-367 Midnight on Bourbon Street

Southland(10″)SLP-205 Sharkey & His Kings of Dixieland

(with LIZZIE MILES)

Cap T-792 A Night in Old New Orleans

168. BOND, CARRIE JACOBS
cm lyr vo

Born August 11, 1862, Janesville, Wis. Died December 28, 1946, Hollywood, ·Calif.

Songwriter with limited output but three all-time popular classics: *Just a-Wearyin' for You* (1901), *I Love You Truly* (1906), *A Perfect Day* (1910). Formed The Bond Shop in 1894, her own publishing company. Sang in vaudeville, entertained troops in World War I. Other compositions: *God Remembers When the World Forgets, I've Done My Work, His Lullaby, Roses Are in Bloom, A Little Pink Rose, My Mother's Voice, A Little Bit o' Honey, Because of the Light, Someone Is Waiting for Me.*

169. BONNEY, BETTY
vo

Good band singer of 40s and early 50s. With Les Brown 1941-2, sang on band's hit novelty record of 1941, *Joltin' Joe DiMaggio.* Worked with Jan Savitt and Jerry Wald in 1943, with Frankie Carle early 1944 for brief period. Then switched to career as single. In 1949 in road show of HIGH BUTTON SHOES. In 1950 with Sammy Kaye. Appeared on TV in early 50s.

RECORDS

LES BROWN

OK 6235 What D'Ya Hear from Your Heart?

OK 6258 Lament to Love/Do You Care?

OK 6323 All That Meat and No Potatoes

OK 6377 Joltin' Joe DiMaggio/The Nickel Serenade

OK 6414 Nothin'/I Got It Bad

OK 6457 Pushin' Along

OK 6500 Baby Mine/He's 1-A in the Army

OK 6573 Everybody's Making Money but Tschaikovsky

OK 6653 Breathless

BETTY JANE BONNEY

Vi 20-1664 How Little We Know/Memphis in June

Vi 20-1678 While You're Away/They Can't Take That Away from Me

Vi 20-1717 Ho Hum/I Can't Make You Love Me

170. BOOKER, BERYL
p vb b vo

Born June 7, 1922, Philadelphia, Pa.

Good jazz pianist in modern style, also vocalist. Early experience playing local bars with combo. Worked with The Toppers, who later became Steve Gibson's Red Caps. In 1946 she joined Slam Stewart, worked with him off and on till 1951. With The Cats and a Fiddle in 1950. Accompanist awhile for Dinah Washington, also played with Austin Powell combo. In early 50s formed own trio, played clubs and recorded, played abroad. Record of *You Better Go Now* attracted particular attention. Still active in 60s and 70s.

RECORDS

BERYL BOOKER

Mer 8279 You Better Go Now

Mer 8297 Love Is the Thing/Stay as Sweet as You Are

Mer 70041 Why Do I Love You?/When a Woman Loves a Man

Dis 176 Thou Swell/Ebony

Vi 40-0147 Low Ceiling/Don't Blame Me

LPs

BERYL BOOKER

EmArcy(10″)MG-26007 Girl Met a Piano

Cad(10″)CLP-1000 Beryl Booker Trio

Dis(10″)DL-3021

(with DON BYAS)

Dis(10″)DL-3022 (recorded in France)

171. BORDONI, IRENE   vo

Born in Corsica

Vivacious singing star of Broadway stage, petite and chic with charming accent. Educated in Paris, first stage appearance there in 1907. New York stage debut in Broadway musical BROADWAY TO PARIS (1912). After supporting roles in several shows, graduated to starring roles. Other Broadway shows MISS INFORMATION (1915), HITCHY-KOO (1917), HITCHY-KOO OF 1918, SLEEPING PARTNERS (1918; nonmusical), AS YOU WERE (1920), THE FRENCH DOLL (1922), LITTLE MISS BLUEBEARD (1923), NAUGHTY CINDERELLA (1925; nonmusical), PARIS (1928), GREAT LADY (1938), LOUISIANA PURCHASE (1940). Also played vaudeville at intervals. Appeared in movies SHOW OF SHOWS (1929), PARIS (1930), LOUISIANA PURCHASE (1941). Played in stock productions at intervals, as late as 1952 appeared in revival of SOUTH PACIFIC.

RECORDS

IRENE BORDONI

Vi 19199 So This Is Love/I Won't Say I Will, I Won't Say I Won't

Vi 19966 Do I Love You?/That Means Nothing to Me

Vi 21742 Land of Going to Be/Don't Look at Me That Way

Co 1983-D My Lover/What's Really on His Mind?

Co 2027-D Just an Hour of Love/Believe Me

172. BOSE, STERLING   t c vo B

Born February 23, 1906, Florence, Ala.
Died June 1958, St. Petersburg, Fla., of
self-inflicted bullet wound

Jazz trumpet player from early 20s into 50s with many good bands. Began professionally in New Orleans, replacing Wingy Manone in jazz group, 1922-3. Manone and several others went to St. Louis and played Arcadia Ballroom 1924-5; band called Arcadian Serenaders. Bose replaced Manone there in 1925, jobbed in St. Louis later. Joined Jean Goldkette in Detroit in 1927. Staff musician on WGN radio in Chicago about two years. Late 1930 joined Ben Pollack, remained on and off till 1933. Studio work in New York awhile. Joe Haymes band in 1934. Tommy Dorsey took over band in late 1935 and Bose remained under Dorsey several months. With Ray Noble awhile in 1936, later that year joined Benny Goodman briefly. In 1937 with Glenn Miller's early band. With Bob Crosby mid-1938 to early 1939. Original member of Bob Zurke's big band, mid-1939 to early 1940. Later in 1940 with Jack Teagarden several months. Jobbed in Chicago awhile, led own combo. Then back to New York in 1943 with George Brunis and Bobby Sherwood. With Miff Mole and Art Hodes in 1944. Various jobs followed in Chicago and New York, then settled in St. Petersburg, Fla. Led own combo at clubs there, including long run at Soreno Lounge 1950-7. Illness curtailed musical activities; finally committed suicide in June 1958.

RECORDS

ARCADIAN SERENADERS

OK 40503 The Co-ed/Just a Little Bit Bad

OK 40517 Ya Gotta Know How/Angry

OK 40538 Back Home in Illinois/Carry It On Down

BEN POLLACK

Pe 15431 Sweet and Hot/I've Got Five Dollars

DUKE WILSON & HIS TEN BLACKBERRIES

Pe 15617 Beale Street Blues

GIL RODIN

Cr 3045 Ninety-Nine Out of a Hundred

Cr 3046 Hello, Beautiful

VIC BERTON

Vo 2915 Jealous/Dardanella

Vo 2964 A Smile Will Go a Long, Long Way

CHICK BULLOCK

Me 12626 Any Time, Any Day, Anywhere/I've Got the World on a String

Pe 15888 Extra!/What's Good for the Goose

Pe 16111 About a Quarter to Nine/I'm Livin' in a Great Big Way

TOMMY DORSEY CLAMBAKE SEVEN

Vi 25201 The Music Goes 'Round and Around/Rhythm in My Nursery Rhymes

MOUND CITY BLUE BLOWERS

Ch 40081 The Music Goes 'Round and Around/The Broken Record

Ch 40098 You Hit the Spot/Spreadin' Rhythm Around

BENNY GOODMAN

Vi 25411 St. Louis Blues

BOB CROSBY BOB CATS

De 2209 Loopin' the Loop

GLENN MILLER

De 1284 Any Time, Any Day, Anywhere/Wistful and Blue

BOB ZURKE

Vi 26317 Hobson Street Blues

Vi 26411 Cuban Boogie Woogie

26420 Peach Tree Street

RAY NOBLE

Vi 25428 One, Two, Button Your Shoe

Vi 25504 Long as You Got Your Health

Vi 25507 Slumming on Park Avenue

ROD CLESS

B&W 29 Froggy Moore/Have You Ever Felt That Way?

B&W 30 I Know That You Know/Make Me a Pallet on the Floor

EDDIE CONDON

VD(12″)211 Ballin' the Jack/Tin Roof Blues

173. BOSTIC, EARL   as vo ar cm B

Born April 25, 1913, Tulsa, Okla.
Died October 28, 1965, Rochester, N.Y.

Alto sax star with hot bands from early 30s into 40s. Attained greatest success with series of recordings of standards in melodious commercial style. Playing in early days marked by good tone and great facility. Early experience with Terrence Holder 1931-2. Attended Xavier University in New Orleans. In 1934-7 worked with Joe Robicheaux, Ernie Fields, Char-

lie Creath, Fate Marable and others. Went to New York in 1938, worked with Don Redman and Edgar Hayes. From late 1938-42 led own band mostly, had long run at Small's Paradise in Harlem. In 40s began arranging for bands including Louis Prima, Hot Lips Page, Lionel Hampton, Jack Teagarden, Ina Ray Hutton, Paul Whiteman, Artie Shaw. In 1943-4 had intervals with Hot Lips Page, Cab Calloway and Lionel Hampton.

In 1945 Bostic formed another combo and worked almost exclusively as leader from that point on. First hard-jazz group, combo later developed commercial style. By 50s many Bostic records good sellers. Recorded a few jump originals but scored with standard ballads played in heavy-toned, melodious style with good beat, appealing to rhythm and blues market. Leading hits included *Flamingo, You Go to My Head, Cherokee, Temptation, Moonglow, Cracked Ice*. Record success enabled him to tour extensively. In late 50s out of music several years due to heart trouble. Tried to resume career on semi-active basis in 1959. In 1965 opened at Rochester's Midtown Tower Hotel, suffered heart attack and died two days later. Composed several jazz numbers; some of best-known were *The Major and the Minor, Let Me Off Uptown, Brooklyn Boogie, Scotch Jam*.

RECORDS

LIONEL HAMPTON

Vi 26423 The Heebie Jeebies Are Rockin' the Town

Vi 26476 I'm on My Way from You/Haven't Named It Yet

DON BYAS

CMS 574 These Foolish Things

HOT LIPS PAGE

CMS 558 You Need Coachin'/Fish for Supper

CMS 574 Six Seven Eight or Nine

EARL BOSTIC

Maj 1055 The Man I Love/Hurricane Blues

Maj 1056 The Major and the Minor/All On

Go 104 Tippin' In/That's the Groovy Thing

Go 154 845 Stomp/Earl's Rhumboogie

Go 160 Temptation/Artistry by Bostic
Go 172 Liza/Scotch Jam
Go 248 The Man I Love/Apollo Theatre Jump
King 4247 Slightly Groovy/Joy Dust
King 4475 Flamingo/I'm Gettin' Sentimental Over You
King 4511 The Moon Is Low/Lover, Come Back to Me
King 4550 Moonglow/Ain't Misbehavin'
King 4586 You Go to My Head/The Hour of Parting
King 4603 Steamwhistle Jump/The Sheik of Araby
King 4623 Cherokee/The Song Is Ended
King 4674 Deep Purple/Smoke Rings
King 4699 Cracked Ice/My Heart at Thy Sweet Voice
King 4829 For All We Know/Beyond the Blue Horizon

LPs

EARL BOSTIC
King 500 The Best of Bostic
King 503 Earl Bostic for You
King 547 (S) Invitation to Dance
King 620 (S) Plays Sweet Tunes of the Roaring 20s
King 632 (S) Sweet Tunes of the Swinging 30s
King(10")295-64 Earl Bostic and His Alto Sax
King(10")295-65 Earl Bostic and His Alto Sax

174. BOSWELL SISTERS   vocal trio
(Connie, Martha, Vet)

All born in New Orleans, La.

Leading vocal trio of 1931-5 period, their style jazz-influenced, their backing consisting regularly of top jazzmen. As youngsters sang in mid-20s. Theatre and radio appearances in New Orleans, also vaudeville tours. In addition to singing, the girls played musical instruments: Connie-cello, Martha-piano, Vet-violin. Performed on radio in Honolulu, San Francisco and eventually New York, where rose to fame. In early 1931 began recording career with Brunswick, soon were recording heavily. For backing on records, sisters used small combos featuring jazz greats Joe Venuti, Dorsey Brothers, Mannie Klein, Eddie Lang, Bunny Berigan, Benny Goodman. Connie also made records as single in this period. Trio appeared on radio during early 30s as guests or on a somewhat regular basis, as on 1932 Chesterfield show (with Arthur Tracy and Ruth Etting) and Bing Crosby show 1934-5. Played England 1933 and 1935. Featured in movies THE BIG BROADCAST OF 1932 (1932), MOULIN ROUGE and TRANSATLANTIC MERRY-GO-ROUND (1934). Group broke up in late 1935 due to marriages of Martha and Vet. Connie, lead singer and principal arranger, went on to long and successful career as single despite handicap that forced her to perform in wheelchair. Occasionally trio appeared together again during next few years, as in 1937 on California radio show.

RECORDS

DON REDMAN
Br(12")20109 Lawd, You Made the Night Too Long
VICTOR YOUNG
Br(12")20112 O.K. America medleys (1 & 2)
RED NICHOLS
Br(12")20107 California Medley (1 & 2)
Br(12")20110 New Orleans Medley, part 1
BOSWELL SISTERS
OK 41444 My Future Just Passed/Heebie Jeebies
OK 41470 Gee, But I'd Like to Make You Happy/Don't Tell Her What Happened to Me
Br 6109 Roll On, Mississippi, Roll On/Shout, Sister, Shout
Br 6173 Shine On Harvest Moon/Heebie Jeebies
Br 6291 Between the Devil and the Deep Blue Sea/There'll Be Some Changes Made
Br 6395 Sentimental Gentleman from Georgia/Down on the Delta
Br 6470 Mood Indigo/Louisiana Hayride
Br 6545 42nd Street/Shuffle Off to Buffalo

607

Br 6733 Song of Surrender/Coffee in the Morning, Kisses at Night

Br 6798 You Oughta Be in Pictures/I Hate Myself

Br 6929 Why Don't You Practice What You Preach?/Don't Let Your Love Go Wrong

Br 7302 Rock and Roll/If I Had a Million Dollars

Br 7348 The Object of My Affection/It's Written All Over Your Face

Br 7412 Alexander's Ragtime Band/Dinah

Br 7467 St. Louis Blues/Travelin' All Alone

De 574 Cheek to Cheek/Top Hat, White Tie and Tails

De 709 Let Yourself Go/I'm Putting All My Eggs in One Basket

LPs

BOSWELL SISTERS

Ace of Hearts (E)AH-116 Nothing Was Sweeter Than the Boswell Sisters (Br RIs)

175. BOSWELL, CONNIE   vo ar cel
(later spelled first name CONNEE)

Born c. 1912, New Orleans, La.

Member of famous Boswell Sisters vocal trio, went on to long and successful singing career as single. Competent on ballads, her jazz-influenced style at best on swing numbers with jazz backing. Polio in infancy, later aggravated by fall, forced her to work in wheelchair during much of her career. (See BOSWELL SISTERS for Connie's activities with trio.) After Boswell Sisters broke up in late 1935, Connie embarked on career as single. Recorded frequently but in more commercial manner than with trio, but still used good backing. Often on radio, regularly on some shows: Refreshment Time (1935-6), Ken Murray show (1937), Richard Himber show (1938), Good News of 1940, Bing Crosby & Kraft Music Hall (1940-1), Kraft Music Hall summer show (1941), Camel Caravan (1942), Connie Boswell Presents (1944). As single appeared in several movies: ARTISTS AND MODELS (1937), KISS THE BOYS GOODBYE (1941), SYNCOPATION (1942), SWING PA-

RADE (1946), SENIOR PROM (1959). Active on records and radio into 50s, occasional TV thereafter.

RECORDS

GLEN GRAY

Br(12")20108 Washboard Blues

RED NICHOLS

Br(12")20110 New Orleans Medley, part 2

CONNIE BOSWELL with BEN POLLACK ORCHESTRA

De 1160 Serenade in the Night/Where Are You?

De 1420 Whispers in the Dark/That Old Feeling

De 1862 Mr. Freddie Blues/Fare Thee Honey, Fare Thee Well

CONNIE BOSWELL with WOODY HERMAN ORCHESTRA

De 2258 Umbrella Man/They Say

De 2259 Deep in a Dream/Thanks for Ev'rything

BING CROSBY-CONNIE BOSWELL-BOB CROSBY'S BOB CATS

De 3689 Tea for Two/Yes Indeed

CONNIE BOSWELL

Br 6297 Lullaby of the Leaves/My Lips Want Kisses

Br 6405 Me Minus You/I'll Never Have to Dream Again

Br 6640 Emperor Jones/Dinner at Eight

Br 6862 Butterfingers/I Knew You When

Br 7303 Lost in a Fog/Isn't It a Shame?

Br 7354 With Every Breath I Take/I'm Growing Fonder of You

De 747 The Panic Is On/Mama Don't Allow It

De 794 You Started Me Dreaming/Mommy

De 829 On the Beach at Bali Bali/I Met My Waterloo

De 2450 Sunrise Serenade/You Grow Sweeter as the Years Go By

De 3366 Blueberry Hill/The Nearness of You

De 3425 Nobody's Sweetheart/Dinah

De 3631 You Forgot About Me/Amapola

De 3893 Sand in My Shoes/Nighty-Night

De 3959 Sweethearts or Strangers/I'll Keep On Loving You
De 18384 Look for the Silver Lining/ Smoke Gets in Your Eyes
De 18913 Ole Buttermilk Sky/Love Doesn't Grow on Trees
De 28498 Singin' the Blues/It Made You Happy When You Made Me Cry
De 28832 I'm Gonna Sit Right Down and Write Myself a Letter/You Need Some Lovin'
De 29148 If I Give My Heart to You/ T-E-N-N-E-S-S-E-E

LPs
CONNIE BOSWELL
Vi LPM-1426 Connie Boswell & The Original Memphis Five in Hi-Fi
Design DLP-68 Connie Boswell Sings Irving Berlin
De DL-8356 Connee

176. BOTHWELL, JOHNNY   as ts B
Born May 26, 1917, Gary, Ind.

Alto sax star of mid-40s, first prominent with Boyd Raeburn band. Good lead man, distinctive soloist with sliding inflection, moody tone. Early experience with Max Miller combo in Chicago in 1940. In early 40s with Gene Krupa, Tommy Dorsey, Bob Chester, Woody Herman, Sonny Dunham. Made mark with progressive band of Boyd Raeburn early 1944 till mid-1945 (with interval away). Left Raeburn in July 1945 to lead combo, then big orchestra in 1946. Band had good arrangements featuring Bothwell's sax, good vocalists in Don Darcy and Claire "Shanty" Hogan, recording contract with Signature. In spite of assets, the band no lasting success. By early 50s Bothwell out of music business.

RECORDS
BOYD RAEBURN
Guild 111 Summertime/March of the Boyds
Guild 133 Out of Nowhere/Boyd's Nest
Guild 134 Blue Prelude/You've Got Me Cryin' Again
JOHNNY BOTHWELL
Si 15001 Lonely Serenade/Laura

Si 15003 I'll Remember April/Ill Wind
Si 15012 I Cover the Waterfront/Street of Dreams
Si 15034 From the Land of the Sky-Blue Water/I Left My Heart in Mississippi
Si 15045 Somewhere in the Night/ Chiquita Banana
Si 15059 My Old Flame/To a Wild Rose
Si 15066 I'll Close My Eyes/I Won't Promise
Si 15071 Dog Patch Boogie/Get a Pin-up Girl
Si 15085 Chelsea Bridge/Dear Max
Si 15139 Ain't Nowhere
Nat 9074 Scotch Plaid/Bolero Balinese

LPs
(miscellaneous bands)
Masterseal MSLP-5013 Hi-Fi Jazz Session
BOYD RAEBURN
Allegro 4028
FTR 1515 (1944-6)
JOHNNY BOTHWELL
Br(10'')BL-58033

177. BOTKIN, PERRY
g bn uk ar cm B

Born July 22, 1907, Richmond, Ind.
Died October 14, 1973, Van Nuys, Calif.

Active career from late 20s through 60s, first as guitarist-sideman, later orchestra leader and musicial supervisor. Extensive radio and recording work. In late 20s and early 30s recorded with many jazz greats. Jobbed with various bands and singers, sometimes led own group. In mid-30s worked with Victor Young and Smith Ballew. Active on radio all during 30s, played many shows of Al Jolson and Eddie Cantor. With John Scott Trotter orchestra on Bing Crosby's Kraft Music Hall. Played on Bob Hope show. In Billy Mills orchestra on Fibber McGee and Molly show, and in Country Washburne band on Curt Massey show. In late 30s and 40s led combos and bands backing singers on records. Prolific, varied recording output, especially aiding in many sessions backing Bing Crosby with Trotter's orchestra. Many years as musical supervisor of Bing Crosby Enterprises,

Inc. In 50s Botkin became studio musician, worked in Hollywood in movies and TV, wrote film background scores. Composer of several songs and instrumentals: *Two Shillelagh O'Sullivan, Duke of the Uke, Uke Ukulele, Pick-a-Lili, Executioner Theme, Waltz of the Hunter.*

RECORDS

COTTON PICKERS
Br 4325 Rampart Street Blues/Kansas City Kitty
Br 4440 St. Louis Gal

RED NICHOLS
Br 6133 Just a Crazy Song/You Rascal You
Br 6149 Moan, You Moaners
Br 6160 Fan It/How Long Blues

WABASH DANCE ORCHESTRA
Duo 4001 That's My Weakness Now
Duo 4005 My Ohio Home
Duo 4012 My Pet

BOSWELL SISTERS
Br 6650 Sophisticated Lady/That's How Rhythm Was Born

HOAGY CARMICHAEL
Br 8250 (with ELLA LOGAN) Two Sleepy People/New Orleans
Br 8255 Riverboat Shuffle/Hong Kong Blues

ELLA LOGAN
Br 8196 The Blue Bells of Scotland/My Bonnie Lies Over the Ocean
Br 8232 Come to the Fair/Ragtime Cowboy Joe

BING CROSBY-JOHNNY MERCER
De 1960 Small Fry/Mr. Crosby and Mr. Mercer

BING CROSBY
De 2535 It Must Be True

FRANCES FAYE
De 916 No Regrets/You're Not the Kind

JACK TEAGARDEN
Br 6716 I Just Couldn't Take It, Baby/A Hundred Years from Today
Br 6741 Love Me/Blue River

FRANKIE LAINE
Mer 1026 Black and Blue/Wrap Your Troubles in Dreams
Mer 1027 Blue, Turning Grey Over You/On the Sunny Side of the Street

PERRY BOTKIN
De 27162 Lover/Uke Ukulele
De 27730 The World Is Waiting for the Sunrise/Botkin's Banjo Band
(as conductor)

MARY HEALY
OK 6002 What Is There To Say?/I'll See You Again

DICK HAYMES
De 24845 Don't Throw Cold Water on the Flame of Love/I Wish I Had a Sweetheart

EVELYN KNIGHT
De 27874 Life Is a Beautiful Thing

LPs

PERRY BOTKIN
WA 2007 Jean Harlow Film Songs

178. BOWERS, ROBIN HOOD   cm B
(ROBERT HOOD BOWERS)
Born May 24, 1877, Chambersburg, Pa.
Died December 29, 1941, New York, N.Y.

Composer for early Broadway shows, later active many years in conducting. Educated at Franklin & Marshall College. Extensive musical training. Wrote scores for Broadway musicals THE MAID AND THE MUMMY (1904), THE VANDERBILT CUP (1906), THE HOYDEN (1907), MARY'S LAMB (1908), THE SILVER STAR (1909), A CERTAIN PARTY, THE RED ROSE and TEMPTATION (1911), A LONELY ROMEO (1919), OH, ERNEST! (1927). Contributed songs to THE SPRING MAID (1911), THE ROSE MAID (1912), BROADWAY BREVITIES OF 1920. Conducted for various record companies 1916-32. Conducted on New York radio 1928-34. Musical director of School of Radio Technique 1935-41. Music attained little popularity outside context of shows. Best-known songs *Chinese Lullaby* and *When the Moon Shines on the Moonshine* (1919).

179. BOWLLY, AL   vo g bn
Born January 7, 1898, Lourenco Marques, Mozambique
Died April 17, 1941, London, England, killed by bomb in World War II

An all-time singing great, noted for many records with Ray Noble orchestra and other English bands through 30s. Smooth singing voice easily identifiable. Consistently first-rate performer on wide range of songs: novelty, torch, humorous or sentimental. Many buffs consider him best singer of 30s. Grew up in Johannesburg, played guitar and banjo and sang. Toured other countries with several bands, recorded in Berlin in 1927. Arrived in England 1928, worked there first with Fred Elizalde. In 1928-9 recorded with Elizalde and others. Extensive recording in 1930 with variety of bands. In 1931 became a leading singer in England thanks to many records with New Mayfair Dance Orchestra (directed by Ray Noble) and with Roy Fox. Regular band singer with Fox, appearing at popular Monseigneur Restaurant in London. In late 1932 Lew Stone took over nucleus of Fox band, featured Bowlly as vocalist, with arrangements made especially for him. Bowlly continued to record 1932-4 with Stone and others, including studio band now under name of Ray Noble. By mid-1934 his records numbered several hundred.

Noble came to U.S. in late 1934, bringing drummer Bill Harty and vocalist Bowlly. With help of Glenn Miller, assembled band of all-star U.S. musicians and began recording with Victor in early 1935. Played New York's Rainbow Room in first important engagement. Bowlly featured prominently on almost every record, also broadcast with Al Goodman. Spot in movie THE BIG BROADCAST OF 1936. Cut last U.S. records in late 1936. Returned to England in early 1937. Developed voice trouble and returned later to U.S. for delicate, successful operation, then returned to England. Busy recording schedule in 1938-9 with several top English bands, including Geraldo's. Also considerable radio work. With England at war, Bowlly's recordings comparatively sparse in 1940. Teamed with Jimmy Mesene, their act alternately billed as Two Greeks and Their Guitars or The Radio Stars with Two Guitars. Played dates, entertained troops in camps, until Bowlly's tragic death.

RECORDS

FRED ELIZALDE
  Br(E) 189 Just Imagine/Wherever You Are

  Br(E) 206 I'm Sorry, Sally/Misery Farm
MARIUS B. WINTER
  Bcst(E) 2599 What a Perfect Night for Love
  Bcst(E) 2600 Beware of Love
ROY FOX
  De(E) 2279 Reaching for the Moon/Lady of Spain
  De(E) 2351 I'm Gonna Get You/It Must Be True
  De(E) 2580 Just One More Chance/Smile, Darn Ya, Smile
  De(E) 2582 You Forgot Your Gloves/Take It from Me
  De(E) 2775 Prisoner of Love/You Didn't Know the Music
  De(E) 2867 Kiss by Kiss/Goodnight, Moon
  De(E) 3099 Ooh, That Kiss!/You're My Everything
  De(E) 3198 Moon
LEW STONE
  De(E) 3534 Three Wishes/Let Me Give My Happiness to You
  De(E) 3675 Blue Prelude/Snowball
  De(E) 3722 Thanks/The Day You Came Along
  De(E) 3734 Experiment/How Could We Be Wrong?
  De(E) 3783 Close Your Eyes/Weep No More, My Baby
  De(E) 5018 Beat o' My Heart/Easy Come, Easy Go
  De(E) 5131 I Never Had a Chance/I've Had My Moments
  De(E) 6890 All Ashore/Penny Serenade
DURIUM DANCE BAND
  Dur(E) 12 Auf Wiedersehen, My Dear/Rain on the Roof
SAVOY HOTEL ORPHEANS
  Co(E) 377 Who Am I?/Linda
GERALDO
  HMV(E) 5427 Heart and Soul/When Mother Nature Sings Her Lullaby
  HMV(E) 5428 Penny Serenade/Never Break a Promise
  HMV(E)5444 My Own/You're as Pretty as a Picture

RAY NOBLE (sometimes billed as New Mayfair Dance Orchestra on HMV)
  HMV(E) 5984 Goodnight, Sweetheart/Shout for Happiness

HMV(E) 6058 Honeymoon Lane/
Hang Out the Stars in Indiana
HMV(E) 6176 With All My Love and
Kisses/Sailing on the Robert E. Lee
HMV(E) 6245 Love Is the Sweetest
Thing
HMV(E) 6283 Please/Here Lies Love
HMV (E) 6306 Lying in the Hay/
Wanderer
HMV(E) 6332 Three Wishes/Let Me
Give My Happiness to You
HMV(E) 6347 Maybe It's Because I
Love You Too Much/It's Within
Your Power
HMV(E) 6380 Roll Up the Carpet/On
the Other Side of Lover's Lane
HMV(E) 6422 This Is Romance/And
So Goodbye
HMV(E) 6471 Not Bad
HMV(E) 6509 It's All Forgotten
Now/I Never Had a Chance
Vi 24571 Who Walks In When I Walk
Out?
Vi 24865 Clouds/Flowers for Madame
Vi 25104 Why Dream?/I Wished on
the Moon
Vi 25277 Yours Truly Is Truly Yours/
The Touch of Your Lips
Vi 25336 When I'm with You/But
Definitely
Vi 25448 Now/Little Old Lady
Vi 25459 There's Something in the
Air/Where the Lazy River Goes By
VICTOR YOUNG
De 278 Say When/When Love Comes
Swinging Along
AL BOWLLY
De(E) 3145 It Was So Beautiful/Hap-
py-Go-Lucky You
De(E) 3956 You Oughta Be in Pic-
tures/Little Dutch Mill
Vi 24849 Blue Moon/In a Blue and
Pensive Mood
Vi 24855 A Little White Gardenia/
You and the Night and the Music
Bb 7319 Outside of Paradise/Every
Day's a Holiday
Bb 7332 I Can Dream, Can't I?/Sweet
Stranger

LPs

AL BOWLLY
Ace of Clubs(E) ACL-1178 With Lew
Stone (RIs)

Ace of Clubs(E) ACL-1204 The Am-
bassador of Song (RIs)
WRC(E) SH146 (RIs of RAY NOBLE,
SAVOY HOTEL ORCHESTRA)
AL BOWLLY-RAY NOBLE (HMV & Vi RIs)
Mon-Ever MES-6816 Vol. 1
Mon-Ever MES-7021 Vol. 2
Mon-Ever MES-7027 Vol. 3
Mon-Ever MES-7039 Vol. 4
Mon-Ever MES-7040 Vol. 5
Mon-Ever MES-7056 Vol. 6
RAY NOBLE (Vi RIs; American band)
Vi LPV-536

180. BOWMAN, DAVE   p
Born September 8, 1914, Buffalo, N.Y.
Died December 28, 1964, Miami, Fla.,
in car accident, by drowning

Pianist associated mostly with dixieland
combos in 40s and 50s. Good soloist,
excellent at backing instrumentalists,
chording modern-influenced. Often used
block chords in unison with soloist in
prearranged melody lines. Worked particularly well with Bud Freeman in
this. Played in style of Jess Stacy.
Raised in Canada by Canadian parents.
Pianist there in early to mid-30s. In
London 1936-7, stint with Jack Hylton.
Settled in New York, worked with Sharkey Bonano briefly. Important jobs with
Bobby Hackett 1937-9 and Bud Freeman
1939-40. With Jack Teagarden in 1940,
Joe Marsala in 1941, Muggsy Spanier
1941-2. Mostly radio staff work for remainder of 40s and early 50s. With Bud
Freeman 1954-5. Settled in Florida and
freelanced in late 50s and 60s until
drowning.

RECORDS

SIDNEY BECHET
Vo 4537 Hold Tight/Jungle Drums
Vo 4575 What a Dream/Chant in the
Night
BUD FREEMAN
Co 35853 At the Jazz Band Ball/Prince
of Wails
Co 35854 That Da Da Strain/Jack
Hits the Road
De 2781 Satanic Blues/The Sail Fish
De 2849 As Long as I Live/Sunday
TEDDY GRACE
De 3428 I'm the Lonesomest Gal in

Town/See What the Boys in the Backroom Will Have
De 3463 Sing/Gee, But I Hate to Go Home Alone

BOBBY HACKETT
Vo 4142 You, You and Especially You.
Motif M-005 Pennies from Heaven

VIC LEWIS
Esq(E) 10-221 Sugar/Keep Smiling at Trouble
Esq(E) 10-230 Early Rising Blues/New York Blues

JOE MARSALA
De 3715 Bull's Eye/Slow Down
De 3764 Lower Register/I Know That You Know

MUGGSY SPANIER
De 4271 Hesitating Blues
VD(12")588 Tin Roof Blues/Cherry

LT. BOB CROSBY
VD(12")480 Pack Up Your Troubles

JOAN BROOKS
Mus 15022 A Little on the Lonely Side/Let Me Love You Tonight
Mus 15023 Waiting/I Think About You

LEE WILEY
Sch 2008 Down with Love/Stormy Weather

DAVE BOWMAN
Si 28126 Cow Cow Boogie/Stars Fell on Alabama

LPs

BUD FREEMAN
Ha HL-7046 Bud Freeman & His All-Star Jazz (Co RIs)
BETH BCP-29 Bud Freeman
GA 33-313 (1 side) Dixieland Jazz

BOBBY HACKETT
Epic LN-3106 The Hackett Horn (Vo RIs)

REX STEWART/WINGY MANONE
Pres 7812 (2nd side) Trumpet Jive!

181. BOYER, ANITA   vo

Band vocalist of 30s and 40s. With Dick Barrie band 1937-9. Joined Tommy Dorsey in September 1939, remained through 1939. Joined Artie Shaw in September 1940, remained through 1940. With Jerry Wald 1942-3, also radio work in 1943. In 1944 played clubs, joined

Jimmy Dorsey for several months later in year. In mid-40s worked with Opie Cates awhile. Married Bob Dukoff (ts, B), remained somewhat active into early 50s. Now lives in Florida.

RECORDS

DICK BARRIE
Cq 9055 My Reverie
Vo 4271 Don't Cross Your Fingers, Cross Your Heart

TOMMY DORSEY
Vi 26386 Baby, What Else Can I Do?
Vi 26404 All in Fun/Heaven in My Arms
Vi 26429 Am I Proud?
Vi 26433 Darn That Dream
Vi 26439 Faithful to You
Vi 26465 It's a Blue World
Vi 26470 I Concentrate on You

VICTOR SALON ORCHESTRA
Vi 26777 Have a Heart
Vi 26778 Rose of Washington Square

ARTIE SHAW
Vi 26760 If It's You/An Old, Old Castle in Scotland
Vi 26790 Love of My Life/A Handful of Stars
Vi 27256 Whispers in the Night/You Forgot About Me
Vi 27315 The Calypso/Beau Night in Hotchkiss Corners

LEO REISMAN
Vi 27344 Bewitched

BILL HEATHCOCK
VD(12")619 My Silent Love

HOAGY CARMICHAEL
ARA 123 How Little We Know

RED NICHOLS
Mer 8015 You Satisfy

SAUTER-FINEGAN ORCHESTRA
Vi 20-5248 Now That I'm in Love

ANITA BOYER
OK 6442 'Tis Autumn/Make Love to Me
Co 40453 Turn the Lights Down Low/I'll Step Aside

182. BRADFORD, PERRY   p vo cm B

Born February 14, 1893, Montgomery, Ala.
Died April 22, 1970, New York, N.Y.

Noted as pianist in 20s accompanying blues singers, bandleader, composer.

Grew up in Atlanta. As teenager toured with minstrel shows. Played jobs in Chicago in 1909. Toured in vaudeville as pianist or part of act. Settled in New York. During 20s recorded with blues singers and hot bands as pianist or vocalist, and led own group. Musical director for Mamie Smith; her recording of his *Crazy Blues* was blues hit. Became composer, publisher, show producer. One of his most successful songs was *It's Right Here for You*. Other songs: *I'll Be Ready When the Great Day Comes, Wicked Blues, Unexpectedly, If You Don't Want Me Blues, That Thing Called Love, Lonesome Blues, Stewin' de Rice, What Have I Done?, What Did Deacon Jones Do?, Keep a-Knockin', You Can't Keep a Good Man Down*.

RECORDS

BOB FULLER
  Ajax 17091 Spread Yo' Stuff/Funny Feelin' Blues
GEORGIA STRUTTERS
  Ha 231 Everybody Mess Around/ Georgia Grind
GULF COAST SEVEN
  Co 14373-D Georgia Sweet Thing
HOWELL, HORSLEY & BRADFORD
  Co 14168-D Harry Wills, the Champion/Wasn't It Nice?
JIMMY JOHNSON
  Co 14417-D Put Your Mind Right on It/Fare Thee Honey Blues
JIMMY WADE
  Ge 6105 All That I Had Is Gone/Original Black Bottom Dance
ALBERTA HUNTER
  OK 8268 Take That Thing Away/ Your Jelly Roll Is Good
  OK 8278 Everybody Does It Now/A Master Man with a Master Mind
  OK 8315 I Don't Want It All
JULIA JONES
  Ge 5177 That Thing Called Love/Liza Johnson's Got Better Bread Than Sally Lee
ETHEL RIDLEY
  Co A-3941 Here's Your Opportunity Blues/Liza Johnson's Got Better Bread Than Sally Lee
  Vi 19111 Memphis, Tennessee/If Anybody Here Wants a Real Kind Mama

LOUISE VANT
  OK 8275 I'm Tired of Everything but You/I Wouldn't Be Where I Am If You Hadn't Gone Away
  OK 8281 Just a Little Bit Bad/Want a Little Lovin'
  OK 8293 Do Right Blues/I've Learned to Do without You Now
COTTONBELT QUARTET
  Vo 1005 Golden Slippers/Lord, I've Done What You Told Me To
BLACKBIRDS OF HARMONY
  Ge 3333 So's Your Old Man
PERRY BRADFORD'S JAZZ PHOOLS
  Vo 15165 Lucy Long/I Ain't Gonna Play No Second Fiddle
  Para 12041 Fade Away Blues/Daybreak Blues
  Para 20309 Charleston, South Carolina/Hoola Boola Dance
PERRY BRADFORD & HIS GANG
  Co 14142-D So's Your Old Man/Just Met a Friend from My Home Town
  OK 8416 Original Black Bottom Dance/Kansas City Blues
  OK 8450 Lucy Long/All That I Had Is Gone

183. BRADLEY, BETTY VO
Born December 13, 1920, Brooklyn, N.Y.

Band singer of late 30s and 40s, good voice and dynamic style. With Gray Gordon 1938-9. In 1940 worked with Sonny James and Johnny McGee, performed on radio. With Bob Chester 1941-2, most productive recording period. Freelanced in mid-40s, worked on radio including period on Rudy Vallee show. Career faded by late 40s.

RECORDS

GRAY GORDON
  Vi 26184 It's Never Too Late
  Vi 26242 I'm in Love with the Honorable Mr. So and So/A Lady Needs a Change
JOHNNY MCGEE
  MW 10067 Sierra Sue/Let There Be Love
BOB CHESTER
  Bb 11034 Blue Echoes
  Bb 11043 Bewitched/My Ship

Bb 11227 There Goes That Song Again/It's So Peaceful in the Country
Bb 11259 You Were Meant for Me/A New Shade of Blue
Bb 11316 This Love of Mine/Joltin' Joe DiMaggio
Bb 11355 I Wish I Had a Sweetheart
Bb 11562 He's My Guy

BETTY BRADLEY
Je 1002 Summertime/Do It Again
Je 1003 The Gypsy
Standard 2048 Who Do You Think You Are?

184. BRADLEY, WILL   tb ar cm B
(WILBUR SCHWICHTENBERG)
Born July 12, 1912, Newton, N.J.

Trombonist who rose to fame in early 40s as leader of good big swing band that featured boogie woogie. Not as widely acclaimed as other jazz trombonists but for all-around ability ranked among best. Beautiful tone, good range and technique, impressive on ballad and lead work. Multinote jazz solos with flowing lines. After early experience in New Jersey, Bradley went to New York in 1928. Freelancing included work with Red Nichols and Milt Shaw. Radio staff musician 1931-4 with bands of Victor Young, Jacques Renard, Nat Shilkret, others. With Ray Noble 1935-6, then more staff work 1936-9.

In mid-1939 formed big band, took name Will Bradley. Ray McKinley drummer and vocalist on jazz-novelty numbers, also co-leader though Bradley got most of the publicity. During 1939 and early 1940 band's typical white swing style attracted little attention. When started featuring big band boogie woogie, however, band caught on. Boogie woogie was pianist Freddie Slack's forte, and Slack and chief arranger Leonard Whitney contributed important arrangements in this style. Band had hit record with *Beat Me, Daddy (Eight to the Bar)*. Other boogie numbers followed and were well received. Popular easy-swing arrangement was *Celery Stalks at Midnight*. Band's themes: *Strange Cargo* and *Think of Me*. Good jazzmen in Peanuts Hucko (cl, ts), Joe Wiedman and Herbie Dell (t). Slack

left at height of his popularity, followed by Bob Holt and Billy Maxted. Steve Lipkins good lead trumpeter for most of band's career. Later good jazzmen Mahlon Clark (cl) and Lee Castle (t). Good vocalists in Carlotta Dale, Jimmy Valentine, Terry Allen, Lynn Gardner and others.

Bradley and McKinley differed over band's style. Bradley favored ballads over boogie woogie. McKinley left in early 1942 and draft caused other personnel changes. Later in 1942 Bradley disbanded, returning to studio work in New York, where active into 70s. In band on TV's late-night Tonight Show. Co-composer of *Celery Stalks at Midnight* and *Strange Cargo*.

RECORDS

RED NICHOLS
Br 6421 My Sweetie Went Away
Br 6767 Slow and Easy
Br(12")20110 New Orleans Medley, part 2

RAY NOBLE
Vi 24849 Blue Moon
Vi 25105 Why Stars Come Out at Night

BILLY BUTTERFIELD
Cap album BD-10 (78's) Gershwin Album

EDDIE CONDON
Atl 661 Time Carries On/Seems Like Old Times

RUTH BROWN with EDDIE CONDON
Atl 879 It's Raining/So Long

ANITA O'DAY with WILL BRADLEY ORCHESTRA
Si 15162 What Is This Thing Called Love?/Boot Whip

WILL BRADLEY
Vo 5130 Memphis Blues/Old Doc Yak
Vo 5182 I Thought About You/Speaking of Heaven
Vo 5210 Make with the Kisses/I'm Fit to Be Tied
Co 35376 Jimtown Blues/A Ghost of a Chance
Co 35530 Beat Me, Daddy (Eight to the Bar) (1 & 2)
Co 35545 (theme) Strange Cargo/Where Do You Keep Your Heart?
Co 35707 Celery Stalks at Midnight

Co 35732 Scramble Two/Rock-a-bye the Boogie
Co 35743 There I Go/Scrub Me, Mama (with a Boogie Beat)
Co 35849 The Lonesome Road/You're Lucky to Me
Co 35939 Star Dust/Chicken Gum-boogie
Co 36044 That's Her Mason-Dixon Line/I Boogie'd When I Should Have Woogied
Co 36101 (theme) Think of Me
Co 36147 Flamingo/Swingin' Down the Lane
Co 36182 When You and I Were Young, Maggie/I'm Misunderstood
Co 36231 Booglie Wooglie Piggy/Love Me a Little Little
Co 36286 From the Land of the Sky-Blue Water/In the Hall of the Mountain King
Co 36401 April in Paris/Stop and Ask Somebody
Co 36470 Who Can I Turn To?/Sleepy Time Gal
Cel 7014 Lightning Boogie/Sugar Hill Boogie Woogie
Si 15111 Celery Stalks at Midnight (No. 2)/If There is Someone Lovelier Than You

LPs

WILL BRADLEY
Epic LN-3115 Boogie Woogie (Co RIs)
Epic LN-3199 The House of Bradley (including numbers by son's combo)
Bandstand BS-1 (1939-41 Co RIs)
WILL BRADLEY-JOHNNY GUARNIERI BAND
Vi LSP-2098 (S) Big Band Boogie
ROYAL GARDEN RAJAHS (one side)
GA 33-313 Dixieland Jazz

185. BRAFF, RUBY   t c B
Born March 16, 1927, Boston, Mass.

Trumpet star of mainstream jazz. Influenced by both traditional and modern styles, worked in all types of combos and big bands. Big brassy tone, melodic and swinging style. Worked in groups in Boston area in late 40s and early 50s. With Pee Wee Russell in Boston and Bud Freeman in St. Louis. Came to New York in 1954, made first recordings that year. Soon became for several years most-

in-demand trumpet player with stars of dixieland and mainstream jazz. In 1955 role in PIPE DREAM on Broadway. Strangely, popularity ebbed in late 50s and 60s. Continued working and recording occasionally but not as prominent. Active into 70s. Formed quartet with guitarist George Barnes, played 1973 Newport-New York Jazz Festival and backed Tony Bennett in concerts.

RECORDS
(All LPs)

RUBY BRAFF
Vi LPM-1332 The Magic Horn
Vi LPM-1510 Hi-Fi Salute to Bunny
Vi LPM-1966 Easy Now
Epic LN-3377 Braff!
Vang VRS-8504 The Ruby Braff Special
Story 320
UA 3045 Blowing Around the World
Stereocraft 507 You're Getting to Be a Habit with Me
Jazztone J-1210 Swinging with Ruby Braff
Beth(10″)BCP-1032 Holiday in Braff
RUBY BRAFF-ELLIS LARKINS
Vang VRS-8507 Two by Two: Ruby and Ellis Play Rodgers and Hart
VIC DICKENSON
Vang VRS-8520 The Vic Dickenson Septet, Vol. 1
Vang VRS-8521 The Vic Dickenson Septet, Vol. 2
BENNY GOODMAN
Cap W-565 Benny Goodman in Hi-Fi
BROTHER JOHN SELLERS
Vang(10″)VRS-8005 Sings Blues and Folk Songs
LEE WILEY
Story(10″)312 Sings Rodgers and Hart
JACK TEAGARDEN
Urania US-41205 (S) Accent on Trombone

186. BRANDWYNNE, NAT   p cm B
Born July 23, 1910, New York, N. Y.

Leader of ideal hotel band with big ensemble sound and good beat. Music warm and danceable, created romantic atmosphere. Enhanced by Brandwynne's featured piano, with its simple and tasteful chords and phrasing. Top band in society circles for years. Early in career, played piano in Leo Reisman band. Pianist Eddy Duchin in band at same time for awhile. In early 30s left Reisman to become musicial director for new singing sensation Russ Columbo. Also worked for Kate Smith. Later formed own band and opened at New York's Waldorf-Astoria Hotel. Long engagements there for years. Theme *If Stars Could Talk*. In 1936 had excellent band with good trumpet by Louis "King" Garcia. Singers Buddy Clark and Barry McKinley on some records. Led band many years, with New York as main base. In late 50s played Las Vegas. Active into 70s in Las Vegas. Composed *Peacock Alley*, *Stars Over Bahia*, *If Stars Could Talk*, *Little Rock Rag*.

RECORDS

NAT BRANDWYNNE

Me 60212 Sailor Beware/My Heart and I

Me 60213 Cling to Me/Just One of Those Things

Me 60313 Misty Islands of the Highlands/That Lovely Night in Budapest

Me 60402 I'd Rather Lead a Band/Let's Face the Music and Dance

Me 70516 They All Laughed/They Can't Take That Away from Me

Me 70527 To a Sweet Pretty Thing/I Dream of San Marino

Br 7655 There's Always a Happy Ending/It's You I'm Talkin' About

Br 7660 The Glory of Love/Lazy Weather

Br 7676 Take My Heart/These Foolish Things

Br 7678 Where Is My Heart?/Long Ago and Far Away

Br 7714 Bye Bye Baby/If We Never Meet Again

Br 7772 In the Chapel in the Moonlight/Never Should Have Told You

Br 7774 Tea on the Terrace/Under Your Spell

De 3914 Amapola/Blue Echoes

Maj 1126 Easy to Love/Sweet and Lovely

Maj 1127 Love for Sale/I'll See You in My Dreams

De album (78's) 24012-3-4-5 Songs of Our Times—1920

De album (78's) 24072-3-4-5 Songs of Our Times—1935

De album (78's) 24096-7-8-9 Songs of Our Times—1941

LPs

NAT BRANDWYNNE

Vik 1078 The Smart Set

Vik 1108 Cole Porter Dance Book

Vo VL-3647 Songs of Our Times—Song Hits of 1935

Cam CAL-301 Dancing at the Waldorf

Co(10")CL-6174 Piano Moods

LENA HORNE (Nat Brandwynne Orchestra, directed by Lennie Hayton)

Vi LOC-1028 At the Waldorf-Astoria

187. BRATTON, JOHN W.

cm lyr vo B

Born January 21, 1867, Wilmington, Del.

Died February 7, 1947, Brooklyn, N. Y.

Composer for Broadway shows in early years of century. Educated at Harkness Academy in Wilmington and Philadelphia College of Music. Early in career sang and acted on stage. Wrote music for Broadway shows STAR AND GARTER and HODGE, PODGE AND CO. (1900), THE LIBERTY BELLES (1901), THE SCHOOL GIRL and THE MAN FROM CHINA (1904), THE PEARL AND THE PUMPKIN (1905), BUSTER BROWN (1908), THE NEWLYWEDS AND THEIR BABY (1909). Later active producer. Songs attained little popularity outside context of shows. Best-known: *I Love You in the Same Old Way*; *My Sunbeam from the South*; *In a Garden of Faded Flowers*; *My Cosey-Corner Girl*; *You'll Always Be Just Sweet Sixteen to Me*; *The Sunshine of Paradise Alley*; *Henrietta, Have You Met Her?*; *Sweetheart, Let's Grow Old Together*; *I Talked to God Last Night*; *The Teddy Bears' Picnic*; *The Rose's Honeymoon*; *Wooden Soldier*; *In a Pagoda*; *One World*; *Only Me*; *I'm on the Water Wagon Now*; *Star of India*; *An American Abroad* (overture).

188. BREEN, BOBBY

vo

Born 1927

Died 1972 in England

Child singer-actor in movies of middle and late 30s. First prominent early 1936 when featured on Eddie Cantor radio show. Clear soprano voice of good quality for youngster. Radio work led to immediate stardom in series of pleasant but unimportant movies. Best featured songs in these were *Rainbow on the River, Let's Sing Again, Put Your Heart in a Song, The Sunny Side of Things*. Movie career ended when voice changed, later found it difficult to shake early image of boy soprano with winsome, childish appearance. Military service, World War II, led show troupe. In later 40s and 50s played clubs in U. S. and abroad in comparative obscurity. In late 50s tried rock and roll. Never able to recapture youthful popularity.

MOVIES

1936—LET'S SING AGAIN; RAINBOW ON THE RIVER
1937—MAKE A WISH
1938—BREAKING THE ICE; HAWAII CALLS
1939—WAY DOWN SOUTH; FISHERMAN'S WHARF; ESCAPE TO PARADISE
1942—JOHNNY DOUGHBOY

RECORDS

BOBBY BREEN
De 798 Let's Sing Again/It's a Sin to Tell a Lie
De 973 The Rosary/M-O-T-H-E-R
De 1053 Rainbow on the River/Flower Song
De 1804 Sleep, My Baby, Sleep/In a Little Dutch Kindergarten
De 1949 Put Your Heart in a Song/Tellin' My Troubles to a Mule
De 1950 The Sunny Side of Things/Happy as a Lark
De 2353 Blue Italian Waters/Fisherman's Chantie
De 2496 Ave Maria/Largo
Bb 7168 Gee, But It's Great to Meet a Friend/My Campfire Dreams
Bb 7320 Hawaii Calls/Song of the Islands
Lon(E) 813 Day of Glory/Royal David's City
A-Bell 834 It's the End of the World/There's a Bell That Rings in My Heart

189. BREEN, MAY SINGHI
cm lyr vo uk
Radio performer many years, known as The Ukulele Lady early in career in 20s.

Later teamed with husband, composer Peter DeRose, for sixteen years on radio series; team known as Sweethearts of the Air. Also aided DeRose in composing. Originated use of ukulele arrangements on sheet music. Taught ukulele many years. Songs: *Bird of Paradise, Cross My Heart, I Love You, I Looked at Norah, Forever and Ever, Ukulele Blues, Texas Star, Back in the Old Sunday School, Way Back Home*.

190. BREESE, LOU
t bn B
(LOU CALABREESE)
Bandleader adept at directing night club and theatre shows. Played with Bert Lown and Paul Specht, also theatre work in New York. Conducted theatre bands in various cities. Formed first band in mid-30s. Impressive front man, sometimes played trumpet. Worked mostly in Chicago area, including famed night club Chez Paree. In mid-1939 took over Bob Baker band (formerly Henry Busse's Chicago band). Disbanded in late 1942, then fronted house band at Chez Paree several years. In 1946 fronted house band at Chicago Theatre. Continued to lead bands through 40s and 50s in Chicago. Usual theme song: *Breezin' Along with the Breeze*.

RECORDS

LOU BREESE
Vs 8259 Where Do I Go from You?/Angel in Disguise
Vs 8265 Swamp Fire/Come to the Fair
Vs 8326 A Latin Tune, a Manhattan Moon and You/Tennessee Fish Fry
Vs 8332 I'm Nobody's Baby/Little Firefly
Hit 7027 Swamp Fire
De 4107 Humpty Dumpty Heart/How Long Did I Dream?
De 4127 Pleasant Dreams/Chiquita
De 4255 Somebody Nobody Loves/Seven Days a Week
De 4269 Loretta/Sweetheart, Wait for Me

LP

LOU BREESE
De DL-4346 His Banjo and Orchestra —Breezing Along

191. BRENNAN, J. KEIRN   lyr vo

Born November 24, 1873, San Francisco, Calif.
Died February 4, 1948, Hollywood, Calif.

Lyricist of popular songs and several show scores. Chief lyricist for famed composer Ernest R. Ball. Collaborated with Ball on best-known songs: *A Little Bit of Heaven, Dear Little Boy of Mine, Let the Rest of the World Go By*. As youth worked as cowboy, took part in Klondike gold rush. Worked as singer for Chicago publishing companies. Wrote for Broadway shows WHITE LILACS (1928), BOOM! BOOM!, BROADWAY NIGHTS, MUSIC IN MAY and A NIGHT IN VENICE (1929), LUANA (1930). Worked in Hollywood as songwriter beginning 1929.

SONGS
(with related shows)

1914—HEART OF PADDY WHACK stage show (A Little Bit of Heaven)
1915—Ireland Is Ireland to Me; That's How the Shannon Flows
1916—Goodbye, Good Luck, God Bless You; Turn Back the Universe and Give Me Yesterday; For Dixie and Uncle Sam
1917—My Sunshine Jane
1918—Dear Little Boy of Mine; One More Day; With All My Heart and Soul
1919—Let the Rest of the World Go By
1922—All Over Nothing at All
1923—Out There in the Sunshine with You; Ten Thousand Years from Now
1926—There's a New Star in Heaven Tonight—Rudolph Valentino
1928-9—(songs for Broadway shows attained no popularity out of context of shows)
1929—SHOW OF SHOWS movie (Dear Little Pup; Meet My Sister; The Only Boy I Know)
1930—LUANA stage show (Luana; A Son of the Sun; Aloha; My Bird of Paradise)
1936—RHYTHM ON THE RANGE movie (Empty Saddles)

Other songs: *I'll Follow the Trail*; *You Hold My Heart*; *When My Boy Comes Home*; *A Little Bit of Love*

192. BREWER, TERESA   vo cm

Born May 7, 1931, Toledo, Ohio

Pert little singing star of the 50s, with baby-type voice but ability to belt out song. Veteran of show business, at 5 Teresa performed on Major Bowes Amateur Hour on radio. Sensational at that age, toured seven years with Bowes road units. Then joined Pick & Pat radio show. Dropped out of show business several years, resumed career at 16 and won success on radio talent shows. Began recording, had first big hit in *Music! Music! Music!* in 1950. Many later records well received. In 1953 good role in movie THOSE RED HEADS FROM SEATTLE. Great popularity in 50s with frequent TV spots. A natural on TV with beauty, showmanship and singing talent. By 60s career waned, but comeback in 1972-3. Composed novelty songs: *I Love Mickey, Down the Holiday Trail, Imp, There's Nothing as Lonesome as Saturday Night, Hush-a-bye Wink-a-bye Do.*

RECORDS

TERESA BREWER

Lon 604 Music! Music! Music!/Copenhagen
Lon 794 Grizzly Bear/Molasses, Molasses
Lon 795 You've Got Me Crying Again/He Can Come Back Anytime He Wants To
Lon 970 Lonesome Gal/Counterfeit Kisses
Lon 1083 The Oceana Roll/The Wang Wang Blues
Lon 1085 If You Don't Marry Me/I Wish I Wuz
Cor 60591 I Don't Care/Sing Sing Sing
Cor 60676 Gonna Get Along without Ya Now/Roll Them Roly Boly Eyes
Cor 60873 Hello Bluebird/Till I Waltz Again with You
Cor 60953 Dancin' with Someone/Breakin' in the Blues
Cor 61043 Ricochet/Too Young to Tango
Cor 61067 Baby Baby Baby/I Guess It Was You All the Time
Cor 61078 Ebenezer Scrooge/I Saw Mommy Kissing Santa Claus

Cor 61152 Jilted/Le Grand Tour de
L'Amour
Cor 61315 Let Me Go, Lover/The
Moon Is on Fire
TERESA BREWER with LES BROWN ORCHES-
TRA
Cor 60994 Into Each Life Some Rain
Must Fall/Too Much Mustard

LPs

TERESA BREWER
Cor CRL-57053 Teresa
Cor CRL-57232 Time for Teresa
Cor CRL-57257 When Your Lover
Has Gone
Cor CRL-57315 Ridin' High
Cor(10″)CRL-56072 Bouquet of Hits
Philips PHS-600062 (S) Teresa Brew-
er's Greatest Hits (not RIs)

193. BRIAN, DONALD   VO

*Born February 17, 1875, St. John's,
Newfoundland
Died December 22, 1948, Great Neck,
N.Y.*

Handsome singing star of Broadway
stage. Greatest success in THE MERRY
WIDOW in 1907, after which became matinee idol. Grew up in Boston. First stage
appearance with touring company in Boston. New York stage debut in 1899, soon
rose to stardom and appeared in many
productions through the years. In 1931
played revival of former triumph THE
MERRY WIDOW.

BROADWAY MUSICALS

1899—ON THE WABASH
1902—THE BELLE OF BROADWAY
1904—LITTLE JOHNNY JONES
1906—FORTY-FIVE MINUTES FROM BROAD-
WAY
1907—THE MERRY WIDOW
1909—THE DOLLAR PRINCESS
1911—THE SIREN
1913—THE MARRIAGE MARKET
1914—THE GIRL FROM UTAH
1916—SYBIL
1917—HER REGIMENT
1918—THE GIRL BEHIND THE GUN
1919—BUDDIES
1922—UP SHE GOES
1927—AIN'T LOVE GRAND
1932—MUSIC IN THE AIR
1939—VERY WARM FOR MAY

193A. BRICE, ELIZABETH   VO

Died January 25, 1965, New York, N.Y.

Beautiful singer-actress of Broadway musicals. Early career singer-dancer in
vaudeville. Small roles in several shows
before supporting role in THE SOCIAL
WHIRL (1906). Other musicals followed.

BROADWAY MUSICALS

1906—THE SOCIAL WHIRL
1908—NEARLY A HERO; MLLE. MISCHIEF
1909—THE MOTOR GIRL
1910—THE JOLLY BACHELORS
1911—THE SLIM PRINCESS
1912—TANTALIZING TOMMY; A WINSOME
WIDOW; ZIEGFELD FOLLIES OF 1912
1913—ZIEGFELD FOLLIES OF 1913
1914—WATCH YOUR STEP
1917—MISS 1917; WORDS AND MUSIC
1919—TOOT SWEET
1920—BUZZIN' AROUND

194. BRICE, FANNY   VO
(FANNIE BORACH)

*Born October 29, 1891, New York, N.Y.
Died May 29, 1951, Los Angeles, Calif.*

Star comedienne of stage and radio.
Known for torch number *My Man* but
mostly performed novelty and dialect
songs. Later in career won great popularity portraying her Baby Snooks, radio's
classic brat. Won amateur contest at 13,
soon entered show business professionally. Played in burlesque and vaudeville,
later played Palace in New York as star.
Performed in ZIEGFELD FOLLIES OF 1910,
which led to many other Broadway revues, particularly for Ziegfeld. Appeared
in nonmusical plays WHY WORRY? (1918)
and FANNY (1925). Starred in two early
movie musicals MY MAN (1929) and BE
YOURSELF (1930). Later movies THE GREAT
ZIEGFELD (1936), EVERYBODY SING (1938),
ZIEGFELD FOLLIES (1946). Career stayed in
high gear during 40s thanks to Baby
Snooks role. For many years her partner
in this skit, playing Daddy, was talented
straight man Hanley Stafford. Guest
spots on radio in 30s. Regular shows
included Ziegfeld Follies of the Air and
Revue de Paree. In late 1939 began playing Baby Snooks on Good News of 1939.
Continued on Maxwell House Coffee

Time in early 40s, starred on shows of similar format through 40s into 1951. Brice inspired title role in 1964 Broadway musical FUNNY GIRL, later starring vehicle for Barbra Streisand in 1968 movie musical.

BROADWAY MUSICALS

1910—ZIEGFELD FOLLIES OF 1910
1911—ZIEGFELD FOLLIES OF 1911
1913—THE HONEYMOON EXPRESS
1916—ZIEGFELD FOLLIES OF 1916
1917—ZIEGFELD FOLLIES OF 1917
1918—ZIEGFELD'S 9 O'CLOCK FROLIC
1919—ZIEGFELD'S MIDNIGHT FROLICS
1920—ZIEGFELD FOLLIES OF 1920; ZIEGFELD GIRLS OF 1920 (or ZIEGFELD'S 9 O'CLOCK REVUE); ZIEGFELD MIDNIGHT FROLIC
1921—ZIEGFELD FOLLIES OF 1921
1923—ZIEGFELD FOLLIES OF 1923
1924—MUSIC BOX REVUE OF 1924
1929—FIORETTA
1930—SWEET AND LOW
1931—BILLY ROSE'S CRAZY QUILT
1934—ZIEGFELD FOLLIES OF 1934
1936—ZIEGFELD FOLLIES OF 1936

RECORDS

FANNY BRICE
Co A-2122 If We Could Only Take Her Word (1 & 2)
Vi 21211 Mrs. Cohen at the Beach (1 & 2)
Vi 21815 I'd Rather Be Blue/If You Want the Rainbow
Vi 22310 Cooking Breakfast for the One I Love/When a Woman Loves a Man
Vi 45263 My Man/Second Hand Rose
Vi 45303 I'm an Indian/Oh, How I Hate That Fellow Nathan
Vi 45323 Becky Is Back in the Ballet/Sheik of Avenue B

LPs

FANNY BRICE
AudFid 707 Fanny Brice (RIs)
(one side) Vi LPV-561 Fanny Brice/ Helen Morgan (RIs)
(miscellaneous artists)
Vi LCT-1112 Old Curiosity Shop (RIs)
Cam CAL-745 Great Personalities of Broadway (RIs)

195. BRIGODE, ACE   B
Died February 3, 1960

Leader of dance band called Ace Brigode & His Virginians from 20s into 50s. Early record hit *Yes, Sir, That's My Baby* in 1925, arrangement by Frank Skinner. Brigode's band did much touring, mostly in midwest and south, played countless one-nighters. Long runs in New York, Chicago, Cleveland, Cincinnati. Modest recording output. Band's appropriate theme song was *Carry Me Back to Ol' Virginny*. By early 30s band had full ensemble sound, was good entertaining unit. Feature number at that time *Goin' Home* (*Largo* theme), with vocal choir of bandsmen and scat vocalist fitting in answering lyrics. Unfortunately, Brigode's better band of 30s never recorded. Band attained no great renown but worked steadily, well known in midwest. Disbanded and retired in early 1945. In late 40s and 50s in charge of publicity and promotion at Chippewa Lake Park near Cleveland.

RECORDS

ACE BRIGODE
Co 282-D Alabamy Bound/A Sun-Kist Cottage
Co 385-D Sleeping Beauty's Wedding
Co 398-D Yes, Sir, That's My Baby
Co 401-D Wait'll It's Moonlight/ Naughty Eyes Behave
Co 426-D Alone at Last/Tired of Everything but You
Co 477-D Normandy/Why Aren't Yez Eatin' More Oranges?
Ca 785 Tweedle-Dee
Linc 2337 Wondering
OK 40008 Dream Daddy
OK 40014 Oklahoma Indian Jazz
OK 40026 You Darlin'
OK 40087 Monnavanna/Colorado
OK 40088 Never Again/Don't Mind the Rain
OK 40153 Only You/Don't Take Your Troubles to Bed
OK 40180 Follow the Swallow
OK 40191 Dreary Weather
OK 40223 Bye Bye, Baby/A Sun-Kist Cottage
Vo 5446 Why Should I Cry Over

You?/You Know You Belong to Somebody Else

196. BRITO, PHIL   VO V
(PHILIP COLOMBRITO)

Born September 15, 1915, Boomer, W. Va.

Good singer with smooth romantic style. Best period with Al Donahue band 1939-42. Began career at 17. Early singing job at Newark hotel, then local radio shows in New York. With Lloyd Huntley in Canada 1933-8 as violinist-vocalist, played radio shows there. Back in U.S., joined Al Donahue, began making a name via appearances, radio and records. In early 1942 went out as single on strength of hit records with Donahue, *Come Back to Sorrento* and *The Shrine of St. Cecelia.* Based in Cincinnati for club and radio work, later played other cities. Various singing shows on radio, sometimes on network. In mid-40s began recording as single. Good role in 1946 movie SWEET-HEART OF SIGMA CHI. Appeared on early TV. Popular 1950 record *Mama,* own composition. Active into 60s. Ill health curtailed activities in later 60s. Settled in West Orange, N.J. Began comeback in 1971.

RECORDS

AL DONAHUE
Vo 5099 The Last Two Weeks in July/Day In—Day Out
Vo 5289 With the Wind and the Rain in Your Hair
Vo 5396 The Sky Fell Down
Vo 5454 Let There Be Love
Vo 5479 Secrets in the Moonlight
Vo 5519 Fools Rush In/I'm Stepping Out with a Memory Tonight
OK 5888 I Hear a Rhapsody
OK 6159 Come Back to Sorrento
OK 6413 The Shrine of St. Cecilia/Under Fiesta Stars
OK 6617 Candles in the Wind/My Heart's on Fire
JAN SAVITT
De 2600 Shabby Old Cabby
De 2614 Running Thru My Mind
PHIL BRITO
Mus 15015 My Heart Tells Me/Little Did I Know

Mus 15018 You Belong to My Heart/I Don't Want to Love You
Mus 15038 I'll See You in My Dreams/After All This Time
Mus 15042 I Used to Love You/A Pretty Girl Is Like a Melody
Mus 15047 A Cottage for Sale/Don't Let Me Dream
Mus 15054 Do You Love Me?/I Wish I Could Tell You
Mus 15080 And Then It's Heaven/Whatta Ya Gonna Do
Mus 15095 Sooner or Later/Years and Years Ago
Mus 15105 Sweet Lorraine/Between the Devil and the Deep Blue Sea
Mus 15112 An Apple Blossom Wedding/I'm Sorry
MGM 10550 Vieni Su/Mattinata
MGM 10591 Mama
MGM 11687 Memories of Sorrento/Darktown Strutters' Ball

197. BRITT, ELTON   vo g cm lyr B
(JAMES BRITT BAKER)

Born July 7, 1912. Marshall, Ark.
Died June 23, 1972, Pennsylvania

Popular country singer and yodeler. Noted for hit record during World War II, *There's a Star Spangled Banner Waving Somewhere* (1942). Combo backing him usually displayed excellent musicianship. Grew up in Osage Hills of Oklahoma, worked on father's farm. Learned to play guitar, sing and yodel. In 1932 talent scouts signed him for radio in Los Angeles. Also worked spots with The Beverly Hillbillies group. Soon popular in California. Several years later he went to New York with Zeke Manners, did radio network shows. After 1942 hit, other popular records: *Chime Bells*(1948), *Candy Kisses* (1949), *Quicksilver* (1950; with Rosalie Allen). Several country and western movies. Often on Grand Ole Opry in Nashville in 50s and 60s. Settled in New York, worked on radio and TV. Later lived on farm in Maryland, raised cattle, worked occasionally at music. Composer of *Chime Bells; Maybe I'll Cry; Cannonball Yodel; Someday; Lorelei; Patent Leather Boots; Weep No More, My Darlin';* others.

RECORDS

ELTON BRITT

Me 12873 Goodnight, Little Girl of My Dreams/Home in Wyoming

Me 13019 Swiss Yodel/Alpine Milkman Yodel

Me 13293 Free Wheelin' Hobo/Take Me Home

Bb 8701 I'll Die Before I Tell You/There's So Much That I Forget

Bb 9000 There's a Star Spangled Banner Waving Somewhere/When the Roses Bloom Again

Bb 9023 I Hung My Head and Cried/Buddy Boy

Bb 33-0521 Weep No More, My Darlin'/Someday

Vi 20-1873 Blue Texas Moonlight/Thanks for Heartaches

Vi 20-1927 Rogue River Valley/Gotta Get Together with My Girl

Vi 20-2027 Too Tired to Care/I Get the Blues When It Rains

Vi 20-2269 Candlelight and Roses/I Wish You the Best of Everything

Vi 20-3090 Chime Bells/Someday

Vi 20-3162 My Mother's Picture/Anyone

Vi 20-4324 Kiss by Kiss/The Tale a Sailor Told

Vi 21-0122 Tears from the Sky/Driftwood on the River

LPs

ELTON BRITT

Vi LPM-1288 Yodel Songs

Vi LPM-2669 Best of Britt

ABC-Para 293 (S) The Wandering Cowboy (with ZEKE MANNERS BAND)

ABC-Para 521 (S) Singing Hills

ABC-Para 744 Sixteen Great Country Performances

(one side) Waldorf 33-1207

198. BRODSZKY, NICHOLAS   cm

Important composer for movie musicals, particularly in early 50s. Hit song, *Be My Love*, for Mario Lanza movie; became Lanza's most featured song.

SONGS

(with related movies)

1950—TOAST OF NEW ORLEANS movie (Be My Love)

1951—RICH, YOUNG AND PRETTY movie (Wonder Why; I Can See You; Paris; Dark Is the Night; We Never Talk Much; How D'ya Like Your Eggs in the Morning?)

1952—BECAUSE YOU'RE MINE movie (Because You're Mine); Jenny Kissed Me

1953—SMALL TOWN GIRL movie (My Flaming Heart); LATIN LOVERS movie (A Little More of Your Amor; I Had to Kiss You)

1954—THE FLAME AND THE FLESH movie (No One but You); I Just Love You; I'll Walk with God

1955—LOVE ME OR LEAVE ME movie (I'll Never Stop Loving You)

199. BROOKMEYER, BOB

v-tb p cl ar cm B

Born December 19, 1929, Kansas City, Mo.

Modern musician with mainstream roots, extremely facile and inventive on valve trombone; also capable pianist. Kansas City Conservatory of Music, then military service. Pianist with Orrin Tucker in 1950. During 1951-2 pianist with Tex Beneke, also worked with Ray McKinley, Louis Prima and Jerry Wald. Switched to slide trombone, then valve trombone in 1952 with Claude Thornhill. In 1953 with Terry Gibbs, Stan Getz, and late 1953-4 with Gerry Mulligan. Several tours abroad. Again with Mulligan in 1957, later in year own group. In early 60s co-led group with trumpet star Clark Terry. Also worked with Mulligan. Several tours abroad. Busy musician, his playing a great asset to any modern group and enlivened many a record session. Extensive record output. In late 60s and into 70s, studio work on west coast.

RECORDS

STAN GETZ

Mer 89059 Erudition/Have You Met Miss Jones?

Mer 89090 Rustic Hop/Cool Mix

BOB BROOKMEYER

PJ 625 Body and Soul/Liberty Belle

LPs

BOB BROOKMEYER
PJ(10″)PJLP-16 Bob Brookmeyer Quartet
Vik LX-1071 Brookmeyer
Mer MG-20600 Jazz Is a Kick
BOB BROOKMEYER-JIMMY GUIFFRE
WP PJ-1233 Traditionalism Revisited
BOB BROOKMEYER-BUD SHANK
PJ(10″)PJLP-20 Bud Shank & Bob Brookmeyer
BOB BROOKMEYER-CLARK TERRY
Mainstream 56043 "Tonight"
BOB BROOKMEYER-ZOOT SIMS
UA 4023 Stretching Out
Story STLP-914 Whooeeee
ZOOT SIMS
Seeco CELP-452 The Art of Jazz
AL COHN
Cor CRL-57118 Al Cohn Quintet
CHET BAKER
PJ(10″)PJLP-15 Chet Baker Sextet
MANNY ALBAM
Vi LPM-1211 The Jazz Workshop
Dot DLP-9004 Jazz New York
Cor CRL-57173 The Jazz Charts of Our Time, Vol. 1
WOODY HERMAN
Everest SDBR-1003 The Herd Rides Again ... In Stereo
RUBY BRAFF
UA 3045 Blowing Around the World
GERRY MULLIGAN
EmArcy MG-36056 Presenting the Gerry Mulligan Sextet
EmArcy MG-36101 Mainstream of Jazz
THAD JONES-MEL LEWIS
Solid State 17003 The Jazz Orchestra

200. BROOKS, NORMAN   vo
(NORMAN JOSEPH ARIE)
Born c. 1928, Canada

Singer noted for voice similar to Al Jolson's. Good entertainer with strong presentation on stage. Grew up in Montreal. In late 40s formed singing act with his sister, played Canadian night clubs. Brooks later became M.C.-singer at Toronto's Casino Theatre. Uncanny Jolson-type voice and style attracted notices, especially on U.S. TV shows in 1950. Brooks stated he sang naturally, did not

try to imitate Jolson. Returned to Canada, had own radio show. Further engagements in U.S. led to recording here. Zodiac label formed to present him on first record hit *Hello Sunshine*. Further records popular. Busy in U.S. in early and mid-50s in night clubs and theatres. Some TV work. Portrayed Jolson in 1956 movie THE BEST THINGS IN LIFE ARE FREE (bit role). Career waned by 60s but continued to play U.S. clubs; popular at Beachcomber in Miami Beach. Mostly active in Canada during later years.

RECORDS

NORMAN BROOKS
Zod 101 Hello Sunshine/You're My Baby
Zod 102 Somebody Wonderful/You Shouldn't Have Kissed Me the First Time
Zod 103 A Sky-Blue Shirt and a Rainbow Tie/This Waltz with You
Zod 104 I'm Kinda Crazy/I'd Like to Be in Your Shoes, Baby
Zod 106 I Can't Give You Anything but Love
Zod 107 Candy Moon/3-D Sweetie
Zod 109 Back in Circulation/Lou-Lou-Louisiana
"X"-0125 Heart/Too Many Heartaches
"X"-0157 If I Had Two Hearts/Lovely Girl
"X"-0179 Goodbye, Gal, Goodbye/Way-Way-Te-Nan-Go
Jamie 1042 I'm Never Satisfied/Two Lovely Blue Eyes
Vi (Can)56-5330 Rockabye Your Baby with a Dixie Melody/April Showers
Vi (Can)56-5365 My Blue Heaven/Toot Toot Tootsie

LPs

NORMAN BROOKS
Spin-O-Rama 3051 Al Jolson Sung by Norman Brooks
Coronet CX-45 The Songs of Al Jolson
Diplomat 2238 Norman Brooks Sings Al Jolson
Verve MGV-2091 I'm Sitting on Top of the World
Promenade 2128 Sings a Musical Tribute to George M. Cohan
Sutton 242 Jolie Was His Name

201. BROOKS, RANDY   t B

Born March 28, 1917
Died March 21, 1967, Springfield,
Maine, in fire

Dynamic trumpet soloist and lead man of 40s. Led good, short-lived big band. Brooks in prime had range and power, rich full tone: ideal lead trumpeter. Rather a child prodigy, at 6 playing trumpet in Salvation Army band. As youngster with Rudy Vallee about two years in early 30s, left to finish high school. With Ruby Newman awhile. Joined Hal Kemp mid-1939, won praise for trumpet work. Remained through Kemp's death in late 1940 and for a time when Art Jarrett took over band. Former Kemp singer Bob Allen led band in early 40s with Brooks as lead trumpet and musical director. In 1943-4 with Les Brown. Own band in 1945, with beautiful arrangements by John Brooks (not related). Band had long run at New York's Roseland for much of 1945. Despite excellent musicianship and Randy's trumpet, band failed to attain much popularity. Brooks disbanded, organized new band in 1949. Suffered stroke in 1950 that ended musical career, later died in fire in Maine home in 1967. Once married to bandleader Ina Ray Hutton.

RECORDS

RANDY BROOKS
    De 18697 Land of the Loon/I'd Do It All Over Again
    De 18752 In the Moon Mist/Don't Let Me Dream
    De 18874 Without You/Strange Love
    De 18897 Surrender/One Love
    De 23869 Tippin' In/After Hours
    De 23935 Harlem Nocturne/A Night at the Three Deuces
    VD(12″)523 To Beat or Not to Beat
    VD(12″)903 A Night at the Three Deuces
(with MARION HUTTON)
    De 18703 I'm Gonna Love That Guy/ No More Toujours L'Amour
(with ELLA FITZGERALD)
    De 18713 A Kiss Goodnight/Benny's Coming Home Saturday
LPs
RANDY BROOKS
    De DL-8201 Trumpet Moods

    FTR 1511 Randy Brooks & His Orchestra

202. BROOKS, SHELTON   p vo cm lyr

Born May 4, 1886, Amesburg, Ontario,
Canada, of Indian-Negro parents

Entertainer during long career, composer of two all-time popular songs, *Some of These Days* (1910) and *Darktown Strutters' Ball* (1910). Grew up in Detroit. Early in career worked as pianist in Detroit cafes, later in Chicago spots. Played ragtime piano style, around 1909 began composing ragtime numbers. Active career in vaudeville in U. S., Canada and England. Good entertainer with humorous style, adept at mimicry, often imitated Bert Williams. Wrote material for Nora Bayes, Al Jolson, Sophie Tucker. Roles in stage shows PLANTATION (1922), DIXIE TO BROADWAY (1924), KEN MURRAY'S BLACKOUTS OF 1949. In 50s less active in show business. Other compositions: *Honey Gal, You Ain't Talking to Me, There'll Come a Time, All Night Long, Walkin' the Dog, If I Were a Bee and You Were a Red Red Rose, Jean.*

RECORDS

(mostly of humorous nature, some billed as Shelton Brooks & Company)

SHELTON BROOKS
    OK 4428 Darktown Court Room
    OK 4682 Collecting Rents/Chicken Thieves
    OK 40137 Buddies/The Old Veterans
    OK 40232 You Got to Go/That's Enough
    OK 40334 Lodge Meeting/The Barber Shop Four
    OK 40385 Work Don't Bother Me/ The Spiritualist
    OK 40528 New Professor/Jailbirds
    OK 40605 The Fortune Teller/Domestic Troubles
    OK 40697 When You're Really Blue/I Am One Sick Man

203. BROONZY, BIG BILL   vo g v cm
(WILLIAM LEE CONLEY BROONZY)

Born June 26, 1893, Scott, Miss.
Died August 14, 1958, Chicago, Ill.

Generally considered best of early male blues singers, kept on singing into modern times. Strong voice and forceful timing. Composed many of songs he performed. Grew up in Arkansas. Military service, World War I. In 1919-20 first important job playing violin in Little Rock. Worked at railroad yard in Chicago in early 20s. In 1924 resumed music career as a sideline, changed to guitar, began to sing the blues. In a few years was working with leading jazzmen and blues singers. In early 30s began recording extensively under name of Big Bill, and through the years his blues records were many and popular. Played Chicago theatres in early 30s. Did nonmusical work in periods between music jobs. In late 30s critic John Hammond helped him obtain New York appearances and some recognition. In 40s Broonzy continued singing, touring, recording. In 50s helped by folk revival, toured Europe, enjoyed rather good LP sales. Favorite accompanying pianists Blind John Davis and Joshua Altheimer.

RECORDS

CRIPPLE CLARENCE LOFTON
   Vo 02951 Monkey Man Blues
   Me 61166 You Done Tore Your Playhouse Down
PETER CHATMAN
   Bb 8945 Whiskey and Gin Blues/You Gonna Worry Too
GEORGIA TOM DORSEY
   Pe 149 Six Shooter Blues/Pig Meat Strut
   Pe 163 My Texas Blues/Broke Man Blues
   Ch 16360 Don't Leave Me Blues
STATE STREET BOYS
   OK 8964 Crazy About You/Midnight Special
   OK 8965 Sweet to Mama/The Dozen
HAM GRAVY (Washboard Sam)
   Vo 03275 Mama Don't Allow It (No. 1)/Who Pumped the Wind in My Doughnut?
   Vo 03375 Jesse James Blues/Mama Don't Allow It (No. 2)
LIL GREEN
   Bb 8464 Cherry Tree Blues/Just Rockin'
   Bb 8524 Romance in the Dark/What Have I Done?

BIG BILL (BROONZY)
   Bb 5535 Mississippi River Blues/Friendless Blues
   Bb 5706 Starvation Blues/Hungry Man Blues
   Bb 5998 Southern Blues/Good Jelly
   Bb 6060 Mountain Blues/Bad Luck Blues
   Pe 0313 C.C. Rider/Prowlin' Ground Hog
   Pe 0335 Hobo Blues/I Wanta See My Baby Cry
   Me 12570 Bull Cow Blues/Too Too Train Blues
   Me 60355 Bricks in My Pillow/Ash Hauler
   Me 60556 Match Box Blues/Big Bill Blues
   Me 70354 Cherry Hill/Seven-Eleven
   Ba 32436 How You Want It Done?/M & O Blues
   Vo 04280 It's Your Time Now/The Mill Man Blues
   Vo 04706 Just a Dream/Baby, I Done Got Wise
   Vo 05259 My Last Goodbye to You/Just a Dream (No. 2)
   Vo 05452 Plow Hand Blues/Looking for My Baby
   OK 05698 Looking Up at Down/Lone Wolf Blues
   OK 06242 Key to the Highway/Green Grass Blues
   Mer 8284 Moppers Blues/I Know She Will
   Mer 70039 South Bound Train/Leavin' Day
   Co 30010 I'm Gonna Move to the Outskirts of Town/Hard Hearted Woman
   Co 30109 San Antonio Blues/Just Rocking

LPs

BIG BILL BROONZY
   Folk FA-2326 Sings Country Blues
   Folk FG-3586 Big Bill Broonzy
   Period(10")SPL-1114 (recorded in Paris)
   Epic EE-22017 Big Bill's Blues (RIs)
   EmArcy MG-36137 The Blues
   Archive FS-213
BIG BILL BROONZY-PETE SEEGER
   Verve Folkways VLP-5006 In Concert

204. BROWN, CLIFFORD   tp ar B

Born October 30, 1930, Wilmington, Del.

Died June 26, 1956, in auto accident

Great young trumpet star of modern school whose career cut short by fatal auto accident. Good tone and taste, fresh ideas, somewhat in style of earlier trumpet great Fats Navarro. Early jobs in Philadelphia area at 17. Attended Maryland State College in 1949. Auto accident kept him out of music about a year. Sidetracked into rhythm and blues field awhile. This period included stint with Chris Powell 1952-3. With Lionel Hampton in later 1953 (including European tour), but little chance to star. Career accelerated when joined drummer Max Roach as co-leader of combo. Acclaimed by fans and critics, hailed as the coming big trumpet star. Early death shocked jazz world, but his reputation endures.

RECORDS
(All LPs)

CLIFFORD BROWN
BN(10")BLP-5032
Jazztone J-1281 Jazz Messages
Mer MG-20827 Remember Clifford
EmArcy MG-36102 Clifford Brown All-Stars

CLIFFORD BROWN-MAX ROACH
EmArcy MG-36070 At Basin Street

CLIFFORD BROWN-ART FARMER
Pres(10")PRLP-167

CLIFFORD BROWN-GIGI GRYCE
BN(10")BLP-5048 (Paris session)

ART BLAKEY
BN 1521 A Night at Birdland, Vol. 1
BN 1522 A Night at Birdland, Vol. 2

ALL-STARS
EmArcy MG-36039 Best Coast Jazz

BOB GORDON-CLIFFORD BROWN
PJ 1214 Arranged by Montrose

DINAH WASHINGTON
EmArcy MG-36000

205. BROWN, LAWRENCE   tb

Born August 3, 1905, Lawrence, Kansas

Featured trombone soloist with Duke Ellington many years, 1932-51 and later in 60s. Known for smooth, warm, melodious style and ability to swing. Extensive recording career with Ellington and with Duke's other star sidemen. Educated on west coast. In addition to trombone, studied piano, violin, tuba and alto sax. Began professional career with various bands on west coast. Worked often with Paul Howard 1927-30 and Les Hite 1930-1. Joined Ellington in early 1932, left to work with Johnny Hodges 1951-5. Freelanced in late 50s, did studio work. In 1960 rejoined Ellington, remained through 60s with intervals away. Busy recording schedule in addition to work with Ellington. Active into 70s.

RECORDS

PAUL HOWARD
Vi 23354 California Swing/Harlem
Vi 23420 Cuttin' Up/Get Ready Blues

LOUIS ARMSTRONG
OK 41422 I'm a Ding Dong Daddy/ I'm in the Market for You

DUKE ELLINGTON
Vi 24521 Stompy Jones
Br 6336 The Sheik of Araby
Br 6432 Ducky Wucky
Br 7752 Yearning for Love (Lawrence's Concerto)
Br 8099 Braggin' in Brass
Br 8186 Rose of the Rio Grande
Br 8204 Lambeth Walk
Co 35291 Little Posey
Vi 27235 Across the Track Blues
Co 38236 Golden Cress

JOHNNY HODGES
Vo 4115 Jeep's Blues
Vo 4335 Swingin' in the Dell
Bb 11021 Day Dream/Junior Hop
Bb 11117 Good Queen Bess/That's the Blues Old Man
Clef 89035 Latino/Through for the Night

REX STEWART
Va 517 Lazy Man's Shuffle
Bb 11057 Linger Awhile
HRS 2005 Solid Rock/Bugle Call Rag
Key(12")1306 Swamp Mist/I'm True to You
Key(12")1307 Zaza/The Little Goose
Cap 48014 'Tain't Like That

JIMMY JONES
HRS 1015 Departure from Dixie

LIONEL HAMPTON
Vi 25575 Buzzin' 'Round with the Bee/Whoa Babe
Vi 25601 Stompology
Vi 26304 Memories of You/The Jumpin' Jive
COOTIE WILLIAMS
Vo 3960 Have a Heart/Echoes of Harlem

LPs

LAWRENCE BROWN
Clef MGC-682 Slide Trombone Featuring Lawrence Brown
Verve V-8067 Slide Trombone
DUKE ELLINGTON
Co C3L27 (3-LP set) The Ellington Era (1927-40 RIs)
Vi LPT-1004 Duke Ellington's Greatest (Vi RIs)
Vi LPV-517 Jumpin' Punkins (Vi RIs)
DUKE ELLINGTON-COUNT BASIE
Co CL-1715 First Time! The Count Meets the Duke
JOHNNY HODGES
Epic LN-3105 Hodge Podge (Vo RIs)
Verve V-8150 Used to Be Duke
Mer(10")MGC-11 Johnny Hodges Collates
REX STEWART
"X"(10")LX-3001 (Bb RIs)
(one side) Jazztone J-1250 Dedicated Jazz
JIMMY RUSHING
Vang VRS-8508 Listen to the Blues

206. BROWN, LES   cl as ts ar cm B
Born March 14, 1912, Reinerton, Pa.

Noted leader of a top dance band from late 30s into 70s, working steadily despite decline of big bands in last decade. Rare solos with band in early days displayed pinch-toned clarinet with jazz feel. Educated at Ithaca College, New York Military Academy and Duke University. Musical start leading dance band at latter school in 1935-6, the Duke Blue Devils; played sax-clarinet and arranged for band. Band played summer 1936 at Budd Lake, N. J., recorded for Decca in fall, broke up early 1937. Brown went to New York, made modest living writing arrangements for publishers and bands, roomed with arranger Glenn Osser. Ar-

ranged for Ruby Newman, Isham Jones, Jimmy Dorsey, Red Nichols, Larry Clinton.

In late 1938 Brown formed big band, played New York's Hotel Edison and made records for Bluebird. Clean-cut, hard-swinging crew with good arrangements by Brown. Featured Herb Muse and Miriam Shaw on vocals. Good engagement at New York World's Fair in 1939. Featured clarinetist Abe Most in early 40s, trumpet star Billy Butterfield briefly, vocalists Betty Bonney, Ralph Young, Doris Day and saxman-novelty singer Butch Stone (who remained band stalwart through the years). 1941 record hit in *Joltin' Joe DiMaggio*. In 1944 recorded all-time hit *Sentimental Journey*. Both composed and arranged by Ben Homer. Joe Petrone another arranger for band. Brown adapted to new progressive sound in late 40s but never had far-out style, so band retained wide following. Arranger Frank Comstock mainly responsible for modern style of band; Skip Martin another arranger. Good soloists in these years and into 50s Ted Nash (ts), Dave Pell (ts, cl), Geoff Clarkson (p), Ray Sims (tb), Ronnie Lang (as), Don Fagerquist (t). Lucy Ann Polk vocalist for a time.

In 1947 band began long association with Bob Hope which continued into 70s. Based in California, band worked on Hope's radio and TV shows, went on overseas tours with Hope to entertain servicemen. Bandsmen also had opportunity to do studio work and freelance recording. Brown recorded steadily, in 1948 had an all-time instrumental hit record, *I've Got My Love to Keep Me Warm*, great arrangement by Skip Martin. In late 50s band on Steve Allen's Sunday night TV show several years, providing excellent backing. Trademark: band's excellent playing of Allen's swinging theme, *This Could Be the Start of Something Big*.

Band never achieved first-rank popularity but, building over the decades, became something of an institution. Always maintained high level of musicianship and kept up with changing styles. One of few bands to survive decline of big bands. After early days Brown seldom played with band but became pleasant, gracious front man adept at directing stage presentations. Band used several theme songs: *Dance of the Blue Devils, Evening Star, Sophisticated Swing,* finally its well-known *Leap Frog.* Band tag line: Les Brown and His Band of Renown. Brown composer or co-composer of songs and instrumentals: *Dance of the Blue Devils, Trylon Stomp, Duckfoot Waddle, Plumber's Revenge, My Number One Dream Came True, Bill's Well, Bill's Ill, We Wish You the Merriest* and hit song *Sentimental Journey.*

RECORDS

LES BROWN

De 991 Swing for Sale/Papa Tree-Top Tall

De 1231 (theme) Dance of the Blue Devils/Swamp Fire

De 1296 Don't You Care What Anyone Says/Ramona

Bb 7858 Star Dust/Boogie Woogie

Bb 10017 This Can't Be Love/Sing for Your Supper

Bb 10161 Don't Worry 'Bout Me/ What Goes Up Must Come Down

Bb 10174 Plumber's Revenge/Duck Foot Waddle

Bb 10314 Trylon Stomp/Perisphere Shuffle

Bb 10381 Makin' Whoopee/Scissors and Knives to Grind

OK 6367 City Called Heaven/It's You Again

OK 6377 Joltin' Joe DiMaggio/The Nickel Serenade

OK 6430 'Tis Autumn/That Solid Old Man

OK 6633 (theme) Evening Star

OK 6696 Mexican Hat Dance/When the Lights Go On Again

Co 36688 A Good Man Is Hard to Find/Bizet Has His Day

Co 36763 Robin Hood/Sleigh Ride in July

Co 36769 Sentimental Journey/Twilight Time

Co 36857 (theme) Leap Frog/Show Me the Way to Go Home

Co 37061 Lover's Leap/High on a Windy Trumpet

Co 38324 I've Got My Love to Keep Me Warm/I'm a-Tellin' You, Sam

Co 38616 Tenderly/Where Are You?

Co 38878 A Foggy Day/Drifting and Dreaming

Cor 60424 Blue Moon/Red Sails in the Sunset

Cor 60583 An American in Paris (1 & 2)

Cor 60918 Ramona/Montoona Clipper

Cor 60959 Midnight Sun/Ruby

LPs

LES BROWN

Co CL-649 Sentimental Journey (Co RIs)

Co CL-1594 Plays Lerner & Loewe

Co(10″)CL-6123 Your Dance Date with Les Brown

Ha HL-7100 The Greatest (Co RIs)

Cor CRL-57030 That Sound of Renown

Cor CRL-57311 Jazz Song Book

Cor CX-1 (2-LP set) Les Brown: Concert at the Palladium

Cor(10″)CRL-56046 You're My Everything

De DL-4607 Les Brown's in Town (Glenn Osser arrangements)

Cap T-1174 The Les Brown Story

207. BROWN, LEW   lyr

Born December 10, 1893, Odessa, Russia
Died February 5, 1958, New York, N.Y.

Lyricist member of famed songwriting team of Henderson-DeSylva-Brown of 20s and 30s. Collaborated with other composers before and after this period to amass array of song hits. Parents brought him to U.S. at 5. As teenager began trying to write lyrics and parodies. Collaborated with veteran composer Albert Von Tilzer for first success, 1912 hit *I'm the Lonesomest Gal in Town.* In ensuing years enjoyed success as lyricist, collaborating with Von Tilzer and others. Began working with composer Ray Henderson in 1922; in 1925 duo joined by lyricist Buddy DeSylva to score for Broadway show GEORGE WHITE'S SCANDALS. Team remained together to produce outstanding body of song hits in 20s and into 1931.

(See biography herein on HENDERSON-DESYLVA-BROWN for details and song listings of songwriting team's career.)

Brown and Henderson continued together several years. Broadway shows GEORGE WHITE'S SCANDALS OF 1931, HOT-CHA (1932), STRIKE ME PINK (1933). Brown teamed with other composers during 30s, mostly for movies. By 40s activities ebbed. Writer-director of his last Broadway show CRAZY WITH THE HEAT in 1941. Other collaborators included Con Conrad, Moe Jaffe, Sidney Clare, Harry Warren, Cliff Friend, Harry Akst, Jay Gorney, Louis Alter, Harold Arlen, Sammy Fain, Sam H. Stept, Charles Tobias.

SONGS
(with related shows—excluding works of Henderson-DeSylva-Brown)

1912—I'm the Lonesomest Gal in Town; Parisienne; Kentucky Sue; Please Don't Take My Lovin' Man Away

1916—If You Were the Only Girl

1917—Give Me the Moonlight, Give Me the Girl

1918—I May Be Gone for a Long Long Time

1919—LINGER LONGER LETTY stage show (Oh, By Jingo); Wait Till You Get Them Up in the Air, Boys

1920—Chili Bean; I Used to Love You

1921—Dapper Dan

1922—GREENWICH VILLAGE FOLLIES OF 1922 stage show (Georgette)

1923—Ain't You Ashamed?; Last Night on the Back Porch; Annabelle

1924—Shine; Why Did I Kiss That Girl?

1925—Don't Bring Lulu; Then I'll Be Happy; If You Hadn't Gone Away

1926—I'd Climb the Highest Mountain; I'm Tellin' the Birds, I'm Tellin' the Bees

1927—One Sweet Letter from You; PIGGY stage show (songs unimportant)

1925-31 (see HENDERSON-DESYLVA-BROWN)

1931—GEORGE WHITE'S SCANDALS OF 1931 stage show (My Song; The Thrill Is Gone; That's Why Darkies Were Born; Life Is Just a Bowl of Cherries; This Is the Missus)

1932—HOT-CHA stage show (There I Go Dreaming Again; You Can Make My Life a Bed of Roses; Conchita;

There's Nothing the Matter with Me)

1933—STRIKE ME PINK stage show (Strike Me Pink; Let's Call It a Day: Love and Rhythm; Restless; It's Great to Be Alive); I May Be Dancing with Somebody Else; I've Got to Pass Your House

1934—CALLING ALL STARS stage show (I'd Like to Dunk You in My Coffee; If It's Love; Just Mention Joe; Stepping Out of the Picture; I Don't Want to Be President); STAND UP AND CHEER movie (Stand Up and Cheer; Baby, Take a Bow; This Is Our Last Night Together; Broadway's Gone Hill Billy; We're Out of the Red; I'm Laughin'; She's 'Way Up Thar)

1936—THE MUSIC GOES 'ROUND movie (Taking Care of You; Suzannah; Rolling Along; There'll Be No South; Life Begins When You're in Love); STRIKE ME PINK movie (new songs: The Lady Dances; Shake It Off; Wind Up with Me; First You Have Me High; Calabash Pipe)

1937—NEW FACES OF 1937 movie (Our Penthouse on Third Avenue; Love Is Never Out of Season; It Goes to Your Feet); VOGUES OF 1938 movie (That Old Feeling)

1938—STRAIGHT, PLACE AND SHOW movie (Why Not String Along with Me?; With You on My Mind); Oh, Ma-Ma

1939—YOKEL BOY stage show (Comes Love; I Can't Afford to Dream; Let's Make Memories Tonight; A Boy Named Lem; Beer Barrel Polka)

1940—Wait Till I Catch You in My Dreams

1941—Don't Cry, Cherie

1942—PRIVATE BUCKAROO movie (Don't Sit Under the Apple Tree; That's the Moon, My Son; Johnny, Get Your Gun); YOKEL BOY movie (original stage score); I Came Here to Talk for Joe

1943—DUBARRY WAS A LADY movie (Madame, I Love Your Crepe

Suzettes); SWING FEVER movie (Mississippi Dream Boat)

1950—On the Outgoing Tide

208. BROWN, NACIO HERB   cm

Born February 22, 1896, Deming, N.M.
Died September 28, 1964, San Fran-
cisco, Calif.

Important composer for movies during early sound years and many years thereafter. Noted for 1929 score of movie BROADWAY MELODY and other movie songs: *Chant of the Jungle, Pagan Love Song, Singin' in the Rain.* Other leading songs: *Doll Dance, Should I?, Paradise, You're an Old Smoothie, Temptation, All I Do Is Dream of You, Alone, Broadway Rhythm, You Are My Lucky Star.* Grew up in Los Angeles. Learned to play piano early, made tour as accompanist. Then set up tailoring business patronized by movie colony, also worked as realtor. Tried composing, had early successes in *Coral Sea* (1920) and *When Buddha Smiles* (1921). Further successes scarce until 1929 when became a top composer in early movie musicals. Several songs for only Broadway musical TAKE A CHANCE in 1932. Producer of some movies. Activities lessened in 40s but continued some writing into 50s. Chief collaborator during career was lyricist Arthur Freed. Others included Buddy DeSylva, Gus Kahn, Leo Robin, Gordon Clifford.

SONGS
(with related shows)

1920—Coral Sea
1921—When Buddha Smiles
1927—Doll Dance
1928—Avalon Town; Rag Doll
1929—BROADWAY MELODY movie (Broadway Melody; You Were Meant for Me; Wedding of the Painted Doll; Love Boat; Harmony Babies from Melody Lane; Boy Friend); HOLLYWOOD REVUE OF 1929 movie (Singin' in the Rain); MARIANNE movie (Blondy); UNTAMED movie (Chant of the Jungle); THE PAGAN movie (Pagan Love Song)
1930—MONTANA MOON movie (The Moon Is Low; Montana Call; Sing a Song of Old Montana; Happy Cowboy); LORD BYRON OF BROADWAY movie (Should I?; The Woman in the Shoe; Only Love Is Real; A Bundle of Old Love Letters); WHOOPEE movie (I'll Still Belong to You)
1932—A WOMAN COMMANDS movie (Paradise); TAKE A CHANCE stage show (Eadie Was a Lady; Turn Out the Lights; You're An Old Smoothie)
1933—THE BARBARIAN movie (Love Songs of the Nile); GOING HOLLYWOOD movie (After Sundown; Temptation; Beautiful Girl; Our Big Love Scene; We'll Make Hay While the Sun Shines; Cinderella's Fella); HOLD YOUR MAN movie (title song)
1934—SADIE MCKEE movie (All I Do Is Dream of You); HOLLYWOOD PARTY movie (Hot Chocolate Soldiers); STUDENT TOUR movie (From Now On; A New Moon Is Over My Shoulder; American Bolero)
1935—A NIGHT AT THE OPERA movie (Alone); BROADWAY MELODY OF 1936 movie (You Are My Lucky Star; Broadway Rhythm; I've Got a Feelin' You're Foolin'; On a Sunday Afternoon; Sing Before Breakfast); CHINA SEAS movie (title song)
1936—SAN FRANCISCO movie (Would You?); THE DEVIL IS A SISSY movie (Say Ah!)
1937—BROADWAY MELODY OF 1938 movie (Yours and Mine; I'm Feelin' Like a Million; Sun Showers; Everybody Sing; Follow in My Footsteps; Your Broadway and My Broadway); AFTER THE THIN MAN movie (Smoke Dreams)
1939—BABES IN ARMS movie (Good Morning)
1940—TWO GIRLS ON BROADWAY movie (My Wonderful One, Let's Dance)
1941—ZIEGFELD GIRL movie (You Stepped Out of a Dream)
1943—WINTERTIME movie (Wintertime; Later Tonight; I Like It Here; Dancing in the Dawn; I'm All a-Twitter Over You; We Always Get Our Girl)

631

1948—THE KISSING BANDIT movie (Love Is Where You Find It; Senorita; If I Steal a Kiss; What's Wrong with Me?); ON AN ISLAND WITH YOU movie (On an Island with You; Takin' Miss Mary to the Ball; Charisse)
1952—SINGIN' IN THE RAIN movie (Make 'Em Laugh; plus many old songs including title song)

209. BROWN, PETE   as ts ss p v B
(JAMES OSTEND BROWN)

Born November 9, 1906, Baltimore, Md. Died September 20, 1963, New York, N.Y.

Alto sax jazzman prominent in 30s and 40s. Clean-cut, jocular, jumping style. Played many instruments. At 12 played violin in local theatre; various theatre jobs later. In mid-20s concentrated on alto sax and tenor sax, worked local dances with several bands. Ended up in New York in 1927, freelanced there. In 1930-7 worked mostly with Charlie Skeets and Fred Moore. With John Kirby 1937-8. Own combo and freelance recording in late 30s, most productive period. He and Frankie Newton led band in 1940, then own band 1941-3. After early 40s dropped from big time due to ill health. Continued to lead band at intervals in Chicago and New York. Active into early 60s.

RECORDS

BUSTER BAILEY
  Va 668 Afternoon in Africa/Dizzy Debutante
  Vo 4089 Planter's Punch/Sloe Jam Fizz
LEONARD FEATHER
  CMS 528 Let's Get Happy/For He's a Jolly Good Fellow
  Vo 4062 Jammin' the Waltz/Clementine
JERRY KRUGER
  Va 666 The Bed Song/So You Won't Sing
JOE MARSALA
  Gen 1717 Wandering Man Blues/Salty Mama Blues
  Gen 3001 Three O'clock Jump/Reunion in Harlem

FRANK NEWTON
  Vo 3811 You Showed Me the Way/Please Don't Talk About Me When I'm Gone
  Vo 3839 Who's Sorry Now?/The Onyx Hop
  Va 616 Easy Living/Where or When
  Bb 10176 Rosetta/The World Is Waiting for the Sunrise
  Bb 10186 Minor Jive/Rompin'
  Bb 10216 Who?/The Blues My Baby Gave to Me
SEXTET OF RHYTHM CLUB OF LONDON
  Bb 10529 Calling All Bars/Mighty Like the Blues
  Bb 10557 You Gave Me the Go-By/Why Didn't William Tell?
WILLIE "THE LION" SMITH
  De 1380 The Old Stamping-Ground/Get Acquainted with Yourself
MIDGE WILLIAMS
  Vo 04026 Love Is Like Whiskey/I'm in a Happy Frame of Mind
PETE BROWN
  De 18118 Tempo di Jump/Ocean Motion
  De 8613 Mound Bayou/Unlucky Woman
  Sess 12-012 Pete's Idea/Jim's Idea
  Sav 522 Bellevue for You/Pete Brown's Boogie
  Sav 579 Midnight Blues/That's It
  Key 1312 It All Depends on You/I May Be Wrong

LPs

PETE BROWN
  Beth BCP-4 (1 side) Jazz Kaleidoscope
  Beth(10")BCP-1011
SAM PRICE
  Jazztone J-1207 Barrelhouse and Blues
JONAH JONES
  Baronet B-103 Trumpet on Tour
WILLIE "THE LION" SMITH
  Ace of Hearts (E)AH-162 The Swinging Cub Men (De RIs)
(miscellaneous artists)
  Verve MGV-8240 At Newport
  Vi LPV-578 Swing, Vol.1 (Vi, Bb RIs)
  EmArcy MG-36018 Alto Altitude

210. BROWN, RAY   b cel
Born October 13, 1926, Pittsburgh, Pa.

A foremost bass man from late 40s into 70s. Strong and beautiful tone. Good knowledge of harmonics, with ability to play jazz solos. Active mostly in modern jazz groups. Gained early experience playing locally, then went to New York in 1945. Early work with Dizzy Gillespie, both in small combo and big band. Own trio at times in late 40s. Accompanied wife Ella Fitzgerald on jobs, including Jazz at the Philharmonic tours. Continued these tours in early 50s with Oscar Peterson trio, joining Peterson in 1951 and remaining through 1965. Took up cello around 1960. Devised cello easier for jazzmen to play, with finger board and tuning similar to bass and with special strings. Settled in California, active in studio work and freelance recording. Late 60s in TV bands, seen often and occasionally featured on Joey Bishop's late-night show. Active into 70s.

RECORDS

DIZZY GILLESPIE
    Vi 40-0130 Night in Tunisia / 52nd Street Theme
    Vi 40-0132 Anthropology/Ol' Man Rebop
    Manor 5000 Salted Peanuts/Be-Bop
    Mus 399 Our Delight/Good Dues Blues
    Mus 404 One Bass Hit (1 & 2)
    Mus 487 Ray's Idea/He Beeped When He Shoulda Bopped

OSCAR PETERSON
    Mer 8959 Love for Sale/Until the Real Thing Comes Along
    Clef 89113 It's Easy to Remember/ Pooper

BUD POWELL
    Mer 11069 Tea for Two/Hallelujah

FLIP PHILLIPS
    Mer 89022 Cottontail/Blues for the Midgets

MILT JACKSON
    DeeGee 3700 Between the Devil and the Deep Blue Sea/Milt Meets Sid

BEN WEBSTER
    Norg 103 That's All/Jive at Six

BILLIE HOLIDAY
    Clef 89108 If the Moon Turns Green/ Autumn in New York

BENNY CARTER
    Norg 111 Gone with the Wind/I've Got the World on a String

ROY ELDRIDGE
    Clef 89110 Willow Weep for Me/ Somebody Loves Me
    Clef 89123 I Can't Get Started/When Your Lover Has Gone

RAY BROWN
    Sav 976 For Hecklers Only
    Mer 8936 Blue Lou/Song of the Volga Boatmen

LPs

RAY BROWN
    Verve MGV-8022 Bass Hit!
    Verve MGV-8290 This Is Ray Brown
    Verve MGV-8390 Jazz Cello
    Verve MGV-8444 With the All-Star Big Band

OSCAR PETERSON
    Verve V-8660 Put on a Happy Face
    Verve V-8681 Something Warm
    Clef MGC-648
    Clef MGC-649
    Clef MGC-650

DIZZY GILLESPIE
    Vi LPM-2398 The Greatest of Dizzy Gillespie (Vi RIs)

BARNEY KESSEL
    Contemp C-3535 The Poll Winners

FRED ASTAIRE
    Mer 1001-2-3-4 (4-LP set) The Fred Astaire Story

FLIP PHILLIPS
    Clef MGC-637 The Flip Phillips Quintet

BLOSSOM DEARIE
    Verve MGV-2037

BUD POWELL
    Verve VSP-37 This Was Bud Powell (1949-56 RIs)

MILT JACKSON
    Impulse 9189 That's the Way It Is

211. BROWN, VERNON   tb B
Born January 6, 1907, Venice, Ill.

Jazz trombonist from mid-20s into 70s. Grew up in East St. Louis, worked with Frankie Trumbauer in St. Louis in mid-20s. Freelanced in Chicago; with Jean Goldkette in 1928. Early 30s with Joe Gill and Benny Meroff. Later freelanced in New York, active in record sessions. Benny Goodman late 1937 to mid-1940, then to Artie Shaw. Left Shaw for brief period with Jan Savitt in early 1941. With Muggsy Spanier's big band 1941-2. Long period of radio studio work in New York in 40s, recorded and played jobs with Goodman in mid-1944. Own band in Seattle in early 50s. Resumed studio work in New York radio and TV in 50s and 60s. Worked with Goodman again in late 1954 and mid-1958 (including European tour). Sideman with Ringling Brothers circus band in New York, early 70s.

RECORDS

BENNY GOODMAN
  Vi 25792 One O'clock Jump/Don't Be That Way
  Vi 25808 Oh Boom!
  Vi 25827 Lullaby in Rhythm
  Vi 25867 Saving Myself for You
EDDIE CONDON
  CMS 515 Sunday/California, Here I Come
HARRY JAMES
  Br 8055 One O'clock Jump/It's the Dreamer in Me
  Br 8067 Texas Chatter/Song of the Wanderer
  Br 8136 Lullaby in Rhythm/Out of Nowhere
  Br 8178 Little White Lies/Wrap Your Troubles in Dreams
RED MCKENZIE
  Vo 3875 Farewell, My Love/Sail Along, Silvery Moon
  Vo 3898 Georgianna/You're Out of This World
PHIL NAPOLEON
  Swan 7511 Sensation Rag/South Rampart Street Parade
  Swan 7512 Livery Stable Blues/That's a-Plenty
  Swan 7513 Bugle Call Rag/Satanic Blues
UNA MAE CARLISLE
  Bea 7174 Teasing Me/You and Your Heart of Stone
  Bea 7175 You're Gonna Change Your Mind
COZY COLE
  Key 656 They Didn't Believe Me
WILD BILL DAVISON
  CMS 563 Confessin'/Big Butter and Egg Man
BUD FREEMAN
  Key 636 Midnight at Eddie Condon's
  Key 638 Inside on the Southside/Town Hall Blues

BOBBY HACKETT
  Melrose 1401 Pennies from Heaven/Rose of the Rio Grande
GEORGE HARTMAN
  Key 613 Always/Darktown Strutters' Ball
  Key 627 Angry/Hindustan

LPs

BUD FREEMAN
  EmArcy MG-36013 Midnight at Eddie Condon's
MEL POWELL
  Co CL-557 Jam Session at Carnegie Hall
BENNY GOODMAN
  Vi LPT-6703 (5-LP set) The Golden Age of Swing (Vi RIs)

212. BRUBECK, DAVE   p ar cm B
Born December 6, 1920, Concord, Calif.

Avant-garde pianist who led a most successful jazz quartet from early 50s into 70s. Known for unorthodox modernistic chords and dynamics. Built solos to rousing climaxes. Used fugue-like patterns with star altoist Paul Desmond. At early age played locally in various types of bands. Attended College of Pacific and Mills College. Military service, World War II. After release led octet, then trio in late 40s without much success. In mid-1951 formed quartet featuring Desmond, quickly hit big. Brubeck and the brilliant Desmond worked together with great rapport, their music tasteful and exciting. Busy recording schedule plus many clubs, festivals and college concerts. Rated top combo of 50s, continued active in 60s. Desmond left group at intervals in 60s and Brubeck worked with various combinations of sidemen, including clarinetist Bill Smith and baritone saxist Gerry Mulligan. Brubeck maintained active schedule as combo leader-soloist-lecturer. Numerous overseas tours during 60s. Jazz works published in series of books.

RECORDS

DAVE BRUBECK OCTET
  Fan 509 The Way You Look Tonight/Love Walked In
DAVE BRUBECK QUARTET
  Fan 517 Crazy Chris/Somebody Loves Me

Fan 520 Frenesi/At a Perfume Counter

Fan 521 Look for the Silver Lining/ This Can't Be Love

Fan 523 Just One of Those Things/My Romance (piano solo)

Fan 527 I May Be Wrong/On a Little Street in Singapore

LPs

DAVE BRUBECK QUARTET

Fan(10″)5,7,8,11,13

Co CL-566 Jazz Goes to College

Co CL-590 At Storyville

Co CL-622 Brubeck Time

Co CL-699 Red Hot and Cool

Co CL-1034 Jazz Goes to Junior College

Co CL-1059 Dave Digs Disney

Co CL-1249 Newport 1958

Co CL-1347 Gone with the Wind

Co CL-2602 Anything Goes

Co CS-8927 (S) Time Changes

Co CS-9012 (S) Impressions of Japan

Co CS-9284 (S) Greatest Hits

Co CS-9672 (S) Last Time We Saw Paris

Jazztone J-1272 The Best of Brubeck

DAVE BRUBECK QUINTET

Fan 3268 Re-Union

213. BRUCE, CAROL   vo

Born November 15, 1919, Great Neck, N.Y.

Excellent singer of stage, screen and radio particularly during 40s. At 17 sang with Lloyd Huntley band in Montreal, later played Canadian clubs. Joined U. S. stage show GEORGE WHITE'S SCANDALS OF 1939. Good role in popular 1940 musical LOUISIANA PURCHASE. Appeared in movies THIS WOMAN IS MINE and KEEP 'EM FLYING (1941), BEHIND THE EIGHT BALL (1942). During 40s performed on radio shows of Ben Bernie, Al Jolson, Henny Youngman. In Broadway revue NEW PRIORITIES OF 1943. In 1946 acclaimed by critics for role of Julie in revival of SHOW BOAT. In 1949 Broadway musical ALONG FIFTH AVENUE. Many club dates in 40s and 50s, stock shows, early TV. In 1961 revival of PAL JOEY, Broadway shows DO I HEAR A WALTZ? (1965) and HENRY, SWEET HENRY (1967).

RECORDS

CAROL BRUCE

De 3557 Wish Me Luck/A Nightingale Sang in Berkeley Square

De 3566 I Should Have Known You Years Ago/If I Feel This Way Tomorrow

De 18185 Misirlou/Red Moon of the "Caribbees"

De 18238 Adios/The Lamp of Memory

De 18431 A Rendezvous in Rio/My Shawl

Co 36471 You Don't Know What Love Is/The Boy with the Wistful Eyes

Sch 507 Louisiana Purchase/The Lord Done Fixed Up My Soul

Sch 510 I Gotta Right to Sing the Blues

VD(12″)87 Something for the Boys/ Abraham/Embraceable You

LPs

CAROL BRUCE

Tops L-1574 Carol Bruce

(original 1946 Broadway revival cast)

Co ML-4058 SHOW BOAT

214. BRUNIS, GEORG   tb cm B
(originally GEORGE BRUNIES)

Born February 6, 1900, New Orleans, La.

A top dixieland trombonist from early 20s into 70s. Pioneer in tailgate-style trombone. As youngster played in New Orleans street parades. Jobbed in area with various groups, worked with Leon Rappolo. Went to Chicago about 1919; period with Elmer Schoebel. In early 20s joined Friars Society Orchestra, which later took name of New Orleans Rhythm Kings. With Ted Lewis 1924-35. Toured U.S. and Europe, did extensive recording work with him. In 1935 led Mills Cavalcade Orchestra. In later 30s worked in New York with leading dixieland groups Sharkey Bonano, Louis Prima, Bobby Hackett. In 1939 with Muggsy Spanier's great combo. In early 40s mostly led own group, worked some with Art Hodes. With Lewis again 1943-46, Eddie Condon 1947-9. Then worked in Chicago with several bands, led own group there and elsewhere 1951-9. In 60s semi-retired due to illness but returned in 70s. Composed several jazz tunes, most notably *Tin Roof Blues*.

RECORDS

FRIARS SOCIETY ORCHESTRA
Ge 4966 Farewell Blues
Ge 4967 Bugle Call Blues/Discontented Blues

NEW ORLEANS RHYTHM KINGS
Ge 5104 Sweet Lovin' Man/Maple Leaf Rag
Ge 5105 That's a-Plenty/Tin Roof Blues
De 161 Tin Roof Blues/San Antonio Shout
De 162 Panama/Jazz It Blues
De 388 Dust Off That Old Pianna/ Since We Fell Out of Love
De 401 Baby Brown/No Lovers Allowed

TED LEWIS
Co 439-D Tin Roof Blues/Milenberg Joys
Co 770-D Tiger Rag/Blues My Naughty Sweetie Gave to Me
Co 1050-D Beale Street Blues/Memphis Blues
Co 1573-D Shim- Me- Sha- Wabble/ Clarinet Marmalade
Co 2113-D San/Aunt Hagar's Blues
Co 2527-D Dallas Blues/Royal Garden Blues

THE WOLVERINES
Ge 5542 Sensation/Lazy Daddy

SHARKEY BONANO
Vo 3450 Old Fashioned Swing/Big Boy Blue
Vo 3470 Swingin' on the Swanee Shore /Swing Like a Rusty Gate

EDDIE CONDON
CMS 500 Love Is Just Around the Corner/Ja-da
CMS 536 Georgia Grind/Dancing Fool

BOBBY HACKETT
Vo 4047 At the Jazz Band Ball/If Dreams Come True
Vo 4142 That Da Da Strain/You, You and Especially You

ART HODES
JR 1001 Royal Garden Blues/103rd Street Boogie

JR 1003 At the Jazz Band Ball/Farewell Blues

WINGY MANONE
Vo 3158 The Broken Record/Rhythm in My Nursery Rhymes
Vo 3192 Shoe Shine Boy/West Wind
Bb 6806 Boo-Hoo/Oh Say, Can You Swing?

MILLS CAVALCADE ORCHESTRA
Co 3066-D Rhythm Lullaby/Lovely Liza Lee

LOUIS PRIMA
Br 7394 Let's Have a Jubilee/Sing It 'Way Low Down
Br 7524 Jamaica Shout/That's Where the South Begins

MUGGSY SPANIER
Bb 10384 That Da Da Strain/Someday Sweetheart
Bb 10417 Big Butter and Egg Man/Eccentric
Bb 10518 Livery Stable Blues/At the Jazz Band Ball

GEORG BRUNIS
CMS 546 Ugle Chile/That Da Da Strain
CMS 556 Tin Roof Blues/Royal Garden Blues
CMS 606 I Used to Love You/I'm Gonna Sit Right Down and Write Myself a Letter

LPs

GEORG BRUNIS
CMS 30015 King of the Tailgate Trombone (RIs)
Maximus 2584 Have a Good Time with Big Georg Brunis
(one side) Southland 210 Dixieland All Stars

TED LEWIS
Epic LN-3170 Everybody's Happy! (Co RIs)

MUGGSY SPANIER
Vi LPM-1295 The Great 16! (Bb RIs)
Ci(10")L-423 This Is Jazz

GEORG BRUNIS with THE NEW ORLEANS RHYTHM KINGS
Riv(10")RLP-1024 (Ge RIs)

215. BRYAN, ALFRED   lyr

Born September 15, 1871, Brantford, Ontario, Canada, of American parents Died April 1, 1958, Gladstone, N.J.

Lyricist whose long career dated from

early years of century. Best-known songs: *Peg o' My Heart*; *Winter*; *Come, Josephine, in My Flying Machine*; *Blue River*; *Japansy*; *My Song of the Nile*; *Lonesome Lover*; *Puddin' Head Jones*. Wrote songs for Broadway musicals SHUBERT'S GAIETIES OF 1919, MIDNIGHT ROUNDERS OF 1920 and 1921. Songs important only in context of shows. Worked for New York publishing houses. Chief collaborators: composers Fred Fisher, George Meyer, Larry Stock. Alfred Gumble, Al Piantadosi, John Klenner.

SONGS

1904—When the Bees Are in the Hive
1906—Bonnie Jean
1907—And a Little Bit More
1908—Are You Sincere?
1909—You Taught Me to Love You, Now Teach Me to Forget
1910—Come, Josephine, in My Flying Machine; Winter; I've Got Your Number
1911—After That I Want a Little More; Bring Back My Golden Dream; If Every Hour Were a Day; Make Me Love You Like I Never Loved Before; That Was Before I Met You
1912—Big Blond Baby; When I Waltz with You
1913—Peg o' My Heart (revived 1947); Tango Town; I'm on My Way to Mandalay
1914—When It's Moonlight on the Alamo; When It's Night Time Down in Burgundy
1915—I Didn't Raise My Boy to Be a Soldier
1916—Come Back to Arizona
1917—Lorraine, My Beautiful Alsace Lorraine; Sweet Little Buttercup
1918—Madelon; Oui, Oui, Marie
1920—Beautiful Anna Bell Lee
1924—Brown Eyes, Why Are You Blue?
1926—Her Beaus Are Only Rainbows
1927—Blue River; Red Lips, Kiss My Blues Away; There's Everything Nice About You
1928—Don't Keep Me in the Dark, Bright Eyes; Japansy; My Window of Dreams
1929—DRAG movie (My Song of the

Nile); CAREERS movie (I Love You, I Hate You)
1930—PARIS movie (Miss Wonderful; Somebody Mighty Like You); Lonesome Lover
1931—Give Me Your Affection, Honey
1933—Puddin' Head Jones
1936—Wintertime Dreams

Other songs: *The Irish Were Egyptians Long Ago*; *Dream Serenade*; *Down in the Old Cherry Orehard*; *When the Harber Lights Are Burning*; *Green Fields and Bluebirds*; *Who Paid the Rent for Mrs. Rip Van Winkle?*; *The High Cost of Loving*; *Joan of Arc*; *Listen to That Jungle Band*; *Daddy, You've Been a Mother to Me*

216. BRYAN, VINCENT   lyr

Lyricist for several Broadway shows during early 1900s. Wrote *Hurray for Baffin's Bay*, big hit in show THE WIZARD OF OZ in 1903. Other leading songs: *Down Where the Wurzburger Flows*, *In the Sweet Bye and Bye*, *In My Merry Oldsmobile*. Mostly inactive in songwriting after 1911. Collaborators included composers Theodore F. Morse, Gus Edwards, Harry Von Tilzer, Manuel Klein, E. Ray Goetz, Irving Berlin.

SONGS
(with related shows)

1902—Down Where the Wurzburger Flows; In the Sweet Bye and Bye
1903—THE WIZARD OF OZ stage show (Hurray for Baffin's Bay)
1904—Down on the Brandywine
1905—FANTANA stage show (Tammany); He's Me Pal; In My Merry Oldsmobile; Napoli
1906—THE MAN FROM NOW stage show (songs unimportant); On San Francisco Bay; I'd Like to See a Little More of You
1907—He Goes to Church on Sunday
1908—THE QUEEN OF THE MOULIN ROUGE stage show (songs unimportant); SCHOOL DAYS stage show (songs unimportant); Don't Take Me Home
1909—The Cubanola Glide
1910—THE KISSING GIRL stage show (songs unimportant)
1911—ZIEGFELD FOLLIES OF 1911 stage

show (Woodman, Woodman, Spare That Tree; Epraham)

1920—AS YOU WERE stage show (songs unimportant)

1927—A NIGHT IN SPAIN stage show (Argentine; International Vamp; My Rose of Spain; Bambazoola)

217. BRYANT, WILLIE   vo B

Born August 30, 1908, New Orleans, La. Died February 9, 1964, Los Angeles, Calif.

Leader of good swing band in mid-30s. Grew up in Chicago. Singer and dancer in clubs and vaudeville from mid-20s to early 30s. Worked with Bessie Smith and Buck & Bubbles. Late 1934 led big swing band. Personnel included Ben Webster, Teddy Wilson, Cozy Cole and later Benny Carter, Taft Jordan. Band produced some memorable recordings, most with Bryant on vocals. Personnel changed, band finally broke up in late 1938. From then into early 40s Bryant worked in New York as entertainer. Served as M.C. for Apollo Theatre's popular weekly special, Amateur Night in Harlem, aired locally. USO tours in World War II. Led another band 1946-8. In late 40s and early 50s disc jockey over Harlem radio. Lived in California in late 50s and 60s, working as disc jockey and M.C.

RECORDS

WILLIE BRYANT

Vi 24847 Throwin' Stones at the Sun/ Chimes at the Meetin'

Vi 24858 A Viper's Moan/It's Over Because We're Through

Vi 25038 Rigamarole/The Sheik

Vi 25045 'Long About Midnight/Jerry the Junker

Vi 25160 Liza/Steak and Potatoes

Bb 6362 Moonrise on the Lowlands/Is It True What They Say About Dixie?

Bb 6374 Ride, Red, Ride/The Glory of Love

Bb 6435 Cross Patch/Mary Had a Little Lamb

De 1772 On the Alamo/Neglected

De 1881 You're Gonna Lose Your Gal/You'll Never Remember

Apo 364 Blues Around the Clock (1 & 2)

Apo 369 Amateur Night in Harlem/ It's Over Because We're Through

218. BUCHANAN, JACK   vo

Born 1891, Scotland Died October 13, 1957

Dancing-singing star of English stage and movies. Performed with typical English smoothness and charm. First appeared in U.S. on Broadway in ANDRE CHARLOT REVUE OF 1924 (brought over from England). Then in 1925 production of same revue. Other stage performances in WAKE UP AND DREAM (1930) and BETWEEN THE DEVIL (1938). Starred in two movie musicals in 1930, MONTE CARLO and PARIS. Starred in important 1936 English movie musical THIS'LL MAKE YOU WHISTLE. After many years performing in England, returned to U.S. for 1953 movie THE BAND WAGON.

RECORDS

GERTRUDE LAWRENCE-JACK BUCHANAN

Co 512-D A Cup of Coffee, a Sandwich and You

JACK BUCHANAN

Co 514-D Gigolette

Co(E) 484 Stand Up and Sing/Night Time

Co(E) 486 I Would If I Could/Take It or Leave It

Co(E) 1483 I Think I Can/One Good Tune Deserves Another

HMV(E) 4083 Living in Clover/Goodnight, Vienna

HMV(E) 8027 So Green/Oh! La! La!

Br(E) 2125 Everything Stops for Tea/ From One Minute to Another

Br(E) 2347 Without Rhythm/There Isn't Any Limit to My Love

JACK BUCHANAN-ELSIE RANDOLPH

Br(E) 2348 This'll Make You Whistle/I'm in a Dancing Mood

FRED ASTAIRE-JACK BUCHANAN

MGM 30795 I Guess I'll Have to Change My Plan

219. BUCK, GENE   lyr
(EDWARD EUGENE BUCK)

*Born August 8, 1885, Detroit, Mich.
Died February 25, 1957, Great Neck,
N.Y.*

Noted lyricist long associated with yearly
ZIEGFELD FOLLIES. Chief aide to Ziegfeld
through the years. Helped Ziegfeld ini-
tiate MIDNIGHT FROLICS series, pioneering
the intimate stage entertainment. Collaborated mostly with composer Dave
Stamper. Also wrote book for some of the
shows. President of ASCAP 1924-41. Educated at University of Detroit and Detroit Art School. Early in career designed
sheet music covers, a pioneer in this field.
Went to New York in 1907. Designed and
directed act for Lillian Russell. Most
songs important only in context of shows.
Best-known songs: *Daddy Has a Sweetheart and Mother Is Her Name*; *Hello,
Frisco!*; *Tulip Time*. Left Ziegfeld in 1926
to produce shows in U.S. and London.
Other collaborators: composers Rudolf
Friml, Jerome Kern, Mischa Elman, Werner Janssen, James Hanley, Raymond
Hubbell, Augustus Thomas, Victor Herbert, Louis Hirsch.

SONGS
(with related shows)

1912—ZIEGFELD FOLLIES OF 1912 stage
show (Daddy Has a Sweetheart
and Mother Is Her Name); Some
Boy
1914—ZIEGFELD FOLLIES OF 1914 stage
show; Everything Is Different
Nowadays
1915—ZIEGFELD FOLLIES OF 1915 stage
show (Hello, Frisco!)
1916—ZIEGFELD FOLLIES OF 1916 stage
show (Have a Heart; others)
1917—ZIEGFELD FOLLIES OF 1917 stage
show (songs unimportant); HAVE A
HEART stage show (title song);
Tiger Rose
1918—ZIEGFELD FOLLIES OF 1918 stage
show (Garden of My Dreams);
ZIEGFELD'S 9 O'CLOCK FROLIC stage
show
1919—ZIEGFELD FOLLIES OF 1919 stage
show (Tulip Time; Sweet Sixteen;
The World Is Going Shimmy

Mad); ZIEGFELD'S MIDNIGHT FROL-
ICS stage show (By Pigeon Post;
Shanghai; Tipperary Mary)
1920—ZIEGFELD FOLLIES OF 1920 stage
show (Sunshine and Shadows;
Any Place Would Be Wonderful
with You; When the Right One
Comes Along; The Love Boat);
ZIEGFELD GIRLS OF 1920 stage
show (songs unimportant); ZIEG-
FELD MIDNIGHT FROLIC stage show
(Shanghai; Dearest; Life Is a
Gambol)
1921—ZIEGFELD FOLLIES OF 1921 stage
show (Princess of My Dreams;
The Legend of the Golden Tree;
Bring Back My Blushing Rose;
Every Time I Hear a Band Play;
Raggedy Rag; Sally, Won't You
Come Back); ZIEGFELD'S MID-
NIGHT FROLIC stage show
1922—ZIEGFELD FOLLIES OF 1922 stage
show ('Neath the South Sea
Moon; My Rambler Rose; Throw
Me a Kiss; It's Getting Dark on
Old Broadway; Some Sweet Day)
1923—ZIEGFELD FOLLIES OF 1923 stage
show (Shake Your Feet; Glorify-
ing the Girls; Swanee River Blues;
Little Old New York; That Old
Fashioned Garden of Mine; I'd
Love to Waltz Through Life with
You; Legend of the Drums)
1924—ZIEGFELD FOLLIES OF 1924 stage
show (Lonely Little Melody; A
Night in June; You're My Happy
Ending; The Beauty Contest)
1925—ZIEGFELD FOLLIES OF 1925 stage
show (Toddle Along; Settle Down
in a One-Horse Town; Everyone
Knows What Jazz Is; I'd Like to
Corral a Gal in the Shade of the
Alamo; I'd Like to Be a Gardener
in a Garden of Girls; Ever Lovin'
Bee; Syncopating Baby; Tonde-
leyo; Eddie, Be Good; Titania)
1926—NO FOOLIN' stage show (No
Foolin'; Florida, the Moon and
You)
1927—TAKE THE AIR stage show (All I
Want Is a Lullaby; Maybe I'll
Baby You)

220. BUCKNER, MILT   p o vb ar B
Born July 10, 1915, St. Louis, Mo.

Swinging pianist and organist, pioneer in block-chord piano style. Grew up in Detroit. Studied at Detroit Institute of Arts, played in local bands. Brother Ted played alto sax. Arranging in early 30s. In Detroit through 30s. First big job with Lionel Hampton in late 1941 as pianist; became chief arranger. Arranged many of Hampton's featured swing numbers, including many versions of *Flying Home*. Other arrangements of note: *The Lamplighter*, *Overtime*, *Slide Hamp Slide*. Big number with band was his piano playing on *Hamp's Boogie Woogie*. Left Hampton in late 1948 to lead combo, later led big band. Again with Hampton 1950-2. In later 50s led small groups in clubs, later switching to organ to enhance popularity in lounge circuit. A happy performer, his swinging organ and bouncy personality delighted patrons. With Roy Eldridge combo awhile in mid-50s. Active into 70s. Buckner credited, along with Phil Moore, with development of popular block-chord or locked-hands piano style in early or mid-40s, later popularized by George Shearing.

RECORDS
LIONEL HAMPTON
De 18613 Chop-Chop/Hamp's Boogie Woogie
De 18669 Loose Wig/Overtime
De 18754 Slide Hamp Slide
De 18830 Chord-a-Re-Bop
De 18910 Tempo's Boogie / The Lamplighter
De 23879 Limehouse Blues/I Want to Be Loved
De 24513 How High the Moon
VD(12")229 I Wonder Boogie/The Major and the Minor
VD(12")404 Vibe Boogie
VD(12")428 Screamin' Boogie
HERBIE FIELDS
Sav 540 Mel's Riff/Buck's Boogie Woogie
Sav 560 Jumpin' for Savoy/How Herbie Feels
ARNETT COBB
Hamp-Tone 102 Shebna/Down Home
(MILT BUCKNER)

DINAH WASHINGTON with LIONEL HAMPTON SEXTET
Key 605 Evil Gal Blues/Homeward Bound
Key 606 Salty Papa Blues/I Know How to Do It
MILT BUCKNER
Sav 693 Fatstuff Boogie/Lazy Joe
Sav 785 Boogie Grunt/Red Red Wine
Scooter 303 Russian Lullaby/By the River Sainte Marie
MGM 10410 Milt's Boogie/Buck's Bop
MGM 10504 Oop-Be-Doop/M.B. Blues

LPs
MILT BUCKNER
Cap T-642 Rockin' with Milt
Cap T-722 Rockin' Hammond
Argo 660 Mighty High
Argo 670 Please, Mr. Organ Player
LIONEL HAMPTON
De DL-79244 "Steppin' Out" Vol. 1 (1942-5 De RIs)
GNP 15 With the Just Jazz All Stars
ILLINOIS JACQUET
Cadet 773 Go Power!

221. BUCKNER, TEDDY   t B
(JOHN EDWARD BUCKNER)
Born July 16, 1909, Sherman, Texas

Dixieland trumpet player, hard-driving and inventive. Lived in Los Angeles most of life. Early professional experience with bands there, including those of Sonny Clay and Curtis Mosby. In 1934 in Buck Clayton's big band in Shanghai. Mid-1936 joined Lionel Hampton band in Los Angeles, took over leadership when Hampton joined Benny Goodman late 1936. Studio work beginning late 30s. With Benny Carter awhile in 1943 and again in 1948. Worked mostly with Kid Ory band 1949-53. From 1954 mostly led band on west coast, active into 70s. Trumpet work in prologue to movie PETE KELLY'S BLUES (1955).

RECORDS
LIONEL HAMPTON
De 24281 Red Top/Giddy Up
De 24505 Goldwyn Stomp
KID ORY
Co 38956 Mahogany Hall Stomp

640

Co 38958 Yaaka Hula Hickey Dula/
   Go Back Where You Stayed Last
   Night

LPs

TEDDY BUCKNER
   Dixieland Jubilee 503 In Concert at
   the Dixieland Jubilee
   Dixieland Jubilee 504 And His Dixie-
   land Band
   Dixieland Jubilee 505 A Salute to
   Louis Armstrong
KID ORY
   GTJ(10″)L-21 Kid Ory's Creole Jazz
   Band
GEORG BRUNIS (one side)
   Southland 210 Dixieland All Stars

222. BULLOCK, CHICK   vo B

Born c. 1904-6, reportedly in Midwest

Perhaps most heavily recorded singer of
30s. Worked with many bands, of all
types, including jazz greats. Husky, virile
voice, easily identifiable, at best on up
tempos. On some records, pseudonyms
were used for his name. On others, Bullock often listed as leader of band. Also
sang on radio at times. After last record
session in early 1941, faded from music
scene. Settled in California, reportedly in
real estate.

RECORDS

BUNNY BERIGAN
   Vo 3179 It's Been So Long/Swing,
   Mister Charlie
   Vo 3224 A Melody from the Sky/A
   Little Bit Later On
VIC BERTON
   Vo 2915 Jealous
   Co 3092-D Imitations of You/Two
   Rivers Flow Through Harlem
HENRY BIAGINI
   Me 351034 Heartstrings
TED BLACK
   Vi 24050 A Shanty in Old Shanty
   Town
BOB CAUSER
   Or 2431 Let's Have Another Cup o'
   Coffee/Soft Lights and Sweet
   Music
   Me 13107 Two Cigarettes in the
   Dark/My Whole Day Is Spoiled

DUKE ELLINGTON
   Vi 22614 The River and Me/Keep a
   Song in Your Soul
   Vi 23036 Sam and Delilah
EDDIE ELKINS
   Pe 15931 May I?/All I Do Is Dream of
   You
   Me 13015 Easy Come, Easy Go/I
   Ain't Lazy—I'm Just Dreamin'
PAUL HAMILTON
   Vo 2721 So Help Me/Easy Come,
   Easy Go
EARL HARLAN
   Me 12840 Our Big Love Scene/After
   Sundown
   Pe 15862 Tired of It All/Just Keep on
   Doin' What You're Doin'
HIGH HATTERS
   Vi 22756 Come to Me/As Long as
   You're There
   Vi 22809 Singin' the Blues/It's the
   Darndest Thing
GENE KARDOS
   Me 12849 Did You Ever See a Dream
   Walking?/You're Such a Comfort
   to Me
DICK MCDONOUGH
   Me 60808 The Scene Changes/On the
   Beach at Bali Bali
   Me 61202 Now or Never/I'm One Step
   Ahead of My Shadow
   Me 70111 Tea on the Terrace/There's
   Frost on the Moon
MIFF MOLE
   Vo 3468 Love and Learn/I Can't
   Break the Habit of You
RUSS MORGAN
   Me 13321 I Threw a Bean Bag at the
   Moon/It's You I Adore
BEN POLLACK
   Pe 15431 I've Got Five Dollars/Sweet
   and Hot
JOE REICHMAN
   Me 13164 Isn't It a Shame?/Some-
   where in Your Heart
ADRIAN ROLLINI
   Vo 2675 A Hundred Years from To-
   day
   Br 6786 Get Goin'/Just Keep On
   Doin' What You're Doin'
TODD ROLLINS
   Me 13143 Sweetie Pie/You Can Put It
   in the Papers

Me 13156 Blue Sky Avenue/Talkin' to Myself

VINCENT ROSE

Me 13203 Happiness Ahead/Pop! Goes Your Heart

JACK SHILKRET

Me 60602 A Little Robin Told Me So/There's Always a Happy Ending

Me 60607 I'm a Fool for Loving You/A Melody from the Sky

Me 70302 Timber/Gee, But You're Swell

NAT SHILKRET

Vi 22623 By Special Permission of the Copyright Owners/I'm One of God's Children

WARING'S PENNSYLVANIANS

Vi 24062 Old Man of the Mountain

CHICK BULLOCK

Pe 12908 Stormy Weather/Have You Ever Been Lonely?

Pe 15643 We Just Couldn't Say Goodbye/My Heart's at Ease

Me 13185 Lost in a Fog/Just Once Too Often

Me 13283 Blue Moon/Haunting Me

Me 351002 So Nice Seeing You Again /Toddlin' Along with You

Me 351019 Without a Word of Warning/I'm in the Mood for Love

Vo 5171 Last Night/Out on a Limb

Vo 5472 Shake Down the Stars/Polka Dots and Moonbeams

Vo 5558 Fools Rush In/The Nearness of You

OK 6100 Amapola/There'll Be Some Changes Made

OK 6261 Indiana/My Melancholy Baby

LPs

BUNNY BERIGAN

Epic LN-3109 Take It, Bunny (Vo, Br RIs)

223. BULLOCK, WALTER   lyr

Born May 6, 1907, Shelburn, Ind.
Died August 19, 1953, Los Angeles, Calif.

Lyricist of songs for movies. Later wrote screen plays. Educated at DePauw University. Collaborated with composers Harold Spina, Alfred Newman, Richard

Whiting, Victor Schertzinger, Jule Styne, Abraham Ellstein. Book and lyrics for Broadway musical GREAT TO BE ALIVE (1950).

SONGS
(with related films)

1936—FOLLOW YOUR HEART movie (Magnolias in the Moonlight; Who Minds About Me?); RHYTHM ON THE RANGE movie (Rhythm on the Range; Hang Up My Saddle); SING, BABY, SING movie (When Did You Leave Heaven?)

1937—FIFTY-SECOND STREET movie (I Still Love to Kiss You Goodnight; Don't Save Your Love; I'd Like to See Samoa of Samoa; Nothing Can Stop Me Now; Sing and Let Your Hair Down); The You and Me That Used to Be

1938—HAPPY LANDING movie (You Appeal to Me); JUST AROUND THE CORNER movie (I Love to Walk in the Rain; This Is a Happy Little Ditty; Brass Buttons and Epaulets); LITTLE MISS BROADWAY movie (Little Miss Broadway; How Can I Thank You?; Swing Me an Old Fashioned Song; If All the World Were Paper; We Should Be Together; Thank You for the Use of the Hall; Be Optimistic); SALLY, IRENE AND MARY movie (I Could Use a Dream; Half Moon on the Hudson)

1940—HIT PARADE OF 1941 movie (Who Am I?; In the Cool of the Evening; Swing Low Sweet Rhythm); THE BLUEBIRD movie (songs unimportant); Where Do I Go from You?

1948—THE THREE MUSKETEERS movie (Viola; My Lady; Song of the Musketeers)

1950—GREAT TO BE ALIVE stage show (songs unimportant)

224. BUNKER, LARRY   vb p d

Born November 4, 1928, Long Beach, Calif.

Good drummer and excellent vibist, playing melodious and happily swinging solos in modern style. In military service 1946-

8. On Mississippi riverboat in modern combo for two years, on drums. Jobbed on west coast, where he picked up vibes. Early jobs with Howard Rumsey, Art Pepper, George Auld, Gerry Mulligan. Period in 1953 with Billy May. By mid-50s recognized as important star on vibes. Heavy freelance recording. In late 50s often worked with singer Peggy Lee. Late 50s included periods with Shorty Rogers and Maynard Ferguson. Active in 60s, including film studio work.

RECORDS

HARRY BABASIN
  Dis 163 Night and Day/Where or When
  NJ 603 How About You?/Sanders Meanders
ART PEPPER
  Dis 157 Brown Gold/These Foolish Things
  Dis 158 Holiday Flight/Surf Ride
LPs
LARRY BUNKER
  Vault 9005 The Larry Bunker Quartette
ABE MOST
  Lib LJH-6004 Mr. Clarinet
GERRY MULLIGAN QUARTET
  PJ(10″)PJLP-2
  PJ(10″)PJLP-5
JOHN GRAAS
  EmArcy MG-36117 Coup de Graas
PETE RUGOLO
  EmArcy MG-36115 Out on a Limb
  Mer PPS-2016 Ten Trumpets and Two Guitars
LOU LEVY
  Vi LPM-1319 Jazz in Four Colors
BOBBY ENEVOLDSEN
  Lib LJH-6008 Smorgasbord
  Tampa TP-14 Reflections in Jazz
HENRY MANCINI
  Vi LSP-2258 Combo!
HARRY BABASIN
  Noc(10″)3
LARRY BUNKER-MARTY PAICH
  Tampa TP-23 Jazz for Relaxation

225. BUNN, TEDDY   g vo B
Born 1909, Freeport, N.Y.
Good jazz guitarist, adept at blues. Early

recognition with The Spirits of Rhythm, group popular in New York clubs and on tour. Bunn was with this group during much of the 30s, with interval away in which he freelanced and led own trio. The Spirits of Rhythm disbanded and resumed several times in the 40s. Bunn did much freelance recording during the years. Beginning in early 40s he was based mostly on west coast, leading own group. Worked periods off and on in 50s with Edgar Hayes and Jack McVea. In late 50s did some work in rock and roll field. Semi-active in 60s but still taking occasional jobs into the 70s.

RECORDS

SIDNEY BECHET
  BN 6 Summertime
  BN 13 Lonesome Blues/Dear Old Southland
LIONEL HAMPTON
  Vi 26739 Martin on Every Block/Charlie Was a Sailor
  Vi 26793 Just for Laffs/Pig Foot Sonata
MILT HERTH QUARTET
  De 1800 The Flat Foot Floogee/Looney Little Tooney
J. C. HIGGINBOTHAM
  BN 501 Weary Land Blues
BOB HOWARD
  De 1698 If You're a Viper/Raggedy but Right
  De 1721 There Ain't Gonna Be No Doggone After Awhile/Baby, It Must Be Love
  De 2263 Sweet Emalina, My Gal/On Revival Day
TOMMY LADNIER
  Bb 10086 Ja-da/Weary Blues
  Bb 10089 Really the Blues/When You and I Were Young, Maggie
RED MCKENZIE with THE SPIRITS OF RHYTHM
  De 186 From Monday On/'Way Down Yonder in New Orleans
  De 243 It's All Forgotten Now/What's the Use of Getting Used to You?
  De 302 As Long as I Live/I've Got the World on a String
MEZZ MEZZROW
  Bb 10085 Comin' On with the Come On (1 & 2)

643

Bb 10088 Revolutionary Blues/Gettin' Together (MEZZROW-LADNIER)

FRANK NEWTON
BN 501 Daybreak Blues

HOT LIPS PAGE TRIO
Bb 8634 Evil Man's Blues/Do It If You Wanna
Bb 8660 Just Another Woman/My Fightin' Gal

THE RAMBLERS
De 2470 'Tain't What You Do/Money Is Honey
De 2499 Honey in the Bee Ball/Lonesome Railroad

TEDDY BUNN
BN 503 King Porter Stomp/Bachelor Blues
BN 504 Guitar in High/Blues without Words
Selective 114 Jackson's Nook/You've Come a Long Ways, Baby

TEDDY BUNN and SPENCER WILLIAMS
Vi 23253 Tampa Twirl/The Chicken and the Worm
Vi 38592 It's Sweet Like So/Pattin' Dat Cat
Vi 38602 Goose and Gander/Clean It Out
Vi 38617 The New Goose and Gander/Blow It Up

SPIRITS OF RHYTHM
De 160 Junk Man/Dr. Watson and Mr. Holmes

LPs

TOMMY LADNIER with MEZZ MEZZROW
"X"(10")LVA-3027 (Bb RIs)
(miscellaneous artists)
Vi LPV-542 The Panassie Sessions (RIs)

SIDNEY BECHET
BN(10")BLP-7002, 7003, 7022

226. BURKE, JOE   cm

Born March 18, 1884, Philadelphia, Pa. Died June 9, 1950, Upper Darby, Pa.

Important composer late 20s through 40s. Wrote for early movie musicals. Two hit songs in 1929, *Tiptoe Through the Tulips with Me* and *Painting the Clouds with Sunshine*. Other leading songs: *Yearning, Carolina Moon, Dancing with Tears in My Eyes, Moon Over Miami*. Educated at University of Pennsylvania. Worked for

New York publishing houses. Chief collaborators: lyricists Al Dubin, Edgar Leslie, Benny Davis, Mark Fisher, Marty Symes, Charles Tobias.

SONGS
(with related shows)

1925—Oh, How I Miss You Tonight; Yearning

1927—Just the Same; Baby Your Mother

1928—EARL CARROLL'S VANITIES OF 1928 stage show (Raquel); Who Wouldn't Be Blue?

1929—GOLD DIGGERS OF BROADWAY movie (Tiptoe Through the Tulips with Me; Painting the Clouds with Sunshine; And They Still Fall in Love; Go to Bed; What Will I Do without You?; In a Kitchenette); APPLAUSE movie (Everybody's Doing It; Doing the New Raccoon; Give Your Little Baby Lots of Lovin'); SHOW OF SHOWS movie (Ping Pongo; If Your Best Friend Won't Tell You); IN THE HEADLINES movie (Love Will Find a Way); Carolina Moon; All That I'm Asking Is Sympathy

1930—HOLD EVERYTHING movie (To Know You Is to Love You; Sing a Little Theme Song; When the Little Roses Get the Blues for You); SALLY movie (If I'm Dreaming); Dancing with Tears in My Eyes; The Kiss Waltz

1931—Crosby, Columbo and Vallee; For You; Many Happy Returns of the Day; When the Rest of the Crowd Goes Home

1933—Goodnight, Little Girl of My Dreams; In the Valley of the Moon

1934—A Little Church Around the Corner; The Moonlight Waltz

1935—In a Little Gypsy Tea Room; Moon Over Miami; A Little Bit Independent; On Treasure Island

1936—ZIEGFELD FOLLIES OF 1936 stage show (Midnight Blue); Cling to Me; Robins and Roses; When a Great Love Comes Along

1937—Getting Some Fun Out of Life; It Looks Like Rain in Cherry Blossom Lane

1938—At a Perfume Counter; Sailing at Midnight; Somewhere with Somebody Else
1939—Rainbow Valley
1940—Dream Valley
1943—By the River of the Roses
1948—Rambling Rose
1950—It Couldn't Happen to a Sweeter Girl

227. BURKE, JOHNNY lyr p

Born October 3, 1908, Antioch, Calif.
Died February 25, 1964, New York, N.Y.

Lyricist with prolific output, mostly for movies. Collaborated with composers James V. Monaco and Jimmy Van Heusen on many songs for Bing Crosby movies. Grew up in midwest, attended Crane College and University of Wisconsin. Worked for publishing houses in Chicago and New York. Began composing in early 30s, by mid-30s concentrated on work for movies. Fabulous number of hit songs through the years. Lyric work outstanding, fit exceptionally well the light, airy, easy-going style Bing adopted in late 30s. Lyrics for Broadway show NELLIE BLY (1946), music and lyrics for DONNYBROOK! (1961). Formed music publishing company with Jimmy Van Heusen in 1944. Other collaborators: composers Arthur Johnston, Victor Schertzinger, Harold Spina.

SONGS
(with related shows)

1930—Yours and Mine
1933—Annie Doesn't Live Here Anymore; Shadows on the Swanee
1934—Beat o' My Heart; Irresistible; It's Dark on Observatory Hill; I've Got a Warm Spot in My Heart for You
1935—Love Dropped in for Tea; You're So Darn Charming; My Very Good Friend the Milkman; Now You've Got Me Doing It
1936—PENNIES FROM HEAVEN movie (Pennies from Heaven; Let's Call a Heart a Heart; One, Two, Button Your Shoe; So Do I; The Skeleton in the Closet); So This Is Heaven; Too Much Imagination

1937—DOUBLE OR NOTHING movie (The Moon Got in My Eyes; It's the Natural Thing to Do; All You Want to Do Is Dance); GO WEST, YOUNG MAN movie (I Was Saying to the Moon; On a Typical Tropical Night)
1938—DOCTOR RHYTHM movie (On the Sentimental Side; My Heart Is Taking Lessons; This Is My Night to Dream; Doctor Rhythm); SING YOU SINNERS movie (I've Got a Pocketful of Dreams; Don't Let That Moon Get Away; Laugh and Call It Love; Where Is Central Park?); Between a Kiss and a Sigh
1939—EAST SIDE OF HEAVEN movie (East Side of Heaven; Sing a Song of Sunbeams; Hang Your Heart on a Hickory Limb; That Sly Old Gentleman); THE STAR MAKER movie (An Apple for the Teacher; Still the Bluebird Sings; Go Fly a Kite; A Man and His Dream); Oh, You Crazy Moon; Scatter-brain; What's New?; Address Unknown
1940—IF I HAD MY WAY movie (April Played the Fiddle; I Haven't Time to Be a Millionaire; Meet the Sun Half-Way; The Pessimistic Character); LOVE THY NEIGHBOR movie (Do You Know Why?; Isn't That Just Like Love?; Dearest, Darest I?); RHYTHM ON THE RIVER movie (Rhythm on the River; That's for Me; Only Forever; The Moon Over Madison Square); ROAD TO SINGAPORE movie (I'm Too Romantic; Sweet Potato Piper; Kaigoon); Polka Dots and Moonbeams; Devil May Care; Imagination
1941—ROAD TO ZANZIBAR movie (It's Always You; Birds of a Feather; You Lucky People You; You're Dangerous; Road to Zanzibar; African Etude)
1942—MY FAVORITE SPY movie (Got the Moon in My Pocket; Just Plain Lonesome); PLAYMATES movie (Humpty Dumpty Heart; How Long Did I Dream?; Thank Your Lucky Stars and Stripes; Romeo

Smith and Juliet Jones; Que Chica); ROAD TO MOROCCO movie (Moonlight Becomes You; Constantly; Road to Morocco; Ain't Got a Dime to My Name; Aladdin's Daughter)

1943—DIXIE movie (If You Please; Sunday, Monday or Always; She's from Missouri; Miss Jemima Walks By; Kinda Peculiar Brown; A Horse That Knows His Way Home)

1944—GOING MY WAY movie (Going My Way; Swinging on a Star; The Day after Forever); BELLE OF THE YUKON movie (Sleigh Ride in July; Like Someone in Love; Every Girl Is Different); AND THE ANGELS SING movie (It Could Happen to You; For the First Hundred Years; His Rocking Horse Ran Away; How Does Your Garden Grow?; Bluebirds in My Belfry; Knockin' on Your Own Front Door); LADY IN THE DARK movie (Suddenly It's Spring)

1945—DUFFY'S TAVERN movie (The Hard Way); BELLS OF ST. MARY'S movie (Aren't You Glad You're You?)

1946—CROSS MY HEART movie (That Little Dream Got Nowhere; Love Is the Darndest Thing; How Do You Do It?); ROAD TO UTOPIA movie (Welcome to My Dream; Personality; It's Anybody's Spring; Good Time Charlie; Put It There, Pal; Would You?); NELLIE BLY stage show (Just My Luck; You May Not Love Me; My Heart Goes Crazy; So Would I

1947—WELCOME STRANGER movie (My Heart Is a Hobo; Country Style; As Long as I'm Dreaming; Smile Right Back at the Sun; Smack in the Middle of Maine); ROAD TO RIO movie (But Beautiful; You Don't Have to Know the Language; Apalachichola, Fla.; For What?; Experience); VARIETY GIRL movie (Harmony)

1948—THE EMPEROR WALTZ movie (The Friendly Mountains; The Kiss in Your Eyes; lyrics added to title song)

1949—A CONNECTICUT YANKEE IN KING ARTHUR'S COURT movie (Busy Doing Nothing; 'Twixt Myself and Me; Once and for Always; If You Stub Your Toe on the Moon; When Is Sometime?); TOP O' THE MORNING movie (Top o' the Morning; You're in Love with Someone)

1950—MISTER MUSIC movie (High on the List; And You'll Be Home; Accidents Will Happen; Life Is So Peculiar); RIDING HIGH movie (Sunshine Cake; The Horse Told Me; Sure Thing; Somewhere on Anywhere Road)

1951—This Is My Night to Dream; Another Human Being of the Opposite Sex

1952—ROAD TO BALI movie (Chicago Style; Moonflowers; Hoot Mon; To See You; The Merry Go Runaround)

1953—LITTLE BOY LOST movie (The Magic Window; Cela M'est Egal (If It's All the Same to You); CARNIVAL IN FLANDERS stage show, Jimmy Van Heusen-cm (Here's That Rainy Day; I'm One of Your Admirers; It's an Old Spanish Custom; Ring the Bell)

1955—Misty

1956—THE VAGABOND KING movie (new lyrics added to some of Rudolf Friml's original songs)

1961—DONNYBROOK! stage show (cm-lyr; songs unimportant)

228. BURKE, SONNY   vb ar cm B
(JOSEPH FRANCIS BURKE)
Born March 22, 1914, Scranton, Pa.

Active as arranger, composer and bandleader. Most prominence in 50s as musical director on record sessions. Attended Duke University, led a band there. Studied composing and arranging, in late 30s sold arrangements to Buddy Rogers, Joe Venuti, Xavier Cugat and others. Took over Sam Donahue's first band in 1939 for about a year when Donahue with Gene Krupa. Wrote swinging arrangements for spirited young band. Band played in New York and recorded there. Burke then arranged for Charlie Spivak

1940-2; co-composer of Spivak's theme *Star Dreams*. Later arranged for Jimmy Dorsey and Gene Krupa. In later years composer or co-composer of *Midnight Sun*; *Black Coffee*; *Somebody Bigger Than You and I*; *They Were Doing the Mambo*; *I Bring You Spring*; *You Was*; and *How It Lies, How It Lies, How It Lies!*. Continued to arrange for various bands. In mid-40s began leading bands backing singers on records. By late 40s musical director for Decca's Hollywood branch. His hit record in 50s, *Mambo Jambo*, contributed to mambo's flurry of popularity. Later musical director for Warner Brothers studio. Scoring for movies and TV, active into 60s.

RECORDS

SONNY BURKE
Vo 5139 The Last Jam Session/Tea for Two
Vo 5356 Lament/I May Be Wrong
Vo 5397 If It Wasn't for the Moon/Easy Does It
Vo 5459 Pick-a-Rib/I Never Purposely Hurt You
OK 5813 Jimmie Meets the Count/Blue Sonata
OK 5873 Can I Be Sure?/Carry Me Back to Old Virginny
OK 5955 The Count Basically/More Than You Know
OK 5989 Jumpin' Salty/Minor DeLuxe
De 24832 Quarantine Sign/Blues Stay Away from Me
De 24993 Mambo Jambo/What, Where and When
De 27541 The Sidewalk Shufflers/That's One for Me
De 27576 Sweetnin' Stuff/I'm Yours to Command
De 27785 Happiness Is This/Cocoanuts
De 27970 I'll Always Be Following You/I Wanna Love You
De 27974 The Grabber/Mambo on My Mind
(as conductor)
KAY THOMPSON
De 24695 Now That I Need You
BILLY ECKSTINE
MGM 10259 Everything I Have Is

Yours/I'll Be Faithful
MEL TORME & HIS MEL-TONES
Mus 397 It Happened in Monterey/Born to Be Blue
DINAH SHORE
Co 37587 You Do/Kokomo, Indiana
JOHNNIE JOHNSTON
MGM 10036 You're Not So Easy to Forget/Ain'tcha Ever Comin' Back?
MGM 10191 Steppin' Out with My Baby/I Bring You Spring
MEL TORME
Mus 15102 You're Driving Me Crazy/It's Dreamtime
LPs
SONNY BURKE
De DL-8090 Let's Mambo

228A. BURNESS, LES   p
Swing pianist with Bunny Berigan early 1937, Artie Shaw spring 1937 to late 1938. Many years with Tony Pastor from 1940.
RECORDS
ARTIE SHAW
Br 7895 All God's Chillun Got Rhythm
Br 7947 The Blues (1 & 2)
Br 7952 Fee Fi Fo Fum
Br 7965 All Alone
Br 7976 Free Wheeling
Br 8019 Free for All
Bb 7759 Back Bay Shuffle
Bb 7772 Comin' On
Bb 7889 You're a Sweet Little Headache
Bb 10055 Thanks for Everything
LPs
ARTIE SHAW
FTR 1501 And His Orchestra, 1937-8, Vol. 1
FTR 1502 And His Orchestra, 1937-8, Vol. 2
FTR 1503 And His Orchestra, 1937-8, Vol. 3
Epic LN-3150 And His Orchestra
Epic EE-22023' Free for All

229. BURNS, RALPH   p ar cm B
Born June 29, 1922, Newton, Mass.
Excellent arranger and composer, important in development of modern jazz in

mid-40s. While in high school, pianist in local bands. Attended New England Conservatory. Went to New York in 1940 with Nick Jerret combo, worked clubs about two years. Arranging job with Charlie Barnet 1942-3 and Red Norvo 1943. Joined Woody Herman in 1944 as arranger and pianist. Arrangements helped set style of first Herman Herd then pioneering in progressive jazz. Composed and arranged famous Herman numbers: *Bijou, Keen and Peachy, Early Autumn, Summer Sequence, Northwest Passage, Lady McGowan's Dream, Rhapsody in Wood, Panacea.* Herman arranger into 50s. Occasionally played other jobs as pianist. Accompanied singers Mildred Bailey and Frances Wayne on tours in early 50s. With Herman on European tour in 1954. In later 50s and 60s freelanced. Recorded with own combo and orchestra. Arranged for Broadway musicals NO STRINGS, LITTLE ME, FUNNY GIRL, GOLDEN BOY. Active into 70s.

RECORDS

(as pianist)

WOODY HERMAN
Co 36789 Caldonia
Co 36835 Northwest Passage
VD(12")411 Somebody Loves Me
VD(12")752 John Hardy's Wife

SONNY BERMAN
Dial 1006 Curbstone Scuffle

CHUBBY JACKSON
Key 616 Cryin' Sands/Northwest Passage

BILL HARRIS
Key 618 Mean to Me/Cross Country

FLIP PHILLIPS
Si 90003 Sweet and Lovely/Bob's Belief

SERGE CHALOFF
Dial 1012 Blue Serge

CHARLIE VENTURA
Nat 9036 Syntheses/Blue Champagne

RALPH BURNS
Dial 1008 Dial-ogue

(as arranger or conductor)

FRAN WARREN
MGM 11270 Wish You Were Here/What Is This Thing Called Love?
MGM 11352 Anywhere I Wander/I Worry 'Bout You

LPs

RALPH BURNS
Jazztone J-1036 Bijou
Mer(10")MGC-115 Free Forms
De DL-8555 The Masters Revisited
De DL-9207 Very Warm for Jazz
Warwick 5001
Epic LN-24015 Swingin' Down the Lane

CHUBBY JACKSON-BILL HARRIS ALL-STARS
Mer(10")MG-25076 Jazz Journey

DON HELLER
Epic LN-3320 Blame It on My Youth

JERI SOUTHERN
De DL-8472 Jeri Gently Jumps

LEE WILEY
Vi LPM-1408 West of the Moon

TONI ARDEN
De DL-8651 Miss Toni Arden

DICK HAYMES
Warwick 2023 Richard the Lion-Hearted

TONY BENNETT
Co CL-1658 My Heart Sings

230. BURNSIDE, R. H.   lyr

Born August 13, 1870, Glasgow, Scotland
Died September 14, 1952, Metuchen, N.J.

Important figure in early Broadway musicals as lyricist-librettist-director-producer. Educated at Great Yarmouth Academy. Left home at early age to become callboy at London's Gaiety Theatre. Worked many years in London theatre in various positions. After Lillian Russell engagement in London, came to U. S. with her as director-producer. Active in Broadway shows beginning 1904 through 20s. Produced, directed and wrote many Hippodrome spectacles. Wrote and staged shows featuring leading stars Fred Stone, Eddie Foy, Jefferson DeAngelis, Fay Templeton, Julia Sanderson, Joseph Coyne, DeWolf Hopper, Virginia Earle. Songs attained little popularity but effective in context of shows. Chief collaborators: composers Raymond Hubbell, Gustav Kerker. Songs included *Ladder of Roses, Annabelle Jerome, Nice to Have a Sweetheart, You Can't Beat the Luck of the Irish.* In later years active in producing Gilbert & Sullivan operettas.

648

BROADWAY MUSICALS
(wrote book & lyrics unless designated otherwise)

1904—SERGEANT KITTY
1906—MY LADY'S MAID (book only); THE TOURISTS
1907—FASCINATING FLORA
1908—THE PIED PIPER (lyrics only)
1910—THE INTERNATIONAL CUP AND THE BALLET OF NIAGARA (book only)
1911—THE THREE ROMEOS
1914—CHIN-CHIN (book only); THE DANCING DUCHESS
1915—HIP-HIP-HOORAY (book only)
1916—THE BIG SHOW (book only)
1917—CHEER UP (book only)
1918—EVERYTHING (book only)
1919—HAPPY DAYS; MISS MILLIONS
1920—TIP TOP
1922—SOME PARTY
1923—STEPPING STONES (book only)
1928—THREE CHEERS

Served as director or producer of many other shows.

231. BURR, HENRY   vo
(HARRY MCCLASKEY)
Born in New Brunswick, Canada

Soft-voiced popular singer of sentimental songs whose career began in or before 1910 and lasted into early 40s. Among first singers to record, continued recording extensively for many years. Sang with Peerless Quartet awhile. Active in early radio, later appeared many times in 30s on popular Cities Service series. Long run on National Barn Dance show from 1935 to early 40s.

RECORDS
ROGER WOLFE KAHN
Vi 20059 Somebody's Lonely
Vi 20071 Cross Your Heart
HENRY BURR
Co A-2308 Silver Threads Among the Gold/The Rosary
Co A-2490 Just a Baby's Prayer at Twilight/Lorraine
Vi 18435 Are You from Heaven?
Vi 18439 Just a Baby's Prayer at Twilight
Vi 18781 When the Corn Is Waving, Annie Dear/I'll Take You Home Again, Kathleen

Vi 19597 Honest and Truly/Dear One
Vi 19959 Always
Vi 20070 I Wish I Had My Old Gal Back Again
Vi 20258 Because I Love You
Vi 20490 What Does It Matter?
Vi 20821 Loved One/Sweet Marie
Vi 20873 Are You Lonesome Tonight?
Co 1515-D Out of the Dawn/Sweetheart Lane
Co 1649-D Cross Roads/Love Dreams
OK 41149 Goodnight, Little Girl, Goodnight/Somewhere a Voice Is Calling
Br 4045-D Memories of France/Out of the Dawn

232. BURTNETT, EARL   p ar lyr cm B
Born February 7, 1896, Harrisburg, Ill.
Died January 2, 1936, Chicago, Ill.

Leader of good dance band in 20s and 30s. Attended Pennsylvania State College. Played piano in dance bands in early 20s, also led band and recorded. Composed some songs that enjoyed considerable popularity: *Canadian Capers* (1915), *Do You Ever Think of Me?* (1920), *Leave Me with a Smile* (1921), *Mandalay* (1924), *'Leven Thirty Saturday Night* (1930). Lesser songs: *Have You Forgotten?*; *Down Honolulu Way*; *Where There's a Will There's a Way*; *This Time Is the Last Time*; *When I Hear an Irishman Sing*; *After Every Party*; *Counting the Days*; *Blue Night*; *Be a Little Sweeter to Me*; *I've Got a New Mama*; *You're the Only One*; *Never Before, Never Again*. Pianist and arranger for Art Hickman in late 20s; took over band in 1929. In 30s the band had good ensemble sound and good hotel-style arrangements. Achieved some popularity in midwest. Played leading ballrooms and Drake Hotel in Chicago. Among sidemen: Bruce Squires (tb), Red Hodgson (t), Hub Lytle (ts). Career of band cut short by Burtnett's death at 39.

RECORDS
EARL BURTNETT
Co 787-D Song of the Wanderer/On the Road to Mandalay
Co 934-D Doll Dance/If I Hadn't You
Co 966-D Just a Rolling Stone/Never Before

Co 1190-D Trees/If I Should Lose You

Co 1361-D Sweet Sue/Stay Out of the South

Br 4231 Broadway Melody/You Were Meant for Me

Br 4232 Wedding of the Painted Doll/ Love Boat

Br 4336 Love Me or Leave Me/A Garden in the Rain

Br 4375 Singin' in the Rain/Orange Blossom Time

Br 4376 Low Down Rhythm/Gotta Feelin' for You

Br 4501 Sunny Side Up/If I Had a Talking Picture of You

Br 4573 Aren't We All?/Turn on the Heat

Br 4577 Your Mother and Mine/Nobody but You

Br 4754 'Leven Thirty Saturday Night/Courtin' Time

Br 4861 Here Comes the Sun

Br 4984 It Must Be True/The Little Things in Life

Br 6034 I Surrender Dear/To Make a Long Story Short

Co 2921-D Ridin' Around in the Rain/Waitin' at the Gate for Katy

Co 2922-D Neighbors/She Reminds Me of You

CHARLES KING with EARL BURTNETT ORCHESTRA

Br 4849 Here Comes the Sun/Leave a Little Smile

233. BURTON, VAL   cm lyr

Born February 22, 1899, London, England

Songwriter who teamed with Will Jason to produce several excellent songs, though output scant. Educated at Oundle School in England. Wrote revues for C. B. Cochrane Productions. Came to U.S. in 1921. Composing work in 30s; also wrote screenplays and radio shows (including Henry Aldrich show). Top song: *When We're Alone (Penthouse Serenade)*.

SONGS
(with related shows)

1930—PUTTIN' ON THE RITZ movie (Singing a Vagabond Song)

1932—When We're Alone (Penthouse Serenade); If It Ain't Love

1933—MELODY CRUISE movie (Isn't This a Night for Love?); Roof Top Serenade

1934—COCK-EYED CAVALIERS movie (The Big Bad Wolf Was Dead; Dilly Dally)

Lesser songs: *Waiting for the Springtime*; *You Alone*; *Lady of the Morning*; *The Day I Met You*; *Some Day Soon*

234. BUSHELL, GARVIN
as ss cl bas f B

Born September 25, 1902, Springfield, Ohio

Versatile reed man with many bands in long career pre-1920 to late 60s. Studied at Wilberforce University. Went to New York in 1919, worked with various bands. Toured with blues singers Mamie Smith and Ethel Waters in early 20s, also toured with various acts. In Europe 1925-7 with Sam Wooding, recorded there. Back in U.S. in late 20s to work with Wooding, Johnny Dunn, Fess Williams and others. With Fletcher Henderson 1935-6, with Cab Calloway 1936-7. On many records with Calloway but seldom featured, though a stalwart in band's sax section. Joined Chick Webb in late 1937. After Webb's death in June 1939 remained six months with band then led by Ella Fitzgerald. 1940-1 jobs included periods with Eddie Mallory and Edgar Hayes. During remainder of 40s and 50s mostly led band in New York and on west coast. Also freelanced. With Wilbur De Paris 1959-64, toured abroad with him. Moved to Puerto Rico in 1967, worked as music teacher.

RECORDS

JOHNNY DUNN

Co A-3541 Bugle Blues/Birmingham Blues

Co A-3579 Put and Take/Moanful Blues

Co 14306-D Sergeant Dunn's Bugle Call Blues/Buffalo Blues

Co 14358-D Ham and Eggs/You Need Some Loving

ROY EVANS

Co 1449-D Georgia's Always on My Mind

LOUISIANA SUGAR BABES

Vi 21346 Thou Swell/Persian Rug

Vi 21348 Willow Tree/'Sippi

MAMIE SMITH'S JAZZ HOUNDS

OK 4254 Royal Garden Blues/Shim-Me King's Blues

SAM WOODING

Pol(G) 20689 Black Bottom/Behind the Clouds

Pol(G) 20690 By the Waters of Minnetonka/Dreaming of a Castle in the Air

ETHEL WATERS

Bb 10517 Baby, What Else Can I Do?/I Just Got a Letter

CHICK WEBB

De(12")15039 I Want to Be Happy

LPs

REX STEWART

Felsted FAJ-7001 Rendezvous with Rex

WILD BILL DAVISON

Riv 12-211 Sweet and Hot

WILBUR DEPARIS

Atl 1363 On the Riviera

Atl 1552 Over and Over Again

235. BUSHKIN, JOE   p t ar cm vo B

Born November 7, 1916, New York, N.Y.

Good jazz pianist in swinging mainstream style, very facile. Good entertainer with playing, singing and flair for showmanship. As teenager played in minor groups in New York. By 1935 worked with name musicians at Famous Door. Jobs with Eddie Condon and Joe Marsala. With Bunny Berigan's big band 1938-9. Later in 1939 briefly with Muggsy Spanier and Joe Marsala. Joined Tommy Dorsey in early 1940, remained two years. Composed *Oh, Look at Me Now*, featured by Dorsey in 1941. Military service, World War II, included stints directing service shows. After discharge played with Benny Goodman latter half of 1946. Composed instrumental, *Benjie's Bubble*, and *Man Here Plays Fine Piano*, both featured by Goodman. In 1947 with Bud Freeman. Worked awhile as radio staff musician. Had role about six months in Broadway play THE RAT RACE 1949-50; also in film version in 1960. In 50s and 60s mostly led own groups, played clubs in New York, Las Vegas and on west coast. On TV occasionally. In mid-60s began playing in

Hawaii, later settled there, returning to continental U.S. at intervals. In later 60s and early 70s worked at music part time. Other compositions: *There'll Be a Hot Time in the Town of Berlin, Whatcha Doin' After the War?, Every Day Is Christmas, If I Knew You Were There, Portrait of Tallulah, Lucky Me, Love Is Everything, Lovely Weather We're Having, Something Wonderful Happens in Summer, Serenade in Thirds.* Chief collaborator Johnny DeVries.

RECORDS

BUNNY BERIGAN

Vi 26068 High Society

Vi 26077 Rockin' Rollers' Jubilee

TOMMY DORSEY

Vi 27208 Another One of Them Things

Vi 27274 Oh, Look at Me Now/You Might Have Belonged to Another

Vi 27701 Who Can I Turn To?

EDDIE CONDON

De 23431 My One and Only

De 24217 Nobody Knows/We Called It Music

Atl 661 Time Carries On/Seems Like Old Times

BENNY GOODMAN

Co 37187 Benjie's Bubble

Co 37207 Man Here Plays Fine Piano

LEE WILEY

LMS 238 'S Wonderful/Sam and Delilah

Gala 3 You Took Advantage of Me/A Little Birdie Told Me So

MUGGSY SPANIER

Bb 10506 Dipper Mouth Blues/I Wish I Could Shimmy Like My Sister Kate

Bb 10518 At the Jazz Band Ball/Livery Stable Blues

Bb 10532 Riverboat Shuffle/Relaxin' at the Touro

BRAD GOWANS

Vi 20-3230 Jazz Me Blues/Singin' the Blues

JOE BUSHKIN

CMS 532 Serenade in Thirds/I Can't Get Started with You

CMS 534 Blue Chips/In a Little Spanish Town

CMS 565 Pickin' at the Pic/Georgia on My Mind

CMS 594 Fade Out/Oh, Lady Be Good

Je 5004 Indian Summer/Mean to Me

Co 39214 Dah'ling / Portrait of Tallulah

LPs

JOE BUSHKIN

Co(10″)CL-6152 Piano Moods

Co(10″)CL-6201 After Hours with Joe Bushkin

Cap T-711 Midnight Rhapsody

Cap T-832 A Fellow Needs a Girl

Cap T-911 Bushkin Spotlights Berlin

De DL-4731 Night Sounds—San Francisco

Epic LN-3345 Piano After Midnight

Atl(10″)108 I Love a Piano

BUNNY BERIGAN

Cam CAL-550 Bunny (Vi RIs)

MUGGSY SPANIER

Vi LPM-1295 The Great 16! (Bb RIs)

LEE WILEY

Co(10″)CL-6169 Night in Manhattan

BRAD GOWANS

Vi(10″)LJM-3000

---

236. BUSSE, HENRY t cm B

Born May 19, 1894, Magdeburg, Germany

Died April 23, 1955, Memphis, Tenn.

Trumpet player noted for theme and showcase tune *Hot Lips*. Distinctive vibrato on soft, muted trumpet work with Paul Whiteman and later with own band became Busse trademark. Came to U.S. in 1912. Joined Whiteman in 1919 and remained into 1928. Rose to some prominence as featured soloist with Whiteman, though not a jazzman. Unique trumpet sound easily identifiable. Famous solo on *When Day Is Done*. Co-composer of *Hot Lips, Wang Wang Blues, Horn Tootin' Blues, Fiesta, Haunting Blues*. In 30s led dance band in sweet style of day. Probably best and most popular recording then was *Have You Forgotten (the Thrill)?* in 1931. In mid-30s important stand at Chicago's Chez Paree boosted popularity. By this time band had developed light-swinging style with shuffle rhythm and mellow sound, very attractive to dancers and listeners. Muted trumpet still fea-

tured. Opening theme, *Hot Lips*, became well known; at times used *When Day Is Done* as closing theme. Substantial recording output. In late 30s he continued popular in Chicago, played New York, toured. Band frequently on radio, including own series. Appeared in a few minor movies. 1941 record of *Stomping Room Only* attained some popularity. Band continued through 40s and into 50s. Died in 1955 shortly before taking the stand at Peabody Hotel in Memphis.

RECORDS

PAUL WHITEMAN

Vi 18690 Whispering/The Japanese Sandman

Vi 18694 The Wang Wang Blues

Vi 18899 Stumbling

Vi 18920 Hot Lips

Vi 21103 Mary

Vi 24105 Love Nest

Vi 27686 Forget-Me-Not

Vi(12″)35828 When Day Is Done

BUSSE'S BUZZARDS

Vi 19727 Deep Elm

Vi 19782 Red Hot Henry Brown/Milenberg Joys

Vi 19934 The Monkey Doodle Doo

HENRY BUSSE

Vi 21674 One Step to Heaven/How About It?

Vi 22651 By the River Sainte Marie/Got the Bench, Got the Park

Vi 22658 I Surrender Dear/Thrill Me

Vi 22677 I'm Thru with Love/You Don't Know What You're Doing

Vi 22678 Fiesta

Vi 22699 Have You Forgotten (the Thrill)?/Faithfully Yours

Co 2932-D All I Do Is Dream of You/Fool That I Am

Co 2937-D (theme) Hot Lips/Jealous

De 198 (theme) Hot Lips/The Wang Wang Blues

De 398 If the Moon Turns Green/Two Seats in the Balcony

De 774 (theme) When Day Is Done/On the Alamo

De 1077 Under Your Spell/Never Should Have Told You

De 1336 Stumbling/It Had to Be You

De 1938 What Goes On Here in My Heart?/A Little Kiss at Twilight

De 3975 Stomping Room Only/The Lady in Red
4-Star 1139 Temptation/For You, For Me, For Evermore
Vita 788 The Lady From 29 Palms/Jalousie
Cor 60242 That Old Gang of Mine/That's the Last Tear

237. BUTTERFIELD, BILLY   t vo B
(CHARLES WILLIAM BUTTERFIELD)

Born January 14, 1917, Middleton, Ohio

Trumpet star of 30s and 40s particularly. Played big-toned lyrical horn and relaxed jazz style. Versatile: excelled equally on ballads, swing and dixieland. Attended Transylvania College, Lexington, Ky., briefly. Left school in 1936 to tour with college band, later taken over by Austin Wylie. Stayed into 1937. Joined Bob Crosby in late 1937, won first fame. Spotlighted on many Crosby records. Left in mid-1940, worked with Artie Shaw on movie SECOND CHORUS, later in 1940 joined Shaw band as regular, to early 1941. With Benny Goodman much of 1941 (and worked brief periods with him through the years). With Les Brown briefly in 1942, then New York radio. In military service awhile in 1945. In late 1945 formed big band, kept it through 1947. Bill Stegmeyer played lead sax and jazz clarinet, did most of arranging, was Butterfield's chief aide. Band made some worthwhile recordings. In late 40s and 50s Butterfield returned to New York studios and freelanced. Led small combos at clubs and for college dates, recorded actively as freelance. In late 60s became charter member of The World's Greatest Jazz Band, group of veteran jazzmen of traditional style led by ex-Crosbyites Yank Lawson and Bob Haggart. Butterfield quit band late in 1972, headed for New Orleans, returned on and off in 1973. With revival of Artie Shaw Gramercy Five led by Johnny Guarnieri in New York 1974.

RECORDS

BOB CROSBY
De 2205 I'm Free (What's New?)

De 2416 Hang Your Heart on a Hickory Limb/Sing a Song of Sunbeams (both BOB CATS)
De 2482 Hindustan/Mournin' Blues (both BOB CATS)
De 2789 Washington & Lee Swing/Peruna (both BOB CATS)
De 3040 Jazz Me Blues/Do You Ever Think of Me? (both BOB CATS)
De 3055 So Far, So Good/You Ought to Hang Your Heart in Shame (both BOB CATS)
De 3248 Spain/All by Myself (both BOB CATS)
De 3271 Embraceable You/Shortenin' Bread

LES BROWN
Co 36724 Sunday

JESS STACY
Vs 8060 What's New?/Melancholy Mood
Vs 8076 Noni/Jess Stay

BILL STEGMEYER
Si 15014 Sentimental Journey/Frantic Rhapsody
Si 15139 I Can't Believe That You're in Love with Me

ARTIE SHAW
Vi 26762 Special Delivery Stomp/Keepin' Myself for You (both GRAMERCY FIVE)
Vi 26763 Cross Your Heart/Summit Ridge Drive (both GRAMERCY FIVE)
Vi 27230 Star Dust

MARTHA TILTON
VD(12")487 Out of Nowhere/Am I Blue? (JO STAFFORD)

BRAD GOWANS
Vi 20-3230 Singin' the Blues/Jazz Me Blues

MEL POWELL
CMS 543 When Did You Leave Heaven?/Blue Skies
CMS 544 Mood at Twilight/The World Is Waiting for the Sunrise

BENNY GOODMAN
Ha 1061 Cherry
Co 36209 Something New (second of three trumpet solos)
Co 36411 I'm Here

BILLY BUTTERFIELD
Cap album BD-10 (78s) Gershwin Album

Cap 182 Moonlight in Vermont/There Goes That Song Again
Cap 305 Star Dust/Sooner or Later
Cap 335 Jalousie/Steamroller
Cap 371 Ain't Misbehavin'/We Could Make Such Beautiful Music
Cap 397 Stella by Starlight/Maybe You'll Be There
Cap 475 Narcissus/Bugle Call Rag
Cap 815 How Am I to Know?/More Than You Know
Cap 15127 Afternoon in August/Malaguena
Cap 15186 What's New?/Wild Oats

LPs

BILLY BUTTERFIELD
Vi LPM-1212 New York Land Dixie
Vi LPM-1590 Thank You for a Lovely Evening
Vi LPM-1699 A Lovely Way to Spend an Evening
Co CL-1673 Golden Horn
Westminister(10")WL-3020 That Butterfield Bounce
Trans-World TWS-200 College Jazz Sampler
Cap(10")H-201 Stardusting
Essex(10")401 Butterfield at Princeton
Essex(10")402 Butterfield at N.Y.U.
Somerset P-2200 I'm in the Mood
ARTIE SHAW
Vi LPM-1241 And His Gramercy Five (Vi RIs)
CONNEE BOSWELL
Vi LPM-1426 And the Original Memphis Five in Hi-Fi
EDDIE CONDON
Co CL-881 Treasury of Jazz
Dot DLP-3141 Dixieland Dance Party
STEVE ALLEN
De 8151-2 (2-LP set) All Star Jazz Concert, Vol. 1 & 2
THE WORLD'S GREATEST JAZZ BAND
Project 3 Stereo PR-5033SD
Project 3 Stereo PR-5039SD Extra!
Atl S-1570 Live at the Roosevelt Grill

238. BUTTERFIELD, ERSKINE

p o vo cm B

Born February 9, 1913, Syracuse, N.Y.
Died July 1961, New York, N.Y.

Good entertainer as pianist-vocalist. Sprightly, light-swinging manner. Leader of good jazz-styled combo. Studied piano

as youngster, began professional career early. Various band jobs included periods with Savoy Sultans and Noble Sissle. Led groups in late 30s, did radio staff work. In early 40s recorded often, using various capable musicians. Especially outstanding: clarinetist Jimmy Lytell. Other jazzmen included Sal Franzella, Al Philburn, Bill Graham, Carl Kress, Yank Lawson, Jerry Jerome. Military service, World War II. After discharge, resumed studio work. More recordings, then faded.

RECORDS

ERSKINE BUTTERFIELD
De 3042 Tuxedo Junction/Salt Butter
De 3043 Darn That Dream/Inconvenience
De 3356 Chocolate/Boogie-Woogie St. Louis Blues
De 3357 Don't Leave Me Now/Pushin' the Conversation Along
De 4360 You Made Me Care/Sleepy Town Train
De 4400 Jumpin' in a Julep Joint/Birmingham Special
De 8510 Beale Street Mama/Whatcha Know, Joe?
De 8524 Missouri Waltz/Stayin' at Home
De 8539 Paradiddle Joe/All the Time
De 8543 Blackberry Jam/Monday's Wash
De 8551 Because of You/You Might Have Belonged to Another
De 8588 Honey Dear/I Was a Fool to Let You Go
De 8620 Crazy Blues/Lovin' Man
Cel 8190 Lighthouse/Part-Time Boogie
DeL 1040 If It's Love You Want, Baby/Is You Too Lazy?
Guild 122 Old Pigeon-Toed Joad/Conversation While Dancing

LPs

ERSKINE BUTTERFIELD
Davis 104 Piano Cocktail

239. BUZZELL, EDDIE   vo lyr

Born November 13, 1900, Brooklyn, N.Y.

Star of several Broadway musicals of 20s: THE GINGHAM GIRL (1922), NO OTHER GIRL (1924), THE DESERT SONG and SWEETHEART TIME (1926), GOOD BOY (1928),

LADY FINGERS (1929). Early experience as child actor in Gus Edwards troupe. In later years wrote and directed movies. Writer and producer of TV films. Compositions included *Mary Had a Little* and *Find 'Em, Feed 'Em, Fool 'Em and Forget 'Em.*

240. BYAS, DON   ts B
(CARLOS WESLEY BYAS)

Born October 21, 1912, Muskogee, Okla.
Died August 23, 1972, Holland

Tenor sax star of 40s. Big-toned, swinging style. Well-conceived, lyrical solos. From the swing school, yet adapted to modern style in mid-40s. In late 20s played in bands in southwest, including those of Terrence Holder, Bennie Moten, Walter Page. Led group in early 30s. Went to west coast, worked with Lionel Hampton, Eddie Barefield, Buck Clayton in mid-30s. To New York in 1937-8 with Eddie Mallory band. Briefly with Lucky Millinder and Don Redman. With Andy Kirk 1939-40. Later in 1940 with Edgar Hayes and Benny Carter. Prestigious job with Count Basie 1941-3. In mid-40s active in progressive groups, fitted in well. Worked with Oscar Pettiford, Coleman Hawkins, Dizzy Gillespie. Busy recording schedule in 1944-5 with own combo. To Europe in 1946 with Don Redman band, decided to stay. Popular in Paris jazz circles, toured several countries, recorded. Returned to visit U.S. occasionally. Lived in Holland in recent years, active till death.

RECORDS

COUNT BASIE
  OK 6564 Harvard Blues
  Co 36709 Sugar Blues/Bugle Blues (Combos)
  Co 36710 Royal Garden Blues (Combo)
  Co 36711 St. Louis Blues (Combo)
HOT LIPS PAGE
  De 18124 Lafayette/South
  Sav 605 Dance of the Tambourine/I Keep Rollin' On
  CMS 558 You Need Coachin'/Fish for Supper
SAVANNAH CHURCHILL
  Manor 1004 All Alone

DIZZY GILLESPIE
  Vi 40-0130 Night in Tunisia/52nd Street Theme
  Manor 1042 Good Bait/I Can't Get Started
EMMETT BERRY
  Nat 9002 Byas'd Opinions/Deep Blue Dream
COZY COLE
  Mer 1099 They Didn't Believe Me
BUCK RAM
  Sav 572 Swing Street/Twilight in Teheran
DON BYAS
  Go 131 Gloomy Sunday/More Than a Mood
  Hub 3022 Poor Butterfly/Double Talk
  Jamb 900 Should I?/You Call It Madness
  Jamb 902 Out of Nowhere/Little White Lies
  Jamb 903 Deep Purple/Them There Eyes
  Super Disc 1006 One O'clock Jump/Three O'clock in the Morning
  Sav 574 Candy/Byas-a-Drink
  Seeco 10-009 Because of You/Vanity
  Seeco 10-012 Too Young/Chlo-e
  Tono(Den) 19000 How High the Moon/Dynamo A
  Sw(Fr) 232 Gloria
  Sw(Fr) 241 Body and Soul/I'm Beginning to See the Light
  Blue Star(Fr) 45 These Foolish Things/Blues for Panassié

LPs

DON BYAS
  Atl(10″)117 Don Byas Solos
  Seeco(10″)35
  Norg(10″)MGN-12
DON BYAS-BERYL BOOKER
  Dis(10″)DL-3022
MARY LOU WILLIAMS (one side)
  Story STLP-906 Messin' 'Round in Montmartre
COUNT BASIE
  Epic LN-3169 Basie's Back in Town (Vo, OK RIs)
EDDIE BARCLAY
  UA 3023 Americans in Paris
(miscellaneous artists)
  Eso ES-548 The Harlem Jazz Scene —1941 (at Minton's and Uptown House)

Masterseal MSLP-5013 Hi-Fi Jazz Session

241. BYERS, BILLY   tb ar cm p B
Born May 1, 1927, Los Angeles, Calif.
Good modern trombonist, talented arranger and composer. Played in local bands, then did movie studio work in early 40s. Military service, World War II. Resumed studio work after discharge as arranger-composer. Played with George Auld and Buddy Rich in 1949, with Benny Goodman and Charlie Ventura in 1950. Staff man on New York radio, working as sideman-arranger-conductor. Periods with Teddy Powell in 1951 and Buddy Rich in 1952. Some writing for TV in early and mid-50s, freelanced in New York. In Paris 1956-7, arranged for Ray Ventura on TV and records. Returned to U.S. in late 1957, continued to freelance in late 50s. With Quincy Jones in early 60s, concentrated on arranging and composing. Many arrangements for Count Basie, Duke Ellington, J. J. Johnson. Movie and TV scoring, including work for Andy Williams TV show.

RECORDS
GEORGE AULD
　　Dis 102 Hollywood Bazaar
　　Dis 109 Darn That Dream
　　Dis 117 Mild and Mellow

LPs
BILLY BYERS
　　Vi LPM-1269 The RCA Victor Jazz Workshop
　　Mer PPS-2028 Impressions of Duke Ellington
　　Concert Hall CHJ-1217 Byers' Guide
GEORGE AULD
　　Dis(10")DL-3007 That's Auld
MOREY FELD
　　Kapp KL-1007 Jazz Goes to Broadway
TONY SCOTT
　　Vi LJM-1022 Scott's Fling
MANNY ALBAM
　　Vi LPM-1211 The Jazz Workshop
RUBY BRAFF
　　Jazztone J-1210 Swinging with Ruby Braff
JIM CHAPIN
　　Pres(10")213

HAL MCKUSICK-BETTY ST. CLAIRE
　　Jub(10")15
RENEE RAFF
　　AudFid AFLP-2142 Among the Stars

242. BYRD, CHARLIE   g cm B
Born September 16, 1925, Suffolk, Va.
Versatile guitarist, accomplished performer in both jazz and classical music. Key figure in rise of bossa nova in U.S. With Sol Yaged in 1947, Joe Marsala and Barbara Carroll in 1948, Freddie Slack in 1949. Interested in classical guitar since 1950, studied with noted virtuoso Segovia in Italy in 1954. Freelanced in 50s. In 60s opened own Showboat Club in Washington, D.C., used it as base. While on tour in South America became acquainted with Brazilian bossa nova music. Later he and saxman Stan Getz married the music to jazz, helped make it popular in 60s. Continued to freelance, appeared as guitar soloist, led combo. Still active in early 70s.

RECORDS
(All LPs)
CHARLIE BYRD
　　Sav MG-12099 Jazz Recital
　　Co CL-2330 Guitar/Guitar (with HERB ELLIS)
　　Co CL-2592 Byrdland
　　Co CL-2692 More Brazilian Byrd
　　Offbeat OJ-3005 Byrd in the Wind
　　Offbeat OLP-3008 At the Village Vanguard
STAN GETZ-CHARLIE BYRD
　　Verve V-8432 Jazz Samba
TOMMY GWALTNEY'S KANSAS CITY NINE
　　Riv RLP-353 Goin' to Kansas City
WOODY HERMAN SEXTET
　　Forum F-9016 At the Roundtable

243. BYRNE, BOBBY   tb vo B
Born October 10, 1918, Columbus, Ohio
Excellent trombonist whose cool jazz solos in 30s were ahead of their time. Also played strong, beautiful lead. Grew up in Detroit. Father an accomplished music teacher, and Byrne studied many instruments but concentrated on trombone. Also studied music in technical high school, well trained at early age. When Tommy quit Dorsey Brothers band in

mid-1935, Jimmy took over and hired Byrne to replace Tommy. Won quick fame with smooth, flowing, fresh, well-conceived jazz solos and confident, silken sweet work.

Left Jimmy Dorsey in mid-1939 to form own big band. Got radio coverage in 1940, recorded, became rather well known. Dorothy Claire featured vocalist; Stuart Wade joined later. Band's theme *Danny Boy*. In 1941 played important dates at Glen Island Casino and Frank Dailey's Meadowbrook, in 1942 had radio show. But band never hit big. Byrne entered military service in 1943. Band thenfronted briefly by Jack Jenney, finally taken over by Dean Hudson. After discharge, Byrne formed another big band but success again eluded him. Disbanded, worked as trombonist in recording studios, later became record company executive. In 1953-4 he led a good small band on Steve Allen's late-night TV show. By 70s had quit music to become businessman. Lives in New Jersey.

RECORDS

JIMMY DORSEY

De 571 Why Shouldn't I?
De 882 In a Sentimental Mood
De 1784 At Your Beck and Call/Who Do You Think I Saw Last Night?
De 1809 If You Were in My Place
De 1970 Love Is Where You Find It/ Garden of the Moon
De 2295 Deep Purple
De 2352 All of Me
De 2523 All I Remember Is You
De 2735 Body and Soul
De 3334 John Silver

BOBBY BYRNE

De 2942 One Cigarette for Two/If It Wasn't for the Moon

De 2956 Can't We Be Friends?/Two Little Doodle Bugs
De 3020 Easy Does It/How Can You Pretend?
De 3028 Busy as a Bee/'Way Back in 1939 A.D.
De 3108 How Many Times?/Barnyard Cakewalk
De 3170 'Deed I Do/Thinking of You
De 3279 Orchids for Remembrance/ Can't Get Indiana Off My Mind
De 3313 That's for Me/Only Forever
De 3325 Love Lies/Trade Winds
De 3392 Maybe/One Look at You
De 3442 (theme) Danny Boy/Maria Elena
De 3613 You Walk By/Chapel in the Valley
De 3648 Bobby's Trombone Blues/ Brazilian Nuts
De 3774 Two Hearts That Pass in the Night/These Things You Left Me
Cos 492 Hymm to the Sun/Hey, Bobby
Rbw 10005 Buttered Roll/Paradise
Rbw 10012 Swingin' Down the Lane/ Upper Fifth Avenue
Waldorf 67 A Tribute to Tommy Dorsey (medleys; 1 & 2)

LPs

BOBBY BYRNE

GA 206 Tribute to the Dorseys
GA 207-SD (S) Great Song Hits of the Glenn Miller Orchestra
GA 33-310 (one side) Dixieland Jazz
GA 33-416 The Jazzbone's Connected to the Trombone
MGM(10″)E-231 (one side) Dixieland vs. Birdland
Comm 33-894 Movie Themes

ROYAL GARDEN RAJAHS

Waldorf(10″)MH-33-121 Dixieland Jazz
GA 33-313 (1 side) Dixieland Jazz

244. CACERES, ERNIE   cl bs ts as B

Born November 22, 1911, Rockport, Texas
Died January 1971 in Texas

Good jazzman, featured on clarinet with big bands in earlier years, then on baritone sax with dixieland bands later in career. Played gutty swing style with excellent tone on all instruments. At 15 played jobs in Corpus Christi, Texas. Left Texas with brother Emilio's small band that featured swing, Latin and Mexican numbers. Emilio good swing violinist. They worked way to New York, scored at Nick's in 1938. Emilio returned to Texas. Ernie remained in New York, played with Bobby Hackett in 1938 and Jack Teagarden most of 1939. With Bob Zurke briefly late 1939-40. Joined Glenn Miller band in early 1940, remained till Miller disbanded and entered military service in late 1942. Caceres on records made by Miller during this period but seldom featured.

Freelanced in New York, in 1943 worked with Johnny Long, Benny Goodman and Tommy Dorsey. With Woody Herman in 1944 on lead alto, also played at Nick's with dixieland bands and did radio work. In military service awhile. Resumed career in 1946, freelanced in New York mostly with dixieland groups, began to concentrate on baritone sax. Heavy recording, many jobs at Nick's. In 1950-6 plum job in combo on Garry Moore's morning TV show, then jazz jobs at night.

Lucrative period. Continued to freelance, worked in early 60s with Bob Crosby and Billy Butterfield. In 1962 Caceres returned to Texas, settled down in San Antonio in semi-retirement. Occasionally played jobs in area with brother Emilio, led own groups.

RECORDS

EMILIO CACERES
    Vi 25710 Humoresque in Swing Time/I Got Rhythm
    Vi 25719 Who's Sorry Now?/What's the Use?
    Vi 26109 Jig in G/Runnin' Wild

JACK TEAGARDEN
    Br 8370 Persian Rug
    OK 6272 United We Swing
    CMS(12")1521 Rockin' Chair/Pitchin' a Bit Short

SIDNEY BECHET
    Vo 4537 Hold Tight/Jungle Drums
    Vo 4575 What a Dream/Chant in the Night

BOBBY HACKETT
    Vo 4565 Ghost of a Chance

VIC LEWIS & HIS AMERICAN JAZZMEN
    Esq(E) 10-231 That's a-Plenty/Muskrat Ramble
    Esq(E) 10-241 Basin Street Blues/Wrap Your Troubles in Dreams

V-DISC ALL-STARS
    VD(12")384 Jack-Armstrong Blues
    VD(12")491 Confessin'

GLENN MILLER
    Bb 10631 My! My! (alto sax)

Bb 10694 I Haven't Time to Be a Millionaire (alto sax)
Bb 10740 Bugle Call Rag
Bb 10982 Anvil Chorus (part 2)
Bb 11063 I Dreamt I Dwelt in Harlem
Bb 11110 Sun Valley Jump
Vi 27943 Long Tall Mama

LOUIS ARMSTRONG
Vi 20-2348 Jack-Armstrong Blues/Rockin' Chair
Vi 20-2530 Some Day/Fifty-Fifty Blues

MIFF MOLE
CMS(12")1518 Peg o' My Heart/St. Louis Blues

EDDIE CONDON
De 23430 'S Wonderful/Somebody Loves Me
De 23718 The Sheik of Araby/Impromptu Ensemble No.1
Atl 661 Time Carries On/Seems Like Old Times

BUD FREEMAN
Key 638 Town Hall Blues

MUGGSY SPANIER
CMS(12")1517 Sweet Lorraine/September in the Rain

LPs

ERNIE & EMILIO CACERES
Audiophile AP-101 (S)

BOB CROSBY
Cor(10")CRL-56018 John Philip Sousa Marches in Dixieland Style

BOBBY HACKETT
Cap T-857 Gotham Jazz Scene

BOBBY HACKETT-JACK TEAGARDEN
Cap T-933 Jazz Ultimate

EDDIE CONDON
De(10")DL-5137 George Gershwin Jazz Concert

DICK CARY
Stereocraft RTN-106 Hot and Cool

JIMMY MCPARTLAND
Br(10")BL-58049 Shades of Bix

GARRY MOORE PRESENTS
Co CL-717 My Kind of Music

245. CADMAN, CHARLES WAKEFIELD
cm lyr p

Born December 24, 1881, Johnstown, Pa.
Died December 31, 1946, Los Angeles, Calif.

Composer noted for songs *At Dawning*

(1906) and *From the Land of the Sky-Blue Water* (1909). Also wrote descriptive pieces. Studied music with various instructors, also at USC and University of Denver. Researched Indian lore and music, lectured on it many years. Other compositions: *I Hear a Thrush at Eve*; *The Far Horizon*; *Four American Indian songs*; *Sayonora*; *Three Songs to Odysseus*; *White Enchantment*; *The Morning of the Year*; *Piano Sonata in A*; *Sonata in G for Violin, Piano*; *Quintet for Strings, Piano*; *Trio in D*; *American Suite*; *Thunderbird Suite*; *Pennsylvania*; *Father of Waters*; *House of Joy*; *Aurora Borealis*; *A Mad Empress Remembers*; *Dark Dancers of the Mardi Gras*; *Trail Pictures*; *Huckleberry Finn Goes Fishing*; *Oriental Rhapsody*; *Hollywood Suite*; many others.

246. CAESAR, IRVING
lyr cm

Born July 4, 1895, New York, N.Y.

A leading lyricist of 20s and 30s. Many songs for stage and movies. Educated at CCNY. Early in career worked in automotive industry. Official stenographer of Henry Ford Peace Ship, World War I. After returning from Europe began songwriting career. Organizer and former president of Songwriters Protective Association. Wrote scores for Broadway musicals GREENWICH VILLAGE FOLLIES of 1922-3-4-5, BETTY LEE and NO, NO, NANETTE (1925), SWEETHEART TIME (1926), YES, YES, YVETTE (1927), HERE'S HOWE (1928), GEORGE WHITE'S SCANDALS OF 1929, NINA ROSA and RIPPLES (1930), THE WONDER BAR (1931), MELODY (1933), WHITE HORSE INN (1936), others with shorter runs. Also contributed songs and partial scores for many other musicals. Wrote for movies in 30s. Best-known songs: *Swanee, I Want to Be Happy, Tea for Two, Sometimes I'm Happy, Crazy Rhythm, Just a Gigolo, Is It True What They Say About Dixie?*. Collaborated with composers George Gershwin, Vincent Youmans, Victor Herbert, Sigmund Romberg, Rudolf Friml, Ray Henderson, Cliff Friend, Louis Hirsch, Roger Wolfe Kahn, Joseph Meyer, Oscar Levant, Gerald Marks.

SONGS
(with related shows)

1918—SINBAD stage show (Swanee)

1920—MORRIS GEST'S MIDNIGHT WHIRL stage show (songs unimportant); KISSING TIME stage show (songs unimportant); THE SWEETHEART SHOP stage show (songs unimportant)

1922—GREENWICH VILLAGE FOLLIES OF 1922 stage show (Sixty Seconds Every Minute); PINS AND NEEDLES stage show (songs unimportant)

1923—GREENWICH VILLAGE FOLLIES OF 1923 stage show (Annabel Lee); POPPY stage show (Someone Will Make You Smile); Chansonette

1924—GREENWICH VILLAGE FOLLIES OF 1924 stage show (wrote book)

1925—GREENWICH VILLAGE FOLLIES OF 1925-6 stage show (songs unimportant); BETTY LEE stage show (songs unimportant); ANDRE CHARLOT'S REVUE OF 1925 (Gigolette); NO, NO, NANETTE stage show (Tea for Two; I Want to Be Happy; No, No, Nanette; Too Many Rings Around Rosie)

1926—NO FOOLIN' stage show (songs unimportant); SWEETHEART TIME stage show (songs unimportant)

1927—YES, YES, YVETTE stage show (I'm a Little Bit Fonder of You; Do You Love as I Love?); HIT THE DECK stage show (Sometimes I'm Happy)

1928—HERE'S HOWE stage show (Crazy Rhythm; Imagination); WHOOPEE stage show (My Blackbirds Are Bluebirds Now); Dear, on a Night Like This; It Goes Like This; You're a Real Sweetheart

1929—POLLY stage show (songs unimportant); GEORGE WHITE'S SCANDALS OF 1929 stage show (Bottoms Up; Bigger and Better Than Ever)

1930—NINA ROSA stage show (Nina Rosa; Your Smiles, Your Tears); RIPPLES stage show (Is It Love?; There's Nothing Wrong with a Kiss; I'm a Little Bit Fonder of You); Lady, Play Your Mandolin

1931—THE WONDER BAR stage show (Elizabeth; Oh, Donna Clara; The Wonder Bar; Something Seems to Tell Me; Lenox Avenue); Just a Gigolo

1932—THE CROONER movie (Sweethearts Forever); THE KID FROM SPAIN movie (Look What You've Done; What a Perfect Combination; In the Moonlight)

1933—MELODY stage show (Melody; Give Me a Roll on a Drum; You Are the Song; Tonight May Never Come Again; I'd Write a Song); Count Your Blessings; If I Forget You

1934—GEORGE WHITE'S SCANDALS movie (Nasty Man; Hold My Hand; My Dog Loves Your Dog; Sweet and Simple; So Nice; Six Women)

1935—CURLY TOP movie (Animal Crackers in My Soup; The Simple Things in Life; It's All So New to Me); I Don't Know Your Name; Dust Off That Old Pianna

1936—STOWAWAY movie (That's What I Want for Christmas); WHITE HORSE INN stage show (White Horse Inn; I Cannot Live without Your Love; The Waltz We Love; It Would Be Wonderful); Is It True What They Say About Dixie?

1937—Vienna Dreams

1941—NO, NO, NANETTE movie (orginal stage score)

1943—MY DEAR PUBLIC stage show (Now That I'm Free; Rain on the Sea; This Is Our Private Love Song; There Ain't No Color Line Around the Rainbow)

1944—You Never Say Yes

1954—And Still I Love You

Other compositions: Sing a Song of Safety (collection); Sing a Song of Friendship (collection); Songs of Health (collection); *Pilgrim of 1940* (suite); *I Was So Young*; *Nashville Nightingale*; *You Can Dance with Any Girl at All*; *There Ought to Be a Law Against That*; *Blue Eyes*; *Love Is Such a Cheat*; *Umbriago*; *What Do You Do Sunday, Mary?*

247. CAHILL, MARIE   vo
Born February 7, 1870, Brooklyn, N.Y.
Died August 23, 1933

Singer-comedienne with ready Irish wit, star of several early Broadway musicals. At 16 first stage experience in minor role in stock production in Brooklyn. Early minor roles on Broadway in EXCELSIOR, JR. (1895), THE GOLD BUG (1896), MONTE CARLO and SPORTING LIFE (1898), STAR AND GARTER (1900). Attained first real success in 1902 popularizing feature songs in two shows, *Under the Bamboo Tree* in SALLY IN OUR ALLEY and *Nancy Brown* in THE WILD ROSE. Her 1903 show NANCY BROWN written around latter song. Further Broadway shows: IT HAPPENED IN NORDLAND (1904), MOONSHINE (1905), MARRYING MARY (1906), THE BOYS AND BETTY (1908), JUDY FORGOT (1910), THE OPERA BALL (1912), 90 IN THE SHADE (1915). In later years top star in vaudeville. In later shows MERRY-GO-ROUND (1927) and THE NEW YORKERS (1930).

RECORDS
MARIE CAHILL
    Vi 45125 Under the Bamboo Tree/ Fare Thee, Honey, Fare Thee Well
    Vi 45265 Washing Baby/Shopping
    Vi 45370 In a Shoe Store/Symphony Concert
    Vi 45386 Jezebel/Mammy's Viny's Lesson
    Vi(12")55081 The Dallas Blues/An Idle Woman's Busy Day

248. CAHN, SAMMY   lyr p v vo B
Born June 18, 1913, New York, N.Y.

A top lyricist with prolific output during long career. Astounding number of hit songs. Collaborated with composer Saul Chaplin from 1936 into early 40s, with Jule Styne during 40s, in later years with Jimmy Van Heusen and others. Wrote night club scores in mid-30s. Scores for Broadway shows HIGH BUTTON SHOES (1947), TWO'S COMPANY (1952), SKYSCRAPER (1965), WALKING HAPPY (1966). Many songs for movies in 40s, huge number in 50s and 60s including numerous title songs. Early in career played violin in bands, worked in vaudeville, also played piano. Co-led dance band with Saul Chaplin in mid-30s. Music publisher since 1955. In 60s and 70s appearances on TV shows, often performing medleys of his songs, also displaying wit. Starred in 1974 Broadway musical WORDS AND MUSIC, revue featuring own patter and songs.

SONGS
(with related shows)

1935—Rhythm Is Our Business (once Jimmie Lunceford theme)

1936—I'm One Step Ahead of My Shadow; Rhythm Saved the World; Shoe Shine Boy; Until the Real Thing Comes Along; Don't Look Now

1937—Bei Mir Bist du Schon; Dedicated to You; If It's the Last Thing I Do; Posin'; Don't You Care What Anyone Says; Love, You're Just a Laugh; Just a Simple Melody; If You Ever Should Leave; Everyone's Wrong but Me

1938—Please Be Kind; Saving Myself for You; Joseph! Joseph!; Wait Till My Heart Finds Out; Laughing Boy Blues

1939—I Want My Share of Love; It's Easy to Blame the Weather; It's My Turn Now; Prosschai; The Girl with the Pigtails in Her Hair; You're a Lucky Guy

1940—LADIES MUST LIVE movie (I Could Make You Care)

1941—TIME OUT FOR RHYTHM movie (As If You Didn't Know)

1943—YOUTH ON PARADE movie (I've Heard That Song Before; You're So Good to Me); Vict'ry Polka

1944—CAROLINA BLUES movie (There Goes That Song Again; Poor Little Rhode Island; You Make Me Dream Too Much; Thanks a Lot); FOLLOW THE BOYS movie (I'll Walk Alone); STEP LIVELY movie (As Long as There's Music; Some Other Time; Come Out, Come Out, Wherever You Are; And Then You Kissed Me; Where Does Love Begin?); KNICKERBOCKER HOLIDAY movie (additional songs); Saturday Night

1945—A SONG TO REMEMBER movie (title

song); ANCHORS AWEIGH movie (I Fall In Love Too Easily; What Makes the Sun Set; The Charm of You; I Begged Her; We Hate to Leave); TONIGHT AND EVERY NIGHT movie (Anywhere); I Should Care; Can't You Read Between the Lines?; It's Been a Long Long Time

1946—KID FROM BROOKLYN movie (You're the Cause of It All; I Love an Old Fashioned Song; Hey, What's Your Name?; Josie; Sunflower Song); THE STORK CLUB movie (Love Me); TARS AND SPARS movie (I'm Glad I Waited for You; Love Is a Merry-Go-Round; Kiss Me Hello); SWEETHEART OF SIGMA CHI movie (Five Minutes More); EARL CARROLL'S SKETCH BOOK movie (I've Never Forgotten); Let It Snow; The Things We Did Last Summer; Day by Day

1947—HIGH BUTTON SHOES stage show (I Still Get Jealous; You're My Girl; Papa, Won't You Dance with Me?); IT HAPPENED IN BROOKLYN movie (I Believe; Time After Time; The Brooklyn Bridge; The Song's Gotta Come from the Heart; Whose Baby Are You?; It's the Same Old Dream); LADIES MAN movie (I Gotta Gal I Love; What Am I Gonna Do About You?)

1948—TWO GUYS FROM TEXAS movie (I Don't Care If It Rains All Night; Hankerin'; Ev'ry Day I Love You Just a Little Bit More; At the Rodeo; There's Music in the Land; I Want to Be a Cowboy in the Movies); ROMANCE ON THE HIGH SEAS movie (It's Magic; Put 'Em in a Box, Tie 'Em With a Ribbon; I'm in Love; It's You or No One; Run Run Run; The Tourist Trade)

1949—IT'S A GREAT FEELING movie (It's a Great Feeling; Fiddle Dee Dee; Blame My Absent Minded Heart; At the Cafe Rendezvous; There's Nothing Rougher Than Love; Give Me a Song with a Beautiful Melody; That Was a Big Fat Lie)

1950—TOAST OF NEW ORLEANS movie (Be

My Love); YOUNG MAN WITH A HORN movie (Melancholy Rhapsody)

1951—RICH, YOUNG AND PRETTY movie (Wonder Why; I Can See You; Paris; Dark Is the Night; We Never Talk Much; How D'Ya Like Your Eggs in the Morning?)

1952—TWO'S COMPANY stage show (It Just Occurred to Me; Esther); BECAUSE YOU'RE MINE movie (Because You're Mine); APRIL IN PARIS movie; Two Wrongs Never Make a Right

1953—Disney's PETER PAN cartoon (Your Mother and Mine); THREE SAILORS AND A GIRL movie (Face to Face; The Lately Song); The Second Star to the Right

1954—IT'S A WOMAN'S WORLD movie (title song); INDISCRETION OF AN AMERICAN WIFE (Indiscretion); THREE COINS IN THE FOUNTAIN movie (title song); Teach Me Tonight

1955—PETE KELLY'S BLUES movie (title song); THE MAN WITH THE GOLDEN ARM movie (title song); THE TENDER TRAP movie (title song); LOVE ME OR LEAVE ME movie (I'll Never Stop Loving You); Love and Marriage; The Impatient Years

1956—WRITTEN IN THE WIND movie (title song); SOMEBODY UP THERE LIKES ME movie (title song); THE LITTLEST REVUE stage show (Good Little Girls); Hey, Jealous Heart; The Test of Time

1957—THE JOKER IS WILD movie (All the Way); DON'T GO NEAR THE WATER movie (title song)

1958—THE LONG HOT SUMMER movie (title song); PARIS HOLIDAY movie (Life Is For Lovin'; Love Won't Let You Get Away; Nothing in Common); SOME CAME RUNNING movie (To Love and Be Loved); INDISCREET movie (title song); Come Fly with Me; How Are You Fixed For Love?; Here Comes Another Song About Texas; Closer Than a Kiss; Fancy Meeting You Here; Straight Down the Middle (golf song)

1959—SAY ONE FOR ME movie (Say One

for Me; You Can't Love 'Em All);
A HOLE IN THE HEAD movie (High
Hopes; All My Tomorrows); THE
BEST OF EVERYTHING movie (The
Best of Everything); A Beautiful
Friendship
1960—HIGH TIME movie (The Second
Time Around); THE WORLD OF
SUZY WONG movie (The World of
Suzy Wong); OCEANS 11 movie
(Ain't That a Kick in the Head)
1961—A POCKETFUL OF MIRACLES movie
(A Pocketful of Miracles)
1962—THE BOYS' NIGHT OUT movie (The
Boys' Night Out; Cathy)
1963—COME BLOW YOUR HORN movie
(Come Blow Your Horn) HOW THE
WEST WAS WON movie (Home in
the Meadow); UNDER THE YUM
YUM TREE movie (Under the Yum
Yum Tree) PAPA'S DELICATE CON-
DITION movie (Call Me Irrespon-
sible)
1964—ROBIN AND THE SEVEN HOODS mov-
ie (My Kind of Town; Style; All
for One and One for All; Mr.
Booze; Charlotte Couldn't
Charleston; Any Man Who Loves
His Mother; Don't Be a Do-
Badder; Bang-Bang); WHERE LOVE
HAS GONE movie (Where Love Has
Gone)
1965—SKYSCRAPER stage show (Every-
body Has the Right to Be Wrong;
I'll Only Miss Her When I Think
of Her)
1966—WALKING HAPPY stage show
(Walking Happy; I Don't Think
I'm in Love; It Might as Well Be
You; Use Your Noggin; How
D'Ya Talk to a Girl?; If I Be Your
Best Chance; What Makes It Hap-
pen?)
1967—THOROUGHLY MODERN MILLIE mov-
ie (Thoroughly Modern Millie;
Tapioca)
1968—STAR! movie (Star); A FLEA IN HER
EAR movie (A Flea in Her Ear)

Also wrote material for movies THE WEST
POINT STORY, YOU'RE NEVER TOO YOUNG,
THE COURT JESTER, MEET ME IN LAS VEGAS,
THE OPPOSITE SEX, TEN THOUSAND BED-
ROOMS, LET'S MAKE LOVE, ROAD TO HONG
KONG, SHE'S WORKING HER WAY THROUGH
COLLEGE, SERENADE, ANYTHING GOES, THE
PLEASURE SEEKERS.

249. CAIN, JACKIE   vo B
(JACQUELINE RUTH CAIN)
Born May 22, 1928, Milwaukee, Wis.

Girl vocalist who teamed with Roy Kral
to form bop-styled singing duo that won
kudos in late 40s and 50s. Jackie jazz-
styled singer with Charlie Ventura in
1948-9. Joined Kral for unusual duets
with Ventura that were acclaimed in jazz
circles. Kral also pianist and arranger,
responsible for many of their routines. In
1949 they married, in late 1949 formed
own combo. Later disbanded, had TV
show in Chicago. Rejoined Ventura in
mid-1953. In later 50s and 60s worked as
act in jazz clubs and smart supper clubs,
mostly in New York and Las Vegas.
Developed entertaining act. Recorded
through the years, did TV appearances,
made commercials for TV and radio.
Active into 70s.

RECORDS
CHARLIE VENTURA
  Nat 9066 Pina Colada
  Nat 9077 'Deed I Do
ROY KRAL-JACKIE CAIN
  Atl 664 Ever Loving Blues/Auld Lang
    Syne
  Atl 668 What Do You Think I Am?/
    Afro-Disia
  Cor 61178 Pa, Take Me to the Cir-
    cus/Banana Split
LPs
CHARLIE VENTURA
  Br BL-54025 Here's Charlie (RIs)
JACKIE CAIN-ROY KRAL
  Roul R-25278 BY JUPITER (and GIRL
    CRAZY) Scores
  ABC-Para 120 The Glory of Love
  ABC-Para 163 Bits and Pieces
  ABC-Para 207 (with BILL HOLMAN OR-
    CHESTRA)
  Co CL-1704 Double Talk
  Verve V6-8668 Changes
  Verve V-8688 Lovesick
  Story STLP-322
  Story STLP-904

249A. CAINE, GEORGIA   vo

Born c. 1876
Died April 4, 1964, Hollywood, Calif.

Beautiful singer-actress of Broadway stage. Character roles in over 30 films 1930-49.

BROADWAY MUSICALS

1899—THE ROGERS BROTHERS IN WALL STREET
1900—FOXY QUILLER
1901—THE MESSENGER BOY
1902—SALLY IN OUR ALLEY
1903—PEGGY FROM PARIS
1904—THE SHO-GUN
1905—THE EARL AND THE GIRL
1906—THE RICH MR. HOGGENHEIMER
1908—MISS HOOK OF HOLLAND; THE MERRY WIDOW (joined during long run)
1909—THE MOTOR GIRL
1910—MADAME TROUBADOUR
1911—THE THREE ROMEOS
1913—ADELE; THE GEISHA (operetta; revival)
1915—TWO IS COMPANY
1920—MARY
1921—THE O'BRIEN GIRL
1922—LITTLE NELLIE KELLY
1924—BE YOURSELF
1930—SMILES

250. CALDWELL, ANNE   lyr vo
(ANNE CALDWELL O'DEA)

Born August 30, 1867, Boston, Mass.
Died October 22, 1936, Hollywood, Calif.

Lyricist-librettist of many Broadway musicals 1907-28. Most songs effective only within context of shows, attained little popularity. *Wait Till the Cows Come Home* a hit from 1917 show JACK O' LANTERN. Other leading songs: *Come and Have a Swing with Me* (1917), *Whose Baby Are You?* and *Left All Alone Again Blues* (1920), *Ka-lu-a* (1921), *In Love with Love, Once in a Blue Moon* and *Raggedy Ann* (1923), *I Know That You Know, In Araby with You* and *You Will, Won't You?* (1926), *Look at the World and Smile* and *Somebody Else* (1927). Chief collaborators Jerome Kern, Vincent Youmans, Hugo Felix, Raymond Hubbell.

BROADWAY MUSICALS
(wrote book and lyrics unless designated otherwise)

1907—THE TOP OF THE WORLD (book only)
1912—THE LADY OF THE SLIPPER (book only)
1914—CHIN-CHIN; WHEN CLAUDIA SMILES
1916—GO TO IT (book only); POM-POM
1917—JACK O' LANTERN
1918—THE CANARY (lyrics only)
1919—THE LADY IN RED; SHE'S A GOOD FELLOW
1920—HITCHY-KOO OF 1920; THE NIGHT BOAT; THE SWEETHEART SHOP; TIP TOP
1921—GOOD MORNING, DEARIE
1922—THE BUNCH AND JUDY
1923—STEPPING STONES
1924—MAGNOLIA LADY; PEG-O'-MY-DREAMS (lyrics only)
1925—THE CITY CHAP (lyrics only)
1926—CRISS CROSS; OH, PLEASE
1927—TAKE THE AIR (book only); YOURS TRULY (lyrics only)
1928—THREE CHEERS

251. CALLENDER, RED   b tu B
(GEORGE CALLENDER)

Born March 6, 1918, Richmond, Va.

Freelance bass man active with jazz groups of 40s and 50s. Plays any style. As teenager with Banjo Bernie in Atlantic City. In California with Louis Armstrong in 1937. Freelanced on west coast with small groups; considerable studio work. Own combo at intervals. In 40s worked with Nat "King" Cole, Lester Young, Erroll Garner, Louis Armstrong, Johnny Otis. Active with bop groups in mid-40s. In late 40s led combo in Hawaii. With Jerry Fielding in early 50s, freelance and studio work in 50s and 60s. Participated in numerous recording sessions through the years.

RECORDS

LOUIS ARMSTRONG
   De 1560 Once in Awhile/On the Sunny Side of the Street
   Vi 40-0136 Sugar
   Vi 20-2087 Do You Know What It Means to Miss New Orleans?

Vi 20-2088 Mahogany Hall Stomp/ Where the Blues Were Born in New Orleans

KAY STARR
Lamp 110 Love Me or Leave Me/Sweet Lorraine
Lamp 104 My Melancholy Baby/Sweet Georgia Brown

HOLLYWOOD HUCKSTERS
Cap 40022 Them There Eyes/Happy Blues

SONNY GREER
Cap 10028 Mood Indigo/The Mooche

LESTER YOUNG
Alad 137 You're Driving Me Crazy/ New Lester Leaps In
Philo 123 D.B. Blues/Lester Blows Again

RED NORVO
Cap 15253 Bop!/I'll Follow You

BABE RUSSIN
Key 630 All the Things You Are/Like Someone in Love

ANDRE PREVIN
Sun 7363 Take the "A" Train/I Got It Bad
Sun 7365 Warm Valley/Subtle Slough

HOWARD MCGHEE
B&W 150 Oodie Coo Bop (1 & 2)

BENNY GOODMAN SEXTET
Cap 15069 The World Is Waiting for the Sunrise

ERROLL GARNER TRIO
Mer 1032 Blue Skies/Don't Blame Me
Mer 1033 Full Moon and Empty Arms/Memories of You
Dial 1016 Pastel/Trio

AL HIBBLER
Alad 154 I Got It Bad/How Long
Alad 155 S'posin'

JAZZ AT THE PHILHARMONIC
Asch 4531 How High the Moon (1 & 2)
Asch 4532 How High the Moon (3)/Lady Be Good (1)
Asch 4533 Lady Be Good (2 & 3)

CHARLIE PARKER
Dial 1014 Dark Shadows/Bird's Nest
Dial 1015 Blow Top Blues/Cool Blues

CHARLIE VENTURA
Lamp 105 Stompin' at the Savoy (1 & 2)

RED CALLENDER
Sun 10056 These Foolish Things/Get Happy
B&W 782 Red Boogie/By the River Sainte Marie
Excl 202 I Wonder/Skyline
Fed 12049 September in the Rain/Tabor-Inn

LPs

RED CALLENDER
Mod LMP-1207 Swingin' Suite
Cr CLP-5012 Callender Speaks Low

ART TATUM-BUDDY DE FRANCO
ARS G-412

BING CROSBY (with Bob Scobey band)
Vi LPM-1473 Bing with a Beat

JOHN GRAAS
EmArcy MG-36117 Coup de Graas

LESTER YOUNG
Alad(10")705 The Lester Young Trio
Score SLP-4028 Swinging Lester Young

WARDELL GRAY
Cr 5004 Way Out Wardell

(miscellaneous artists)
ModRec LMP-1202 Groovin' High
Cr CLP-5129 Kings of Dixieland, Vol. 2
Tops(10")L-928-69 Junior Jazz at the Auditorium

252. CALLOWAY, CAB   d vo cm lyr B
(CABELL CALLOWAY)

Born December 25, 1907, Rochester, N.Y.

Famed scat singer-bandleader of 30s and 40s. Exciting showman, led excellent big band with outstanding soloists. "Hi-De-Ho" scat singing his trademark, but handled ballads capably too. Grew up in Baltimore. Attended law school awhile in Chicago but quit when began singing in Chicago clubs. Worked stage revues, toured, worked with sister Blanche. In late 20s fronted The Alabamians in Chicago. 1929 role in New York revue CONNIE'S HOT CHOCOLATES. Later in 1929 led The Alabamians at Savoy in Harlem. Then fronted The Missourians, soon using own name as bandleader. First real success early 1931-2 at Harlem's Cotton Club, where his uninhibited style and hot band were naturals. By 1932 a sensation, aided by good radio coverage and records. Known for such numbers as *Minnie the Moocher* (theme), *Kickin' the Gong Around*, *St. James Infirmary*, *Reefer Man*, *Eadie Was a Lady*. Band in movie BIG BROADCAST OF 1932. Other movies: INTERNATIONAL HOUSE (1933), THE SINGING KID (1936), MANHATTAN MERRY-GO-ROUND (1937), STORMY WEATHER (1943), SENSATIONS OF 1945 (1944), ST. LOUIS BLUES (1958). Band recorded extensively over the years. Toured England 1934.

Cab famed for frantic gyrations in front of band, with long black hair awry, sometimes clad in white tuxedo. Handled most vocals, specializing in swingers and novelties. Almost overlooked: his distinctive way with ballads. Through the years band maintained high level of musicianship, showcased good jazz soloists. Star the great Chu Berry on tenor sax, with him from mid-1937 until death in late 1941. Other outstanding jazzmen with band: Eddie Barefield, Benny Payne, Doc Cheatham, Ben Webster, Walter Thomas, Claude Jones, Keg Johnson, Milt Hinton, Tyree Glenn, Dizzy Gillespie, Hilton Jefferson, Quentin Jackson, Cozy Cole, Jonah Jones, Shad Collins. Good singer June Richmond with band awhile in late 30s. Cab composed many numbers featured by band: *Minnie the Moocher*; *The Scat Song*; *The Jumpin' Jive*; *Lady with the Fan*; *Zaz Zuh Zaz*; *Chinese Rhythm*; *Are You in Love with Me Again?*; *That Man's Here Again*; *Peck-a-Doodle-Doo*; *I Like Music*; *Rustle of Swing*; *Three Swings and Out*; *Are You Hep to the Jive?*; *Boog-It*; *Come On with the "Come On"*; *Silly Old Moon*; *Sunset*; *Rhapsody in Rhumba*; *Are You All Reet?*; *Hi-De-Ho Man*; *Levee Lullaby*; *Hot Air*; *Geechy Joe*; *Let's Go, Joe*. Chief collaborators Irving Mills, Clarence Gaskill, Buck Ram, Andy Gibson, Jack Palmer, Paul Mills. Broke up band in 1948, led new band briefly in 1951.

George Gershwin wrote role of Sportin' Life in famed opera PORGY AND BESS with Cab in mind. Cab didn't play in original 1935 show but during 1952-4 played the role in road show version touring U.S.

and abroad, returning to role occasionally in later years. In later 50s and 60s less active, occasionally led combo or orchestra or played as single, sometimes on TV. In late 60s played in all-Negro version of show HELLO, DOLLY. One of most successful and best-liked bandleaders, his contributions to popular and jazz music of major importance in 30s and 40s.

RECORDS

THE MISSOURIANS
    Vi 38067 Market Street Stomp/Missouri Moan
    Vi 38071 You'll Cry for Me, but I'll Be Gone/Ozark Mountain Blues
CAB CALLOWAY
    Pe 15457 Mood Indigo/Farewell Blues
    Pe 15490 Levee Low Down/Blues in My Heart
    Pe 15551 Down Hearted Blues/Corrine Corrina
    Pe 15623 Dinah/I'm Now Prepared to Tell the World It's You
    Br 6074 Minnie the Moocher/Doin' the Rhumba
    Br 6105 St. James Infirmary/Nobody's Sweetheart
    Br 6209 Kickin' the Gong Around/Between the Devil and the Deep Blue Sea
    Br 6272 The Scat Song/Cabin in the Cotton
    Br 6340 Reefer Man/You Gotta Hi-De-Ho
    Br 7638 I Love to Sing-a/Save Me, Sister
    Br 7685 When You're Smiling/Are You in Love with Me Again?
    Vi 24414 Evenin'/Harlem Hospitality
    Vi 24659 Emaline/Margie
    Vi 24690 Moonglow/Hotcha Razz-Ma-Tazz
    Va 593 Congo/My Gal Mezzanine
    Va 643 She's Tall, She's Tan, She's Terrific/I'm Always in the Mood for You
    Vo 4477 April in My Heart/Do You Wanna Jump, Children?
    Vo 4498 Angels with Dirty Faces/F.D.R. Jones
    Vo 4511 Deep in a Dream/I'm Madly in Love with You

Vo 5005 The Jumpin' Jive/Trylon
Swing
OK 5687 Come On with the "Come
On"/A Ghost of a Chance
OK 6084 Bye Bye Blues/Run Little
Rabbit
OK 6109 Willow Weep for Me/Jonah
Joins the Cab
OK 6305 Take the "A" Train/Chatta-
nooga Choo Choo
OK 6341 I See a Million People/We
Go Well Together
OK 6717 I'll Be Around/Virginia,
Georgia and Caroline
OK 6720 Let's Go Joe/A Smo-o-oth
One
Co 36786 Let's Take the Long Way
Home/Foo a Little Ballyhoo

LPs

CAB CALLOWAY
Epic LN-3265 Cab Calloway (Vo, Br
RIs)
Br(10")BL-58010 Cab Calloway (Br
RIs)
Ace of Hearts(E) AH-106 (Br RIs)
(miscellaneous artists)
Sutton 270 BLACKBIRDS OF 1928 (RIs)

253. CAMARATA, TOOTS

t ar cm lyr B

(SALVADOR TUTTI
CAMARATA)

Born May 11, 1913, Glen Ridge, N.J.

Arranger and orchestra leader for record
sessions, best known for work in 40s and
50s. Studied at Juilliard. In early 30s on
trumpet with Frank Dailey, Scott Fisher,
Charlie Barnet. With Hale Hamilton
1935-6. Joined Jimmy Dorsey in late 1936
on trumpet, also arranged. Starting 1938
concentrated solely on arranging for Jimmy. Composed several numbers used by
band: *Mutiny in the Brass Section*; *Hollywood Pastime*; *Dixieland Detour*; *Finger-
bustin'*; *What Makes Sammy Run?*; *A Man
and His Drum*; *Shoot the Meat Balls to
Me, Dominick Boy*. Arranged band's biggest hits, famed Bob Eberly-Helen O'Connell duets on tunes like *Green Eyes*,
Tangerine, *Yours*. Other compositions:
1941 pop song, *Moonlight Masquerade*,
and later numbers *Trumpeter's Prayer*,
Louis, *No More*, *Verdiana Suite*, *Rhum-
balero*, *Story of the Stars*, *Rhapsody for*

Saxophone, Who Knows?. In late 30s, in
addition to work for Dorsey, also arranged for Paul Whiteman and for Bing
Crosby's Kraft Music Hall radio show. In
early 40s Camarata formed his own large
orchestra for radio and records. In mid-
40s musical director for Decca Records.
In 1948-50 to England as musical director
for London Records, where he managed
to adapt music on English pop records to
U.S. market. In early 50s active in U.S.
recording work. In 1954 arranger and
musical director for Decca house band
The Commanders, an excellent, swinging
band featuring good brass. Eddie Grady
later became leader and took band on
road. Active in late 50s and 60s with Walt
Disney studios as musical director.

RECORDS

TOOTS CAMARATA
De 27850 Never/My Concerto
De 27909 Heaven Drops Her Curtain
Down/Only Fools
De 28332 Mandolino-Mandolino/Who
Knows?
De 28367 Jambalaya/Mademoiselle
De 28376 Brief Interlude/Veradero
De 28528 Flashing Pearls/The Singing
Zither
De 28714 All I Desire/Return to Par-
adise
De 28882 Willow Weep for Me/Waltz
Theme
THE COMMANDERS
De 28966 I Want a Little Girl/Davey
Jones
De 29048 Kentucky Boogie/Make
Love to Me
(as conductor)
JOHN RAITT
De 28337 Because You're Mine/The
Song Angels Sing
BERYL DAVIS
Vi 20-2268 If My Heart Had a Win-
dow/I Want to Be Loved
Vi 20-3036 Just Once More/Down the
Stairs and Out the Door
BING CROSBY
De 23678 Till the Clouds Roll By/Ol'
Man River
BILLY HOLIDAY
De 23391 Lover Man/That Old Devil
Called Love
De 23483 No More

LPs

TOOTS CAMARATA
  Vista 4027 MAN OF LA MANCHA (with
    MIKE SAMMES SINGERS)
  Vista 4047 (S) Tutti's Trumpets
  Vista 4048 (S) Tutti's Trombones
  De DL-8112 Music for a Lazy After-
    noon
  De(10″)DL-5461 Fiddlesticks
  Vo VL-3660   Rendezvous with
    Camarata
THE COMMANDERS
  De(10″)DL-5525 Meet the Command-
    ers
(as conductor)
JERI SOUTHERN
  De DL-8394 When Your Heart's on
    Fire

254. CAMPBELL, JAMES   cm lyr

English songwriter who teamed with
countryman Reg Connelly on several
songs popular in U.S. Pair usually collaborated with another composer on its
songs. Leading hits in U.S. were *If I Had
You* (1929), *When the Organ Played at
Twilight* (1930), *Goodnight Sweetheart*
(1931), *By the Fireside, Just an Echo in the
Valley* and *Till Tomorrow* (1932), *Try a
Little Tenderness* (1933).

255. CANDIDO, CANDY   b vo B

Born c. 1905, New Orleans, La.

Bassist-comic known for comical voice
ranging from extremely high to extremely
low notes, with antics accompanying.
Dubbed voice for Popeye in many movie
cartoons of 30s. Worked with Ted Fio
Rito band, in movies with band. Early
start in dance bands, toured with carnival,
led own band. In early 30s worked with
Peck Kelley, Russ Columbo. In 1932
teamed with guitarist Otto Heimel to
form duo known as Candy & Coco,
accompanied singer Gene Austin (and at
various times in later years). In 1934-6
featured with Fio Rito band, which made
movie shorts and appeared in two Dick
Powell movies TWENTY MILLION SWEET-
HEARTS (1934) and BROADWAY GONDO-
LIER (1935). Candido appeared in other
movies, including GIFT OF GAB (1934),
SOMETHING TO SING ABOUT (1937), CAM-

PUS RHYTHM (1943). Led own group
1937-9, returned to Fio Rito 1940-2. In
military service. With Fio Rito again
briefly in 1945. Played clubs in late 40s
and 50s as single or with combo. On
Jimmy Durante radio show 1950-1.

RECORDS

CANDY CANDIDO & THE KIDS
  De 1590 Ma/Big Bass Fiddle
CANDY & COCO
  Vo 2833 Kingfish Blues/New Orleans
  Vo 2849 China Boy/Bugle Call Rag
GENE AUSTIN
  De 1656 Dear Old Southland/China
    Boy
TED FIO RITO (as bassist; possibly some
  vocals)
  Br 6902 Soft Green Seas/King Kame-
    hameha
  Br 6924 Hot Dogs and Sasparella/
    Thank You for a Lovely Evening
  Br 6928 Crickets in the Grass/The Big
    Bad Wolf Was Dead
  Br 7315 Blue Moon/Were You
    Foolin'?
  Br 7327 June in January/With Every
    Breath I Take
  Br 7364 On the Good Ship Lollipop/
    Ting-a-ling
  Br 7392 Got Me Doin' Things/Let Me
    Sing You to Sleep
  Br 7451 Outside of You/The Rose in
    Her Hair
  Br 7452 Lulu's Back in Town/You
    Can Be Kissed
  Br 7478 I Want to Learn to Speak
    Hawaiian/Sweet and Slow
JOE "FINGERS" CARR-CANDY CANDIDO
  Cap 1847 Cecilia/Snuggle Bug

256. CANDOLI, CONTE   t B
(SECONDO CANDOLI)

Born July 12, 1927, Mishawaka, Ind.

Trumpet player in modern style, facile,
with good range. Younger brother of Pete
Candoli, also trumpet star. Began professionally in South Bend area in 1942. With
Woody Herman briefly in 1943, then
completed high school and rejoined Herman in early 1945. Left September 1945
for military service. Worked with Chubby
Jackson combo in 1947, Stan Kenton
1948 and Charlie Ventura 1949. Another

period with Herman in 1950. With Charlie Barnet in 1951 and again with Kenton 1952-3. In early 1954 led combo in Chicago. In 1955 settled in California, began period of several years with Howard Rumsey's Lighthouse All-Stars. Also played jobs with brother Pete and Shelly Manne. In 1959 he and Pete formed band, played on west coast. Freelanced on jobs and record sessions. During 1961-6 period mostly with Shelly Manne group in California, played nightly TV show. Active into 70s.

RECORDS

CHUBBY JACKSON
Rbw 111 Crown Pilots/Lemon Drop
Rbw 112 Boomsie/Dee Dee's Dance
Rbw 113 Begin the Beguine/Crying Sands
MGM 10228 The Happy Monster/ L'ana
CHARLIE VENTURA
Vi 20-3552 Boptura/Yankee Clipper
Mer 8942 Avalon
Mer 8949 Bugle Call Rag/That Old Feeling
Mer 8995 Rose Room
SHELLY MANNE
DeeGee 3801 The Count on Rush Street/All of Me

LPs

CONTE CANDOLI
Cr CLP-5162 Little Band, Big Jazz
Beth(10″)BCP-1016 Conte Candoli
Mode 109 Conte Candoli Quartet
CONTE CANDOLI-PETE CANDOLI
Mer MG-20515 The Brothers Candoli: Sextet
Dot DLP-3062 The Brothers Candoli
Dot DLP-3168 Bell, Book, and Candoli
CONTE CANDOLI-LOU LEVY
Atl 1268 West Coast Wailers
CONTE CANDOLI-STAN LEVEY
REP 205 West Coasting
SHELLY MANNE
Cap 2313 That's Gershwin!
HOWARD LUCRAFT
De DL-8679 Showcase for Modern Jazz
RICHIE KAMUCA
Hi-Fi Record 12-604 Jazz Erotica

HOWARD RUMSEY
Contemp C-3504 Lighthouse All-Stars, Vol. 6
STAN KENTON
Cap(10″)L-383 New Concepts of Artistry in Rhythm
STAN LEVEY
Beth BCP-71 Grand Stan
Mode 101 Stan Levey/5

257. CANDOLI, PETE   t ar cm B
(WALTER JOSEPH CANDOLI)
Born June 28, 1923, Mishawaka, Ind.
Trumpet player in modern style. Big-toned, powerful soloist, high-note specialist and good arranger. Older brother of Conte Candoli, also trumpet star. Got early start with name bands, first big job with Sonny Dunham in 1940. With Will Bradley 1941 and Ray McKinley 1942. Joined Tommy Dorsey for one year, 1943-4. In mid-40s with Freddie Slack, Alvino Rey, Charlie Barnet, Teddy Powell and Woody Herman (did screamer trumpet bits with latter band). With Boyd Raeburn 1947, later in year joined Tex Beneke for 1947-8 period. With Jerry Gray 1950-1. Settled on west coast for freelance and studio work. Periods with Les Brown and Stan Kenton, and in 1954-5 led own band. Jobs included some with brother Conte, and in 1959 he and Conte led band on west coast. Freelanced on jobs and record sessions in 60s. Active into 70s, in band on Merv Griffin's late-night TV show, sometimes featured. Co-starred as actor with wife Edie Adams in 1973 tour of 30s Broadway musical ANYTHING GOES.

RECORDS

WOODY HERMAN
Co 36803 Apple Honey
Co 36815 Goosey Gander
Co 36835 Northwest Passage
Co 36949 Wild Root
BILL HARRIS
Key 618 Mean to Me/Cross Country
Key 626 Characteristically B.H.
METRONOME ALL-STAR BAND
Vi 40-4000 Look Out/Metronome All Out

LPs

PETE CANDOLI
De DL-74761 (S) Moscow Mule and Many More Kicks
Somerset 17200 Blues, When Your Lover Has Gone

PETE CANDOLI-CONTE CANDOLI
Mer MG-20515 The Brothers Candoli: Sextet
Dot DLP-3062 The Brothers Candoli
Dot DLP-3168 Bell, Book, and Candoli

TOOTS CAMARATA
Vista 4047 (S) Tutti's Trumpets

PEGGY LEE
De(10")DL-5482 Black Coffee

JERRY FIELDING
De DL-8450 Fielding's Formula

RUSS GARCIA & MARTY PAICH
Beth 6039 Jazz Music for the Birds and the Hep Cats

PETE RUGOLO
Co CL-604 Adventures in Rhythm
Mer PPS-2016 Ten Trumpets and Two Guitars

ELMER BERNSTEIN
Choreo A-11 Movie and TV Themes

GLEN GRAY
Cap W-1022 Sounds of the Great Bands, Vol. 1

HENRY MANCINI
Vi LSP-2258 (S) Combo!

258. CANDULLO, JOE   tu v vo ar B

Bandleader from mid-20s into 40s. 20s band played semi-hot style, many arrangements by Candullo himself. Extensive recording during this period. Jazzman Red Nichols believed to play on many Candullo records. Information on personnel almost completely lacking, but solos performed by capable jazzmen. Band based in New York mostly. Later in 30s Candullo fronted hotel-type band, in mid-30s played Rainbow Grill, Manhattan. In late 30s played outside New York, including long engagements in Florida.

RECORDS

(*probable Red Nichols solo)

JOE CANDULLO
Ed 51848 Battle of Blues*
Ed 51852 Brown Sugar*

Ge 3316 Spanish Mama/The Nightmare*
Ge 3392 For You and Me/Don't Be Angry*
Ge 3402 Bogadillo*
Ge 3405 Tomboy Sue*
Ba 1784 Deep Henderson/Jackass Blues*
Ba 1796 Black Bottom / Messin' Around
Ba 7169 A Jazz Holiday
Ba 7218 When Sweet Susie Goes Stepping By*
Ca 1048 Brown Sugar*
Pat 36461 Mary Lou/I Wish You Were Jealous of Me*
Ve 1361 My Sunday Gal/Yes Flo*
Ve 1397 Go Wash an Elephant/Fifty Million Frenchmen Can't Be Wrong
Pe 14667 Down by the Old Sea Shore/Baby Face*
Pe 14668 Turkish Towel/Crazy Quilt
Pe 14831 It's a Million to One You're in Love
Re 8109 Black Bottom / Nervous Charlie Stomp
Ha 235 Sadie Green/Me Too
Ha 286 Blowin' Off Steam/Brown Sugar

259. CANOVA, JUDY   vo

Born November 20, 1916, Jacksonville, Fla.

Popular hillbilly singer-comedienne of late 30s and 40s, active on radio and in movies. Could sing straight but usually affected cornball style and high voice gyrations for laughs. Sang on Florida radio at 12. Attended Cincinnati Conservatory of Music to study for opera, gave it up. In 1934 with sister Annie and brother Zeke to New York, landed job in Greenwich Village club doing mountaineer act. Judy star of act, later won small role in Broadway musical CALLING ALL STARS. Show opened in December 1934, ran only 36 performances. Good role in ZIEGFELD FOLLIES OF 1936, which opened in January 1936 and had good run of 115 performances. Later in 1936 Canovas scored with antics and singing on Paul Whiteman radio show. Early 1937 starred on Rippling Rhythm Revue on radio, with Shep Fields band and Frank Parker. Here Judy became well known as comic hillbilly singer also adept at comic dialogue. Later Canovas broke up and Judy continued as single. In mid-1939 starred in successful Broadway musical YOKEL BOY. Had appeared in a few movies previously but in 40s movie career flourished, continued through 50s. Had long-running radio show, 1943-53, with attractive theme song *Go to Sleepy, Little Baby* which she helped compose. In later years less active in show business, occasionally appeared on TV.

MOVIES

1935—GOING HIGH BROW
1936—IN CALIENTE
1937—ARTISTS AND MODELS; THE THRILL OF A LIFETIME
1940—SCATTERBRAIN
1941—SIS HOPKINS; PUDDIN' HEAD
1942—SLEEPYTIME GAL; THE QUEEN OF SPIES; JOAN OF THE OZARKS; TRUE TO THE ARMY
1943—CHATTERBOX; SLEEPY LAGOON
1944—LOUISIANA HAYRIDE
1945—HIT THE HAY
1946—SINGIN' IN THE CORN
1951—HONEYCHILE
1952—OKLAHOMA ANNIE; THE WAC FROM WALLA WALLA
1954—UNTAMED HEIRESS
1955—CAROLINA CANNONBALL; LAY THAT RIFLE DOWN
1960—THE ADVENTURES OF HUCKLEBERRY FINN

RECORDS

ANNIE, JUDY & ZEKE CANOVA
  Cq 7724 The Fatal Shot
JUDY CANOVA
  OK 6683 Is It True?/Some One
  Vs 8094 Time for Jookin'/St. Louis Blues
  ARA 138 It Couldn't Be True/You Stole My Heart
  Mer 6149 (theme) Go to Sleepy, Little Baby/I Ain't Got Nobody
  Sterling 106 Time for Jookin'/St. Louis Blues

LPs

JUDY CANOVA
  Sutton 296 Judy Canova and Esmereldy Sing Country Favorites
  Coronet CXS-239 Country Cousin
  Cam CAL-662 Judy Canova
  Tops L-1613 Judy Canova in Hi-Fi

260. CANTOR, EDDIE   vo lyr
(EDDIE ISRAEL ISKOWITZ, nicknamed Banjo Eyes)

Born January 31, 1892, New York, N.Y. Died October 10, 1964, Hollywood, Calif.

All-time great entertainer. Noted for talent as comedian, soft vaudeville-type singing, light, skipping dance steps. Nicknamed Banjo Eyes because of wide, expressive eyes. Parents immigrants from Russia. Eddie orphaned at early age, raised by grandmother. As child appeared in amateur contests. Joined Gus Edwards troupe of youngsters and played vaudeville; George Jessel in same troupe. Later toured with Lila Lee in Cantor & Lee act. Became important vaudeville star, featured blackface routine, played New York's Palace Theatre. Reached stardom with performances on Broadway in ZIEGFELD FOLLIES OF 1917-1918-1919 (and later in 1923 and 1927). Appeared in shows BROADWAY BREVITIES OF 1920, MIDNIGHT ROUNDERS OF 1921, MAKE IT SNAPPY (1922). Starred in KID BOOTS (1924) and WHOOPEE (1928). Last Broadway show BANJO EYES (1942). Associated with songs *You'd Be Surprised, Dinah, Ida, That's the Kind of a Baby for Me, My Baby Just Cares for Me, Makin' Whoopee, Now's the Time to Fall in Love* and his most famous, *If You Knew Susie.* Lost heavily in 1929 stock market crash, renewed efforts in show business.

Began Hollywood career in 1930, made popular movies in 30s and 40s. On early radio in 20s, late 1931 began own big show for Chase & Sanborn. Show quickly projected Cantor into top popularity of career. Show featured and made famous bandleader Dave Rubinoff (billed as Rubinoff & His Violin), also featured comic Bert Gordon (The Mad Russian) and later Parkyakarkus. Show's well-known theme song, *One Hour with You*, sung dramatically at each closing by Cantor. In comic routines Cantor quipped frequently about wife Ida and five daughters. Radio shows of varying formats in 30s and 40s. Helped child singers Deanna Durbin and Bobby Breen attain stardom in mid-30s, later helped singers Dinah Shore and Eddie Fisher early in careers. Radio shows in 50s, and in 1961 had show Ask Eddie Cantor. On TV with own shows in early 50s, but heart trouble curtailed activity in new medium, eventually caused retirement. 1953 movie THE EDDIE CANTOR STORY featured Keefe Brasselle effectively playing title role, Cantor lyricist for several songs including *Merrily We Roll Along*, *There's Nothing Too Good for My Baby*, *Get a Little Fun Out of Life*, *The Old Stage Door*, *It's Great to Be Alive*. Wrote autobiographies *My Life Is in Your Hands* and *Take My Life*; other books: *As I Remember Them; Ziegfeld, the Great Glorifier; The Way I See It* and *Caught Short!*.

MOVIES

1930—WHOOPEE; GLORIFYING THE AMER-
     ICAN GIRL
1931—PALMY DAYS
1932—THE KID FROM SPAIN
1933—ROMAN SCANDALS
1934—KID MILLIONS
1936—STRIKE ME PINK
1937—ALI BABA GOES TO TOWN
1940—FORTY LITTLE MOTHERS
1943—THANK YOUR LUCKY STARS
1944—SHOW BUSINESS; HOLLYWOOD CAN-
     TEEN
1948—IF YOU KNEW SUSIE
1952—THE STORY OF WILL ROGERS

RECORDS

EDDIE CANTOR
    Emer 10102 You'd Be Surprised
    Emer 10301 Margie
    Co A-3624 I'm Hungry for Beautiful
      Girls/I Love Her—She Loves Me
    Co A-3934 Oh Gee, Oh Gosh, Oh
      Golly I'm in Love/Eddie
    Co A-3964 No, No, Nora/I've Got the
      Yes We Have No Bananas Blues
    Co 364-D If You Knew Susie

Co 415-D Row, Row, Rosie
Co 457-D Oh! Boy, What a Girl
Co 2723-D What a Perfect Combina-
    tion/Look What You've Done
Co 35428 Margie/Little Curly Hair in
    a High Chair
Vi 18342 That's the Kind of a Baby for
    Me/The Modern Maiden's Prayer
Vi 21831 Makin' Whoopee/Hungry
    Women
Vi 22189 My Wife Is on a Diet/Can-
    tor's Tips on the Stock Market
Me 13001 Over Somebody Else's
    Shoulder/The Man on the Flying
    Trapeze
Me 13183 Mandy/An Earful of Music
Me 13184 Okay, Toots/When My Ship
    Comes In
De 3798 Makin' Whoopee/Yes, Sir,
    That's My Baby
De 3873 They Go Wild Simply Wild
    Over Me/Oh Gee, Oh Gosh, Oh
    Golly I'm in Love
De 23985 Makin' Whoopee/Now's the
    Time to Fall in Love
De 23987 Ida/You'd Be Surprised
LEO REISMAN (Cantor vocalist but unlist-
ed)
    Vi 22851 There's Nothing Too Good
    for My Baby

LPs

EDDIE CANTOR
    Vik LV-1119 The Best of Eddie Cantor
      (RIs)
    Cam CAL-531 The Best of Eddie Can-
      tor (RIs)
    Cam CAL-870 Sings "Ida" and His
      Other Hits
    (one side) Ace of Hearts(E) AH-25 (De
      RIs)
    AudFid 702 Date with Eddie Cantor

261. CAREY, MUTT   t B
(THOMAS CAREY)

Born 1891, New Orleans, La.
Died September 3, 1948, San Francisco,
*   Calif.*

Jazz trumpet man whose career started about 1914 and continued to 40s, with time away from music. Much of career spent with Kid Ory. Early experience in parade and band work in New Orleans before joining Ory in 1914. Toured with various bands and road shows, played in Chicago. With Wade Whaley in New Orleans in 1918. To California in 1919 to join Ory again. Took over band in 1925 when Ory left. Remained in California, jobbing and leading bands at intervals. Music became sideline as he worked at other jobs to make ends meet. He and Ory reunited in 1944, continued together until late 1947. Carey then to New York, led group of veteran jazzmen on a few recordings. Returned to California, resumed musical activities there for several months until death. Played good traditional trumpet but unfortunately left few records for posterity.

RECORDS

ORY'S SUNSHINE ORCHESTRA
  Sunshine 3003 Ory's Creole Trombone/Society Blues
ROBERTA DUDLEY
  Sunshine 3001 Krooked Blues/When You're Alone Blues
RUTH LEE
  Sunshine 3002 Maybe Some Day/That Sweet Something
KID ORY
  Cres 1 South/Creole Song
  Cres 2 Blues for Jimmy/Get Out of Here
  Cres 5 Careless Blues/Do What Ory Say
  Cres 7 Panama/Under the Bamboo Tree
  Exner 3 Dippermouth Blues/Savoy Blues
  Exner 4 High Society/Ballin' the Jack
  Co 37274 Tiger Rag/Bucket Got a Hole in It
  Co 37276 Creole Bo Bo/Bill Bailey, Won't You Please Come Home?
HOCIEL THOMAS
  Ci 1014 Go Down Sunshine
MUTT CAREY & HIS NEW YORKERS
  Cen 4007 The Entertainer/Joplin's Sensation
  Cen 4008 Chrysanthemum/Fidgety Feet
  Cen 4013 Ostrich Walk/Indiana
  Cen 4017 Cake Walking Babies/Shim-Me-Sha-Wabble
  Cen 4018 Slow Drivin' (1 & 2)

262. CARLE, FRANKIE   p ar cm B
Born March 25, 1903, Providence, R.I.

Well-known pianist-composer of late 30s and bandleader of 40s and 50s. Best-known composition *Sunrise Serenade* became popular standard. Pianist with light and buoyant touch, always melody first but embellished it slightly with strong rhythm—a very attractive style. As youngster tutored by uncle Nicholas Colangelo, famed pianist. Professional by 18, accompanied vaudeville performers and played in dance bands. Early job with Ed J. McEnelly band. In mid-30s joined Mal Hallett for four years, with interval leading own group around 1935. Was leading own band again in 1939 when joined Horace Heidt in July, remained until late 1943. Featured by Heidt, also received plaudits for hit songs: *Georgianna* (1937), *Sunrise Serenade* and *Shadows* (1939), *Falling Leaves* and *A Lover's Lullaby* (1940), *Oh, What It Seemed to Be* (1946), *Roses in the Rain*, *Dreamy Lullaby* and *Moonlight Whispers* (1947). Lesser numbers: *Carle Boogie*, *Lollipop Ball*, *Sunrise Boogie*, *Sunrise in Napoli*, *Blue Fantasy*, *I Didn't Know*, *The Golden Touch*, *The Apple Valley Waltz*.

In early 1944 organized big band, successful through 40s and into 50s. Good band, theme song *Sunrise Serenade*. Featured Carle's piano predominately. First vocalists Betty Bonney and Phyllis Lynne. Carle's daughter, Marjorie Hughes, sang with band several years. Excellent singer, made hit record with Carle in 1946, *Oh, What It Seemed to Be*. Gregg Lawrence good singer in later 40s. Band had radio series, recorded often. Carle also recorded frequently with only his piano and rhythm. By late 40s band was excellent, vastly underrated. Great ensemble sound and solid beat, outstanding arrangements of ballads with light swing, good sax section. Appeared in 1949 movie MY DREAM IS YOURS. In later 50s Carle ceased as regular bandleader, worked still less in 60s. On occasion led small groups or bands, made recordings. Rare appearances on TV. Spot on Merv Griffin's TV show in 1971 revealed that Carle retained amiable professional manner and deft touch on keyboard. Returned to tour with Big Band Calvalcade show late 1973-early 1974.

RECORDS

MAL HALLETT
  De 1163 Ridin' High
  De 1190 Humoresque

HORACE HEIDT
  Co 35446 A Lover's Lullaby
  Co 35709 Falling Leaves
  Co 36100 Toy Piano Jump/Toy Piano Minuet
  Co 36275 Sunrise Serenade/Donkey Serenade
  Co 36450 Carle Meets Mozart

FRANKIE CARLE (piano with rhythm)
  De 1456 (medleys)
  De 1457 (medleys)
  De(12")29215 "Damsel in Distress" Medley/"I'd Rather Be Right" Medley
  Co 35570-1-2-3
  Co 36331-2-3-4

FRANKIE CARLE ORCHESTRA
  Vo 5155 Chico's Love Song/It's a Whole New Thing
  Vo 5241 Blue Fantasy/Night Glow
  Co 36826 I'd Rather Be Me/I Was Here When You Left Me
  Co 36892 Oh, What It Seemed to Be/As Long as I Live
  Co 36906 I'm Glad I Waited for You/No, Baby, Nobody but You
  Co 37069 Rumors Are Flying/Without You
  Co 37222 We Could Make Such Beautiful Music/Too Many Times
  Co 37269 (theme) Sunrise serenade/Carle Boogie
  Co 37930 Peggy O'Neil/I'll Hate Myself in the Morning
  Co 38354 Little Jack Frost Get Lost/I Couldn't Stay Away from You
  Co 38573 I'm Gonna Let You Cry for a Change
  Co 38690 Whistling in the Dark/I Still Care
  Co 38783 Dream a Little Dream of Me/Tell Me
  Vi 20-3732 I Wish I Didn't Love You So/Spring Will Be a Little Late This Year

  Vi 20-3952 The One-Finger Melody/The Winter Waltz
  Vi 20-4538 Tell Me Why/Any Time

LPs

FRANKIE CARLE
  De(10")DL-5087 Piano Magic
  Cam CAL-478 The Piano Style of Frankie Carle (Vi RIs)
  Co CL-531 Frankie Carle's Piano Party
  Vi LPM-1868 37 Favorites for Dancing
  Vi LPM-1963 Show Stoppers in Dance Time
  Vi LPM-2148 A Carle-Load of Hits
  Vi LPM-2592 30 Hits of the Tuneful 20s
  Vi(10")LPM-3024 Top Pops

263. CARLE, RICHARD   vo cm lyr

Born 1871, Somerville, Mass.
Died 1941

A top comedian and star of Broadway musicals beginning pre-1900 and continuing over twenty years. Also wrote book and lyrics for several shows. Known for 1906 show song *A Lemon in the Garden of Love*. Performed on stage in England. Broadway career ended in early 20s, except for appearance in 1930 show. In silent movies of 1928-9, continued in sound films. Character roles and bit parts in over 80 movies 1928-41.

BROADWAY MUSICALS
*(*also wrote book and lyrics)*

1896—IN GAY NEW YORK; THE LADY SLAVEY
1900—MAM'SELLE 'AWKINS*
1901—THE LADIES' PARADISE
1904—THE MAID AND THE MUMMY* THE TENDERFOOT*
1905—THE MAYOR OF TOKIO*
1906—THE SPRING CHICKEN* (and music)
1908—MARY'S LAMB* (and music)
1911—JUMPING JUPITER*
1912—THE GIRL FROM MONTMARTRE
1913—THE DOLL GIRL
1915—90 IN THE SHADE
1916—THE COHAN REVUE OF 1916
1917—WORDS AND MUSIC
1921—THE BROADWAY WHIRL
1923—ADRIENNE
1930—THE NEW YORKERS

Also book and lyrics for THE HURDY-GURDY GIRL (1907) and THE BOY AND THE GIRL (1909), also music for latter.

264. CARLISLE, KITTY   vo
Born 1914

Soprano active on stage, in movies and radio in 30s and 40s. Studied voice in U. S. and Europe. First singing role in 1932 show RIO RITA. In 1933 Broadway musical CHAMPAGNE SEC. First movie MURDER AT THE VANITIES (1934). Became popular when beauty and singing enhanced two important Bing Crosby movies, SHE LOVES ME NOT (1934) and HERE IS MY HEART (1935). Sang with Allan Jones in 1935 Marx Brothers movie A NIGHT AT THE OPERA. Strangely, made only two more movies, LARCENY WITH MUSIC (1943) and HOLLYWOOD CANTEEN (1944). In Broadway shows WHITE HORSE INN (1936), THE THREE WALTZES (1938), WALK WITH MUSIC (1940). Various stage and stock productions in years following, including SHOW TIME vaudeville revue (1942), RAPE OF LUCRETIA (1948), ANNIVERSARY WALTZ (1954). On radio at intervals. In 50s and 60s well-known personality on TV as regular on long-running panel show To Tell the Truth. Widow of playwright Moss Hart.

RECORDS
KITTY CARLISLE
   De 23320 I'll Remember April/I'll Get By
   De 23359 The Very Thought of You/ Sweet Dreams, Sweetheart

265. CARLISLE, UNA MAE
                       p vo cm B
Born December 26, 1918, Xenia, Ohio Died 1956, New York, N.Y. (either November 7 or December 12)

Pianist-singer in jazz-phrased style, noted for recording of own composition, *Walkin' by the River*, very popular in early 1941. Played in Cincinnati as youngster, discovered by Fats Waller, coached and aided by him. Appeared at Radio City Music Hall in New York. To Europe with a show in late 30s. Stayed several years, recorded, played clubs, did radio and film work. In early 40s she played clubs in U.S., did radio work, became known in 1941 via aforementioned record hit. Later in 1941 composed and recorded another popular song, *I See a Million People*. In 1945 on Gloom Dodgers radio show. Own radio and TV series in late 40s and early 50s. Continued to play clubs, made a few recordings. Retired in 1954 because of ill health.

RECORDS
UNA MAE CARLISLE
   Vo(E) 162 Don't Try Your Jive on Me/Love Walked In
   Vo(E) 198 Hangover Blues/Mean to Me
   Vo (E)199 I'm Crazy 'Bout My Baby/ Anything for You
   Bb 10898 You Made Me Love You/If I Had You
   Bb 11033 Walkin' by the River/I Met You Then, I Know You Now
   Bb 11120 Blitzkrieg Baby/It's Sad but True
   Bb 11159 Oh I'm Evil/You Mean So Much to Me
   Bb 11181 I See a Million People/The Booglie Wooglie Piggy
   Bb 11257 Can't Help Lovin' Dat Man/Anything
   Bb 11507 So Long Shorty/Sweet Talk
   Bea 7170 'Tain't Yours/Without Your Baby
   Bea 7171 You Gotta Take Your Time/I Like It 'Cause I Love You
   Co 38864 Tired Hands/Strange
   Co 38881 Long/Gone
   Co 38979 Three Little Bugs/We've All Got a Lesson to Learn

LPs
(miscellaneous artists)
   Vi LPV-578 Swing, Vol. 1 (Vi, Bb RIs)

266. CARLSON, FRANKIE   d
Born May 5, 1914, New York, N.Y.

Good big-band drummer, best known for work with Woody Herman. First big job with Todd Rollins in 1933. Later jobs with Gene Kardos, Mills Cavalcade Orchestra, Clyde McCoy. Joined first Herman band in late 1936, remained until early 1942—band's blues-dominated period. Featured on Herman's big clarinet-

and-drum feature, *Golden Wedding*. With Horace Heidt in 1944 awhile, also in 1944 with Lew Gray and Red Nichols on west coast. Settled in Los Angeles to do studio work, played with Nelson Riddle, Sonny Burke, Skip Martin and others. Continued active in studios through 50s and 60s.

RECORDS

WOODY HERMAN

De 1801 Twin City Blues/Laughing Boy Blues

De 1879 Caliope Blues/The Flat Foot Floogie

De 1900 Lullaby in Rhythm/Don't Wake Up My Heart

De 2250 Indian Boogie Woogie/Blue Evening

De 2440 Woodchopper's Ball/Big Wig in the Wigwam

De 2539 Paleface/The Sheik of Araby

De 2664 Jumpin' Blue/Big Morning

De 2933 Blues on Parade/Love's Got Me Down

De 2979 Pick-a-Rib/Say "Si-Si"

De 3332 Deep Night/Whistle Stop

De 3436 Golden Wedding / Five O'clock Whistle

De 3577 Chips' Boogie Woogie/Chips' Blues (both FOUR CHIPS)

De 4176 A String of Pearls/Las Chiapanecas

De 4353 Elise/Yardbird Shuffle (both FOUR CHIPS)

RAFAEL MENDEZ

Pan-Am 111 I Know That You Know/Tea for Two

Pan-Am 112 In a Little Spanish Town/Kitten on the Keys

GLENN MILLER

Bb 10201 The Chestnut Tree/And the Angels Sing

Bb 10214 Moonlight Serenade

Bb 10229 The Lady's in Love with You

MILLS CAVALCADE ORCHESTRA

Co 3066-D Lovely Liza Lee/Rhythm Lullaby

CONNIE BOSWELL (with Woody Herman)

De 2258 They Say/The Umbrella Man

De 2259 Deep in a Dream/Thanks for Everything

RED NICHOLS

Cap 15150 If I Had You

Cap 40062 Little by Little

EDDIE MILLER

Cap 40039 You Oughta Be in Pictures

LPs

WOODY HERMAN

De DL-8133 Woodchoppers' Ball (De RIs)

Cor(10")CRL-56005 Blue Prelude (De RIs)

Cor(10")CRL-56010 Souvenirs (De RIs)

FOUR FRESHMEN

Cap T-763 And Five Trumpets

267. CARLYLE, RUSS   vo v cm B

Born July 4, 1921, Cleveland, Ohio

Good band vocalist, best known for work with Blue Barron in late 30s. Later led own band. Early in career played violin with society bands, with some singing. Joined Barron in 1936 and remained until 1940. Military service awhile, World War II. After discharge worked as single in Cleveland clubs several years. In 1949 formed band, played hotels and ballrooms. Recorded to small extent in 50s, had some success with *In a Little Spanish Town* late 1954-5. Led band into 60s, later worked on and off. Composed several songs, mostly novelty: *If I Ever Love Again, Stashu Pandowski, Studola Pumpa, Sing a Lumma Lay*.

RECORDS

BLUE BARRON

Va 582 And Then They Called It Love/Don't Ever Change

Bb 7419 At a Perfume Counter/Did an Angel Kiss You?

Bb 7608 I Hadn't Anyone Till You

Bb 7872 Heart and Soul

Bb 10394 Little Old Band of Gold/When I Climb Down from My Saddle

Bb 10444 I Didn't Know What Time It Was

Bb 10487 I'm Fit to Be Tied

Bb 10905 The Bells of Monterey

RUSS CARLYLE

Cor 60053 You're So Understanding/The Gang That Sang "Heart of My Heart"

Cor 60081 Golden Sands of Hawaii/On the Roly Coaster

Cor 60135 When You Wore a Tu-
lip/Sing a Lumma Lay
Mer 5788 Cross Me Off Your List/
Only You
"X"-0055 In a Little Spanish Town/
Nice Knowing You
LP

Recar RCS-2014 (S) Plays Today's
Hits

268. CARMICHAEL, HOAGY
cm lyr ar p vo B
(HOAGLAND HOWARD
CARMICHAEL)

Born November 22, 1899, Bloomington, Ind.

Great composer of immense popularity, noted especially for *Star Dust*, probably most popular song of era. Other leading compositions: *Rockin' Chair, Georgia on My Mind, Lazy River, Lazybones, Little Old Lady, Small Fry, Two Sleepy People, Skylark, Ole Buttermilk Sky* and Academy Award winner *In the Cool Cool Cool of the Evening*. Good entertainer as pianist-singer with simple, casual style. Attended Indiana University, played in college bands and with jazzmen like Bix Beiderbecke. Passed up career as lawyer for songwriting. First real success his immortal *Star Dust*. Written 1927, it emerged with lyrics in early 1931 to become overnight sensation. String of successful songs in 30s and 40s. Wrote for movies, also score for 1940 Broadway musical WALK WITH MUSIC. Beginning mid-40s seen in several movies, a natural in character roles. Guest spots on radio shows, had own series at intervals. Own TV show in early 50s. Collaborators included lyricists Mitchell Parish, Frank Loesser, Johnny Mercer, Sammy Lerner, Stanley Adams, Ed Heyman, Paul Francis Webster, Jack Brooks, Ned Washington, Jo Trent. Wrote autobiographies *The Stardust Road* and *Sometimes I Wonder*.

SONGS
(with related shows)

1925—Riverboat Shuffle; Washboard Blues; Boneyard Shuffle
1930—Rockin' Chair
1931—Star Dust; Georgia on My Mind; Lazy River
1932—Thanksgivin'; Come Easy Go Easy Love; Sing It Way Down Low
1933—Lazybones; Ole Faithful; Snowball
1934—Judy; Moon Country; One Morning in May
1935—Ballad in Blue; Down t' Uncle Bill's
1936—ANYTHING GOES movie (Moonburn); Sing Me a Swing Song; Sing a Song of Nonsense; Lyin' to Myself
1937—THE SHOW IS ON stage show (The Show Is On; Little Old Lady); Old Man Moon
1938—EVERY DAY'S A HOLIDAY movie (Jubilee); THANKS FOR THE MEMORY movie (Two Sleepy People); SING YOU SINNERS movie (Small Fry); ST. LOUIS BLUES movie (Kinda Lonesome); Heart and Soul; April in My Heart
1939—Blue Orchids; I Get Along without You Very Well; Vagabond Dreams; Hong Kong Blues
1940—ROAD SHOW movie (I Should Have Known You Years Ago); WALK WITH MUSIC stage show (I Walk with Music; The Rhumba Jumps; Ooh, What You Said; Way Back in 1939 A.D.; What'll They Think of Next?); Can't Get Indiana Off My Mind; Poor Old Joe; The Nearness of You
1941—We're the Couple in the Castle
1942—Skylark; Lamplighter's Serenade
1943—TRUE TO LIFE movie (The Old Music Master; There She Was; Mister Pollyana)
1944—TO HAVE AND HAVE NOT movie (How Little We Know)
1945—JOHNNY ANGEL movie (Memphis in June); Baltimore Oriole
1946—THE STORK CLUB movie (Doctor, Lawyer and Indian Chief); CANYON PASSAGE movie (Ole Buttermilk Sky; Rogue River Valley)
1947—IVY movie (Ivy); Put Yourself in My Place, Baby; Things Have Changed; Don't Forget to Say "No," Baby
1949—The Three Rivers

1950—Follow the Swallow to Hide-a-Way Hollow
1951—HERE COMES THE GROOM movie (In the Cool Cool Cool of the Evening)
1952—Watermelon Weather
1953—GENTLEMEN PREFER BLONDES movie (two songs added to Jule Styne's original stage score: Anyone Here for Love?; When Love Goes Wrong); Love Will Soon Be Here
1962—HATARI! movie (Just for Tonight)

MOVIES
(as actor)

1937—TOPPER
1944—TO HAVE AND HAVE NOT
1945—JOHNNY ANGEL
1946—CANYON PASSAGE; THE BEST YEARS OF OUR LIVES
1947—NIGHT SONG
1949—JOHNNY HOLIDAY
1950—YOUNG MAN WITH A HORN
1952—THE LAS VEGAS STORY; BELLES ON THEIR TOES
1955—TIMBERJACK

RECORDS

JEAN GOLDKETTE (as vocalist)
  Vi 21150 So Tired
PAUL WHITEMAN (as pianist)
  Vi(12″)35877 Washboard Blues
HITCH'S HAPPY HARMONISTS (as pianist)
  Ge 3066 Boneyard Shuffle/Washboard Blues
HOAGY CARMICHAEL
  Ge 6311 Star Dust/One Night in Havana
  Ge 6474 March of the Hoodlums/Walkin' the Dog
  Vi 38139 Rockin' Chair/Barnacle Bill the Sailor
  Vi 22864 Bessie Couldn't Help It
  Vi 23013 Georgia on My Mind/One Night in Havana
  Vi 24119 I Was Taken by Storm/After Twelve O'clock
  Vi 24182 Thanksgivin'/Sing It Way Down Low
  Vi 24402 Lazybones/Snowball
  Vi 24505 One Morning in May
  Vi 24627 Moon Country/Judy
  Br 8255 Hong Kong Blues/Riverboat Shuffle

ARA 123 How Little We Know/Hong Kong Blues
ARA 124 Memphis in June/Billy-a-Dick
ARA 128 Doctor, Lawyer and Indian Chief/Am I Blue?
Cap 2593 Love Will Soon Be Here/When Love Goes Wrong
HOAGY CARMICHAEL-ELLA LOGAN
  Br 8250 Two Sleepy People/New Orleans
HOAGY CARMICHAEL with MATTY MATLOCK ALL-STARS
  De 24871 Darktown Strutters' Ball/That's a-Plenty

LPs

HOAGY CARMICHAEL
  Vi(10″)LPT-3072 Old Rockin' Chair (Vi RIs)
  Jazztone J-1266 Hoagy Sings Carmichael (with Pacific Jazzmen)
  Ace of Hearts(E) AH-92 Mr. Music Master (De RIs)

269. CARMINATI, TULLIO   vo

Born September 21, 1894, Zara, Dalmatia

Singer-actor who attained some success in early and mid-30s on stage and screen. Smooth, sophisticated style. Born in Zara, Dalmatia (Italian possession). Left home at 15 to join road company as actor. Played all over Italy for bare existence. Worked up to prominent stage roles. Came to U.S. after World War I. In several silent movies. Starred on Broadway in popular 1929 comedy STRICTLY DISHONORABLE. Later in 1929 starred in movie version, scored well with singing in this early sound movie. Appeared in Broadway musicals MUSIC IN THE AIR (1932) and GREAT LADY (1938). Became well known in mid-30s via several movies: MOULIN ROUGE and ONE NIGHT OF LOVE (1934; co-starred in latter with opera star Grace Moore), PARIS IN SPRING and LET'S LIVE TONIGHT (1935). Other movies: GALLANT LADY (1933), THREE MAXIMS (1936), GIRL OF THE STREETS (1938), SAFARI (1940). Small roles in occasional movies 1949-63.

RECORDS

TULLIO CARMINATI
  Co 3023-D Love Passes By/I Live in
  My Dreams

270. CARNEY, HARRY   bs as cl b-cl
Born April 1, 1910, Boston, Mass.

Top jazz baritone sax soloist, famed as
stalwart in Duke Ellington band over 40
years. Rich tone and powerful, ambling
style with Ellington early established him
as all-time great. As youngster, Carney
played in Boston bands. Heard by Duke
Ellington and hired in late 1926. Association, practically unparalleled for lon-
gevity in jazz field, extended almost continuously through 1973 (with brief intervals away from band). Key Ellington
soloist through the years. Also heavy
freelancing on recordings with other jazz
groups, including other stars of Ellington's band.

RECORDS

DUKE ELLINGTON
  Vi 38035 Doin' the Voom Voom
  Vi 38045 Harlemania
  Vi 23022 Old Man Blues
  Br 6404 Lightnin'
  Br 6638 Jive Stomp
  Br 7310 Saddest Tale (b-cl)
  Br 8213 Exposition Swing
  Br 8297 Slap Happy
  Br 8411 Way Low
  De 880 Chicago/Harlem Speaks
  Co 35776 Country Gal
  Vi 27356 Jumpin' Punkins
  Vi 27880 Perdido
  Mus 465 Golden Feather
  Co 39670 VIP's Boogie
BARNEY BIGARD
  Va 515 Caravan/Stompy Jones
  Va 525 Clouds in My Heart/Frolic
  Sam
  Va 655 Jazz a la Carte/Demi-Tasse
  Bb 11581 "C" Blues/Brown Suede
REX STEWART
  Vo 3844 Sugar Hill Shim Sham/Love
  in My Heart
  Key(12")1306 Swamp Mist/I'm True
  to You
  Key(12")1307 Zaza/The Little Goose
  Bb 10946 Without a Song/My Sunday
  Gal

COOTIE WILLIAMS
  Va 555 I Can't Believe That You're in
  Love with Me/Diga Diga Doo
JIMMY JONES
  HRS 1015 Departure from Dixie
SANDY WILLIAMS
  HRS 1007 Chili Con Carney
  HRS 1008 Sumpin' Jumpin' 'Round
  Here/After Hours on Dream Street
LIONEL HAMPTON
  Vi 26304 The Jumpin' Jive
ED HALL
  BN 511 It's Been So Long/I Can't Be-
  lieve That You're in Love with Me
BILLY TAYLOR'S BIG EIGHT
  Key 615 Carney-Val in Rhythm/Night
  Wind
HARRY CARNEY
  HRS 1020 Minor Mirage/Candy Cane
  HRS 1021 Jamaica Rumble/Shadowy
  Sands
  Wax 115 Why Was I Born?/Triple
  Play

LPs

HARRY CARNEY
  Clef MGC-640 Harry Carney with
  Strings
  Verve V-2028 Mood for Girl and Boy
DUKE ELLINGTON
  Co C3L27 (3-LP set) The Ellington
  Era, Vol. 1 (1927-40 RIs)
  Vi LPV-517 Jumpin' Punkins (Vi RIs)
  Vi LPT-1004 Duke Ellington's Great-
  est (Vi RIs)
  Vi LPM-1364 In a Mellotone (Vi RIs)
  Vi LPM-3782 Far East Suite
  Beth BCP-60 Historically Speaking
  —The Duke
JOHNNY HODGES
  Epic LN-3105 Hodge Podge (Vo RIs)
  Verve V-8150 Used to Be Duke
JOHNNY HODGES-REX STEWART
  Vi LPV-533 Things Ain't What They
  Used to Be (Bb RIs)
REX STEWART
  "X"(10")LX-3001 (Bb RIs)
  CBS(E) 52628 (Vo RIs)

271. CARPENTER, THELMA   vo
Excellent singer, especially popular in 40s.
Beautifully controlled and warm voice,
good phrasing. While in high school sang
in small clubs in New York. Later worked

with Jack Jenney, Teddy Wilson, Coleman Hawkins. In 1942 attracted attention with successful stay at Kelly's Stable. Joined Count Basie in 1943, remained till early 1945—unfortunately, mostly during recording ban. Recorded in mid-40s. On Eddie Cantor radio show 1945-6. Played clubs in late 40s and 50s. Semiactive in later years. In 1968, after three years out of music, New York club date.

RECORDS
COUNT BASIE
Co 36766 I Didn't Know About You
COLEMAN HAWKINS
Bb 10477 She's Funny That Way
THELMA CARPENTER
Maj 1017 These Foolish Things/My Guy's Come Back
Maj 1023 Hurry Home/Just a-Sittin' and a-Rockin'
Maj 1028 Bill/Can't Help Lovin' Dat Man
Maj 1030 Seems Like Old Times/Jug of Wine
Maj 1104 Harlem on My Mind/Joshua Fit de Battle of Jericho
Co 30141 I'm a Fool About Someone/ Just You, Just Me
THELMA CARPENTER with HERMAN CHITTISON TRIO
Mus 320 I Should Care/All of My Life

LPs
THELMA CARPENTER
Cor CRL-57433

272. CARR, JOE "FINGERS"   p B
(LOUIS F. BUSCH)
Rose to fame in 50s as pianist in ragtime and honkytonk style. In 30s with George Olsen and Hal Kemp bands. Married to Kemp vocalist Janet Blair, later to singer Margaret Whiting. Records in 50s sold well.

RECORDS
JOE "FINGERS" CARR
Cap 1311 Rocky's Rag/Lovebug Itch
Cap 1484 Bye Bye Blues/Tom's Tune
Cap 1558 Ballin' the Jack/It Must Be True
Cap 1777 Down Yonder/Ivory Rag
Cap 2009 Noodlin' Rag/Yes Yes

Cap 2081 That Ever Lovin' Rag/ Goodtime Charlie
Cap 2187 Stumbling/Boogie Woogie Rag
Cap 2257 Headin' for Home/Rattlesnake Rag
Cap 2359 Doo-Wacky Rag/Aloha Oe
Cap 2557 Doodle-Doo-Doo/San Antonio Rose
Cap 2581 Collegiate/The One Called Reilly
Cap 2665 Istanbul/Maple Leaf Rag
Cap 2730 Until Sunrise/Humoresque
JOE "FINGERS" CARR-EWING SISTERS
Cap 1733 I Love a Piano/Ventura Boulevard Boogie

LPs
JOE "FINGERS" CARR
Cap T-443 Joe "Fingers" Carr & His Ragtime Band
Cap T-760 Mr. Ragtime
Cap T-2019 The Hits of Joe "Fingers" Carr
WB 1406 Giant Hits of the Small Combos
JOE "FINGERS" CARR with PEE WEE HUNT
Cap T-783 "Pee Wee" and "Fingers"
(miscellaneous artists)
WB SY-1425 (S) Flappers, Speakeasies & Bathtub Gin

273. CARR, LEROY   vo p cm
Born 1905
Died 1935

Blues singer with prolific recording career 1928-35. Accompaniment by own piano, plus guitarist Scrapper Blackwell on most records. Bittersweet vocal quality. Piano had light blues touch. Influenced contemporary and later blues singers. Composed many songs he featured, some light and amusing. Most featured number *How Long How Long Blues*. Died at early age of nephritis caused by heavy drinking.

RECORDS
LEROY CARR
Vo 1191 My Own Lonesome Blues/ How Long How Long Blues
Vo 1200 Broken Spoke Blues/Tennessee Blues
Vo 1241 How Long How Long Blues (No. 2)/Prison Bound Blues
Vo 1279 How Long How Long Blues

(No. 3)/You Don't Mean Me No
Good
Vo 1290 Straight Alky Blues (1 & 2)
Vo 1412 Gambler's Blues/There Ain't
Nobody Got It Like She Got It
Vo 1435 The New How Long How
Long Blues/Love Hides All Faults
Vo 1473 Rainy Day Blues/ Won't Miss
You When You're Gone
Vo 1541 Sloppy Drunk Blues/Hard
Times Done Drove Me to Drink
Vo 1549 Four Day Rider/Alabama
Woman Blues
Vo 1585 Big House Blues/New How
Long How Long Blues (No. 2)
Vo 1709 Lonesome Nights/I Keep the
Blues
Vo 02657 Mean Mistreater Mama/
Blues Before Sunrise
Vo 02762 Mean Mistreater Mama (No.
2)/Shady Lane Blues
Vo 02922 Stormy Weather Blues/
Moanful Blues
Vo 03107 Muddy Water/Southbound
Blues
Vo 03349 Big Four Blues/You Got Me
Grieving
Bb 5877 Ain't It a Shame?/When the
Sun Goes Down
Bb 5915 Rocks in My Bed/Big Four
Blues
Bb 5946 Bad Luck All the Time/Just a
Rag
Bb 5963 Going Back Home/Six Cold
Feet in the Ground

LPs

LEROY CARR
Co CL-1799 Blues Before Sunrise
RBF 1 The Country Blues
RBF 202 Rural Blues

274. CARR, MICHAEL   cm lyr
Songwriter whose work was scant but
worthwhile, with several songs enjoying
considerable popularity.

SONGS
1933—Ole Faithful
1934—Because it's Love; Strange
1935—The Gentleman Obviously Doesn't
Believe
1936—Dinner for One, Please, James;
Did Your Mother Come from Ireland?; The Sunset Trail

1938—Two Bouquets
1939—Cinderella, Stay in My Arms;
South of the Border
1941—Until You Fall in Love
1942—He Wears a Pair of Silver Wings
1948—The Little Old Church in Leicester
Square

275. CARROLL, BARBARA   p cm
(BARBARA CAROLE
COPPERSMITH)

*Born January 25, 1925, Worcester,
Mass.*

Outstanding modern jazz pianist. Tasteful
style with beautiful chords and developing patterns. Training at New England
Conservatory, early professional experience in girl trio on USO tour. In late 40s
led trio in New York, by early 50s was
working top clubs. Well known for LPs.
In 1953 Broadway musical ME AND JUL-
IET; had acting role and performed with
her trio. Husband-bassist Joe Shulman in
trio during 50s until sudden death in
1957. Active in 60s and 70s with appearances and some recording. Composer
of several jazz numbers: *Barbara's Carol,
Fancy Pants, Just Plain Blue, Lost in a
Crowded Place.*

RECORDS
STAN HASSELGARD
VD(12")900 Cottontop
SERGE CHALOFF
Fut 3003 Chickasaw/Bop Scotch
Fut 3004 The Most!/Chasin' the Bass
BARBARA CARROLL
Dis 129 Barbara's Carol/You Stepped
Out of a Dream
Dis 130 Dancing on the Ceiling/The
Puppet That Dances Be-Bop
Dis 174 Morocco (1 & 2)

LPs

BARBARA CARROLL
Vi LJM-1001
Vi LJM-1023 Lullabies in Rhythm
Vi LPM-1296 We Just Couldn't Say
Goodbye
Vi LPM-1396 It's a Wonderful World
Verve MGV-2095 Barbara
Atl(10")132 Piano Panorama, Vol. 3
OSCAR PETTIFORD
Pres PRLP-7813 Memorial Album
(1949 & 1954 RIs)

276. CARROLL, BOB   vo
Born June 18, 1918

Big-voiced baritone with dance bands, later on musical stage. At start of career sang on radio commercials, later on radio shows. Joined Charlie Barnet band in late 1940 and remained for a year. Military service, World War II. After discharge with Jimmy Dorsey 1946-7. Freelance recording, career as single. Strong voice was always held under control so as not to overpower a dance band (similar case to that of Vaughn Monroe). In later years turned to stage where voice heard to best advantage. Performed in stock and stage presentations through the years. In early 60s appeared as guest vocalist on late-night talk shows. Active into 70s, starring in road version of FIDDLER ON THE ROOF in 1971.

RECORDS
CHARLIE BARNET
Bb 10934 I Hear a Rhapsody
Bb 10975 I Can't Remember to Forget
Bb 11004 These Things You Left Me
Bb 11051 Afraid to Say Hello
Bb 11111 Harmony Haven
Bb 11202 When the Sun Comes Out/I'll Never Let a Day Pass By
Bb 11223 Be Fair/Wasn't It You?
Bb 11292 The Heart You Stole from Me
Bb 11321 You Were There
Bb 11327 Isle of Pines
Bb 11417 I'll Remember April
TED FIO RITO
De 4258 Lily of Laguna
JIMMY DORSEY
De 18917 The Whole World Is Singing My Song
De 18923 The Language of Love
MGM 10001 Heartaches/No Greater Love
MGM 10010 Time After Time
MGM 10035 Ballerina
MGM 10316 Angela Mia
KAY KYSER
Co 38527 My One, My Only, My All/Just for Fun
Co 38596 On the Trail
HENRY KING
De 3084 I Fall All Over Myself

GORDON JENKINS
Cap 124 White Christmas/Heaven for Two
TOOTS CAMARATA
De 27909 Heaven Drops Her Curtain Down
BOB CARROLL
Comet 5203 Where/Say It with Your Heart
Derby 814 Where/Say It with Your Heart
Derby 821 A Little Love/Where Did You Go?
Derby 831 Am I to Blame?/Why Break the Heart That Loves You?
Derby 840 I Really Don't Want to Know/There Is Danger
De 24309 Pianissimo/One Raindrop Doesn't Make a Shower

277. CARROLL, EARL   cm lyr
Born September 16, 1893, Pittsburgh, Pa.
Died June 17, 1948, Mt. Carmel, Pa., in plane crash

Important figure in theatrical world 1912-33. Produced and directed many revues. Also worked as composer-lyricist-librettist. At 10 worked as program boy in theatres. At 16 worked his way around world. Staff writer for New York publishing firm 1912-17. Military service, World War I. Built two Earl Carroll theatres in New York in 1922-3 and 1931. Also built Earl Carroll Restaurant in Hollywood in 1939, became movie producer. Leading compositions: *So Long, Letty*; *Isle d'Amour*; *One Look at You*; *Dreams of Long Ago*; *Give Me All of You*; *While We Dance*; *Just the Way You Are*; *Dreaming*; *Blue Bird*.

BROADWAY MUSICALS
(with which connected in various capacities)
1912—THE PASSING SHOW OF 1912
1913—ZIEGFELD FOLLIES OF 1913
1914—PRETTY MRS. SMITH
1916—SO LONG LETTY
1917—CANARY COTTAGE
1918—THE LOVE MILL
1919—THE LITTLE BLUE DEVIL
1923—EARL CARROLL'S VANITIES OF 1923
1924—EARL CARROLL'S VANITIES OF 1924
1925—EARL CARROLL'S VANITIES OF 1925

1929—EARL CARROLL'S SKETCH BOOK; FIORETTA

1933—MURDER AT THE VANITIES

Also involved with other productions off Broadway and with movies A NIGHT AT EARL CARROLL'S (1940), EARL CARROLL'S VANITIES (1945), EARL CARROLL'S SKETCH BOOK (1946).

278. CARROLL, HARRY   cm ar p

Born November 28, 1892, Atlantic City, N.J.
Died December 26, 1962, Mt. Carmel, Pa.

Composer who contributed to Broadway stage, also composed independently. Early career as pianist in theatres, cafes and vaudeville. Arranged for music publishers in New York. Leading compositions: *The Trail of the Lonesome Pine* and *There's a Girl in the Heart of Maryland* (1913), *By the Beautiful Sea* (1914), *She Is the Sunshine of Virginia* (1916), and his most famous, *I'm Always Chasing Rainbows* (1918). Other compositions: *On the Mississippi, Down in Bom-Bombay, Somewhere on Broadway, I Take a Little Rain with the Sunshine, The Land of My Best Girl, Our Home Town, Tip Top Tipperary Mary, Roll On River Missouri, Smother Me with Kisses and Kill Me with Love, A Kiss for Cinderella, Wherever There's Music and Beautiful Girls, Japanese Toyland.* Contributed music for Broadway shows THE BELLE OF BOND STREET and DANCING AROUND (1914), MAID IN AMERICA (1915), OH, LOOK! (1918), ZIEGFELD'S 9 O'CLOCK FROLIC (1921). Wrote occasional music for other shows.

279. CARROLL, JOHN   vo

Born 1913

Handsome baritone who appeared in movie musicals of early 40s, later did many comedy and dramatic roles. Appeared in about 50 movies. Most important movie musicals included SUNNY (1941), RIO RITA (1942), HIT PARADE OF 1943, FIESTA (1947), THE SONG PARADE (1950), HIT PARADE OF 1951, THE FARMER TAKES A WIFE (1953).

280. CARROLL, NANCY   vo
(ANN VERONICA LAHIFF)

Born November 19, 1906, New York, N.Y.
Died August 6, 1965, New York, N.Y.

Beautiful star of early movie musicals 1929-30, later turned to dramatic and comedy roles. Early in career had supporting role in Al Jolson's Broadway show BIG BOY in 1925. Worked in silent movies, first appearance late 1927 in LADIES MUST DRESS. After other silent movies 1928-9 she became popular star during hectic transition from silent to sound movies. Early successes: THE DANCE OF LIFE, CLOSE HARMONY and SWEETIE (1929), FOLLOW THROUGH, PARAMOUNT ON PARADE and HONEY (1930). Appeared in about 30 other movies 1930-8 including 1934 musical TRANSATLANTIC MERRY-GO-ROUND. Then popularity dimmed, roles minor. Active in show business at intervals later in career. As late as 1965 toured with plays.

281. CARSON, JACK   vo

Born October 27, 1910, Carmen, Manitoba, Canada
Died January 3, 1963

Brash, wisecracking star of movies and radio, sang occasionally and adequately. Early in career did singing and M.C. work. House M.C. at Tower Theatre in Kansas City in mid-30s. Minor roles in movies about eight years before star status in mid-40s. Co-starred with Dennis Morgan in musical movies. Later developed into good dramatic actor. Appeared in over 80 movies. Had own popular radio show from 1943 through 40s. TV appearances and own series briefly during 50s. Most important movie musicals: THE HARD WAY (1942; drama-musical), SHINE ON HARVEST MOON (1944), THE TIME, THE PLACE AND THE GIRL (1946), LOVE AND LEARN (1947), APRIL SHOWERS, ROMANCE ON THE HIGH SEAS and TWO GUYS FROM TEXAS (1948), IT'S A GREAT FEELING and MY DREAM IS YOURS (1949). Outstanding dramatic performances in A STAR IS BORN (1954), CAT ON A HOT TIN ROOF (1958). Died in 1963 of cancer.

## 282. CARSON, MINDY					vo

Born July 16, 1927, New York, N.Y.

Popular singer of late 40s and 50s, excellent night club entertainer. First break in 1946: won singing spot on Paul Whiteman's Stairway to the Stars radio show, also worked concerts with him. Later same year joined Harry Cool band. Began recording with success, launched career as single. Played clubs and theatres, worked with Whiteman on radio. Later own radio show, also own show on early TV. In early 50s on various TV shows. In 1958 Broadway show THE BODY BEAUTIFUL. In 60s faded from music scene.

RECORDS

MINDY CARSON

Mus 527 Pianissimo/What Do You Want to Make Those Eyes at Me For?

Mus 574 You Took Advantage of Me/Some Things Will Never Change

Vi 20-3508 Blame My Absent-Minded Heart/Song of Surrender

Vi 20-3681 My Foolish Heart/Candy and Cake

Vi 20-3944 If I Were a Bell/Just for a While

Vi 20-4039 Button Up Your Overcoat/Together

Vi 20-4040 Thank Your Father/Just a Memory

Vi 20-4041 The Best Things in Life Are Free/You're the Cream in My Coffee

Vi 20-4119 When You and I Were Young, Maggie/Gotta Find Somebody to Love

Vi 20-4151 You Only Want Me When You're Lonesome/Lonely Little Robin

Vi 20-4259 Out in the Cold Again/Hangin' Around with You

Vi 20-4457 Allegheny Fiddler/Dance Me Loose

Co 39889 All the Time and Everywhere/Barrels 'n' Barrels of Roses

Co 39989 Three Red Roses/I Cry Your Name

Co 40057 Darling, Darling/I Never Let You Cross My Mind

MINDY CARSON-GUY MITCHELL

Co 39950 So Am I/I Want You for a Sunbeam

Co 39992 Tell Us Where the Good Times Are/There's Nothing as Sweet as My Baby

LPs

MINDY CARSON

Roy(10″)18168 Mindy Carson and Orchestra

## 283. CARTER FAMILY					vocal group

Original members:
Alvin Pleasant (A.P.) Carter, born Maces Springs, Va.
Sara (his wife), born July 21, 1889, Wise County, Va.
Maybelle Carter (his sister-in-law), born May 10, 1909, Nickelsville, Va.

Famed country singing group, influential in development of country music in late 20s and early 30s. Established style of close-harmony singing, with Maybelle's Autoharp providing unique accompaniment. Trio formed in 1926, worked in Maces Springs and general area at all types of jobs and social events. After auditioning for talent scout, made first recordings in Bristol, Tenn., in 1927. Records well received; recorded steadily through the years. Made many personal appearances. Later in 30s A.P. and Sara divorced but trio still worked together. In late 30s children Jeanette and Joe joined group. In Del Rio, Texas, 1938-41, performed on Mexican radio station, later on Charlotte, N.C., station. In 1943 group broke up. Maybelle then formed new group with daughters June, Helen and Anita, during 1943-8 performed on radio in Richmond, Va. Later performed on Grand Ole Opry in Nashville. Group broke up in 50s but Maybelle continued to appear on Grand Ole Opry into 60s. In 70s on Johnny Cash's TV show with three daughters; June married Johnny Cash.

RECORDS

CARTER FAMILY

Vi 40058 My Clinch Mountain Home/Foggy Mountain Top

Vi 40126 Sweet Fern/Lulu Wall

Vi 20877 Poor Orphan Child/Wandering Boy

Vi 21074 Little Log Cabin by the Sea/Bury Me Under the Weeping Willow

Vi 21638 Will You Miss Me When I'm Gone?/Little Darling, Pal of Mine

Me 13113 Lumberton Wreck/New River Train

Me 13431 Broken Hearted Lover/Will You Miss Me When I'm Gone?

Me 350923 Let's Be Lovers Again/I'm Thinking Tonight of My Blue Eyes

MW 4225 Keep on the Sunny Side/Church in the Wildwood

MW 4432 Wildwood Flower

MW 7444 Wabash Cannon Ball/If One Won't Another One Will

MW 8004 Just Another Broken Heart/Answer to Weeping Willow

Bb 5058 River of Jordan/Where We'll Never Grow Old

Bb 5243 Green Fields of Virginia/Spirit of Love Watches

Bb 5529 Hello, Central/I'll Be All Smiles Tonight

Bb 8350 Wabash Cannon Ball/I Never Will Marry

Bb 9026 Keep on the Firing Line/Fifty Miles of Elbow Room

De 5240 My Dixie Darling/Are You Lonesome Tonight?

Cq 8693 God Gave Noah the Rainbow Sign/On the Rock Where Moses Stood

Vo 03112 Lonesome Valley/The Little Black Train

Vo 04390 Don't Forget Me, Little Darling/Gathering Flowers from the Hillside

Vo 05475 My Virginia Rose Is Blooming/The Homestead on the Farm

LPs

CARTER FAMILY

De DL-4404 A Collection of Favorites by the Carter Family (RIs)

Vi LPM-2772 'Mid the Green Fields of Virginia (RIs)

Cam CAL-586 Original and Great Carter Family (RIs)

Co HL-7396 Great Sacred Songs (RIs)

Co HL-7422 Country Sounds of the Original Carter Family (RIs)

284. CARTER, BENNY
as ts cl t tb p ar cm B

Born August 8, 1907, New York, N.Y.

An all-time great alto sax star as soloist and section leader, versatile musician on many instruments, excellent arranger, masterful at scoring for reed sections. Led band in 30s and 40s. Great facility on alto sax, with beautiful tone and most tasteful solo style. Essentially from mainstream jazz school, absorbed some modern jazz elements into style in later years. As teenager played jobs in small clubs. In 1924 worked with June Clark, Lois Deppe and Earl Hines among others. Intended to enroll at Wilberforce College in Ohio, instead left with Horace Henderson and the college band to play in New York. Worked with Fletcher Henderson brief periods, with Charlie Johnson 1927-8 over a year. Toured with own band late 1928-9. Important year with Fletcher Henderson 1930-1 during which also arranged for band. With Chick Webb briefly in 1931; later arranged *Liza* as showcase for Webb's drumming. In mid-1931 joined famed McKinney's Cotton Pickers for about a year. Own band 1932-4. During early 30s arranged for McKinney's Cotton Pickers, Duke Ellington, Fletcher Henderson, Teddy Hill, Benny Goodman. In late 1934-5 briefly with Fletcher Henderson and Willie Bryant. Late in 1935 to Europe, joined Willie Lewis in Paris. 1936-8 in London as staff arranger for Henry Hall's BBC band. During these two years Carter toured Europe, hailed by jazz musicians and fans.

Returned to U.S. in mid-1938. Led band from 1939 into early 40s. As bandleader Carter never real success. Bands suffered frequent changes in personnel. Recorded with his bands and freelance through the years. At times in 40s led combo. Played mostly in New York and on west coast, finally settled on west coast in mid-40s. Continued active arranging schedule; at one stretch in 1942 arranged for Lucky Strike Hit Parade radio show. In later 40s heavy studio work as musician-arranger-composer. In 50s many LPs, recording with top jazz stars, sometimes as leader. In 50s and 60s composed and scored for TV shows. Freelanced through 60s and into 70s in all types of music, occasionally fronted band on special dates such as 1972 Newport-New York Jazz Festival.

In addition to many compositions for movies and TV, wrote numerous jazz tunes including *Hot Toddy*, *Shoot the Works*, *Everybody Shuffle*, *Dream Lullaby*, *Take My Word* (also known as *Lonesome Nights*),*When Lights Are Low*, *My Favorite Blues*, *Nightfall*, *Devil's Holiday*, *Kansas City Suite*, *Deep South Mood*, *Symphony in Riffs*, *Harlem Mood*, *Manhattan Mood*, *Hollyridge Drive*, *I'm in the Mood for Swing*, *Malibu*. Also composed good bluesy ballads: *Blues in My Heart* (1931), *Blue Interlude* (1933), *Melancholy Lullaby* (1939), *Hurry Hurry* (1943). Band in 1943 movie THOUSANDS CHEER. Carter in 1952 movie THE SNOWS OF KILIMANJARO. Active in film composing in later years.

RECORDS

FLETCHER HENDERSON
Co 14392-D Easy Money/Come On, Baby
Co 1913-D Blazin'/Wang Wang Blues
Co 2329-D Chinatown, My Chinatown
De 555 Liza/Hotter Than 'Ell

MCKINNEY'S COTTON PICKERS
Vi 38097 Gee, Ain't I Good to You
Vi 38102 Miss Hannah (cl)
Vi 38133 I'd Love It

WILLIE LEWIS
Co(E) 5002 Star Dust (t)

CHOCOLATE DANDIES
De 18255 Blue Interlude/Once Upon a Time
Co 36008 Dee Blues/Bugle Call Rag

LIONEL HAMPTON
Vi 26011 I'm in the Mood for Swing/ Shoe Shiner's Drag

UNA MAE CARLISLE
Bb 11033 Walkin' by the River/I Met You Then, I Know You Now

BOB HOWARD
De 343 Throwin' Stones at the Sun/ You Fit into the Picture

VARSITY SEVEN
Vs 8135 Scratch My Back/Save It, Pretty Mama
Vs 8147 It's Tight Like That/Easy Rider

RED NORVO
Cap 15083 Under a Blanket of Blue/ Hollyridge Drive

JULIA LEE
Cap 40056 My Sin/Doubtful Blues
Cap 40082 When You're Smiling/King Size Papa

BEN WEBSTER
Mer 8298 King's Riff

BENNY CARTER
Co 2898-D Devil's Holiday/Symphony in Riffs
OK 41567 Lonesome Nights/Blue Lou
Vo(E) 4 Nightfall/Swingin' at Maida Vale
Vo(E) 11 When Day Is Done/Just a Mood
Sw(Fr) 20 Blue Light Blues/I'm Coming Virginia
Vo 4984 Melancholy Lullaby/Plymouth Rock
Vo 5112 Scandal in A Flat/Savoy Stampede
Vo 5224 Vagabond Dreams/Love's Got Me Down Again
Vo 5399 Sleep/Slow Freight
Bb 10962 All of Me/The Very Thought of You
Bb 11288 Midnight/My Favorite Blues
Bb 11341 Sunday/Back Bay Boogie
Cap 144 Hurry Hurry/Poinciana
Cap 200 I Surrender Dear/Malibu
Cap 48015 I Can't Get Started
Mer 89026 Isn't It Romantic?/Key Largo
Clef 89109 Flamingo/Can't We Be Friends?
Norg 111 Gone with the Wind/I've Got the World on a String

LPs

BENNY CARTER
UA 4017 Aspects
Verve MGV-8148 Alone Together
20th Fox TFM-3134 Benny Carter in Paris
Contemp M-3561 Swingin' the 20s
Pres PR-7643 (early RIs)

ARNOLD ROSS (one side)
EmArcy(10")MG-26029 Holiday in Piano

LIONEL HAMPTON
Cam CAL-402 Jivin' the Vibes (Vi RIs)

DAVE PELL
Cap T-1687 I Remember John Kirby

BEN WEBSTER
Norg MGN-1001 The Consummate Artistry of Ben Webster

COLEMAN HAWKINS
Vi LJM-1017 The Hawk in Flight (Bb, Vi RIs)

MEZZ MEZZROW
"X"(10")LVA-3015 (Vi RIs)

BENNY CARTER-ROY ELDRIDGE
ARS G-413 The Urbane Jazz of Benny Carter and Roy Eldridge

285. CARTER, BOB   b cm ar
(ROBERT KAHAKALAU)

Born February 11, 1922, New Haven, Conn.

Prominent bass man with top bands and combos from late 40s into 60s. Parents Hawaiian. Taught music by father, early experience in his orchestra. In late 30s played in Boston area. In early 40s toured, sometimes led own group. Military service, World War II. After discharge settled in New York, freelanced, became well known. Worked with such jazzmen as Charlie Parker, Dizzy Gillespie, Charlie Shavers, Tony Scott, Stuff Smith. With Charlie Ventura 1947-8, Benny Goodman 1949-50. In later 1950-1 with Tommy Dorsey and Goodman again. In late 1951 with Buddy Morrow. In 1953 briefly with Marian McPartland, then another stint with Charlie Ventura 1953-4. In 50s studied composing and arranging. Jobs with Red Norvo, Bob Harrington, Shelly Manne, Billy May, Charlie Barnet, Elliot Lawrence. Also did arranging. In Honolulu awhile, then back to New York in 1958. With Bobby Hackett in 1959. Active into 60s.

RECORDS
(All LPs)

BOBBY HACKETT
Cap T-1235 The Bobby Hackett Quartet

LOU STEIN
Br(10")BL-58053

BOB ALEXANDER (one side)
GA 33-325 Progressive Jazz (b-ar-cm)

RED NORVO
Vi LPM-1240 Hi-Five

ALLEN EAGER
Sav(10")MG-9015 New Trends in Modern Music, Vol. 2

CHARLIE VENTURA
Cor(10")56067
Norg(10")20

JOHNNY SMITH
Roost(10")413

286. CARTER, WILF   vo g cm lyr
(worked mostly as MONTANA SLIM)

Born December 18, 1904, Guysborough, Nova Scotia

Country and western star from early 30s to 60s. During early life worked as cowboy and rodeo performer. Began as professional entertainer, performed on Canadian radio in early 30s. In 1933 on New York radio. Announcer Bert Parks dubbed him Montana Slim and Carter adopted name for professional career. Some recordings under real name but mostly as Montana Slim. Composed much of material he featured, mostly plaintive cowboy ballads and yodels. In 60s settled in Florida, dropped out of show business.

RECORDS

WILF CARTER
Bb 5545 Take Me Back to Old Montana/Round-up in the Fall
Bb 5871 Gonna Ride to Heaven on Streamline/Two Gun Cowboy
Bb 6107 Sundown Blues/Cowboy Lullaby
Bb 6210 Deep Ocean/These Women
Bb 8696 I Bought a Rock for a Rocky Mountain Gal/Streamlined Yodel Song

MONTANA SLIM
Bb 6826 Round-up Time in Heaven/Dreamy Prairie Moon
Bb 6827 Roamin' My Whole Life Away/Yodeling Cowgirl
Bb 8202 When It's Twilight Over Texas/Memories of My Little Old Log Shack
Bb 8491 You Are My Sunshine/What a Wonderful Mother of Mine
Bb 8566 My Old Canadian Home/Back Ridin' the Old Trail Again
Bb 8743 Call of the Range/It's Great to Be Back in the Saddle Again
Bb 8842 Why Did We Ever Part?/The Last Letter
Bb 8924 If You Don't Really Care/My Lulu

Bb 33-0510 Sittin' by the Old Corral/
That First Love of Mine
Vi 27785 Old Montana Blues/Pete
Knight's Last Ride
Vi 27786 I'm Hittin' the Trail/Brown-
Eyed Prairie Rose
Vi 20-2561 Hang the Key on the Bunk-
house Door/Rye Whiskey
Vi 21-0392 Jolly Old St. Nicholas/
Rudolph the Red-Nosed Reindeer

LPs

MONTANA SLIM
Cam CAL-527 Montana Slim
Cam CAL-847 32 Wonderful Years
Cam CAL-2171 No Letter Today
Cam CAL Walls of Memory
Starday 300 Living Legend

287. CARY, DICK   p t v mel ar cm B
Born July 10, 1916, Hartford, Conn.

A leading arranger for dixieland combos.
Gave structure to a band and still left
room for soloists. Adept on several instruments. As child studied violin, played
in Hartford Symphony Orchestra in high
school. Learned other instruments, concentrated on piano, later played in local
dance bands. Played in New York clubs
in early 40s, including Nick's. In 1943
worked with Benny Goodman and Glen
Gray. In military service awhile during
World War II. In 1946 with Billy Butterfield, later led own band. In 1947-8 with
Louis Armstrong, with Jimmy Dorsey late
1949-50. During these years worked
mostly as pianist. In early 50s began
working mostly with dixieland groups,
arranging and frequently playing mellophone and trumpet. Well-conceived writing gave these groups added dimension,
established him as top arranger in dixieland field. With Jerry Jerome and Eddie
Condon in early 50s, including TV work.
Pianist-arranger for Wild Bill Davison in
1952. Arranged for Bud Freeman and
Tommy Dorsey, worked with Bobby
Hackett 1956-7 and Max Kaminsky 1958.
Settled on west coast in 1959, maintained
busy schedule through 60s with arranging-composing assignments and freelance
playing on jobs and records. Worked with
Ben Pollack, Bob Crosby, Red Nichols,
Eddie Condon, Matty Matlock and other
leading dixieland jazzmen. Also taught.

RECORDS

JIMMY DORSEY
Co 38655 Struttin' with Some Barbe-
cue/Chimes Blues
Co 38731 When You Wore a Tulip
RUTH BROWN
Atl 879 It's Raining/So Long

LPs

DICK CARY
Co CL-1425 And the Dixieland Dood-
lers
Stereocraft RTN-106 Hot and Cool
EDDIE CONDON
Dot DLP-3141 Dixieland Dance Party
BOBBY HACKETT
Cap T-857 Gotham Jazz Scene
LOUIS ARMSTRONG
Vi LPM-1443 Town Hall Concert Plus
LOU MCGARITY
Jub 1108 Some Like It Hot
REX STEWART
Felsted FAJ-7001 Rendezvous with
Rex
JIMMY MCPARTLAND
Br(10'')BL-58049 Shades of Bix
JIMMY DORSEY
Co(10'')CL-6095 Dixie by Dorsey
MAX KAMINSKY
Vi(10'')LJM-3003

288. CARYLL, IVAN   cm B
(FELIX TILKEN)

Born 1861, Liege, Belgium
Died November 28, 1921, New York,
N.Y.

Composer of scores for many Broadway
musicals pre-1900 to 1920. Best songs: *My
Beautiful Lady* in THE PINK LADY (1911),
Goodbye, Girls, I'm Through in CHIN-CHIN
(1914), *Come and Have a Swing with Me*
and *Wait Till the Cows Come Home* in
JACK O' LANTERN (1917). Educated at
Liege Conservatory, also studied in Paris.
Wrote for French stage, then to London
to become conductor at Gaiety Theatre.
Wrote for London stage, his shows then
imported to U.S. for successful runs
1891-1910. First U.S. show LA CIGALE
(1891). Settled in U.S. permanently in
1911 to continue illustrious career. Songs
fresh, light, well constructed. Other leading songs: *By the Saskatchewan; Kiss
Waltz; Oh! Oh! Delphine; Venus Waltz;
There's a Light in Your Eyes; There's Life*

689

in the Old Dog Yet; *The Soldiers in the Park*; *Oh, How I Love Society*. Chief lyricists Owen Hall, C. M. S. McLellan, Anne Caldwell.

BROADWAY MUSICALS

1891—LA CIGALE
1894—LITTLE CHRISTOPHER COLUMBUS
1897—THE GIRL FROM PARIS
1898—THE RUNAWAY GIRL
1901—THE LADIES' PARADISE; THE MESSENGER BOY
1902—THE TOREADOR
1903—THE GIRL FROM KAY'S
1905—THE DUCHESS OF DANTZIC; THE EARL AND THE GIRL
1906—THE LITTLE CHERUB
1907—THE ORCHID
1908—THE GIRLS OF GOTTENBURG
1910—OUR MISS GIBBS
1911—THE PINK LADY; MARRIAGE A LA CARTE
1912—OH! OH! DELPHINE
1913—THE LITTLE CAFE
1914—THE BELLE OF BOND STREET; CHIN-CHIN; PAPA'S DARLING
1917—JACK O' LANTERN
1918—THE CANARY; THE GIRL BEHIND THE GUN
1920—KISSING TIME; TIP TOP

## 289. CASE, RUSS					t ar cm B

Born March 19, 1912, Hamburg, Iowa
Died October 10, 1964, Miami, Fla.

Conductor on radio and record sessions, most prominent during 40s and 50s. On Des Moines radio in early 30s. In 1932 to Chicago with Frankie Trumbauer on trumpet. Later that year joined Paul Whiteman, also arranged for him. With Benny Goodman briefly in Billy Rose Music Hall band in summer of 1934. Freelanced in radio and arranged for various bands. With Hal Kemp band late 1934 to early 1936. Arranged for Andre Kostelanetz orchestra. In 1939 with Raymond Scott Quintet. Continued freelance trumpet work till mid-40s, then concentrated on career as conductor-arranger. During much of 40s served as pop music director for Victor Records. Conductor of many radio series; stints on Seven-Up Show and Kraft Music Hall. In 40s and 50s busy with recording sessions directing orchestra backing singers or recording on

his own. Also conducting-arranging for TV, active in early 60s. Composed several jazz numbers and descriptive works including *Midnight Oil, Sliphorn Sam, La Valse, Frantic Fiddles, Gambler's Ballet, Little Genius Ballet, Gabriel's Heater*.

RECORDS

(as sideman)
RAYMOND SCOTT QUINTET
   Br 8404 In an Eighteenth Century Drawing Room/Boy Scout in Switzerland
   Br 8452 Siberian Sleigh Ride/The Tobacco Auctioneer
   Co 35247 New Year's Eve in a Haunted House/The Girl with the Light Blue Hair
   Co 37360 A Little Bit of Rigoletto/The Quintet Plays Carmen
BOSWELL SISTERS
   De 574 Cheek to Cheek/Top Hat, White Tie and Tails
   De 671 I'm Gonna Sit Right Down and Write Myself a Letter/The Music Goes 'Round and Around
JOHNNY WILLIAMS
   Vo 5077 Milenberg Joys/Ma Curly-Headed Baby
   Vo 5213 Clarinet Marmalade/Memory Lane

(as conductor)
BETTY RHODES
   Vi 20-1885 This Is Always/Somewhere in the Night
BILLY DANIELS
   Mer 5721 That Old Black Magic/I Concentrate on You
   Mer 5806 Diane/September Song
BILL FARRELL
   MGM 10519 You've Changed
   MGM 10637 It Isn't Fair/Bamboo
BILLY ECKSTINE
   MGM 10825 I've Never Been in Love Before/I'll Know
DINAH SHORE
   Vi 20-1732 But I Did/As Long as I Live
BERYL DAVIS
   Vi 20-3019 The Blue Room/Don't Blame Me
PERRY COMO
   Vi 20-1709 Till the End of Time/That Feeling in the Moonlight
   Vi 20-3099 By the Way/For You

RUSS CASE
Vi 20-1940 Night and Day/Begin the Beguine
Vi 20-2344 Secrets/As Years Go By
MGM 10554 Envy/A Thousand Violins
MGM 10852 Wild Card/Margot
Vi(12")28-0407 Great Day/Sometimes I'm Happy
Vi(12")28-0408 Tea for Two/Hallelujah

LPs

RUSS CASE
"X"(10")LXA-3014 Sleepy Serenades
"X"(10")LXA-1007 Yesterdays
Vik LX-1027 Gypsy Moods

(as conductor)
BILLY DANIELS
Mer MG-20104 Around That Time
GIGI DURSTON with RUSS CASE ORCHESTRA
Rondo-lette 865 Miss You

290. CASEY, AL   g

Born September 15, 1915, Louisville, Ky.

Good rhythm guitarist and soloist. Best known for work with Fats Waller combo in 30s and 40s. Moved to New York in 1930, studied guitar there. Professional career began at top when joined Waller in 1933. Starred with Waller on a host of Victor records. With Waller till 1943 except for interval with Teddy Wilson big band 1939-40 and briefly with Buster Harding 1940. Beginning in 1943, led own trio in 40s, playing clubs in New York, Chicago, Los Angeles and other spots. With Clarence Profit Trio 1944. Also freelance and recording work. Most rhythm and solo work with unamplified guitar. Active in 50s and 60s, though comparatively obscure since early 50s. During 1957-61 period played rock and roll with King Curtis. Played in New York area with No Gap Generation Jazz Band in 1973.

RECORDS

FATS WALLER
Vi 24648 Do Me a Favor
Vi 24737 Sweetie Pie
Vi 24742 Let's Pretend There's a Moon
Vi 24801 Dream Man
Vi 24867 Baby Brown
Vi 24888 Dust Off That Old Pianna

Vi 24892 Whose Honey Are You?
Vi 25026 I Ain't Got Nobody
Vi 25348 Let's Sing Again/The More I Know You
Vi 25359 Black Raspberry Jam
Vi 25363 Why Do I Lie to Myself About You?/You're Not the Kind
Vi 25563 Boo-Hoo
Bb 10008 You Look Good to Me
Bb 10035 Yacht Club Swing
Bb 11078 Mamacita/Shortnin' Bread
Bb 11324 Buck Jumpin'

FRANKIE NEWTON
Bb 10216 Who?/The Blues My Baby Gave to Me

EARL HINES
Si 28109 Squeeze Me/I've Got a Feeling I'm Falling
Si 28110 Honeysuckle Rose/My Fate Is in Your Hands

PETE BROWN
Sav 522 Pete Brown's Boogie/Bellevue for You

BIG SID CATLETT
Cap 10032 Love for Scale/I Never Knew

JIMMY JOHNSON
Vo 4768 Harlem Woogie/After Tonight

CHU BERRY
CMS(12")1508 Gee, Baby, Ain't I Good to You?/On the Sunny Side of the Street

UNA MAE CARLISLE
Bb 10853 Now I Lay Me Down to Dream/Papa's in Bed with His Britches On

LEONARD FEATHER'S ALL-STARS
CMS 547 Esquire Bounce/Esquire Blues
CMS 548 My Ideal/Mop-Mop

ED HALL
CMS(12")1512 Downtown Cafe Boogie/Uptown Cafe Boogie

MEZZ MEZZROW
Bb 6319 The Panic Is On/Mutiny in the Parlor
Bb 6320 Lost/A Melody from the Sky

AL CASEY
Cap 10034 Sometimes I'm Happy/How High the Moon

LPs

AL CASEY
Pres MVLP-12 The Al Casey Quartet

691

Pres SVLP-2007 (S) Buck Jumpin'
FATS WALLER
Vi LPM-537 Fractious Fingering (Vi
RIs)
Vi LPM-1502 Handful of Keys (Vi
RIs)
Jazztone J-1247 Plays and Sings (Bb
RIs)
FLETCHER HENDERSON ALL-STARS
Jazztone J-1285 The Big Reunion
TEDDY WILSON
MGM(10")E-129 Runnin' Wild (Mus
RIs)
(miscellaneous artists)
Vi LPV-578 Swing, Vol. 1 (Vi, Bb RIs)

291. CASTLE, IRENE and VERNON
(IRENE FOOTE and VERNON BLYTHE)

Famed early dancing team, popular sensation several years until Vernon's entry into World War I and subsequent death. Performed in Broadway productions, invented dances that influenced the music scene. A former English magician, Vernon began career in U. S. on stage as dancer-actor. Minor roles in shows ABOUT TOWN (1906), THE GIRL BEHIND THE COUNTER (1907), THE MIMIC WORLD (1908), OLD DUTCH and THE MIDNIGHT SONS (1909), SUMMER WIDOWERS (1910). Vernon had good role in 1911 Lew Fields show THE HEN PECKS, in which Irene had small part. They married and formed dance team. In Paris in cafe act in 1912. Featured dance Castle Rock, rose to international fame. Returned to U. S. where Vernon appeared in Broadway shows THE LADY OF THE SLIPPER (1912), THE SUNSHINE GIRL (1913). Castles rose to great popularity through performances in theatres and cafes, capped by starring roles in 1914 show WATCH YOUR STEP. Originators of dance specialties The Texas Tommy, Bunny Hug, Turkey Trot, Castle Polka, The Maxixe, Castle Tango, The Gavotte. Performed in smooth, elegant manner. Whirlwind tour increased their popularity to fetish proportions, with public imitating their dress and habits. Castles also organized string of dance studios. At height of success, Vernon joined British flying unit in France during World War I, did aerial photography at the front. Transferred to U. S. as flying instructor. At Fort Worth Flying School in 1918 killed in crash with student. Irene appeared in 1917 show MISS 1917, soon retired. 1939 movie STORY OF VERNON AND IRENE CASTLE starred Castles' counterparts of 30s, Fred Astaire and Ginger Rogers.

292. CASTLE, LEE   t B
(LEE CASTALDO)

Born February 28, 1915, New York, N.Y.

Trumpeter from 30s into 70s. Good lead man and jazz soloist in swing and dixieland groups. Started career at 18. First big jobs in 1936 with Joe Haymes, Dick Stabile and Artie Shaw (with latter into 1937). In 1937 briefly with Red Norvo, joined Tommy Dorsey late 1937 and remained through 1938. With Jack Teagarden most of 1939, late in year rejoined Dorsey briefly. Own band most of 1940. With Will Bradley much of 1941, late in year joined Artie Shaw and remained several months into 1942. Own band awhile, then joined Benny Goodman in late 1942 and remained a year. Then active in studio work. Again fronted band in mid-40s. Worked briefly with Artie Shaw in 1950. With the Tommy Dorsey band featuring Jimmy Dorsey during 1953-6, featured trumpet soloist. After Tommy's death in late 1956, Castle remained in band as assistant leader to Jimmy. After Jimmy's death in mid-1957, Castle took over leadership. Has led band ever since. Billed as Jimmy Dorsey Band directed by Lee Castle, features Jimmy's old hit numbers.

RECORDS

ARTIE SHAW
Br 7735 Sugar Foot Stomp
TOMMY DORSEY
Vi 25813 I Never Knew
WILL BRADLEY
Co 36340 Basin Street Boogie
GLENN HARDMAN
Co 35263 Upright Organ Blues/Jazz
Me Blues
Co 35341 China Boy/On the Sunny
Side of the Street

LEE CASTLE
  Mus 15031 Dream/Story of Two Cig-
    arettes
  Mus 15035 Jump It, Mr. Trumpet/La
    Rosita
  Jay-Dee 666 Stars and Stripes Forev-
    er/Alabama Blues
  VD(12″)274 I Get the Blues When It
    Rains
  VD(12″)293 Uptown Express
JIMMY DORSEY
  Fraternity F755 So Rare/Sophisticated
    Swing

LPs

LEE CASTLE
  Davis 105 Dixieland Heaven
  Epic LN-3560
  Epic LN-3579
  Epic LN-3681
LEE CASTLE & THE JIMMY DORSEY OR-
  CHESTRA
  Pickwick SPC-3125 Play Bacharach
    and David
TOMMY DORSEY (his last band)
  Co CL-1190 The Fabulous Dorseys in
    Hi-Fi
  Co CL-1240 Sentimental and Swinging
ARTIE SHAW
  Epic LN-3112 With Strings (Br, Vo
    RIs)
RAY MCKINLEY
  Waldorf(10″)MH-33-161 The Swingin'
    30s
  (one side) GA 33-333 The Swinging
    Thirties

293. CATHCART, DICK   t vo B
(CHARLES RICHARD
CATHCART)

*Born November 6, 1924, Michigan City,
Ind.*

Excellent trumpet soloist in the Bix
Beiderbecke tradition—beautiful tone,
fresh ideas, easy swing. At best in dixieland groups. From musical family; three
brothers professional musicians. Early
start with name bands, first big job with
Ray McKinley several months in 1942.
With Alvino Rey late 1942-3. In mid-1943
entered military service. After discharge
with Bob Crosby most of 1946. Studio
work at MGM for three years. With Ben
Pollack group 1949-50 and Ray Noble

1950-1. In mid-1951 on Jack Webb's
radio show, Pete Kelly's Blues, as member of outstanding dixieland band. In
1951 led group in Los Angeles. In 1952 on
California TV with Frank DeVol. Good
run in mid-50s on Bob Crosby's daytime
TV show, also sang with Modernaires
awhile there and later. In 1955 on soundtrack of movie PETE KELLY'S BLUES, did
trumpet work for Jack Webb. In 1959
musical director of short-lived TV series,
Pete Kelly's Blues. During 50s considerable freelance recording with leading
west coast dixieland stars. Several years in
60s with Lawrence Welk on ballroom
jobs, concerts and weekly TV show, often
featured on trumpet or in vocal group.
Left when Lennon Sisters left (had married Peggy Lennon), and 1969-70 was
musical director on Lennons' TV series.
Active into 70s.

RECORDS

PETE KELLY'S BIG SEVEN
  Cap 1753 Louisiana (classic Bix-like
    solo)
  Cap 1780 Till We Meet Again
RAY MCKINLEY
  Hit 7005 Who Wouldn't Love You?
BEN POLLACK
  Dis 131 San Sue Strut/I Can't Give
    You Anything but Love
  Dis 132 Tin Roof Blues/San Antonio
    Shout
  Mod Holly 203 Royal Garden Blues/
    Third Man Theme
ART LUND
  MGM 10648 Sugarfoot Rag
HOAGY CARMICHAEL
  De 24871 That's a-Plenty/Darktown
    Strutters' Ball

LPs

JOHNNY BEST ALL-STARS & DICK CATHCART
  ALL-STARS
  Mer PPS-2009 Dixieland Left and
    Right
DICK CATHCART with WARREN BARKER
  ORCHESTRA
  WB 12750 Bix MCMLIX
MATTY MATLOCK
  Co CL-690 Pete Kelly's Blues
  Mayfair 9569 Dixieland
  Tops 1569 Matty Matlock & His
    Dixie-Men

(miscellaneous artists)
   Golden Tone C-4021 Dixieland
   Cr CLP-5129 Kings of Dixieland, Vol. 2
   Vi LPM-1126 Pete Kelly's Blues
   WB 1303 Authentic Music from TV Production of PETE KELLY'S BLUES

294. CATLETT, SID   dB
(nicknamed BIG SĪD)

Born January 17, 1910, Evansville, Ind.
Died March 25, 1951, Chicago, Ill.

A leading drummer of 30s and 40s in traditional and swing styles. Extensive freelance recording career. Grew up in Chicago. Early jobs in late 20s with Darnell Howard, then with Sammy Stewart at Michigan Theatre and toured with him. Worked in New York in early 30s with Elmer Snowden, Benny Carter, Rex Stewart, Sam Wooding, McKinney's Cotton Pickers. With Jeter-Pillars band in St. Louis in 1935. Back in New York with Fletcher Henderson about six months in 1936. Joined Don Redman in late 1936, remained two years. With Louis Armstrong off and on, late 1938-41. During 1941 brief periods with Roy Eldridge and Benny Goodman. Rejoined Armstrong late 1941-2 for several months, then with Teddy Wilson 1942-4. Led combo next three years in various cities. With Louis Armstrong All-Stars 1947-9, much touring. During 1949-50 played many jobs at Jazz Ltd., Chicago, as house drummer (with intervals away). Active until sudden death from heart attack.

RECORDS

FLETCHER HENDERSON
   Vi 25297 Moonrise on the Lowlands/I'm a Fool for Loving You
   Vi 25317 Jangled Nerves/I'll Always Be in Love with You
   Vo 3213 Grand Terrace Swing/Stealin' Apples
DON REDMAN
   Vo 3354 Too Bad/Bugle Call Rag
CHOCOLATE DANDIES
   Sw(Fr) 226 What'll It Be/Out of My Way
   CMS(12")1506 I Surrender Dear/I Can't Believe That You're in Love with Me

TEDDY WILSON
   Br 7684 Warmin' Up/Blues in C Sharp Minor
   VD(12")16 How High the Moon/Russian Lullaby
LESTER YOUNG
   Key 603 Just You, Just Me/I Never Knew
   Key 604 Afternoon of a Basieite/Sometimes I'm Happy
LOUIS ARMSTRONG
   De 2267 Jeepers Creepers/What Is This Thing Called Swing?
   De 2615 Confessin'/Our Monday Date
   De 2934 You're a Lucky Guy/You're Just a No Account
   De 4106 Leap Frog/I Used to Love You
   Vi 40-4005 Ain't Misbehavin'/Pennies from Heaven
BENNY GOODMAN
   Co 36254 Tuesday at Ten
   Co 36379 The Count
   Co 36421 Pound Ridge
ED HALL
   BN(12")28 High Society/Blues at Blue Note
   BN(12")29 Night Shift Blues/Royal Garden Blues
HOT LIPS PAGE
   CMS 571 Rockin' at Ryan's/You'd Be Frantic Too
EDDIE CONDON
   Atl 661 Time Carries On/Seems Like Old Times
AL CASEY
   Cap 10034 Sometimes I'm Happy/How High the Moon
DON BYAS
   Super Disc 1010 Super Session/Melody in Swing
   Super Disc 1011 Embraceable You/The Sheik of Araby
SIDNEY BECHET
   BN 502 Bechet's Steady Rider/Saturday Night Blues
SID CATLETT
   CMS 564 Sleep/Linger Awhile
   CMS(12")1515 Memories of You/Just a Riff
   Regis 5000 Blues in Room 920/Blue Skies
   Cap 10032 I Never Knew/Love for Scale

LPs

SIDNEY BECHET
"X"(10")LVA-3024 (Bb, Vi RIs)
LOUIS ARMSTRONG
Vi LPM-1443 Town Hall Concert Plus
CHU BERRY
CMS(10")20024 (CMS RIs)
COLEMAN HAWKINS
CMS(10")20025 (CMS RIs)

295. CAUSER, BOB   B

There is considerable myth about this person. Many good hotel-band records issued under this name during 1931-6 period. Some undoubtedly by Freddy Martin band featuring Martin's distinctive lead tenor sax and vocalists Elmer Feldkamp and Terry Shand. Majority by studio groups of excellent musicians, many with good hot solos. Other vocalists on these records include Chick Bullock, Dick Robertson, Tony Sacco, Smith Ballew, Johnny Hauser, Buddy Clark. Bunny Berigan, Dorseys, Mannie Klein, other jazzmen said to appear on some records. One theory: Bob Causer was booking agent and/or hotel manager in Ithaca, N.Y. (home of Cornell University—hence name Bob Causer & His Cornellians on some records), and name was used on records in return for bookings. Band news in music magazines listed Bob Causer band playing at Westwood Supper Club, Richmond, Va., 1938-9, and in Syracuse, N.Y., in mid-1939. Hence there apparently *was* a real Bob Causer band, at least in late 30s.

RECORDS
*(*probably Freddy Martin)*

BOB CAUSER
Pe 15556 Delishious/Somebody from Somewhere
Pe 15557 I Found You/Oh, What a Thrill
Pe 15583 One Hour with You/What Would You Do?
Pe 15616 My Silent Love/If I Could Call You Sweetheart
Pe 15639 Rain, Rain, Go Away/The One-Note Trumpet Player
Pe 15746 What Have We Got to Lose?/Maybe It's Because I Love You Too Much*

Pe 15769 Sweetheart Darlin'/Love Songs of the Nile
Pe 15782 Learn to Croon/Moonstruck*
Pe 15890 Why Do I Dream These Dreams?/Don't Say Goodnight
Pe 15969 Say It/Then I'll Be Tired of You*
Pe 16062 Because of Once Upon a Time/Tiny Little Fingerprints
Me 12532 You'll Get By/More Beautiful Than Ever
Me 12631 Love Tales/Farewell to Arms
Me 12671 Let's Call It a Day/Stormy Weather
Me 12791 Give Me Liberty or Give Me Love/Dinner at Eight
Me 12848 Puddin' Head Jones/My Old Man
Me 13010 No More Heartaches, No More Tears/Riptide*
Me 13138 Don't Let It Bother You/When He Comes Home to Me
Me 13206 Irresistible/Were You Foolin'?
Me 13392 Flowers for Madame/Seein' Is Believin'
Me 60409 I'm Building Up to an Awful Letdown/Alone at a Table for Two
Me 60505 Welcome Stranger/Every Minute of the Hour
Me 60514 Hills of Old Wyomin'/Love Came Out of the Night
Me 61209 Did You Mean It?/When Is a Kiss Not a Kiss?

296. CAVALLARO, CARMEN
p ar cm B

Born May 6, 1913, New York, N.Y.

Flashy society-style pianist, rather flowery but with excellent touch and technique, beautiful chords. Leader of good sweet-styled dance band many years. As youngster had considerable training as classical pianist, played many concerts in U.S. and abroad. Then dance jobs, long period with Al Kavelin 1933-7 where billed simply as Carmen and featured prominently with band. Later did some arranging for band. Joined Rudy Vallee in 1937 for about a year, then with Abe

Lyman in 1938 for awhile. Freelanced, worked with Enric Madriguera, Meyer Davis dance units, and on radio. In 1939 led five-piece combo at St. Louis hotel. By mid-1940 to Detroit with eight-piece group, then in late 1940 to New York. Popular wherever he played, and recordings helped. In 40s played top hotels in big cities, including long stays in Chicago and New York, and appeared in many theatres. Late 1943-4 change to swing band failed. In mid-1944 formed band in former style. In several movies: HOLLYWOOD CANTEEN (1944), OUT OF THIS WORLD and DIAMOND HORSESHOE (1945), THE TIME, THE PLACE AND THE GIRL (1946). In late 40s had Sunday afternoon radio show The Schaeffer Parade. Recorded heavily both with band and as soloist with rhythm section. In 1956 did an excellent job on soundtrack of movie THE EDDY DUCHIN STORY, imitating Duchin piano style (with Tyrone Power portraying Duchin). Active in 60s, in later years concentrating on concerts. Composer of several songs, including *Wanda, While the Nightwind Sings, Masquerade Waltz*.

RECORDS

CARMEN CAVALLARO (piano with rhythm)
  De 3110 Cocktails for Two/The Very Thought of You
  De 3113 Body and Soul/You're Mine, You
  De 3114 Alone Together/Night and Day
  De 3505 My Silent Love/I'm Gettin' Sentimental Over You
  De 3506 I Can't Get Started/Temptation
  De 3800 All the Things You Are/Lovely to Look At
  De 3804 You're Just a Flower from an Old Bouquet/You're My Everything
  De 4057 Day Dreaming/I Dream Too Much
  De 18539 You and You/Voices of Spring
  De 24060-1-2-3 Songs of Our Times—1932

CARMEN CAVALLARO ORCHESTRA
  De 3899 'Til Reveille/A Romantic Guy, I

De 18631 In the Middle of Nowhere/Wouldn't It Be Nice?
De 18671 The More I See You/In Acapulco
De 18742 A Love Like This/Warsaw Concerto
De 24953 Sweetheart of All My Dreams/So in Love
De 27655 Wanda/Every Little Movement
De 28085 Blue Tango/Serenade in the Night

BOB EBERLY with CARMEN CAVALLARO ORCHESTRA
  De 18813 Come Closer to Me/Full Moon and Empty Arms

BING CROSBY with CARMEN CAVALLARO
  De 23457 I Can't Believe That You're in Love with Me/I Can't Begin to Tell You

LPs

CARMEN CAVALLARO
  De DL-4669 The Magic Music of Hollywood
  De DL-8289 THE EDDY DUCHIN STORY (soundtrack)
  De DL-8305 THE KING AND I—and Other Rodgers-Hammerstein Songs
  De DL-8805 Cocktails with Cavallaro
  De(10")DL-5007 Dancing in the Dark (De RIs)
  De(10")DL-5199 For Sweethearts Only (De RIs)

DICK HAYMES with CARMEN CAVALLARO
  De(10")DL-5023 Irving Berlin Songs

297. CAVANAUGH, DAVE   ts ar B

Tenor saxist with various groups early in career but best known in late 40s and 50s as orchestra director backing singers on records, then A & R man and producer for Capitol Records. In early 1946 saxman-arranger with Bobby Sherwood band. Freelanced on record sessions, began leading combo or band backing singers on records. Arrangements tasteful, made small group sound clean-cut and compact. Also led dixieland group in clubs and on dance jobs. In early 1951 named eastern A & R director for Capitol in New York. In late 1952 went to west coast to head their Kidisc department, later became producer in 60s for Capitol.

RECORDS

(as sideman)

JULIA LEE

Cap 340 On My Way Out

Cap 379 Young Girl's Blues

Cap 40008 Since I've Been with You

Cap 40028 Snatch and Grab It/I Was Wrong

Cap 40082 When You're Smiling/King Size Papa

Cap 15106 Wise Guys/All I Ever Do Is Worry

HOLLYWOOD HUCKSTERS (ts-ar)

Cap 40022 Them There Eyes/Happy Blues

JOE ALEXANDER

Cap 15100 If I Should Lose You/Blue Holiday

Cap 15274 I Never Had a Chance/So Long Darling

Cap 40079 Hold Me

SAMMY DAVIS, JR.

Cap 57-70045 Smile, Darn Ya, Smile/Azure

JESSE PRICE

Cap 40047 Jump It with a Shuffle/Nagasaki

(as conductor)

KAY STARR

Cap 1677 Wheel of Fortune/Angry

Cap 15087 Snuggled on Your Shoulder/Don't Let Your Love Go Wrong

Cap 15288 There Ain't No Sweet Man/Please Love Me

Cap 15504 It's the First Time/You've Got to See Mama Every Night

ELLA MAE MORSE

Cap 2539 Oh, You Crazy Moon

VICKI YOUNG

Cap 2478 I Love You So Much/Let Me Hear You Say (I Love You)

Cap 2543 Affair with a Stranger/Ricochet

Cap 2704 Somebody Else Is Talking My Place/Forever Yours

BOB EBERLY

Cap 2103 Isn't This a Night for Love/Hills of Pride

HOAGY CARMICHAEL

Cap 2593 Love Will Soon Be Here/When Love Goes Wrong

LPs

DAVE CAVANAUGH

Cap 640 Arthur Murray Rock and Roll Dance Party

298. CAVANAUGH, JAMES   lyr

Born in New York, N.Y.

Lyricist of 30s and 40s with several song successes. Early in career played vaudeville, wrote own material. Chief collaborators John Redmond, Nat Simon, Frank Weldon, Vincent Rose, Larry Stock, Dick Robertson.

SONGS

1933—I Like Mountain Music

1934—Neighbors; You're in My Power

1935—Why Have a Falling Out?

1938—The Umbrella Man

1939—The Man with the Mandolin; Whistling in the Wildwood

1940—Crosstown; The Gaucho Serenade; Goody Goodbye; The Sidewalk Serenade; On a Simmery Summery Day

1944—A Little on the Lonely Side; You're Nobody 'Til Somebody Loves You

1945—That Feeling in the Moonlight; I'd Do It All Over Again

1947—Dreams Are a Dime a Dozen

1948—The Man on the Carousel; A Lovely Rainy Afternoon

299. CAVANAUGH, PAGE

p vo ar cm B

Born January 26, 1922, Cherokee, Kansas

Leader of Page Cavanaugh Trio, popular in 40s and early 50s. Group featured soft-voiced unison singing predominantly with Cavanaugh's full chords and tasteful piano style giving excellent backing. Capable solo pianist, modern style. Cavanaugh's career began locally, then to Los Angeles about 1940 to job. Military service, World War II, where trio originated in 1943 and continued after discharge. Al Viola (guitar) and Lloyd Pratt (bass) original members with Cavanaugh. Close-knit, entertaining group. Popularity began on west coast then spread nationally through records, radio and movies.

Latter included A SONG IS BORN, BIG CITY and ROMANCE ON THE HIGH SEAS (1948), LULLABY OF BROADWAY (1951). Busy schedule playing clubs, hotels and theatres. On west coast TV. In later years personnel changed to Dave Porrazzo(guitar) and Jack Smalley (bass). Cavanaugh continued with trio, also used larger combo at times through 50s. Composed some of novelty and jazz-flavored numbers featured by group. In early 60s opened night club.

RECORDS
PAGE CAVANAUGH TRIO
ARA 151 Air Mail Special/Saipan
ARA 160 After You've Gone/Fish and Chips
Encore 504 Crazy Rhythm/Too Soon
Encore 506 Don't Blame Me/When the Gooses Come Back to Massachusetts
Encore 516 You Go to My Head/Jump Easy
Mastertone 7519 The Three Bears/Autumn in New York
Mastertone 7523 Saipan/Vine Street Hayride
Si 15190 Blue Moon/Body and Soul
Si 15195 The Man I Love/I'll Remember April
VD(12″)530 The Shivers/When the Gooses Come Back to Massachusetts
Ray 113 Has-Been Heart/Look! Look! It's Raining Sunshine Drops
Vaya 901 Homer's Hymn/You Don't Know What Love Is
Vi 20-2085 All of Me/The Three Bears
Vi 20-2246 Walkin' My Baby Back Home/Heartbreakin'
Vi 20-2646 Anything for You/Ok'l Baby Dok'l
Vi 20-3290 I'm Gonna Get Lost from You/The Gal Who's Got My Heart
JANE HARVEY with PAGE CAVANAUGH TRIO
Vi 20-2149 Foggy River/My Number One Dream Came True
JOHNNY DESMOND with PAGE CAVANAUGH TRIO
Vi 20-2109 Guilty/I'll Close My Eyes

LPs
PAGE CAVANAUGH TRIO (and combos)
Vaya(10″)103-4 After Hours

"X"(10″)LVA-3027 The Page Cavanaugh Trio
Tops L-1523 Page Cavanaugh
Time S-2121 (S) Softly
Cap T-879 Fats Sent Me (6-piece combo)
Vi LSP-2734 (S) The Page 7 (7-piece combo)
DORIS DAY-GENE NELSON-PAGE CAVANAUGH TRIO
Co(10″)CL-6149 Tea for Two

300. CAWTHORN, JOSEPH   vo lyr
Born March 29, 1867, New York, N.Y.
Died 1949

Actor-comedian in Broadway musicals 1898-1925. In about 50 movies many years beginning 1928, comic and character roles. Most important movie musicals THE CAT AND THE FIDDLE and TWENTY MILLION SWEETHEARTS (1934), GOLD DIGGERS OF 1935, HARMONY LANE, MUSIC IN THE AIR, NAUGHTY MARIETTA, SWEET ADELINE and SWEET MUSIC (1935), THE GREAT ZIEGFELD (1936), LILLIAN RUSSELL (1940). Film career ended in 1942. Wrote lyrics to two featured songs in Broadway shows, *You Can't Play Every Instrument in the Band* in THE SUNSHINE GIRL (1913) and *I Can Dance with Everybody but My Wife* in SYBIL (1916).

BROADWAY MUSICALS
1898—THE FORTUNE TELLER
1899—THE SINGING GIRL
1901—THE SLEEPING BEAUTY AND THE BEAST
1903—MOTHER GOOSE
1905—FRITZ IN TAMMANY HALL
1906—THE FREE LANCE
1907—THE HOYDEN
1908—LITTLE NEMO
1910—GIRLIES
1911—THE SLIM PRINCESS
1913—THE SUNSHINE GIRL
1914—THE GIRL FROM UTAH
1916—SYBIL
1917—RAMBLER ROSE
1918—THE CANARY
1920—THE HALF MOON
1921—TANGERINE
1922—THE BLUE KITTEN
1925—SUNNY

RECORDS

JOSEPH CAWTHORN

Vi(12")55074 I Can Dance with Everybody but My Wife/It's a Small World

Vi(12")70098 You Can't Play Every Instrument in the Band

301. CELESTIN, PAPA   c vo B
(OSCAR CELESTIN)

Born January 1, 1884, parish of La-Fourche, La.
Died December 15, 1954, New Orleans, La.

Pioneer in development of jazz as cornetist and leader in New Orleans. Moved to New Orleans in 1906 after music experience elsewhere. First played mostly in brass bands. Formed band in 1910 to play Tuxedo Hall, continued as bandleader after hall closed in 1913. In later years called group The Original Tuxedo Jazz Orchestra, included good jazzmen. Remained in New Orleans area entire career, sometimes touring the Gulf coast. Recorded in New Orleans 1925-7. After early 30s in music only part-time. Worked in New Orleans shipyards during World War II. In dixie revival period of late 40s and early 50s, became more active in music, leading combo and making records. Appeared in movie CINERAMA HOLIDAY in 1953.

RECORDS

ORIGINAL TUXEDO JAZZ ORCHESTRA

OK 8198 Black Rag/Careless Love

OK 8215 Original Tuxedo Rag

CELESTIN'S ORIGINAL TUXEDO JAZZ ORCHESTRA

Co 636-D My Josephine/Station Calls

Co 14200-D Give Me Some More/I'm Satisfied You Love Me

Co 14220-D Dear Almanzoer/Papa's Got the Jim-Jams

Co 14259-D As You Like It/Just for You, Dear, I'm Crying

Co 14323-D When I'm with You/It's Jam Up

Co 14396-D The Sweethearts of T.K.O./Ta-Ta Daddy

DeL 1123 Hey-La-Ba/My Josephine

Re 1201 Maryland, My Maryland/Marie Laveau

RWP 9-10 When the Saints Go Marching In/Little Liza Jane

RWP 11-12 Oh, Didn't He Ramble/High Society

Co 48009 Darktown Strutters' Ball/Tiger Rag (from soundtrack of CINERAMA HOLIDAY)

LPs

CELESTIN'S ORIGINAL TUXEDO JAZZ ORCHESTRA

Southland(10")SLP-206 Papa Celestin's Golden Wedding

Melodisc(E) MLP-506 Papa Celestin & His New Orleans Band (last records)

302. CHALLIS, BILL   p ar B
Born July 8, 1904, Wilkes-Barre, Pa.

Talented arranger, principally in late 20s to 40s, influential in development of big band arranging. Gained most fame during period with star-studded Paul Whiteman band of late 20s. Outstanding arrangements fashioned good ensemble sound with nice shadings and interludes. Could orchestrate for large, rather ponderous band such as Whiteman's and showcase jazzmen effectively. Attended Bucknell University. With Dave Harmon band in 1925 as pianist-arranger. Joined Jean Goldkette in late 1926 for a year; his arrangements greatly improved band. Then joined Whiteman early 1928, became his most important arranger. Scoring gave jazz greats Bix Beiderbecke and Frankie Trumbauer good backgrounds for jazz solos, gave equally good backing to vocalists Bing Crosby, Jack Fulton and Rhythm Boys. In late 20s arranged for Trumbauer record sessions, Cass Hagan and others. After Whiteman band completed movie THE KING OF JAZZ, Challis left band in spring of 1930. Became freelance arranger in New York and in early 30s wrote for Nat Shilkret, Glen Gray, Dorsey Brothers, and Willard Robison radio show. Some conducting on radio; in 1935-6 had show, Bill Challis and His Music. During later 30s wrote arrangements for Fletcher Henderson, Richard Himber, Lennie Hayton, Claude Hopkins and others. In 40s assignments for Glen Gray and Jerry Wald. Continued arranging in 50s and 60s, although less active.

ARRANGEMENTS

JEAN GOLDKETTE

Sunday; I'd Rather Be the Girl in Your Arms; Hoosier Sweetheart; Idolizing; My Pretty Girl; Slow River; Lane in Spain; I'm Proud of a Baby Like You

PAUL WHITEMAN

Lonely Melody; When You're with Somebody Else; San; Coquette; My Pet; Sugar; Louisiana; Changes; Dardanella; Ol' Man River; Sweet Sue; Oh, You Have No Idea; Love Nest; My Heart Stood Still; Back in Your Own Backyard; Out O' Town Gal; 'Tain't So, Honey, 'Tain't So; Because My Baby Don't Mean "Maybe" Now; Oh, Miss Hannah; Reaching for Someone; That's My Weakness Now; Cradle of Love; Let's Do It; Great Day; Without a Song; Washboard Blues

FRANKIE TRUMBAUER

Ostrich Walk; Three Blind Mice

FLETCHER HENDERSON

Singing the Blues (Vi label); Clarinet Marmalade; My Gal Sal

DORSEY BROTHERS

The Blue Room

GLEN GRAY

Dardanella; I Love You Truly; For You; Time on My Hands; Blue Rhapsody

RECORDS
(featuring his arrangements)

BOBBY HACKETT

Br B-1026 album (78s)

LPs

PAUL WHITEMAN

Vi LPV-570 Paul Whiteman, Vol. 2 (RIs)

"X"(10″)LVA-3040 Featuring Bix Beiderbecke (RIs)

JEAN GOLDKETTE

"X"(10″)LVA-3017 (RIs)

BIX BEIDERBECKE with PAUL WHITEMAN

Co CL-846 The Bix Beiderbecke Story, Vol. 3 (RIs)

Vi LPM-2323 The Bix Beiderbecke Legend (RIs)

303. CHALOFF, SERGE   bs B

Born November 24, 1923, Boston, Mass.
Died July 16, 1957, Boston, Mass.

Important figure in development of bop. Exciting soloist and all-time great on baritone sax. Facile, inventive, hard-swinging, great command of instrument. First big job with Tommy Reynolds in 1939. With Dick Rogers 1941-2, Shep Fields 1943, Ina Ray Hutton 1944. In 1945 with Boyd Raeburn and George Auld, then with Jimmy Dorsey later 1945-6. With Woody Herman 1947-9, where became star. Also freelance record sessions during this period. With Count Basie combo briefly in 1950. Later in 1950 returned to Boston, taught music. Led groups in Boston, also in 1952 in Chicago for a time. With Herb Pomeroy big band in Boston in 1956. Died in 1957 of cancer; had been stricken a year earlier but still worked when able.

RECORDS

WOODY HERMAN

Co 38304 Four Brothers

Cap 616 Keeper of the Flame

Cap 15365 Lemon Drop

SONNY BERMAN

Dial 1006 Curbstone Scuffle

COUNT BASIE

Co 38888 The Golden Bullet

METRONOME ALL-STARS

Co 38734 No Figs/Double Date

Cap 1550 Early Spring/Local 802 Blues

RED RODNEY

Mer 1065 Fine and Dandy/Elevation

SERGE CHALOFF

Sav 906 A Bar a Second

Sav 956 Serge's Urge/Pumpernickel

Sav 978 Gabardine and Serge

Fut 3003 Chickasaw/Bopscotch

Fut 3004 The Most!/Chasin' the Bass

Motif 002 Pat/King Edward the Flatted Fifth

Dial 1012 Blue Serge

LPs

SERGE CHALOFF

Cap T-742 Blue Serge

Cap T-6510 Boston Blow-up!

Story(10″)310 Serge Chaloff and Boots Mussulli

Story(10″)317 Fable of Mable

Sav(10″)XP8087 Lestorian Mode
SERGE CHALOFF-OSCAR PETTIFORD
Mercer(10″)103 New Stars, New
Sounds
THE FOUR BROTHERS (Sims-Cohn-Stew-
ard-Chaloff)
Vik LX-1096 Together Again!
(miscellaneous artists)
Dial(10″)210 The Woodchoppers
WOODY HERMAN
Cap T-324 (1948-50 RIs)
OSCAR PETTIFORD
Pres 7813 Memorial Album (1949 &
1954 RIs)

304. CHANDLER, KAREN   vo
Excellent singer, worked last half of 1946
with Benny Goodman under name of Eve
Young. Recorded several vocals with
band, appeared on radio also. In later 40s
worked as single in clubs and on records,
later used name of Karen Chandler. In
1952 had hit record, *Hold Me, Thrill Me,
Kiss Me*, followed with other recordings.
Husband Jack Pleis often arranged for
her, accompanied her as pianist-bandleader. By later 50s career waned.

RECORDS
BENNY GOODMAN (as Eve Young)
Co 37149 For You, for Me, for Ev-
ermore
Co 37187 A Gal in Calico
Co 37207 Man Here Plays Fine Piano
Co(Aus) 3129 That's the Beginning of
the End
EVE YOUNG
Vi 20-3077 Cuanto Le Gusta/Say
Something Sweet to Your Sweet-
heart
Vi 20-3335 Laughing Boy/I Can't
Think of a Thing to Do
Vi 20-3412 Cabaret/It's Me
KAREN CHANDLER
Cor 60831 Hold Me, Thrill Me, Kiss
Me/One Dream
Cor 60911 I Hear the Music Now/The
Old Sewing Machine
Cor 60958 I'd Love to Fall Asleep/
Goodbye, Charlie, Goodbye
Cor 60995 Rosebud/I Wouldn't Want
It Any Other Way
Cor 61034 Transfer/Madonna
Cor 61088 Flash in the Blue/Why?

Cor 61137 Positively No Dancing/Hit
the Target, Baby
Cor 61181 Why Didn't You Tell Me?/
Out in the Middle of the Night
LPs
KAREN CHANDLER
Strand SL-1028 Dear Mr. Gable

305. CHANNING, CAROL   vo
Born January 31, 1921, Seattle, Wash.
Wide-eyed, husky-voiced comedienne of
stage, screen and TV. Attended Benning-
ton College in Vermont, studied dance
and drama. Played small clubs in New
York area. Landed job as understudy in
Broadway show LET'S FACE IT (1941).
Worked as model in Los Angeles awhile.
Played in Hollywood revue LEND AN EAR,
gained notice when it ran on Broadway in
1948. Starring role in show GENTLEMEN
PREFER BLONDES (1949), long-running suc-
cess. Permanently associated with show's
hit, *Diamonds Are a Girl's Best Friend*.
Bookings in clubs, theatre and TV in 50s.
In 1956 movie THE FIRST TRAVELING
SALESLADY. Starred on Broadway in SHOW
GIRL (1961) and biggest hit HELLO, DOLLY!
(1964). With latter road show in 1965.
Featured role in 1967 movie THOROUGHLY
MODERN MILLIE, also 1968 movie SKIDOO.
Occasional appearances on TV in later
60s and 70s. Starred in 1974 revival
of Broadway musical LORELEI. Distinctive sound and style led to many imi-
tations by comedian-mimics.

RECORDS
(all LPs)
(original Broadway cast)
Co ML-4290 GENTLEMEN   PREFER
BLONDES
Roul R-80001 SHOW GIRL
(movie soundtrack)
De DL-1500 THOROUGHLY   MODERN
MILLIE

306. CHAPLIN, SAUL   cm lyr ar p B
Born February 19, 1912, Brooklyn, N.Y.
Composer of hit songs beginning mid-30s.
Later important conductor-executive in
films. Collaborated on many songs with
lyricist Sammy Cahn. Leading songs:
Shoe Shine Boy, Until the Real Thing

Comes Along, Bei Mir Bist du Schon, Please Be Kind, The Anniversary Song. Educated at NYU School of Commerce. Played in dance bands, co-led band in mid-30s with Cahn. Began composing in 1935 with Cahn. Wrote special material for vaudeville and night club acts. In 1941 began Hollywood career as composer-arranger, later became musical director and producer. Scored movies COVER GIRL (1944), THE JOLSON STORY (1946), ON THE TOWN (1949), SUMMER STOCK (1950), AN AMERICAN IN PARIS (1951), KISS ME KATE (1953), SEVEN BRIDES FOR SEVEN BROTHERS (1954), HIGH SOCIETY (1956), THE TEAHOUSE OF THE AUGUST MOON (1956), MERRY ANDREW (1958), WEST SIDE STORY (1961). Musical director of several movies. Produced movie STAR! (1968). Wrote score late 1947 for unsuccessful show BONANZA BOUND which did not reach Broadway.

SONGS
(with related movies and shows)

1935—Rhythm Is Our Business (once Jimmie Lunceford theme)
1936—I'm One Step Ahead of My Shadow; Rhythm Saved the World; Shoe Shine Boy; Until the Real Thing Comes Along; Don't Look Now
1937—Bei Mir Bist du Schon; Dedicated to You; If It's the Last Thing I Do; Posin'; Just a Simple Melody; Love, You're Just a Laugh; If You Ever Should Leave; Don't You Care What Anyone Says; Everyone's Wrong but Me
1938—Please Be Kind; Saving Myself for You; Joseph! Joseph!; Wait Till My Heart Finds Out; Laughing Boy Blues
1939—I Want My Share of Love; It's Easy to Blame the Weather; It's My Turn Now; You're a Lucky Guy; Prosschai; The Girl with the Pigtails in Her Hair
1940—LADIES MUST LIVE movie (I Could Make You Care)
1941—TIME OUT FOR RHYTHM movie (As If You Didn't Know); The End of the Rainbow
1945—A SONG TO REMEMBER movie (title song)

1946—THE JOLSON STORY movie (The Anniversary Song)
1947—BONANZA BOUND unsuccessful stage show (Tell Me Why; Up in Smoke; Fill 'Er Up; I Know It's True)
1950—SUMMER STOCK movie (You Wonderful You)
1958—MERRY ANDREW movie
1968—STAR! movie (In My Garden of Joy)

307. CHARIOTEERS, THE   vo
Popular vocal group from mid-30s to late 40s. Organized at Wilberforce College in Ohio. On Cincinnati radio two years. To New York in late 30s for radio, theatres, records. Personnel: William B. Williams (tenor), Edward Jackson (tenor), Ira Williams (baritone), Howard B. Daniel (bass), Jimmy Sherman (pianist-arranger). In 1938 in highly successful show HELLZAPOPPIN.

RECORDS
THE CHARIOTEERS
OK 6220 All Alone and Lonely/Careless Love
OK 6247 Daddy/Down, Down, Down
OK 6292 Wrap Your Troubles in Dreams/I Heard of a City Called Heaven
OK 6310 The Cowboy Serenade/Yes Indeed
OK 6332 I Don't Want to Set the World on Fire/One, Two, Three, O' Lairy
OK 6390 Elmer's Tune/Hawaiian Sunset
OK 6424 Nothin'/Call It Anything, It's Love
OK 6509 I Got It Bad/Cancel the Flowers
Co 35424 So Long/The Gaucho Serenade
Co 35736 Calling Romance/Je Vous Aime
Co 35741 All God's Chillun Got Shoes/I'm in His Care
Co 35779 I Should Have Known You Years Ago/Caliope Jane
Co 35811 Call of the Canyon/We'll Meet Again
Co 35942 May I Never Love Again/

Why Is a Good Gal So Hard to Find?
Co 36027 Braggin'/You Walk By
Co 36094 I Understand/Dream for Sale
Co 36730 Sylvia/This Side of Heaven
Co 37074 On the Boardwalk in Atlantic City/You Make Me Feel So Young
Co 37399 Ride, Red, Ride/So Long
Co 38065 Oooh! Look-a There, Ain't She Pretty?/What Did He Say?
Co Album C-156 (78s) Sweet and Low
(with MILDRED BAILEY)
Vo 5209 Don't Dally with the Devil/Sometimes I Feel Like a Motherless Child
(with FRANK SINATRA)
Co 36854 Don't Forget Tonight Tomorrow/Lily Belle

LPs

THE CHARIOTEERS
Co(10")CL-6014 Sweet and Low

308. CHARLES, TEDDY

vb p d ar cm B

(THEODORE CHARLES COHEN)

Born April 13, 1928, Chicopee Falls, Mass.

Modern vibes star of late 40s and 50s. Avant-garde musician who experimented in advanced patterns and sounds, called music New Directions. Worked as Teddy Cohen until early 1952, changed to Teddy Charles as leader of combo. Studied at Juilliard. Early work with Bob Astor band. With Randy Brooks in 1948, with Chubby Jackson and Buddy DeFranco in 1949. In Artie Shaw's big band in 1950. Jobbed with various groups 1951-2, later in 1952 formed own group. Since then has led various sized groups off and on, has done jazz composing, has freelanced on jobs and record sessions. A & R man for several record companies. Played concerts at colleges in 60s but gradually worked less in music.

RECORDS

BUDDY DEFRANCO
Cap 57-757 Extrovert/When We're Alone

CHUBBY JACKSON
Co 38451 Father Knickerbopper/Godchild
Co 38623 Tiny's Blues/All Wrong
TEDDY CHARLES
Pres 838 The Lady Is a Tramp/I'll Remember April
Pres 889 So Long, Broadway

LPs

TEDDY CHARLES
Pres(10")PRLP-132 Teddy Charles & His Trio
Pres(10")PRLP-143 New Directions, Vol. 1
Pres(10")PRLP-164 New Directions, Vol. 3
Pres(10")PRLP-178 (featuring BOB BROOKMEYER)
Elektra 136 Vibe-rant
Warwick 2033
NJ(10")1106
BUDDY DEFRANCO
Cap(10")H-322
Cap(10")H-325
Cap(10")H-371
RUSTY DEDRICK
Mon-Ever MES-7035(S) The Many Friends of Rusty Dedrick
MANHATTAN JAZZ ALL-STARS
Co CL-1426 Swinging GUYS AND DOLLS
RALPH SHARON
Lon(E) LL-1488 All Star Sextet
WARDELL GRAY·
Pres PRLP-7343 (2-LP set) Memorial Album

309. CHATTAWAY, THURLAND

cm lyr p

Born April 18, 1872, Springfield, Mass. Died November 12, 1947, Milford, Conn.

Early songwriter, worked mostly alone on both music and lyrics. Best-known song *Red Wing* (lyrics only). To New York in 1896, wrote for music magazine edited by Theodore Dreiser.

SONGS

1899—Mandy Lee; Little Black Me
1901—I've Grown So Used to You; When I Gave My Heart to You; When the Blue Sky Turns to Gold
1904—My Honey Lou
1905—My Guiding Star

1906—In a Little House That's Built for Two
1907—My Honey Bee; Red Wing; The Sweetest Flower the Garden Grew

Other songs included *Can't You Take It Back and Change It for a Boy?*; *Kerry Mills Barn Dance*; *We've Been Chums for Fifty Years*; *Singing Baby's Toes to Sleep*; *Outside the Heavenly Gates*; *Pals, Good Old Pals*

310. CHEATHAM, DOC   t B
(ADOLPHUS ANTHONY CHEATHAM)

Born June 13, 1905, Nashville, Tenn.

Good lead trumpet and jazz soloist in tasteful traditional style; underrated musician. Began professionally in early 20s playing locally and on tour. To Chicago in mid-20s, worked with Albert Wynn, also led own band. In Philadelphia with Bobby Lee and Wilbur DeParis. With Chick Webb for brief period. Toured Europe with Sam Wooding 1929-30, recorded abroad. Back in U.S., in early 30s worked with Alabamians and McKinney's Cotton Pickers. Joined Cab Calloway in 1932, remained until mid-1939 with intervals away. Lead trumpet with Calloway, hot solos few. With Teddy Wilson big band late 1939-40. Freelanced in early 40s, then with Eddie Heywood 1943-4. Mostly teaching next several years in New York. With Marcelino Guerra band 1948-50. In 50s with such Latin-American bands as Perez Prado, Machito, Vincentico Valdez, also considerable work with Vic Dickenson and Wilbur DeParis. Several tours abroad. During 1960-5 led band in New York. Active through 60s and into 70s freelancing, including stint with Benny Goodman mid-1966 to early 1967, and more tours abroad.

RECORDS

SAM WOODING
  Pa(Sp) 25424 Indian Love/Bull Foot Stomp
  Pat(Fr) 8684 Downcast Blues/Weary River
CAB CALLOWAY
  Br 6424 I've Got the World on a String
  Br 6460 I've Gotta Right to Sing the Blues
PUTNEY DANDRIDGE
  Vo 3399 I'm in a Dancing Mood/With Plenty of Money and You
  Vo 3409 That Foolish Feeling/Gee, But You're Swell
EDDIE HEYWOOD
  CMS 554 'Tain't Me/Save Your Sorrow
  CMS 570 Blue Lou/Carry Me Back to Old Virginny
  CMS 578 Just You, Just Me/'Deed I Do
  CMS(12")1514 Begin the Beguine/I Cover the Waterfront
BILLIE HOLIDAY
  CMS 559 I Cover the Waterfront/Lover, Come Back to Me
  CMS 585 My Old Flame/I'm Yours

LPs

ADOLPHUS "DOC" CHEATHAM
  Jezebel JZ-102 (S) 2-LP set
EDDIE HEYWOOD
  CMS(10")20007 (CMS RIs)
BILLIE HOLIDAY
  CMS(10")20006 (CMS RIs)
PEE WEE RUSSELL
  Story 308
WILBUR DEPARIS
  Atl 1363 On the Riviera
JUANITA HALL
  Counterpoint CSPT-556 Sings the Blues
HAROLD BAKER-DOC CHEATHAM
  Swingsville SVLP2021 Shorty and Doc
MACHITO
  Roul 52006 Kenya
JOHN HANDY
  Vi LSP-3762 Introducing Cap'n John Handy

311. CHERRY, DON   vo

Good pop singer of 50s and 60s. First hit record *Vanity* in 1951 led to many more recordings during 50s. On TV, including shows of Arthur Godfrey, Dean Martin and late-night hosts. Good amateur golfer, at one period tried pro circuit without success. In later years leaned toward country and western music, his voice well suited to it. Career waned after 50s, worked semi-actively. Recording of *Take a Message to Mary* well received in 1969.

RECORDS

DON CHERRY

De 27128 Here in My Arms/Thinking of You
De 27484 I Apologize/Bring Back the Thrill
De 27618 Vanity/Powder Blue
De 27626 I Can See You/My Life's Desire
De 27836 I Can't Help It/Grievin'
De 27944 My Sentimental Heart/I'll Sing to You
De 28368 It's Been So Long, Darlin'/Silver Dew on the Blue Grass Tonight
De 28452 I Don't Want to Set the World on Fire/From Your Lips Only
De 28477 How Long/The Second Star to the Right
De 28548 Changeable/A Lover's Quarrel
De 28635 All by Myself/If They Should Ask Me
De 28768 If You See Sally/I've Got to Pass Your House
De 28789 No Stone Unturned/Till the Moon Turns Green
De 29005 I'm Through with Love/You Didn't Have to Tell Me

DON CHERRY with TOMMY DORSEY ORCHESTRA

De 27247 Strangers/Music, Maestro, Please

LPs

DON CHERRY

Strand SL-1048 Don Cherry and Strings
Monument 8049 Cherry Smashes
Monument 18088 Let It Be Me
Monument 18109 Take a Message to Mary
Co CL-893 Swingin' for Two

312. CHESTER, BOB   ts cm B

Born March 20, 1908, Detroit, Mich.

Leader of excellent, underrated band in late 30s and 40s. In earlier years used Glenn Miller reed sound frequently, but band drove harder than Miller's. Born into wealthy family, educated at universities of Detroit and Dayton. In early and mid-30s played sax with Russ Morgan, Ben Pollack, Paul Specht, Arnold Johnson, Ben Bernie, Irving Aaronson. In middle and late 30s at various times led hotel-style band in Detroit. 1939 band built along swing lines, with excellent arrangements. Handled ballads beautifully in sweet-swing style. Excellent vocalists in Dolores O'Neill, later Betty Bradley, Bob Haymes, Bill Darnell. Alec Fila lead trumpet awhile. Band's first theme *Slumber*. Later theme, *Sunburst*, composed by Chester (who also composed *The Octave Jump*, featured by band). By early 40s band dropped Miller sound. During this period personnel at times included Joe Harris (tb), Johnny Bothwell (as), John LaPorta (as), Bill Harris (tb), Herbie Steward (as). Mid-1944-5 Chester was out of band business about a year, came back in late 1945, continued into early 50s (with period as disc jockey in Detroit in 1948-9). Lou Gardner, good vocalist, featured in later 40s. Chester now successful in automotive business in Detroit.

RECORDS

BOB CHESTER

Bb 10378 Judy/El Rancho Grande
Bb 10470 After All/Love Never Went to College
Bb 10513 57th Street Drag/Aunt Hagar's Blues
Bb 10614 With the Wind and the Rain in Your Hair/I Walk with Music
Bb 10649 The Octave Jump/You Little Heart Breaker You
Bb 10735 The Moon Won't Talk/Orchids for Remembrance
Bb 10780 Chester's Choice/River, Stay 'Way from My Door
Bb 10842 There Shall Be No Night/One Look at You
Bb 10865 We Three/Off the Record
Bb 10916 Old, Old Castle in Scotland/Talkin' to the Wind
Bb 10941 Who Am I?/When I Leave the World Behind
Bb 11227 There Goes That Song Again/It's So Peaceful in the Country

Bb 11478 (theme) Sunburst/Tomor-
row's Sunrise
Bb 11562 He's My Guy/By the Light
of the Silv'ry Moon
Son 2006 Linda/Roses in the Rain
Son 3011 Surrender
Son 3020 Years and Years Ago
(with UNA MAE CARLISLE)
Co 38979 Three Little Bugs/We've All
Got a Lesson to Learn
(with ALAN FOSTER)
Co 38959 Forgive Me/Have You?

LPs

BOB CHESTER
Bandstand BSR-7103 (1939-42 Bb RIs)

313. CHEVALIER, MAURICE   vo

Born September 12, 1888, Paris, France
Died January 1, 1972, Paris, France

Noted French entertainer, star of early
movie musicals in U.S. Long, successful
career in show business. Famed for jaunty
air and French charm; straw hat became
trademark. Began singing in Paris as
youth in second-rate cafes around 1900.
Worked up to 1909 appearance in FOLIES
BERGERE; then had broad comic style.
Joined Mistinguette to form dance team
1909-13, became popular in Paris. Military service, World War I; wounded and
in prison camp. Resumed career, worked
up to good club bookings and stage revue
roles. Developed into sophisticated and
charming entertainer, by end of 20s one
of France's most popular. Appeared with
British bandleader Jack Hylton in Paris
1930. Burst upon American scene in 1929,
starring in two movie musicals INNOCENTS
OF PARIS and THE LOVE PARADE. Handsome, personable, popular in U.S. during
early 30s as more movie musicals followed. Associated with songs *Louise* and
Mimi particularly. By mid-30s popularity
waned. In late 30s back in France for club
and movie work. During World War II in
seclusion; at one time rumored killed.
After war, revived career in France, returned to U.S. in 1947, performed in clubs
and concerts. Career boosted by 1958
movie GIGI; more movies and frequent
TV spots followed. In 60s, concert tours
in U.S. and Europe. Later years inactive.

MOVIES

1929—INNOCENTS OF PARIS; THE LOVE
PARADE
1930—THE BIG POND; PLAYBOY OF PARIS;
PARAMOUNT ON PARADE
1931—THE SMILING LIEUTENANT
1932—LOVE ME TONIGHT; ONE HOUR WITH
YOU
1933—A BEDTIME STORY; THE WAY TO
LOVE
1934—THE MERRY WIDOW
1935—FOLLIES BERGERE
1937—THE BELOVED VAGABOND
1957—LOVE IN THE AFTERNOON
1958—GIGI
1959—COUNT YOUR BLESSINGS
1960—PEPE; A BREATH OF SCANDAL; CAN-
CAN
1961—FANNY
1962—JESSICA; IN SEARCH OF THE CAST-
AWAYS; BLACK TIGHTS (narration)
1963—A NEW KIND OF LOVE
1964—PANIC BUTTON; I'D RATHER BE RICH
1967—MONKEYS GO HOME!

RECORDS

MAURICE CHEVALIER with JACK HYLTON
ORCHESTRA
HMV(E)3686 Maurice Chevalier Med-
ley (1 & 2)
MAURICE CHEVALIER
Vi 21918 Louise/Wait Till You See Ma
Cherie
Vi 22007 It's a Habit of Mine/On Top
of the World Alone
Vi 22093 Valentine/Los Ananas
Vi 22285 My Love Parade/Nobody's
Using It Now
Vi 22294 You've Got That Thing/
Paris, Stay the Same
Vi 22378 All I Want Is Just One Kiss/
Sweeping the Clouds Away
Vi 22405 You Brought a New Kind of
Love to Me/Livin' in the Sunlight,
Lovin' in the Moonlight
Vi 22542 My Ideal/It's a Great Life
Vi 22634 Hello, Beautiful/Walking My
Baby Back Home
Vi 22723 Moonlight Saving Time/
Right Now
Vi 22941 What Would You Do?/Oh,
That Mitzi
Vi 24063 Mimi/Poor Apache

Vi 24882 I Was Lucky/Singing a Happy Song
Vi 25-0092 Hello, Beautiful/Wait Till You See Ma Cherie
Vi 25-0093 Louise/Just a Bum
(sung in French)
Co(Fr) 12020 Un Bon Mouvement/Pour Vous Mesdames
Co(Fr) 12021 Je Ne Dis Pas Non/Mon Coeur
HMV(Fr) 7766 Mon Vieux Paris/Vous Valez Mieux Qu'un Sourire
HMV(Fr) 8015 Les Moutons/Dans Un Coin De Paname

LPs

MAURICE CHEVALIER
MGM E-3702 Yesterday
MGM E-3703 Today
MGM E-3738 Sings Broadway
MGM E-3773 A Tribute to Al Jolson
MGM E-3801 Life Is Just a Bowl of Cherries
MGM E-4205 The Very Best of Chevalier
Vi LPV-564 Maurice Chevalier, Vol. 1 (Vi RIs)
Vi LPM-2076 Thank Heaven for Maurice
·Mon-Ever MES-7028 You Brought a New Kind of Love to Me
Vi(10")LPT-3042 Maurice Chevalier
(movie soundtrack)
MGM E-3641 GIGI

314. CHILDS, REGGIE   v B

Born in England

Leader of a sweet-styled hotel and ballroom band of 30s. Sometimes used arrangements along Hal Kemp lines. Before career as bandleader, worked as violinist with Paul Whiteman, Vincent Lopez, Wayne King. Continued with band through 40s into 50s. In later years dubbed music "rolling style."

RECORDS

REGGIE CHILDS
Bb 5269 Did You Ever See a Dream Walking?/Many Moons Ago
Bb 5278 You're Gonna Lose Your Gal
Bb 5279 After Sundown/Our Big Love Scene

Bb 5292 One Minute to One
De 978 Did You Mean It?/Close to Me
De 979 If We Never Meet Again/Love Is a Powerful Thing
De 987 I Was Saying to the Moon/On a Typical Tropical Night
De 1249 Sweet Heartache/Just to Remind You
De 1262 No More Tears/Maybe
De 1269 At a Carnival in Venice/Honeybunch
De 1582 Sweet Stranger/I'm the One Who Loves You
De 1588 Just a Sweet Old Gentleman and a Quaint Old Lady/Scrapin' the Toast
De 1673 Goodnight Angel/There's a New Moon Over the Old Mill
Vs 8095 Speaking of Heaven/Yogi Yogi

315. CHITTISON, HERMAN   p B

Born 1909, Flemingsburg, Ky.
Died March 8, 1967, Cleveland, Ohio

Excellent jazz pianist, combined strong rhythm and chords with tasteful melodic approach. Self-taught on piano, played at early age. Attended Kentucky State College briefly in 1927. At 19 joined Zach Whyte and remained over two years in late 20s, playing in Cincinnati area. In early 30s he toured theatres as accompanist for comedian Stepin Fetchit, later for singers Adelaide Hall and Ethel Waters. In Europe 1934-40, mostly with Willie Lewis band. Also toured with Louis Armstrong, led own band, worked in Egypt. Recorded often while abroad. Back in U.S. in 1940, worked New York's top jazz clubs. Became prominent via solo spot on every program of long-running radio series, Casey, Crime Photographer. In 1945 on radio on Gloom Dodgers show, in 1946 on Lanny Ross show. On early TV. Continued playing in 50s and 60s, last several years in Cleveland.

RECORDS

WILLIE LEWIS
Pa(Fr) 591 Nagasaki/I Can't Dance
Pa(Fr) 803 Rhythm Is Our Business/I've Got a Feelin' You're Foolin'

Pa(Fr) 817 All of Me/Star Dust
Pa(Fr) 898 Stompin' at the Savoy/
Christopher Columbus
Pa(Fr) 1030 Sweet Sue / Organ
Grinder's Swing

LOUIS ARMSTRONG
Br(G) A-9683 St. Louis Blues/Tiger
Rag
Br(Fr) A-500492 Song of the Vipers/
Will You, Won't You Be My Baby?

GEORGE WETTLING
Key(12″)1318 You Brought a New
Kind of Love to Me/Somebody
Loves Me

MILDRED BAILEY
De 3888 All Too Soon/Everything
Depends on You
De 3953 Lover, Come Back to Me/It's
So Peaceful in the Country

EDDIE BRUNNER
Sw(Fr) 30 I Double Dare You/
Montmartre Blues
Sw(Fr) 41 Margie/Bagatette

GRETA KELLER
De(Fr) 6821 Goodbye to Summer/I'm
Gonna Lock My Heart

HERMAN CHITTISON
Sw(Fr) 33 My Melancholy Baby/I'm
Putting All My Eggs in One Basket
Sw(Fr) 51 My Own Blues/My Last Af-
fair/No More Tears
Bb 11333 Flamingo/The Man I Love
Mus 315 How High the Moon/The
Song Is Ended
Mus 320 I Should Care/All of My Life
Br 80127 Frasquita Serenade/My Old
Flame
(with ETHEL WATERS)
Vi 20-2459 Blues in My Heart/Care-
less Love
(with EVELYN KNIGHT)
VD(12″)559 There Will Never Be An-
other You

LPs

HERMAN CHITTISON
Co(10″)CL-6134 Keyboard Capers
Co(10″)CL-6182 Herman Chittison
Trio
Jansara 83001 Epitome of a Beat

316. CHRISTIAN, CHARLIE   g

Born c. 1916-19, Dallas, Texas
Died March 2, 1942, New York, N.Y.

Great jazz guitarist, pioneer in emergence
of guitar as solo instrument and in use of
electrical amplification. Also pioneer in
development of modern jazz. Recognized
by top jazzmen as major talent, career cut
short by early death from tuberculosis.
Grew up in Oklahoma, learned guitar as
youngster, by 1934 was playing professionally in southwest. Later worked up to
northwest, played also in Minneapolis
and with Jeter-Pillars band in St. Louis.
In 1939 jazz critic John Hammond heard
about Christian, stopped at Oklahoma
City to hear him, urged Benny Goodman
to hire him. Christian joined Goodman in
August 1939. Benny immediately impressed, using Christian to build his Quintet to
Sextet. Record sessions by this group
among Goodman's most admired, sparked by Christian's fresh guitar—both solo
ideas and chord feeding. Quickly rose to
renown in jazz circles. Active in sessions
at Minton's, club in Harlem managed by
former bandleader Teddy Hill, who encouraged top musicians to stop in and
jam. Here Christian a top attraction, and
at these sessions bop was born. Christian
came down with tuberculosis at peak of
career, in mid-1941 entered New York
sanitarium. In February 1942 caught
pneumonia and died in a few weeks, a
tragic loss to music.

RECORDS

BENNY GOODMAN SEXTET
Co 35254 Flying Home/Rose Room
Co 35319 Honeysuckle Rose
Co 35349 Seven Come Eleven/Shivers
Co 35466 Poor Butterfly/The Sheik of
Araby
Co 35553 Six Appeal/These Foolish
Things
Co 35810 Wholly Cats/Royal Garden
Blues
Co 35901 As Long as I Live/Benny's
Bugle
Co 36099 A Smo-o-o-oth One/Air
Mail Special
Co 36684 Solo Flight (ORCHESTRA)

METRONOME ALL-STAR BAND
Vi 27314 Bugle Call Rag/One O'clock
Jump

IDA COX
Vo 05336 Deep Sea Blues/Death Letter Blues

JIMMY MUNDY
VD(12″)701 Air Mail Special

EDDY HOWARD
Co 35915 Exactly Like You/Wrap Your Troubles in Dreams

CHARLIE CHRISTIAN
Vox Album 302 Charlie's Choice, 1-2-3/Stompin' at the Savoy, 1-2-3

LPs

BENNY GOODMAN
Co CL-500 Benny Goodman Combos (Co RIs)

Co CL-524 Benny Goodman Presents Fletcher Henderson Arrangements (Co RIs)

Jazz Archives JA-6 Charlie Christian/Lester Young—Together 1940 (unissued 1940-1 Goodman Sextet Co takes)

CHARLIE CHRISTIAN
Co CL-652 With Benny Goodman Sextet and Orchestra (Co RIs)

Archive FS-219 With Dizzy Gillespie, Thelonious Monk

Eso(10″)ESJ-1 Jazz Memorial (miscellaneous artists)

Eso ES-548 The Harlem Jazz Scene —1941 (at Minton's and Uptown House)

ED HALL
BN B-6505 Celestial Express (BN RIs)

317. CHRISTY, JUNE   vo
(SHIRLEY LUSTER)

Born November 20, 1925, Springfield, Ill.

Husky-voiced jazz-styled singer in style of Anita O'Day, later evolved own style. Rose to fame with Stan Kenton. First sang for local bands and in hotel bands in Chicago area, including Benny Strong and Boyd Raeburn (in hotel-band days). Joined Kenton in mid-1945, replacing Anita O'Day. First hit: *Tampico*. Left several years later for career as single, returning at intervals. Married saxman Bob Cooper, sometimes worked jobs with him, including tour abroad. Toured with Ted Heath show in mid-50s. Good recording career. Played clubs, concerts and festivals through the years but less active in 60s.

RECORDS

STAN KENTON
Cap 202 Tampico
Cap 219 It's Been a Long, Long Time
Cap 229 Just a-Sittin' and a-Rockin'
Cap 235 I Been Down in Texas/Shoo Fly Pie
Cap 250 4 Months, 3 Weeks, 2 Days, 1 Hour Blues
Cap 298 It's a Pity to Say Goodnight
Cap 387 Across the Alley from the Alamo
Cap 911 How High the Moon/Willow Weep for Me
Cap 912 Soothe Me
Cap 10125 Lonely Woman
Cap 15327 He Was a Good Man
Cap 20089 Ain't No Misery in Me
Cap 28010 June Christy
VD(12″)590 Ride On
VD(12″)596 I Never Thought I'd Sing the Blues

JUNE CHRISTY
Cap 436 If I Should Lose You
Cap 578 The Way You Look To-night/Everything Happens to Me
Cap 1823 Daddy
Cap 2384 I've Got a Letter/Let Me Share Your Name
Cap 2590 Whee Baby/Not I

LPs

STAN KENTON
Cap T-167 Artistry in Rhythm (Cap RIs)

JUNE CHRISTY with STAN KENTON
Cap T-656 Duet
Cap TBO-1327 (2-LP set) Road Show

JUNE CHRISTY
Cap T-725 The Misty Miss Christy
Cap T-833 Fair and Warmer
Cap T-1006 This Is June Christy
Cap T-1114 The Song Is June
Cap T-1202 Those Kenton Days
Cap T-1398 Cool School
Cap T-1498 Off Beat

318. CHURCHILL, FRANK   cm

Born October 20, 1901, Rumford, Maine
Died May 14, 1942, Castaic, Calif.

Composer of 30s and early 40s, best known for 1933 novelty song hit *Who's Afraid of the Big Bad Wolf?* and memorable score for 1938 cartoon movie SNOW WHITE AND THE SEVEN DWARFS. Educated

709

at University of California. Early in career worked as movie theatre pianist. Under contract with Walt Disney Studios 1930 until death, furnished background music for movie cartoons. Chief collaborators Ann Ronell, Larry Morey, Ned Washington.

SONGS
(and related shows)

1933—THREE LITTLE PIGS movie cartoon (Who's Afraid of the Big Bad Wolf?)
1938—SNOW WHITE AND THE SEVEN DWARFS full-length movie cartoon (Whistle While You Work; Heigh-Ho; One Song; Someday My Prince Will Come; With a Smile and a Song; I'm Wishing; Isn't This a Silly Tune?); BREAKING THE ICE movie (Put Your Heart in a Song; The Sunny Side of Things; Happy as a Lark; Tellin' My Troubles to a Mule; Goodbye, My Dreams, Goodbye)
1939—Blue Italian Waters
1941—DUMBO full-length movie cartoon (Baby Mine; When I See an Elephant Fly; Look Out for Mr. Stork; Song of the Roustabouts)
1942—BAMBI full-length movie cartoon (Love Is a Song)

319. CHURCHILL, SAVANNAH   VO

Born August 21, 1919, New Orleans, La. Died April 19, 1974, Brooklyn, N.Y.

Good jazz-styled singer, specializing in commercial blues. Grew up in Brooklyn, early experience in church choirs. First professional job at Small's Paradise, club in Harlem. Worked with Benny Carter 1942-4. Then clubs and theatres as single, plus recording. After early 50s career waned.

RECORDS

BENNY CARTER
  Cap 144 Hurry Hurry
  Cap 165 Just a Baby's Prayer at Twilight
JIMMY LYTELL & HIS ALL-STAR SEVEN
  Bea 104 Fat Meat Is Good Meat/Tell Me Your Blues and I Will Tell You Mine
  Bea 106 Two-Faced Man/He's Commander-in-Chief of My Heart
SAVANNAH CHURCHILL
  Manor 1004 All Alone/Daddy, Daddy
  Manor 1014 Too Blue to Cry/I Can't Get Enough of You
  Manor 1046 Foolishly Yours/I Want to Be Loved
  Manor 1093 Is It Too Late?/I Understand
  Manor 1142 Try to Forget/I'll Never Belong to Anyone Else
  Co 30146 The Best of Friends/The Things You Do to Me
  Arco 1202 I'll Never Be Free/Get Another Guy
  Arco 1259 Can Anyone Explain?/The Devil Sat Down and Cried
  Arco 1263 Changeable You
  Vi 20-4280 It's No Sin
  Vi 20-4448 In Spite of Everything You Do/Don't Grieve, Don't Sorrow, Don't Cry
  Vi 20-4773 Don't Worry 'Bout Me/I'm Waiting for a Guy Named Joe
  Vi 20-5031 Walking by the River/If I Didn't Love You So

320. CLAIRE, INA   VO

Born October 15, 1893, Washington, D.C.

Beautiful singer-actress of stage and screen. Began career in vaudeville in 1907, sang and did impersonations. New York stage debut in 1911 show JUMPING JUPITER in supporting role. Performed in TEMPTATION and THE QUAKER GIRL (1911), LADY LUXURY (1914), ZIEGFELD FOLLIES OF 1915 and 1916 (sang hit song *Hello, Frisco* in 1915 show). Reached stardom in non-musical show THE GOLD DIGGERS (1919). Thereafter in comedies or dramas rather than musicals. Plays included BLUEBEARD'S EIGHTH WIFE (1921), THE AWFUL TRUTH (1922), GROUNDS FOR DIVORCE (1924), THE LAST OF MRS. CHENEY (1925), OUR BETTERS (1928), BIOGRAPHY (1932), ODE TO LIBERTY (1934), END OF SUMMER (1936), ONCE IS ENOUGH (1938), THE TALLEY METHOD (1941), THE FATAL WEAKNESS (1946), THE CONFIDENTIAL CLERK (1954). In movies THE AWFUL TRUTH (1929), ROYAL FAMILY OF BROAD-

WAY (1930), REBOUND (1931), THE GREEKS HAD A WORD FOR THEM (1932), BIOGRAPHY (1933), NINOTCHKA (1939), CLAUDIA and STAGE DOOR CANTEEN (1943).

321. CLARE, SIDNEY　　　　　　lyr
Born August 15, 1892, New York, N.Y.
Died August 29, 1972, California

Lyricist of 20s and 30s. Best known songs: *Ma, Then I'll Be Happy, I'd Climb the Highest Mountain, Miss Annabelle Lee, Please Don't Talk About Me When I'm Gone, On the Good Ship Lollipop.* Began career at 15 as dancer. Later became comedian in vaudeville, wrote special material for vaudeville acts. First song hit *Ma* in 1921. Several others popular in 20s. In 1929 began writing for movie musicals. During career collaborated with composers Oscar Levant, Con Conrad, Cliff Friend, Richard Whiting, Harry Akst, others.

SONGS
(with related shows)

1921—MIDNIGHT ROUNDERS OF 1921 stage show (Ma)
1924—Me and the Boy Friend
1925—Then I'll Be Happy; We're Back Together Again
1926—I'd Climb the Highest Mountain
1927—Cobblestones; One Sweet Letter from You; What Do I Care What Somebody Said?; Miss Annabelle Lee
1929—STREET GIRL movie (Lovable and Sweet; My Dream Memory); THE DELIGHTFUL ROGUE movie (Gay Love); TANNED LEGS movie
1930—HIT THE DECK movie (Keepin' Myself for You)
1931—At Last I'm Happy; Under Your Window Tonight; Please Don't Talk About Me When I'm Gone
1933—I May Be Dancing with Somebody Else
1934—BRIGHT EYES movie (On the Good Ship Lollipop); 365 NIGHTS IN HOLLYWOOD movie (My Future Star; Yes to You); TRANSATLANTIC MERRY-GO-ROUND movie (It Was Sweet of You; Oh, Leo; Rock and Roll); You're My Thrill

1935—MUSIC IS MAGIC movie (Music Is Magic; La Locumba; Love Is Smiling at Me; Honey Chile)
1937—SING AND BE HAPPY movie (Sing and Be Happy; What a Beautiful Beginning)
1938—RASCALS movie

322. CLARK, BOBBY　　　　　　vo
Comic star of Broadway musicals. First appeared with Paul McCullough in comic team of Clark & McCullough, continued solo after McCullough's death in 1935. Team played vaudeville, made first Broadway appearance in 1922. Clark's greatest successes MEXICAN HAYRIDE (1944) and AS THE GIRLS GO (1948).

BROADWAY MUSICALS
(CLARK & MCCULLOUGH)
1922—MUSIC BOX REVUE OF 1922
1924—MUSIC BOX REVUE OF 1924
1926—THE RAMBLERS
1930—STRIKE UP THE BAND
1932—WALK A LITTLE FASTER
1935—THUMBS UP

(BOBBY CLARK)
1936—ZIEGFELD FOLLIES OF 1936
1939—STREETS OF PARIS
1942—STAR AND GARTER
1944—MEXICAN HAYRIDE
1948—AS THE GIRLS GO

323. CLARK, BUDDY　　　　　　vo
(SAMUEL GOLDBERG)
Born July 26, 1912, Dorchester, Mass.
Died October 1, 1949, Los Angeles,
Calif., from injuries received in plane
crash

An all-time great pop vocalist. Straightforward style, good phrasing and intonation, a smooth and pleasant voice, easily identifiable. Logged heavy air time on top radio shows in 30s and 40s, including Hit Parade and own popular show. Career was cut short at peak by fatal plane crash. Grew up in Boston. Attended Northeastern Law School but in 1932 turned to singing. On Boston radio two years. In late 1934-early 1935 with Benny Goodman on now historic Let's Dance radio show, also recorded two numbers with him. Radio staff singer on CBS, at times had own 15-minute singing shows in mid-30s. Heavy free-lance recording with name and studio bands, sometimes without label credit. Most regular singer on Hit Parade 1936-8. On this show worked with several bands: Fred Rich, Harry Sosnik, Bob Haring, Al Goodman, Richard Himber, Peter Van Steeden, Mark Warnow, Carl Hoff. In 1938 on radio shows of Ben Bernie, Richard Himber's Melody Puzzles, American Tobacco Company show on Mutual, and a Sunday afternoon show. On Wayne King show 1940-1 and Vincent Lopez show 1940. Did memorable voice dubbing in 1937 for Jack Haley in movie WAKE UP AND LIVE. Plot centered around Haley's sensational singing voice, and Clark's voice made it credible.

In spite of heavy schedule, to this point Clark virtually unknown. Became better known in early 40s from his radio show Here's to Romance, eventually replaced by Dick Haymes in mid-1943. Military service awhile, World War II. Own show late 1945, The Contented Hour, quickly became popular. Showcased Buddy's singing, featured good big orchestra and guest stars. Sudden popularity brought highly successful series of recordings for Columbia; *Linda* especially big in 1947. In 1947 movie I WONDER WHO'S KISSING HER NOW, voice dubbed for Mark Stevens. Heard on soundtrack of two other movies, MELODY TIME (1948) and SONG OF SURRENDER (1949). By late 1949 Clark peaked. Radio show and records still very popular. Then tragedy. Clark passenger on small private plane returning from Stanford-Michigan football game. Plane lost altitude, crashed on Los Angeles street. Clark thrown from plane, died hours later.

RECORDS

FREDDY MARTIN
Br 6976 Stars Fell on Alabama
Br 6982 Isn't It a Shame?/In the Quiet of an Autumn Night

JOE MOSS
Br 7617 West Wind/Saddle Your Blues to a Wild Mustang

BENNY GOODMAN
Co 2988-D Like a Bolt from the Blue

Vi 25011 I'm Livin' in a Great Big Way

RUBY NEWMAN
Br 7633 On Your Toes/Quiet Night

LUD GLUSKIN
Co 2987-D Sweet Music
Br 7592 I'm Shooting High/I've Got My Fingers Crossed

NAT BRANDWYNNE
Br 7678 Where Is My Heart?/Long Ago and Far Away
Me 70527 I Dream of San Marino/To a Sweet Pretty Thing

BOB CAUSER
Me 60514 Hills of Old Wyomin'/Love Came Out of the Night

JOE REICHMAN
Me 60810 But Definitely

EDDY DUCHIN
Vi 25589 A Star Is Born/Ten O'clock Town

DICK MCDONOUGH
Me 60907 Summer Holiday / I'm Grateful to You
Me 60908 Dear Old Southland/'Way Down Yonder in New Orleans
Me 61104 Midnight Blue/When the Moon Hangs High

XAVIER CUGAT
Vi 25561 A Love Song of Long Ago

WAYNE KING
Vi 27373 A Broken Melody
Vi 27516 Time and Time Again

BUDDY CLARK
Vo 4191 Spring Is Here/I Married an Angel
OK 6403 Delilah/A Sinner Kissed an Angel
Vs 8233 I Walk with Music/This Is the Beginning of the End
Co 37215 Linda/Love Is a Random Thing
Co 37223 How Are Things in Glocca Morra?/If This Isn't Love
Co 37985 I'll Dance at Your Wedding/All Dressed Up with a Broken Heart
Co 38040 Ballerina/It Had to Be You
Co 38294 Here I'll Stay/Green-Up Time
Co 38491 If You Were Only Mine/It Had to Be You
Co 38546 Song of Surrender/You're Breaking My Heart

CORPORAL BUDDY CLARK
  VD(12″)215 How Little We Know
BUDDY CLARK-DORIS DAY
  Co 38174 Love Somebody/Confess
  Co 38353 My Darling, My Darling/
    That Certain Party
BUDDY CLARK-DINAH SHORE
  Co 37921 Let's Do It

LPs

BUDDY CLARK
  Co(10″)CL-6007 For You Alone
  Co(10″)CL-6054 Songs of Romance
  Co(10″)CL-6084 Encores
  Ha HL-7081 Girl of My Dreams
  Co CL-2634 Buddy Clark's Greatest
    Hits (Co RIs)

324. CLARK, DICK   ts

Hot tenor sax soloist with Benny Goodman in early period of band. First big job
with Joe Haymes band mid-1932 to mid-
1933. With Buddy Rogers band before
joining Goodman at start of 1935 (possibly a month earlier), working on the
now historic Let's Dance radio show and
recording with him. With Goodman until
August 1936. Settled in California, joined
Phil Ohman band, then did studio work
including Kraft Music Hall with John
Scott Trotter orchestra and Fibber
McGee & Molly with Billy Mills orchestra, late 30s and early 40s. Briefly with
Artie Shaw in 1940.

RECORDS

DUKE WILSON AND HIS TEN BLACKBERRIES
  (Joe Haymes)
  Pe 15662 Pray for the Lights to Go
    Out/When I Put On My Long
    White Robe
JOE HAYMES
  Co 2704-D The Old Man of the Moun-
    tain
  Co 2716-D Toll/When I Put On My
    Long White Robe
REGINALD FORESYTHE
  Co 3012-D Dodging a Divorce
BENNY GOODMAN
  Vi 25024 Japanese Sandman (probable
    Clark solo)
  Vi 25363 There's a Small Hotel
GENE KRUPA
  De 18114 Three Little Words/Blues of
    Israel

  De 18115 Jazz Me Blues/The Last
    Round-up
JIMMY MCPARTLAND
  De 3363 Panama/Eccentric
  De 18441 Original Dixieland One-
    Step/I'm All Bound 'Round with
    the Mason-Dixon Line
ARTIE SHAW
  Vi 26542 Frenesi (probable Clark solo)

LPs

BENNY GOODMAN
  Sunbeam SB-132 From the Congress
    Hotel (1936 airchecks)

325. CLARK, MAHLON   cl as ts f B
(sometimes spelled MAYLON)

Born March 7, 1923, Portsmouth, Va.

Capable reed man with name bands of
40s and 50s, good jazz clarinetist. First
big job with Dean Hudson in 1939-40.
Joined Will Bradley in early 1941, remained about a year. In 1942 with Louis
Prima and Ray McKinley. Military service, World War II. In mid-40s studio work
in Hollywood and freelance jobs, also led
groups of varying sizes. Worked with Pee
Wee Hunt, Sonny Burke. With Lawrence
Welk several years in middle and late 60s,
featured prominently on TV. Active into
70s.

RECORDS

WILL BRADLEY
  Co 36340 Basin Street Boogie
RAY MCKINLEY
  Cap 117 Without a Song
RAY LINN
  Encore 510 Caravan/Tea Time
  Encore 512 Serenade in Sevenths/Es-
    cape
  Atomic 220 Eastside Jump/Where's
    Pres?
  Atomic 221 The Mad Monk/Blop
    Blah
DAN GRISSOM (with Mahlon Clark Sextet)
  Je 2007 Dinah/You Don't Know What
    Love Is
CATALINA SEXTETTE
  VD(12″)761 The Sphinx/Skrontch
MAHLON CLARK
  Je 5000 I'm a Dreamer (Aren't We
    All?)/Atomic Did It
  Je 5001 Can't We Be Friends?/East
    Lynne Jump

713

LPs

MEMBERS OF BENNY GOODMAN'S BRUSSELS WORLD'S FAIR ORCHESTRA (with Mahlon Clark-cl)

Cr CLP-5090 Salute to Benny Goodman

GUS BIVONA

Mer MG-20304 Plays the Music of Steve Allen

326. CLARK, MARGUERITE   vo

Born February 22, 1887, Cincinnati, Ohio
Died September 25, 1940, New York, N.Y.

Beautiful singer-actress of Broadway stage. Small roles in musicals, worked up to stardom. In plays BABY MINE and JIM THE PENMAN (1910), THE LIGHTS O' LONDON (1911; all-star revival), SNOW WHITE AND THE SEVEN DWARFS (1912; 72 matinee performances only), ARE YOU A CROOK? and PRUNELLA (1913). Later in movies.

BROADWAY MUSICALS

1900—BELLE OF BOHEMIA
1901—THE NEW YORKERS
1902—THE WILD ROSE
1903—MR. PICKWICK
1905—HAPPYLAND
1906—THE MAN FROM NOW
1908—THE PIED PIPER
1909—THE BEAUTY SPOT
1910—THE KING OF CADONIA

327. CLARKE, GRANT   lyr

Born May 14, 1891, Akron, Ohio
Died May 16, 1931, Calif.

Lyricist 1912-31, career cut short by death at 40. Most famous songs: *Ragtime Cowboy Joe, He'd Have to Get Under—Get Out and Get Under, Second Hand Rose, Blue (and Broken Hearted), Am I Blue?, Weary River.* Early in career actor in stock companies. Wrote for music publishing firms in New York, later became publisher. Wrote special material for Bert Williams, Fanny Brice, Eva Tanguay, Nora Bayes, Al Jolson. Score for 1924 Broadway show DIXIE TO BROADWAY, also songs for movie musicals 1929-30. Collaborators included composers George Meyer, Harry Akst, James V. Monaco, Fred Fisher, Harry Warren, Al Piantadosi, Milton Ager, Archie Gottler, James Hanley, Arthur Johnston.

SONGS
(with related shows)

1911—ZIEGFELD FOLLIES OF 1911 stage show (Dat's Harmony)
1912—Ragtime Cowboy Joe
1913—He'd Have to Get Under—Get Out and Get Under; Oh, You Million Dollar Doll; Sit Down, You're Rocking the Boat!
1914—Back to the Carolina You Love; He's a Devil in His Own Home Town; I Love the Ladies
1916—The Honolulu Blues; There's a Little Bit of Bad in Every Good Little Girl; You Can't Get Along with 'Em or without 'Em
1918—Everything Is Peaches Down in Georgia; I Hate to Lose You; If He Can Fight Like He Can Love, Good Night Germany; In the Land of Beginning Again
1920—My Little Bimbo Down on the Bamboo Isle; I Love the Land of Old Black Joe
1921—ZIEGFELD FOLLIES OF 1921 stage show (Second Hand Rose; Now I Know)
1922—Blue (and Broken Hearted)
1924—DIXIE TO BROADWAY stage show (Mandy, Make Up Your Mind; I'm a Little Blackbird Looking for a Bluebird)
1928—Avalon Town
1929—BROADWAY BABIES movie (Wishing and Waiting for Love; Broadway Baby Dolls); IS EVERYBODY HAPPY? movie (Wouldn't It Be Wonderful?; I'm the Medicine Man for the Blues); ON WITH THE SHOW movie (Am I Blue?; Let Me Have My Dreams; Birmingham Bertha; In the Land of Let's Pretend; others); WEARY RIVER movie (Weary River)
1930—NO, NO, NANETTE movie (new songs instead of original score); BRIGHT LIGHTS movie (Nobody Cares If I'm Blue)
1931—Thanks to You

Other songs: *When You're in Love with Someone; Beatrice Fairfax; Oogie Oogie Wa Wa; Home in Pasadena; Just for Me and Mary; Sahara Rose; Yokohama Lullaby; Regretful Blues*

328. CLARKE, KENNY   d vb B
(nicknamed Klook)

Born January 9, 1914, Pittsburgh, Pa.

Foremost drummer in development of bop in early and mid-40s. Important in establishing different style of drumming to fit the new music, veering from steady four-beat rhythm to give bass drum accent off beat as well. Began professional career in early 30s, with Leroy Bradley band several years. With Roy Eldridge in 1935, then in St. Louis with Jeter Pillars band. Joined Edgar Hayes in New York 1937-8, took Scandinavian tour with him in 1938. Later in 1938 with Claude Hopkins, then 1939-40 with Teddy Hill. Part of Hill's band played Minton's club in Harlem in early 40s, with Clarke in combo. Participated in seminal jam sessions there with Charlie Christian, Charlie Parker, Dizzy Gillespie, Thelonious Monk and others that laid groundwork for bop. In next several years Clarke with Benny Carter in New York and Red Allen in Chicago. Own band in New York, then military service several years. Active from 1946 into 50s with bop combos. Recognized as a leading figure in movement. With Dizzy Gillespie for much of 1946-8, including work in Europe. Also with Tadd Dameron and Billy Eckstine, and freelance. Charter member of Modern Jazz Quartet during 1952-5. In 1956 to France, remained, worked with various jazz groups there and toured. Six-year stay at Blue Note in Paris to 1967. In late 60s and into 70s, co-leader of big band with pianist Francy Boland.

RECORDS
EDGAR HAYES
   De 1444 So Rare/Love Me or Leave Me
   De 1509 I Know Now/When You and I Were Young, Maggie
   De 1684 Blue Skies/Sweetheart
   De 1940 Meet the Band/Barbary Coast Blues
MILDRED BAILEY
   Co 35532 How Can I Ever Be Alone?/Tennessee Fish Fry

Co 35589 I'll Pray for You/Blue and Broken-Hearted
COUNT BASIE
   OK 6221 You Betcha My Life/Down, Down, Down
SIDNEY BECHET
   Vi 27204 One O'clock Jump
   Vi 27574 Swing Parade/I Know That You Know
   Bb 10623 Indian Summer/Preachin' Blues
CHARLIE CHRISTIAN
   Vox album 302 Charlie's Choice (1-2-3)/Stompin' at the Savoy (1-2-3)
ELLA FITZGERALD
   De 4007 Jim/This Love of Mine
BILLIE HOLIDAY
   OK 5831 I Hear Music/I'm All for You
   OK 6134 Let's Do It/Georgia on My Mind
BUDDY JOHNSON
   De 8562 Troyon Swing/Southern Exposure
COLEMAN HAWKINS
   Mercer 1962 Sophisticated Lady/It's Only a Paper Moon
CAL TJADER
   Sav 1117 Tangerine/Love Me or Leave Me
MILT JACKSON
   Hi-Lo 1405 Heart and Soul/Love Me Pretty Baby
   Hi-Lo 1412 True Blues/Softly, as in a Morning Sunrise
   DeeGee 3700 Milt Meets Sid/Between the Devil and the Deep Blue Sea
DIZZY GILLESPIE
   Mus 399 Our Delight/Good Dues Blues
   Mus 447 Things to Come
   Vi 20-2603 Two Bass Hit/Stay on It
   Vi 20-3145 Cubana Be/Cubana Bop
KENNY CLARKE
   Vi 20-3144 Royal Roost/Epistrophy
   Emanon 9601 Out of Nowhere/Confirmation
   Ce 1501 Roll 'Em Bags/You Go to My Head
   DeeGee 3602 Klook Returns
   DeeGee 3606 I'll Get You Yet
   Sw(Fr) 277 Confirmation/A la Colette
   Sw(Fr) 281 Jay Mac/Maggie's Draw

LPs

KENNY CLARKE
  Sav MG-12006 Kenny Clarke
  Sav MG-12017 Bohemia After Dark
  Epic LN-3376 Plays Andre Hodier
  Pres 7605 The Paris Bebop Sessions
    (RIs)
KENNY CLARKE-FRANCY BOLAND
  Co 2314 Now Hear Our Meanin'
  Atl 1401 Jazz Is Universal
  Pres 7634 Fire, Heat, Soul and Guts!
MILT JACKSON
  Sav MG-12070 The Jazz Skyline
(miscellaneous artists)
  Vi LPV-519 The Be-Bop Era (Vi RIs)
  Eso ES-548 The Harlem Jazz Scene
    —1941 (at Minton's and Uptown
    House)
DEXTER GORDON
  BN 4146 Our Man in Paris

329. CLARKSON, GEOFFREY   p cm
(nicknamed Jeff or Geoff)

Born September 2, 1914, Yonkers, N.Y.

Modern pianist with tasteful block-chord style. Gained attention with Les Brown band in 40s. Parents English. As teenager good pianist, worked at composing. Wrote 1931 hit *Home*, with lyrics by father and help of bandleader Peter Van Steeden. Attended Juilliard. In late 30s jobbed around New York. Worked with Bob Sylvester, Bobby Hackett. With McFarland Twins orchestra in early 40s. Joined Les Brown in mid-1943, important figure during years band adapting to progressive style. With Brown into 1954. Worked with Ray Anthony. Entered studio work and performed for movies, TV and record sessions. Active into 70s, mainly as TV musical director. Other compositions: *I Struck a Match in the Rain*; *No Sun*; *The Organ, the Monkey and Me*; *Goodbye to Love*; *Sitting on a Rainbow*.

RECORDS

LES BROWN
  Co 37061 Lover's Leap/High on a
    Windy Trumpet
  Co 38250 Sophisticated Swing/Blue
    Danube
  Co 38324 I've Got My Love to Keep
    Me Warm

Co 38381 Just One of Those Things
  Cor 60424 Blue Moon/Red Sails in the
    Sunset
  Cor 60785 You Forgot Your Gloves
  Cor 60918 Ramona
TED NASH
  Key 628 I've Got a Pocketful of
    Dreams/The Girl in My Dreams
    Tries to Look Like You

LPs

LES BROWN
  Co(10″)CL-6123 Dance Date with Les
    Brown
  Cor(10″)CRL-56026 Over the Rain-
    bow
  Cor(10″)CRL-56077 Musical Weather
    Vane
VAN ALEXANDER
  Cap T-1243 The Home of Happy Feet
    (The Savoy)

330. CLAYTON, BUCK   t ar cm B
(WILBUR CLAYTON)

Born November 12, 1911, Parsons, Kansas

Trumpet star over long career dating from 30s. Rose to eminence in Count Basie band. Good swing style, inventive solos, muted work very effective. Excellent arranger. Worked with several bands on west coast in early 30s, including Earl Dancer. Led big band in Los Angeles. Teddy Weatherford booked band in Shanghai, appeared with it sometimes, 1934-6. Returned to Los Angeles in 1936 and re med leading band there, later freelanced. Joined Basie in late 1936, his clean-cut swinging solos featured with band many years until military service late 1943. With Basie, Clayton contributed arrangements in simple and swinging lines, including *H and J*; *Love Jumped Out*; *What's Your Number?*; *Down for Double*; *It's Sand, Man*; *Taps Miller*; *Seventh Avenue Express*. Composed jazz numbers *Red Bank Boogie*, *Swingin' at the Copper Rail*, *Stan's Dance*, *Night Ferry*, *Avenue C*, *Buckini*, *Love Jumped Out*, *Seventh Avenue Express*. Late 1946 toured with Jazz at the Philharmonic. Freelance arranging for Benny Goodman among others and jobbing in New York. With combos of J. C. Heard, Ike Quebec,

Charlie Ventura, Don Byas, Trummy Young. In late 1949-50 led band on European tour. In early 50s worked with singer Jimmy Rushing, long runs with pianist Joe Bushkin. With Benny Goodman in 1956 movie THE BENNY GOODMAN STORY. With Goodman, Sidney Bechet, Eddie Condon in late 50s. Several tours abroad in 50s and 60s. In early 60s with Jimmy Rushing and clarinetist Peanuts Hucko. Appeared at many concerts and festivals, recorded. Active into 70s.

RECORDS

COUNT BASIE
De 1121 Swinging at the Daisy Chain
De 1252 Exactly Like You/Boogie Woogie
De 1446 Good Morning Blues
De 1682 Blues in the Dark
De 1770 Topsy/Don't You Miss Your Baby
De 1965 Doggin' Around
De 2212 Jumpin' at the Woodside
Vo 4860 Miss Thing (1 & 2)
Vo 4886 12th Street Rag
OK 6244 9:20 Special/Goin' to Chicago
OK 6440 Fiesta in Blue
OK 6508 Platterbrains
Co 36710 Royal Garden Blues (combo)

TEDDY WILSON
Br 7824 This Year's Kisses/He Ain't Got Rhythm
Br 7859 Why Was I Born?/I Must Have That Man
Br 7917 Sun Showers/Yours and Mine
Br 8070 When You're Smiling/I Can't Believe That You're in Love with Me
Mus 547 The Sheik of Araby

BILLIE HOLIDAY
Vo 3593 Me, Myself and I/Without Your Love
Vo 3605 Born to Love/A Sailboat in the Moonlight

KANSAS CITY FIVE/SIX
CMS 510 I Know That You Know/Laughing at Life
CMS 511 Good Mornin' Blues/Them There Eyes

BERNIE LEIGHTON
Mello-Roll 5004 Whispering/Smooth Sailing

JOHNNY GUARNIERI
Mer 1119 All My Life/Groovin' with J.G.

BUCK CLAYTON
Melrose 1201 Diga Diga Doo/Love Me or Leave Me
Melrose 1202 We're in the Money/B.C. Blues
HRS 1027 Saratoga Special/Sentimental Souvenir
HRS 1028 Harlem Cradle Song/My Good Man Sam
RJ 719 High Tide/Don's Blues
RJ 720 Who's Sorry Now?/Sugar Blues
RJ 721 Blues in First/Blues in Second

LPs

BUCK CLAYTON
Co CL-548 A Buck Clayton Jam Session
Co CL-701 Jumpin' at the Woodside
Co CS-8123(S) Songs for Swingers
Vang VRS-8514 Buckin' the Blues

FRANKIE LAINE
Co CL-808 Jazz Spectacular

COUNT BASIE
Epic LN-3169 Basie's Back in Town (Vo, OK RIs)
Epic LG-3107 Lester Leaps In (Vo RIs)

PEE WEE RUSSELL
Pres 7672 Memorial Album

JAZZ AT THE PHILHARMONIC
Clef(10″)MG-6 JATP Blues

BENNY GOODMAN
De DL8253/4 THE BENNY GOODMAN STORY (movie soundtrack)
Co CL2572 The Benny Goodman Sextet/Trio with Rosemary Clooney

331. CLEARY, MICHAEL H.   cm o p

Born April 27, 1902, Weymouth, Mass.
Died June 15, 1954, New York, N.Y.

Composer of late 20s and 30s. Output sparse but included a few popular songs. Attended West Point, wrote songs there, chapel organist. Left army in 1926, reporter awhile in Boston. Began composing late 20s. Contributed material for Broadway shows and early movie musicals. Special material for night clubs. Military service, World War II, as captain, promoted to major. Discharged but never returned to songwriting. Collaborated with lyricists Nat and Max Lief, Herb Magidson, Maurice Sigler, Arthur Swanstrom, Ned Washington.

SONGS
(with related shows)

1928—EARL CARROLL'S VANITIES OF 1928 stage show (Vaniteaser; My Arms Are Wide Open; Getting the Beautiful Girls); Is There Anything Wrong in That?
1929—SHOW OF SHOWS movie (Singin' in the Bathtub); H'lo Baby
1931—SHOOT THE WORKS stage show (songs unimportant); THE THIRD LITTLE SHOW stage show (songs unimportant)
1932—HEY NONNY NONNY stage score (songs unimportant); Here It Is Monday and I've Still Got a Dollar
1936—When a Lady Meets a Gentleman Down South
1937—SEA LEGS stage show (unsuccessful show, songs unimportant)

Other songs: *Ten O'clock Town*; *Deep in the Blue*; *It's in the Stars*; *My Impression of You*

332. CLESS, ROD   cl
(GEORGE RODERICK CLESS)

Born May 20, 1907, Lennox, Iowa
Died December 8, 1944, New York,
N.Y., from injuries received in a fall

Dixieland clarinetist of 30s and 40s, played with top jazzmen but remained comparatively obscure. Early experience with bands in Iowa, to Chicago in 1927 to freelance. Jobbed with Bud Freeman, Frank Teschemacher, Charles Pierce, Louis Panico. Toured with Frankie Quartell in 1928. Played in 30s with many groups, including hotel bands. Long runs at High Hat Club and Silhouette Club in Chicago. In early 1939 joined Muggsy Spanier's outstanding dixieland combo, produced memorable records. With combo to New York, where disbanded late 1939. Remained in New York, in early 40s worked with Art Hodes, Marty Marsals, Ed Farley, Georg Brunis, Bobby Hackett, Wild Bill Davison. Last engagement with Max Kaminsky at Pied

Piper December 4, 1944. Suffered serious fall leaving club, died four days later.

RECORDS

MUGGSY SPANIER
   Bb 10384 Someday Sweetheart/That Da Da Strain
   Bb 10506 Dipper Mouth Blues/Sister Kate
   Bb 10518 At the Jazz Band Ball/Livery Stable Blues
   Bb 10719 At Sundown/Bluin' the Blues
   Bb 10766 Lonesome Road/Mandy, Make Up Your Mind
ART HODES
   De 18437 Georgia Cake Walk/Liberty Inn Drag
   De 18438 Indiana/Get Happy
   Si 101 I Found a New Baby/Four or Five Times
   Si 102 Diga Diga Doo/Tin Roof Blues
CHICAGO RHYTHM KINGS
   Si 104 Song of the Wanderer/There'll Be Some Changes Made
   Si 105 Sugar/Randolph Street Rag
YANK LAWSON
   Si 28103 Squeeze Me/The Sheik of Araby
THE LION'S JAZZ BAND (Willie Smith)
   B&W 6 Let's Mop It/How Could You Put Me Down?
   B&W 24 Muskrat Ramble/Bugle Call Rag
MAX KAMINSKY
   CMS 561 Eccentric/Guess Who's in Town
   CMS 595 Love Nest/Everybody Loves My Baby
ROD CLESS
   B&W 29 Froggy Moore/Have You Ever Felt That Way?
   B&W 30 I Know That You Know/Make Me a Pallet on the Floor

LPs

MUGGSY SPANIER
   Vi LPM-1295 The Great 16! (Bb RIs)
ART HODES
   BN(10″)7004 Art Hodes & His Chicagoans (BN RIs)
   Riv(10″)RLP-1012 (Si RIs)
MAX KAMINSKY
   CMS(10″)FL-20019
YANK LAWSON
   Br(10″)58035 (RIs)

333. CLEVELAND, JIMMY   tb B

Born May 3, 1926, Wartrace, Tenn.

Modern trombonist of 50s and 60s, rapid-note style with light, swinging touch. Attended University of Tennessee. First big job with Lionel Hampton, remained till late 1953 and toured Europe with band. Freelanced in New York, worked with James Moody, Eddie Heywood, Lucky Thompson, Oscar Pettiford and Seldon Powell-Tony Aless group. Toured Europe 1959-60 with Quincy Jones band and musical show. Studio work and freelance recording on west coast later. Own combo at times. In pit band 1965-6 for Broadway show FUNNY GIRL. Active into 70s in New York and on west coast.

RECORDS
(all LPs)

JIMMY CLEVELAND
    EmArcy MG-36066 Introducing Jimmy Cleveland & His All-Stars
    EmArcy MG-36126 Cleveland Style
    EmArcy SRE-66003 (S) Rhythm Crazy
    Mer MG-20442 A Map of Jimmy Cleveland
GEORGE WALLINGTON
    BN(10")5045 George Wallington Showcase
JOE NEWMAN
    Vi LPM-1324 Salute to Satch
THE BIRDLAND DREAM BAND
    Vik LX-1070
MAYNARD FERGUSON
    Vik LX-1077 Birdland Dream Band, Vol. 2
HAL MCKUSICK
    Vi LPM-1366 Jazz Workshop
SELDON POWELL
    Roost 2220 The Seldon Powell Sextet
MUNDELL LOWE
    Cam CAL-522 TV Action Jazz!
OSCAR PETTIFORD
    Beth(10")BCP-1019 Basically Duke
ART FARMER
    Pres(10")162
QUINCY JONES
    Pres(10")172

334. CLINTON, LARRY .t tb cl ar cm B

Born August 17, 1909, Brooklyn, N.Y.

Outstanding bandleader-arranger-composer of 30s and 40s. First fame as excellent arranger, then as composer of swing music, finally as leader of a top band of late 30s. Noted for ability to adapt classics to popular music as ballads or swing numbers. Band boasted impeccable musicianship, with polished swing style and delicately shaded treatment of ballads. Early job with Ferde Grofe briefly in 1932 as sideman-arranger. Later in 30s arranged for Isham Jones, Glen Gray, Tommy and Jimmy Dorsey, Claude Hopkins, Bunny Berigan. Composed numbers, mostly swing, featured by many bands: *Satan Takes a Holiday*; *Whoa Babe*; *My Silent Mood*; *Midnight in a Madhouse*; *Boogie Woogie Blues*; *Strictly for the Persians*; *Study in Brown* (theme); *Study in Surrealism*; *Study in Green*; *Study in Blue*; *Study in Red*; *An Empty Ballroom*; *Calypso Melody*; *Abba Dabba*; *The Campbells Are Swinging*; *Molasses, Molasses*; *Bolero in Blue*; *Dodging the Dean*; *The Big Dipper*; *Dusk in Upper Sandusky*; *Shades of Hades*; *Shalimar*; *Dreamy Melody*. Several compositions made Hit Parade: *The Dipsy Doodle* (1937), *My Reverie* (1938), *It Took a Million Years* and *Our Love* (1939). Arrangements on classics *Martha* and *I Dreamt I Dwelt in Marble Halls* became famous.

In late 1937 Clinton formed own big band, began heavy recording for Victor. Outstanding vocalist in Bea Wain, key figure in band's rise. Used several theme songs; *The Dipsy Doodle* most famous. Good jazzmen featured: Tony Zimmers, Babe Russin, Toots Mondello, Skeets Herfurt, Wolfe Tannenbaum (later Tayne). Later outstanding vocalist Terry Allen, plus capable Peggy Mann and Ford Leary (jazz and novelty numbers). In early 1939 Clinton's band helped make hit of *Deep Purple*, rose in band polls. Records well received. Maintained popularity in 1940-1, broke up in late 1941 as Clinton entered military service. In late 40s Clinton again led band but never regained former popularity. In 50s owned publishing and record business, served awhile as A&R man for Kapp Records.

RECORDS

LARRY CLINTON
    Vi 25697 The Big Dipper/Midnight in a Madhouse

719

Vi 25706 True Confession/I've Got My Heart Set on You
Vi 25707 Abba Dabba/The Campbells Are Swinging
Vi 25761 I Was Doing All Right/Love Is Here to Stay
Vi 25775 I Fall in Love with You Every Day/How'dja Like to Love Me?
Vi 25789 Martha/I Dreamt I Dwelt in Marble Halls
Vi 25837 I Married an Angel/How to Win Friends and Influence People
Vi 26006 My Reverie/Boogie Woogie Blues
Vi 26046 Dodging the Dean/Heart and Soul
Vi 26076 Chant of the Jungle/Design for Dancing
Vi 26100 My Heart Belongs to Daddy/Most Gentlemen Don't Like Love
Vi 26112 Temptation/Variety Is the Spice of Life
Vi 26141 Deep Purple/A Study in Red
Vi 26283 In a Persian Market/Poor Little Rich Girl
Vi 26341 The Moon Is Low/'S Wonderful
Vi 26417 My Silent Mood/Toselli's Serenade
Vi 26582 A Study in Modernism/Missouri Scrambler
Vi 26626 Blue Lovebird/How Can I Ever Be Alone?
Bb 10850 A Brown Bird Singing/Dance of the Candy Fairy
Bb 10984 Moonlight and Tears/You Forgot About Me
Bb 11140 Estrellita/Essential to Me
De 24301 Oooh! Look-a There, Ain't She Pretty?/The Dickey-Bird Song
Rbw 10099 The Wheels Keep Spinning Around/Walk Before You Run

(as conductor)
KAY ARMEN
King 15168 Love Me a Little Bit Less/I Can't Afford Another Broken Heart
PAULETTE SISTERS
Co 40030 Shalimar/Tell Me You Don't Love Me
SYLVIA SIMS
Bell 1035 Darktown Strutters' Ball

LPs
LARRY CLINTON
Bandstand BSR-7102 (1939-41 Vi, Bb RIs)
Vi LPM-1342 Larry Clinton in Hi-Fi
Vi VPM-6085 (2-LP set) This Is Larry Clinton (Vi RIs)
Cam CAL-434 Dance Date with Larry Clinton (Vi RIs)
MGM E-3567 Music for Tired Golfers
Tops(10″)L-920 Plays for Dancing
ROBERT ASHLEY (as arranger)
MGM E-3485 Music from Italian Films

335. CLOONEY, BETTY   vo
Born April 12, c. 1930-1, Maysville, Ky.
Good singer but overshadowed by success of elder sister Rosemary. Active in 40s and early 50s. Teamed with Rosemary early in amateur contests and various events. Family moved to Cincinnati. In high school sisters landed nightly radio show on WLW in mid-40s, Moon River, worked with Barney Rapp. Several years later joined Tony Pastor band as vocal duo, remained over two years. In 1949 Betty returned home awhile and Rosemary embarked upon career as single. Betty resumed singing in 1950, worked with Clyde Trask. In early 50s appeared on TV shows of Robert Q. Lewis, Jack Paar and others, also made a few records. However, by mid-50s career waned.

RECORDS
TONY PASTOR (all by Clooney Sisters)
Co 37839 Tira-Lira Li
Co 38068 The Secretary Song/I'm My Own Grandpaw
Co 38355 The Chowder Social
Co 38383 Saturday Night Mood
Co 38577 If I Had a Million Dollars
Co 38962 Bread and Butter Woman
BETTY CLOONEY
King 15071 Anyone Can Fall in Love
King 15102 Would I Love You/Faithful
King 15103 Alone/Haven't Seen You in a Month of Sundays
"X"-0076 Whisper/Si, Si, Senor
Cor 60930 I Idolize You/You're All I See

Cor 61000 Sin in Satin/A Great Big City Boy Like You
Cor 61050 My Love Is a Wanderer/ How Many Sweethearts Have I?

ROSEMARY CLOONEY-BETTY CLOONEY
Co 39185 I Still Feel the Same About You
Co 40305 Sisters

336. CLOONEY, ROSEMARY   vo

Born May 23, 1928, Maysville, Ky.

Excellent singer with strong, melodious style, very popular in 50s. Teamed early with younger sister Betty in amateur contests and various events. Family moved to Cincinnati. In high school sisters landed nightly radio show on WLW in mid-40s, Moon River, worked with Barney Rapp. Several years later joined Tony Pastor band as vocal duo, remained over two years. In 1949 Betty returned home awhile and Rosemary embarked on career as single. Landed TV job on Songs for Sale, began recording for Columbia with success, had big 1951 hit with *Come on-a My House*. Other popular records *Tenderly, This Ole House, Hey There*. On various TV shows in early 50s, late 1954 started radio show, 1956 had TV film series featuring The Hi-Lo's. Important roles in several movies THE STARS ARE SINGING and HERE COME THE GIRLS (1953), RED GARTERS and WHITE CHRISTMAS (1954), DEEP IN MY HEART (1955). Married Jose Ferrer. Appeared on all the top TV variety shows and late-night shows through 50s and early 60s. Since then semi-active.

RECORDS

TONY PASTOR (by Clooney Sisters, except *Rosemary alone)
Co 37839 Tira-Lira Li/My O' Darlin', My O' Lovely, My O' Brien*
Co 38068 The Secretary Song/I'm My Own Grandpaw
Co 38355 The Chowder Special/It's Like Taking Candy from a Baby*
Co 38383 Saturday Night Mood
Co 38577 If I Had a Million Dollars
Co 38962 Bread and Butter Woman

ROSEMARY CLOONEY
Co 39467 Come on-a My House/Rose of the Mountain
Co 39648 Tenderly/Did Anyone Call?
Co 39710 Half as Much/Poor Whip-Poor-Will
Co 39813 Blues in the Night/Who Kissed Me Last Night?
Co 39931 What Would You Do?/I Laughed Until I Cried
Co 40003 When I See You/It Just Happened to Happen to Me
Co 40142 When You Love Someone
Co 40266 This Ole House/Hey There
Co 40305 Love, You Didn't Do Right by Me/Sisters (with BETTY CLOONEY)
Co 40370 Count Your Blessings/White Christmas

ROSEMARY CLOONEY-BETTY CLOONEY
Co 39185 I Still Feel the Same About You

ROSEMARY CLOONEY-GUY MITCHELL
Co 39052 Marrying for Love/You're Just in Love

ROSEMARY CLOONEY with HARRY JAMES ORCHESTRA
Co 39905 The Continental/You'll Never Know

LPs

ROSEMARY CLOONEY
Co CL-1230 Rosie's Greatest Hits
Co(10")CL-6297 While We're Young
Ha HL-7123 Rosemary Clooney in High Fidelity
Reprise R-6088 Love
Reprise R-6108 Thanks for Nothing
Cor CRL-57266 Swing Around Rosie

ROSEMARY CLOONEY-HI LO'S
Co CL-1006 Ring Around Rosie

ROSEMARY CLOONEY-BING CROSBY
Vi LPM-1854 Fancy Meeting You Here

ROSEMARY CLOONEY with DUKE ELLINGTON ORCHESTRA
Co CL-872 Blue Rose

BENNY GOODMAN SEXTET with ROSEMARY CLOONEY
Co CL2572

(movie soundtrack)
Co(10")CL-6282 RED GARTERS

337. COAKLEY, TOM   d B

Leader of good hotel band in 1932-6. Attended University of California, co-leader of dance band there, attended law school. Formed band in 1929 with personnel mostly from California colleges, played college and club dates on west coast. In 1932 band scored at Oakland's Athens Club, appeared on Lucky Strike remote broadcast, toured west coast and northwest. Good runs 1933-4 at Palace Hotel in San Francisco with wide radio coverage. In 1934-6 band featured vocalist Carl Ravazza, in 1934 Kay Thompson briefly. Used theme *Haunting Me* (not the 1935 pop tune), composed by Jack Swales. Toured in mid-30s, playing top hotels from coast to coast. Returned to San Francisco in 1936. Final job there at St. Francis Hotel, quit band business in April to practice law. Turned band over to Carl Ravazza, who continued it in late 30s.

RECORDS

TOM COAKLEY
Br 6577 Here Is My Heart/I Had It, and I Lost It, and It's Gone
Br 6702 Clean as a Whistle/Lucky Fella
Vi 24480 Many Moons Ago/Good Morning Glory
Vi 24489 We Were the Best of Friends/Sing a Little Low Down Tune
Vi 24600 I'll String Along with You/Fair and Warmer
Vi 24610 I'm Satisfied
Vi 24621 That's What Makes the World Go 'Round/Call It Anything (It Isn't Love)
Vi 24741 Okay Toots/Your Head on My Shoulder
Vi 24744 Take a Number from One to Ten/Let's Give Three Cheers for Love
Vi 25058 I'm Just an Ordinary Human/Rainbow
Vi 25062 Rhythm Is Our Business/Simply Grand

338. COBB, ARNETT   ts B

Born August 10, 1918, Houston, Texas

Big-toned tenor sax star of 40s and 50s. Could swing in tasteful style or honk and play wild. Began locally in 1933, with Chester Boone band 1934-6. In Texas area 1936-42 with Milt Larkin. Did some touring, ended up in Chicago in late 1942. With Lionel Hampton early 1943 to 1947. Formed combo, recorded, become popular. Illness forced retirement in late 40s. Comeback in early 50s. Made several record singles, small combo swingers with commercial appeal, later turned to LPs. In 1956 auto accident interrupted career several months. At end of 50s Cobb settled in Houston, led big band there into 60s.

RECORDS

LIONEL HAMPTON
De 18669 Overtime
De 18880 Air Mail Special (1 & 2)
De 23639 Flying Home (No. 2)
De 23792 Blow Top Blues
DINAH WASHINGTON
Key 605 Evil Gal Blues/Homeward Bound
Key 606 I Know How to Do It/Salty Papa Blues
ARNETT COBB
Apo 772 Cobb's Idea/Still Flying
Apo 775 When I Grow Too Old to Dream (1 & 2)
Apo 778 Dutch Kitchen Bounce/Go Red Go
Apo 781 Cobb Boogie/Arnett Blows for 1300
Hamp-Tone 102 Shebna
OK 6823 Cocktails for Two
OK 6851 Charmaine/I'm in the Mood for Love
OK 6872 Without a Word of Warning/Jumping the Blues
OK 6912 Someone to Watch Over Me/The Shy One
OK 6928 Linger Awhile/Li'l Sonny
Atl 1042 Horse Laff/Mr. Pogo
Mer 70171 The Traveler/Apple Wine
Co 39040 Smooth Sailing/Your Wonderful Love
Co 39369 Lunar Moon/Holy Smoke

LPs

ARNETT COBB
Pres 7151 Blow, Arnett, Blow
Pres 7165 Party Time
Pres 7175 More Party Time
Pres 7216 Movin' Right Along
Pres 7711 The Best of Arnett Cobb
LIONEL HAMPTON
De DL-79244 "Steppin' Out", Vol. 1 (1942-5 De RIs)

339. COBB, WILL D.   lyr

Born July 6, 1876, Philadelphia, Pa.
Died January 20, 1930, New York, N.Y.

Lyricist 1899-1917, collaborated with composer Gus Edwards on many songs including big hit *School Days*. Other important songs: *I Can't Tell Why I Love You, but I Do*; *Waltz Me Around Again, Willie*; *I Just Can't Make My Eyes Behave* (Anna Held's featured song); *Sunbonnet Sue*; *Yip-I-Addy-I-Ay*. Attended Girard College in New York. Worked as sales clerk in New York department store before songwriting.

SONGS
(with related shows)

1899—The Singer and the Song; You Are the Only Girl I'll Ever Care About
1900—All for a Man Whose God Was Gold; Goodbye, Dolly Gray; I Can't Tell Why I Love You, but I Do
1901—I Don't Want Money; I'll Be with You When the Roses Bloom Again; Mamie; I'm Dreaming of a Bygone Day
1902—Could You Be True to Eyes of Blue?; Fare Thee Well, Molly Darling
1904—The Girl Who Cares for Me; Goodbye, Little Girl, Goodbye; In Zanzibar
1905—If a Girl Like You Loved a Boy Like Me; Somebody's Sweetheart I Want to Be
1906—HIS HONOR THE MAYOR stage show (Waltz Me Around Again, Willie); I Just Can't Make My Eyes Behave; Rose Bud; Two Dirty Little Hands
1907—Laddie Boy
1908—SCHOOL DAYS stage show (title song); Sunbonnet Sue; Yip-I-Addy-I-Ay
1910—If I Was a Millionaire
1913—I'll Get You
1916—I Lost My Heart in Honolulu
1917—Just a Simple Country Maiden; For You a Rose

340. COBURN, JOLLY   B

Leader of hotel band in middle and late 30s. Good band with better arrangements than most of this school. Unfortunately, band did not attain great popularity or record much. Graduate of U.S. Naval Academy.

RECORDS

JOLLY COBURN
  Vi 24735 The Continental/Irresistible
  Vi 24743 Stay as Sweet as You Are/ College Rhythm
  Vi 25396 Organ Grinder's Swing/Out Where the Blue Begins
  Vi 25399 Fancy Meeting You/It Can Happen to You
  Bb 7038 Bluebonnet/Don't You Know or Don't You Care?
  Bb 7049 Gone with the Dawn/Having Wonderful Time
  Bb 7081 Am I Dreaming?/Have You Got Any Castles, Baby?
  Bb 7083 Afraid to Dream/The Loveliness of You
  Bb 7100 Remember Me?/Am I in Love?

341. COHAN, GEORGE M. . cm lyr vo

Born July 3, 1878, Providence, R.I.
Died November 5, 1942, New York, N.Y.

An all-time great of Broadway stage as performer-composer-lyricist-librettist-director-producer. Pioneer in veering from European operettas which American writers copied. Shows brash and energetic, American to the core, with unabashed nostalgic and patriotic songs. Dynamic stage performer with distinctive style of dancing, singing and acting. Leading songs endured through the years: *Give My Regards to Broadway*, *The Yankee Doodle Boy*, *You're a Grand Old Flag*, *Forty-Five Minutes from Broadway*, *Harrigan*, *Mary's a Grand Old Name*. Wrote greatest of all war songs during World War I, *Over There*, for which received Congressional Medal. First professional appearance as Little Georgie, child violinist, at Keith's Bijou in Boston. First dramatic role in show DANIEL BOONE. Starred in PECK'S BAD BOY in 1890. Parents Jeremiah (Jerry) and Helen (Nellie), vaudeville performers. He and sister Josephine (Josie) joined them to form act known as The Four Cohans. Played vaudeville and became top act, aided by George's material, performance, business ability. Later George's wife Ethel Levey joined act. George also wrote material for other vaudeville acts, over 150 sketches by age 21. First Broadway shows short-lived: THE GOVERNOR'S SON (1901), RUNNING FOR OFFICE (1903), LITTLE JOHNNY JONES (1904; unsuccessful despite good score). Subsequent shows ran longer, but early shows with best songs had surprisingly modest runs. Nonetheless, Cohan starred in and produced steady string of shows, built reputation. 15-year partner, producer Sam Harris, helped put on these shows. Josie left Four Cohans at intervals later. Other three Cohans last appeared together in Broadway show THE LITTLE MILLIONAIRE (1911). George performed alone in other musicals and dramas. In later years turned mostly to writing and producing. By late 20s semi-active in theatre, returned in 1937 to star in musical I'D RATHER BE RIGHT with considerable success. Cohan appeared in movies THE PHANTOM PRESIDENT (1932) and GAMBLING (1934). In 1940 his old play adapted for Judy Garland movie LITTLE NELLIE KELLY. On radio occasionally during 30s. Outstanding movie YANKEE DOODLE DANDY (1942) based on Cohan's life, with James Cagney winning Academy Award for portrayal of Cohan. 1968 Broadway musical GEORGE M! also based on Cohan's life, with Joel Grey portraying Cohan. Both productions featured many Cohan songs.

During career Cohan in Broadway musicals THE GOVERNOR'S SON (1901); RUNNING FOR OFFICE (1903); LITTLE JOHNNY JONES (1904); GEORGE WASHINGTON, JR. (1906); THE HONEYMOONERS (1907); THE YANKEE PRINCE (1908); THE LITTLE MILLIONAIRE (1911); HELLO, BROADWAY! (1915); THE MERRY MALONES (1927); I'D RATHER BE RIGHT (1937). Associated with other musicals as writer or producer: FORTY-FIVE MINUTES FROM BROADWAY (1906); THE TALK OF NEW YORK (1907); FIFTY MILES FROM BOSTON (1908); THE AMERICAN IDEA (1908); THE MAN WHO OWNS BROADWAY (1909); THE COHAN REVUE OF 1916; THE COHAN REVUE OF 1918; THE ROYAL VAGABOND (1919); THE VOICE OF MCCONNELL (1919); LITTLE NELLIE KELLY (1922); THE RISE OF ROSIE O'REILLY (1924); BILLIE (1928).

Cohan associated with nonmusical Broadway plays: BROADWAY JONES (1912; actor); SEVEN KEYS TO BALDPATE (1913; author); GENIUS AND THE CROWD (1920; producer); THE MEANEST MAN IN THE WORLD (1920; actor); THE TAVERN (1921; actor); THE SONG AND DANCE MAN (1923; actor); AMERICAN BORN (1925; actor); GAMBLING (1929; actor); PIGEONS AND PEOPLE (1933; author, actor); AH! WILDERNESS (1933-4, long run; actor); SEVEN KEYS TO BALDPATE revival (1935; author, actor); FULTON OF OAK FALLS (1937; actor); RETURN OF THE VAGABOND (1940; actor, last stage appearance).

SONGS
(with related shows)

1897—The Warmest Baby in the Bunch
1898—I Guess I'll Have to Telegraph My Baby
1899—My Little Lady; Telephone Me, Baby
1900—I Won't Be an Actor No More
1901—THE GOVERNOR'S SON stage show (Too Many Miles from Broadway; The Story of the Wedding March)
1902—Then I'd Be Satisfied with Life
1903—RUNNING FOR OFFICE stage show (I'll Be There in the Public Square; I Want to Go to Paree, Papa); MOTHER GOOSE stage show (Always Leave Them Laughing When You Say Goodbye)
1904—LITTLE JOHNNY JONES stage show (The Yankee Doodle Boy; Give My Regards to Broadway; Goodbye, Flo; Life's a Funny Proposition After All)
1906—FORTY-FIVE MINUTES FROM BROADWAY stage show (Forty-Five Minutes from Broadway; Mary's a Grand Old Name; So Long, Mary; Stand Up and Fight Like H ...); GEORGE WASHINGTON, JR. stage show (You're a Grand Old Flag; I Was Born in Virginia; All Aboard for Broadway)
1907—THE HONEYMOONERS stage show (I'll Be There in the Public Square; I'm a Popular Man; If I'm Going

to Die I'm Going to Have Some Fun); THE TALK OF NEW YORK stage show (When a Fellow's on the Level with a Girl That's on the Square; Under Any Old Flag at All; I Want the World to Know I Love You; When We Are M-A-Double R-I-E-D)

1908—FIFTY MILES FROM BOSTON stage show (Harrigan; A Small Town Girl; Ain't It Awful); THE AMERICAN IDEA stage show (Too Long from Longacre Square; F-A-M-E; That's Some Love); THE YANKEE PRINCE stage show (Come On Down Town; I'm Awfully Strong for You; I'm to Marry a Nobleman; The ABC's of the U.S.A.)

1909—THE MAN WHO OWNS BROADWAY stage show (The Man Who Owns Broadway; There's Something About a Uniform; I've Always Been a Good Old Sport)

1911—THE LITTLE MILLIONAIRE stage show (Any Old Place the Old Flag Flies; Barnum Had the Right Idea; Oh, You Wonderful Girl); VERA VIOLETTA stage show (That Haunting Melody)

1915—HELLO, BROADWAY! stage show (Hello Broadway!; I Wanted to Come to Broadway; That Old-Fashioned Cakewalk; My Flag; Barnum and Bailey Rag; Pygmalion Rose)

1916—THE COHAN REVUE OF 1916 stage show (It's a Long Way from Broadway to Edinboro Town; You Can Tell That I'm Irish)

1917—Over There

1918—THE COHAN REVUE OF 1918 stage show (The Eyes of Youth See the Truth; Their Hearts Are Over Here); When You Come Back

1919—THE ROYAL VAGABOND stage show (Opera, Comic Opera; In a Kingdom of Our Own); THE VOICE OF MCCONNELL stage show (Ireland, the Land of My Dreams; You Can't Deny You're Irish; When I Look in Your Eyes; Mavourneen)

1922—LITTLE NELLIE KELLY stage show (Nellie Kelly, I Love You; Till

Good Luck Comes Rolling Along; You Remind Me of My Mother; The Voice in My Heart)

1924—THE RISE OF ROSIE O'REILLY stage show (When June Comes Along with a Song; Born and Bred in Brooklyn; Let's You and I Say Goodbye; The Ring to the Name of Rosie)

1927—THE MERRY MALONES stage show (Molly Malone; God's Good to the Irish; Like a Wandering Minstrel; The Bronx Express); When Lindy Comes Home

1928—BILLIE stage show (Billie; Every Boy in Town's My Sweetheart; Where Were You, Where Was I?; Go Home Every Once in a While)

RECORDS

GEORGE M. COHAN

Vi 60042 Life's a Funny Proposition After All

Vi 60043 You Won't Do Any Business If You Haven't Got a Band

Vi 60044 I'm Mighty Glad I'm Living, That's All!

Vi 60045 I Want to Hear a Yankee Doodle Tune

Vi 60049 Hey There! May There

Vi 60052 The Small Town Gal

Vi(12'')70039 P.S.—Mr. Johnson Sends Regards

342. COHN, AL   ts ar cm B

Born November 24, 1925, Brooklyn, N.Y.

Leading modern musician from late 40s into 70s. Excellent tenor sax soloist with swinging, inventive modern style. Even more important as arranger; became one of the best. Early in career arranged for radio (including Hit Parade) and for bands of George Auld and Woody Herman. In early 40s played with Joe Marsala and Auld. In 1947 with Alvino Rey and Buddy Rich. With Herman 1948-9. During 1950 built book for big Jerry Wald band, also arranged for Herman. In mid-1950 with Charlie Ventura. Out of music beginning around mid-1951. In early 1952 joined Elliot Lawrence as sideman-arranger. Since that point has worked as freelance sideman and arranger. In later 50s extensive arranging for Jack Sterling radio show. Much in demand as performer through 60s. Worked with top musicians on many recording sessions, led own band on occasion. Arranged for TV shows of Andy Williams, Pat Boone, Steve Allen. Composed jazz originals performed by various bands. Active into 70s; arrangements for 1974 Broadway revue MUSIC! MUSIC!.

RECORDS

SERGE CHALOFF
Fut 3003 Chickasaw/Bop Scotch
Fut 3004 The Most!/Chasin' the Bass
MARY ANN MCCALL
Roost 511 After I Say I'm Sorry/The Sky Is Crying
AL COHN
Triumph 812 Groovin' with Gus/Let's Get Away from It All

LPs

AL COHN
Vi LJM-1024 Mr. Music
Vi LJM-1116 The Natural Seven
Vi LPM-1161 The Jazz Workshop
Vi LPM-1207 That Old Feeling
Epic LN-3278 The Sax Section
Cor CRL-57118 The Al Cohn Quintet
Dawn DLP-1110 Cohn on the Saxophone
AL COHN-BILL PERKINS-RICHIE KAMUCA
Vi LPM-1162 The Brothers!
AL COHN-ZOOT SIMS-HERBIE STEWARD-SERGE CHALOFF
Vik LX-1096 The Four Brothers—Together Again!
WOODY HERMAN
Everest SDBR-1003 The Herd Rides Again ... In Stereo
DICK COLLINS
Vi LJM-1027 King Richard the Swing Hearted
TEDDI KING
Vi LPM-1147 Bidin' My Time
URBIE GREEN
"X"(10")LXA-3026 A Cool Yuletide
ABC-Para 137 All About Urbie Green & His Big Band
ANDY KIRK
Vi LPM-1302 A Mellow Bit of Rhythm

ELLIOT LAWRENCE
Fan 3-206 Plays Gerry Mulligan Arrangements
Fan 3-219 Plays Tiny Kahn and Johnny Mandel Arrangements
Fan 3-236 Swinging at the Steel Pier
OSCAR PETTIFORD
Pres 7813 Memorial Album (1949 & 1954 RIs)

343. COKER, HENRY   tb
Born December 24, 1919, Dallas, Texas

Jazz trombonist in swing style, best known for work with Count Basie in 50s. Good lead on powerhouse arrangements, fresh and inventive as soloist. Attended Wiley College in Texas. With Nat Towles in 1937. Went to Hawaii, played with native bands there in late 30s and during war years. Returned to U.S. in 1945. With Benny Carter several months, then with Eddie Heywood combo late 1945-6 almost a year. Freelanced on west coast. During 1949-52 mostly with Illinois Jacquet combo and big band. Joined Basie in 1952, remained till 1963. Freelanced in New York during next years. In Ray Charles band late 60s and early 70s.

RECORDS

EDDIE HEYWOOD
De 23812 It's Only a Paper Moon
De 24604 Pom Pom
ILLINOIS JACQUET
Alad 101 Flying Home (1 & 2)
Alad 102 Uptown Boogie
Vi 22-0037 Big Foot/B-Yat
Vi 22-0097 Hot Rod
COUNT BASIE
Clef 89115 Peace Pipe

LPs

COUNT BASIE
Clef MGC-647 Dance Session Album No. 2
Clef MGC-666
PAUL QUINICHETTE
Dawn DLP-1109 The Kid from Denver
FRANK WESS
CMS(10")FL-20031 Frank Wess Quintet
CMS(10")FL-20032 Frank Wess Sextet

JOE NEWMAN
  Story(10″)318 And the Boys in the
    Band
KENNY CLARKE
  Sav(10″)MG-15053 (Vol. 2)
TADD DAMERON
  Pres 7037 Fontainebleau
OSIE JOHNSON
  Jazztone J-1234 Swingin' Sounds
FREDDIE GREEN
  Vi LPM-1210

344. COLE, BOB   lyr cm

Talented early Negro songwriter active mostly in 1897-1909 period. Formed songwriting team with J. Rosamond Johnson in 1899, also performed with him in vaudeville. Team played in short-run Broadway shows THE SHOO-FLY REGIMENT (1907) and THE RED MOON (1909). Biggest hit song *Under the Bamboo Tree* in show SALLY IN OUR ALLEY (1902). Wrote scores for several Broadway shows and additional material for others.

SONGS
(with related shows)

1897—The Wedding of the Chinee and the Coon
1899—Chicken
1900—THE BELLE OF BRIDGEPORT stage show (songs unimportant); I Must-a Been a-Dreamin'
1901—THE LITTLE DUCHESS stage show (Maiden with the Dreamy Eyes); THE SLEEPING BEAUTY AND THE BEAST stage show (The Owl and the Moon; Tell Me, Dusky Maiden); My Castle on the Nile
1902—SALLY IN OUR ALLEY stage show (Under the Bamboo Tree); Oh, Didn't He Ramble (under Will Handy pseudonym)
1903—A GIRL FROM DIXIE stage show (songs unimportant); MR. BLUEBEARD stage show (songs unimportant); NANCY BROWN stage show (Congo Love Song; Under the Bamboo Tree—interpolated); Lazy Moon; Magdaline, My Southern Queen; My Mississippi Belle
1904—HUMPTY DUMPTY stage show (songs unimportant); IN NEWPORT stage show (songs unimportant); AN ENGLISH DAISY stage show (song unimportant)
1907—THE SHOO-FLY REGIMENT stage show (book only)
1909—THE RED MOON stage show (also wrote book)

345. COLE, BUDDY   p o ar cm B
(EDWIN LEMAR COLE)

Born December 15, 1916, Irving, Ill.
Died November 5, 1964, North Holly-
wood, Calif.

Freelance pianist-organist-leader on west coast. Known for backing of leading singers on jobs and records. Good rhythmic piano-organ style with full, beautiful chords, ideal as accompanist. Grew up in Los Angeles. Learned piano and organ at early age, worked theatres in early 30s. Later with society bands Jay Whidden, Garwood Van, Johnny Bittick, Bob Grant. With Frankie Trumbauer 1939-40. Played organ on NBC radio in Hollywood and at Radio City Music Hall in New York. With Alvino Rey 1941-3. Freelanced as studio musician in Hollywood through the years. Played on radio shows of Hoagy Carmichael, Ginny Simms, Bing Crosby, Phil Harris; also had own show. Piano work for movies. Many record sessions as leader of combo or accompanying singers. Arranged for many singers.

RECORDS

EDDIE LEMAR (Buddy Cole)
  Cap 20095 Fine and Dandy/You Do Something to Me
  Cap 20097 The Lady Is a Tramp/I Guess I'll Have to Change My Plan
BUDDY COLE
  Cap 1104 Mona Lisa/The Peanut Vendor
  Cap 1403 Somebody Stole My Gal
  Cap 20053 Temptation/Smoke Gets in Your Eyes
  Cap 20054 Body and Soul/Begin the Beguine
  Cap 20056 The Song Is You/I've Got You Under My Skin
  Cap 20135 Cheek to Cheek/Sophisticated Lady

Cap 20136 The Moon Was Yellow/Orchids in the Moonlight
Cap 20138 This Is Romance/I've Got the World on a String

(as pianist)

ALVINO REY
Bb 11108 Amapola
Bb 11136 Hindustan
Bb 11476 Little Hawk
Bb 11573 The Major and the Minor

DAVE BARBOUR
Cap 358 Forever Nicki/Forever Paganini

KING SISTERS
Mer 5431 I'll Get By/Somedays There Just Ain't No Fish

MAHLON CLARK
Je 5000 I'm a Dreamer/Atomic Did It
Je 5001 Can't We Be Friends?/East Lynne Jump

(as leader of combo or orchestra backing)

CHAMP BUTLER
Co 39935 Kaw-Liga

ELLA MAE MORSE
Cap 424 Old Shank's Mare/Get Off It and Go

GISELE MACKENZIE
Cap 1983 Wishin'/Goodbye Sweetheart
Cap 2110 Whistle My Love/Johnny

CLARK DENNIS
Cap 15403 Galway Bay/O'Leary Is Leery of Fallin' in Love

BUDDY STARK
De 28039 Be Anything/Sincere

THE STARLIGHTERS
Cap 1481 I Whistle a Happy Tune/Sweet, Sweet Pauline

JOHNNY RAY
Co 39908 The Touch of God's Hands/I'm Gonna Walk and Talk with My Lord

BING CROSBY
De 29850 In a Little Spanish Town/Ol' Man River

KING SISTERS
Vi 20-1672 Sweetheart of All My Dreams/A Tender Word Will Mend It All

LPs

EDDIE LEMAR (Buddy Cole)
Cap(10")176 Music for Dancing

BUDDY COLE
Co CL-874 Organ Moods in Hi-Fi

728

Co CS-8065 (S) Pipes, Pedals and Fidelity
WB W-1265 Sleepy Time Gal
WB W-1384 Backgrounds to Love
WB W-1397 Love Between Goodbyes, 1941-5
Cap(10")175 Keys to Romance

BING CROSBY
De DL-8575 New Tricks

ROSEMARY CLOONEY
Cor CRL-57266 Swing Around Rosie

346. COLE, COZY   d B
(WILLIAM RANDOLPH COLE)
Born October 17, 1909, East Orange, N.J.

A leading swing band drummer. Good technique and showmanship. Fit into any jazz style. First big job with Wilbur Sweatman in New York about 1928, then own band awhile. 1931-3 with Blanche Calloway, 1933-4 with Benny Carter. With Willie Bryant's excellent swing band 1935-6, then joined swinging Stuff Smith combo 1936-8. With Cab Calloway in late 1938 till late 1942. Radio studios 1942-3, including work with Raymond Scott. Also led own group and worked with Miff Mole and Johnny Guarnieri. Appeared late 1943-4 in Broadway musical CARMEN JONES and in 1945 his combo replaced Benny Goodman's awhile in musical SEVEN LIVELY ARTS. During later 40s freelanced, studio work, own combo, recording. Joined Louis Armstrong All-Stars in early 1949, remained till late 1953. In 1954 opened successful drum school with Gene Krupa in New York. In mid-50s with Joe Bushkin, Sol Yaged, many jobs at Metropole in New York. Jazz tours in later 50s including Europe 1957 with Jack Teagarden-Earl Hines band. Had record hit in 1958, *Topsy*, featuring his drumming. This revived his name, enabled him to tour in late 50s and 60s with combo. Led group at Metropole and on Arthur Godfrey show several years. In 1968 joined Jonah Jones combo. Active into 70s.

RECORDS

WILLIE BRYANT
Vi 24847 Throwin' Stones at the Sun/Chimes at the Meetin'
Vi 25038 Rigamarole/The Sheik

Bb 6362 Moonrise on the Lowlands/Is It True What They Say About Dixie?

Bb 6374 Ride, Red, Ride/The Glory of Love

STUFF SMITH

Vo 3201 After You've Gone/You'se a Viper

Vo 3234 Robins and Roses/I've Got a Heavy Date

CAB CALLOWAY

Vo 4700 Ratamacue/Ad-De-Dey

Vo 5005 Trylon Swing/The Jumpin' Jive

Vo 5062 Crescendo in Drums/Utt-Da-Zay

Vo 5467 Paradiddle/Pickin' the Cabbage

OK 5664 Rhapsody in Rhumba/Fifteen Minute Intermission

OK 5874 Feelin' Tip Top/The Workers' Train

OK 5950 Hot Air/Levee Lullaby

OK 6084 Bye Bye Blues/Run Little Rabbit

OK 6305 Take the "A" Train/Chattanooga Choo Choo

REX STEWART

Key(12")1306 Swamp Mist/I'm True to You

Key(12")1307 Zaza/The Little Goose

HANK D'AMICO

Nat 9006 Cole Heat Warm Feet/Over the Rainbow

DON BYAS

Jamb 900 Should I?/You Call It Madness

Jamb 901 Jamboree Jump/Pennies from Heaven

LIONEL HAMPTON

Vi 25658 Drum Stomp/Confessin'

Vi 25699 The Object of My Affection/Judy

JOHNNY GUARNIERI

Maj 1054 All the Things You Are/Carioca

COLEMAN HAWKINS

Key 609 'S Wonderful/I Only Have Eyes for You

Key 611 Flame Thrower/Night and Day

COZY COLE

Sav 502 Jericho/Nice and Cozy

Sav 519 Jersey Jump-Off/On the Sunny Side of the Street

Cont 6000 Look Here/A Ghost of a Chance

Cont 6001 Willow Weep for Me/Take It Back

Guild 130 Night Wind/Now's the Time

Love 5003 (45-RPM) Topsy (1 & 2)

LPs

COZY COLE

Beth BCP-21 At Metropole Cafe

CP 403 A Cozy Conception of Carmen (one side) GA 33-334 After Hours (one side) Felsted FAJ-7002 Earl's Backroom and Cozy's Caravan (first side by EARL HINES)

CHU BERRY

Epic LN-3124 "Chu" (Va, Vo RIs)

LOUIS ARMSTRONG & THE ALL-STARS

De DL-8329 New Orleans Nights

De(10")DL-5280 Jazz Concert, Vol. 2

LIONEL HAMPTON

Cam CAL-402 Jivin' the Vibes (Vi RIs)

Cam CAL-517 Open House (Vi RIs)

JOHNNY GUARNIERI

Roy(10")VLP-6047

347. COLE, NAT "KING"

p o vo cm B

(NATHANIEL ADAMS COLES)

Born March 17, 1917, Montgomery, Ala.

Died February 15, 1965, Santa Monica, Calif.

A leading pop singer of 40s and 50s. Warm ballad style, smooth and melodious. First a talented jazz pianist of early modern school. Led King Cole Trio, dropped it for highly successful singing career. Grew up in Chicago; brothers Eddie, Fred and Isaac professional musicians. Led own band in Chicago in 1934. Toured with "Shuffle Along" road show, settled in California. Played clubs as piano soloist. In 1939 formed Trio, beginning long association with capable guitarist Oscar Moore. Wesley Prince on bass, replaced several years later by Johnny Miller. Cole played in Earl Hines style with modern chord structure. He and Moore integrated playing neatly, fashioned tasteful sound. Trio early featured instrumentals and unison singing, with occasional Nat vocal. In later years

Nat's vocals so popular that they got spotlight. Early record hit *Straighten Up and Fly Right* in 1944, followed next year with *It's Only a Paper Moon*. In 1944-5 group toured with Benny Carter. Appeared in several movies: HERE COMES ELMER (1943), STARS ON PARADE (1944), BREAKFAST IN HOLLYWOOD (1946), MAKE BELIEVE BALLROOM (1949). Brief radio show in 1946, later series 1948-9. Cole composed several novelty numbers: *I'm a Shy Guy, Straighten Up and Fly Right, That Ain't Right, It's Better to Be by Yourself, Just for Old Time's Sake, Calypso Blues.*

In later 40s Moore and Miller replaced by Irving Ashby and Joe Comfort. Nat's voice now main feature, piano and Trio secondary, sometimes augmented by lush strings. Nat's big record hit *Nature Boy* in 1948 accompanied by Frank DeVol's orchestra. By late 1951 Trio dissolved and Cole became a single. Constant flow of recordings in 50s very popular. Hits: *Mona Lisa, Too Young, Pretend, Ramblin' Rose*, many others. Nat appeared in several movies: BLUE GARDENIA and SMALL TOWN GIRL (1953), ISTANBUL and CHINA GATE (1957), ST. LOUIS BLUES (1958; portrayed composer W. C. Handy), NIGHT OF THE QUARTER MOON (1959), CAT BALLOU (1965). Many tours in U.S., Europe, South America. Many TV appearances, own TV show 1956-7. In early 60s often on Hollywood Palace TV show. Last performance in 1964; career curtailed by lung cancer.

RECORDS

KING COLE TRIO (later ones billed Nat Cole & His Trio)
  De 8520 Sweet Lorraine/This Side Up
  De 8604 Call the Police/Are You Fer It?
  De 8630 That Ain't Right/Hit That Jive, Jack
  Atlas 100 F.S.T./My Lips Remember Your Kisses
  Atlas 106 Let's Pretend/Got a Penny
  Excel 106 Beautiful Moons Ago/Let's Spring One
  Cap 154 Straighten Up and Fly Right/I Can't See for Lookin'
  Cap 169 Gee, Baby, Ain't I Good to You?/I Realize Now

Cap 256 Route 66/Everyone Is Sayin' Hello Again
Cap 304 For Sentimental Reasons/The Best Man
Cap 20010 Body and Soul/The Man I Love
Cap 20012 It's Only a Paper Moon/Easy Listening Blues
Cap 20063 To a Wild Rose/I'm in the Mood for Love
Cap 1010 Mona Lisa/The Greatest Inventor
Cap 1449 Too Young/That's My Girl
Cap 1669 Makin' Whoopee/This Is My Night to Dream
Cap 2069 Somewhere Along the Way/What Does It Take?
Cap 2130 Walkin' My Baby Back Home/Funny
Cap 2230 Faith Can Move Mountains/The Ruby and the Pearl
Cap 2346 Pretend/Don't Let Your Eyes Go Shopping
Cap 2754 It Happens to Be Me/Alone Too Long
Cap 3027 Darling, Je Vous Aime Beaucoup/The Sand and the Sea
(as pianist with various groups)
CAPITOL INTERNATIONAL JAZZMEN
  Cap 283 You Can Depend on Me/Stormy Weather
  Cap 10031 Riffamarole/If I Could Be with You
THE KEYNOTERS
  Key 629 Airiness a la Nat/The Way You Look Tonight
JO STAFFORD
  Cap 259 Cindy
METRONOME ALL-STARS
  Cap 15039 Metronome Riff/Leap Here
  Co 37293 Nat Meets June/Sweet Lorraine

LPs

KING COLE TRIO
  De DL-8260 In the Beginning (De RIs)
  Cap(10″)H-177 (Cap RIs)
  Cap(10″)H-220 (Cap RIs)
  Cap T-592 Instrumental Classics (Cap RIs)
NAT "KING" COLE
  Cap WCL-1613 (3-LP set) The Nat "King" Cole Story
  Cap T-332 Penthouse Serenade (piano)

Cap W-824 Love Is the Thing
Cap W-903 Just One of Those Things
Cap T-1793 Ramblin' Rose

348. COLEMAN, BILL   t fl-h vo B
Born August 4, 1904, Paris, Ky.

Trumpet star in mainstream style. Delicate tone, jaunty swing. Little recognized in U.S., built reputation in Europe, spent most of career there. Grew up in Cincinnati, early professional jobs there in early 20s. To New York in mid-20s. With Lloyd and Cecil Scott much of 1926-30. With Luis Russell part of 1929. In early 30s with Charlie Johnson and Ralph Cooper, rejoined Luis Russell 1932-3. With Lucky Millinder in 1933, including European tour. With Benny Carter 1933-4, Fats Waller and Teddy Hill 1934-5. In September 1935 back to Europe. played with leading foreign stars including 1937-8 with Willie Lewis. Own band at times, toured India 1937. To U.S. in late 1939. With Benny Carter and Fats Waller briefly. Joined Teddy Wilson combo mid-1940, remained about a year. With Andy Kirk late 1941-2. Led combo at times. In mid-40s with Noble Sissle, Mary Lou Williams, John Kirby. With Sy Oliver big band late 1946-7 and Billy Kyle combo late 1947-8. Late 1948 settled in France. Active career 50s into 70s, toured many countries as bandleader or soloist, played jazz festivals.

RECORDS
CECIL SCOTT
Vi 38098 Lawd, Lawd/In a Corner
Vi 38117 Bright Boy Blues/Springfield Stomp
EDDIE BRUNNER
Sw(Fr) 30 I Double Dare You/ Montmartre Blues
Sw(Fr) 41 Margie/Bagatelle
CHICK BULLOCK
OK 6013 Smiles/It Had to Be You
OK 6261 My Melancholy Baby/Indiana
GARNET CLARK
HMV(Fr) 7618 Rosetta/The Object of My Affection
FATS WALLER
Vi 24801 Dream Man/I'm Growing Fonder of You

Vi 24808 Believe It, Beloved/If It Isn't Love
Vi 24846 Because of Once Upon a Time/Baby Brown
Vi 24863 I'm a Hundred Percent for You/You Fit into the Picture
DICKY WELLS
Sw(Fr) 16 Sweet Sue/Hangin' Around Boudon
Sw(Fr) 27 Japanese Sandman/I Got Rhythm
Si 23115 Linger Awhile/Hello Babe
EDDY HOWARD
Co 35915 Exactly Like You/Wrap Your Troubles in Dreams
TEDDY WILSON
Co 35905 I Never Knew/Embraceable You
Co 36084 Oh, Lady Be Good/But Not for Me
INTERNATIONAL JAZZMEN
Cap 10031 Riffamarole/If I Could Be with You
JIMMY JONES
Wax 103 Five O'clock Drag
COLEMAN HAWKINS
Si 28101 Voodte/Hawkins Barrel House
Si 28102 Stumpy/How Deep Is the Ocean?
BILL COLEMAN
Sw(Fr) 22 Bill Street Blues/After You've Gone
Sw(Fr) 42 Indiana/Bill Coleman Blues
Philips(Fr) 72128 Muskrat Ramble/ Black and Blue

LPs
FATS WALLER
Vi(10")LPT-3040 (Vi RIs)
DICKY WELLS
Pres 7593 In Paris 1937 (Sw RIs)
BILL COLEMAN-BUDDY TATE
Pat(Fr) CPTX-240863 (S) Together at Last

349. COLEMAN, EMIL   p B
Born June 19, 1894

Leader of hotel band from early 20s into 60s, polite dance music with taste and musicianship. Played top hotels throughout country. On various radio shows, including own show. On TV show series in early 50s. Recorded on LPs in later 50s and 60s. Still playing hotels in 60s.

731

RECORDS

EMIL COLEMAN

Vo 14458 Teddy Bear Blues/Bee's Knees

Vo 14462 Pack Up Your Sins/Porcelain Maid

Br 4977 Overnight/I Love Love

Br 6006 Where Have You Been?/I'm Getting Myself Ready for You

Br 6036 I've Got Five Dollars/We'll Be the Same

Co 2831-D Mine/Let 'Em Eat Cake

Co 2846-D Let's Begin/Smoke Gets in Your Eyes

Co 2859-D Moon About Town/What Is There to Say?

Co 2882-D I Was in the Mood/Without That Certain Thing

Co 2893-D Music Makes Me/In a Shelter from a Shower

Co 2930-D Little Man, You've Had a Busy Day/So Help Me

Co 2933-D I Wish I Were Twins/I'm Counting on You

Co 2960-D It Was Sweet of You/If I Had a Million Dollars

Co 2961-D An Earful of Music/When My Ship Comes In

De 365 A Little White Gardenia/When My Prince Charming Comes Along

De 366 Clouds/Be Careful, Young Lady

LPs

EMIL COLEMAN

Vi(10")LPM-3009 Sambas by Emil Coleman

King(10")199-8 Tangos and Rhumbas

Philips PHM-200041 Lights Up The Plaza

Audio Lab 1570 Invites You To Dance, and Dance and Dance!

GISELE MACKENZIE (Emil Coleman Orchestra directed by Al Pellegrini)

Sun SUS-5155 (S) In Person at the Empire Room of the Waldorf-Astoria

350. COLLETTE, BUDDY

ts f cl as p ar B

(WILLIAM MARCEL COLLETTE)

Born August 6, 1921, Los Angeles, Calif.

Versatile reed man, best known on flute. As youngster learned several instruments, soon led own band. In late 30s played with various bands; own band 1940-1. With Cee Pee Johnson 1941-2 and Les Hite 1942. Military service, World War II. In 1946 in Los Angeles formed co-op group with Lucky Thompson and others for awhile. In late 40s worked with The Treniers, Edgar Hayes, Johnny Otis, Louis Jordan, Benny Carter. With Gerald Wilson 1949-50. In early 50s studio work with Jerry Fielding and on Groucho Marx radio and TV show many years. Own group awhile. With Chico Hamilton in 1956. Later that year formed own group. Active through 60s and into 70s mostly as bandleader, also freelance. Taught reeds and arranging, also worked in Italy in 60s. Composing and background music for movies (including THE GEORGE WASHINGTON CARVER STORY; TRAUMA; A COMEDY TALE OF FANNY HILL). Composed *Blue Sands, Santa Monica, Soft Touch, Room with Skies.*

RECORDS
(all LPs)

BUDDY COLLETTE

Mer MG-20447 At the Cinema!

EmArcy MG-36133 Buddy Collette's Swinging Shepherds

ABC-Para 179 Calm, Cool and Collette

Contemp C-3522 Man of Many Parts

Contemp C-3531 Nice Day with Buddy Collette

RED NORVO

Contemp C-3534 Music to Listen to Red Norvo By

Lib LRP-3035 Red Norvo Ad Lib Featuring Buddy Collette

RED CALLENDER

Mod LMP-1207 Singin' Suite

Cr CLP-5012 Callender Speaks Low

HOWARD LUCRAFT

De DL-8679 Showcase for Modern Jazz

JOHN GRAAS

EmArcy MG-36117 Coup de Graas

DICK MARX

Omega OSL-2(S) Marx Makes Broadway

LOUIS BELLSON

Verve MGV-8280 Music, Romance and Especially Love

LEONARD FEATHER'S STARS
MGM E-3390 West Coast vs. East Coast
JERRY FIELDING
De DL-8450 Fielding's Formula
CONTE CANDOLI ALL-STARS
Cr CLP-5162 Little Band, Big Jazz

351. COLLINS, ARTHUR   vo

Novelty and dialect singer active in vaudeville and on records. One of best singers specializing in "coon" songs, with good voice and sympathetic treatment. Teamed with Byron G. Harlan in comic-singing duo. Early member of Peerless Quartet. Career began around 1900 and lasted well into 20s. Prolific recording output 1910-16, earliest years of recording industry in present form.

RECORDS

ARTHUR COLLINS
Vi 16103 If I'm Goin' to Die/That Welcome on the Mat
Vi 16110 Moving Day
Vi 16171 I Got to See the Minstrel Show
Vi 16211 All In, Down and Out
Vi 16215 Any Rags/Every Little Bit Added to What You've Got
Vi 16293 Hot Tamale Man
Vi 16498 Let Me Down Easy
Vi 16845 I'll Lend You Everything Except My Wife
Vi 16867 Steamboat Bill
Vi 16897 Chicken Reel
Vi 17011 Ghost of the Banjo Coon
Vi 17118 When Uncle Joe Plays a Rag on His Old Banjo
Vi 18072 I'm Going Way Back Home
COLLINS AND HARLAN (with Byron G. Harlan)
Ed 50248 Auntie Skinner's Chicken Dinner
Co A-724 My Wife's Gone to the Country
Co A-801 That Mesmerizing Mendelssohn Tune
Co A-1246 When the Midnight Choo-Choo Leaves for Alabam'
Co A-1626 Do the Funny Fox Trot
Co A-1675 Ruff Johnson's Harmony Band/On the 5:15
Vi 16426 On a Monkey Honeymoon
Vi 16540 Sugar Moon

Vi 16708 Put Your Arms Around Me, Honey
Vi 16908 Alexander's Ragtime Band
Vi 16937 Steamboat Bill/Mississippi Dippy Dip
Vi 17020 Everybody's Doing It Now
Vi 17221 Preacher and the Bear/Bake Dat Chicken Pie
Vi 17256 Niggah Loves His 'Possum
Vi 17300 At the Levee on Revival Day
Vi 17825 Alabama Jubilee
Vi 18038 Honey Bunch
Vi 18128 Two-Key Rag/Honest Injun

352. COLLINS, DOROTHY   vo
(MARJORIE CHANDLER)

Born c. 1927, Windsor, Ontario, Canada

Good pop singer with strong, melodious voice, equally competent on ballads or up-tempo novelties. Rose to fame as star of Hit Parade TV show in 50s. As youngster appeared on Canadian radio. Bandleader Raymond Scott heard her when she visited Chicago in early 40s, hired her to sing with band as his protege. Brought her along slowly, developed voice and style for many years with him. In 1950 Scott bandleader on TV Hit Parade. Dorothy first sang commercial for sponsor, Lucky Strike, soon became one of four singers featured on show. Married Scott 1953. Hit Parade, popular in mid-50s, faded out in late 50s when poor quality of popular songs caused drop in public interest. Dorothy played clubs, appeared as guest on many TV shows through 50s and early 60s. Career waned and she disappeared from TV. In later 60s played summer stock and road shows. Comeback in 70s with role in Broadway musical FOLLIES.

RECORDS

(with RAYMOND SCOTT)
MGM 10006 We Knew It All the Time
MGM 10132 I Love You, Yes I Do
MGM 10282 You'd Be Surprised
MGM 11036 Mountain High, Valley Low/Yesterday's Ice Cubes
Audivox 100 My Heart Stood Still/To Make a Long Story Short
Audivox 102 Mother Talk/Tico Tico
Audivox 104 Singin' in the Rain/Tiger Rag

Audivox 107 Crazy Rhythm/Mountain High, Valley Low
Audivox 108 Break My Heart Gently/Can This Be the End of a Dream?

DOROTHY COLLINS
MGM 10753 I'm Playing with Fire/My Imagination
MGM 11020 How Many Times?/Did I Remember?
De 28251 From the Time You Say Goodbye/So Madly in Love
De 28421 If'n/Puppy Love
De 28574 Small World/Silly Heart

DOROTHY COLLINS-SNOOKY LANSON
De 28461 I Will Still Love You/Jump Back, Honey

LPs

DOROTHY COLLINS
Cor CRL-57106 Songs by Dorothy Collins
Vo 3724

353. COLLINS, JOHN   g

Born September 20, 1913, Montgomery, Ala.

Underrated guitarist, rhythm and solo. Long career from early 30s into 70s. Moved to Chicago, played early jobs there, including several years in mother's band in early 30s (pianist Georgia Corham). Worked with Art Tatum in 1935, then late 1936-40 with Roy Eldridge; to New York with latter in 1940. Jobbed there early 40s with Lester Young, Dizzy Gillespie, Benny Carter, Fletcher Henderson. Military service 1942-6. With Slam Stewart 1946-8 and Billy Taylor 1949-51. With Nat "King" Cole beginning late 1951 until 1964 when Cole retired due to illness. Active freelance remainder of 60s and into 70s, including long stint with Bobby Troup trio.

RECORDS

MILDRED BAILEY
Vo 3449 My Last Affair/Trust in Me
Vo 3456 Where Are You?/You're Laughing at Me
Co 35463 Fools Rush In/From Another World

UNA MAE CARLISLE
Bb 11096 Beautiful Eyes/There'll Be Some Changes Made
Bb 11120 Blitzkrieg Baby/It's Sad but True

ROY ELDRIDGE
Vo 3458 After You've Gone/Where the Lazy River Goes By
Vo 3479 Wabash Stomp/Florida Stomp
Vo 3577 Heckler's Hop/That Thing
Vs 8084 It's My Turn Now/You're a Lucky Guy
Vs 8107 Pluckin' the Bass/I'm Gettin' Sentimental Over You

FLETCHER HENDERSON
Co 36214 Let's Go Home/I Like My Sugar Sweet
Co 36289 A Pixie from Dixie/We Go Well Together

BILLIE HOLIDAY
OK 5806 The Same Old Story/Practice Makes Perfect
OK 5831 I Hear Music/I'm All for You
OK 6134 Let's Do It/Georgia on My Mind

PETE JOHNSON
De 18121 627 Stomp/Piney Brown Blues (JOE TURNER)

HOT LIPS PAGE
De 18124 Lafayette/South

ART TATUM
De 8526 Wee Baby Blues/Battery Bounce
De 8536 Stompin' at the Savoy/Last Goodbye Blues

SLAM STEWART
Mus 367 Dr. Foo/Oh My, Oh My, Oh Gosh
Mus 396 Blues Collins/Coppin' Out

ESQUIRE ALL-AMERICAN AWARD WINNERS
Vi 40-0134 Blow Me Down
Vi 40-0135 Buckin' the Blues
Vi 40-0136 Indian Summer
Vi 40-0137 Indiana Winter

KENNY CLARKE
Vi 20-3144 Epistrophy/52nd Street Theme

VIC DICKENSON
BN 1600 Lion's Den/Tenderly

BERYL BOOKER
Mer 8297 Love Is the Thing/Stay as Sweet as You Are

LPs

BILLY TAYLOR
Atl(10")113 Piano Panorama, Vol. 1
BERYL BOOKER
EmArcy(10")MG-26007 Girl Met a Piano
(miscellaneous artists)
Vi LPV-519 The Be-Bop Era (Vi RIs)
Vi LPV-578 Swing, Vol. 1 (Vi, Bb RIs)

354. COLLINS, LEE   t B

Born October 17, 1901, New Orleans, La.
Died July 3, 1960, Chicago, Ill.

Jazz trumpeter in New Orleans style. Played parades and dances locally at early age. Mostly in New Orleans through 20s, worked with Pops Foster, Papa Celestin, Zutty Singleton. Led own band at intervals. Replaced Louis Armstrong in King Oliver's band in Chicago for a few months in 1924, also recorded there with Jelly Roll Morton. Toured in south in late 20s, sometimes with own band. Co-leader of Jones-Collins Astoria Hot Eight for recordings. In 1930 with Luis Russell awhile in New York, then freelanced in Chicago in early 30s, including stints with Johnny Dodds, Zutty Singleton. In mid-30s led band, toured country. In late 30s and 40s jobbed and led band mostly in Chicago area. In 50s with Art Hodes, two European tours with Mezz Mezzrow (1951 and 1954), led own band. In later 50s ill health forced him out of music.

RECORDS

RICHARD M. JONES
Bb 6569 Trouble in Mind/Black Rider
JELLY ROLL MORTON
Autograph 606 Fish Tail Blues/High Society
Autograph 607 Weary Blues/Tiger Rag
VICTORIA SPIVEY
Vo 03314 Dreaming of You/I Can't Last Long
Vo 03366 Any Kind-a-Man/I Ain't Gonna Let You See My Santa Claus
Vo 03405 Detroit Moan/Hollywood Stomp

JONES-COLLINS ASTORIA HOT EIGHT
Vi 38576 Duet Stomp/Astoria Strut
Bb 10952 Tip Easy Blues/Damp Weather Blues

LPs

(miscellaneous artists)
"X"(10")3029 (Vi, Bb RIs)
JACK DELANEY
Southland SLP-201
Southland SLP-214
MEZZ MEZZROW
BN(10")BLP-7023
JELLY ROLL MORTON
Riv(10")1027

355. COLLINS, SHAD   t
(LESTER RALLINGSTON COLLINS)

Born June 27, 1910, Elizabeth, N.J.

Good swing trumpet player in 30s and 40s. Grew up in Lockport, N.Y. After some professional work in 1929-30, broke through with name bands. In early 30s with Chick Webb, Benny Carter, Tiny Bradshaw. With Teddy Hill 1936-7, including European trip. Briefly with Don Redman. With Cab Colloway off and on 1936-38. Joined Count Basie late 1938 until early 1940. Worked with Freddy Moore, Lester Young, Buddy Johnson. Joined Cab Calloway September 1941, remained almost two years, later rejoined 1944-6. With Buster Harding in 1948, Al Sears 1950. In 50s toured with Jimmy Rushing and worked with Cab Calloway, Sam "The Man" Taylor and several rhythm and blues bands. Freelanced in New York through 50s, less active in 60s.

RECORDS

CAB CALLOWAY
Br 7685 Are You in Love with Me Again?/When You're Smiling (probable Collins solo)
Vo 3995 Three Swings and Out
Vo 4019 Bugle Blues
OK 6547 Tappin' Off
COUNT BASIE
De 2631 You Can Depend on Me
Vo 5085 Pound Cake
Vo 5169 Nobody Knows

BENNY CARTER
Co(E) 628 Swing It
BILLIE HOLIDAY
OK 6134 Let's Do It/Georgia on My Mind
OK 6214 Romance in the Dark/All of Me
BUDDY JOHNSON
De 8562 Troyon Swing/Southern Exposure
De 8573 It's the Gold/I'm My Baby's Baby
DICKY WELLS
SW(Fr) 25 I Got Rhythm (second trumpet solo; fourth chorus)
Sw(Fr) 39 Nobody's Blues but My Own
KING COLE QUINTET
Disc 2010 Heads/It Had to Be You
Disc 2011 Pro-sky/I Can't Give You Anything but Love
IKE QUEBEC
BN 539 The Masquerade Is Over/Basically Blue
BROTHER JOSHUA
Si 1012 Bachelor's Blues/Stop to Conquer
Si 1013 Come Down Baby/Don't Pay Me No Mind

LPs

DICKY WELLS
Pres 7593 In Paris 1937 (Sw RIs)
BENNY CARTER
Pres 7643 (early RIs)
VIC DICKENSON
Vang(10")VRS-8012
Vang(10")VRS-8013
(miscellaneous artists)
Vi LPV-578 Swing, Vol. 1 (Vi, Bb RIs)

356. COLUMBO, RUSS

vo v acc cm lyr B

Born in 1908
Died September 2, 1934, killed accidentally by pistol

Singing star of 1931-4 whose brief but popular career cut short by tragic shooting accident. High baritone voice with silken quality, highly romantic style. At 17 played violin and accordion well. In late 20s worked as singer-violinist with bands in California, got big break with Gus Arnheim at Hollywood's Cocoanut Grove in 1929. Famous movie and radio stars became aware of his good looks and smooth singing. Several bit parts in movies. Featured at times by Arnheim but not a star. Then fronted own band in 1931, received good radio coverage, quickly became a sensation. Theme song, *You Call It Madness*, captured his style and mood. Popular records for Victor. Had a hand in writing several songs he featured: *You Call It Madness, Prisoner of Love, Let's Pretend There's a Moon, Too Beautiful for Words, My Love, When You're in Love, Just Another Dream of You*. Band toured U.S., and briefly Europe. Made a few movie shorts and appeared in three films: BROADWAY THROUGH A KEYHOLE (1933), MOULIN ROUGE and WAKE UP AND DREAM (1934; latter released after death). People always speculate on how big a star Columbo might have become. His three films give little clue.

Fatal accident occurred at friend's home. Friend's desk had an ancient set of dueling pistols used as paperweights or curios. They had long been there and were believed to be unloaded. Friend struck a match against one pistol to light a cigarette. Gun fired, bullet ricocheted off desk and struck Columbo in head. Before death Columbo linked romantically with actress Carole Lombard. His mother, blind and in precarious health, wasn't told of death. For years members of family and Miss Lombard pretended he was alive, read mother "letters from Russ" explaining that pressing work kept him from visiting her. Mother died never knowing the truth.

RECORDS

GUS ARNHEIM
OK 41037 Back in Your Own Backyard
LEO REISMAN
Vi 22546 A Peach of a Pair
RUSS COLUMBO
Vi 22801 Guilty/I Don't Know Why
Vi 22802 (theme) You Call It Madness/Sweet and Lovely
Vi 22826 Goodnight Sweetheart/Time on My Hands
Vi 22861 You Try Somebody Else/Call Me Darling

Vi 22867 Prisoner of Love/Where the Blue of the Night

Vi 22903 All of Me/Save the Last Dance for Me

Vi 22909 Just Friends/You're My Everything

Vi 22976 Auf Wiedersehen, My Dear/ Paradise

Vi 24045 Just Another Dream of You/Living in Dreams

Vi 24076 As You Desire Me/The Lady I Love

Vi 24077 Lonesome Me/My Love

Vi 24194 Lost in a Crowd/Street of Dreams

Vi 24195 I Called to Say Goodnight/ Make Love the King

Br 6972 When You're in Love/Let's Pretend There's a Moon

SE 5001 Too Beautiful for Words/I See Two Lovers

(RIs)

Bb 6503 Time on My Hands/You Call It Madness

Bb 7118 Sweet and Lovely

Vi 27634-5-6-7 (album of Vi RIs)

LPs

RUSS COLUMBO (all RIs)

Vi LPM-2072 Love Songs by Russ Columbo

Vik LX-996 Love Songs by Russ Columbo

"X"-LVA-1002

357. COMDEN, BETTY   lyr vo

Born May 3, 1915, New York, N.Y.

Important lyricist beginning mid-40s, teamed with Adolph Green for lyrics and book of major Broadway musicals. Duo joined composers Jule Styne and Leonard Bernstein for several successful scores. Miss Comden attended NYU. Teamed with Green and young actress Judy Holliday at Village Vanguard in late 30s. Later at New York's Rainbow Room and Blue Angel. Comden and Green teamed with longtime friend Bernstein on 1945 Broadway show ON THE TOWN, their first success. Duo wrote book and lyrics, also performed in show. Collaborated again with Bernstein on WONDERFUL TOWN (1953). Collaborated with composers Morton Gould on BILLION DOLLAR

BABY (1946) and Saul Chaplin on unsuccessful BONANZA BOUND (1947). In 1947 they began association with composer Jule Styne for important Broadway musicals HIGH BUTTON SHOES (1947), TWO ON THE AISLE (1951), PETER PAN (1954), BELLS ARE RINGING (1956), SAY DARLING (1958), DO RE MI and SUBWAYS ARE FOR SLEEPING (1961), FADE OUT—FADE IN (1964), HALLELUJAH, BABY! (1967). Comden and Green also wrote songs for several movies, collaborated with Roger Edens and Andre Previn. During 60s team appeared occasionally on late-night TV talk shows, wrote screenplays for movies ON THE TOWN, GOOD NEWS, THE BARKLEYS OF BROADWAY, SINGIN' IN THE RAIN, THE BAND WAGON, AUNTIE MAME, BELLS ARE RINGING, WHAT A WAY TO GO. Team wrote songs for 1974 revival of Broadway musical LORELEI. Best-known songs: *New York, New York; Just in Time; The Party's Over; Make Someone Happy.*

SONGS
(with related shows and films)

1945—ON THE TOWN stage show (New York, New York; Lonely Town; Lucky to Be Me; Some Other Time)

1946—BILLION DOLLAR BABY stage show (Broadway Blossom; I'm Sure of Your Love; Bad Timing)

1947—GOOD NEWS movie (The French Lesson); BONANZA BOUND unsuccessful stage show (Tell Me Why; Up in Smoke; Fill 'Er Up; I Know It's True)

1949—ON THE TOWN movie (original stage score, some new material); TAKE ME OUT TO THE BALL GAME movie (The Right Girl for Me; Strictly U.S.A.; It's Fate, Baby, It's Fate; Yes Indeedy; O'Brien to Ryan to Goldberg)

1951—TWO ON THE AISLE stage show (Hold Me, Hold Me, Hold Me; There Never Was a Baby Like My Baby; If You Hadn't but You Did; How Will He Know?; Everlasting; Give a Little, Get a Little Love; So Far, So Good)

1952—SINGIN' IN THE RAIN movie (Moses)

1953—WONDERFUL TOWN stage show

737

(Ohio; It's Love; A Quiet Girl; A Little Bit in Love; Wrong Note Rag)
1954—PETER PAN stage show (partial score: Wendy; Captain Hook's Waltz; Distant Melody; Never Never Land)
1955—IT'S ALWAYS FAIR WEATHER movie
1956—BELLS ARE RINGING stage show (Just in Time; The Party's Over; Long Before I Knew You; Drop That Name; It's a Simple Little System; I'm Goin' Home; Hello, Hello There!)
1958—SAY DARLING stage show (Say Darling; The River Song; Dance Only with Me)
1961—DO RE MI stage show (Make Someone Happy; I Know About Love; Cry Like the Wind; Adventure; What's New at the Zoo?); SUBWAYS ARE FOR SLEEPING stage show (Comes Once in a Lifetime; I'm Just Taking My Time; Girls Like Me; Ride Through the Night; Be a Santa)
1964—FADE OUT—FADE IN stage show (Fade Out—Fade In; You Mustn't Be Discouraged; Call Me Savage; Close Harmony)
1967—HALLELUJAH, BABY! stage show (Hallelujah, Baby!; My Own Morning; Talking to Yourself; Being Good Isn't Good Enough; Not Mine; I Don't Know Where She Got It)

RECORDS
(all LPs)

BETTY COMDEN-ADOLPH GREEN
Cap WAO-1197 A Party with Betty Comden and Adolph Green
(original Broadway cast)
Co OL-5540 ON THE TOWN

358. COMO, PERRY   vo
Born May 18, 1912, Canonsburg, Pa.
Leading singer and TV star of 50s and 60s who rose to fame after years as band vocalist. In younger years Como was a barber, owned shop in home town. Won singing job with Freddy Carlone band in 1933, touring southwestern Pennsylvania. Big break in 1936, joined Ted Weems

band. Virile baritone voice along Bing Crosby lines won some attention. With Weems on Beat the Band radio show 1940-1. Remained with band until it broke up in 1942. Worked as single on radio, in clubs and theatres. In four movies (not important ones, but voice and looks registered well with fans): SOMETHING FOR THE BOYS (1944), DOLL FACE and IF I'M LUCKY (1946), WORDS AND MUSIC (1948). 1945 hit record, *Till the End of Time*, followed by *Prisoner of Love* and *Temptation*. Other hits: *Because* and *When You Were Sweet Sixteen*. Through middle and late 40s, popular Supper Club series of 15-minute shows on radio. TV in early 50s, top-rated hour show by 1955 which continued till 1963. Theme song *Dream Along with Me*. Acquired reputation as casual, relaxed performer. Worked at this easy-going image, conformed vocal style somewhat to it. Continued to record, during later 60s occasionally did specials, guest spots or commercials on TV. Gradually became less active in entertainment. Featured on 1973 TV special, "Cole Porter in Paris."

RECORDS

TED WEEMS
De 820 You Can't Pull the Wool over My Eyes
De 895 Until Today
De 958 Picture Me without You
De 959 Darling, Not without You/Out Where the Blue Begins
De 969 Rainbow on the River
De 1695 A Gypsy Told Me/In My Little Red Book
De 2019 Simple and Sweet
De 2794 Two Blind Loves/Goody Goodbye
De 3627 May I Never Love Again/It All Comes Back to Me Now
De 4131 Angeline/Having a Lonely Time
PERRY COMO
Vi 20-1709 Till the End of Time/That Feeling in the Moonlight
Vi 20-1814 Prisoner of Love/All Through the Day
Vi 20-1919 Temptation/Goodbye Sue
Vi 20-1945 If I'm Lucky/One More Vote

Vi 20-2653 Because/If I Had All the World and Its Gold

Vi 20-3402 Bali Ha'i/Some Enchanted Evening

Vi 20-3747 On the Outgoing Tide/ Hoop-Dee-Doo

Vi 20-4033 More Than You Know/ Without a Song

Vi 20-4112 We Kiss in a Shadow/Hello, Young Lovers

Vi 20-5064 Lies/Don't Let the Stars Get in Your Eyes

Vi 20-5317 No Other Love/Keep It Gay

Vi 47-5647 Wanted/Look Out the Window

Vi 20-6590 (theme) Dream Along with Me/Somebody Up There Likes Me

LPs

PERRY COMO

Vi LOP-1004 Saturday Night with Mr. C

Vi LMP-1176 Relaxing with Perry Como

Vi LPM-1463 We Get Letters

Vi LOP-1007 Como's Golden Records

Vi PR-138 Perry at His Best

Vi(10″)LPM-3013 TV Favorites

Cam CAL-440 Sings Just for You

359. COMSTOCK, FRANK

p tb ar cm B

Born September 20, 1922, San Diego, Calif.

Top arranger in modern style, best known for long association with Les Brown band. Consistently smooth and tasteful on swing numbers; full, beautiful sound on ballads. Studied arranging and sold arrangements in high school. Trombonist-arranger for Sonny Dunham in 1939, arranged for Benny Carter in 1941. Began arranging for Les Brown in 1942, did work for him through 50s. Important in development of Brown band and in adapting it to modern style in middle and late 40s. His arrangements gave band good modern sound but not far-out. Also arranged and conducted for singers Doris Day, Rosemary Clooney, The Hi-Lo's, Margaret Whiting, others. Arranged for TV shows of Bob Hope, Steve Allen, Pete Kelly's Blues, The D.A.'s Man, Rocky

and His Friends, Ensign O'Toole, McHale's Navy. Conducted on TV shows. Some writing for movies. Active through 60s and into 70s.

RECORDS
(all LPs)

FRANK COMSTOCK

Co CL-8003 Patterns

WB 1463 Music from Outer Space

(as arranger and/or conductor)

PHIL SILVERS and SWINGING BRASS

Co CL-1011

FRANKIE LAINE

Co CL-1317 You Are My Love

THE HI-LO'S

Co CL-952 Suddenly It's the Hi-Lo's

Co CL-1023 Now Hear This

Co CL-1121 Love Nest

ROSEMARY CLOONEY & THE HI-LO'S

Co CL-1006 Ring Around Rosie

LES BROWN

Cor CX-1 (2-LP set) Concert at the Palladium

Cor(10″)CRL-56026 Over the Rainbow

Co(10″)CL-6008 Sentimental Journey (Co RIs)

Co(10″)CL-6060 Dance Parade (Co RIs)

(movie soundtrack featuring GOGI GRANT)

Vi LOC-1030 THE HELEN MORGAN STORY

(movie soundtrack)

Dot DLP-3714 THE LAST OF THE SECRET AGENTS

360. CONDON, EDDIE   g bn cm B
(ALBERT EDWIN CONDON)

Born November 16, 1905 or 1906, Goodland, Ind.

Died August 4, 1973, New York, N.Y. of bone cancer

Famed jazz organizer and combo leader, highly successful at promoting jazz. Rhythm guitarist who played with or hired scores of jazz greats. Leading spokesman for jazz via articles, books, interviews and celebrated wisecracks. Grew up in Chicago Heights, Ill., first played professionally there on banjo. Worked in Chicago in mid-20s, began half-century association with jazzmen like

Bud Freeman, Gene Krupa, Jimmy McPartland. Worked with many groups including those of Charles Pierce, Louis Panico, Jack Gardner, Red Nichols. With Red McKenzie on record sessions in late 20s and jobs in early 30s. During mid-30s worked part-time at music with Riley-Farley band, Red McKenzie, Joe Marsala. With Bobby Hackett in 1938 and Bud Freeman in 1939-40. Jobbed mostly at Nick's in Greenwich Village, in 1942 began promoting jazz concerts at Town Hall in New York and elsewhere, by middle 40s very successful. Through the years on dozens of record sessions as sideman or leader. Wrote some jazz numbers; best known: *We Called It Music*, *Home Cooking*, *That's a Serious Thing*. In late 1945 opened own jazz club, Eddie Condon's, in Greenwich Village, moved to upper East Side in 1958, finally closed in mid-1967. Usually played at this jazz mecca himself, always featured standout dixieland artists. Had jazz series, Floor Show, on early TV, late 40s. In 50s made outstanding LPs, toured abroad in 1957 and 1964. In late 60s became ill, recovered, returned to music part-time into 70s. Wrote or edited books on jazz: *We Called It Music* (autobiography), *Eddie Condon's Treasury of Jazz* (anthology), *Eddie Condon's Scrapbook of Jazz*. Final public performance July 1973 at New York-Newport jazz festival.

RECORDS

LOUIS ARMSTRONG
   OK 8669 I Can't Give You Anything but Love
   OK 8680 Mahogany Hall Stomp
CHICAGO RHYTHM KINGS
   Br 4001 I've Found a New Baby/There'll Be Some Changes Made
MCKENZIE-CONDON CHICAGOANS
   OK 40971 Liza/Nobody's Sweetheart
   OK 41011 Sugar/China Boy
MOUND CITY BLUE BLOWERS
   Co 1946-D Indiana/Firehouse Blues
   Vi 38087 Tailspin Blues/Never Had a Reason to Believe in You
   Vi 38100 Hello, Lola/One Hour
FATS WALLER
   Vi 38050 Harlem Fuss/The Minor Drag

THE RHYTHMAKERS
   Co 35882 Mean Old Bed Bug Blues/Yellow Dog Blues
BUD FREEMAN
   De 18112 The Buzzard/Tillie's Downtown Now
   Bb 10370 I've Found a New Baby/Easy to Get
   Bb 10386 China Boy/The Eel
BOBBY HACKETT
   Vo 4047 At the Jazz Band Ball/If Dreams Come True
   Vo 4565 A Ghost of a Chance/Doin' the New Lowdown
ART HODES
   De 18437 Georgia Cake Walk/Liberty Inn Drag
   De 18438 Indiana/Get Happy
TEMPO KING
   Bb 6534 William Tell/Anything for You
   Bb 6535 Papa Tree Top Tall/I'll Sing You a Thousand Love Songs
JOE MARSALA
   Va 565 Wolverine Blues/Jazz Me Blues
RED MCKENZIE
   De 507 Murder in the Moonlight/Let's Swing It
   De 521 Double Trouble/That's What You Think
EDDIE CONDON
   Br 6743 The Eel/Home Cooking
   CMS 536 Georgia Grind/Dancing Fool
   CMS(12")1500 Carnegie Drag/Carnegie Jump
   CMS(12")1509 Mammy o' Mine/Tortilla B Flat
   De 23430 'S Wonderful/Somebody Loves Me
   De 23433 Swanee/I'll Build a Stairway to Paradise
   De 23719 Stars Fell on Alabama/Farewell Blues
   De 27035 Jazz Me Blues/Maple Leaf Rag
   De 27095 Charleston/Black Bottom
   Atl 661 Time Carries On/Seems Like Old Times

LPs

EDDIE CONDON
   De(10")DL-5195 Jazz Band Ball, Vol. 1

De(10″)DL-5196 Jazz Band Ball, Vol. 2
Co CL-616 Jammin' at Condon's
Co CL-719 Bixieland
Co CL-881 Treasury of Jazz
Co CL-1089 The Roaring Twenties
Dot DLP-3141 Dixieland Dance Party
(miscellaneous artists)
"X"(10″)LX-3005 (Bb, Vi RIs)
BUD FREEMAN
Ha HL-7046 Bud Freeman & His All-Star Jazz
BOBBY HACKETT
Epic LN-3106 The Hackett Horn (Vo RIs)
BILLY BANKS & THE RHYTHMAKERS
IAJRC 4 (1932 Me-Pe RIs)

361. CONFREY, ZEZ   p cm lyr B
(EDWARD ELZEAR CONFREY)
Born April 3, 1895, Peru, Ill.
Died 1972

Pianist-bandleader-composer of 20s whose solo pieces for piano became standards. Studied at Chicago Musical College. Cut many early piano rolls. Military service, World War I. Led band throughout 20s, appeared on radio. Mainly famous for compositions which showcased piano but could also be played by orchestra. Best works include *Kitten on the Keys, Dizzy Fingers, Stumbling, Buffoon, Jack in the Box, Grandfather's Clock, Dumbell, Nickel in the Slot, Mississippi Shiver, Charleston Chuckles, Humorestless, Valse Mirage, Three Little Oddities, Concert Etude, Oriental Fantasy, Parade of the Jumping Beans, Ultra Ultra, Rhythm Venture, Champagne, Tune for Mademoiselle, Pickle Pepper Polka, Poor Buttermilk, You Tell 'Em Ivories.* Wrote good popular song of 1934, *Sittin' on a Log.*

RECORDS
ZEZ CONFREY
Emer 10486 Kitten on the Keys/Poor Buttermilk
Br 2082 Kitten on the Keys/My Pet
Br 2112 Poor Buttermilk/You Tell 'Em Ivories
Br 2167 Greenwich Witch/Coaxing the Piano
Vi 18900 Kitten on the Keys/True Blue Sam

Vi 18902 I Love Her—She Loves Me
Vi 18921 Are You Playing Fair?
Vi 18962 Cow Bells
Vi 18973 All Muddled Up/True Blue Sam
Vi 18981 I'm Goin' to Plant Myself in My Old Plantation Home
Vi 19008 When All Your Castles Come Tumbling Down
Vi 19037 The Fuzzy Wuzzy Bird/Some Little Someone
Vi 19090 Oh Harold/Rosetime and You
Vi 19430 Mississippi Shiver/Nickel in the Slot
Vi 20777 Dizzy Fingers/Kitten on the Keys
Vi 21010 Polly/Trudy
Ba 2059 Greenwich Witch/You Tell 'Em Ivories

362. CONNELLY, REG   cm lyr

English songwriter who teamed with countryman James Campbell on several songs popular in U.S. Pair usually collaborated with another composer. Leading hits in U.S. *If I Had You* (1929), *When the Organ Played at Twilight* (1930), *Goodnight Sweetheart* (1931), *By the Fireside, Just an Echo in the Valley* and *Till Tomorrow* (1932), *Try a Little Tenderness* (1933). Connelly credited with *Underneath the Arches* (1933) without Campbell.

363. CONNIFF, RAY   tb ar cm B
Born November 6, 1916, Attleboro, Mass.

Talented trombonist-arranger with name bands, rose to fame beginning in 1956 as conductor-arranger on LPs featuring choral group blending voices with orchestra in unusual, tasteful manner. Started playing professionally in Boston at early age. With Dan Murphy and Henry Biagini in 1936. With Jack Marshard 1937. With Bunny Berigan 1938-9 over a year. Joined Bob Crosby late 1939, remained till late 1940. Led band awhile in early 1941. Later in 1941 with Vaughn Monroe as trombonist-arranger. In late 1941 joined Artie Shaw, remained till early 1942. In 1943 arranged for Jerry Wald. Military service, World War II, in Artie Shaw's navy band. Trombonist-arranger for Shaw's 1945 band. Worked with Harry James as arranger-composer, his jazz numbers featured prominently by band in later 40s. In 1951 arranged for Jerry Wald, worked with Sonny Burke as trombonist-arranger. In 1952 with Frank DeVol on California TV. Signed with Columbia Records as arranger-conductor for leading singers. Then in later 50s came success with own series of LPs. Active in 60s and 70s with records, conducting and arranging. Toured England 1973.

RECORDS

ARTIE SHAW
　Vi 27860 Needlenose
　Vi 20-1638 'S Wonderful/I'll Never Be the Same
COZY COLE
　Sav 501 Talk to Me/Body and Soul
　Sav 502 Jericho/Concerto for Cozy
ART HODES
　BN 505 Maple Leaf Rag/Yellow Dog Rag
　BN 506 She's Crying for Me/Slow 'Em Down Blues
　BN 507 Doctor Jazz/Shoe Shiner's Drag
　BN 508 There'll Be Some Changes Made/Clark and Randolph
JERRY JEROME
　Asch 500 Girl of My Dreams/Rainbow Blues
　Asch 501 Arsenic and Old Face/When I Grow Too Old to Dream
　Asch 502 Misty Blues
RAY CONNIFF
　Br 80240 Super Chief/Beanie Boy Boogie

LPs

RAY CONNIFF
　Co CL-925 'S Wonderful!
　Co CL-1074 'S Marvelous
　Co CL-1137 'S Awful Nice
　Co CL-1252 Broadway in Rhythm
　Co CL-1334 It's the Talk of the Town
　Co CL-2118 You Make Me Feel So Young
RAY CONNIFF-BILLY BUTTERFIELD
　Co CL-1346 Conniff Meets Butterfield
ART HODES (as trombonist)
　BN(10″)7004 Art Hodes & His Chicagoans (BN RIs)

EILEEN ROGERS (as conductor)
　Co CL-1096 Blue Swing

364. CONNOR, CHRIS   VO
Born November 8, 1927, Kansas City, Mo.

Jazz-styled singer who won fame with Stan Kenton following style of predecessors June Christy and Anita O'Day, but tone, dynamics and rhythm gave her individuality. Sang with college band at University of Missouri. In late 40s sang awhile with Bob Brookmeyer combo in Kansas City, picked up valuable experience. To New York in 1949, worked in Snowflakes vocal group with Claude Thornhill band, later as soloist for band over two years. With Jerry Wald awhile in 1952, then with Kenton 1952-3 where singing became known. Began as single later in 1953, worked clubs and recorded. At best in small clubs with combos. Active through 50s and into 70s.

RECORDS

STAN KENTON
　Cap 2388 Jeepers Creepers/And the Bull Walked Around, Olay!
　Cap 2511 All About Ronnie
JERRY WALD
　De 28203 You're the Cream in My Coffee
CHRIS CONNOR
　Beth 1291 Blue Silhouette/Gimme Gimme

LPs

CHRIS CONNOR
　Beth BCP-20 This Is Chris
　Beth BCP-6004 Sings Lullabys of Birdland
　Atl 2-601 (2-LP set) Sings the George Gershwin Almanac of Song
　Atl 1228 Chris Connor RC)Atl 1286 A Jazz Date with Chris Connor
　Atl 1290 Chris Craft/Chris Connor
　Atl 1307 Ballads of the Sad Cafe
　Atl 8032 Witchcraft/Chris Connor
　Atl 8046 Portrait of Chris
　Atl 8061 Free Spirits
　ABC-Para 529 Sings Gentle Bossa Nova
　Clar 611 Sings George Gershwin
CHRIS CONNOR-MAYNARD FERGUSON
　Roul R-52068 Two's Company

365. CONRAD, CON   cm p
(CONRAD K. DOBER)

Born June 18, 1891, New York, N.Y.
Died September 28, 1938, Van Nuys,
Calif.

Composer of 20s and 30s, wrote for stage
and movies. Novelty hit *Barney Google* in
1923. Enduring songs: *Margie, Ma, Memory Lane, Lonesome and Sorry, Champagne
Waltz, You Call It Madness, The Continental, Midnight in Paris.* Theatre pianist
early in career, also vaudeville in U.S. and
Europe. Songs for Broadway shows during 20s. Music publisher. To Hollywood
in 1929 to write for movie musicals.
Collaborators included Herb Magidson,
Buddy DeSylva, Benny Davis, J. Russel
Robinson, Archie Gottler.

SONGS
(with related shows)

1918—Oh! Frenchy
1920—Margie; Palesteena; Singin' the
Blues
1921—MIDNIGHT ROUNDERS OF 1921 stage
show (Ma); Mandy 'n' Me
1922—California
1923—Barney Google; Steppin' Out;
You've Gotta See Mama Ev'ry
Night
1924—MOONLIGHT stage show (In a Bungalow; Forever; Honeymoon
Blues; On Such a Night; others);
Mah Jong; She's Everybody's
Sweetheart; Memory Lane
1925—BETTY LEE stage show (songs unimportant); BIG BOY stage show
(Miami); MERCENARY MARY stage
show (songs unimportant)
1926—AMERICANA stage show (songs unimportant); KITTY'S KISSES stage
show (Kitty's Kisses; I'm in Love;
Early in the Morning; Stepping on
the Blues; others); Lonesome and
Sorry
1927—TAKE THE AIR stage show (Ham
and Eggs in the Morning)
1928—Dear, on a Night Like This; The
Song I Love
1929—FOX MOVIETONE FOLLIES OF 1929
movie (Big City Blues; Breakaway; Walking with Susie; That's
You, Baby); BROADWAY movie
(Hittin' the Ceiling; Sing a Little

Love Song); THE COCK-EYED
WORLD movie (So Long; Elenita;
So Dear to Me); Look What
You've Done to Me
1930—HAPPY DAYS movie (Mona; Crazy
Feet); Here Comes Emily Brown;
Nine Little Miles from Ten-Ten-
Tennessee
1931—PALMY DAYS movie (Bend Down,
Sister); At Last I'm Happy; You
Call It Madness
1932—Lonesome Me
1933—I May Be Dancing with Somebody
Else
1934—GIFT OF GAB movie (Blue Sky Avenue; Talking to Myself); THE GAY
DIVORCEE movie (The Continental;
Needle in a Haystack); Champagne Waltz
1935—HERE'S TO ROMANCE movie (Here's
to Romance; Midnight in Paris)

366. COOK, JOE   vo
(real name Lopez)

*Born 1890, Evansville, Ind.; orphaned at
3, adopted by Cook family of Evansville*
*Died May 16, 1959, Clinton Hollow,
N.Y.*

Star of important Broadway shows. Primarily comic-juggler-dancer-acrobat, also
sang. Started in local amateur shows, at
14 left town to repeat act in similar
contests throughout U.S. Entered vaudeville, worked up to top bookings such as
New York's Palace Theatre. Broadway
debut in HITCHY-KOO OF 1919, made hit
singing *When I Had a Uniform On.* Starred in EARL CARROLL'S VANITIES OF 1923-
1924-1926. Two long-running shows, RAIN
OR SHINE (1928) and FINE AND DANDY
(1930). Less successful shows HOLD YOUR
HORSES (1933) and BROADWAY SHOW-WINDOW (1936). Long-running show IT HAPPENS ON ICE (1940). Starred in 1930 movie
RAIN OR SHINE (converted from original
stage show), also later minor movie work.
Guest spots on radio during 30s, own
shows at intervals in mid-30s. Early 1937
replaced Smith Ballew briefly as host of
The Chateau show. Suffered from Parkinson's Disease; forced to retire 1942.

367. COOK, WILL MARION
cm lyr v B

Born January 27, 1869, Washington, D.C.
Died July 19, 1944, New York, N.Y.

Negro composer-lyricist, wrote music for first Negro musical to play Broadway, CLORINDY (or THE ORIGIN OF THE CAKEWALK; 1898). Educated at Oberlin College, plus musical training. Wrote for Broadway shows THE WILD ROSE (1902), IN DAHOMEY (1903), THE SOUTHERNERS (1904), ABYSSINIA (1906), BANDANA LAND (1908). Conducted for some shows. In 1919 led Negro group, American Syncopated Orchestra, on tour of U.S. and Europe. Most popular compositions *Bon Bon Buddy* (1907), *Lovey Joe* (1910), *I'm Coming Virginia* (1927 jazz standard). Other songs: *Good Evenin', My Little Gypsy Maid, Swing Along, Who Dat Say Chicken in Dis Crowd?, Darktown Is Out Tonight, Exhortation, On Emancipation Day, That's How the Cakewalk's Done, The Rain Song, Happy Jim, I May Be Crazy but I Ain't No Fool, Down the Lover's Lane, Mandy Lou, Red Red Rose, A Little Bit of Heaven Called Home.*

368. COOL, HARRY
vo B

Born June 28, 1913

Excellent pop singer. First prominent with Dick Jurgens band, later bandleader. Consistent performer with strong baritone voice. In show business and radio several years before joining Jurgens as virtual unknown. Replaced popular Eddy Howard around late 1939, fast achieved recognition. Left Jurgens around 1943-4 to work as single. In 1944 replaced Dick Haymes on Here's to Romance radio show. Bandleader mid-1945, taking over Carl Ravazza band, smooth hotel type. Through 40s and into early 50s played widely, recorded. Became night club manager after leaving band business.

RECORDS

DICK JURGENS
OK 5628 Avalon/A Million Dreams Ago
OK 5825 There Shall Be No Night/I Want to Live
OK 6022 My Silent Love

OK 6331 There Goes That Song Again
OK 6456 The Bells of San Raquel
OK 6535 I'll Never Forget
Vo 5478 From Another World
Co 36643 Why Don't You Fall in Love with Me?
Co 36669 You'd Be So Nice to Come Home To

HARRY COOL
Si 15007 Symphony/My Guy's Come Back
Si 15036 It Had to Be You
Si 15043 Rumors Are Flying/The Whole World Is Singing My Song
Si 15062 Bless You/Either It's Love or It Isn't
Si 15069 It's a Good Day/Are You Kiddin'?
Mer 3054 It's Dreamtime/Cecilia
Mer 3063 Forgive Me/I'm a-Rollin'
Mer 3066 Ragtime Cowboy Joe/Who Takes Care of the Caretaker's Daughter?
Mer 3070 My Baby Just Cares for Me/Mama's Gone, Goodbye
Mer 5080 I Wouldn't Be Surprised/Pass That Peace Pipe
Mer 5126 Baby Face/I Went Down to Virginia
Fredlo 52066 Ace in the Hole/A Cottage for Sale

369. COOLEY, SPADE
v vo cm lyr B

Born in Grande, Okla.
Died 1972

Country and western bandleader known as King of Western Swing. Gained fame leading good large-sized western swing band with outstanding arrangements of that type. Often played violin fronting band. As youngster played violin at square dances. Had classical aspirations but began working with western groups. During career was based on west coast. In mid-30s Hollywood extra and musician. In 1939 small role in first of several Roy Rogers movies, by 1945 had made many films. During one period sang with Riders of the Purple Sage vocal group. Own band in 1942. In 1946 leased Santa Monica Ballroom as band's base many years. Own radio show in late 40s. Early TV in California. Band reached musical peak in early 50s, played jazz and ballad standards capably. Tragedy struck Cooley in later life: jailed many years for slaying wife. After lengthy period released, died soon after. Composer of several numbers, notably *Shame on You.*

RECORDS

SPADE COOLEY

Co 36935 Detour/You Can't Break My Heart

Co 37237 Oklahoma Stomp/You Better Do It Now

Co 20071 Shame on You/A Pair of Broken Hearts

Co 20375 Cow Bell Polka/Troubled Over You

Co 20431 Yodeling Polka/Hide Your Face

Vi 20-2181 Minuet in Swing/It's Dark Outside

Vi 20-2295 Boggs Boogie/Red Hair and Green Eyes

Vi 20-2668 Spanish Fandango/The Best Deal in Town

Vi 21-0150 Foolish Tears/Send Ten Pretty Flowers

Vi 47-3195 The Last Round-up/ Wagon Wheels

Vi 47-3196 In the Chapel in the Moonlight/Lights Out

De 28253 Swingin' the Devil's Dream/Crazy 'Cause I Love You

De 46310 Chew Tobacco Rag/Rhumba Boogie

LPs

SPADE COOLEY

Co(10″)HL-9007 Sagebrush Swing

370. COON, CARLETON   d vo cm B

Born February 5, 1894, Rochester, Minn.

Died May 4, 1932, Chicago, Ill.

Co-leader of popular Coon-Sanders Orchestra in 20s and early 30s. (For details, see following biography on orchestra.) Co-composer of 1926 song *Hi-Diddle-Diddle* which stayed popular through the years.

371. COON-SANDERS ORCHESTRA

Popular dance band of 20s and early 30s, co-led by Carleton Coon and Joe Sanders (see biographies of both). Top dance band, particularly in late 20s; good

musicianship and lively, happy, uninhibited music. Many arrangements by Sanders in distinctive semi-hot style featuring jazz breaks. Two leaders handled vocals capably either solo or duet. Especially effective: exuberant tenor voice of Sanders, and his showmanship. The two grew up in Missouri, met in Kansas City, formed band there in 1920. After several years mostly in Kansas City area, band got big break as early radio remotes from the Muehlbach Hotel in middle and late 20s made it famous throughout midwest. Band's late-night shows earned it the name of the Kansas City Night Hawks.

Band played Chicago date in 1924, again in late 1926 at Blackhawk Restaurant with many radio wires. Long return engagements followed. Began recording in mid-20s, by late 20s recorded frequently. Toured, kept Kansas City as base. Own show on NBC radio awhile. Two big numbers: *Here Comes My Ball and Chain* and *Slue Foot.* Personnel remained constant during last five years of band—a happy family. In late 1931-2 band went east for lengthy stay at Hotel New Yorker. Band at Hotel Sherman's College Inn in Chicago in 1932 when tragedy struck. Carleton Coon had abscessed tooth, died suddenly May 4. Band never recovered. Sanders tried to carry on as leader, played tour already booked, but band broke up year after. Sanders later formed own band, had long career.

RECORDS

COON-SANDERS ORCHESTRA

Co A-3403 Some Little Bird

Vi 19316 Night Hawk Blues/Red Hot Mama

Vi 19745 Yes, Sir, That's My Baby

Vi 19750 That's All There Is/Everything Is Hotsy Totsy Now

Vi 19922 Flamin' Mamie

Vi 20015 Sittin' Around

Vi 20390 Brainstorm/My Baby Knows How

Vi 21148 Mine—All Mine/Is She My Girl Friend?

Vi 21258 Stay Out of the South

Vi 21305 Slue Foot/The Wail

Vi 21546 Too Busy/Down Where the Sun Goes Down

Vi 21562 Indian Cradle Song
Vi 21680 Blazin'
Vi 21803 What a Girl, What a Night/
My Suppressed Desire
Vi 21812 Here Comes My Ball and
Chain/Who Wouldn't Be Jealous
of You?
Vi 21891 Rhythm King/Mississippi,
Here I Am
Vi 21895 Little Orphan Annie/Bless
You, Sister
Vi 22300 Harlem Madness
Vi 22342 Darktown Strutters' Ball/Af-
ter You've Gone
Vi 22950 What a Life!/Let That Be a
Lesson to You
Vi 22951 Lo and Behold/Sing a New
Song
Vi 38083 Louder and Funnier/Smilin'
Skies

LPs

COON-SANDERS ORCHESTRA
Vi LPV-511 Radio's Aces—The Coon-
Sanders Night Hawks (Vi RIs)
TOM 32 (Vi RIs)
TOM 33 (Vi RIs)

372. COOPER, BOB
ts f cl E-h oboe cm B

Born December 6, 1925, Pittsburgh, Pa.

Modern-style jazzman talented on many
reeds. Especially able jazz soloist on tenor
sax and leading exponent of oboe in jazz.
Early in career joined Stan Kenton, remained stalwart in band 1945-51. Married
Kenton vocalist June Christy, often
worked with her through the years. In
early 50s freelanced on west coast,
worked with Jerry Gray, Shorty Rogers,
Pete Rugolo, among others. In 1954 with
Howard Rumsey's Lighthouse All-Stars,
remained many years. Freelance recordings and movie-radio-TV work. Active
through 60s into 70s. Played in bands on
late-night TV. Jazz compositions include
*Bossa Nova, Gone for the Day, Jazz Theme
and Variations, Tequila Time.*

RECORDS

STAN KENTON
Cap 888 Blues in Riff
Cap 906 Harlem Holiday
Cap 1279 Viva Prado

THE POLL CATS
Atl 851 Sa-frantic
JUNE CHRISTY
Cap 406 If I Should Lose You/Skip-
Rope
Cap 578 The Way You Look To-
night/Everything Happens to Me
SHELLY MANNE
DeeGee 3801 The Count on Rush
Street/All of Me

LPs

BOB COOPER
Cap T-6513 Shifting Winds
Contemp C-3544 Coop!
WP 1226 Flute 'n' Oboe
PJ 35 Barefoot Adventure
BUD SHANK-BOB COOPER
PJ 1226 The Flute and the Oboe
BUD SHANK
PJ 1219 Jazz at Cal-Tech
HOWARD RUMSEY
Contemp(10")C-2501 Lighthouse All-
Stars, Vol. 2
Contemp(10")C-2506 Lighthouse All-
Stars, Vol. 3
Contemp(10")C-2510 Lighthouse All-
Stars, Vol. 4
JOHN GRAAS
EmArcy MG-36117 Coup de Graas
Trend(10")TL-1005 The French Horn
LAURINDO ALMEIDA
Cap ST-1759 (S) Viva Bossa Nova!
BARNEY KESSEL
Contemp(10")C-2511
MAYNARD FERGUSON
EmArcy(10")MG-26024 Dimensions
HOWARD LUCRAFT
De DL-8679 Showcase for Modern
Jazz

373. COOPER, JERRY
vo g tb B

Strong-voiced baritone popular in 30s.
Early in career led band awhile. In 1933
appearing in Studio Club in New Orleans
when bandleader Roger Wolfe Kahn
heard him singing over radio, encouraged
him to come to New York. Cooper landed
singing job on CBS radio in 1934. Recorded with several bands in mid-30s.
Active on radio, own shows at intervals in
late 30s. Appeared on Musical Toast
show 1935-6 and mid-1937, in 1938 singing host on Hollywood Hotel. In 1938

movie HOLLYWOOD HOTEL. In Broadway musicals BOYS AND GIRLS TOGETHER (1940) and GENTLEMEN PREFER BLONDES (1949). Continued to play clubs, recorded occasionally. Active into 50s.

RECORDS

BEN SELVIN
    Co 2844-D My Dancing Lady
EMIL COLEMAN
    Co 2847-D You're Devastating
    Co 2859-D Moon About Town/What Is There to Say?
    Co 2869-D Song of Surrender/Lovely
EDDY DUCHIN
    Vi 25318 I'll Stand By/Love Came Out of the Night
    Vi 25343 Guess Who/Take My Heart
    Vi 25429 To Mary, with Love/I've Got Something in My Eye
    Vi 25432 It's De-Lovely/You've Got Something
    Vi 25472 Love and Learn/Seal It with a Kiss
    Vi 25517 Too Marvelous for Words/Just a Quiet Evening
    Vi 25520 Our Song/Whistling Boy
    Vi 25569 Let's Call the Whole Thing Off/Without Your Love
JERRY COOPER
    Vi 25485 Timber/Goodnight My Love
    Rbw 141 Be Fair with Me/If You Were Mine
    Abbey 15014 Wasted Words/I'm Always in Love with Someone
    Anchor 14 Have You Ever Been Lonely?/I'm Sorry I Made You Cry

LPs

EDDY DUCHIN
    Vik LX-1043 The Fabulous Eddy Duchin (Vi RIs)

374. COOTS, J. FRED   cm p
Born May 2, 1897, Brooklyn, N.Y.

Important composer of 20s and 30s with numerous hit songs. Most famous: *A Precious Little Thing Called Love, Love Letters in the Sand, Santa Claus Is Comin' to Town, A Beautiful Lady in Blue, You Go to My Head*. Early in career worked as song plugger, then pianist in vaudeville and night clubs. Wrote for Broadway musicals SALLY, IRENE AND MARY (1922),

ARTISTS AND MODELS OF 1924-1925, JUNE DAYS (1925), THE MERRY WORLD and A NIGHT IN PARIS (1926), WHITE LIGHTS (1927), SONS O' GUNS (1929). Songs for other Broadway shows on lesser scale. Wrote for three editions of Cotton Club revues in 30s and for a few movies. Collaborators included lyricists Haven Gillespie, Benny Davis, Lou Davis, Sam M. Lewis, Joe Young, Clifford Grey.

SONGS
(with related shows)

1922—SALLY, IRENE AND MARY stage show (I Wonder Why; Something in Here; Time Will Tell)
1924—ARTISTS AND MODELS OF 1924 stage show (Who's the Lucky Fellow?; I Love to Dance When I Hear a March)
1925—ARTISTS AND MODELS OF 1925 stage show (Follow Your Stars; Take a Little Baby Home with You); GAY PAREE stage show (songs unimportant); JUNE DAYS stage show (songs unimportant); MAYFLOWERS stage show (songs unimportant)
1926—THE MERRY WORLD stage show (Sunday); A NIGHT IN PARIS stage show (songs unimportant)
1927—WHITE LIGHTS stage show (songs unimportant)
1928—SHOPWORN ANGEL movie (A Precious Little Thing Called Love); Doin' the Raccoon; It Was the Dawn of Love; Moonlight Madness; A Love Tale of Alsace Lorraine
1929—SONS O' GUNS stage show (Cross Your Fingers; Why?; It's You I Love; May I Say "I Love You"?; Red Hot and Blue Rhythm); Here Comes My Ball and Chain
1930—RIPPLES stage show (You Never Can Tell About Love); I Miss a Little Miss; I Still Get a Thrill
1931—Love Letters in the Sand
1932—Here's Hoping; Strangers; You'll Get By
1933—I Want to Ring Bells; One Minute to One; This Time It's Love; Two Tickets to Georgia
1934—For All We Know; I Knew You When; Santa Claus Is Comin' to Town

1935—It Never Dawned on Me; Louisiana Fairy Tale; Things Might Have Been So Diff'rent; Whose Honey Are You?; Is It Just a Summer Romance?

1936—SONS O' GUNS movie (some songs from original stage score); A Beautiful Lady in Blue; That's What You Mean to Me; Doin' the Suzy Q; I'll Stand By; I'm Grateful to You; In My Estimation of You; Isn't Love the Strangest Thing?; Until Today; Who Loves You?; The More I Know You; A Little Robin Told Me So; Why Do I Lie to Myself About You?; You Started Me Dreaming; Yours Truly Is Truly Yours; Copper Colored Gal

1937—In Your Own Little Way; Alabama Barbecue; My Day Begins and Ends with You

1938—Summer Souvenirs; There's Honey on the Moon Tonight; You Go to My Head; I'm Madly in Love with You

1939—Let's Stop the Clock

1940—I'll Wait for You Forever; Poor Ballerina; Wait Till I Catch You in My Dreams

1947—Encore, Cherie

1950—Little Johnny Chickadee

1952—The Bluest Word I Know Is "Lonesome"

1954—If I Should Love Again

Others songs: *What's Gonna Be with You and Me?*; *There's Oceans of Love by the Beautiful Sea*; *Me and My Teddy Bear*; *When the Teddy Bears Go Marching on Parade*; *Goodbye, Mama, I'm Off to Yokohama*

375. CORCORAN, CORKY   ts B
(GENE PATRICK CORCORAN)
Born July 28, 1924, Tacoma, Wash.

Swinging, warm-toned tenor sax soloist, prominent with Harry James band in 40s and beyond. At 16 joined Sonny Dunham band 1940-1. At start of 1942 joined James, became most featured sideman. Remained till 1947, with Tommy Dorsey 1947-8. In 1949 freelanced, led band awhile. Late 1949-57 rejoined James several times. In late 50s led combo on west coast, particularly in Seattle and Los Angeles. Active in 60s freelancing, leading combo. Back with James on and off in 60s, with him steadily in early 70s.

RECORDS
HARRY JAMES
Co 36533 Skylark/The Clipper
Co 36632 Let Me Up
Co 36838 Autumn Serenade
Co 36996 Easy
Co 37301 I Can't Get Up the Nerve to Kiss You
Co 37351 Moten Swing
Co 38134 All the Way
Co 38300 Ab-Mur
Co 39419 Tango Blues
HELEN HUMES
Alad 121 Did You Ever Love a Man?/Voo It
Alad 122 Central Avenue Boogie
SHORTY SHEROCK
Si 28113 It's the Talk of the Town
CORKY CORCORAN
Key 621 Minor Blues/What Is This Thing Called Love?
Key 654 You Know It

LPs
CORKY CORCORAN
Epic LN-3319 The Sound of Love
HARRY JAMES
MGM E-4265 New Version of Down Beat Favorites
MGM E-4274 In a Relaxed Mood
Cap T-874 Wild About Harry
LIONEL HAMPTON
De DL-4194 Star Dust ("Just Jazz" Concert)
GNP 15 With the Just Jazz All-Stars
GENE NORMAN PRESENTS
De DL-9055 Just Jazz
(miscellaneous artists)
EmArcy MG-36018 Alto Altitude
EmArcy MG-36023 Battle of the Saxes

376. CORNELL, DON   vo g
Born in New York, N.Y.

Singer with smooth, high baritone voice similar to sound and style of legendary Russ Columbo. Successful career in 50s launched by 1950 hit record *It Isn't Fair* as vocalist with Sammy Kaye band. Early in career played guitar and sang in bands in New York area. Jobs in late 30s with Bobby Hayes, Al Kavelin, Red Nichols, Mickey Alpert, Michael Zarin, Lennie Hayton. With McFarland Twins band in 1941. Joined Sammy Kaye early 1942 as singer-guitarist. Military service, World War II. Rejoined Kaye in 1946, remained through 40s. After 1950 hit played night clubs and theatres, appeared on early TV. First records for Victor produced no hits. Switched to Coral Records late 1951, had more success with *I'm Yours, Hold My Hand, I'll Walk Alone, This Is the Beginning of the End*. By early 60s career waned.

RECORDS

BOBBY HAYES
Me 70309 Trust in Me
MCFARLAND TWINS
Bb 11449 When Day Is Done/Hey Zeke!
SAMMY KAYE
Vi 27972 If I Cared a Little Bit Less/ Taboo
Vi 20-2601 A Bed of Roses/Fool That I Am
Vi 20-3063 Here I'll Stay
Vi 20-3321 Careless Hands
Vi 20-3609 It Isn't Fair/My Lily and My Rose
DON CORNELL
Vi 20-3776 I Surrender Dear/You Dreamer You
Vi 20-3909 Au Revoir Again/A Whistle and a Prayer
Vi 20-3950 Take Me in Your Arms/ The Breeze
Vi 20-3991 Sue Me/Velvet Lips
Vi 20-4043 That Old Feeling/Was That the Human Thing to Do?
Vi 20-4044 When I Take My Sugar to Tea/I'll Be Seeing You
Cor 60690 I'm Yours/My Mother's Pearls
Cor 60748 This Is the Beginning of the End/I Can't Cry Anymore
Cor 60903 If You Were Only Mine/ S'posin'
Cor 61206 Hold My Hand/I'm Blessed
Cor 61253 No Man Is an Island/All at Once

LPs

DON CORNELL
Cor CRL-57055 Don
Dot DLP-3160 Don's Greatest Hits
SAMMY KAYE
"X" LX-1014 Featuring Don Cornell (RIs)

377. COSLOW, SAM   cm lyr vo

Born December 27, 1902, New York, N.Y.

Important composer-lyricist of 20s and 30s, many popular songs. Most famous: *Sing You Sinners, Was It a Dream?, Just One More Chance, Thanks, Moon Song, Learn to Croon, Cocktails for Two, My Old Flame*. Wrote lyrics for Broadway musical ARTISTS AND MODELS OF 1924, also wrote for many movies. Began songwriting after high school. Later partner in publishing firm Spier & Coslow. To Hollywood in 1929 to write songs for movies, continued during 30s. In 1933 collaborated with composer Arthur Johnston on excellent scores for Bing Crosby's first two starring movies COLLEGE HUMOR and TOO MUCH HARMONY. Made a few recordings as vocalist during 30s. In partnership with Col. James Roosevelt in 1940 founded "Soundies": song-movie shorts for coin machines. Movie producer in 40s. Chief collaborators Arthur Johnston, Harry Woods, Fred Hollander, Abner Silver. On many songs Coslow wrote music and lyrics. Left music, became successful publisher of investment services. Retired to Florida.

SONGS
(with related shows)

1920—It Might Have Been You
1923—Bebe
1926—Hello, Swanee, Hello
1928—Lonely Melody; Was It a Dream?
1929—THE DANCE OF LIFE movie (True Blue Lou; The Flippity Flop); You Want Lovin'; Daddy, Won't You Please Come Home?
1930—HONEY movie (Sing You Sinners; In My Little Hope Chest; I Don't Need Atmosphere); PARAMOUNT ON PARADE movie (Sweepin' the Clouds Away); THE VAGABOND KING movie (If I Were King)

1931—Just One More Chance; You Didn't Know the Music

1933—HELLO, EVERYBODY movie (Moon Song; Twenty Million People); COLLEGE HUMOR movie (Learn to Croon; Moonstruck; Down the Old Ox Road); TOO MUCH HARMONY movie (Thanks; The Day You Came Along; Black Moonlight; Bucking the Wind); I Guess It Had to Be That Way; This Little Piggie

1934—BELLE OF THE NINETIES movie (My Old Flame; When a St. Louis Woman Comes Down to New Orleans; Troubled Waters; My American Beauty); MURDER AT THE VANITIES movie (Cocktails for Two; Live and Love Tonight)

1935—ALL THE KING'S HORSES movie (A Little White Gardenia; Be Careful, Young Lady); CORONADO movie (How Do I Rate with You?; You Took My Breath Away); GOIN' TO TOWN movie (Now I'm a Lady); In the Middle of a Kiss

1936—RHYTHM ON THE RANGE movie (You'll Have to Swing It); IT'S LOVE AGAIN movie (I Nearly Let Love Go Slipping Through My Fingers; Gotta Dance My Way to Heaven; It's Love Again; Tony's in Town)

1937—MAKE WAY FOR TOMORROW movie (title song); DOUBLE OR NOTHING movie (After You; It's On, It's Off); SWING HIGH, SWING LOW movie (I Hear a Call to Arms); A HUNDRED MEN AND A GIRL movie (It's Raining Sunbeams); MOUNTAIN MUSIC movie (Good Mornin'; If I Put My Heart in a Song); TURN OFF THE MOON movie (Turn Off the Moon; Jammin'; Easy on the Eyes; That's Southern Hospitality); THIS WAY PLEASE movie (Love or Infatuation?); TRUE CONFESSION movie (title song); LOVE ON TOAST movie (I Want a New Romance; I'd Like to Play a Love Scene); Tea on the Terrace

1938—EVERY DAY'S A HOLIDAY movie (title song); THRILL OF A LIFETIME movie (title song); ST. LOUIS BLUES movie (Kinda Lonesome); YOU AND ME movie (The Right Guy for Me); Beside a Moonlit Stream; Have You Forgotten So Soon?

1939—At a Little Hot Dog Stand; An Old Curiosity Shop; I'm in Love with the Honorable Mr. So and So; A New Moon and an Old Serenade; A Table in a Corner; Tomorrow Night

1940—DREAMING OUT LOUD movie (title song); Make-Believe Island; Last Night's Gardenias

1947—COPACABANA movie (most of score, including Je Vous Aime); CARNEGIE HALL movie (Beware, My Heart)

1950—SUMMER STOCK movie (Heavenly Music)

1953—AFFAIR WITH A STRANGER movie (title song)

RECORDS
(as vocalist)

SAM COSLOW

Vo 25001 Learn to Croon/Moonstruck

Vo 25002 Down the Old Ox Road/ Where Have I Heard That Melody?

Vi 21631 You're a Real Sweetheart/ King for a Day

Vi 24143 Say It Isn't So/Give Her a Kiss

Vi 24144 Here Lies Love/Please

Vi 24386 Learn to Croon/Moonstruck

(with THE HIGH HATTERS ORCHESTRA)

Vi 21682 I Wanna Be Loved by You/ Some Sweet Someone

(with GERALDO ORCHESTRA)

De(E) 5806 The Morning After/Some Other Time

378. COSTA, EDDIE vb p o B

Born August 14, 1930, Atlas, Pa.
Died July 28, 1962, New York, N.Y., in auto crash

Swinging vibes star; modern jazz style with traditional roots. Active in 50s with leading modern jazzmen. Brother Bill taught him piano at early age. At 17 with Frank Victor Trio in Pennsylvania for two years. He and Victor joined Joe Venuti in Chicago for several months. Then in brother Bill's combo in New York. Military service 1951-2. After discharge concentrated on vibes, made a name. With Sal Salvador, Johnny Smith, Kai Winding, Don Elliott, Tal Farlow. In late 50s led group at intervals. With Woody Herman off and on during 1958-9. Freelance and studio work. Tragic death at 31 cut short a most promising career.

RECORDS
(all LPs)

EDDIE COSTA
Cor CRL-57230 GUYS AND DOLLS Like Vibes
(one side) Verve MGV-8237 At Newport
Mode 118 Eddie Costa Quintet
EDDIE COSTA-VINNIE BURKE
Jub JGM-1025 The Eddie Costa-Vinnie Burke Trio
THE FIRST MODERN PIANO QUARTET
Cor CRL-59102 A Gallery of Gershwin
MANHATTAN JAZZ SEPTETTE
Cor CRL-57090
CHUCK WAYNE
Vik LX-1098 String Fever
SAL SALVADOR
Beth BCP-74 A Tribute to the Greats
MUNDELL LOWE
Cam CAL-522 TV Action Jazz!
Cam CAL-627 Themes from TV Action Shows
FRANK SOCOLOW
Beth BCP-70 Sounds by Socolow
WOODY HERMAN SEXTET
Forum 9016 At the Roundtable
AARON BELL
Lion 70113 "Victory at Sea" in Jazz
BILLY VER PLANCK
Sav MG-12121 Jazz for Play Girls
TUBBY HAYES
Epic LA-16023 Tubby the Tenor
SHELLY MANNE
Impulse A-20 Two, Three, Four

379. COTTON, BILLY   d vo B

Born 1899, Westminster, England
Died March 25, 1969

Leading English bandleader. Long career from early 20s through 60s. Consistently good band capable of playing sweet or semi-hot, but known more for novelty numbers and showmanship. Cotton began career as teenage drummer in British army. First band in early 20s, a few years later played top London spots such as Astoria Ballroom and Ciro's. Began radio broadcasts in 1931, active on radio through the years. Band had crisp, full ensemble sound, versatile. Stressed showmanship and entertainment, carried several singers capable of handling ballads but particularly good on novelties. Cotten large, plump man, ideal front for band with singing, dancing, talking, wisecracking. Band maintained popularity till Cotton's death.

RECORDS

BILLY COTTON
OK 41576 Man from Harlem/I Can't Dance
OK 41578 The Tattooed Lady (1 & 2)
OK 41588 Rhythm Mad
Co 2649-D Oh, Monah
Co 3039-D Spring Doesn't Mean a Thing
ReZono(E) 1458 Two Cigarettes in the Dark/I Saw Stars
ReZono(E) 1812 I'll Never Say "Never Again" Again/Ev'ry Single Little Tingle of My Heart
ReZono(Aus) 22134 Little Man, You've Had a Busy Day/The Show Is Over
Lon(E) 462 Rolling 'Round the World/Hang on the Bell, Nellie
Lon(E) 643 The French Can-Can Polka/Oh Nicholas! Don't Be So Ridiculous
Lon(E) 704 Rain/My Thanks to You
Lon(E) 1025 The Music Man/The Chicken Song
Lon(E) 1313 Coronation Bells March/In a Golden Coach

LPs

BILLY COTTON
Philips(E) SBL-7730 Band Show
WRC(E) SH-141 Billy Cotton & His Band (1930-6 RIs)

380. COTTON, LARRY   vo

Band vocalist of 30s and early 40s, tenor noted mostly for period with Horace Heidt. Began career in early 30s. After several years with Jimmie Grier, joined Heidt in late 30s, featured prominently. Appeared with Heidt on popular Pot o' Gold radio show 1938-41 and in 1941 movie of same title. Military service, World War II.

RECORDS

JIMMIE GRIER
Br 7381 I'm Keeping Those Keepsakes You Gave Me
HORACE HEIDT
Br 8021 There's a Gold Mine in the Sky
Br 8148 I'll Still Be Loving You
Br 8329 The Masquerade Is Over
Br 8334 Don't Worry 'Bout Me
Br 8382 This Is No Dream/Wishing
Br 8414 Let's Make Memories Tonight
Br 8430 If I Were Sure of You/The Man with the Mandolin
Br 8441 Over the Rainbow/Address Unknown
Co 35213 Goodnight, My Beautiful/ Our First Kiss

381. COUNCE, CURTIS   b B

Born January 23, 1926, Kansas City, Mo.
Died July 31, 1963, Los Angeles, Calif.

Bass man active on west coast, mostly in modern groups. Also combo leader. As youngster with Nat Towles 1941-4. Settled on west coast, with Edgar Hayes several years. Later with Wardell Gray, Billy Eckstine, Benny Carter, Bud Powell. By mid-50s busy freelance. Stints with Shorty Rogers, Buddy DeFranco, Stan Kenton. In late 50s led groups at intervals, continued to freelance. Active in early 60s until death from heart attack.

RECORDS

HERB GELLER
EmArcy 16016 Sleigh Ride/Silver Rain
CLAUDE WILLIAMSON
Cap 7-65003 All God's Chillun Got Rhythm/Woodyn' You
BILL HOLMAN
Cap 7-65000 Plain Folks/Cousin Jack
JOHNNY OTIS
Excel 141 Preston Love's Mansion/My Baby's Business
Excel 142 Jimmy's 'Round the Clock Blues/Harlem Nocturne

ILLINOIS JACQUET
Clef 89164 Learnin' the Blues/Honeysuckle Rose

LPs

CURTIS COUNCE
Contemp C-3526 The Curtis Counce Group
SHORTY ROGERS
Vi LJM-1004 Shorty Rogers Courts the Count
CLIFFORD BROWN
EmArcy MG-36102 Clifford Brown All-Stars
CHET BAKER-ART PEPPER
WP PJ-1234 Playboys
LEONARD FEATHER'S STARS
MGM E-3390 West Coast vs. East Coast
LESTER YOUNG
Score SLP-4028 Swinging Lester Young
(miscellaneous artists)
EmArcy MG-36039 Best Coast Jazz
PJ 18 Picture of Heath
HERB GELLER
EmArcy(10")MG-26045 Herb Geller Plays
TEDDY CHARLES
Pres(10")164
Pres(10")169

382. COURTNEY, ALAN   cm

Born November 29, 1912, New York, N.Y.

Radio disc jockey in 30s and 40s, TV host later in career. Began on radio 1930. Disc jockey on stations WOR in Newark, WOV in New York. Later dubbed 1280 Club; chief rival to Martin Block's Make Believe Ballroom early 40s. Beginning late 40s pioneered radio talk show and call-in format. Composed novelty *Joltin' Joe DiMaggio*, Les Brown 1941 hit. Other compositions *Hereafter*; *Shhh, It's a Military Secret*; *Smile for Me*. Collaborated with Lanny Grey, John Jacob Loeb, Walter Bishop. Later in career settled in Miami. Still active there on radio and TV in 60s and 70s.

383. COURTNEY, DEL   B

Born 1910, Oakland, Calif.

Leader of popular hotel band in 30s and 40s. Featured a combination of sweet styles with lightweight arrangements. Theme *Three Shades of Blue*. Attended St. Mary's College, had first band there. Later graduated from University of California in 1933. Formed band after college, played Oakland and Seattle in mid-30s. By late 30s playing top hotels such as New York's Ambassador and New Yorker, Edgewater Beach in Chicago, Roosevelt in New Orleans, Cocoanut Grove in Los Angeles, Royal Hawaiian in Honolulu. Also played Harrah's Club at Lake Tahoe. In 40s band faded. In early 50s still active, led band at west coast spots and on west coast TV. Later less active as bandleader. In 60s appeared on some King Family TV shows. Produced halftime shows for Oakland Raiders football team in 70s.

RECORDS
DEL COURTNEY
    Vo 4850 This Is No Dream/I'm in Love with the Honorable Mr. So and So
    Vo 4864 The Lamp Is Low/Somebody Told Me They Loved Me
    Vo 4992 Over the Rainbow/How Lovely You Are
    Vo 5046 Put That Down in Writing/To You, Sweetheart, Aloha
    Vo 5061 An Angel in a Furnished Room/A Table in a Corner
    Vo 5212 I Hear a Dream/It's a Hap-Hap-Happy Day
    Vo 5279 Blue Rain/Out of Space
    Vo 5291 When Love Beckoned/It Was Written in the Stars
    Vo 5306 At the Balalaika/In Our Little Part of Town
    Vo 5332 Oh, What a Lovely Dream/My Rosary of Broken Dreams
    Vo 5354 The Singing Hills/Hawaiian War Chant
    Vo 5608 All This and Heaven Too/You Think of Ev'rything
    OK 5720 Now I Lay Me Down to Dream/Basket Weaver
    Dot 15106 Blue Mist (1 & 2)
    Radiotone 25313-4 I'm Terribly Lonesome without You/Just a Bundle of Dreams

LPs
DEL COURTNEY
    Cap T-1070 Dancing 'Till Daybreak

384. COVINGTON, WARREN
tb ar cm vo B

Born August 7, 1921, Philadelphia, Pa.

Trombonist active in bands and studios in 40s and 50s; reached fame in late 50s as leader of the Tommy Dorsey Orchestra after Dorsey's death. Early in career worked with Isham Jones in 1939, in early 40s with Mitchell Ayres and Horace Heidt. Military service, World War II. After discharge with Les Brown, Gene Krupa and Boyd Raeburn. From late 1946 until 1956 CBS staff musician in New York. In 1957 led The Commanders, studio band formed by Toots Camarata and led awhile by Eddie Grady. In early 1958 Covington took over as leader of Tommy Dorsey orchestra, continued on and off into 70s, perpetuated TD's style and hits. Covington handled Tommy's trombone solos well. Also led band under own name. During career also did vocal-arranging-composing work. Toured England 1974 featuring Dorsey arrangements, ex-Dorsey sidemen Sy Oliver, Skeets Herfurt, Johnny Mince, Pee Wee Erwin, trumpeter Chris Griffin, Bernie Privin.

RECORDS
(all LPs)

WARREN COVINGTON—THE COMMANDERS
    De DL-8408 Shall We Dance?
WARREN COVINGTON and THE TOMMY DORSEY ORCHESTRA
    De DL-4120 Dance to the Songs Everybody Knows
    De DL-8802 The Fabulous Arrangements of Tommy Dorsey in Hi-Fi
    De DL-8904 Dance and Romance
    De DL-8914 The Swingin' Era
    De DL-8996 It Takes Two to ...
WARREN COVINGTON
    Vo 73810
    Recar RCS-2038(S) Plays Hits of the 60s, Vol. 2

385. COWARD, NOEL
cm lyr vo p

Born December 16, 1899, Teddington, near London, England
Died March 26, 1973, Jamaica, West Indies

Glittering English performer-songwriter-playwright, prodigiously productive. Probably England's greatest songwriter, his songs well received in U.S. as well. Excellent stage and screen performer in musicals or drama. Suave, sophisticated, witty writer, tuneful melodist. Most popular songs: *I'll See You Again, Zigeuner, I'll Follow My Secret Heart, Mad About the Boy, Someday I'll Find You.* At early age joined stage troupe, toured England. Military service, World War I. After discharge again on stage in song and dance roles as well as dramatic. Began writing scores and books for English productions. First hit HAY FEVER in London in 1924. First U.S. hit play THE VORTEX in 1925, in which he starred. Later same year plays HAY FEVER and EASY VIRTUE ran in U.S., followed by THE MARQUISE in 1927. First Broadway musicals well received: THIS YEAR OF GRACE (1928; Coward performed) and BITTER SWEET (1929). Starred in own plays PRIVATE LIVES (1931) and DESIGN FOR LIVING (1933). Show CONVERSATION PIECE (1934) popular but POINT VALAINE (1935) flopped. Co-starred with Gertrude Lawrence in series of short plays, TONIGHT AT 8:30 (1936). Other Coward plays: BLITHE SPIRIT (1941), QUADRILLE (1954), FALLEN ANGELS (1956), NUDE WITH VIOLIN (1957; Coward starred). Other musicals: SET TO MUSIC (1939), SAIL AWAY (1961), THE GIRL WHO CAME TO SUPPER (1963). Great Broadway team of Alfred Lunt and Lynn Fontanne starred in several Coward plays. Musicals written first for London, usually but not always followed in U.S. Appeared in U.S. movies THE SCOUNDREL (1935), THE ASTONISHED HEART (1950), OUR MAN IN HAVANA and SURPRISE PACKAGE (1960), PARIS WHEN IT SIZZLES (1964), BUNNY LAKE IS MISSING (1965), BOOM! (1968), THE ITALIAN JOB (1969). Played in and directed 1942 British award-winning film IN WHICH WE SERVE. Several of his plays made into movies, including CAVALCADE, PRIVATE LIVES, DESIGN FOR LIVING, BLITHE SPIRIT, THE HAPPY BREED, BRIEF ENCOUNTER. Coward's protean talents spanned half a century. His best music captured brilliantly in 1972-3 New York revue OH, COWARD!.

SONGS
(with related shows)
1924—ANDRE CHARLOT REVUE OF 1924

stage show (Parisian Pierrot; There's Life in the Old Girl Yet)
1925—ANDRE CHARLOT REVUE OF 1925 stage show (Poor Little Rich Girl; The Roses Have Made Me Remember; The Girls I Am Leaving in England Today)
1928—THIS YEAR OF GRACE stage show (A Room with a View; Dance, Little Lady; World Weary; This Year of Grace)
1929—BITTER SWEET stage show (I'll See You Again; Zigeuner; If Love Were All; Tokay)
1930—Someday I'll Find You (interpolated in English play PRIVATE LIVES)
1931—THE THIRD LITTLE SHOW stage show (Mad Dogs and Englishmen); ZIEGFELD FOLLIES OF 1931 stage show (Half Caste Woman)
1932—Mad About the Boy
1933—CAVALCADE movie (Twentieth Century Blues)
1934—CONVERSATION PIECE stage show (I'll Follow My Secret Heart; Nevermore)
1936—TONIGHT AT 8:30 stage show (You Were There)
1939—SET TO MUSIC stage show (Weary of It All; Never Again; I've Been to a Marvelous Party; The Stately Homes of England; The Party's Over Now)
1940—BITTER SWEET movie (original stage score)
1961—SAIL AWAY stage show (Sail Away; Later Than Spring; Go Slow, Johnny; Something Very Strange; Where Shall I Find Him?; others)
1963—THE GIRL WHO CAME TO SUPPER stage show (I've Been Invited to a Party; Lonely; This Time It's True Love; I'll Remember Her; Here and Now; My Family Tree; Soliloquies; others)

Other compositions include *Any Little Fish, London Pride, Matelot, Nina, Lover of My Dreams*

RECORDS
NOEL COWARD
  Vi 22819 Any Little Fish/Half Caste Woman
  Vi 24332 Mad Dogs and Englishmen/

Lover of My Dreams
Vi 24772 World Weary/Zigeuner
Vi 25079 The Party's Over Now/Let's Say Goodbye
Vi 25230 We Were So Young/Mrs. Worthington
Vi 25439 We Were Dancing/Parisian Pierrot
Vi 27228 I'll See You Again/Dearest Love
HMV(E) 2719 A Room with a View/Mary Make Believe
HMV(E) 9198 The Last Time I Saw Paris/London Pride
HMV(E) 9210 It's Only You/Imagine the Duchess' Feelings
HMV(E) 9433 Sigh No More/What Happened to Him
HMV(E) 9434 Matelot/Nina

NOEL COWARD with NEW MAYFAIR ORCHESTRA
HMV(E)(12")2289 CAVALCADE, 1 & 2 (songs of 1899-1910 and 1912-30)

LPs

NOEL COWARD
Co ML-5063 At Las Vegas
NOEL COWARD and GERTRUDE LAWRENCE
Mon Ever MES7042 We Were Dancing
THE NOEL COWARD ALBUM
Co MG 30088 (1-LP set; RIs)

386. COX, IDA   vo

Born in 1889, Cedartown, Ga.
Died November 10, 1967, Knoxville, Tenn.

Leading blues singer with extensive recording career in 20s. At 14 sang in minstrel shows in south. Began recording in 1923 for Paramount, clicked. Often accompanied by Lovie Austin & Her Blues Serenaders. Married to pianist Jesse Crump, often worked with him on records and jobs. Star of Negro vaudeville and tent shows of southwest and midwest into early 30s. Retired from music for several years, brief comeback in New York in 1939 for club, concert and record work. Settled in Knoxville, again in obscurity. Brought back in 1961 to record.

RECORDS

IDA COX
Para 12044 Graveyard Dream Blues/Weary Way Blues

Para 12045 Bama Bound Blues/Love Is the Thing I'm Wild About
Para 12063 Chattanooga Blues/I've Got the Blues for Rampart Street
Para 12212 Last Time Blues/Blues Ain't Nothin' Else But!
Para 12220 Death Letter Blues/My Mean Man Blues
Para 12251 Graveyard Bound Blues/Mississippi River Blues
Para 12282 Cold Black Ground Blues/Someday Blues
Para 12291 Black Crepe Blues/Fare Thee Well Poor Gal
Para 12298 Mistreatin' Daddy Blues/Southern Woman's Blues
Para 12307 Long Distance Blues/Lonesome Blues
Para 12318 Coffin Blues/Rambling Blues
Para 12344 Trouble Trouble Blues/I'm Leaving Here Blues
Para 12353 Do Lawd Do/Night and Day Blues
Para 12488 'Fore Day Creep/Gypsy Glass Blues
Para 12513 Lost Man Blues/Pleading Blues
Para 12582 Midnight Hour Blues/Give Me a Break Blues
Para 12727 Separated Blues/Sobbin' Tears Blues
Para 12965 I'm So Glad/Jailhouse Blues
Vo 05258 Take Him Off My Mind/Pink Slip Blues
Vo 05336 Deep Sea Blues/Death Letter Blues
OK 6405 Last Mile Blues/I Can't Quit That Man

LPs

IDA COX
Riv RLP-147 The Moanin', Groanin' Blues (Para RIs)
Riv RLP-374 Blues for Rampart Street
Riv(10")RLP-1019 (Para RIs)

387. CRAIG, FRANCIS   p ar cm lyr B

Born September 10, 1900, Dickson, Tenn.

Prominent bandleader in Nashville for years, rose to fame in late 40s with two record hits *Near You* and *Beg Your Pardon*. As pianist played simple, rhythmic style with emphasis on melody. Attended Vanderbilt. Military service, World War I. Began leading band in mid-20s, mostly based in Nashville and popular there. One main spot: The Hermitage. Radio broadcasts starting in late 20s. Irene Beasley and James Melton sang with band in late 20s; Kenny Sargent replaced Melton. Phil Harris played drums in band. Craig become nationally prominent in 1947 with record hit *Near You*, followed in 1948 with sequel *Beg Your Pardon*. Both featured Craig's piano in distinctive lilting style, inspired imitators. Craig co-composer of both songs. Sudden popularity brought on brief flurry of recordings. Continued in Nashville long after his short day in the sun. Active in 50s and 60s. Other compositions include *Red Rose* (theme), *Tennessee Tango, A Broken Heart Must Cry, Foolin', Do Me a Favor, Play Them Bones.*

RECORDS
FRANCIS CRAIG
>Co 495-D Forgiveness/Mighty Lak' a Rose
>Co 567-D Marble Halls/Steady Roll Blues
>Co 649-D Ting-a-ling/In the Middle of the Night
>Co 709-D Hard-to-Get Gertie/Believe
>Co 1266-D That Florida Low-Down/Moonlight in Mandalay
>Co 1440-D All Day Long/Dream River
>Co 1544-D Red Rose/Coon-Tail
>Bullet 1001 Near You/Red Rose
>Bullet 1012 Beg Your Pardon/Looking for a Sweetheart
>Bullet 1013 Foolin'/Do Me a Favor
>Bullet 1040 I Still Get a Thrill/Disillusioned
>MGM 10378 Tennessee Tango/I Thought I Was Dreaming
>MGM 10468 Away from You/Forgiveness
>MGM 10558 The Whole Year 'Round/My Tears Are Still Falling for You
>De 27937 For the First Time/Play Them Bones
>De 28089 Near You/Stars and Stripes Medley

388. CRAWFORD, CLIFTON
vo cm lyr

Early star of Broadway musical comedies. Wrote hit *Nancy Brown* for 1902 show THE WILD ROSE. Collaborated on book and lyrics for SEEING NEW YORK (1906) and on music for MY BEST GIRL (1912).

BROADWAY MUSICALS
1902—FOXY GRANDPA
1903—THE JEWEL OF ASIA; MOTHER GOOSE
1906—SEEING NEW YORK
1908—THREE TWINS
1911—THE QUAKER GIRL
1912—MY BEST GIRL
1915—NED WAYBURN'S TOWN TOPICS; THE PEASANT GIRL; A WORLD OF PLEASURE
1916—HER SOLDIER BOY
1918—FANCY FREE
1919—MY LADY FRIENDS (non-musical)

389. CRAWFORD, JAMES
d B
Born January 14, 1910, Memphis, Tenn.

Drummer with Jimmie Lunceford band through its greatest years. Important feature of band was lightly swinging beat and Crawford a stalwart in providing it. Attended LeMoyne College. Worked with Lunceford band first in summer of 1928, then regularly in 1929. Left in 1943—the only big band he had ever played with. With Ben Webster combo in 1943. Military service 1943-5. In late 1945-9 mostly with Ed Hall combo in New York and Boston. Freelanced in New York, many jobs at Cafe Society. Led group at times in later years. In late 40s began unusual phase for jazz musician—playing Broadway musicals in pit bands. Played for many in next two decades. Toured in 1958 with show JAMAICA. With Tyree Glenn in 1969. Active into 70s.

RECORDS
JIMMIE LUNCEFORD
>Vi 38141 In Dat Mornin'/Sweet Rhythm
>Vi 24522 Jazznocracy/Chillun, Get Up
>Vi 24568 White Heat/Leaving Me
>De 131 Rose Room/Mood Indigo
>De 299 Stratosphere/Solitude
>De 415 Rain/Because You're You
>De 682 I'm Walking Through Heaven

with You/I'm Nuts About Screwy Music
De 765 Dream of You/Hittin' the Bottle
De 915 Me and the Moon/On the Beach at Bali Bali
De 980 Harlem Shout/I Can't Escape from You
De 1035 My Last Affair/Running a Temperature
De 1229 Honest and Truly/Linger Awhile
De 1617 Margie/Like a Ship at Sea
De 1808 By the River Sainte Marie/My Melancholy Baby
Vo 4831 Mandy/The Lonesome Road
Vo 4875 What Is This Thing Called Swing?/Ain't She Sweet?
Vo 4979 I Love You/Oh Why, Oh Why
Vo 5326 Wham/Lunceford Special
Co 35700 Pavanne / Minnie the Moocher Is Dead
De 18534 You're Always in My Dreams/Easy Street

MILDRED BAILEY
Maj 1101 At Sundown/Lover, Come Back to Me

HARRY CARNEY
HRS 1020 Minor Mirage/Candy Cane
HRS 1021 Jamaica Rumble/Shadowy Sands

MEZZ MEZZROW
Vi 25612 Hot Club Stomp/The Swing Session's Called to Order
Vi 25636 Blues in Disguise/That's How I Feel Today

DICKY WELLS
HRS 1018 Drag Nasty/Opera in Blue

TRUMMY YOUNG
Cos 901 Rattle and Roll/Behind the Eight Bar

LPs

JIMMIE LUNCEFORD
Co CL-2715 Lunceford Special (Co, Vo RIs)
De DL-8050 Jimmie Lunceford and His Band (De RIs)
De DL-9238 Harlem Shout (De RIs)
"X"(10")LX-3002 (Vi RIs)

FLETCHER HENDERSON ALL-STARS
Jazztone J-1285 The Big Reunion

GEORGE WILLIAMS
Vi LPM-1301 A Salute to Jimmie Lunceford
DON REDMAN
Roul R-25070 Dixieland in High Society
ANDY GIBSON
Cam CAL-554 Mainstream Jazz
LOU STEIN
Epic LG-3101 House Hop

390. CRAWFORD, JESSE o p cm B
Born December 2, 1895, Woodland, Calif.
Died May 28, 1962, Sherman Oaks, Calif.

Most famous of organists, very popular in 20s and 30s. Reached peak about 1928-31 when records played frequently on radio. Most popular record probably *At Dawning/Roses of Picardy*. Began career around 1908, toured as pianist with dance band in northwest. First organ job at Gem Theatre, Spokane, 1911. Other theatres followed. First organ soloist at Grauman's Theatre in Los Angeles in 1918. Worked in Chicago in early 20s. Got coveted organist job at New York's Paramount Theatre, during 1926-33 entertained crowds nightly, sometimes with talented wife Helen at twin organ console. Toured English theatres. Later in U.S. turned more to concert and radio work, provided background music for dramas on NBC and CBS. Led sweet-styled dance orchestra 1937-8, featured self and wife on twin electric organs. Recording output through the years extensive. Active in 40s and 50s on radio and records. Wrote instruction books on organ. Compositions include *Starlight Rendezvous, Harlem Holiday, Louisiana Nocturne, Mood Tragic, Vienna Violins, March of the Matadors, The Swiss Doll, Lonely, Hawaiian Honeymoon.*

RECORDS

JESSE CRAWFORD
Vi 19906 Remember/Sleepy Time Gal
Vi 20110 At Dawning/Roses of Picardy
Vi 20560 Song of the Wanderer/What Does It Matter?

Vi 20791 At Sundown/Russian Lullaby

Vi 20838 When Day Is Done/Dawn of Tomorrow

Vi 21171 Mary/Dancing Tambourine

Vi 21850 I'll Get By/How About Me?

Vi 21933 Carolina Moon/A Precious Little Thing Called Love

Vi 22066 My Sin/Singin' in the Rain

Vi 22129 How Am I to Know?/Miss You

Vi 22242 Chant of the Jungle/Tiptoe Through the Tulips with Me

Vi 22333 Gypsy Love Song/Ah! Sweet Mystery of Life

Vi 22394 Stein Song/Song of the Islands

Vi 22413 It Happened in Monterey/Moonlight Reminds Me of You

Vi 22510 When the Organ Played at Twilight/The Kiss Waltz

Vi 24035 Masquerade/I'd Love to Be Loved

Vi 24329 L'Amour Toujours L'Amour/Song of Songs

Vi 24450 My Beautiful Lady/Auf Wiedersehen, My Dear

De 178 Toselli's Serenade/Kiss Me Again

De 3923 When the Organ Played at Twilight/The Perfect Song

De 3924 When Day Is Done/Goin' Home

De 27905 Jalousie/I'll See You in My Dreams

De 28234 Kiss of Fire/I'm Yours

JESSE CRAWFORD & HIS ORCHESTRA

Bb 7105 Dancing Under the Stars/Me, Myself and I

Bb 7107 It's the Natural Thing to Do/After You

Bb 7117 On with the Dance/Love Is on the Air Tonight

LPs

JESSE CRAWFORD

De DL-8071 The Waltzes of Irving Berlin

De DL-8300 When the Organ Played at Twilight

De DL-8565 Poet at the Pipe Organ

De DL-8649 An Enchanted Evening (Richard Rodgers Melodies)

De DL-8758 Pops by the Poet

De DL-8790 The Melodies of Jimmy McHugh

391. CREAMER, HENRY   lyr cm vo
Born June 21, 1879, Richmond, Va.
Died October 14, 1930, New York, N.Y.

Writer of several all-time song hits. Usually collaborated as lyricist with composer Turner Layton. Most famous songs: *That's a-Plenty* (1909), *After You've Gone* (1918), *Dear Old Southland* (1921), *'Way Down Yonder in New Orleans* (1922), *If I Could Be with You* (1930). Worked for Gotham-Attucks Music Company in New York. Played vaudeville in U.S. and Europe; sang, danced, clowned, usually with pianist Layton. Wrote material for minor Broadway shows including THREE SHOWERS (1920), STRUT MISS LIZZIE (1922), KEEP SHUFFLIN' (1928). Other compositions: *Go 'Long Mule*; *Alabama Stomp*; *Sweet Emalina, My Gal*; *Everybody's Gone Crazy 'Bout the Doggone Blues*; *Strut Miss Lizzie*; *Whoa, Tillie, Take Your Time*; *Down by the River*; *Jersey Walk*; *I Need Lovin'*; *Goodbye, Alexander, My Honey*.

392. CRISS, SONNY   as B
(WILLIAM CRISS)
Born October 23, 1927, Memphis, Tenn.

Alto sax star in modern idiom; early influence in bop style of late 40s. Facile, clean-cut swinging style somewhat along Charlie Parker lines. Moved to Los Angeles in 1942, graduated from high school there. In late 40s active in bop on west coast. With Johnny Otis, Al Killian, Howard McGhee, Gerald Wilson. Toured with Jazz at the Philharmonic show. With Billy Eckstine in early 50s. Freelanced on west coast in later 50s, worked with Buddy Rich, led own band. In 60s spells of obscurity, came back with series of LPs, became more active, remained so in early 70s.

RECORDS

FLIP PHILLIPS

Mer 8929 Swingin' for Julie and Brownie

SONNY CRISS

Bop 104 The Hunt (pt. 2)

Bop 108 Bopera (pt. 4)

Mer 8910 The First One/Calidad
Mer 8915 Blues for the Boppers/Tornado

LPs

SONNY CRISS
Pres 7511 This Is Criss!
Pres 7526 Portrait of Sonny Criss
Pres 7530 Up, Up and Away
Pres 7576 Sonny's Dream
Pres 7628 I'll Catch the Sun
Imp 9006
Imp 9020
WARDELL GRAY
Pres 7343 (2-LP set) Memorial Album (RIs)
Pres(10")PRLP-128
SONNY CRISS-TOMMY TURK
Clef(10")122
(miscellaneous artists)
Cr 284 Groovin' High

393. CROSBY, BING   vo cm lyr
(HARRY LILLIS CROSBY)

Born May 2, 1901 or 1904, Tacoma, Wash.

One of the greatest of entertainers, beloved figure in show business with long, fabulous career. Epic popularity as singer and actor in major media. Singing sensation of early 30s, his husky, virile voice contrasted with soft-voiced style previously dominant. Jazz-influenced, especially by Louis Armstrong and Bix Beiderbecke. Often sang in up tempo with offbeat style, sometimes whistled a few bars. Records through the years sold multi-millions. Perennial favorite *White Christmas* an all-time best seller.

Grew up in Spokane. Attended Gonzaga University briefly, there teamed with Al Rinker as novelty singing duo. They worked their way to Los Angeles, were heard by Paul Whiteman and hired for band late 1926. Duo joined by Harry Barris to form trio called The Rhythm Boys, became top attraction with band. Bing also soloed. Trio and Bing appeared on dozens of records with Whiteman in late 20s. After 1930 movie KING OF JAZZ, Rhythm Boys and Whiteman parted. Later in year trio with Gus Arnheim at Cocoanut Grove in Los Angeles. Bing's solos attracted attention which prompted

him to launch career as a single. By early 1931 his fifteen-minute shows several nights a week for Cremo Cigars were a sensation. Theme: *Where the Blue of the Night*.

Began to record frequently, later in 1931 made movie shorts. Radio shows grew to thirty minutes, then sixty minutes, became weekly programs with varying formats. In late 1932 featured in movie THE BIG BROADCAST OF 1932. In 1933 first starring movie COLLEGE HUMOR great success, launched parade of outstanding musicals over next quarter century. Every movie featured excellent songs by top composers. James Monaco and Johnny Burke contributed heavily 1938-40, with Jimmy Van Heusen and Johnny Burke taking over for many years thereafter.

In late 30s style changed from romantic, emotional crooning to light, airy style, with songs and arrangements to match. Arrangements of John Scott Trotter (musical director on radio and records) and songs of Burke-Van Heusen captured new mood well. Other notable scores on movies GOING HOLLYWOOD (1933; by Nacio Herb Brown and Arthur Freed), MISSISSIPPI (1935; by Richard Rodgers and Lorenz Hart), HOLIDAY INN (1942; by Irving Berlin—blockbuster score including *White Christmas*, charming film, one of Bing's best).

In January 1936 Bing became permanent host of Kraft Music Hall on radio, remained well into 40s. In mid-40s pioneered in use of taped rather than live broadcasts. Bing and comedian Bob Hope carried on good-natured feud through the years, co-starred with Dorothy Lamour in 1940 movie THE ROAD TO SINGAPORE, which launched series of popular "ROAD" pictures.

After early classic Brunswick records, Bing recorded mostly for Decca. Hits included *Pistol Packin' Mama* and *Don't Fence Me In* with Andrews Sisters; *Sweet Leilani, Now Is the Hour, Too-Ra-Loo-Ra-Loo-Ral, I'll Be Home for Christmas, Galway Bay, Swinging on a Star, New San Antonio Rose, Dear Hearts and Gentle People*; and *Play a Simple Melody* with son Gary. Bing introduced scores of excellent songs in movies and made hit records of them, including *Please, Learn to Croon, Temptation, Thanks, The Day You Came Along, May I?, Love Thy Neighbor, Love in Bloom, June in January, With Every Breath I Take, Love Is Just Around the Corner, Soon, It's Easy to Remember, Without a Word of Warning, I'm an Old Cowhand, Pennies from Heaven, Sweet Leilani, Blue Hawaii, Small Fry, I've Got a Pocketful of Dreams, Moonlight Becomes You, Swinging on a Star, But Beautiful, White Christmas.*

Academy Award for acting in 1944 movie GOING MY WAY. Later outstanding performances in movies LITTLE BOY LOST (1953), COUNTRY GIRL (1954), MAN ON FIRE (1957). Four sons from first marriage to singer-actress Dixie Lee active in show business, sometimes worked as quartet; Gary most successful as single. After wife's death Bing married actress Kathryn Grant and raised another family.

Few appearances on early TV. In late 50s some excellent specials. Own non-musical TV show in 1964-5. In following years frequent M.C. of the Hollywood Palace, also guest appearances on various TV shows. In these years, activities slowed. Credited as composer or lyricist of noteworthy songs including *From Monday On* (1928), *At Your Command* and *Where the Blue of the Night* (1931), *Waltzing in a Dream* (1932), *A Ghost of a Chance* (1933).

MOVIES

1930—KING OF JAZZ
1932—THE BIG BROADCAST OF 1932
1933—COLLEGE HUMOR; TOO MUCH HARMONY; GOING HOLLYWOOD
1934—WE'RE NOT DRESSING; SHE LOVES ME NOT
1935—HERE IS MY HEART; MISSISSIPPI; TWO FOR TONIGHT; THE BIG BROADCAST OF 1936
1936—ANYTHING GOES; RHYTHM ON THE RANGE; PENNIES FROM HEAVEN
1937—WAIKIKI WEDDING; DOUBLE OR NOTHING
1938—DOCTOR RHYTHM; SING YOU SINNERS
1939—EAST SIDE OF HEAVEN; PARIS HONEYMOON; THE STAR MAKER
1940—THE ROAD TO SINGAPORE; RHYTHM

ON THE RIVER; IF I HAD MY WAY
1941—THE ROAD TO ZANZIBAR; BIRTH OF THE BLUES
1942—THE ROAD TO MOROCCO; STAR SPANGLED RHYTHM; HOLIDAY INN
1943—DIXIE
1944—GOING MY WAY; HERE COME THE WAVES
1945—DUFFY'S TAVERN; OUT OF THIS WORLD (singing voice only); BELLS OF ST. MARY'S
1946—THE ROAD TO UTOPIA; BLUE SKIES
1947—WELCOME STRANGER; THE ROAD TO RIO; VARIETY GIRL
1948—THE EMPEROR WALTZ
1949—A CONNECTICUT YANKEE IN KING ARTHUR'S COURT; TOP O' THE MORNING; ADVENTURES OF ICHABOD AND MR. TOAD (narration)
1950—RIDING HIGH; MISTER MUSIC
1951—HERE COMES THE GROOM
1952—JUST FOR YOU; THE ROAD TO BALI
1953—LITTLE BOY LOST
1954—WHITE CHRISTMAS; COUNTRY GIRL
1956—ANYTHING GOES; HIGH SOCIETY
1957—MAN ON FIRE
1959—SAY ONE FOR ME
1960—HIGH TIME; PEPE
1962—THE ROAD TO HONG KONG
1964—ROBIN AND THE SEVEN HOODS
1966—STAGECOACH

RECORDS

PAUL WHITEMAN (*with The Rhythm Boys)
  Vi 20627 Side by Side*/Pretty Lips*
  Vi 20679 Magnolia*
  Vi 21218 Ol' Man River/Make Believe
  Vi 21365 I'm Winging Home
  Vi 21389 I'm Afraid of You/My Pet
  Co 1444-D 'Tain't So, Honey, 'Tain't So
  Co 1683-D Makin' Whoopee
  Co 1974-D Waiting at the End of the Road
  Co 2010-D (I'm a Dreamer) Aren't We All?/If I Had a Talking Picture of You
  Co 2023-D Great Day/Without a Song
PAUL WHITEMAN'S RHYTHM BOYS
  Vi 21302 From Monday On/What Price Lyrics?
  Co 1455-D That's Grandma/Wa Da Da
  Co 1819-D Louise/So the Bluebirds

and the Blackbirds Got Together
Co 2223-D A Bench in the Park

GUS ARNHEIM
Vi 22561 It Must Be True/Fool Me
Some More
Vi 22618 I Surrender Dear
Vi 22691 Ho Hum/I'm Gonna Get
You
Vi 22700 Thanks to You/One More
Time

DORSEY BROTHERS ORCHESTRA
OK 41188 My Kinda Love

IPANA TROUBADOURS
Co 1694-D I'll Get By/Rose of Mandalay

BING CROSBY
Co 1773-D My Kinda Love/Till We
Meet
Vi 22701 Just a Gigolo/Wrap Your
Troubles in Dreams
Br 6120 Just One More Chance/Were
You Sincere?
Br 6145 Many Happy Returns of the
Day/At Your Command
Br 6226 (theme) Where the Blue of the
Night/I'm Sorry Dear
Br 6394 Please/Waltzing in a Dream
Br 6406 Here Lies Love/How Deep Is
the Ocean?
Br 6414 Brother, Can You Spare a
Dime?/Let's Put Out the Lights
Br 6472 I'm Young and Healthy/
You're Getting to Be a Habit with
Me
Br 6594 Learn to Croon/Moonstruck
Br 6643 Thanks/Black Moonlight
Br 6644 The Day You Came Along/I
Guess It Had to Be That Way
Br 6695 Temptation/We'll Make Hay
While the Sun Shines
Br 6852 Love Thy Neighbor/Riding
Around in the Rain
Br 6853 May I?/She Reminds Me of
You
Br 6936 Love in Bloom/Straight from
the Shoulder
De 309 With Every Breath I Take/
Maybe I'm Wrong Again
De 310 June in January/Love Is Just
Around the Corner
De 391 It's Easy to Remember/
Swanee River
De 392 Soon/Down by the River

De 547 I Wish I Were Aladdin/From
the Top of Your Head
De 548 Without a Word of Warning/
Takes Two to Make a Bargain
De 871 I'm an Old Cowhand/I Can't
Escape from You
De 947 Pennies from Heaven/Let's
Call a Heart a Heart
De 1175 Sweet Leilani/Blue Hawaii
De 1376 It's the Natural Thing to Do/
All You Want to Do Is Dance
De 1648 My Heart Is Taking Les-
sons/On the Sentimental Side
De 2201 I Have Eyes/The Funny Old
Hills
De 2359 East Side of Heaven/Sing a
Song of Sunbeams
De 2535 It Must Be True/I Surrender
Dear
De 3161 April Played the Fiddle/I
Haven't Time to Be a Millionaire
De 3300 Only Forever/When the
Moon Comes Over Madison
Square
De 3309 Rhythm on the River/That's
for Me
De 4065 Shepherd Serenade/Anniver-
sary Waltz
De 18429 White Christmas/Let's Start
the New Year Right
De 18513 Moonlight Becomes You/
Constantly
De 18561 Sunday, Monday or Al-
ways/If You Please
De 18570 I'll Be Home for Christmas/
Danny Boy
De 18597 Going My Way/Swinging
on a Star
De 18621 Too-Ra-Loo-Ra-Loo-Ral/I'll
Remember April
De 23849 Country Style/My Heart Is a
Hobo
De 24279 Now Is the Hour/Silver
Threads Among the Gold
De 24283 But Beautiful/One I Love
De 24295 Galway Bay/My Gal's an
Irish Girl
De 28969 Y' All Come/Changing Part-
ners
De 29024 My Love, My Love/Secret
Love
BING CROSBY-DIXIE LEE CROSBY
De 907 A Fine Romance/The Way
You Look Tonight

BING CROSBY-ANDREWS SISTERS

De 23277 Pistol Packin' Mama/Victory Polka

De 23281 Jingle Bells/Santa Claus Is Comin' to Town

De 23364 Don't Fence Me In/The Three Caballeros

BING CROSBY-CARMEN CAVALLARO

De 23457 I Can't Believe That You're in Love with Me/I Can't Begin to Tell You

BING CROSBY-BOB HOPE

De 40000 Put It There, Pal/The Road to Morocco

BING CROSBY-DONALD O'CONNOR

De 29035 Back in the Old Routine/If There's Anybody Here

BING CROSBY-GARY CROSBY

De 27112 Play a Simple Melody/Sam's Song

LPs

BING CROSBY

"X" LVA-1000 Young Bing Crosby (Vi RIs)

Co CL-6027 Crosby Classics (Br RIs)

Epic (S) E2E 202 The Bing Crosby Story, Vol. 1: The Early Jazz Years

Br BL-54005 The Voice of Bing in the 1930s (Br RIs)

Co C2L 43 Bing Crosby in Hollywood, 1930-1934

De DX-151 (5-LP set) Bing (De RIs)

De DL-8575 New Tricks

De(10")DL-5520 Bing Sings the Hits

MGM E-4929 Bing Sings the Great Standards!

PAUL WHITEMAN

Co CL-2830 Featuring Bing Crosby (Co RIs)

(movie soundtrack)

Reprise FS-2021 (S) ROBIN AND THE SEVEN HOODS

394. CROSBY, BOB   vo B
(GEORGE ROBERT CROSBY)

Born August 23, 1913, Spokane, Wash.

Younger brother of all-time great entertainer Bing Crosby. Successful career leading dixieland-styled big band many years beginning 1935. Husky singing voice with family resemblance to Bing's but with slight quaver, at best on uptempo songs. Attended Gonzaga University, while there took singing jobs including radio work. Vocalist with Anson Weeks 1933-4 and with Dorsey Brothers 1934-5. Began to front own band, formed from nucleus of Ben Pollack band. When Pollack disbanded in 1934, saxman Gil Rodin organized new group as corporation. With him: Yank Lawson (t), Matty Matlock (cl), Eddie Miller (ts), Nappy Lamare (g), Ray Bauduc (d), Gil Bowers (p), Deane Kincaide (ts, ar). They jobbed till early 1935, recorded under names of Gil Rodin and Clark Randall, landed job on Ruth Etting radio show with augmented group. Rodin hired Bob Crosby as front man and singer, signed with Decca mid-1935. Arrangements by Matlock, Kincaide and bassist Bob Haggart gave band distinctive sound. First big band with strong dixieland lines. Handled ballads well, and outstanding jazzmen made it one of the greatest of the big bands. Theme song *Summertime.* Later jazz stars included Billy Butterfield (t), Muggsy Spanier (t), Irving Fazola (cl), Warren Smith (tb), Floyd O'Brien (tb), Bob Zurke (p), Joe Sullivan (p), Jess Stacy (p), Buddy Morrow (tb; then Moe Zudecoff), Bill Stegmeyer (cl), Hank D'Amico (cl). Best-known numbers included *The Old Spinning Wheel, Little Rock Getaway, March of the Bob Cats, South Rampart Street Parade, The Big Noise from Winnetka, Skaters Waltz, Honky Tonk Train Blues, I'm Free* (later popular as: *What's New?*), *My Inspiration, Boogie Woogie Maxixe.* Bob Cats, eight-piece combo within band, helped popularize authentic dixieland on broad scale.

Band perked up in 1939 when clarinet great Irving Fazola joined. Beautiful clarinet enhanced ensemble sound on lead work, gave warmth to ballads and lilt to jazz. He, Miller, Zurke, Lawson and Butterfield band's top soloists. Clarinetist Matlock concentrated on arranging when Fazola (and later D'Amico) joined. Good female vocalists: Kay Weber, Marion Mann, Teddy Grace, Bonnie King, Liz Tilton, and Doris Day briefly in mid-1940. In 1938-9 long run at Chicago's Black Hawk Restaurant boosted band, as did subbing for Benny Goodman on 1939 summer Camel Caravan: so successful Camel continued band into 1939-40 season. Band style more commercial in early 40s when Jimmy Mundy and Paul Weston took over some arranging, reverted more to earlier dixieland when Lawson rejoined summer 1941. Disbanded in December 1942.

Then movie work for Crosby. Military service, World War II; led bands, conducted shows. After discharge resumed as bandleader in modern style with no great success. Later reverted to dixieland, hired former key men. Recordings infrequent but much radio, including Jack Benny show early 50s and own Club 15 series. On early TV, and outstanding daytime 1953-6 show featured good jazz combo and singers Joanie O'Brien, Carol Richards and Modernaires. Night-time TV shows. Active in 60s, often led combo modeled after Bob Cats. In 1972 became part of stage show featuring former bandleaders and singers. Appeared in movies as single or with band: LET'S MAKE MUSIC (1940), SIS HOPKINS and ROOKIES ON PARADE (1941), PRESENTING LILY MARS, THOUSANDS CHEER, YOUTH ON PARADE, REVEILLE WITH BEVERLY (1943), THE SINGING SHERIFF, MEET MISS BOBBY SOCKS, PARDON MY RHYTHM, KANSAS CITY KITTY, MY GAL LOVES MUSIC, SEE HERE PRIVATE HARGROVE (1944), WHEN YOU'RE SMILING (1950), TWO TICKETS TO BROADWAY (1951), THE ROAD TO BALI (1952), SENIOR PROM (1958), THE FIVE PENNIES (1959).

RECORDS

ANSON WEEKS
Br 6661 You've Got Everything
Br 6727 Sittin' on a Log/Sittin' Up Waitin' for You
Br 6795 Waitin' at the Gate for Katy/ Oh Me! Oh My! Oh You!

DORSEY BROTHERS ORCHESTRA
De 118 Basin Street Blues
De 195 Lost in a Fog/I Couldn't Be Mean to You
De 206 Out in the Cold Again/Day Dreams
De 311 Here Is My Heart/Love Is Just Around the Corner
De 320 Blame It on My Youth
De 376 Dinah/Night Wind

BOB CROSBY (* Bob Cats)
De 478 Flowers for Madame/In a Little Gypsy Tea Room
De 614 On Treasure Island/At Your Service, Madame
De 727 Goody Goody/What's the Name of That Song?
De 896 Pagan Love Song/Come Back, Sweet Papa
De 1196 The Old Spinning Wheel/Between the Devil and the Deep Blue Sea
De 1552 Little Rock Getaway/Vieni Vieni
De 1747 Yancey Special/At the Jazz Band Ball
De 1865 March of the Bob Cats*/ Who's Sorry Now?*
De 2205 (theme) Summertime/I'm Free (What's New?)
De 2208 The Big Noise from Winnetka/Honky Tonk Train Blues
De 2209 My Inspiration/Loopin' the Loop*
De 2282 Skaters Waltz/Eye Opener
De 2464 I Never Knew Heaven Could Speak/Rose of Washington Square
De 2657 Over the Rainbow/You and Your Love
De 2825 The Love Nest*/Till We Meet Again*
De 2848 Boogie Woogie Maxixe/High Society
De 3154 Fools Rush In/Sympathy
De 3248 Spain*/All by Myself*
De 4027 I'm Trusting in You/From One Love to Another
De 4415 Black Zephyr/Blue Surreal
De 18355 It's a Long Way to Tipperary*/Sweethearts on Parade*
De(12")15038 South Rampart Street Parade/Dogtown Blues

LPs

BOB CROSBY
De DL-8061 Bob Crosby's Bob Cats (De RIs)
Cor CRL-57060 Bob Cats' Blues
Cor CRL-57062 Bob Crosby in Hi-Fi
Cor CRL-57089 (De RIs)
Dot DLP-3278 Bob Crosby's Great Hits
Co CL-766 The Bob Crosby Show (TV Cast)
Mon-Ever 6815 Live at the Rainbow Grill

Mon-Ever 7026 Mardi Gras Parade
DORSEY BROTHERS ORCHESTRA
De(10″)DL-6016 Dixieland Jazz (De RIs)
Design DLP-147 Spotlight on the Dorsey Brothers (De RIs)

395. CROSBY, ISRAEL   b

Born January 19, 1919, Chicago, Ill.
Died August 11, 1962, Chicago, Ill.

Bass man with leading jazz groups from mid-30s into 60s. Active freelance career. Started playing professionally in Chicago in mid-30s, including work with Albert Ammons. Important period with Fletcher Henderson 1936-8. With Three Sharps and a Flat in 1939. Freelance work, joined Horace Henderson late 1940-1, then Teddy Wilson 1941-3. With Raymond Scott big band on radio in 1944, then several years as studio musician. In early 50s with Ahmad Jamal combo. More freelance including trip to Far East with Benny Goodman late 1956-7. In late 50s rejoined Jamal, remained till 1962. Last few months of life with George Shearing combo.

RECORDS

ALBERT AMMONS
De 749 Nagasaki/Boogie Woogie Stomp
GENE KRUPA
Vi 25263 Mutiny in the Parlor/I'm Gonna Clap My Hands
Vi 25276 I Hope Gabriel Likes My Music/Swing Is Here
De 18114 Blues of Israel/Three Little Words
De 18115 The Last Round-up/Jazz Me Blues
Clef 89099 Capital Idea/Overtime
Mer 89057 Coronation Hop/Paradise
JIMMIE NOONE
De 18439 Sweet Georgia Brown/'Way Down Yonder in New Orleans
De 18440 He's a Different Type of Guy/The Blues Jumped a Rabbit
JESS STACY
De 18110 The World Is Waiting for the Sunrise
De 18119 Barrelhouse
FLETCHER HENDERSON
Vi 25297 Moonrise on the Lowlands/I'm a Fool for Loving You

Vi 25317 Jangled Nerves/I'll Always Be in Love with You
Vi 25339 Grand Terrace Rhythm/Riffin'
Vi 25379 Jimtown Blues/You Can Depend on Me
Vo 3511 Rose Room/Back in Your Own Backyard
Vo 3534 Stampede/Great Caesar's Ghost
TEDDY WILSON
Br 7663 Mary Had a Little Lamb/Too Good to Be True
Br 7684 Blues in C Sharp Minor/Warmin' Up
CHU BERRY
Va 532 Too Marvelous for Words/Now You're Talking My Language
Va 587 Limehouse Blues/Indiana
AULD-HAWKINS-WEBSTER SAXTET
Apo 754 Pick Up Boys/Porgy
Apo 755 Uptown Lullaby/Salt Peanuts
ED HALL
BN(12″)28 High Society/Blues at Blue Note
BN(12″) 29 Night Shift Blues/Royal Garden Blues
ISRAEL CROSBY
Apo 390 I Know the Blues/The Death of Piney Brown
Apo 405 I Feel the Blues/I Deal in Cats

LPs

GENE KRUPA
Clef(10″)MGC-152 The Gene Krupa Sextet No. 2
CHU BERRY
Epic LN-3124 "Chu" (Va, Vo RIs)
JIMMY YANCEY
Atl(10″)134
ED HALL
BN 6505 Celestial Express (BN RIs)
GEORGE SHEARING
Cap T-1827 Jazz Moments
(miscellaneous artists)
Vi LPV-578 Swing, Vol. 1 (Vi, Bb RIs)

396. CRUMIT, FRANK   vo uk cm lyr

Born September 26, 1889, Jackson, Ohio
Died September 7, 1943, Longmeadow, Mass.

Entertainer on stage, radio and records, active in 20s and 30s. Known for novelty numbers, notably *Abdul Abulbul Amir* and

Gay Caballero (his compositions). Educated at Culver Military Academy and University of Ohio. Vaudeville early in career; periods in act, The Three Comedians, and as single, The One Man Glee Club. Played ukulele, sang in soft voice, stressed novelty material. Brief run in 1920 Broadway show BETTY BE GOOD, more success later in GREENWICH VILLAGE FOLLIES OF 1920. In TANGERINE (1921) which starred future wife Julia Sanderson. Composed hit song of show, *Sweet Lady*. In NIFTIES OF 1923. He and Miss Sanderson took over leads in MOONLIGHT (1924) after show started. Married Julia Sanderson in 1927; they retired from show business two years. Came back in 1929 to star together on radio, continuing through 30s in musical shows of varying formats. Became known as The Singing Sweethearts. Reached peak of radio popularity with entertaining, tuneful show 1933-4. In 1939 began Battle of the Sexes game show which ran until Crumit's death in 1943. Other songs by Crumit as composer or lyricist included *My Lady*; *Tale of the Ticker*; *Song of the Prune*; *King of Borneo*; *A Parlor Is a Pleasant Place to Sit In*; *Donald the Dub*; *There's No One with Endurance Like the Man Who Sells Insurance*; *Get Away, Old Man, Get Away*; *Pretty Little Dear*; *The Buckeye Battle Cry* (for Ohio State University).

RECORDS

FRANK CRUMIT
Co A-2973 The Love Nest
Co A-3388 I Used to Love You/No Wonder I'm Blue
Co A-3415 All by Myself
Co A-3431 Three O'clock in the Morning/Moonlight
Co A-3475 Sweet Lady/You're Just the Type for a Bungalow
Co A-3573 Ha! Ha! Ha!/She's Mine, All Mine
Vi 19365 Ida/Roll Them Roly Boly Eyes
Vi 19945 Billy Boy/Grandfather's Clock
Vi 20124 The Girl Friend/Mountain Greenery
Vi 20462 Crazy Words—Crazy Tune/High-High-High Up in the Hills
Vi 20486 Sunny Disposish/My Lady

Vi 20715 Abdul Abulbul Amir/Frankie and Johnny
Vi 21466 No News/Three Trees
Vi 21735 Gay Caballero/I Learned About Women
Vi 22859 I'm a Specialist/Lady of My Dreams
Vi 24092 Little Brown Jug/Life Is Only a Merry-Go-Round
De 205 Harry Von Tilzer song medleys (1 & 2)
De 1697 Josephine/Connie's Got Connections in Connecticut

FRANK CRUMIT with JACQUES RENARD ORCHESTRA
Vi 21811 Everybody Loves You

FRANK CRUMIT-JULIA SANDERSON
Vi 22630 Would You Like to Take a Walk?
De 18154 Sweet Lady/Hello, I've Been Looking for You
De 18155 We'll Never Grow Old/Same Sort of Girl
De 18156 You're Here and I'm Here/Bring Me a Rose
De 18157 They Didn't Believe Me/The Girl with a Brogue

LPs

FRANK CRUMIT
"X" LVA-1005 The Gay Caballero (Vi RIs)
Ace of Hearts(E) AH-96 The Gay Caballero (Vi RIs)

397. CUGAT, XAVIER   v cm lyr ar B
Born January 1, 1900, Barcelona, Spain

Best-known bandleader in rhumba and other Latin-American dance styles, also composer of hauntingly beautiful tunes that fitted his type of band. Long, successful career. Family moved to Cuba when Cugat young. Studied violin, played in Grand Opera Company of Havana and concerts, earned money to send parents to New York. Studied in Berlin, played concert tours, worked with Berlin Symphony. To U.S., concert at Carnegie Hall, worked with opera singers. Also learned to draw caricatures. Tours took him to west coast, where worked for awhile as caricaturist on *Los Angeles Times*. In late 20s organized orchestra specializing in Spanish and Latin-American music, opened at Cocoanut Grove in Los Angeles. Active in early sound movies, writing and scoring, notably for 1930 movie IN GAY MADRID starring Ramon Novarro. In 30s band had many successful engagements at New York's Waldorf-Astoria. In late 1934-5 one of three bands on historic Let's Dance radio show. During 1941-6 often on radio, including spell on Garry Moore-Jimmy Durante show; also own series at times. During this period featured good singers Lina Romay and Miguelito Valdes. In 50s Abbe Lane (one of several beautiful wives) featured singer. Lovely compositions included theme song *My Shawl* (1934), *Rain in Spain* (1934), *Night Must Fall* (1939), *Nightingale* (1942).

In 40s band in many movies, notably those of Esther Williams and Jane Powell. Received most footage ever given dance band in films GO WEST, YOUNG MAN (1937), YOU WERE NEVER LOVELIER (1942), THE HEAT'S ON, TROPICANA and STAGE DOOR CANTEEN (1943), BATHING BEAUTY and TWO GIRLS AND A SAILOR (1944), WEEKEND AT THE WALDORF (1945), HOLIDAY IN MEXICO and NO LEAVE NO LOVE (1946), THIS TIME FOR KEEPS (1947), A DATE WITH JUDY, LUXURY LINER, and ON AN ISLAND WITH YOU (1948), NEPTUNE'S DAUGHTER (1949), CHICAGO SYNDICATE (1955), THE PHYNX (1969). Band on early TV, in later years limited to occasional spots. Cugat on late-night talk shows with Abbe Lane in 60s, then in late 60s and 70s with next wife, Spanish guitarist-singer Charo. Less active in show business in later years.

RECORDS

XAVIER CUGAT
    Vi 24387 Rain in Spain/Caminito
    Vi 24508 (theme) My Shawl/Silencio
    Vi 24813 Isle of Capri/Vous! Qu'avez-vous
    Vi 25012 The Lady in Red/Adios Muchachos
    Vi 25133 Begin the Beguine/Waltz Down the Aisle
    Vi 25207 Little Rose of the Rancho/Cosi Cosa
    Vi 25389 Mi Sombrero/La Bomba
    Vi 25407 Love, What Are You Doing to My Heart?/Say "Si Si"

Vi 25561 A Love Song of Long Ago/It's No Secret I Love You
Vi 26074 Night Must Fall/Cui Cui
Vi 26334 Perfidia/Nana
Vi 26641 The Breeze and I/When the Swallows Come Back to Capistrano
Vi 26769 Frenesi/Cuatro Personas
Vi 26794 Adios/Green Eyes
Co 35857 Two Dreams Met/A Million Dreams Ago
Co 36041 Intermezzo/A Rendezvous in Rio
Co 36091 Tony's Wife/La Cucaracha
Co 36559 Nightingale/Sleepy Lagoon
Co 36718 Amor/Let Me Love You Tonight
Co 37523 I'm Old Fashioned/Ev'rything I Love
Co 37541 (theme) My Shawl
Co 38558 Thrill Me/Nocturnal Chaperone

LPs

XAVIER CUGAT
    Co CL-537 Dance with Cugat
    Co CL-579 Cugat's Favorite Rhumbas
    Co CL-1094 Cugat Cavalcade
    Co CL-1143 Waltzes—But by Cugat!
    Mer PPS-2003 Viva Cugat!
    Mer PPS-6021 (S) Plays Continental Hits

398. CUMMINS, BERNIE   d vo B

Leader of popular dance band of 30s. First worked as dancer in home town of Akron. Later became drummer, led combo. In late 20s augmented group to hotel-style dance band. Theme song *Dark Eyes*. Early, important engagements at New York's Hotel Biltmore and Hotel New Yorker, also at Chicago's Trianon Ballroom. Brother Walter handled many of vocals for several years. Band recorded regularly. Cummins led band, less successfully, in 40s and 50s. In later years settled in Florida.

RECORDS

BERNIE CUMMINS
    Br 3750 Funny Face/'S Wonderful
    Br 3772 Lonely Melody/When You're with Somebody Else
    Br 3952 'Cause I'm in Love/Out o'-Town Gal
    Br 3996 Out of the Dawn/Chiquita

Vi 21907 Just an Old Love Affair/Till We Meet

Vi 22088 Little by Little/Every Day Away from You

Vi 22331 Lucky Little Devil/Everybody Tap

Vi 22351 A Cottage for Sale

Vi 22354 Exactly Like You/On the Sunny Side of the Street

Vi 22355 Minnie the Mermaid/You Will Come Back to Me

Vi 22425 Absence Makes the Heart Grow Fonder

Vi 22494 F'r Instance/Lonely

Co 2827-D I'll Be Faithful/You've Got Everything

Co 2828-D Beautiful Girl/I'm Dancin' on a Rainbow

Co 2844-D I Guess It Had to Be That Way

Vo 3714 The Lady Is a Tramp/Getting Some Fun Out of Life

Vo 3749 Goodbye Jonah/Dreams for Sale

Vo 3851 Everything You Said Came True/I Told Santa Claus to Bring Me You

Vo 3889 You're My Dish/More Power to You

Me 71106 Have You Ever Been in Heaven?/Mama, I Wanna Make Rhythm

Bb 10777 I'm Losing My Mind/Seems Like a Month of Sundays

Bb 10815 Ragtime Cowboy Joe/So Deep Is the Night

399. CURTIS, KEN   vo
(CURTIS GATES)

Nationally known actor in 60s and 70s, famed for character role as Festus on TV's popular Gunsmoke show. Public generally unaware of earlier career as singer. Early experience singing western songs but could sing pop songs as well. With Shep Fields band in 1942, later in year briefly with Tommy Dorsey after Frank Sinatra left. In mid-40s began movie career with good acting and singing roles in country variety and western movies, small roles in better movies. In late 40s and early 50s sang with Sons of the Pioneers vocal group as featured performer. Had series Ripcord on TV in

mid-50s before Gunsmoke. Occasionally sang on TV in later years, displayed good voice and professional manner.

RECORDS
SHEP FIELDS

Bb 11464 Let's Say Goodnight with a Dance

Bb 11497 Breathless

Bb 11537 Wonder When My Baby's Coming Home/This Is Worth Fighting For

Bb 11552 You're Easy to Dance With/You're Too Good for Good-for-Nothing Me

KEN CURTIS

Cry 657 Hannah Lee/Are You

Cry 658 Go and Leave Me/He Was There

Mer 6009 I Learned to Love You Too Late/Idaho-Ho

MGM 11510 Call of the Far-Away Hills

400. CUTSHALL, CUTTY   tb
(ROBERT DEWEES CUTSHALL)
Born December 29, 1911, Huntington County, Pa.
Died August 16, 1968, Toronto, Canada

Trombonist with dixieland groups; forceful, uninhibited style. Jobs in Pittsburgh in early 30s, including classical work. Began touring in 1934 with Charles Dornberger band. With Jan Savitt 1939-40. Joined Benny Goodman late 1940, remained till spring of 1942. Military service, World War II. Rejoined Benny Goodman in 1946 for about six months. Prominent in dixieland revival of late 40s, freelanced in New York, played jazz spots with top dixielanders. With Billy Butterfield, Eddie Condon, Peanuts Hucko, Jimmy Dorsey; also studio work. Brief jobs in 50s with Goodman, mostly with Eddie Condon at his club, late 40s to late 60s. Also with Yank Lawson, Max Kaminsky, Peanuts Hucko, Bob Crosby in 60s. Last job with Condon in Toronto, where suffered fatal heart attack.

RECORDS
BENNY GOODMAN

Co 36421 The Count

Co 37091 Put That Kiss Back Where You Found It

Co 37149 For You, for Me, for Evermore

JIMMY DORSEY

Co 38649 Charley My Boy/Johnson Rag

Co 38654 Jazz Me Blues/Panama

Co 38655 Chimes Blues/Struttin' with Some Barbecue

Co 38657 Tin Roof Blues/South Rampart Street Parade

EDDIE CONDON

De 24987 At the Jazz Band Ball/Dill Pickles

De 27035 Jazz Me Blues

De 27095 Charleston/Black Bottom

GENE KRUPA

Vi 20-3766 Bonaparte's Retreat/My Scandinavian Baby

Vi 20-3816 At the Jazz Band Ball/I Want Gold in My Pocket

Vi 20-3965 Walkin' with the Blues/I'm Forever Blowing Bubbles

Vi 20-4026 Panhandle Rag/Blues My Naughty Sweetie Gave to Me

BOBBY HACKETT

VD(12″)871 My Honey's Lovin' Arms

VD(12″)880 Fidgety Feet

LPs

EDDIE CONDON

Co CL-616 Jammin' at Condon's

Co CL-719 Bixieland

Co CL-881 Treasury of Jazz

Co CL-1089 The Roaring Twenties

Dot DLP-3141 Dixieland Dance Party

BOB CROSBY

Cor CRL-56018 John Philip Sousa Marches in Dixieland Style

HENRY JEROME

De DL-4307 Strings in Dixieland

YANK LAWSON

ABC-Para 567 Ole Dixie

FRANK HUBBELL & THE STOMPERS

Atco 33-196 Penny Candy and Other Treats

WILD BILL DAVISON

Co CL-983 With Strings Attached

DON REDMAN

Roul R-25070 Dixieland in High Society

D

400A. DAFFAN, TED　　g v ar cm B
(THERON EUGENE DAFFAN)

Born September 21, 1912, Beauregarde Parish, La.

Successful composer and bandleader in country and western field. Billed as Ted Daffan & His Texans. Compositions plaintive and moving, recorded successfully by various artists. Most famous songs *Truck Drivers Blues* (1939), *A Worried Mind* (1941), *Born to Lose* (1942), *No Letter Today* (1942). Others include *Always Alone, Don't Be Blue for Me, Take Me Back Again, I'm a Fool to Care, Blue Steel Blues, Look Who's Talkin', Time Won't Heal My Broken Heart, Baby You Can't Get Me Down, Broken Vows, Trouble Keeps Hangin' 'Round My Door, You'd Better Change Your Ways, Weary Steel Blues, Two of a Kind, Walkin' in the Cold Cold Rain, Just Born That Way, Shut That Gate, Headin' Down the Wrong Highway, Shadow on My Heart.* Sometimes used pseudonym Frankie Brown as composer. Big hit record on own compositions *Born to Lose/No Letter Today.* Grew up in Houston; radio and dance jobs there with Blue Ridge Playboys 1934-5, Bar X Cowboys 1936-40. Led band early 40s into late 50s. Good run at Venice Pier in Los Angeles mid-40s. Left band behind in 1946, led new band remainder of 40s in Dallas-Fort Worth-Houston. 1958-61 in Nashville in publishing business with Hank Snow. Houston in 60s.

RECORDS

TED DAFFAN

OK 05573 I'm a Fool to Care/Put Your Little Arms Around Me
OK 05668 A Worried Mind/Blue Steel Blues
OK 06311 Always Alone/Weary Steel Blues
OK 06452 Breakin' My Heart Over You/Car Hop's Blues
OK 6706 Born to Lose/No Letter Today
OK 6719 Bluest Blues/Look Who's Talkin'
OK 6744 Headin' Down the Wrong Highway/Shadow on My Heart
Co 20462 Just Born That Way/Two of a Kind
Co 20567 I'm That Kind of a Guy/Flame of Love
Co 20668 Strangers Passing By/So Dissatisfied
Co 20679 I've Got Five Dollars and It's Saturday Night/I'm Gonna Leave This Darned Old Town
Co 37087 Broken Vows/Shut That Gate
Co 38092 Bury Me Deep/The Straight and Narrow Way

401. DAILEY, DAN　　vo
(DAN DAILEY, JR.)

Born December 14, 1917, New York, N.Y.

Star of movie musicals as song and dance

man, also developed into excellent actor. Early vaudeville and club experience. First movie THE MORTAL STORM (1940), minor role. Gradually worked up to stardom. Co-starred with Betty Grable in several films. Greatest performance as entertainer-actor probably in WHEN MY BABY SMILES AT ME (1948). Other important movie musicals LADY BE GOOD and ZIEGFELD GIRL (1941), PANAMA HATTIE (1942), MOTHER WORE TIGHTS (1947), GIVE MY REGARDS TO BROADWAY and YOU WERE MEANT FOR ME (1948), YOU'RE MY EVERYTHING (1949), I'LL GET BY and MY BLUE HEAVEN (1950), CALL ME MISTER (1951), THE GIRL NEXT DOOR (1953), THERE'S NO BUSINESS LIKE SHOW BUSINESS (1954), IT'S ALWAYS FAIR WEATHER (1955), THE BEST THINGS IN LIFE ARE FREE and MEET ME IN LAS VEGAS (1956), PEPE (1960; strong role in latter). Outstanding performance in THE PRIDE OF ST. LOUIS (1952) as baseball star Dizzy Dean. On TV in 60s, had own series.

RECORDS
(LPs)

DAN DAILEY
  Tops L-1598 Dan Dailey

402. DAILEY, FRANK   B

Born c. 1901
Died February 27, 1956, Montclair, N.J.

Bandleader of 30s, most noted as proprietor of famous Meadowbrook in Cedar Grove, N.J., key spot for name bands. After years as bandleader, by mid-30s led good sweet band regularly at Meadowbrook. Later in 1936 when Meadowbrook began booking other bands, Dailey toured. By late 30s band had gimmick. At end of number band would stop, Dailey would say "Stop and Go!" and band would resume for half chorus or so in same tempo. Billed as Frank Dailey and His Stop and Go Orchestra. Disbanded in 1939 and became owner of Meadowbrook. Leading bands booked there for years; prestigious spot with lots of airtime. Popular radio feature for years was regular Saturday afternoon broadcast from there, which gave bands valuable showcase.

RECORDS
FRANK DAILEY
  Bb 5953 Paris in Spring/Bon Jour, Mam'selle
  Bb 5954 Gypsy Violin/I'll Never Say "Never Again" Again
  Bb 5955 Rhythm Is Our Business/Time Will Tell
  Bb 6027 I'm in the Mood for Love/I Feel a Song Comin' On
  Bb 6028 I Wished on the Moon/Double Trouble
  Bb 6030 Cheek to Cheek/Isn't This a Lovely Day?
  Bb 6663 No Use Pretending/You Are All I've Wanted
  Bb 6664 Let's Put Our Heads Together/With Plenty of Money and You
  Bb 7477 An Old Straw Hat/I Love to Whistle
  Bb 7479 Toy Trumpet/In Bad with Sinbad
  Bb 7491 By the Shalimar/Sissy
  Bb 7646 I Wish I Was the Willow/Great Camp Meetin' Ground
  Bb 7648 A Little Kiss at Twilight/What Goes On Here in My Heart?
  Bb 10004 April in My Heart/While a Cigarette Was Burning
  Vo 3794 Purple Mood/Quicksands
  Vo 3798 Everything You Said Came True/Something to Sing About
  Vo 3822 Scattin' at the Kit Kat/Southland Serenade

403. DAILY, PETE   c tu v-tb B

Born May 5, 1911, Portland, Ind.

Dixieland cornetist, gained prominence as combo leader in 40s and 50s. In early years worked jobs on tuba, then switched to cornet. Began in Chicago in 1930, remained there into early 40s. With Frank Melrose, Bud Freeman, Boyce Brown, Art Van Damme. Own band in early 40s. In 1942 to California, with Mike Riley and Ozzie Nelson. Military service, World War II. Late in 1945 rejoined Nelson. In 1946 own dixieland combo, spirited group based on west coast. Popular there many years, recorded often. Continued as bandleader through 50s into 60s. Took up valve trombone. In early 60s worked in Chicago again, then back to California in late 60s.

RECORDS

EDDIE MILLER
Cap 40039 You Oughta Be in Pictures

PETE DAILY
Cap 728 Green Light Rag/Sailing Down the Chesapeake Bay
Cap 760 O Katharina/Down Home Rag
Cap 1055 Red Rose Romp/Minnie the Mermaid
Cap 1370 Johnson Rag/Louisiana
Cap 1486 Walkin' the Dog/Roamin' in the Gloamin'
Cap 1588 Take Me Out to the Ball Game/Harmony Rag
Cap 2041 North/China Boy
Cap 15315 Circus Slide/When the War Breaks Out in Mexico
Cap 15433 Dixieland Shuffle/Careless Love
Cap 15434 At a Georgia Camp Meeting/When the Saints Go Marching In
Cap 60008 South/She Looks Like Helen Brown
Sun 7559 Redlight Rag/Sugarfoot Strut
JM 14 Bluin' the Blues/5:30 A.M. Blues
JM 29 Jazz Man Strut/Sobbin' Blues
JM 30 Yelping Hound Blues/Clarinet Marmalade
Jump 12 Wolverine Blues/Livery Stable Blues
Jump 24 Lazy Daddy/Shake It and Break It
GTJ 61 Sobbin' Blues/Jazz Man Strut
GTJ 68 Yelping Hound Blues/Clarinet Marmalade

LPs

PETE DAILY
Cap T-385 Dixie by Daily
Cap(10")H-183 Pete Daily's Dixieland Band
De(10")DL-5261 Dixieland Jazz Battle, Vol. 1
Camay CA-3035 The Bobcats and Pete Daily

404. DALE, ALAN vo

Born July 9, 1926, Brooklyn, N.Y.

Leading pop singer of late 40s and 50s. Excellent singer with smooth baritone voice. At 16 had singing job at Coney Island. Joined Carmen Cavallaro late 1943, with George Paxton 1944-6. In early 1946 began as single. Two recording hits in *Oh, Marie* and *Darktown Strutters' Ball*. On TV in late 40s, good show in 1951. Played clubs in 40s and 50s, then tired of the grind and retired from show business. Returned; semi-active in 70s.

RECORDS

GEORGE PAXTON
Hit 7121 Ev'ry Time We Say Goodbye/Only Another Boy and Girl
VD(12")553 My Devotion
Guild 131 Out of This World
Guild 132 I'll See You in My Dreams

ALAN DALE-CONNIE HAINES
Cor 60700 Darktown Strutters' Ball

ALAN DALE
Si 15163 It's a Lonesome Old Town/My Melancholy Baby
Si 15166 Papa, Won't You Dance with Me?/Hold Me in Your Heart
Si 15169 The Wildest Gal in Town/I Never Loved Anyone
Si 15174 All Dressed Up with a Broken Heart/My Cousin Louella
Si 15175 Judy/An Old Sombrero
Cor 60699 Oh, Marie
Cor 60754 Faith/I'm Sorry
Cor 60809 My Thrill/You're My Destiny
Cor 60850 Laugh, Clown, Laugh/Toddling the Todalo
Cor 61435 You Still Mean the Same to Me/Sweet and Gentle
De 27961 Broken Hearted/Silver and Gold
Co 38814 Today, Tomorrow and Forever/Ride Magic Carpet
Co 38874 You Wonderful You/Of All Things
Co 39033 Let's Do It Again/Rainbow Gal
Co 39391 A Robin and a Rainbow and a Red Red Rose/Tell Me
Hi-Tone 202 Goodnight Sweetheart/Shine On Harvest Moon

405. DALE, CARLOTTA vo

Excellent band singer of late 30s and early 40s; impressive delivery. Best known for work with Jan Savitt in late 30s; heard on his Music for Moderns show on New York radio. In late 1939 joined new Will Bradley band. By early 40s faded from limelight.

RECORDS

JAN SAVITT
Bb 7504 Lovelight in the Starlight
Bb 7670 When Twilight Comes
Bb 7748 Love of My Life
Bb 10013 Hurry Home
De 2391 I Want My Share of Love
De 2614 You Taught Me to Love Again
De 2739 Twilight Interlude

WILL BRADLEY
Vo 5182 I Thought About You
Vo 5210 Make with the Kisses/Fit to Be Tied
Vo 5262 This Changing World
Co 35376 A Ghost of a Chance
Co 35399 Gotta Get Home
Co 35414 It's a Wonderful World/ Watching the Clock
Co 35542 So Far So Good

JESS STACY
Vs 8060 What's New?/Melancholy Mood

406. DALE, JIMMY   p v ar cm
Born June 18, 1901, Bronx, N.Y.

Arranger for dance bands, best known as a leading stock arranger of early and mid-30s. As teenager played in bands of Paul Tremaine, Mike Speciale and Dave Harmon, studied arranging. Attended Columbia University. Toured in vaudeville as pianist. Began working as stock arranger in 1930; hot arrangements soon widely used. Arranged also for name bands including Tommy Dorsey, Benny Goodman, Frankie Carle. Arranged for singer Al Jolson and songwriters George Gershwin, Irving Berlin, Oscar Hammerstein II. Wrote for TV shows. Taught in later years. Composing credits include *The Smugglers' Nightmare, Navy Bounce, Russian Dressin', I've Got a Cookie in Kansas, Suzanne, Just Say I Love Her, Blue Silhouette.*

407. DALEY, CASS   vo
(CATHERINE DAILEY)
Born July 17, 1915

Comedienne-singer of movies and radio

during 40s. Shouting style along Martha Raye lines. Hat-check girl in New Jersey night club in 1933, began singing in floor show. Then played clubs on east coast. Worked with Ozzie Nelson band. Played vaudeville late 30s till 1942, developed comic act. First movie role in musical THE FLEET'S IN (1942); then STAR SPANGLED RHYTHM (1942), CRAZY HOUSE and RIDING HIGH (1943), DUFFY'S TAVERN and OUT OF THIS WORLD (1945), LADIES MAN and VARIETY GIRL (1947). Active on radio beginning mid-40s on Maxwell House and Fitch Bandwagon shows, also own show. Small roles in later movies HERE COMES THE GROOM (1951), RED GARTERS (1954), THE SPIRIT IS WILLING (1967), THE PHYNX (1969), NORWOOD (1970). Played stock at times, including early 70s.

RECORDS

HOAGY CARMICHAEL-CASS DALEY
De 27474 Golden Rocket/Aba Daba Honeymoon
De 27743 A Woman Is a Five Letter Word/I'm Waiting Just for You

CASS DALEY
De 3051 Where Were You Last Night?/It's the Last Time I'll Fall in Love
De 23758 That's the Beginning of the End/Mama's Gone, Goodbye

407A. DALHART, VERNON   vo
(MARION T. SLAUGHTER)
Born April 6, 1883, Jefferson, Texas
Died September 15, 1948, Bridgeport, Conn.

Prolific recording artist from around 1917 into 30s. Early singer of folk-country-western-Negro songs. Often sang of tragic events. Formed professional name from Texas towns Vernon and Dalhart. Recorded under nearly 40 pseudonyms including Mack Allen, Tobe Little, Al Craver, Bill Vernon, Tom Watson, Bob White, Jeff Calhoun. Early career recorded popular and nostalgic songs. By early 1924 career sagged; recorded hillbilly tune *The Prisoner's Song*, Victor best-seller. Other leading numbers *The Death of Floyd Collins, The Wreck of the Old 97, In the Baggage Coach Ahead, The Letter Edged in Black, The Mississippi Flood.*

RECORDS

MACK ALLEN (Vernon Dalhart)
Ha 351 Muddy Water/Song of the Wanderer
Ha 721 Treasure Untold/Mother Was a Lady
Ha 1095 Eleven More Months and Ten More Days/There's a Rainbow in the Sky (with ADELYNE HOOD)

BOB WHITE (Vernon Dalhart)
Do 3466 The Prisoner's Song/Doin' the Best I Can

AL CRAVER (Vernon Dalhart)
Co 15031-D The Death of Floyd Collins/Little Mary Phagan
Co 15044-D Sinking of the Submarine S-51/Little Birdie
Co 15046-D Convict and the Rose/Dream of the Miner's Child

VERNON DALHART with ROSS GORMAN ORCHESTRA
Co 563-D The Prisoner's Song

VERNON DALHART with TENNESSEE TOOTERS
Co 144-D Ground Hog Blues / Chattanooga

VERNON DALHART-CHARLIE WELLS
Co 15152-D Death's Shadow Song/My Blue Ridge Mountain Home

VERNON DALHART-CARSON ROBISON
Br 149 When the Moon Shines Down Upon the Mountain/Sing On, Brother, Sing (with ADELYNE HOOD)
Co 15282-D Drifting Down the Trail of Dreams/Bring Me a Leaf from the Sea
Vi 20539 My Blue Mountain Home/Oh Dem Golden Slippers

VERNON DALHART
Vi 18512 Rock-a-bye Your Baby with a Dixie Melody
Vi 19427 The Prisoner's Song/The Wreck of the Old 97
Vi 19627 In the Baggage Coach Ahead/I Will Ne'er Forget My Mother and My Home
Vi 19837 The Letter Edged in Black/The Lightning Express
Vi 20611 The Mississippi Flood/I'll Be with You When the Roses Bloom Again
Co 267-D De Clouds Gwine Roll Away/I'm Doing the Best I Can

Co 2102-D Calamity Jane/Out in the Great North West
Co 15041-D Wreck of the Shenandoah/Stone Mountain Memorial
Re 9621 Mr. Radio Man/In the Evening
Chal 155 The Engineer's Child/The Great Titanic
Supertone 9227 The Death of Floyd Collins/The Letter Edged in Black
Ve 1982 My Kentucky Mountain Girl/Going Down to New Orleans
Br 102 Billy Richardson's Last Ride/Little Home in Tennessee
Br 3572 Lucky Lindy/The Lost French Flyers
OK 40156 Boll Weevil Blues
OK 40487 When the World Turns You Down/The Sailor Boy's Farewell

408. DAMERON, TADD   p ar cm B
(TADLEY EWING DAMERON)

Born February 21, 1917, Cleveland, Ohio
Died March 8, 1965, New York, N.Y.

Important early figure in development of bop particularly as arranger and composer. Wrote outstanding charts for hard-swinging bop combos, later for large bands. Began professionally as pianist in 1938-9 in Ohio area with bands and accompanying singers, even then experimenting with unorthodox, innovating piano chords and structures. Worked with Video Musso in New York in 1940, also arranged. Later in 1940 joined Harlan Leonard in Kansas City as arranger, scored *Dameron Stomp, Rock and Ride, A La Bridges, 400 Swing, Keep Rockin'*. Defense work, World War II. Later in 40s arranged for Jimmie Lunceford, Count Basie, George Auld. Period with Billy Eckstine's bop-styled big band in mid-40s furthered his arranging style. Arranged for Dizzy Gillespie; outstanding numbers *Hot House, Emanon, Our Delight*. Own combo in New York in 1948. Co-leader with Miles Davis at Paris Jazz Festival in 1949, then composed and arranged for Ted!) Heath band in England. In 1951 to Cleveland as promoter, also managed restaurant. Late 1951-2 with Bull Moose Jackson as pianist-arranger, then led big bop band. Freelanced, concentrating on

773

arranging and composing. In late 50s career interrupted by narcotics. Resumed in 1961 as arranger. Illness forced retirement in late 1964. Compositions included *Good Bait, If You Could See Me Now, Hot House, Cool Breeze, Our Delight, The Squirrel, Fountainebleau, Stay on It, Casbah, Lady Bird, Dial B for Beauty*.

RECORDS

SARAH VAUGHAN
  Cont 6008 What More Can a Woman Do?/I'd Rather Have a Memory Than a Dream
BABS' 3 BIPS AND A BOP
  BN 534 Oop-Pop-A-Da/Stomping at the Savoy
  BN 535 Lop-Pow/Pay Dem Blues
  BN 536 Dob Bla Bli/Weird Lullaby
DEXTER GORDON
  Sav 913 Settin' the Pace (1 & 2)
  Sav 960 So Easy/Dexter's Riff
  Sav 955 Dextrose
TADD DAMERON
  BN 540 The Squirrel/Our Delight
  BN 541 The Chase/Dameronia
  BN 559 Jahbero/Lady Bird
  BN 1564 Symphonette
  Sav 931 A Be-Bop Carol/The Tadd Walk
  Cap 57-60006 Sid's Delight/Casbah
  Cap 57-60015 Focus/John's Delight

LPs

TADD DAMERON
  Riv 419 The Magic Touch
  Pres 7037 Fontainebleau
  Pres(10″)159 A Study in Dameronia
  Jazzland 50 Fats Navarro with the Tadd Dameron Quintet (RIs)
TADD DAMERON-JOHN COLTRANE
  Pres 7070 Mating Call
FATS NAVARRO
  BN 1531 The Fabulous Fats Navarro, Vol. 1 (RIs)
DEXTER GORDON
  Sav MG-12130 Dexter Rides Again
CARMEN MCRAE (as conductor)
  De DL-8347 Blue Moon
SONNY STITT (as arranger-conductor)
  Atl 1395 Sonny Stitt and the Top Brass
HARLAN LEONARD (as arranger)
  Vi LPV-531 (Bb RIs)

409. D'AMICO, HANK   cl as B
(HENRY D'AMICO)
Born March 21, 1915, Rochester, N.Y.
Died December 3, 1965, New York, N.Y.

Good jazz soloist on clarinet; Goodman style with clear, strong tone. Grew up in Buffalo, early musical experience there included jobs on excursion boats. With Paul Specht in 1936. Joined Red Norvo in fall 1936, remained till spring 1939. With Richard Himber spring 1939 to spring 1940, then joined Bob Crosby and remained till mid-1941. In early 40s led big band awhile, then beginning mid-1942 had periods with Les Brown, Red Norvo and Benny Goodman. In 1943 with Raymond Scott on radio and with Johnny Guarnieri, Cozy Cole, Miff Mole and Tommy Dorsey. In 1944 staff musician on ABC, stayed about ten years. Own band at times on radio. In later 50s freelanced in New York and led groups. Continued into 60s; last job with Morey Feld group.

RECORDS

RED NORVO
  Br 7767 Peter Piper/Now That Summer Is Gone
  Br 7815 Smoke Dreams/A Thousand Dreams of You
  Br 7868 Liza/I Would Do Anything for You
  Br 7896 Remember/Jiving the Jeep
  Br 7928 Everyone's Wrong but Me
  Br 7932 The Morning After/Do You Ever Think of Me?
  Br 7970 Worried Over You/Tears in My Heart
  Br 7975 Russian Lullaby/Clap Hands (Here Comes Charlie)
  Br 8068 Love Is Here to Stay/I Was Doing All Right
  Br 8085 More Than Ever/A Serenade to the Stars
  Br 8088 Please Be Kind
  Br 8171 A Cigarette and a Silhouette/After Dinner Speech
  Br 8202 Garden of the Moon
  Br 8227 I Have Eyes
  Br 8230 This Is Madness
  Vo 4698 We'll Never Know

MILDRED BAILEY
Vo 3758 Right or Wrong
Vo 4036 At Your Beck and Call
Vo 4109 If You Were in My Place/ Moonshine Over Kentucky
Vo 4253 So Help Me
Vo 4282 Now It Can Be Told / I Haven't Changed a Thing
Vo 4432 Old Folks

BOB CROSBY
VD(12″)480 Pack Up Your Troubles
De 3431 You're Bound to Look Like a Monkey (BOB CATS)
De 3576 Take Me Back Again/I'll Come Back to You (both BOB CATS)
De 3752 Flamingo/Far Away Music
De 3808 I'll Keep Thinking of You/ I've Nothing to Live for Now (both BOB CATS)
De 3815 Call It Anything/Something I Dreamed, No Doubt
De 3929 The Angels Came Thru
De 4398 These Things I Can't Forget/A Precious Memory (both BOB CATS)

COZY COLE
Cont 6000 A Ghost of a Chance/Look Here
Cont 6001 Willow Weep for Me/Take It Back

JOHNNY GUARNIERI
Sav 509 Exercise in Swing/Basie English
Sav 511 These Foolish Things/Salute to Fats

JESS STACY
Vs 8076 Noni/Jess Stay

JO STAFFORD
VD(12″)487 Am I Blue?

GEORGE WETTLING
Key(12″)1311 Home/Too Marvelous for Words
Key(12″)1318 Somebody Loves Me/ You Brought a New Kind of Love to Me

HANK D'AMICO
Nat 9003 Gone at Dawn
Nat 9004 Shy Little Witch from Greenwich
Nat 9005 East of the Sun/Between the Devil and the Deep Blue Sea
Nat 9006 Over the Rainbow/Cole Heat Warm Feet

MGM 10638 Anything for You/I Only Have Eyes for You
MGM 10639 Deep Purple/You're the Cream in My Coffee
MGM 10641 Poor Butterfly / If Dreams Come True

LPs

HANK D'AMICO
Beth(10″)BCP-1006

BILLY BUTTERFIELD
Vi LPM-1590 Thank You for a Lovely Evening

JAZZ RENAISSANCE QUINTET
Mer MG-20605 Movin' Easy

WINGY MANONE
De DL-8473 Trumpet on the Wing (one side) Pres 7812 Trumpet Jive!

LESTER YOUNG
Sav MG-12068 The Immortal Lester Young (Sav RIs)

MAX KAMINSKY
Vi(10″)LJM-3003

ERSKINE BUTTERFIELD
Livingston 1062-BN Just for Kicks

MILDRED BAILEY
Co C3L22 (3-LP set) Her Greatest Performances (1929-46 RIs)

410. DAMONE, VIC   vo
(VITO FARINOLA)

Born June 12, 1928, Brooklyn, N.Y.

Handsome singing star of movies-radio-TV-records. Excellent singing voice with strong, smooth delivery and straightforward Sinatra style. Took vocal lessons while usher at New York's Paramount Theatre. Milton Berle helped him land early job at La Martinique Club. Later sang at Paramount Theatre and on radio. Own radio show Saturday Night Serenade for CBS 1947-8, then 1949 summer show. A sensation at Hollywood's Mocambo Club. This led to records and films. In 1951 movies RICH, YOUNG AND PRETTY and THE STRIP. Military service, later 1951-3. After discharge did radio work, appeared in 1953 film ATHENA. Later movies DEEP IN MY HEART, KISMET and HIT THE DECK (1955), HELL TO ETERNITY (1960), SPREE (1967), THE TRACK OF THE SEVENTEEN (1969). During 50s and 60s played top clubs, many appearances on TV, including own series.

RECORDS

VIC DAMONE

Mer 5053 Ivy/I Have but One Heart
Mer 5090 Serenade of the Bells/I'll Dance at Your Wedding
Mer 5261 Again/I Love You So Much It Hurts
Mer 5271 You're Breaking My Heart/ The Four Winds and the Seven Seas
Mer 5391 This Is the Night
Mer 5429 I Hadn't Anyone Till You/ Vagabond Shoes
Mer 5444 Operetta/Mama
Mer 5454 I Love That Girl/Tzena, Tzena, Tzena
Mer 5486 Take Me in Your Arms/Beloved Be Faithful
Mer 5669 Wonder Why/I Can See You
Mer 70022 April in Paris/My Love Song

LPs

VIC DAMONE

Mer MG-20163 Yours for a Song
Mer(10″)MG-25133 April in Paris
Co CL-900 That Towering Feeling
Co CL-1174 Closer Than a Kiss
Co CL-1368 This Game of Love
WB 1607 (S) Country Love Songs
(movie soundtracks)
MGM E-3163 HIT THE DECK
MGM E-3281 KISMET
MGM(10″)E-86 RICH, YOUNG AND PRETTY

411. DANDRIDGE, PUTNEY   p vo B
(LOUIS DANDRIDGE)

Born c. 1900, Richmond, Va.
Died c. 1946, New York, N.Y.

Pianist-vocalist best known for a series of combo records in 1935-6: happy, swinging jazz on worthy pop tunes of period featuring good jazzmen. Swinging pianist and jazz-phrased, humorous singer. Began professionally about 1918, toured with shows into mid-20s. Based in Buffalo in later 20s. In early 30s accompanist for dancer Bill Robinson. Led band in Cleveland 1932-4. In early 1935 in New York at Adrian's Tap Room, later at other clubs including Hickory House. But apart from swinging records, won little attention in music world, soon faded into obscurity.

RECORDS

ADRIAN & HIS TAP ROOM GANG (Rollini)

Vi 25072 I Got a Need for You/ Weather Man
Vi 25085 Jazz o' Jazz/Nagasaki
Vi 25208 Bouncin' in Rhythm/Honeysuckle Rose

PUTNEY DANDRIDGE

Vo 2935 You're a Heavenly Thing/Mr. Bluebird
Vo 2982 Chasing Shadows/When I Grow Too Old to Dream
Vo 3006 Cheek to Cheek/Isn't This a Lovely Day?
Vo 3122 No Other One/A Little Bit Independent
Vo 3252 It's a Sin to Tell a Lie/All My Life
Vo 3277 These Foolish Things/Cross Patch
Vo 3287 A Star Fell Out of Heaven/Mary Had a Little Lamb
Vo 3304 Sing, Baby, Sing/You Turned the Tables on Me
Vo 3351 Easy to Love/You Do the Darndest Things, Baby
Vo 3399 With Plenty of Money and You/I'm in a Dancing Mood
Vo 3409 That Foolish Feeling/Gee, But You're Swell

LPs

ADRIAN ROLLINI

"X"(10″)LVA-3034 Swing Session: 1935 (Vi RIs)

412. DANIELS, BEBE   vo
(VIRGINIA DANIELS)

Born January 14, 1901, Dallas, Texas
Died early 1971 in England

Beautiful star of silent and sound movies, sang in several movie musicals 1929-31. Began silent movie career in 1917 with Harold Lloyd in JUST NUTS. Many shorts with Lloyd and Snub Pollard. By mid-20s a star in silents. Most important MISS BREWSTER'S MILLIONS and VOLCANO (1926), A KISS IN A TAXI (1927), TAKE ME HOME and FEEL MY PULSE (1928). A hit in sound musical RIO RITA (1929), DIXIANA (1930) and REACHING FOR THE MOON

(1931). In important 1933 movie musical 42ND STREET, also 1933 English movie THE SONG YOU GAVE ME. In 1935 movie musical MUSIC IS MAGIC, also several dramatic films in 30s. She and husband, actor Ben Lyon, toured in plays during 30s in U.S. and England. Team popular in England, settled there. Popular during World War II entertaining troops. Lyon became film executive. They had long-running radio show in England, later on TV. Returned occasionally to U.S. for visits. Bebe retired from show business in 1963 due to stroke and subsequent ill health.

RECORDS

BEBE DANIELS
Vi 22132 You're Always in My Arms/ If You're in Love, You'll Waltz
Vi 22283 Night Winds/Until Love Comes Along
Br 7402 Dream Shadows/Hollywood Holiday (with BEN LYON, SKEETS GALLAGHER)

LPs

Epic LN-3188 Here Come the Girls (RIs) (miscellaneous artists; one song)
Vi LPV-538 Stars of the Silver Screen, 1929-1930 (RIs)
Mon-Ever MES-7030 A Nostalgia Trip to the Stars 1920-1950, Vol. 1 (RIs)
Mon-Ever MES-7031 A Nostalgia Trip to the Stars 1920-1950, Vol. 2 (RIs)

413. DANIELS, BILLY   vo

Popular singing stylist and excellent showman, noted for vocal and body gyrations. Rose to fame on rendition of *That Old Black Magic*. Attended Florida Normal College, began singing on Jacksonville radio. Later landed job at Ubangi Club in New York, soon played top clubs there. By the mid-40s Daniels well known. Supporting roles in several movies: HOLD 'EM, NAVY (1937), FRENCHMAN'S CREEK (1944), MASQUERADE IN MEXICO (1945), WHEN YOU'RE SMILING (1950), CRUISIN' DOWN THE RIVER (1953), THE BEAT GENERATION (1959). Records well received in late 40s and 50s. During much of career used former Cab Calloway pianist Benny

Payne as accompanist. Payne also contributed comedy and vocalizing. Their showmanship excellent. In 1964 important role for Daniels in Broadway musical GOLDEN BOY starring Sammy Davis, Jr. Occasional appearances on TV. By later 60s less active in show business.

RECORDS

BILLY DANIELS
Mer 1207 Too Marvelous for Words/I Get a Kick Out of You
Mer 1211 September Song/Just One of Those Things
Mer 1235 That Old Black Magic/ Diane
Mer 5614 I Never Knew/I'll Never Know Why
Mer 5721 That Old Black Magic/I Concentrate on You
Mer 5806 September Song/Diane
Mer 5868 After You've Gone/Must You Go?
Mer 70291 I Still Get a Thrill/The Game of Love

LPs

BILLY DANIELS
Mer MG-20047 Love Me or Leave Me
Mer MG-20104 Around That Time
Mer-Wing MGW-12116 Love Songs for a Fool
Craftsmen C-8025 The Fabulous Billy Daniels
Jub JGM-5011 At Basin Street East

414. DANKWORTH, JOHNNY
                                as ar cm B

Born September 20, 1927, London, England

Excellent alto sax soloist, early influence in development of modern jazz in England. Soft-toned but driving style. Early in career played in ship bands on crossings to U.S., became interested in modern jazz. With various groups in England in late 40s, formed band in 1950. Groups in early 50s had inventive, tightly knit arrangements, featured his alto sax. Soon a top jazz star in England. In 1959 brought band to U.S. In 60s extensive arranging and composing. Jobbed with wife, jazz-styled singer Cleo Laine, including U.S. appearances. Composing-arranging-conducting for English movies and TV. His later works took on deep, descriptive tone and unorthodox style, strived for new horizons. On Queen Elizabeth's Honors List for music 1974.

RECORDS

ALAN DEAN BE-BOPPERS
De(E)9188 Gone with the Windmill/ Barbados

MELODY MAKER ALL-STARS
Esq(E)10-353 For Victors Only/Gallop Poll

JAZZ AT TOWN HALL
JC 1000 Buzzy (1 & 2)

JOHNNY DANKWORTH
Esq(E) 5-056 Wedding of the Painted Doll/Sin
Esq(E) 10-093 Cherokee/Seven Not Out
Esq(E) 10-163 The Slider/I Hear Music
Esq(E) 10-173 Webb City/Leon Bismarck
Esq(E) 10-193 Strictly Confidential/Allen's Alley
Esq(E) 10-223 Our Delight/Bopscotch
Pa(E) 3694 Moon Flowers/Two Ticks
Pa(E) 3719 Easy Living/I Get a Kick Out of You
Pa(E) 3836 My Buddy/Jerky Thing
Pa(E) 3850 Oo-Be-Doop/Runnin' Wild
Pa(E) 3871 I Got Rhythm/I Know You're Mine
BN 1611 Leapin' in London/Birdland Bounce

LPs

JOHNNY DANKWORTH
Fon 27531 Shakespeare and All That Jazz (with CLEO LAINE)
Fon 67603 The Sophisticated Johnny Dankworth
Roul R-52096 Jazz from Abroad
(one side) BN(10″)BLP-5019 Johnny Dankworth's Cool Britons

THE COOL BRITONS
BN(10″)5052
(movie soundtracks as composer-conductor)
20th Fox S-4182(S) MODESTY BLAISE
UA 5187 (S) SALT & PEPPER

415. DARCY, DON   vo
(JOHN ARCESI; sometimes as DON D'ARCY)
Born February 11, 1918, Sayre, Pa.

Good baritone with name bands of 30s and 40s. Beginning in 1935 with Charlie Barnet, then King Garcia, Dick Gasparre, Joe Marsala, Lud Gluskin, Joe Venuti. 1943-4 with Sonny Dunham. Later 1944 joined Boyd Raeburn, then Johnny Bothwell and Art Mooney. Also worked as single. In late 40s and early 50s recorded under real name. Career faded, never having achieved popularity he deserved.

RECORDS

LOUIS "KING" GARCIA
Bb 6302 Love Is Like a Cigarette/It's Great to Be in Love
Bb 6303 No Greater Love

BOYD RAEBURN
Grand 1004 Starlight Avenue
Grand 1005 I Dream of You
Grand 1006 This Must Be Love
Grand 1007 It Could Happen to You
Guild 104 Prisoner of Love
Guild 107 I Didn't Know About You

JOHNNY BOTHWELL
Si 15034 I Left My Heart in Mississippi
Si 15045 Somewhere in the Night
Si 15059 My Old Flame
Si 15066 I'll Close My Eyes

JOHN ARCESI
Cap 711 Noah's Ark/Spooks
Cap 2206 Wild Honey/Moonlight Brings Memories
Cap 2270 I'm Alone Because I Love You/I Promise You
Cap 2300 It's Over/Lost in Your Love

416. DARENSBOURG, JOE .cl as ts B
Born July 9, 1906, Baton Rouge, La.

Clarinetist in traditional New Orleans style. After many years as professional musician, first prominent in 50s. Early experience locally in mid-20s, also toured with road show. Played riverboats to St. Louis, worked there with Fate Marable and Charlie Creath. Toured with band in Al G. Barnes circus, winding up on west coast. Worked there with Mutt Carey in late 20s. Played on liners leaving west coast. Led band at intervals. After early 30s mostly out of music. Returned in early 40s. Several periods with Kid Ory beginning in mid-40s. In early 50s with Gene Mayl, with Teddy Buckner 1956-7. Led own band during later 50s. In early 1961 with John St. Cyr, later that year joined Louis Armstrong's All Stars. Remained till mid-1964, won some attention during this period. Through later 60s again led band on west coast.

RECORDS

KID ORY
Exner 3 Dippermouth Blues/Savoy Blues
Exner 4 Ballin' the Jack/High Society
De 25133 Muskrat Ramble/The Girls Go Crazy About the Way I Walk
De 25134 High Society / Blanche Touquatoux
Co 38958 Go Back Where You Stayed Last Night/Yaaka Hula Hickey Dula

BURT BALES
GTJ 36 Down Among the Sheltering Palms

JEANNE GAYLE & GIN BOTTLE FOUR
GTJ 35 Angry

JOE DARENSBOURG
Hot Rod 1001 Hot Rod Harry/Hot Rod Cowboy
Lark 782 Yellow Dog Blues

LPs

GENE MAYL'S DIXIELAND RHYTHM KINGS
Audiophile AP-18

LOUIS ARMSTRONG
Kapp KS-3364 (S) Hello, Dolly!

TEDDY BUCKNER
Dixieland Jubilee 503 In Concert at the Dixieland Jubilee
Dixieland Jubilee 504 And His Dixieland Band

417. DARNELL, BILL   vo
(later spelled last name DARNEL)

Born June 20, 1920, Loraine, Ohio

Singer with name bands in 30s, later a single. Strong, husky, easily identifiable voice. Began professionally in mid-30s. Early job with Bobby Grayson, sustaining shows on New York radio. In late 30s

with Red Nichols about two years, in early 40s with Al Kavelin and Bob Chester. Military service, World War II. Resumed career as single. First records as crooner not popular, so began belting out songs with more success. Records in early 50s well received, especially *Chattanooga Shoe Shine Boy* and *Sugarfoot Rag*. One of best: *That's the Way Love Goes*. By end of 50s Darnell had faded.

RECORDS

EDGAR HAYES
De 1382 High, Wide and Handsome
De 1444 So Rare/Love Me or Leave Me

FRANK FROEBA
De 1500 Tears in My Heart
De 1525 Miles Apart

RED NICHOLS
Bb 10179 Our Love/You're So Desirable
Bb 10200 I Never Knew Heaven Could Speak
Bb 10328 Poor Loulie Jean
Bb 10332 It's 'Way Past My Dreaming Time

AL KAVELIN
OK 5734 I Give You My Word/Willie, Willie
OK 5746 Practice Makes Perfect/The Swiss Bellringer
OK 5829 Who Dreamed You Up?/Whatever Happened to You?

BOB CHESTER
Bb 11017 I Could Write a Book
Bb 11034 Waterloo Bridge
Bb 11088 My Sister and I

BILL DARNELL
Key 665 Let's Fall in Love/Walkin' My Baby Back Home
Abbey 53 Do You Miss Me?/Under the Linden Tree
Standard 2048 Stars Will Fade
De 28706 Come to Me/Tonight, Love
Cor 60093 So Much/Hoe Cake Hominy and Sassafras Tea
Cor 60147 Chattanooga Shoe Shine Boy/Sugarfoot Rag
Cor 60295 Three Little Words/Blues My Naughty Sweetie Gave to Me
Cor 60369 Once There Lived a Fool/Lovesick Blues

779

"X"-0001 That's the Way Love Goes/ For You
"X"-0031 Teardrop Avenue/You Can Betcha Life

LPs

BILL DARNELL
"X"(10″)LXA-3033 Bill Darnell Sings

418. DAVENPORT, COW COW
p o vo cm lyr
(CHARLES DAVENPORT)
Born April 23, 1894, Anniston, Ala.
Died December 2, 1955, Cleveland, Ohio

Early ragtime pianist, pioneer in boogie woogie style. Played church organ early, then piano in honkytonks. Vaudeville act with Dora Carr. Much touring in carnivals and vaudeville from 1914 through 20s. Also sang. In 30s worked in Cleveland, then more touring. Inactive intervals in later years, worked off and on in New York, Nashville, Cleveland until death. Wrote lasting jazz and novelty numbers: *Mama Don't Allow It, You Rascal You, Cow Cow Blues, Do You Call That Religion?*. Lesser songs: *Low Down Man Blues, I Ain't No Ice Man, Buckwheat Cakes, State Street Jive, Hobson City Stomp* and other blues. In 1942-3 Freddie Slack and vocalist Ella Mae Morse had hit record, *Cow Cow Boogie*, adapted from Davenport's earlier *Cow Cow Blues*. After some controversy Davenport sold out rights to tune.

RECORDS
DORA CARR-CHARLES DAVENPORT
OK 8130 You Might Pizen Me
OK 8244 Good Woman's Blues/He Don't Mean Me No Harm
OK 8284 Fifth Street Blues
OK 8306 You Got Another Thought Coming/Alabama Mis-Treater
HOUND HEAD HENRY
Vo 1208 Freight Train Special/Steam boat Blues
Vo 1209 Hound Head Blues/Rooster Crowin' Blues
Vo 1210 Cryin' Blues/Laughin' Blues
MEMPHIS SAM AND JOHN
Ge 6978 It's Just All Right/Everybody Likes That Thing

COW COW DAVENPORT
Para 12439 Jim Crow Blues/Goin' Home Blues
Para 12452 New Cow Cow Blues/ Stealin' Blues
Vo 1198 Cow Cow Blues/State Street Jive
Vo 1253 Alabama Strut/Chimin' the Blues
Vo 1291 Texas Shout/We Gonna Rub It
Ge 6869 Atlanta Rag/Slow Drag
De 7462 I Ain't No Ice Man/Railroad Blues
De 7486 Don't You Loud Mouth Me/ That'll Get It
De 7813 The Mess Is Here
Comet 3 Run into Me/Hobson City Stomp
Comet 4 Gin Mill Stomp/Cow Cow's Stomp
Br 80022 Cow Cow Blues/State Street Jive
CHARLIE DAVENPORT-IVY SMITH
Ge 6994 He Don't Mean Me No Harm/You Got Another Thought Coming to You
COW COW DAVENPORT-SAM THEARD
Vo 1408 That'll·Get It/I'm Gonna Tell You in Front So You Won't Feel Hurt Behind

419. DAVID, HAL   lyr
Born May 25, 1921, New York, N.Y.
Lyricist beginning late 40s. Successful career from late 50s through 70s collaborating with composer Burt Bacharach on many popular songs. Younger brother of lyricist Mack David. Attended NYU. Best-known songs *The Four Winds and the Seven Seas, Walk On By, Alfie, The Look of Love, Raindrops Keep Fallin' on My Head, Do You Know the Way to San Jose?, What the World Needs Now Is Love.* Other collaborators Arthur Altman, Lee Pokriss, Sherman Edwards, Redd Evans, Don Rodney, Henry Mancini.

SONGS
(with related shows; *in collaboration with Burt Bacharach)
1942—Candles in the Wind

1949—The Four Winds and the Seven Seas; Single Saddle; Blue for a Boy, Pink for a Girl
1950—American Beauty Rose
1951—Wonderful, Wasn't It?
1952—More or Less
1953—Hug Me a Hug
1954—A Walkin' Tune; Chain Reaction
1957—The Story of My Life*; Winter Warm*; Magic Moments*; Warm and Tender*
1959—Broken-Hearted Melody; My Heart Is an Open Book; In Times Like These*; With Open Arms*; Loving Is a Way of Living*; That Kind of Woman*
1960—Outside My Window
1961—You'll Answer to Me; Sea of Heartbreak; Forever My Love*; Don't Envy Me*
1962—Johnny Get Angry; Don't Make Me Over*; The Man Who Shot Liberty Valance*; Make It Easy on Yourself*; Only Love Can Break a Heart*; Wonderful to Be Young*
1963—WIVES AND LOVERS movie (title song)*; Anyone Who Had a Heart*; Blue on Blue*
1964—A HOUSE IS NOT A HOME movie (title song)*; First Night of the Full Moon; Walk On By*; Reach Out for Me*; Wishin' and Hopin'*; I Fell in Love with Your Picture*
1965—WHAT'S NEW, PUSSYCAT? movie (title song)*; What the World Needs Now Is Love*; Here I Am*
1966—ALFIE movie (title song)*; PROMISE HER ANYTHING movie (title song)*
1967—The Look of Love*; Do You Know the Way to San Jose?* (c. 1967-8)
1969—BUTCH CASSIDY AND THE SUNDANCE KID movie (Raindrops Keep Fallin' on My Head)*

Other songs: They Long to Be Close to You*; Blue Guitar*; Send Me No Flowers*; What Do You See in Her?; La Charanga; Our Concerto; True Love Never Runs Smooth*; 24 Hours from Tulsa*; I Wake Up Cryin'*; Any Old Time of the Day*; Trains and Boats and Planes*; Magic Potion*; Always Something There to Remind Me*; This Empty Place*; You'll Never Get to Heaven*; Baby Elephant Walk; A Lifetime of Loneliness*; Woodland Symphony; Over the Hills; Remember Me in Your Dreams; Who's Been Sleeping in My Bed?*

420. DAVID, MACK   lyr cm
Born July 5, 1912, New York, N.Y.

Important lyricist from early 30s through 60s. Best-known songs *Moon Love, On the Isle of May, The Singing Hills, A Sinner Kissed an Angel, Candy, La Vie en Rose, I Don't Care If the Sun Don't Shine.* Older brother of lyricist Hal David. Attended Cornell University and St. John's Law School. Wrote TV themes for 77 Sunset Strip, Bourbon Street Beat, Hawaiian Eye, Surfside 6, The Roaring Twenties, Lawman, Casper the Friendly Ghost. Wrote scores and title songs for movies. Collaborators included composers Jerry Livingston, Al Hoffman, Alex Kramer, Joan Whitney, Frankie Carle, Count Basie, Burt Bacharach, Ernest Gold, Elmer Bernstein, Frank DeVol, Henry Mancini.

SONGS
(with related shows)

1932—Rain, Rain, Go Away
1936—Quicker Than You Can Say Jack Robinson
1938—Just a Kid Named Joe; Sixty Seconds Got Together; There's Honey on the Moon Tonight; Blue and Sentimental
1939—Moon Love; But It Didn't Mean a Thing; What Do You Know About Love?
1940—Falling Leaves; On the Isle of May; The Singing Hills
1941—POT O' GOLD movie (Do You Believe in Fairy Tales?; A Knife, a Fork and a Spoon; When Johnny Toots His Horn; Pete the Piper; Hi, Cy, What's a-Cookin'?); A Sinner Kissed an Angel
1942—Sweet Eloise; Take Me
1944—It's Love, Love, Love; Candy; Don't You Know I Care?
1946—I'm Just a Lucky So and So; I'm Gonna Lasso a Dream; You're Too Dangerous, Cherie

1947—Chi-Baba, Chi-Baba; That's What Every Young Girl Should Know; At the Candlelight Cafe; You Are Everything to Me; Serenade to Love

1948—Sunflower; Don't You Love Me Anymore?; Baby, Don't Be Mad at Me

1949—CINDERELLA movie cartoon (Cinderella; A Dream Is a Wish Your Heart Makes; The Cinderella Work Song; So This Is Love; Bibbidi, Bobbidi, Boo); I Don't Care If the Sun Don't Shine

1950—AT WAR WITH THE ARMY movie (The Navy Gets the Gravy but the Army Gets the Beans; Tonda Wanda Hoy; You and Your Beautiful Eyes); La Vie en Rose

1951—The Mill on the Floss

1952—SAILOR BEWARE movie (Never Before; Sailors' Polka; Merci Beaucoup; The Old Calliope; Today, Tomorrow, Forever)

1953—SHANE movie (title song); THOSE RED HEADS FROM SEATTLE movie (Baby, Baby, Baby; I Guess It Was You All the Time); When Someone Wonderful Thinks You're Wonderful

1954—My Own True Love (lyrics added to Max Steiner's Tara's Theme)

1955—Cherry Pink and Apple Blossom White; Dawn

1959—THE HANGING TREE movie (title song); The Blues Country Style

1961—BACHELOR IN PARADISE movie (title song)

1962—WALK ON THE WILD SIDE movie (title song)

1963—HUD movie (title song); IT'S A MAD, MAD, MAD, MAD WORLD movie (title song)

1964—HUSH, HUSH, SWEET CHARLOTTE movie (title song); LOVE GODDESS movie (title song)

1965—CAT BALLOU movie score (The Ballad of Cat Ballou; others)

1966—HAWAII movie (Hawaii; My Wishing Doll); It Must Be Him

1967—THE DIRTY DOZEN movie (The Dirty Dozen)

Other songs: *Bermuda Buggyride*; *It Only Hurts for a Little While*; *I Like It, I Like It*; *The Call of the Faraway Hills*; *The Willow*; *Room for One More*; *Bimbombay*; *Young Emotions*; *Spellbound*; *Johnny Zero*

421. DAVIS, BENNY   lyr vo
Born August 21, 1895, New York, N.Y.

Lyricist with prolific output early 20s into 60s. Best-known songs *Margie, I'm Nobody's Baby, Angel Child, Yearning, Baby Face, Carolina Moon, Chasing Shadows, With These Hands*. Chief collaborators composers J. Fred Coots, Milton Ager, Harry Akst. Others included Con Conrad, Arthur Swanstrom, J. Russel Robinson, Billy Baskette, Nat Shilkret, Murray Mencher. At 14 in vaudeville. Several years later in act with Blossom Seeley and Benny Fields. Wrote lyrics for 1929 Broadway musical SONS O' GUNS, also for three editions of Cotton Club revues in 30s.

SONGS
(with related shows)

1917—Goodbye Broadway, Hello France

1920—Margie

1921—I'm Nobody's Baby (revived 1940); Make Believe

1922—Angel Child; Say It While Dancing

1923—First, Last and Always; Indiana Moon; A Smile Will Go a Long Long Way; Dearest, You're the Dearest to My Heart

1924—Main Street Wasn't Big Enough for Mary

1925—Are You Sorry?; Yearning; Oh, How I Miss You Tonight

1926—Baby Face; Everything's Gonna Be All Right; Lonesome and Sorry; Sleepy Head; If I'd Only Believed in You; Somebody's Lonely; That's My Girl

1927—Gorgeous; I'm Gonna Meet My Sweetie Now; It's a Million to One You're in Love; No Wonder I'm Happy

1928—Mary Ann; Who Wouldn't Be Blue?; That's How I Feel About You

1929—SONS O' GUNS stage show (Cross Your Fingers; Why?; It's You I

Love; May I Say "I Love You"?; Red Hot and Blue Rhythm); Carolina Moon; Takes You; All That I'm Asking Is Sympathy

1930—I Still Get a Thrill
1931—If You Haven't Got a Girl; Little Mary Brown; Nothing's Too Good for My Baby; I'm Happy When You're Happy
1932—So Ashamed
1934—There Goes My Heart; I Hate Myself; Wish Me Good Luck, Kiss Me Goodbye
1935—Chasing Shadows
1936—That's What You Mean to Me; Copper Colored Gal; Doin' the Suzy Q; I'll Stand By; I'm Grateful to You; In My Estimation of You; The More I Know You; Isn't Love the Strangest Thing?; Until Today; Why Do I Lie to Myself About You?; Who Loves You?; You Started Me Dreaming; Yours Truly Is Truly Yours; A Little Robin Told Me So; Alabama Barbecue
1937—My Day Begins and Ends with You
1938—Let This Be a Warning to You, Baby; I'm Madly in Love with You
1939—This Is No Dream; To You; Sweet Dreams, Sweetheart; All in Favor of Swing Say "Aye"
1940—Where Were You Last Night?
1942—All I Need Is You; Please Think of Me
1946—Far Away Island
1948—She's a Home Girl
1949—How Green Was My Valley
1950—Every Moment of My Life
1951—A Kiss and a Promise
1952—When
1953—With These Hands; False Love; You Fooled Me
1954—Endless
1961—Baby's First Christmas; Don't Break the Heart That Loves You
1963—FOLLOW THE BOYS movie (title song)

Other songs: *Lost a Wonderful Girl*; *When Will the Sun Shine for Me?*; *Patricia*; *The Old Mill Wheel*; *This Is My Happiest Moment*; *There's No Other Girl*.

422. DAVIS, BERYL   VO
Born c. 1925

Good English singer who performed in U.S. from late 40s. Melodious style. Started in England at 9 as singer-dancer. Played vaudeville, appeared on radio. In later years with dance bands, including Ted Heath in mid-40s. Came to U.S. in 1947, signed with Victor Records. Later in 1947 began appearing on Lucky Strike Hit Parade radio show. In late 40s married and retired awhile. Came back in late 1950 for more recordings and radio work, had early TV show in 1951. In later 50s teamed with Jane Russell, Connie Haines and Della Russell to form female quartet specializing in gospel songs.

RECORDS
STEPHANE GRAPPELLY
  De(E) 8375 Star Eyes/Heavenly Music
  Lon(E) 101 Don't You Know I Care?/No One Else Will Do
  Lon(E) 154 That Old Black Magic/Star Eyes
  Lon(E) 155 Confessin'/Heavenly Music
ART YOUNG
  Lon(E) 153 I Cried for You/Blue Skies
DAVID ROSE
  MGM 30858 Sleepy Lagoon
BERYL DAVIS
  Vi 20-2268 If My Heart Had a Window/I Want to Be Loved
  Vi 20-2426 It All Came True/One Little Tear Is an Ocean
  Vi 20-2483 The Best Things in Life Are Free/Pass That Peace Pipe
  Vi 20-2685 Strangers in the Dark
  Vi 20-3019 The Blue Room/Don't Blame Me
  Vi 20-3036 Just Once More/Down the Stairs and Out the Door
  MGM 11515 You/Nowhere Guy
  MGM 30724 Suddenly/Beautiful Music to Love By
BERYL DAVIS-JANE RUSSELL-CONNIE HAINES-DELLA RUSSELL
  Cor 61113 Make a Joyful Noise Unto the Lord/Do Lord

423. DAVIS, BILL   o p g ar cm
(WILLIAM STRETHEN DAVIS; known as WILD BILL DAVIS)
Born November 24, 1918, Glasgow, Mo.

Pioneer jazz organist. Grew up in Parsons, Kan. Attended Tuskegee Institute and Wiley College. Early musical work in late 30s as guitarist-arranger with Milt Larkin. To Chicago in early 40s for freelance jobs and arranging. With Louis Jordan 1945-8 as pianist-arranger, sometimes played organ. In late 40s organist in Chicago and New York clubs. In early 50s began leading combo. Records soon caught public fancy. Continued arranging; charts for Duke Ellington and Count Basie. His arrangement of *April in Paris* for Basie big hit in mid-50s. In later years his powerful, swinging organ style moved from jazz to rhythm and blues. Active through 60s, took European tour with Ellington in 1969.

RECORDS
WILD BILL DAVIS
- Mercer 1955 Things Ain't What They Used to Be/Make No Mistake
- OK 6867 Rough Ridin'/Azure Te
- OK 6879 Picadilly Circus/Without a Song
- OK 6913 Alexandria, Va./Ooh Ah-De-De-De
- OK 6946 Lullaby of Birdland/April in Paris
- OK 7013 Indian Summer/Theme from "The Joe Louis Story"
- OK 7021 Ain't Feeling So Good/Bring the Money In

DOLORES HAWKINS (trio backing)
- OK 6903 Each Time

LPs
WILD BILL DAVIS
- Epic N-3118 Wild Bill Davis at Birdland
- Epic N-5094 Dance the Madison
- Cor CRL-57417 One More Time
- Vi LSP-3799(S) Midnight to Dawn
- Everest SDBR-1052 Flying High with Wild Bill Davis
- Tangerine S-1509 Wonderful World of Love

JOHNNY HODGES-WILD BILL DAVIS
- Vi LSP-3706(S) In Atlantic City

- Verve V-8570 Mess of Blues
- Verve V-8617 Joe's Blues

EDDIE SHU-JOE ROLAND-WILD BILL DAVIS
- Mercer(10″)1002

424. DAVIS, EDDIE "LOCKJAW"
ts B

Born March 2, 1921, New York, N.Y.

Tenor sax star with powerful, hard-driving style. Ability to fit with mainstream, modern and rhythm-and-blues bands. Also effective on ballads. With Cootie Williams 1942-4. With Lucky Millinder, Andy Kirk and Louis Armstrong during 1944-5. Mostly led combo in New York 1945-52, also freelanced. Joined Count Basie mid-1952 and remained a year. Then freelanced, led combo. Organist Shirley Scott teamed with his group beginning 1955 into 60s. In mid-60s rejoined Basie as sideman-road manager.

RECORDS
COOTIE WILLIAMS
- Hit 8088 Sweet Lorraine/Honeysuckle Rose
- Hit 8089 You Talk a Little Trash/Floogie Boo

COUNT BASIE
- Mer 89014 Paradise Squat/Hobnail Boogie
- Mer 89085 Bread

GENE KRUPA
- Clef 89119 Windy/Meddle My Minor

EDDIE "LOCKJAW" DAVIS
- Sav 904 Hollerin' and Screamin'/Maternity
- Sav 907 Calling Dr. Jazz/Stealin' Trash
- Sav 933 Spinal/Fracture
- Haven 800 Lockjaw/Afternoon in a Doghouse
- Haven 801 Surgery/Athlete's Foot
- Apo 767 Lover/Licks a-Plenty
- Apo 779 Foxy/Sheila
- Lenox 515 Minton's Madhouse/Ravin' at Haven
- Roost 553 My Blue Heaven/Bewitched
- Roost 559 Please Don't Talk About Me When I'm Gone/Blues in My Heart

LPs

EDDIE "LOCKJAW" DAVIS
Pres 7141 Cookbook, Vol. 1
Pres 7161 Cookbook, Vol. 2
Pres 7171 "Jaws" in Orbit
Vi LPM-3652 Lock, the Fox
Vi LPM-3741 The Fox and the Hounds

EDDIE "LOCKJAW" DAVIS-SHIRLEY SCOTT
Moodsville 30 Misty

EDDIE "LOCKJAW" DAVIS-PAUL GONSALVES
Vi LSP-3882 Love Calls

COUNT BASIE
Roul R-52003 Basie

TINY GRIMES
Pres 7144 Callin' the Blues

ARNETT COBB
Pres 7151 Blow, Arnett, Blow

425. DAVIS, JANETTE   vo
Born in Memphis, Tenn.

Low, husky-voiced singer who rose to fame in 50s as star of Arthur Godfrey shows on radio and TV. Sang on radio at 14. Later to Chicago, on radio there, worked with Caesar Petrillo and others. In mid-40s own nightly network shows. Joined Godfrey radio show in 1946 and remained over ten years. Became well known through his shows, especially on TV in early and mid-50s: daily morning show (simultaneously on radio) and weekly variety show. Sometimes sang duets with Godfrey. When shows faded in late 50s, she retired from show business.

RECORDS

JANETTE DAVIS
Co 38096 There Ought to Be a Society/They Can't Make a Lady Out of Me
Co 38223 Put the Blame on Mame/Just a Shade on the Blue Side
Co 38677 Poison Ivy/I Don't Know Whether to Laugh or Cry over You
Co 38815 Cross Your Heart/Darn It, Baby, That's Love (with ARTHUR GODFREY)
Co 39537 You
Co 39689 Gonna Get Along without Ya Now
Ha 1048 Some Enchanted Evening/A Wonderful Guy

JANETTE DAVIS with LARRY CLINTON ORCHESTRA
Rbw 10099 Walk Before You Run

JANETTE DAVIS-BILL LAWRENCE
Co 39025 Longing/Li'l Ol' You

JANETTE DAVIS-JERRY WAYNE
Co 38386 If That Isn't Love, What Is?/A Little Bird Told Me
Co 38387 You Say the Nicest Things, Baby/I Got Lucky in the Rain

JANETTE DAVIS-ARTHUR GODFREY
Co 40251 After You've Gone

LPs

ARTHUR GODFREY
Co GL-521 Arthur Godfrey's TV Calendar Show

425A. DAVIS, JIMMIE   vo g cm lyr B
Born September 11, 1902, Quitman, La.

Country and western star from 30s into 50s. Two-term governor of Louisiana. Composer or co-composer of important songs including *Nobody's Darlin' but Mine* (1935), *When It's Roundup Time in Heaven* (1936), *You Are My Sunshine* (1940), *A Worried Mind* and *Sweethearts or Strangers* (1941), *Columbus Stockade Blues* (1943), *There's a New Moon Over My Shoulder* (1944). Grew up in Beech Springs, La. Educated at Louisiana College and LSU. Professor of history and social science at Dodd College. Composed and performed country music as sideline, then left teaching to become full-time professional. Signed mid-30s with new Decca Records. Sang on Shreveport radio, attained popularity. Police commissioner of Shreveport, then state public service commissioner. Governor of Louisiana 1944-8. Helped write, starred and sang in movie on life story LOUISIANA around late 1946-7. In several western movies early 40s. Late 40s returned to entertaining; in 50s leading gospel singer. Second term as governor 1960-4.

RECORDS

JIMMIE DAVIS
Bb 5006 Bear Cat Mama/She's a Hum Dum Dinger
Bb 5425 Alimony Blues/You've Been Tom Cattin' Around

Bb 5496 Shotgun Wedding/Arabella Blues

De 5206 High Geared Mama/Bed Bug Blues

De 5779 My Blue Heaven/Why Should I Care?

De 5794 What Else Can I Do?/I'm Still a Fool Over You

De 5813 You Are My Sunshine/Old Timer

De 5902 Sweethearts or Strangers/On the Sunny Side of the Rockies

De 5989 Pay Me No Mind/I'm Knocking at Your Door Again

De 6062 You Told Me a Lie/Don't You Cry Over Me

De 6070 I Dreamed of an Old Love Affair/A Sinner's Prayer

De 6100 Is It Too Late?/There's a Chill on the Hill Tonight

De 6105 There's a New Moon Over My Shoulder/Love, Don't Let Me Down

De 14590 Mansion Over the Hilltop/I Ain't Gonna Study War No Mo'

De 14596 Someone to Care/I Won't Have to Cross Jordan Alone

De 46003 Nobody's Darlin' but Mine/Sweethearts or Strangers

De 46381 Fifteen Miles from Dallas/Bayou Pon Pon

Cap 40281 Sometimes Late at Night/White Lace, Red Clay

LPs

JIMMIE DAVIS

De DL-4432 Highway to Heaven

De DL-4495 Jimmie Davis Sings

De DL-8896 You Are My Sunshine

De DL-8953 Suppertime

De DL-74819 Gospel Hour

De DL-75387 Memories Coming Home

425B. DAVIS, JOHNNY "SCAT"

t vo B

Born c. 1915, Brazil, Ind.

Scat singer and trumpet player with Fred Waring band. Some prominence in late 30s movies. Exuberant personality. Raspy scat vocals effective at up tempos. Began career as teenager. Early 30s with Jimmy Joy, Red Nichols, Will Osborne, Smith Ballew. Briefly fronted Casa Loma band 1932. Joined Waring 1932, remained almost constantly through mid-30s, featured on Waring radio show. Left at intervals to lead band 1935 to 1937. Briefly with Frankie Trumbauer early 1937. Waring band and singers featured in big 1937 movie VARSITY SHOW starring Dick Powell. Davis registered as comic, made more movies with Powell, HOLLYWOOD HOTEL and COWBOY FROM BROOKLYN (1938). Other movies GARDEN OF THE MOON and BROTHER RAT (1938), MR. CHUMP (1939), SARONG GIRL (1943), KNICKERBOCKER HOLIDAY and YOU CAN'T RATION LOVE (1944). Toured 1939 with big band; key engagement at Chicago's Blackhawk Restaurant. Theme *Hooray for Hollywood* (song he sang in HOLLYWOOD HOTEL). Excellent front man. Leader of bands and combos in 40s and 50s. Sometimes played good dixieland, always stressed showmanship and sound musicianship. Less prominent later years.

RECORDS

RED NICHOLS

Br 6219 Get Cannibal/Junk Man Blues

WARING'S PENNSYLVANIANS

Vi 22966 You're the One

Vi 22978 Rhymes/How'm I Doin'?

Vi 24030 I Heard

DECCA ALL-STAR REVUE

De 345 You're the Top (1 & 2)

De 473 'Way Back Home (1 & 2)

JOHNNY "SCAT" DAVIS

Cr 3208 Sugar

Cr 3210 Blue Kentucky Moon

De 256 Were You Foolin'?/Don't Stop Me If You've Heard It Before

De 257 A Hundred to One It's You/Congratulate Me

De 271 Between Showers/You Gotta Give Credit to Love

De 272 College Rhythm/Take a Number from One to Ten

De 573 Truckin'/Loafin' Time

De 583 I Feel a Song Comin' On/Everything Is Okey-Dokey

Hit 7012 Hip Hip Hooray/White Christmas

Universal 17 (theme) Hooray for Hollywood/How Can You Pretend?

LPs

JOHNNY "SCAT" DAVIS
King 626 Here's Lookin' Atcha

426. DAVIS, MAXWELL   ts as v ar B

Born January 14, 1916, Independence, Kansas
Died October 1970, Los Angeles, Calif.

Competent reed man best known as conductor on records or A & R man. Led band in Wichita in mid-30s, played alto sax and violin. In 1936 on tenor sax with Gene Coy. Freelanced in Los Angeles in late 30s. Developed as arranger, worked for Jimmie Lunceford in early 40s among others. In late 40s and 50s led group at intervals. Worked with Lee Young combo in Los Angeles, with Ray Anthony 1952-3. Concentrated on career as A & R man for record companies. With Aladdin label eight years, also period with Modern. On Crown label produced series of LP tributes to famous bandleaders, with all-star jazzmen playing arrangements simulating various bands. Results good, demonstrated ability of Davis as arranger-conductor.

RECORDS

FELIX GROSS
DB 180 Can't Make You, Can't Buy You/Peaceful Loving
HELEN HUMES
Philo 125 He Don't Love Me Anymore/Pleasin' Man Blues
Philo 126 See See Rider/It Is Better to Give Than Receive
Dis 519 Sad Feeling/Rock Me to Sleep
Dis 520 This Love of Mine/He May Be Yours
PETE JOHNSON
DB 168 Skidrow Boogie/Half Tight Boogie
DB 169 Rocket Boogie "88" (1 & 2)
DB 175 Wrinkle Head Boogie/Roadhouse Boogie
RAY ANTHONY
Cap 2293 Idaho
RED CALLENDER
Fed 12049 September in the Rain/Tabor-Inn

MARSHALL ROYAL
Supreme 1544 September in the Rain
Swing Time 313 Little White Lies
IKE CARPENTER
Alad 3172 Sandu
BOBBY PITTMAN
Supreme 101 Deep in a Dream/Don't Mention Love to Me
MAXWELL DAVIS
Swing Time 313 Don't Worry 'Bout Me
RPM 382 The Way You Look Tonight/Side Car
B&W 785 Goody Goody Baby/Root of All My Evil
B&W 858 M.T. Boogie

LPs

MAXWELL DAVIS
Alad 804
Alad(10")709
(as arranger-conductor)
Cr CST-134 A Tribute to Artie Shaw
Cr CLP-5047 A Toast to Tommy & Jimmy Dorsey
Cr CLP-5050 A Tribute to Glenn Miller
Cr CLP-5093 A Salute to Stan Kenton
Cr CLP-5111 Compositions of Count Basie and Others
Cr CLP-5153 Compositions of Duke Ellington and Others

427. DAVIS, MEYER   B

Born c. 1895-6

Well-known leader and booker of society bands from pre-1920 into 70s. Organized first band in high school. By 20 had bands at Willard in Washington, D.C., and Bellevue-Stratford in Philadelphia at same time, fronting each band on alternate weeks. This gave him idea of furnishing dance bands on mass scale. Through the years he gradually built up booking facilities and reputation, was able to furnish band for any occasion on 24-hour notice. Sometimes dozens of units worked for him on same night at different locations. Based mainly in New York, furnished bands in other cities too. These included Washington, where played many formal affairs for six Presidents. His units first and foremost *dance* bands, with lilting, accentuated beat that drew dancers onto floor. Davis units flexible in size and style, could play any type of job. Kept libraries up to date with latest show tunes, popular songs and novelties. In later years seldom appeared himself as leader, but continued active as booker into 70s.

RECORDS

MEYER DAVIS

Co A3883 South Sea Eyes/I'd Love to Have Ya

Vi 19526 Washington & Lee Swing/ Nobody Loves You Like I Do

Br 3938 I Can't Give You Anything but Love/In the Evening

Br 4112 My Old Girl's My New Girl Now

Br 4134 Happy Days and Lonely Nights/When Summer Is Gone

Br 4470 True Blue Lou/The Flippity Flop

Br 4561 He's So Unusual/A Year from Today

Br 4588 Lonely Troubadour/That's Why I'm Jealous of You

Br 4603 If I Had My Way/There Must Be Somebody Waiting for Me

Br 4618 My Fate Is in Your Hands

Br 4748 Blue Is the Night

Br 4802 Nobody Cares If I'm Blue/ Ro-Ro-Rollin' Along

Co 2815-D Thanks/The Day You Came Along

Co 2816-D By a Waterfall/Honey-moon Hotel

Co 2821-D Heat Wave/Lonely Heart

Co 2822-D How's Chances?/Easter Parade

Co 2852-D Did You Ever See a Dream Walking?/Many Moons Ago

Co 36425 Tea for Two/Hallelujah

Co 36426 Time on My Hands/Carioca

Co 36427 I Know That You Know/I Want to Be Happy

Co 36428 Great Day/Without a Song

LPs

MEYER DAVIS

Vi LPM-1756 Meyer Davis & His Or-chestra

ABC-Para 176 Meyer Davis Cordially Invites You ...

ABC-Para 197 On with the Dance

788

428. DAVIS, MILES   t fl-h cm B
Born May 25, 1926, Alton, Ill.

Considered by many to be top modern jazz trumpeter of 50s and 60s. Style very soft, cool, understated, with unorthodox solo lines. Grew up in East St. Louis, Ill. At 15 with Eddie Randall band in St. Louis. After high school with Adam Lambert combo in Chicago; filled in with Billy Eckstine band in St. Louis. To New York in 1945 to study at Juilliard. Modern greats Dizzy Gillespie and Charlie Parker took interest in Davis; soon playing in Parker's combo and with others. Left Juilliard late 1945, went with Benny Carter band to Los Angeles. Worked there again with Parker, attracted following via Parker's Dial recordings. Back east with Eckstine. Another period with Parker in New York during 1947-8. Led combos in late 40s, made memorable recordings. Freelanced in early 50s. Since mid-50s own combo, many LPs. Busy here and abroad into 70s.

RECORDS

CHARLIE PARKER

Sav 573 Billie's Bounce/Now's the Time

Sav 597 Ko-Ko

Dial 1002 A Night in Tunisia/Orni-thology

Dial 1003 Yardbird Suite

Dial 1021 Little Bo-Peep/Don't Blame Me

METRONOME ALL-STARS

Cap 1550 Early Spring/Local 802 Blues

BE-BOP BOYS

Sav 903 Thriving from a Riff

MILES DAVIS

Sav 934 Milestones/Sippin' at Bells

Sav 977 Little Willie Leaps

Cap 15404 Move/Budo

Cap 57-60005 Jeru/Godchild

Cap 57-60011 Boplicity/Israel

Cap 7-1221 Venus de Milo/Darn That Dream

BN 1595 Woody'n You/Dear Old Stockholm

Pres 734 Blue Room/Morpheus

Pres 742 Whispering/Down

Pres 777 Dig? (1 & 2)

MILES DAVIS-LEE KONITZ

Pres 755 Yesterdays

LPs

MILES DAVIS

Cap T-1974 Birth of the Cool (Cap RIs)
Pres 7044 Collector's Items (Pres RIs)
Pres 7094 Cookin'
Co CL-949 'Round About Midnight
Co CL-1041 Miles Ahead
Co CL-2051 Seven Steps to Heaven
Co CL-2306 In Concert
Co CL-2350 Miles Davis/E.S.P.
Co CL-2601 Miles Smiles
BN 1501 Miles Davis, Vol. 1
BN 1502 Miles Davis, Vol. 2

CHARLIE PARKER

Baronet 107 The Early Bird (Dial RIs)
Jazztone J-1214 The Fabulous Bird (Dial RIs)
Sav(10″)MG-9000 Charlie Parker, Vol. 1 (Sav RIs)
Sav(10″)MG-9001 Charlie Parker, Vol. 2 (Sav RIs)
Sav MG-12014 The Genius of Charlie Parker (Sav RIs)

429. DAVIS, PAT   ts cl as
(FRANK ALLEN DAVIS)

Born May 26, 1909, Little Rock, Ark.

Tenor sax soloist with Glen Gray & the Casa Loma Orchestra 1929-43. Dance jobs in mid-20s, including period with Blue Steele. Joined Casa Loma in 1929 as charter member. Had worked with key men in group when it was formed from nucleus of a Jean Goldkette unit and played at Casa Loma in Toronto, before reorganizing as co-op group. Featured on tenor sax solos. In mid-1943 left to return to Little Rock.

RECORDS

THELMA TERRY & HER PLAY-BOYS

Co 1588-D Dusky Stevedore/When Sweet Susie Goes Stepping By

ROY WILSON & HIS GEORGIA CRACKERS

Me 12026 Swamp Blues/Deserted Blues

GLEN GRAY

Vi 24256 Casa Loma Stomp
Br 6486 The Lady from St. Paul
Br 6588 Wild Goose Chase/Buji
Br 6800 I Got Rhythm
Vo 4258 Put on Your Old Grey Bonnet/Alexander's Ragtime Band

De 199 Chinatown, My Chinatown/When Will I Know?
De 286 Stompin' Around
De 986 Royal Garden Blues/Shades of Hades
De 1048 Copenhagen/Jungle Jitters
De 1412 Casa Loma Stomp
De 2031 Mindin' My Business/Song of India

LPs

GLEN GRAY

Cor CRL-56006 Hoagy Carmichael Songs (De RIs)
Ha HL-7045 The Great Recordings of Glen Gray (Br RIs)
De DL-8570 (De RIs)
De(10″)DL-5089 Musical Smoke Rings (De RIs)

430. DAVISON, WILD BILL   c B

Born January 5, 1906, Defiance, Ohio

Jazz cornetist, dixieland style, with 50-year career as sideman and bandleader. Began playing professionally in Ohio in early 20s. During 1924-6 with Chubb-Steinberg band and Seattle Harmony Kings. Freelanced in Chicago 1927-32, including periods with Benny Meroff, Charles Dornberger, Ray Miller. In late 1931 organized band featuring rising clarinet star Frank Teschemacher. Tragedy struck on March 1, 1932, when Davison's car (with Teschemacher a passenger) collided with taxi. Teschemacher killed. Band soon folded. Davison moved to Milwaukee, led band and freelanced during 1933-41. In early 40s led bands in New York and Boston, worked with Brad Gowans and others in New York. Military service about two years, World War II. In late 1945 began playing at Eddie Condon's club, worked regularly there in late 40s and 50s. English tour with Condon in 1957. Beginning 1960 on west coast several years, led band and freelanced. Later 60s toured Europe several times as jazz soloist. Led Jazz Giants group in east 1968-9. Active in 70s leading own band, jobbing.

RECORDS

CHUBB-STEINBERG

OK 40106 Walking Talking Dolly/From One Till Two

OK 40107 Blue Evening Blues/Horsey, Keep Your Tail Up

Ge 3058 Mandy, Make Up Your Mind/Steppin' in Society

BENNY MEROFF

OK 41171 Smiling Skies/Me and the Man in the Moon

GEORG BRUNIS

CMS 546 Ugly Chile/That Da Da Strain

CMS 556 Royal Garden Blues/Tin Roof Blues

CMS 608 Sweet Lovin' Man/Wang Wang Blues

EDDIE CONDON

De 23600 Improvisation for the March of Time/She's Funny That Way

De 23719 Farewell Blues

De 24219 Ida/Down Among the Sheltering Palms

De 24220 Aunt Hagar's Blues/Rose of the Rio Grande

De 24987 At the Jazz Band Ball/Jazz Me Blues

BUD FREEMAN

Key 637 Sentimental Baby

ART HODES

BN 532 Memphis Blues/Shine

BN 533 'Way Down Yonder in New Orleans/St. James Infirmary

ALL-STAR STOMPERS

Ci 1023 Eccentric/Tishomingo Blues

Ci 1024 Baby, Won't You Please Come Home?/Big Butter and Egg Man

EDDIE EDWARDS

CMS 610 Tiger Rag/Barnyard Blues

CMS 612 Ostrich Walk/Lazy Daddy

GEORGE WETTLING

Co 39497 Collier's Clambake/Collier's Climb

WILD BILL DAVISON

CMS 549 Clarinet Marmalade/Original Dixieland One-Step

CMS 563 Confessin'/Big Butter and Egg Man

CMS 628 High Society/Wrap Your Troubles in Dreams

CMS(12")1511 That's a-Plenty/Panama

Ci 1032 Just a Gigolo/Why Was I Born?

Ci 1033 A Ghost of a Chance/Yesterdays

LPs

WILD BILL DAVISON

CMS(10")FL-20000 Wild Bill Davison & His Commodores (CMS RIs)

Jazzology J-2 Wild Bill Davison's Jazzologists

Riv 12-211 Sweet and Hot

Sav 12055 Ringside at Condon's

Co CL-871 (with strings) Pretty Wild

WILD BILL DAVISON with FAT CAT MCREE'S MANASSAS ALL STARS

Fat Cat Jazz 106 "I'll Be a Friend with Pleasure"

TONY PARENTI

Riv 12-205 Tony Parenti's Ragtime Band

Jazzology J-1 Tony Parenti & His New Orleanians

EDDIE CONDON

Co CL-547 (one side) Jam Session Coast-to-Coast

Co CL-616 Jammin' at Condon's

Co CL-719 Bixieland

Co CL-881 Treasury of Jazz

GEORGE WETTLING

Kapp KL-1028 Jazz Trios

ALL-STAR STOMPERS

Ci(10")L-402

431. DAWN, DOLLY   vo cm lyr
(THERESA MARIA STABILE)

Born February 3, 1919, Newark, N.J.

Personable singer with George Hall band, very popular in 30s. Excellent voice, effective on ballads and outstanding in belting out novelties and swingers, good showman. Replaced Hall's star singer Loretta Lee after coaching by Hall. With band 1935-41. Ties with Hall so close he adopted her after several years. Also recorded under own name, sometimes as Dolly Dawn & Her Dawn Patrol. Hall band fixture at New York's Hotel Taft in 30s, and great radio coverage from there made Dolly and band popular. In 1941 Hall retired and turned band over to Dolly awhile. In 1942 she turned to career as single, played clubs and theatres, sang on radio. Record output declined and career faded in late 40s. Worked occasionally in 50s, made a few recordings. Some composing, including *Keep Dreaming* and *The Little Birdies*.

RECORDS

GEORGE HALL

Bb 6015 My Very Good Friend the Milkman
Bb 6099 Accent on Youth
Bb 6101 Will Love Find a Way?
Bb 6127 A Picture of Me without You/Got a Bran' New Suit
Bb 6172 Santy, Bring My Mommy Back to Me
Bb 6173 You Took My Breath Away
Bb 6214 Moon Over Miami
Bb 6282 Every Minute of the Hour
Bb 6379 Love Came Out of the Night
Bb 6509 Please Keep Me in Your Dreams
Va 569 Our Penthouse on Third Avenue/Love Is Never Out of Season
Va 663 You're My Dish
Cq 9045 Says My Heart/You Leave Me Breathless
Vo 3943 I Simply Adore You/Always and Always
Vo 4018 I Fall in Love with You Every Day/How'dja Like to Love Me?
(DOLLY DAWN)
Vo 4297 My Own/You're as Pretty as a Picture

DOLLY DAWN

Bb 6098 As Long as the World Goes 'Round/No Strings
Bb 6216 I'm Sittin' High on a Hilltop/Eeny Meeny Miney Mo
Bb 6381 Robins and Roses/I'll Stand By
Va 557 Alibi Baby/The You and Me That Used to Be
Va 621 You've Got Something There/Have You Got Any Castles, Baby?
Vo 3790 Blossoms on Broadway/You Can't Stop Me from Dreaming
Vo 3874 You're a Sweetheart/Let's Pitch a Little Woo
Vo 3908 Two Dreams Got Together/Bei Mir Bist du Schon
Vo 5160 Goody Goodbye/Shine
El 5018 She'll Always Remember/There Won't Be a Shortage of Love
Jub 6002 Be Anything/You're Not Worth My Tears
Jub 6006 I'm Gettin' Sentimental Over You/Smooth as Silk

432. DAWN, HAZEL   VO
(HAZEL LATOUT)

Born March 23, 1891, Ogden, Utah

Singing star of Broadway musicals, a sensation in debut in 1911 show THE PINK LADY. Associated with show's hit song *My Beautiful Lady*. From musical family; two sisters opera singers (Cecile Arden, Margaret Romaine), one in musical comedy (Eleanor Dawn). Studied voice in London. First stage experience there with small role in DEAR LITTLE DENMARK in 1909. After long-run success in 1911, starred in THE LITTLE CAFE (1913), THE DEBUTANTE (1914), THE CENTURY GIRL (1916). Later, lesser roles in NIFTIES OF 1923, KEEP KOOL (1924), GREAT TEMPTATIONS (1926). In nonmusical plays UP IN MABEL'S ROOM (1919), GETTING GERTIE'S GARTER and THE DEMI-VIRGIN (1921). During 1914-17 appeared in several silent movies. Married in 1927 and retired several years. In unsuccessful 1931 play WONDER BOY. Settled in California, returned to New York in 1947 with daughter Hazel Dawn, Jr., whose stage aspirations soon terminated by marriage. During much of 50s and 60s worked as well-known receptionist in New York talent agency's casting department.

433. DAY, DENNIS   VO
(EUGENE MCNULTY)

Born May 21, 1917, New York, N.Y.

Tenor who became prominent on Jack Benny radio show in 40s. Little professional experience before landing coveted job with Benny late 1939. Sang on New York radio earlier in year. Replaced Kenny Baker with Benny. Instant success thanks to clear Irish tenor and flair for comedy. Military service awhile, World War II. Regular on Benny show in 40s and early 50s, then moved to TV with show. Own shows on radio and TV; talented at impersonations and comedy. On various TV specials and Benny series in later 50s and 60s. In movies BUCK BENNY RIDES AGAIN (1940), POWERS GIRL and SLEEPY LAGOON (1943), MELODY TIME (1948), I'LL GET BY (1950), GOLDEN GIRL (1951), THE GIRL NEXT DOOR (1953). By late 60s largely inactive in show business.

RECORDS

DENNIS DAY

Vi 20-1947 You Keep Coming Back Like a Song/Remember When You Sang "Oh Promise Me"

Vi 20-2451 My Wild Irish Rose/By the Light of the Silv'ry Moon

Vi 20-2737 If It Were Easy to Do/A Few More Kisses

Vi 20-3015 I Love You/I'd Love to Live in Loveland

Vi 20-3323 The Streets of Laredo/Tarra-Ta-Larra Ta-Lar

Vi 20-3900 There Will Never Be Another You/Beautiful Land of My Dreams

Vi 20-3953 And You'll Be Home/The Place Where I Worship

Vi 20-4052 Silver Moon/When Hearts Are Young

Vi 20-4053 Serenade/Deep in My Heart, Dear

Vi 20-4140 Mister and Mississippi/A Trinket of Shiny Gold

Vi 20-4214 Maybe It's Because I Love You Too Much/Mary Rose

Vi 20-4285 California Moon/Never

Vi 20-4560 I Hear a Rhapsody/Mistakes

Cap 125 I'm Glad There Is You

Cap 10013 All the Things You Are/Smoke Gets in Your Eyes

Cap 10014 I've Got You Under My Skin/When Day Is Done

Cap 10015 Danny Boy/With a Song in My Heart

Cap 10016 My Heart Stood Still/Falling in Love with Love

LPs

DENNIS DAY

Vi——— Sings Songs from MY WILD IRISH ROSE

Masterseal MS-3 At Hollywood's Moulin Rouge

Design DLPX-1 Christmas Is for the Family

434. DAY, DORIS   vo
(DORIS KAPPELHOFF)

Born April 3, 1922, Cincinnati, Ohio

Band singer who entered movies in late 40s, became top star in late 50s and 60s. Excellent singer with soft, ingratiating voice. In movies displayed considerable ability in dramatic and comedy roles, especially latter. Studied dancing early, at 12 toured with Fanchon & Marco stage show. Early partner Jerry Doherty. Broken leg turned her to singing. Sang on radio station WLW in Cincinnati and with local bands including Jimmy James around 1937-8, Barney Rapp 1939 and briefly with Bob Crosby in 1940. Some movie work at intervals during 1939-42, small roles in minor films: SAGE OF DEATH VALLEY, VILLAGE BARN DANCE, THOU SHALT NOT KILL, FEDERAL FUGITIVES, MR. CELEBRITY. With Les Brown mid-1940 to early 1941. Quit to give birth to son. In 1943 on Cincinnati station WSAI. Rejoined Les Brown 1943, gained fame in 1944 with hit record of *Sentimental Journey*. Much record work with Brown band. Left in late 1946 for career as single. On radio shows of Bob Hope and Jack Kirkwood. In late 1947 worked briefly with Frank Sinatra on Hit Parade radio show. Good role in 1948 movie ROMANCE ON THE HIGH SEAS (featuring hit tune *It's Magic*). Starred in musicals in early 50s, occasionally played dramatic parts. Mostly lightweight All-American-girl roles. Gordon MacRae, Gene Nelson, Dennis Morgan, Jack Carson worked with her in musicals. In 1955 starred in Ruth Etting role in big musical-drama LOVE ME OR LEAVE ME. Performance outstanding, established her as top star. More important movies followed: good dramas, a few major musicals, a series of popular comedies. Movie career lasted through 60s. In late 60s and early 70s on TV in own situation-comedy show. During two decades of movie work, Doris recorded frequently and her records sold well.

MOVIES

1948—ROMANCE ON THE HIGH SEAS

1949—IT'S A GREAT FEELING; MY DREAM IS YOURS

1950—YOUNG MAN WITH A HORN; TEA FOR TWO; THE WEST POINT STORY; STORM WARNING

1951—LULLABY OF BROADWAY; ON MOONLIGHT BAY; I'LL SEE YOU IN MY DREAMS; STARLIFT

1952—THE WINNING TEAM; APRIL IN PARIS
1953—BY THE LIGHT OF THE SILVERY MOON; CALAMITY JANE
1954—LUCKY ME; YOUNG AT HEART
1955—LOVE ME OR LEAVE ME
1956—JULIE; THE MAN WHO KNEW TOO MUCH
1957—PAJAMA GAME
1958—TEACHER'S PET; TUNNEL OF LOVE
1959—PILLOW TALK; IT HAPPENED TO JANE
1960—MIDNIGHT LACE; PLEASE DON'T EAT THE DAISIES
1961—LOVER COME BACK
1962—JUMBO; THAT TOUCH OF MINK
1963—THE THRILL OF IT ALL; MOVE OVER, DARLING
1964—SEND ME NO FLOWERS
1965—DO NOT DISTURB
1966—GLASS BOTTOM BOAT
1967—CAPRICE
1968—WHERE WERE YOU WHEN THE LIGHTS WENT OUT?; WITH SIX YOU GET EGGROLL

RECORDS

LES BROWN
OK 5964 While the Music Plays On/ Dig It
OK 6011 Between Friends
OK 6062 Amapola/Easy as Pie
Co 36769 Sentimental Journey
Co 36875 Aren't You Glad You're You?/The Last Time I Saw You
Co 36884 You Won't Be Satisfied/ Come to Baby Do
Co 36977 I Got the Sun in the Morning
Co 37066 The Whole World Is Singing My Song
Co 37153 Sooner or Later

DORIS DAY
Co 38302 Just Imagine/Pretty Baby
Co 38507 Now That I Need You
Co 39031 If I Were a Bell/I've Never Been in Love Before
Co 39423 Shanghai/My Life's Desire
Co 39637 Baby Doll/Oops
Co 39786 When I Fall in Love/Take Me in Your Arms
Co 39881 April in Paris/The Cherries
Co 40020 Kiss Me Again, Stranger
Co 40108 Secret Love/The Deadwood Stage

Co 40300 Anyone Can Fall in Love/If I Give My Heart to You
Co 40408 There's a Rising Moon/Till My Love Comes to Me
Co 40505 Never Look Back/I'll Never Stop Loving You
Co 40704 Que Sera, Sera/I've Gotta Sing Away These Blues

DORIS DAY-FRANK SINATRA
Co 38513 Let's Take an Old Fashioned Walk

DORIS DAY-BUDDY CLARK
Co 38394 I'll String Along with You/ Powder Your Face with Sunshine

LPs

DORIS DAY
Co CL-749 Day in Hollywood
Co CL-1053 Day by Night
Co CL-1210 Doris Day's Greatest Hits
Co CL-8066 (S) Hooray for Hollywood
Co(10") CL-6071 You're My Thrill

DORIS DAY-GENE NELSON-PAGE CAVANAUGH TRIO
Co(10") CL-6149 Tea for Two

DORIS DAY-HARRY JAMES ORCHESTRA
Co(10") CL-6106 Young Man with a Horn

DORIS DAY-ANDRE PREVIN
Co CL-1752 Duet

(movie soundtracks)
Co CL-710 LOVE ME OR LEAVE ME
Co OL-5210 PAJAMA GAME
Co OL-5860 JUMBO
Co(10") CL-6273 CALAMITY JANE

435. DAY, EDITH   VO

Born April 10, 1896, Minneapolis, Minn.
Died May 1, 1971, London, England

Singing-acting star of important Broadway musicals and London productions. Starred in hit show IRENE (1919), sang *Alice Blue Gown*. Sang *A Kiss in the Dark* in show ORANGE BLOSSOMS (1922). Later 20s began performing in U.S. shows at London's Drury Lane Theatre, became known as The Queen of Drury Lane. In musicals ROSE-MARIE, DESERT SONG, SHOW BOAT, RIO RITA. In Noel Coward shows WAITING IN THE WINGS and SAIL AWAY. Lived in London after retirement.

BROADWAY MUSICALS

1916—FOLLOW ME

1918—GOING UP
1919—IRENE
1922—ORANGE BLOSSOMS
1923—WILDFLOWER

436. DAYE, IRENE   vo

Born c. 1918
Died November 1, 1971, Greenville, S.C.

Band singer of 30s and 40s with strong, melodious voice. Early jobs with Jan Murphy and Mal Hallett. Joined Gene Krupa band in mid-1938, remained till early 1941. Joined Charlie Spivak in late 1943 (later marrying him), continued singing till early 50s.

RECORDS

GENE KRUPA
  Br 8205 My Own/Any Time at All
  Br 8280 Say It with a Kiss
  Br 8292 An Old Curiosity Shop/I Won't Believe It
  Br 8340 The Lady's in Love with You/Some Like It Hot
  Br 8400 You Taught Me to Love Again
  Br 8448 Moonlight Serenade/You and Your Love
  Co 35218 Take Your Love/Sweetheart, Honey, Darlin', Dear
  Co 35304 After All/Vagabond Dreams
  Co 35324 Drummin Man
  Co 35336 You're a Lucky Guy
  Co 35474 My Wonderful One, Let's Dance
  Co 35508 Six Lessons from Madame LaZonga
  OK 5802 I Hear Music
  OK 5961 Deep in the Blues/You Forgot About Me
  OK 6021 There'll Be Some Changes Made
  OK 6034 Boogie Woogie Bugle Boy
  OK 6046 Drum Boogie
SAM DONAHUE
  Bb 11198 Do You Care?
  Bb 11285 Beat the Band to the Bar
CHARLIE SPIVAK
  Vi 20-1636 Ev'ry Time We Say Goodbye
  Vi 20-1646 Sweetheart of All My Dreams/My Baby Said Yes
  Vi 20-2585 Golden Earrings
  Vi 20-2600 The Gentleman Is a Dope

  Vi 20-2777 But None Like You
  Vi 20-2864 Inner Sanctum

437. DeANGELIS, JEFFERSON   vo

Born November 30,1859, San Francisco, Calif.
Died March 20, 1933, Orange, N.J.

Star of Broadway musicals and plays. Early performance in THE BEGUM (1887), first genuine American comic opera. Long run in POOR JONATHAN (1890) co-starring with Lillian Russell. Appeared in BRIAN BORU (1896), THE HIGHWAYMAN (1897), THE ROYAL ROGUE (1900), THE EMERALD ISLE (1902). First big success in 1905 musical FANTANA. In 1907 starred in failure THE GIRL AND THE GOVERNOR, later in year had more success in THE GAY WHITE WAY. In short-running THE BEAUTY SPOT (1909). In operetta THE MIKADO (1910) and MARIE DRESSLER'S ALL STAR GAMBOL (1913). Other Broadway musicals: THE PEARL MAIDEN (1912), THE PASSING SHOW OF 1917, SOME PARTY (1922), CHINA ROSE (1925).

438. DEDRICK, RUSTY   t ar B
(LYLE DEDRICK)

Born July 12, 1918, Delevan, N.Y.

Trumpet man with big horn sound in traditional and swing styles with modern influence. Attended Fredonia State Teachers College. With Dick Stabile in 1938-9. In early 1940 with Red Norvo, then with Claude Thornhill later 1940-1. Military service, World War II. With Ray McKinley and Shep Fields in 1946. Rejoined Thornhill late 1946-7, did some arrangements. Sideman-arranger with Art Waner in New York, 1950-1. Settled in New York as studio musician, active in TV work especially. In 60s his LPs made him better known.

RECORDS
(all LPs)

RUSTY DEDRICK
  Mon-Ever MES-6918 (S) Harold Arlen in Hollywood
  Mon-Ever MES-7035 (S) The Many Friends of Rusty Dedrick
  Mon-Ever MES 6809-10-11 (3-LP set) (S) Irving Berlin

4 Corners FCL-4207 The Big Band
Sound
Counterpoint CPT-552 Salute to
Bunny
Eso(10″)EST-9

DON ELLIOTT-RUSTY DEDRICK
Riv 12-218 Counterpoint for Six
Valves

RICHARD MALTBY
Vik LX-1068 Manhattan Bandstand

MAXINE SULLIVAN
Mon-Ever MES-7038 (S) Shakespeare

439. DeFRANCO, BUDDY   cl ar cm B
(BONIFACE FERDINAND
LEONARDO DEFRANCO)

Born February 17, 1923, Camden, N.J.
Top modern-style clarinetist from mid-
40s into 70s. Great facility and drive, cool
and vibrato-less tone. Grew up in Philadelphia. At 14 won Major Bowes com-
petition and Tommy Dorsey swing contest. Co-leader of teenage band, played on
Philadelphia radio. In late 1939 with Scat
Davis. In early 40s with Gene Krupa, Ted
Fio Rito, Charlie Barnet. Joined Tommy
Dorsey band in late 1944, remained till
mid-1946. Won kudos for swinging clarinet work with Dorsey. In later 40s with
Boyd Raeburn, again with Dorsey. With
Count Basie combo in 1950. Led big band
in 1951, quartet in 1952. Led combo in
later 50s. Won *Down Beat* poll as top
clarinetist for unprecedented string of
years, 1945-55. Strangely, new jazz critics
began to call DeFranco's work "emotion-
less," panned records. Career suffered for
a time. In mid-60s teamed with accordionist Tommy Gumina awhile. In 1965
replaced Ray McKinley as leader of
Glenn Miller Orchestra, continued into
70s. Band perpetuated Miller sound and
hits, featured DeFranco's still outstanding
clarinet. Left band early 1974 to lead jazz
combo. Composer of jazz numbers including *Strings Have Strung, Really Swell,
Warm Evening.*

RECORDS
TOMMY DORSEY
Vi 20-1608 Opus No. 1
Vi 20-1938 The Song Is You/Then I'll
Be Happy

METRONOME ALL-STARS
Cap 15039 Leap Here/Metronome
Riff
Co 38734 No Figs/Double Date

CHARLIE SHAVERS
Vogue 754 She's Funny That Way/
Dizzy's Dilemma
Vogue 755 Serenade to a Pair of Ny-
lons/Broadjump

COUNT BASIE
Co 38888 The Golden Bullet/Blue-
beard Blues

BUDDY DEFRANCO
Cap 57-747 Extrovert/When We're
Alone
MGM 10946 Out of Nowhere/Danc-
ing on the Ceiling
MGM 11043 Make Believe/Why Do I
Love You?
MGM 11250 Get Happy/Samia Shuf-
fle
MGM 11303 Just One of Those
Things/Carioca
MGM 11453 Oh, Lady Be Good/Easy
Living
Clef 89076 Show Eyes/Autumn in
New York

LPs
BUDDY DEFRANCO
Verve MGV-2089 Plays Benny
Goodman
Verve MGV-8221 Cooking the Blues
Verve MGV-8315 Bravura
Cap(10″)H-322
Cap(10″)H-325
Norg MGN-1085 The Buddy DeFranco
Wailers

BUDDY DEFRANCO-ART TATUM
ARS G-412

BUDDY DEFRANCO-TOMMY GUMINA
De DL-4031 Pacific Standard
(Swingin') Time
Mer MG-20743 Kaleidoscope
Mer MG-20833 Polytones

**BUDDY DEFRANCO & THE GLENN MILLER
ORCHESTRA**
Comm 940-S Do You Wanna Dance?
Vi LPM-3819 In the Mod

TOMMY DORSEY
20th Fox TCF-101-2 (2-LP set)
Tommy Dorsey's Greatest Band
(transcription RIs)

440. DeHAVEN, GLORIA   vo

Born July 23, 1924, Los Angeles, Calif.

Beautiful singing star of movie musicals in 40s and 50s. Daughter of stage performer Carter DeHaven. Good singing voice and strong presentation. Early experience with Jan Savitt band in 1942. Small roles in several movies of early 40s, first good singing role in BROADWAY RHYTHM (1944). Starred in numerous movies, most for MGM. Developed into capable dramatic actress, performed in non-musicals. Frequently on TV in 50s as singer or actress. In 1955 Broadway musical SEVENTH HEAVEN (revival of old play/movie). Semi-active in 60s, occasional TV work.

MOVIES

1940—WHEN LADIES MEET; THE GREAT DICTATOR; SUSAN AND GOD
1941—KEEPING COMPANY; TWO-FACED WOMAN; THE PENALTY
1943—BEST FOOT FORWARD; THOUSANDS CHEER
1944—BROADWAY RHYTHM; STEP LIVELY; TWO GIRLS AND A SAILOR; THE THIN MAN GOES HOME; MANHATTAN SERENADE
1945—BETWEEN TWO WOMEN
1948—SUMMER HOLIDAY
1949—YES, SIR, THAT'S MY BABY; SCENE OF THE CRIME; THE DOCTOR AND THE GIRL
1950—I'LL GET BY; SUMMER STOCK; THREE LITTLE WORDS; THE YELLOW CAB MAN
1951—TWO TICKETS TO BROADWAY
1953—DOWN AMONG THE SHELTERING PALMS
1955—SO THIS IS PARIS; THE GIRL RUSH

RECORDS

JAN SAVITT
   Bb 11584 If You Ever, Ever Loved Me
   Bb 30-0800 Romance a la Mode
GLORIA DEHAVEN with GUY LOMBARDO ORCHESTRA
   De 27666 Out o' Breath/Because of You
   De 27741 Hold Me—Hold Me—Hold Me/I Wish I Wuz
GLORIA DEHAVEN
   MGM 30242 Who's Sorry Now?
   MGM 30252 Mem'ry Island

De 27086 There Isn't Very Much to Do Now/Don't Be Afraid
De 27328 I See a Million People/If I Were a Blackbird
De 27731 Let the Worrybird Worry for You/The Closer You Are

LPs

(movie soundtracks)
   MGM(10")E-516 THREE LITTLE WORDS
   MGM(10")E-519 SUMMER STOCK
   Metro M-615 THREE LITTLE WORDS
   De(10")DL-5553 SO THIS IS PARIS
(original Broadway cast)
   De DL-9001 SEVENTH HEAVEN

441. DeKOVEN, REGINALD   cm B

Born April 3, 1859, Middletown, Conn.
Died January 16, 1920, Chicago, Ill.

Composer-director with prolific career in Broadway musicals 1887-1913. Specialized in operettas, recognized as top talent. Few of his songs popular outside context of shows. His 1890 production ROBIN HOOD featured immortal *Oh, Promise Me*, also *Brown October Ale*. Educated abroad, including period at Oxford. Returned to U.S. in 1882. Worked in brokerage firm awhile, also had dry-goods business. Collaborated with lyricist Harry B. Smith, composed first genuine American comic opera THE BEGUM (1887). Scored for Broadway shows in ensuing years. Wrote heavy operas THE CANTERBURY PILGRIMS (1917) and RIP VAN WINKLE (1920). Music critic for *Chicago Evening Post* 1889-90, *Harper's Weekly* 1895-7, *New York Journal* 1898-1906, *New York World* 1907-12. Organized and conducted Washington, D.C., Symphony Orchestra 1902-4.

BROADWAY MUSICALS
(wrote music)

1887—THE BEGUM
1889—DON QUIXOTE
1890—ROBIN HOOD
1892—THE KNICKERBOCKERS
1893—THE ALGERIAN; THE FENCING MASTER
1894—ROB ROY
1896—THE MANDARIN
1897—THE HIGHWAYMAN
1899—PAPA'S WIFE; THE THREE DRAGOONS
1900—BROADWAY TO TOKIO; FOXY QUILLER

1901—THE LITTLE DUCHESS
1902—MAID MARIAN
1903—THE JERSEY LILY; THE RED FEATHER
1905—HAPPYLAND
1907—THE STUDENT KING; THE GIRLS OF HOLLAND
1908—THE GOLDEN BUTTERFLY
1909—THE BEAUTY SPOT
1912—THE WEDDING TRIP
1913—HER LITTLE HIGHNESS

442. DeLANGE, EDDIE   vo lyr B
(EDGAR DELANGE)

Born January 12, 1904, Long Island City, N.Y.
Died July 13, 1949, Los Angeles, Calif.

Bandleader and lyricist of 30s and 40s. Attended University of Pennsylvania. First worked in Hollywood; bit roles in several movies. To New York about 1934 to concentrate on songwriting. Wrote lyrics to two popular songs, Will Hudson's *Moonglow* (1934) and Duke Ellington's *Solitude* (1935). Formed band with Hudson in early 1936 called Hudson-DeLange Orchestra, lasted till early 1938. DeLange fronted band and sang, had crowd-pleasing personality. Band had excellent arrangements (many by Hudson), performed ballads and swing numbers equally well, featured Ruth Gaylor as vocalist. DeLange led own band in 1938-9, featured novelties predominately, but band could swing. Theme *Don't Forget*. On 1939 radio show Honolulu Bound with Phil Baker and Andrews Sisters. Wrote book and lyrics for 1939 Broadway musical SWINGIN' THE DREAM (only 13 performances). Broke up band, continued songwriting in 40s. Collaborated with composers Josef Myrow, Jimmy Van Heusen, Louis Alter, Joseph Meyer, Sam H. Stept.

RECORDS

HUDSON-DELANGE ORCHESTRA
Br 7598 Tormented/It's a Lot of Idle Gossip
Br 7656 Organ Grinder's Swing/ You're Not the Kind
Br 7708 I Never Knew/When It's Sleepy Time Down South
Br 7715 Mr. Ghost Goes to Town/ Mint Julep
Br 7809 How Was I to Know?/Am I Intruding?
Br 8077 Doin' the Reactionary/Sunday in the Park
Br 8147 Why Pretend?/China Clipper
Ma 125 Star Dust/Bugle Call Rag
Ma 138 Yours and Mine/I'm Feelin' Like a Million

EDDIE DELANGE
Bb 7837 Button Button/Jump Jump's Here
Bb 7841 Popcorn Man/Willie the Weeper
Bb 7855 New Shoes Blues/What Are Little Girls Made Of?
Bb 10027 Copenhagen/You Can't Kiss a Frigidaire
Bb 10035 Muskrat Ramble
Bb 10080 My Heart Belongs to Daddy/Three Little Kittens
Bb 10094 Livery Stable Blues/Cockeyed Mayor of Kaunakai
Bb 10199 Serenade to a Wild Cat/Beer Barrel Polka
Bb 10368 Jelly Roll Polka/The Merry Old Land of Oz
Bb 10441 Stop! It's Wonderful/Jiminy Cricket

LP

HUDSON-DELANGE ORCHESTRA
Bandstand 7105 (1936-9 RIs)

SONGS
(with related shows)

1934—I Wish I Were Twins; Moonglow
1935—Haunting Me; Solitude
1937—You're Out of This World to Me; What Are Little Girls Made Of?
1938—At Your Beck and Call; So Help Me; Deep in a Dream; This Is Madness
1939—All I Remember Is You; Can I Help It?; Heaven Can Wait; Good for Nothin' but Love; SWINGIN' THE DREAM stage show (Swingin' a Dream; Darn That Dream; Peace, Brother)
1940—All This and Heaven Too; And So Do I; Flower of Dawn; Looking for Yesterday; Shake Down the Stars; No Love Blues
1941—A String of Pearls
1942—WHEN JOHNNY COMES MARCHING HOME movie (This Is Worth Fight-

ing For); Just as Though You Were Here; Velvet Moon

1945—Who Threw the Whiskey in the Well?; Land of the Loon; Along the Navajo Trail

1946—IF I'M LUCKY movie (If I'm Lucky; One More Vote; Bottom Dollar; Follow the Band); NO LEAVE, NO LOVE movie (When It's Love); ONE MORE TOMORROW movie (title song); Man with a Horn; Afternoon Moon; Passé

1947—NEW ORLEANS movie (Do You Know What It Means to Miss New Orleans?; Endie; Blues Are Brewin'); Arizona Sundown; When Am I Gonna Kiss You Good Morning?; Strange What a Song Can Do; THE BISHOP'S WIFE movie (Lost April)

443. DeLEATH, VAUGHN . vo p cm lyr

Born September 26, 1896, Mt. Pulaski, Ill.
Died May 28, 1943, Buffalo, N.Y.

Singer with extensive radio and recording career in 20s and 30s. Sometimes credited with originating "crooning." Grew up in California. Concert singer and composer in early teens. Attended Mills College in California. Reportedly first woman on radio, active from mid-20s to early 30s on Wrigley show 1926-7, Firestone Hour 1929-30, various NBC shows. Managed New York station WDT. On Broadway in LAUGH, CLOWN, LAUGH in 1923. Returned to network radio in early 1935, continued through 30s. In 1936 ran night club in Stamford, Conn. During career played vaudeville and recorded frequently. Composer or lyricist for several songs: *Drive Safely*; *Hi-Yo, Silver!*; *I Wasn't Lying When I Said I Loved You*; *Little Bit of Sunshine*; *The Gingerbread Brigade*; *Blue Bonnets Underneath the Texas Skies*; *At Eventide*; *Bye Lo*; *Ducklings on Parade*; *If It Hadn't Been for You*; *My Lover Comes a-Riding*; *Rosemary for Remembrance*; *Madonna's Lullaby*; *Cherokee* (1920; not Ray Noble song).

RECORDS

FRED RICH
    Co 1241-D The Man I Love

DON VOORHEES
    Co 1284-D Can't Help Lovin' Dat Man
MOANA ORCHESTRA
    Co 1251-D Aloha Oe Blues
BROADWAY NITELITES
    Co 1604-D I Wanna Be Loved by You
BEN BERNIE
    Br 3808 Can't Help Lovin' Dat Man
SAM LANIN
    OK 40754 Yankee Rose/Blue Skies
LOUIS KATZMAN
    Br 4213 My Man
PAUL WHITEMAN
    Co(12")50068-D The Man I Love
HAROLD LEONARD
    Co 1105-D Joy Bells
VAUGHN DELEATH
    Ed 52192 Keep Sweeping the Cobwebs off the Moon/My Blue Heaven
    Ed 52222 Sunshine/I Just Roll Along
    Co 361-D Ukulele Lady/Banana Oil
    Co 711-D Cross Your Heart/Whadda You Say?
    Co 915-D My Hap-Happiness/I Wonder How I Look When I'm Asleep
    Co 1556-D Dirty Hands, Dirty Face/Little Brown Shoe
    Vi 20600 Song of the Wanderer
    Vi 20787 Sing Me a Baby Song
    Vi 21042 Together, We Two
    Br 3443 Crazy Words—Crazy Tune/Since I Found You
    Br 3608 Sometimes I'm Happy/Baby Feet Go Pitter Patter
    Br 3683 Mr. Aeroplane Man/Tin Pan Parade
    Br 4533 Chant of the Jungle/He's So Unusual
VAUGHN DELEATH-FRANKLYN BAUR
    Co 1236-D Up in the Clouds/Thinking of You

443A. DELMORE BROTHERS
vo v g cm lyr
(ALTON DELMORE)

Born December 25, 1908, Elkmont, Ala.
Died July 4, 1964, Nashville, Tenn.

(RABON DELMORE)

Born December 3, 1910, Elkmont, Ala.
Died December 4, 1952, Athens, Ala.

Entertaining country and western duo from 30s to early 50s. Prolific recording and composing. On radio in many cities. Often on Nashville's Grand Ole Opry. Toured U.S., Canada, Mexico. Last recordings early 50s. After Rabon's death late 1952, Alton settled in Huntsville, Ala and taught music.

RECORDS

DELMORE BROTHERS
- Bb 5338 The Frozen Girl/Bury Me Out on the Prairie
- Bb 5403 Brown's Ferry Blues
- Bb 5467 Got Nowhere to Travel/ Ramblin' Minded Blues
- Bb 5531 Got the Big River Blues/Blue Railroad Train Blues
- Bb 5589 Girls Don't Worry My Mind/Smoky Mountain Bill
- Bb 5857 I'm Memphis Bound/I Believe, for Mother Told Me So
- Bb 7337 Heavenly Light Is Shining on Me/Lead Me
- Bb 7383 The Farmer's Girl/Look Up Look Down the Lonesome Road
- Bb 7436 Goodbye Booze/Careless Love
- Bb 7496 In a Vine Covered Chapel in Valley/'Cause I Don't Mean to Cry When You're Gone
- Bb 7560 Ain't It Hard to Love?/Big Ball in Texas
- Bb 7913 Leavin' on That Train/Git Along
- King 518 Be My Little Pet/Lonely Moon
- King 525 Fast Express/I've Found an Angel
- King 548 Don't Forget Me/Midnight Train
- King 592 Brown's Ferry Blues/Mississippi Shore
- King 599 Boogie Woogie Baby/Born to Be Blue
- King 769 Calling to That Other Shore/The Wrath of God
- King 784 Down Home Boogie/Weary Day

LPs
(miscellaneous artists)
- Vi LPM-6015 Stars of the Grand Ole Opry (RIs)
- Cam CAL-898 "Maple on the Hill" and Other Old Time Country Favorites (RIs)

444. DELTA RHYTHM BOYS   vo

Singing quartet in gospel-blues style. Attained some popularity in 40s. Played clubs and theatres, recorded. In movie shorts and low-budget films including CRAZY HOUSE (1943), SWINGTIME HOLIDAY (1944), EASY TO LOOK AT (1945). Lasted into 50s, with some touring abroad.

RECORDS

DELTA RHYTHM BOYS
- De 4406 Praise the Lord and Pass the Ammunition/Dry Bones
- De 4440 Travelin' Light/Do Nothin' 'Til You Hear from Me
- De 8530 Star Dust/Would It Be Asking Too Much?
- De 8554 The Things I Love/I Do, Do You?
- De 23771 Just Squeeze Me/Hello, Goodbye, Just Forget It
- Vi 20-2855 You're Mine, You/Never Underestimate the Power of a Woman
- Vi 20-5217 Dancin' with Someone/ Long Gone Baby
- Metronome(Sw) 521 Begin the Beguine/On the Sunny Side of the Street
- Metronome(Sw) 522 Gypsy in My Soul/I've Got You Under My Skin

DELTA RHYTHM BOYS-GULF COAST FIVE
- De 18650 Is There Somebody Else?/ Gee, Ain't I Good to You?

DELTA RHYTHM BOYS with JIMMIE LUNCEFORD ORCHESTRA
- De 23451 Honeydripper/Baby, Are You Kidding?

DELTA RHYTHM BOYS with CHARLIE BARNET ORCHESTRA
- De 23541 Just a-Sittin' and a-Rockin'/No Pad to Be Had

MILDRED BAILEY-DELTA RHYTHM BOYS
- De 3661 Jenny/When That Man Is Dead and Gone
- De 3691 Georgia on My Mind/I'm Afraid of Myself
- De 3755 Sometimes I'm Happy/Rockin' Chair

ELLA FITZGERALD-DELTA RHYTHM BOYS
- De 23452 It's Only a Paper Moon/Cry You Out of My Heart

445. DeLUGG, MILTON

acc p ar cm B

Born December 2, 1918, Los Angeles, Calif.

Accordionist-composer-bandleader who achieved some prominence on TV in 50s and 60s, especially on Johnny Carson show. Attended U.C.L.A. Staff musician in Los Angeles for radio and movies. With Matty Malneck combo in late 30s, attracted attention in several movies as capable but goofy-acting accordionist. Pioneer in elevating accordion to respectable place in jazz. Military service, World War II. In 1946-7 led combo on west coast, worked with Frankie Laine mid-1946. Conductor-arranger for Abe Burrows radio show in late 40s, later on TV. Similar work on early TV for Broadway Open House and Herb Shriner show. In 50s composed popular songs *Hoop-Dee-Doo* and *Orange Colored Sky* (1950), *Shanghai* and *Be My Life's Companion* (1951), *Just Another Polka* (1953). Lesser songs: *My Lady Loves to Dance*; *Wrong Wrong Wrong*; *Send My Baby Back to Me*; *The Little White Horse*; *Roller Coaster*; *The Big Beat*; *Gee, I'm Glad I Married You*; *Zone 28*; *Pin Wheel*; *Soft Shoe Sam*; *Wings Over Mars*; *Frantic for Five*; *Mr. Honky Tonk*; *Rumpus Room*. Chief collaborators: wife Anne, Bob Hilliard, Sammy Gallop, William Stein, Allan Roberts. In mid-60s led excellent big band on Carson show. In late 60s and 70s more TV conducting on special programs.

RECORDS

THE SOPHISTICATES
De 1818 Swing Low, Sweet Chariot/ Liebestraum
De 1883 Dark Eyes/Song of the Volga Boatmen

MATTY MALNECK
De 2060 Sing You Sinners/Hearts and Flowers
De 2182 St. Louis Blues/Humoresque
Co 36174 Green Eyes/I Take to You
Co 36184 Little Girl Blue/Hurry Back to Sorrento

FRANKIE LAINE (combo backing)
Mer 5028 I May Be Wrong

ROBERT SCOTT (orchestra backing)
Mer 3069 My Future Just Passed/Hills of Colorado

MILTON DELUGG
Mer 1127 Jalousie/Hora Staccata
Mer 3016 I May Be Wrong/Pickle in the Middle
King 15037 Hoop-Dee-Doo/Zone 28
LP
MILTON DELUGG
Vi LPM-3809 And the Tonight Show Big Band

446. DENNIS, CLARK

vo

Born December 19, 1911, Flint, Mich.

Tenor especially good on Irish songs. In 1930 played local clubs, performed on radio. On west coast 1933-4 with Raymond Paige and Orville Knapp bands. In Chicago in 1935 with Ben Pollack. On NBC's Breakfast Club on radio 1936-7. Later 1937 also on Club Matinee, Wednesday Night Minstrel and Jamboree radio shows. Late 1937-8 on Fibber McGee & Molly show. With Paul Whiteman orchestra in 1939. In 40s worked as single in clubs, theatres and radio (at times on own singing series). After Harmonicats record hit of *Peg o' My Heart* in 1947, Dennis recording of same also well received. Career later waned a bit, revived in 1953 when several recordings plus club and TV appearances led to more radio work in 1954.

RECORDS

CLARK DENNIS
Cap 346 Peg o' My Heart/Bless You
Cap 485 You Are Never Away/I'll Never Say I Love You
Cap 871 Patsy Fagan/How Can You Buy Killarney?
Cap 971 Summer Night/Kathy
Cap 1301 Love's Old Sweet Song/The Lorelei
Cap 10073 All the Things You Are
Cap 15075 On the Little Village Green/Jalousie
Cap 15307 Tenderly/I'm So Lonesome I Could Cry
Cap 15403 Galway Bay/O'Leary Is Leery of Fallin' in Love
Tiffany 1302 Granada/My Love for You
Tiffany 1303 My Buddy/You and Your Smile

CLARK DENNIS-JOAN EDWARDS
    De 2692 Say It Isn't So/Easter Parade
CLARK DENNIS with GORDON JENKINS ORCHESTRA
    De 28148 It Only Takes a Moment/If
        They Ask Me

447. DENNIS, MATT   cm p ar vo
Born February 11, 1914, Seattle, Wash.
Composer of hit songs particularly in
early 40s, mostly featured by Tommy
Dorsey band and Frank Sinatra. Chief
collaborator lyricist Tom Adair. Songs
had sophisticated, mod touch ahead of
their time. Excellent entertainer as
singer-pianist. Vocal style relaxed and
jazz-influenced with rare feel for lyrics.
Good pianist in modern style. Born into
vaudeville family, learned to play piano
early. Worked as pianist with Horace
Heidt in 1933. Settled in Hollywood,
worked as single in clubs. Accompanied
singers Martha Tilton, Merry Macs, Six
Hits and a Miss, Pied Pipers (with them
when they joined Tommy Dorsey).
Worked for Dorsey as vocal coach-arranger-composer. Biggest hits, all recorded by Dorsey: *Will You Still Be Mine?*,
Let's Get Away from It All, *Everything
Happens to Me*. Military service, World
War II. There did radio work, arranging,
had stint with Glenn Miller's AAF orchestra. After discharge worked as entertainer in clubs, on radio and TV. Still
active into late 60s.

SONGS
1940—Love Turns Winter to Spring;
    Who's Yehoodi?; Relax
1941—Everything Happens to Me; Let's
    Get Away from It All; Will You
    Still Be Mine?; Little Man with a
    Candy Cigar; Nine Old Men; Violets for Your Furs
1942—That Soldier of Mine; The Night
    We Called It a Day
1950—Show Me the Way to Get Out of
    This World
1953—Angel Eyes

Other songs: *We Belong Together*; *Junior
and Julie*; *New in Town*; *Mine Eyes*; *It's
Over, It's Over, It's Over*; *This Tired
Routine Called Love*; *The Spirit of Christmas*; *We've Reached the Point of No
Return*; *Snuggle Up, Baby*; *You Can Believe Me*

RECORDS
MATT DENNIS with PAUL WESTON ORCHESTRA
    Cap 285 Ole Buttermilk Sky/Just
        Squeeze Me
    Cap 329 At Sundown/So Would I
MATT DENNIS
    Cap 362 Linda/Roses in the Rain
    Cap 425 Lazy Mood/A Trout, No
        Doubt
    Cap 20130 Mean to Me
    VD(12")739 Just Squeeze Me
LPs
MATT DENNIS
    Vi LPM-1065 She Dances Overhead
    Vi LPM-1322 Play Melancholy Baby
    Vi LPM Dennis Anyone?
    Jub 1105 Welcome Matt Dennis
    Kapp KL-1024 Matt Dennis Plays and
        Sings
    (one side) Spinorama S-160

448. DENNY, JACK   p B
*Born c. 1894 (probably in Canada)
Died September 15, 1950, Los Angeles,
Calif.*
Leader of good sweet band in 30s and
40s; hotel style with full ensemble sound.
Early in career led band in Canada. Key
engagement at Montreal's Mount Royal.
In late 20s became popular in U.S. via
records and hotel jobs. Sweet-styled arrangements distinctive. Some used oboe,
innovation for dance bands. Long runs at
New York's Waldorf-Astoria and Chicago's Drake Hotel. Band in 1933 movie
MOONLIGHT AND PRETZELS. In 1934 radio
show with Ethel Waters, Harry Richman
and others. In late 1934-5 with Harry
Richman show. Led band through 30s
into 40s. Theme *Under the Stars*. Entertaining group for theatres. Occasionally
played in Canada.

RECORDS
JACK DENNY
    Br 3011 Forever and Ever with You/
        Smile a Little Bit
    Br 3400 Song of Shanghai/I Love the
        Moonlight
    Br 3445 Roses for Remembrance/All I
        Want Is You

Br 3884 Hello, Montreal/Always a Way to Remember
Br 4170 My Mother's Eyes/Sun at My Window
Br 4594 Blondy/Hang On to Me
Br 4604 Congratulations/Climbing the Stairs
Br 4697 Beside an Open Fireplace/ Can't Be Bothered with Me
Br 4698 Hangin' On the Garden Gate/Night of Happiness
Br 4789 Girl Trouble/Leave It That Way
Br 6088 Out of Nowhere/Say a Little Prayer for Me
Br 6114 Nevertheless/Stories
Vi 22906 Goodnight Moon/Starlight
Vi 22907 Just Friends/Oh, What a Thrill
Vi 22916 How Can You Say You Love Me?/Snuggled on Your Shoulder
Vi 22917 Auf Wiedersehen, My Dear/A Million Ways to Say "I Love You"
Vi 24012 Lazy Day/Sharing
Vi 24023 Why Can't This Night Go On Forever?/Hello, Sweetheart
Vi 24183 The Song Is You/I've Told Ev'ry Little Star
Vi 24213 I'm Playing with Fire
Vi 24217 Moon Song/Twenty Million People
Ma 113 Just to Remind You/Swing, Swing, Mother-in-Law

449. DePARIS, SIDNEY   t fl-h B

Born May 30, 1905, Crawfordsville, Ind. Died September 13, 1967, New York, N.Y.

Jazz trumpet star with hot tone and driving style. Adept in use of plunger mute. Younger brother of jazz trombonist Wilbur DeParis. Boys taught music by father, traveled with various bands in mid-20s. Sidney to New York in late 20s, with Charlie Johnson, Benny Carter and McKinney's Cotton Pickers. With Don Redman 1932-6. In later 30s jobbed in New York, periods with Willie Bryant, Johnson, Mezz Mezzrow, Redman. With Zutty Singleton late 1939-40. Worked on memorable recording sessions in Jelly Roll Morton's comeback in 1939 and with

Sidney Bechet in 1940. In early 40s played with Carter, Singleton, Art Hodes. In 1943-4 co-led combo with brother at Jimmy Ryan's in New York. Then freelanced, led own band. In late 40s joined Wilbur's band to play again at Ryan's and at Child's Restaurant through 50s. In 60s brothers played other locations. In later years Sidney slowed down by illness.

RECORDS

CHARLIE JOHNSON
Vi 21712 The Boy in the Boat/Walk That Thing
Vi 38059 Harlem Drag/Hot Bones and Rice

MCKINNEY'S COTTON PICKERS
Vi 38097 Gee, Ain't I Good to You
Vi 38102 Miss Hannah

DON REDMAN
Br 6368 Hot and Anxious
Br 6429 Nagasaki

JELLY ROLL MORTON
Bb 10429 Oh, Didn't He Ramble/ Winin' Boy Blues
Bb 10434 High Society/I Thought I Heard Buddy Bolden Say
Bb 10450 Ballin' the Jack/Don't You Leave Me Here

MEZZ MEZZROW
Bb 10088 Revolutionary Blues

SIDNEY BECHET
Vi 26640 Shake It and Break It/Wild Man Blues
BN(12")43 Blue Horizon/Muskrat Ramble

ART HODES
De 18437 Georgia Cake Walk/Liberty Inn Drag
De 18438 Indiana/Get Happy

ED HALL
BN(12")28 High Society/Blues at Blue Note
BN(12")29 Night Shift Blues/Royal Garden Blues

DEPARIS BROTHERS' ORCHESTRA
CMS 552 Black and Blue/I've Found a New Baby
CMS 567 Change o' Key Boogie/The Sheik of Araby

SIDNEY DEPARIS
BN(12")40 Everybody Loves My Baby/The Call of the Blues
BN(12")41 Who's Sorry Now?/Ballin' the Jack

LPs

SIDNEY DEPARIS
BN 6501 Jazz Classics—DeParis Dixie (BN RIs)

WILBUR DEPARIS
Atl 1336 The Wild Jazz Age
Atl 1363 On the Riviera
Atl 1552 Over and Over Again
Atl(10″)141 Wilbur DeParis & His Rampart Street Ramblers

SIDNEY BECHET
"X"(10″)LVA-3024 (Bb, Vi RIs)

CHARLIE JOHNSON
"X"(10″)LVA-3026 (Vi RIs)

450. DePARIS, WILBUR   tb B

Born January 11, 1900, Crawfordsville, Ind.
Died January 3, 1973, New York, N.Y.

Jazz trombonist with good tone, tasteful style. Led traditional-styled small bands that stressed ensemble sound and good soloists. Older brother of jazz trumpeter Sidney DeParis. Boys taught music by father. As youngster Wilbur played in father's carnival band. In early 20s with various bands, including work in New Orleans. In middle and late 20s led band at times in Philadelphia, also freelanced in other locations. In early 30s with Leroy Smith, Dave Nelson, Benny Carter and others. On Spike Hughes all-star recording sessions in 1933. Played in Europe with Noble Sissle and Teddy Hill. In 1937 with Mills Blue Rhythm Band awhile. Late 1937 joined Louis Armstrong, remained three years. In early 40s freelanced, period with Roy Eldridge big band. In 1943-4 co-led combo with brother at Jimmy Ryan's in New York. With Duke Ellington 1945-7. In later 40s led combo featuring brother at Ryan's again and at Child's Restaurant. Continued with band in 50s mostly at Ryan's, then in 60s at various spots.

RECORDS

BUBBER MILEY
Vi 38138 I Lost My Gal from Memphis/Without You, Emaline
Vi 38146 Black Maria/Chinnin' and Chattin' with May

JELLY ROLL MORTON
Vi 23019 That'll Never Do

Vi 23321 If Someone Would Only Love Me
Vi 38135 Little Lawrence/Harmony Blues

DAVE NELSON
Vi 22639 I Ain't Got Nobody/When Day Is Done
Vi 23039 Some of These Days

CLIFF JACKSON
B&W(12″)1204 Quiet Please/Walking and Talking to Myself
B&W(12″)1205 Cliff's Boogie Blues/Jeepers Creepers

SIDNEY BECHET
Ci 1057 Who?/September Song
Ci 1058 I Got Rhythm/Song of the Medina

DEPARIS BROTHERS ORCHESTRA
CMS 552 Black and Blue/I've Found a New Baby
CMS 567 Change o' Key Boogie/The Sheik of Araby

LPs

WILBUR DEPARIS
Atl 1233 Marchin' and Swingin'
Atl 1253 At Symphony Hall
Atl 1318 That's a-Plenty
Atl 1336 The Wild Jazz Age
Atl 1363 On the Riviera
Atl 1552 Over and Over Again
Atl(10″)141 Wilbur DeParis & His Rampart Street Ramblers
Clar 614

SIDNEY BECHET (one side)
CMS(10″)FL-20020 New Orleans Style, Old and New

451. DePAUL, GENE   cm p ar vo

Born June 17, 1919, New York, N.Y.

Composer of 40s and 50s, collaborated with Don Raye for much of earlier work. Teamed with lyricist Johnny Mercer on excellent scores for movie SEVEN BRIDES FOR SEVEN BROTHERS (1954) and Broadway musical LI'L ABNER (1956). Early in career worked as pianist in dance bands, in theatres as pianist-singer. Arranged for vocal groups. Began songwriting at start of 40s; much of work for movies. Military service two years, World War II. Leading songs *I'll Remember April, Star Eyes, Irresistible You, Mr. Five by Five, Cow Cow Boogie, He's My Guy, Teach Me Tonight.*

SONGS
(with related shows)

1940—Your Red Wagon
1941—KEEP 'EM FLYING movie (Pig Foot Pete; You Don't Know What Love Is; Let's Keep 'Em Flying; The Boy with the Wistful Eyes); IN THE NAVY movie (We're in the Navy; Starlight, Starbright)
1942—BEHIND THE EIGHT BALL movie (Mr. Five by Five); RIDE 'EM, COWBOY movie (I'll Remember April; Rockin' and Reelin'; Give Me My Saddle; Wake Up Jacob; Beside the Rio Tonto); HELLZAPOPPIN' movie (You Were There); He's My Guy
1943—I DOOD IT movie (Star Eyes); WHAT'S BUZZIN', COUSIN? movie (Ain't That Just Like a Man); FOLLOW THE BAND movie (He's My Guy); Cow Cow Boogie
1944—BROADWAY RHYTHM movie (Irresistible You; Milkman, Keep Those Bottles Quiet)
1947—LOVE THAT BOY movie (The Night Has a Thousand Eyes)
1948—A DATE WITH JUDY movie (Judaline); A SONG IS BORN movie (A Song Is Born; Daddy-O); SO DEAR TO MY HEART movie cartoon (It's Whatcha Do with Whatcha Got)
1949—ICHABOD AND MR. TOAD movie cartoon (Katrina; The Headless Horseman)
1950—Your Eyes; I'm in Love with You
1952—ALICE IN WONDERLAND movie cartoon ('Twas Brillig); I Love to Hear a Choo Choo Train
1954—SEVEN BRIDES FOR SEVEN BROTHERS movie (Spring, Spring, Spring; Bless Your Beautiful Hide; Sobbin' Women; June Bride; When You're in Love; Lament; Goin' Courtin'); Teach Me Tonight
1956—LI'L ABNER stage show (Namely You; If I Had My Druthers; Love in a Home; Jubilation T. Cornpone; Oh Happy Day; The Country's in the Very Best of Hands)
1959—LI'L ABNER movie (original stage score)

452. DeROSE, PETER   cm ar p
Born March 10, 1900, New York, N.Y.
Died April 23, 1953, New York, N.Y.

Composer with career lasting over 30 years. Best-known songs *When Your Hair Has Turned to Silver, Somebody Loves You, Have You Ever Been Lonely?, Wagon Wheels, Rain, Deep Purple, Lilacs in the Rain, Starlit Hour.* Teamed with wife May Singhi Breen for 16 years on radio series (1923-39) Sweethearts of the Air. Worked for publishing companies early in career. Wrote a few songs for Broadway shows. During career collaborators included wife, Harry Richman, Jo Trent, Billy Hill, Charles Tobias, Mitchell Parish, Benny Davis, Al Stillman, Sam M. Lewis, Sammy Gallop, Stanley Adams, Carl Sigman. Active songwriter until death.

SONGS
(with related shows)

1918—Now All the World's at Peace
1920—Gretchen; When I'm Gone I Won't Forget
1922—Suez
1926—Muddy Water
1927—Lazy Weather
1928—EARL CARROLL'S VANITIES OF 1928 stage show (Watch My Baby Walk); Dixie Dawn; I Just Roll Along
1930—When Your Hair Has Turned to Silver; Somewhere in Old Wyoming
1931—I'm Just a Dancing Sweetheart; You'll Be Mine in Apple Blossom Time
1932—Nightfall; Somebody Loves You; You'll Always Be the Same Sweetheart
1933—Have You Ever Been Lonely?; Louisville Lady; There's a Home in Wyomin'
1934—ZIEGFELD FOLLIES OF 1934 stage show (Wagon Wheels); Rain
1935—The Oregon Trail; When Love Knocks at Your Heart; Moonlight and Magnolias
1936—Close to Me; Now or Never
1938—So Little Time; When Twilight Comes
1939—Deep Purple; The Lamp Is Low; Lilacs in the Rain

1940—EARL CARROLL'S VANITIES stage show (Starlit Hour; Angel); IT HAPPENS ON ICE stage show (The Moon Fell in the River); On a Little Street in Singapore; Orchids for Remembrance

1941—ICE CAPADES OF 1941 skating revue (Somewhere; I Hear America Singing; Swing Me a Lullaby; Oriental Moonrise); Orange Blossom Lane

1942—All I Need Is You; Moonlight Mood

1945—Autumn Serenade

1946—That's Where I Came In; Put That Kiss Back Where You Found It

1947—As Years Go By

1948—On the Little Village Green; In the Market Place of Old Monterey

1949—Who Do You Know in Heaven?; Twenty-Four Hours of Sunshine

1950—Cross My Heart, I Love You; A Marshmallow World; The Breeze Is My Sweetheart

1951—ON MOONLIGHT BAY movie (Love Ya); How Thoughtful of You; That's How Our Love Will Grow

1952—ABOUT FACE movie (No Other Girl for Me; If Someone Had Told Me); Sunday Is for My Darling

1953—You Can Do It

Other compositions: *Just Say Aloha*; *That's Life, I Guess*; *In a Mission by the Sea*; *Royal Blue*; *Maytime in Vienna*; *Evening Star*; *American Waltz*; *Buena Sera*; *God of Battles*; *I Hear a Forest Praying*

RECORDS

PETER DEROSE ORCHESTRA

Elec 1922 Underneath the Harlem Moon/I'm Sure of Everything but You

Elec 1925 A Boy and a Girl Were Dancing/My River Home

453. DERWYN, HAL   vo g B
(sometimes spelled DERWIN)
Born August 7, 1914

Popular singer of late 40s, excellent on ballads. Rich baritone voice. Guitarist-vocalist with Shep Fields 1938-40. With Boyd Raeburn and Les Brown in early 40s. Later in 40s worked as single; popular 1947-9, records sold well. Led hotel-style band with excellent arrangements into 50s. Entered agency work in 1957.

RECORDS

SHEP FIELDS

Bb 7697 Don't Let That Moon Get Away

Bb 10056 An Old Curiosity Shop

Bb 10589 Burn, Firewood, Burn

Bb 10670 Day Dreams Come True at Night/Cecilia

ARTIE SHAW

Vi 20-1716 That's for Me/Yolanda

HAL DERWYN-MARTHA TILTON

Cap 57-618 Take Me Back/Ballin' the Jack

HAL DERWYN

Cap 288 The Old Lamplighter/I Guess I'll Get the Papers

Cap 336 You'll Always Be the One I Love/Another Night Like This

Cap 377 It Might Have Been a Different Story/Take My Word for It

Cap 430 Blue and Broken-Hearted/An Apple Blossom Wedding

Cap 446 On the Avenue/How Lucky You Are

Cap 469 Little Old Mill/How the Time Goes By

Cap 498 We Just Couldn't Say Goodbye/Worry Worry Worry

Cap 502 One Dozen Roses/No One but You

Cap 15071 Always/Melody Time

Cap 15160 At the Flying "W"/Sissy

Cap 15282 Louise/I Go In When the Moon Comes Out

454. DESLYS, GABY   vo
Born c. 1883-4, Marseilles, France
Died February 11, 1920, Paris, France

French musical comedy star; in several Broadway musicals 1911-16. U.S. debut in REVUE OF REVUES [1911]. Later in year VERA VIOLETTA with Al Jolson. Two more with Jolson: THE WHIRL OF SOCIETY (1912) and THE HONEYMOON EXPRESS (1913). Then THE BELLE OF BOND STREET (1914) and STOP! LOOK! LISTEN! (1916).

455. DESMOND, JOHNNY

vo p cm lyr

(GIOVANNI ALFREDO
DESIMONS)

Born November 14, 1920, Detroit, Mich.

Popular singer of 40s and 50s. Baritone with smooth delivery, showmanship, romantic ballad style; also capable of belting out songs. Attended Detroit Conservatory of Music. On Detroit radio, also song and dance man in Detroit clubs. Organized vocal quartet The Downbeats, which joined Bob Crosby in mid-1940 as The Bob-O-Links. In late 1941 Desmond joined Gene Krupa as solo vocalist, remained several months. Military service World War II. In 1943 with Glenn Miller's AAF band in U.S. and overseas, established himself as featured singer. Radio series in England, A Soldier and a Song. After service worked as single; in 1946 on radio shows The Teenagers' Club and Philip Morris, later own singing shows. In early 50s began long run on Breakfast Club show. During these years also recorded. On TV in the 50s on Face the Music and Hit Parade, also with Ray McKinley and the Glenn Miller Orchestra. In 1958 starred in Broadway musical SAY DARLING. Played in FUNNY GIRL as later replacement. Occasional TV appearances in 60s, played clubs and stock shows. Active into 70s. Composer or lyricist of several songs: *How Much Will I Miss You?*; *Oh, My Darlin'*; *Please Don't Forget Me, Dear*; *I Wonder What Little Dogs Dream Of*; *Dancing Man*; *When.*

RECORDS

BOB CROSBY (with The Bob-O-Links vocal group)
De 3417 You Forgot About Me
De 3451 Drummer Boy
De 3488 Dry Bones

GENE KRUPA
OK 6447 This Time the Dream's on Me/Two in Love
OK 6517 Tropical Magic/Day Dreaming
OK 6563 All Through the Night
OK 6619 Me and My Melinda

MAJOR GLENN MILLER'S AAF OVERSEAS ORCHESTRA
VD(12")601 Symphony

JOHNNY DESMOND
Vi 20-1810 Do You Love Me?/In the Moon Mist
Vi 20-2109 Guilty/I'll Close My Eyes
Co 38269 Lillette/Bella Bella Marie
Cor 60736 How Much Will I Miss You?/Battle Hymn of the Republic
Cor 61031 It's So Nice to Be Nice to Your Neighbor
Cor 61069 The River Seine/Woman
MGM 10358 Peggy Dear/While the Angelus Was Ringing
MGM 10451 The Four Winds and the Seven Seas/If I Only Had One Day to Live
MGM 10480 Fiddle Dee Dee/Two Little New Little Blue Little Eyes
MGM 10518 Don't Cry, Joe/The Longest Mile
MGM 10613 C'est Si Bon/If You Could Care
MGM 10850 C'est La Vie/You're the Only One for Me
MGM 10947 Because of You/Andiamo

LPs

JOHNNY DESMOND
Co CL-1477 Blue Smoke
MGM(10")E-186 Hands Across the Table
Lion L-70061 Dreams of Paris
Mayfair 9635 (S) Johnny Desmond Swings in Magnificent Stereo

GLENN MILLER AAF ORCHESTRA
Vi LPM-1494 Those Marvelous Miller Moods
Vi LPT-6702 (5-LP set) (Third Limited Edition)

456. DESMOND, PAUL

as B

(real name BREITENFELD)

Born November 25, 1924, San Francisco, Calif.

Most popular alto saxist of cool jazz. Winner of many polls from mid-50s through 60s. Rose to fame in Dave Brubeck Quartet with cool, fluent sax solos. He and pianist Brubeck formed perfectly integrated team. Desmond tasteful and inventive on ballads, light-swinging and subtle on up-tempo numbers. Attended San Francisco State College. Military service, late 40s. With Jack Fina and Jack Sheedy in 1950, Alvino Rey in 1951. Also freelanced on west coast during this period. Joined Brubeck in mid-1951. Soon group rose to top. Group active many years. In 60s Desmond left and returned at intervals, also working with others and recording on his own. Maintained status as star on modern alto sax.

RECORDS

DAVE BRUBECK OCTET
Fan 509 Love Walked In/The Way You Look Tonight

DAVE BRUBECK QUARTET
Fan 517 Crazy Chris/Somebody Loves Me
Fan 520 Frenesi/At a Perfume Counter
Fan 521 Look for the Silver Lining/ This Can't Be Love
Fan 523 Just One of Those Things
Fan 527 I May Be Wrong/On a Little Street in Singapore

LPs

DAVE BRUBECK QUARTET
Fan(10″)5,7,8,11,13
Co CL-566 Jazz Goes to College
Co CL-590 At Storyville
Co CL-622 Brubeck Time
Co CL-699 Red Hot and Cool
Co CL-1034 Jazz Goes to Junior College
Co CL-1249 Newport 1958
Co CL-2602 Anything Goes
Jazztone J-1272 The Best of Brubeck

DAVE BRUBECK QUINTET
Fan 3268 Re-Union

PAUL DESMOND
Fan(10″)3-21 Desmond
Vi LPM-2438 Desmond Blue
Vi LSP-3407 (S) Glad to Be Unhappy
WB 1356 Paul Desmond and Friends
A&M 3015 Summertime
A&M 3032 Bridge Over Troubled Waters

PAUL DESMOND-GERRY MULLIGAN
Vi LPM-2624 Two of a Mind

PAUL DESMOND-DON ELLIOTT
Fan 3235

457. DeSYLVA, BUDDY   lyr cm
(or B. G.; GEORGE GARD DeSYLVA)

Born January 27, 1895, New York, N.Y.
Died July 11, 1950, Los Angeles, Calif.

Lyricist in famed songwriting team of Henderson-DeSylva-Brown of 20s and 30s. Collaborated with other composers before and after to amass big batch of hit songs. Grew up in California, attended USC awhile. Early interest in show business, tried writing songs. Al Jolson took him to New York, used several of his songs in 1918 Broadway show SINBAD. Jolson and DeSylva collaborated on several hits in ensuing years. DeSylva wrote for shows LA, LA, LUCILLE (1919), SALLY and BOMBO (1921), ORANGE BLOSSOMS and THE YANKEE PRINCESS (1922), GEORGE WHITE'S SCANDALS OF 1922-1923-1924, SWEET LITTLE DEVIL (1924), BIG BOY and CAPTAIN JINKS (1925). Miscellaneous songs for other productions. Famous early songs: *Avalon*; *April Showers*; *Look for the Silver Lining*; *A Kiss in the Dark*; *Somebody Loves Me*; *Alabamy Bound*; *California, Here I Come*; *If You Knew Susie*. Joined composer Ray Henderson and lyricist Lew Brown in 1925 to write score for show GEORGE WHITE'S SCANDALS. Team remained together to produce outstanding array of song hits in 20s into 1931.

(See biography herein on HENDERSON-DESYLVA-BROWN for details and song listings of team's career.)

After leaving Henderson and Brown, wrote lyrics for 1932 Broadway musical TAKE A CHANCE. Became movie producer, wrote music for movies. In mid-30s produced popular Shirley Temple films: THE LITTLE COLONEL, THE LITTLEST REBEL, CAPTAIN JANUARY, POOR LITTLE RICH GIRL, STOWAWAY. Also produced Broadway shows DUBARRY WAS A LADY (1939), LOUISIANA PURCHASE and PANAMA HATTIE (1940). Head of Paramount Pictures several years. Music publisher, later recording executive with Capitol Records. In later years ill health curtailed activities. Other song collaborators included Gus Kahn, George and Ira Gershwin, Jerome Kern, Vincent Rose, Joseph Meyer, Victor Herbert, Ballard MacDonald, Lewis Gensler, James Hanley, Nacio Herb Brown, Richard Whiting, Vincent Youmans, Emmerich Kalman, Louis Silvers.

807

SONGS
(with related shows, excluding works of Henderson-DeSylva-Brown)

1918—SINBAD stage show ('n Everything; I Gave Her That; I'll Say She Does)

1919—LA, LA, LUCILLE stage show (songs unimportant); You Ain't Heard Nothin' Yet

1920—Avalon

1921—BOMBO stage show (April Showers; Yoo Hoo); THE BROADWAY WHIRL stage show (songs unimportant); SALLY stage show (Sally; Look for the Silver Lining; Wild Rose; On with the Dance; Whip-Poor-Will; The Lorelei); Down South

1922—THE FRENCH DOLL stage show (Do It Again); GEORGE WHITE'S SCANDALS OF 1922 stage show (I'll Build a Stairway to Paradise); ORANGE BLOSSOMS stage show (A Kiss in the Dark; This Time It's Love; The Lonely Nest; A Dream of Orange Blossoms); THE YANKEE PRINCESS stage show (Roses, Lovely Roses; In the Starlight; I Still Can Dream)

1923—GEORGE WHITE'S SCANDALS OF 1923 stage show (songs unimportant); LITTLE MISS BLUEBEARD stage show (I Won't Say I Will, I Won't Say I Won't); NIFTIES OF 1923 stage show (songs unimportant)

1924—GEORGE WHITE'S SCANDALS OF 1924 stage show (Somebody Loves Me; Rose of Madrid; Night Time in Araby); SWEET LITTLE DEVIL stage show (Sweet Little Devil; Virginia; Someone Believes in You); Alabamy Bound; California, Here I Come; Oh Baby; May Time; Memory Lane

1925—BIG BOY stage show (If You Knew Susie; Hello 'Tucky; Miami; Keep Smiling at Trouble; California, Here I Come); CAPTAIN JINKS stage show (Fond of You; I Do; Kiki; Sea Legs); Headin' for Louisville; Save Your Sorrow; Just a Cottage Small

1926—QUEEN HIGH stage show (Cross Your Heart; Gentlemen Prefer Blondes; Queen High); When Day Is Done

1925-31 (see HENDERSON-DESYLVA-BROWN)

1930—Minnie the Mermaid

1932—TAKE A CHANCE stage show (Eadie Was a Lady; Turn Out the Lights; You're an Old Smoothie; Oh How I Long to Belong to You; So Do I; Rise 'n' Shine; Should I Be Sweet?; My Lover)

1933—TAKE A CHANCE movie (Rise 'n' Shine—from original stage score); MY WEAKNESS movie (Gather Lip Rouge While You May; Be Careful; How Do I Look?)

1939—LOVE AFFAIR movie (Wishing)

458. DEUTSCH, ADOLPH   cm ar B
Born October 20, 1897, London, England

Composer-arranger for movie background music beginning late 30s. Studied music at Royal Academy of London. To U.S. in 1910, citizen in 1920. Early work as bandleader and arranger for other bands. Worked at Paul Whiteman's Music Hall three years. Movie composing produced no popular songs but good background music. Also arranger and conductor for movies. Founder of Screen Composers Association, president 1943-53. Compositions include *March of the United Nations, Margot, Clarabelle, Three Sisters, Piano Echoes, Skyride, Stairways, March Eccentrique, The Scottish Suite, Lonely Room* (theme from THE APARTMENT).

MOVIES
(as composer, scorer, conductor or musical director; partial listing)

1937—THEY WON'T FORGET

1940—THEY DRIVE BY NIGHT

1941—HIGH SIERRA

1942—THE MALTESE FALCON

1944—THE MASK OF DIMITRIOS

1948—JULIA MISBEHAVES

1949—THE STRATTON STORY; TAKE ME OUT TO THE BALL GAME; INTRUDER IN THE DUST

1950—FATHER OF THE BRIDE; ANNIE GET YOUR GUN

1951—SHOW BOAT
1952—MILLION DOLLAR MERMAID
1953—THE BAND WAGON
1954—THE LONG LONG TRAILER; SEVEN BRIDES FOR SEVEN BROTHERS
1955—OKLAHOMA!
1957—FUNNY FACE; LES GIRLS
1959—SOME LIKE IT HOT
1960—THE APARTMENT

459. DEUTSCH, EMERY   v cm B

Born September 10, 1907, Budapest, Hungary

Violinist-bandleader of 30s and 40s, prominent in radio. Studied violin at Budapest's Royal Academy of Music. Also studied at Fordham University and Juilliard. Appeared on radio in mid-20s, became staff conductor for CBS (c. 1930-42). In early years led gypsy-styled bands featuring own violin. Wrote two famous numbers *Play, Fiddle, Play* (1932) and *When a Gypsy Makes His Violin Cry* (1935); latter theme song. Through 30s on many broadcasts, also played theatres and hotels. In mid-1937 formed good sweet-styled band. Recorded, used Barry McKinley and Frank Parrish as vocalists. Entered U.S. Maritime Service as musical conductor in late 1942. After service again led dance band through 40s into late 50s. Other compositions: *My Gypsy Rhapsody, Moon of Desire, Stars and Soft Guitars, Halgato, Budapest Suite, Beautiful Danube, No Wonder You're Blue, The Old Gypsy Fiddler, 'Til Now* and 1937 pop tune *Stardust on the Moon*.

RECORDS

EMERY DEUTSCH
Br 7862 It's Swell of You/Never in a Million Years
Br 7871 Sweet Heartache/Heart and Soul
Br 7886 He's a Gypsy from Poughkeepsie/It Looks Like Rain in Cherry Blossom Lane
Br 7894 The First Time I Saw You/You Can't Run
Br 7905 A Sailboat in the Moonlight/Moonlight on the Highway
Br 7909 Love Is Never Out of Season/Our Penthouse on Third Avenue

Br 7961 Harbor Lights/Stardust on the Moon
Br 7972 Vieni Vieni/You Can't Stop Me from Dreaming
Br 7979 You Started Something/When the Organ Played O Promise Me
Br 8109 I Want a New Romance/I'd Love to Play a Love Scene
Br 8118 Joseph, Joseph!/Who'll Buy My Bublitchki?
Bb 10340 Vol Vistu Gaily Star/Hungarian Dance No. 1
Bb 10357 None but the Lonely Heart/Troika
Bb 10440 If I Knew Then/Bonnie with the Big Blue Eyes
Bb 10571 Long Hair Swing/Isle of Bong Bong
Maj 1154 (theme) When a Gypsy Makes His Violin Cry/Once Upon a Time

LPs

EMERY DEUTSCH
ABC-Para 281
ABC-Para 354 Play, Emery, Play

460. DeVOL, FRANK   as v vo ar cm B

Born September 20, 1911, Moundsville, W.Va.

Talented musician-arranger-composer who became well-known orchestra leader in 50s and 60s. Grew up in Ohio, attended Miami University of Ohio. Played violin in father's orchestra. Early jobs with Emerson Gill and George Olsen. Played lead alto sax and arranged for Horace Heidt in late 30s. Arranged for Alvino Rey's band in 1939 and early 40s. In 1943 staff conductor on radio shows in Los Angeles. In later 40s was active in leading bands behind singers on radio and records. Own network show. Musical director for shows of Ginny Simms, Jack Smith, Jack Carson. On early TV as bit actor and personality in addition to leading bands on shows. Active recording in 50s. Arranged and composed for TV and movies, wrote TV theme for My Three Sons and movie title songs *Lylah* and *Hush, Hush, Sweet Charlotte*. Other compositions include *Friendly Tavern Polka, I and Claudie, My Chinese Fair Lady, The Chaperone*. Film credits as musical director and/or composer of background music include THE BIG KNIFE (1955), PILLOW TALK (1959), THE BRAMBLE BUSH (1960), BOYS' NIGHT OUT and WHATEVER HAPPENED TO BABY JANE? (1962), UNDER THE YUM YUM TREE (1963), GOOD NEIGHBOR SAM and SEND ME NO FLOWERS (1964), HUSH, HUSH, SWEET CHARLOTTE and CAT BALLOU (1965), THE GLASS BOTTOM BOAT (1966), THE DIRTY DOZEN and GUESS WHO'S COMING TO DINNER (1967).

RECORDS
(as lead alto sax)
HORACE HEIDT
  Br 8043 Sweet as a Song/Half Moon on the Hudson
  Br 8048 History of Sweet Swing/Toy Trumpet
  Br 8073 I Fall in Love with You Every Day/How'dja Like to Love Me?
  Br 8096 Shadows on the Moon/Who Are We to Say?
  Br 8110 Lovelight in the Starlight/Where Have We Met Before?
  Br 8184 I've Got a Date with a Dream/This May Be the Night
(as conductor and/or arranger)
MARGARET WHITING
  Cap 20116 Little Girl Blue/Thou Swell
KAY STARR
  Cap 1072 Mississippi/He's a Good Man to Have Around
  Cap 1492 Then You've Never Been Blue
GORDON MACRAE
  Cap 2352 Congratulations to Someone/How Do You Speak to an Angel?
HAL DERWYN
  Cap 336 You'll Always Be the One I Love/Another Night Like This
MARTHA TILTON-HAL DERWYN
  Cap 57-618 Take Me Back/Ballin' the Jack
BOB CARROLL
  Derby 840 I Really Don't Want to Know/There Is Danger
DORIS DAY
  Co 40300 Anyone Can Fall in Love
JAYE P. MORGAN
  Derby 828 Just a Gigolo/Wasted Tears

  Derby 837 Life Is Just a Bowl of Cherries/Operator 299
FRANK DEVOL
  Cap 57-752 Lotta Pizzicato/Southwest Territory
  Cap 1178 Love Letters in the Sand/This Year's Kisses
LPs
FRANK DEVOL
  Co CL-1371 Fabulous Hollywood!
  Co CS-8010 (S) Portraits
  ABC-Para 563 The New Old Sweet Songs
  Cap(10")H-208 Waltzing on Air
(as conductor; probably arranger on some)
ELLA FITZGERALD
  Verve MGV-4004 Like Someone in Love
  Verve MGV-4034 Hello Love
ROBERT GOULET
  Co CS-8476 (S) Always You
DORIS DAY
  Co CS-8066 (S) Hooray for Hollywood
VIC DAMONE
  Co CL-1174 Closer Than a Kiss
DENNIS DAY
  Masterseal MS-3 At Hollywood's Moulin Rouge
TONY BENNETT
  Co CL-1186 Long Ago ...

461. DeWITT, ALLAN   vo B
Good band singer of 30s and 40s, smooth baritone voice with quality. With Tiny Hill in late 30s. Interim vocalist with Tommy Dorsey in late 1939, after Jack Leonard left and before Frank Sinatra joined. With Jan Savitt 1940-1 for most productive period on records. In early 1945 in Chicago with Jimmy Jackson and Wayne King. Mid-1945 military service awhile. In later 40s sang in Chicago area with various groups, worked as single. Booked own band in late 40s and early 50s in Chicago and midwest.
RECORDS
TINY HILL
  Vo 4957 In Love with Love
TOMMY DORSEY
  Vi 26433 Careless
  Vi 26465 Angel

Vi 26470 I've Got My Eyes on You
JAN SAVITT
De 3153 Where Was I?
De 3178 It's a Lovely Day Tomor-
row/You Can't Brush Me Off
De 3196 I'm Stepping Out with a
Memory Tonight
De 3695 April Showers
De 3937 Tell Me
Vi 27403 The Things I Love
Vi 27423 I Went Out of My Way
Vi 27464 It's So Peaceful in the Coun-
try
Vi 27573 As We Walk into the Sunset
Vi 27577 I See a Million People
Vi 27643 'Tis Autumn/Who Calls?

461A. DEXTER, AL   g v vo cm lyr B
(ALBERT POINDEXTER)
Born May 4, 1902, Jacksonville, Texas

Country and western performer, rose to
fame 1943 with hit record of own composition *Pistol Packin' Mama*. Important
song in helping country and western
break into pop music field. Early years
house painter with music as sideline.
Early 30s led group Texas Troopers. Began recording later 30s. Fame of hit
record led to better bookings in 40s.
Active in 50s and 60s but less prominent.
Played in own night spot Bridgeport Club
in Dallas. Composed many songs featured by his group including *Rosalita,
Triflin' Gal, Honky Tonk Blues, Too Late
to Worry, Guitar Polka, Saturday Night
Boogie, Car Hoppin' Mama, Rose of Mexico, Sundown Polka, One More Day in
Prison, Alimony Blues, Down at the Road-
side Inn, New Broom Boogie, Little Sod
Shanty, My Careless Heart, Move Over
Rover.*

RECORDS
AL DEXTER
Vo 03435 New Jelly Roll Blues/Honky
Tonk Blues
Vo 03636 Car Hoppin' Mama/Broken
Hearted Blues
Vo 03719 Honky Tonk Baby/Don't
Cry for Me When I'm Gone
Vo 04277 My Baby Loves Me/Gypsy
Swing
Vo 04405 One More Day in Prison/
I'm Happy When You're Happy

Vo 05121 Bar Hotel/Daddy's in the
Dog House Now
Vo 05572 When We Go a-Honky-Ton-
kin'/Wine, Women and Song
OK 05783 Come Back to Me, My Dar-
ling/You May Be Sorry
OK 06127 New Soldier's Farewell/
Down at the Roadside Inn
OK 06397 Darling, It's All Over
Now/Who's Been Here?
OK 6708 Pistol Packin' Mama/Rosa-
lita
OK 6718 So Long Pal/Too Late to
Worry
OK 6727 I'll Wait for You, Dear/Los-
ing My Mind Over You
OK 6740 Triflin' Gal/I'm Lost without
You
Co 20010 Guitar Polka/Honey Do
You Think It's Wrong?
Co 20062 I'm Losing My Mind Over
You/I'll Wait for You, Dear
Co 20267 Pistol Packin' Mama/Rosa-
lita
Co 20438 Rose of Mexico/Calico Rag
De 28739 My Careless Heart/Move
Over Rover

LPs
AL DEXTER
Co (10'')HL-9005 Songs of the
Southwest
Ha HL-7293 Pistol Packin' Mama
Cap T-1701
Hilltop 6070 Pistol Packin' Mama

462. DICKENSON, VIC   tb vo B
Born August 6, 1906, Xenia, Ohio

Jazz trombonist with humorous slant to
his playing; raspy tone sometimes called
slushbucket sound. Very inventive, easily
identifiable. Able to fit in any type of
band, but most work with dixieland
groups. Jobbed in Columbus, Ohio in
early 20s. Later played in Madison, Wis.,
and other locations. With Speed Webb in
late 20s and Zach Whyte in early 30s.
After other jobs,with Blanche Calloway
band 1933-6. With Claude Hopkins
1936-9 mostly at New York's Roseland
Ballroom. With Benny Carter in late 1939
and Count Basie early 1940 to early 1941.
Then periods with Carter, Sidney Bechet,
Hot Lips Page, Frankie Newton, Cole-

man Hawkins. With Eddie Heywood 1943-7. In later 40s freelanced in California, led band at times. During 1949-56 based mostly in Boston. Many jobs with Bobby Hackett there, also led band for long runs at Savoy Club. 1957 stint with Red Allen at New York's Metropole. In later 50s played in New York, also abroad. In early 60s periods with George Wein's All-Stars and Wild Bill Davison. Then with Saints and Sinners group, also abroad on several tours. Co-led group with Bobby Hackett 1968-70, then in mid-1970 joined World's Greatest Jazz Band. Left 1973, jobbed.

RECORDS

SIDNEY BECHET
    Vi 27663 Rip Up the Joint/Laughin' in Rhythm
    Vi 20-1510 Blues in the Air/The Mooche

JAMES P. JOHNSON
    BN(12″)32 Blue Mizz/Victory Stride
    BN(12″)33 Joy-Mentin'/After You've Gone

EDDIE HEYWOOD
    CMS 570 Blue Lou/Carry Me Back to Old Virginny
    CMS 578 Just You, Just Me/'Deed I Do
    De 23427 Blue Lou/Please Don't Talk About Me When I'm Gone

ED HALL
    BN(12″)28 High Society/Blues at Blue Note
    BN(12″)29 Night Shift Blues/Royal Garden Blues

ART HODES
    BN(12″)34 Sweet Georgia Brown/Sugar Foot Stomp
    BN(12″)35 Squeeze Me/Bugle Call Rag

HOT LIPS PAGE
    Cont 6003 It Ain't Like That/Big "D" Blues

COLEMAN HAWKINS
    Cap 10036 Hollywood Stampede/I'm Thru with Love

LESTER YOUNG
    Philo 123 D.B. Blues/Lester Blows Again

JIMMY MCPARTLAND
    Pres 303 Come Back Sweet Papa/Manhattan

Pres 304 Use Your Imagination/Davenport Blues

JULIA LEE
    Cap 15106 Wise Guys
    Cap 15367 I Didn't Like It the First Time
    Cap 40082 When You're Smiling/King Size Papa

VIC DICKENSON
    BN 1600 Lion's Den/Tenderly
    BN 1601 In a Mellotone/I'm Gettin' Sentimental Over You

LPs

VIC DICKENSON
    Vang VRS-8520 The Vic Dickenson Septet, Vol. 1
    Vang VRS-8521 The Vic Dickenson Septet, Vol. 2
    Story 920 Vic's Boston Story

BOBBY HACKETT-VIC DICKENSON
    Project 3-PR/5034SD This Is Our Bag

BOBBY HACKETT
    Chiaroscuro CR-105 Live at the Roosevelt Grill with Vic Dickenson

RUBY BRAFF
    Vang VRS-8504 The Ruby Braff Special

JIMMY MCPARTLAND
    Jazztone J-1227 The Middle Road

THE SAINTS AND SINNERS
    MPS 15174 In Europe

THE WORLD'S GREATEST JAZZ BAND
    Atl SD-1570 Live at the Roosevelt Grill
    Atl SD-1582 What's New?
    World Jazz Records WJLP-5-1 Century Plaza
    World Jazz Records WJLP-5-2 Hark the Herald Angels Swing

463. DIETRICH, MARLENE   VO
(MARIA MAGDALENE DIETRICH VON LOSCH)
Born December 27, 1904, Weimar, Germany

Sexy German actress who became important star in U.S. movies of 30s and 40s. Usually played hardened, world-weary woman, poised and sophisticated. Sang in low, husky voice, half-talking style, in a few movies. Actress in German silents during 20s. Sensation in early German sound film THE BLUE ANGEL (1930). By

1931 film acclaimed in U.S., its haunting song *Falling in Love Again* becoming popular. Miss Dietrich won reputation for beautiful legs in this film but displayed them rarely thereafter. First U.S. movie MOROCCO (1931). Starred in top movies during next 20 years. Continued in 50s and 60s at slower pace but in important movies. At intervals performed in night clubs and recorded. In 1967 presented own show on Broadway. Other famous featured song *See What the Boys in the Back Room Will Have* in movie DESTRY RIDES AGAIN (1939). Starred in 1973 TV special.

MOVIES

1930—THE BLUE ANGEL (German)
1931—MOROCCO; DISHONORED
1932—SHANGHAI EXPRESS; BLONDE VENUS
1933—THE SONG OF SONGS
1934—THE SCARLET EMPRESS
1935—THE DEVIL IS A WOMAN
1936—DESIRE; THE GARDEN OF ALLAH
1937—KNIGHT WITHOUT HONOR; ANGEL
1939—DESTRY RIDES AGAIN
1940—SEVEN SINNERS
1941—FLAME OF NEW ORLEANS; MANPOWER
1942—THE LADY IS WILLING; THE SPOILERS; PITTSBURGH
1944—FOLLOW THE BOYS; KISMET
1947—GOLDEN EARRINGS
1948—A FOREIGN AFFAIR
1950—STAGE FRIGHT
1951—NO HIGHWAY IN THE SKY
1952—RANCHO NOTORIOUS
1956—AROUND THE WORLD IN 80 DAYS (cameo)
1957—THE MONTE CARLO STORY; WITNESS FOR THE PROSECUTION
1958—TOUCH OF EVIL
1961—JUDGMENT AT NUREMBERG
1964—PARIS WHEN IT SIZZLES

RECORDS

MARLENE DIETRICH
Vi 22593 Falling in Love Again/ Naughty Lola
Br 7723 Allein in Einer Grossen Stadt/Mein Blonde Baby
Br 7724 Wo Ist Der Mann?/Ja, So Bin Ich
Br 7725 Assez/Moi Je M'Ennuie
Br 7726 Jonny/Peter

HMV(G) 3490 Quand　　　L'Amour Meurt/Give Me the Man
Br(E) 3045 You Do Something to Me/You Go to My Head
De 11059 (also 23141) Falling in Love Again/See What the Boys in the Back Room Will Have
De 23140 You've Got That Look/You Go to My Head
De 24582 Black Market/Illusions
De 40497 Peter/Ich Hab' Noch
Br 85018 Wo Ist Der Mann?/Ja, So Bin Ich
MARLENE DIETRICH-ROSEMARY CLOONEY
Co 39812 Good for Nothin'/Too Old to Cut the Mustard

LPs

MARLENE DIETRICH
Cap ST-10937 (S) Marlene
De DL-8465 Marlene Dietrich
Co 4975
Co(10″)GL-105 Marlene Dietrich Overseas
Vox(10″)PL-3040 Songs
Ace of Hearts(E) AH-131 Marlene Dietrich (De RIs)
Adventures in Sound 164 Dietrich in Rio

464. DIETZ, HOWARD　　　　lyr
Born September 8, 1896, New York, N.Y.

Important lyricist from 20s into 60s. Collaborated in early years with composer Arthur Schwartz on memorable scores for Broadway musicals, notably THE LITTLE SHOW (1929), THREE'S A CROWD (1930), THE BAND WAGON (1931), FLYING COLORS (1932), REVENGE WITH MUSIC (1934), AT HOME ABROAD (1935), BETWEEN THE DEVIL (1938), INSIDE U.S.A. (1948). Wrote for other shows, also for movies. Librettist for many Broadway shows. Collaborated with composers Jerome Kern, Vernon Duke, Jimmy McHugh, Ralph Rainger. Best-known songs *I Guess I'll Have to Change My Plan, Dancing in the Dark, Louisiana Hayride, Moanin' Low, Something to Remember You By, A Shine on Your Shoes, You and the Night and the Music, By Myself, I See Your Face Before Me, That's Entertainment.* Attended Columbia University briefly. Early in career wrote newspaper columns and ads. Military service, World War I. In 1924 began long association with MGM as ad and publicity director, years later served in similar capacity for Loew's, Inc. Wrote some material for radio, later TV. Wrote English lyrics for operas DER FLEDERMAUS and LA BOHEME. In 60s collaborated with Arthur Schwartz again on Broadway musicals THE GAY LIFE (1961) and JENNIE (1963). Wrote 1974 autobiography *Dancing in the Dark*.

SONGS
*(with related shows; *also wrote book)*

1923—POPPY stage show (Alibi Baby)
1924—DEAR SIR stage show (songs unimportant)
1927—THE MERRY-GO-ROUND stage show* (Hogan's Alley; Gabriel Is Blowing His Horn; What D'Ya Say?; Tampa)
1929—THE LITTLE SHOW stage show* (I Guess I'll Have to Change My Plan; I've Made a Habit of You; Moanin' Low; Little Old New York); GRAND STREET FOLLIES stage show (I Need You So)
1930—THREE'S A CROWD stage show (The Moment I Saw You; Right at the Start of It; Something to Remember You By; All the King's Horses); THE SECOND LITTLE SHOW stage show (Lucky Seven; What a Case I've Got on You; Sunrise; I Like Your Face)
1931—THE BAND WAGON stage show* (Dancing in the Dark; I Love Louisa; High and Low; New Sun in the Sky; Where Can He Be?; Hoops; White Heat; Sweet Music)
1932—FLYING COLORS stage show* (Louisiana Hayride; A Shine on Your Shoes; Alone Together)
1934—REVENGE WITH MUSIC stage show* (You and the Night and the Music; If There Is Someone Lovelier Than You; When You Love Only One; That Fellow Manuelo); HOLLYWOOD PARTY movie (Feelin' High); Born to Be Kissed
1935—AT HOME ABROAD stage show* (Got a Bran' New Suit; Farewell, My Lovely; Thief in the Night; Love

Is a Dancing Thing; Oh, Leo!; That's Not Cricket; What a Wonderful World)
1937—UNDER YOUR SPELL movie (title song)
1938—BETWEEN THE DEVIL stage show* (I See Your Face Before Me; By Myself; You Have Everything; I'm Against Rhythm; Triplets)
1940—KEEP OFF THE GRASS stage show* (On the Old Park Bench; others)
1944—SADIE THOMPSON stage show* (The Love I Long For; Fisherman's Wharf; When You Live on an Island; Garden in the Sky; Siren of the Tropics); JACKPOT stage show (What Happened?; Sugar Foot; What's Mine is Yours; The Last Long Mile; It Was Nice Knowing You)
1948—INSIDE U.S.A. stage show (Haunted Heart; Rhode Island Is Famous for You; My Gal Is Mine Once More; First Prize at the Fair); THREE DARING DAUGHTERS movie (The Dickey-Bird Song)
1950—DANCING IN THE DARK movie (title song; other old songs)
1953—THE BAND WAGON movie (original stage score; new song: That's Entertainment)
1961—THE GAY LIFE stage show, Arthur Schwartz-cm (Magic Moment; Why Go Anywhere at All?; Who Can? You Can!; Something You Never Had Before; You're Not the Type; Come a-Wanderin' with Me)
1963—JENNIE stage show, Arthur Schwartz-cm (Waitin' for the Evening Train; When You're Far Away from New York Town; Where You Are; I Still Look at You That Way; Before I Kiss the World Goodbye)

465. DILLARD, BILL   t vo B
Born July 20, 1911, Philadelphia, Pa.

Trumpeter-vocalist, best known for vocals with Teddy Hill, where big baritone voice featured. Played in local bands as teenager. To New York in 1929, jobbed. In early 30s with Jelly Roll Morton, Luis Russell, Benny Carter and Lucky Millinder among others. With Teddy Hill 1934-8, including European tour in 1937. With Dave Martin 1938-9, in late 1939 with Coleman Hawkins. With Louis Armstrong most of 1940. After freelancing, including brief period with Red Norvo, in 1943 Dillard became actor. Minor acting-singing roles on Broadway in CARMEN JONES (1943), ANNA LUCASTA (1945), MEMPHIS BOUND and BEGGARS' HOLIDAY (1946), LOST IN THE STARS (1950), GREEN PASTURES (1951), MY DARLIN' AIDA (1952). In 1949 played in Europe accompanying blues singer Huddie Ledbetter. In 50s acting roles on TV dramatic shows. With Machito band in 1951. In later years semi-active in music; occasional jobs as trumpeter-vocalist or leading band.

RECORDS

CLARENCE WILLIAMS
  Pe 15387 Papa De Da Da/Baby, Won't You Please Come Home?
  Pe 15403 Hot Lovin'
SPIKE HUGHES
  De(E) 3606 Pastorale
TEDDY HILL (vocals on all)
  Me 13351 Got Me Doin' Things
  Me 13364 When Love Knocks at Your Heart
  Bb 6908 Big Boy Blue
  Bb 6941 The You and Me That Used to Be
  Bb 6954 I Know Now/The Lady Who Couldn't Be Kissed
  Bb 6988 San Anton'
  Bb 6989 I'm Happy, Darling, Dancing with You
  Bb 7013 Yours and Mine/I'm Feelin' Like a Million
LITTLE RAMBLERS
  Bb 6220 I'm Shooting High/The Music Goes 'Round and Around
  Bb 6232 I've Got My Fingers Crossed/I'm Building Up to an Awful Letdown
DICKY WELLS
  Sw(Fr) 3 Hot Club Blues/I've Found a New Baby
  Sw(Fr) 27 I Got Rhythm
  Sw(Fr) 39 Dinah/Nobody's Blues but My Own

LPs

BENNY CARTER
  Pres 7643 (early RIs)
TEDDY HILL
  "X"(10")LVA-3030 (RIs)
DICKY WELLS
  Pres 7593 In Paris 1937 (Sw RIs)

466. DINNING SISTERS   VO
(Ginger, Lou and Jean)

Popular singing trio of late 40s and 50s. Musicianly group somewhat in tradition of Boswell Sisters. In early 40s regulars on National Barn Dance radio show. During 1943-5 numerous shows on Chicago radio; played clubs in Chicago. In low-budget movie musicals. In later 40s their records attained some popularity. Lou Dinning also recorded on her own; excellent singer. By mid-50s trio's career waned.

RECORDS

DINNING SISTERS
  Cap 389 If I Had My Life to Live Over/My Adobe Hacienda
  Cap 1473 San Antonio Rose/Please Don't Talk About Me When I'm Gone
  Cap 1511 Somebody/Very Good Advice
  Cap 1726 Tennessee Blues/I Can't Forget
  Cap 2082 I'm Lost/Love Me Sweet and Love Me Long
  Cap 15184 Buttons and Bows/San Antonio Rose
  Cap 15339 Harlem Sandman/Oh Monah
  Cap 20017 Sentimental Gentleman from Georgia/Please Don't Talk About Me When I'm Gone
  Cap 20019 You're a Character, Dear/Once in Awhile
  Cap 20020 Brazil/The Way You Look Tonight
  Cap 20131 I Get the Blues When It Rains
  VD(12")905 Harlem Sandman
LOU DINNING
  Cap 1892 The Little White Cloud That Cried/Blue December
  Cap 1927 Trust in Me/I'll Still Love You

Cap 2013 Just Friends/Sick, Sad, Sorry and Blue
Cap 2076 Again and Again/Torment
PAUL WESTON (Lou Dinning vo)
Cap 245 Nobody Else but Me

LPs

DINNING SISTERS
Somerset P-3800 Songs by the Dinning Sisters

467. DIXON, JOE   cl as ts b-s vo B
Born April 21, 1917, Lynn, Mass.

Good jazz clarinetist in mainstream style. Attended New England Conservatory. To New York in 1934. First big band job with Bill Staffon 1935-6; also with Adrian Rollini. Joined Tommy Dorsey early 1936, remained one year. Worked briefly in 1937 with Gus Arnheim. Joined Bunny Berigan in May 1937, remained over a year as featured soloist. Clarinet tone at this time thin and reedy; played multinote solos. In later years tone became fuller, lost rasp; solos swung in more leisurely fashion. With Fred Waring about five years, 1938-43. In 1943 military service. After discharge mostly with dixieland groups in New York, Eddie Condon and Miff Mole among others. In 50s freelanced, led combo in New York. In early 60s career curtailed by auto accident. Taught music, worked as disc jockey. In later 60s again led combo.

RECORDS

BILL STAFFON
Bb 6048 Heartstrings (vo)
TOMMY DORSEY
Vi 25326 Royal Garden Blues
Vi 25508 The "Goona Goo"
Vi 25467 After You've Gone
BUNNY BERIGAN
Vi 25653 A Study in Brown
Vi 25667 Sweet Varsity Sue
Vi 25811 Sophisticated Swing
Vi 25848 Azure
Vi 26001 Russian Lullaby
Vi 26138 Black Bottom
EMPERORS OF JAZZ
Swam 7507 Muskrat Ramble/Clarinet Marmalade
Swam 7508 At the Jazz Band Ball
BRAD GOWANS
Vi 20-3230 Singin' the Blues/Jazz Me Blues

EDDIE CONDON
De 23431 Oh, Lady Be Good
De 23433 Swanee
De 23719 Stars Fell on Alabama
MARTHA TILTON
VD(12")524 Beyond the Blue Horizon
BING CROSBY
De 24114 Blue/After You've Gone

LPs

JOE DIXON
Golden Crest CR-3036 Joe Dixon "Boom Chicks"
BUNNY BERIGAN
Cam CAL-550 Bunny (Vi RIs)
BRAD GOWANS
Vi(10")LJM-3000
EDDIE CONDON
De(10")DL-5137 George Gershwin Jazz Concert
PHIL NAPOLEON
EmArcy(10")MG-26008 Dixieland Classics, Vol. 1 (Swan RIs)
BUNNY BERIGAN
Vi LPV-581 His Trumpet and Orchestra, Original 1937-9 Recordings (Vi RIs)

468. DIXON, MORT   lyr
Born March 20, 1892, New York, N.Y.
Died March 23, 1956, Bronxville, N.Y.

Lyricist of 20s and 30s. Famous songs: *That Old Gang of Mine*; *Bye Bye Blackbird*; *I'm Looking Over a Four-Leaf Clover*; *Just Like a Butterfly*; *Would You Like to Take a Walk?*; *I Found a Million Dollar Baby*; *River, Stay 'Way from My Door*; *You're My Everything*; *Flirtation Walk*; *The Lady in Red*; *Happiness Ahead*. In early years actor in vaudeville. Military service, World War I. Directed army show WHIZ BANG in France after war. Began songwriting early 20s, wrote many hits. Scored a few Broadway musicals and movies. Chief collaborators composers Ray Henderson, Harry Warren, Harry Woods, Allie Wrubel, lyricist Billy Rose.

SONGS
(with related shows)

1923—That Old Gang of Mine
1924—Follow the Swallow; I Wonder Who's Dancing with You Tonight
1925—Bam, Bam, Bamy Shore; Too Many Parties and Too Many Pals; If I Had a Girl Like You

1926—Bye Bye Blackbird; Under the Ukulele Tree; I'm in Love with You, That's Why
1927—Cover Me Up with Sunshine; Nesting Time; I'll Take Care of Your Cares; I'm Looking Over a Four-Leaf Clover; Is It Possible?; Just Like a Butterfly; Moonbeam, Kiss Her for Me; Where the Wild Wild Flowers Grow
1928—Hello, Montreal; In the Sing Song Sycamore Tree; Nagasaki; Old Man Sunshine; If You Want the Rainbow
1929—Where the Sweet Forget-Me-Nots Remember; Where You Are
1930—SWEET AND LOW stage show (Would You Like to Take a Walk?; He's Not Worth Your Tears)
1931—BILLY ROSE'S CRAZY QUILT stage show (I Found a Million Dollar Baby; Sing a Little Jingle); THE LAUGH PARADE stage show (You're My Everything; Ooh! That Kiss); River, Stay 'Way from My Door
1932—Pink Elephants
1933—I Raised My Hat; Marching Along Together
1934—FLIRTATION WALK movie (Flirtation Walk; Mr. and Mrs. Is the Name); HAPPINESS AHEAD movie (Happiness Ahead; Pop! Goes Your Heart)
1935—SWEET MUSIC movie (Fare Thee Well, Annabelle; I See Two Lovers); IN CALIENTE movie (The Lady in Red); I LIVE FOR LOVE movie (I Live for Love; Mine Alone); WE'RE IN THE MONEY movie (So Nice Seeing You Again); BRIGHT LIGHTS movie (Toddlin' Along with You)
1936—Did You Mean It?; Every Once in Awhile
1937—I Can't Lose That Longing for You
1939—Tears from My Inkwell

469. DODDS, BABY d B
(WARREN DODDS)

Born December 24, 1898, New Orleans, La.
Died February 14, 1959, Chicago, Ill.

Leading drummer in New Orleans jazz style. Long career playing Chicago spots. Built variations on his basic press roll, used auxiliary equipment. Younger brother of great clarinetist Johnny Dodds. As youngster played parades and dances in New Orleans. With Papa Celestin awhile. With Fate Marable on riverboat jobs 1918-21. In 1922 with King Oliver in San Francisco and Chicago. Left Oliver in late 1923, continued in Chicago with Honore Dutrey and Freddie Keppard. During 20s many jobs with brother Johnny, especially in late 20s. Also with Lil Armstrong, Charlie Elgar, Dave Peyton, Louis Armstrong, many others. During much of 30s with brother Johnny in Chicago. At times he and Johnny drove cabs to earn living. Frequent runs at Three Deuces as house drummer in later 30s. In 40s with Jimmie Noone, Bunk Johnson, Art Hodes, mostly freelance. Featured on This Is Jazz radio series, mid-40s. Left Chicago to work at intervals in New York and abroad in middle 40s through early 50s. With Bob Wilber, Natty Dominique, Lee Collins, Don Frye. Two strokes curtailed career awhile. Resumed until further illness caused final retirement in 1957.

RECORDS

KING OLIVER
 OK 4933 Snake Rag/High Society Rag
 Ge 5134 Mandy Lee Blues/I'm Going to Wear You Off My Mind
 Ge 5135 Froggie Moore/Chimes Blues
JELLY ROLL MORTON
 Vi 20772 Hyena Stomp/Billy Goat Stomp
 Vi 20948 Beale Street Blues/The Pearls
 Bb 10256 Wild Man Blues/Jungle Blues
LOUIS ARMSTRONG
 OK 8474 Wild Man Blues/Gully Low Blues
 OK 8482 Willie the Weeper/Alligator Crawl
 Co 35661 S.O.L. Blues
BEALE STREET WASHBOARD BAND
 Vo 1403 Forty and Tight/Piggly Wiggly
CHICAGO FOOTWARMERS
 OK 8533 Ballin' the Jack/Grandma's Ball

DIXIELAND THUMPERS
Para 12525 Weary Way Blues/There'll
Come a Day
RICHARD M. JONES
Sess 12006 New Orleans Hop Scop
Blues/29th & Dearborn
Sess 12007 Jazzin' Babies Blues/Canal
Street Blues
SIDNEY BECHET
Vi 27204 Blues in Thirds
Vi 27240 Stompy Jones/Save It, Pretty
Mama
LIL ARMSTRONG
B&W(12")1210 Confessin'/East Town
Boogie
B&W(12")1211 Lady Be Good/Little
Daddy Blues
MEZZROW-BECHET QUINTET
KJ 146 Really the Blues (1 & 2)
TUT SOPER
SD 5000 Oronics/Stardust Stomp
SD 5001 Thou Swell/It's a Ramble
BABY DODDS
BN 518 Careless Love/Winin' Boy
Blues
BN 519 High Society/Feelin' at Ease
Ci 1001 Wolverine Blues/Drum Im-
provisation No. 1
Ci 1039 Buddy Bolden's Blues/Drum
Improvisation No. 2
Disc 6007 Spooky Drums/Rudiments
with Drumstick: Nerve Beat
Disc 6006 Maryland/Rudiments with
Drumstick: Tom-Tom Workout

LPs

BABY DODDS
Folk(10")FP-30 Talking and Drum
Solos (with narration)
KING OLIVER
Epic LN-3208 (OK RIs)
LOUIS ARMSTRONG
Co CL-852 Louis Armstrong & His
Hot Seven (OK RIs)
JOHNNY DODDS & KID ORY
Epic LN-3207 (RIs)
JOHNNY DODDS
"X"(10")LX-3006 Johnny Dodds'
Washboard Band (Vi RIs)
JELLY ROLL MORTON
"X"(10")LVA-3028 Jelly Roll
Morton's Red Hot Peppers (Vi RIs)
BUNK JOHNSON & KID ORY
Riv(10")1047 New Orleans Revival

ALL-STAR STOMPERS
Ci(10")L-402 This Is Jazz
WILD BILL DAVISON
Riv 12-211 Sweet and Hot
TONY PARENTI
Riv 12-205 Tony Parenti's Ragtime
Band

470. DODDS, JOHNNY   cl as B

Born April 12, 1892, New Orleans, La.
Died August 8, 1940, Chicago, Ill.

Jazz great on clarinet in traditional New
Orleans style. Long career in Chicago.
Warm tone and forceful solo attack; fit in
well in small-band ensembles. Older
brother of drummer Baby Dodds. Took
up clarinet at 17. Parade and dance jobs
locally till 1920, including periods with
Kid Ory and Fate Marable on riverboats.
With King Oliver in Chicago, remained
1920-4. Made Chicago base thereafter,
worked with Honore Dutrey and Freddie
Keppard. Led band from late 1924
through 20s, mostly at Kelly's Stables.
Brother Baby Dodds worked often with
him, especially in late 20s. Much freelance recording, including jazz classics
with Louis Armstrong. Also recorded
under own name. In 30s led band at
Chicago clubs. At times during 30s he and
brother had to drive cab to earn living.
One trip to New York in 1938, soon
returned to Chicago. Heart attack in 1939
caused inactivity. In 1940 played occasionally until death.

RECORDS

KING OLIVER
OK 4933 Snake Rag/High Society Rag
Ge 5133 Canal Street Blues/Just Gone
LOUIS ARMSTRONG
OK 8299 You're Next/Oriental Strut
OK 8300 Muskrat Ramble
OK 8320 Yes, I'm in the Barrel
OK 8551 Got No Blues/I'm Not
Rough
Co 35661 S.O.L. Blues
LIL'S HOT SHOTS
Vo 1037 Drop That Sack/Georgia Bo
Bo
LOVIE AUSTIN
Para 12361 Jackass Blues / Frog
Tongue Stomp

BEALE STREET WASHBOARD BAND
  Vo 1403 Forty and Tight/Piggly Wiggly
CHICAGO FOOTWARMERS
  OK 8533 Ballin' the Jack/Grandma's Ball
BLYTHE'S WASHBOARD RAGAMUFFINS
  Para 12428 Ape Man/Your Folks
DIXIELAND JUG BLOWERS
  Vi 20415 Memphis Shake
  Vi 20420 House Rent Rag
  Vi 20480 Carpet Alley
FREDDIE KEPPARD
  Para 12399 Stock Yards Strut/Salty Dog
JELLY ROLL MORTON
  Vi 20948 Beale Street Blues/The Pearls
  Vi 21064 Wolverine Blues/Mr. Jelly Lord
  Bb 10256 Wild Man Blues
STATE STREET RAMBLERS
  Ge 6232 Weary Way Blues/Cootie Stomp
  Ge 6249 There'll Come a Day
JOHNNY DODDS
  Br 3567 Wild Man Blues/Melancholy
  Br 3568 After You've Gone/Come On and Stomp, Stomp, Stomp
  Vi 21552 Bull Fiddle Blues/Blue Washboard Stomp
  Vi 21554 Blue Clarinet Stomp/Blue Piano Stomp
  Vi 38004 Bucktown Stomp/Weary City
  Bb 10240 Goober Dance/Too Tight
  De 2111 Wild Man Blues/29th & Dearborn
  De 7413 Blues Galore/Shake Your Can
  De 18094 Red Onion Blues/Gravier Street Blues

LPs

JOHNNY DODDS
  Vi LPV-558 (Vi RIs)
  "X"(10″)LX-3006 (Vi RIs)
  Riv 12-104 New Orleans Clarinet (RIs)
JOHNNY DODDS & KID ORY
  Epic LN-3207 (RIs)
KING OLIVER
  Epic LN-3208 (OK RIs)
LOUIS ARMSTRONG with KING OLIVER
  Riv(10″)1029 (Ge RIs)

LOUIS ARMSTRONG
  Co CL-851 (Hot Five OK RIs)
  Co CL-852 (Hot Seven OK RIs)

471. DOGGETT, BILL   or p ar cm B
Born February 16, 1916, Philadelphia, Pa.

Leading jazz organist, successful in rhythm and blues field in 50s. Excellent in combos and in providing backing for soloists. In late 30s in various groups, led band. With Jimmy Mundy and Lucky Millinder in 1940. With Ink Spots 1942-4 as pianist-arranger. With Illinois Jacquet 1945-7. With Louis Jordan 1950-1 as pianist, then switched to organ. Free-lanced on organ, then formed combo. LPs well received. Hit record *Honky Tonk*. Active in 60s playing dates and recording occasionally.

RECORDS

VIC DICKENSON
  BN 1600 Lion's Den/Tenderly
JOHNNY OTIS
  Excel 141 Preston Love's Mansion/My Baby's Business
  Excel 142 Jimmy's 'Round the Clock Blues/Harlem Nocturne
ILLINOIS JACQUET
  Sav 593 Jumpin' Jacquet/Blue Mood
  Sav 911 Illinois Goes to Chicago/Jacquet and No Vest
  Apo 766 Jumpin' at Apollo/Jacquet Bounce
  Alad 179 You Left Me All Alone/Jivin' with Jack the Bellboy
ELLA FITZGERALD
  De 27693 Smooth Sailing
  De 28126 Airmail Special
LOUIS JORDAN
  De 28088 Slow Down/Never Trust a Woman
  De 28335 All of Me/There Goes My Heart
HELEN HUMES
  Philo 105 He May Be Your Man/Blue Prelude
  Philo 106 Every Now and Then/Be-Baba-Leba
EARL BOSTIC
  King 4954 Indiana/Bubbins Rock
BILL DOGGETT
  King 4530 Big Dog (1 & 2)

819

King 4605 Moondust/Early Bird
King 4650 Percy Speaks/Ready Mix
King 4702 The Song Is Ended/It's a Dream
King 4711 There's No You/Easy
King 4738 Honey/The Nearness of You
King 4742 Winter Wonderland/Christmas Song
King 4950 Honky Tonk (1 & 2)

LPs

BILL DOGGETT
  King 633 High and Wide
  King 641 Big City Dance Party
  King 395-502 Moondust
  King 395-531 Everybody Dance the Honky Tonk
  Co CL-1814 Oops!
  Co CL-1942 Prelude to the Blues
(as conductor)
JIMMY RUSHING & AL HIBBLER
  Grand Prix K-407 Big Boy Blues
(as conductor-arranger)
ELLA FITZGERALD
  Verve V-4056 Rhythm Is My Business

472. DOLAN, ROBERT EMMETT
cm ar p B

*Born August 3, 1906, Hartford, Conn.
Died September 26, 1972, California*

Conductor of stage, movies and radio, also arranger and composer. Collaborated with lyricist Johnny Mercer on Broadway musicals TEXAS, LI'L DARLIN' (1949) and FOXY (1964). Attended Loyola College, also extensive music training later. Active on radio from mid-30s, conducted on many shows. Conductor or musical director for Broadway shows GOOD NEWS, FOLLOW THROUGH, FLYING COLORS, STRIKE ME PINK, HOT-CHA, MAY WINE, HOORAY FOR WHAT?, LEAVE IT TO ME, VERY WARM FOR MAY, LOUISIANA PURCHASE. In 40s composer, scorer, conductor or musical director for films including STAR SPANGLED RHYTHM, LADY IN THE DARK, BELLS OF ST. MARY'S, INCENDIARY BLONDE, BLUE SKIES, ROAD TO RIO. Score for Broadway musical TEXAS, LI'L DARLIN' included title song, *Big Movie Show in the Sky*, *Horseshoes Are Lucky*, *They Talk a Different Language*, *It's Great to Be Alive*.

Other songs: *Hullabaloo, At Last I'm in Love, Song of the Highwayman, Out of the Past, Glamour Waltz, Your Heart Will Tell You So.*

473. DOLLY SISTERS
vo

Twins, born October 25, 1892, in Hungary
JANSZIEKA (or YANSCI) DEUTSCH (nicknamed Jenny)
ROSZICKA (or ROZISKA) DEUTSCH (nicknamed Rosie)

Headline act of vaudeville and revues. Beautiful, glamorous, chic entertainers; excelled in elaborate production numbers. Known primarily as dancers, also sang and acted. In Broadway musicals THE ECHO (1910), ZIEGFELD FOLLIES OF 1911, A WINSOME WIDOW and THE MERRY COUNTESS (1912), GREENWICH VILLAGE FOLLIES OF 1924, also in play HIS BRIDAL NIGHT (1916). Played leading theatres in U.S. and abroad. Popular in Paris revues early 20s, also starred in revue THE LEAGUE OF NOTIONS in London in 1921. Names revived in 1945 with movie THE DOLLY SISTERS starring Betty Grable and June Haver in many song and dance numbers.

474. DOMNERUS, ARNE
as cl B

Born December 20, 1924, Stockholm, Sweden

Outstanding Swedish modern jazz star on alto sax. Beautiful soft tone, light swinging style, well-conceived solos. Good clarinetist too, with cool tone and modern style. Became known in Sweden in late 40s; played in Simon Brehm band. By early 50s had group, became top star in Sweden. LPs appeared in U.S. in mid-50s, won recognition here for Domnerus and other Swedish stars. Played New York 1974 with 7-piece combo.

RECORDS

ARNE DOMNERUS
  HMV(Sw) 7709 Favor of a Fool/The Man I Love
  HMV(Sw) 7710 Yours and Mine/Hallelujah
  HMV(Sw) 7832 I Never Knew/I Should Care
  Metro(Sw) 103 More Than You Know/Conversation

Pres 792 Anytime for You/Let's Cool
One
EXPRESSENS ELITORKESTER 1952
Musica(Sw) 9215 Laura/Nice Work If
You Can Get It
SWINGIN' SWEDES
BN 1605 Pick Yourself Up/Summer-
time
SWEDISH STARS
Cup(Sw) 9007 Cream of the Crop (1 &
2)
Son(Sw) 7433 Indiana (1 & 2)
Son(Sw) 7434 Don't Blame Me/All the
Things You Are
ROLF ERICSON
Dis 1732 Perdido/Miles Away

LPs

ARNE DOMNERUS
Pres(10″) 133 New Sounds from
Sweden, Vol. 3
Pres(10″) 134 Clarinet Solos
Cam CAL-417
Vi(10″) LPT-3032 Around the World
in Jazz—Sweden
SWEDISH ALL-STARS
Pres(10″) 119 New Sounds from
Sweden, Vol. 1
BENGT HALLBERG
· Pres(10″) 176
ROLF ERICSON
Dis(10″) DL-2008 Swedish Pastry
HARRY ARNOLD
Jazztone J-1270 The Jazztone Mystery
Band
Mer MG-36139 Plus Big Band Plus
Quincy Jones Equals Jazz!

475. DONAHUE, AL   v ar cm B

Born June 12, 1904, Boston, Mass.

Leader of popular dance band in 30s and
40s. Band played with verve, crispness,
full ensemble sound; could swing but
better on ballads. Donahue attended
Boston University and New England
Conservatory. Started as bandleader in
late 20s. Played several years in early 30s
in Bermuda; popular there. Donahue
worked year as M.C. in Detroit theatres.
Moved back and forth from Bermuda to
U.S. By mid-30s band known in U.S.
Billed as *Low Down Rhythm in a Top Hat*
(also title of theme song, of which Don-

ahue was co-composer). Popular at New
York's Rainbow Room, also played top
spots in other cities. Good vocalists Barry
McKinley and Paula Kelly in 30s, Phil
Brito in 40s. Donahue wrote some of
band's arrangements. Co-composer of
popular 1938 tune *Don't Cross Your Fingers, Cross Your Heart*. In mid-40s band
played west coast as well as New York
and other locations. In 1954 had TV show
on west coast. In later years faded but
continued as bandleader as late as 1971.

RECORDS

AL DONAHUE
De 599 Twenty-Four Hours a Day/
Love Makes the World Go 'Round
De 626 Alone/The Winter Waltz
De 630 You Took My Breath Away/
How Do I Rate with You?
De 981 It's Love I'm After/To Mary
—with Love
De 989 Bermuda Buggyride/I Want
the Whole World to Love You
Vo 4195 Beside a Moonlit Stream/
Naturally
Vo 4513 Hurry Home / Jeepers
Creepers
Vo 4550 Between a Kiss and a Sigh/I
Won't Believe It
Vo 4846 Stairway to the Stars/Cinder-
ella, Stay in My Arms
Vo 4888 Moon Love/To You
Vo 4956 White Sails/Persian Rug
Vo 4993 Oh, You Crazy Moon/This
Heart of Mine
Vo 5099 The Last Two Weeks in
July/Day In—Day Out
Vo 5264 Darn That Dream/Kiss and
Remember
Vo 5314 (theme) Low Down Rhythm
in a Top Hat/Copenhagen
Vo 5351 Temptation/Pinch Me
Vo 5519 Fools Rush In/I'm Stepping
Out with a Memory Tonight
OK 5660 Southern Fried/Route 23
OK 5888 Frenesi/I Hear a Rhapsody
OK 6017 Candles in the Wind/My
Heart's on Fire
OK 6413 The Shrine of St. Cecilia/
Under Fiesta Stars
4-Star 1081 It Couldn't Be True/And
Two Is Eight
4-Star 1121 My Serenade/Texas Moon

476. DONAHUE, JACK   vo

Born c. 1892, Charleston, Mass.
Died October 1, 1930, New York, N.Y.

Song and dance man, starred in Broadway musicals ZIEGFELD FOLLIES OF 1920, MOLLY DARLING (1922), BE YOURSELF (1924), SUNNY (1925), ROSALIE (1928), SONS O' GUNS (1929; also collaborated on book), AMERICA'S SWEETHEART (1931). Wrote book for PRINCESS CHARMING (1930). Starred in vaudeville, developed into comedian to add to singing and dancing. "Shadow dance" routine featured in act.

477. DONAHUE, SAM   ts ar cm B

Born March 8, 1918, Detroit, Mich.
Died March 22, 1974, Reno, Nevada,
of cancer.

Bandleader and tenor saxist with powerful jumping style and distinctive warm tone. In late 30s led good young band in Detroit. Sonny Burke took over when Donahue joined Gene Krupa in mid-1938 for two years. Also in 1940 briefly with Harry James and Benny Goodman. In early 1941-2 took back former band. Excellent band; in 1942 played Glen Island Casino in New Rochelle, N.Y. Donahue composed numbers featured by band: *Lonesome, It Counts a Lot, Skooter, I Never Purposely Hurt You, Six Mile Stretch, Sax-a-Boogie*. Military service, took over Artie Shaw's big Navy band upon Shaw's discharge. Outstanding band, made impressive V-Discs.

After discharge formed great band in 1946: contagious beat, swung, good arrangements and soloists. Donahue sax featured. Career going well when called back into service in 1951 for about six months. Joined Tommy Dorsey in late 1951, left in 1953 to form another band. In early 1954 bandleader Ray Anthony bought Billy May band, turned it over to Donahue to lead. Lasted several years. Donahue led own band again in late 50s. Worked with Stan Kenton about a year during 1960-1. In late 1961 became leader of Tommy Dorsey Orchestra (Dorsey having died in 1956). This unit perpetuated Dorsey name, featured his arrangements. Also featured: trumpet star Charlie Shavers, vocal group Pied Pipers, singers Helen Forrest, Frank Sinatra, Jr. Unit later billed as Frank Sinatra Jr. Show, became showcase for latter, and size of band shrank. Became music director of New York's Playboy Club. Led band in Reno from 1969.

RECORDS

GENE KRUPA
     Br 8335 The Madam Swings It
     Co 35387 Marcheta/Symphony in Riffs
     OK 5921 Feelin' Fancy

SAM DONAHUE
     OK 6334 It Counts a Lot/Lonesome
     OK 6358 Skooter/Four or Five Times
     Bb 11131 They Still Make Love in London/Au Reet
     Bb 11169 Saxophone Sam/Loafin' on a Lazy Day
     Bb 11198 Do You Care?/Six Mile Stretch
     Bb 11479 Flo Flo/I'll Never Tire of You
     Encore 500 Hollywood Hop/Encore Essence
     Cap 260 Dinah/Take Five
     Cap 293 Scufflin'/Put That Kiss Back
     Cap 325 A Rainy Night in Rio/Anybody's Love Song
     Cap 357 My Melancholy Baby/I Can't Believe It Was All Make Believe
     Cap 472 Red Wing/The Whistler
     Cap 15081 I'll Get Along Somehow/ Sax-a-Boogie
     Cap 15340 Gypsy Love Song/Out in the Cold Again
     Si 15192 Encore Essence/Round the Block

MUS 1/C SAM DONAHUE & THE NAVY BAND
     VD(12")522 Dinah
     VD(12")533 My Melancholy Baby
     VD(12")553 Moten Swing/Just You, Just Me
     VD(12")583 Deep Night/I've Found a New Baby

SAM DONAHUE & BILLY MAY ORCHESTRA
     Cap 2759 Bill and Sam/Rose-Marie

LPs

SAM DONAHUE
     Cap T-613 Young Moderns in Love
     Cap T-626 Sam Donahue

Musirama Remington RE-33-1847-8
Dance Date with Sam Donahue
SAM DONAHUE & TOMMY DORSEY ORCHES-
TRA
Vi LSP-2830 (recorded live from
Americana Hotel in New York)
WOODY HERMAN
Everest SDBR-1003 (S) The Herd
Rides Again ... In Stereo
STAN KENTON
Cap ST-1796 (S) Adventures in Jazz
JERRY FIELDING
Trend(10″)1004
Kapp KL-1026 Dance Concert

478. DONALDSON, WALTER
cm lyr ar p

*Born February 15, 1893, Brooklyn, N.Y.
Died July 15, 1947, Santa Monica,
Calif.*

Top composer with numerous hits. Most
famous: *My Buddy*; *My Blue Heaven*;
Yes, Sir, That's My Baby; *At Sundown*;
Carolina in the Morning; *Love Me or Leave
Me*; *Makin' Whoopee*; *Little White Lies*;
My Mammy; *You're Driving Me Crazy*.
Fabulous output during 1925-8; com-
posed dozens of leading songs then.
Wrote for Broadway shows, including
memorable score for WHOOPEE (1928).
Collaborators included lyricists Gus
Kahn, Sam M. Lewis, Joe Young, Edgar
Leslie, Harold Adamson, Johnny Mercer.
In early years worked for New York
brokerage firm. Pianist for music pub-
lisher. During World War I entertained
troops 19 months at Camp Upton, N.Y.
Later worked for Irving Berlin's publishing company. Had own publishing company, Donaldson, Douglas & Gumble, by
1928. To Hollywood in early 30s as composer-arranger for movies.

SONGS
(with related shows)

1915—Back Home in Tennessee; Just Try
to Picture Me Down Home in
Tennessee; You'd Never Know the
Old Home Town of Mine
1918—SINBAD stage show (My Mammy);
The Daughter of Rosie O'Grady
1919—THE LADY IN RED stage show
(China Dragon Blues; Play Me
That Tune); How Ya Gonna Keep
'Em Down on the Farm?; I'll Be
Happy When the Preacher Makes
You Mine; You're a Million Miles
from Nowhere
1920—ED WYNN'S CARNIVAL stage show (I
Love the Land of Old Black Joe);
My Little Bimbo Down on the
Bamboo Isle
1921—Down South
1922—THE PASSING SHOW OF 1922 stage
show (Carolina in the Morning);
Dixie Highway; Georgia; My
Buddy; Sweet Indiana Moon; On
the 'Gin 'Gin 'Ginny Shore; Tell
Her at Twilight
1923—Mindin' My Business; Beside a
Babbling Brook
1924 ROUND THE TOWN stage show (Chi-
quita); Back Where the Daffodils
Grow; In the Evening; My Best
Girl; Oh, Baby
1925—I Wonder Where My Baby Is To-
night; Isn't She the Sweetest
Thing; That Certain Party; The
Midnight Waltz; Let It Rain, Let
It Pour; My Sweetie Turned Me
Down; Swanee Butterfly; Yes, Sir
That's My Baby; In the Middle of
the Night
1926—SWEETHEART TIME stage show (One
Way Street; Marian; Two by
Four; Actions Speak Louder Than
Words); After I Say I'm Sorry;
For My Sweetheart; But I Do
—You Know I Do; Don't Be An-
gry with Me; I've Got the Girl; It
Made You Happy When You
Made Me Cry; Just a Bird's-Eye
View of My Old Kentucky Home;
Let's Talk About My Sweetie;
That's Why I Love You; There
Ain't No Maybe in My Baby's
Eyes; Thinking of You; Where'd
You Get Those Eyes?
1927—At Sundown; Changes; Dixie Vag-
abond; He's the Last Word; If
You See Sally; Just Once Again;
Mary; Just the Same; My Blue
Heaven; My Ohio Home; A Shady
Tree; Sam, the Old Accordion
Man; Sing Me a Baby Song;
Someday You'll Say O.K.
1928—WHOOPEE stage show (Makin'
Whoopee; I'm Bringing a Red Red

Rose; Love Me or Leave Me; My Baby Just Cares for Me; Come West, Little Girl, Come West); Anything You Say; Just Like a Melody out of the Sky; Because My Baby Don't Mean Maybe Now; Out of the Dawn; Out of Town Gal; Say "Yes" Today

1929—Junior; Reaching for Someone; Romance

1930—SMILES stage show (Youre Driving Me Crazy); WHOOPEE movie (original stage score); Kansas City Kitty; Lazy Lou'siana Moon; Little White Lies; Sweet Jennie Lee; 'Tain't No Sin; There's a Wah-Wah Girl in Agua Caliente

1931—ZIEGFELD FOLLIES OF 1931 stage show (I'm with You); Blue Kentucky Moon; An Evening in Caroline; Goodnight Moon; Hello, Beautiful; Without That Gal; You Didn't Have to Tell Me

1932—My Mom; I'm So in Love; You're Telling Me

1933—You've Got Everything

1934—HOLLYWOOD PARTY movie (I've Had My Moments; Feelin' High); KID MILLIONS movie (An Earful of Music; Okay, Toots; When My Ship Comes In; Your Head on My Shoulder); Dancing in the Moonlight; A Thousand Goodnights; Sleepy Head; Riptide

1935—Clouds; Tender Is the Night

1936—THE GREAT ZIEGFELD movie (You; You Never Looked So Beautiful; You Gotta Pull Strings); SUZY movie (Did I Remember?); SINNER TAKE ALL movie (I'd Be Lost without You); It's Been So Long

1937—AFTER THE THIN MAN movie (Blow That Horn); SARATOGA movie (Saratoga; The Horse with the Dreamy Eyes)

1938—Why'd Ya Make Me Fall in Love?; Rainbow 'Round the Moon

1939—THAT'S RIGHT—YOU'RE WRONG movie (I'm Fit to Be Tied); Could Be; Cuckoo in the Clock; Gotta Get Some Shut-eye; Basket Weaver Man

1940—Mister Meadowlark

1943—WHAT'S BUZZIN', COUSIN? movie (Nevada)

479. DONEGAN, DOROTHY   p o
Born April 6, 1924, Chicago, Ill.

Pianist-entertainer in 40s and 50s. Strong, uninhibited style, swinging beat, excellent chord construction, facile. Good showman and entertainer, ideal for intimate rooms. Worked early as church organist. In 1942 caught on with piano work in Chicago clubs, at same time attended Chicago Conservatory for classical training. Worked on west coast, appeared in 1944 movie SENSATIONS OF 1945. Played various cities. Hit peak in 50s. Active in 60s. Played New York 1974.

RECORDS

DOROTHY DONEGAN

  Bb 8979 Piano Boogie/Every Day Blues

  Cont 6033 Yesterdays/Dorothy's Boogie Woogie

  Cont 6034 Limehouse Blues/Tiger Rag

  Cont 6051 Jumpin' Jack Boogie/Little Girl from St. Louis

  Cont 6056 Some of These Days/Kilroy Was Here

  Cont 6057 How High the Moon/Schubert's Boogie Woogie

  Cont 6058 The Man I Love/Two Loves Wuz One Too Many for Me

LPs

DOROTHY DONEGAN

  MGM(10″)E-278

  Jub(10″)11

  Roul R-25010 At the Embers

  Cap T-1155 Dorothy Donegan Live!

  Cap T-1226 Donneybrook with Donegan

  Regina 285 Swingin' Jazz in Hi-Fi

480. DONNELLY, DOROTHY   lyr
Born January 28, 1880, New York, N.Y.
Died January 3, 1928, New York, N.Y.

Lyricist-librettist of Broadway musicals, notably Sigmund!) Romberg shows BLOSSOM TIME (1921), THE STUDENT PRINCE (1924) and MY MARYLAND (1927). Other shows FANCY FREE (1918), POPPY (1923), MY PRINCESS 1927]. Educated in convent.

Actress in brother Henry Donnelly's stock company. In Broadway plays SOL-DIERS OF FORTUNE (1902) and CANDIDA (1903]. Toured in plays, starred in MA-DAME X 1909-11. In successful collabora-tion with Romberg, lyricist for enduring songs *Deep in My Heart, Dear; Drinking Song; Golden Days; Serenade; Song of Love; Silver Moon; Your Land and My Land.*

481. DOOLEY, RAY   vo
Performer in Broadway musicals, Noted for portrayal of mischievous infant. Low comic style. Star in several ZIEGFELD FOLLIES; next to Fanny Brice, most pop-ular comedienne of series. Early in career in family act in native England; played music halls. In later years married tal-ented entertainer Eddie Dowling, played vaudeville with him around 1911-19. Their Broadway careers mostly separate, except for shows SIDEWALKS OF NEW YORK (1927) and THUMBS UP (1935). They co-starred in 1931 movie HONEYMOON LANE, appeared as team with Benny Goodman band on Elgin radio show in spring 1936. After Broadway shows 1917-1935 Ray mostly inactive in show business. Eddie stayed busy many years as performer-writer-director-producer.

BROADWAY MUSICALS
1917—WORDS AND MUSIC
1918—HITCHY-KOO OF 1918
1919—ZIEGFELD FOLLIES OF 1919
1920—ZIEGFELD FOLLIES OF 1920
1921—ZIEGFELD FOLLIES OF 1921
1922—THE BUNCH AND JUDY
1923—NIFTIES OF 1923
1924—ZIEGFELD FOLLIES OF 1924
1925—ZIEGFELD FOLLIES OF 1925
1926—NO FOOLIN' (later titled ZIEGFELD'S AMERICAN REVUE OF 1926)
1927—SIDEWALKS OF NEW YORK
1928—EARL CARROLL'S VANITIES OF 1928
1935—THUMBS UP

482. DORHAM, KENNY   t ts B
(MCKINLEY HOWARD DORHAM)
Born August 30, 1924, Fairfield, Texas
Modern-style trumpet jazzman. Born into musical family, studied music at early age. Grew up in Austin, Texas. Attended Wiley College, played in band there. Military service briefly, World War II. With Russell Jacquet in Houston in 1943. In mid-40s with early bop groups of Dizzy Gillespie, Billy Eckstine, others. With Lionel Hampton 1947, Mercer Ellington 1948. Two years with Charlie Parker 1948-50, including trip to Paris in 1949. Freelanced 1951-5, based in New York. Took up tenor sax. Joined Art Blakey & Jazz Messengers in 1955. Own group in 1956, then joined Max Roach awhile. In later 50s and 60s continued to lead groups and freelance. In later years worked inter-mittently.

RECORDS
BE-BOP BOYS
   Sav 900 Webb City (1 & 2)
   Sav 901 Fat Boy (1 & 2)
KENNY CLARKE
   Vi 20-3144 Royal Roost/Epistrophy
   Cen 1501 Roll 'Em Bags/You Go to My Head
   Cen 1502 Bruz/Don't Blame Me
J. J. JOHNSON
   NJ 803 Elysses
   NJ 806 Hilo/Opus V
   NJ 810 Foxhunt
THELONIOUS MONK
   BN 1602 Let's Cool One/Skippy
CHARLIE PARKER
   Mer 11022 Passport/Visa

LPs
KENNY DORHAM
   BN 1524 'Round About Midnight at the Cafe Bohemia
   BN 1535
   BN 4036 Whistle Stomp
   BN(10")5035 Afro-Cuban
   Debut(10")9
MAX ROACH
   EmArcy MG-36098 Max Roach Plus Four
   BN(10")5010
MATTHEW GEE
   Riv 12-221 Jazz by Gee!
THELONIOUS MONK
   BN 1511 Genius of Modern Music, Vol. 2
TADD DAMERON
   Pres 7037 Fontainebleau

J. J. JOHNSON
  Pres(10″)109
SONNY ROLLINS
  Pres(10″)186
LOU DONALDSON
  BN(10″)5055
(miscellaneous artists)
  Vi LPV-519 The Be-Bop Era (Vi RIs)

483. DORSEY BROTHERS ORCHESTRA

Separate careers of brothers Jimmy and Tommy listed under own names. This account covers periods when they joined to lead Dorsey Brothers band.

By late 20s, musical talents of Dorseys placed them among leading musicians of day. Organized band for recording and special engagements, employed excellent musicians. Sporadic recording began 1928 and continued into 1934, producing good records. Outstanding sidemen included Mannie Klein (t), Mickey Bloom (t), Arthur Schutt (p), Phil Napoleon (t), Glenn Miller (tr, ar), Eddie Lang (g), Muggsy Spanier (c), Bunny Berigan (t). Vocalists included Smith Ballew, Scrappy Lambert, Mildred Bailey, Bing Crosby, Kay Weber. In late 1931-2 led band in Broadway musical EVERYBODY'S WELCOME.

In April 1934 Dorseys organized permanent band. Played swing and ballads; most arrangements by Glenn Miller. After one-nighters, in summer 1934 played Sands Point Beach Club in Long Island, got generous remotes on NBC. In August began heavy recording with Decca. By late 1934 band established. Tommy fronted. Outstanding sidemen included Glenn Miller, George Thow (t), Charlie Spivak (t), Skeets Herfurt (ts), Ray McKinley (d), Bobby Van Eps (p). Vocalists: Kay Weber, Don Matteson, Bob Crosby (replaced in spring 1935 by Bob Eberly). Theme song *Sandman*.

In May 1935 band opened at Glen Island Casino in New Rochelle, N.Y. Brothers often fought. Tommy had intense drive while Jimmy was inclined to be easygoing. On Memorial Day they had a violent argument and separated, to remain distant for most of next ten years.

Jimmy took over the band, with Bobby Byrne handling Tommy's trombone solos. Tommy took over nucleus of Joe Haymes band that September. Each became successful as bandleader.

In mid-40s brothers worked together on 1947 biographical movie THE FABULOUS DORSEYS. Reunited in mid-1953 when Jimmy joined Tommy's band, remained together until Tommy's death in late 1956. The band billed as The Tommy Dorsey Orchestra Featuring Jimmy Dorsey. With emphasis on nostalgia, former hits of both featured heavily. But repertoire also included current songs and new jazz originals. Summer TV show in 1954, another in 1955-6 on which rock singer Elvis Presley introduced. Vocalists: Lynn Roberts, Johnny Amoroso, Gordon Polk. Arrangements mostly by Neal Hefti and Howard Gibeling. Band in long run at New York's Hotel Statler when Tommy died. Jimmy took over although in bad health. Jimmy died in mid-1957 and trumpet star Lee Castle became leader.

RECORDS

DORSEY BROTHERS ORCHESTRA
  OK 40995 Persian Rug/Mary Ann
  OK 41007 Coquette/The Yale Blues
  OK 41083 Was It a Dream? (1 & 2)
  OK 41188 My Kinda Love
  OK 41210 Mean to Me/Button Up Your Overcoat
  Re 8931 Congratulations/Beside an Open Fireplace
  Co 2581-D Ooh, That Kiss!/By the Sycamore Tree
  Br 6537 Mood Hollywood/Shim Sham Shimmy
  Br 6624 By Heck/Old Man Harlem
  Br 6938 Judy/Annie's Cousin Fanny
  De 115 I'm Gettin' Sentimental Over You/Long May We Love
  De 118 By Heck/Basin Street Blues
  De 208 Stop, Look and Listen/Heat Wave
  De 291 Hands Across the Table/Dream Man
  De 296 Honeysuckle Rose (1 & 2)
  De 297 (theme) Sandman/Missouri Misery
  De 335 I Believe in Miracles/Dancing with My Shadow

De 370 Lullaby of Broadway/The Words Are in My Heart
De 376 Night Wind/Dinah
De 480 I'll Never Say "Never Again" Again/Every Little Moment
De 520 You're So Darn Charming/ You Saved My Life
De 560 Tailspin/I've Got a Feelin' You're Foolin'

TOMMY DORSEY ORCHESTRA, Featuring JIMMY DORSEY
Bell(7")1024 You're My Everything
Bell(7")1028 Marie/Green Eyes
Bell(7")1041 Wanted
Bell(7")1044 Three Coins in the Fountain
Bell(7")1053 The High and the Mighty

LPs

DORSEY BROTHERS ORCHESTRA
De DL-8217 Tenderly (De RIs)
De(10")DL-6016 Dixieland Jazz (De RIs)
Design DLP-147 Spotlight on the Dorsey Brothers (De RIs)

TOMMY DORSEY ORCHESTRA FEATURING JIMMY DORSEY
Co CL-1190 The Fabulous Dorseys in Hi-Fi, Vol. 1
Co CL-1240 Sentimental and Swinging
Colpix CP-436 The Golden Era, Vol. 4
Urania UJ-1215 Last Moments of Greatness, Vol. 3

484. DORSEY, JIMMY   as cl t cm B

Born February 29, 1904, Shenandoah, Pa.
Died June 12, 1957, New York, N.Y.

All-time great jazz soloist and bandleader. Facile on both his instruments, excellent technique. Usually played ballads on alto sax in beautifully flowing style, jazz on clarinet. Distinctive vibrato on both, especially on clarinet, made work easily identifiable. Beginning in 1935 led big band until early 50s in sweet-swing style. Older brother of trombonist Tommy. Brothers learned music as youngsters, played in father's band for parades and concerts, had own dance band. In early 20s they played with Scranton Sirens and California Ramblers. Beginning about 1925 they freelanced in New York, became established as excellent section men

and hot soloists. Recordings prolific. Jimmy and Benny Goodman friendly rivals for hot clarinet spots in recording studios in late 20s and early 30s. Dorseys with Jean Goldkette band in 1926, Paul Whiteman in 1927. Jimmy with Ted Lewis in mid-1930, toured Europe. In early 30s on radio with Fred Rich, Nat Shilkret, Victor Young, Jacques Renard, Andre Kostelanetz, Rudy Vallee, Lennie Hayton and others.

(See DORSEY BROTHERS ORCHESTRA biography for details of brothers as co-leaders and for record sessions 1928-35 and dance band 1934-5.)

Jimmy immediately successful as bandleader in 1935. Featured many swing arrangements, handled ballads well. Vocalists Kay Weber and Bob Eberly. Recorded heavily for Decca 1935-1946. In January 1936 landed plum job on Bing Crosby's Kraft Music Hall on radio. In 1936 swing became the rage, and each show featured Dorsey band in swing number. Young Bobby Byrne outstanding soloist on trombone. Other good sidemen through the years: Skeets Herfurt (ts), Ray McKinley (d), Shorty Sherock (t), Herbie Haymer (ts), Freddie Slack (p), Buddy Schutz (d), Joe Lippman (p, ar), Sonny Lee (tb), Babe Russin (ts). Don Matteson with band years as trombonist and occasional vocalist. Arrangers included Larry Clinton, Bobby Van Eps, Skeets Herfurt, Fud Livington, Toots Camarata (who wrote several swing numbers featured by band). Theme song *Contrasts*, beautiful showcase for the Dorsey sax. Early instrumental hits: *John Silver, Parade of the Milk Bottle Caps, Dusk in Upper Sandusky.*

Band built name through 30s, hit peak in early 40s with record hits of Latin-American songs *Green Eyes, Yours, Maria Elena, Amapola.* Vocalist Helen O'Connell joined band in early 1939, teamed with Eberly on many hits. Other popular records *Blue Champagne, Time Was, Embraceable You, Tangerine.* During this period chief arrangers Toots Camarata and Joe Lippman, with assists from Hal Mooney and Don Redman. Band in several movies: THE FLEET'S IN (1942), I

DOOD IT (1943), LOST IN A HAREM, FOUR JILLS IN A JEEP and HOLLYWOOD CANTEEN (1944). In 1947 Dorseys starred in biographical movie THE FABULOUS DORSEYS. Jimmy used various vocalists when O'Connell and Eberly departed after early 40s. In late 40s and early 50s had good band along semi-modern lines, also featured dixieland combo during dixieland revival, records of which well received.

(See DORSEY BROTHERS ORCHESTRA biography for details of 1953-6 period.)

After death of Tommy in late 1956, Jimmy took over band. In 1957 ill health, first reported as neuritis, forced him to leave band. Trumpet star Lee Castle took over, used altoist Dick Stabile on some records. Jimmy died of cancer in mid-1957 with hit record *So Rare* then going strong. Composed swing numbers *John Silver, Parade of the Milk Bottle Caps, Dusk in Upper Sandusky, Mood Hollywood, Shim Sham Shimmy, Beebe, Waddlin' at the Waldorf, Contrasts* (originally *Oodles of Noodles*). Composed popular songs *Just Lately* (1937), *It's the Dreamer in Me* (1938), *It's Anybody's Moon* and *So Many Times* (1939), *Talkin' to My Heart* (1940), *Isle of Pines* and *Once and for All* (1941), *I'm Glad There Is You* (1942), *Two Again* (1944).

RECORDS

FRED RICH
Co 1893-D Don't Hang Your Dreams on a Rainbow/Song of the Moonbeams

ED LOYD
Me 12696 Remember My Forgotten Man
Pe 15761 Look What I've Got

RED NICHOLS
Br 3407 Washboard Blues/That's No Bargain
Br 3477 Buddy's Habits/Boneyard Shuffle
Br 4724 Tea for Two/I Want to Be Happy
Br 6012 Rockin' Chair/My Honey's Lovin' Arms
Br 6133 Just a Crazy Song/You Rascal You
Br 6138 Slow But Sure/Little Girl

Br 6219 Junk Man Blues/Get Cannibal

TED LEWIS
Co 2088-D You've Got That Thing/Harmonica Harry
Co 2113-D San/Aunt Hagar's Blues
Co 2181-D Dinah/The Lonesome Road

MOUND CITY BLUE BLOWERS
OK 41526 Darktown Strutters' Ball/You Rascal You

BING CROSBY
BT 6533 Someone Stole Gabriel's Horn/Stay on the Right Side of the Road

CHICK BULLOCK
Pe 12933 Shadows on the Swanee/Louisiana Lullaby
Pe 15678 Mighty River/Underneath the Harlem Moon
Pe 15743 Low Down Upon the Harlem River/Going! Going!! Gone!!!

BEN SELVIN
Co 2150-D Let Me Sing And I'm Happy/Across the Breakfast Table

BOSWELL SISTERS
Br 6335 Hand Me Down My Walkin' Cane/Doggone, I've Done It!
Br 6442 It Don't Mean a Thing/Minnie the Moocher's Wedding Day

CHARLESTON CHASERS
Co 861-D Someday Sweetheart/After You've Gone
Co 909-D Davenport Blues/Wabash Blues
Co 1891-D Ain't Misbehavin'/Moanin' Low

ED LANG
OK 8696 Freeze an' Melt/Hot Heels

MIFF MOLE
OK 40784 A Hot Time in the Old Town Tonight/Darktown Strutters' Ball
OK 40848 Davenport Blues
OK 41232 That's a-Plenty/I've Got a Feeling I'm Falling

NAPOLEON'S EMPERORS
Vi 38057 My Kinda Love/Mean to Me
Vi 38069 Anything/You Can't Cheat a Cheater

JOE VENUTI
OK 41144 The Blue Room/Sensation

OK 41469 I've Found a New Baby/ Sweet Sue

ADRIAN ROLLINI

Me 12630 Hustlin' and Bustlin' for Baby/You've Got Me Cryin' Again

JACK TEAGARDEN

Br 6716 I Just Couldn't Take It, Baby/A Hundred Years from Today

ORIGINAL MEMPHIS FIVE

Co 2577-D St. Louis Gal/My Honey's Loving Arms

Co 2588-D Jazz Me Blues/Anything

COTTON PICKERS

Br 4404 Sweet Ida Joy/Sugar Is Back in Town

Br 4440 No Parking/St. Louis Gal

JIMMY DORSEY

De 882 In a Sentimental Mood/ Stompin' at the Savoy

De 1200 Hollywood Pastime/Jamboree

De 1508 I Got Rhythm/Flight of the Bumble Bee

De 1724 At a Perfume Counter/Love Walked In

De 1809 If You Were in My Place/I Let a Song Go Out of My Heart

De 1834 There's a Faraway Look in Your Eye/I Hadn't Anyone Till You

De 1939 Dusk in Upper Sandusky/ Darktown Strutters' Ball

De 1970 Love Is Where You Find It/ Garden of the Moon

De 2002 Change Partners/The Yam

De 1295 Deep Purple/Fate

De 2553 An Old Fashioned Tune Always Is New/I Poured My Heart into a Song

De 2554 Back to Back/Especially for You

De 2735 Dixieland Detour/Body and Soul

De 2810 You're the Greatest Discovery/My Prayer

De 3150 The Breeze and I/Little Curly Hair in a High Chair

De 3152 Six Lessons from Madame La Zonga/Boog It

De 3198 (theme) Contrasts/Perfidia

De 3334 John Silver/Parade of the Milk Bottle Caps

De 3435 The Bad Humor Man/You've Got Me This Way

De 3585 I Understand/High on a Windy Hill

De 3629 Amapola/Donna Maria

De 3657 Yours/When the Sun Comes Out

De 3698 Green Eyes/Maria Elena

De 3775 Blue Champagne/All Alone and Lonely

De 3859 Time Was/Isle of Pines

De 3928 Embraceable You/Fingerbustin'

De 4123 Tangerine/Ev'rything I Love

De 18372 Sorghum Switch/My Devotion

De 18376 Take Me/This Is Worth Fighting For

De 18571 Star Eyes/They're Either Too Young or Too Old

MGM 10001 Heartaches/No Greater Love

MGM 10098 On Green Dolphin Street/I Still Get Jealous

MGM 10316 At Sundown/Angela Mia

Co 38649 Charley My Boy/Johnson Rag

Co 38774 Sweet Georgia Brown/Kiss Me

Co 39138 By Heck/Lily of the Valley

LPs

JIMMY DORSEY

De DL-4248 Remember Jimmy (De RIs)

De DL-4853 Jimmy Dorsey's Greatest Hits (De RIs)

De DL-8153 Latin American Favorites (De RIs)

De DL-8609 The Great Jimmy Dorsey (De RIs)

Dot DLP-3437 So Rare

Lion L-70063 Jimmy Dorsey & His Orchestra

Co Cl-608 Dixie by Dorsey

Frat F-1008 The Fabulous Jimmy Dorsey

TED LEWIS

Epic LN-3170 Everybody's Happy! (Co RIs)

PHIL NAPOLEON

TOM 13 (early RIs)

BEN SELVIN

TOM 17 Vol. 2 (1929-30 Co RIs)

JACK TEAGARDEN
  Jolly Roger(10″)5026 (Br RIs)
THE DORSEY BROTHERS
  TOM 14 (RIs, with various bands)

485. DORSEY, TOMMY   tb t cm B

Born November 19, 1905, Shenandoah, Pa.

Died November 26, 1956, Greenwich, Conn.

All-time great trombonist and band-leader. As studio musician in early days played in light-swinging style, later concentrated on straight solo work, became famous for smooth phrasing and beautiful tone. As bandleader, one of most popular. Younger brother of Jimmy, bandleader and star on alto sax and clarinet. Brothers learned music as youngsters, played in father's band for parades and concerts, had own dance band. In early 20s they played with Scranton Sirens and California Ramblers. Beginning about 1925 they freelanced in New York, became established as excellent section men and hot soloists. Recordings prolific. With Jean Goldkette band in 1926, Paul Whiteman 1927. Tommy with Eddie Elkins, Vincent Lopez, Roger Wolfe Kahn, Rudy Vallee, Lennie Hayton, Andre Kostelanetz, Victor Young, Nat Shilkret, Fred Rich (including radio work with some).

(See DORSEY BROTHERS ORCHESTRA biography for details of brothers as co-leaders for record sessions 1928-35 and dance band 1934-5.)

Using nucleus of the Joe Haymes band, Tommy opened at New York's Hotel Lincoln and in September 1935 began recording with Victor. Immense output over next 15 years. Early outstanding sidemen Sterling Bose (t), Joe Dixon (cl), Dave Tough (d), Bud Freeman (ts), Bunny Berigan (t), Pee Wee Erwin (t), Johnny Mince (cl), Howard Smith (p), Skeets Herfurt (as), Max Kaminsky (t). In 30s featured dixieland combo within band, Clambake Seven. Later sidemen Babe Russin (ts), Yank Lawson (t), Buddy Rich (d), Don Lodice (ts), Joe Bushkin (p), Ziggy Elman (t), Buddy DeFranco (cl),

Charlie Shavers (t), Boomie Richman (ts). Vocalists in 30s Jack Leonard and Edythe Wright. In 1940-2 Frank Sinatra star vocalist. Other vocalists in early 40s Connie Haines, Jo Stafford, Pied Pipers, Dick Haymes; Bob Allen in mid-40s. In later 40s Stuart Foster featured vocalist. Most important arranger Sy Oliver; joined 1939, gave band many hits. Other arrangers Deane Kincaide, Paul Weston, Axel Stordahl, Bill Finegan. Theme *I'm Getting Sentimental Over You* fit Tommy's trombone style perfectly, became famous. Popular feature of band: series of arrangements in *"Marie* cycle" (*Who?*; *Blue Moon*; *Yearning*; *East of the Sun*; etc.) with male vocal and band answering in background, followed by jazz solos.

1936 summer radio show featuring swing music, especially Bud Freeman's hot work. Later that year on Jack Pearl radio show, own 1937 summer show. In fall 1937 began radio series for Raleigh-Kool which lasted three years. Band hit big early 1937 with record coupling *Marie* and *Song of India* featuring outstanding arrangements and Bunny Berigan solos. Another hit, *Boogie Woogie*, attracted little notice when released in 1938 but became all-time hit when reissued in 1943 during record ban. Other hit records *Once in a While*; *Music, Maestro, Please*; *Yes, Indeed!*; *I'll Be Seeing You*; *I'll Never Smile Again*; *This Love of Mine*; *Will You Still Be Mine?*; *Easy Does It*; *Just as Though You Were Here*; *On the Sunny Side of the Street*.

In 1942 strings added, large-sized band maintained awhile. Under disciplined leadership band consistently impeccable with excellent sidemen-arrangers-vocalists.

During 40s band on radio series of varying formats. In movies LAS VEGAS NIGHTS (1941), SHIP AHOY (1942), DUBARRY WAS A LADY, GIRL CRAZY and PRESENTING LILY MARS (1943), BROADWAY RHYTHM (1944), THRILL OF A ROMANCE (1945), DISC JOCKEY (1951). In 1947 Dorseys starred in biographical movie THE FABULOUS DORSEYS. Tommy in A SONG IS BORN (1948). During hectic days of late 40s and 50s when many bands died, Tommy's kept working.

(See DORSEY BROTHERS ORCHESTRA biography for details of 1953-6 period).

Tommy died tragically: after heavy meal, choked to death in sleep. A few days later Jackie Gleason presented TV tribute to Tommy. Former star sidemen and singers played Tommy's old hits. Jimmy also appeared. Tommy co-composer of several songs popular in 1939: *In the Middle of a Dream, To You, This Is No Dream, You Taught Me to Love Again.*

RECORDS

FRED RICH
Co 1893-D Don't Hang Your Dreams on a Rainbow/Song of the Moonbeams

RED NICHOLS
Br 4695 Soon/Strike Up the Band
Br 4701 Sometimes I'm Happy/Hallelujah

NAPOLEON'S EMPERORS
Vi 38057 My Kinda Love/Mean to Me
Vi 38069 Anything/You Can't Cheat a Cheater

ORIGINAL MEMPHIS FIVE
Co 2577-D St. Louis Gal/My Honey's Lovin' Arms
Co 2588-D Jazz Me Blues/Anything

COTTON PICKERS
Br 4325 Rampart Street Blues/Kansas City Kitty
Br 4440 St. Louis Gal/No Parking

ADRIAN ROLLINI
Me 12630 Hustlin' and Bustlin' for Baby/You've Got Me Crying Again

RUBE BLOOM & HIS BAYOU BOYS
Co 2103-D The Man from the South/St. James Infirmary
Co 2186-D Mysterious Mose/Bessie Couldn't Help It
Co 2218-D On Revival Day/There's a Wah-Wah Girl in Agua Caliente

CHARLESTON CHASERS
Co 2133-D Cinderella Brown/Sing You Sinners

ED LANG
OK 8696 Freeze an' Melt/Hot Heels

LITTLE RAMBLERS
Co 346-D Cross Words Between My Sweetie and Me/Don't Bring Lulu
Co 403-D Look Who's Here!/Got No Time

JOE VENUTI
OK 41056 Because My Baby Don't Mean Maybe Now/Just Like a Melody Out of the Sky
OK 41192 Weary River/That's the Good Old Sunny South

TOMMY DORSEY
Vi 25183 Don't Give Up the Ship/At a Little Church Affair
Vi 25236 (theme) I'm Getting Sentimental Over You/I've Got a Note
Vi 25314 Rhythm Saved the World/At the Codfish Ball (both CLAMBAKE SEVEN)
Vi 25476 Tea on the Terrace/I'm in a Dancing Mood
Vi 25508 The Goona Goo/If My Heart Could Only Talk
Vi 25523 Marie/Song of India
Vi 25591 Our Penthouse on Third Avenue/Love Is Never Out of Season
Vi 25657 Smoke Gets in Your Eyes/Night and Day
Vi 25686 Once in a While/If It's the Last Thing I Do
Vi 25695 You're a Sweetheart/Nice Work If You Can Get It
Vi 25815 Yearning/Deed I Do
Vi 25866 Music, Maestro, Please/All Through the Night
Vi 26054 Boogie Woogie/Weary Blues
Vi 26126 Hawaiian War Chant/Midnight on the Trail
Vi 26145 Cocktails for Two/Old Black Joe
Vi 26185 Blue Moon/Panama
Vi 26346 March of the Toys/By the River Sainte Marie
Vi 26429 Easy Does It/Am I Proud?
Vi 26433 Careless/Darn That Dream
Vi 26437 Milenberg Joys (1 & 2)
Vi 26439 Losers Weepers/Faithful to You
Vi 26508 The Lonesome Road (1 & 2)
Vi 26539 I'll Be Seeing You/Polka Dots and Moonbeams
Vi 26628 I'll Never Smile Again/Marcheta
Vi 26666 Trade Winds/Only Forever
Vi 26736 Our Love Affair/That's for Me
Vi 27274 Oh, Look at Me Now/You Might Have Belonged to Another
Vi 27317 Dolores/I Tried

Vi 27359 Everything Happens to Me/ Whatcha Know, Joe?

Vi 27377 Let's Get Away from It All (1 & 2)

Vi 27421 Will You Still Be Mine?/Yes, Indeed!

Vi 27508 This Love of Mine/Neiani

Vi 27887 Well, Git It!/Somewhere a Voice Is Calling

Vi 27903 Just as Though You Were Here/Street of Dreams

Vi 10-1045 Melody/By the Sleepy Lagoon

Vi 20-1522 Mandy, Make Up Your Mind/It Started All Over Again

Vi 20-1608 Opus No. 1/I Dream of You

Vi 20-1648 On the Sunny Side of the Street/Any Old Time

Vi 20-3492 Pussy Willow/Dream of You

De 27973 May I?/One Morning in May

LPs

TOMMY DORSEY

Vi LPM-1433 Tribute to Dorsey, Vol. 2 (Vi RIs)

Vi LPM-1569 Frankie and Tommy (Vi RIs)

Cam CAL-800 Dedicated to You (Vi RIs)

De DL-8217 Tenderly (De RIs)

Vo VL-3613 Tommy Dorsey's Dance Party (De RIs)

20th Fox TCF-101-2 (2-LP set) Tommy Dorsey's Greatest Band (transcription RIs)

PHIL NAPOLEON

TOM 13 (early RIs)

BEN SELVIN

TOM 16 Vol. 1 (1931 Co RIs)

BOSWELL SISTERS

Ace of Hearts(E) AH-116 (Br RIs)

THE DORSEY BROTHERS

TOM 14 (RIs with various bands)

486. DOUGLAS, BOOTS   d ar B

Leader of hard-swinging big band in San Antonio in 30s; called Boots & His Buddies. During 1935-7 period band made over twenty records on Bluebird. Displayed great drive, uninhibited style, capable soloists, good arrangements (many

by Douglas). Star soloist Baker Millens on tenor sax. Theme *Wild Cherry*. Unusual feature: band often changed song titles of standards. *The Somebody* was *Somebody Loves Me*, *The Weep* was *Willow Weep for Me*, *The Goo* was *The Goona Goo*, *Sleepy Gal* was *Sleepy Time Gal*, etc.

RECORDS

BOOTS & HIS BUDDIES

Bb 6063 (theme) Wild Cherry/Rose Room

Bb 6081 Riffs/I Love You Truly

Bb 6132 Anytime/How Long, pt. 1

Bb 6301 Georgia/How Long, pt. 2

Bb 6307 Marie/Coquette

Bb 6333 Swing/Vamp

Bb 6357 Sweet Girl

Bb 6862 Jealous/I Like You Best of All

Bb 6880 Haunting Memories/When the Time Has Come

Bb 6914 Swanee River Blues/Rhythmic Rhapsody

Bb 7005 San Anton Tamales

Bb 7187 Blues of Avalon/The Raggle Taggle

Bb 7217 The Goo/The Weep

Bb 7236 The Sad

Bb 7241 Ain't Misbehavin'

Bb 7245 The Happy

Bb 7269 The Somebody

Bb 7556 Chubby/Deep South

Bb 7596 True Blue Lou/Gone

Bb 7669 Lonely Moments

Bb 7944 A Salute to Harlem/Do Re Mi

Bb 10036 Careless Love/East Commerce Stomp

Bb 10106 Boots Stomp/A Ghost of a Chance

Bb 10113 Lonesome Road Stomp/Remember

LPs

BOOTS & HIS BUDDIES (one side)

IAJRC 3 (Bb RIs)

487. DOUGLAS, MIKE   vo
(MICHAEL DOWD)

Host of syndicated TV variety show in 60s and 70s. Good singer with smooth, high baritone. Military service, World War II. Joined Kay Kyser band as vocalist in mid-1945, remained through 40s. On Kyser's radio show. Sang as single in clubs, in early 50s became staff singer on Chicago radio, then TV. Rose to fame with daily TV variety show, 90 minutes of talk, comedy, music. Likable host with talent for comedy and interviews, plus excellent singing. Occasionally on top TV shows as guest singer. His version of song *The Men in My Little Girl's Life* popular in late 60s.

RECORDS

KAY KYSER
  Co 36824 Rosemary
  Co 36844 That's for Me
  Co 36882 Angel/Coffee Time
  Co 36900 Slowly
  Co 36979 All the Time
  Co 36989 I Love an Old Fashioned Song
  Co 37073 Ole Buttermilk Sky
  Co 37095 The Old Lamplighter
  Co 38641 Altar in the Pines/I'm Startin' Sweetheartin' Again
  Co 38712 My Lily and My Rose/Open Door—Open Arms
  Co 38713 Wilhelmina
  Co 38914 The Dixieland Jamboree
MIKE DOUGLAS
  De 24584 She's a Home Girl

LPs

MIKE DOUGLAS
  Epic LN-24169 It's Time for Mike Douglas
  Epic LN-24186 The Men in My Little Girl's Life

488. DOWELL, SAXIE   ts vo cm B
(HORACE K. DOWELL)

Born May 29, 1904, North Carolina

Sideman-singer-bandleader of 30s and 40s. Attended University of North Carolina. In Hal Kemp band from mid-20s to spring of 1939 (including European tour in 1930). Occasionally featured on tenor sax and novelty vocals. Wrote popular novelty hits *Three Little Fishies* (1939) and *Playmates* (1940). Own band in 1939. Military service, World War II. Led navy band aboard U.S.S. Franklin when torpedoed. After discharge formed band in 1946 along Kemp lines with muted, clip-ped-note brass and low-register clarinets. Dowell handled novelty vocals. In 1948 worked as songplugger, remained in song publishing for a time.

RECORDS

HAL KEMP
  Br 7587 The Music Goes 'Round and Around
  Vi 26204 The Chestnut Tree
SAXIE DOWELL
  Son 3026 The Old Lamplighter/Rumors Are Flying
  Son 3029 Rugged but Right/She Told Him Emphatically No
  Son 3036 It's Dreamtime/All I've Got Is Me
  Son 3039 Serenade to Love/Lulu Had a Sweetheart

489. DOWLING, EDDIE   vo cm lyr
(JOSEPH NELSON GOUCHER)

Born December 11, 1895, Woonsocket, R.I.

Performer of many talents, active on stage as actor-composer-lyricist-director-producer. Big hit roles SALLY, IRENE AND MARY (1922), HONEYMOON LANE (1926). Wrote book and lyrics for latter and for SIDEWALKS OF NEW YORK (1927). At 10 had job as ship's cabin boy, in spare time sang for passengers. World tour as member of St. Paul's Cathedral Choir. Entered vaudeville, became headliner in a few years. Married English entertainer Ray Dooley. They played vaudeville around 1911-19. Wife starred in various Broadway shows. Dowling began Broadway career in THE VELVET LADY (1917), followed by ZIEGFELD FOLLIES OF 1919. After successes in 1922 and 1926 shows, appeared with wife in SIDEWALKS OF NEW YORK (1927) and THUMBS UP (1935). Starred in 1929 movie THE RAINBOW MAN. He and wife co-starred in 1931 movie HONEYMOON LANE (adapted from 1926 stage success), also appeared as team with Benny Goodman band on Elgin radio show in spring 1936. Dowling became important producer of Broadway plays THE TIME OF YOUR LIFE, SHADOW AND SUBSTANCE, THE WHITE STEED, GLASS MENAGERIE, HERE COME THE CLOWNS, HIS DOUBLE LIFE, BIG HEARTED HERBERT, RICHARD II,

MADAME CAPET, THE ICEMAN COMETH. Acted in plays HERE COME THE CLOWNS, BLAZE O' GLORY, THE RAINBOW MAN, THE TIME OF YOUR LIFE, ANGEL IN THE PAWNSHOP, MAGIC, HELLO OUT THERE, others. Starred in 1930 movie BLAZE O' GLORY, collaborated on score. Founder-president of USO Camp Shows during World War II. M.C. of We the People radio show in early 40s and Talent Scouts in 1948. By late 50s mostly inactive in show business. Lyricist or composer for songs *The Little White House (at the End of Honeymoon Lane), Jersey Walk, Heading for Harlem, Playground in the Sky, Wherever You Are, Half a Moon, Little Log Cabin of Dreams, Dreams for Sale, High Up on a Housetop, Mary Dear, Row Row with Roosevelt, Did God Die in Dixie?, Welcome Home, May God Keep You in the Palm of His Hand, Do You Remember?, Logic, Suzie from Sioux City, Oh You Rag, Time Will Tell.* Chief collaborators James F. Hanley, J. Fred Coots, Victor Herbert, Bernie Wayne.

490. DOWNEY, MORTON .vo p cm lyr

Born November 14, 1901, Wallingford, Conn.

Tenor singing star of 30s and 40s, noted particularly for radio shows. Began professional singing in Greenwich Village movie theatre. In 1919 hired by Paul Whiteman, was featured with band till mid-20s (including stint aboard S.S. Leviathan). By 1926 playing clubs and theatres. Irish-style tenor, soft and melodious. Sometimes mixed in whistling, often accompanied himself on piano. Success in European clubs in 1927. Opened own club in New York, the Delmonico, a success for years.

Three early sound films: SYNCOPATION and MOTHER'S BOY (1929), LUCKY IN LOVE (1930). On early radio, rose to prominence in 1931 with 15-minute singing show several nights a week. Popular theme *Wabash Moon* which he sang and whistled. Through the years radio shows of varying lengths and formats, including Studio Party (1934) and Pall Mall show with Eddy Duchin band (1939). Began popular Coca Cola series in 1941, continued during most of 40s. Guest appearances on other shows. In 1939-40 featured singer at Billy Rose's Aquacade at New York World Fair. In 1949 own show on TV with Roberta Quinlan, other shows in early 50s. Continued on radio in 50s. From mid-20s to late 40s recorded at intervals. Co-composer of popular songs *Wabash Moon* and *Now You're in My Arms* (1931). Lesser compositions *California Skies, All I Need Is Someone Like You, In the Valley of the Roses, That's How I Spell Ireland, Sweeten Up Your Smile, There's Nothing New.* After early 50s less active in show business. Astute businessman, through the years built interests in several successful companies.

RECORDS

MORTON DOWNEY

Br 2887 When the One You Love Loves You/The Melody That Made You Mine
Br 2973 Let the Rest of the World Go By/The World Is Waiting for the Sunrise
Vi 21806 I'm Sorry Sally/How About Me?
Vi 21860 I'll Always Be in Love with You/My Inspiration Is You
Vi 21940 I'll Always Be Mother's Boy/There'll Be You and I
Vi 22673 (theme) Wabash Moon/Mother's Apron Strings
Vi 22674 Say a Little Prayer for Me/Church in the Valley
Pe 12783 Just Friends/Save the Last Dance for Me
Pe 12797 Paradise/One Hour with You
Pe 12865 A Boy and a Girl Were Dancing/I May Never Pass Your Way Again
Pe 12874 Street of Dreams/Strange Interlude
Pe 12888 I Wake Up Smiling/Just So You'll Remember
Pe 12923 Love Is the Thing/Hold Your Man
Pe 13048 I Saw Stars/Two Cigarettes in the Dark
Pe 13115 I Was Lucky/A Little White Gardenia

Me 12644 Farewell to Arms/I Bring a Song

Me 12710 Sweetheart Darlin'/Isn't It Heavenly?

Me 13374 The Words Are in My Heart/Would There Be Love?

Me 13437 In the Middle of a Kiss/You're an Angel

Ba 32372 Auf Wiedersehen, My Dear/Snuggled on Your Shoulder

Maj 1046 Blue Skies/All by Myself

Maj 1047 My Romance/More Than You Know

Maj 1061 The Whole World Is Singing My Song/The Old Lamplighter

491. DOWNS, JOHNNY   VO
Born 1913

Juvenile star of low-budget movies from 1935 to early 40s. Many were musicals in which he played lead role, sang and danced. As youngster played in Our Gang comedies. Minor role in Broadway musical STRIKE ME PINK (1933), starring roles in ARE YOU WITH IT? (1945) and HOLD IT! (1948). Roles minor in movies of late 40s. In 50s on children's TV in San Diego. In 60s and 70s in real estate in Coronado, Calif.

MOVIES

1934—BABES IN TOYLAND

1935—CORONADO; COLLEGE SCANDAL; SO RED THE ROSE; THE VIRGINIA JUDGE; THE CLOCK STRIKES EIGHT

1936—PIGSKIN PARADE; EVERYBODY'S OLD MAN; THE FIRST BABY; THE ARIZONA RAIDERS; THE PLAINSMAN

1937—COLLEGE HOLIDAY; TURN OFF THE MOON; CLARENCE; BLONDE TROUBLE

1938—THRILL OF A LIFETIME; ALGIERS; HUNTED MEN; HOLD THAT COED!; SWING, SISTER, SWING

1939—HAWAIIAN NIGHTS; LAUGH IT OFF; BAD BOY; PARENTS ON TRIAL

1940—I CAN'T GIVE YOU ANYTHING BUT LOVE, BABY; MANIA FOR MELODY; A CHILD IS BORN; SLIGHTLY TEMPTED; MELODY AND MOONLIGHT; SING DANCE PLENTY HOT

1941—MOONLIGHT IN HAWAII; ALL-AMERICAN COED; ADAM HAD FOUR SONS; RED HEAD; SING ANOTHER CHORUS; HONEYMOON FOR THREE

1942—BEHIND THE EIGHT BALL; THE MAD MONSTER

1943—CAMPUS RHYTHM; HARVEST MELODY; WHAT A MAN!

1944—TWILIGHT ON THE PRAIRIE

1945—RHAPSODY IN BLUE; FOREVER YOURS; THE RIGHT TO LOVE

1946—THE KID FROM BROOKLYN

1949—SQUARE DANCE JUBILEE

1950—HILLS OF OKLAHOMA

1953—CRUISIN' DOWN THE RIVER; GIRLS OF PLEASURE ISLAND; COLUMN SOUTH; LAST OF THE PONY RIDERS

492. DRAGONETTE, JESSICA   VO
Born in Calcutta, India

Soprano singing star of radio from late 20s into early 40s. Repertoire dominated by light classical and occasionally operatic material, did show tunes and popular songs ably too. Brought to U.S. and settled in convent school near Plainfield, N.J. Studied singing, played small roles on stage. Featured in Broadway shows EARL CARROLL'S VANITIES OF 1925 and GRAND STREET FOLLIES OF 1926. Began on NBC radio in late 1926. Shows included The Cycle of Romance, Coca Cola show, Philco's Theatre of Memories, Hoover Sentinels. Many appearances on popular Cities Service Concerts on radio in early and mid-30s. Poll elected her Queen of Radio for 1935. Left Cities Service show at end of 1936; own show with Al Goodman orchestra during most of 1937. Late 1941-5 many appearances on Saturday Night Serenade show. Only movie BIG BROADCAST OF 1936, although singing voice used in 1940 full-length cartoon GULLIVER'S TRAVELS. During World War II toured camps to entertain troops, appeared at war bond rallies. Active through 40s into 50s. Still popular, drew huge crowds at outdoor concerts. Wrote autobiography *Faith Is a Song* c. 1957.

RECORDS

JESSICA DRAGONETTE

Br 3874 Shepherd of the Hills/Mem'ries

Br 4355 Lover, Come Back to Me/Vagabond King Waltz

Br 4437 Love's Old Sweet Song/Old
Folks at Home
Br 4601 Italian Street Song/Giannina
Mia
Br 4702 Moonbeams/L'Amour, Tou-
jours, L'Amour
Br 4904 Lullaby/When You're Away
Br 7433 Bells Across the Meadows/
First Love
Br 7444 Italian Street Song/Giannina
Mia
Br 7481 Through Doorway of Dreams/
Alice Blue Gown
Vi 2141 Lullaby for a Doll/The Owl
and the Pussy Cat
Vi 2215 Before the Crucifix/Songs My
Mother Taught Me
Vi 4457 Ciribiribin/Love's Own Waltz
Vi 4463 Siboney/Estrellita

493. DRAKE, ALFRED   vo
(ALFRED CAPURRO)
Born October 7, 1914, New York, N.Y.

Baritone with strong melodious voice, star
of Broadway musicals and plays. Mem-
orable performances in hit musicals OK-
LAHOMA! (1943), KISS ME, KATE (1949),
KISMET (1953). Attended Brooklyn Col-
lege. Debut on New York stage in 1933 in
chorus of Gilbert & Sullivan operetta.
More operettas in New York in 1935,
chorus singer and understudy in WHITE
HORSE INN (1936). Minor role in BABES IN
ARMS (1937), better roles in TWO BOU-
QUETS (1938), ONE FOR THE MONEY and
STRAW HAT REVUE (1939). Acting roles in
plays AS YOU LIKE IT and OUT OF THE
FRYING PAN (1941), YESTERDAY'S MAGIC
(1942). After smash hit in OKLAHOMA!
(1943), starred in musicals SING OUT
SWEET LAND (1944) and BEGGAR'S HOL-
IDAY (1947), movie musical TARS AND
SPARS (1946), then in play JOY TO THE
WORLD (1948). Starred in long-running
shows KISS ME, KATE (1949) and KISMET
(1953). In later years acted in Shakespeare
plays OTHELLO, MUCH ADO ABOUT NOTH-
ING, HAMLET. Starred in TV productions
of THE ADVENTURES OF MARCO POLO, VOL-
PONE, NAUGHTY MARIETTA, THE YEOMEN
OF THE GUARD. Other TV appearances in
50s and 60s. Starred in Broadway musical

KEAN (1961). Talented performer in musicals or plays with warm personality and
great stage presence.

RECORDS
ALFRED DRAKE
De 40206 The World Is Mine To-
night/Till the Sands of the Desert
Grow Cold
Vi 20-3352 So in Love/Were Thine
That Special Face
Cad 1238 The Happy Wanderer/Des-
tiny's Darling
ALFRED DRAKE-JOAN ROBERTS
De 23287 People Will Say We're in
Love
ALFRED DRAKE-HOWARD DASILVA
De 23286 Pore Jud Is Daid

LPs
ALFRED DRAKE
De DL-4239 DOWN IN THE VALLEY
Co ML-5111 THE ADVENTURES OF MAR-
CO POLO
(original Broadway casts)
De 79017 OKLAHOMA!
Co OL-4140 KISS ME, KATE
Co OL-4850 KISMET
Co KOL-5720 KEAN

494. DRAKE, MILTON   cm lyr v vo
Born August 3, 1916, New York, N.Y.

Composer of several popular songs in-
cluding *Pu-leeze, Mr. Hemingway!* (1932),
Bless Your Heart (1933), *I'm Counting on
You* and *Champagne Waltz* (1934), *Pardon
My Love* (1935), *If It's You* (1940), *Java
Jive* (1941), *Mairzy Doats* (1944). Attend-
ed NYU, also had musical training. As
child in vaudeville, silent films and radio.
Several song hits while still teenager.
Singer and announcer on radio. Wrote
material for night club and theatre revues.
Wrote music for movies THE AWFUL
TRUTH, CHAMPAGNE WALTZ, THE BIG
STORE, MY LITTLE CHICKADEE, HE STAYED
FOR BREAKFAST, MURDER IN SWINGTIME,
ALL THE ANSWERS, GOOD GIRLS GO TO
PARIS, TOAST OF THE TOWN, BLONDIE
MEETS THE BOSS, YOUNG AND BEAUTIFUL,
EVERYTHING'S ON ICE, START CHEERING.
Became active in market and media re-
search, was research manager for

McGraw-Hill. Author of *Almanacs of the United States 1639-1875.* Other songs *I Don't Like Music, My Dreams Have Gone with the Wind, Great Guns* (official Coast Artillery song), *Nina Never Knew, Fuzzy Wuzzy, Don't Change Horses* (Roosevelt campaign song, 1944), *Kiss Me Sweet, For Whom the Bell Tolls* (movie title song), *I'm a Big Girl Now, Felicia No Capicia, Heaven Only Knows, Li'l Abner, The Town Crier, If Wishes Were Kisses, She Broke My Heart in Three Places, Instant Love, The Man with the Weird Beard, Golden Wedding Waltz, Ashby de la Zooch, Early to Bed, I Loved You Wednesday, Jack-in-the-Box, Whippoorwill Hill, Jack-of-All-Trades, Wake Up and Dream, Boomerang, The Hobo Song, Miracle on Main Street.*

495. DRESSER, PAUL   cm lyr vo
(PAUL DREISER)

Born April 1857, Terre Haute, Ind.
Died January 30, 1906, New York, N.Y.

Important early composer; much of his work pre-1900. Brother of famed novelist Theodore Dreiser. Changed name to Dresser upon beginning musical career. Most famous songs *On the Banks of the Wabash* and *My Gal Sal*. Early education at St. Meinrad's, Indiana, studying for priesthood. Left while teenager to work in medicine shows and vaudeville as blackface comedian. First song hit, *The Letter That Never Came* in 1886, performed in Brooklyn in minstrel show he was working in. Convinced Dresser to abandon performing and concentrate on songwriting. At turn of century member of publishing company Howley, Haviland & Dresser. Wrote, produced and starred in plays A GREEN GOODS MAN, THE DANGER SIGNAL, THE TWO JOHNS, THE MIDNIGHT BELL, A TIN SOLDIER. 1942 movie MY GAL SAL portrayed life of Dresser; latter's role played by Victor Mature.

SONGS

1886—The Letter That Never Came
1887—The Outcast Unknown
1888—The Convict and the Bird
1890—Little Jim; The Lone Grave
1891—The Pardon Came Too Late

1894—Once Ev'ry Year; Take a Seat, Old Lady
1895—I Was Looking for My Boy, She Said; Jean; Just Tell Them That You Saw Me; We Were Sweethearts for Many Years
1896—Don't Tell Her That You Love Her; A Dream of My Boyhood Days; He Brought Home Another; He Fought for a Cause He Thought Was Right
1897—If You See My Sweetheart; On the Banks of the Wabash; You're Goin' Far Away, Lad
1898—Come Tell Me What's Your Answer, Yes or No; Every Night There's a Light; The Old Flame Flickers, and I Wonder Why; The Path That Leads the Other Way; Our Country, May She Always Be Right; Sweet Savannah; We Fight Tomorrow, Mother
1899—The Curse of the Dreamer; I Wonder Where She Is Tonight; In Good Old New York Town; That's Where My Heart Is Tonight; We Come from the Same Old State
1900—I'd Still Believe You True; Calling to Her Boy Just Once Again
1901—In the Great Somewhere; Mr. Volunteer; There's No North or South Today; Way Down in Old Indiana; When the Birds Have Sung Themselves to Sleep; My Heart Still Clings to the Old First Love
1902—In Dear Old Illinois
1903—Where Are the Friends of Other Days?; The Boys Are Coming Home Today; Lincoln, Grant or Lee
1904—She Went to the City; When I'm Away from You, Dear
1905—My Gal Sal; The Day That You Grew Colder; The Town Where I Was Born; Jim Judson—from the Town of Hackensack

496. DRESSLER, MARIE   vo
(LEILA VON KOERBER)

Born November 9, 1869, Coburg, Canada
Died July 28, 1934

Queen of low comedy, rose to fame in

movies of early 30s. Many years in vaudeville, then successful career on Broadway in musicals and plays. Primarily raucous comedienne, sang occasionally in rough novelty style. Minor role in 1892 play ROBBERS OF THE RHINE. In 1893 important role with Lillian Russell in PRINCESS NICOTINE. Other Broadway shows MADELEINE (1895), THE LADY SLAVEY (1896), THE MAN IN THE MOON (1899), THE BOY AND THE GIRL (1909), TILLIE'S NIGHTMARE (1910), ROLY-POLY (1912), A MIX-UP (1914), THE PASSING SHOW OF 1921, THE DANCING GIRL (1923). In 1913 arranged and planned own stage revue MARIE DRESSLER'S ALL STAR GAMBOL. Worked in silent movies, then became popular comedienne during early sound movies. Teamed with Wallace Beery to form comic couple in movies MIN AND BILL and TUGBOAT ANNIE.

MOVIES
(sound)

1929—HOLLYWOOD REVUE OF 1929; THE VAGABOND LOVER; ROAD SHOW; DIVINE LADY
1930—CHASING RAINBOWS; THE GIRL SAID NO; CALL OF THE FLESH; ONE ROMANTIC NIGHT; ANNA CHRISTIE; CAUGHT SHORT; LET US BE GAY; MIN AND BILL; DERELICT
1931—REDUCING; POLITICS
1932—EMMA; PROSPERITY
1933—DINNER AT EIGHT; CHRISTOPHER BEAN; SINGER OF SEVILLE; TUGBOAT ANNIE

RECORDS
(LPs)

(miscellaneous artists; one song)
  Audio Rarities LPA-2290 They Stopped the Show (RIs)

497. DREW, KENNY   p
Born August 28, 1928, New York, N.Y.
Modern pianist with rhythmic beat, influenced by earlier styles of piano. Good accompanist. Studied classical music as well as early jazz piano greats. In late 40s in New York with leading modern jazzmen Howard McGhee, Coleman Hawkins, Lester Young, Charlie Parker. With Buddy DeFranco quartet 1952-3. Freelanced on west coast three years, led

combo. In late 50s freelanced in New York. With Buddy Rich 1958-9. To France in 1961, played there in early 60s. In 1964 settled in Copenhagen, continued to play abroad.

RECORDS
(all LPs)

KENNY DREW
  BN(10")5023 Kenny Drew Trio
  Jazz-West 4 Talkin' and Walkin' with the Kenny Drew Quartet
  Riv 12-224 The Kenny Drew Trio
  Riv 12-236 This Is New: Kenny Drew
CLIFFORD BROWN
  EmArcy MG-36102 Clifford Brown All-Stars
JEAN THIELEMANS
  Riv 1125 Man Bites Harmonica
JOHN COLTRANE
  BN 1577 Blue Train
DEXTER GORDON
  Pres 7763 A Day in Copenhagen
BUDDY DEFRANCO
  MGM(10")E-177
  Norg(10")3
HOWARD MCGHEE
  BN(10")5012
SONNY ROLLINS
  Pres(10")137
SONNY STITT
  Pres(10")127
(miscellaneous artists)
  EmArcy MG-36039 Best Coast Jazz

498. DREYER, DAVE   cm lyr p
Born September 22, 1894, Brooklyn, N.Y.
Songwriter of 20s and 30s, collaborated on enduring hits. Early work as pianist for publishing companies. Accompanist for singers Al Jolson, Sophie Tucker, Belle Baker, Frank Fay. Wrote background music for movies during 30s. Founded publishing company in 1947. Chief collaborators Al Jolson, Billy Rose, Herman Ruby, Ballard MacDonald.

SONGS

1924—When I Was the Dandy and You Were the Belle
1925—Cecilia
1927—Me and My Shadow; Four Walls
1928—Back in Your Own Backyard; THE

SINGING FOOL movie (Golden Gate; There's a Rainbow 'Round My Shoulder)
1929—A Year from Today
1930—I'm Following You
1931—I Wanna Sing About You; I'm Keepin' Company; Wabash Moon
1933—In a Little Second Hand Store
1936—I'll Never Let You Go

498A. DUBIN, AI   lyr

Born June 10, 1891, Zurich, Switzerland
Died February 11, 1945, New York, N.Y.

Leading lyricist. Prolific career began 1917. With composer Harry Warren formed ace movie songwriting team of 30s. Astonishing output included songs for important Dick Powell movie musicals. During pre-Warren period collaborated with composers Jimmy McHugh, Irving Mills, J. Russel Robinson and mostly Joe Burke. Pioneer songwriter for sound movies 1929-30. Most famous songs *Tiptoe Through the Tulips with Me, 42nd Street, Dancing with Tears in My Eyes, Shuffle Off to Buffalo, You're Getting to Be a Habit with Me, Shadow Waltz, I'll String Along with You, I Only Have Eyes for You, She's a Latin from Manhattan, With Plenty of Money and You, The Anniversary Waltz, Lullaby of Broadway, Lulu's Back in Town, September in the Rain, Indian Summer, Feudin' and Fightin'.* To U.S. 1893, settled in Pennsylvania, educated at Perkiomen Seminary. Worked for New York publishing companies. Military service, World War I. Moderate success at songwriting before collaboration with Warren. Team's early songs included *Along Came Sweetness* (1928) and *The River and Me* (1931). Regular association 1932 till 1939. Dubin added lyrics to old Victor Herbert melody for 1939 hit *Indian Summer*. Limited collaboration with McHugh and others 1939-45. With James V. Monaco wrote large score for 1943 movie STAGE DOOR CANTEEN but songs unimportant.

SONGS
(with related shows)

1917—All the World Will Be Jealous of Me
1920—Tripoli
1921—Crooning
1923—Just a Girl That Men Forget
1925—ANDRE CHARLOT REVUE OF 1925 stage show (A Cup of Coffee, a Sandwich and You); The Lonesomest Girl in Town; Nobody Knows What a Red Headed Mama Can Do
1926—My Dream of the Big Parade
1927—TAKE THE AIR stage show (Ham and Eggs in the Morning); WHITE LIGHTS stage show (songs unimportant); All by My Ownsome
1928—Half-Way to Heaven; I Must Be Dreaming; Memories of France; Along Came Sweetness
1929—GOLD DIGGERS OF BROADWAY movie (Tiptoe Through the Tulips with Me; Painting the Clouds with Sunshine; And They Still Fall in Love; Go to Bed; What Will I Do without You?; In a Kitchenette); SHOW OF SHOWS movie (Ping Pongo; If Your Best Friend Won't Tell You); IN THE HEADLINES movie (Love Will Find a Way); Ev'rybody Loves You
1930—HOLD EVERYTHING movie (To Know You Is to Love You; Sing a Little Theme Song; When the Little Roses Get the Blues for You); SALLY movie (If I'm Dreaming); Dancing with Tears in My Eyes; The Kiss Waltz
1931—Crosby, Columbo and Vallee; For You; Many Happy Returns of the Day; When the Rest of the Crowd Goes Home; The River and Me
1932—THE CROONER movie (Three's a Crowd); Too Many Tears
1933—ROMAN SCANDALS movie (No More Love; Build a Little Home; Keep Young and Beautiful; Rome Wasn't Built in a Day); 42ND STREET movie (42nd Street; Shuffle Off to Buffalo; You're Getting to Be a Habit with Me; I'm Young and Healthy; It Must Be June); GOLD DIGGERS OF 1933 movie (Gold Digger's Song; I've Got to Sing a Torch Song; Shadow Waltz; Pettin' in the Park; Remember My Forgotten Man);

FOOTLIGHT PARADE movie (Shanghai Lil; Honeymoon Hotel); My Temptation

1934—WONDER BAR movie (Come to the Wonder Bar; Why Do I Dream Those Dreams?; Goin' to Heaven on a Mule; Don't Say Goodnight; Viva La France; Fairer on the Riviera; Tango Del Rio); MOULIN ROUGE movie (Boulevard of Broken Dreams; Coffee in the Morning, Kisses at Night; Song of Surrender); TWENTY MILLION SWEETHEARTS movie (I'll String Along with You; Fair and Warmer; What Are Your Intentions?; Is My Baby Out for No Good?); DAMES movie (Dames; I Only Have Eyes for You; Try to See It My Way; The Girl at the Ironing Board)

1935—GO INTO YOUR DANCE movie (Go Into Your Dance; She's a Latin from Manhattan; About a Quarter to Nine; The Little Things You Used to Do); GOLD DIGGERS OF 1935 movie (Lullaby of Broadway; The Words Are in My Heart; I'm Goin' Shoppin' with You); BROADWAY GONDOLIER movie (Lulu's Back in Town; The Rose in Her Hair; Outside of You; You Can Be Kissed; Lonely Gondolier); SHIPMATES FOREVER movie (Don't Give Up the Ship; I'd Love to Take Orders from You; I'd Rather Listen to Your Eyes); PAGE MISS GLORY movie (Page Miss Glory); SWEET MUSIC movie (Sweet Music); STARS OVER BROADWAY movie (Where Am I?; You Let Me Down; At Your Service, Madame; Broadway Cinderella)

1936—COLLEEN movie (You Gotta Know How to Dance; I Don't Have to Dream Again; Boulevardier from the Bronx); HEARTS DIVIDED movie (Two Hearts Divided; My Kingdom for a Kiss); SING ME A LOVE SONG movie (Summer Night; The Little House That Love Built; That's the Least You Can Do for a Lady); CAIN AND MABEL movie (I'll Sing You a Thousand Love Songs)

1937—MELODY FOR TWO movie (Melody for Two; September in the Rain); GOLD DIGGERS OF 1937 movie (With Plenty of Money and You; All's Fair in Love and War); THE SINGING MARINE movie (I Know Now; 'Cause My Baby Says It's So; The Lady Who Couldn't Be Kissed; You Can't Run Away from Love Tonight; Song of the Marines); MR. DODD TAKES THE AIR movie (Am I in Love?; Remember Me?); MARKED WOMAN movie (My Silver Dollar Man); How Could You?

1938—GOLD DIGGERS IN PARIS movie (A Stranger in Paree; I Wanna Go Back to Bali; The Latin Quarter); GARDEN OF THE MOON movie (Garden of the Moon; Love Is Where You Find It; The Girl Friend of the Whirling Dervish; Confidentially; The Lady on the Two-Cent Stamp)

1939—STREETS OF PARIS stage show (Is It Possible?; Rendezvous Time in Paree; South American Way; Doin' the Chamberlain; Danger in the Dark; Robert the Roué); Put That Down in Writing; Indian Summer; An Angel in a Furnished Room

1940—KEEP OFF THE GRASS stage show (Clear Out of This World; A Latin Tune, a Manhattan Moon and You); TILL WE MEET AGAIN movie (Where Was I?); ALONG THE SANTA FE TRAIL movie (Along the Santa Fe Trail)

1941—The Angels Came Thru; It Happened in Hawaii; The Anniversary Waltz

1943—STAGE DOOR CANTEEN movie (We Mustn't Say Goodbye; many more)

1945—LAFFING ROOM ONLY stage show (Feudin' and Fightin'—popular in 1947)

499. DUCHIN, EDDY   p B

Born April 10, 1910, Cambridge, Mass.
Died February 9, 1951, New York, N.Y.

Popular pianist-bandleader in 30s and 40s. Known for unique piano introductions to band's numbers and for light, flowery style. Solos simple, sometimes one-finger melody line; remained close to melody, made some use of dynamics. Style imitated by many. Hotel-type band with average musicianship. Attended pharmacy school, turned to music. Began professionally about 1929. Early, important job about two years with Leo Reisman at New York's Central Park Casino. Piano style and handsome looks attracted fans. In late 1931 formed band, later played Central Park Casino as bandleader. Important early engagement at Chicago's Congress Hotel in 1934. During 30s band vocalist Lew Sherwood; also trumpeter and chief Duchin aide. Themes *Be My Love* and *My Twilight Dream*, latter adapted from Chopin. In 30s Milt Shaw provided many arrangements, also played violin with band.

Band had sustaining radio shows in early 1934. Late 1934-5 on Ed Wynn Texaco show. In 1936 on Burns & Allen show. During 1937-9 on La Salle show, Kopper's Coke show, Hour of Romance, and Pall Mall show with Morton Downey. In movies CORONADO (1935) and THE HIT PARADE (1937). Recordings numerous. By late 30s band changed: slightly larger, better musically. But peak years of popularity around 1934-6. Military service, 1942-5. Joined Kraft Music Hall radio show in 1946, with Eddie Foy & The Music Hall in 1947, own show in 1949. Led good band these years, also intervals as single. Never regained former popularity, and career curtailed by illness. Died in 1951 from leukemia.

In 1956 excellent movie on Duchin life, THE EDDY DUCHIN STORY. Tyrone Power portrayed Duchin capably, with Carmen Cavallaro's piano on soundtrack. Eddy's son Peter successful society pianist-bandleader, adopts a little of father's style but far more advanced musically.

RECORDS

EDDY DUCHIN

Vi 24280 Hold Me/I Can't Remember
Vi 24479 A Hundred Years from To-day/I Just Couldn't Take It, Baby
Vi 24492 Song of Surrender/Coffee in the Morning, Kisses at Night

Vi 24510 Let's Fall in Love/Love Is Love Anywhere
Vi 24591 May I?/She Reminds Me of You
Vi 24736 Flirtation Walk/I See Two Lovers
Vi 25318 I'll Stand By/Love Came Out of the Night
Vi 25472 Love and Learn/Seal It with a Kiss
Vi 25514 Moonlight and Shadows/Love Is Good for Anything That Ails You
Vi 25517 Too Marvelous for Words/Just a Quiet Evening
Vi 25583 You're Looking for Romance/Moonlight on the Highway
Vi 25595 Heaven Help This Heart of Mine/The Camera Doesn't Lie
Br 6425 The Song Is You/I've Told Ev'ry Little Star
Br 6445 Night and Day/After You
Br 6481 Try a Little Tenderness/I May Never Pass Your Way Again
Br 8130 Ride, Tenderfoot, Ride/I'll Dream Tonight
Br 8155 Ol' Man Mose/Between the Devil and the Deep Blue Sea
Br 8224 My Reverie/How Can We Be Wrong?
Br 8238 Heart and Soul/It's a Lonely Trail
Br 8252 Get Out of Town/From Now On
Br 8287 September Song/It Never Was You
Co 2625-D Can't We Talk It Over?/Snuggled on Your Shoulder
Co 2626-D Soft Lights and Sweet Music/By the Fireside
Co 35314 (theme) My Twilight Dream/Parade of the Little White Mice
Co 35628 Trade Winds/It Was Music
Co 35703-4-5-6 (piano solos)
Co 35724 Same Old Story/Our Love Affair
Co 35867 It All Comes Back to Me Now/The Old Jalop
Co 35903 You Walk By/Here's My Heart
Co 36076-7-8-9 (piano solos)
Co 36400 Brazil/Carinhose
Co 36454 'Tis Autumn/Madelaine

Co 38740 Let's Go West Again/I Never Knew I Loved You

LPs

EDDY DUCHIN
Co CL-790 The Eddy Duchin Story (Co RIs, piano solos)
Co(10")CL-6010 Eddy Duchin Reminisces
Vik LX-1043 The Fabulous Eddy Duchin (Vi RIs)

500. DUKE, VERNON   cm lyr p
(VLADIMIR DUKELSKY)

Born October 10, 1903, Parafianovo, Russia
Died January 16, 1969, Santa Monica, Calif.

Popular-song composer of 30s and 40s with distinctive flair and substance. Most famous songs *April in Paris, I Can't Get Started, What Is There to Say?, Autumn in New York, Cabin in the Sky, Taking a Chance on Love*. Musical training as youth in Russia; attended Kiev Conservatory of Music at 13. In 1920 family fled to U.S. from revolution in Russia. Duke had little success in U.S. at first, went back to Europe in 1923. During 20s successful writing for London musicals including THE YELLOW MASK, KATJA THE DANCER, YVONNE, BLUE MAZURKA, THE POW WOWS, TWO LITTLE GIRLS IN BLUE, OPEN YOUR EYES. Returned to U.S. in 1929. First American song *I'm Only Human After All* in Broadway musical GARRICK GAIETIES OF 1930. Wrote music for shows WALK A LITTLE FASTER (1932), ZIEGFELD FOLLIES OF 1934 and 1936, CABIN IN THE SKY and IT HAPPENS ON ICE (1940), BANJO EYES (1942), JACKPOT and SADIE THOMPSON (1944), TWO'S COMPANY (1952), THE LITTLEST REVUE (1956); fewer songs for other shows. Chief collaborators lyricists John Latouche, E. Y. Harburg, Ira Gershwin, Ogden Nash, Howard Dietz. Wrote autobiography *Passport to Paris*. Military service, World War II; Lt. Commander in Coast Guard.

SONGS
(with related shows)

1930—GARRICK GAIETIES OF 1930 stage show (I'm Only Human After All);

THREE'S A CROWD stage show (Talkative Toes)
1931—SHOOT THE WORKS stage show (Muchacho)
1932—AMERICANA stage show (Let Me Match My Private Life with Yours); WALK A LITTLE FASTER stage show (April in Paris; Where Have We Met Before?; others)
1933—This Is Romance
1934—ZIEGFELD FOLLIES OF 1934 stage show (Suddenly; I Like the Likes of You; What Is There to Say?)
1935—THUMBS UP stage show (Autumn in New York)
1936—ZIEGFELD FOLLIES OF 1936 stage show (I Can't Get Started; That Moment of Moments; An Island in the West Indies; Words without Music)
1937—THE SHOW IS ON stage show (Now; What Has He Got?; Casanova)
1940—CABIN IN THE SKY stage show (Cabin in the Sky; Taking a Chance on Love; Honey in the Honeycomb; others); IT HAPPENS ON ICE stage show (Double or Nothing; Long Ago; Adagio Dan; Don't Blow That Horn, Gabriel)
1942—BANJO EYES stage show (Not a Care in the World; A Nickel to My Name)
1943—CABIN IN THE SKY movie (original stage score; title song and Taking a Chance on Love first popular this year)
1944—JACKPOT stage show (What Happened?; Sugar Foot; What's Mine Is Yours; The Last Long Mile; It Was Nice Knowing You); SADIE THOMPSON stage show (The Love I Long For; Fisherman's Wharf; When You Live on an Island; Garden in the Sky; Siren of the Tropics); HOLLYWOOD CANTEEN movie (We're Having a Baby)
1952—TWO'S COMPANY stage show, Ogden Nash-lyr (Out of the Clear Blue Sky; Roundabout; others); APRIL IN PARIS movie (old title song plus new material with lyricist Sammy Cahn)
1956—THE LITTLEST REVUE stage show, Ogden Nash-lyr (Madly in Love;

Love Is Still in Town; You're Far from Wonderful); (John Latouche-lyr: Summer Is a-Comin' In); (Sammy Cahn-lyr: Good Little Girls)

1957—TIME REMEMBERED stage play, cm-lyr (Time Remembered; Ages Ago; Waltz Codetta)

(year unknown) London in July

Serious works: *Zephyr and Flora* (ballet); *Violin Concerto, Cello Concerto, Sonata in D for Violin and Piano*; *Parisian Suite*; *String Quartet in C*; *Surrealist Suite*; *Souvenirs de Monte Carlo*; *Ode to the Milky Way*; *Lady Blue* (ballet); *Souvenir de Venise*; *The Silver Shield* (U.S. Coast Guard Fighting Song)

501. DUKES OF DIXIELAND

jazz combo

Co-leaders:
FRANK ASSUNTO (t) (born January 29, 1932, New Orleans, La.; died February 25, 1974, New Orleans, La.)
FRED ASSUNTO (tb) (born December 3, 1929, New Orleans, La.)

Popular dixieland band of 50s and 60s. Brothers Frank and Fred Assunto formed band in New Orleans in 1947 called Basin Street Four (or Five, or Six, according to size). In early 1949 band on Horace Heidt talent show on radio, later toured with him, adopting name Dukes of Dixieland. Band popular in New Orleans, then toured. Jacob, father of brothers, played trombone and banjo in band, also served as manager. Personnel changed at times but Assuntos remained nucleus. Featured Pete Fountain on clarinet in band's early years. Although arrangements worked, sounded spontaneous. Began recording for Audio Fidelity Records in Chicago in 1956, waxed popular LPs in late 50s and 60s. Active through 60s into 70s.

RECORDS

FRANK ASSUNTO
NOB 9 The Dukes Stomp/Hindustan
NOB 10 Wailin' Blues/After You've Gone
NOB 12 Samson's Delight/St. James Infirmary

DUKES OF DIXIELAND
OK 6958 Bourbon Street Parade/339 Rag
OK 6969 What's the Matter?/Quand Mo T'est Petite
OK 6978 April in Portugal/Darkness on the Delta

LPs

DUKES OF DIXIELAND
Vi LPM-2097 Featuring Pete Fountain
Co CL-1728 Breakin' It Up on Broadway
Ha HL-7349 The Best of the Dukes of Dixieland
AudFid AFLP-1964 More Best of the Dukes of Dixieland, Vol. 2
AudFid AFSD-5823 (S) You Have to Hear It to Believe It!
AudFid AFSD-5924 (S) Louie (Armstrong) and the Dukes of Dixieland
AudFid AFSD-6172 (S) Tailgating
AudFid AFSD-6174 (S) On Parade
Vo 73846 Hello, Dolly!
De 74708 Come On and Hear
De 74863 Come to the Cabaret
De 74864 Thoroughly Modern Millie
De 74975 Dixieland's Greatest Hits

502. DuLANY, HOWARD

vo

Good baritone with Frank Dailey 1935-9 and Gene Krupa 1940-1. Musical career curtailed by military service, World War II. Married dancer Anne Middleton, quit music after discharge, settled in Florida and raised family.

RECORDS

FRANK DAILEY
Bb 6028 I Wished on the Moon
Bb 6029 You're So Darn Charming/ Broken-Hearted Troubadour
Bb 7646 I Wish I Was the Willow
Bb 7648 A Little Kiss at Twilight
Bb 7668 Isn't It Wonderful, Isn't It Swell?/There's a Village in a Valley
Bb 10004 April in My Heart/While a Cigarette Was Burning
Bb 10204 Have Mercy/Let's Tie the Old Forget-Me-Not
GENE KRUPA
Co 35444 Moments in the Moonlight
Co 35520 All This and Heaven Too/ When the Swallows Come Back to Capistrano

OK 5686 Love Lies/Only Forever
OK 5760 I'm Waiting for Ships That Never Come In
OK 5802 A Nightingale Sang in Berkeley Square
OK 5826 Two Dreams Met
OK 5883 It All Comes Back to Me Now
OK 5961 You Forgot About Me
OK 6021 These Things You Left Me
OK 6165 Maria Elena/A Rendezvous in Rio
OK 6187 Where You Are
OK 6198 Don't Cry, Cherie
OK 6210 Flamingo
OK 6255 Love Me as I Am/Afraid to Say Hello
OK 6266 The Cowboy Serenade/'Til Reveille
OK 6411 Who Can I Turn To?
HOWARD DULANY
Bb 10007 Until the End/Mexicali Rose

503. DUNCAN SISTERS   vo cm lyr
ROSETTA DUNCAN
Born November 23, 1900, Los Angeles, Calif.
Died December 4, 1959, Chicago, Ill.
VIVIAN DUNCAN
Born June 17, 1902, Los Angeles, Calif.
Popular sister act of 20s and early 30s. Noted for Topsy and Eva routine. Starred in TOPSY AND EVA (1925) on Broadway stage, wrote music and lyrics for show. Associated with show's hit song *Rememb'ring.* Other shows DOING OUR BIT (1917), SHE'S A GOOD FELLOW (1919), TIP TOP (1920). Starred in early sound movie IT'S A GREAT LIFE [1930]. Active in vaudeville throughout career. Much entertaining in London in 20s and 30s. Appeared in clubs and various theatrical productions in mid-30s. Became music publishers. Composed *Rememb'ring, I Never Had a Mammy, Do Re Mi, The Moon Am Shinin', Someday Soon.*

RECORDS
DUNCAN SISTERS
Vi 19050 The Music Lesson/Baby Sister Blues
Vi 19113 Stick in the Mud/The Argentines, Portuguese

Vi 19206 Rememb'ring/I Never Had a Mammy
Vi 19311 Aunt Susie's Picnic Day/Um-Um-Da-Da
Vi 19352 Tom Boy Blues/Bull Frog Patrol
Vi 19527 Mean Cicero Blues/Cross-Word Puzzle Blues
Vi 19987 Happy-Go-Lucky Days/Kinky Kids Parade
Vi 20963 Dawning/Baby Feet Go Pitter Patter
Vi 21226 Lickens/Black and Blue Blues
Vi 22269 I'm Following You/Hoosier Hop

504. DUNCAN, WILLIAM CARY   lyr
Born February 6, 1874, North Brookfield, Mass.
Died November 21, 1945, North Brookfield, Mass.
Lyricist-librettist of Broadway shows 1910-1929. Educated at Amherst. Teacher at Brooklyn Polytechnic School 1897-1917. Author of *The Amazing Madame Jumel* and *Golden Hoofs.* Editor of *American Kennel Gazette* and *Outdoor Life* (dog department). Songs attained little popularity outside context of shows. Included *Katy Did, When the Cherry Blossoms Fall, Love of Mine, I Love the Love That's New, The Heart of a Crimson Rose, The Best I Ever Get Is the Worst of It, A Twelve O'clock Girl in a Nine O'clock Town, No One Else but You, What Do You Do When I'm Gone?.* Collaborators included composers Karl Hoschna, Jean Schwartz, Clifford Grey, Rudolf Friml.

BROADWAY MUSICALS
(wrote book and lyrics unless designated otherwise)

1910—KATY DID
1913—THE PURPLE ROAD
1917—HIS LITTLE WIDOWS (lyrics only)
1918—FIDDLERS THREE (book only)
1919—THE ROYAL VAGABOND (lyrics only)
1920—THREE SHOWERS (book only)
1921—THE ROSE GIRL
1922—THE BLUE KITTEN
1924—MARY JANE MCKANE; MOLLY DARLING (book only); PRINCESS APRIL (book only)

1927—TALK ABOUT GIRLS (book only); YES, YES, YVETTE (book only)
1928—SUNNY DAYS
1929—GREAT DAY! (book only)

505. DUNHAM, SONNY

t tb ar cm vo B
(ELMER LEWIS DUNHAM)
Born November 16, 1914, Brockton, Mass.

Trumpeter-bandleader of 30s and 40s. Attained prominence as soloist with Glen Gray, particularly on showcase *Memories of You*. Began studying music at 7, played in local bands as teenager. In late 20s worked in New York. With Ben Bernie about six months, then two years with Paul Tremaine 1929-31. In late 1931 led own band called Sonny Lee & His New York Yankees. Joined Glen Gray in early 1932, remained until early 1940 except for unsuccessful venture as bandleader several months in 1937. Formed big band in early 1940 notable for good musicianship and arrangements by George Williams. Included Corky Corcoran on tenor sax and vocalist Ray Kellogg. Theme *Memories of You*. Band in 1942 movies BEHIND THE EIGHT BALL and OFF THE BEATEN TRACK. Band played top spots but attained no great popularity. In 1951 Dunham disbanded, worked awhile with Bernie Mann and Tommy Dorsey. In later 50s led band off and on. In 60s settled in Miami, freelanced, occasionally fronted band.

RECORDS

GLEN GRAY
Vi 24256 Casa Loma Stomp
Br 6486 The Lady from St. Paul
Br 6513 Blue Prelude
Br 6800 I Got Rhythm
Br 7521 Narcissus
De 1672 Memories of You
De 2399 Georgia on My Mind/Bone Yard Shuffle
ALL-STAR BAND
Vi 26144 Blue Lou
SONNY DUNHAM
Vs 8205 Just a Memory/Estrellita
Vs 8227 Little White Lies/Dark Eyes
Vs 8234 (theme) Memories of You/ Blue Skies

Bb 11124 I Understand/Mighty Lak' a Rose
Bb 11148 Bar Babble/Throwing Pebbles in the Millstream
Bb 11200 Sand in My Shoes/Easy Street
Bb 11214 Lament to Love/Down, Down, Down
Bb 11253 Hi, Neighbor!/The Nickel Serenade
Bb 11289 (theme) Memories of You/ As We Walk into the Sunset
Bb 11305 Nothin'/My Foolish Heart and I
Bb 11337 Watch the Birdie/When I Grow Too Old to Dream
Bb 11504 Heavenly Hideaway/Deliver Me to Tennessee
Hit 7073 I'll Be Around/When They Ask About You
Hit 7074 Holiday for Strings/Don't Worry, Mom
Vogue 774 Desert Fantasy/Save Me a Dream
Vogue 775 Clementine/I Love You in the Daytime Too
Embassy 1010 (theme) Memories of You/It's Just a Matter of Time

LPs

GLEN GRAY
Cor(10")CRL-56006 Hoagy Carmichael Songs (De RIs)
Ha HL-7045 The Great Recordings of Glen Gray (Br RIs)
Extreme Rarities LP-1005 Glen Gray and the Casa Loma Orchestra on the Air—1934 (transcription RIs)

506. DUNN, JOHNNY

c B
Born February 19, 1897, Memphis, Tenn.
Died August 20, 1937, Paris, France

Early jazz cornetist and bandleader. Attended Fisk University. As teenager worked at Memphis theatre as solo act. Played with W. C. Handy band several years around 1917-20. Worked in revues, also with Mamie Smith band. Led band, Johnny Dunn's Original Jazz Hounds, off and on during most of 20s; band accompanied blues singer Lena Wilson at times. Played in Europe in 1923 with Plantation Orchestra, later with same in U.S. At times worked solo act. Played in Europe with BLACKBIRDS OF 1926 show. In 1927-8 led band in New York and Chicago. Later in 1928 to Europe with Noble Sissle band, remained abroad. Led band and played with others, mostly in Paris. Settled in Holland. Returned to Paris in 1937, died there.

RECORDS

GULF COAST SEVEN
  Co A-3916 Fade Away Blues/Daybreak Blues
  Co A-3978 Memphis, Tennessee/Papa, Better Watch Your Step
W. C. HANDY
  Lyratone 4211 Beale Street Blues/Joe Turner Blues
  Lyratone 4212 Hesitating Blues/Yellow Dog Blues
LEW LESLIE'S BLACKBIRDS ORCHESTRA
  Br 4030 Bandana Babies/Magnolia's Wedding Day
PLANTATION ORCHESTRA
  Co(E) 4185 Silver Rose/Smiling Joe
  Co(E) 4238 Arabella's Wedding Day/For Baby and Me
MAMIE SMITH'S JAZZ HOUNDS
  OK 4254 Royal Garden Blues/Shim-Me King's Blues
  OK 4296 That Thing Called Love/Old-Time Blues
  OK 4305 Baby, You Made Me Fall for You/You Can't Keep a Good Man Down
JOHNNY DUNN
  Co A-3541 Bugle Blues/Birmingham Blues
  Co A-3579 Put and Take/Moanful Blues
  Co A-3878 Dixie Blues/Sugar Blues
  Co A-3893 Sweet Lovin' Mama/Vampin' Sal
  Co 124-D Dunn's Cornet Blues/You've Never Heard the Blues
  Co 14306-D Sergeant Dunn's Bugle Call Blues/Buffalo Blues
  Co 14358-D Ham and Eggs/You Need Some Loving
  Vo 1176 Original Bugle Blues/What's the Use of Being Alone?

LPs

JOHNNY DUNN'S ORIGINAL JAZZ HOUNDS
  VJM(E) 11 (1921-3 Co RIs)

507. DUNNE, IRENE   VO
Born December 20, 1904, Louisville, Ky.

Leading movie actress of 30s and 40s, talented at light comedy as well as drama. Delicate soprano singing voice, performed in some musical movies as well as on Broadway stage early in career. Grew up in Madison, Ind. Studied at Chicago College of Music. First real stage experience touring with road show at 16. Minor or supporting roles in Broadway shows THE CLINGING VINE (1923), LOLLIPOP (1924), THE CITY CHAP (1925), SWEETHEART TIME (1926). Starred in YOURS TRULY (1927), SHE'S MY BABY and LUCKEE GIRL (1928). In 1929 toured country in road company of SHOW BOAT. To Hollywood in 1930. After several movies, co-starred with Richard Dix in important 1931 movie CIMARRON, reached stardom. Mostly dramatic roles until late 30s, then leading star of light comedy. Sang in several movies including LEATHERNECKING (1930), STINGAREE (1934), ROBERTA and SWEET ADELINE (1935), SHOW BOAT (1936), HIGH, WIDE AND HANDSOME (1937), JOY OF LIVING (1938). Other leading movies included BACK STREET (1932), SILVER CORD (1933), AGE OF INNOCENCE (1934), MAGNIFICENT OBSESSION (1935), THEODORA GOES WILD (1936), THE AWFUL TRUTH (1937), LOVE AFFAIR (1939), MY FAVORITE WIFE (1940), A GUY NAMED JOE (1943), LIFE WITH FATHER (1947), I REMEMBER MAMA (1948). Mostly inactive since mid-50s; turned down many offers of roles in all media.

RECORDS

IRENE DUNNE
  Br 7420 Lovely to Look At/When I Grow Too Old to Dream
  De 18201 Smoke Gets in Your Eyes/I've Told Ev'ry Little Star
  De 18202 Why Was I Born?/All the Things You Are
  De 18203 They Didn't Believe Me/Babes in the Wood

LPs

(miscellaneous artists; one song)
  Epic LN-3188 Here Come the Girls (RIs)
(movie soundtrack)
  S-T 204 ROBERTA

508. DUNSTEDTER, EDDIE

o ar cm B

Born August 2, 1897, Edwardsville, Ill.

Leading organist from 20s to 60s. Attended Washington University. Through the years performed in theatres and did considerable radio work. In military service, World War II; conducted orchestra. In later years movie and TV work. Composed *San Francisco Beat*; *Hello, Mom*; *Pi Ka Ke*.

RECORDS

EDDIE DUNSTEDTER
Br 3928 Ramona/Girl of My Dreams
Br 3978 Kiss Me Again/Serende
Br 4148 Neapolitan Nights/Sonny Boy
Br 4292 Marie/Carolina Moon
Br 4293 Parade of the Wooden Soldiers/Ah, Sweet Mystery of Life
Br 4320 If I Had My Way/That's How I Feel About You
Br 4746 Aloha/Song of the Islands
Br 4902 Ciribiribin/O Sole Mio
De 1572 Nola/Parade of the Wooden Soldiers
De 1843 The Donkey Serenade/La Cumparsita
De 3635 Flapperette/The Doll Dance
De 3928 Ramona/Girl of My Dreams
KENNY BAKER with EDDIE DUNSTEDTER
De 2189 O Holy Night/O Little Town of Bethlehem
De 2190 It Came Upon the Midnight Clear/Hark! The Herald Angels Sing
DONALD NOVIS with EDDIE DUNSTEDTER
De 2047 Diane/Alice Blue Gown

LPs

EDDIE DUNSTEDTER
Cap T-1410 Pipes and Power
Cap T-1545 Where Dreams Come True
(miscellaneous artists; as arranger)
Foremost FML-S-1 My Square Laddie

509. DURANTE, JIMMY .vo p cm lyr B
(nicknamed Schnoz or Schnozzola)

Born February 10, 1893, New York, N.Y.

Lovable little comedian with long and popular career in all phases of show business. Big nose butt of many jokes. Pianist and singer of songs in patter style; composed many of his featured numbers. "Sang" in raspy, choppy manner, half talking. Purposely murdered language as part of act. Studied piano at early age; first club job at Coney Island at 17. In 1916 organized combo called Original New Orleans Jazz Band, featured dixieland. First played in New York area, then other locales. In 1923 joined Lou Clayton and Eddie Jackson to form vaudeville team of Clayton, Jackson & Durante. Team featured song, dance and comedy, became one of New York's favorites. Team in Broadway shows SHOW GIRL (1929) and THE NEW YORKERS (1930) and in movie ROADHOUSE NIGHTS (1930). Durante star of trio, resisted solo offers until Depression hit vaudeville. Then signed movie contract with Clayton as manager and Jackson contributing material. Durante immediate hit in NEW ADVENTURES OF GET-RICH-QUICK WALLINGFORD and CUBAN LOVE SONG (1931), THE PASSIONATE PLUMBER and SPEAK EASILY (1932). Prominent roles in movie musicals BROADWAY TO HOLLYWOOD (1933), GEORGE WHITE'S SCANDALS, HOLLYWOOD PARTY and STUDENT TOUR (1934). Movie career waned late 30s to early 40s.

Starred in Broadway musicals STRIKE ME PINK (1933), JUMBO (1935), RED HOT AND BLUE (1936), STARS IN YOUR EYES (1939), KEEP OFF THE GRASS (1940). Many guest spots on radio during 30s, popularized own song *Inka Dinka Doo* in 1933. Starred on 1934 Chase & Sanborn Hour, also on Billy Rose's Jumbo Show in 1936. Co-starred with Garry Moore on popular radio show 1943-6. Own show 1947 into early 50s. Good roles in several movies of middle and late 40s, more popular than ever. Suffered loss in 1950 when Lou Clayton died. Busy schedule in 50s and 60s. Own show on early TV, many guest spots and specials through the years. Sometimes Sonny King and chorus girls worked with him on production numbers, occasionally Jackson. Co-starred with Lennon Sisters on 1969-70 show. Continued club work, in 60s often with Sonny King. Well known but mysterious closing on radio and TV shows was "Goodnight, Mrs. Calabash, wherever you are." Less active in 70s.

Composer or lyricist of songs *Inka Dinka Doo*; *Jimmy, the Well-Dressed Man*; *Can Broadway Do without Me?*; *Who Will Be with You When I'm Far Away?*; *I Ups to Him and He Ups to Me*; *Umbriago*; *Start Off Each Day with a Song*; *Any State in the Forty-Eight Is Great*; *I'm Jimmy's Girl*; *Daddy, Your Mama Is Lonesome for You.* Chief collaborators Jackie Barnett and Ben Ryan. Biography of Durante, *Schnozzola*, written by Gene Fowler. Confined to wheelchair after stroke early 1974.

MOVIES

1929—ROADHOUSE NIGHTS
1931—NEW ADVENTURES OF GET-RICH-QUICK WALLINGFORD; CUBAN LOVE SONG; HER CARDBOARD LOVER
1932—THE PASSIONATE PLUMBER; THE PHANTOM PRESIDENT; SPEAK EASILY; WET PARADE; BLONDIE OF THE FOLLIES
1933—HELL BELOW; WHAT! NO BEER?; BROADWAY TO HOLLYWOOD; MEET THE BARON
1934—PALOOKA; STRICTLY DYNAMITE; HOLLYWOOD PARTY; GEORGE WHITE'S SCANDALS OF 1934; SHE LEARNED ABOUT SAILORS; STUDENT TOUR
1935—CARNIVAL
1936—LAND WITHOUT MUSIC
1938—START CHEERING; LITTLE MISS BROADWAY; SALLY, IRENE AND MARY; FORBIDDEN MUSIC
1940—MELODY RANCH
1941—YOU'RE IN THE ARMY NOW; THE MAN WHO CAME TO DINNER
1944—TWO GIRLS AND A SAILOR
1945—MUSIC FOR MILLIONS
1946—ZIEGFELD FOLLIES; TWO SISTERS FROM BOSTON
1947—IT HAPPENED IN BROOKLYN; THIS TIME FOR KEEPS
1948—ON AN ISLAND WITH YOU; YOU'RE BEAUTIFUL
1950—THE GREAT RUPERT; THE YELLOW CAB MAN; THE MILKMAN
1960—PEPE (cameo)
1962—JUMBO
1963—IT'S A MAD, MAD, MAD, MAD WORLD

RECORDS

CLAYTON, JACKSON & DURANTE
Co 1860-D Can Broadway Do without Me?/So I Ups to Him
JIMMY DURANTE
Br 6774 Inka Dinka Doo/Hot Patatta
Co 36732 Inka Dinka Doo/Hot Patatta
De 23351 Inka Dinka Doo/Umbriago
De 23566 Start Off Each Day with a Song/Durante, the Patron of the Arts
De 23567 Who Will Be with You When I'm Far Away?/So I Ups to Him
De 23568 Jimmy, the Well-Dressed Man/Joe Goes Up—I Come Down
Maj 1059 G'wan Home, Your Mudder's Callin'/There Are Two Sides to Every Girl
MGM 30207 Fugitive from Esquire/My Nose's Birthday
JIMMY DURANTE-EDDIE JACKSON
MGM 30255 Bill Bailey/What You Goin' to Do When the Rent Comes 'Round?
JIMMY DURANTE-DANNY KAYE-JANE WYMAN-GROUCHO MARX
De 27748 Black Strap Molasses/How Di Ye Do
JIMMY DURANTE-BETTY GARRETT
MGM 30176 Any State in the Forty-Eight Is Great/The Pussy Cat Song
JIMMY DURANTE-HELEN TRAUBEL
Vi(12")12-3229 The Song's Gotta Come from the Heart/A Real Piano Player

LPs

JIMMY DURANTE
Lion L-70053 In Person
De DL-9049 Club Durant
De(10")DL-5116 Durante Sings
WB 1655 One of Those Songs
MGM E-4207 The Very Best of Jimmy Durante
(one side) Ace of Hearts(E) AH-25 (De RIs)
(movie soundtrack)
Co OL-5860 JUMBO
(miscellaneous artists)
De DEA-7-2 (2-LP set) Those Wonderful Thirties

510. DURBIN, DEANNA   vo
(EDNA MAE DURBIN)
Born December 4, 1921, Winnipeg, Canada

Beautiful singing star of movies from 1937 to late 40s, from teenager to adult. Clear soprano voice, at home with classical and pop music. Appearances on Eddie Cantor radio show of mid-30s brought attention, led to movie career. First film 1935 short EVERY SUNDAY with Judy Garland. Starred in 1937 movie THREE SMART GIRLS, followed with other popular films. Usually played self-assured, sometimes precocious teenager in late 30s. In 40s matured to light romantic roles. Dramatic role in 1944 movie CHRISTMAS HOLIDAY. Married French film director late 1950, retired from show business to live in France.

MOVIES

1937—THREE SMART GIRLS; A HUNDRED MEN AND A GIRL
1938—MAD ABOUT MUSIC; THAT CERTAIN AGE
1939—THREE SMART GIRLS GROW UP; FIRST LOVE
1940—IT'S A DATE; SPRING PARADE
1941—NICE GIRL?; IT STARTED WITH EVE
1943—THE AMAZING MRS. HOLIDAY; HERS TO HOLD; HIS BUTLER'S SISTER
1944—CAN'T HELP SINGING; CHRISTMAS HOLIDAY
1945—LADY ON A TRAIN
1946—BECAUSE OF HIM
1947—I'LL BE YOURS; SOMETHING IN THE WIND
1948—UP IN CENTRAL PARK; FOR THE LOVE OF MARY

RECORDS

DEANNA DURBIN
De 1097 Someone to Care for Me/Il Bacio (The Kiss)
De 1471 It's Raining Sunbeams/La Traviata
De 2274 My Own/Les Filles de Cadix
De 2757 Because/Ave Maria
De 2758 The Last Rose of Summer/Home Sweet Home
De 3061 Ave Maria/Alleluja
De 3062 Loch Lomond/Musetta's Waltz Song
De 3063 Love Is All/Amapola
De 3414 Waltzing in the Clouds/When April Sings
De 3655 Thank You, America/Old Folks at Home
De 18199 My Hero/Kiss Me Again
De 18261 When the Roses Bloom Again/Love's Old Sweet Song
De 18297 Poor Butterfly/Annie Laurie
De 18575 Say a Prayer for the Boys Over There/God Bless America
De 23389 More and More/Any Moment Now
De 23397 Spring Will Be a Little Late/Always
De 24167 Something in the Wind/It's Only Love
De(12")15044 One Fine Day/Spring in My Heart

LPs

DEANNA DURBIN
Ace of Hearts(E) AH-93 A Date with Deanna Durbin (De RIs)
Ace of Hearts(E) AH-147 A Date with Deanna Durbin, Vol. 2 (De RIs)
De DL-8785 Deanna Durbin (De RIs)

511. DURHAM, EDDIE   g tb ar cm B
Born August 19, 1906, San Marcos, Tex.

Prominent jazzman of 30s and 40s, important arranger-composer of swing numbers. Pioneer on amplified guitar. Several brothers musicians, formed Durham Brothers orchestra locally. In mid-20s Eddie toured with circus band. Active in Kansas City jazz scene in late 20s. With Bennie Moten mostly during 1929-33, wrote some arrangements. With Willie Bryant briefly as arranger, then with Jimmie Lunceford 1935-7 as trombonist-arranger, also featured on guitar. Arrangements for Lunceford included *Harlem Shout*; *Avalon*; *Bird of Paradise*; *Oh, Boy*; *Blues in the Groove*; *Swingin' on C*; *Wham*; *Count Me Out*; *Pigeon Walk*; *Lunceford Special*; *Hittin' the Bottle*; *Running a Temperature*; *It's Time to Jump and Shout*. With Count Basie 1937-8 as sideman-arranger; scores included *Topsy*, *Out the Window, Swinging the Blues, Time Out*. In 1938-9 arranged for Ina Ray Hutton's all-girl band. Furnished Glenn

Miller arrangements for *Slip Horn Jive, Wham, Glen Island Special, Baby Me, I Want to Be Happy*. Arranged for Artie Shaw, Jan Savitt, Lunceford again. In 1940 led tightly knit eight-piece combo featuring altoist Buster Smith and Durham's mellow, swinging amplified guitar. Only two records made by this excellent group. Musical director in 1941 for singer Bon Bon, later 1941-3 for all-girl band International Sweethearts of Rhythm. Led own all-girl band awhile. In 50s concentrated on arranging, also freelanced. In late 50s and 60s led band in New York area, continued arranging. Active into 70s. Composer or co-composer of swing numbers *John's Idea, Every Tub, Out the Window, Good Morning Blues, Time Out, Topsy, Blues in the Groove, Glen Island Special, Wham, Four Letters, Swinging the Blues, Don't You Miss Your Baby?, Sent for You Yesterday, Swingin' on C*, also 1941 popular song *I Don't Want to Set the World on Fire*.

RECORDS

BON BON
> De 3980 I Don't Want to Set the World on Fire/Sweet Mama, Papa's Getting Mad
> De 8567 Blow, Gabriel, Blow/All That Meat and No Potatoes

HARRY JAMES
> Br 8035 When We're Alone/Life Goes to a Party
> Br 8038 Jubilee/I Can Dream, Can't I?

KANSAS CITY FIVE/SIX
> CMS 509 Countless Blues/I Want a Little Girl
> CMS 510 Laughing at Life/I Know that You Know
> CMS 511 Good Mornin' Blues/Them There Eyes
> CMS 512 Pagin' the Devil/'Way Down Yonder in New Orleans

EDDIE DURHAM
> De 8529 Magic Carpet/Fare Thee Honey Fare Thee Well
> De 18126 I Want a Little Girl/Moten's Swing

LPs

JIMMIE LUNCEFORD
> De DL-79238 Harlem Shout (De RIs)

512. DUVIVIER, GEORGE   b ar cm
Born August 17, 1920, New York, N.Y.

Bassist active with many bands beginning in 40s. Studied at N.Y.U. and Conservatory of Music and Art. First big job with Coleman Hawkins late 1940-1. With Lucky Millinder in late 1941-2. Military service, World War II. Joined Jimmie Lunceford as arranger in late 1945, remained till leader's death in mid-1947. Later in 1947 joined Sy Oliver's big band as sideman-arranger. Also arranged for Joe Thomas sextet. With Nellie Lutcher 1950-2, including trips abroad. Freelanced in New York. In 1953-4 with singers Billy Eckstine, Pearl Bailey, Lena Horne (trips abroad with latter). With Louis Bellson, Bernard Peiffer, Terry Gibbs, Don Redman, Bud Powell, Stan Getz, Tony Scott, Benny Carter, Gerry Mulligan, Benny Goodman (in band for 1956 movie THE BENNY GOODMAN STORY). Remained active with freelance jobs and recordings. Composed jazz numbers; best-known *Open House* and *Lunar*.

RECORDS

LUCKY MILLINDER
> De 4099 Let Me Off Uptown/How About That Mess
> De 4146 Hey Huss
> De 18353 Savoy
> De 18386 I Want a Tall Skinny Papa
> De 18496 That's All

JIMMIE LUNCEFORD
> De 18655 I'm Gonna See My Baby/That Someone Must Be You

DUSTY FLETCHER
> Nat 4013 Dusty Fletcher's Mad Hour (1 & 2)

HAL MITCHELL FOUR
> Debut 104 Mitch's Blues/Confidentially

SY OLIVER
> MGM 10004 Slow Burn
> MGM ———— Scotty

LPs

JACK TEAGARDEN
> Verve V-8495

BUD POWELL
> Vi LPM-1423 Strictly Powell
> Vi LPM-1507 Swingin' with Bud
> Norg MGN-1077 Piano Interpretations by Bud Powell

ART FARMER
Mer MG-20766 Listen to Art Farmer and The Orchestra

PHIL BODNER
Cam CAL-985 A Lover's Concerto

JOHNNY SMITH
Verve V-8737 Kaleidoscope

LEE WILEY
Mon-Ever MES-7041 (S) Back Home Again

MAXINE SULLIVAN-BOB WILBER
Mon-Ever MES 6919 Close as Pages in a Book

RUSTY DEDRICK
4 Corners FCL-4207 The Big Band Sound

RUSTY DEDRICK (and singers)
Mon-Ever ME 6809-10-11 (3-LP set) Irving Berlin

LOUIS BELLSON
Norg MGN-1011 Louis Bellson Quintet

BENNY GOODMAN
Cap W565 B.G. In Hi-Fi
De DL8252-3 (2-LP set) THE BENNY GOODMAN STORY (soundtrack)

513. EAGER, ALLEN   ts as B

Born January 10, 1927, New York, N.Y.

Modern-styled tenor sax star, active in developing period of bop in mid-40s. Strong-toned, driving style. At 15 first important job with Bobby Sherwood. Brief stints 1943-5 with Sonny Dunham, Woody Herman, Hal McIntyre, Shorty Sherock, Tommy Dorsey, Johnny Bothwell. In mid-40s led combo at intervals, played with leading bop groups in New York jazz clubs. In 1948 with Tadd Dameron. Over next several years with Buddy Rich at intervals. Retired from music awhile, then led combo in mid-50s. In early 1956 co-led combo with Howard McGhee on west coast. Played in Paris 1956-7; late 1957 returned to U.S. In a few years less active; name faded.

RECORDS

COLEMAN HAWKINS
Vi 40-0131 Spotlite/Say It Isn't So
Vi 40-0133 Allen's Alley/Low Flame
RED RODNEY
Key 670 Elevation/Fine and Dandy
TADD DAMERON
BN 559 Jahbero/Lady Bird
BN 1564 Symphonette
DAVE LAMBERT-BUDDY STEWART
JS(Fr) 627 Hot Halavah
JS(Fr) 674 Bopelground
TEDDY REIG ALL-STARS
Sav 975 Mr. Dues
GERRY MULLIGAN
Pres 763 Funhouse/Mullenium

STAN GETZ TENOR SAX STARS
NJ 802 Five Brothers/Four and One Moore
NJ 811 Speedway
NJ 818 Battleground
ALLEN EAGER
Sav 611 Booby Hatch/Rampage
Sav 621 Vot's Dot
Sav 908 Donald Jay/Meeskite
Sav 909 Symphony Sid's Idea
Sav 932 Jane's Bounce
Sav 948 And That's for Sure/All Night, All-Frantic
Sav 958 Nightmare Allen/Church Mouse

LPs

ALLEN EAGER
Sav(10″) MG-9015 New Trends in Modern Music, Vol. 2
Sav(10″) MG-15044 Vol. 2 (1946-7 sessions)
EmArcy MG-36016 Advance Guard of the 40s
STAN GETZ
NJ(10″) 102 Vol. 1
FATS NAVARRO
BN(10″) 5004 (BN RIs)
GERRY MULLIGAN
Pres(10″) PRLP-141
COLEMAN HAWKINS
Vi LJH-1017 The Hawk in Flight (Bb, Vi RIs)
GERRY MULLIGAN-ALLEN EAGER
Pres (10″) PRLP-120
GEORGE HANDY
"X" LXA-1004 Handyland U.S.A.

514. EATON, MARY   VO

Born 1902
Died 1946

Singing and dancing star of Broadway musicals of 20s. Began stage career in THE ROYAL VAGABOND (1919). Became popular with work in ZIEGFELD FOLLIES OF 1920-1921-1922. Co-starred with Eddie Cantor in important musical KID BOOTS (1924). Starred in LUCKY (1927) for modest run. Later in year successful in long-running FIVE O'CLOCK GIRL. In movie musicals THE COCOANUTS (1929) and GLORIFYING THE AMERICAN GIRL (1930).

515. EBERLE, RAY   VO B

Born January 19, 1919, Hoosick Falls, N.Y.

Well-known featured vocalist with Glenn Miller band during heyday. Younger brother of Bob Eberly, star vocalist with Jimmy Dorsey. Ray a natural for Miller band. Voice pitched slightly higher than Bob's; its melodious, slightly fragile quality fit perfectly with Miller muted brass and reeds. Ray's spelling of last name correct; Bob had changed spelling earlier to "Eberly." Ray had no professional experience when joined Miller in late 1938 on brother's recommendation. Miller helped coach him in early days. Ray consistently good on vocals, handsome asset to band. Featured on band's Chesterfield radio series and on dozens of records. Two most famous *At Last* and *Moonlight Cocktail*. Remained till mid-1942, shortly before Miller entered service. In late 1942 briefly with Gene Krupa, then to Hollywood for Universal shorts and movies including FOLLOW THE BAND, MISTER BIG and HI YA, SAILOR (1943), THIS IS THE LIFE (1944). Worked as single in late 1944-5. Military service awhile in 1945. Led band in later 40s and 50s, featured Miller-styled arrangements and former Miller hits. Billy Maxted wrote some of band's arrangements. By late 50s Eberle less active in music. Occasional TV appearances in 60s and early 70s on nostalgic shows. Around 1970 began singing regularly with Tex Beneke's Miller-style band, mostly on west coast.

RECORDS

GLENN MILLER
Bb 7853 My Reverie
Bb 10276 To You/Stairway to the Stars
Bb 10290 Blue Evening/The Lamp Is Low
Bb 10303 Moon Love/Stay in My Arms, Cinderella
Bb 10329 Oh, You Crazy Moon
Bb 10366 Over the Rainbow
Bb 10372 Blue Orchids
Bb 10404 My Prayer/Blue Moonlight
Bb 10423 Last Night/Melancholy Lullaby
Bb 10486 Blue Rain
Bb 10495 Indian Summer
Bb 10520 Careless/Vagabond Dreams
Bb 10536 Faithful to You/It's a Blue World
Bb 10638 Sierra Sue/Moments in the Moonlight
Bb 10684 Hear My Song, Violetta/Starlight and Music
Bb 10728 Fools Rush In
Bb 10768 Blueberry Hill/A Million Dreams Ago
Bb 10893 Yesterthoughts/A Handful of Stars
Bb 10970 Along the Santa Fe Trail
Bb 11063 A Stone's Throw from Heaven
Bb 11215 You and I/The Angels Came Thru
Bb 11235 The Cowboy Serenade
Bb 11401 Moonlight Cocktail
Bb 11462 The Story of a Starry Night/Skylark
Vi 27934 At Last
Vi 27935 Serenade in Blue
RAY EBERLE
Si 15214 Serenade in Blue/Easy Ride
Apo 1014 More Than You Know/It's a Wonderful Night

LPs

RAY EBERLE
Golden Tone C-4030 Plays Glenn Miller
Tops L-1573 Plays a Tribute to Glenn Miller
Tiara 7530
Design 48

GLENN MILLER
  Vi LPT-1016 Juke Box Saturday Night
    (Bb, Vi RIs)
  Vi LPT-1031 The Nearness of You
    (Bb, Vi RIs)
  Vi LPM-2080 (Bb RIs)
(miscellaneous artists)
  WB 1505 Something Old, Something
    New

516. EBERLY, BOB   VO
(ROBERT EBERLE)

Born July 24, 1916, Mechanicville, N.Y.

Prominent vocalist with Jimmy Dorsey
band. Rich baritone with excellent phrasing, regarded by many as top male band
vocalist 1938-42. Older brother of Ray
Eberle, featured singer with Glenn Miller.
Bob changed spelling of last name early
in career. First gained attention with
vocals for Dorsey Brothers Orchestra in
spring of 1935, during last few months of
band's existence. When Dorseys separated Jimmy continued with band as leader.
Eberly stayed until 1943. Vocalist Helen
O'Connell joined band early 1939, teamed
with Bob on big Dorsey hits in early 40s:
*Green Eyes, Yours, Amapola, Time Was,
Tangerine.* Bob sang popular *Blue Champagne* and *The Breeze and I.* Eberly featured with Dorsey band in movies THE
FLEET'S IN (1942) and I DOOD IT (1943). In
1947 biographical movie THE FABULOUS
DORSEYS. Had offers to become a single
but remained with Dorsey until military
service 1943. During service hitch lost
popularity, never really regained it as
single in postwar years. In 1953 he and
Helen O'Connell with Ray Anthony band
on TV series. In 1955 on TV show in New
York. Infrequent TV appearances in 50s
and 60s, sometimes reuniting with Helen
O'Connell on nostalgic shows. Led band
on and off, sang mostly at clubs in New
York area into 70s.

RECORDS

DORSEY BROTHERS ORCHESTRA
  De 476 Chasing Shadows
  De 482 You're All I Need
  De 559 You Are My Lucky Star
  De 560 I've Got a Feelin' You're
    Foolin'

JIMMY DORSEY
  De 764 You/You Never Looked So
    Beautiful
  De 951 Pennies from Heaven/One,
    Two, Button Your Shoe
  De 1660 I Was Doing All Right/Love
    Is Here to Stay
  De 1671 I Fall in Love with You Every
    Day
  De 1724 Love Walked In/At a Per-
    fume Counter
  De 1746 Lost and Found
  De 1970 Love Is Where You Find
    It/Garden of the Moon
  De 2002 Change Partners
  De 2536 This Is No Dream
  De 2735 Body and Soul
  De 2814 If I Had You/A Table in a
    Corner
  De 3150 The Breeze and I
  De 3391 Whispering Grass/Talkin' to
    My Heart
  De 3446 A Handful of Stars/Falling
    Leaves
  De 3570 I Hear a Rhapsody/The
    Mem'ry of a Rose
  De 3629 Amapola/Donna Maria
  De 3657 Yours
  De 3698 Green Eyes/Maria Elena
  De 3710 My Sister and I/In the Hush
    of the Night
  De 3775 Blue Champagne/All Alone
    and Lonely
  De 3859 Time Was/Isle of Pines
  De 4123 Tangerine/Ev'rything I Love
  De 18372 My Devotion
  De 18433 Serenade in Blue
  De 18460 Daybreak/Brazil
  De 18532 Let's Get Lost

BOB EBERLY
  De 18896 Cynthia's in Love/And Then
    I Looked at You
  Cap 1533 Alone/I Made a Promise
  Cap 1887 I Can't Help It/Somebody's
    Been Beatin' My Time
  Cap 2103 Isn't This a Night for
    Love?/Hills of Pride

BOB EBERLY-HELEN O'CONNELL
  Cap 1802 It's Dark on Observatory
    Hill/In a Little Spanish Town

LPs

BOB EBERLY
  GA 33-341 Sings Tender Love Songs
BOB EBERLY-HELEN O'CONNELL
  WB 1403 Recapturing the Excitement of the Jimmy Dorsey Era (recreations)
JIMMY DORSEY
  De DL-4248 Remember Jimmy (De RIs)
  De DL-4853 Jimmy Dorsey's Greatest Hits (De RIs)
  De DL-8153 Latin American Favorites (De RIs)
  De DL-8609 The Great Jimmy Dorsey (De RIs)

517. EBSEN, BUDDY   cm lyr vo
(CHRISTIAN EBSEN, JR.)

Born April 2, 1908, Orlando, Fla.

Known primarily as eccentric dancer and actor. On rare occasions vocalized on stage, in movies and on TV. Educated at University of Florida. Early in career worked with sister Vilma as dance team in vaudeville. Team in Broadway musicals FLYING COLORS (1932) and ZIEGFELD FOLLIES OF 1934, in movie BROADWAY MELODY OF 1936 (1935). After Vilma retired, Buddy worked as dancer-actor. In movie musicals BORN TO DANCE and CAPTAIN JANUARY (1936), BROADWAY MELODY OF 1938 (1937), GIRL OF THE GOLDEN WEST and MY LUCKY STAR (1938), THEY MET IN ARGENTINA (1941), also in film drama-with-music BANJO ON MY KNEE (1936). On Broadway again in YOKEL BOY (1939) and revival of SHOW BOAT (1946). Career waned during 40s. Returned to movies in 50s, developed into competent dramatic actor. Important later movies RED GARTERS (1954) and BREAKFAST AT TIFFANY'S (1961). Big hit during 60s in long-running TV series The Beverly Hillbillies. This led to guest spots on other TV shows, where sometimes sang and danced. Early 70s starred in own TV series Barnaby Jones.

RECORDS
(LP)

(movie soundtrack)
  Vista 5002 THE ONE AND ONLY GENUINE ORIGINAL FAMILY BAND

518. ECKSTINE, BILLY   vo t v-tb B
(WILLIAM CLARENCE ECKSTEIN; nicknamed Mr. B)

Born July 8, 1914, Pittsburgh, Pa.

Handsome top singer of late 40s and early 50s. Big baritone voice, smooth and tasteful style despite occasional exaggerated phrasing. Attended Howard University, Washington, D.C. Began singing in small Washington clubs, then in Buffalo, Detroit and Chicago. First prominent as vocalist with Earl Hines 1939-43. Learned to play trumpet with Hines. Left band in late 1943, worked a few months as single. With aid of saxman Budd Johnson in early 1944 formed big band. From mid-1944 to early 1947 band important pioneer of bop. Dizzy Gillespie served awhile as sideman-arranger-musical director. Personnel included at times Charlie Parker, Gene Ammons, Lucky Thompson, Dexter Gordon, Leo Parker, Art Blakey, Fats Navarro, Howard McGhee, Kenny Dorham, Miles Davis. Trombonist Jerry Valentine with band entire period. Sarah Vaughan vocalist about a year. Arrangements by Dizzy Gillespie, Tadd Dameron and Budd Johnson, who later replaced Gillespie as musical director. Eckstine was featured prominently on vocals, sometimes on trombone; excellent front man. The band toured, had good location jobs, but by early 1947 hit lean times and broke up. Unfortunately group not well recorded. Eckstine took up career as single, quickly reached great heights. Records popular and numerous in early 50s. So well known disc jockeys called him simply "Mr. B." Played top clubs, appeared in 1952 movie SKIRTS AHOY!. Popularity faded in late 50s and 60s but work continued in clubs and on records; also occasional TV appearances. Long runs in Las Vegas and other Nevada spots. Several tours of Europe, Australia and Asia. Active in early 70s.

RECORDS

EARL HINES
  Bb 10763 My Heart Beats for You
  Bb 10985 Wait 'Til It Happens to You
  Bb 11065 I'm Falling for You/Jelly, Jelly

Bb 11199 Julia
Bb 11329 Water Boy
Bb 11374 I Got It Bad
Bb 11394 You Don't Know What Love Is
Bb 11512 Skylark
Bb 11567 Stormy Monday Blues

BILLY ECKSTINE ORCHESTRA
DeL 2001 Blowin' the Blues Away/If That's the Way You Feel
DeL 2002 Opus X/The Real Thing Happened to Me
Nat 9014 A Cottage for Sale/I Love the Rhythm in a Riff
Nat 9017 Prisoner of Love/All I Sing Is Blues
Nat 9018 Blue/Second Balcony Jump
Nat 9052 Cool Breeze/You're My Everything
Nat 9121 Jelly Jelly/My Deep Blue Dream

BILLY ECKSTINE
MGM 10259 Everything I Have Is Yours/I'll Be Faithful
MGM 10311 Blue Moon/Fools Rush In
MGM 10368 Caravan/A Senorita's Bouquet
MGM 10778 You've Got Me Crying Again/The Show Must Go On
MGM 10799 Be My Love/Only a Moment Ago
MGM 10825 I've Never Been in Love Before/I'll Know
MGM 10903 I Apologize/Bring Back the Thrill
MGM 10982 Love Me/I'm a Fool to Want You
MGM 11028 Enchanted Land/I've Got My Mind on You
MGM 11073 Out in the Cold Again/Once
MGM 11177 A Room with a View/Carnival
MGM 11655 Rendezvous/I'm in a Mood

BILLY ECKSTINE-SARAH VAUGHAN
MGM 11144 I Love You/Evry Day

LPs

BILLY ECKSTINE
Nat(10″)2001 Billy Eckstine Sings (Nat RIs)
Regent MG-6052 Prisoner of Love

Lion L-70057 The Best of Billy Eckstine
Mer MG-20674 At Basin Street East (with QUINCY JONES)
EmArcy MG-36129 Billy Eckstine's Imagination
Roul 25104 (with BILLY MAY)

BILLY ECKSTINE-SARAH VAUGHAN
Mer MG-20316 Sing the Best of Irving Berlin

519. EDDY, NELSON   VO

Born June 29, 1901, Providence, R.I.
Died March 6, 1967

Singing star of movies and radio in 30s and 40s. Teamed with Jeanette MacDonald in series of popular movie musicals in operetta style. Rich baritone voice with excellent diction. Learned to sing by listening to opera records. As young man worked odd jobs to pay for vocal lessons. Early experience with Philadelphia Civic Opera. In 1924 New York operatic debut in small role. Some singing on radio. Obscure concert singer in early 30s when signed by MGM head Louis B. Mayer. Minor singing roles in movies DANCING LADY and BROADWAY TO HOLLYWOOD (1933), STUDENT TOUR (1934). Co-starred with Miss MacDonald in NAUGHTY MARIETTA (1935), won instant stardom. Pair's subsequent movies top box office draws. Eddy starred 1934-5 on Voice of Firestone and other radio shows. Own radio show 1935-6. In late 1937 joined Don Ameche and Dorothy Lamour on Chase & Sanborn show, remained till late 1939. In 40s own radio shows at intervals. Movie contract ended in 1947, radio shows several years later. Worked night clubs and stock musical productions. Teamed often with singer Gale Sherwood. On TV occasionally. Active until death.

MOVIES
*(*with Jeanette MacDonald)*

1933—DANCING LADY; BROADWAY TO HOLLYWOOD
1934—STUDENT TOUR
1935—NAUGHTY MARIETTA*
1936—ROSE-MARIE *
1937—MAYTIME*; ROSALIE
1938—GIRL OF THE GOLDEN WEST*; SWEETHEARTS*

1939—BALALAIKA; LET FREEDOM RING
1940—BITTER SWEET*; NEW MOON*
1941—THE CHOCOLATE SOLDIER
1942—I MARRIED AN ANGEL*
1943—PHANTOM OF THE OPERA
1944—KNICKERBOCKER HOLIDAY
1946—MAKE MINE MUSIC (voice on sound-track)
1947—NORTHWEST OUTPOST

RECORDS

NELSON EDDY-JEANETTE MACDONALD
  Vi 4323 Indian Love Call/Ah! Sweet Mystery of Life
  Vi 4329 Will You Remember?/Farewell to Dreams
NELSON EDDY-RISE STEVENS
  Co 4281-M Sympathy/My Hero
  Co 4283-M Forgive/The Chocolate Soldier
  Co 4508-M Golden Days/Come Boys
NELSON EDDY-JO STAFFORD
  Co——— With These Hands/Till We Meet Again
NELSON EDDY
  Vi 4280 I'm Falling in Love with Someone/Tramp, Tramp, Tramp Along the Highway
  Vi 4281 'Neath the Southern Moon/Ah! Sweet Mystery of Life
  Vi 4284 Love's Old Sweet Song/Auf Wiedersehen
  Vi 4285 When I Grow Too Old to Dream/You Are Free
  Vi 4305 Rose-Marie/The Mounties
  Vi 4313 Through the Years/Dusty Road
  Vi 4366 By the Waters of Minnetonka/Trees
  Vi 4389 Soldiers of Fortune/Senorita
  Co 4241-M Stout Hearted Men/Wanting You
  Co 4314-M Oh, What a Beautiful Mornin'/Surrey with the Fringe on Top
  Co 4315-M Great Day/Without a Song
  Co 4335-M Danny Boy/The Old Refrain
  Co 17173-M At the Balalaika/The Magic of Your Love
  Co 17329-M Shortnin' Bread/Water Boy

LPs

NELSON EDDY
  Co CL-828 OKLAHOMA!
  Co CL-831 THE DESERT SONG
  Co(10")ML-2094 NAUGHTY MARIETTA
  Ha HL-7142 Stouthearted Men
  Ha HL-7151 Because
  Cam CAL-492 Nelson Eddy Favorites (Vi RIs)
  Sun 1143 'Til the End of Time
NELSON EDDY-JEANETTE MACDONALD
  Vi LPV-526 (Vi RIs)
  Vi LPM-1738 Favorites in Hi-Fi (Vi RIs)
NELSON EDDY-GALE SHERWOOD
  Sun 1176 Our Love

520. EDENS, ROGER   cm lyr ar p

Born November 9, 1905, Hillsboro, Tex.
Songwriter-arranger for MGM in 30s and 40s; producer in later years. Pianist in pit band for Broadway musical GIRL CRAZY late 1930-1. Then with Ethel Merman as accompanist-arranger. Began with MGM in 1933, wrote special material for movies. Scored movies STRIKE UP THE BAND, FOR ME AND MY GAL, EASTER PARADE, ON THE TOWN, ANNIE GET YOUR GUN, TAKE ME OUT TO THE BALL GAME. Did musical adaptation for movies of GIRL CRAZY, MEET ME IN ST. LOUIS, ZIEGFELD FOLLIES. Chief collaborators on songs Hugh Martin, Ralph Freed, Betty Comden, Adolph Green, James V. Monaco, Sigmund Romberg.

SONGS
(with related shows)

1937—BROADWAY MELODY OF 1938 movie (special material for Dear Mr. Gable, combining it with old song You Made Me Love You)
1938—LOVE FINDS ANDY HARDY movie (In Between)
1940—LITTLE NELLIE KELLY movie (It's a Great Day for the Irish); STRIKE UP THE BAND movie (Our Love Affair; Nobody); TWO GIRLS ON BROADWAY movie (My Wonderful One, Let's Dance)
1941—LADY BE GOOD movie (You'll Never Know; Your Words and

My Music); ZIEGFELD GIRL movie (Minnie from Trinidad; Ziegfeld Girls; Laugh! I Thought I'd Split My Sides; Caribbean Love Song); BABES ON BROADWAY movie (Hoe Down)

1943—THOUSANDS CHEER movie (Carnegie Hall)

1946—ZIEGFELD FOLLIES movie (Bring on the Wonderful Men; Here's to the Girls)

1947—GOOD NEWS movie (The French Lesson; Pass That Peace Pipe)

1949—ON THE TOWN movie (added new material to original stage score); TAKE ME OUT TO THE BALL GAME movie (The Right Girl for Me; Strictly U.S.A.; It's Fate, Baby, It's Fate; Yes Indeedy; O'Brien to Ryan to Goldberg)

1952—SINGIN' IN THE RAIN movie (Moses)

1957—FUNNY FACE movie (collaborated with Leonard Gershe on new songs; Think Pink; On How to Be Loved; Bonjour Paris; Basal Metabolism; Marche Funebre)

Other compositions: *A Pretty Girl Milking Her Cow*; *Figaro*; *Sawdust, Spangles and Dreams*; *You're Awful*; *Main Street*. Wrote numbers Judy Garland sang at Palace Theatre and in concerts: *Judy at the Palace*; *This Is the Time of the Evening*.

521. EDISON, HARRY   t cm B
(nicknamed Sweets)

Born October 10, 1915, Columbus, Ohio

Trumpet star from late 30s into 70s; long period in Count Basie band. Admired for warm style, interesting ideas somewhat in modern idiom. Worked in St. Louis 1933-6, mostly with Jeter-Pillars band. In New York in 1937 with Lucky Millinder & Blue Rhythm Band. Joined Basie in 1938, stayed till 1950. With Jimmy Rushing, also toured with Jazz at the Philharmonic. In early 50s many jobs with Buddy Rich, including tours in U.S. and South America accompanying Josephine Baker. Settled on west coast, did studio work, led combo at intervals. In late 50s led combo in New York and on tour. Led group accompanying singer Joe Williams on tour in 1961. On west coast again to freelance and play studios. European tour in 1964 with Jazz at the Philharmonic. With Basie at intervals in 60s; European tour with Basie in 1970. Occasionally in bands on late-night TV shows. Credited as composer or co-composer of jazz numbers, most of which featured by Basie band: *Jive at Five, Beaver Junction, Center Piece, Pound Cake, Shorty George, Sweet, Evil Blues, Free Eats, Mutton Leg, Every Tub*.

RECORDS

COUNT BASIE
De 1880 Swinging the Blues
De 2224 Panassie Stomp
De 2922 Jive at Five
Vo 4747 Rockabye Basie
Co 35448 Easy Does It (2nd trumpet solo)/Louisiana
OK 6095 Broadway
OK 6244 9:20 Special

RED CALLENDER
Sun 10056 Get Happy/These Foolish Things

ILLINOIS JACQUET
Clef 89164 Learnin' the Blues/Honeysuckle Rose

BILLIE HOLIDAY
Vo 5377 The Man I Love

DEXTER GORDON
Mer(12")8900 Rosetta/I've Found a New Baby

HARRY EDISON
Philo 119 Laura/I Blowed and Gone
Philo 120 Ain'tcha Gonna Do It?/Exit Virginia Blues
PJ 613 These Foolish Things/Indiana

LPs

HARRY EDISON
Verve MGV-8211 Gee, Baby, Ain't I Good to You
Verve MGV-8295 The Swinger: Harry Edison
Roul R-52023 "Sweetenings"
Clef MGC-717 Sweets

HARRY EDISON-JOE WILLIAMS
Roul R-52069 Together

BUDDY RICH-HARRY EDISON
Norg MGN-1038 Buddy and Sweets

COUNT BASIE
Epic LN-3169 Basie's Back in Town (Vo, OK RIs)

BARNEY KESSEL
Contemp C-3513 Barney Kessel, Vol. 3
CY TOUFF
PJ 1211 Cy Touff, His Octet and Quintet
BUDDY DEFRANCO
Verve MGV-8315 Bravura
Norg MGN-1085 The Buddy DeFranco Wailers
PAUL QUINICHETTE
UA 4054 Like Who?
BILLIE HOLIDAY
Verve V-8257 Songs for Distingue Lovers

522. EDWARDS, CLIFF   vo uk d
(nicknamed and often billed as
UKULELE IKE)
Born 1895, Hannibal, Mo.
Died July 1971, Hollywood, Calif.

Soft-voiced singer and ukulele player popular in 20s and 30s. Got start performing in St. Louis saloons. Travelled, worked at carnivals and various odd jobs. Later as drummer in Chicago teamed with Joe Frisco, played vaudeville, worked up to top engagements. In Broadway musicals LADY BE GOOD (1924), SUNNY (1925), ZIEGFELD FOLLIES OF 1927, GEORGE WHITE'S SCANDALS OF 1936. Popular in movies during transition from silents to sound. Played supporting light comedy and musical roles. Appeared in 23 movies 1929-31, most important HOLLYWOOD REVUE OF 1929 (sang hit song *Singin' in the Rain*), GOOD NEWS, LORD BYRON OF BROADWAY, MONTANA MOON, THOSE THREE FRENCH GIRLS, MARIANNE, SO THIS IS COLLEGE, THE SOUTHERNERS. During remainder of 30s and 40s appeared in 47 additional movies; most important musicals TAKE A CHANCE, GEORGE WHITE'S SCANDALS OF 1934 and 1935, GIRL OF THE GOLDEN WEST. In movie cartoon PINOCCHIO his squeaky voice used for Jiminy Cricket character. Performed on radio, made many records. Died in nursing home in 1971.

RECORDS
CLIFF EDWARDS or UKULELE IKE
Pe 11593 Oh Lovey Be Mine/Say, Who Is That Baby Doll?

Pe 11594 How She Loves Me/Lonesomest Girl in Town
Pe 11598 Dinah/Keep On Crooning
Pe 11640 Side by Side/Oh Baby, Don't We Get Along
Pe 12126 It Had to Be You/California, Here I Come
Pat 25126 Fascinating Rhythm/I'll Take Her Back
Pat 32074 June Night/Insufficient Sweetie
Harmo 1014 Alabamy Bound
Harmo 1015 Let It Rain, Let It Pour
Co 1295-D Together/Mary Ann
Co 1471-D I Can't Give You Anything but Love/That's My Weakness Now
Co 1523-D Half-Way to Heaven/It Goes Like This
Co 1869-D Singin' in the Rain/Orange Blossom Time
Co 1907-D Just You, Just Me/Hang On to Me
Br 6307 Dream Sweetheart/All of a Sudden
Br 6319 Crazy People/A Great Big Bunch of You
Vo 2587 It's Only a Paper Moon/Night Owl
Ba 33436 I Was Born Too Late/I Got Shoes, You Got Shoesies
De 1106 If I Had You/The Night Is Young and You're So Beautiful
De 1166 Somebody Loves Me/St. Louis Blues
De 3000-1-2-3 (songs from PINOCCHIO, with VICTOR YOUNG ORCHESTRA)
De 18837 Give a Little Whistle/Turn on the Old Music Box
Mer 5309 Singin' in the Rain/June Night

LPs
CLIFF EDWARDS
Vista BV-4043 Ukulele Ike Happens Again
(movie soundtrack; one side)
De DL-8387 PINOCCHIO

523. EDWARDS, EDDIE   tb B
Born May 22, 1891, New Orleans, La.
Died April 9, 1963, New York, N.Y.

Trombonist with pioneer jazz group, Original Dixieland Jazz Band, 1916-25.

Learned violin and trombone as youngster (self-taught). First worked as violinist in theatre orchestra, soon concentrated on trombone and played in local bands. Worked in Chicago in 1916.

(See biography herein on NICK LAROCCA for details on Original Dixieland Jazz Band.)

After break-up of Original Dixieland Jazz Band, Edwards led band in New York ballrooms in late 20s. Out of music about six years, then joined reassembled Original Dixieland Jazz Band late 1936 to early 1938. Freelanced in New York 1938-42, at times inactive or in society orchestras. In 1943-4 toured with Katherine Dunham show. Continued to freelance, at times led band, as on 1946 recordings. In various groups during dixieland revival in late 40s and early 50s. In later years worked at intervals. Co-composer of jazz standards *Tiger Rag*, *Livery Stable Blues*, *Clarinet Marmalade*, *Fidgety Feet*.

RECORDS

ORIGINAL DIXIELAND JAZZ BAND
Co A-2297 Darktown Strutters' Ball/ Indiana
Co(E) 735 Barnyard Blues/At the Jazz Band Ball
Co(E) 736 Ostrich Walk/Sensation Rag
Co(E) 759 Satanic Blues/'Lasses Candy
Vi 18255 Livery Stable Blues/Dixie Jazz Band One-Step
Vi 18457 At the Jazz Band Ball/Ostrich Walk
Vi 18472 Skeleton Jangle/Tiger Rag
Vi 18483 Bluin' the Blues/Sensation Rag
Vi 18513 Mournin' Blues/Clarinet Marmalade
Vi 18564 Fidgety Feet/Lazy Daddy
Vi 18717 Margie/Palesteena
Vi 18722 Broadway Rose / Sweet Mama
Vi 18729 Home Again Blues/Crazy Blues
Vi 18772 Jazz Me Blues/St. Louis Blues
Vi 18798 Royal Garden Blues/Dangerous Blues

Vi 18850 Bow Wow Blues
Vi 25502 Barnyard Blues/Original Dixieland One-Step
Vi 25524 Tiger Rag/Skelton Jangle
Vi 25525 Clarinet Marmalade/Bluin' the Blues
VD(12")214 Tiger Rag/Sensation
EDDIE EDWARDS' ORIGINAL DIXIELAND JAZZ BAND
CMS 610 Tiger Rag/Barnyard Blues
CMS 611 Mournin' Blues/Skeleton Jangle
CMS 612 Ostrich Walk/Lazy Daddy
CMS 613 Shake It and Break It/When You and I Were Young, Maggie

LPs

EDDIE EDWARDS' ORIGINAL DIXIELAND JAZZ BAND
CMS(10")FL-20003 (CMS RIs)
ORIGINAL DIXIELAND JAZZ BAND
"X"(10")LX-3007 (Vi RIs)
Vi LPV-547 (Vi RIs)

524. EDWARDS, GUS   cm vo

> Born August 18, 1879, Hohensaliza, Germany
> Died November 7, 1945, Los Angeles, Calif.

Composer-performer-producer important in musical scene beginning just after turn of century. Composed famous songs *School Days*, *In My Merry Oldsmobile*, *I Just Can't Make My Eyes Behave* (Anna Held's feature song), *Sunbonnet Sue*, *By the Light of the Silvery Moon*. Brought to U.S. in 1881, grew up in New York. Sang in vaudeville, later directed and produced children's troupes to play vaudeville featuring youngsters Eddie Cantor, George Jessel, Walter Winchell, Lila Lee, Elsie Janis, Georgie Price, Duncan Sisters, Sally Rand, Jack Pearl, Ray Bolger, Eleanor Powell, Lane Sisters, Paul Haakon, Ina Ray Hutton, Herman Timberg, Hildegarde, Mae Murray, Eddie Buzzell, Groucho Marx, Bert Wheeler, Louis Silvers, Mervin LeRoy, Louise Groody, Ricardo Cortez, Helen Menken. Edwards troupes played top spots including Palace Theatre in New York. Edwards wrote scores for Broadway musicals WHEN WE WERE FORTY-ONE (1905), HIP-HIP-HOORAY (1907), THE MERRY-GO-ROUND and SCHOOL DAYS

861

(1908), ZIEGFELD FOLLIES OF 1910, SUN-
BONNET SUE (1923), BROADWAY SHOW
WINDOW (1936). Contributed songs for
other shows, bulk of score for important
movie musical HOLLYWOOD REVUE OF
1929. Chief collaborators lyricists Will D.
Cobb, Edward Madden, Robert B. Smith,
Joe Goodwin. Established Gus Edwards
Music Hall in New York, also publishing
company. Produced cabaret revues. After
retiring from vaudeville in 1928, returned
1930-7. Ill health forced retirement 1939.
In same year movie appeared on his life,
THE STAR MAKER, starring Bing Crosby in
Edwards role and featuring many old
Edwards songs.

SONGS
(with related shows)

1899—The Singer and the Song; You Are
the Only Girl I'll Ever Care About
1900—All for a Man Whose God Was
Gold; I Can't Tell Why I Love
You, But I Do
1901—I Don't Want Money; I'll Be with
You When the Roses Bloom
Again; I'm Dreaming of a Bygone
Day; Mamie
1902—Could You Be True to Eyes of
Blue?
1903—MR. BLUEBEARD stage show (songs
unimportant); THE WIZARD OF OZ
stage show (I Love Only One Girl
in the Wide, Wide World)
1904—THE MEDAL AND THE MAID stage
show (In Zanzibar); The Girl Who
Cares for Me; Goodbye, Little
Girl, Goodbye
1905—WHEN WE WERE FORTY-ONE stage
show (songs unimportant); FAN-
TANA stage show (Tammany); He's
Me Pal; If a Girl Like You Loved
a Boy Like Me; In My Merry
Oldsmobile; Somebody's Sweetheart I Want to Be
1906—ABOUT TOWN stage show (When
Tommy Atkins Marries Dolly
Gray); HIS HONOR THE MAYOR
stage show (Come Take a Skate
with Me); I Just Can't Make My
Eyes Behave; Two Dirty Little
Hands; I'd Like to See a Little
More of You
1907—HIP-HIP-HOORAY stage show (songs

unimportant); ZIEGFELD FOLLIES
OF 1907 stage show (In the Grand
Old Sands; Bye Bye, Dear Old
Broadway); Laddie Boy
1908—SCHOOL DAYS stage show (School
Days); THE MERRY-GO-ROUND
stage show (songs unimportant);
MISS INNOCENCE stage show (My
Cousin Carus'); Sunbonnet Sue
1909—BREAKING INTO SOCIETY stage show
(songs unimportant); ZIEGFELD
FOLLIES OF 1909 stage show (By
the Light of the Silvery Moon;
Come On and Play Ball with Me;
Up, Up, Up in My Aeroplane; My
Cousin Carus')
1910—ZIEGFELD FOLLIES OF 1910 stage
show (Sweet Kitty Bellaires; Look
Me Over Carefully; Kidland; A
Woman's Dream); If I Was a
Millionaire
1911—Jimmy Valentine
1913—I'll Get You; Little Miss Killarney
1916—I Lost My Heart in Honolulu
1917—For You a Rose; Just a Simple
Country Maiden
1923—SUNBONNET SUE stage show ('Mem-
ber When; Love Is a Garden of
Roses; Where the Bluebells Grow;
Same Old Sunbonnet Sue; School
Days Are Over; Sunbonnet Sue)
1929—HOLLYWOOD REVUE OF 1929 movie
(Orange Blossom time; Your
Mother and Mine; Strolling
Through the Park One Day; No-
body but You; Lon Chaney Will
Get You If You Don't Watch Out;
Minstrel Days; I Never Knew I
Could Do a Thing Like That);
SHOW OF SHOWS movie (Your
Mother and Mine)
1936—BROADWAY SHOW WINDOW stage
show (Spring Is in the Air; Hitch
Your Wagon to a Star; Poverty
Row; plus old songs)

525. EDWARDS, JOAN   vo p cm lyr
*Born February 13, 1919, New York,
N.Y.*

Singer of late 30s and 40s best known for
work with Paul Whiteman band and on
radio show Lucky Strike Hit Parade; also
composer-lyricist. Attended Hunter Col-

lege. In 1937-8 on radio shows. Joined Whiteman on Chesterfield show mid-1938, remained with Whiteman into 1940. In late 1940 good run in Broadway show IT HAPPENS ON ICE. On 1941 radio show Girl About Town. In late 1941 on Hit Parade; appeared on more than 200 over next several years. On other radio shows; played night clubs and hotels. In movie HIT PARADE OF 1947. In 50s concentrated on composing. In 1950 with collaborator Lyn Duddy wrote score for Broadway musical TICKETS PLEASE (best song *Darn It, Baby, That's Love*). Other compositions include *Heart of Stone—Heart of Wood, And So It Ended, Let's Make Up Before We Say Goodnight, Do You Still Feel the Same?, Television's Tough on Love*. Wrote for Copacabana revues in New York. At intervals on radio in 50s.

RECORDS

PAUL WHITEMAN
De 2083 While a Cigarette Was Burning
De 2578 Moon Love/To You
De 2913 Heaven in My Arms
De 2937 My Fantasy/Darn That Dream
JOAN EDWARDS
De 2693 How Deep Is the Ocean/ Russian Lullaby
De 3562 There Shall Be No Night/ Isola Bella
De 3580 Lamplight/Some of Your Sweetness
LMS 292 How High the Moon/House with a Little Red Barn
LMS 304 Fools Fall in Love/Latins Know How
LMS 322 Bewitched/In Our Little Den
VD(12″)328 Always
Vogue 761 More Than You Know/Go West, Young Man
Vogue 782 Maybe You'll Be There/ What Am I Gonna Do About You?
JOAN EDWARDS-CLARK DENNIS
De 2692 Say It Isn't So/Easter Parade

LPs
(as composer-lyricist with Lyn Duddy)
ARTHUR GODFREY
Co GL-521 Arthur Godfrey's TV Calendar Show

526. EDWARDS, JULIAN   cm
Born 1855 in England
Died 1910 in U.S.

English composer; came to U.S. in 1888 and had successful career. Scores for Broadway musicals; active until death. Most successful show DOLLY VARDEN (1902). Most of his songs important only within context of shows. Best-known songs *My Own United States* in WHEN JOHNNY COMES MARCHING HOME (1902) and *Sweet Thoughts of Home* in LOVE'S LOTTERY (1904). Chief collaborator lyricist Stanislaus Stange.

BROADWAY MUSICALS
(wrote music)
1892—JUPITER
1893—FRIEND FRITZ
1895—MADELEINE
1896—THE GODDESS OF TRUTH; BRIAN BORU
1898—THE JOLLY MUSKETEER
1902—DOLLY VARDEN; WHEN JOHNNY COMES MARCHING HOME
1904—LOVE'S LOTTERY
1906—HIS HONOR THE MAYOR
1907—THE BELLE OF LONDON TOWN; THE GIRL AND THE GOVERNOR
1908—THE GAY MUSICIAN
1909—THE GIRL AND THE WIZARD; THE MOTOR GIRL
1910—MOLLY MAY

527. EGAN, RAYMOND B.   lyr vo
Born November 14, 1890, Windsor, Ontario, Canada
Died October 13, 1952, Westport, Conn.

Lyricist mostly active during 20s and early 30s. Major songs *Japanese Sandman, Till We Meet Again, Ain't We Got Fun, I Never Knew (I Could Love Anybody), Sleepy Time Gal, Three on a Match*. Wrote minor material for a few Broadway musicals and movies. Collaborators included composers Walter Donaldson, Ted Fio Rito, Harry Tierney, Richard Whiting. Grew up in Detroit. Boy soprano seven years in St. John's Episcopal Choir. Educated at University of Michigan. Early in career bank clerk, then staff writer for publishing company, both in Detroit.

SONGS
(with related shows)

1916—Mammy's Little Coal Black Rose
1917—Some Sunday Morning; Where the Morning Glories Grow
1918—Till We Meet Again
1919—TOOT SWEET stage show (songs unimportant)
1920—SILKS AND SATINS stage show (This Is the End of Me Now); Japanese Sandman; I Never Knew (I Could Love Anybody)
1921—Ain't We Got Fun; Biminy Bay; When Shall We Meet Again?; Tea Leaves
1922—Song of Persia
1923—Rocky Mountain Moon
1925—HOLKA POLKA stage show (In a Little While); Sleepy Time Gal
1926—There Ain't No Maybe in My Baby's Eyes; There's a Boatman on the Volga
1927—If You See Sally
1930—PARAMOUNT ON PARADE movie (My Marine)
1932—RED HEADED WOMAN movie (title song); Tell Me Why You Smile, Mona Lisa; Three on a Match
1935—EARL CARROLL'S SKETCH BOOK OF 1935 stage show (Let the Man Who Makes the Gun)
1936—Knick Knacks on the Mantel
1938—Juliana
1940—Poor Ballerina

Other songs: *They Called It Dixieland*; *You're Still an Old Sweetheart of Mine*; *Somebody's Wrong*; *Dear Old Gal, Who's Your Pal Tonight?*; *Mighty Blue*; *Downstream Drifter*

528. ELDRIDGE, ROY   t fl-h vo B
(DAVID ROY ELDRIDGE; nicknamed LITTLE JAZZ)

Born January 30, 1911, Pittsburgh, Pa.

Outstanding trumpet star of 30s and 40s. Powerful swing style, good tone, great facility. As youngster he learned several instruments. After local experience, left home in 1927 to lead combo in road show, later played in carnival band. Led band awhile back in Pittsburgh. First big job in 1928 with Fletcher Henderson's Dixie Stompers (under direction of Horace Henderson). With Speed Webb 1929-30. In early 30s with Cecil Scott, Elmer Snowden, Charlie Johnson, Teddy Hill. In 1933 led band in Pittsburgh with brother Joe. With McKinney's Cotton Pickers in Baltimore in 1934, then with Teddy Hill in New York 1935. He and brother again led combo in late 1935-6 in New York. With Fletcher Henderson much of 1936, where solo work brought him national attention. During remainder of 30s led bands of varying sizes. In 1940 good run at Kelly's Stables in New York; late 1940-1 led band in Chicago. Theme *Little Jazz.*

With Gene Krupa two years, 1941-3 (until band broke up); gained great prominence with solos and vocals. 1943-4 freelanced, studio work, led band. Joined Artie Shaw in late 1944 (after Shaw's discharge from Navy) as featured soloist, remained till late 1945. Again led big band, later combos. In 1949 with Krupa, toured with Jazz at the Philharmonic. Toured Europe in 1950 with Benny Goodman, remained abroad as single; long stay in Paris. As bop emerged in middle and late 40s Eldridge lost some popularity—and some faith in himself. Paris restored confidence. Returned to U.S. in April 1951, maintained busy schedule with own groups, freelance, Jazz at the Philharmonic, festivals, recordings. Many dates with Coleman Hawkins and with Sol Yaged in late 50s. Many jobs 1963-5 with Ella Fitzgerald. Several tours abroad with various units. Active into 70s with festivals, clubs, concerts. In 1971-4 at Jimmy Ryan's in New York. Another European tour 1972 in combo from Count Basie band.

RECORDS

TEDDY HILL
    Me 13351 Here Comes Cookie/Got Me Doin' Things
    Me 13364 When the Robin Sings His Song Again/When Love Knocks at Your Heart
FLETCHER HENDERSON
    Vo 3211 Blue Lou/Christopher Columbus
    Vo 3213 Stealin' Apples/Grand Terrace Swing

Vi 25297 I'm a Fool for Loving You/
Moonrise on the Lowlands
Vi 25375 Shoe Shine Boy
Vi 25379 Jimtown Blues
TEDDY WILSON
Br 7498 What a Little Moonlight Can
Do/A Sunbonnet Blue
Br 7501 Miss Brown to You/I Wished
on the Moon
Br 7554 If You Were Mine/Eeny
Meeny Miney Mo
Br 7663 Mary Had a Little Lamb/Too
Good to Be True
DELTA FOUR
De 737 Farewell Blues/Swingin' on the
Famous Door
FRED RICH
Vo 5420 How High the Moon/A
House with a Little Red Barn
MILDRED BAILEY
Vo 3449 My Last Affair/Trust in Me
Vo 3456 Where Are You?/You're
Laughing at Me
CHU BERRY
CMS 516 Sittin' In/46 West 52
CMS(12")1502 Star Dust/Body and
Soul
CHOCOLATE DANDIES
CMS(12")1506 I Surrender Dear/I
Can't Believe That You're in Love
with Me
PUTNEY DANDRIDGE
Vo 2982 Chasing Shadows/When I
Grow Too Old to Dream
Vo 3024 Nagasaki
BILLIE HOLIDAY
OK 5481 Body and Soul/What Is This
Going to Get Us?
OK 5719 Laughing at Life/Tell Me
More
GENE KRUPA
Vi 25263 Mutiny in the Parlor/I'm
Gonna Clap My Hands
Vi 25276 I Hope Gabriel Likes My
Music/Swing Is Here
OK 6210 Let Me Off Uptown
OK 6255 Afraid to Say Hello
OK 6278 After You've Gone
OK 6352 Rockin' Chair/Tunin' Up
OK 6563 Ball of Fire/All Through the
Night
Co 36591 Knock Me a Kiss
ARTIE SHAW
Vi 20-1638 I'll Never Be the Same

Vi 20-1647 The Sad Sack/The Grab-
town Grapple (both GRAMERCY
FIVE)
Vi 20-1668 Little Jazz
ROY ELDRIDGE
Vo 3458 After You've Gone/Where
the Lazy River Goes By
Vo 3479 Wabash Stomp/Florida
Stomp
Vo 3577 Heckler's Hop/That Thing
Vs 8144 Who Told You I Cared?/Does
Your Heart Beat for Me?
Vs 8154 High Society/Muskrat Ram-
ble
Br 80117 The Gasser/Jump Through
the Window
Key 607 Don't Be That Way/St. Louis
Blues
De 24417 I Can't Get Started/After
You've Gone
VD(12")612 Roy Meets Horn
Mer 89056 Love for Sale/Dale's Wail
KING DAVID (Roy Eldridge)
Vogue(Fr) 5041 It Don't Mean a
Thing/The Man I Love
Vogue(Fr) 5044 Easter Parade/Wild
Driver

LPs

ROY ELDRIDGE
Clef MGC-683 Little Jazz
Clef MGC-704 Rockin' Chair
ARS G-404 Jam Session
EmArcy MG-36084 Roy's Got
Rhythm
GENE KRUPA
Cam CAL-340 Mutiny in the Parlor
(Vi RIs)
Verve MGV-2008 Drummer Man
ROY ELDRIDGE-BENNY CARTER
ARS G-413 The Urbane Jazz of Roy
Eldridge and Benny Carter
ARTIE SHAW
Vi LPV-582 Featuring Roy Eldridge

529. ELGART, LARRY   as ss B
*Born March 20, 1922, New London,
Conn.*

Good lead alto saxman featured in band
of brother Les, also co-leader of band and
leader of own band. Sax distinctively
modern in sound, important asset of
bands' sound and style. At 16 summer job
with Bob Astor, at 17 with Charlie Spiv-

ak, then with Woody Herman, Red Norvo, Freddie Slack. With Jerry Wald 1941-2, there played third sax for only time in career (Les Robinson first sax). With Bobby Byrne later in 1942-3. This band fronted by Jack Jenney awhile, then taken over by Dean Hudson; Les Elgart joined in later period. Studio work in New York in mid-40s. Lead soprano sax in brother's band early 1945-6, later own band at intervals. With Bobby Byrne 1950. In pit band of Broadway show TOP BANANA, late 1951-2.

(See biography on LES ELGART herein for details of Larry with that band.)

RECORDS

(See LES ELGART biography; Larry on all records listed.)

LARRY ELGART
De 29043 More Than You Know/ You're Driving Me Crazy

LPs

LARRY ELGART
Vi LSP-2045 (S) New Sounds at the Roosevelt
Cam CAL-575 Easy Goin' Swing

530. ELGART, LES   t B
Born August 3, 1918, New Haven, Conn.
Leader of popular 50s and 60s dance band with distinctive sound and style. Good lead trumpeter and front man. In early 40s briefly with Bunny Berigan, Hal McIntyre, Charlie Spivak, Harry James, Muggsy Spanier. With Woody Herman briefly in 1943; late 1943-4 with Dean Hudson. Bandleader early 1945-6 with brother Larry on soprano sax lead. Then each brother led own band, with little success. Brothers freelanced late 40s and early 50s, experimented with new arrangements and sounds. In 1953 joined with arranger Charles Albertine to launch Les Elgart band. Larry's distinctive lead alto sax combined with unusual Albertine arrangements gave the band its own sound and style: modern, mellow, haunting sound with subtle swing and good beat (despite absence of piano). Almost all ensemble; rarely featured soloists. Band acclaimed by critics and especially fans, quickly rose to popularity. Well

received LPs followed. Brothers split into separate bands in late 50s. Later reunited, sometimes billed as Les and Larry Elgart. Band active in 60s, playing top spots and recording; occasionally on TV.

RECORDS

LES ELGART
Mus 15079 Mabel! Mabel!/Nobody Knows the Trouble I've Seen
Bullet 1028 I Went Down to Virginia/What Do You Want to Make Those Eyes at Me For?
Co 40137 The Gang That Sang Heart of My Heart/Geronimo
Co 40179 Varsity Drag/Rocky's Prelude
Co 40214 Charleston/Meet Me Tonight in Dreamland
Co 40249 Wedding Bells/Spending the Summer in Love
Co 40388 Charlie's Dream/Bazoom!

LPs

LES ELGART
Co CL-536 Sophisticated Swing
Co CL-594 Just One More Dance
Co CL-619 The Band of the Year
Co CL-684 The Dancing Sound
Co CL-875 The Elgart Touch
Co CL-904 The Most Happy Fella
Co CL-1008 For Dancers Only
Ha HL-7374 The Greatest Dance Band in the Land
LES AND LARRY ELGART
Co CL-1052 Les and Larry Elgart and Their Orchestra
Co CS-8002 (S) Sound Ideas
Co CS-8092 (S) Les and Larry Elgart

531. ELISCU, EDWARD   lyr
Born April 2, 1902, New York, N.Y.
Lyricist-actor-playwright-producer active on Broadway and in Hollywood. Collaborated on important songs *Great Day, More Than You Know, Without a Song, Carioca, Flying Down to Rio.* Educated at CCNY. Acted in Broadway plays THE RACKET, QUARANTINE, THE DYBBUK. Wrote plays THE HOLDUP MAN, THEY CAN'T GET YOU DOWN. Co-producer of MEET THE PEOPLE (1941). Wrote scores for GREAT DAY! and LADY FINGERS (1929), A LITTLE RACKETEER (1932), FREDERIKA (1937; also

librettist), MEET THE PEOPLE (1941; also librettist), THE BANKER'S DAUGHTER (1962). Wrote music for movies, notably score for FLYING DOWN TO RIO (1933). Wrote screenplays THE GAY DIVORCEE, THREE HUSBANDS, OUT OF THE BLUE. Collaborators included songwriters Vincent Youmans, Billy Rose, Jay Gorney, Henry Myers, Johnny Green, Gus Kahn, Vernon Duke, Manning Sherwin, Richard Myers, Ned Lehac, Billy Hill, Franz Lehar.

SONGS
(with related shows)

1929—GREAT DAY! stage show (Great Day; More Than You Know; Without a Song); LADY FINGERS stage show (songs unimportant)
1930—WHOOPEE movie (I'll Still Belong to You); They Cut Down the Old Pine Tree
1931—THE THIRD LITTLE SHOW stage show (You Forgot Your Gloves)
1932—A LITTLE RACKETEER stage show (songs unimportant)
1933—FLYING DOWN TO RIO movie (Flying Down to Rio; Carioca; Music Makes Me; Orchids in the Moonlight)
1937—FREDERIKA stage show (Kiss to Remind You; Rose in the Heather; One; Rising Star; Why Did You Kiss My Heart Awake?; Wayside Rose; Oh Maiden, My Maiden)
1941—MEET THE PEOPLE stage show (Meet the People; Four Freedoms)
1943—THE MORE THE MERRIER movie (Damn the Torpedoes—Full Speed Ahead)
1962—THE BANKER'S DAUGHTER stage show, Sol Kaplan-cm (songs unimportant)

532. ELLINGTON, DUKE   p cm ar B
(EDWARD KENNEDY ELLINGTON)
Born April 29, 1899, Washington, D.C. Died May 24, 1974, New York, N.Y., of cancer and pneumonia

Musical giant as bandleader, composer and arranger. Long career from 1918 into 70s. Composed staggering number of jazz works through the years, as well as many songs of lasting popularity. As pianist played modified stride style, tasteful and easy-swinging, with own brand of unorthodox chord structures and ornate patterns. Highly successful bandleader for half a century with immense body of recorded work. Personnel in band more constant than in most. As teenager played in Washington, D.C., area. Led small band in 1918; early members Otto Hardwick (as) and Arthur Whetsol (t), joined in 1919 by Sonny Greer (d). With them and Elmer Snowden (bn), Ellington went to New York in 1922 to join Wilbur Sweatman awhile. Left, returned to New York in 1923, played Hollywood Club (later Kentucky Club) with Snowden as leader. Fred Guy replaced Snowden, Ellington became leader, called group The Washingtonians. 1924-7 band toured New England many times, returned to Kentucky Club, played other Harlem clubs and theatres.

In December 1927 Ellington opened Harlem's Cotton Club under own name as leader. Band increased gradually to full size. This engagement established band, which fit "jungle" atmosphere of club, got heavy radio coverage. Played there off and on into 1931, with periods at other spots and touring. In 1929 band in Broadway musical SHOW GIRL. Irving Mills, Ellington's manager, asset in booking clubs and record dates. In late 1930 band got publicity from spot in much heralded movie CHECK AND DOUBLE CHECK starring Amos 'n' Andy. Best-known early records *East St. Louis Toodle-Oo* (theme), *The Mooche, Creole Love Call, Mood Indigo, Black and Tan Fantasy*. First European tour great success 1933; later tour 1939, several in 50s and 60s plus trips to other continents.

Public became aware of excellent sidemen who stayed with band many years: Johnny Hodges (as), Barney Bigard (cl), Harry Carney (bs), Sonny Greer (d), Bubber Miley (t), Cootie Williams (t), Tricky Sam Nanton (tb), Juan Tizol (tb), Lawrence Brown (tb). Later: Rex Stewart (t), Ben Webster (ts), Jimmy Blanton (b), Cat Anderson (t), Ray Nance (t v), Jimmy Hamilton (cl), Paul Gonsalves (ts), Clark

Terry (t) and others briefly. Sidemen with band many years: Otto Hardwick (as), Fred Guy (g), Arthur Whetsol (t), Freddy Jenkins (t). In 50s and 60s personnel changed more often.

Most arranging by Ellington. In 1939 Billy Strayhorn joined as composer-arranger; style similar to Ellington's, contributed importantly. Strayhorn's *Take the "A" Train* featured number, later band theme. Band had unique sound; arrangements and compositions conformed to soloists, featured unorthodox voicing, chords and patterns to set moods. Many critics and fans regard the 1940-3 years as band's most creative period. Unfortunately, recording ban in effect latter part of period. Ivy Anderson was principal vocalist 1931-42. Various sidemen sang. Al Hibbler featured in late 40s. Beginning early 50s little emphasis on vocals as band concentrated on instrumentals.

Band in movies CHECK AND DOUBLE CHECK (1930), BELLE OF THE NINETIES, SYMPHONY IN BLACK and MURDER AT THE VANITIES (1934), THE HIT PARADE (1937), CABIN IN THE SKY and REVEILLE WITH BEVERLY (1943). Ellington composed and recorded soundtrack for movies THE ASPHALT JUNGLE (1950), ANATOMY OF A MURDER (1959), PARIS BLUES (1961), ASSAULT ON A QUEEN (1966), CHANGE OF MIND, German film JANUS. Wrote score for Broadway musical BEGGAR'S HOLIDAY (1946), pageant of Negro history MY PEOPLE (1963), TIMON OF ATHENS. The band played first concert at Carnegie Hall in 1943, others there in later years. Busy schedule of tours, festivals, formal concerts, sacred concerts, recordings, occasional TV. In later years Ellington frequently on TV as single, usually playing own compositions on piano. Composed *The River* 1970 for American Ballet Theatre. Wrote autobiography *Music Is My Mistress* 1973.

Band maintained high level of musicianship, kept abreast of times. New members absorbed Ellington spirit. Son Mercer assistant 1955-9 but mostly on his own as bandleader-arranger-composer. Duke remarkably successful composer.

Jazz numbers featured by own band, sometimes by other bands. Many songs become standards. Collaborators included lyricists Irving Mills, Mitchell Parish, Paul Francis Webster, Eddie DeLange, John Latouche. Composed longer, more serious works, particularly in 50s and 60s. Seemed no end to his vast talent as band flourished in 70s. Band slated to continue after Duke's death under son Mercer's leadership. Most important compositions listed below; all recorded by Ellington.

POPULAR SONGS

1931—Mood Indigo
1932—It Don't Mean a Thing
1933—Sophisticated Lady
1935—Solitude
1936—In a Sentimental Mood
1937—Caravan
1938—I Let a Song Go Out of My Heart; If You Were in My Place; Prelude to a Kiss
1939—Something to Live For; I Never Felt This Way Before
1940—All Too Soon
1941—I Got It Bad
1942—Don't Get Around Much Anymore; Things Ain't What They Used to Be
1943—Do Nothin' Till You Hear from Me
1944—Don't You Know I Care?; I Didn't Know About You; I'm Beginning to See the Light
1945—Just a-Sittin' and a-Rockin'
1946—I'm Just a Lucky So and So; Afternoon Moon; It Shouldn't Happen to a Dream
1958—Satin Doll

SELECTED INSTRUMENTALS
(in alphabetical order)
Across the Track Blues
Awful Sad
Azure
Baby, When You Ain't There
Bakiff
Best Wishes
Birmingham Breakdown
Black and Tan Fantasy
Black Beauty
Blue Goose

Blue Harlem
Blue Light
Blue Ramble
Blue Reverie
Blue Serge
Blues with a Feelin', The
Bojangles
Bouncing Buoyancy
Boy Meets Horn
Braggin' in Brass
Buffet Flat
Bundle of Blues
Carnival in Caroline
Chatterbox
Chocolate Shake
C Jam Blues
Clarinet Lament
Conga Brava
Cotton Club Stomp
Cotton Tail
Country Gal
Creole Love Call
Creole Rhapsody
Crescendo in Blue
Daybreak Express
Delta Serenade
Dicty Glide, The
Diminuendo in Blue
Doin' the Voom Voom
Double Check Stomp
Drop Me Off in Harlem
Ducky Wucky
Duke Steps Out, The
Dusk
Dusk in the Desert
East St. Louis Toodle-oo
Echoes of Harlem
Echoes of the Jungle
Fancy Dan
Flaming Sword, The
Flaming Youth
Gal from Joe's, The
Giddybug Gallop, The
Grievin'
Gypsy without a Song, A
Happy-Go-Lucky Local
Harlem Air-Shaft
Harlem Speaks
Harlemania
Harmony in Harlem
High Life
I'm Checkin' Out—Goom'bye
In a Jam
In a Mellotone

I've Got to Be a Rug Cutter
Jack the Bear
Jazz Convulsions
Jeep Is Jumpin', The
Jubilee Stomp
Jump for Joy
Just Squeeze Me
Lament for a Lost Love
Lazy Rhapsody
Lightnin'
Lost in Meditation
Magenta Haze
Main Stem
Me and You
Merry-Go-Round
Misty Mornin'
Mooche, The
Moon Mist
Morning Glory
Mystery Song, The
Oh, Babe! Maybe Someday
Old King Dooji
Old Man Blues
Portrait of Bert Williams
Pyramid
Reminiscing in Tempo
Ring Dem Bells
Rockin' in Rhythm
Rude Interlude
Rumpus in Richmond
Saratoga Swing
Saturday Night Function
Scattin' at the Kit Kat
Scrounch
Sentimental Lady
Sepia Panorama
Serenade to Sweden
Sergeant Was Shy, The
Showboat Shuffle
Slippery Horn
Stevedore Stomp
Stevedore's Serenade
Subtle Lament
Sultry Serenade
Sump'n' 'Bout Rhythm
Swampy River
Swing Low
Three Cent Stomp
Tootin' Through the Roof
Transblucency
Trumpet in Spades
Warm Valley
Way Low
What Am I Here For?

EXTENDED WORKS

Black, Brown and Beige; Perfume Suite; New World a-Comin'; The Liberian Suite; The Tattooed Bride; Deep South Suite; Blutopia; Blue Belles of Harlem; Night Creature; Impressions of the Far East; Ad Lib on Nippon; Virgin Islands Suite; Suite Thursday; The Golden Broom and the Green Apple; Blue Mural; In the Beginning God; Such Sweet Thunder; The River; Good News for Modern Man

RECORDS

DUKE ELLINGTON

Ge 3342 Animal Crackers/Li'l Farina
Vo 1077 Immigration Blues / The Creeper
OK 8602 Diga Diga Doo/Doin' the New Low Down
OK 41013 Take It Easy/Jubilee Stomp
Vi 38007 Bandana Babies/I Must Have That Man
Vi 38036 Saturday Night Function/ High Life
Vi 38058 Saratoga Swing / Misty Mornin'
Br 3480 (theme) East St. Louis Toodle-oo/Birmingham Breakdown
Br 4110 Awful Sad/Louisiana
Br 4705 Jazz Convulsions/Jolly Wog
Br 6038 Rockin' in Rhythm/12th Street Rag
Br 6265 It Don't Mean a Thing/Rose Room
Br 6600 Sophisticated Lady/Stormy Weather
Br 7461 In a Sentimental Mood/ Showboat Shuffle
Br 7514 Truckin'/Accent on Youth
Br 8099 Braggin' in Brass/Carnival in Caroline
Br 8108 I Let a Song Go Out of My Heart/The Gal from Joe's
Br 8168 Pyramid/Rose of the Rio Grande
Br 8306 Boy Meets Horn/Old King Dooji
Vi 21137 Black and Tan Fantasy/Creole Love Call
Vi 22528 Three Little Words/Ring Dem Bells

Vi 22587 Mood Indigo/When a Black Man's Blue
Vi 24755 Solitude/Delta Serenade
Vi 26536 Jack the Bear/Morning Glory
Vi 26610 Cotton Tail/Never No Lament
Vi 26788 In a Mellotone/Rumpus in Richmond
Vi 26796 Warm Valley / Flaming Sword
Vi 27380 (theme) Take the "A" Train/ Sidewalks of New York
Vi 27531 I Got It Bad/Chocolate Shake
Vi 27740 Chelsea Bridge/What Good Would It Do?
Vi 20-1598 What Am I Here For?/I Don't Mind
Vi 20-1618 Don't You Know I Care?/ I'm Beginning to See the Light
Ma 123 Scattin' at the Kit Kat/The New Birmingham Breakdown
Ma 131 Caravan/Azure
Co 35214 The Sergeant Was Shy/Serenade to Sweden
Co 35310 Tootin' Through the Roof/ Grievin'
Co 38165 Air Conditioned Jungle/It's Monday Every Day
Co 39428 The Hawk Talks/Fancy Dan
Mus 484 Trumpet No End (Blue Skies)/It Shouldn't Happen to a Dream

LPs

DUKE ELLINGTON

Co C3L27 (3-LP set) The Ellington Era, Vol. 1 (1927-40 RIs)
Co CL-825 Masterpieces by Ellington
Vi LPV-506 Daybreak Express (Vi RIs)
Vi LPV-517 Jumpin' Punkins (Vi RIs)
Vi LPV-541 Johnny Come Lately (1942-5 Vi RIs)
Vi LPT-1004 Duke Ellington's Greatest (Vi RIs)
Vi LPM-1364 In a Mellotone (Vi RIs)
Vi LPM-3906 ... And His Mother Called Him Bill
Br BL-54007 Early Ellington (Br RIs))
Cam CAL-459 At the Cotton Club (RIs)
Cap T-679 Ellington Showcase

Reprise 6185 Concert in the Virgin Islands

Reprise 6234 Duke Ellington's Greatest Hits ("live" in concert)

Solid State SS-19000 (S) (2-LP set) Duke Ellington's 70th Birthday Concert (recorded live in England)

DUKE ELLINGTON-CHARLIE MINGUS-MAX ROACH

UA 14017 Money Jungle

DUKE ELLINGTON-JOHN COLTRANE

Impulse A-30

JOHNNY HODGES

Epic LN-3105 Hodge Podge (Vo RIs)

REX STEWART

"X"(10")LX-3001 (Bb RIs)

THE DUKE'S MEN

Epic EE22005 Barney Bigard/Rex Stewart/Johnny Hodges/Cootie Williams (1936-9 Vo RIs)

533. ELLINGTON, MERCER

t cm ar B

Born March 11, 1919, Washington, D.C.
Son of Duke Ellington, had career mostly on his own, away from father. Attended Columbia University, Juilliard and N.Y.U. Formed band in 1939. Joined father in 1941 to study and work at composing-arranging. Military service, World War II. Led band in late 40s. Worked briefly with Duke in 1950. Mercer Record Company in 1950-2. With Cootie Williams in 1954 as sideman-manager. Chief aide to father 1955-9. Led band at intervals in 60s and recorded with all-star personnel. Disc jockey on New York radio, 1962-5. Joined father's band in 1965 as sideman-manager, assumed leadership after Duke's death 1974. During career arranged for Charlie Barnet, Duke Ellington, Count Basie, Cootie Williams, others. Composer or co-composer of *Things Ain't What They Used to Be, The Girl in My Dreams Tries to Look Like You, Blue Serge, Moon Mist, John Hardy's Wife, Jumpin' Punkins.*

RECORDS
(all LPs)

MERCER ELLINGTON

Cor CRL-57225 Stepping into Swing Society

Cor CRL-57293 Colors in Rhythm

DUKE ELLINGTON

Co ML-4418

534. ELLIOTT, DON

mel t vb vo ar cm B

(DON ELLIOTT HELFMAN)

Born October 21, 1926, Somerville, N.J.
Modern musician of many talents. Started in local bands. Studied at Juilliard. Military service, World War II. Attended University of Miami awhile, studied arranging. In late 40s in vocal group Hi, Lo, Jack & the Dame, played clubs and theatres. Joined George Shearing combo on vibes in 1950, remained into late 1951. With Teddy Wilson and Terry Gibbs. With Benny Goodman briefly in 1952. In 1953 with Buddy Rich on mellophone; joined Gibbs again. For balance of 50s and 60s freelanced, led groups at intervals. During 60s concentrated on composing for movies and Broadway. Stage credits include A THURBER CARNIVAL (1960), HAPPIEST MAN ALIVE (1962), THE BEAST IN ME (1963).

RECORDS

GEORGE SHEARING

MGM 10956 I'll Be Around/Quintessence

MGM 10986 I Remember You/The Breeze and I

MGM 11282 Five O'clock Whistle/Simplicity

DON ELLIOTT

Sav 882 Oh! Look at Me Now/Mighty Like a Rose

Sav 883 Darn That Dream/Jeepers Creepers

LPs

DON ELLIOTT

Co CL-1724 Love Is a Necessary Evil

Vi LJM-1007 The Don Elliott Quintet

Design DLP-69 Music of the Sensational Sixties

ABC-Para 142 At the Modern Jazz Room

Sav(10")9003

DON ELLIOTT-RUSTY DEDRICK

Riv 12-218 Counterpoint for Six Valves

DON ELLIOTT-CAL TJADER

Sav MG-12054 Vib-rations

GEORGE SHEARING
MGM(10″)E-90
TERRY GIBBS
Br 54018
PAUL DESMOND-DON ELLIOTT
Fan 3-235
MOREY FELD
Kapp KL-1007 Jazz Goes to Broadway
RUBY BRAFF
Stereocraft RCS-507 You're Getting to Be a Habit with Me
LOUIS BELLSON
Verve MGV-8137 Skin Deep
JOE PUMA
Beth(10″)BCP-1012
SONNY STITT
Roost(10″)415
(original Broadway cast)
Co KOL-5500 A THURBER CARNIVAL

535. ELLIOTT, JACK　　　　lyr ar vo

Born May 7, 1914, Gowanda, N.Y.

Lyricist active mostly in movies. Early in career sang in night clubs, theatres, vaudeville, radio. Wrote special material for other acts as well as his own. Began songwriting in 1940, for movies in 1943. Wrote or arranged background scores for over 100 movies, also conducted on soundtracks. Later some writing for TV. Collaborators included composers Lew Quadling, Harold Spina, Victor Young.

SONGS

1941—Do You Care?; I Think of You
1948—You're a Character, Dear; In the Wee Small Hours of the Morning
1949—I Don't Wanna Be Kissed by Anyone but You
1950—Sam's Song; Timeless; Waitin' at the Station; It's So Nice to Have a Man Around the House; Be Mine; Our Very Own; Driftin' Down the Dreamy Ol' Ohio
1952—A Weaver of Dreams; Don't Tempt Me; Tears; Let Me Kiss Your Tears Away; Funny Melody; If They Ask Me
1954—Putty in Your Hands; Summer Vacation

Other songs: *Ivory Rag*; *The Pansy*; *Sugar Coated Lies*; *Drop Me a Line*; *Toot Whistle Plunk and Boom*; *Mornin' on the Farm*; *Coffee in the Morning*

536. ELLIS, ANITA　　　　vo

Born in Montreal, Canada

Excellent singer, known for dubbing for stars in movies. At 16 singer on Los Angeles radio. Later played Hollywood clubs. Attended Cincinnati School of Music, sang on Cincinnati radio. Also attended U.C.L.A. Own radio show in Hollywood in early 40s, Songs for Overseas; on Tommy Riggs show and others. In 1944 on Andy Russell radio show, then on Red Skelton show two years, one year on Jack Carson show. Became behind-the-scenes singing star in movies when singing dubbed for non-singing actresses, particularly for Rita Hayworth in movies GILDA (1946), DOWN TO EARTH (1947), THE LADY FROM SHANGHAI (1948). Dubbed for Vera-Ellen in THREE LITTLE WORDS (1950) and THE BELLE OF NEW YORK (1952). Famous rendition of *Put the Blame on Mame* in GILDA, dubbed for Rita Hayworth. Also played supper clubs in New York and all over U.S.

RECORDS

ANITA ELLIS
Mer 3068 How Lucky You Are/They Can't Take That Away from Me
Mer 3072 Golden Earrings/Love for Love
Mer 5530 I'm Yours/Ask Anyone Who Knows
MGM 30519 Naughty but Nice/Bride's Wedding Day Song

LPs

ANITA ELLIS
Epic LN-3280 I Wonder What Became of Me
Epic LN-3419 Hims
(movie soundtrack)
Metro 615 THREE LITTLE WORDS

537. ELLIS, HERB　　　　g ar cm B

Born August 4, 1921, McKinney, Texas

Good rhythm guitarist and tasteful soloist in modern vein. Excellent at providing background for jazz soloists and singers. Attended North Texas State College. In 1944 with Glen Gray on first big job. With Jimmy Dorsey early 1945-early 1947. For several years member of Soft Winds group, then freelance. With Oscar Peterson 1953-8, attained prominence.

Toured with Peterson trio in Jazz at the Philharmonic shows. Accompanied singers Ella Fitzgerald and Julie London. In 60s active in TV bands: on Steve Allen show in early 60s, Joey Bishop show in late 60s, Merv Griffin show in 70s.

RECORDS

JIMMY DORSEY
De 18777 J.D.'s Boogie Woogie
BEN WEBSTER
Norg 103 That's All/Jive at Six
ROY ELDRIDGE
Clef 89110 Willow Weep for Me/ Somebody Loves Me
Clef 89123 I Can't Get Started/When Your Lover Has Gone
SOFT WINDS
Maj 1180 I Told Ya I Loved Ya/ They're Mine, They're Mine
Maj 1181 To Be Continued/That's My Kind of Girl
Maj 1206 P.S., I Love You/Two Loves Have I

LPs

HERB ELLIS
Norg MGN-1081 Ellis in Wonderland
Epic LA-16034 The Midnight Roll
Verve MGV-8252 Nothing but the Blues
HERB ELLIS-CHARLIE BYRD
Co CL-2330 Guitar/Guitar
HERB ELLIS-STUFF SMITH
Epic BA-17039 Together!
BEN WEBSTER
Norg MGN-1001 The Consummate Artistry of Ben Webster
BLOSSOM DEARIE
Verve MGV-2037
TERRY GIBBS
Verve MGV-2136 Music from Cole Porter's CAN-CAN
FLIP PHILLIPS
Clef MGC-637 The Flip Phillips Quintet
RAY BROWN
Verve MGV-8290 This Is Ray Brown
OSCAR PETERSON
Clef MGC-623
Clef MGC-624
Clef MGC-625

538. ELLIS, SEGER   vo p cm lyr B
Born July 4, 1904, Houston, Texas
Singer of 20s and 30s; used outstanding

musicians in bands backing him. Attended University of Virginia. Singer-pianist in vaudeville and night clubs. Soft voice on many records 1925-31; sessions sometimes included jazzmen Louis Armstrong, Joe Venuti, Eddie Lang, Tommy and Jimmy Dorsey, Mannie Klein. Own radio series at intervals. In later 30s led good swing band Called Seger Ellis & His Choir of Brass; featured as many as eight brass, as few as one reed. Wife, Irene Taylor, excellent vocalist, worked with band in late 30s and early 40s. Later Ellis led combo awhile. Military service, World War II. In later years composer or lyricist. Songs: *Little Jack Frost Get Lost*; *My Beloved Is Rugged*; *Eleven Sixty P.M.*; *After You*; *What You Don't Know Won't Hurt You*; *You're All I Want for Christmas*; *Christmas Will Be Here*; *You Don't Have to Be a Santa Claus*; *It Hurts Me More Than It Hurts You*; *No, Baby, Nobody but You*; *I Need You Like I Need a Hole in the Head*; *Unless You're Free*; *Goin' Steady Anniversary*; *I'm Never the Lover*; *I Wish I Had My Old Time Sweetheart Back Again*; *You Be You*; *It's All Over but the Crying*; *If You've Got Someplace to Go*. Also wrote *Oilers*, official song of Houston Oilers pro football team. Compositions early in career: *Prairie Blues* and *Sentimental Blues*.

RECORDS

BENNY MEROFF
OK 40967 Lonely Melody
FRED RICH
Co 1299-D I'm Walkin' on Air
SOUTHERN MELODY ARTISTS
OK 41129 My Window of Dreams
ROYAL MUSIC MAKERS
OK 41020 Auf Wiedersehen/I Can't Do without You
JIMMY DORSEY
De 782 It's No Fun/Moonrise on the Lowlands
SEGER ELLIS
Vi 19755 Prairie Blues/Sentimental Blues (piano)
OK 41061 Sweet Sue/Beloved
OK 41077 I Can't Give You Anything but Love/Don't Keep Me in the Dark, Bright Eyes
OK 41221 Coquette/Louise
OK 41225 S'posin'/To Be in Love

OK 41274 Singin' in the Rain/Your Mother and Mine
OK 41291 Ain't Misbehavin'/There Was Nothing Else to Do
OK 41321 I'm a Dreamer/If I Had a Talking Picture of You
OK 41349 A Little Kiss Each Morning/Have a Little Faith in Me
OK 41413 The Moon Is Low/Montana Call
OK 41467 Body and Soul/Sweet Jennie Lee
Co 2362-D Cheerful Little Earful/I Miss a Little Miss
Br 6022 It's a Lonesome Old Town/ My Love for You
Br 6076 Heartaches/One Little Raindrop
Br 6135 Nevertheless/As Long As You're There
De 1275 Shivery Stomp/Three Little Words
De 1350 Bee's Knees/Sometimes I'm Happy
Br 8261 I Wish I Had You/What Do You Know About Love?
Br 8290 A Room with a View/Your Eyes Are Bigger Than Your Heart
Br 8321 We Speak of You Often/The Moon Is a Silver Dollar
OK 5721 Happy Travelin'/Cuddle Up a Little Closer
OK 5966 No Jug, No Jazz/When It's Sleepy Time Down South

539. ELMAN, ZIGGY   t cm B
(HARRY FINKELMAN)

Born May 26, 1914, Philadelphia, Pa.
Died June 26, 1968, Van Nuys, Calif.

Leading trumpet star of late 30s and 40s; powerful swing style. Attained fame with solo on Benny Goodman band recording of Elman composition *And the Angels Sing*. Grew up in Atlantic City. As youngster learned trombone and reeds in addition to trumpet; at 13 played clubs. Local job early in career; most important at Steel Pier in early and mid-30s. Joined Benny Goodman in fall of 1936. When trumpet star Harry James left band at end of 1938, Elman became leading trumpet soloist. Sometimes incorporated Jewish fralich style in solos. Wrote fralich show-case for himself, 1939's big hit *And the Angels Sing* (originally *Fralich in Swing*). In 1939 a series of recordings released under Elman's name: tasteful swing, tightly knit arrangements. Elman featured with four-man sax section and rhythm section, mostly from Goodman band. Series included his later showcase number *You're Mine, You*. Left Goodman July 1940, joined Tommy Dorsey August. Trumpet featured. Remained till military service, 1943. Rejoined Dorsey 1946-7 save for interval leading own band early 1947. In late 40s settled on west coast, led own band at times, did studio work and freelancing. In early 50s TV work. Rejoined Goodman for tour 1953, fronted band when Goodman took sick. Seen in 1956 movie THE BENNY GOODMAN STORY but solo on *And the Angels Sing* played by Mannie Klein on soundtrack. Active through 50s into 60s, until illness curtailed playing. Bought music store. Three other jazz compositions by Elman: *Forgive My Heart, Zaggin' with Zig, Who'll Buy My Bublitchki?*.

RECORDS
BENNY GOODMAN
Vi 25467 Bugle Call Rag
Vi 25492 Swing Low, Sweet Chariot/ When You and I Were Young, Maggie
Vi 25497 Jam Session
Vi 25751 Bei Mir Bist du Schon (pt. 2)
Vi 25840 Feelin' High and Happy
Vi 26170 And the Angels Sing/Sent for You Yesterday
Vi 26187 I'll Always Be in Love with You
Vi 26211 Show Your Linen, Miss Richardson
Vi 26230 The Siren's Song
Vi 26263 Who'll Buy My Bublitchki?
Co 35210 There'll Be Some Changes Made
Co 35319 Honeysuckle Rose
Co 35356 Zaggin' with Zig
Co 35497 Crazy Rhythm / Mister Meadowlark
Co 35527 The Hour of Parting/Cocoanut Grove
TOMMY DORSEY
Vi 27233 Swanee River

Vi 27249 Swing High/Swing Time Up in Harlem
Vi 27876 Moonlight on the Ganges
Vi 27887 Well, Git It!
Vi 27962 Blue Blazes
Vi 36396 Deep River
Vi 36399 For You/Swing Low, Sweet Chariot

LIONEL HAMPTON
Vi 25699 Judy/The Object of My Affection
Vi 26362 Ain'tcha Comin' Home
Vi 26423 Gin for Christmas
Vi 26447 I've Found a New Baby/Four or Five Times
Vi 26595 Flying Home/Save It Pretty Mama

MILDRED BAILEY
Vo 3367 For Sentimental Reasons/It's Love I'm After
Vo 3378 More Than You Know/'Long About Midnight

TOOTS MONDELLO
Vs 8110 Sweet Lorraine/Beyond the Moon
Vs 8118 St. Louis Gal/Louisiana

METRONOME ALL STAR BAND
Co 35389 King Porter Stomp
Vi 27314 One O'clock Jump/Bugle Call Rag

ZIGGY ELMAN
Bb 10103 Fralich in Swing (And the Angels Sing)/Bublitchki
Bb 10316 You're Mine, You/Zaggin' with Zig
Bb 10342 Let's Fall in Love/I'll Never Be the Same
Bb 10413 You Took Advantage of Me/I'm Yours
Bb 10563 Tootin' My Baby Back Home/What Used to Was Used to Was
Bb 10741 Forgive My Heart/Love Is the Sweetest Thing
MGM 10047 And the Angels Sing/Three Little Words
MGM 10332 How High the Moon/The Night Is Young and You're So Beautiful
MGM 10902 I'd Climb the Highest Mountain
MGM 11089 Sunny Disposish/Birth of the Blues

MGM 11197 All I Do Is Dream of You/With a Song in My Heart

LPs

ZIGGY ELMAN
MGM E-3389 Sentimental Trumpet
MGM(10")E-163
MGM(10")E-535
Swing Era LP-1015 (RIs)

BENNY GOODMAN
Vi LPT-1005 (Vi RIs)
Co SL-180 (2-LP set) 1937/38 Jazz Concert No. 2 (airchecks)
MGM 3E9 (3-LP set) Treasure Chest Performance Recordings 1937-1938

LIONEL HAMPTON
Cam CAL-402 Jivin' the Vibes (Vi RIs)
Vi LJM-1000 (Vi RIs)

TOMMY DORSEY
Vi LPM-1433 Tribute to Dorsey, Vol. 2 (Vi RIs)
Vi LPM-6003

JESS STACY
Atl 1225 Tribute to Benny Goodman

PAUL WESTON
Co CL-693 Mood for 12
Co CL-879 Solo Mood
Cap T1154 Music for Dreaming

540. ENEVOLDSEN, BOB

v-tb cl ts b ar cm

Born January 11, 1920, Billings, Montana

Versatile modern musician best known for work on valve trombone. Attended University of Montana. Military service, World War II. Played clarinet in Utah Symphony in late 40s. Went to Los Angeles, became known in early 50s as versatile section man and capable soloist. Freelanced on club jobs and recording sessions. In 60s arranged for TV shows, commercials, bands and singers. Played in band on Steve Allen TV show in early 60s. Active into 70s.

RECORDS
(all LPs)

BOB ENEVOLDSEN
Noc(10")6
Lib LJH-6008 Smorgasbord
Tampa TP-14 Reflections in Jazz

LENNIE NIEHAUS
  Contemp C-3503 Vol. 3: The Octet,
  No. 2
  Contemp C-3540 Zounds! The Lennie
  Niehaus Octet!
  Contemp(10″)C-2517 Vol. 2: The Oc-
  tet
HARRY BABASIN
  Noc(10″)3
SHORTY ROGERS
  Vi LPH-1561 Portrait of Shorty
LEONARD FEATHER'S STARS
  MGM E-3390 West Coast vs. East
  Coast
JIMMY GUIFFRE
  Cap(10″)H-549
JIMMY COOK
  Cam CAL-670 The Best New Band of
  the Year
RUSS GARCIA-MARTY PAICH
  Beth 6039 Jazz Music for the Birds and
  the Hepcats
GERRY MULLIGAN
  Cap(10″)H-439
SHELLY MANNE
  Contemp(10″)C-2503
BOBBY TROUP
  Cap(10″)H-484
HOWARD RUMSEY
  Contemp(10″)C-2515 Lighthouse All
  Stars, Vol. 5
(miscellaneous artists)
  WB 1272 (S) The Trombones,Inc.
  Interlude ST-1009 (S) Revel Without a
  Pause

541. ENGLANDER, LUDWIG   cm B
Born 1859 in Austria
Died September 13, 1914

Composer of scores for Broadway musicals; main period 1900-14. Best THE
STROLLERS (1901). Led small orchestras in
Vienna early in career. Came to U.S. in
1880s. First operetta THE PRINCESS CON-
SORT unsuccessful. In 1894 wrote music
for THE PASSING SHOW, forerunner of
revue-type shows of later years. Songs
important within context of shows but
attained little popularity.

BROADWAY MUSICALS
(wrote music)
1894—THE PASSING SHOW
1895—A DAUGHTER OF THE REVOLUTION
1899—THE ROUNDERS; IN GAY PAREE
1900—BELLE OF BOHEMIA; THE CADET
  GIRL; THE CASINO GIRL; THE MONKS
  OF MALABAR
1901—THE NEW YORKERS; THE STROLLERS
1902—SALLY IN OUR ALLEY
1903—THE JEWEL OF ASIA; THE OFFICE
  BOY
1904—A MADCAP PRINCESS; THE TWO
  ROSES
1905—THE WHITE CAT
1906—THE RICH MR. HOGGENHEIMER
1907—THE GAY WHITE WAY
1908—MISS INNOCENCE
1914—MADAME MOSELLE (unsuccessful
  show)

542. ENNIS, SKINNAY   d t vo B
(ROBERT ENNIS)
Born August 13, 1909, Salisbury, N.C.
Died June 3, 1963, Beverly Hills, Calif.;
choked to death on bone while dining
in restaurant

Well-known singer with Hal Kemp in 30s,
later bandleader. Noted for intimate,
breathless singing style. Enrolled at University of North Carolina about 1927,
worked there with Kemp band as drum-
mer-singer, continued professionally with
band in late 20s, playing in Europe several months in 1930. Featured vocalist,
most famous member of band because of
unique singing. Most popular numbers
with Kemp *Got a Date with an Angel,
Lamplight, A Heart of Stone.* Left Kemp
early 1938. In movie COLLEGE SWING.
Became bandleader on west coast, taking
over Gil Evans band. Evans remained as
arranger until 1941; Claude Thornhill
pianist-arranger-musical director in early
years. Theme song *Got a Date with an
Angel.* Band promptly landed prestige job
on Bob Hope radio show 1938. Ennis
featured on a vocal on each show, also
did comedy. On show till 1943, simultaneously played top hotels in California.
Ennis movies SLEEPY TIME GAL and SWING
IT, SOLDIER (1942), FOLLOW THE BAND
(1943), RADIO STARS ON PARADE (1945).
Military service 1943-4, led service band.
Upon release late 1944 rejoined Hope
show, remained till late 1946. On Abbott
& Costello show late 1946-7. Played ho-

tels, ballrooms and theatres in late 40s and 50s. In late 50s began long run at Statler-Hilton Hotel in Los Angeles.

RECORDS

CAROLINA CLUB ORCHESTRA (Hal Kemp)
Me 12177 I Found a Million Dollar Baby/Sing a Little Jingle

HAL KEMP
Br 3937 Lovable
Br 4212 My Lucky Star/You Wouldn't Fool Me, Would You?
Br 6087 I Had to Lose You/I'm Mad About You
Br 6616 Shadows on the Swanee/It Might Have Been a Diff'rent Story
Br 6974 Strange
Br 7317 Flirtation Walk/Hands Across the Table
Br 7319 Got a Date with an Angel
Br 7437 In the Middle of a Kiss
Br 7745 I've Got You Under My Skin
Br 7783 One Never Knows, Does One?
Br 7958 Got a Date with an Angel/A Heart of Stone
Vi 25598 Stop! You're Breaking My Heart
Vi 25651 Got a Date with an Angel/ Lamplight

SKINNAY ENNIS
Vi 26047 Garden of the Moon/Girl Friend of the Whirling Dervish
Vi 26094 Deep in a Dream/Gardenias
Vi 26207 Strange Enchantment/That Sentimental Sandwich
Vi 26212 Wishing/Hooray for Spinach
Vi 27586 I Don't Want to Set the World on Fire/Don't Let Julia Fool Ya
Vi 27747 I Found You in the Rain/ You Are the Lyric
ARA 110 Sleigh Ride in July/Jumpin' Jiminy
Si 15032 Remember Me?/The Iggedy Song
Si 15033 (theme) Got a Date with an Angel/I Don't Know Why
Si 15056 Oh, But I Do/So Would I

LPs

SKINNAY ENNIS
MGM E-3531 Got a Date with an Angel
Philips 200002 Salutes Hal Kemp

HAL KEMP
Vi(10″)LPT-3016 This Is Hal Kemp (ViRIs)

543. ERICSON, ROLF   t fl-h B

Born August 29, 1922, Stockholm, Sweden

Swedish modern trumpet star who played many years in U.S. Relaxed, tasteful style, good tone, inventive modern patterns. Played with Swedish modern jazzmen in mid-40s; to U.S. in 1947. Briefly with Benny Carter, Dick Mulliner, Art Mooney, Roy Stevens, others. With Charlie Barnet most of 1949. In 1950 with Charlie Ventura, Elliot Lawrence and Benny Goodman briefly, then several months with Woody Herman. Returned to Sweden in late 1950. In early 50s U.S. jazz fans became aware of top Swedish jazzmen when LPs released here. Ericson star soloist on many. In late 1952 back to U.S., in 1953 with Charlie Spivak and Howard Rumsey. With Stan Kenton in 1954, Les Brown 1955-6. To Sweden later in 1956; U.S. stars in his combo. In later 50s worked on west coast with Harry James, Les Brown, Howard Rumsey. With Stan Kenton again in 1959. In 60s with Charles Mingus, Rod Levitt, Duke Ellington. Continued freelancing on west coast.

RECORDS

SWINGIN' SWEDES
BN 1605 Pick Yourself Up/Summertime

LARS GULLIN
Gazell(Sw) 2018 All God's Chillun/ Danny-O

EXPRESSENS ELITORKESTER
Musica(Sw) 9204 Stompin' at the Savoy/How High the Moon
Musica(Sw) 9215 Laura/Nice Work If You Can Get It

HOWARD RUMSEY
Contemp 359 Witch Doctor/Mambo Los Feliz

ROLF ERICSON
Artist(Sw) 3050 Lullaby in Rhythm/ The Nearness of You
Artist(Sw) 3073 The Way You Look Tonight/The World Is Waiting for the Sunrise

Dis 1731 Strike Up the Band/The Nearness of You

Dis 1732 Perdido/Miles Away

LPs

ROLF ERICSON

Dis(10")DL-2008 Swedish Pastry

EmArcy MG-36106 And His American All-Stars

SWEDISH ALL-STARS

Pres(10")PRLP-119 New Sounds from Sweden, Vol. 1

ARNE DOMNERUS

Vi(10")LPT-3032 Around the World in Jazz—Sweden

HOWARD RUMSEY

Contemp(10")C-2506 Lighthouse All-Stars, Vol.3

ROD LEVITT

Vi LPM-3372 The Man and His Music

STAN KENTON

Cap TBO-1327 (2-LP set) Road Show

HAROLD LAND

Contemp C-3550 Harold in the Land of Jazz

544. ERROL, LEON   vo

Born July 3, 1881, Sydney, Australia
Died October 12, 1951 in U.S.

Excellent comedian and rubber-legged dancer featured in Broadway musicals and movies. On rare occasions did novelty singing. Played nervous, henpecked husbands. Bald, known for frantic gestures and eccentric slipping and sliding. Popular performer, sure laugh-getter. Began in vaudeville 1910, worked up to good roles in Broadway shows. In musicals A WINSOME WIDOW (1912), ZIEG-FELD FOLLIES OF 1911-1912-1913-1914-1915, THE CENTURY GIRL (1916), HITCHY-KOO and DANCE AND GROW THIN (1917), HITCHY-KOO OF 1918, SALLY and ZIEG-FELD'S MIDNIGHT FROLIC (1921), LOUIS THE 14TH (1925), YOURS TRULY (1927), FIORETTA (1929). In early sound movies 1930, went on to appear in over 60 until death. Many comedy shorts. Most notable movie musicals WE'RE NOT DRESSING (1934), CORONADO (1935), THE GREAT ZIEGFELD (1936), MAKE A WISH (1937), DANCING CO-ED (1939), MOONLIGHT IN HAWAII (1941), FOLLOW THE BAND (1943),

HIGHER AND HIGHER (1944). During 40s featured in MEXICAN SPITFIRE movie series starring Lupe Velez.

RECORDS
(LP)

(miscellaneous artists; one song with Marilyn Miller)

Pelican 102 Stars of the Ziegfeld Follies (RIs)

545. ERWIN, PEE WEE   t cm lyr B
(GEORGE ERWIN)

Born May 30, 1913, Falls City, Neb.

Good jazz trumpet man in dixieland and swing style, strongly influenced by Bunny Berigan. Grew up in Kansas City. As youngster toured in vaudeville, played in local bands. To New York in 1931. 1931-4 with Joe Haymes, Isham Jones, Freddy Martin. With Benny Goodman late 1934 to mid-1935, including work on Let's Dance radio show. With Ray Noble's first U.S. band 1935-6. With Goodman several months in 1936, including Elgin broadcasts. Worked awhile on west coast. Joined Tommy Dorsey early 1937, replacing Bunny Berigan; remained till mid-1939, with intervals away. With Raymond Scott Quintet and Johnny Green, then own band in early 40s. With Bob Allen awhile in 1942. Active in radio studio work several years. In 1949 and through most of 50s based in New York, played mostly at Nick's. Became prominent among dixieland jazzmen, played with top groups. With Tony Parenti in later 50s. In 60s active on TV; shows included Garry Moore, Carol Burnett, Jackie Gleason. In late 60s teamed with Chris Griffin to form the Griffin-Erwin School of Music in Teaneck, N.J. Composer-lyricist of several jazz numbers including *Piano Man, Creole Rag, Music Southern Style, Jazz Frappe, Stay On the Train*. Featured with Warren Covington-Tommy Dorsey band on 1974 British tour.

RECORDS

BENNY GOODMAN

Co 3033-D Down Home Rag

TOMMY DORSEY

Vi 25568 Twilight in Turkey/The

Milkmen's Matinee (both CLAM-
BAKE SEVEN)
Vi 25693 Who?/The Dipsy Doodle
Vi 25750 Little White Lies/Just a Sim-
ple Melody
Vi 25815 Yearning
Vi 26023 Chinatown, My Chinatown/
The Sheik of Araby (both CLAM-
BAKE SEVEN)
Vi 36207(12") Stop, Look and Listen/
Beale Street Blues
RAY NOBLE
Vi 25223 Dinah
SIX BLUE CHIPS
De 740 Steel Roof/Cheatin' Cheech
SANDY WILLIAMS
HRS 1022 Tea for Me/Sandy's Blues
HRS 1023 Sam-Pan/Frost on the
Moon
HRS 1029 Gee, Baby, Ain't I Good to
You
PEE WEE ERWIN
King 15073 Eccentric/Music Southern
Style
King 15074 Shake It and Break It/
Mashuga Over You
King 15075 When the Saints Go
Marching In/Tin Roof Blues

LPs

PEE WEE ERWIN
Br BL-54011 The Land of Dixie
Urania 1202 Accent on Dixieland
UA 3071 Down by the Riverside
Jazztone J-1237 New York Dixieland
RAY NOBLE
Vi(10")LPT-3015 (Vi RIs)
SAMMY SPEAR
Lon LA-38001 Plays a Little Traveling
Music
BENNY GOODMAN
Sunbeam SB 101-2-3 Thesaurus
Rhythm Makers Orchestra (6/6/35
ET RIs)
HENRY JEROME
De DL-4307 Strings in Dixieland
TOMMY REYNOLDS
King 395-510 Jazz for Happy Feet
BOBBY BYRNE (one side)
GA 33-310 Dixieland Jazz
ROYAL GARDEN RAJAHS (one side)
GA 33-313 Dixieland Jazz
(miscellaneous artists)

Design DLP-38 Golden Era of Dixieland Jazz

546. ETTING, RUTH   vo cm lyr
*Born November 23, c. 1903, David City,
Neb.*

Singing star of 20s and 30s. Active in
night clubs, theatre, radio and records.
Leading song stylist of era, able on sentimental ballads and rhythm tunes. At 17
got job in Chicago night club working on
costumes. Later landed spot in chorus line
at another club. Had to work hard at
dancing but was a natural as a singer.
Soon featured singer at various clubs. In
1920 met Martin (Moe the Gimp) Snyder,
who helped her get better bookings, married her in 1922. She sang on early radio
in Chicago, eventually winning title of
"Chicago's Sweetheart." Snyder continued battling to further her career. She
played top clubs and theatres. Began for
Columbia Records in mid-20s.

In 1927 big break starring on Broadway
in ZIEGFELD FOLLIES OF 1927. Other shows
followed: WHOOPEE (1928), SIMPLE SIMON
(1930), ZIEGFELD FOLLIES OF 1931. In 1930
in short-lived NINE-FIFTEEN REVUE. In early 30s guest star on many radio shows.
Radio appearances and her performance
in 1931 FOLLIES sparked revival of old
song *Shine On Harvest Moon*. On 1932
Chesterfield radio show. Own show for
Oldsmobile in 1934 and Kellogg College
Prom in 1935. In movies ROMAN SCAN-
DALS (1933), GIFT OF GAB and HIPS HIPS
HOORAY (1934). In 1936 starred on London stage. By later 30s career waned but
worked at intervals. In late 40s tried
comeback in clubs and on radio. New
York sustaining radio show 1947-8. In
earlier years composer or lyricist of pop-
ular songs *Wistful and Blue* (1927), *When
You're with Somebody Else* (1928), *Maybe
—Who Knows?* (1929). Miss Etting hon-
ored with 1955 movie on her life, LOVE ME
OR LEAVE ME. Doris Day outstanding in
Etting role, sang many songs associated
with Etting career. James Cagney played
Snyder. Movie theme: turbulent Etting-
Snyder relationship.

RECORDS

RUTH ETTING

Co 644-D Lonesome and Sorry/But I Do—You Know I Do

Co 865-D 'Deed I Do/There Ain't No Maybe in My Baby's Eyes

Co 908-D Sam, the Old Accordion Man/It All Depends on You

Co 995-D My Man/After You've Gone

Co 1288-D When You're with Somebody Else/Back in Your Own Backyard

Co 1680-D Love Me or Leave Me/I'm Bringing a Red, Red Rose

Co 1762-D Button Up Your Overcoat/Mean to Me

Co 1958-D Ain't Misbehavin'/At Twilight

Co 2146-D Ten Cents a Dance/Funny, Dear, What Love Can Do

Co 2172-D Let Me Sing and I'm Happy/A Cottage for Sale

Co 2216-D Dancing with Tears in My Eyes/I Never Dreamt

Co 2300-D Body and Soul/If I Could Be with You

Co 2529-D Guilty/Now That You're Gone

Co 3014-D March Winds and April Showers/Things Might Have Been So Diff'rent

Co 3085-D Shine On Harvest Moon/ Ten Cents a Dance

Pe 12739 Just One More Chance/Have You Forgotten?

Pe 12754 Me/Love Letters in the Sand

Ba 32398 Can't We Talk It Over?/ Love, You Funny Thing

Ba 32499 It Was So Beautiful/I'll Never Be the Same

Br 6697 Build a Little Home/No More Love

Br 6719 Everything I Have Is Yours/ Dancing in the Moonlight

Br 6761 Keep Romance Alive/Tired of It All

Br 6769 This Little Piggie/Smoke Gets in Your Eyes

Br 7646 Lost/It's Been So Long

De 1084 There's Something in the Air/In the Chapel in the Moonlight

De 1107 Goodnight My Love/May I Have the Next Romance with You?

LPs

RUTH ETTING

Co ML-5050 The Original Recordings of Ruth Etting (Co RIs)

Biograph C-11 "Hello, Baby" (1926-31 Co RIs)

(miscellaneous artists)

Co C3L35 (3-LP set) The Original Sound of the 20s

547. EVANS, DALE   vo p cm lyr

Born October 1912, Uvalde, Texas

Excellent singer of radio, movies and TV, rose to greatest prominence after marrying cowboy film star Roy Rogers. Co-starred with Rogers in all media, including rodeos and special events. Attended high school in Osceola, Ark. Business college training, also studied voice, piano and dancing. Early in career sang on radio in Memphis, Dallas, Louisville, also worked with Anson Weeks and Herman Waldman bands. Worked in Chicago clubs in 1940, joined CBS radio there. Sang with Caesar Petrillo orchestra on radio shows of early 40s. Collaborated with pianist-husband (before Rogers) Dale Butts on minor songs in that period. In 1943 sang with Ray Noble on California radio. Sang on Jack Carson radio show 1944. Began movie career in early 40s, sang and acted mostly in westerns. By early 1945 had appeared in nine Roy Rogers movies. Made over 40 movies during career. In mid-40s on Jimmy Durante-Garry Moore radio show, also on Saturday Night Roundup with Roy Rogers. Married Rogers in 1947. Rogers-Evans team top-rated western series on TV in early 50s. Later TV specials, guest appearances, own show again in 1962. Active through 60s into 70s, popular pair. Generous in charity work, adopted children, received citations for humanitarian efforts. Dale wrote articles and book, *Angel Unaware*, about her retarded child Robin. Composer or lyricist of songs *Will You Marry Me, Mr. Laramie?*; *Aha, San Antone*; *Down the Trail to San Antone*; *Lo Dee Lo Di; T for Texas; Buckeye Cowboy; I'm Gonna Lock You Out-a My Heart, No Bed of Roses; I Wish I Had Never Met Sunshine; The Bible Tells Me So; Happy Trails.* Last song often theme of team.

RECORDS

ABE LYMAN
Bb 10887 Help Me

DALE EVANS
Maj 11025 Under a Texas Moon/His Hat Cost More Than Mine

LPs

DALE EVANS
Cap T-399 Get to Know the Lord

ROY RODGERS-DALE EVANS
Vi LPM-1439 Sweet Hour of Prayer

Other books: *Christmas Is Always; Dearest Debbie; Cool It or Lose It!; Salute to Sandy; The Woman at the Well; Time Out, Ladies!; My Spiritual Diary; To My Son; No Two Ways About It!; Dale.*

548. EVANS, DOC   c ar B
(PAUL WESLEY EVANS)

Born June 20, 1907, Spring Valley, Minn.

Dixieland cornet star and bandleader, active mostly in Minneapolis area. Excellent ensemble horn, solo style in Beiderbecke-Nichols tradition, very creative. Learned several instruments as youngster but concentrated on cornet. Attended Carleton College. Began playing in Minneapolis-St. Paul area in early 30s, also did arranging. Led dixieland band mostly, but out of music at intervals. Stayed in Minnesota until mid-40s. In 1946-8 well received in Chicago and New York. In 1949 with Miff Mole in Chicago; 1950 played in Los Angeles. In 50s and 60s based again in Minneapolis. Records popular with dixieland fans. Played clubs, concerts, radio, TV. In 60s and 70s recorded for Audiophile Records, used pianist Knocky Parker frequently.

RECORDS

DOC EVANS
Disc 6070 Original Dixieland One-Step/Barnyard Blues
Disc 6073 Bugle Call Rag/Tin Roof Blues
Disc 6074 That's a-Plenty/That Da Da Strain
Disc 6075 Panama Rag/Farewell Blues
AFRS 102 High Society/That Eccentric Rag

Dublin's 1 Lulu's Back in Town/One Sweet Letter
Dublin's 2 S'posin'/Walkin' My Baby Back Home
Dublin's 3 Parker House Roll/Hindustan
Dublin's 4 Doc's Ology/I Can't Believe That You're in Love with Me
Joco 105 Blues Doctor/Doctor Jazz
Joco 107 Milenberg Joys/Memphis Blues
Joco 108 Walkin' the Dog/Ostrich Walk
Joco 111 Sidewalk Blues/Buddy Bolden Blues
Joco 113 Beale Street Blues/Weary Blues
Joco 117 Singin' the Blues/When It's Sleepy Time Down South

LPs

DOC EVANS
Para(10")106 Doc Evans' Jazzmen (Dublin's RIs)
Audiophile AP-31 Cornet Artistry
Audiophile AP-33 Dixieland Classics
Audiophile AP-34 Dixieland Classics
Audiophile AP-44 Dixieland Classics
Audiophile AP-50 Classics of the 20s
Audiophile AP-56 Muskrat Ramble
Audiophile AP-57 The Sweetest Since Gabriel
Audiophile AP-63 Spirituals and Blues
Audiophile AP-68 Reminiscing in Dixieland

TURK MURPHY
Co CL-793 New Orleans Jazz Festival (miscellaneous artists)
Audiophile 68 Reminiscing in Dixieland, Vol. 1
Audiophile 69 Reminiscing in Dixieland, Vol. 2

549. EVANS, GEORGE   vo cm
(nicknamed HONEY BOY)

Leading comedian around turn of century. Starred in vaudeville and minstrel shows. Burnt-cork minstrel with great comic routine, starred in Lew Dockstader's Minstrels among others. In 1894 composed popular song *I'll Be True to My Honey Boy*, from which grew permanent nickname Honey Boy. With lyricist Ren Shields composed all-time hit *In the Good Old Summertime* (1902). Other compositions *In the Merry Month of May* (1903), *Come Take a Trip in My Air-Ship* (1904), *You'll Have to Wait Till My Ship Comes In* (1906), *Come to the Land of Bohemia* (1907).

550. EVANS, GIL   p ar cm B
(IAN ERNEST GILMORE GREEN)
Born May 13, 1912, Toronto, Canada

Leading arranger in modern style, in later years capable pianist. Family left Canada, lived in Stockton, Calif. Led big band there 1933-8. Skinnay Ennis took over band in 1938; Evans remained as arranger. Band began long run on Bob Hope radio show, played top hotels on west coast. Evans with Claude Thornhill 1941-2, in military service 1943-5, rejoined Thornhill 1946-8. Arrangements for Thornhill in early 40s innovative, with delicate shading and tonal coloring. Utilized French horns and clarinets. In late 40s Evans leading arranger for bop combos and big bands, including Billy Butterfield and Gene Williams. Arranged two sides of famous 1949 Miles Davis "Birth of the Cool" record sessions for Capitol. Arranged for night club acts, radio, TV, Peggy Lee, the Dorseys, Tony Bennett, Benny Goodman. Outstanding arrangements backing Miles Davis on LPs in 50s and 60s. In 1952 took up serious study of piano, became competent. Arranging-composing made him in demand in late 50s and 60s. Led big bands at times. Continued active in 70s.

RECORDS
(all LPs)

GIL EVANS
    WP 1246 New Bottle, Old Wine
    WP 1270 Great Jazz Standards
    NJ 8215 Big Stuff
    Verve V-68555
    Impulse S-4 Out of the Cool
    Impulse S-9 Into the Hot

(as arranger)
CLAUDE THORNHILL
    Co(10")CL-6164
    Ha 7088 (Co RIs)

MILES DAVIS
    Cap DT-1974 Birth of the Cool (two arrangements)
    Co CL-1041 Miles Ahead
    Co CL-1274 PORGY AND BESS
    Co CS-8271 Sketches of Spain
    Co CS-8612 At Carnegie Hall
    Co CS-8906 Quiet Nights

(as arranger-conductor)
ASTRUD GILBERTO
    Verve V-8643 Look to the Rainbow

551. EVANS, HERSCHEL   ts cl ar cm
Born 1909, Denton, Texas
Died February 9, 1939, New York, N.Y.

Tenor sax jazzman most noted for years with Count Basie. Career cut short by early death. Played warm-toned sax in Coleman Hawkins vein; tasteful, well conceived solos. Began professionally in Texas about 1926. In late 20s with Edgar Battle, Terrence Holder, others. With Troy Floyd late 20s into early 30s. With Benny Moten 1933-5 in Kansas City and elsewhere. Briefly with Hot Lips Page in Kansas City mid-1935. Worked in Los Angeles late 1935-6 with Charlie Echols, Lionel Hampton and Buck Clayton. Joined Basie in late 1936, featured soloist. Lester Young also featured on tenor sax; he and Evans offered sharp contrast in styles. Arranging-composing for Basie included *Doggin' Around* and *Texas Shuffle*. Noted for sax solo on *Blue and Sentimental*. Remained with band until heart trouble led to untimely death.

RECORDS

COUNT BASIE
    De 1121 Swingin' at the Daisy Chain
    De 1363 One O'clock Jump (1st tenor sax solo)/John's Idea
    De 1379 Smarty
    De 1538 Time Out
    De 1682 Georgianna (1st tenor sax solo)
    De 1880 Swinging the Blues (2nd tenor sax solo)/Sent for You Yesterday
    De 1965 Doggin' Around (1st tenor sax solo)/Blue and Sentimental
    De 2030 Texas Shuffle

De 2212 Jumpin' at the Woodside (clarinet solo)
De 2224 Panassie Stomp

MILDRED BAILEY
Vo 3615 If You Ever Should Leave/ Heaven Help This Heart of Mine
Vo 3626 The Moon Got in My Eyes/ It's the Natural Thing to Do

LIONEL HAMPTON
Vi 26011 Shoe Shiner's Drag
Vi 26017 Muskrat Ramble

HARRY JAMES
Br 8067 Texas Chatter
Br 8055 One O'clock Jump

LPs

COUNT BASIE
Br BL-54012 (De RIs)
De DL-8049 (De RIs)
Ace of Hearts(E) AH-119 Blues I Love to Sing (De RIs)

LIONEL HAMPTON
Cam CAL-402 Jivin' the Vibes (Vi RIs)

552. EVANS, RAY   lyr reeds
Born February 4, 1915, Salamanca, N.Y.

Lyricist of many popular songs, mostly for movies. Partner composer Jay Livingston. Best-known songs *To Each His Own*; *Golden Earrings*; *Buttons and Bows*; *Mona Lisa*; *Silver Bells*; *Que Sera, Sera*; *Dear Heart*; *Tammy*. Attended Wharton School at University of Pennsylvania. Played clarinet and sax in college bands in clubs and on cruise ships. Met pianist Jay Livingston in college; later formed team. Evans worked as clerk and accountant during hard days getting started. Early important work for team: special material for Olsen & Johnson hit show HELLZAPOPPIN' in late 30s. Also wrote for comedians' later show SONS O' FUN in early 40s. First successful song *G'Bye Now* in 1941. Songwriting interrupted when Livingston entered military service, World War II. Evans worked in aircraft plant, also wrote for radio. Pair reunited, landed movie contract, began successful song writing in later 40s. Many movie scores, title songs and miscellaneous

songs through 50s into 60s. In 1954 big score for movie RED GARTERS, close to operetta style. Wrote for TV, including theme songs for shows Bonanza, Mr. Lucky, Mr. Ed. Wrote for night club acts of Mitzi Gaynor, Betty Hutton, Cyd Charisse. Scored Broadway show OH, CAPTAIN! (1958) and later unsuccessful LET IT RIDE (1961). Team formed publishing company, at times collaborated with composers Victor Young, Henry Mancini, Max Steiner.

SONGS
(with related shows; all with Jay Livingston)

1941—G'Bye Now
1945—THE CAT AND THE CANARY movie (Why Girls Leave Home); ON STAGE EVERYBODY movie (Stuff Like That There)
1946—THE STORK CLUB movie (A Square in the Social Circle); TO EACH HIS OWN movie (title song); On the Other End of a Kiss
1947—MY FAVORITE BRUNETTE movie (My Favorite Brunette; Beside You); DREAM GIRL movie (title song); GOLDEN EARRINGS movie (title song)
1948—WHISPERING SMITH movie (Laramie); The Streets of Laredo; Cincinnati
1949—SAMSON AND DELILAH movie (Song of Delilah); BITTER VICTORY movie (You're Wonderful); SONG OF SURRENDER movie (title song); COPPER CANYON movie (title song); THE GREAT LOVER movie (A Thousand Violins); THE PALEFACE movie (Buttons and Bows); THE HEIRESS movie (My Love Loves Me); SORROWFUL JONES movie (Having a Wonderful Wish; Rock-a-bye Bangtail); MY FRIEND IRMA movie (My Friend Irma; Here's to Love; Just for Fun; My One, My Only, My All)
1950—CAPT. CAREY, U.S.A. movie (Mona Lisa); FANCY PANTS movie (Home Cookin'; Fancy Pants; Yes, M'Lord); MY FRIEND IRMA GOES WEST movie (I'll Always Love You)

1951—THE LEMON DROP KID movie (Silver Bells; It Doesn't Cost a Dime to Dream; They Obviously Want Me to Sing); HERE COMES THE GROOM movie (Your Own Little House; Bonne Nuit; Misto Christofo Columbo); AARON SLICK FROM PUNKIN CRICK movie (My Beloved; Marshmallow Moon; Still Water; Why Should I Believe in You?; Life Is a Beautiful Thing)

1952—THUNDER IN THE EAST movie (The Ruby and the Pearl); SON OF PALEFACE movie (Wing Ding Tonight; California Rose; What a Dirty Shame); WHAT PRICE GLORY movie (My Love, My Life)

1953—THE STARS ARE SINGING movie; HERE COME THE GIRLS movie (When You Love Someone; Girls Are Here to Stay; Ya Got Love; You Never Looked So Beautiful; Heavenly Days; See the Circus); HOUDINI movie (The Golden Years); SOMEBODY LOVES ME movie (Thanks to You)

1954—RED GARTERS movie (Red Garters; A Dime and a Dollar; Meet a Happy Guy; Brave Man; Good Intentions; Bad News; Man and Woman)

1956—THE MAN WHO KNEW TOO MUCH movie (Que Sera, Sera)

1957—TAMMY AND THE BACHELOR movie (Tammy)

1958—OH, CAPTAIN! stage show (Femininity; You Don't Know Him; All the Time; Give It All You Got; Double Standard); HOUSEBOAT movie (Almost in Your Arms; Bing! Bang! Bong!); ANOTHER TIME, ANOTHER PLACE movie (title song); SADDLE THE WIND movie (title song)

1961—BREAKFAST AT TIFFANY'S movie (Lovers in New York)

1964—LET IT RIDE stage show; DEAR HEART movie (title song)

1967—WAIT UNTIL DARK movie (title song)

Also wrote material for movies MONSIEUR BEAUCAIRE, ALL HANDS ON DECK, PARIS SMILES, THE OSCAR, others.

553. EWELL, DON   p ar cm

Born November 14, 1916, Baltimore, Md.

Jazz pianist adept at New Orleans style, played others well too. Studied art at Maryland Institute of Fine Arts and music at Peabody Conservatory, took music jobs at same time. Played with trio in Atlantic City, then with The Townsmen band 1936-40 in Baltimore (also wrote arrangements). Military service, World War II. In later 40s with Bunk Johnson, Doc Evans, Sidney Bechet, Muggsy Spanier. With Miff Mole 1949-50. In Chicago in early 50s with Doc Evans, Georg Brunis, Eddie Wiggins, Lee Collins, Kid Ory. Led combo at intervals. With Turk Murphy in 1956, mostly with Jack Teagarden later 1956-60. Worked in Toronto during 1965-6. In 60s and early 70s mostly soloist or leader of combo.

RECORDS
(all LPs)

DON EWELL
   Atl 1261 Dixieland at Jazz, Ltd.
   GTJ 10043 Plays Fine Piano!
   GTJ 12021 Music to Listen to Don Ewell By
   Audiophile AP-66 Yellow Dog Blues
   Fat Cat's Jazz 109 Jazz on a Sunday Afternoon
   Chiaroscuro CR-106 (S) A Portrait of Don Ewell
   GHB 30 In New Orleans
DON EWELL-WILLIE "THE LION" SMITH
   Exel 501 Grand Piano
LEWIS-EWELL BIG FOUR
   GHB 68
KID ORY
   GTJ(10")L-21 Kid Ory's Creole Jazz Band
TURK MURPHY
   Co CL-927 New Orleans Shuffle
JACK TEAGARDEN
   Cap T-1095 Big T's Dixieland Band
   Verve V-8416 Mis'ry and the Blues
   Sounds 1203 In Concert
CLAIRE AUSTIN
   GTJ(10")L-24
EDDIE CONDON
   Jazzology J-50 Jazz as It Should Be Played

554. FABRAY, NANETTE   VO
(NANETTE FABARES)
Born 1922

Singer-dancer-actress of stage, screen and
TV, talented performer. Child star in Our
Gang movie comedies. Minor roles in
movies THE PRIVATE LIVES OF ELIZABETH
AND ESSEX (1939) and A CHILD IS BORN
(1940), featured role in THE BAND WAGON
(1953). Starred in MEET THE PEOPLE musical revue in Hollywood from December
25, 1939, well into 1940, gained notice
when show opened on Broadway December 25, 1940. In 1941 minor role in show
LET'S FACE IT. Starred in Broadway musicals MY DEAR PUBLIC (1943), JACKPOT
(1944), HIGH BUTTON SHOES (1947), LOVE
LIFE (1948), ARMS AND THE GIRL (1950),
MAKE A WISH (1951), MR. PRESIDENT
(1962). Appeared frequently on TV from
late 50s into 70s.

RECORDS
NANETTE FABRAY
  MGM 30795 Louisiana Hayride
(with JACK MCCAULEY and "HIGH BUTTON
SHOES" CAST)
  Vi 45-0038 I Still Get Jealous/There's
    Nothing Like a Model "T"
LPs
(original Broadway casts)
  Vi LSO-1107 HIGH BUTTON SHOES
  Co KOL-5870 MR. PRESIDENT
  De(10")DL-5200 ARMS AND THE GIRL
(movie soundtrack)
  MGM E-3051 THE BAND WAGON

555. FAGERQUIST, DON   t
*Born February 6, 1927, Worcester,
Mass.*
*Died January 24, 1974, Los Angeles,
Calif., of kidney disease*

Excellent modern jazz trumpet soloist;
beautiful tone, tasteful, facile and driving.
First big job with Mal Hallett 1943.
Mostly with Gene Krupa 1944-50. With
Artie Shaw awhile in 1949. In 1952 with
Woody Herman, also accompanying
panying singer Anita O'Day. Joined Les
Brown in early 1953, attracted attention
with solos. Became better known in later
50s and 60s from outstanding work on
Dave Pell LPs. In 1956 started studio
work on west coast, also freelanced. Vastly underrated jazz star.

RECORDS
(all LPs)
DAVE PELL OCTET
  Trend TL-1501 Plays a Folio of Sel-
    dom Heard Tunes by Rodgers &
    Hart
  Trend(10")T-1003 Plays a Gallery of
    Seldom Heard Tunes by Irving Ber-
    lin
  Kapp KL-1034 Plays Burke & Van
    Heusen
  Vi LPM-1320 Jazz Goes Dancing
LES BROWN
  Cor CRL-57000-1 (2 LPs) Concert at
    the Palladium, 1 & 2
  Cor CRL-57311 Jazz Song Book
  Cap T-659 Les Brown All-Stars
  De DL-4607 Les Brown's in Town

MEMBERS OF BENNY GOODMAN'S BRUSSELS
  WORLD'S FAIR ORCHESTRA
  Cr CLP-5090 Salute to Benny Good-
  man
PETE RUGOLO
  EmArcy MG-36115 Out on a Limb
LEONARD FEATHER'S STARS
  MGM E-3390 West Coast vs. East
  Coast
BUDDY DEFRANCO
  Verve MGV-2089 Plays   Benny
  Goodman
LAURINDO ALMEIDA
  Cap ST-1759 (S) Viva Bossa Nova!
HARRY BETTS
  Choreo A-6 The Jazz Soul of Doctor
  Kildaire and Other TV Themes
HEINIE BEAU
  Cor CRL-57247 And the Hollywood
  Jazz Stars
(miscellaneous artists)
  Interlude ST-1009 (S) Revel without a
  Pause
ANITA O'DAY
  Verve VG-2157 (S) Trav'lin' Light

556. FAIN, SAMMY   cm vo p
Born June 17, 1902, New York, N.Y.

Important composer with prolific career from late 20s into 60s. Most famous songs *Wedding Bells (Are Breaking Up That Old Gang of Mine)*; *You Brought a New Kind of Love to Me*; *When I Take My Sugar to Tea*; *By a Waterfall*; *I Can Dream, Can't I?*; *That Old Feeling*; *I'll Be Seeing You*; *Secret Love*; *Love Is a Many-Splendored Thing*. Early in career worked for New York publishing company, then entertained as pianist-singer. Teamed with Artie Dunn on radio. Began songwriting in mid-20s. Recorded occasionally as singer-pianist c. 1930. Wrote music for Broadway shows EVERYBODY'S WELCOME (1931), HELLZAPOPPIN' and RIGHT THIS WAY (1938), GEORGE WHITE'S SCANDALS OF 1939, BOYS AND GIRLS TOGETHER (1940), SONS O' FUN (1941), ALIVE AND KICKING (1950), FLAHOOLEY (1951), ANKLES AWEIGH (1955). Wrote for movies beginning 1930. Chief collaborators lyricists Irving Kahal, Lew Brown, Jack Yellen, Mitchell Parish, E. Y. Harburg, Harold Adamson, Bob Hilliard, Paul Francis

Webster. Appeared on TV occasionally in later years on shows honoring composers; played and sang his songs effectively.

SONGS
(with related shows)

1925—Nobody Knows What a Red Headed Mama Can Do
1927—I Ain't That Kind of a Baby; I Left My Sugar Standing in the Rain
1928—Let a Smile Be Your Umbrella; There's Something About a Rose
1929—Wedding Bells (Are Breaking Up That Old Gang of Mine)
1930—THE BIG POND movie (You Brought a New Kind of Love to Me; Mia Cara)
1931—EVERYBODY'S WELCOME stage show (Even as You and I; Is Rhythm Necessary?); When I Take My Sugar to Tea
1932—Hummin' to Myself; Was That the Human Thing to Do?
1933—FOOTLIGHT PARADE movie (By a Waterfall; Sittin' on a Backyard Fence; Ah, the Moon Is Here); COLLEGE COACH movie (Lonely Lane)
1934—HAROLD TEEN movie (How Do I Know It's Sunday?; Simple and Sweet; Two Little Flies on a Lump of Sugar); HAPPINESS AHEAD movie (Beauty Must Be Loved); HERE COMES THE NAVY movie (Hey, Sailor!); FASHIONS OF 1934 movie (Spin a Little Web of Dreams); MANDALAY movie (When Tomorrow Comes)
1935—SWEET MUSIC movie (Ev'ry Day; There's a Different "You" in Your Heart); GOIN' TO TOWN movie (Now I'm a Lady)
1936—Am I Gonna Have Trouble with You?; That Never-to-Be-Forgotten Night
1937—NEW FACES OF 1937 movie (Our Penthouse on Third Avenue; Love Is Never Out of Season; It Goes to Your Feet); VOGUES OF 1938 movie (That Old Feeling); Don't You Know or Don't You Care?; Bluebonnet
1938—HELLZAPOPPIN' stage show (It's

886

Time to Say Aloha; Fiddle Dee Duddle); RIGHT THIS WAY stage show (I Can Dream, Can't I?; I'll Be Seeing You); Who Blew Out the Flame?

1939—GEORGE WHITE'S SCANDALS OF 1939 stage show (Are You Havin' Any Fun?; Mexiconga; Goodnight, My Beautiful; In Waikiki; Something I Dreamed Last Night); The Moon Is a Silver Dollar

1940—BOYS AND GIRLS TOGETHER stage show (Such Stuff as Dreams Are Made Of; I Want to Live); Love Song of Renaldo

1941—SONS O' FUN stage show (Happy in Love; Let's Say Goodnight with a Dance)

1943—SWING FEVER movie (Mississippi Dream Boat)

1944—TWO GIRLS AND A SAILOR movie (You Dear)

1945—ANCHORS AWEIGH movie (The Worry Song); THRILL OF A ROMANCE movie (Please Don't Say No); WEEKEND AT THE WALDORF movie (And There You Are; Guadalajara)

1946—NO LEAVE, NO LOVE movie (All the Time; Old Sad Eyes); TWO SISTERS FROM BOSTON movie (After the Show; Down by the Ocean; others)

1948—THREE DARING DAUGHTERS movie (The Dickey-Bird Song)

1949—Dear Hearts and Gentle People

1950—ALIVE AND KICKING stage show (songs unimportant); MICHAEL TODD'S PEEP SHOW stage show (Violins from Nowhere)

1951—FLAHOOLEY stage show, E. Y. Harburg-lyr (Flahooley; Here's to Your Illusions; He's Only Wonderful; many more); CALL ME MISTER movie (I Just Can't Do Enough for You)

1952—ALICE IN WONDERLAND movie cartoon, Bob Hilliard-lyr (I'm Late; Very Good Advice; All in the Golden Afternoon)

1953—PETER PAN movie cartoon, Sammy Cahn-lyr (Your Mother and Mine); THE JAZZ SINGER movie, Jerry Seelen-lyr (I Hear the Music Now; Living the Life I Love; Hush-a-Bye); CALAMITY JANE movie, Paul Francis Webster-lyr (Secret Love; The Deadwood Stage; Black Hills of Dakota; others); THREE SAILORS AND A GIRL movie, Sammy Cahn-lyr (Face to Face; The Lately Song); The Second Star to the Right

1954—LUCKY ME movie, Paul Francis Webster-lyr (I Speak to the Stars; The Blue Bells of Broadway)

1955—LOVE IS A MANY-SPLENDORED THING movie (title song); ANKLES AWEIGH stage show, Dan Shapiro-lyr

1957—APRIL LOVE movie (title song)

1958—MARJORIE MORNINGSTAR movie (A Very Precious Love); A CERTAIN SMILE movie (title song)

1962—TENDER IS THE NIGHT movie (title song)

1972—Strange Are the Ways of Love

RECORDS
(as vocalist)

LLOYD KEATING
Ve 2053 Turn On the Heat

SAMMY FAIN
Ve 1843 Wedding Bells (Are Breaking Up That Old Gang of Mine)/Love Me or Leave Me
Ve 1943 To Be in Love/What a Day!
Ve 1961 Why Can't You?
Ve 1993 Liza/Ain't Misbehavin'
Ve 2014 Lovable and Sweet/Painting the Clouds with Sunshine
Ve 2163 Mia Cara/I'm in the Market for You
Ha 1179 You Brought a New Kind of Love to Me/Ro-Ro-Rollin' Along
Di 2904 What Didja Wanna Make Me Love You For?/Things That Were Made for Love
Di 3078 Navy Blues/My Sweeter Than Sweet

557. FAITH, PERCY   p v ar cm B
Born April 7, 1908, Toronto, Canada

Noted radio and record conductor from 40s through 60s. Learned violin and piano, as youngster played silent movie houses in Canada. Attended Toronto

Conservatory. Arranged for bands in Toronto. Active on Canadian radio middle and late 30s, became staff conductor and arranger for Canadian Broadcasting Corp. Own radio show, carried in U.S. To U.S. in 1940, conductor on popular Contented Hour radio show for years. Also on Buddy Clark show 1946 and Coca Cola show beginning 1947. Well known on radio through 40s with large orchestra; his excellent arrangements string-dominated but with effective brass and sax also. In 1950 joined Columbia Records as conductor-arranger. Worked with leading singers Tony Bennett, Rosemary Clooney, Doris Day, Johnny Mathis, others. Later in 50s in movie studios. Arranger-conductor for 1955 Doris Day movie LOVE ME OR LEAVE ME, all-time great musical on life of Ruth Etting. Scored background for movies THE LOVE GODDESSES, THE OSCAR, THE THIRD DAY, I'D RATHER BE RICH. Hit record in 1953: *The Song from Moulin Rouge (Where Is Your Heart?)*. 1950 hit song *My Heart Cries for You*. Other compositions include *Manon* (1950); *No One but You* (1951); *There's Always My Heart* and *Did Anyone Call?* (1952); *An Angel Made of Ice* (1953); *Be Patient, My Darling*; *That's How It Goes* and *Why Does It Have to Be Me?* (1954). Descriptive works and themes included *Music Thru the Night, March of the Junior Scouts, Buy a Bond for Victory, The Snow Goose, Aphrodite, Noche Caribe, Perpetual Notion, Nervous Gavotte, Brazilian Sleighbells, Cheerio, Carefree, The Virginian Theme.* Chief collaborator Carl Sigman. Still active in movie studios and recording into early 70s.

RECORDS

PERCY FAITH
Co 38862 They Can't Take That Away from Me
Co 38918 This Is the Time/All My Love
Co 39011 Sleigh Ride/Christmas in My Heart
Co 39790 Jamaican Rhumba/Da-Du
Co 39944 The Song from Moulin Rouge/Swedish Rhapsody
(as conductor-arranger)

TONY BENNETT
Co 39555 Blue Velvet/Solitaire
Co 40004 I'll Go/Someone Turned the Moon Upside Down
Co 40048 Rags to Riches/Here Comes That Heartache Again
FELICIA SANDERS
Co 39965 I May Not Remember Your Name
DOROTHY KIRSTEN
Co 4620-M Mine/Embraceable You
TONI ARDEN
Co 39440 If You Turn Me Down/Invitation to a Broken Heart
Co 39737 I'm Yours/Kiss of Fire
JERRY VALE
Co 39929 And No One Knows/You Can Never Give Me Back My Heart
Co 40058 Ask Me/A Tear, a Kiss, a Smile
ROSEMARY CLOONEY
Co 39333 Mixed Emotions/Kentucky Waltz
Co 39648 Tenderly/Did Anyone Call?
DORIS DAY
Co 40505 Never Look Back/I'll Never Stop Loving You
MARION MARLOWE
Co 40149 If You Love Me/You're Not Living in Vain
FRANK PARKER-MARION MARLOWE
Co 40032 An Old Fashioned Picture/The Melba Waltz
SARAH VAUGHAN
Co 39932 I Confess/A Lover's Quarrel
ALAN DALE
Co 38874 You Wonderful You/Of All Things

LPs

PERCY FAITH
Co CL-895 MY FAIR LADY
Co CL-955 LI'L ABNER
Co CL-1081 The Columbia Album of George Gershwin, Vol. 1
Co CL-1201 The Columbia Album of Victor Herbert, Vol. 1
Co CL-1322 Bouquet
Co CL-1493 Percy Faith's Greatest Hits
Co CL-2023 Themes for Young Lovers
Co CL-2650 Plays the Academy Award Winner

Co CS-8005(S) SOUTH PACIFIC
Co CS-9835(S) Windmills of Your Mind
(as conductor-arranger)
HELEN WARD
Co(10")CL-6271 It's Been So Long
JOHNNY MATHIS
Co CL-1078 Warm
EARL WRIGHTSON-LOIS HUNT
Co CL-1302 A Night with Sigmund Romberg
WILD BILL DAVISON
Co CL-871 Pretty Wild
(movie soundtrack)
Co CL-710 LOVE ME OR LEAVE ME

558. FARLEY, EDDIE   t vo cm lyr B

Born July 16, 1905, Newark, N.J.

Co-leader of Riley-Farley band which rose to quick fame in early 1936 with fantastic novelty hit *The Music Goes 'Round and Around*. Band competent combo specializing in swing and dixieland. Farley with Bert Lown 1931-3, with Will Osborne in early 30s. He and trombonist Mike Riley formed band 1935, played jazz clubs in New York, a hit at Onyx Club. Two leaders plus Red Hodgson composed *Music Goes 'Round*. Caught on during last week of 1935, and during first two weeks of 1936 enjoyed probably greatest popularity ever attained by song for a like period. This brought renown for awhile, led to spot in 1936 movie THE MUSIC GOES 'ROUND. Team composed 1936 pop tunes *I'm Gonna Clap My Hands* and *Looking for Love*. In late 1936 team split and each led own band. Farley continued leading in 40s and 50s; long runs in 50s at club in Irvington, N.J.

RECORDS

BERT LOWN
Bb 5068 Mississippi Basin (vo)
RILEY-FARLEY ORCHESTRA (Riley sometimes spelled Reilly)
De 578 The Music Goes 'Round and Around/Lookin' for Love
De 619 South/I Never Knew
De 641 Blue Clarinet Stomp/Wabash Blues
De 683 I'm Gonna Clap My Hands/Not Enough

De 684 I Wish I Were Aladdin/You're Wicky, You're Wacky, You're Wonderful
De 994 Trouble Don't Like Music/A High Hat, a Piccolo and a Cane
De 1041 Hey-Hey/With Thee I Swing
De 3364 The Music Goes 'Round and Around/I'm Gonna Clap My Hands (RIs)
EDDIE FARLEY
De 1165 Nero/I Can't Break the Habit of You
De 1168 The Mood That I'm In/You're Everything Sweet
De 1237 To a Sweet Pretty Thing/There's No Two Ways About It
De 1250 I'm Bubbling Over/I Hum a Waltz
Token 201 Jazz Me Blues/Margie
Delvar 111 The Music Goes 'Round and Around/Ida
Delvar 116 Song of the Islands/Ophelia
NOTE: following records reported as actually Riley-Farley Orchestra:
TED RUSSELL
Ch 40040, 40041, 40042, 40056, 40057, 40065, 40066, 40079, 40089, 40109, 40110
TOP HATTERS
Ch 40067

559. FARLOW, TAL   g

Born June 7, 1921, Greensboro, N.C.

Good modern guitarist, facile and inventive. Took up guitar 1943. First good job with Dardanelle Trio. In late 40s with combos of Marge Hyams, Buddy De-Franco and Marshall Grant. Made impact 1950-3 with Red Norvo trio. With Artie Shaw's Gramercy Five late 1953-4, again with Norvo 1954-5. By late 50s semi-active in music, away from New York 1958-68. In late 60s led trio in New York.

RECORDS

RED NORVO
Dis 134 Time and Tide/Cheek to Cheek
Dis 135 Swedish Pastry/Night and Day

889

Dis 147 Zing! Went the Strings of My Heart/September Song

ARTIE SHAW'S GRAMERCY FIVE
Clef 89117 Sunny Side Up/Imagination

LPs

RED NORVO
Fan 3-218 Red Norvo with Strings
Fan 3-244 The Red Norvo Trios

ARTIE SHAW'S GRAMERCY FIVE
Clef(10")MGC-159 Album No. 1
Clef(10")MGC-160 Album No. 2

BUDDY DEFRANCO
Verve MGV-8221 Cooking the Blues

SONNY CRISS
Pres 7530 Up, Up and Away

OSCAR PETTIFORD
Pres 7813 Memorial Album (1949 & 1954 RIs)

TAL FARLOW-BARNEY KESSEL-OSCAR MOORE
Norg MGN-1033 Swing Guitars

TAL FARLOW
Norg MGN-1014 The Artistry of Tal Farlow
Norg MGN-1027 The Interpretations of Tal Farlow
Norg MGN-1030 A Recital by Tal Farlow
Norg(10")MGN-19 The Tal Farlow Album
Verve MGV-8289 This Is Tal Farlow
Verve MGV-8371 Plays Harold Arlen
ARS 418
Pres 7732 The Return of Tal Farlow/1969

560. FARMER, ART   t fl-h cm B

Born August 21, 1928, Council Bluffs, Ark.

Modern jazz trumpeter active as freelancer and combo leader. Grew up in Phoenix. To Los Angeles in 1945 to seek musical career. With Horace Henderson, Floyd Ray, Johnny Otis. Freelanced in New York 1947-8. Returned to west coast, worked with Benny Carter, Wardell Gray, others. With Lionel Hampton late 1952-3, including 1953 European tour. Based in New York in mid-50s. With Charlie Mingus and Horace Silver; teamed with Gigi Gryce awhile. Led groups at times. Composed and often featured jazz number *Farmer's Market*. With Gerry Mulligan late 50s. Teamed with Benny Golson 1959-62. Led combo in early 60s featuring guitarist Jim Hall. In mid-60s concentrated on fluegelhorn, his work enhanced by its mellow sound. Since 1965 divided time between U.S. and Austria (based there, sometimes toured other countries).

RECORDS

WARDELL GRAY
Pres 770 Farmer's Market
Pres 840 Bright Boy/April Skies

ART FARMER
Pres 875 Mau Mau (1 & 2)
Pres 891 Wildwood/Tiajuana
Pres 894 Elephant Walk/Evening in Paris
Pres 906 Autumn Nocturne/I Walk Alone

LPs

ART FARMER
UA 4062 The Aztec Suite
Atl 1442 Sing Me Softly of the Blues
Scepter 521 The Many Faces of Art Farmer
Status ST-8258 Early Art
NJ 8203 (including *Farmer's Market*)
Mer MG-20766 Listen to Art Farmer and the Orchestra
Pres 7031 Plays the Compositions and Arrangements of Gigi Gryce and Quincy Jones
Co CL-2649 The Time and the Place

ART FARMER-BENNY GOLSON JAZZTET
Mer MG-20737 Another Git Together

CLIFFORD BROWN-ART FARMER
Pres(10")167

GENE AMMONS
Pres 7039 The Happy Blues
Pres 7083 Funky

JOE HOLIDAY
De DL-8487 Holiday in Jazz

HAL MCKUSICK
Vi LPM-1366 Jazz Workshop
Cor CRL-57131 Hal McKusick Quintet

WARDELL GRAY
Pres 7343(2-LP set) Memorial Album
Pres(10")147

GERRY MULLIGAN QUARTET
Co CS-8116(S) What Is There to Say?

OSCAR PETTIFORD
ABC-Para 227 The Oscar Pettiford Orchestra in Hi-Fi
JIMMY CLEVELAND
EmArcy SRE-66003(S) Rhythm Crazy

561. FARRELL, BILL vo b
(WILLIAM FIORELLI)
Born c. 1926, Cleveland, Ohio

Big-voiced baritone; played night clubs, on radio and records. Began in mid-40s as bassist and singer in local combos. Working as single in Buffalo club, heard and hired by Bob Hope. Featured singer on Hope's radio show in September 1948, continued several years. Guest spots on other radio shows, continued to play night clubs. Record contract with MGM 1949, recorded into early 50s. Billy Eckstine, also with MGM, popular during same period. He and Farrell feuded mildly over similar singing style. By later 50s Farrell faded.

RECORDS

BILL FARRELL
MGM 10488 Circus/Through a Long and Sleepless Night
MGM 10519 You've Changed/And It Still Goes
MGM 10576 Some Hearts Sing/Your Eyes
MGM 10637 It Isn't Fair/Bamboo
MGM 10757 'Deed I Do/You're Not in My Arms Tonight
MGM 10840 Love Locked Out/Don't You Know or Don't You Care?
MGM 10948 Wonderful, Wasn't It?/My Prayer
MGM 11062 Blue Velvet/Be Mine Tonight
MGM 11113 Cry/Shrimp Boats
MGM 11146 Call Me a Dreamer/What Good Am I without You?
MGM 11193 Sincere/Heaven Knows Why
MGM 11234 Please/Here's to Us
MGM 11310 A Sinner Kissed an Angel/Maria Mia
MGM 11374 I Wish I Knew/Commandments of Love
MGM 11500 Farewell to Arms/Is It a Crime?

561A. FARRELL, CHARLES vo
Born c. 1901-2

Performer in movie musicals 1929-31. Began in silent movies. Primarily actor, sang adequately. Co-starred with Janet Gaynor in big movie musical SUNNY SIDE UP (1929) with popular score by Henderson-DeSylva-Brown. In movie musicals HAPPY DAYS and HIGH SOCIETY BLUES (1930), DELICIOUS (1931). Co-starred with Miss Gaynor in these and in eight non-musicals. Leading team in early 30s movies. Other important Farrell films: SEVENTH HEAVEN (1927), STREET ANGEL (1928), THE MAN WHO CAME BACK and BODY AND SOUL (1931), TESS OF THE STORM COUNTRY (1932), MOONLIGHT SONATA (1937). In about 50 movies, few after 30s. Many years mayor of Palm Springs, Calif., beginning late 40s. Co-starred with Gale Storm in TV series My Little Margie early 50s. Also associated many years with Racquet Club. Not the Farrell of the Jim Miller-Charlie Farrell records of late 20s-early 30s.

562. FARRELL, EILEEN vo

Classical singer with beautiful soprano, also effective on popular songs. After radio appearances, own show beginning 1947, The Family Hour. Theme: *Let My Song Fill Your Heart*. In 1955 began on operatic stage, made Metropolitan Opera debut in 1960. Appeared with New York Philharmonic Orchestra numerous times in concert. Sang at musical festivals and concerts U.S. and abroad. In 60s appeared occasionally on TV shows displaying talent at comedy and pop singing as well as classical numbers.

RECORDS

EILEEN FARRELL
Co 4443-M The Last Rose of Summer/The Kerry Dance
Co 4444-M Come Back to Erin/Killarney
Co 4445-M Danny Boy/The Rose of Tralee
De 27206 (theme) Let My Song Fill Your Heart/Bless This House

LPs

EILEEN FARRELL
Co CL-1465 I've Got a Right to Sing the Blues!
Co CL-1653 Here I Go Again
Co CL-1739 This Fling Called Love
Lon(E) 25920 Songs America Loves
Ha(E) 11235

AL GOODMAN
Vi LK-1004 Franz Lehar Memorial Album

563. FATOOL, NICK   d

Born January 2, 1915, Milbury, Mass.

Drummer with dixieland and swing bands. Attended high school in Providence, R.I.; early band jobs there. First big job with Joe Haymes 1937. With George Hall and Don Bestor in 1938. With Bobby Hackett early 1939, Benny Goodman spring 1939-40 and with Artie Shaw mid-1940 and 41. With Claude Thornhill, Les Brown and Jan Savitt before joining Alvino Rey late 1942-3. Settled in California mid-40s to do studio work. Played with west coast dixieland groups of Eddie Miller, Matty Matlock, Bob Crosby, others. With Harry James at intervals. In early and mid-50s in excellent dixieland group Pete Kelly's Big Seven for radio and 1955 movie PETE KELLY'S BLUES. In later 50s and 60s often with Bob Crosby, including 1964 Oriental tour. Much freelance recording. Active on west coast into 70s.

RECORDS

BENNY GOODMAN
Co 35210 There'll Be Some Changes Made/Jumpin' at the Woodside
Co 35254 Rose Room/Flying Home (both SEXTET)
Co 35362 Stealin' Apples/Opus Local 802
Co 35466 The Sheik/Poor Butterfly (both SEXTET)

ARTIE SHAW
Vi 26762 Special Delivery Stomp/Keepin' Myself for You (both GRAMERCY FIVE)
Vi 26763 Cross Your Heart/Summit Ridge Drive (both GRAMERCY FIVE)
Vi 27230 Temptation/Star Dust

Vi 27343 Pyramid/This Is Romance
Vi 36383(12″) Concerto for Clarinet (1 & 2)

LIONEL HAMPTON
Vi 26595 Flying Home/Save It Pretty Mama
Vi 26604 Shades of Jade/Till Tom Special

PETE KELLY'S BIG SEVEN
Cap 1780 Till We Meet Again

CAPITOL JAZZMEN
Cap 10011 Sugar/Ain't Goin' No Place
Cap 10012 Someday Sweetheart/That Old Feeling

CHARLIE VENTURA
Sun 10051 Tea for Two/A Ghost of a Chance
Sun 10054 "C.V." Jump/I Surrender Dear

WINGY MANONE
Kem 2700 Riders in the Sky/Round Square Dance

JO STAFFORD
Cap 1039 Pagan Love Song/Simple Melody

ZEP MEISSNER
MGM 30166 Dixie Downbeat/Who's Sorry Now?

FLOYD O'BRIEN
Jump 4 Carolina in the Morning/Royal Garden Blues

HARRY JAMES
Co 38557 Ultra

LPs

ARTIE SHAW
Vi LPM-1241 And His Gramercy Five (Vi RIs)

JACK TEAGARDEN
Cap T-721 This Is Teagarden!

CHARLIE CHRISTIAN
Co CL-652 With Benny Goodman Sextet and Orchestra (Co RIs)

MATTY MATLOCK
Co CL-690 Pete Kelly's Blues
Mayfair 9569 Dixieland

GLEN GRAY
Cap W-1022 Sounds of the Great Bands, Vol. 1

MUGGSY SPANIER
Ava A-12 Columbia—The Gem of the Ocean

RAY ANTHONY
Cap T-678 Big Band Dixieland
RAMPART STREET PARADERS
Co CL-648 Rampart & Vine
Co CL-785 Dixieland, My Dixieland
Co CL-1061 Texas! U.S.A.
MAXWELL DAVIS
Cr CST-134 Tribute to Artie Shaw
PETE KELLY'S BIG SEVEN
Vi LPM-1126 Pete Kelly's Blues
BING CROSBY (with Bob Scobey Band)
Vi LPM-1473 Bing with a Beat

564. FAUST, LOTTA   vo

Born 1881
Died January 25, 1910, New York, N.Y.
Beautiful singing star of Broadway musicals; most important THE GIRL BEHIND THE COUNTER (1907) and THE MIDNIGHT SONS (1909). Earlier supporting roles in THE CASINO GIRL (1900), THE LIBERTY BELLES and MY LADY (1901), WONDERLAND (1905). Other leading roles in THE WHITE HEN (1907) and THE MIMIC WORLD (1908).

565. FAY, FRANK   vo

Born November 17, 1897, San Francisco, Calif.
Died 1961
Personable comedian on Broadway stage; sang occasionally in musicals. In vaudeville many years; played top spots including New York's Palace Theatre. Graduated into roles on musical stage. He and wife Barbara Stanwyck headed intimate revue TATTLE TALES (1933); closed after 28 performances. Fay in early sound movies SHOW OF SHOWS (1929), UNDER A TEXAS MOON and THE MATRIMONIAL BED (1930), BRIGHT LIGHTS and GOD'S GIFT TO WOMEN (1931), A FOOL'S ADVICE (1932) in several later movies; good role in LOVE NEST (1951). After early 30s career waned because of drinking problem. Revived in mid-30s as appearances on Rudy Vallee radio show led to own show 1936. Put on stage presentation FRANK FAY VAUDEVILLE in 1939. In 1943 stage revues LAUGH TIME and NEW PRIORITIES OF 1943. Greatest role in hit play HARVEY (1944).

BROADWAY MUSICALS

1918—GIRL O' MINE; THE PASSING SHOW OF 1918
1919—OH, WHAT A GIRL
1920—JIM JAM JEMS
1922—FRANK FAY'S FABLES
1923—ARTISTS AND MODELS OF 1923
1927—HARRY DELMAR'S REVELS
1933—TATTLE TALES

566. FAYE, ALICE   vo
(ALICE JEANNE LEPPERT)

Born May 5, 1912, New York, N.Y.
Beautiful blonde singer and movie actress; top star from mid-30s to mid-40s. At 14 in chorus line at New York's Capitol Theatre. Danced in other theatres and night clubs. Chorus girl in Broadway show GEORGE WHITE'S SCANDALS OF 1931, starring singing idol Rudy Vallee. He discovered Alice could sing in sexy, throaty manner, took charge of her career. She toured with Vallee band, sang for first time on his radio show May 1933. Continued on show about a year, took name of Faye. Vallee starred in 1934 movie GEORGE WHITE'S SCANDALS, helped Alice get big break in same. Her sex appeal registered strongly, particularly in hit song *Nasty Man*. In three minor movies 1934, shot up to stardom with 1935 movies GEORGE WHITE'S SCANDALS OF 1935, EVERY NIGHT AT EIGHT, MUSIC IS MAGIC. In ensuing years starred in excellent movie musicals, occasional dramas. Worked with stars Don Ameche, Tyrone Power, Shirley Temple, Dick Powell, Betty Grable, John Payne. Among best films: big musicals ALEXANDER'S RAGTIME BAND and IN OLD CHICAGO (1938), ROSE OF WASHINGTON SQUARE (1939), LILLIAN RUSSELL (1940; played title role of famous buxom beauty). Her movies had excellent scores, yielded hits like *Sing, Baby, Sing*; *Goodnight My Love*; *Never in a Million Years*; *There's a Lull in My Life*; *I'm Shooting High*; *You're a Sweetheart*; *I Never Knew Heaven Could Speak*; *You'll Never Know*. Retired from movies 1945, later came back with effective role in remake of STATE FAIR 1962. On radio frequently as guest singer or dramatic

actress. In 1937 starred awhile on Music from Hollywood, with Hal Kemp band. In 1946-54 co-starred with husband, bandleader-singer Phil Harris, in long-running radio series. (Married first to singer Tony Martin.) In late 50s and 60s occasionally on TV, sometimes with Harris, sometimes in own specials. Slated for 1974 comeback in revival of Broadway musical GOOD NEWS.

MOVIES

1934—GEORGE WHITE'S SCANDALS; NOW I'LL TELL; SHE LEARNED ABOUT SAILORS; 365 NIGHTS IN HOLLYWOOD
1935—GEORGE WHITE'S SCANDALS OF 1935; EVERY NIGHT AT EIGHT; MUSIC IS MAGIC
1936—KING OF BURLESQUE; POOR LITTLE RICH GIRL; SING, BABY, SING; STOWAWAY
1937—ON THE AVENUE; WAKE UP AND LIVE; YOU CAN'T HAVE EVERYTHING; YOU'RE A SWEETHEART
1938—SALLY, IRENE AND MARY; ALEXANDER'S RAGTIME BAND; IN OLD CHICAGO
1939—TAIL SPIN; ROSE OF WASHINGTON SQUARE; HOLLYWOOD CAVALCADE; BARRICADE
1940—LITTLE OLD NEW YORK; LILLIAN RUSSELL; TIN PAN ALLEY
1941—THAT NIGHT IN RIO; THE GREAT AMERICAN BROADCAST; WEEKEND IN HAVANA
1943—HELLO, FRISCO, HELLO; THE GANG'S ALL HERE
1944—FOUR JILLS IN A JEEP
1945—FALLEN ANGEL
1962—STATE FAIR

RECORDS

RUDY VALLEE
  Bb 5171 Honeymoon Hotel
  Bb 5175 Shame on You
  Bb 5182 Happy Boy—Happy Girl
ALICE FAYE
  Me 13220 My Future Star/Yes to You
  Me 13346 According to the Moonlight/Oh, I Didn't Know
  Me 60308 I'm Shooting High/Spreadin' Rhythm Around
  Me 60309 I've Got My Fingers Crossed/I Love to Ride the Horses on the Merry-Go-Round

  Br 7821 Goodnight My Love/I've Got My Love to Keep Me Warm
  Br 7825 This Year's Kisses/Slumming on Park Avenue
  Br 7860 Never in a Million Years/It's Swell of You
  Br 7876 There's a Lull in My Life/ Wake Up and Live

LPs

ALICE FAYE
  Co CL-3068 Alice Faye in Hollywood (1934-7) (RIs)
  Reprise R-6029 Sings Her Famous Movie Hits
(movie soundtrack)
  Dot DLP-9011 STATE FAIR
  Curtain Calls 100-3
(miscellaneous artists; one song)
  Epic LN-3188 Here Come the Girls (RIs)

567. FAZOLA, IRVING   cl reeds B
(IRVING HENRY PRESTOPNIK)
Born December 10, 1912, New Orleans, La.
Died March 20, 1949, New Orleans, La.

All-time great clarinetist, at home with dixieland, blues, ballads and swing. Beautiful tone. Sometimes played notes sparingly, always movingly. Originally a dixielander, absorbed swing elements into style. Early jobs in 1927 with Candy Candido and Louis Prima. Jobbed in New Orleans in late 20s. With Sharkey Bonano 1930-4 off and on. In late 1934 discovered by Ben Pollack playing in Hotel Roosevelt's Blue Room. With Pollack late 1934-early 1937. Featured on Pollack's theme *Song of the Islands*. With Gus Arnheim several months mid-1937, with Glenn Miller's early band last two months 1937. Rejoined Pollack briefly early 1938 in New Orleans, toured. Joined Bob Crosby about March 1938, remained till May 1940, won fame as a leading jazz soloist with band. Beautiful tone in ensemble and lyric solos sparked band into its greatest period. Fazola a natural for big-band dixieland style of Crosby crew. Featured in showcase *My Inspiration*. Later in 1940 with Jimmy McPartland awhile in Chicago, then with Tony Almerico in New Orleans. Joined Claude Thornhill in early 1941, remained most of year. Clarinet featured, fit perfectly with Thornhill's delicately shaded arrangements. With Muggsy Spanier's big band early 1942, featured with Teddy Powell 1942-3 about a year. With Horace Heidt about five months 1943. Returned to New Orleans October 1943, played there 1944-8 with Tony Almerico, Louis Prima and Leon Prima. Active until death 1949. A huge man, suffered from high blood pressure, died of heart attack.

RECORDS

BEN POLLACK

Va 504 Deep Elm/The Moon Is Grinning at Me
Va 556 In a Sentimental Mood/Peckin'
Br 7764 Song of the Islands/Jimtown Blues

GUS ARNHEIM

Br 7904 Exactly Like You/Schubert's Serenade
Br 7930 My Cabin of Dreams

GLENN MILLER

Br 8062 Humoresque/Doin' the Jive

BOB CROSBY

De 1962 Milk Cow Blues/Squeeze Me
De 2209 My Inspiration/Loopin' the Loop (BOB CATS)
De 2282 Skater's Waltz/Eye Opener
De 2464 I Never Knew Heaven Could Speak/Rose of Washington Square
De 2465 If I Were Sure of You/The Lady's in Love with You
De 2657 Over the Rainbow/You and Your Love
De 2734 Blue Orchids/The World Is Waiting for the Sunrise
De 2776 Can I Help It?/The Little Man Who Wasn't There
De 2789 Washington & Lee Swing/Peruna (both BOB CATS)
De 3018 With the Wind and the Rain in Your Hair/You, You Darlin'
De 3154 Sympathy/Fools Rush In
De 3248 Spain/All by Myself (both BOB CATS)

CLAUDE THORNHILL

OK 6168 Stack of Barley/Hungarian Dance No. 5
OK 6178 Sleepy Serenade/Do I Worry?
Co 36391 Orange Blossom Lane/Moonlight Masquerade

Co 36435 Autumn Nocturne/Where Has My Little Dog Gone?

TEDDY POWELL

Bb 11554 Midsummer Matinee/Be Careful, It's My Heart
Bb 11575 Why Don't You Fall in Love with Me?/Helpless

JESS STACY

Vs 8121 Breeze (1 & 2)
Vs 8132 Clarinet Blues/I Can't Believe That You're in Love with Me

MUGGSY SPANIER

De 4168 Can't We Be Friends?/Chicago
De 4271 Hesitating Blues / Little David, Play on Your Harp

IRVING FAZOLA

Key 624 Sweet Lorraine/Clarinet Marmalade
Key 660 Isle of Capri/When Your Lover Has Gone
Vi 40-0140 Original Dixieland One-Step/Bluin' the Blues
Vi 40-0141 Satanic Blues/Ostrich Walk

LPs

IRVING FAZOLA

Mer(10")MG-25016 (Key RIs)
EmArcy MG-36022 New Orleans Express (RIs)

BOB CROSBY

De DL-8061 (De RIs)

MUGGSY SPANIER

De DL-8250 (De RIs)

568. FEATHER, LEONARD p ar cm B

Born September 13, 1914, London, England

Jazz critic; came to U.S. from England in 1939. Leading jazz spokesman as writer-lecturer-organizer-leader-pianist-composer. Editor *Metronome* in 40s, author of *Down Beat's* "Blindfold Test" feature column for about 25 years. Feather and Barry Ulanov chief critics heralding modern jazz. Author of magazine articles, jazz columns, books on jazz. Organized record sessions, concerts and festivals. Served as leader, played competent piano on record sessions. Arranged and wrote material for singers Lena Horne, Dinah Shore, Pearl Bailey, Frankie Laine, Eartha Kitt. Own network radio show Platterbrains 1953-8, also series Jazz Club, U.S.A. Books include *The Encyclopedia of Jazz, The Encyclopedia of Jazz in the Sixties, The Encyclopedia Yearbook of Jazz, The Book of Jazz.* Compositions include *Mighty Like the Blues, Jamming the Waltz, Dinah's Blues, Panacea, I Left My Heart in Your Hand, Meet Me Half-Way, Lonesome as the Night Is Long, Bebop Waltz, Bass Reflex, Signing Off, You Can't Go Home Again, Salty Papa Blues, You're Crying, Get Rich Quick, Where Were You?, Love Is a Word for the Blues, Mound Bayou, A Whole Lot o' Woman, Blowtop Blues, Snafu, Evil Gal Blues, The Bossa Nova, Sounds of Spring, Twelve Tone Blues, Winter Sequence, Hi Fi Suite.* Chief collaborators Andy Razaf, Steve Allen, Milton Raskin, Dick Hyman, Dory Langdon Previn. Active from late 30s into 70s performing valuable services to jazz. Wrote jazz column for *Los Angeles Times* into 70s.

RECORDS
(as pianist)

HOT LIPS PAGE
  Bb 8634 Evil Man's Blues/Do It If You Wanna
  Bb 8660 Just Another Woman/My Fightin' Gal
  Bb 8981 Dirty Mama Blues
GEORGE SHEARING (accordion)
  De(E) 7038 Squeezin' the Blues
LOUIS ARMSTRONG
  Vi 20-2456 Blues for Yesterday/Blues in the South
BARNEY BIGARD
  B&W(12")1206 Blues Before Dawn
WILLIE BRYANT
  Apo 364 Blues Around the Clock (1 & 2)
  Apo 369 It's Over Because We're Through/Amateur Night in Harlem
SARAH VAUGHAN
  Cont 6024 Signing Off
  Cont 6031 East of the Sun/Interlude
JOE MARSALA
  B&W(12")1203 Blues in the Storm/Unlucky Woman
CLYDE BERNHART with LEONARD FEATHER'S BLUE SIX
  Mus 345 Lost Weekend Blues/The Lady in Bed

Mus 348 Blues in the Red/Scandalmonger Mama
Mus 506 Blues Behind Bars/Blues without Booze
COUSIN JOE with LEONARD FEATHER'S HIPTET
  Alad 117 Just Another Woman
  Alad 118 Post War Future Blues
HELEN HUMES with LEONARD FEATHER'S HIPTET
  Sav 5513 I Would If I Could/Fortune Tellin' Man
  Sav 5514 Suspicious Blues/Keep Your Mind on Me
LEONARD FEATHER'S ALL-STARS
  Cont 6009 Esquire Stomp/Esquire Jump
  Cont 6016 Scram/Thanks for the Memory
LEONARD FEATHER-DAN BURLEY
  Cont 6006-7 Suite in Four Comfortable Quarters (1-2-3-4)

LPs

LEONARD FEATHER'S STARS
  VJ 6878 Encyclopedia of Jazz (of the 60s)
  MGM E-3390 West Coast vs. East Coast
LEONARD FEATHER-DICK HYMAN ALL-STARS
  MGM E-3650 OH, CAPTAIN

569. FEATHERSTONHAUGH, BUDDY
ts B

(RUPERT EDWARD LEE FEATHERSTONHAUGH)

Born October 4, 1909, Paris, France

Tenor sax star in England in 30s and 40s. Gutty-toned, hard-swinging. Led compact jazz group featuring swinging, tightly knit arrangements. Attended school in Sussex, England. With Spike Hughes 1930-1, various English groups during 30s and early 40s. Led group, recording excellent jazz series on HMV. Band on London radio. By late 40s less active in music. In mid-50s came back with combo, embraced modern jazz. Active into 60s.

RECORDS

BUDDY FEATHERSTONHAUGH
  De(E) 3649 I've Got the World on a String/Royal Garden Blues

De(E) 3650 When Buddha Smiles/
Sheik of Araby
HMV(E) 9331 Rug Cutter's Swing/
Clarinet Marmalade
HMV(E) 9339 Washboard Blues/Woo
Woo
HMV(E) 9347 Sweet Georgia Brown/
Christopher Columbus
HMV(E) 9350 Heartbreak Blues/295
Jump
HMV(E) 9361 King Porter Stomp/Big
Noise from Winnetka
HMV(E) 9367 One O'clock Jump/
Ain't Misbehavin'
HMV(E) 9372 Stevedore Stomp/Ain't-
cha Got Music
HMV(E) 9383 It's the Talk of the
Town/Soft Winds
HMV(E) 9384 I Wish I Were
Twins/How Am I to Know?
HMV(E) 9426 Air in D Flat/Between
the Devil and the Deep Blue Sea

LPs

BUDDY FEATHERSTONHAUGH
Vi(10")LPT-3034 Around the World in
Jazz—England (HMV RIs)

570. FELD, MOREY   d B

*Born August 15, 1915, Cleveland, Ohio
Died March 28, 1971, Denver, Colo., in
a fire at his home*

Drummer with swing and dixieland
bands. With Ben Pollack 1936, Joe
Haymes 1938. In late 1939-40 with Bud
Freeman. Freelanced in New York,
mostly with combos. Briefly with Benny
Goodman early 1944, joined again later
1944-5. In 1946 with Buddy Morrow and
Eddie Condon. Freelanced in New York
in late 40s. In early 50s with Bobby
Hackett, Peanuts Hucko, Phil Olivella,
Joe Bushkin, Billy Butterfield. Led groups
at intervals. Brief periods with Goodman
1952-3-4. In middle and later 50s studio
work. In 60s played at Condon's, some
jobs with Goodman. Led trio at New
York World's Fair 1964. Toured with
George Wein's Newport All-Stars.
Worked in California awhile 1968, then
with Peanuts Hucko in Denver 1968-9.
With World's Greatest Jazz Band briefly
as first drummer.

RECORDS

BUD FREEMAN
De 18064 Big Boy/Copenhagen
De 18065 Oh Baby/Sensation
De 18066 Tia Juana/I Need Some
Pettin'
De 18067 Fidgety Feet/Susie
BENNY GOODMAN
Co 36767 Ev'ry Time We Say
Goodbye/Only Another Boy and
Girl (both QUINTET)
Co 36781 After You've Gone (SEX-
TET)/Body and Soul (TRIO)
Co 36787 You Brought a New Kind of
Love to Me/Close as Pages in a
Book
Co 36813 Gotta Be This or That (1 &
2)
Co 36817 Slipped Disc/Oomph Fah
Fah (both SEXTET)
Co 36908 Give Me the Simple Life/I
Wish I Could Tell You
BUDDY CLARK
Vs 8230 Nothing but You/From An-
other World
Vs 8233 I Walk with Music/This Is the
Beginning of the End
SARAH VAUGHAN
Cont 6024 Signing Off
Cont 6031 East of the Sun/Interlude
TONY MOTTOLA
Maj 1106 Guilty/Trigger Fantasy
Maj 1125 Coquette/Tony's Touch
SLAM STEWART
Cont 10001 Voice of the Turtle/Time
on My Hands
Cont 10003 Honeysuckle Rose/Jingle
Bells
TEDDY WILSON
Mus 316 Just You, Just Me/Just for
You Blues
Mus 317 Ev'ry Time We Say Goodbye
JOHNNIE GUARNIERI
Maj 1094 Beyond the Moon/My Gal
Sal
Maj 1095 Flying Home/Believe It, Be-
loved
JACKSON-HARRIS HERD
Mer 89052 Tutti Frutti/Sue Loves
Mabel
CONNIE HAINES (with Morey Feld combo)
Cor 60308 Swingin' Doors/Everybody
Knows You by Your First Name

Cor 60309 Guys and Dolls/A Bushel and a Peck

LPs

MOREY FELD
Kapp KL-1007 Jazz Goes to Broadway

BERNIE LEIGHTON
Co(10")CL-6112

TEDDY WILSON
MGM(10")E-129 Runnin' Wild (Mus RIs)

WILD BILL DAVISON
Riv 12-211 Sweet and Hot

PEANUTS HUCKO
(one side) Jazztone J-1250 Dedicated Jazz
(one side) GA 33-333 The Swinging Thirties

THE WORLD'S GREATEST JAZZ BAND
Project PR/5033SD (S)

571. FELDKAMP, ELMER   vo ts

Died September 27, 1938, San Francisco, Calif.

Soft-voiced singer of 30s, best known for vocals with Freddy Martin. Sideman-singer with Bert Lown 1931-2. Freelance recording in early 30s. Sideman and featured vocalist with Martin 1933-8, featured on band's radio shows American Revue (1934), Vick's Open House (1935), Penthouse Serenade (1936-7).

RECORDS

BERT LOWN
Vi 22623 By My Side/I'm So Afraid of You
Vi 22689 Now You're in My Arms
Vi 22795 I Can't Get Mississippi Off My Mind
Vi 22908 Was That the Human Thing to Do?/The More You Hurt Me
Vi 24087 I'm Yours for Tonight/Over the Weekend

RUSS CARLSON
Cr 3373 Everyone Says "I Love You"/Goodnight Vienna

DEL LAMPE
Cr 3429 Street of Dreams/It's Within Your Power

ADRIAN SCHUBERT
Cr 3493 Sweetheart Darlin'/Love Songs of the Nile

ED LOYD
Me 12326 Too Many Tears

ALLEN BURNS
Pe 15732 A Tree Was a Tree/Why Can't This Night Go On Forever?

EDDIE KIRKEBY
Or 2348 There's Nothing Too Good for My Baby

CLIFF MARTIN
Pe 15645 Through My Tears

BOB CAUSER (probably Freddy Martin)
Pe 15746 What Have We Got to Lose?/Maybe It's Because I Love You Too Much
Pe 15969 Say It/Then I'll Be Tired of You
Me 13010 No More Heartaches, No More Tears/Riptide

HOTEL BOSSERT ORCHESTRA (Freddy Martin)
Me 12737 Trouble in Paradise/Can't We Meet Again?

FREDDY MARTIN
Br 6717 April in Paris/Count Your Blessings
Br 6905 So Help Me/Your Love
Br 6948 I Saw Stars/Then I'll Be Tired of You
Br 6998 Be Still, My Heart/What a Difference a Day Made
Br 7337 Sweet Music/Ev'ry Day
Br 7439 Reckless/Give a Broken Heart a Break
Br 7604 A Melody from the Sky/So This Is Heaven

ELMER FELDKAMP
Cr 3374 Sweethearts Forever/Three's a Crowd
Cr 3391 I'll Never Have to Dream Again/When Mother Played the Organ
Cr 3466 Lover
Cr 3521 It Isn't Fair/Let's Make Up

572. FELICE, ERNIE   acc vo B

Talented, facile jazz accordionist in modern style. Originator of distinctive combo sound: his accordion doubled clarinet lead, provided lush modern-chord backing. Sound soon imitated throughout U.S. by numerous combos with similar instrumentation. Led combo in this style when hired by Benny Goodman in January 1947; featured in Goodman combos on radio and records. Left Goodman after about four months, resumed leading combo. Recorded in late 40s, again using distinctive sound and now popularizing it because of his new prominence. Unfortunately faded from music scene in 50s.

RECORDS

BENNY GOODMAN (combos)
Cap 394 Fine and Dandy
Cap 15768 Sweet Georgia Brown
Cap 20126 How High the Moon
Cap 20127 Music, Maestro, Please/ The Bannister Slide
ERNIE FELICE
Cap 413 Dream a Little Dream of Me/Carolina Moon
Cap 453 Stumbling/O Sole Mio
Cap 486 Solitude/Love Is So Terrific
Cap 561 Popcorn Polka/You Gotta Stop
Cap 15228 Love Me or Leave Me/Oodles of Boodle

LPs

ERNIE FELICE
Cap(10″)H-192 Cocktail Time
BENNY GOODMAN (combos)
Cap(10″)H-479

573. FENTON, CARL   p B

Bandleader of 20s and 30s. Started recording around 1920, continued through 20s. Band played ballrooms and theatres and on early radio in 20s. Backed Bing Crosby on nightly Cremo Cigar radio show on CBS late 1931-early 1932 with good band often including Joe Venuti, Eddie Lang, Manny Klein, Phil Napoleon, Jerry Colonna, Tommy Dorsey, Artie Shaw, Frank Signorelli, Lennie Hayton. In 1935-6 played on New York radio; in late 1936-7 had show with singer Sid Garry.

RECORDS

AL JOLSON with CARL FENTON ORCHESTRA
Br 2671 Follow the Swallow/I Wonder What's Become of Sally
Br 3013 Miami/Remember
AL BERNARD with CARL FENTON ORCHESTRA
Br 3553 Memphis Blues/Hesitation Blues

CARL FENTON
Br 2048 The Love Boat/Cuban Man
Br 2067 Rosie
Br 2603 Limehouse Blues/Worried
Br 2640 I Want to Be Happy/"No, No, Nanette" Medley
Br 2739 All Alone/At the End of a Winding Lane
Br 2759 Rose-Marie/A Little Bit of This
Br 2913 Collegiate
Br 2943 Footloose/I Miss My Swiss
Br 3033 Song of the Flame/Cossack Love Song
Br 3472 Rio Rita/Following the Sun Around
Br 3519 Doll Dance/Delirium
Br 3537 Silver Moon/Your Land and My Land
Br 4421 What a Day/Maybe—Who Knows?
Br 4467 Smiling Irish Eyes/The World's Greatest Sweetheart Is You
Br 4557 Sweetness/Laughing Marionette
Br 4574 I Came to You/When You Are Mine
Br 4734 Song of the Vagabonds
Br(12″)20047 "Queen High" Medley (1 & 2)
Va 529 Beginner's Luck/They Can't Take That Away from Me

574. FERGUSON, MAYNARD
t tb fl-h v-tb vo B

Born May 4, 1928, Montreal, Canada

Modern trumpet star noted for incredible high-register work. Rough-hewn, undisciplined style early in career, evolved into excellent modern style and retained great power. Studied in Canada at French Conservatory of Music. At 15 with Stan Woods band in Montreal. At 16 formed band with brother, played three years in Montreal area. In 1949 in U.S. with Boyd Raeburn, Jimmy Dorsey, Charlie Barnet. Joined Stan Kenton in early 1950, created a sensation with powerful highnote work; big hit in concerts. With Kenton about two years, then freelanced with modern groups. Another period with Kenton mid-1952 to early 1953. Studio work in

899

California. Led exciting groups, in 1956 took Dream Band of Birdland (all-stars) into New York's Birdland. Led various-sized groups in late 50s and 60s. Sometimes worked as single, appeared occasionally as soloist on late-night TV. Based in England since 1968, awhile in India. Brought excellent young band from England to U.S. in 1972.

RECORDS

CHARLIE BARNET
  Cap 843 All the Things You Are (also on LeeJay 8007)
LOUIS BELLSON
  Clef 89083 Caxton Hall Swing/Phalanges
BEN WEBSTER
  Mer 8298 King's Riff
KAY BROWN with MAYNARD FERGUSON ORCHESTRA
  Mer 5863 Roses All the Way/Wow
STAN KENTON
  Cap(12″)8-28009 Maynard Ferguson
MAYNARD FERGUSON
  Cap 1269 Love Locked Out/Band Ain't Draggin'
  Cap 1713 What's New?/Hot Canary
  EmArcy 16002 The Way You Look Tonight/Lonely Town
  EmArcy 16013 All God's Chillun Got Rhythm/Over The Rainbow

LPs

MAYNARD FERGUSON
  EmArcy MG-36076 Around the Horn
  EmArcy MG-36114 Boy with Lots of Brass
  EmArcy(10″)MG-26024 Dimensions
  Roul R-52064 Maynard '61
  Vik LX-1070 Birdland Dream Band
  Vik LX-1077 Birdland Dream Band, Vol. 2
  Cameo C-1066 Come Blow Your Horn
  Mainstream 56031 Color Him Wild
  Mainstream 56045 The Blues Roar
CHRIS CONNER-MAYNARD FERGUSON
  Roul R-52068 Two's Company
STAN KENTON
  Cap(10″)L-248
  Cap(10″)H-325
BEN WEBSTER
  EmArcy(10″)MG-26006
DINAH WASHINGTON
  EmArcy MG-36000

(miscellaneous bands)
  Cap T-667 Battle of the Big Bands

575. FIELDING, JERRY   p ar cm B
(JOSHUA FELDMAN)
Born June 17, 1922, Pittsburgh, Pa.

Talented arranger-conductor, in modern idiom. Scores boast beautiful chord structures and patterns. Also capable arranger in more simplified style for singers and radio-TV shows. As youngster arranged for bands at Pittsburgh's Stanley Theatre. At 18 became arranger for Alvino Rey in New York, then went with him to west coast. Based there, arranged for Tommy Dorsey, Charlie Barnet, Kay Kyser and other bands. In 40s arranged for radio shows of Kay Kyser, Hoagy Carmichael, Kate Smith, Bob Crosby, Andrews Sisters. First conducting job on Jack Paar radio show. In early 50s directed band on own TV show. Led dance band, toured awhile. Arranger and/or conductor on TV shows of Groucho Marx, Betty Hutton, Bewitched, Farmer's Daughter, Hogan's Heroes, Life of Riley. Movie scoring. Wrote or conducted for night club performers Betty Hutton, Eddie Fisher, Teresa Brewer, Ritz Brothers, Mitzi Gaynor, Juliet Prowse, Vic Damone, Cyd Charisse, Tony Martin, Debbie Reynolds, Polly Bergen, Barry Sisters, McGuire Sisters, Steve Lawrence. In 50s and 60s led groups on records, showcased his outstanding arrangements. Compositions include *City of Brass, Polynesian Peace Chant, Paris Magicque, The Essence of Calculated Calm.*

RECORDS
(all LPs)

JERRY FIELDING
  De DL-8371 Swingin' in Hi-Fi
  De DL-8450 Fielding's Formula
  De DL-8669 Hollywood Jazztet
  Trend(10″)1000
  Kapp KL-1026 Play a Dance Concert
  Time 2059 Bit of Ireland
  Time 2119
  Comm S-922(S) Near East Brass
THE HI-LO'S and JERRY FIELDING ORCHESTRA
  Kapp KL-1027

TERESA BREWER (as conductor)
  Cor CRL-57315 Ridin' High
(movie soundtrack; as composer-conductor)
  Vi LOC-1068 ADVISE AND CONSENT
KATHY BARR (as arranger-conductor)
  Vi LPM-1562 Follow Me
HOGAN'S HEROES
  Sun SUS-5137 (S) Sing the Best of World War II

576. FIELDS, ARTHUR   vo cm lyr

Born August 6, 1888, Philadelphia, Pa.
Died March 29, 1953, Largo, Fla.

Popular vocalist and performer of 20s specializing in novelty, minstrel and rhythmic numbers. Child singer, professional at 11. In minstrel shows and vaudeville, later on radio. Extensive freelance recording plus records under own name. Vocalist with Fred "Sugar" Hall in late 20s, daily morning radio show with Hall in 1937. Composer or lyricist of popular songs and novelties: *Aba Daba Honeymoon, On the Mississippi, Auntie Skinner's Chicken Dinner, There's a Blue Sky 'Way Out Yonder, Who Else but God?, Eleven More Months and Ten More Days, Our Hometown Mountain Band, I Got a Code Id By Dose, There Shall Be No More Tears.* Also wrote serious works called *48 Hymns of Happiness.*

RECORDS

HOLLYWOOD DANCE ORCHESTRA
  Do 3991 Who's That Pretty Baby?
SAM LANIN
  Do 3644 Sweet Child/I Want Somebody to Cheer Me Up
  Ba 1961 Side by Side/Hello, Cutie
PERRY'S HOT DOGS
  Re 9917 There Ain't No Flies on Auntie/Show Me the Way to Go Home
DUBIN'S DANDIES
  Je 5759 Gettin' Along
BAILEY'S LUCKY SEVEN
  Ge 3125 On a Night Like This
CALIFORNIA RAMBLERS
  Co 669-D Ya Gotta Know How to Love
  Ed 51737 What a Man!
  Pe 14609 Horses
JOE CANDULLO
  Pe 14650 As Long as I Have You

FIVE BIRMINGHAM BABIES
  Pe 14623 What a Man!
ROSS GORMAN
  Co 460-D Hugo, I'll Go Where You Go
FRED "SUGAR" HALL
  OK 40891 Is It Possible?/Someday You'll Say "O.K."
  OK 41008 The Grass Grows Greener/It's Bologney
LITTLE RAMBLERS
  Co 679-D I Wonder What's Become of Joe?/Hot Henry!
UNIVERSITY SIX
  Ha 296 My Baby Knows How
ARTHUR FIELDS
  Vi 18489 Oh, How I Hate to Get Up in the Morning/Oh, Frenchy
  Vi 18522 Ja-da
  Re 8081 I Wish You Were Jealous of Me
  Re 9417 Toot Toot Tootsie
  Ba 6315 Geraldine
  Pe 15055 When Sweet Susie Goes Steppin' By/Ho-Ho-Ho-Hogan
  OK 40146 Why Live a Lie?
  Co 290-D Cross Words/I Never Knew How Much I Loved You
  Br 6367 Temperance Is Coming (1 & 2)

577. FIELDS, CARL "KANSAS"   d B

Born December 5, 1915, Chipman, Kansas

Drummer with jazz bands in 40s and early 50s; later years mostly abroad. Grew up in Chicago, studied drums, began professionally in mid-30s. In late 30s with Jimmie Noone, Johnny Long and Walter Fuller. With King Kolax in 1940, joined Roy Eldridge late in year and remained several months. Led band awhile in 1941; also with Ella Fitzgerald, Andy Kirk and Benny Carter. In 1942 with Edgar Hayes, Charlie Barnet, and bop experimentalists Dizzy Gillespie and Charlie Parker. Military service, late 1942-5. In later 40s periods with Cab Calloway, Claude Hopkins, Willie "The Lion" Smith, Roy Eldridge, Hot Lips Page, Sidney Bechet, Dizzy Gillespie, Eddie Condon. In early 50s led group in New York at intervals, also freelanced. European tour in 1953 with Mezz Mezzrow. Returned to Europe in 1954, settled in France. Active in music abroad in later 50s and 60s. Later in 60s returned to U.S. to work.

RECORDS

MEL POWELL
   CMS 543 When Did You Leave Heaven?/Blue Skies
   CMS 544 The World Is Waiting for the Sunrise/Mood at Twilight
JONAH JONES
   Sw(Fr) 228 That's the Lick/I Can't Give You Anything but Love
   Sw(Fr) 243 I'm Headin' for Paris/Jonah's Wail

LPs

BUD POWELL
   Reprise R-6098 Bud Powell in Paris
MEZZ MEZZROW
   Vogue(Fr) 3 Jazz Time Paris (1953)
DIZZY GILLESPIE
   Dee Gee(10")1000
LIONEL HAMPTON
   EmArcy(10")MG-26038
(miscellaneous artists)
   Pax 6015 Americans Abroad

578. FIELDS, DOROTHY   lyr

Born July 15, 1905, Allenhurst, N.J.
Died March 28, 1974, New York, N.Y.,
of heart attack

Important lyricist of many popular songs, noted for early collaboration with composer Jimmy McHugh. Daughter of Lew Fields of famous Weber & Fields comedy team. Best-known songs *I Can't Give You Anything but Love, On the Sunny Side of the Street, Exactly Like You, Don't Blame Me, Lovely to Look At, I Won't Dance, I'm in the Mood for Love, A Fine Romance, The Way You Look Tonight.* Scored for Broadway shows BLACKBIRDS OF 1928, HELLO DADDY (1929), INTERNATIONAL REVUE (1930), SINGIN' THE BLUES and RHAPSODY IN BLACK (1931), STARS IN YOUR EYES (1939), UP IN CENTRAL PARK (1945), ARMS AND THE GIRL (1950), A TREE GROWS IN BROOKLYN (1951), BY THE BEAUTIFUL SEA (1954), REDHEAD (1959), SWEET CHARITY (1966), THE HAROLD ARLEN SCRAPBOOK (1967), SEE-SAW (1973). Co-librettist with brother Herbert for LET'S FACE IT (1941), SOMETHING FOR THE BOYS (1943),

MEXICAN HAYRIDE (1944), UP IN CENTRAL PARK (1945), ANNIE GET YOUR GUN (1946), ARMS AND THE GIRL (1950), BY THE BEAUTIFUL SEA (1954), REDHEAD (1959). Wrote for movies during most of 1930-9, in later years at intervals. Other collaborators composers Jerome Kern, Oscar Levant, Arthur Schwartz, Fritz Kreisler, Sigmund Romberg, Morton Gould, Burton Lane, Albert Hague, Max Steiner, Cy Coleman. First woman elected to Songwriters' Hall of Fame.

SONGS
(with related shows; with Jimmy McHugh 1928-35)

1928—BLACKBIRDS OF 1928 stage show (I Can't Give You Anything but Love; Diga Diga Doo; I Must Have That Man; Porgy; Doin' the New Low Down; Baby; Bandanna Babies); Collegiana

1929—HELLO DADDY stage show (In a Great Big Way; Let's Sit and Talk About You; Out Where the Blues Begin; Futuristic Rhythm)

1930—INTERNATIONAL REVUE stage show (On the Sunny Side of the Street; Exactly Like You); VANDERBILT REVUE stage show, unsuccessful (Blue Again; Button Up Your Heart); LOVE IN THE ROUGH movie (Go Home and Tell Your Mother; One More Waltz)

1931—RHAPSODY IN BLACK stage show (I'm Feelin' Blue); SHOOT THE WORKS stage show (How's Your Uncle?); CUBAN LOVE SONG movie (title song); SINGIN' THE BLUES play with two songs (Singin' the Blues; It's the Darndest Thing)

1933—DANCING LADY movie (My Dancing Lady); Dinner at Eight; Don't Blame Me; Hey, Young Fella

1934—Lost in a Fog; Thank You for a Lovely Evening

1935—THE NITWITS movie (Music in My Heart); ROBERTA movie (Lovely to Look At; I Won't Dance); EVERY NIGHT AT EIGHT movie (I'm in the Mood for Love; I Feel a Song Comin' On; Speaking Confidentially; Take It Easy); HOORAY FOR LOVE movie (Hooray for Love;

Livin' in a Great Big Way; I'm in Love All Over Again; You're an Angel); Every Little Moment

(not with Jimmy McHugh)

1935—IN PERSON movie (Don't Mention Love to Me; Out of Sight, Out of Mind; I've Got a New Lease on Life); I DREAM TOO MUCH movie (I Dream Too Much; I'm the Echo; I Got Love; The Jockey on the Carousel); ALICE ADAMS movie, Max Steiner-cm (I Can't Waltz Alone)

1936—SWING TIME movie (The Way You Look Tonight; A Fine Romance; Pick Yourself Up; Bojangles of Harlem; Never Gonna Dance; Waltz in Swing Time); THE KING STEPS OUT movie (Stars in My Eyes; Madly in Love)

1937—WHEN YOU'RE IN LOVE movie (Our Song; Whistling Boy)

1938—JOY OF LIVING movie (You Couldn't Be Cuter; Just Let Me Look at You; What's Good About Good-Night?; A Heavenly Party)

1939—STARS IN YOUR EYES stage show (This Is It; It's All Yours; Okay for Sound; A Lady Needs a Change)

1940—ONE NIGHT IN THE TROPICS movie (Remind Me; You and Your Kiss; Ferendola; Simple Philosophy)

1945—UP IN CENTRAL PARK stage show (Close as Pages in a Book; April Snow; When You Walk in the Room; It Doesn't Cost You Anything to Dream)

1950—ARMS AND THE GIRL stage show (Nothin' for Nothin'; There Must Be Somethin' Better Than Love; A Cow, and a Plow, and a Frau)

1951—A TREE GROWS IN BROOKLYN stage show, Arthur Schwartz-cm (If You Haven't Got a Sweetheart; I'll Buy You a Star; Make the Man Love Me; Payday; Look Who's Dancing; Love Is the Reason); TEXAS CARNIVAL movie (Young Folks Should Get Married; Whoa, Emma); MR. IMPERIUM movie (Let Me Look at You; Andiamo; My Love an' My Mule)

1953—THE FARMER TAKES A WIFE movie (Today I Love Ev'rybody)

1954—BY THE BEAUTIFUL SEA stage show, Arthur Schwartz-cm (Hang Up; Happy Habit; Alone Too Long; More Love Than Your Love; Coney Island Boat; I'd Rather Wake Up by Myself)

1959—REDHEAD stage show, Albert Hague-cm (Merely Marvelous; Look Who's in Love; others)

1965—SWEET CHARITY stage show, Cy Coleman-cm (Big Spender; Baby Dream Your Dreams; If My Friends Could See Me Now; I Love to Cry at Weddings)

1973—SEE-SAW stage show, Cy Coleman-cm

579. FIELDS, GRACIE   VO

Born January 9, 1898, Rochdale, Lancashire, England

English comedienne and singing star who played often in U.S. Melodious soprano effective on ballads, sacred songs and novelties such as famous *The Biggest Aspidastra in the World*. As child played in touring companies. Became popular, later played music halls and clubs, recorded, appeared in English movies. First trip to U.S. 1930. 1940 to Canada on behalf of war effort, then to U.S. in night clubs, on stage and screen. In 1942 joined vaudeville show KEEP 'EM LAUGHING after it opened, also in TOP NOTCHERS stage show. During career in England and U.S., in movies SALLY OF OUR ALLEY (1931), LIVING ON THE BRIGHT SIDE (1932), SING AS WE GO (1934), QUEEN OF HEARTS (1936), THE SHOW GOES ON and IT'S LOVE I'M AFTER (1937), WE'RE GOING TO BE RICH (1938), SMILING ALONG (1939), SHIPYARD SALLY (1940), STAGE DOOR CANTEEN and HOLY MATRIMONY (1943), MOLLY AND ME (1944), PARIS UNDERGROUND (1945). Radio show in U.S. 1942-4, again in 1951-2. Recorded in U.S., and English recordings popular here, particularly *Now Is the Hour* in 1947. Active into 50s, later semi-active, mostly in England.

RECORDS

GRACIE FIELDS

HMV(E) 8209 In My Little Bottom Drawer/Sing as We Go

Rex(E) 8558 (medleys) Life Is a Song/The Words Are in My Heart/Lullaby of Broadway, etc.

Rex(E) 9166 Little Old Lady/The First Time I Saw You

Lon(E) 110 Now Is the Hour/Come Back to Sorrento

Lon(E) 115 The Lord's Prayer/Bless This House

Lon(E) 129 Red Sails in the Sunset/Au Revoir

Lon(E) 362 Forever and Ever/Underneath the Linden Tree

Lon(E) 514 Happy Valley/Echoes

Lon(E) 844 Bon Voyage/When You Return

De(H) 33015 ANNIE GET YOUR GUN Medley (1 & 2)

Vi 26377 Danny Boy/Wish Me Luck

Vi 26507 Swing Your Way to Happiness/I've Got the Jitterbugs

De 18183 The Biggest Aspidastra in the World/He's Dead—But He Won't Lie Down

De 18218 Rose O'Day/O'Brien Has Gone Hawaiian

De 18458 Walter, Walter/That Lovely Weekend

De 18459 Ave Maria/An Old Violin

LPs

GRACIE FIELDS
Ace of Clubs(E) ACL-1107 Sing as We Go

580. FIELDS, HERBIE
as ts ss bs cl f vo ar B

Born May 24, 1919, Elizabeth, N.J.
Died September 17, 1958, Miami, Fla.,
by suicide

A most underrated musician, talented and versatile. Complete command of most reeds, excellent tone on all. Jazz solos in modern style, exuberant and facile clarinetist in Artie Shaw vein. Attended Juilliard 1936-8 where extensively trained on many instruments. First professional job with Reggie Childs 1937. Led group 1939-40. In 1940-1 with Leonard Ware, Slam Stewart and Raymond Scott. Made name as leader of good army band at Fort Dix, N.J., 1941-2, then led air force band in Atlantic City 1942-3. Medical discharge late 1943, led band

awhile. With Lionel Hampton late 1944 to early 1946, only white musician in band. Led big band 1946-1947, mostly combos remainder of 40s. Played clubs in Chicago and New York, recorded. In 50s settled in Florida, became less active in music. Committed suicide with overdose of sleeping pills; left note saying his work in this world completed.

RECORDS

LIONEL HAMPTON
De 24513 Ribs and Hot Sauce

GLADYS HAMPTON
Hamp-Tone 105 Four Squares Only/Star Time

HAMPTON ALL-STARS
Hamp-Tone 107 Gate Serene Blues/Jenny

HERBIE FIELDS
Sav 540 Mel's Riff/Buck's Boogie Woogie

Sav 560 How Herbie Feels/Jumpin' for Savoy

Sav 591 Camp Meeting/Run Down

Sav 592 Just Relaxin'/Four O'clock Blues

Sav 654 O.K. Sarge/Star Dust

Si 90004 These Foolish Things/You Can Depend on Me

Vi 20-1961 Among My Souvenirs/Jalousie

Vi 20-1962 I Guess I'll Get the Papers/There's Nothing the Matter with Me

Vi 20-2054 Cherokee/Moon Nocturne

Vi 20-2179 Soprano Boogie/I Wanna

Vi 20-2274 Rainbow Mood/Dardanella

Vi 20-2581 Chinese Lullaby/Come Back to Sorrento

Vi 20-2747 You Turned the Tables on Me/I Wish I Knew the Name

Vi 20-3052 In a Persian Market

Cor 60867 Everything I Have Is Yours/Dardanella

Cor 60959 Bobbin' in the Surf/Rio Rita

De 29752 Makin' Whoopee/St. Louis Blues

LPs

HERBIE FIELDS
(one side) De DL-8130 Blow Hot—Blow Cool

RKO ULP-146 A Night at Kitty's

LIONEL HAMPTON
De(10″)DL-5230

581. FIELDS, LEW vo
(MOSES SCHANFIELD)

Born January 1, 1867, New York, N.Y.
Died July 20, 1941, Beverly Hills, Calif.

(See biography herein on famous comedy team of WEBER & FIELDS.)

582. FIELDS, SHEP ts cl B

Born September 12, 1910, Brooklyn, N.Y.

Leader of 30s dance band known for "rippling rhythm." First led band while attending St. John's University in Brooklyn. Led band professionally in early 30s; important 1934 engagements in Miami and New York. First big break in 1936 touring with Veloz & Yolanda dance team; band known as Veloz & Yolanda Dance Orchestra. Important Chicago engagement at Palmer House with good radio coverage. "Rippling rhythm" began to catch on. Band went out on its own, recorded. By late 1936 band on radio show—*Radio Guide's* Court of Honor. Own show early 1937, Rippling Rhythm Revue; comedian Bob Hope joined in May as MC. Band played New York, Chicago, Los Angeles, elsewhere. In movie BIG BROADCAST OF 1938.

Unique "rippling rhythm" had several ingredients. Each number opened with introductory attention-getting sound made by blowing through a straw into a glass of water, close to microphone. Then followed a tinkling piano, muted and clipped brass, mellow saxes and facile accordionist doing arpeggio-like fill-ins. Glissing viola used on breaks. Arrangers Sal Gida and Lou Halmy; latter featured on only trumpet in band. Mac Miller viola, Murray Golden accordion (later Caesar Muzzioli). Theme *Rippling Rhythm*. Band had good vocalists in Bob Goday, later Hal Derwyn.

In early 40s Fields pioneered another style: nine reeds, no brass. Good arrangements cleverly disguised absence of brass. Men doubled on 35 reeds. Arrangers Glenn Osser, Lew Harris, Freddy Noble. During wartime, hard to find musicians capable of handling arrangements. In 1947 reverted to Rippling Rhythm, continued into 50s but without 30s popularity. Excellent band late 1950, commercially and musically pleasing; arrangements mostly by Freddy Noble. Settled in Houston 1955, worked mostly as disc jockey, fronted band on occasion.

RECORDS

SHEP FIELDS

Bb 6417 On the Beach at Bali Bali/Do You or Don't You Love Me?
Bb 6418 Us on a Bus/Rendezvous with a Dream
Bb 6548 Me and the Moon/Out Where the Blue Begins
Bb 6592 Easy to Love/I've Got You Under My Skin
Bb 6640 In the Chapel in the Moonlight/You're Everything Sweet
Bb 6662 Swamp Fire/Now That Summer Is Gone
Bb 6665 Where Are You?/That Foolish Feeling
Bb 6685 Goodnight My Love/One Never Knows, Does One?
Bb 6747 Serenade in the Night/Little Old Lady
Bb 6749 Love and Learn/I Adore You
Bb 6757 This Year's Kisses/The Girl on the Police Gazette
Bb 6759 (theme) Rippling Rhythm/Basin Street Blues
Bb 6779 Too Marvelous for Words/Just a Quiet Evening
Bb 7016 Gone with the Wind/A Star Is Born
Bb 7304 You Took the Words Right Out of My Heart/This Little Ripple Had Rhythm
Bb 7318 Thanks for the Memory/Mama, That Moon Is Here Again
Bb 7355 Goodnight Angel/There's a New Moon Over the Old Mill
Bb 10670 Day Dreams Come True at Night/Cecilia
Bb 11325 Autumn Nocturne/Who Can I Turn To?
Bb 11537 Wonder When My Baby's Coming Home/This Is Worth Fighting For
Bb 11583 When the Lights Go On Again/Better Not Roll Those Blue, Blue Eyes

Vogue 764 I Guess I'll Get the Papers/Whatta Ya Gonna Do?

MGM 10454 Havin' a Wonderful Wish/Don't Call Me Sweetheart Anymore

MGM 10823 Harbor Lights/I'm Forever Blowing Bubbles

LPs

SHEP FIELDS

Cam CAL-388 (Bb RIs)

Lion(10″)E-70008 Designed for Dancing

Golden Crest CR-3037 Rippling Rhythm in Hi-Fi

(one side) Roy(10″)18142 (with TONI ARDEN)

583. FINA, JACK   p ar cm B

Born August 13, 1913, Passaic, N.J.
Died May 14, 1970, California

Pianist-bandleader, first famous with Freddy Martin band as pianist-arranger of Martin's 1941 all-time hit *Tonight We Love*. Studied piano early, attended New York College of Music. Radio staff pianist, played awhile with Clyde McCoy. Joined Martin 1936, featured on piano; some arranging. With Martin into early 40s. In mid-1946 formed big band; record hit *Bumble Boogie* late 1946 (own arrangement). Band featured Fina piano, often on boogie woogie and ragtime. Active bandleader into 60s. Composed *Piano Portrait, Dream Sonata, Samba Caramba, Rhumbanera, Chango, Bumble Boogie*.

RECORDS

FREDDY MARTIN

Bb 7712 Milenberg Joys/Wolverine Blues

Bb 11211 Piano Concerto in B Flat (Tonight We Love)

Bb 11328 Symphonie Moderne

Bb 11430 Grieg Piano Concerto

JACK FINA

Mer 1023 Tonight We Love/My Reverie

Mer 3046 I'll Close My Eyes/Save Me a Dream

Mer 5001 Bumble Boogie/Now and Forever

Mer 5021 Maybe You'll Be There/That's Where I Came In

MGM 10085 Golden Earrings/So Far

MGM 10122 Music from Beyond the Moon/Song of New Orleans

MGM 10149 At the Candlelight Cafe/The Gypsy Polka

MGM 10289 Canadian Capers/Siesta

MGM 10372 Just Reminiscing/It's a Big Wide Wonderful World

MGM 10379 Love Me! Love Me! Love Me!/When Is Sometime?

MGM 10447 Twilight/Lora-Belle Lee

MGM 10610 Shangri-la/Spaghetti Rag

MGM 10671 Dreamboat Rendezvous/That's a-Plenty

MGM 10869 Song of the Bayou/Baltimore Rag

LPs

JACK FINA

Mer(10″)MG-25017

Mer(10″)MG-25033

Dot DLP-3243 Jack Fina Plays Boogie Woogie

Dot DLP-3374 Great Hits in Boogie Woogie

584. FINEGAN, BILL   p ar cm B

Born April 3, 1917, Newark, N.J.

Brilliant arranger and co-leader of unique Sauter-Finegan band of 50s. Extensive formal musical training, including Paris Conservatory. Gorgeous score for Tommy Dorsey, *The Lonesome Road*, won him spot as arranger for Glenn Miller during band's great years 1939-42. Integral part of band excellence. Scored for band's two movies SUN VALLEY SERENADE (1941) and ORCHESTRA WIVES (1942), also for THE FABULOUS DORSEYS (1947). After Miller went into service in late 1942, Finegan rejoined Dorsey, worked for him off and on into early 50s. Furnished arrangements for Horace Heidt 1942-3. In 1946 some arrangements for Les Elgart. In France and England studying music 1948-50. On return to U.S. resumed arranging for Dorsey. In mid-1952 joined with Eddie Sauter to form Sauter-Finegan band, which did well for several years despite early doubts about commercial appeal due to elaborate, unconventional style. Arrangements of two leaders provided a riot of color and quick changes of mood, featured seldom-used piccolo, flute, oboe, bass clarinet, English horn and recorders (which imparted light, feathery touch). Tympani and other unusual percussion effects utilized. Sally Sweetland and Andy Roberts featured singers. Band broke up early 1957. Finegan freelance arranger. In 1959 and into 60s he and Sauter produced jingles for TV and radio. Finegan continued to write for TV and radio. Composed jazz numbers during career; one of best *Pussy Willow*. Arranged for Glenn Miller Orchestra under direction of Buddy DeFranco 1973.

ARRANGEMENTS

GLENN MILLER

Sunrise Serenade; Little Brown Jug; Pavanne; Runnin' Wild; Song of the Volga Boatmen; Rhapsody in Blue; Johnson Rag; My Isle of Golden Dreams; Ciribiribin; My Melancholy Baby; The Sky Fell Down; Rug Cutter's Swing; Slow Freight; Star Dust (with Glenn Miller); Danny Boy (with Chummy McGregor); Yours Is My Heart Alone; Alice Blue Gown; When the Swallows Come Back to Capistrano; Blueberry Hill; A Million Dreams Ago; Be Happy; Angel Child; Yesterthoughts; The Call of the Canyon; A Handful of Stars; Frenesi; A Nightingale Sang in Berkeley Square; It's Always You; A Stone's Throw from Heaven; Under Blue Canadian Skies; I Know Why (with Jerry Gray); The Cowboy Serenade; It Happened in Sun Valley; I'm Thrilled; Day Dreaming; From One Love to Another; Moonlight Sonata; Slumber Song; Skylark; When Johnny Comes Marching Home; Serenade in Blue (with Billy May); A Story of a Starry Night; At Last (with Billy May)

TOMMY DORSEY

The Lonesome Road; Chlo-e; The Continental; Pussy Willow; Hollywood Hat; Wagon Wheels

RECORDS

SAUTER-FINEGAN ORCHESTRA

Vi 20-4866 Doodletown Fifers/Azure-Te

Vi 20-4927 Moonlight on the Ganges/April in Paris
Vi 20-4995 Midnight Sleighride/When Hearts Are Young
Vi 20-5065 Nina Never Knew/Love Is a Simple Thing
Vi 20-5248 Yankee Doodletown/Now That I'm in Love
Vi 20-5506 Joey's Theme/Doodletown Races
Vi 47-5359 "O"/The Moon Is Blue

LPs

SAUTER-FINEGAN ORCHESTRA

Vi LPM-1003 Inside Sauter-Finegan
Vi LPM-1051 Concert Jazz
Vi LPM-1240 Adventure in Time
Vi LPM-1634 Memories of Goodman and Miller
Vi LPM-2474 Inside Sauter-Finegan Revisited
Vi LPM-3115 New Directions in Music

THE SONS OF SAUTER-FINEGAN

Vi LPM-1104

(as conductor-arranger)

AMES BROTHERS

Vi LSP-1487 Sweet Seventeen

585. FIO RITO, TED   p o ar cm B

Born December 20, 1900, Newark, N.J.
Died July 22, 1971, Scottsdale, Ariz.

Pianist-bandleader with career of about 50 years; composer of many important songs. At 16 first job playing piano in nickelodeon. Worked in music publishing house. At 18 with Ross Gorman band. Formed band with Dan Russo in early 20s known as Oriole Terrace Orchestra, later Russo-Fio Rito Orchestra. Played in Chicago and midwest in mid-20s. Bought out Russo's interest in later 20s. Several years at Edgewater Beach Hotel in Atlantic City. Played piano and organ with band. Theme *Rio Rita*. Band sweet-styled and pleasant, not outstanding, but commercially successful. Muzzy Marcellino featured vocalist most of 30s. Comic-bassist Candy Candido also featured. Future movie star Betty Grable sang with band briefly as youngster around 1933, also June Haver, probably in early 40s. Peak popularity in mid-30s through radio and records, spots in Dick Powell movies

907

TWENTY MILLION SWEETHEARTS (1934) and BROADWAY GONDOLIER (1935). Also in movie SILVER SKATES (1943). Radio included 1934 show with Dick Powell; also with Powell on Hollywood Hotel late 1934-5. On Frigidaire show 1936. 1937-9 on Jack Haley's Variety Show; also on Lady Esther and Al Jolson shows. Band based on west coast much of 30s, popular there. Active in 40s but less prominent; recordings infrequent. In late 1956 Fio Rito took over house band at Chicago's Chez Paree. By 60s led band at own club in Scottsdale, Ariz. Later less active, led band occasionally. In 1970 led four-piece combo in Sacramento, Las Vegas and other spots. Compositions, especially those in 20s, enjoyed wide popularity; a few became standards.

SONGS

1921—By the Pyramids
1922—Doo Dah Blues; Toot Toot Tootsie
1923—No, No, Nora; When Lights Are Low
1924—Charley, My Boy; The Little Old Clock on the Mantel
1925—Alone at Last; Dreamer of Dreams; When I Dream of the Last Waltz with You; I Never Knew; Sometime
1927—After We Kiss
1928—I'm Sorry, Sally; King for a Day; Laugh, Clown, Laugh
1929—Then You've Never Been Blue; I Used to Love Her in the Moonlight
1930—Hangin' on the Garden Gate
1931—Now That You're Gone
1932—Three on a Match
1934—How Can It Be a Beautiful Day?; A Pretty Girl—a Lovely Evening
1935—Roll Along Prairie Moon; Alone at a Table for Two
1936—Yours Truly Is Truly Yours; When the Moon Hangs High; Knick Knacks on the Mantel
1937—Goodnight Kisses
1939—An Angel in a Furnished Room
1940—Now I Lay Me Down to Dream
1942—Lily of Laguna
1952—Funny Melody

Chief collaborators Gus Kahn, Ernie Erdman, Robert King, Cecil Mack, Sam M. Lewis and Joe Young.

RECORDS

RUSSO-FIO RITO ORCHESTRA
Vi 19917 That Certain Party/Then I'll Be Happy
Vi 20046 Sweet Southern Breeze

TED FIO RITO
Co 1967-D Then You've Never Been Blue/On Candle-light Lane
Vi 22252 Under a Texas Moon
Vi 22300 There Will Never Be Another Mary
Vi 22301 Hangin' on the Garden Gate
Br 6422 Willow Weep for Me/More Beautiful Than Ever
Br 6478 Darkness on the Delta/Baby
Br 6503 You Are Too Beautiful/Hallelujah, I'm a Bum
Br 6505 A Ghost of a Chance/I'll Take an Option on You
Br 6555 Hold Me/Sweetheart Darlin'
Br 6556 In the Park in Paree/Look What I've Got
Br 6736 My Little Grass Shack/What's Good for the Goose
Br 6924 Thank You for a Lovely Evening/Hot Dogs and Sasparella
Br 7315 Blue Moon/Were You Foolin'?
Br 7327 June in January/With Every Breath I Take
Br 7380 My Heart Is an Open Book/Here Comes Cookie
Br 7451 Outside of You/The Rose in Her Hair
Br 7452 Lulu's Back in Town/You Can Be Kissed
De 677 The Broken Record/Hypnotized
De 679 Cling to Me/Alone at a Table for Two
De 697 It's Been So Long/Let's Face the Music and Dance
De 746 Yours Truly Is Truly Yours/Honey
De 771 Knick Knacks on the Mantel/You Gotta Know How to Dance
De 777 Every Minute of the Hour/I'm a Fool for Loving You

De 1176 Sweet Leilani/Hawaiian Hospitality
De 2220 They Say / Everybody's Laughing
De 3936 No, No, Nora/King for a Day
De 4258 (theme) Rio Rita/Lily of Laguna
(with DICK POWELL, 1st side)
Br 6859 Fair and Warmer/I'll String Along with You

586. FIREHOUSE FIVE PLUS TWO

Dixieland combo. Played free-wheeling, uninhibited, happy music, rose to popularity in the dixieland revival of late 40s. Original personnel Ward Kimball (tb, B), Clarke Mallory (cl), Harper Goff (bn), Frank Thomas (p), Ed Penner (b, sax), Jim MacDonald (d), Johnny Lucas (t). Later Monte Mountjoy (d) and Danny Alguire (t). Group began in Hollywood 1945 when Kimball and other employees of Disney Studios played occasional jobs in spare time. As publicity gimmick, sometimes used old firetruck to travel to jobs. Group signed with Les Koenig of Good Time Jazz Records, made numerous popular sides 1949. Clancy Hayes later featured vocalist-banjoist. In 1951 band in movies HIT PARADE OF 1951 and GROUNDS FOR MARRIAGE. On TV in early 50s. Active into 60s.

RECORDS

FIREHOUSE FIVE PLUS TWO

GTJ 1 Firehouse Stomp/Blues My Naughty Sweetie Gave to Me
GTJ 2 San/Fireman's Lament
GTJ 5 Brass Bell/Everybody Loves My Baby
GTJ 6 Riverside Blues/Red Hot River Valley
GTJ 13 Tiger Rag/The World Is Waiting for the Sunrise
GTJ 14 Pagan Love Song/Yes, Sir, That's My Baby
GTJ 23 Copenhagen/Frankie and Johnny
GTJ 24 St. Louis Blues/Down Where the Sun Goes Down
GTJ 33 Lonesome Mama Blues/Sweet Georgia Brown

GTJ 46 San Antonio Rose/Show Me the Way to the Fire
GTJ 52 Mississippi Rag/Five Foot Two
GTJ 67 Chinatown, My Chinatown/ When You Wore a Tulip
GTJ 73 Lonesome Railroad Blues/ Runnin' Wild

LPs

FIREHOUSE FIVE PLUS TWO

GTJ L-10038 Crashes a Party!
GTJ L-10049 At Disneyland
GTJ L-10052 Goes to a Fire
GTJ L-11144 Around the World
GTJ L-12010 The Firehouse Five Story, Vol. 1
GTJ L-12011 The Firehouse Five Story, Vol. 2
GTJ L-12012 The Firehouse Five Story, Vol. 3
GTJ L-12018 Firehouse Five Plus Two Goes South
GTJ(10″)33-2

587. FISCHER, CARL   p ar cm B

*Born April 9, 1912, Los Angeles, Calif.
Died March 28, 1954, Sherman Oaks, Calif.*

Musician of many talents; in later career musical director for popular singer Frankie Laine. Earlier, pianist in bands on west coast and in Honolulu. Did arranging, including stock arrangements. Studio work in Hollywood. Assistant director of maritime service band, World War II. Resumed civilian career early 1945, with Pee Wee Hunt combo 1946. In 1947 with Laine, from sensational rise until Fischer's death. Pianist-arranger-conductor for Laine. Modest success as composer; leading songs *You've Changed* (1941), *It Started All Over Again* and *Who Wouldn't Love You?* (1942), *We'll Be Together Again* (1945). Lesser songs *A Kiss for Tomorrow; When You're in Love; Could Ja?; Black Lace; Promise; Baby, Just for Me; How Cute Can You Be?; Fool Am I; Where Is Our Love?; Minuet; Thanks for Your Kisses.*

RECORDS
(as conductor and/or pianist)

FRANKIE LAINE

Mer 1026 Black and Blue/Wrap Your Troubles in Dreams

Mer 1027 Blue, Turning Grey Over You/On the Sunny Side of the Street

Mer 5007 That's My Desire/By the River Sainte Marie

Mer 5028 Stay as Sweet as You Are

Mer 5091 We'll Be Together Again/ Shine

Mer 5130 Baby, Don't Be Mad at Me/Put 'Em in a Box, Tie 'Em with a Ribbon

Mer 5174 Singing the Blues/Thanks for You

Mer 5293 Georgia on My Mind/ You're Just the Kind

Mer 5390 A Kiss for Tomorrow/ Swamp Girl

Mer 5500 If I Were a Bell/Sleepy Ol' River

Mer 5656 You Left Me Out in the Rain/The Gang That Sang Heart of My Heart

Mer 5733 Anything for You/Get Happy

588. FISHER, DORIS   cm lyr vo
Born May 2, 1915, New York, N.Y.

Songwriter of 40s, teamed almost entirely with Allan Roberts on both music and lyrics. Daughter of famed composer Fred Fisher, collaborated with him on first hit song *Whispering Grass* (1940). Educated at Juilliard. Sang in night clubs and on radio, also with Eddy Duchin band in 1943. Recorded with own group as Penny Wise & Her Wise Guys.

SONGS
(with related shows)

1940—Whispering Grass

1941—Invitation to the Blues

1944—A SMALL WORLD movie (A Tender Word Will Mend It All); Into Each Life Some Rain Must Fall; You Always Hurt the One You Love; Saltin' Away My Sweet Dreams; Angelina

1945—Tampico; Jodie Man; Good, Good, Good; Benny's Coming Home on Saturday; You Can't See the Sun When You're Crying; Gee, It's Good to Hold You

1946—GILDA movie (Put the Blame on Mame; Amado Mio); DEAD RECKONING movie (Either It's Love or It Isn't); THRILL OF BRAZIL movie (A Man Is a Brother to a Mule)

1947—DOWN TO EARTH movie (They Can't Convince Me; Let's Stay Young Forever; People Have More Fun Than Anyone); VARIETY GIRL movie (Tired); That's Good Enough for Me

1948—THE LADY FROM SHANGHAI movie (Please Don't Kiss Me)

Other songs; *Tutti Frutti*; *I Wish*; *That Ole Devil Called Love*; *Fla-Ga-La-Pa*.

589. FISHER, EDDIE   vo
Born August 10, 1928, Philadelphia, Pa.

Leading popular singer of 50s. Strong melodic voice, straightforward style, excellent musicianship. Adept at show songs, also sang well in Al Jolson style at times. Sang in local amateur shows, and on radio in high school. Singing jobs with Buddy Morrow and Charlie Ventura in 1946. Singing at Grossinger's in New York State's Borscht Belt when heard by Eddie Cantor, joined Cantor's radio show in 1949. Instant hit, began successful recordings. Widely popular when career interrupted by military service 1952-3. After discharge zoomed to stardom 1953-4. Song series on TV, also many guest appearances throughout 50s. In late 50s had show with George Gobel, each starring on alternate weeks and working together occasionally. Highly publicized marriages to actresses Debbie Reynolds, Elizabeth Taylor and Connie Stevens. In movies ALL ABOUT EVE (1950), BUNDLE OF JOY (1956) and BUTTERFIELD 8 (1960). Leading record hits included *Many Times*; *I'm Walking Behind You*; *Oh, My Papa*; *Anytime*. In 60s infrequently on TV, top night clubs occasionally. In late 60s record hit *The Games Lovers Play*. Comeback tries in 70s, never regained 50s popularity.

RECORDS

EDDIE FISHER

Vi 20-3829 Just Say I Love Her/Give a Broken Heart a Chance to Cry
Vi 20-3901 Thinking of You/If You Should Leave Me
Vi 20-4036 My Mammy/My Blue Heaven
Vi 20-4037 My Mom/After I Say I'm Sorry
Vi 20-4038 At Sundown/My Buddy
Vi 20-4120 Unless/I Have No Heart
Vi 20-4359 Anytime/Never Before
Vi 20-4444 Trust in Me/Tell Me Why
Vi 20-4680 I'm Yours/Just a Little Lovin'
Vi 20-4830 Wish You Were Here/The Hand of Fate
Vi 20-5137 Downhearted/How Do You Speak to an Angel?
Vi 20-5293 I'm Walking Behind You/Just Another Polka
Vi 20-5365 With These Hands/When I Was Young
Vi 20-5552 Oh, My Papa/Until You Said Goodbye
Vi 20-6529 On the Street Where You Live/Sweet Heartaches

LPs

EDDIE FISHER

Vi LPM-1097 I Love You
Vi LPM-1181 May I Sing to You?
Vi LPM-1647 As Long as There's Music
Vi LPM-3726(S) Games That Lovers Play
Vi LSP-3820(S) People Like You
Vi LSP-3914 (S) You Ain't Heard Nothin' Yet
Vi(10″)LPM-3058 I'm in the Mood for Love
Vi(10″)LPM-3122 Sings Irving Berlin Favorites
Ramrod RRS-1-2 (S) (2-LP set) At the Winter Garden
Dot DLP-3631 Eddie Fisher Today!
Dot DLP-3670 Young and Foolish
Dot DLP-25785 His Greatest Hits

590. FISHER, FRED   cm lyr

Born September 30, 1875, Cologne, Germany, of American parents
Died January 14, 1942, New York, N.Y.

Prolific composer from 1904-1940. Most famous songs *Come, Josephine, in My Flying Machine*; *Peg o' My Heart*; *Dardanella*; *They Go Wild, Simply Wild, Over Me*; *Chicago*. Father of composer-lyricist Doris Fisher. Educated in Germany. Served in German navy and French Foreign Legion. Came to U.S. 1900, began songwriting in Chicago, later New York. Active in own and other publishing houses. Special material for movies in 30s, also for vaudeville and night clubs. Resumed publishing activities in New York. Wrote music and lyrics for some songs. Collaborators included lyricists Joseph McCarthy, Billy Rose, Grant Clarke, Howard Johnson, Alfred Bryan. Last song *Whispering Grass* (1940) in collaboration with daughter Doris. 1949 movie OH, YOU BEAUTIFUL DOLL featured life story and songs, with S. Z. ("Cuddles") Sakall in Fisher role.

SONGS
(with related shows)

1904—Ev'ry Little Bit Helps
1905—If the Man in the Moon Were a Coon
1907—And a Little Bit More
1909—In Sunny Italy
1910—Come, Josephine, in My Flying Machine; Oh! You Chicken; Any Little Girl That's a Nice Little Girl Is the Right Little Girl for Me
1911—After That I Want a Little More; If Every Hour Were a Day; Make Me Love You Like I Never Loved Before
1912—Big Blond Baby
1913—Peg o' My Heart (revived 1947); I'm on My Way to Mandalay
1914—There's a Little Spark of Love Still Burning; When It's Moonlight on the Alamo
1915—Norway; Siam; There's a Broken Heart for Every Light on Broadway
1916—Ireland Must Be Heaven, for My Mother Came from There; There's a Little Bit of Bad in Every Good Little Girl; You Can't Get Along with 'Em or without 'Em
1917—Lorraine, My Beautiful Alsace Lorraine; Night Time in Little

Italy; They Go Wild, Simply Wild, Over Me
1918—Happiness; Oui, Oui, Marie
1919—Dardanella
1920—Daddy, You've Been a Mother to Me
1921—I Found a Rose in the Devil's Garden; When the Honeymoon Was Over
1922—Chicago
1924—Savannah
1925—Sonya
1926—If All the Stars Were Pretty Babies
1927—Fifty Million Frenchmen; When the Morning Glories Wake Up in the Morning
1928—There Ain't No Sweet Man
1929—HOLLYWOOD REVUE OF 1929 movie (Bones and Tambourines; Strike Up the Band; Tableaux of Jewels); MY MAN movie (I'd Rather Be Blue); SO THIS IS COLLEGE movie (I Don't Want Your Kisses; Until the End); Happy Days and Lonely Nights
1930—CHILDREN OF PLEASURE movie (Girl Trouble; Dust); Blue Is the Night
1935—Georgia Rockin' Chair
1936—Moon Rose; Your Feet's Too Big
1938—Angels with Dirty Faces
1939—Two Fools in Love
1940—Whispering Grass

591. FISHER, FREDDIE "SCHNICK-LEFRITZ"   cl vo B

Born 1904, Lourdes, Iowa

Leader of band in late 30s and early 40s that specialized in unabashed, "outrageous" cornball music. Featured George Rock on trumpet and vocals. Band quickly gained attention with spirited, bumptious, purposely corny recordings. Played theatres, presenting hilarious comedy along with music. In movies GOLD DIGGERS IN PARIS (1938) and SEVEN DAYS ASHORE (1944). Some members left Fisher in early 40s to form rival Korn Kobblers band. In early 50s Fisher led a dixieland combo.

RECORDS

FREDDIE "SCHNICKLEFRITZ" FISHER
De 1309 Tiger Rag/Red Hot Mama

De 1501 When My Baby Smiles at Me/Nobody's Got the Blues but Me
De 1537 Listen to the Mocking Bird/ Washboard Man
De 1771 Colonel Corn/Wild Wild Women
De 1814 The Latin Quarter/I Wanna Go Back to Bali
De 1861 Turkey in the Straw/Land Where Sweet Daddies Grow
De 1929 Red Wing/When They Played the Polka
De 2034 Goofus/Silver Bell
De 2095-6-7-8-9 (album)
De 2168 Some of These Days/Hot Time in the Old Town Tonight
De 2409 Sugar Loaf Waltz/Winona Waltz
De 2511 Horsie, Keep Your Tail Up/ My Pony Boy
De 2741 They Go Wild Simply Wild Over Me/At The Moving Picture Ball
De 2965 Swingin' at the Hoedown/ Everything Is Hotsy Totsy Now
De 3295 My Black Hen/My Little Girl
De 3327 Bluebird/Wienerwurst Polka
De 3766 Are You from Dixie?/Between You and Me and the Lamp Post
De 3788 Bye Bye Blackbird/The Old Grey Mare
De 4425 Pistol Packin' Mama/- Wilberforce, Get Off That Horse!
De 27510 The Aba Daba Honeymoon/Wild Wild Women
King 15009 Dixie Lament/Oleo

592. FISHER, SALLIE   vo

Born c. 1881
Died June 8, 1950, Twenty-Nine Palms, Calif.

Beautiful star of Broadway musicals 1903-14. Appeared with George M. Cohan in 1912 revival of FORTY-FIVE MINUTES FROM BROADWAY in addition to first-run musicals.

BROADWAY MUSICALS

1903—THE BILLIONAIRE
1905—SERGEANT BRUE
1907—THE TATTOOED MAN
1908—A KNIGHT FOR A DAY

1909—THE PRINCE OF TONIGHT; A STUB-
BORN CINDERELLA .
1912—MODEST SUZANNE; THE WOMAN
HATERS
1913—EVA
1914—WATCH YOUR STEP

593. FITZGERALD, ELLA   vo cm B

Born April 25, 1918, Newport News, Va.

All-time great popular singer, jazz-styled.
Highly respected by musicians and jazz
fans. Clear voice with good quality, fine
beat, harmonics and musicianship. In
later years used voice as musical instrument to project progressive jazz patterns.
Orphaned young, she lived in New York
with aunt. Won Harlem Amateur Hour,
joined Chick Webb band in 1934. Immediate hit with jazz public but not until
1938 with general public via big record hit
with Webb *A-Tisket A-Tasket*. After
Chick's death mid-1939 Ella assumed
leadership of band. Theme *Let's Get Together*. In 1942 began career as single,
played clubs and theatres, recorded.
Toured with Jazz at the Philharmonic at
various periods from 1946 into 50s, made
concert tours in U.S. and abroad. In
movies RIDE 'EM, COWBOY (1942), PETE
KELLY'S BLUES (1955), ST. LOUIS BLUES
(1958), LET NO MAN WRITE MY EPITAPH
(1960). In demand on TV in late 50s and
60s, busy at clubs, concerts, festivals. Still
active in early 70s despite eye operation.
Co-composer of popular songs *You
Showed Me the Way* (1937) and *A-Tisket
A-Tasket* (1938), and lesser numbers *I Fell
in Love with a Dream*; *I Found My Yellow
Basket*; *Spinnin' the Webb*; *Chew, Chew,
Chew*; *Please Tell the Truth*; *Just One of
Those Nights*.

RECORDS

CHICK WEBB
De 830 Sing Me a Swing Song
De 831 A Little Bit Later On/Under
the Spell of the Blues
De 1032 You'll Have to Swing It/Vote
for Mr. Rhythm
De 1114 Love, You're Just a Laugh
De 1123 Take Another Guess/When I
Get Low I Get High
De 1220 You Showed Me the Way

De 1356 Love Is the Thing, So They
Say
De 1586 Rock It for Me
De 1587 The Dipsy Doodle
De 1840 A-Tisket A-Tasket
De 2021 Wacky Dust
De 2105 F.D.R. Jones/I Love Each
Move You Make
De 2556 Little White Lies/One Side of
Me
De 2665 Sugar Pie/That Was My
Heart

BENNY GOODMAN
Vi 25461 Goodnight My Love/Take
Another Guess
Vi 25469 Did You Mean It?

TEDDY WILSON
Br 7640 All My Life
Br 7729 My Melancholy Baby

ELLA FITZGERALD
De 2826 After I Say I'm Sorry/Baby,
What Else Can I Do?
De 2988 Starlit Hour/Is There Some-
body Else?
De 3199 I Fell in Love with a Dream/
Shake Down the Stars
De 3490 Taking a Chance on Love/
Cabin in the Sky
De 3608 Three Little Words/The One
I Love
De 4007 Jim/This Love of Mine
De 18605 Once Too Often/Time
Alone Will Tell
De 23546 Stone Cold Dead in de Mar-
ket/Patootie Pie
De 23866 A Sunday Kind of Love/
That's My Desire
De 23956 Lady Be Good/Flying
Home
De 24387 You Turned the Tables on
Me/How High the Moon
De 28774 You'll Have to Swing It (1 &
2)
De 29746 The Tender Trap/My One
and Only Love

LPs

ELLA FITZGERALD
Verve MGV-4001-2 (2-LP set) Sings
the Cole Porter Song Book
Verve MGV-4002-2 (2-LP set) Sings
the Rodgers & Hart Song Book
Verve MGV-4004 Like Someone in
Love

Verve MGV-4024 Sings Gershwin Song Book, Vol. 1
Verve MGV-4046-2 (2-LP set) Sings the Harold Arlen Song Book
Verve MGV-4054 Swings Brightly with Nelson (Riddle)
Verve MGV-4056 Rhythm Is My Business
De DXS-7156 (2-LP set) Best of Ella
De DL-8695 First Lady of Song

ELLA FITZGERALD-LOUIS ARMSTRONG
Verve MGV-4011-2 (2-LP set) PORGY AND BESS

CHICK WEBB
De DL-9223 King of the Savoy, Vol. 2 (1937-9 De RIs)

594. FLANAGAN, RALPH   p ar cm B

Born April 7, 1919, Loraine, Ohio

Leader of popular dance band of 50s and 60s featuring Glenn Miller reed sound. Chiefly responsible for Miller revival during that period. As teenager played piano in local bands. In 1940 pianist-arranger with Sammy Kaye. Joined merchant marine 1942, arranged for service band. Back in civilian life, arranged for Sammy Kaye, Charlie Barnet, Tony Pastor, Hal McIntyre, Gene Krupa, Boyd Raeburn, Alvino Rey, Blue Barron. Arranged for Perry Como Supper Club radio show and for singers Tony Martin and Mindy Carson. Began forming band in 1949 with young musicians comparatively unknown, booked engagements in 1950. Quickly rose to fame with well-received records, heavy club, ballroom and prom dates, radio spots. Although no connection with Glenn Miller, became prominent using Miller sound. Soon other bands followed, notably Jerry Gray, Art Mooney, Ray Anthony. Thus began Miller revival. Band's theme *Singing Winds*. Popular record hit *Hot Toddy*. Harry Prime excellent vocalist. Active into 60s, Flanagan fronted bands of varying sizes. In later years featured himself on piano. Credited as composer of *Singing Winds*, *Hot Toddy*, *Flanagan's Boogie*, *Albuquerque*.

RECORDS

RALPH FLANAGAN
Rbw 30401 Always/Make Believe

Rbw 30402 Low Gear/Come On In
Rbw 30403 Goodbye/Gettin' Sentimental Over You
Rbw 30404 St. Louis Blues/Basin Street Blues
Bb 30-0006 My Hero/Tell Me Why
Bb 30-0007 Don't Cry, Joe/Swing to 45
Bb 30-0008 Penthouse Serenade/ Whispering Hope
Bb 30-0017 'Way Back Home/The Trail of the Lonesome Pine
Vi 20-3724 Spring Will Be a Little Late This Year/Joshua
Vi 20-3888 Mona Lisa/Toreador
Vi 20-3911 (theme) Singing Winds/ Harbor Lights
Vi 20-3949 I've Never Been in Love Before/The Billboard March
Vi 20-4008 I Remember the Cornfields/Beautiful
Vi 20-4656 (theme) Singing Winds/ Honest and Truly
Vi 20-4703 I'll Walk Alone/Just a Little Lovin'
Vi 20-4705 I'm Yours/Kiss of Fire
Vi 20-4885 Tippin' In/I Should Care
Vi 20-5095 Hot Toddy/Serenade
Vi 20-5237 Moon/Albuquerque

LPs

RALPH FLANAGAN
Rbw(10")702 A Tribute to Glenn Miller (Rbw RIs)
Cam CAL-322 Dancing Down Broadway
Vi(10")LPM-1 Let's Dance Again with Flanagan

595. FLANAGAN, TOMMY   p

Born March 16, 1930, Detroit, Mich.

Jazz pianist, swinging bop style. Tasteful, inventive soloist, excellent accompanist. With Dexter Gordon in 1945. In later 40s and early 50s with Lucky Thompson, Milt Jackson, Billy Mitchell, Miles Davis and others. Military service awhile, early 50s. In later 50s with J. J. Johnson, Kenny Burrell and Tyree Glenn. At times led trio. Freelanced, in demand for records. With Coleman Hawkins in 1961, including tour abroad. Accompanied Ella Fitzgerald 1963-5, then Tony Bennett, Ella again in 1970 and later. Several tours abroad. Active in early 70s.

RECORDS
(all LPs)

TOMMY FLANAGAN
Pres MVLP-9 The Tommy Flanagan Trio
Pres S-7632 Trio Overseas

J. J. JOHNSON
Co CL-1030 First Place
Co CS-8109 (S) Blue Trombone

MILT JACKSON
Impulse S-70 (S) Jazz 'n' Samba
Atl 1294 Bags and Flutes
UA 4022 Bags' Opus

ART FARMER
Scepter 521 The Many Faces of Art Farmer
Mer MG-20766 Listen to Art Farmer and the Orchestra

KENNY BURRELL
Pres S-7308 (S) Blue Moods

SONNY ROLLINS
Pres PRLP-7079 Saxophone Colossus

THAD JONES
UA 4025 Motor City Scene
BN 1513 Detroit-New York Function

COLEMAN HAWKINS
Verve V-8509 Alive! At the Village Gate

COLEMAN HAWKINS-ROY ELDRIDGE-JOHNNY HODGES
Verve V-8504 Alive! At the Village Gate

BENNY GREEN
VJ 1005 The Swingin'est

DEXTER GORDON
Pres S-7829 (S) The Panther

595A. FLATT, LESTER
g bn vo cm lyr B

Born June 28, 1914, Overton County, Tenn.

Country and western performer. Teamed with Earl Scruggs to form group Foggy Mountain Boys. Excellent musicians, leading exponents of bluegrass style of folk music. Style's antecedents in pioneer artists Gid Tanner, Charlie Poole, Fisher Hendley, Frank Blevins. Flatt-Scruggs style formulated with Bill Monroe group 1945-8. Five-string banjo important as lead and background instrument. Fiddle, banjo and "dobro" guitar (using metal resonator to amplify sound) interwoven in playing. No other amplification. Style had drive, vigor, strong syncopation. Early career Flatt on Roanoke radio. Flatt-Scruggs group formed 1948, toured south. Often on Nashville's Grand Ole Opry. Huge popularity by late 50s. Flatt handled most vocals. Scruggs banjo exceptional, gave group identifying sound. Other members Paul Warren (v), Buck Graves ("dobro" g), Cousin Jake Tullock (b). LPs well received. Appearances on network TV, own shows on Nashville TV and radio. During prime years group toured about 100,000 miles per year, performed abroad. Recorded famous theme *The Ballad of Jed Clampett* for long-running TV series The Beverly Hillbillies. Duo separated early 1969; Flatt continued to lead Foggy Mountain Boys. Composer or co-composer of country songs including *Bouquet in Heaven, Someone You Have Forgotten, Little Girl in Tennessee, Crying My Heart Out Over You, Building on Sand, The Old Home Town, Why Don't You Tell Me So?, I'll Never Lose Another, I Won't Be Hanging Around, Petticoat Junction* (TV theme), *Nashville Cats.*

RECORDS

FLATT & SCRUGGS
Co 20830 Jimmy Brown/Somehow To-night
Co 21091 Why Did You Wander?/Thinking About You
Mer 6181 My Cabin in Caroline/We'll Meet Again, Sweetheart
Mer 6200 Bouquet in Heaven/Baby Blue Eyes

LPs

LESTER FLATT
Nugget 104 The One and Only Lester Flatt

FLATT & SCRUGGS
Co CL-1564 Foggy Mountain Banjo
Co CL-1664 Songs of Famous Carter Family
Co CL-1951 Hard Travelin'
Co CL-2045 At Carnegie Hall
Co CL-2570 Greatest Hits

Co CS-8630 (S)
Co CS-9443 (S) Strictly Instrumental
Co CS-9596 (S) Changin' Times
Co CS-9741 (S) Nashville Airplane
Ha HL-7340 Great Original Recordings
Ha HL-11265 Songs to Cherish
Archive FS-259
Mer 61162 Bonnie and Clyde

596. FLIPPEN, JAY C.   vo

Born c. 1898-1901
Died February 3, 1971, Los Angeles, Calif.

Versatile singer-comedian-actor of vaudeville, stage, radio, TV, movies. Played vaudeville early years. In Broadway musicals JUNE DAYS (1925), HELLO, LOLA and GREAT TEMPTATIONS (1926), PADLOCKS OF 1927, THE SECOND LITTLE SHOW (1930), TAKE A BOW (1944). Recordings of novelty and rhythm numbers during 20s. Used hot accompaniment, said to include cornetist Red Nichols. On radio at intervals as comedian-actor. In mid-30s replaced Major Bowes on WGN's Amateur Show when Bowes moved to network, filled in on Phil Baker show. In 1937 headed Broadway Melody Hour awhile. Most success in Hollywood as able character actor. Effective roles in more than 50 movies 1947-69.

RECORDS

JAY C. FLIPPEN & HIS GANG
Pe 12277 How Many Times?/Who Wouldn't?
Pe 12302 Short and Sweet/For My Sweetheart
Pe 12308 Hello Bluebird/He Didn't Know
Pe 12367 Clementine/You Don't Like It—Not Much
Pe 12373 I Ain't Got Nobody/An' Furthermore
Pe 12392 My Operation/Did You Mean It?
Pat 32218 How Could Red Riding Hood?
Pat 32260 South Wind
Pat 32321 Is She My Girl Friend?/I Told Them All About You

596A. FOLEY, RED   vo cm
(CLYDE JULIAN FOLEY)

Born June 17, 1910, Blue Lick (or possibly Berea), Ky.
Died September 19, 1968, Fort Wayne, Ind.

Country and western singer popular in 40s and 50s on radio and records. Good baritone, excellent gospel singer. Most famous number *Peace in the Valley*. Attended Georgetown College briefly. With Cumberland Ridge Runners group 1932 on Chicago's National Barn Dance radio show. Sang on Cincinnati radio awhile, returned to National Barn Dance show as single. Late 30s starred on radio on The Renfro Valley Show and Avalon Time. Often on Nashville's Grand Ole Opry. Top artist by early 40s. Reputedly first star to record from Nashville (1945). 1950 hits *Chattanooga Shoe Shine Boy*, also *Goodnight, Irene* in duet with Ernest Tubb. Starred several years on Ozark Jubilee radio and TV from Springfield, Mo. Occasionally on network TV; regular spot on Fess Parker show around 1962-3. Performed several times with son-in-law Pat Boone. Own publishing firm; composed country and western songs.

RECORDS

RED FOLEY & CUMBERLAND RIDGE RUNNERS
Ba 33021 Blonde Headed Girl/The Dying Rustler
RED FOLEY
De 5962 I Ain't Lazy—I'm Just Dreamin'/A Rose and a Prayer
De 6010 Will You Wait for Me, Little Darlin'?/Chiquita
De 6069 Pals of the Saddle/Someday Somewhere Sweetheart
De 6102 Smoke on the Water/Blue Star Shining Bright
De 6108 Hang Your Head in Shame/I'll Never Let You Worry My Mind
De 14505 Just a Closer Walk with Thee/Steal Away
De 14573 Peace in the Valley/Where Could I Go but to the Lord?
De 27810 Alabama Jubilee/Dixie
De 27981 Salty Dog Rag/Milk Bucket Boogie

De 28694 I Believe/Mansion Over the Hilltop
De 28944 Peace of Mind/Goodbye, Bobby Boy
De 29626 Blue Guitar/Just Call Me Lonesome
De 46035 Freight Train Boogie/Rockin' Chair Boogie
De 46205 Chattanooga Shoe Shine Boy/Sugarfoot Rag
De 46285 Music by the Angels/Someone Else, Not Me
De 46292 Tennessee Polka/Tennessee Saturday Night
De 46319 Peace in the Valley/Old Soldiers Never Die

RED FOLEY with LAWRENCE WELK ORCHESTRA
De 18698 Shame on You/At Mail Call Today

RED FOLEY-ERNEST TUBB
De 46255 Goodnight, Irene/Hillbilly Fever, #2

RED FOLEY-ROBERTA LEE
De 27763 Night Train to Memphis/If I Had a-Knowed, You Could-a Goed
De 28343 I Gotta Have You/Don't Believe Everything You Hear

RED FOLEY-ANDREWS SISTERS
De 14566 It Is No Secret/He Bought My Soul at Calvary

RED FOLEY-EVELYN KNIGHT
De 27378 My Heart Cries for You/ 'Tater Pie
De 27599 Idle Rumors/Crawdad Song

LPs

RED FOLEY
De DL-4107 Golden Favorites
De DL-8847 Let's All Sing with Red Foley
De DL-74849 Songs for the Soul
De DL-75003 Greatest Hits
De DL-75154 The Old Master
De DX-177 (2-LP set) The Red Foley Story
Vo 1351 Red Foley
Vo 3751

597. FORAN, DICK   vo
Born 1910

Actor in about 80 movies since 1934, many of them westerns. Starred in low-budget films, usually secondary roles in better ones. Sang in many movies in smooth Irish tenor. Non-western musicals included IN THE NAVY and KEEP 'EM FLYING (1941), BEHIND THE EIGHT BALL, PRIVATE BUCKAROO and RIDE 'EM, COWBOY (1942), HE'S MY GUY (1943). Best role probably in 1945 light comedy GUEST WIFE, co-starring with Don Ameche and Claudette Colbert. Sang on Burns & Allen radio show 1937. In 1943 starred in Broadway revival of musical A CONNECTICUT YANKEE. On TV occasionally in dramatic or comedy roles.

RECORDS

DICK FORAN
De 1039 Mexicali Rose/Moonlight Valley

DICK FORAN-VIVIENNE SEGAL
De 23315 Can't You Do a Friend a Favor?

598. FORD, HELEN   vo

Beautiful star of Broadway musicals, mostly during 20s. Also in non-musical plays, including THE RIVALS as late as 1942.

BROADWAY MUSICALS

1920—THE SWEETHEART SHOP
1922—FOR GOODNESS SAKE; THE GINGHAM GIRL
1923—HELEN OF TROY, NEW YORK
1924—NO OTHER GIRL
1925—DEAREST ENEMY
1927—PEGGY ANN
1928—CHEE-CHEE
1933—CHAMPAGNE SEC
1938—GREAT LADY

599. FORD, TENNESSEE ERNIE
vo cm
(ERNEST JENNINGS FORD)
Born February 13, 1919, Bristol, Tenn.

Singing star and TV personality of 50s and 60s. Specialized in gospel, country and western music, also capable singer of pop and contemporary music. Good ad-lib comic, used country humor and corn-ball expressions, in reality suave and polished. Began in Bristol radio late 30s. Announcer in Atlanta, singer-announcer in Knoxville. Military service, World War II. Resumed radio in California. On Pasadena radio worked with Capitol recording stars Cliffie Stone and Merle Travis, landed Capitol contract later. Early record hits *Shotgun Boogie* and *Mule Train*, also hit with Kay Starr on *I'll Never Be Free*. Solid comedy roles on Lucille Ball TV shows, also own summer show 1954. In mid-50s daily morning show popular several years. From late 1956 into 60s weekly night show. Continued to record; hit *Sixteen Tons* 1955 sold millions, became Ford trademark. Inactive in show business several years, came back semi-active in later 60s and into 70s. Occasionally on TV as guest or M.C. or on own specials. Composed songs including *Hogtied Over You, Kiss Me Big, Softly and Tenderly*.

RECORDS

KAY STARR-TENNESSEE ERNIE FORD
Cap 1124 I'll Never Be Free/Ain't Nobody's Business but My Own
TENNESSEE ERNIE FORD-DINNING SISTERS
Cap 1911 Rock City Boogie/Streamlined Cannon Ball
TENNESSEE ERNIE FORD
Cap 1295 Shotgun Boogie/I Ain't Gonna Let It Happen No More
Cap 1470 Kentucky Waltz/Strange Little Girl
Cap 1521 Mr. and Mississippi/She's My Baby
Cap 1775 Kissin' Bug Boogie/Woman Is a Five-Letter Word
Cap 2338 Sweet Temptation/I Don't Know
Cap 2810 River of No Return/Give Me Your Word
Cap 3262 Sixteen Tons/You Don't Have to Be a Baby to Cry
Cap 32173 Ballad of Davy Crockett/Farewell
Cap 40258 Mule Train/Anticipation Blues
Cap 40280 Cry of the Wild Goose

LPs

TENNESSEE ERNIE FORD
Cap T-1380 Sixteen Tons
Cap T-1473 Come to the Fair
Cap T-1680 Sing a Spiritual with Me
Cap T-2444 My Favorite Things
Cap ST-127 (S) Songs I Like to Sing
Cap ST-218 (S) New Wave

Cap ST-2896 (S) World of Pop and Country
Cap STCL-2942 (S) (3-LP set) Deluxe Set
Cap ST-583 (S) Everything Is Beautiful
Pick S-3047 (S) Bless Your Pea Pickin' Heart
Pick S-3066 (S) I Love You So Much
Pick S-3118 (S) I Can't Help It

600. FORDE, HAL   vo

Handsome actor-singer of Broadway stage.

BROADWAY MUSICALS

1911—THE ENCHANTRESS
1913—ADELE
1915—MAID IN AMERICA
1916—THE GIRL FROM BRAZIL
1917—OH, BOY!
1920—HONEYDEW
1922—MOLLY DARLING
1924—HASSARD SHORT'S RITZ REVUE
1927—OH, ERNEST!
1933—AS THOUSANDS CHEER
1936—GEORGE WHITE'S SCANDALS OF 1936

601. FORESYTHE, REGINALD

p ar cm B

Born May 28, 1907, London, England, of West Indian descent

Noted avant-garde composer-arranger of mid-30s. Jazz-novelty numbers *Dodging a Divorcee* and *Serenade for a Wealthy Widow* popular at dawn of swing era. In California movie studios late 20s, Chicago in early 30s. Returned to England, led band 1933. Four unusual records in U.S. 1935 featuring Benny Goodman, all-star personnel, all reeds plus rhythm. Returned 1935 to England to stay, lead band. RAF, World War II. Again led band awhile in London clubs. Foresythe's works modernistic, ahead of their time. Used unusual instrumentation, voicing, harmony and melody lines, tightly knit arrangements. Up-tempo numbers swing lightly; slow pieces moody, descriptive. Other compositions *Deep Forest* (theme of Earl Hines), two good pop songs *Mississippi Basin* (1933) and *Because It's Love*

(1934), numerous instrumentals recorded by own band (sometimes billed The New Music of Reginald Foresythe).

RECORDS

REGINALD FORESYTHE (piano solos)
  Co(E) 1407 Because It's Love/St. Louis Blues
REGINALD FORESYTHE-ARTHUR YOUNG (piano duets)
  Co(E) 1264 Camembert/Chromolithograph
  Vi 26224 Mood Indigo/Solitude
  Vi 26274 Tiger Rag/St. Louis Blues
  De(E) 770 Anything Goes
  De(E) 779 With the Duke
  De(E) 5758 Cheek to Cheek/The Piccolino
  De(E) 5759 BROADWAY MELODY OF 1936 Medley/BROADWAY GONDOLIER Medley
REGINALD FORESYTHE ORCHESTRA
  Co(E) 675 Angry Jungle/Serenade for a Wealthy Widow
  Co(E) 726 Garden of Weed/Berceuse for an Unwanted Child
  Co(E) 744 Bit/The Duke Insists
  Co(E) 787 Volcanic/Autocrat Before Breakfast
  Co 2916-D Serenade for a Wealthy Widow/Angry Jungle
  Co 3000-D The Duke Insists/Garden of Weed
  Co 3012-D Dodging a Divorcee/Lullaby
  Co 3060-D Melancholy Clown/The Greener the Grass
  De(E) 5660 Landscape/Homage to Armstrong
  De(E) 5711 Tea for Two/Sweet Georgia Brown
  De(E) 6203 Swing for Roundabout/The Revolt of the Yes Men
  De(E) 6363 Aubade/Burlesque

602. FORREST, GEORGE   lyr cm p
(nicknamed CHET)

Born July 31, 1915, Brooklyn, N.Y.

Songwriter who teamed with Robert Wright on music and lyrics. Their specialty: adapting old or classical material to popular versions. Prime example: collaboration with composer Rudolf Friml to adapt his *Chansonette* to popular song *Donkey Serenade* for 1937 movie THE FIREFLY. Other well-known songs of team *Always and Always*; *It's a Blue World*; *At the Balalaika*; *Strange Music*; *Stranger in Paradise*; *Baubles, Bangles and Beads*. Active in writing for movies mid-30s into 40s. Other collaborators Walter Donaldson, Edward Ward, Franz Waxman, Herbert Stothart, George Posford. Later wrote and adapted scores for Broadway shows SONG OF NORWAY (1944), MAGDALENA (1948), KISMET (1953), KEAN (1961).

SONGS
(with related shows; all with Robert Wright)

1936—SINNER TAKE ALL movie, Walter Donaldson-cm (I'd Be Lost without You)
1937—THE FIREFLY movie, Rudolf Friml-cm (The Donkey Serenade); MAYTIME movie, Herbert Stothart-cm (Vive L'Opera; Street Singer); AFTER THE THIN MAN movie, Walter Donaldson-cm (Blow That Horn); SARATOGA movie, Walter Donaldson-cm (title song; The Horse with the Dreamy Eyes)
1938—MANNEKIN movie, Edward Ward-cm (Always and Always); THREE COMRADES movie, Franz Waxman-cm (Comrade Song; Yankee Ragtime College Jazz; How Can I Leave Thee; Mighty Forest); SWEETHEARTS movie (new lyrics for several old Victor Herbert songs)
1939—BALALAIKA movie, Herbert Stothart and George Posford-cm (At the Balalaika; Ride, Cossack, Ride; The Volga Boatman; Toreador Song); THE WOMEN movie, Edward Ward-cm (Forevermore)
1940—MUSIC IN MY HEART movie (It's a Blue World; Ho! Punchinello)
1942—FLYING WITH MUSIC movie (Pennies for Peppino)
1944—SONG OF NORWAY stage show (adapted Edvard Grieg melodies; best song Strange Music)
1948—MAGDALENA stage show, Villa-Lobos-cm (lavish score, songs unimportant)

1953—KISMET stage show (adapted Alexander Borodin melodies; songs: Stranger in Paradise; Baubles, Bangles and Beads; And This Is My Beloved; Night of My Nights; He's in Love; Sands of Time)
1955—KISMET movie (original stage score)
1961—KEAN stage show (Sweet Danger; Chime In!; Elena; The Fog and the Grog; others)
1965—ANYA stage show (adapted Rachmaninoff melodies; unsuccessful show)

603. FORREST, HELEN   vo
Born April 12, 1918, Atlantic City, N.J.
A leading band vocalist of 30s and 40s. Featured with Artie Shaw, Benny Goodman and Harry James during their prime years. Voice strong and warm, interpreted lyrics sensitively. Early in career sang on radio as Bonnie Blue, The Blue Lady, Marlene, other names. Sang with brother's band in club in Washington, D.C. Rose fast after joining Artie Shaw late summer 1938. Shaw zoomed and Miss Forrest helped. Joined Benny Goodman December 1939 after Shaw abruptly quit, remained till August 1941. Joined Harry James, another band rising to the top. Sang on several James hits: *I Don't Want to Walk without You, I Had the Craziest Dream, I've Heard That Song Before.* In movies with band: SPRINGTIME IN THE ROCKIES (1942), BATHING BEAUTY and TWO GIRLS AND A SAILOR (1944). Also sang *Time Waits for No One* in 1944 movie SHINE ON HARVEST MOON and *Out of Nowhere* in 1945 movie YOU CAME ALONG. Became a single late 1943, played clubs and theatres. In late 1944 teamed with singing star Dick Haymes on radio show which continued as popular series several years. She also recorded through the years. By mid-50s less active in show business. In early 60s toured with Sam Donahue & The Tommy Dorsey Orchestra. In later 60s occasionally on TV on nostalgic shows. In later years worked clubs again; still active in 70s.

RECORDS
ARTIE SHAW
  Bb 7889 I Have Eyes/You're a Sweet Little Headache

Bb 10075 They Say/A Room with a View
Bb 10079 Say It with a Kiss/It Took a Million Years
Bb 10188 I'm in Love with the Honorable Mr. So and So
Bb 10195 You Grow Sweeter as the Years Go By/If You Ever Change Your Mind
Bb 10307 I Poured My Heart into a Song
Bb 10319 All I Remember Is You
Bb 10334 Melancholy Mood/Moon Ray
Bb 10345 I'll Remember/Easy to Say
Bb 10468 Without a Dream to My Name/A Table in a Corner

BENNY GOODMAN
  Co 35391 How High the Moon/The Fable of the Rose
  Co 35420 The Sky Fell Down/It Never Entered My Mind
  Co 35461 Ev'ry Sunday Afternoon/Devil May Care
  Co 35472 I'm Nobody's Baby/Buds Won't Bud
  Co 35487 The Moon Won't Talk/I Can't Love You Any More
  Co 35574 Dreaming Out Loud/I Can't Resist You
  Co 36022 My Sister and I
  Co 35863 Hard to Get
  Co 35869 Cabin in the Sky/Taking a Chance on Love
  Co 35910 These These You Left Me/Yes, My Darling Daughter
  Co 35944 Bewitched/This Is New
  Co 35962 Perfidia
  Co 36209 When the Sun Comes Out
  Co(12")55001 The Man I Love
  Co(12")55002 More Than You Know

HARRY JAMES
  Co 36478 I Don't Want to Walk without You
  Co 36518 I Remember You
  Co 36533 Skylark
  Co 36599 But Not for Me
  Co 36650 That Soldier of Mine/Mr. Five by Five
  Co 36659 I Had the Craziest Dream
  Co 36668 I've Heard That Song Before
  Co 36677 I Heard You Cried Last Night

LIONEL HAMPTON
Vi 26751 I'd Be Lost without You
DICK HAYMES-HELEN FORREST
De 23317 Long Ago and Far Away/ Look for the Silver Lining
De 23434 I'll Buy That Dream/Some Sunday Morning
De 23472 I'm Always Chasing Rainbows/Tomorrow Is Forever
HELEN FORREST
De 18600 Time Waits for No One/In a Moment of Madness
De 18624 Every Day of My Life/I Learned a Lesson I'll Never Forget
De 18723 I'm Glad I Waited for You/ My Guy's Come Back
MGM 10040 Don't Tell Me/I Wish I Didn't Love You So
MGM 10050 You Do/Baby, Come Home
MGM 10105 Don't Take Your Love from Me/Don't You Love Me Anymore?
MGM 10373 Why Is It?/I Don't See Me in Your Eyes Anymore
MGM 11128 Swingin' Down the Lane/Snowman
Bell(7")1017 Changing Partners/ Lover, Come Back to Me

LPs

HELEN FORREST
Cap T-704 Voice of the Name Bands
BENNY GOODMAN
Co GL-523 (Co Ris)
Co CL-534 (Co RIs)
SAM DONAHUE & THE TOMMY DORSEY ORCHESTRA
Vi LSP-2830 (Recorded Live from Americana Hotel in New York)
HARRY JAMES
Ha HL-7159 And His Great Vocalists
DICK HAYMES
De(10")DL-5243 Songs with Helen Forrest
ARTIE SHAW
Vi LPM-1570 Any Old Time
Cam CAL-515 Artie Shaw Swings Show Tunes
Cam CAL-584 One Night Stand

604. FORREST, JIMMY   ts cm B
Born January 24, 1920, St. Louis, Mo.
Composer of all-time jazz standard *Night*

Train. Underrated jazzman on tenor sax; strong tone, great facility, hard-driving modern style. In late 30s worked in St. Louis area with Fate Marable, Jeter-Pillars band, Dewey Jackson and others. New York in early 40s; period with Jay McShann. With Andy Kirk 1943-7. Led combo awhile in St. Louis. With Duke Ellington late 1949-50. Freelanced in 50s and 60s, led group at intervals.

RECORDS

JIMMY FORREST
United 110 Night Train/Bolo Blues

LPs

JIMMY FORREST
Delmark DL-404 All the Gin Is Gone
Pres 7218 (S) Most Much
Pres 7235 (S) Sit Down and Relax
Pres 7712 (S) The Best of Jimmy Forrest
HARRY EDISON
Verve V-8295
BENNY GREEN
Time 52021
BLUE MITCHELL
Mainstream MRL-315
THE MAINSTREAM SEXTET
Cam CAL-554 Mainstream Jazz

605. FOSDICK, DUDLEY   mel
Born 1902, Liberty, Ind.
Died June 27, 1957

Early jazzman on mellophone, unusual instrument for jazz. Early experience in brother's band, also with Ted Weems awhile. With Red Nichols in 20s on memorable record sessions. In late 20s with Tommy Gott, Don Voorhees, Roger Wolfe Kahn. Freelanced, radio staff musician in early 30s. Joined Guy Lombardo in 1936, remained into early 40s. Resumed studio work, remained active into early 50s.

RECORDS

RED NICHOLS
Br 3854 Nobody's Sweetheart/Avalon
Br 3855 Japanese Sandman
Br 3955 Whispering/There'll Come a Time
Br 3961 Margie/Panama
Br 3989 Imagination/Original Dixieland One-Step

Br(12″)20066 Poor Butterfly/Can't You Hear Me Calling, Caroline?

LOUISIANA RHYTHM KINGS
Vo 15779 Futuristic Rhythm/Out Where the Blues Begin
Vo 15784 That's a-Plenty

IRVING MILLS & HIS HOTSY TOTSY GANG
Br 4014 Doin' the New Low Down/ Diga Diga Doo

MIFF MOLE
OK 41098 Crazy Rhythm/You Took Advantage of Me

GENE FOSDICK'S HOOSIERS
Vo 14535 Farewell Blues/Aunt Hagar's Blues

606. FOSTER, CHUCK　　cl as ts vo B

Born August 26, 1912, Jeanette, Pa.

Leader of hotel-style band from late 30s into 70s. Early experience locally, then in California beginning 1935. Formed band 1939. Popular in Los Angeles, toured west coast. Later played midwest. Theme *Oh, You Beautiful Doll*. Military service awhile, World War II. In late 1944 reorganized band, played Chicago's Black Hawk Restaurant. Foster sang, also featured vocalists Jimmy Castle, Ray Robbins, Dottie Dotson, Jean Gordon, Tommy Ryan in 40s. Active into 70s.

RECORDS

CHUCK FOSTER
VD(12″)19 She Don't Wanna/Night Train to Memphis//Leave Us Face It
OK 5915 (theme) Oh, You Beautiful Doll/Sleepy Time Gal
OK 6003 All I Desire/Spring Fever
OK 6304 The Kiss Polka/I've Been Drafted
OK 6333 If It's You/Just Once Again
Mer 3054 (theme) Oh, You Beautiful Doll/My Cousin Louella
Mer 3058 Linda/Roses in the Rain
Mer 3064 On the Avenue/Just Around the Corner
Mer 5085 The Foggy Foggy Dew/My Cousin Louella
Mer 5125 Dardanella/Who Put That Dream in Your Eyes?
Vo 55013 Room Full of Roses/There's Yes Yes in Your Eyes

Vo 55034 Zing! Went the Strings of My Heart/I Love My Baby
Vo 55035 That Lucky Old Sun/My Bolero

LPs

CHUCK FOSTER
Phillips 1965 At the Peabody

607. FOSTER, FRANK　　ts cl ar cm B

Born September 23, 1928, Cincinnati, Ohio

Gained fame as star tenor saxist with Count Basie. Big-toned, swinging, facile modern style. Attended Wilberforce University. Worked in Cincinnati with Jack Jackson and Andrew Johnson. With Snooky Young band in Detroit 1949-50, also arranged. Job at Bluebird Inn in Detroit 1950. Military service 1951-2 in Korea. Joined Basie in 1953, remained till 1964. Wrote originals and arrangements for Basie, including backgrounds for singer Joe Williams. Freelanced in later 60s, worked with Lloyd Price, Lionel Hampton, Woody Herman, again with Basie. Freelance arranging, composing. Led big band or combo at intervals. In early 70s with Elvin Jones combo. Composed jazz numbers *Shiny Stockings*; *Vested Interest*; *May We*; *Who, Me?*; *Blues for Daddy-O*; *Blues in Hoss' Flat*.

RECORDS
(all LPs)

COUNT BASIE
Clef MGC-647 Dance Session Album No. 2
Clef MGC-666 Basie
Clef MGC-678 Count Basie Swings, Joe Williams Sings
Roul R-52106 Basie Easin' It

DUKE ELLINGTON/COUNT BASIE
Co CL-1715 First Time! The Count Meets the Duke

JOE NEWMAN
Vang VRS-8007 Joe Newman & His Band
Story STLP-905 I Feel Like a Newman

MATTHEW GEE
Riv 12-221 Jazz by Gee!

BENNY GREEN
VJ 1005 The Swingin'est

GEORGE WALLINGTON
BN(10″)5045 George Wallington Showcase

THELONIOUS MONK
Pres(10″)180 Thelonious Monk Quintet

(miscellaneous artists)
Jazztone J-1220 The Count's Men
VJ 3024 Juggin' Around

ELVIN JONES
BN 84369 (S) Genesis

FRANK FOSTER
Vogue LD-209 Frank Foster Quartet
Mainstream MRL-349 The Silent Minority
Pres 7461 (S) Fearless
Pres 7479 (S) Soul Outing
BN 84278 (S) Manhattan Fever
BN(10″)5043 New Faces—New Sounds

608. FOSTER, POPS   b tu
(GEORGE MURPHY FOSTER)

Born 1892, McCall, La.
Died October 30, 1969, San Francisco, Calif.

Bass man with 60-year career in music from pioneer jazz days into late 60s. Mostly with dixieland combos. Played tuba in early days, switched to string bass late 20s (an early influence in use of bass in dance bands). Grew up in New Orleans. Began professionally around 1906, worked parade and dance jobs in area. A few years later jobbed with Kid Ory, Armand Piron, King Oliver. With Fate Marable band on riverboats 1918-21. Joined Charlie Creath in St. Louis 1921, later with Dewey Jackson there. To California 1923, worked with Kid Ory, Mutt Carey, others. In mid-20s to St. Louis; periods again with Creath and Jackson. Joined Luis Russell in New York 1929. Louis Armstrong took over leadership 1935. Foster remained till 1940, with intervals away. In early 40s with Teddy Wilson, Happy Caldwell and Norman Langlois (as duo). Less active in music 1942-5, then with Sidney Bechet and Art Hodes, in Europe with Mezz Mezzrow. In 1948 joined Bob Wilber dixieland group, remained when Jimmy Archey assumed leadership 1950, including 1952 European

tour. With Conrad Janis combo, then late 1955-6 long European tour with Sam Price. In later 50s and early 60s on west coast with Earl Hines combo; based there, freelanced in later 60s. 1966 European tour. Activities curtailed by leg operation.

RECORDS

HENRY ALLEN
Vi 38080 Swing Out/Feeling Drowsy
Vi 38088 Funny Feathers Blues/How Do They Do It That Way?

LUIS RUSSELL
OK 8734 Jersey Lightning/New Call of the Freaks
Vo 1579 Saratoga Drag/Case on Dawn
Vi 22789 Goin' to Town/Say the Word

LOUIS ARMSTRONG
OK 8680 Mahogany Hall Stomp
OK 8774 Dallas Blues
OK 41375 Blue, Turning Grey over You/Song of the Islands
De 685 The Music Goes 'Round and Around/Rhythm Saved the World
De 1661 Struttin' with Some Barbecue
De 2267 Jeepers Creepers/What Is This Thing Called Swing?

WILTON CRAWLEY
Vi 38094 Snake Hip Dance/She's Driving Me Wild

CHARLES CREATH
OK 8477 Crazy Quilt/Butter Finger Blues

J. C. HIGGINBOTHAM
OK 8772 Give Me Your Telephone Number/Higginbotham Blues

DEWEY JACKSON
Vo 1040 Capitol Blues/She's Cryin' for Me

JELLY ROLL MORTON
Vi 23402 Jersey Joe/Sweet Peter
Vi 23424 Mississippi Mildred

MOUND CITY BLUE BLOWERS
Vi 38087 Tailspin Blues/Never Had a Reason to Believe in You
Vi 38100 One Hour/Hello, Lola

CARNIVAL THREE
Disc 6001 Harlem Hotcha/Lorenzo's Blues
Disc 6002 Bandana Days/Creole Lullaby

MEZZ MEZZROW
Vi 25636 Blues in Disguise/That's How I Feel Today

SIDNEY BECHET
BN(12″)43 Blue Horizon/Muskrat Ramble
BN(12″)44 St. Louis Blues/Jazz Me Blues

ART HODES
BN(12″)45 Shake That Thing/Apex Blues

TONY PARENTI
Jazzology 3 Sunday/There'll Be Some Changes Made
Jazzology 4 Dippermouth Blues/ Moonlight on the Ganges

CONRAD JANIS
Ci 1076 K.C. Stomps/Oriental Man

BOB WILBER
Ci 1062 Sweet Georgia Brown/Coal Black Shine
Ci 1063 The Mooche/When the Saints Go Marching In
Ci 1064 Zig Zag/Limehouse Blues

LPs

MUGGSY SPANIER
Ci(10″)L-423 This Is Jazz

TONY PARENTI
Jazzology J-1 And His New Orleanians

SIDNEY BECHET
Co CL-836

CONRAD JANIS
Ci(10″)L-404 Conrad Janis' Tailgate Jazz Band

BOB WILBER and SIDNEY BECHET
Ci(10″)L-406

WILD BILL DAVISON
Riv 12-211 Sweet and Hot

LUIS RUSSELL
Pa(E)PMC-7025 (OK RIs)

MEZZ MEZZROW
"X"(10″)LVA-3015 Swing Session (Vi RIs)

609. FOSTER, STUART   vo d

Born June 30, 1918, Binghamton, N.Y.

Vocalist best known for period with Tommy Dorsey. Strong baritone, melodious and straightforward style. Early jobs locally as drummer, also sang. To New York 1940, got vocal job in Ina Ray Hutton's all-male band, remained till 1944. With Guy Lombardo several months. Joined Dorsey early 1945, carried on tradition of great Dorsey male singing stars. In 1947 movie THE FABULOUS DORSEYS. Prominent with Dorsey, stayed till mid-1947. Began career as single, played clubs and radio shows. In 1951 sang with Johnny Guarnieri combo on radio. Occasional appearances on TV. Freelance recording with various bands. Career in 50s and 60s no great success.

RECORDS

INA RAY HUTTON
El 5007 A Sinner Kissed an Angel/ Madelaine
OK 5830 A Handful of Stars
OK 6335 At Last

GUY LOMBARDO
De 18634 Always/The Trolley Song

TOMMY DORSEY
Vi 20-1657 A Friend of Yours
Vi 20-1669 Out of This World/June Comes Around Every Year
Vi 20-1710 Nevada
Vi 20-1728 A Door Will Open/Aren't You Glad You're You?
Vi 20-1787 Why Do I Love You?
Vi 20-1809 If I Had a Wishing Ring/ We'll Gather Lilacs
Vi 20-1901 I Don't Know Why/Remember Me?
Vi 20-1985 There Is No Breeze/This Time
Vi 20-2122 How Are Things in Glocca Morra?/When I'm Not Near the Girl I Love
Vi 20-2210 Time After Time/It's the Same Old Dream
Vi 20-2870 The Story of a Starry Night
Vi 20-2871 The Things I Love
Vi 20-2872 Our Love

HUGO WINTERHALTER
Vi 20-4087 I'll Never Know Why
Vi 20-4212 Blow, Blow, Winds of the Sea/Make Believe Land
Vi 20-5092 Your Mother and Mine

LEROY HOLMES
MGM 11569 Julie

RUSS CASE
MGM 10528 Wishing Star
MGM 10554 A Thousand Violins

XAVIER CUGAT
Vi 47-5391 You Too, You Too

GORDON JENKINS
    De 28806 Fury/Afternoon Dream
STUART FOSTER
    Abbey 15065 Take Me/Chimney Smoke

LPs

TOMMY DORSEY
    20th Fox TCF-101-2 (2-LP set) Tommy Dorsey's Greatest Band (transcription RIs)

610. FOUNTAIN, PETE   cl ts B

Born July 3, 1930, New Orleans, La.
Fat-toned dixieland clarinetist with commercial appeal. Influenced by Benny Goodman and Irving Fazola. First professional job in New Orleans 1949; played clubs. Briefly with Assunto brothers before group named Dukes of Dixieland. With Phil Zito and Basin Street Six 1950-4; late 1956-7 with Al Hirt. Led group awhile. Hired by Lawrence Welk mid-1957 for TV; instant success. Featured weekly on Welk show, became popular even among listeners who cared little for jazz. Featured on Welk LPs. Left Welk early 1959 at height of popularity, returned to New Orleans to form combo. Big attraction, began recording well received LPs. Opened club in New Orleans, The French Quarter Inn, based there most of 60s and early 70s. Played concerts in various cities; occasional TV.

RECORDS

BASIN STREET SIX
    Ci 1072 Margie/Farewell Blues
PETE FOUNTAIN
    Southland 7018 Cherry/Song of the Wanderer
    Southland 7019 Home/Struttin' with Some Barbecue

LPs

PETE FOUNTAIN
    Cor CRL-57200 Lawrence Welk Presents Pete Fountain
    Cor CRL-57313 Pete Fountain Day
    Cor CRL-57314 At the Bateau Lounge
    Cor CRL-57333 Salutes the Great Clarinetists
    Cor CRL-57389 Bourbon Street
    Cor CRL-57440 South Rampart Street Parade

    Cor CRL-57453 Pete's Place
    Cor CRL-57460 Licorice Stick
    Cor CRL-57473 Mr. Stick Man
    Cor CRL-57474 Standing Room Only
PETE FOUNTAIN-AL HIRT
    Verve V-1028 Blockbustin' Dixie
AL HIRT
    Verve V-1012 Jazz Band Ball
JACK DELANEY
    Southland SLP-214
DUKES OF DIXIELAND
    Vi LPM-2097 Featuring Pete Fountain

611. FOUR FRESHMEN   vocal quartet

> **ROSS BARBOUR** *(d t; born December 31, 1928)*
>
> **DON BARBOUR** *(g; born April 19, 1927)*
>
> **BOB FLANIGAN** *(tb b; born August 22, 1926)*
>
> **KEN ERRAIR** *(t b Fr-h; born January 23, 1928)*
>
> [Errair replaced 1956 by Ken Albers (t mel)]

Singing group, pioneers in progressive jazz harmonics and patterns by vocal units. Carried group singing beyond style of Modernaires, Pied Pipers and Merry Macs. Arrangements featured by turns soft unison singing, full harmony, modern voicing, strong phrasing, varied dynamics. Men adept instrumentalists in modern style—great asset for concerts, festivals and club jobs. Group formed 1948 while members attending Arthur Jordan Conservatory of Music in Indianapolis. Performed in midwest, attained some popularity. Big boost from Stan Kenton in getting contract with Capitol. Records caught on, thanks to innovative sounds. In 1951 movie RICH, YOUNG AND PRETTY. Busy through 50s; occasional spots on TV. Not as prominent during 60s and into 70s but still worked.

RECORDS

FOUR FRESHMEN
    Cap 1293 Then I'll Be Happy/Mr. B's Blues
    Cap 2152 It's a Blue World/Tuxedo Junction
    Cap 2286 The Day Isn't Long Enough/Stormy Weather

Cap 2398 Poinciana/Baltimore Oriole
Cap 2564 Holiday/It Happened Once Before
Cap 2745 Seems Like Old Times
Cap 2832 I'll Be Seeing You/Please Remember
Cap 2898 We'll Be Together Again/ My Heart Stood Still
Cap 3154 Day by Day/How Can I Tell Her?

LPs

FOUR FRESHMEN
Cap T-522 Voices in Modern
Cap T-683 And Five Trombones
Cap T-743 Freshmen Favorites
Cap T-763 And Five Trumpets
Cap T-844 And Five Saxes
Cap T-1485 The Freshman Year
Lib 7590 Class by Themselves
Lib 7630 Different Strokes
STAN KENTON
Cap TBO-1327 (2-LP set) Road Show

612. FOX, HARRY   vo

Born 1882, Pomona, Calif.
Died July 20, 1959, Woodland Hills, Calif.

Handsome leading man and singer in vaudeville and on Broadway. Married awhile to Yansci Dolly of Dolly Sisters; couple performed in vaudeville together.

BROADWAY MUSICALS

1912—THE PASSING SHOW OF 1912
1913—THE HONEYMOON EXPRESS
1915—MAID IN AMERICA
1916—STOP! LOOK! LISTEN!
1918—OH, LOOK!
1924—ROUND THE TOWN (unsuccessful show)
1925—GEORGE WHITE'S SCANDALS OF 1925

RECORDS

HARRY FOX
Co A-2557 I'm Always Chasing Rainbows
Co A-2600 Oh! You La! La!
Co A-2732 Anything Is Nice If It Comes from Dixieland
Co A-2769 I'm Goin' to Break That Mason-Dixon Line
Co A-2787 Alexander's Band Is Back in Dixieland

Co A-2828 I Lost My Heart in Dixieland/Bless My Swanee River Home
Co A-2942 'Way Down Barcelona Way
Co A-2964 I'd Love to Fall Asleep and Wake Up in My Mammy's Arms/ Rock-a-bye Lullaby Mammy

613. FOX, ROY   c B

Born c. 1902-3, Denver, Colo.

American bandleader of late 20s who went on to greater fame in England during 30s. Early cornet work on summer job at Santa Monica, Calif.; soon after joined Abe Lyman. At 19 led 19-piece band at Club Royale in Culver City, Calif. Later played choice spots in Los Angeles, Miami, New York. 15-month run at Hollywood's Cocoanut Grove, later at Montmartre Cafe. Recorded in late 20s, including sides co-featured with singer June Pursell. Supervisor of music at Fox Studios for nascent sound movies late 20s. In 1929 took seven-piece American band to England; first job at Cafe de Paris in London. Remained in England, became musical director of Decca Records. Formed outstanding sweet-swing band that quickly became one of England's most popular, 1931-2. Played London's Monseigneur Restaurant. Al Bowlly featured vocalist, Lew Stone (p) and Nat Gonella (t,vo) in band. Active recording. Used *Whispering* for theme song.

Stone took over leadership in late 1932. Illness curtailed Fox's career then and at other times in 30s. Back soon with another good band, continued to 1939. Then to Australia for health. During World War II Fox lived in California. At war's end back to England, attempted to resume as bandleader. Postwar economics wouldn't support big band. Late 1947 music-hall tour unsuccessful, hampered by snowstorms. In 1952 abandoned comeback try, later became agent in English show business. Active through 60s.

RECORDS

JUNE PURSELL with ROY FOX ORCHESTRA
Br 4230 If I Had You/That's the Good Old Sunny South

Br 4412 From Sunrise to Sunset/I'm Walkin' Around in a Dream

Br 4504 Marianne/When I See My Sugar

ROY FOX

Vo 15770 Makin' Whoopee/Sweetheart of All My Dreams

Br 4384 Nobody's Fault but My Own/My Melody Man

Br 4419 Tiptoe Through the Tulips with Me/Painting the Clouds with Sunshine

Br 6955 My Hat's on the Side of My Head

De(E) 2279 Reaching for the Moon/Lady of Spain

De(E) 2341 Fiesta/By My Side

De(E) 2396 Lazy Day/Poor Kid

De(E) 2404 I Found You/Love for Sale

De(E) 2514 Sweet and Lovely/Sing Another Chorus, Please

De(E) 2580 Just One More Chance/Smile, Darn Ya, Smile

De(E) 2582 You Forgot Your Gloves/Take It from Me

De(E) 2775 Prisoner of Love/You Didn't Know the Music

De(E) 2867 Kiss by Kiss/Goodnight Moon

De(E) 2922 Somebody Loves You/When We're Alone

De(E) 2923 I'm for You a Hundred Percent/Can't We Talk It Over?

De(E) 3029 Lullaby of the Leaves/Gone Forever

De(E) 3093 Marta/One More Affair

De(E) 3099 Ooh, That Kiss!/You're My Everything

De(E) 3151 If You Were Only Mine/Call It a Day

De(E) 3198 Moon

De(E) 3617 I Raised My Hat/I Cover the Waterfront

De(E) 3731 Love Locked Out/Happy and Contented

De 326 Ole Faithful/Carry Me Back to the Lone Prairie

Bb 7594 Trusting My Luck/Souvenir of Love

Vi 25593 Harbor Lights

HMV(E) 5230 Blue Hawaii/Sweet Is the Word for You

LPs

ROY FOX

Ace of Clubs(E) 1172 Roy Fox & The Monseigneur Band (De[E] RIs)

614. FOY, EDDIE   VO
(EDWARD FITZGERALD)

Born March 9, 1854, New York, N.Y.
Died February 16, 1928, Kansas City, Mo.

Dancer-comic in vaudeville and on Broadway over 30 years. Known for hoarse, hissing voice and eccentric dancing, and for song *He Goes to Church on Sunday*. Grew up in Chicago. At early age sang and danced in beer halls and restaurants. Then toured in minstrels and vaudeville. In 1884 starred in HENDERSON'S EXTRAVAGANZAS, later in string of Broadway shows. During one vaudeville period act included his children, billed as Eddie Foy & The Seven Little Foys. Eddie Foy, Jr. went on to career as stage-movie performer. 1955 movie THE SEVEN LITTLE FOYS starred Bob Hope as Foy.

BROADWAY MUSICALS

1898—HOTEL TOPSY TURVY
1901—THE STROLLERS
1902—THE WILD ROSE
1903—MR. BLUEBEARD
1904—PIFF! PAFF!! POUF!!!
1905—THE EARL AND THE GIRL
1907—THE ORCHID
1908—MR. HAMLET OF BROADWAY
1910—UP AND DOWN BROADWAY
1912—OVER THE RIVER

615. FOY, EDDIE, JR.   VO

Born c. 1905-1908, possibly in New Rochelle, N.Y.

Son of famed performer Eddie Foy; as youngster a member of vaudeville act Eddie Foy & The Seven Little Foys. Later followed in father's footsteps as eccentric dancer and comic. Vaudeville in 20s, then in Broadway shows and movies. Strong secondary roles in stage shows as actor-dancer-singer. Similar roles in early sound movies. On radio occasionally; in 1936 regularly on Hammerstein's Music Hall show. In 1947 had show Eddie Foy & The

Music Hall with Eddy Duchin band. In movies off and on; active period 1939-44, mostly small roles as comic or character actor. Portrayed famous father in important movies LILLIAN RUSSELL (1940) and YANKEE DOODLE DANDY (1942). In 1942 starred in YOKEL BOY, movie version of stage hit. Achieved greatest success as a featured star of Broadway musical THE PAJAMA GAME (1954), later played same role in movie version 1957. Good movie roles in LUCKY ME (1954) and BELLS ARE RINGING (1960). In 1961 Broadway show DONNYBROOK!. Occasional TV in 50s and 60s; usually displayed smooth, offbeat dancing. Active through 60s. Career in movies about 40 features and a dozen shorts.

BROADWAY MUSICALS

1929—SHOW GIRL
1930—RIPPLES; SMILES
1931—THE CAT AND THE FIDDLE
1935—AT HOME ABROAD
1937—ORCHIDS PREFERRED (unsuccessful show)
1945—THE RED MILL (revival)
1954—THE PAJAMA GAME
1961—DONNYBROOK!

RECORDS
(all LPs)

(original Broadway casts)
Co OL-4840 THE PAJAMA GAME
Kapp KDL-8500 DONNYBROOK!
(movie soundtrack)
Co OL-5210 THE PAJAMA GAME

616. FRANKLIN, DAVE   cm lyr p
Born September 28, 1895, New York, N.Y.

Composer of 30s and 40s; best-known songs *When My Dream Boat Comes Home, I Must See Annie Tonight, The Anniversary Waltz, The Merry-Go-Round Broke Down.* Left school at 13 to work as pianist in publishing house. Later in vaudeville accompanying performers. Played night clubs in New York, London, Paris, elsewhere. Songwriting in mid-30s, having written minor material as early as 1930. Wrote special material for Connie's Inn and Paradise Restaurant revues and for bandleader Ben Bernie. For some

songs wrote music and lyrics. Chief collaborator Cliff Friend, others Isham Jones, Al Dubin, Irving Taylor.

SONGS
(with related shows)

1930—PARAMOUNT ON PARADE movie (I'm Isadore the Toreador)
1934—I Ain't Lazy—I'm Just Dreamin'; It's Funny to Everyone but Me
1935—Give a Broken Heart a Break; I Woke Up Too Soon
1936—When My Dream Boat Comes Home; I Hope Gabriel Likes My Music; Breakin' in a Pair of Shoes
1937—Everything You Said Came True; The Merry-Go-Round Broke Down; Never Should Have Told You; Two Dreams Got Together; You Can't Stop Me from Dreaming
1938—I Must See Annie Tonight; There's a Brand New Picture in My Picture Frame; Who Do You Think I Saw Last Night?; I Come from a Musical Family
1939—THAT'S RIGHT—YOU'RE WRONG movie (Happy Birthday to Love); Concert in the Park; I'm Building a Sailboat of Dreams; You Don't Know How Much You Can Suffer
1941—The Anniversary Waltz
1942—The Penny Arcade
1946—One-zy Two-zy
1947—Lone Star Moon
1949—The Golden Sands of Hawaii; California Orange Blossom
1950—You Are My Love; A Man Wrote a Song; A Good Time Was Had by All
1954—Still You'd Break My Heart

617. FRANKLIN, IRENE   vo
Star performer in vaudeville and on Broadway as singer, dancer and actress. Later played character roles in over 20 movies 1934-9.

BROADWAY MUSICALS
1907—THE ORCHID
1910—THE SUMMER WIDOWERS
1915—HANDS UP
1917—THE PASSING SHOW OF 1917

1921—GREENWICH VILLAGE FOLLIES OF 1921
1929—SWEET ADELINE

RECORDS
(LP; one song)

(miscellaneous artists)
Audio Rarities LPA-2290 They Stopped the Show (RIs)

618. FRANZELLA, SAL   cl ts as

Born April 25, 1915, New Orleans, La.
Died November 8, 1968, New Orleans, La.

Underrated jazz musician with good tone and fluent style, at best on dixieland. Had classical talent, excellent technique. Good formal training on several instruments. At 14 pit band work. Played New Orleans spots into 1936. With Louis Prima mid-1936. In early 1937 toured with Benny Meroff band, then studio work in New York. With Isham Jones in New York and Louis Prima in Chicago. With Paul Whiteman 1938-41 where solos drew some attention. Staff musician 1941-7 in New York on NBC radio. With Phil Napoleon 1946. Moved to west coast for studio work in 50s and 60s. In later 60s returned to New Orleans, active there in symphonic work and jazz.

RECORDS

PAUL WHITEMAN
  De 2698 Blue Skies/What'll I Do?
ERSKINE BUTTERFIELD
  De 3209 What's Cooking?/Your Feet's Too Big
  De 3252 Nothin' to Do/The Down Home Blues
FRANK FROEBA
  De 1500 My Swiss Hilly Billy/Tears in My Heart
  De 1525 Danger, Love at Work/Miles Apart
  De 1545 Who?/Goblins in the Steeple
TEDDY GRACE
  De 1524 Goodbye, Jonah/Tears in My Heart
  De 1602 I've Taken a Fancy to You/I'll Never Let You Cry
PHIL NAPOLEON'S EMPERORS
  Swan 7510 Sister Kate/I'll Never Be the Same

Swan 7511 Sensation Rag/South Rampart Street Parade
Swan 7512 Livery Stable Blues/That's a-Plenty
Swan 7513 Satanic Blues/Bugle Call Rag
SAL FRANZELLA
  Swan 7514 Clarinet Impromptu/Dizzy Fingers
  Maj 1199 Yesterdays/Valse Bluette
  Maj 1207 Lazy River/Minute Samba
  "X"-0008 Impossible Motion/Fantastic Impromptu

LPs

PHIL NAPOLEON
EmArcy (10") MG-26009 Dixieland Classics, Vol. 2

619. FRAZEE, JANE   vo
(MARY JANE FRAHSE)

Born c. 1919

Singer-actress who starred in low-budget musicals during war years. Attractive, vivacious, sang capably.

MOVIES

1940—MELODY AND MOONLIGHT
1941—BUCK PRIVATES; MOONLIGHT IN HAWAII; SAN ANTONIO ROSE; ANGELS WITH BROKEN WINGS
1942—HELLZAPOPPIN'; WHAT'S COOKIN'?; WHEN JOHNNY COMES MARCHING HOME; ALMOST MARRIED; MOONLIGHT MASQUERADE; MOONLIGHT IN HAVANA; GET HEP TO LOVE; DON'T GET PERSONAL
1943—HI YA, CHUMP; RHYTHM OF THE ISLAND
1944—KANSAS CITY KITTY; BEAUTIFUL BUT BROKE; COWBOY CANTEEN; SWING AND SWAY; SWING IN THE SADDLE; ROSIE THE RIVETER; PRACTICALLY YOURS; SHE'S A SWEETHEART
1945—SWINGIN' ON A RAINBOW; THE BIG BONANZA; SWINGIN' ON BROADWAY; TEN CENTS A DANCE
1946—A GUY COULD CHANGE
1947—CALENDAR GIRL; SPRINGTIME IN THE SIERRAS; ON THE OLD SPANISH TRAIL
1948—THE GAY RANCHERO; UNDER CALIFORNIA STARS; GRAND CANYON

TRAIL; INCIDENT; LAST OF THE WILD HORSES
1951—RHYTHM INN

620. FREED, ARTHUR   lyr

Born September 9, 1894, Charleston, S.C.
Died April 12, 1973, Los Angeles, Calif.

Lyricist with long, active career in movie work. Collaborated mostly with composer Nacio Herb Brown. Brother of lyricist Ralph Freed. Noted for 1929 score of movie BROADWAY MELODY and other movie songs *Chant of the Jungle, Pagan Love Song, Singin' in the Rain.* Other leading songs *I Cried for You, Should I?, Fit as a Fiddle, Temptation, All I Do Is Dream of You, Alone, Broadway Rhythm, You Are My Lucky Star.* Grew up in Seattle. Early in career wrote material for Gus Edwards acts and various vaudeville performers. Played vaudeville with Louis Silvers, later collaborated with him on material for New York cafe revues. Military service, World War I. Returned to vaudeville awhile. Became theatre manager in Los Angeles, produced shows. Began writing for movie musicals 1929. Other collaborators include composers Gus Arnheim, Al Hoffman, Harry Warren, Burton Lane, Roger Edens. Later producer of outstanding movie musicals including BABES IN ARMS, ZIEGFELD FOLLIES, THE WIZARD OF OZ, FOR ME AND MY GAL, GIRL CRAZY, MEET ME IN ST. LOUIS, THE HARVEY GIRLS, TILL THE CLOUDS ROLL BY, GOOD NEWS, THE PIRATE, EASTER PARADE, WORDS AND MUSIC, THE BARKLEYS OF BROADWAY, ON THE TOWN, ROYAL WEDDING, ANNIE GET YOUR GUN, SHOW BOAT, AN AMERICAN IN PARIS, BRIGADOON, IT'S ALWAYS FAIR WEATHER, THE BAND WAGON, SILK STOCKINGS, GIGI, THE BELLS ARE RINGING. In 60s president of Academy of Motion Picture Arts and Sciences, appeared on several Academy Award TV specials.

SONGS
(with related shows)

1921—When Buddha Smiles
1923—I Cried for You
1924—In the Land of Shady Palm Trees
1929—BROADWAY MELODY movie (Broadway Melody; You Were Meant for Me; Wedding of the Painted Doll; Love Boat; Harmony Babies from Melody Lane; Boy Friend); HOLLYWOOD REVUE OF 1929 movie (Singin' in the Rain); MARIANNE movie (Blondy); UNTAMED movie (Chant of the Jungle); THE PAGAN movie (Pagan Love Song)
1930—MONTANA MOON movie (The Moon Is Low; Montana Call; Sing a Song of Old Montana; Happy Cowboy); LORD BYRON OF BROADWAY movie (Should I?; The Woman in the Shoe; Only Love Is Real; A Bundle of Old Love Letters); THOSE THREE FRENCH GIRLS movie (You're Simply Delish); Here Comes the Sun
1931—It Looks Like Love
1932—THE BIG BROADCAST OF 1932 movie (It Was So Beautiful); Fit as a Fiddle; It's Winter Again
1933—THE BARBARIAN movie (Love Songs of the Nile); GOING HOLLYWOOD movie (After Sundown; Temptation; Beautiful Girl; Our Big Love Scene; We'll Make Hay While the Sun Shines; Cinderella's Fella); HOLD YOUR MAN movie (title song); Meet Me in the Gloaming
1934—SADIE MCKEE movie (All I Do Is Dream of You); HOLLYWOOD PARTY movie (Hot Chocolate Soldiers); STUDENT TOUR movie (From Now On; A New Moon Is Over My Shoulder; American Bolero)
1935—A NIGHT AT THE OPERA movie (Alone); BROADWAY MELODY OF 1936 movie (Broadway Rhythm; You Are My Lucky Star; I've Got a Feelin' You're Foolin'; On a Sunday Afternoon; Sing Before Breakfast); CHINA SEAS movie (title song)
1936—SAN FRANCISCO movie (Would You?); THE DEVIL IS A SISSY movie (Say Ah!)
1937—BROADWAY MELODY OF 1938 movie (Yours and Mine; I'm Feelin' Like a Million; Sun Showers; Everybody Sing; Follow in My Footsteps; Your Broadway and My

Broadway); AFTER THE THIN MAN movie (Smoke Dreams); HER HUSBAND LIES movie (No More Tears)
1939—BABES IN ARMS movie (Good Morning)
1940—TWO GIRLS ON BROADWAY movie (My Wonderful One, Let's Dance); STRIKE UP THE BAND movie (Our Love Affair)
1945—YOLANDA AND THE THIEF movie (Yolanda; Coffee Time; Angel; Will You Marry Me?; This Is a Day for Love); This Heart of Mine
1946—ZIEGFELD FOLLIES movie (This Heart of Mine; There's Beauty Everywhere)
1950—PAGAN LOVE SONG movie score
1952—SINGIN' IN THE RAIN movie (Make 'Em Laugh; many old songs including title song)

621. FREED, RALPH   lyr cm

Born May 1, 1907, Vancouver, British Columbia, Canada
Died February 13, 1973, California

Lyricist of 30s and 40s, much of work for movies. Brother of lyricist Arthur Freed. Best-known songs *Little Dutch Mill, How About You?, Who Walks In When I Walk Out?, You Leave Me Breathless*. Grew up in Seattle. Began songwriting in 1934; began movie work 1937. Collaborators include composers Sammy Fain, Burton Lane, Harry Barris.

SONGS
(with related shows)

1934—Little Dutch Mill; Who Walks In When I Walk Out?
1935—Sandman; Yankee Doodle Never Went to Town
1936—Guess Who; Hawaiian War Chant
1937—CHAMPAGNE WALTZ movie (When Is a Kiss Not a Kiss?; Blue Danube Waltz); COLLEGE HOLIDAY movie (Who's That Knocking at My Heart?; The Sweetheart Waltz); DOUBLE OR NOTHING movie (Listen, My Children, and You Shall Hear); SWING HIGH, SWING LOW movie (Swing High, Swing Low; Panamania; Spring Is in the Air); Smarty; Stop, Look and Listen

1938—HER JUNGLE LOVE movie (Lovelight in the Starlight); COCOANUT GROVE movie (You Leave Me Breathless); YOU AND ME movie (title song); Stolen Heaven
1939—SHE MARRIED A COP movie (I'll Remember); RIO movie (Heart of Mine)
1940—IT'S A DATE movie (It Happened in Kaloha); Love Lies
1941—BABES ON BROADWAY movie (Babes on Broadway; How About You?; Anything Can Happen in New York; Hoe-Down); ZIEGFELD GIRL movie (Caribbean Love Song)
1943—DUBARRY WAS A LADY movie (Madame, I Love Your Crepe Suzettes); SWING FEVER movie (Mississippi Dream Boat); THOUSANDS CHEER movie (I Dig a Witch in Wichita)
1944—TWO GIRLS AND A SAILOR movie (In a Moment of Madness; The Young Man with a Horn)
1945—ANCHORS AWEIGH movie (The Worry Song); THRILL OF A ROMANCE movie (Please Don't Say No)
1946—NO LEAVE, NO LOVE movie (All the Time); TWO SISTERS FROM BOSTON movie (After the Show; Down by the Ocean; many more); ZIEGFELD FOLLIES movie (Here's to the Girls)
1950—My Next Romance; Just the Way You Are
1952—Fifty Years Ago
1954—Come Back to My Arms; Jesse James
1957—I Never Felt More Like Falling in Love

622. FREEMAN, BUD   ts cl cm B
(LAWRENCE FREEMAN)

Born April 13, 1906, Chicago, Illinois

All-time great jazzman on tenor sax. Gutty, bouncing style all his own, easily identifiable. Brother of actor Arnie Freeman. Learned jazz early as member of Chicago's famed Austin High Gang. Frank Teschemacher, Dick and Jimmy McPartland, Dave Tough also in group, called Blue Friars. Husk O'Hare took over as leader late 1924, named group

Husk O'Hare's Red Dragons, later Husk O'Hare's Wolverines. Continued into 1926. Freeman toured awhile 1926 with Art Kassel. Played with jazz groups in Chicago, joined Ben Pollack late 1927 and went with him to New York. Left Pollack mid-1928, later played aboard ship to France. In 1929 mostly in New York with Zez Confrey, Red Nichols and others. In early 30s with Paul Whiteman, Gene Kardos, Roger Wolfe Kahn. With Joe Haymes 1934-5. Joined Ray Noble's all-star U.S. band in early 1935, remained a year. With Tommy Dorsey 1936-8, where attained first public eminence as featured soloist. With Benny Goodman most of 1938. Led combo in New York 1939-40 called Summa Cum Laude Orchestra. In late 1939 group in short-lived Broadway musical SWINGIN' THE DREAM (13 performances). From mid-1940 to 1943 led various groups, mostly in Chicago. Military service 1943-5, led service bands, mostly in Aleutians.

From mid-40s through 60s mostly led groups and freelanced. Played Chicago and New York, toured U.S. and abroad. Operated and played in own Gaffer Club in Chicago 1949. Prolific recording career, many concerts and festivals. In early 60s toured with Newport Jazz Festival All-Stars. In late 60s became charter member of group of outstanding veteran jazzmen, The World's Greatest Jazz Band, still with them in early 70s. Freeman a great jazzman who didn't stand still; improved through the years, probably hit peak in late 50s and early 60s. Composer of jazz numbers *The Eel, The Sail Fish, The Octopus, Crazeology, Inside on the Southside, The Atomic Era*. Collected autobiographical essays into 1974 book *You Don't Look Like a Musician.*

RECORDS

JOE HAYMES
Me 13225 Wild Honey/Singing Between Kisses
Me 13286 In My Country That Means Love/Throwin' Stones at the Sun
RAY NOBLE
Vi 25070 Chinatown, My Chinatown
TOMMY DORSEY
Vi 025314 At the Codfish Ball (CLAMBAKE SEVEN)

Vi 25363 Thats a-Plenty
Vi 25539 Mendelssohn's Spring Song
Vi 25556 Dark Eyes/Blue Danube
Vi 25568 The Milkmen's Matinee/ Twilight in Turkey (both CLAMBAKE SEVEN)
Vi 25573 Sleep
Vi 26632 Are All My Favorite Bands Playing or Am I Dreaming? (issued anonymously; spoof of "Mickey Mouse" bands by Tommy Dorsey featuring Bud Freeman on vocal and tenor sax)
Vi 25657 Smoke Gets in Your Eyes/ Night and Day
Vi 25676 If the Man in the Moon Were a Coon/Josephine (both CLAMBAKE SEVEN)
Vi 25750 Little White Lies/Just a Simple Melody
Vi 25824 What'll I Do?/Oh! How I Hate to Get Up in the Morning
Vi 26259 Hymn to the Sun
Vi(12″)36207 Stop, Look and Listen/ Beale Street Blues

RED NICHOLS
Br 4925 Who?/Carolina in the Morning
Br 4778 Rose of Washington Square
THE CELLAR BOYS
Vo 1503 Wailing Blues/Barrel House Stomp
MCKENZIE-CONDON CHICAGOANS
OK 40971 Nobody's Sweetheart/Liza
BENNY GOODMAN
Br 4968 After Awhile/Muskrat Ramble
Vi 25827 Lullaby in Rhythm/That Feeling Is Gone
Vi 26087 Bumble Bee Stomp/Ciri-biribin
Vi 26095 My Honey's Lovin' Arms
LEE WILEY
LMS 281 How Long Has This Been Going On?/My One and Only
TEDDY GRACE with BUD FREEMAN ORCHESTRA
De 3428 I'm the Lonesomest Gal in Town/See What the Boys in the Backroom Will Have
De 3463 Sing/Gee, But I Hate to Go Home Alone
EDDIE CONDON
Co 35680 The Eel/Home Cooking

932

Br 6743 The Eel/Home Cooking
CMS 500 Ja-da/Love is Just Around the Corner
CMS(12″)1500 Carnegie Drag/Carnegie Jump
De 23719 Stars Fell on Alabama

LOUIS ARMSTRONG
De 29102 Basin Street Blues (1 & 2)

BUD FREEMAN
CMS 501 You Took Advantage of Me/Three's No Crowd
CMS 507 LIFE Spears a Jitterbug/What's the Use?
CMS 513 The Blue Room/Exactly Like You
Bb 10370 I've Found a New Baby/Easy to Get
Bb 10386 China Boy/The Eel
De 2781 The Sail Fish/Satanic Blues
De 18064 Big Boy/Copenhagen
De 18066 Tia Juana/I Need Some Pettin'
De 18112 The Buzzard/Tillie's Downtown Now
De 18113 Keep Smilin' at Trouble/What Is There to Say?
Co 35855 Muskrat Ramble/47th and State
Co 35856 After Awhile/Shim-Me-Sha-Wabble
Maj 1018 I Got Rhythm/Where Have You Been?
Key 636 Tea for Two/Midnight at Eddie Condon's
SD 504 Taking a Chance on Love/You Took Advantage of Me

LPs

BUD FREEMAN
Beth 29
Cap(10″)H-625 Classics in Jazz
Ha HL-7046 Bud Freeman & His All-Star Jazz (Co RIs)
UA 15033 (S) Something Tender
Dot DLP-3166 Bud Freeman & His Summa Cum Laude Trio
Mon-Ever MES-7022 The Compleat Bud Freeman

TOMMY DORSEY
Vi LPM-1432 Tribute to Dorsey, Vol. 1 (Vi RIs)

JACK TEAGARDEN
Verve V-8495

JIMMY MCPARTLAND
Jazztone J-1241 Dixieland Now and Then
EDDIE CONDON
Dot DLP-3141 Dixieland Dance Party
THE WORLD'S GREATEST JAZZ BAND
Project 3 Stereo PR5033SD
Project 3 Stereo PR5039SD Extra!
Atl S-1570 Live at the Roosevelt Grill

623. FREEMAN, RUSS   p ar cm
Born May 28, 1926, Chicago, Ill.

Modern swinging pianist, good accompanist, popular in west coast jazz scene. Grew up in California; formal musical training there. In 1947 with Howard McGhee and Dexter Gordon. Freelanced, by 50s playing and arranging for leading west coast jazzmen Shorty Rogers, Art Pepper, Howard Rumsey, Chet Baker, Wardell Gray. In demand for records. Led trio at times. From 1955 to early 60s mostly with Shelly Manne, including 1960 European tour. Freelance arranging. In late 1959 with Benny Goodman on European tour. In early 60s founded musical publishing firm, published own compositions including *The Wind, Nothin' to Do with Love, Summer Sketch, Fan Tan, No Ties, Say When, Maid in Mexico, Happy Little Sunbeam, Speak Easy, Double Play, Sound Effects Manne, Slight Minority, Hugo Hurwhey*. Active into 70s.

RECORDS
(all LPs)

RUSS FREEMAN
PJ(10″)8 Russ Freeman Trio
RUSS FREEMAN-SHELLY MANNE
Contemp(10″)C-2518
RUSS FREEMAN-CHET BAKER
PJ 1232 Quartet
(miscellaneous combos)
WP 404 Jazz Swings Broadway
CHET BAKER
PJ(10″)9 Chet Baker Ensemble
PJ(10″)15 Chet Baker Sextet
BENNY GOODMAN
Co CL-1579 Goodman Swings Again
SERGE CHALOFF-BOOTS MUSSULLI
Story(10″)310
ART PEPPER
Tampa RS-1001

BUDDY BREGMAN
  WP 1263 Swingin' Standards
CY TOUFF
  PJ 1211 His Octet and Quintet
JOHN GRAAS
  Trend(10″)TL-1005 The French Horn
HARRY BETTS
  Choreo A-6 The Jazz Soul of Doctor
    Kildaire and Other TV Themes
HOWARD RUMSEY
  Contemp C-3501
SHELLY MANNE
  Contemp(10″)C-2511

624. FREEMAN, STAN   p vo cm
Born April 3, 1920, Waterbury, Conn.
Master pianist brilliant on jazz, pop, show
tunes, classical music. Studied classical
piano at Hartt School of Music. Military
service, World War II. In 1946 with Tex
Beneke band. Classical debut at Carnegie
Hall in 1947. Guest pianist with sympho-
ny orchestras in New York, Buffalo, Cin-
cinnati and Washington, D.C. Piano
Playhouse show on radio, own shows.
Teamed often with pianist Cy Walter.
Active on TV early 50s. Worked clubs as
pianist, also sang, used jokes and patter;
clever entertainer. Played harpsichord on
Rosemary Clooney's record hit *Come on-a
My House.* Composer of *Miss Satan, My
Heart Will Tell You So, Guy with the
Voodoo, Faith, The Fickle Finger of Fate,
The Other Half of Me.* Scored 1964 Broad-
way musical I HAD A BALL; Jack Lawrence
lyricist. Active into 70s.

RECORDS
ROSEMARY CLOONEY
  Co 39467 Come on-a My House
STAN FREEMAN
  Epic 9052 My Old Heart Throb/Poor
    Papa
  Co 39541 Perdido/The Blue Room
  OK 6833 Come on-a Stan's House/St.
    Louis Blues

LPs
STAN FREEMAN
  Co CL-1126 Oh Captain!
  Co(10″)CL-6158 Piano Moods
  Co(10″)CL-6193 Come on-a Stan's
    House
  Epic LN-3224 At the Blue Angel

Ha HL-7067 Plays 30 All-Time Hits
Project PR-5012-SD (S) Fascination
STAN FREEMAN-CY WALTER
  MGM(10″)E-52
LEE WILEY
  Co(10″)CL-6216 Sings Irving Berlin
TEX BENEKE
  FTR 1510 Tex Beneke & His Orches-
    tra (1946)

625. FREY, FRAN   vo
Featured male vocalist with George Olsen
from mid-20s to mid-30s. Also sang in
band trio. Some freelance, also worked as
single.

RECORDS
GEORGE OLSEN
  Vi 19852 A Little Bit Bad
  Vi 19977 Horses
  Vi 20060 Hello, Aloha, How Are
    You?/Let's Make Up
  Vi 20112 Where'd You Get Those
    Eyes?/Hi-Diddle-Diddle
  Vi 20875 Good News/The Varsity
    Drag
  Vi 21452 Because My Baby Don't
    Mean "Maybe" Now
  Vi 21816 Makin' Whoopee/Until You
    Get Somebody Else
  Vi 21819 Where the Shy Little Violets
    Grow
  Vi 21927 Walking with Susie
  Vi 21942 A Garden in the Rain/
    Dream Mother
  Vi 21954 Little Pal/I'm in Seventh
    Heaven
  Vi 22035 Reaching for Someone
  Vi 22065 If You Believed in Me/Song
    of the Moonbeams
  Vi 22937 You Can Make My Life a
    Bed of Roses
  Vi 22947 Love, You Funny Thing
  Vi 24125 All-American Girl
  Vi 24139 It's Gonna Be You
  Vi 24220 The Girl in the Little Green
    Hat/My Fraternity Pin
BENNIE KRUEGER
  Br 6334 Come On and Sit Beside the
    Sea
VICTOR YOUNG
  Br 6281 You Can Make My Life a Bed
    of Roses
  Br(12″)20112 O.K. America Medleys
    (1 & 2)

FRAN FREY
Co 2788-D Moonstruck/Learn to Croon
Co 2814-D Be Careful/Gather Lip Rouge While You May
Co 2841-D Sittin' on a Log/Puddin' Head Jones

625A. FRIEDHOFER, HUGO

cm ar cello B

Born May 1902, San Francisco, Calif.

Composer-arranger of movie background music 1929 into 70s. As youth played cello in San Francisco theatre orchestras, also with The People's Symphony. Studied harmony and composition with Domenico Brescia, later with Ernest Toch, Nadia Boulanger. Began movie work as arranger on important early sound musical SUNNY SIDE UP (1929). Continued arranging for Fox studio early 30s, changed to Warner Brothers 1935. Outstanding arranging for CAPTAIN BLOOD (1935), THE CHARGE OF THE LIGHT BRIGADE (1936). Achieved renown as master arranger; worked on many scores of composers Max Steiner and Erich Wolfgang Korngold. Began composing portions of movie backgrounds; first complete work THE ADVENTURES OF MARCO POLO (1938). By early 40s steadily engaged as composer-arranger for complete backgrounds. Outstanding work for THE BEST YEARS OF OUR LIVES (1946), THE BISHOP'S WIFE (1947), ACE IN THE HOLE (1951), THE YOUNG LIONS (1958).

MOVIES

(as composer and probable arranger-conductor of background music; partial listing)

1938—THE ADVENTURES OF MARCO POLO
1943—CHINA GIRL; THEY CAME TO BLOW UP AMERICA; PARIS AFTER DARK
1944—LIFEBOAT; THE LODGER; HOME IN INDIANA
1945—BREWSTER'S MILLIONS; GETTING GERTIE'S GARTER
1946—GILDA; SO DARK THE NIGHT; THE BEST YEARS OF OUR LIVES
1947—BODY AND SOUL; THE BISHOP'S WIFE; WILD HARVEST
1948—A SONG IS BORN; JOAN OF ARC; ADVENTURES OF CASANOVA; SEALED VERDICT
1949—BRIDE OF VENGEANCE

1950—CAPTAIN CAREY, U.S.A.; THE SOUND OF FURY; BROKEN ARROW; TWO FLAGS WEST
1951—ACE IN THE HOLE
1952—RANCHO NOTORIOUS; THE OUTCASTS OF POKER FLAT; LYDIA BAILEY; ABOVE AND BEYOND
1953—THUNDER IN THE EAST; ISLAND IN THE SKY; HONDO
1954—VERA CRUZ
1955—THE RAINS OF RANCHIPUR; SOLDIER OF FORTUNE
1956—THE HARDER THEY FALL; THE REVOLT OF MAMIE STOVER; BETWEEN HEAVEN AND HELL
1957—BOY ON A DOLPHIN; THE SUN ALSO RISES; AN AFFAIR TO REMEMBER
1958—THE YOUNG LIONS; IN LOVE AND WAR; THE BARBARIAN AND THE GEISHA
1959—WOMEN OBSESSED; THE BLUE ANGEL; THIS EARTH IS MINE
1961—ONE-EYED JACKS; HOMICIDAL
1962—GERONIMO; BEAUTY AND THE BEAST
1964—THE SECRET INVASION
1971—RICHTOFEN AND BROWN

RECORDS
(all LPs)

(movie soundtracks; as composer and probable arranger-conductor)
Lib LOM-16001 ONE EYED JACKS
Kapp KDL-7001 THE SUN ALSO RISES
De DL-7029 ISLAND IN THE SKY
De DL-8580 BOY ON A DOLPHIN
De DL-8719 THE YOUNG LIONS
De DL-8915 THIS EARTH IS MINE
20th-Fox 3004 THE BARBARIAN AND THE GEISHA

626. FRIEDMAN, IZZY   cl as ts
(IRVING FRIEDMAN)

Born December 25, 1903, Linton, Ind.

Featured hot clarinetist with jazz greats in 20s. Early dance jobs in New York 1924. With Vincent Lopez 1925-6. Freelanced; period with Isham Jones. Joined Paul Whiteman early 1928 to mid-1930. In Whiteman 1930 movie KING OF JAZZ. Remained in Hollywood for studio work. Later conducting and supervisory work in studios. Long career in movie industry 30s and 40s; rose to executive positions. In 1950 formed company to furnish music and sound effects for movies and TV, continued into early 60s.

RECORDS

BIX BEIDERBECKE

  Ok 41040 Thou Swell/Somebody Stole My Gal

  OK 41088 Ol' Man River/Wa-Da-Da

  OK 41173 Rhythm King/Louisiana

  Pa(E) 2833 Margie

EDDIE LANG

  OK 41344 Walkin the Dog/March of the Hoodlums

  Pa(E) 840 What Kind o' Man Is You?

MASON-DIXON ORCHESTRA

  Co 1861-D What a Day!/Alabamy Snow

FRANKIE TRUMBAUER

  OK 41019 Our Bungalow of Dreams/ Lila

  OK 41039 Borneo/My Pet

  OK 41100 Bless You, Sister/Dusky Stevedore

  OK 41145 Take Your Tomorrow/Love Affairs

  OK 41252 Nobody but You/Got a Feelin' for You

  OK 41268 Shivery Stomp/Reaching for Someone

JOE VENUTI

  OK 41320 That Wonderful Something/Chant of the Jungle

PAUL WHITEMAN

  Vi 21274 Mississippi Mud/From Monday On

  Vi 21389 My Pet

  Vi 21438 Louisiana

  Co 1491-D Oh! You Have No Idea

  Co 1496-D Is It Gonna Be Long?

LPs

BIX BEIDERBECKE

  Co CL-844-6 (3-LP set) The Bix Beiderbecke Story (RIs)

PAUL WHITEMAN

  "X"(10")LVA-3040 Featuring Bix Beiderbecke (Vi RIs)

626A. FRIEND, CLIFF   cm lyr p

Born October 1, 1893, Cincinnati, Ohio

Prolific songwriter from early 20s into 50s. Many hits; best-known *June Night, Then I'll Be Happy, Give Me a Night in June, The Broken Record, Wah-Hoo,*

When My Dream Boat Comes Home, The Merry-Go-Round Broke Down, I Must See Annie Tonight, You Can't Stop Me from Dreaming. Wrote score for GEORGE WHITE'S SCANDALS OF 1929, songs for Broadway shows and movies. Educated at Cincinnati College and Conservatory. Test pilot at Wright Field. Pianist for Harry Richman and other vaudeville performers in U.S. and in English music halls. Collaborators included Dave Franklin, Lew Brown, Sidney Clare, Billy Rose, Irving Caesar, Abel Baer, Charles Tobias, Carmen Lombardo.

SONGS
(with related shows)

1921—BOMBO stage show (Oh, How She Can Dance; Some Beautiful Morning; Let the Little Joy Bells Ring; songs possibly added during show's 1922-4 tour)

1922—California; Lovesick Blues; Bow Wow Blues; You Tell Her—I Stutter

1923—Mamma Loves Pappa

1924—June Night; Let Me Linger Longer in Your Arms; When the One You Love Loves You; Where the Dreamy Wabash Flows; Where the Lazy Daisies Grow; There's Yes Yes in Your Eyes

1925—Then I'll Be Happy; Let It Rain, Let It Pour

1926—Hello, Bluebird; Tamiami Trail; I'm Tellin' the Birds, I'm Tellin' the Bees; Oh, If I Only Had You

1927—PIGGY stage show (songs unimportant); Give Me a Night in June; The Whisper Song; Joy Bells

1928—WHOOPEE stage show (My Blackbirds Are Bluebirds Now); You're a Real Sweetheart; It Goes Like This

1929—GEORGE WHITE'S SCANDALS OF 1929 stage show (Bottoms Up; Bigger and Better Than Ever); Bashful Baby; The Same Old Moon

1930—THE GOLDEN CALF movie (Can I Help It?; Modernistic; I'm Tellin' the World About You; Maybe, Someday)

1931—EARL CARROLL'S VANITIES OF 1931 stage show (It's Great to Be in Love); At Last I'm Happy; Freddy the Freshman; I Wanna Sing About You

1932—GEORGE WHITE'S MUSIC HALL VARIETIES stage show (There'll Never Be Another Girl Like You); THE CROONER movie (Sweethearts Forever); Just Because You're You; Let's Have a Party; The Language of Love; You've Got Me in the Palm of Your Hand

1934—MANY HAPPY RETURNS movie (The Sweetest Music This Side of Heaven); DOWN TO THE LAST YACHT movie (There's Nothing Else to Do in Na-La-Ka-Mo-Ka-Lu); Freckle Face, You're Beautiful; What's Good for the Goose

1935—GEORGE WHITE'S SCANDALS OF 1935 movie (Hunkadola)

1936—The Broken Record; Out Where the Blue Begins; Wah-Hoo; Wake Up and Sing; When My Dream Boat Comes Home

1937—Everything You Said Came True; Never Should Have Told You; The Merry-Go-Round Broke Down; Two Dreams Got Together; You Can't Stop Me from Dreaming

1938—I Must See Annie Tonight; Who Do You Think I Saw Last Night?; There's a Brand New Picture in My Picture Frame

1939—Concert in the Park; I'm Building a Sailboat of Dreams; You Don't Know How Much You Can Suffer; My Rosary of Broken Dreams

1940—Confucius Say; Trade Winds

1941—Below the Equator

1942—BANJO EYES stage show (We Did It Before); Wherever You Are

1943—Don't Sweetheart Me

1944—SHINE ON HARVEST MOON movie (Time Waits for No One); Gonna Build a Big Fence Around Texas

1947—Lone Star Moon

1950—You Are My Love

1951—Everything's Gonna Be All Right

1955—Still You'd Break My Heart

627. FRIGANZA, TRIXIE   vo
(BRIGID O'CALLAGHAN)

Born November 29, 1870, Grenola, Kansas
Died February 27, 1955, Flintridge, Calif.

Comedienne-singer-mimic with beauty and engaging personality. Headliner in vaudeville and star of Broadway musicals. First introduction to Broadway THE MASCOT in 1892. Supporting roles in shows JUPITER (1892), BELLE OF BOHEMIA (1900), THE CHAPERONS (1902), THE DARLING OF THE GALLERY GODS (1903), TWIDDLE-TWADDLE (1906). By now a star; top roles in THE ORCHID (1907), THE AMERICAN IDEA (1908), THE PASSING SHOW OF 1912, NED WAYBURN'S TOWN TOPICS (1915), CANARY COTTAGE (1917) and years later JOHN MURRAY ANDERSON'S ALMANAC (1929). In 1908 early film work for Cameraphone. Between shows played vaudeville, toured with stock companies. Cameo role in 1940 Bing Crosby movie IF I HAD MY WAY.

628. FRILEY, VERN   tb

Born July 5, 1924, Marshall, Mo.

Trombonist; agile modern style. With Ray McKinley 1946-50. Later in 1950 with Woody Herman briefly, then joined Tommy Tucker. In 1951 with Gene Williams and again McKinley. With Sauter-Finegan in 1952, Les Brown 1954-5. Beginning 1955 freelanced in Hollywood, including movie and TV work; continued into 60s.

RECORDS
RAY MCKINLEY
  Maj 7206 Borderline
SAUTER-FINEGAN ORCHESTRA
  Vi 20-4866 Azure-Te
  Vi 20-5065 Nina Never Knew
WOODY HERMAN
  Mars 1003 Four Others
LPs
RAY MCKINLEY
  Cam CAL-295 (Vi RIs)
  Allegro(10″)4015
WOODY HERMAN
  Co CL-592 The Three Herds (Co RIs)

937

629. FRIML, RUDOLF   cm p

Born December 7, 1879, Prague, Czech.
Died November 12, 1972, Hollywood,
Calif.

Great composer of Broadway stage. Scored many shows, Created all-time popular songs. Two greatest successes with popular scores ROSE-MARIE (1924; 557 performances) and THE VAGABOND KING (1925; 511 performances). Other notable shows THE FIREFLY (1912), HIGH JINKS (1913), KATINKA (1916), SOMETIME (1918), THE LITTLE WHOPPER (1919), THE THREE MUSKETEERS (1928). Friml not infallible, had several flops. Failures included last two shows LUANA (1930) and MUSIC HATH CHARMS (1935). Most memorable songs include *Sympathy*; *Giannina Mia*; *Allah's Holiday*; *L'Amour, Toujours, L'Amour*; *Chansonette* (later altered to become *The Donkey Serenade*); *Rose-Marie*; *Indian Love Call*; *Only a Rose*; *Song of the Vagabonds*; *March of the Musketeers*. Collaborators included lyricists Otto Harbach, P. G. Wodehouse, Rida Johnson Young, Oscar Hammerstein II, Brian Hooker, Clifford Grey, Harold Atteridge, Dailey Paskman. Operettas became stage standards performed by road companies over and over. Several made into movies.

Educated at Prague Conservatory, became concert pianist. Toured Europe several years with violinist Jan Kubelik. After U.S. tours 1901 and 1906, Friml made home here. Worked at composing; first big break as substitute for Victor Herbert in writing score for THE FIREFLY in 1912. Popular score launched Broadway career. Friml and Sigmund Romberg soon joined Herbert as leading composers of operetta-style musicals; major influences on Broadway stage. After 1935 less active. In 1937 THE FIREFLY became popular movie; old composition *Chansonette* converted into movie's hit song *The Donkey Serenade*. Wrote score for movie NORTHWEST OUTPOST in 1947. During last years appeared on several Merv Griffin TV shows honoring composers, displayed amazing vigor for his advanced years, even played compositions on piano.

SONGS
(with related shows)

1912—THE FIREFLY stage show (Giannina Mia; Sympathy; When a Maid Comes Knocking at Your Door; The Dawn of Love; Love Is Like a Firefly)

1913—HIGH JINKS stage show (High Jinks; The Bubble; Love's Own Kiss; Something Seems Tingle-ingling; Not Now but Later)

1915—THE PEASANT GIRL stage show (Listen, Dear; Love Is Like a Butterfly; And the Dream Came True; The Flame of Love)

1916—KATINKA stage show (Katinka; Allah's Holiday; My Paradise)

1917—YOU'RE IN LOVE stage show (You're in Love; I'm Only Dreaming; That's the Only Place Where Our Flag Shall Fly); KITTY DARLIN' stage show (unsuccessful)

1918—GLORIANNA stage show (When a Girl; Toodle-oo; My Climbing Rose); SOMETIME stage show (Sometime; Keep On Smiling; The Tune You Can't Forget)

1919—TUMBLE INN stage show (I've Told My Love; Snuggle and Dream; The Thoughts I Wrote on the Leaves of My Heart); THE LITTLE WHOPPER stage show (You'll Dream and I'll Dream; 'Round the Corner; Oh, What a Little Whopper)

1921—JUNE LOVE stage show (June Love; Don't Keep Calling Me Dearie; Dear Love, My Love; The Flapper and The Vamp); ZIEGFELD FOLLIES OF 1921 stage show (Bring Back My Blushing Rose; Every Time I Hear a Band Play)

1922—THE BLUE KITTEN stage show (Cutie; I Found a Bud Among the Roses; When I Waltz with You; Blue Kitten Blues); L'Amour, Toujours, L'Amour

1923—CINDERS stage show (Cinders; Belles of the Bronx; One Good Time; I'm Simply Mad About the Boys); ZIEGFELD FOLLIES OF 1923 stage show (Chansonette)

1924—ROSE-MARIE stage show (Rose-Marie; Indian Love Call; Song of the Mounties; Totem Tom-Tom; The Door of My Dreams)
1925—THE VAGABOND KING stage show (Song of the Vagabonds; Only a Rose; Some Day; Huguette Waltz)
1926—THE WILD ROSE stage show (The Wild Rose; Brown Eyes; One Golden Hour; We'll Have a Kingdom); NO FOOLIN' stage show (later titled ZIEGFELD'S AMERICAN REVUE OF 1926; Florida, the Moon and You; Wasn't It Nice?; I Want a Girl to Call My Own)
1928—THE THREE MUSKETEERS stage show (March of the Musketeers; Ma Belle; Heart of Mine; Queen of My Heart; All for One, One for All; Your Eyes); WHITE EAGLE stage show (Give Me One Hour; Gather the Rose; Silver Wing; Regimental Song)
1930—LUANA stage show (unsuccessful); THE VAGABOND KING movie (original stage score)
1935—MUSIC HATH CHARMS stage show (unsuccessful)
1936—ROSE-MARIE movie (original stage score)
1937—THE FIREFLY movie (original stage score; old composition Chansonette converted to new song, The Donkey Serenade)
1947—NORTHWEST OUTPOST movie (songs not popular)
1954—ROSE-MARIE movie (original stage score plus new songs by other writers)
1956—THE VAGABOND KING movie (original stage score; Johnny Burke wrote some new lyrics)

RECORDS
(as pianist)

RUDOLF FRIML
  Co 533-D Song of the Vagabonds/ Chansonette
  Co 2112-D Song of the Vagabonds/ Vagabond King Waltz
  Vi 22540 Huguette Waltz/Indian Love Call
  Sch 2007 Barcelona

LPs
RUDOLF FRIML
  Westminster 6069 Friml Plays Friml

630. FROEBA, FRANK   p o cm B
Born c. 1907, New Orleans, La.

Swing-era pianist active with leading jazzmen of period. Played professionally at 15. Worked solo and with local jazzmen, also as theatre organist. To New York in 1924. With Johnny Dedroit and freelanced. Led first band in Atlantic City, N.J. Various jobs in New York early 30s included Irving Aaronson and Will Osborne 1933-4. With Benny Goodman band in formative stage, late 1934 to mid-1935. Worked with Goodman on Let's Dance radio show. In late 1935-6 led outstanding jazzmen on record sessions. Remainder of 30s with Riley-Farley Band and organist Milt Herth. Joined Merle Pitt's WNEW house band on New York radio late 30s. Many record sessions for Decca house bands. Led combo in New York clubs later 30s and 40s. Radio work in 40s. In late 40s and 50s recorded in ragtime and honky-tonk style with some success. In later 50s worked Miami spots as soloist or combo leader. Composer of *It All Begins and Ends with You* (1936) and *The Jumpin' Jive* (1939).

RECORDS
JOHNNY DEDROIT
  OK 40240 Eccentric
  OK 40285 Lucky Kentucky/When My Sugar Walks Down the Street
JACK PURVIS
  OK 8782 Poor Richard/Down Georgia Way
  OK 8808 Dismal Dan/Be Bo Bo
BENNY GOODMAN
  Co 2845-D Texas Tea Party/Dr. Heckle and Mr. Jibe
  Co 3011-D Music Hall Rag
  Co 3033-D Down Home Rag
  Vi 25136 Dear Old Southland
MILT HERTH QUARTET
  De 2046 The Lambeth Walk/Rockin' in Rhythm
  De 2623 Jump Jump's Here/The Spider and the Fly

BOB HOWARD
De 1698 If You're a Viper/Raggedy but Right

RILEY-FARLEY BAND
De 578 Looking for Love
De 619 South

DICK ROBERTSON
De 1407 Ebb Tide/In a Little Carolina Town
De 1415 Blossoms on Broadway/You Can't Stop Me from Dreaming
De 1498 Rollin' Plains/I Want You for Christmas

JOE SODJA
Va 609 Limehouse Blues/I Never Knew

ANDREWS SISTERS
De 1496 Why Talk About Love?/Just a Simple Melody
De 1562 Bei Mir Bist du Schon/Nice Work If You Can Get It

LIL ARMSTRONG
De 1904 Oriental Swing/Let's Get Happy Together

THE RHYTHMAKERS
Co 35841 Who Stole the Lock on the Hen House Door?

JOHNNIE DAVIS
De 573 Truckin'/Loafin' Time
De 583 I Feel a Song Comin' On/Everything Is Okey-Dokey

FRANK FROEBA
Co 3110-D The Music Goes 'Round and Around/There'll Be a Great Day in the Morning
Co 3131-D Just to Be in Caroline/'Tain't Nobody's Biz'ness What I Do
Co 3151-D Organ Grinder's Swing/Rhythm Lullaby
Co 3152-D It All Begins and Ends with You/Whatcha Gonna Do When There Ain't No Swing?
De 1401 The Big Apple/Josephine
De 1525 Miles Apart/Danger, Love at Work
De 1545 Who?/Goblins in the Steeple
De 23601 Sugar Blues/St. Louis Blues
De 24234 Ma/In a Little Spanish Town
De 24385 Bye Bye Blackbird/If You Were the Only Girl

LPs

FRANK FROEBA
De(10″)DL-5043 Back Room Piano
De(10″)DL-5455 Moonlight Playing Time
Vs(10″)VLP-6031 Boys in the Back Room
ABC-Para 199 Honky-Tonk Piano

BENNY GOODMAN
Co CL-821 The Vintage Goodman (Co RIs)
Sunbeam SB 101-2-3 Thesaurus Rhythm Makers Orchestra (6/6/35 ET RIs)

631. FROMAN, JANE   VO

Born November 10, 1907, St. Louis, Mo.

Outstanding singer with strong, melodious voice, excellent phrasing. Most active in 30s and 40s. Much formal training, attended University of Missouri and Cincinnati Conservatory of Music. In early 30s sang over WLW radio in Cincinnati. To Chicago several months with Paul Whiteman. Sustaining radio show on NBC from Chicago, also played clubs there. To New York radio, by 1934 well established. In Broadway musicals ZIEGFELD FOLLIES OF 1934, KEEP OFF THE GRASS (1940), ARTISTS AND MODELS (1943) and 1942 vaudeville show LAUGH, TOWN, LAUGH with Ed Wynn. In movies STARS OVER BROADWAY (1935) and RADIO CITY REVELS (1938). On radio shows The Seven Star Revue early 1934, Bromo Seltzer Hour late 1934-5, Pontiac show 1935, 1937 summer Jello show, 1939 show with Jan Peerce and Erno Rapee orchestra, Star Theatre 1942. Also guest spots on various shows. Continued to play clubs in later 30s and early 40s, also recorded.

Miss Froman seriously injured February 1943 in Lisbon plane crash; with group of show business volunteers to entertain overseas troops. Broke bones, and serious leg damage required many operations through the years. In November 1943 managed to appear in Broadway musical ARTISTS AND MODELS; show folded after 28 performances. Career often interrupted for treatmant of injury. In 1945 played New York's Copacabana, later U.S.O.

tour. Career waned. Comeback with records and club dates early 50s a tribute to her courage and determination. 1952 movie of her life WITH A SONG IN MY HEART. Outstanding musical, with Susan Hayward brilliantly playing role of Miss Froman. Jane in good voice on soundtrack. After several years, career again waned.

RECORDS

HENRY THIES
    Vi 22460 June Kisses
    Vi 22461 Sharing
JANE FROMAN
    De 180 Lost in a Fog/My Melancholy Baby
    De 181 I Only Have Eyes for You/A New Moon Is Over My Shoulder
    De 710 But Where are You?/Please Believe Me
    De 725 If You Love Me/It's Great to Be in Love Again
    Co 36414 Tonight We Love/What Love Done to Me
    Co 36460 Baby Mine/When I See an Elephant Fly
    Maj 1048 You, So It's You/Linger in My Arms a Little Longer, Baby
    Maj 1049 I Got Lost in His Arms/Millionaires Don't Whistle
    Maj 1086 For You, for Me, for Evermore/A Garden in the Rain
    Vi(12")12333 The Man I Love
    Cap 2044 I'll Walk Alone/With a Song in My Heart
    Cap 2154 Wish You Were Here/Mine
    Cap 2219 My Love, My Life/No!
    Cap 2496 My Shining Hour/If I Love You a Mountain
    Cap 2639 Robe of Calvary/The Sound of Love
    Cap 2755 I Solemnly Swear/Backward, Turn Backward
(medleys, SONNY SCHUYLER on some vocals)
    Vi(12")12332 Of Thee I Sing/I Got Rhythm/Bidin' My Time etc.
    Vi(12")12335 Do-Do-Do/Someone to Watch Over Me/Swanee etc.
    Vi(12")12336 Lady Be Good/Fascinating Rhythm/Strike Up the Band/ etc.

LPs

JANE FROMAN
    Vi(10")LPT-3055 Gems from Gershwin
    Cap T-889 Songs at Sunset
    Cap(10")309
    De(10")DL-6021 (De RIs)
(movie soundtrack)
    Cap T-309 WITH A SONG IN MY HEART
(revival Broadway cast)
    Cap S-310 PAL JOEY

632. FULLER, WALTER   t vo B

Born February 15, 1910, Dyersburg, Tenn.

Trumpet star and vocalist, best known for work with Earl Hines in 30s. Left home as youngster, toured in carnival and vaudeville shows. Worked in Chicago middle and late 20s. Mostly with Sammy Stewart in late 20s, including spells in New York. With Hines 1931-7, where work attracted attention as featured performer. Joined Horace Henderson late 1937 for a year, rejoined Hines and remained till late 1940. Freelanced, formed combo 1941. Long runs in Chicago in early to mid-40s. In 1946 settled in San Diego, led band there through the years, mostly at Club Royal. Continued active through 60s.

RECORDS

EARL HINES
    Br 6541 Rosetta
    Br 6872 Julia
    Br 6960 We Found Romance
    Vo 3379 Darkness
    De 182 That's a-Plenty
    De 183 Cavernism
    De 218 Fat Babes
    De 337 Rosetta/Copenhagen
    De 577 Wolverine Blues/Rock and Rye
    De 654 Julia
    De 714 Bubbling Over
    Bb 10351 Ridin' and Jivin'
    Bb 10467 After All I've Been to You
    Bb 10763 'Gator Swing
    Bb 10792 You Can Depend on Me
    Bb 10835 Call Me Happy
    Bb 10870 Topsy Turvy
LIONEL HAMPTON
    Vi 26114 Rock Hill Special/Down Home Jump

Vi 26173 Fiddle Diddle

JIMMY MUNDY
Va 598 I Surrender Dear/Ain't Misbehavin'

LPs

EARL HINES
De DL-9221 South Side Swing (1934-5 De RIs)

633. FULTON, JACK   tb vo cm lyr B

Born June 13, 1903, Philipsburg, Pa.

Gained most fame as soft-voiced tenor featured with Paul Whiteman in late 20s and 30s. With George Olsen six months 1926 as trombonist-vocalist. Joined Whiteman later in 1926 as trombonist-vocalist, became well known as band's leading vocalist. On many Whiteman records and radio shows. Left band late 1934 for career as single. Sang on morning radio shows 1935. Long tenure on Franklin MacCormack's Poetic Melodies show 1936-8. Mid-1938 on Just Entertainment show with Andrews Sisters several months, later on The Laugh Liner show. In 1936 led band working with singer Sophie Tucker. In 1939 in band led by Ramona, former Whiteman vocalist. In early to mid-40s active on Chicago radio as a staff trombonist-vocalist. Played clubs and theatres in 40s, mostly in Chicago. Continued as radio staff musician in 50s. Composer or lyricist of popular songs *Last Night I Said a Prayer* (1942), *Until* (1945; popular 1948), *My Baby Didn't Even Say Goodbye* (1948), *Wanted* (1954), *Times Two, I Love You* (1955), *Ivory Tower* (1956), *Silence Is Golden* (1957). Lesser songs *My Greatest Mistake, Peace, Make America Proud of You, Mrs. Santa Claus*. Chief collaborator Lois Steele.

RECORDS

PAUL WHITEMAN
Co 2047-D Should I?

Co(12")50068-D My Melancholy Baby
Co(12")50103-D Sweet Sue
Vi 22827 A Faded Summer Love/Old Playmate
Vi 22834 Cuban Love Song/Tell Me with a Love Song
Vi 22879 By the Sycamore Tree
Vi 22882 Don't Suppose/A Rose and a Kiss
Vi 22885 Sylvia
Vi 22998 The Voice in the Old Village Choir
Vi 24089 Here's Hoping
Vi 24096 Nightfall
Vi 24097 You'll Always Be the Same Sweetheart
Vi 24141 How Deep Is the Ocean?
Vi 24364 My Moonlight Madonna
Vi 24365 Ah, But Is It Love?
Vi 24566 True

RUSS MORGAN
Me 13390 Have You Written Home to Mother?

VINCENT ROSE
Or 3140 Tell Me That You Love Me

EARL BACKUS
Epic 9012 On the Trail

JACK FULTON
Pe 13139 It's Easy to Remember/ When I Grow Too Old to Dream
Pe 350903 The Rose in Her Hair/In a Little Gypsy Tea Room
Vo 2522 My Moonlight Madonna/It Isn't Fair
Vo 2546 Love Is the Sweetest Thing/ This Is Romance
Vo 2793 Two Cigarettes in the Dark/ One Night of Love
Vo 2800 P.S. I Love You/If I Had a Million Dollars
De 3302 My Moonlight Madonna/ When Day Is Done
Mer 70349 If You Ever Get to My Home Town/True Blue Sue
Tower 1454 Sunflower/Tell Me the Truth

634. GAILLARD, SLIM

g p vb vo cm lyr B

(BULEE GAILLARD)

Born January 14, 1916, Detroit, Mich.

Pianist and combo leader, swinging musician, composer of novelty songs featuring jive lyrics, excellent entertainer. Played vaudeville as solo act in early 30s: danced, played instruments, sang. Based in New York 1937. Teamed with bassist Slam Stewart to form combo known as Slim & Slam, with drums and piano added. Won popularity with 1938 novelty hit *Flat Foot Floogie*. In 1939 Gaillard formed combo called Slim Gaillard & His Flat Foot Floogie Boys. He and Stewart worked together on occasions later. Gaillard in military service awhile, World War II. Early 1945-6 had combo on west coast, toured, ended up in New York 1947. Other novelty hits *Cement Mixer* (1946) and *Down by the Station* (1948). Composed a string of novelty tunes with jive lyrics. Combos on record sessions in middle and late 40s featured his novelties but sometimes spotted good jazz by Charlie Parker, Dizzy Gillespie, Dodo Marmarosa, Howard McGhee, Marshall Royal, Lucky Thompson. Small roles in several movie musicals. In 50s mostly vocalist and M.C. Semi-active in show business in 60s. Other compositions: *Tutti Frutti, Vol Vist du Gaily Star, Jump Session, Chicken Rhythm, Soony Roony, Laughing in Rhythm, Dunkin' Bagel, Arabian Boogie,* *Tip Light, Minuet in Vout, Opera in Vout,* many other novelties.

RECORDS

SLIM & SLAM
- Vo 4021 Flat Foot Floogie/Chinatown, My Chinatown
- Vo 4225 Tutti Frutti/Look-a There
- Vo 4346 Jump Session/Vol Vist du Gaily Star
- Vo 4521 Dopey Joe/Buck Dance Rhythm

SLIM GAILLARD
- Vo 5138 Chicken Rhythm/A-Well-a-Take-'Em Joe
- Vo 5483 Look Out/Beatin' the Board
- Vo 5557 Windy City Hop/Fitzwater Street
- OK 6015 Rhythm Mad/Bongo
- OK 6260 Lookin' for a Place to Park/Hit That Mess
- OK 6382 Champagne Lullaby/Bingie-Bingie-Scootie
- Queen 4104 Vout Oreenie/Please Wait for Me
- Cadet 201 Cement Mixer/Scotchin' with Soda
- Bel-Tone 753 Dizzy Boogie/Popity Pop
- Bel-Tone 761 Santa Monica Jump/Slim's Jam
- Bel-Tone 762 Chicken Rhythm/Mean Pretty Mama
- MGM 10017 Tip Light / Arabian Boogie

MGM 10309 Down by the Station/A Ghost of a Chance

Maj 9005 School Kids Hop/Chicken Rhythm

Mer 5606 Laughing in Rhythm/Soony Roony

Melodisc 1013 Dunkin' Bagel/Don't Blame Me

LPs

SLIM GAILLARD

Mer(10")MGC-126 Mish Mash (RIs)

Dot DLP-3190 Slim Gaillard Rides Again

Norg(10")MGN-13 Slim Gaillard & His Musical Aggregations Wherever They May Be

Clef(10")506 Opera in Vout

CHARLIE PARKER

Sav MG-12014 The Genius of Charlie Parker (1944-8 RIs)

635. GALBRAITH, BARRY   g

Born December 18, 1919, Pittsburgh, Pa.

Guitarist with tasteful modern style. In 1941 with Red Norvo, Teddy Powell, Babe Russin. Joined Claude Thornhill early 1942; later in year with Vaughn Monroe and Hal McIntyre. With Jerry Wald 1943. Military service, World War II. Again with Thornhill 1946-7. Studio musician in New York late 40s, also freelance. By mid-50s in demand for records. With Jimmy Lyon trio 1953. Continued studio work in 50s and 60s.

RECORDS
(all LPs)

HAL MCKUSICK

Vi LPM-1164 In a 20th-Century Drawing Room

Vi LPM-1366 Jazz Workshop

Beth BCP-16 East Coast Jazz, Vol. 8

Cor CRL-57116 Jazz at the Academy

WILL BRADLEY (one side)

GA 33-310 Dixieland Jazz

JOE NEWMAN

Vik LX-1060 The Midgets

SAM MOST

Beth BCP-18 East Coast Jazz, Vol. 9

JIMMY HAMILTON

Jazztone J-1238 Accent on Clarinet

RUBY BRAFF

UA 3045 Blowing Around the World

RUSTY DEDRICK

4 Corners FCL-4207 The Big Band Sound

RUSTY DEDRICK (and singers)

Mon-Ever MES-6809-10-11 (S) Irving Berlin (His Songs)

JOE PUMA

Beth(10")BCP-1012

AARON SACHS

Beth(10")BCP-1008

CLAUDE THORNHILL

Co(10")CL-6164 Encores

TAL FARLOW

Norg(10")MGN-19 The Tal Farlow Album

636. GALLAGHER & SHEAN
vocal team
(ED GALLAGHER)
(AL SHEAN; *born 1868, died 1949*)

Famed comic team of one stage Irishman and one stage Jew; stars of vaudeville and musical stage. Composed hit song of 1922, *Mr. Gallagher and Mr. Shean*. Patter song with questions and answers endured, lent itself to parodies and topical lines added later. Team formed in 1910, played burlesque and vaudeville. Featured comedy and songs. In Broadway show THE ROSE MAID in 1912. Team split. Shean in Broadway shows PRINCESS PAT (1915) and CINDERELLA ON BROADWAY (1920). Team reunited, achieved greatest success in ZIEGFELD FOLLIES OF 1922, which featured their hit song. Number soon widely imitated. Stock lines ("Absolutely, Mr. Gallagher?" and "Positively, Mr. Shean!") became trademark. Team won top vaudeville bookings, played New York's Palace Theatre. Split permanently 1925. Shean on stage in BETSY (1927; short run) and MUSIC IN THE AIR (1932). Also in nonmusicals such as FATHER MALACHY'S MIRACLE (1937). Comic and character parts in 25 movies 1934-44, including musicals MUSIC IN THE AIR and SWEET MUSIC (1935), SAN FRANCISCO (1936), 52ND STREET (1937), THE GREAT WALTZ (1938), ZIEGFELD GIRL (1941). In 1944 movie ATLANTIC CITY famed team portrayed by Jack Kenny and Al Shean.

RECORDS

GALLAGHER & SHEAN
Vi 18941 Mr. Gallagher & Mr. Shean
(1 & 2)

637. GALLODORO, AL   as cl

Alto sax virtuoso, great technique, beautifully controlled tone. Adept at classical music. Best known in popular music and jazz as lead sax with Paul Whiteman. Joined Whiteman around early 1937, remained about four years. Featured in Whiteman's "Sax Soctette" within band. In later years taught, played concerts and music clinics. Occasional recording as soloist. In 1950 led swing combo awhile in New York. For years, through 1973, starred in New York with Seuffert Band, Sousa-type band led by George F. Seuffert.

RECORDS

PAUL WHITEMAN (as lead sax)
De 2075 All Ashore/My Reverie
De 2083 While a Cigarette Was Burning/Heart and Soul
De 2467 After You've Gone/I Kiss Your Hand, Madame
De 2578 To You/Moon Love
De 2694 Crinoline Days/Tell Me Little Gypsy
De 2698 Blue Skies/What'll I Do?
De 2913 Heaven in My Arms/That Lucky Fellow
De 2937 My Fantasy/Darn That Dream
De(12″)29051 Rhapsody in Blue (1 & 2)
De(12″)29052 Second Rhapsody (1 & 2)
De(12″)29058 Manhattan Serenade/Manhattan Moonlight
De(12″)29060 Side Street in Gotham (1 & 2)
BERNIE GREEN
Vi 20-4716 Linger Awhile/Lonesome and Sorry

LPs

AL GALLODORO
Co(10″)CL-6188 Saxophone Contrasts
JACK SHAINDLIN
——— Academy Award Favorites

638. GALLOP, SAMMY   lyr cm
Born March 16, 1915, Duluth, Minn.
Died February 26, 1971, Hollywood, Calif.

Songwriter of 40s and 50s, best known for *Elmer's Tune, Holiday for Strings, There Must Be a Way, Count Every Star, Somewhere Along the Way, Wake the Town and Tell the People.* Quit as surveyor-draftsman for composing 1940. Wrote scores for New York night clubs and obscure material for minor Broadway shows. Collaborators Peter DeRose, David Rose, Guy Wood, Jerry Livingston, Rube Bloom, Steve Allen, Milton DeLugg, Jimmy Van Heusen, David Saxon, Elmer Albrecht, Howard Steiner, Chester Conn.

SONGS
1941—Elmer's Tune
1943—Holiday for Strings
1945—There Must Be a Way; Autumn Serenade
1946—Shoo Fly Pie and Apple Pan Dowdy; I Guess I Expected Too Much
1947—Maybe You'll Be There; Oh! What I Know About You
1948—Starlight Rendezvous
1949—The Blossoms on the Bough; A Bluebird Singing in My Heart; All Year 'Round; Have a Little Sympathy
1950—Count Every Star; Vagabond Shoes; Crazy Little Moonbeam
1951—I'll Never Know Why; Velvet Lips; Forgetful
1952—Somewhere Along the Way; Outside of Heaven
1953—Bring Back the Sunshine; My Heart Is a Kingdom; My Lady Loves to Dance; Mighty Lonesome Feelin'; Will-o'-the-Wisp Romance
1954—It Happens to Be Me; Boulevard of Nightingales; Guessing; Paraguay
1955—Wake the Town and Tell the People

Other songs: *Outside of Heaven; Make Her Mine; Half as Lovely; No Good Man; Night Lights; The Right Thing to Say; Meet Me Where They Play the Blues; I Bow My Head in Silent Prayer; The Little Guppy; My Mama Said No, No; Are Yuh*

Spoken Fer?; *Inspiration Time*; *You Ain't Got No Romance*; *We Shall Be Free*; *Featherhead*; *Free*; *That Wonderful Girl of Mine*

639. GANNON, KIM   lyr
(JAMES KIMBLE GANNON)

Born November 18, 1900, Brooklyn, N.Y.

Died April 29, 1974, Lake Worth, Fla.

Lyricist of popular songs of 40s and 50s, best known *I Understand, Moonlight Cocktail, I'll Be Home for Christmas, A Dreamer's Holiday, Under Paris Skies*. Wrote score for 1951 Broadway show SEVENTEEN, songs for movies. Collaborators composers Max Steiner, J. Fred Coots, Mabel Wayne, Walter Kent, Jule Styne, Josef Myrow. Attended Albany Law School, admitted to New York bar in 1934. Five years later began songwriting.

SONGS
(with related shows)

1939—For Tonight
1940—Angel in Disguise; The Five O'clock Whistle; I Understand; Half-Way Down the Street
1941—Make Love to Me; Be Fair
1942—ALWAYS IN MY HEART movie (title song); I'll Pray for You; Moonlight Cocktail; The Singing Sands of Alamosa; South Wind; Autumn Nocturne
1943—POWERS GIRL movie (Three Dreams Are One Too Many; The Lady Who Didn't Believe in Love; Out of This World); NOW, VOYAGER movie (It Can't Be Wrong); OLD ACQUAINTANCE movie (title song); I'll Be Home for Christmas
1944—SHINE ON HARVEST MOON movie (new material); SONG OF THE OPEN ROAD movie (Too Much in Love)
1945—EARL CARROLL'S VANITIES movie (Endlessly); Sweet Dreams, Sweetheart
1947—IF WINTER COMES movie (title song); Say So
1949—A Dreamer's Holiday
1951—SEVENTEEN stage show, Walter Kent-cm (This Was Just Another Day; Summertime Is Summertime; Reciprocity; Ode to Lola; After All, It's Spring; Headache and Heartache; others)
1952—So Madly in Love
1953—I'm Wond'rin'; Under Paris Skies
1956—Croce di Oro (Cross of Gold)
1958—Same Old Moon
1960—I Want to Be Wanted

640. GARBER, JAN   v B

Born November 5, 1897, Morristown, Pa.

Leader of dance band especially popular in 30s. Long career from 20s into 60s. Attended University of North Carolina. Talented violinist, played in Philadelphia Symphony Orchestra. Military service, World War I; band director. Formed dance band early 20s with pianist Milton Davis; called the Garber-Davis Orchestra under the direction of Jan Garber. In late 20s Garber led own band, featured good semi-hot style. In early 30s band fading; playing Cleveland when Garber heard sweet band led by Freddie Large. Offered to take over band and get good bookings, was accepted. Thus was born Garber's famous sweet style. Featured mellow sax section with accentuated vibrato, muted brass, guitar obligatos. Garber and Large composed famous theme *My Dear*. Key early job at Cincinnati's Netherland Plaza. Band popular 1933-5, especially in midwest. Heard often on radio; numerous records. Garber billed as The Idol of the Air Lanes. Leading vocalist romantic, deep-voiced Lee Bennett; trumpet man Fritz Heilbron handled novelty vocals, provided comedy. Pianist Rudy Rudisill with band 15 years. Band popular through 30s. In 1942 Garber surprised music world, switched to swing band, arrangements mostly by Gray Rains. Vocalists Liz Tilton and Bob Davis. Played swing about two years, but few records due to record ban and no great popularity. Reverted to sweet style 1945. Recorded in later 40s and 50s, kept busy. Band in movies HERE COMES ELMER (1943) and MAKE BELIEVE BALLROOM (1949). In 60s Garber less active; recorded and played occasionally.

RECORDS

GARBER-DAVIS ORCHESTRA

Vi 19164 First, Last and Always/Oh Gee, Oh Gosh, Oh Golly, I'm in Love

Vi 19216 You're in Kentucky, Sure as You're Born/That Bran' New Gal o' Mine

JAN GARBER

Vi 20676 Positively—Absolutely/You Don't Like It—Not Much

Vi 20754 What Do I Care What Somebody Said?/Under the Moon

Co 1334-D Back in Your Own Backyard

Co 1372-D She's a Great Great Girl/Was It a Dream?

Co 1724-D Weary River/Caressing You

Co 2115-D Puttin' on the Ritz/When a Woman Loves a Man

Vi 24412 And So Goodbye/I'll Be Faithful

Vi 24444 You're Gonna Lose Your Gal/You've Got Everything

Vi 24498 Temptation/Boulevard of Broken Dreams

Vi 24629 All I Do Is Dream of You/Grandfather's Clock

Vi 24636 (theme) My Dear

Vi 24727 Isn't It a Shame?/Blue in Love

Vi 24730 Blue Sky Avenue/Rain

Vi 24809 Blame It on My Youth/The Object of My Affection

Vi 24880 It's Easy to Remember/Here Comes Cookie

Vi 25013 In a Little Gypsy Tea Room/In the Merry Month of May

Vi 25025 In the Middle of a Kiss

Vi 25110 Accent on Youth/Ridin' Up the River Road

De 647 I'm Shooting High/I Feel Like a Feather in the Breeze

De 651 A Beautiful Lady in Blue/Moon Over Miami

De 693 Love Came Out of the Night/A Little Rendezvous in Honolulu

De 733 (theme) My Dear/If You Love Me

De 851 Take My Heart/Afterglow

De 1294 A Kiss in the Dark/The Siren's Song

Br 7870 The Blue Room/Moonlight and Roses

Br 7906 Yours and Mine/I'm Feelin' Like a Million

Br 7929 Roses in December/Let's Have Another Cigarette

Br 7969 Rosalie/If I Can Count on You

Br 8060 Love Walked In/Ten Pretty Girls

Vo 4687 It's Never Too Late/It's an Old Fashioned Locket

Vo 4900 I Poured My Heart into a Song/An Old Fashioned Tune Always Is New

OK 6039 I Can't Remember to Forget/Come Down to Earth, My Angel

Vs 8216 It's a Wonderful World/Gotta Get Home

Hit 7070 No Love, No Nothin'/My Heart Tells Me

Cap 719 Now That I Need You/You're Breaking My Heart

Cap 1325 If I Were a Bell/Nobody's Chasing Me

Cap 15305 (theme) My Dear/Soft Shoe Shuffle

LPs

JAN GARBER

Cam CAL-297 (Vi RIs)

Cor(10″)CRL-56007 Among My Souvenirs (De RIs)

De DL-8793 Music from the Blue Room

De(10″)DL-4730

Vo 3694 (De RIs)

Ridgeway RLP-500 Satin Touch

De 74841 (S) The Shadow of Your Smile

De 74971 (S) Mello Medleys

641. GARCIA, RUSS   t Fr-h cm ar B

Born April 12, 1916, Oakland, Calif.

Best known for conducting-arranging for singers on 50s and 60s records. Attended San Francisco State Teachers College, also much classical music training. Played trumpet in local dance bands, also in Los Angeles with Horace Heidt and Al Donahue. Studio work for radio and movies as musician-arranger. By mid-50s busy on record sessions with top singers. In later 50s and 60s composed and arranged for radio-TV-movies. Wrote film backgrounds for THE TIME MACHINE, CARNIVAL IN APRIL, ATLANTIS. TV backgrounds included Rawhide, Laredo, The Virginian. Composed orchestral number *Adventures in Emotion*.

RECORDS
(all LPs)

RUSS GARCIA
Beth BCP-46 Four Horns and a Lush Life
Kapp KL-1050 Listen to the Music of Russ Garcia & His Orchestra
RUSS GARCIA-MARTY PAICH
Beth 6039 Jazz Music for the Birds and the Hep Cats

(as conductor-arranger)

RAY BROWN
Verve MGV-8390 Jazz Cello
NELLIE LUTCHER
Lib LRP-3014 Our New Nellie
BUDDY DEFRANCO-OSCAR PETERSON
Norg MGN-1016 Play George Gershwin
ANITA O'DAY
Verve MGV-2145 Waiter, Make Mine Blues
Verve MGV-8485 Sings the Winners
HERB JEFFRIES
Beth BCP-72
LOUIS ARMSTRONG
Verve MGV-4012 Under the Stars
BUDDY DEFRANCO
Verve MGV-2033 Broadway Showcase
PEGGY CONNELLY
Beth BCP-53

642. GARDNER, FREDDY   as cl bs B
Born c. 1911 (probably in England)
Died July 26, 1950, London, England

Lead alto sax and soloist with Ray Noble band in its great musical period in England, early 30s. On many Noble records on England's HMV label, later issued in U.S. on Victor. Lilting tone and vibrato important in band's beautiful ensemble sound (never duplicated by Noble's U.S. bands). After Noble went to U.S. 1934, Gardner continued active in England as freelance, also led groups. Attracted some attention in U.S. in late 40s and early 50s when several alto sax solo records issued

here. Working in England with Peter Yorke orchestra as featured soloist at death.

RECORDS

RAY NOBLE
HMV(E) 5893 I've Got a Feeling
HMV(E) 5956 Sunny Days
HMV(E) 6040 Roll On, Mississippi, Roll On
HMV(E) 6098 Got a Date with an Angel
HMV(E) 6147 Blues in My Heart
HMV(E) 6321 Look What You've Done
HMV(E) 6332 Three Wishes
HMV(E) 6347 It's Within Your Power
HMV(E) 6366 A Couple of Fools in Love
HMV(E) 6375 I've Got to Sing a Torch Song
HMV(E) 6379 There's a Cabin in the Pines
HMV(E) 6396 It's Bad for Me
HMV(E) 6413 Thanks
HMV(E) 6440 You Ought to See Sally on Sunday/On a Steamer Coming Over
HMV(E) 6453 Who Walks In When I Walk Out?
HMV(E) 6471 Not Bad
HMV(E) 6484 My Sweet
HMV(E) 6499 Nasty Man
HMV(E) 6508 All I Do Is Dream of You
Vi 24624 My Hat's On the Side of My Head
Vi 25262 Rock Your Cares Away
FREDDY GARDNER
Pa(E) 2153 China Boy
Pa(E) 2189 Japanese Sandman (1 & 2)
Rex(E) 9207 You Can't Stop Me from Dreaming/That Old Feeling
Rex(E) 9225 I Want to Be Happy/ Limehouse Blues
Rex(E) 9244 The Snake Charmer/The Dipsy Doodle
Rex(E) 9396 Music, Maestro, Please/ It's De-Lovely
Rex(E) 9513 Jeepers Creepers/Tom, Tom, the Piper's Son
Rex(E) 9935 Someday Sweetheart/10 A.M. Blues
Vi 20-3121 Tea Leaves/Where Apple Blossoms Fall

Co 38346 I'm in the Mood for Love/I
Only Have Eyes for You
Co 38975 Body and Soul/Valse Vanite

LPs

FREDDY GARDNER
Co(10″)CL-6187
Mon-Ever MES-7044 Freddy Gardner
(Co and other RIs)

RAY NOBLE
Mon-Ever MES-6816 (HMV, Vi RIs)
Mon-Ever MES-7021 (HMV, Vi RIs)
Mon-Ever MES-7027 (HMV, Vi RIs)
Mon-Ever MES-7039 (HMV, Vi RIs)
Mon-Ever MES-7040 (HMV, Vi RIs)

642A. GARDNER, KENNY   VO

Featured vocalist with Guy Lombardo
from 40s into 70s. First period around late
1940-2; absent several years (military
service?). Rejoined 1946 into 70s. Featured with Lombardo on New Year's Eve
TV shows.

RECORDS

GUY LOMBARDO
De 3586 Tea for Two
De 3616 Corn Silk
De 3665 Blue Afterglow/Sing Song
Serenade
De 3674 Star Dust
De 3753 After You've Gone/Nobody's
Sweetheart
De 3880 You and I/Yip-I-Addy-I-Ay
De 3890 Sweethearts on Parade/After
the Ball
De 3999 I Don't Want to Set the
World on Fire
De 4066 Easy Street/Sailboat in the
Sky
De 4155 You Made Me Love You/
Mandy Is Two
De 23799 Anniversary Song
De 23865 It Takes Time
De 24226 I Still Get Jealous
De 24258 Serenade of the Bells
De 24288 Frankie and Johnny/I'm My
Own Grandpaw
De 24704 Hop-Scotch Polka/Danger-
ous Dan McGrew
De 24792 The Music Goes 'Round and
Around/Hot Time in the Old Town
Tonight
De 24825 Enjoy Yourself/Rain or
Shine

De 27336 Get Out Those Old
Records/Tennessee Waltz
De 27645 Lonesome and Sorry
De 28352 Sunshowers/You Like?
De 28476 Why Don't You Believe Me?

LPs

GUY LOMBARDO
De DL-4177 New Year's Eve with Guy
Lombardo
De DL-8097 Lombardo Land, U.S.A.
De (10″)DL-5329 Enjoy Yourself
Cap T-1393 At Harrah's Club

643. GARLAND, JOE

ts bs-s bs p cel ar cm B
Born August 15, 1903, Norfolk, Va.

Composer of famous instrumentals *In the
Mood* (inspired by or similar to four
earlier jazz tunes: *Tar Paper Stomp,
There's Rhythm in Harlem, Hot and Anxious, Jumpy Nerves*) and *Leap Frog* (Les
Brown's theme). Long career as sideman-
musical director-arranger-composer. Attended Shaw University and Aeolian
Conservatory, Baltimore. Played classical
music with Cosmopolitan Brass Band of
Baltimore and Excelsior Military Band of
Norfolk. Early jobs with Elmer Snowden
and Joe Steele. Freelanced in New York
late 20s, worked with Jelly Roll Morton.
With Mills Blue Rhythm Band 1932-6,
also did some arranging. With Edgar
Hayes 1937-8, later in 1938 with Don
Redman. With Louis Armstrong 1939-42;
musical director and sideman. Freelanced
in New York. Again musical director for
Armstrong 1945-7. With Claude Hopkins
and Herbie Fields. Musical director for
Earl Hines band 1948-9. In 50s less active; led band at intervals, did freelancing, arranging-composing. Other compositions: *The Stuff Is Here, Harlem After
Midnight, Jazz Martini, Congo Caravan,
Easy Go, Brown Sugar Mine, Once in Ev'ry
Heart, Keep the Rhythm Going, Serenade
to a Savage, What's Your Hurry?, There's
Rhythm in Harlem*.

RECORDS

JELLY ROLL MORTON
Vi 38055 Red Hot Pepper/Deep Creek
Blues

MILLS BLUE RHYTHM BAND
Co 2994-D Keep the Rhythm Going/
  Solitude
Co 3087-D Congo Caravan
EDGAR HAYES
De 1416 Stomping at the Renny/
  Laughing at Life
RED ALLEN
Vo 3097 Red Sails in the Sunset/I
  Found a Dream
Vo 3098 On Treasure Island/Boots
  and Saddle
Vo 3261 On the Beach at Bali Bali/
  Take My Heart
Vo 3262 You're Not the Kind/Chlo-e
SEMINOLE SYNCOPATORS
OK 40228 Sailing on Lake Pontchar-
  train

LP

LOUIS ARMSTRONG
De DL-9225 Louis Armstrong: Rare
  Items 1935-1944 (De RIs)

644. GARLAND, JUDY   vo
(FRANCES GUMM)

*Born June 10, 1922, Grand Rapids,
Mich.
Died January 22, 1969, London, Eng-
land*

Singer-movie star, darling of MGM musicals as teenager. Troubled figure in
turbulent later life. Parents in show business. Judy and sisters formed singing
group, Gumm Sisters, worked locally,
graduated to bookings in larger cities.
Appeared with George Jessel at Chicago's
Oriental Theatre. Jessel suggested that
Judy adopt name of Garland. Family
moved to California, sisters worked spots
there. When sisters married, Judy became
a single, adopted Garland name. Given
screen test, signed by MGM. First film
with Deanna Durbin in 1935 short EVERY
SUNDAY. First feature movie was musical
PIGSKIN PARADE in fall of 1936; performance adequate in cast of veterans. In 1937
movie BROADWAY MELODY OF 1938, Judy
registered strongly singing *You Made Me
Love You* to photo of Clark Gable. Quickly became star. Made attractive team with
Mickey Rooney in big movies late 30s
and early 40s. As youngster Judy fresh
and natural, with strong, clear voice. In

1939 career zoomed with lead in THE
WIZARD OF OZ, in which she sang *Over the
Rainbow.* Movie became classic; shown
many times on TV. In 1937 sang on Jack
Oakie's Caravan radio show, in 1940 on
Bob Hope show. Many appearances on
radio. Began recording in late 30s, continued through the years. In 40s starred in
nostalgic movies FOR ME AND MY GAL
(1942), MEET ME IN ST. LOUIS (1944), THE
HARVEY GIRLS (1946).

Career waned a bit due to ill health,
alcoholism, weight problem. Sensational
comeback concerts at London's Palladium and New York's Palace. Opened latter
October 1951 during vaudeville revival,
booked four weeks, stayed 19. In 1954
starred in heralded remake of movie A
STAR IS BORN: a triumph, though cost
time, money, heartaches. Judy identified
with film's feature song *The Man That
Got Away.* In late 50s and 60s more ill
health and drinking, weight gains and
losses, all took toll. On TV and stage,
often had to rely on reputation and
showmanship to carry her performance.
Occasionally on TV in 50s and 60s, more
frequently later. Own show 1963-4. Used
hand microphone, flung cord around,
draped it over her shoulder, used jerky,
nervous motions—but always scored
heavily. In 1967 own show on New York
stage. Despite ill health, public shocked at
news of her death in 1969. In 60s and 70s
daughter Liza Minnelli carved out successful career on stage and TV, later in
movies.

MOVIES

1936—PIGSKIN PARADE
1937—BROADWAY MELODY OF 1938;
    THOROUGHBREDS DON'T CRY
1938—EVERYBODY SING; LOVE FINDS
    ANDY HARDY; LISTEN, DARLING
1939—THE WIZARD OF OZ; BABES IN ARMS
1940—ANDY HARDY MEETS DEBUTANTE;
    STRIKE UP THE BAND; LITTLE
    NELLIE KELLY
1941—ZIEGFELD GIRL; LIFE BEGINS FOR
    ANDY HARDY; BABES ON BROAD-
    WAY
1942—FOR ME AND MY GAL
1943—PRESENTING LILY MARS; GIRL CRA-
    ZY; THOUSANDS CHEER

1944—MEET ME IN ST. LOUIS
1945—THE CLOCK
1946—THE HARVEY GIRLS; ZIEGFELD FOL-
LIES
1947—TILL THE CLOUDS ROLL BY
1948—THE PIRATE; EASTER PARADE;
WORDS AND MUSIC
1949—IN THE GOOD OLD SUMMERTIME
1950—SUMMER STOCK
1954—A STAR IS BORN
1960—PEPE (voice)
1961—JUDGMENT AT NUREMBERG
1962—GAY PURR-EE (voice)
1963—A CHILD IS WAITING; I COULD GO
ON SINGING

RECORDS

JUDY GARLAND
De 1432 All God's Chillun Got
Rhythm/Everybody Sing
De 1463 You Can't Have Ev'rything/
You Made Me Love You
De 2672 Over the Rainbow/The Jitter-
bug
De 2873 Oceans Apart/Figaro
De 2881 Swanee/Embraceable You
De 3174 I'm Nobody's Baby/Buds
Won't Bud
De 3231 The End of the Rainbow
De 3593 Our Love Affair/I'm Always
Chasing Rainbows
De 18543 Zing! Went the Strings of
My Heart/Fascinating Rhythm
De 23309 But Not for Me
De 23361 The Trolley Song/Boys and
Girls Like You
De 23688 Love/Changing My Tune
De 23746 There Is No Breeze/Don't
Tell Me That Story
De 40270 The Man That Got Away/
Here's What I'm Here For
MGM 30002 Look for the Silver Lin-
ing
MGM 30098 You Can Do No
Wrong/Love of My Life
MGM 30172 Johnny One-Note/I
Wish I Were in Love Again (with
MICKEY ROONEY)
MGM 50025 Meet Me Tonight in
Dreamland/Put Your Arms
Around Me, Honey
JUDY GARLAND-GENE KELLY
De 18480 For Me and My Gal/When
You Wore a Tulip

MGM 30097 Be a Clown
JUDY GARLAND-DICK HAYMES
De 23687 Aren't You Kind of Glad
We Did?/For You, For Me, For
Evermore

LPs

JUDY GARLAND
De DL-8190 Greatest Performances
(RIs)
De DXB-172 (2-LP set) The Best of
Judy Garland (RIs)
Cap T-734 Judy
Cap T-835 Alone
Cap WBO-1569 (2-LP set) At Carnegie
Hall (April 23, 1961)
(movie soundtracks)
De DL-8387 (one side) THE WIZARD OF
OZ
MGM(10″)E-502 EASTER PARADE
MGM(10″)E-519 SUMMER STOCK
Co BL-1201 A STAR IS BORN
MGM E-3464 WIZARD OF OZ
JUDY GARLAND-LIZA MINELLI
Cap WBO-2295 (2-LP set) "Live" at
the London Palladium

645. GARNER, ERROLL   p cm
Born June 15, 1923, Pittsburgh, Pa.

Popular jazz pianist with distinctive style.
Left hand provided full chords while right
played melody line with lagging beat:
sometimes with abandon but always in
excellent taste. Swinging semi-modern
style, lush on ballads. Happy music, attractive even to those with no love for
jazz. Self-taught, couldn't read music.
Played locally on radio and at clubs as
teenager. During 1939-44 moved from
Pittsburgh to New York frequently,
played one-nighters elsewhere. Joined
Slam Stewart trio in New York 1944.
Soon after formed trio, continued with
trio or as single for 30 years. Popular by
late 40s. In 50s and 60s on TV more than
any other jazz musician: a video natural
with elfin appearance, sly humor, gra-
ciousness, tasteful piano. So small had to
sit on big telephone directory atop piano
bench. Several tours abroad in 60s. Composer of standard *Misty*. Other compositions: *Play, Piano, Play*; *Solitaire*;
Dreamy; *Blues Garni*; *Trio*; *Turquoise*;
Other Voices; *No More Shadows*; *Passing*

Through; *Dreamstreet*; *Erroll's Bounce*.
Composed for 1963 movie A NEW KIND OF
LOVE. Active into 70s.

RECORDS

CHARLIE PARKER
Dial 1014 Dark Shadows/Bird's Nest
Dial 1015 Blow Top Blues/Cool Blues
SLAM STEWART
Manor 1012 Hop Skip and Jump/
Three Blind Micesky
Manor 1028 Sherry Lynn Flip/Blue
Brown and Beige
ERROLL GARNER
B&W 16 Movin' Around/Twistin' the
Cat's Tail
Si 15136 Loot to Boot/Sweet Lorraine
Mer 1001 Embraceable You/Lover,
Come Back to Me
Mer 1032 Blue Skies/Don't Blame Me
Mer 2040 Symphony/Bouncin' with
Me
Mer 70442 Misty/Exactly Like You
Sav 571 Laura/Somebody Loves Me
Sav 688 I Cover the Waterfront/Pent-
house Serenade
Sav 728 Body and Soul/It's Easy to
Remember
Dial 1016 Pastel/Trio
Dial 1026 Play, Piano, Play/Frankie
and Garni
Vogue(Fr) 5003 Lover Man/What Is
This Thing Called Love?
Co 39580 Robbins Nest/It's the Talk
of the Town
Co 39996 Lullaby of Birdland/Easy to
Love

LPs

ERROLL GARNER
Co CL-583 Erroll Garner Gems
Co CL-883 Concert by the Sea
Dial(10″)208 Piano Moods
Mer MG-20063 Solitaire
Mer MG-20090 Afternoon of an Elf
Mer MG-20859 A NEW KIND OF LOVE
Movie Music
Mer SR-61308 Feeling Is Believing
MGM E-4335 A Night at the Movies
MGM E-4361 Campus Concert
MGM E-4463 That's My Kick
CHARLIE PARKER
Jazztone J-1214 The Fabulous Bird
(Dial RIs)
Baronet 107 The Early Bird (Dial RIs)

646. GARRETT, BETTY   VO
Born 1919

Attractive, lively performer of stage and
movies during 40s and 50s. Supporting
roles in Broadway musicals LET FREEDOM
RING (1942; unsuccessful), SOMETHING
FOR THE BOYS (1943), JACKPOT (1944),
LAFFING ROOM ONLY (1945). Starred in
long-running show CALL ME MISTER
(1946). Second leads in movies but able to
display dynamic singing style. Later years
in road shows with husband Larry Parks,
still active in early 70s.

MOVIES

1945—ANCHORS AWEIGH
1948—THE BIG CITY; WORDS AND MUSIC
1949—TAKE ME OUT TO THE BALL GAME;
ON THE TOWN; NEPTUNE'S DAUGH-
TER
1950—THE SKIPPER SURPRISED HIS WIFE
1955—MY SISTER EILEEN
1957—THE SHADOW ON THE WINDOW; THE
MISSING WITNESS

RECORDS

BETTY GARRETT
Allied 5024 The Soft Shoe/Go
MGM 10147 Ok'l, Baby, Dok'l/There
Ought to Be a Society
MGM 10288 It's a Quiet Town/I'm
Strictly on the Corny Side
MGM 10621 Poison Ivy/Don't Throw
Cold Water on the Flame of Love
MGM 30173 There's a Small Hotel
BETTY GARRETT-MILTON BERLE
Vi 45-0015 This Can't Be Love
BETTY GARRETT-JIMMY DURANTE
MGM 30176 Any State in the Forty-
Eight Is Great/The Pussy Cat Song
BETTY GARRETT-LARRY PARKS
MGM 10629 You Missed the Boat/
Can I Come in for a Second?

LPs

(movie soundtrack)
Metro M-580 WORDS AND MUSIC

647. GARRY, SID   VO
(SID GARFUNKEL; sometimes
spelled SID GARY)
Born c. 1901
Died April 5, 1973, New York, N.Y.

Strong-voiced baritone in theatrical style
of Al Jolson and Harry Richman. Active

in 20s and 30s. Played clubs and vaudeville, recorded, sang on radio. Active into late 30s; sang on New York radio.

RECORDS

DUKE ELLINGTON
 Vi 22603 Blue Again
HOTEL PENNSYLVANIA MUSIC
 Diva 3120 Stein Song
CALIFORNIA RAMBLERS
 Pe 15052 Talkin' to Myself
RED NICHOLS
 Br(12″)20110 New Orleans Medley, pt. 2
SID GARRY
 Ha 380 Rio Rita/Nesting Time
 Ha 1103 Singing a Vagabond Song/ Cryin' for the Carolines
 Ha 1117 There's Danger in Your Eyes, Cherie/If I Were King
 Ha 1266 Just a Gigolo/I'm Happy When You're Happy
 Ca 8327 Sonny Boy
 Ca 8344 High Up on a Hill Top
 Ca 8359 There's a Rainbow 'Round My Shoulder
 Ca 9089 Makin' Whoopee
 Re 8900 Aren't We All?
 Ve 2130 Let Me Sing and I'm Happy/To My Mammy
 Do 4473 My Sweeter Than Sweet
 Pe 12525 Mean to Me/The Things That Were Made for Love
 Pe 12562 Through
 Me 12029 Song of the Fool/My Love for You
 Me 12044 I'd Rather Have You/To Whom It May Concern
 Me 12069 At Last I'm Happy/The River and Me

648. GASKILL, CLARENCE   cm lyr p
Born February 1892, Philadelphia, Pa.
Died April 29, 1947, Fort Hill. N.Y.

Songwriter with limited output but several important songs. Teenage pianist in local theatres. At early age owned publishing company. Toured in vaudeville as the Melody Monarch. Military service, World War I. Composing at intervals. Songs included *I Love You Just the Same, Sweet Adeline* (1919); *Doo Wacka Doo* (1924); *I Can't Believe That You're in Love with Me* (1927); *I'm Wild About Horns on Automobiles* (1928); *Prisoner of Love* (1931). Score for unsuccessful stage show FRANK FAY'S FABLES (1922). Music and lyrics for long-running stage success EARL CARROLL'S VANITIES OF 1925: over 20 songs, none popular. At intervals wrote material for night club revues.

649. GAXTON, WILLIAM   vo
(ARTURO ANTONIO GAXIOLA)
Born December 2, 1893, San Francisco, Calif.
Died 1963

Stage star of 20s and 30s. Most famous role as President Wintergreen in 1932 hit OF THEE I SING. Early in career performed with partner in vaudeville. Military service, World War I. Returned to vaudeville 1918 as single, worked up to top spots including New York's Palace Theatre. Broadway debut in MUSIC BOX REVUE OF 1922. Starred in important musicals ensuing years. In 1926 silent movie IT'S THE OLD ARMY GAME. In sound movies FIFTY MILLION FRENCHMEN (1931), THEIR BIG MOMENT (1934), BEST FOOT FORWARD, SOMETHING TO SHOUT ABOUT and THE HEAT'S ON (1943), TROPICANA (1944), DIAMOND HORSESHOE (1945). In later years retired to farm in Stamford, Conn.

BROADWAY MUSICALS
1922—MUSIC BOX REVUE OF 1922
1927—A CONNECTICUT YANKEE
1929—FIFTY MILLION FRENCHMEN
1932—OF THEE I SING
1933—LET 'EM EAT CAKE
1934—ANYTHING GOES
1936—WHITE HORSE INN
1938—LEAVE IT TO ME
1940—LOUISIANA PURCHASE
1946—NELLIE BLY (unsuccessful)

650. GAYLOR, RUTH   vo
Born May 5, 1918, Brooklyn, N.Y.
Died March 21, 1972, New York, N.Y.

Band vocalist 1935-45. Eloquent, underrated singer with warm, melodious voice, sensitive treatment of lyrics. First important job with Hudson-Delange orchestra late 1935-7. With Mitchell Ayres 1937-8; several months with Bunny Berigan 1938.

Late 1939-41 with Teddy Powell. Married and retired awhile 1941-3. 1943-5 with Hal McIntyre, including tour overseas to entertain troops. Then left music for family life.

RECORDS

HUDSON-DELANGE ORCHESTRA

Br 7598 Tormented/It's a Lot of Idle Gossip

Br 7656 You're Not the Kind

Br 7700 The Moon Is Grinning at Me/It Seems I've Done Something Wrong Again

Br 7727 What the Heart Believes/ Looking Down at the Stars

Ma 112 Never in a Million Years/ Wake Up and Live

Ma 132 You're My Desire

MITCHELL AYRES

Va 540 To a Sweet Pretty Thing

BUNNY BERIGAN

Vi 25833 Moonshine Over Kentucky/I Got a Guy

Vi 25858 'Round the Old Deserted Farm/Never Felt Better, Never Had Less

Vi 25868 It's the Little Things That Count

Vi 25872 Wacky Dust

Vi 25877 And So Forth

Vi 25881 The Pied Piper/Ten Easy Lessons

TEDDY POWELL

De 3034 The One I Love

Bb 11016 Taking a Chance on Love/ Here's My Heart

Bb 11089 Two Hearts That Pass in the Night

Bb 11092 Talking to the Wind

Bb 11152 I Went Out of My Way

Bb 11213 Jim

Bb 11276 Mickey

Bb 11358 Hereafter/You're Not the Kind

HAL MCINTYRE

Bb 30-0831 I'm Making Believe

Bb 30-0837 Saturday Night/My Funny Valentine

651. GAYNOR, JANET   vo
(LAURA GAINER)

Born October 6, 1907, Philadelphia, Pa.

Important figure in early movie musicals 1929-31, though primarily dramatic ac-

tress. Sang and danced in co-starring role with Charles Farrell in big movie musical SUNNY SIDE UP (1929), with popular score by songwriting team Henderson-DeSylva-Brown. Co-starred with Farrell in movie musicals HAPPY DAYS and HIGH SOCIETY BLUES (1930), DELICIOUS (1931) and in eight non-musicals: top movie team early 30s. As child Janet lived with family in several locales, ended up in California. In 1925 extra in silent movies. First good role in THE JOHNSTOWN FLOOD (1926). Three important silent movies SUNRISE and SEVENTH HEAVEN (1927), STREET ANGEL (1928). Received first Oscar awarded as best actress in SEVENTH HEAVEN. Starred in three part-sound 1929 films, then big hit SUNNY SIDE UP. Singing voice natural and charming, not strong or well-trained. Disliked musicals, demanded serious roles. Beginning late 20s voted top star eight consecutive years by theatre managers. Starred in important 1937 movie A STAR IS BORN. Career waned after two movies in 1938. Thereafter mostly in retirement. Role in 1957 movie BERNADINE and in unsuccessful play MIDNIGHT SUN in 1959.

652. GAYNOR, MITZI   vo
(FRANCESCA MITZI GERBER; of Hungarian descent)

Born September 4, 1930, Chicago, Ill.

Bright star of movie musicals, talented dancer and singer. Earlier training for ballet and opera. Burst upon movie scene with secondary role in MY BLUE HEAVEN (1950). Beauty, personality, talent quickly projected her to stardom. Capable comedienne and dramatic actress. Portrayed musical-comedy star Eva Tanguay in movie THE "I DON'T CARE" GIRL (1953), had lead in movie version of SOUTH PACIFIC (1958). As movie work waned for stars during 60s, fashioned outstanding night club act. Guest on TV occasionally, several excellent specials of her own. Active at intervals in early 70s.

MOVIES

1950—MY BLUE HEAVEN

1951—TAKE CARE OF MY LITTLE GIRL; GOLDEN GIRL

1952—WE'RE NOT MARRIED; BLOODHOUNDS OF BROADWAY

1953—THE "I DON'T CARE" GIRL; DOWN AMONG THE SHELTERING PALMS
1954—THERE'S NO BUSINESS LIKE SHOW BUSINESS; THREE YOUNG TEXANS
1956—ANYTHING GOES; THE BIRDS AND THE BEES
1957—THE JOKER IS WILD; LES GIRLS
1958—SOUTH PACIFIC
1959—HAPPY ANNIVERSARY
1960—SURPRISE PACKAGE
1963—FOR LOVE OR MONEY
1969—FOR THE FIRST TIME

RECORDS
(all LPs)

MITZI GAYNOR
  Verve MGV-2115 Sings the Lyrics of Ira Gershwin
(movie soundtracks)
  Vi LSO-1032 SOUTH PACIFIC
  MGM E-3590 LES GIRLS
  De DL-8091 THERE'S NO BUSINESS LIKE SHOW BUSINESS

652A. GEAR, LUELLA   vo

Born September 5, 1897, New York, N.Y.

Attractive singing star of Broadway stage. Vaudeville, club and theatre work between Broadway shows and later in career. Some radio and TV to mid-60s.

BROADWAY MUSICALS

1917—LOVE O' MIKE
1923—POPPY
1926—QUEEN HIGH
1928—THE OPTIMISTS; UPS-A-DAISY
1932—GAY DIVORCE
1934—LIFE BEGINS AT 8:40
1936—ON YOUR TOES
1939—STREETS OF PARIS
1941—CRAZY WITH THE HEAT
1942—COUNT ME IN
1948—MY ROMANCE
1953—SABRINA FAIR

653. GELLER, HERB   as cm B

Born November 2, 1928, Los Angeles, Calif.

Modern jazzman on alto sax, popular mid-50s to early 60s on west coast. Underrated elsewhere. Facile, inventive, beautiful tone, tasteful. Early work on west coast with Joe Venuti 1946 and Jimmy Zito 1948. To New York 1949, with Jack Fina, Claude Thornhill, Jerry Wald, Lucky Millinder. Returned to west coast 1951, became important in jazz colony there. With Billy May, Howard Rumsey, Shorty Rogers, Maynard Ferguson, Chet Baker, Bill Holman, Dan Terry. In 1954 formed combo, including wife Lorraine (competent pianist), continued until her death 1958. Worked in east again, including jobs with Benny Goodman and Louis Bellson. Settled in West Berlin early 60s; 1963-5 staff member of Radio Free Berlin Orchestra. In 1965 opened own club featuring himself and foreign jazz stars.

RECORDS
(all LPs)

HERB GELLER
  Jub 1044 Fire in the West
  Jub 1094 Stax of Sax
  EmArcy MG-36024 The Gellers
  EmArcy(10″)MG-26045 Herb Geller Plays
MAYNARD FERGUSON
  EmArcy MG-36076 Around the Horn
  Vik LX-1070 Birdland Dream Band
  Vik LX-1077 Birdland Dream Band, Vol. 2
DINAH WASHINGTON
  EmArcy MG-36065 Dinah!
MARTY PAICH
  Cad 3010
CLIFFORD BROWN
  EmArcy MG-36102 Clifford Brown All-Stars
ALL-STARS
  EmArcy MG-36039 Best Coast Jazz
  De(12″)DL-8079 Jazz Studio 2
CHET BAKER
  PJ 9 Chet Baker Ensemble
HOWARD RUMSEY
  Contemp(10″)C-2506 Lighthouse All-Stars, Vol. 3
SHORTY ROGERS
  Vi LJM-1004 Shorty Rogers Courts the Count
  Vi LPM-1561 Portrait of Shorty

654. GENE & GLENN
(GENE CARROLL and GLENN ROWELL)

Radio team of 30s, created popular characters Jake and Lena. Began radio series on WTAM, Cleveland, about 1931.

Shows had simple homey atmosphere, featured light comedy, patter, piano, songs. Theme song *Hello, Hello, Hello*. Rowell played piano, Carroll harmonica, guitar, drums and jews' harp. Second radio series 1934. In 1937-8 broadcasting from west coast. To Hartford's WTIC, where showed folded early 40s. Collaborated as composers, mostly of religious songs.

GENE CARROLL

vo cm lyr har d g

Born April 18, 1898, Chicago, Ill.
Died March 5, 1972

Compositions *Next Door to Jesus; Like His Dad; Have You Made Somebody Happy Today?; At the Husking Bee; Little Tired Mother of Mine; Tune Jesus into Your Heart; Moonlight Lane; A Canoe, the Wabash and You; If You See Margie; Bluebell Valley*. Played Lena, Fibber McGee's maid. On Cleveland TV with Gene Carroll Show featuring amateurs.

GLENN ROWELL

p o vo cm lyr ar

Born November 2, 1899, Pontiac, Mich.
Died October 9, 1965

Attended Strausberger's Conservatory of Music in St. Louis. Pianist-arranger for St. Louis publishing house. Song demonstrator in Chicago store. Pianist-organist in Chicago theatres 1922-23. On radio beginning 1924. Member of Ford & Glenn team on radio and records 1925-30. After decade in Gene & Glenn team, active in radio many years, later TV. In 60s ragtime piano records with Johnny Maddox. Compositions *I Wish You Were Jealous of Me; But Do You?; Next Door to Jesus; Like His Dad; Some of Your Sweetness; At the Husking Bee; If You See Margie; Little Tired Mother of Mine; Tune Jesus into Your Heart; Moonlight Lane; Your Kids and Mine; Help the Kid Around the Corner; Daddy's Lullaby; Don't You Cry, Little Darlin'; Seven Little Stars and the Man in the Moon; Open the Window of Your Heart; Where in the World but America?; Schoolday Sweethearts; Read Your Bible Every Day*.

RECORDS

GENE & GLENN

Vi 22385 Whippoorwill/They Cut Down the Old Pine Tree
Vi 22396 Searching for You in My Dreams/Toy Town Admiral
Vi 22402 Home Is Heaven/Are You Ashamed of Me?

FORD & GLENN

Co 303-D I'll See You in My Dreams/Made a Hit with Kit-Kit-Kitty
Co 572-D Behind the Clouds/Tie Me to Your Apron Strings Again
Co 583-D Sleepy Head/Talking to the Moon
Co 608-D I Wish You Were Jealous of Me/Truly I Do
Co 749-D Mary Lou/I'd Love to Call You My Sweetheart
Co 768-D Schoolday Sweethearts/Won't You
Co 920-D Log Cabin Lullaby/Along Miami Shore
Co 1720-D Dream Train/I Get the Blues When It Rains
Co 1828-D The Utah Trail/When It's Springtime in the Rockies
Co 2013-D Piccolo Pete/That's Why I'm Jealous of You

655. GENSLER, LEWIS E.   cm

Born December 4, 1896, New York, N.Y.

Composer of 20s and 30s. Wrote for Broadway shows and movies. Best-known songs *Cross Your Heart, Love Is Just Around the Corner*. Later became movie producer.

SONGS
(with related shows)

1922—QUEEN O' HEARTS stage show (Queen o' Hearts; You Need Someone; Tom-Tom)
1924—BE YOURSELF stage show (songs unimportant)
1925—BIG BOY stage show (Keep Smiling at Trouble); CAPTAIN JINKS stage show (Fond of You; I Do; Kiki; Sea Legs)
1926—QUEEN HIGH stage show (Queen High; Cross Your Heart; Gentlemen Prefer Blondes)
1928—UPS-A-DAISY stage show (Ups-a-

Daisy; Will You Remember, Will You Forget?; Hot!)

1931—THE GANG'S ALL HERE stage show (By Special Permission of the Copyright Owners, I Love You; It Always Takes Two; Speak Easy; Speaking of You)

1932—BALLYHOO OF 1932 stage show (Thrill Me; Riddle Me This; Nuts and Noodles; How Do You Do It?)

1934—MELODY IN SPRING movie (Melody in Spring; Ending with a Kiss)

1935—HERE IS MY HEART movie (Love Is Just Around the Corner); OLD MAN RHYTHM movie (I Never Saw a Better Night)

656. GERALDO   p o B
(GERALD BRIGHT)

Born 1904, London, England
Died May 4, 1974, Vevey, Switzerland of heart attack

Popular English bandleader. At early age played piano and organ in theatres. Trip around world; studied popular music in many countries. After return to England, formed band. Long engagement at Hotel Majestic, St. Anne's, stayed five years as north country favorite. Also on radio. In South America awhile, mostly Brazil; became devotee of tango music, introduced it in London. Adopted name of Geraldo, became popular as a leading society band late 30s. Popular radio shows on BBC such as Chateau de Madrid, Romance in Rhythm, Dancing Through, The Music Shop, Band Box, Milestones of Melody. Great vocalist Al Bowlly, after leaving Ray Noble in U.S., recorded often with Geraldo 1938-9. During World War II Geraldo band entertained troops. Active into 50s and 60s. Later arrangements had modern touch, mixed styles, afforded spots for jazz soloists.

RECORDS
GERALDO
Co(E) 436 Thrill of the Tango/You Could Never Be True
Co(E) 2364 Good Morning/Where or When
Co 2983-D Isle of Capri/Madonna Mine

Co 3007-D "Evergreen" Selections (1 & 2)
Co 39967 The Ecstasy Tango/La Cumparsita
De(E) 6201 Valencia/Isle of Capri//Oh, Donna Clara
De(E) 6411 September in the Rain/Will You Remember?
HMV(E) 5394 You Couldn't Be Cuter/Just Let Me Look at You
HMV(E) 5428 Penny Serenade/Never Break a Promise
HMV(E) 5437 Two Sleepy People/While a Cigarette Was Burning
HMV(E) 5443 Summer's End/Any Broken Hearts to Mend?
HMV(E) 5444 My Own/You're as Pretty as a Picture
HMV(E) 5449 One Day When We Were Young/I'm in Love with Vienna
Pa(E) 1799 Our Love Affair/And So Do I
Pa(E) 1848 There Goes That Song Again/No.10 Lullaby Lane
Pa(E) 2040 Swinging on a Star/Don't Sweetheart Me
Pa(E) 2072 Meadowlands/I'm Confessin'
Pa(E) 2312 Taps Miller/All of Me

LPs
GERALDO
Pa(E) PMC-7139 Hello Again
Cam CAL-442 Dance, Dance, Dance!
Cam CAL-555 Dance, Dance, Dance! (Vol. 2)
Cam CAL-652 Dance, Dance, Dance! (Vol. 3)

657. GERSHWIN, GEORGE   cm p

Born September 26, 1898, Brooklyn, N.Y.
Died July 11, 1937, Beverly Hills, Calif.

Among greatest popular composers. Productive life cut short at 38. Scores for numerous Broadway shows, notably LADY BE GOOD (1924), OH, KAY! (1926), FUNNY FACE (1927), STRIKE UP THE BAND and GIRL CRAZY (1930), OF THEE I SING (1932; first musical to win Pulitzer Prize), PORGY AND BESS (1935). Had begun writing for movies just before death. Most famous songs *Swanee*; *Fascinating Rhythm*; *Oh,*

Lady Be Good; *Somebody Loves Me*; *The Man I Love*; *Liza*; *Someone to Watch Over Me*; *'S Wonderful*; *I Got Rhythm*; *Strike Up the Band*; *I've Got a Crush on You*; *How Long Has This Been Going On?*; *Embraceable You*; *Of Thee I Sing*; *Summertime*; *A Foggy Day*; *They Can't Take That Away from Me*; *Love Is Here to Stay*; *Love Walked In*; and concert piece *Rhapsody in Blue*. Work often had a special quality above ordinary popular songs. Brother Ira chief lyricist beginning 1925. Sons of Jewish immigrants from Russia. Extensive early musical training. At 15 pianist and songplugger for Remick Music Company in New York. Accompanist for Louise Dresser and Nora Bayes. In 1917 signed by Max Dreyfus as staff composer for Harms Publishing Company. First hit *Swanee* 1918, featured by Al Jolson in Broadway show SINBAD. First stage score for LA, LA, LUCILLE (1919). Several scores for GEORGE WHITE'S SCANDALS and other shows.

Acclaimed for *Rhapsody in Blue*, performed by Paul Whiteman orchestra at New York's Aeolian Hall February 12, 1924. Whiteman used main theme as own theme in later years. Gershwin's other serious music included *An American in Paris*, written in Paris 1928, and *Concerto in F*. In 1934 Gershwin had own radio show Music by Gershwin, conducted large orchestra. Negro opera PORGY AND BESS on Broadway stage 1935 won further acclaim.

Other collaborators lyricists Arthur Jackson, Irving Caesar, Buddy DeSylva, Oscar Hammerstein II, Otto Harbach, Gus Kahn. Music world stunned at 1937 death from brain tumor. Career probably hadn't peaked; might have became most successful of movie composers. Biographies of Gershwin include *A Journey to Greatness* by David Ewen, *Gershwin* by Isaac Goldberg, *The Gershwin Years* by Edward Jablonski and Lawrence Stewart, *George Gershwin* by Robert Payne, *The Gershwins* by Robert Kimball and Alfred E. Simon. Popular 1945 movie RHAPSODY IN BLUE based on Gershwin's life, featured his songs, starred Robert Alda as Gershwin.

SONGS

*(with related shows; *with lyricist Ira Gershwin)*

1916—THE PASSING SHOW OF 1916 stage show (The Making of a Girl)

1918—SINBAD stage show (Swanee); LADIES FIRST stage show* (The Real American Folk Song; Some Wonderful Sort of Someone)

1919—LA, LA, LUCILLE stage show* (Nobody but You; There's More to a Kiss Than a Sound; Tee-Oodle-Um-Bum-Bo); GOOD MORNING JUDGE stage show (I Am So Young and You Are So Beautiful; There's More to a Kiss Than the X-X-X); THE LADY IN RED stage show (Something About Love)

1920—GEORGE WHITE'S SCANDALS OF 1920 stage show (Idle Dreams; Scandal Walk; On My Mind the Whole Night Long); MORRIS GEST'S MIDNIGHT WHIRL stage show (Baby Dolls; I'll Show You a Wonderful World; Limehouse Nights; Poppyland); THE SWEETHEART SHOP stage show (We're Pals; Waitin' for the Sun to Come Out); BROADWAY BREVITIES OF 1920 stage show (I Love to Dance; Love, Honor and Oh Baby; Spanish Love; I'm a Dancing Fool); ED WYNN'S CARNIVAL stage show (Oh, I'd Love to Be Loved by You)

1921—GEORGE WHITE'S SCANDALS OF 1921 stage show (Drifting Along with the Tide; South Sea Isles)

1922—GEORGE WHITE'S SCANDALS OF 1922 stage show (I'll Build a Stairway to Paradise; I Found a Four Leaf Clover); OUR NELL stage show (Innocent Ingenue Baby; Walking Home with Angeline; Bye and Bye; My Old New England Home); FOR GOODNESS SAKE stage show (Someone; Tra-La-La); THE FRENCH DOLL stage show (Do It Again); PINS AND NEEDLES stage show (No One Else but That Girl of Mine); SPICE OF 1922 stage show (The Yankee Doodle Blues)

1923—GEORGE WHITE'S SCANDALS OF

1923 stage show (The Life of a Rose; Let's Be Lonesome Together; There Is Nothing Too Good for You; You and I in Old Versailles); THE DANCING GIRL stage show (That American Boy of Mine; Cuddle Me as We Dance; Pango Pango; Why Am I Sad?); LITTLE MISS BLUEBEARD stage show* (I Won't Say I Will, I Won't Say I Won't); NIFTIES OF 1923 stage show (At Half Past Seven; Nashville Nightingale; Sunshine Trail)

1924—GEORGE WHITE'S SCANDALS OF 1924 stage show (Somebody Loves Me; Rose of Madrid; Night Time in Araby); LADY BE GOOD stage show* (Oh, Lady Be Good; Fascinating Rhythm; Hang on to Me; So Am I; The Man I Love, hit song of later years, dropped from show); SWEET LITTLE DEVIL stage show (Sweet Little Devil; Virginia; Someone Believes in You); Rhapsody in Blue

1925—TELL ME MORE stage show* (Tell Me More; Kickin' the Clouds Away; Why Do I Love You So?; My Fair Lady)

1926—TIP TOES stage show* (Tip Toes; That Certain Feeling; Sweet and Low Down; Looking for a Boy; Lady Luck); OH, KAY! stage show* (Someone to Watch Over Me; Do-Do-Do; Clap Yo' Hands; Oh, Kay; Maybe; Fidgety Feet); SONG OF THE FLAME stage show (Song of the Flame; Cossack Love Song); AMERICANA stage show* (Blowing the Blues Away; The Lost Barber Shop Chord)

1927—FUNNY FACE stage show* (Funny Face; 'S Wonderful; My One and Only; High Hat; Let's Kiss and Make Up; He Loves and She Loves)

1928—ROSALIE stage show* (How Long Has This Been Going On?; Say So; Oh Gee, Oh Joy); TREASURE GIRL stage show* (A Place in the Country; Oh, So Nice; Feeling I'm

Falling; K-ra-zy for You; I've Got a Crush on You—popular later in 1930 show STRIKE UP THE BAND)

1929—SHOW GIRL stage show* (Liza; Do What You Do; So Are You; An American in Paris—used as background music)

1930—STRIKE UP THE BAND stage show* (Strike Up the Band; Soon; I've Got a Crush on You; The Man I Love—tried and dropped from show); GIRL CRAZY stage show* (I Got Rhythm; Bidin' My Time; But Not for Me; Embraceable You; Could You Use Me?; Treat Me Rough; Sam and Delilah); NINE-FIFTEEN REVUE stage show* (Toddlin' Along; unsuccessful show); SONG OF THE FLAME movie (original stage score)

1931—DELICIOUS movie* (Delishious; Somebody from Somewhere; You Started It; New York Rhapsody)

1932—OF THEE I SING stage show* (Of Thee I Sing; Love Is Sweeping the Country; Who Cares?; Wintergreen for President); GIRL CRAZY movie* (original stage score)

1933—LET 'EM EAT CAKE stage show* (Let 'Em Eat Cake; Mine; many lesser songs); PARDON MY ENGLISH stage show* (My Cousin in Milwaukee; Lorelei; Isn't It a Pity?)

1935—PORGY AND BESS stage show* (Summertime; I Got Plenty o' Nuttin'; It Ain't Necessarily So; I Love You, Porgy; Bess, You Is My Woman Now; My Man's Gone Now; Where Is My Bess?; A Woman Is a Sometime Thing; There's a Boat Dat's Leavin' Soon for New York)

1937—THE SHOW IS ON stage show* (By Strauss); A DAMSEL IN DISTRESS movie* (A Foggy Day; Nice Work If You Can Get It; Things Are Looking Up Now); SHALL WE DANCE? movie* (Shall We Dance?; Let's Call the Whole Thing Off; They All Laughed; They Can't Take That Away from Me; Beginner's Luck; Slap That Bass)

1938—GOLDWYN FOLLIES movie* (Love Is Here to Stay; Love Walked In; I Was Doing All Right; I Love to Rhyme; Just Another Rhumba)

1943—GIRL CRAZY movie* (original stage score)

1947—THE SHOCKING MISS PILGRIM movie* (some old, heretofore unpublished songs of Gershwin: For You, For Me, For Evermore; Aren't You Kind of Glad We Did?; Changing My Tune; The Back Bay Polka; Waltzing Is Better Sitting Down)

1949—THE BARKLEYS OF BROADWAY movie (old song: They Can't Take That Away from Me)

1951—AN AMERICAN IN PARIS movie* (old Gershwin songs featured: An American in Paris; I Got Rhythm; Embraceable You; By Strauss; Our Love Is Here to Stay; I'll Build a Stairway to Paradise; Tra-La-La)

1957—FUNNY FACE movie* (original stage score plus: Clap Yo' Hands; How Long Has This Been Going On?)

1959—PORGY AND BESS movie* (original stage score)

Serious works: *Piano Concerto in F; Preludes for Piano; Second Piano Rhapsody; Cuban Overture*

RECORDS
(as pianist)

GEORGE GERSHWIN
Co 809-D Clap Yo' Hands/Do-Do-Do
Co 812-D Someone to Watch Over Me/Maybe

LPs

GEORGE GERSHWIN
20th Fox 1004 Plays the Rhapsody in Blue
20th Fox 3013 At the Piano

658. GERSHWIN, IRA   lyr
Born December 6, 1896, New York, N.Y.

Outstanding lyricist with prolific output over long career. Noted for teaming with brother George, brilliant composer, on many all-time great songs. Also collaborated with composers Louis Alter, Harold Arlen, Vernon Duke, Jerome Kern, Joseph Meyer, Sigmund Romberg, Arthur Schwartz, Harry Warren, Richard Whiting, Kurt Weill, Burton Lane, Vincent Youmans. Wrote scores for Broadway shows and movies, some in collaboration with brother. Gershwins sons of Jewish immigrants from Russia. Ira attended CCNY and Columbia University Extension. Worked for touring carnival and publishing company. Began songwriting about same time as George, teamed with him regularly beginning 1925, shared many triumphs. After George's death 1937 wrote with other composers, including movie scores. Best-known songs with composers other than George: *I Can't Get Started, Cheerful Little Earful, You're a Builder Upper, Let's Take a Walk Around the Block, My Ship, Long Ago and Far Away, The Man That Got Away.* Wrote book *Lyrics on Several Occasions.* Life portrayed in books *The Gershwin Years* by Edward Jablonski and Lawrence Stewart and *The Gershwins* by Robert Kimball and Alfred E. Simon.

SONGS
*(with related shows; *collaborated with brother—see* GEORGE GERSHWIN *biography for song listings)*

1918—LADIES FIRST stage show*

1919—LA, LA, LUCILLE stage show*

1921—TWO LITTLE GIRLS IN BLUE stage show (used pseudonym Arthur Francis; Two Little Girls in Blue; Oh Me, Oh My, Oh You; Dolly)

1923—LITTLE MISS BLUEBEARD stage show*

1924—LADY BE GOOD stage show*; BE YOURSELF stage show

1925—TELL ME MORE stage show*

1926—TIP TOES stage show*; OH, KAY! stage show*; AMERICANA stage show* (plus: Sunny Disposish)

1927—FUNNY FACE stage show*

1928—ROSALIE stage show*; TREASURE GIRL stage show*

1929—SHOW GIRL stage show*

1930—STRIKE UP THE BAND stage show*; GIRL CRAZY stage show*; NINE-FIFTEEN REVUE stage show*; GARRICK GAIETIES OF 1930 stage show (I'm Only Human After All);

SWEET AND LOW stage show (Cheerful Little Earful)

1931—DELICIOUS movie*

1932—OF THEE I SING stage show*; GIRL CRAZY movie*

1933—LET 'EM EAT CAKE stage show*; PARDON MY ENGLISH stage show*

1934—LIFE BEGINS AT 8:40 stage show (You're a Builder Upper; Let's Take a Walk Around the Block; Fun to Be Fooled; What Can You Say in a Love Song?; Shoein' the Mare)

1935—PORGY AND BESS stage show*

1936—ZIEGFELD FOLLIES OF 1936 stage show (I Can't Get Started; That Moment of Moments; An Island in the West Indies; Words without Music)

1937—THE SHOW IS ON stage show*; A DAMSEL IN DISTRESS movie*; SHALL WE DANCE? movie*

1938—GOLDWYN FOLLIES movie* (plus: Spring Again; I'm Not Complaining)

1941—LADY IN THE DARK stage show (My Ship; Jenny; This Is New; One Life to Live; The Princess of Pure Delight; Tschaikowsky)

1943—GIRL CRAZY movie*

1944—COVER GIRL movie (Long Ago and Far Away; Sure Thing; Put Me to the Test; Cover Girl; The Show Must Go On; Who's Complaining?; Make Way for Tomorrow); LADY IN THE DARK movie (original stage score)

1945—FIREBRAND OF FLORENCE stage show (Sing Me Not a Ballad; You're Far Too Near Me; A Rhyme for Angela); WHERE DO WE GO FROM HERE? movie (All at Once; If Love Remains; Song of the Rhineland; Morale; Columbus)

1946—PARK AVENUE stage show (For the Life of Me; Sweet Nevada; Goodbye to All That; There's No Holding Me)

1947—THE SHOCKING MISS PILGRIM movie*

1949—THE BARKLEYS OF BROADWAY movie (My One and Only Highland Fling; You'd Be Hard to Replace; Shoes with Wings On; Manhattan Downbeat; Weekend in the Country; plus old song They Can't Take That Away from Me)

1951—AN AMERICAN IN PARIS movie*

1954—A STAR IS BORN movie, Harold Arlen-cm (The Man That Got Away; Here's What I'm Here For; Gotta Have Me Go with You; Born in a Trunk; That Long Face); THE COUNTRY GIRL movie, Harold Arlen-cm (Live and Learn; The Search Is Through; The Pitchman)

1957—FUNNY FACE movie*

1959—PORGY AND BESS movie*

659. GERUN, TOM   B
(THOMAS GERUNOVITCH)

Leader of good dance band late 20s and 30s. Sometimes played semi-hot. Sidemen in early 30s included saxmen Woody Herman and Tony Martin. Vocalist Ginny Simms with band awhile. In mid-30s had dance spot on west coast, Bal Tabarin.

RECORDS

TOM GERUN

Br 4050 My Gal Sal/There's a Rainbow 'Round My Shoulder

Br 4429 Am I Blue?/Let Me Have My Dreams

Br 4520 Every Now and Then/I'm in Love with You

Br 4521 One Sweet Kiss/Some Day Soon

Br 4628 My Love Parade/Dream Lover

Br 4727 Sing, You Sinners/In My Little Hope Chest

Br 4829 Around the Corner/Absence Makes the Heart Grow Fonder

Br 4859 Rollin' Down the River/My Sweetheart Serenade

Br 4895 If I Could Be with You/A Big Bouquet for You

Br 4916 Memories of You/You're Lucky to Me

Br 4999 What Good Am I without You?/Nine Little Miles from Ten-Ten-Tennessee

Br 6002 You're the One I Care For/Come a Little Closer

Br 6064 By My Side/If You Should Ever Need Me

Br 6282 By the Fireside/Now That I Have You

Br 6353 The Lady I Love/A Shanty in Old Shanty Town

Br 6364 My Heart's at Ease/Lonesome Me

Br 6365 Sweethearts Forever/Three's a Crowd

Br 6371 Sentimental Gentleman from Georgia/We Were Only Walking in the Moonlight

660. GETZ, STAN　　　　　ts B

Born February 2, 1927, Philadelphia, Pa.

Great tenor sax star in modern style. Cool, delicate tone, facile, solos consistently inventive and tasty. Long reign at top of jazz popularity polls in 50s and 60s. Moved to New York when youngster. At 15 with Dick Rogers band. Next with Jack Teagarden and Bob Chester. Important year with Stan Kenton 1944-5. In mid-1945 led trio in Hollywood, then with Benny Goodman late 1945 to early 1946. Also with Jimmy Dorsey, Randy Brooks, Herbie Fields. With Woody Herman's Second Herd 1947-9 attained stardom. From that point led groups. Busy schedule, extensive recording. Scandinavian tour 1951. Europe 1958 with Jazz at the Philharmonic; remained abroad through 1960. Great popularity in 1962 when he and guitarist Charlie Byrd combined to become leading exponents of new bossanova style in U.S. Blended Brazilian music with light jazz—a most attractive sound. On several TV shows thanks to new popularity. Worked with bossa-nova artists Luiz Bonfa, Joao Gilberto and Astrud Gilberto. Won awards for bossanova recordings. Maintained jazz activities also. Career remained in high gear through 60s into 70s, here and in Europe.

RECORDS

BENNY GOODMAN

36908 Give Me the Simple Life

WOODY HERMAN

Cap 616 Early Autumn/Keeper of the Flame

Co 38304 Four Brothers

AL HAIG

Seeco 10-005 Ante-Room/Skull Buster

Seeco 10-006 Pennies from Heaven/Poop Deck

KAI WINDING

Sav 602 Sweet Miss/Loaded

JOHNNY SMITH

Roost 547 Moonlight in Vermont/Tabu

Roost 568 Jaguar/Tenderly

TERRY GIBBS

NJ 800 T & S/Terry's Tune

NJ 803 Cuddles/Elysses

METRONOME ALL-STARS

Cap 1550 Early Spring/Local 802 Blues

Co 38734 No Figs/Double Date

STAN GETZ

NJ 802 Five Brothers/Four and One Moore

NJ 818 Battleground/Prezervation

NJ 829 My Old Flame/The Lady in Red

Pres 724 Battle of Saxes/Wrap Your Troubles in Dreams

Pres 740 What's New?/Indian Summer

Roost 520 Tootsie Roll/Strike Up the Band

Roost 529 Flamingo/Don't Get Scared

Roost 532 Dear Old Stockholm/I Only Have Eyes for You

Roost 562 Lullaby of Birdland/Autumn Leaves

Mer 89025 The Way You Look Tonight/Stars Fell on Alabama

Mer 89042 Lover, Come Back to Me/'Tis Autumn

Norg 119 Down by the Sycamore Tree/I Hadn't Anyone 'Til You

Metro(Sw) 554 S'cool Boy/Ack, Varmeland Du Skona

LPs

STAN GETZ

Pres(10″)102 Stan Getz, Vol. 1

Pres(10″)104 Stan Getz, Vol. 2

Jazztone J-1230

Roost 2209 At Storyville, Vol. 1

Roost 2225 At Storyville, Vol. 2

Verve V-8200 The Cool Sounds

Verve V-8412 Focus

Verve V-8494 Big Band Bossa Nova

Verve V-8554 Reflections

Verve V-8707 Voices

STAN GETZ-CHARLIE BYRD
Verve V-8432 Jazz Samba
STAN GETZ-GERRY MULLIGAN
Verve V-8249 Gerry Mulligan Meets Stan Getz
HERB ELLIS
Verve V-8252 Nothing but the Blues (movie soundtrack)
De DL-8252 THE BENNY GOODMAN STORY Vol. 1
De DL-8253 THE BENNY GOODMAN STORY Vol. 2

661. GIBBS, GEORGIA   vo
(FREDDA GIBSON; born GIB-BONS)

Born August 17, 1920, Worcester, Mass.
Excellent singer; strong voice with good showmanship. As youngster sang on local radio, worked weekends in Boston clubs and theatres. First band job with Perley Stevens in Boston. Sang on Lucky Strike radio show 1937-8. With Richard Himber on Melody Puzzles show in 1938, also on Tim & Irene show 1938. Toured with Hudson-DeLange band almost a year. Briefly with Frankie Trumbauer (1940) and Artie Shaw (1942). In early 40s sang on Herb Shriner radio show, Hit Parade again, Camel Caravan, own singing series. Up to this point used professional name Gibson with various first names Fredda, Freddye, Freddie. In later 1942 adopted name of Georgia Gibbs. In later 40s on popular Garry Moore-Jimmy Durante radio show, where Moore dubbed her "Her Nibs, Miss Georgia Gibbs." On Tony Martin show 1946. Club and theatre work throughout career. Recorded frequently later 40s and 50s, record hits *Kiss of Fire* (1952) and *Tweedle Dee* (1955). TV appearances in 50s and 60s.

RECORDS
HUDSON-DELANGE ORCHESTRA
Br 7785 Remember When/I'll Never Tell You I Love You
Br 7795 If We Never Meet Again
FRANKIE TRUMBAUER
Vs 8223 Laziest Gal in Town
HAL KEMP
Vi 26215 If It's Good

ARTIE SHAW
Vi 27779 Not Mine/Absent Minded Moon
GEORGIA GIBBS
Vi 20-1660 The More I See You/In Acapulco
Maj 12000 You Keep Coming Back Like a Song/Willow Road
Maj 12008 So Would I/Wrap Your Troubles in Dreams
Maj 12009 How Are Things in Glocca Morra?/Necessity
Maj 12010 Ballin' the Jack/As Long as I'm Dreaming
Maj 12014 Ol' Man Mose/Put Yourself in My Place, Baby
Mer 5681 While We're Young/While You Danced, Danced, Danced
Mer 5823 Kiss of Fire/A Lasting Thing
Mer 70218 He's Funny That Way/Say It Isn't So
Mer 70238 The Bridge of Sighs/A Home Lovin' Man
Mer 70274 Under Paris Skies/I Love Paris
Mer 70298 Baubles, Bangles and Beads/Somebody Bad Stole de Wedding Bell
Mer 70339 My Sin/I'll Always Be Happy with You
Mer 70517 Tweedle Dee / You're Wrong, All Wrong
Mer 70572 Dance with Me, Henry/Every Road Must Have a Turning
Cor 60353 Get Out Those Old Records/I Still Feel the Same About You
GEORGIA GIBBS-BOB CROSBY
Cor 60227 A Little Bit Independent/Simple Melody
LPs
GEORGIA GIBBS
Mer MG-20170 Swingin' with Her Nibs
Mer(10")MG-25199 The Man That Got Away
Cor CRL-57183 Her Nibs, Georgia Gibbs
Rondo-lette 876 "Her Nibs" (Maj RIs)
Bell 6000

662. GIBBS, PARKER   vo ts
Featured singer with Ted Weems band

from 1925 to late 30s; also played tenor sax in band. Good at novelty and rhythm tunes. Vocalist on Weems hit record *Piccolo Pete* late 1929.

RECORDS

TED WEEMS

Vi 20120 My Cutey's Due at Two-to-Two Today/I'm Gonna Park Myself in Your Arms

Vi 20829 She's Got "It"

Vi 21767 You're the Cream in My Coffee

Vi 21809 My Troubles Are Over

Vi 22037 Piccolo Pete

Vi 22038 What a Day!

Vi 22137 Miss Wonderful

Vi 22238 Harmonica Harry

Vi 22304 Talk of the Town

Vi 22499 A Girl Friend of a Boy Friend of Mine

Vi 22515 Sing

Vi 22564 The One-Man Band

Vi 22637 Walkin' My Baby Back Home/I Lost My Gal Again

Vi 22838 I'm for You a Hundred Percent/That's What I Like About You

Vi 22881 She's So Nice

Vi 24219 At the Baby Parade/The Old Kitchen Kettle

Vi 24308 Look Who's Here!/Hats Off, Here Comes a Lady

Bb 5235 I'm a Lover of Paree

Bb 5236 Doin' the Uptown Lowdown/Buckin' the Wind

Co 2976-D Winter Wonderland

De 895 Bye Bye Baby

De 1704 What Are You Doing the Rest of Your Life?

LPs

TED WEEMS

TOM 23 (1928-30 Vi RIs)

663. GIBBS, TERRY   vb d p cm B
(JULIUS GUBENKO)

Born October 13, 1924, Brooklyn, N.Y.

Leading modern jazz star on vibes in 50s and 60s. Swinging style, fresh solo lines. Toured with Major Bowes unit at 12 as drummer. Other drumming experience before military service, World War II. Joined New York jazz scene primarily as vibist. In 1947 with Bill DeArango, Tommy Dorsey, Chubby Jackson. With Buddy Rich 1948, Woody Herman late 1948-9. With Tommy Dorsey mid-1950; brief periods with Benny Goodman in early 50s. Stardom in mid-50s freelancing and leading combo or big band. Mostly on west coast since late 50s; 1963-4 in New York. Frequent recording. Led band on west coast TV. Original jazz compositions *T & S, Terry's Tune, Peaches, Shaine Une Zees, That Feller McKeller*.

RECORDS

ALLEN EAGER

Sav 908 Meeskite/Donald Jay

SERGE CHALOFF

Fut 3004 The Most!/Chasin' the Bass

CHUBBY JACKSON

Rbw 10093 Crown Pilots/Lemon Drop

Rbw 10098 Boomsie/Dee Dee's Dance

BENNY GOODMAN SEXTET

Co 39564 Farewell Blues

WOODY HERMAN

Cap 616 Early Autumn/Keeper of the Flame

Cap 720 Jamaica Rhumba

Cap 15365 Lemon Drop

METRONOME ALL-STARS

Cap 1550 Early Spring/Local 802 Blues

TERRY GIBBS

Sav 818 I've Got You Under My Skin/Serenade in Blue

Br 80219 Cheerful Little Earful/Lollypop

Br 80224 Swinging the Robert A.G./I May Be Wrong

Br 80243 That Feller McKeller/Fabulous Figs

NJ 800 Terry's Tune/T & S

NJ 803 Cuddles/Elysses

NJ 804 Michelle (1 & 2)

LPs

TERRY GIBBS

Mer MG-20440 Terry Gibbs & His Orchestra

Mer MG-20704 Explosion!

EmArcy MG-36064 Vibes on Velvet

EmArcy MG-36103 Swingin' with Terry Gibbs

EmArcy MG-36128 Plays the Duke

Verve MGV-2136 Music from Cole Porter's CAN-CAN

Mainstream 6048 It's Time We Met
Impulse S-58 Take It from Me
TERRY GIBBS-BILL HARRIS
Premier PS-2006 Woodchoppers' Ball
ALLEN EAGER
Sav(10″)MG-15044 Vol. 2
Sav(10″)MG-9015 New Trends of
Jazz, Vol. 2
BENNY GOODMAN
Co CL-552 The New Benny Goodman
Sextet

664. GIFFORD, GENE   bn g ar cm
(HAROLD EUGENE GIFFORD)
*Born May 31, 1908, Americus, Ga.
Died November 12, 1970, Memphis,
Tenn.*

Chief arranger for Glen Gray & the Casa
Loma Orchestra 1930-5. Set band's style,
which became popular and influential in
public acceptance of swing. Composed
swing numbers featured by band. Grew
up in Memphis. Played banjo as youngster. Toured southwest with Lloyd
Williams band, played with Watson's Bell
Hops in Mississippi. Led band touring
Texas. With Blue Steele 1928-9, switched
to guitar. On Detroit date hired by Jean
Goldkette to write arrangements for his
units. With Goldkette unit led by Henry
Biagini, which evolved into Casa Loma
Orchestra later led by Glen Gray. Played
guitar with band several years, then concentrated on arranging and composing.
Composed band's famous theme *Smoke
Rings*. Other compositions featured by
band: *Casa Loma Stomp, Black Jazz,
White Jazz, Dance of the Lame Duck,
Maniac's Ball, San Sue Strut, Stompin'
Around, Out of Space*. Wrote riff-styled
arrangements on swing numbers for
Gray, pretty, danceable arrangements on
ballads. Led noteworthy record session
1935 with Bunny Berigan and all-star jazz
personnel. For session wrote four numbers: *Nothin' but the Blues, Squareface,
Dizzy Glide, New Orleans Twist*. Left Gray
for freelance arranging and studio work.
Arranged for Freddy Martin, Mal Hallett,
Tommy Reynolds, Jimmy Joy, Ada Leonard. With Bob Strong 1943 as guitarist-
arranger. U.S.O. tour mid-40s. With Gray
again as arranger 1948-9. In 50s and 60s

mostly in New York at various jobs
outside of music. Settled in Memphis
1969 to teach music.

RECORDS
GENE GIFFORD
Vi 25041 Nothin' but the Blues/New
Orleans Twist
Vi 25065 Squareface/Dizzy Glide
LPs
GENE GIFFORD (one side)
"X"(10″)LVA-3034 Swing Session (Vi
RIs)

665. GILBERT, JEAN   cm
Composer for successful Broadway
shows. Songs attained no popularity, were
effective within context of shows.

BROADWAY MUSICALS
1912—MODEST SUZANNE
1914—QUEEN OF THE MOVIES
1915—A MODERN EVE
1922—LADY IN ERMINE
1926—KATJA, THE DANCER
1929—THE RED ROBE; THE STREET SINGER
1932—MARCHING BY (unsuccessful)

666. GILBERT, L. WOLFE   lyr
*Born August 31, 1886, Odessa, Russia
Died July 13, 1970*

Popular song lyricist in 20s and early 30s.
Best known: *Waiting for the Robert E.
Lee; Down Yonder; O, Katharina!; Ramo-
na; Jeannine, I Dream of Lilac Time; My
Mother's Eyes; The Peanut Vendor*. To
U.S. at age one; grew up in Philadelphia.
Vaudeville and cafe entertainer. Began
composing. Success mid-20s; several hit
songs. Founded own publishing compa-
ny. Wrote for radio and TV. Autobiog-
raphy: *Without Rhyme or Reason*. Chief
collaborators composers Lewis Muir,
Mabel Wayne, Abel Baer, Ben Oakland,
Jay Gorney, Nat Shilkret, Richard Fall,
Anatole Friedland.

SONGS
(with related shows)

1912—Here Comes My Daddy Now;
Hitchy-Koo; Waiting for the Robert E. Lee
1913—You Did, You Know You Did;
Mammy Jinny's Jubilee

1915—By Heck; My Sweet Adair
1916—Hawaiian Sunshine; My Own Iona
1917—Lily of the Valley; Oriental Nights; Are You from Heaven?
1918—Singapore
1920—Dance-o-Mania
1921—Down Yonder (revived in 50s)
1924—O, Katharina!
1925—I Miss My Swiss; Don't Wake Me Up, Let Me Dream
1926—Hello, Aloha, How Are You?
1927—Lucky Lindy
1928—Chiquita; Gypsy; Ramona; Jeannine, I Dream of Lilac Time; When You're with Somebody Else
1929—If You Believed in Me; My Mother's Eyes
1930—HAPPY DAYS movie (I'm on a Diet of Love); PARAMOUNT ON PARADE movie (Dancing to Save Your Sole; I'm in Training for You; Drink to the Girl of My Dreams); Chimes of Spring; The Peanut Vendor
1931—Green Eyes; Mama Inez; Maria, My Own; Marta; Poor Kid; Mama Don't Want No Peas and Rice and Cocoanut Oil
1933—ROMAN SCANDALS movie (Tax on Love)
1940—My Son, My Son
1946—Dixieland Rendezvous

Other songs: *Take Me to That Swanee Shore*; *Shades of Night*; *My Little Dream Girl*; *La Golondrina*; *The Right Kind of Man*; *Hopalong Cassidy March*; *Forever and a Day*; *African Lament*; *In the Land of Make Believe*; *No One Can Take Your Place*; *Astronaut of Space*; *I Laughed at Love*

667. GILLESPIE, DIZZY   t vo cm ar B
(JOHN BIRKS GILLESPIE)

Born October 21, 1917, Cheraw, S.C.

Trumpet star, giant of jazz; one of the originators of bop in 40s. Trumpet style brilliantly facile and inventive. Studied music early, attended Laurinburg Institute in North Carolina. Later lived in Philadelphia. Played jobs locally beginning about 1935-6. First big job with Teddy Hill in New York 1937; European tour with him. Freelanced in New York,

then important period with Cab Calloway over two years, 1939-41. At this time began experimenting with style later known as bop: unorthodox chord progressions and rhythmic accents. In early 40s arranged for Woody Herman, Jimmy Dorsey, Earl Hines, others. Briefly with Ella Fitzgerald, Benny Carter, Charlie Barnet, Les Hite, Lucky Millinder. With Earl Hines late 1942-3, as was Charlie Parker. Pair worked on formulating bop style, in band and in late-hour jam sessions at Minton's club in Harlem. In 1943 Gillespie co-led combo with Oscar Pettiford. Joined Billy Eckstine's big band mid-1944 as sideman-arranger-musical director. Important, pioneer bop band. Later 1944 Gillespie led combo, worked with Parker as duo became most famous boppers. Dizzy led big band most of 1945-50. Several tours abroad late 40s and early 50s. Toured with Jazz at the Philharmonic. Partner in DeeGee record company awhile. Busy through 50s into 70s, mostly leading combos and recording. Two 1956 foreign tours heading big band sponsored by U.S. government, an innovation. Sometimes commercialized groups with comedy and vocals. Invented trumpet with bell extending upward from middle of horn at 45-degree angle. Occasional TV. By later 60s solos seldom displayed former fire and facility. Composer of numerous jazz numbers including *A Night in Tunisia*; *Con Alma*; *Woody'n You*; *Ow*; *Groovin' High*; *Tour de Force*; *Manteca*; *Anthropology*; *Swing Low Sweet Cadillac*; *Something Old, Something New*; *Lorraine*; *Cool World*; *Blue 'n' Boogie*; *Interlude*; *Bye*; *Kush*; *Blue Mood*; *Sugar Hips*; *Hey Pete*; *Devil and the Fish*; *Rails*; *Rumbola*; *Cool Breeze*.

RECORDS

TEDDY HILL
  Bb 6988 King Porter Stomp
CAB CALLOWAY
  Vo 5467 Pickin' the Cabbage
  OK 5566 Hard Times
  OK 5950 Hot Air
  OK 6084 Bye Bye Blues
  OK 6305 Take the "A" Train
LES HITE
  Hit 7001 Jersey Bounce

JOE MARSALA
  B&W 18 Cherokee/My Melancholy Baby
METRONOME ALL-STARS
  Co 38734 Double Date
  Cap 15039 Metronome Riff/Leap Here
SLIM GAILLARD
  Bel-Tone 753 Dizzy Boogie/Popity Pop
LIONEL HAMPTON
  Vi 26371 Hot Mallets/When Lights Are Low
  Vi 26393 Early Session Hop/One Sweet Letter from You
JAZZ AT THE PHILHARMONIC
  Disc 2003 Crazy Rhythm (1 & 2)
RED NORVO
  Comet(12")6 Slam Slam Blues/Hallelujah
  Comet(12")7 Congo Blues/Get Happy
TONY SCOTT
  Go 105 Ten Lessons with Timothy
TEMPO JAZZMEN
  Dial 1001 Dynamo (A & B)
  Dial 1003 'Round About Midnight
  Dial 1005 Diggin' for Diz
CHARLIE PARKER
  Mer 11058 Bloomdido/My Melancholy Baby
  Mer 11082 Mohawk/An Oscar for Treadwell
GEORGE AULD
  Guild 128 Co-Pilot
DIZZY GILLESPIE
  Mus 399 Our Delight/Good Dues Blues
  Mus 447 Emanon/Things to Come
  Mus 485 Groovin' High/A Hand Fulla Gimme
  Mus 488 Dizzy Atmosphere/All the Things You Are
  Vi 40-0130 52nd Street Theme/Night in Tunisia
  Vi 40-0132 Ol' Man Rebop/Anthropology
  Manor 1042 Good Bait/I Can't Get Started
  Cap 797 Say When
  DeeGee 3601 Birk's Works/Tin Tin Daeo
  DeeGee 3604 The Champ (1 & 2)
  DeeGee 3607 Umbrella Man/Star Dust

  Norg 107 It's the Talk of the Town (1 & 2)

LPs

DIZZY GILLESPIE
  Sav MG-12020 Groovin' High (Mus RIs)
  Vi LPM-2398 The Greatest of Dizzy Gillespie (Vi RIs)
  Vi LJM-1009 Dizzier and Dizzier (some Vi RIs)
  Reprise R-6072 Dateline: Europe
  Philips(E) 652021 New Wave
  Verve MGV-8313 Have Trumpet, Will Excite
  Verve MGV-8386 A Portrait of Duke Ellington
DIZZY GILLESPIE-CHARLIE PARKER
  Jazztone J-1204 Giants of Modern Jazz (Dial RIs)
MODERN JAZZ SEXTET
  Norg MGN-1076
(miscellaneous artists)
  Vi LPV-519 The Be-Bop Era (Vi RIs)
  Masterseal 5013 Hi-Fi Jazz Session (RIs)
  Eso ES-548 The Harlem Jazz Scene— 1941 (at Minton's and Uptown House)

668. GILLESPIE, HAVEN   lyr cm

Born February 6, 1888, Covington, Ky.

Songwriter active mostly in 20s and 30s; primarily lyricist. Best-known songs *Drifting and Dreaming, Breezin' Along with the Breeze, Honey, Santa Claus Is Comin' to Town, You Go to My Head, That Lucky Old Sun.* Early in career journeyman printer with newspapers, including *New York Times.* Began composing mid-20s. Chief collaborator composer J. Fred Coots. Others Richard Whiting, Larry Shay, Egbert Van Alstyne, Seymour Simons. Beasley Smith. Received Freedoms Foundation Award 1950 for song *God's Country.*

SONGS

1924—You're in Kentucky, Sure as You're Born
1925—Drifting and Dreaming
1926—Breezin' Along with the Breeze
1927—Beautiful; Tin Pan Parade
1929—Honey; Who Wouldn't Be Jealous of You?

1930—Do Ya Love Me?
1931—Beautiful Love; By the Sycamore Tree; The Sleepy Town Express
1934—Santa Claus Is Comin' to Town
1935—Louisiana Fairy Tale; Moonlight and Magnolias; Whose Honey Are You?
1936—The Wedding of Jack and Jill
1938—It's the Little Things That Count; There's Honey on the Moon Tonight; You Go to My Head
1939—Let's Stop the Clock
1942—Seeing You Again Did Me No Good
1949—The Old Master Painter; That Lucky Old Sun; My Bashful Nashville Gal from Tennessee
1950—God's Country
1952—Love Me Sweet and Love Me Long
1953—Kiss

Other songs: *You Happened to Me; Come Home; Our Silver Anniversary; This Holy Love; Don't Forget; Sleepy Ol' River; I'm Just a Little Blue for You*

669. GILLHAM, ART   p vo B

Born January 1, 1895, Fulton County, Ga.
Died June 6, 1961

Pianist-singer of 20s and 30s. Very light voice, billed as The Whispering Pianist. Grew up in St. Louis. Military service, World War I. Travelled for sheet music company in mid-20s, sang and played its songs on radio. Successful recording for Columbia in 20s and early 30s. Early records mostly used only rhythm section backing. Made a few records as Art Gillham & His Southland Syncopators, featured Red Nichols, Miff Mole, Eddie Lang, other jazzmen. Records in early 30s used smooth studio bands. Played theatres and many radio stations throughout U.S. In late 30s quit music, settled in Atlanta, served as principal of business college many years.

RECORDS
(*Southland Syncopators)

ART GILLHAM
Co 238-D Way Out West in Kansas/ How Do You Do?
Co 328-D You May Be Lonesome/I

Had Someone Else Before I Had You
Co 343-D Second Hand Love/Hesitation Blues
Co 411-D Angry/Smile All the While
Co 425-D Cecilia/If You Leave Me I'll Never Cry
Co 626-D Say It Again/I'd Climb the Highest Mountain
Co 710-D Tenderly/Thinking
Co 1051-D I'm Waiting for Ships That Never Come In/Pretty Little Thing
Co 1194-D Twiddlin' My Thumbs*/ The Pal You Left at Home
Co 1253-D Now I Won't Be Blue*/ What a Wonderful Night This Would Be
Co 1282-D So Tired/You'd Rather Forget Than Forgive
Co 1726-D Some Sweet Day* /Sweetheart of All My Dreams*
Co 2119-D Absence Makes the Heart Grow Fonder/Have a Little Faith in Me
Co 2265-D Confessin'/My Heart Belongs to a Girl Who Belongs to Somebody Else
Co 2291-D Good Evenin'/I'm Drifting Back to Dreamland
Co 2349-D To Whom It May Concern/Gazing at the Stars
Co 2374-D Shine On Harvest Moon/If You're Happy, I'll Be Glad
Co 2506-D You Are the Rose of My Heart/Just a Minute More

670. GIUFFRE, JIMMY
ts cl bs ar cm B

Born April 26, 1921, Dallas, Texas

Modern-styled jazz musician whose arranging-composing surpassed solo work in importance. Not a facile soloist, had gutty, simple style on tenor sax. His clarinet work, though simple, brought him first real prominence due to cool, vibratoless tone, predominately in lower register, and lagging-beat style. Attended North Texas State Teachers College, studied composing in Los Angeles. In AAF orchestra 1944. With Jimmy Dorsey 1947, Buddy Rich 1948, Woody Herman 1949. In 1950 with Garwood Van and Spade Cooley. With Howard Rumsey's Lighthouse All-Stars 1951-2. Mostly with

Shorty Rogers 1953-5. Freelanced, part of west coast jazz scene. In later 50s led combos, recorded with them. Writing talents established him as important figure in modern jazz. Won fame writing-arranging *Four Brothers* for a 1948 Woody Herman record. Voicing of sax section cool, innovative; became known as the Four Brothers sound. Giuffre concentrated on clarinet, abandoned tenor sax several years. Led combos on foreign tours in 60s. In one period had trio which played abstract jazz, works he composed for group. In later 60s returned to more orthodox modern jazz. Composed numerous jazz numbers, some lengthy and serious for concerts. Active into 70s.

RECORDS
(all LPs)

JIMMY GIUFFRE
Cap T-634 Tangents in Jazz
Cap(10″)H-549 Jimmy Giuffre
Atl 1238 The Giuffre Clarinet
Atl 1254 Jimmy Giuffre Three
Co CL-1964 Free Fall
Verve V-8397 Fusion
Verve V-8402 Thesis
SHORTY ROGERS
Cap(10″)H-294 Modern Sounds
Vi LJM-1004 Shorty Rogers Courts the Count
Atl 1212 The Swinging Mr. Rogers
Atl 1232 Martians Come Back
SHELLY MANNE
Contemp C-3584 The Three
PETE JOLLY
Vi LPM-1105
LENNIE NIEHAUS
Contemp C-3503 Vol.3: The Octet, No.2
JOHN GRAAS
Trend(10″)TL-1005 The French Horn
BOB BROOKMEYER-JIMMY GIUFFRE
World Pac PJ-1233 Traditionalism Revisited
HOWARD RUMSEY
Contemp(10″)C-2501 Lighthouse All-Stars Vol. 2

670A. GLASER, LULU   vo

Born June 2, 1874, Allegheny, Pa.
Died September 5, 1958, Norwalk, Conn.

Attractive performer of early Broadway musicals, later vaudeville headliner. Excellent singer-actress-comedienne. Co-starred with husband Ralph Herz in MISS DOLLY DOLLARS (1905), LOLA FROM BERLIN (1907). Turned to vaudeville after last Broadway show 1912, retired 1918.

BROADWAY MUSICALS
1899—CYRANO DE BERGERAC
1900—SWEET ANNE PAGE
1901—THE PRIMA DONNA
1902—DOLLY VARDEN
1904—A MADCAP PRINCESS
1905—MISS DOLLY DOLLARS
1907—LOLA FROM BERLIN
1908—MLLE. MISCHIEF; THE MERRY WIDOW BURLESQUE (farce)
1910—THE GIRL AND THE KAISER
1912—MISS DUDELSACK (non-musical)

671. GLEASON, JACKIE   vo cm B

Born February 26, 1916, Brooklyn, N.Y.

Leading TV performer in 50s and 60s after many years in show business. Top comedian; plump frame butt of jokes. Also singer, composer, leader of large studio orchestras on mood-music LPs. As youngster worked as M.C. in amateur shows, carnival barker, daredevil driver, disc jockey. Comedian in night clubs beginning around 1940. Small roles in movies 1941-2. In unsuccessful Broadway show ARTISTS AND MODELS (1943), then starred in hit FOLLOW THE GIRLS (1944). More night clubs during 40s. Starred in Broadway show ALONG FIFTH AVENUE (1949); modest run. Clicked on early TV as character on popular show The Life of Riley, got own show and quick popularity early 50s. Featured various skits, characters, formats. Most popular skit The Honeymooners, widely featured in later years. Early co-stars of skit Art Carney, Audrey Meadows, Joyce Matthews. Latter two replaced mid-60s by Sheila MacRae and Betty Kean. Gleason wrote shows' theme *Melancholy Serenade*. Other compositions *Lovers' Rhapsody*, *Glamour*, *To a Sleeping Beauty*, *On the Beach*. Last shows of late 60s used musical comedy format featuring original songs by Lyn Dutty and others. Issued series of 50s LPs: dreamy mood music, large orchestras, lush strings, often featured cornetist

Bobby Hackett or other jazzmen. Later varied styles of music. Gleason gave music good exposure on TV. In mid-50s one summer hour-long replacement show presented name bands, all styles. Also presented Tommy Dorsey band featuring Jimmy Dorsey on summer show, continued it during regular season. When Tommy died Gleason sponsored tribute show starring former Dorsey sidemen and singers. In 1959 starred in Broadway musical TAKE ME ALONG. Starred in several 60s movies, become excellent character actor. By late 60s tired of show-biz grind, retired voluntarily.

MOVIES

1941—NAVY BLUES
1942—ALL THROUGH THE NIGHT; LARCENY, INC.; ORCHESTRA WIVES; SPRINGTIME IN THE ROCKIES
1950—THE DESERT HAWK
1961—THE HUSTLER
1962—BLOOD MONEY; GIGOT (also wrote music)
1963—SOLDIER IN THE RAIN; REQUIEM FOR A HEAVYWEIGHT
1965—PAPA'S DELICATE CONDITION
1968—HOW TO COMMIT MARRIAGE
1969—DIAMOND JIM BRADY; DON'T DRINK THE WATER; LET ME COUNT THE WAYS

RECORDS

JACKIE GLEASON ORCHESTRA

Cap 2361 (theme) Melancholy Serenade/You're Getting to Be a Habit with Me
Cap 2437 Body and Soul/Alone Together
Cap 2438 My Funny Valentine/Love Is Here to Stay
Cap 2439 But Not for Me/Love, Your Spell Is Everywhere
Cap 2507 Peg o' My Heart/Limelight
Cap 2515 White House Serenade/The President's Lady
Cap 2659 Golden Violins/Mystery Street

LPs

JACKIE GLEASON ORCHESTRA

Cap(10″)H-352 Music for Lovers Only
Cap W-509 Music, Martinis and Memories

Cap W-568 Plays Romantic Jazz
Cap W-632 Music to Change Her Mind
Cap SW-859 (S) Presents Velvet Brass
Cap SW-2684 (S) Taste of Brass
Cap STCL-2816 (3-LP set) (S) DeLuxe Set
Cap SW-2880 (S) Doublin' in Brass (original Broadway cast)
Vi LSO-1050 TAKE ME ALONG

672. GLENN, TYREE   tb vb cm B
(EVANS TYREE GLENN)

Born November 23, 1912, Corsicana, Texas

Died May 18, 1974, Englewood, N.J., of cancer

Excellent performer on trombone and vibes in mainstream style. Led groups later in career, injected humor and commercialism at times. First played locally, then toured with blues singer Ma Rainey c. 1928. In Washington, D.C., 1934-6 with Tommy Mills. On west coast 1936-7 with Eddie Barefield, Lionel Hampton and others. With Eddie Mallory 1937-9, touring with Ethel Waters much of the time. With Benny Carter most of 1939. Most important period with Cab Calloway 1940-6, where solo talents flourished. In fall 1946 to Europe with Don Redman, remained almost a year in Copenhagen as soloist. Joined Duke Ellington mid-1947, remained till 1951. Late 1951 toured Scandinavia as soloist. In early 50s freelance, studio work. On Jack Sterling radio show late 50s to 1964. Led combo at times. 1957 began long run at the Embers in New York. Musical director of Louis Armstrong All-Stars 1964-71. Early 70s again led group in New York, worked at the Roundtable. Composer of jazz numbers *Waycross Walk, Sterling Steel, After the Rain, Roulette.*

RECORDS

ETHEL WATERS

De 1613 You're a Sweetheart/I'll Get Along Somehow

CAB CALLOWAY

OK 5687 Comin' On with the "Come On"
OK 5911 North of the Mohawk Trail

OK 5950 Hot Air
OK 6084 Bye Bye Blues
MILT HINTON
Key 639 Everywhere/Beefsteak Charlie
SID CATLETT
Super Disc 1022 Just a Riff/Mop de Mop Mop
Super Disc 1023 What's Happenin'?/Before Long
DUKE ELLINGTON
Co 38234 Hy'a Sue
Co 38237 Three Cent Stomp
Co 38363 Sultry Serenade
SIMON BREHM
Musica(Sw) 9203 Sweet Lorraine/My Melancholy Baby
HOT LIPS PAGE
Ci 3004 Main Street
TYREE GLENN
Abbey 5001 Dusty Serenade/Sultry Serenade
Roost 557 Sugar/Wrap Your Troubles in Dreams
Sw(Fr) 232 Working Eyes
Blue Star(Fr) 25 The Hour of Parting/I Surrender Dear

LPs

TYREE GLENN
Forum SF-9068 (S) At the Embers
Roul 25050 At the Roundtable
Roul 25075 With Strings
Roul 25115 Let's Have a Ball
Roul 25184 The Trombone Artistry of Tyree Glenn
EDGAR SAMPSON
Cor CRL-57049 Swing Softly Sweet Sampson
TONY PARENTI
Jazztone J-1215 Happy Jazz
GEORGE WEIN & STORYVILLE SEXTET
Beth 6050 Jazz at the Modern
JACK STERLING QUINTET
Ha HL-7202 Cocktail Swing
REX STEWART-WINGY MANONE (one side)
Pres 7812 Trumpet Jive!

673. GLUSKIN, LUD   ar B
Born 1901, New York, N.Y.

Well-known bandleader on radio, principally in 30s. Attended Yale. Led band abroad late 20s, recorded extensively in France and Germany. Began on U.S. radio early 30s. Usually served as or-chestra backing star performers. Radio shows included own show 1934, The Big Show late 1934-5, Block & Sully show 1935, On the Air with Lud Gluskin 1936, Ken Murray show and Hollywood Show Case 1937-8, own show 1938, Al Jolson show 1938-9, Tuesday Night Party 1939. Movie scoring, including THE MAN IN THE IRON MASK (1939). Used excellent singer Buddy Clark on some recordings mid-30s. Busy radio schedule in 40s, including Ed Wynn and Burns & Allen shows as well as own show. In early 50s on Burns & Allen TV show.

RECORDS

LUD GLUSKIN
Hom(G) 4-3021 Tiger Rag
Pol(G) 22041 Crazy Rhythm
Pol(G) 22192 High Tension
Pol(G) 22833 Doin' the New Low Down
Pol(G) 22939 Milenberg Joys
Co 2951-D One Night of Love/Moonlight on the River Danube
Co 2952-D The Continental/La Cucaracha
Co 2970-D Hands Across the Table/Speak to Me with Your Eyes
Co 2987-D Sweet Music/Just Mention Joe
Co 3008-D Pardon My Love/It's You I Adore
Br 7535 Red Sails in the Sunset/Rhythm and Romance
Br 7536 Here's to Romance/Midnight in Paris
Br 7590 Moon Over Miami/Ghost of the Rhumba
Br 7592 I've Got My Fingers Crossed/I'm Shooting High
Br 7658 She Shall Have Music/My First Thrill
Br 7664 On the Air/Sunshine at Midnight
Br 7779 Rainbow on the River/You're Too Good to Be True
Br 7788 Head Over Heels in Love/May I Have the Next Romance with You?

674. GODFREY, ARTHUR   vo g uk bn
Born August 31, 1903, New York, N.Y.

Top entertainer on radio in late 40s and

on TV during 50s. Host of popular variety shows. Sang in husky baritone with trace of Irish brogue, became known as ukulele player. Left home at 14, travelled, worked odd jobs. Entered vaudeville 1924 as banjoist. Served in coast guard. Educated at Naval Radio School, Great Lakes, Ill., and Green Lakes Material School, Bellevue, D.C. On radio 1929 as "The Warbling Banjoist." Baltimore radio 1930 as announcer-personality-disc jockey. About 1934 had 15-minute radio shows in homey patter style of popular Smilin' Ed McConnell. On radio Washington, D.C., 1935, on show Arthur Godfrey and All the Little Godfreys, with excellent band in sweet-swing style. In 1937-8 on Barbasol and Professor Quiz shows, own show for Cremo Cigars. Hosted variety shows on radio early 40s. Rose to prominence postwar with network morning show and as host of popular Talent Scouts show (later on TV). By late 40s a household name to millions of housewives. In 1946 Broadway show THREE TO MAKE READY.

Godfrey entered TV in late 40s; show Arthur Godfrey and His Friends popular in early to mid-50s. Theme *Seems Like Old Times*. TV family well-known, chiefly announcer Tony Marvin, singers Frank Parker, Marion Marlowe, McGuire Sisters, Janette Davis; others Carmel Quinn, Haleloke, Mariners, Lu Ann Simms, Julius LaRosa. Godfrey dropped LaRosa from show, created a flap. Pat Boone given early boost from regular stints on show mid-50s. Though bothered by old hip injury and sometimes hardly able to walk, Godfrey worked anyway. Later overcame lung cancer to return to vigorous health. Record hits *Too Fat Polka*, *Candy and Cake*, *The Thousand Islands Song*. One of best vocal efforts *Scattered Toys*. By late 50s popularity waned on TV, bowed out as TV regular, occasionally appeared in 60s as host or guest star, did TV commercials. Continued daily radio show through 60s. On this, as on TV, had excellent small orchestra, sometimes featured talented sidemen. Quit radio, continued active in early 70s on TV commercials.

RECORDS

ARTHUR GODFREY

Bb 7829 Old Folks/There's No Place Like Your Arms

Bb 7842 Indiana Moonlight/Song of Old Hawaii

De 2958 and 25348 I'd Love to Live in Loveland/Back Home on Saturday Night

De 3014 I'd Give a Million Tomorrows/Lay My Head Beneath a Rose

Co 37921 Too Fat Polka/For Me and My Gal

Co 38081 The Thousand Islands Song/I'm Looking Over a Four-Leaf Clover

Co 38246 The Trail of the Lonesome Pine/Turkish Delight

Co 38721 Candy and Cake/Dear Old Girl

Co 38785 Scattered Toys/C'n I Canoe You Up the River?

Co 38882 Hawaii/Driftin' Down the Dreamy Ol' Ohio

Co 39632 Slow Poke/Dance Me Loose

Co 39792 Honey/I Love Girls

ARTHUR GODFREY-JANETTE DAVIS

Co 38815 Darn It, Baby, That's Love

Co 40251 After You've Gone

ARTHUR GODFREY-MARY MARTIN

Co 38991 A Rainy Day Refrain/C'est Tout

LPs

ARTHUR GODFREY

Co CL-1575 Arthur Godfrey's Greatest Hits (Co RIs)

Co GL-521 Arthur Godfrey's TV Calendar Show

Co(10")CL-6113 Arthur Godfrey and His Friends

Contempo 3900 Arthur Godfrey's Golden Hits

675. GOERING, AL   p ar cm B

Born December 20, 1898, Chicago, Ill.
Died April 16, 1963, Chicago, Ill.

Pianist-arranger with Ben Bernie 1922-39. At 17 played in trio at Chicago's Friar Inn. Led trio, jobbed around Peoria, Ill.

Five years in Jacksonville and Miami, developed as arranger. Joined Ben Bernie late 1922. Besides records with Bernie, in late 20s recorded with Jack Pettis on important jazz sessions. Name used on some labels as by Al Goering & His Collegians. Stayed with Bernie, did many arrangements. In 1938 remained in California when Bernie went to New York. Arranged for and played in Frankie Trumbauer band, continued to send Bernie arrangements. Rejoined awhile 1939. Then concentrated on arranging, mainly for Bernie on Chicago's Wrigley Gum radio show (later for Caesar Petrillo on same show). Active in 40s. Co-composer of 1931 hit *Who's Your Little Who-zis?*. Lesser compositions *Holding My Honey's Hand, One of Us Was Wrong, Paradise Isle, Face to Face, Sweetest Melody, Looks Like a Cold Cold Winter, Heads You Do (and Tails You Don't)*, and jazz numbers *Up and at 'Em, Bag o' Blues, Stockholm Stomp, Freshman Hop*.

RECORDS

BEN BERNIE
(see BERNIE biography for records on Br, Co, De)
JACK PETTIS
  Ba 1907 Stockholm Stomp
  Ba 7001 Once Over Lightly
  Ba 7005 Steppin' It Off
  Do 4080 Candied Sweets
  Vo 15703 Dry Martini/Hot Heels
  Vo 15761 Broadway Stomp
  Vi 21559 Spanish Dream/Doin' the New Low Down
  Vi 21793 Bag o' Blues/Freshman Hop
  OK 41410 Bag o' Blues
  OK 41411 Freshman Hop/Sweetest Melody
IRVING MILLS & HIS HOTSY TOTSY GANG
  Br 4838 Railroad Man/Crazy 'Bout My Gal
  Br 4998 I Wonder What My Gal Is Doin'/What a Night!
  Vo 15860 St. Louis Blues
MILLS MUSICAL CLOWNS
  Pe 15136 Sweetest Melody
TEN FRESHMEN
  Pe 15235 Freshman Hop/Bag o' Blues

676. GOETZ, E. RAY   cm lyr

Born June 12, 1886, Buffalo, N.Y.
Died June 12, 1954, Greenwich, Conn.

Songwriter who contributed to many Broadway musicals as composer or lyricist. Best-known songs *For Me and My Gal, Yaaka Hula Hickey Dula, Who'll Buy My Violets?*. Collaborators included A. Baldwin Sloane, Vincent Bryan, Silvio Hein, Raymond Hubbell, George Meyer, Jean Schwartz, Pete Wendling. Later producer of shows including AS YOU WERE, THE FRENCH DOLL, LITTLE MISS BLUEBEARD, PARIS, FIFTY MILLION FRENCHMEN, THE NEW YORKERS.

SONGS
(with related shows)

1906—THE BABES AND THE BARON stage show (Could You Learn to Love?) Don't Go in the Lion's Cage To-night

1907—ZIEGFELD FOLLIES OF 1907 stage show (Reincarnation; I Think I Oughtn't Auto Anymore); He Goes to Church on Sunday

1910—A MATINEE IDOL stage show; PRINCE OF BOHEMIA stage show; I Love It; I'm Waiting Here for Winnie; In the Shadows; Havana; Oh! You Chicken

1911—THE HEN PECKS stage show (June; White Light Alley; Little Italy; Toddling the Todalo); THE NEVER HOMES stage show (There's a Girl in Havana; Tonight's the Night; The Kiss Burglar; Take Me Along with You, Dearie); Take Me Back to the Garden of Love; When You Hear Love's Hello

1912—HANKY-PANKY stage show (Where the Edelweiss Is Blooming; Rose of Pyramid Land; Million Dollar Ball); HOKEY-POKEY stage show (La Belle Paree; The Minstrel Parade; The Singer and the Song; The Garden of Yesterday; On the Stage; Senorita; Rosie); ROLY-POLY stage show (Dear Old Heidelberg; I'm a Lonesome Romeo; Steinland; When I'm Waltzing); THE SUN DODGERS stage show (unsuccessful)

973

1913—ALL ABOARD stage show (Asia; In My Garden of Eden for Two; Mr. Broadway, U.S.A.; The Ragtime Yodeling Man; Under the China Moon); THE PLEASURE SEEKERS stage show (Switzerland; Love Me to a Viennese Melody; The Alpine Girl)

1915—HANDS UP stage show (I'm Simply Crazy Over You; Cute Little Summertime; Ginger; Pirate's Rag; Tiffany Girl; Cling a Little Closer)

1916—ROBINSON CRUSOE, JR. stage show (Yaaka Hula Hickey Dula); STEP THIS WAY stage show (Step This Way; Keep Up the Pace; Romany; Heart of the Golden West; You Ought to Go to Paris)

1917—HITCHY-KOO stage show (The Isle of Lost Romance; Dreamy Parisian Tune; If You Were Here; Lady of the Sea); WORDS AND MUSIC stage show (Everything Looks Rosy and Bright; Lady Romance; It's All Right If You're in Love; I May Stay Away a Little Longer); For Me and My Gal (revived 1942)

1918—HITCHY-KOO OF 1918 stage show

1920—AS YOU WERE stage show (If You Could Care; Helen of Troy; If You'll Say It with Flowers; Washington Square)

1922—GEORGE WHITE'S SCANDALS OF 1922 stage show (Argentina; Cinderelatives); THE FRENCH DOLL stage show (You Don't Have to Do as I Do)

1923—GEORGE WHITE'S SCANDALS OF 1923 stage show (Let's Be Lonesome Together; Life of a Rose); LITTLE MISS BLUEBEARD stage show (Who'll Buy My Violets?; So This Is Love; The Gondola and the Girl)

1925—NAUGHTY CINDERELLA stage show (Nothing But "Yes" in My Eyes; Do I Love You?; Mia Luna)

1928—PARIS stage show (Paris; The Land of Going to Be)

676A. GOLD, ERNEST   cm ar p B
Born July 13, 1921, Vienna, Austria

Composer-arranger of movie background music 40s through 60s. Best-known songs from this work *On the Beach, Exodus, It's a Mad Mad Mad Mad World.* To U.S. 1938, settled in New York. To Hollywood 1945, many years composing-arranging for B movies and westerns. Prominence 1959 with excellent work on important film ON THE BEACH. Followed by classic scoring job on EXODUS (1960).

MOVIES
(as composer and probable arranger-conductor of background music; partial listing)

1945—THE GIRL OF THE LIMBERLOST
1946—THE FALCON'S ALIBI; SMOOTH AS SILK
1947—EXPOSED; LIGHTHOUSE
1948—OLD LOS ANGELES
1951—UNKNOWN WORLD
1953—MAN CRAZY; JENNIFER
1954—THE OTHER WOMAN
1955—THE NAKED STREET
1956—RUNNING TARGET; EDGE OF HELL
1957—AFFAIR IN HAVANA
1958—TOO MUCH, TOO SOON; THE DEFIANT ONES; WINK OF AN EYE
1959—THE YOUNG PHILADELPHIANS; ON THE BEACH; BATTLE OF THE CORAL SEA
1960—INHERIT THE WIND; EXODUS
1961—JUDGMENT AT NUREMBERG; THE LAST SUNSET; A FEVER IN THE BLOOD
1962—PRESSURE POINT; A CHILD IS WAITING
1963—IT'S A MAD MAD MAD MAD WORLD
1965—SHIP OF FOOLS
1969—THE SECRET OF SANTA VITTORIA

RECORDS
(all LPs)

(movie soundtracks; as composer and probable arranger-conductor)

Lon LL-3320 (themes from various movies)
UA 5095 JUDGMENT AT NUREMBERG
UA 5110 IT'S A MAD MAD MAD MAD WORLD
UA 5200 THE SECRET OF SANTA VITTORIA
Vi LSO-1058 EXODUS
Vi LM-2817 SHIP OF FOOLS (re-orchestrated; conducted by Arthur Fiedler)
Roul 25098 ON THE BEACH
Mer MG-20381 TOO MUCH, TOO SOON

677. GOLD, LOU p B

Bandleader best known for recordings in late 20s and early 30s. Bandleader in mid-20s, based mostly in New York. Contractor for band jobs and record sessions. Extensive recording, although name possibly used as pseudonym on some records. Competent bands in typical studio style.

RECORDS

LOU GOLD

Ca 683 O, Katharina!
Ca 735 The Flapper Wife
Pe 14570 Smile a Little Bit
Pe 14656 Black Bottom/Lucky Day
Pe 14862 The Varsity Drag/Lucky in Love
Pe 15182 Big City Blues
Pe 15236 If I Had a Talking Picture of You
Pe 15318 Across the Breakfast Table/Reminiscing
Pe 15377 Three Little Words
Pe 15489 I'm Thru with Love/Dancing in the Dark
Pe 15574 Rain on the Roof/Kiss Me Goodnight
Pe 15614 Hummin' to Myself/The Night Shall Be Filled with Music
Di 2502 Baby Your Mother/Here Comes the Show Boat
Di 2768 When Summer Is Gone
Di 2924 Breakaway/That's You, Baby
Di 3056 My Fate Is in Your Hands
OK 40779 The Dixie Vagabond/If You See Sally
Clar 5178 Underneath the Sunlit Skies
Re 8800 Am I Blue?/Let Me Have My Dreams
Re 10337 I'm Mad About You/Oh, How I Miss You
Ha 64 I Never Knew
Ha 1133 'Leven Thirty Saturday Night
Ba 6258 Avalon Town
Cr 3060 The River and Me/Would You Like to Take a Walk?
Cr 3063 I'm Afraid of You/Walking My Baby Back Home
Cr 3109 I Surrender Dear/Thrill Me
Cr 3229 You're My Everything/An Evening in Caroline
Cr 3252 Delishious/When We're Alone

678. GOLDEN, JOHN cm lyr

Born June 27, 1874, New York, N.Y.
Died June 17, 1955, New York, N.Y.

Songwriter who scored for several Broadway musicals. Most songs attained no popularity, effective only within context of shows. Two biggest hits *Goodbye, Girls, I'm Through* in CHIN-CHIN (1914) and *Poor Butterfly* in THE BIG SHOW (1916). Other notable songs *You Can't Play Every Instrument in the Band* in THE SUNSHINE GIRL (1913) and *I Can Dance with Everyone but My Wife* in SYBIL (1916). Scores for Broadway shows MISS PRINNT (1900), THE CANDY SHOP (1909), OVER THE RIVER (1912), THE BIG SHOW (1916), CHEER UP (1917). Contributed material to HIP-HIP-HOORAY (1915), GO TO IT (1916), EVERYTHING (1918). Educated at NYU. Began career as actor, later newspaper reporter and humorist. After songwriting produced Broadway plays, including TURN TO THE RIGHT, THREE WISE FOOLS, LIGHTNIN', THE FIRST YEAR, SEVENTH HEAVEN, COUNSELOR-AT-LAW, SUSAN AND GOD, WHEN LADIES MEET, AS HUSBANDS GO, LET US BE GAY, CLAUDIA, SKYLARK. Playwright, also wrote autobiography *Stagestruck*. A founder of Stage Relief Fund and Stage Door Canteen.

679. GOLDKETTE, JEAN p B

Born March 18, 1899, Valenciennes, France
Died March 24, 1962, Santa Barbara, Calif.

Noted for all-star band and recordings 1926-9. Lived in Greece and Russia, came to U.S. 1911. Pianist in Chicago and Detroit, settled in latter. Bought Greystone Ballroom there, booked bands. Formed big band 1924, recorded for Victor. Russ Morgan joined 1926 as arranger and organizer, helped get outstanding musicians. Excellent band 1926-7 at times featured Don Murray, Joe Venuti, Bix Beiderbecke, Frankie Trumbauer, Eddie Lang, Danny Polo, Andy Secrest, Tommy and Jimmy Dorsey, Sterling Bose, Bill Rank, others. Used Detroit as base, travelled, played New York. Payroll large, probably a factor in band's demise. Goldkette also booked McKinney's Cotton Pickers, other units including one that evolved into Casa Loma Orchestra (later led by Glen Gray). In early 30s some radio. Gave up booking, later worked as agent. Occasional work as classical pianist. In mid-1939 presented concert of American music at New York's Carnegie Hall with 90-piece orchestra, no great success. In 1944 led combo in Detroit. Occasionally active in music in later 40s and 50s. Settled in California 1961.

RECORDS

JEAN GOLDKETTE
Vi 19947 Dinah/After I Say I'm Sorry
Vi 20031 Lonesome and Sorry/Gimme a Little Kiss
Vi 20256 Don't Be Angry with Me
Vi 20270 Idolizing/Hush-a-Bye
Vi 20273 Sunday/I'd Rather Be the Girl in Your Arms
Vi 20466 I'm Looking Over a Four-Leaf Clover
Vi 20469 I'm Proud of a Baby Like You
Vi 20471 Hoosier Sweetheart
Vi 20472 Look at the World and Smile
Vi 20491 A Lane in Spain
Vi 20493 Sunny Disposish
Vi 20588 My Pretty Girl/Cover Me Up with Sunshine
Vi 20926 Slow River
Vi 20981 Blue River
Vi 20994 Clementine
Vi 21150 So Tired/Just a Little Kiss from a Little Miss
Vi 21166 Here Comes the Show Boat/My Ohio Home
Vi 21565 Just Imagine
Vi 21800 Sweethearts on Parade/That's What Puts the "Sweet" in Home Sweet Home
Vi 21805 Don't Be Like That/My Blackbirds Are Bluebirds Now
Vi 21853 She's Funny That Way
Vi 22027 Tiptoe Through the Tulips with Me/Painting the Clouds with Sunshine
Bilt 1012 In My Merry Oldsmobile

LPs

JEAN GOLDKETTE
"X"(10")LVA-3017 (Vi RIs)
Cam CAL-548 Dance Hits of the 20s (updated versions)

BIX BEIDERBECKE
Vi LPM-2323 The Bix Beiderbecke Legend (RIs)

680. GONELLA, NAT   t vo B

Born March 7, 1908, London, England

English trumpet star and vocalist in Louis Armstrong style. In early 30s with top English bands of Billy Cotton, Roy Fox, Lew Stone and Ray Noble. Formed group in 1935 featuring jazz and good showmanship, became popular; billed as Nat Gonella & His Georgians. Busy schedule with stage shows, film work and tours in England, Holland and Sweden. Extensive recording. In U.S. late 1938-9, recorded. At outbreak of war 1939 in Sweden awhile. In 1940 New Georgians band, entertained British troops. Entered military service. In later 40s led band, then career waned.

RECORDS

RAY NOBLE
HMV(E) 5819 Crazy Feet
HMV(E) 6308 Wanderer
HMV(E) 6319 Love Tales
HMV(E) 7331 Hustlin' and Bustlin' for Baby
HMV(E) 6375 I've Got to Sing a Torch Song/Pettin' in the Park
HMV(E) 6450 The Sun Is Around the Corner
HMV(E) 6459 Have a Heart
LEW STONE
De 247 Isle of Capri
NAT GONELLA
De(E) 3292 Rockin' Chair/When You're Smiling
De(E) 3992 Georgia on My Mind/Sweet Sue
De(E) 5108 Moon Country/Troublesome Trumpet
Pa(E) 117 Basin Street Blues/E Flat Blues
Pa(E) 132 Star Dust/Mr. Rhythm Man
Pa(E) 161 Nagasaki/Tiger Rag
Pa(E) 193 Hot Lips/Blow, Gabriel, Blow
Pa(E) 210 Black Coffee/Lazy River
Pa(E) 318 New Orleans Twist/Chicago
Pa(E) 386 Sweet Music Man/The Music Goes 'Round and Around

Pa(E) 392 Singin' the Blues/Junk Man's Blues
Pa(E) 503 Ride, Red, Ride/Harlem Hokum Blues
Pa(E) 594 Crazy Valves/Trumpetous
Pa(E) 731 Blow That Horn/Smoke Dreams
Pa(E) 908 The Big Apple/Peckin'
Pa(E) 1029 Jubilee/The Dipsy Doodle
Pa(E) 1237 It's the Rhythm in Me/ Small Fry
Pa(E) 1376 Just a Kid Named Joe/ Jeepers Creepers
Co(E) 2492 The Jumpin' Jive/Plucking on a Golden Harp
Co(E) 2620 Mean to Me/The Sheik
Co(E) 2754 Kansas City Moods/Blues Upstairs and Downstairs

LPs

NAT GONELLA
Co(E) 33SX1380 The Nat Gonella Story
RAY NOBLE
Mon-Ever MES-6816 (HMV, Vi RIs)
Mon-Ever MES-7021 (HMV, Vi RIs)
Mon-Ever MES-7027 (HMV, Vi RIs)
Mon-Ever MES-7039 (HMV, Vi RIs)
Mon-Ever MES-7040 (HMV, Vi RIs)

681. GONSALVES, PAUL   ts

Born July 12, 1920, Boston, Mass.

Died May 15, 1974, in North London, England, of unknown causes

Tenor sax soloist with Duke Ellington 50s into 70s. Strong-toned, driving style created excitement on swing numbers; warm ballad style. Grew up in Pawtucket, R.I. Early experience with Sabby Lewis in Boston early 40s. Military service, World War II. With Count Basie 1946-9, Dizzy Gillespie late 1949-50. Later in 1950 joined Ellington, began most important phase of career. Leading soloist with Ellington, remained almost continuously through 1973. Brief intervals away included period in 1953 with Tommy Dorsey.

RECORDS

COUNT BASIE
Vi 20-2314 I Ain't Mad at You
Vi 20-2677 Robbins' Nest
Vi 20-2695 Basie's Basement

THE CORONETS
Mercer 1969 Night Walk/The Happening
DUKE ELLINGTON
Co 39428 Fancy Dan
Co 39712 Bensonality
PAUL GONSALVES
EmArcy 16008 Don't Blame Me/It Don't Mean a Thing

LPs

COUNT BASIE
Vi LPM-1112 (1947-50 Vi RIs)
DUKE ELLINGTON
Cap W-521 Ellington '55
Cap T-637
Co CL-1282 At The Bal Masque
Co ML-4639
Vi LSP-3782 (S) Far East Suite
Reprise S-6154 (S) Ellington '66
Reprise S-6185 (S) Concert in the Virgin Islands
PAUL GONSALVES
Impulse S-41 (S) Cleopatra Feelin' Jazzy
Impulse S-55 (S) The Way It Is

681A. GOODHART, AL   cm p

Born January 26, 1905, New York, N.Y.
Died November 30, 1955, New York, N.Y.

Composer of 30s and 40s. Best-known songs *I Apologize*; *Fit as a Fiddle*; *Auf Wiedersehen, My Dear*; *I Saw Stars*; *Who Walks In When I Walk Out?*; *I'm in a Dancing Mood*; *She Shall Have Music*; *Johnny Doughboy Found a Rose in Ireland*; *Serenade of the Bells*. Early career as radio announcer, vaudeville pianist, special material writer. On radio in piano duo. After 1931 hit *I Apologize* concentrated on composing. Productive mid-30s. In England 1934-7 with Al Hoffman and Maurice Sigler, scored for stage and movies. World War II with USO entertaining troops in U.S. and abroad. Chief collaborators included Hoffman, Sigler, Mann Curtis, Sammy Lerner, Ed Nelson, Kay Twomey, Allan Roberts.

SONGS
(with related shows)

1930—DANGEROUS NAN MCGREW movie

(Dangerous Nan McGrew; I Owe You)
1931—I Apologize
1932—Auf Wiedersehen, My Dear; Happy-Go-Lucky You; Fit as a Fiddle; It's Winter Again
1933—Roll Up the Carpet; Meet Me in the Gloaming; Two Buck Tim from Timbuctoo
1934—I Saw Stars; Jimmy Had a Nickel; Who Walks In When I Walk Out?; Why Don't You Practice What You Preach?; Your Guess Is Just as Good as Mine
1935—Black Coffee
1936—THIS'LL MAKE YOU WHISTLE English stage show (Crazy with Love; I'm in a Dancing Mood; There Isn't Any Limit to My Love; My Red Letter Day); SHE SHALL HAVE MUSIC English movie (She Shall Have Music; My First Thrill); FIRST A GIRL English movie (Everything's in Rhythm with My Heart; Say the Word and It's Yours; I Can Wiggle My Ears); JACK OF ALL TRADES English movie (Where There's You There's Me); COME OUT OF THE PANTRY English movie (Everything Stops for Tea); There's Always a Happy Ending
1937—GANGWAY English movie (Gangway; Lord and Lady Whoozis)
1939—Romance Runs in the Family
1942—Johnny Doughboy Found a Rose in Ireland; Better Not Roll Those Blue, Blue Eyes
1947—Serenade of the Bells; Who Were You Kissing?
1948—In a Little Book Shop
1949—Festival of Roses
1950—The Place Where I Worship

682. GOODMAN, AL   p ar cm B

Born August 12, 1890, Nikopol, Russia
Died January 10, 1972, New York, N.Y.

Composer-conductor of 20s Broadway musicals; active in 30s and 40s radio. Studied at Peabody Conservatory in Baltimore. As teenager played in nickelodeons; also vaudeville act with brothers. Pianist in movie houses. Began working for show producer Earl Carroll in California 1915. Conductor for Al Jolson awhile, then with Shubert musical productions. Conducted orchestra for Broadway musicals BLOSSOM TIME, MY DREAM GIRL, GOOD NEWS, THE BAND WAGON, THE NEW MOON, also ZIEGFELD FOLLIES and GEORGE WHITE'S SCANDALS shows. Wrote music for Broadway musicals LINGER LONGER LETTY (1919), CINDERELLA ON BROADWAY (1920), THE LAST WALTZ (two songs) and THE WHIRL OF NEW YORK (1921), THE PASSING SHOW OF 1922 and LADY IN ERMINE (1922), ARTISTS AND MODELS OF 1923, TOPICS OF 1923, CAROLINE and DEW DROP INN (1923), ARTISTS AND MODELS OF 1925 and GAY PAREE (1925), NAUGHTY RIQUETTE (one song; 1926). Songs effective in shows, little known otherwise. Best-known song *When Hearts Are Young* with Sigmund Romberg, from show LADY IN ERMINE. Goodman's chief collaborators Edgar Smith, Cyrus Wood, Clifford Grey.

Conductor for THE JAZZ SINGER in 1927, first part-sound movie starring Al Jolson. Began to concentrate on radio 1932; important conductor-arranger in 30s and 40s. On Irving Berlin show 1934, Bromo Seltzer Hour late 1934-5, Music at the Haydns 1935, Ziegfeld Follies of the Air 1936, Show Boat late 1936-7, Jessica Dragonette's new show 1937, Your Hollywood Parade starring Dick Powell 1938. Early 40s conducted on Fred Allen show, Family Hour and Star Theatre. On various shows through 40s into early 50s, sometimes own show featuring orchestra and guest singers. Recording through the years, LPs in 50s.

RECORDS

ZELMA O'NEAL with AL GOODMAN
  Br 4207 I Want to Be Bad/Button Up Your Overcoat
AL GOODMAN
  Br 4362 I'm Just a Vagabond Lover/ I'm Still Caring
  Br 4383 Or What Have You?/I've Made a Habit of You
  Br 4487 Marianne/Just You, Just Me
  Br 4488 Lovable and Sweet/My Dream Memory
  Br 4623 Mary/Lonesome Little Doll

Br 4726 Thank Your Father/Without Love
Co 35418 Voices of Spring/Tales from the Vienna Woods
Co 35619 That Naughty Waltz/Three O'clock in the Morning
Co 35759 Who?/All the Things You Are
Co 35760 Look for the Silver Lining/They Didn't Believe Me
Co 36218 Little Grey Home in the West/Roses of Picardy
Co 36449 Lady of the Evening/Alexander's Ragtime Band
Co 36450 Say It with Music/Remember
Co 36451 Blue Skies/Say It Isn't So
Co 36556 When I Grow Too Old to Dream/Deep in My Heart, Dear
Vi 28-0412 Hymn to the Sun/Gypsy Dance
Vi 45-0048 The Desert Song/One Alone
Vi 45-0057 Rose-Marie/Indian Love Call

LPs

AL GOODMAN

Co(10″)CL-6041 The Music of Irving Berlin
Cam CAL-382 THE STUDENT PRINCE
Ambassador S-98070 (S) CAMELOT
Spinorama MK-3045 THE KING AND I
Vi LK-1012 ROSE-MARIE
Promenade 2092 SOUTH PACIFIC
Diplomat 2214 MY FAIR LADY
Diplomat 2255 Irving Berlin Songbook
NORMAN BROOKS with AL GOODMAN ORCHESTRA
Spinorama S-3051 Al Jolson Sung by Norman Brooks

683. GOODMAN, BENNY
cl as bs t cm vo B

Born May 30, 1909, Chicago, Ill.

Jazz giant, all-time great on clarinet, King of Swing. Playing typified by strong, full tone, great facility, inventive ideas. Also accomplished classical musician. Man most responsible for rise of swing in mid-30s. Led big swing band many years with consistently high jazz standard, rarely yielded to commercialism. Good formal musical training, including study at Chicago's Hull House. First professional performance as youngster imitating Ted Lewis at Chicago theatre. Dance dates in Chicago area with Charles "Murph" Podolsky at remarkably early age of 13. Summer excursion jobs 1923, later in year with Jules Herbevaux. Late 1923-4 with Arnold Johnson, 1924-5 with Art Kassel. Excellent musician at 16, with valuable experience. In California with Ben Pollack beginning summer 1925; to Chicago with band early 1926. Featured soloist with this star-studded band; solos on records attracted attention in jazz circles. Mostly with Pollack until fall 1929, left band in New York, began recording heavily as sideman 1928-33 with varied studio name bands. Hot clarinet featured in solos on many records; tone and style easily identifiable. Also played alto sax in section and solo work. Pit band work for Broadway shows, also in radio bands of Don Voorhees, Dave Rubinoff, Nat Shilkret, Andre Kostelanetz, Paul Whiteman, others. September 1931 led pit band for Broadway show FREE FOR ALL (15 performances). In summer 1932 organized band accompanying singer Russ Columbo. Jazz buff-critic John Hammond arranged record sessions for Goodman and all-star personnel late 1933 and early 1934 with memorable results.

In summer 1934 formed big band to play Billy Rose's Music Hall, had excellent personnel. In late 1934 band won job on now-historic Let's Dance radio show for National Biscuit Company, December 1934 to May 1935. Show an innovation: three bands playing alternate sets for three hours late Saturday nights coast to coast. Other bands Xavier Cugat (Latin music) and Kel Murray (sweet). Goodman's hot band a delayed sensation. Mid-1935 tour mediocre; four weeks in Denver a fiasco. To amazement of Benny and sidemen, band a huge success at Palomar Ballroom in Los Angeles: earlier Let's Dance broadcasts had built following there. Next milestone at Chicago's Congress Hotel, November 1935 to May 1936 with nightly radio coverage. Furnished biggest impetus to swing craze early 1936; Benny hailed as King of Swing. Theme song exciting, swinging

Let's Dance, one of best of all themes. Different closing theme, pretty and mournful *Goodbye*. Clarinet featured. Art Rollini and Dick Clark handled tenor sax solos, then Vido Musso, Bud Freeman. Jack Lacey trombone soloist, followed by Joe Harris and Murray McEachern. Early trumpet stars Bunny Berigan, Pee Wee Erwin, Chris Griffin, Ziggy Elman. Harry James joined January 1937 as chief trumpet soloist. Trumpet section of James, Elman and Griffin 1937-8 among greatest. Lead altoist Hymie Schertzer sparked sax section, which achieved smooth, swinging sound. Band had great swing beat: distinctive thudding sound laid down by rhythm section of Gene Krupa (d), brother Harry Goodman (b), Allen Reuss (g), Jess Stacy (p). Benny's younger brother Irving played trumpet for brief periods with band. Helen Ward excellent vocalist during formative years late 1934 through 1936. Fletcher Henderson wrote many arrangements; notable work by Jimmy Mundy, Spud Murphy, Horace Henderson, Edgar Sampson. Pianist Teddy Wilson began with Goodman in Trio 1935, vibist Lionel Hampton made it Quartet 1936. Band played Elgin radio show spring 1936. Later in year on Camel Caravan show, sharing honors with Nat Shilkret orchestra. Later Shilkret dropped out. Jack Oakie became host awhile. In mid-1937 Goodman took over show, continued as its star through 30s; important part of band's career. Carnegie Hall concert on January 16, 1938, a first for jazz and a sensation. LPs of concert, issued 1950, all-time bestseller among jazz albums.

Personnel changed through the years. Sidemen Harry James and Gene Krupa left in late 30s to form bands. Ziggy Elman rose to prominence with solo on own composition *And the Angels Sing*, big hit for Goodman 1939. Martha Tilton featured vocalist 1937-9. Mildred Bailey sang with band briefly late 1939, followed by Helen Forrest 1940-1, Peggy Lee 1941-3. Peggy scored with late 1942-3 record hit *Why Don't You Do Right?*. Male singer Art London with Goodman in 1942, came back 1946 as Art Lund. In November-December 1939 Goodman

Sextet in short-lived Broadway musical SWINGIN' THE DREAM (13 performances only). In early 1941 band starred on Old Gold radio show. Band changed sound early 40s with modern arrangements of Eddie Sauter predominating. Star sidemen Lou McGarity (tb), George Auld (ts), Charlie Christian (g), Billy Butterfield (t), Cootie Williams (t), Vido Musso (ts), Mel Powell (p ar). By mid-40s personnel changes frequent but band always maintained high level of musicianship until disbanded early 1944.

In late 1944 Goodman reorganized Sextet for Broadway musical SEVEN LIVELY ARTS. Reorganized big band early 1945, later in year had two-sided record hit *Gotta Be This or That*. Band on Socony radio show summer 1946, later joined comedian Victor Borge as show continued to summer 1947. Benny had protege, young Swedish modern clarinetist Stan Hasselgard, in spring 1948, gave him solo spots. Later in year Hasselgard formed combo, died in auto accident. In late 1948-9 band bop-flavored, with Chico O'Farrell arranging (foremost effort *Undercurrent Blues*). By early 50s Goodman no longer had permanent band; organized various-sized groups for special jobs, featured leading jazzmen. In late 50s and 60s played top TV shows, featured on several specials. Clarinet soloist with symphony orchestras. Numerous trips abroad with bands: Europe spring 1950, Japan-Thailand-Burma late 1956-7, Brussels World's Fair and other countries mid-1958, Canada spring 1959, Europe late 1959, South America late 1961, Russia mid-1962, Japan early 1964, Belgium summer 1966, Europe early 1970, plus several appearances in England through the years. Semiactive in early 70s; played New York's Rainbow Grill, occasionally on TV. 1956 movie THE BENNY GOODMAN STORY starred Steve Allen in Goodman role. Benny's clarinet and all-star band on soundtrack.

Goodman and band had prominent roles in movies HOLLYWOOD HOTEL (1938), THE POWERS GIRL and THE GANG'S ALL HERE (1943), SWEET AND LOWDOWN (1944). Performed special numbers in BIG BROADCAST OF 1937 (1936), STAGE DOOR CANTEEN (1943), MAKE MINE MUSIC (1946;

soundtrack only). Goodman appeared as single in SYNCOPATION (1942; in jam session sequence), A SONG IS BORN (1948).

Goodman composer or co-composer of jazz numbers featured by his and other bands, including *Flying Home*; *LIFE Goes to a Party*; *Stompin' at the Savoy*; *Lullaby in Rhythm*; *Don't Be That Way*; *House Hop*; *Seven Come Eleven*; *Air Mail Special*; *Dizzy Spells*; *If Dreams Come True*; *Georgia Jubilee*; *Gone with "What" Wind*; *Soft Winds*; *A Smo-o-o-oth One*; *Smoke House*; *Swingtime in the Rockies*; *Texas Tea Party*; *Till Tom Special*; *Wholly Cats*; *Board Meeting*; *Pound Ridge*; *Opus Local 802*; *Opus 1/2*; *Opus 3/4*; *Kingdom of Swing*; *Four Once More*; *Clarinetitis*; *Fiesta in Blue*; *Bannister Slide*; *Benjie's Bubble*; *Pick-a-Rib*; *Rattle and Roll*; *Rachel's Dream*; *Scarecrow*; *Bedlam*; *Balkan Mixed Grill*; *Solo Flight*; *Macedonia Lullaby*; *Killer Diller*; *Swing Angel*; *Tattletale*; *Rock Rimmon*. Goodman wrote autobiography 1939, *Kingdom of Swing* with Irving Kolodin. Career treated in detail in *BG On the Record: A Bio-Discography of Benny Goodman* by D. Russell Connor and Warren Hicks. More active in 1973. Revived original Quartet for New York-Newport Jazz Festival and other appearances.

RECORDS

BEN POLLACK
Vi 20425 He's the Last Word
Vi 21184 Waitin' for Katie/Memphis Blues
Vi 21437 Singapore Sorrows

JACK PETTIS
OK 41411 Freshman Hop/Sweetest Melody

THE LUMBERJACKS
Ca 9030 Whoopee Stomp

BROADWAY BROADCASTERS
Ca 9130 Honey

RED NICHOLS
Br 4363 Chinatown, My Chinatown/ On the Alamo
Br 4373 Indiana/Dinah
Br 4877 Peg o' My Heart/China Boy

RUDY MARLOW
Di 3088 Do Ya' Love Me?

RUBE BLOOM & HIS BAYOU BOYS
Co 2186-D Mysterious Mose/Bessie Couldn't Help It

REGINALD FORESYTHE
Co 3012-D Dodging a Divorcee

THE KNICKERBOCKERS
Co 2502-D Me!

LEE MORSE
Co 2497-D It's the Girl/I'm an Unemployed Sweetheart

HOAGY CARMICHAEL
Vi 38139 Barnacle Bill the Sailor/ Rockin' Chair

BEN SELVIN
Co 2356-D I Miss a Little Miss/Cheerful Little Earful
Co 2421-D Smile, Darn Ya, Smile/The One Man Band

EDDIE LANG-JOE VENUTI
Me 12277 Farewell Blues/Someday Sweetheart
Me 12294 Beale Street Blues/After You've Gone

JOHNNY WALKER
Co 2404-D When Your Lover Has Gone/Walkin' My Baby Back Home

TED LEWIS
Co 2428-D Egyptian Ella/I'm Crazy 'Bout My Baby
Co 2527-D Dallas Blues/Royal Garden Blues

ROY CARROLL
Ha 1322 Roll On, Mississippi, Roll On/Moonlight Saving Time

ADRIAN ROLLINI
Me 12829 Sweet Madness/Savage Serenade
Me 12893 Who Walks In When I Walk Out?/Got the Jitters
De 265 Riverboat Shuffle/Sugar
De 359 Davenport Blues/Somebody Loves Me

VINCENT ROSE (Benny Goodman)
Me 13158 Stars Fell on Alabama/ Learning

THE MODERNISTS (Benny Goodman)
Me 13159 Solitude/I'm Getting Sentimental Over You

TEDDY WILSON
Br 7498 What a Little Moonlight Can Do
Br 7501 I Wished on the Moon/Miss Brown to You

MEL POWELL
CMS 543 Blue Skies/When Did You Leave Heaven?

CMS 544 The World Is Waiting for the Sunrise/Mood at Twilight

HOLLYWOOD HUCKSTERS

Cap 40022 Them There Eyes/Happy Blues

ETHEL WATERS with BENNY GOODMAN ORCHESTRA

Co 2853-D One Hundred Years from Today/I Just Couldn't Take It, Baby

BENNY GOODMAN

Me 12205 Slow But Sure/You Can't Stop Me from Lovin' You

Co 2845-D Texas Tea Party/Dr. Heckle and Mr. Jibe

Co 2907-D Emaline/Georgia Jubilee

Co 3003-D Blue Moon/Throwin' Stones at the Sun

Co 3011-D Cokey/Music Hall Rag

Vi 25009 The Dixieland Band/Hunkadola

Vi 25090 Sometimes I'm Happy/King Porter

Vi 25136 Blue Skies/Dear Old Southland

Vi 25145 Jingle Bells

Vi 25215 (closing theme) Goodbye/Sandman

Vi 25245 It's Been So Long/Goody Goody

Vi 25247 Stompin' at the Savoy/Breakin' in a Pair of Shoes

Vi 25258 When Buddha Smiles/Basin Street Blues

Vi 25411 St. Louis Blues

Vi 25461 Goodnight, My Love/Take Another Guess

Vi 25510 I Want to Be Happy/Rosetta

Vi 25792 Don't Be That Way/One O'clock Jump

Vi 25871 Big John Special/The Flat Foot Floogie

Vi 25880 Wrappin' It Up/My Melancholy Baby

Vi 26130 Bach Goes to Town/Whispering

Vi 26170 And the Angels Sing/Sent for You Yesterday

Vi(12")36205 Sing, Sing, Sing (1 & 2)

Co(12")55001 Benny Rides Again/The Man I Love

Co 35301 (theme) Let's Dance/Boy Meets Horn

Co 35410 Beyond the Moon/Night and Day

Co 35869 Cabin in the Sky/Taking a Chance on Love

Co 36652 Why Don't You Do Right?/Six Flats Unfurnished

Co 36813 Gotta Be This or That (1 & 2)

Co 36908 Give Me the Simple Life/I Wish I Could Tell You

Co 39416 Down South Camp Meetin'/South of the Border

Co 39976 What a Little Moonlight Can Do/I'll Never Say "Never Again" Again

OK 6497 Somebody Else Is Taking My Place/That Did It Marie

OK 6544 Clarinet a la King/How Long Has This Been Going On?

OK 6590 Jersey Bounce/A String of Pearls

Cap 15409 Undercurrent Blues

BENNY GOODMAN (combos)

Vi 25333 (TRIO) China Boy/Oh, Lady Be Good

Vi 25398 (QUARTET) Dinah/Moonglow

Vi 25644 (QUARTET) Avalon/The Man I Love

Co 35254 (SEXTET) Rose Room/Flying Home

Co 35320 (SEXTET) Soft Winds/Memories of You

Co 36099 (SEXTET) Air Mail Special/A Smo-o-o-oth One

Co 36684 (QUARTET) The World Is Waiting for the Sunrise

Co 36767 (QUINTET) Ev'ry Time We Say Goodbye/Only Another Boy and Girl

OK 6486 (SEXTET) Limehouse Blues/If I Had You

Cap 20127 (QUINTET) Music, Maestro, Please/The Bannister Slide (Sextet)

Cap 10173 (SEPTET) Stealin' Apples

LPs

BENNY GOODMAN

Co OSL-160 (2-LP set) Carnegie Hall Jazz Concert

Co SL-180 (2-LP set) Benny Goodman 1937/38 Jazz Concert No. 2 (airchecks)

Co GL-500 Benny Goodman Combos (Co RIs)

Co GL-523 Presents Eddie Sauter Arrangements (Co RIs)
Co CL-524 Presents Fletcher Henderson Arrangements (Co RIs)
Co CL-552 The New Benny Goodman Sextet
Co CL-821 The Vintage Goodman (1931-4 Co RIs)
Co CL-1324 Happy Session
Sunbeam SB 101-2-3 Thesaurus Rhythm Makers Orchestra June 6, 1935 (ET RIs)
Vi LPM-1099 The Golden Age of Benny Goodman (Vi RIs)
Vi LPT-6703 (5-LP set) The Golden Age of Swing (Vi RIs)
Cam CAL-624 Swing, Swing, Swing (choice Vi RIs)
Cam CAL-872 Featuring Great Vocalists of Our Times (choice Vi RIs)
Cap W-565 Benny Goodman in Hi-Fi
Cap(10″)H-409 The Benny Goodman Band (Cap RIs)
Ha HL-7190 Swing with Benny Goodman (later Co RIs)
Lon SPB-21 Benny Goodman Today (1970)
BEN POLLACK
"X"(10″)LX-3003 (Vi RIs)
TED LEWIS
Epic LN-3170 Everybody's Happy! (Co RIs)
ADRIAN ROLLINI-JOE VENUTI-EDDIE LANG
Br(10″)BL-58039 Battle of Jazz (1934 De RIs)//(1931 Me RIs)
BEN SELVIN
TOM 16 Vol. 1 (1931 Co RIs)
TOM 17 Vol. 2 (1929-30 Co RIs)
THE HOTSY TOTSY GANG
TOM 12 (Br RIs)

684. GOODMAN, HARRY   b tu
Born c. 1906-8, Chicago, Ill.

Older brother of jazz great-bandleader Benny Goodman. Stalwart on bass in Benny's band from formative years to late 30s. Early musical training at Chicago's Hull House. Often with Benny's early recording groups. Joined Ben Pollack in Chicago early 1926 after Benny had joined in California 1925. Played tuba with Pollack until switching to string bass 1928. Left Pollack in New York late 1929. Had extensive recording with studio bands and jazz groups late 20s and early 30s, also on radio. Again with Pollack late 1933-4; period with Smith Ballew 1934. Joined Benny's early band late 1934, played now-historic Let's Dance radio show to May 1935. With band from rough beginnings until mid-1939. Important cog in band's great rhythm section. Left to settle in New York, manage his Pick-a-Rib restaurant, enter music publishing.

RECORDS
BEN POLLACK
Vi 20425 He's the Last Word
Vi 21437 Singapore Sorrows/Sweet Sue
Vi 21944 My Kinda Love/On with the Dance
Co 2870-D Got the Jitters/I'm Full of the Devil
Co 2879-D Deep Jungle/Swing Out
HOAGY CARMICHAEL
Vi 38139 Barnacle Bill the Sailor/ Rockin' Chair
JOHNNY WALKER
Co 2404-D When Your Lover Has Gone/Walkin' My Baby Back Home
IRVING MILLS & HIS HOTSY TOTSY GANG
Br 4838 Railroad Man/Crazy 'Bout My Gal
Br 4998 I Wonder What My Gal Is Doin'
NEW ORLEANS RAMBLERS
Me 12133 I'm One of God's Children/ No Wonder I'm Blue
RED NICHOLS
Br 6014 Blue Again/When Kentucky Bids the World "Good Morning"
THE CAPTIVATORS
Me 12049 What Good Am I without You?/We're Friends Again
JACK PETTIS
Vi 38105 Bugle Call Blues
ZIGGY ELMAN
Bb 10096 Sugar/29th & Dearborn
Bb 10103 Fralich in Swing/Bublitchki
WINGY MANONE
Br 6911 No Calling Card/Strange Blues
Br 6940 Send Me/Walkin' the Streets
HARRY ROSENTHAL (Benny Goodman)

Co 2982-D   Say When/When Love Comes Swingin' Along

TEDDY WILSON

Br 7736 Sing, Baby, Sing/You Turned the Tables on Me

Br 7943 The Hour of Parting/Coquette

DIXIE DAISIES

Ro 808 'Cause I'm in Love/Diga Diga Doo

LOUISIANA RHYTHM KINGS

OK 41189 In a Great Big Way/Let's Sit and Talk About You

KENTUCKY GRASSHOPPERS

Ba 6295 It's Tight Like That/Four or Five Times

VINCENT ROSE (Benny Goodman)

Me 13158 Stars Fell on Alabama/Learning

THE MODERNISTS (Benny Goodman)

Me 13159 Solitude/I'm Getting Sentimental Over You

BENNY GOODMAN

Me 12090 You Didn't Have to Tell Me/I'm Happy When You're Happy

Co 2923-D I Ain't Lazy—I'm Just Dreamin'/As Long as I Live

Co 2927-D Moonglow/Breakfast Ball

Co 3003-D Blue Moon/Throwin' Stones at the Sun

Co 3011-D Cokey/Music Hall Rag

Co 3015-D Clouds/Night Wind

Vi 25009 Hunkadola/The Dixieland Band

Vi 25024 Japanese Sandman/Always

Vi 25090 Sometimes I'm Happy/King Porter

Vi 25136 Blue Skies/Dear Old Southland

Vi 25145 Jingle Bells

Vi 25215 Goodbye/Sandman

Vi 25245 It's Been So Long/Goody Goody

Vi 25247 Stompin' at the Savoy/Breakin' in a Pair of Shoes

Vi 25268 Madhouse/Between the Devil and the Deep Blue Sea

Vi 25355 Swingtime in the Rockies/I've Found a New Baby

Vi 25411 St. Louis Blues

Vi 25510 I Want to Be Happy/Rosetta

Vi 25792 Don't Be That Way/One O'clock Jump

Vi 26060 Russian Lullaby/Margie

Vi 26099 This Can't Be Love/Sing for Your Supper

Vi 26170 And the Angels Sing/Sent for You Yesterday

LPs

BENNY GOODMAN

Vi LPM-1099 The Golden Age of Benny Goodman (Vi RIs)

Vi LPT-6703 (5-LP set) The Golden Age of Swing (Vi RIs)

Cam CAL-624 Swing, Swing, Swing (choice Vi RIs)

Cam CAL-872 Featuring Great Vocalists of Our Times (choice Vi RIs)

Co OSL-160 (2-LP set) Carnegie Hall Jazz Concert

Co CL-821 The Vintage Goodman (1931-4 Co RIs)

BEN POLLACK

"X"(10″)LX-3003 (Vi RIs)

685. GOODMAN, IRVING   t

Born February 6, 1914, Chicago, Ill.

Younger brother of jazz great-bandleader Benny Goodman and bassist Harry. Good trumpet section man in leading bands of 30s and 40s. Joined Charlie Barnet in mid-1936 for a year; brief period with brother Benny late 1936. With Bunny Berigan later 1937 through most of 1938. Rejoined Goodman about four months early 1939. With Teddy Powell later 1939 into early 1940. Rejoined Benny for brief periods early 1940 and 1941. With Vaughn Monroe and Alvino Rey in early 40s. Military service, World War II. Joined Tommy Dorsey several months, late 1946-7. With Benny again most of remainder of 1947. In 50s Irving became studio musician on west coast. In mid-1956 with Benny in all-star movie THE BENNY GOODMAN STORY.

RECORDS
(solo work)

ADRIAN ROLLINI

De 787 Tap Room Swing/Lessons in Love

De 807 Swing Low/Stuff, etc.

686. GOODWIN, JOE   lyr

Born June 6, 1889, Worcester, Mass.
Died July 31, 1943, Bronx, N.Y.

Lyricist best known for songs *Tie Me to*

Your Apron Strings Again, Everywhere You Go, Your Mother and Mine, When You're Smiling. Early in career monologist in vaudeville. Later worked for publishing companies. Song output modest; most successful late 20s. Wrote for early movie musicals. Collaborators Louis Alter, Gus Edwards, George Meyer, Al Piantadosi, Mark Fisher, Larry Shay. Wrote for London revues with Nat Ayer.

SONGS
(with related shows)

1911—Billy
1912—Love, Honor and Obey; That's How I Need You
1913—Melinda's Wedding Day; When You Play in the Game of Love
1915—The Little House Upon the Hill; What a Wonderful Mother You'd Be
1916—Baby Shoes
1917—One Day in June
1918—Three Wonderful Letters from Home
1920—All That I Want Is You
1922—THE FRENCH DOLL stage show (Gee, But I Hate to Go Home Alone)
1925—What Do We Care If It's One O'clock; I'm Knee Deep in Daisies; Tie Me to Your Apron Strings Again
1927—Everywhere You Go; Hoosier Sweetheart
1929—HOLLYWOOD REVUE OF 1929 movie (Orange Blossom Time; Your Mother and Mine; Strolling Through the Park One Day; Nobody but You; Lon Chaney Will Get You If You Don't Watch Out; Minstrel Days; I Never Knew I Could Do a Thing Like That); SHOW OF SHOWS movie (Your Mother and Mine); UNTAMED movie (That Wonderful Something); Love Ain't Nothin' but the Blues
1930—When You're Smiling

Other songs: *They're Wearing Them Higher in Hawaii*; *Breeze*; *A Girlie Was Just Made to Love*; *When I Get You Alone Tonight*; *Liberty Bell, It's Time to Ring Again*

687. GORDON, BOB   bs ts B
Born June 11, 1928, St.Louis, Mo.
Died August 28, 1955, in auto crash enroute from Hollywood to San Diego, Calif.

Talented baritone sax star in modern style. Promising career cut short at 27. Attended Westlake College of Music in Los Angeles 1948. 1949-52 mostly with Alvino Rey on tenor sax; also with Billy May and Horace Heidt early 50s. Switched to baritone sax, became part of west coast jazz scene. Capable soloist. Freelanced; enroute to play Pete Rugolo concert job in San Diego when fatal accident occurred.

RECORDS
(all LPs)

BOB GORDON
  PJ(10")12 Meet Mr. Gordon
BOB GORDON-CLIFFORD BROWN
  PJ 1214 Arranged by Montrose
JACK MONTROSE
  PJ-1208 Jack Montrose Sextet
LENNIE NIEHAUS
  Contemp C-3540 Zounds! The Lennie Niehaus Octet!
  Contemp(10")C-2513
  Contemp(10")C-2517
HERBIE HARPER
  Noc(10")1
MAYNARD FERGUSON
  EmArcy(10")MG-26024 Dimensions
CHET BAKER
  PJ(10")9 Chet Baker Ensemble
PETE RUGOLO
  Co CL-604 Adventures in Rhythm
  Co CL-689
SHELLY MANNE
  DeeGee(10")1003
HOWARD RUMSEY
  Contemp(10")C-2515 Lighthouse All Stars, Vol. 5
DUANE TATRO
  Contemp C-3514
JACK MILLMAN
  De DL-8156
TAL FARLOW
  Norg MGN-1030 A Recital by Tal Farlow
(miscellaneous artists)
  Cap T-659 Les Brown All-Stars
  De DL-8130 Blow Hot, Blow Cool

985

688. GORDON, DEXTER   ts B

Born February 27, 1923, Los Angeles, Calif.

Swinging tenor sax star of early bop era. Maintained good tone and easy swinging style through the years. Played locally 1940, late in year joined Lionel Hampton for three years. 1943-4 in Los Angeles with Lee Young, Jesse Price, Louis Armstrong. In mid-40s with Billy Eckstine's bop-styled band over a year; featured in tenor sax duels with Gene Ammons. With bop combos in New York and on west coast in later 40s. Led combo in 50s mostly on west coast in relative obscurity. Comeback 1960-2 in New York; waxed well-received LPs. Late 1962 to Copenhagen; remained, worked throughout Europe in 60s, returned to U.S. for periods in 1964-5 and 1969. Continued to record. Active abroad into 70s.

RECORDS

BILLY ECKSTINE
DeL 2001 Blowin' the Blues Away
RED NORVO
Cap 15253 Bop!/I'll Follow You
DIZZY GILLESPIE
Mus 486 Blue 'n Boogie
SIR CHARLES & HIS ALL-STARS
Apo 757 Takin' Off/If I Had You
Apo 759 20th Century Blues/The Street Beat
DEXTER GORDON
Sav 576 Blow Mr. Dexter/Dexter's Deck
Sav 603 Long, Tall, Dexter/Dexter Digs In
Sav 612 Dexter's Cuttin' Out/Dexter's Minor Mad
Sav 623 Dexter Rides Again
Sav 913 Settin' the Pace (1 & 2)
Sav 955 Dextrose
Sav 960 So Easy/Dexter's Riff
Dial 1018 Mischievous Lady/A Ghost of a Chance
Dial 1022 Bikini
Dial 1038 Lullaby in Rhythm/It's the Talk of the Town
Dial 1042 Sweet and Lovely
Mer(12″)8900 Rosetta/I've Found a New Baby
DEXTER GORDON-WARDELL GRAY
Dial 1017 The Chase (1 & 2)

Bop 102 The Hunt (1 & 2)
DEXTER GORDON-TEDDY EDWARDS
Dial 1028 The Duel (1 & 2)

LPs

DEXTER GORDON
Sav(10″)MG-9016 New Trends in Modern Music, Vol. 3
Sav MG-12130 Dexter Rides Again
BN 4112 Go!
BN 4133 A Swingin' Affair
BN 4146 Our Man In Paris
BN 4176 One Flight Up
Pres 7623 The Tower of Power
Pres 7763 A Day in Copenhagen
Pres 7829 The Panther!
WARDELL GRAY
Pres 7343 (2-LP set) Memorial Album (RIs)
LEO PARKER
Sav(10″)MG-9009 Leo Parker—All-Star Series
STAN LEVEY
Beth BCP-37

689. GORDON, GRAY   cl as ts B

Leader of sweet-styled dance band in late 30s featuring Tic-Toc Rhythm gimmick. Early in career played with and fronted Elmo Mack & His Purple Derbies band, a somewhat hot-styled group mostly based in midwest. First big bandleader job 1933 Chicago World's Fair. Played there again 1934 and at Chicago's Merry Garden Ballroom. By 1938 developed Tic-Toc Rhythm: clocklike sound. Band had good sweet ensemble sound, used muted and clipped brass and mellow clarinet section. Rhythm often accentuated with temple blocks establishing "tick-tock" sound. Theme song *One Minute to One*. Cliff Grass featured vocalist in late 30s. Band often played New York's Hotel Edison. In 40s Gordon abandoned Tic-Toc style for swing, improved musically but not commercially. Disbanded during World War II, entered music publishing. Later in personal management, associated with Les Paul and Mary Ford several years.

RECORDS

GRAY GORDON
Bb 7775 When a Prince of a Fella Meets a Cinderella/You're the

Very Last Word in Love
Bb 7845 (theme) One Minute to One
Bb 10020 After Looking at You/I Kissed You in a Dream Last Night
Bb 10132 Blue Italian Waters/Sell Your Cares for a Song
Bb 10142 It's All So New to Me/The Moon Is a Silver Dollar
Bb 10575 Gone with the Wind/'Way Back in 1939 A.D.
Bb 10648 No More Rain/I Was Watching a Man Paint a Fence
Bb 10711 Clear Out of This World/It Wouldn't Be Love
Bb 10739 I Can't Resist You/My Enchantress of the Night
Bb 10819 I Could Make You Care/ Ferryboat Serenade
Bb 10873 I Hear Music/Dancing on a Dime
Bb 11077 You Waited Too Long/ Granada
Bb 11138 Why Do I Love You?/Make Believe
Vi 26184 It's Never Too Late/Chopsticks
Vi 26193 Sing a Song of Sunbeams/ Hang Your Heart on a Hickory Limb
Vi 26232 Beer Barrel Polka/But It Didn't Mean a Thing
Vi 26242 I'm in Love with the Honorable Mr. So and So/A Lady Needs a Change
Vi 26295 Especially for You/Rumpel-Stilts-Kin
Vi 26328 If I Only Had a Brain/We're Off to See the Wizard
Vi 26350 It's Funny to Everyone but Me/Lingering on Your Doorstep
Vi 26396 Goody Goodbye/To You, Sweetheart, Aloha

689A. GORDON, KITTY vo
Born 1877 or 1878, England
Died May 26, 1974, Brentwood, N.Y.

Beautiful English singer-actress, performed on Broadway. U.S. debut in VERONIQUE (1904). Other musicals THE GIRL AND THE WIZARD (1909); ALMA, WHERE DO YOU LIVE? (1910); THE ENCHANTRESS (written for her by Victor Herbert) and LA BELLE PAREE (1911); A WORLD OF PLEAS-

URE (1915). Performed in vaudeville. In early silent films. Last appearance 1952 in TV's Life Begins at 80.

690. GORDON, MACK lyr vo
Born June 21, 1904, Warsaw, Poland
Died March 1, 1959, New York, N.Y.

Lyricist with numerous hit songs, mostly for movies. He and composer Harry Revel important movie songwriting team during 30s. Teamed successfully with Harry Warren in 40s movies. Other collaborators composers Josef Myrow, Ray Henderson, Vincent Youmans, Jimmy Van Heusen, James V. Monaco, Edmund Goulding. Most famous songs *Did You Ever See a Dream Walking?*; *Time on My Hands*; *May I?*; *Love Thy Neighbor*; *With My Eyes Wide Open, I'm Dreaming*; *Stay as Sweet as You Are*; *Without a Word of Warning*; *Goodnight, My Love*; *Never in a Million Years*; *Chattanooga Choo Choo*; *I Had the Craziest Dream*; *At Last*; *Serenade in Blue*; *There Will Never Be Another You*; *You'll Never Know*; *I Can't Begin to Tell You*; *You Make Me Feel So Young*; *Mam'selle*. Brought to U.S. at early age, grew up in Brooklyn and Bronx. With minstrel show as boy soprano. Later comedian-singer in vaudeville. Began songwriting early 30s, collaborated with Harry Revel almost at outset. Team to Hollywood 1933, quickly became established.

SONGS
(with related shows and films, divided according to three sets of collaborators)

(all songs 1931-9 with HARRY REVEL)

1930—SMILES stage show (Time on My Hands); POINTED HEELS movie (Ain't-cha?)

1931—ZIEGFELD FOLLIES OF 1931 stage show (Help Yourself to Happiness; Cigarettes, Cigars); EVERYBODY'S WELCOME stage show (All Wrapped Up in You); FAST AND FURIOUS stage show (unsuccessful)

1932—SMILING FACES stage show (unsuccessful); MARCHING BOY stage show (unsuccessful); And So to Bed; A Boy and a Girl Were Dancing; I Played Fiddle for the Czar; Listen to the German Band; Underneath the Harlem Moon

1933—BROADWAY THROUGH A KEYHOLE movie (Doin' the Uptown Low-down; You're My Past, Present and Future); It Was a Night in June; An Orchid to You; It's Within Your Power; A Tree Was a Tree

1934—SHOOT THE WORKS movie (With My Eyes Wide Open, I'm Dreaming); SITTING PRETTY movie (Did You Ever See a Dream Walking?; You're Such a Comfort to Me; Many Moons Ago; Good Morning Glory); WE'RE NOT DRESSING movie (May I?; Love Thy Neighbor; She Reminds Me of You; Goodnight, Lovely Little Lady; Once in a Blue Moon); THE GAY DIVORCEE movie (Don't Let It Bother You; Let's Knock K-neez); SHE LOVES ME NOT movie (Straight from the Shoulder; I'm Hummin', I'm Whistlin', I'm Singin'; Put a Little Rhythm in Everything You Do); COLLEGE RHYTHM movie (College Rhythm; Stay as Sweet as You Are; Take a Number from One to Ten; Let's Give Three Cheers for Love)

1935—LOVE IN BLOOM movie (Here Comes Cookie; Got Me Doin' Things; My Heart Is an Open Book); TWO FOR TONIGHT movie (Two for Tonight; Without a Word of Warning; I Wish I Was Aladdin; Takes Two to Make a Bargain; From the Top of Your Head); PARIS IN SPRING movie (Paris in Spring); Would There Be Love?

1936—COLLEGIATE movie (You Hit the Spot; I Feel Like a Feather in the Breeze); POOR LITTLE RICH GIRL movie (When I'm with You; But Definitely; You Gotta Eat Your Spinach, Baby; Oh, My Goodness; I Like a Military Man; Where There's Life There's Soap); STOW-AWAY movie (Goodnight, My Love; One Never Knows, Does One?; I Wanna Go to the Zoo); A Star Fell Out of Heaven

1937—WAKE UP AND LIVE movie (Wake Up and Live; Never in a Million Years; There's a Lull in My Life; It's Swell of You; I'm Bubbling Over); HEAD OVER HEELS IN LOVE movie (English film; May I Have the Next Romance with You?; Looking Around Corners for You; There's That Look in Your Eyes Again; Don't Give a Good Gosh Darn); THIN ICE movie (I'm Olga from the Volga); YOU CAN'T HAVE EVERYTHING movie (You Can't Have Everything; Afraid to Dream; The Loveliness of You; Danger, Love at Work; Please Pardon Us, We're in Love); ALI BABA GOES TO TOWN movie (I've Got My Heart Set on You; Swing Is Here to Sway)

1938—IN OLD CHICAGO movie (title song); JOSETTE movie (Where in the World; In Any Language; May I Drop a Petal in Your Glass of Wine?); LOVE AND HISSES movie (Sweet Someone; I Wanna Be in Winchell's Column; Be a Good Sport; Broadway's Gone Hawaii); THANKS FOR EVERYTHING movie (title song; others); LOVE FINDS ANDY HARDY movie (Meet the Beat of My Heart; What Do You Know About Love?; It Never Rains but It Pours); TAILSPIN movie (Are You in the Mood for Mischief?); MY LUCKY STAR movie (I've Got a Date with a Dream; Could You Pass in Love?; This May Be the Night; By a Wishing Well; The All American Swing); SALLY, IRENE AND MARY movie (Sweet as a Song; Got My Mind on Music); REBECCA OF SUNNYBROOK FARM movie (An Old Straw Hat)

1939—ROSE OF WASHINGTON SQUARE movie (I Never Knew Heaven Could Speak); THE RAINS CAME movie (title song)

(all songs with HARRY WARREN)

1940—DOWN ARGENTINE WAY movie (Down Argentina Way; Two Dreams Met); YOUNG PEOPLE movie (Young People; Fifth Avenue; I Wouldn't Take a Million; Tra-La-La-La; The Mason-Dixon Line); TIN PAN ALLEY movie (You

Say the Sweetest Things, Baby)
1941—THAT NIGHT IN RIO movie (They
Met in Rio; Boa Noite; Chica
Chica Boom Chic; I, Yi, Yi, Yi, Yi,
I Like You Very Much; The Baron
Is in Conference); THE GREAT
AMERICAN BROADCAST movie
(Where You Are; I Take to You;
The Great American Broadcast;
Long Ago Last Night; It's All in a
Lifetime; I've Got a Bone to Pick
with You); WEEKEND IN HAVANA
movie (Tropical Magic; A Week-
end in Havana; The Man with the
Lollypop Song; The Nango; When
I Love I Love; Romance and
Rhumba); SUN VALLEY SERENADE
movie (I Know Why; Chattanooga
Choo Choo; It Happened in Sun
Valley; The Kiss Polka)
1942—ORCHESTRA WIVES movie (At Last;
Serenade in Blue; I've Got a Gal
in Kalamazoo; People Like You
and Me); SPRINGTIME IN THE
ROCKIES movie (I Had the Craziest
Dream; A Poem Set to Music;
Pan-American Jubilee); ICELAND
movie (There Will Never Be An-
other You; Let's Bring New Glory
to Old Glory; You Can't Say No
to a Soldier)
1943—SWEET ROSIE O'GRADY movie (My
Heart Tells Me; The Wishing
Waltz; Get Your Police Gazette;
Going to the Country Fair; My
Sam; Where Oh Where Oh Where
Is the Groom?); HELLO, FRISCO,
HELLO movie (You'll Never Know;
I Gotta Have You)
1945—DIAMOND HORSESHOE movie (I
Wish I Knew; The More I See
You; In Acapulco; Play Me an
Old Fashioned Melody; Welcome
to the Diamond Horseshoe; A
Nickel's Worth of Jive; Moody;
Cook Me Up a Show)
1950—SUMMER STOCK movie (If You Feel
Like Singing, Sing; Friendly Star;
Happy Harvest; Mem'ry Island;
Dig-Dig-Dig for Your Dinner;
Blue Jean Polka)
(songs with miscellaneous composers)
1939—Speaking of Heaven; If What You
Say Is True

1940—LILLIAN RUSSELL movie (Adored
One; Waltz Is King); LITTLE OLD
NEW YORK movie (Who Is the
Beau of the Belle of New York?);
In an Old Dutch Garden; Some-
body Told Me; Secrets in the
Moonlight; This Is the Beginning
of the End
1942—SONG OF THE ISLANDS movie (Sing
Me a Song of the Islands; Blue
Shadows and White Gardenias;
What's Buzzin', Cousin?; O'Brien
Has Gone Hawaiian; Down on
Ami Ami Oni Oni Isle; Maluna
Malolo Mawaena)
1944—PIN-UP GIRL movie (Time Alone
Will Tell; Once Too Often; Don't
Carry Tales Out of School); SWEET
AND LOWDOWN movie (I'm Mak-
ing Believe; Ten Days with Baby;
Hey, Bub, Let's Have a Ball; Chug
Chug, Choo-Choo, Chug); IRISH
EYES ARE SMILING movie (Bessie in
a Bustle; I Don't Want a Million
Dollars)
1945—THE DOLLY SISTERS movie (I Can't
Begin to Tell You; Don't Be Too
Old Fashioned; We Have Been
Around; Powder, Lipstick and
Rouge)
1946—THREE LITTLE GIRLS IN BLUE movie
(You Make Me Feel So Young;
This Is Always; Somewhere in the
Night; On the Boardwalk in At-
lantic City)
1947—MOTHER WORE TIGHTS movie (You
Do; Kokomo, Indiana; This Is My
Favorite City; There's Nothing
Like a Song; On a Little Two-Seat
Tandem; Rolling Down to Bowl-
ing Green; Fare-Thee-Well Dear
Alma Mater; Tra-La-La-La);
Mam'selle
1948—WHEN MY BABY SMILES AT ME movie
(By the Way; What Did I Do?)
1949—THE BEAUTIFUL BLONDE FROM
BASHFUL BEND movie (Every Time
I Meet You; others); COME TO THE
STABLE movie (Through a Long
and Sleepless Night)
1950—WABASH AVENUE movie (Baby,
Won't You Say You Love Me?;
Wilhelmina; Down on Wabash
Avenue)

989

1951—CALL ME MISTER movie, Sammy Fain-cm (I Just Can't Do Enough for You)
1953—THE GIRL NEXT DOOR movie, Josef Myrow-cm (The Girl Next Door; Nowhere Guy; You; If I Love You a Mountain); I LOVE MELVIN movie, Josef Myrow-cm (Where Did You Learn to Dance?; A Lady Loves to Love; I Know What He'll Look Like; Saturday Afternoon Before the Game)
1956—BUNDLE OF JOY movie, Josef Myrow-cm (unimportant songs)

691. GORMAN, ROSS   as ts bs cl B

Born c. 1890-1
Died February 28, 1953, New York, N.Y.

Leader of good hot-styled band in mid-20s. As youngster performed with father in vaudeville. With Vincent Lopez probably pre-1920. With Paul Whiteman at times 1921-25. Featured clarinet soloist on Whiteman's *Rhapsody in Blue*, introduced at 1924 Aeolian Hall concert, and on Victor recording. Sideman and musical director for The Virginians, early 20s hot group extensively recorded. Also led Ross Gorman & His Novelty Syncopaters in early 20s. In 1922 co-composer of popular *Rose of the Rio Grande* which became a standard. In 1924-5 conducted band for Broadway show EARL CARROLL'S VANITIES. Band recorded, included jazzmen Red Nichols and Miff Mole. Led other good bands on jobs and records into 1927. In late 20s and early 30s Gorman on radio with B. A. Rolfe and other bands, specializing in many reed instruments. Staff musician on NBC radio, played many top shows.

RECORDS

BUSSE'S BUZZARDS
  Vi 19727 Deep Elm
  Vi 19782 Red Hot Henry Brown/ Milenberg Joys
PAUL WHITEMAN
  Vi 19671 Charleston
  Vi 19720 Footloose
  Vi 19773 Rhythm Rag
  Vi(12")55225 Rhapsody in Blue (1 & 2)
YERKES' NOVELTY FIVE
  Co A-6116 Easy Pickin's

Vo 14024 Swanee/Mystery
(as musical director and sideman)
THE VIRGINIANS
  Vi 18933 Blue/Why Should I Cry Over You?
  Vi 19001 Rose of the Rio Grande/ Who Did You Fool After All?
  Vi 19419 Superstitious Blues
  Vi 19965 I Wish I Could Shimmy Like My Sister Kate/Gee! But I Hate to Go Home Alone
ROSS GORMAN & HIS EARL CARROLL ORCHESTRA
  Co 435-D Oh Boy! What a Girl/Remember
  Co 459-D A Kiss in the Moonlight/ Somebody's Crazy About You
  Co 460-D Hugo, I'll Go Where You Go/Want a Little Lovin'
  Co 498-D Rhythm of the Day/I'm Sitting on Top of the World
  Co 516-D I Never Knew/Sleepy Time Gal
ROSS GORMAN
  Co 631-D Valencia/Cherie, I Love You
  Ca 1063 Idolizing
  Ha 322 Come Day—Go Day/Sidewalk Blues
  Ha 350 You're the One for Me
  Ha 403 Pardon the Glove/My Wife's in Europe Today
  Ge 6118 Kickapoo Trail/Phantom Blues

692. GORNEY, JAY   cm lyr B

Born December 12, 1896, Bialystok, Russia

Composer for Broadway shows mostly in 20s, later for movies. In 1932 wrote memorable Depression song *Brother, Can You Spare a Dime?*, moody theme with outstanding lyrics by E. Y. Harburg. Other notable songs *What Wouldn't I Do for That Man?*, *You're My Thrill*. To U.S. in 1906, educated in Detroit. Attended University of Michigan, also extensive musical training. Wrote music in college, including operettas, also led band. In navy World War I, became bandleader. Studied again later, earned law degree. Began composing mid-20s. During new sound era music department head at Paramount Pictures Astoria Studios in

New York 1929-30. To Hollywood 1933, worked for 20th Century-Fox. Produced films for Columbia early 40s. Active in TV as writer-director-producer. Collaborators E. Y. Harburg, Henry Myers, Edward Eliscu, Lew Brown, Sidney Clare, Howard Dietz, Walter and Jean Kerr.

SONGS
(with related shows)

1924—GREENWICH VILLAGE FOLLIES OF 1924 stage show (Zulu Lou; Bom-Bom-Beedle-Um-Bo); VOGUES OF 1924 stage show (many songs, unimportant); TOP HOLE stage show (Dance Your Way to Paradise; In California; Is It Any Wonder; The Girls)

1925—EARL CARROLL'S VANITIES OF 1925 stage show (Somebody's Crazy About You); GREENWICH VILLAGE FOLLIES OF 1925-6 stage show (Garden of Used-to-Be; When Evening Shadows Fall)

1926—SWEETHEART TIME stage show (A Girl in Your Arms)

1927—THE MERRY-GO-ROUND stage show (Gabriel Is Blowing His Horn; What D'Ya Say?; Yes Girl; New York Town; Tampa)

1929—EARL CARROLL'S SKETCH BOOK stage show (Like Me Less, Love Me More; Kinda Cute); APPLAUSE movie (What Wouldn't I Do for That Man?)

1930—EARL CARROLL'S VANITIES OF 1930 stage show (Knee Deep in Daisies; I Came to Life); GLORIFYING THE AMERICAN GIRL movie (What Wouldn't I Do for That Man?)

1931—SHOOT THE WORKS stage show (Muchacha; Hot Moonlight; My Heart's a Banjo)

1932—AMERICANA stage show (Brother, Can You Spare a Dime?)

1933—MOONLIGHT AND PRETZELS movie (Moonlight and Pretzels; Ah, But Is It Love?)

1934—STAND UP AND CHEER movie (Baby, Take a Bow; This Is Our Last Night Together; Broadway's Gone Hillbilly; We're Out of the Red; I'm Laughin'); You're My Thrill

1935—REDHEADS ON PARADE movie (I Found a Dream)

1941—MEET THE PEOPLE stage show (Meet the People; The Stars Remain)

1943—THE MORE THE MERRIER movie (Damn the Torpedoes—Full Speed Ahead)

1948—HEAVEN ON EARTH stage show (unsuccessful)

1949—TOUCH AND GO stage show (songs unimportant)

693. GOTTLER, ARCHIE   cm p
Born May 14, 1896, New York, N.Y.
Died June 24, 1959, California

Composer for several Broadway shows and early sound movies. Attended CCNY and Long Island Business College. As youth played piano in silent movie theatres. Pioneer in early sound movies as composer and director. During World War II in Signal Corps Training Film Program. Collaborators Edgar Leslie, Con Conrad, Sidney D. Mitchell, Johnny Lange, George Meyer, Jerome Gottler (son).

SONGS
(with related shows)

1915—America, I Love You; In the Gold Fields of Nevada

1916—Rolling Stones

1918—ZIEGFELD FOLLIES OF 1918 stage show (Would You Rather Be a Colonel with an Eagle on Your Shoulder or a Private with a Chicken on Your Knee?); I Hate to Lose You; Mammy's Soldier Boy

1920—BROADWAY BREVITIES OF 1920 stage show (book only)

1928—GOOD BOY stage show (Don't Be Like That); That's How I Feel About You

1929—FOX MOVIETONE FOLLIES OF 1929 movie (Big City Blues; Breakaway; Walking with Susie; That's You, Baby); BROADWAY movie (Hittin' the Ceiling; Sing a Little Love Song); THE COCK-EYED WORLD movie (So Long; Elenita; So Dear to Me)

1930—HAPPY DAYS movie (Mona; Crazy Feet); To Whom It May Concern

1939—Baby Me

Other songs: *What Do You Mean by Loving Somebody Else?*; *Easter Sunday on the Prairie*; *Santa Claus Is Riding the*

Trail; *Kiss Me Goodnight*; *Love Me or Leave Me Alone*; *Oogie Oogie Wa Wa*; *Wine, Women and Song*; *Girl on the Isle of Man*; *All American*; *Bye Bye, Mr. Dream Man*; *How's About It?*; *Mammy's Chocolate Soldier*; *I Didn't Expect It from You*

694. GOULD, MORTON   cm ar p B

Born December 10, 1913, Richmond Hill, L.I., N.Y.

Composer of semi-classical numbers notably *Pavanne*. Wrote scores for Broadway shows BILLION DOLLAR BABY (1946) and ARMS AND THE GIRL (1950). Child prodigy, at 6 first composition *Just Six* published. Pianist in concerts, vaudeville and radio as child. Studied at Juilliard. At 17 got job at Radio City Music Hall in New York as staff arranger. Later arranged and conducted for NBC radio shows. In 1938 *Pavanne* popular. In 1939-40 his radio show Music for Today featured symphonic jazz. Conducted orchestra on Major Bowes radio show 1941, Jack Pearl show 1942. Own show 1943 and later 40s, featured concert music. Guest conductor for symphony orchestras throughout U.S., often played his semi-classical works. Appeared with orchestra in movie DELIGHTFULLY DANGEROUS (1945), wrote musical score. In two Broadway shows collaborated with Betty Comden and Adolph Green 1946, Dorothy Fields 1950. Recorded serious works as well as pop tunes in semi-classical style.

SONGS
(with related shows)

1945—DELIGHTFULLY DANGEROUS movie (I'm Only Teasin'; In a Shower of Stars; Through Your Eyes to Your Heart)
1946—BILLION DOLLAR BABY stage show (Broadway Blossom; I'm Sure of Your Love; Bad Timing; One Track Mind)
1950—ARMS AND THE GIRL stage show (Nothin' for Nothin'; There Must Be Somethin' Better Than Love; A Cow, and a Plow, and a Frau)

Other compositions: *Pavanne*; *Jericho*; *Lincoln Legend*; *Chorale and Fugue in Jazz*; *Spirituals for String Choir and Orchestra*; *A Cowboy Rhapsody*; *Caricatones*; *Foster Gallery*; *St. Lawrence Suite*; *Inter-*

play for Piano and Orchestra; *Latin American Symphonette*; *Ballad for Band*; *Fall River Legend*; *Satirical Dance*; *American Symphonette* No. 1 and No. 2; *Concertette for Viola and Orchestra*; *Viola Concerto*; *Derivations for Clarinet*; *American Caprice*; *American Salute*; *Guaracha*; *Tropical*; *Minstrel Show*; *Holiday Music*; *Philharmonic Waltzes*; *Serenade of Carols*; *Harvest for Strings, Harp and Vibraphone*; *Little Symphony*; *Homespun Overture*

RECORDS

MORTON GOULD (as pianist)
Vi 24205 Bolero/Satirical Dance
MORTON GOULD ORCHESTRA
De 18204 Summertime/Deep River
De 18205 Swing Low Sweet Chariot/ Sometimes I Feel Like a Motherless Child
De 18206 Home on the Range/La Estrellita
De 18207 The Man I Love/Solitude
Co 4364-M Laura/Body and Soul
Co 4365-M Sophisticated Lady/Holiday for Strings
Co 4366-M Over the Rainbow/Solitude
Co 4426-M Brazil/Cielito Lindo
Co 4449-M Surrey with the Fringe on Top/Stormy Weather
Co 7555-M Tea for Two/What Is This Thing Called Love?
Co 7577-M Two Guitars/Birth of the Blues
Co 7578-M The Peanut Vendor/Masquerade

LPs

MORTON GOULD
Co CL-560 Symphonic Serenade
Co CL-664 Starlight Serenade
Co(10")ML-2015 South of the Border
Co(10")ML-2021 Soft Lights and Sweet Music
Co(10")DL-5067 At the Piano
Vi LM-1884 OKLAHOMA! — CAROUSEL Suites
Vi LM-1956 SCHEHERAZADE in High Fidelity
Vi LM-1994 Jungle Drums
Vi LM-2002 AN AMERICAN IN PARIS/ PORGY AND BESS
Vi LM-2006 Music for Summertime
Vi LM-2080 Brass and Percussion
Vi LSC-2217 Baton and Bows

695. GOWANS, BRAD v-tb cl as c ar
(ARTHUR BRADFORD GOWANS)

Born December 3, 1903, Billerica, Mass.
Died September 8, 1954, Los Angeles, Calif.

Dixieland jazzman on valve trombone, most active in 40s and 50s. Began professionally mid-20s, played clarinet and cornet. In late 20s with Mal Hallett and Bert Lown. Out of music early and mid-30s, came back to join Bobby Hackett combo in Boston 1936. Concentrated on valve trombone remainder of career. Also with Frank Ward in Boston. To New York 1938; periods with Hackett again and Wingy Manone. In 1939 with Hackett big band (v-tb, ar) and Bud Freeman, late 1939-40 with Joe Marsala. In 40s mostly with dixieland groups, except period in 1942 with Ray McKinley's big band (v-tb, ar). With Art Hodes, Eddie Condon, Max Kaminsky. With Jimmy Dorsey's big band 1948. With Nappy Lamare 1949-50, on early TV. Settled on west coast and freelanced early 50s. Last job with Eddie Skrivanek 1953-4. Often arranged for bands he played in.

RECORDS
PERLEY BREED (on clarinet)
  Ge 3059 Honey, I'm in Love with You
  Ge 5608 Tell Me, Dreamy Eyes/ Where's My Sweetie Hiding?
NEW ORLEANS JAZZ BAND (on clarinet)
  Ba 1618 The Camel Walk
  Ba 1624 Melancholy Lou
ORIGINAL DIXIELAND JAZZ BAND (on clarinet)
  VD(12")214 Tiger Rag/Sensation
THE REDHEADS (on cornet)
  Pe 14738 Heebie Jeebies
BUD FREEMAN
  Bb 10370 I've Found a New Baby/ Easy to Get
  Bb 10386 China Boy/The Eel
  De 2781 The Sail Fish/Satanic Blues
  De 2849 Sunday/As Long as I Live
  De 18064 Big Boy/Copenhagen
  De 18067 Susie/Fidgety Feet
ART HODES
  De 18437 Georgia Cake Walk/Liberty Inn Drag
  De 18438 Indiana/Get Happy
JAM SESSION AT COMMODORE
  CMS(12")1504 A Good Man Is Hard to Find (1 & 2)
  CMS(12")1505 A Good Man Is Hard to Find (3 & 4)
WINGY MANONE
  Bb 7621 Martha/Flat Foot Floogie
  Bb 7622 Heart of Mine/Little Joe from Chicago
  Bb 7633 Manone Blues/Let's Break the Good News
EDDIE CONDON
  De 18040 Nobody's Sweetheart/Friar's Point Shuffle
  De 18041 There'll Be Some Changes Made/Someday Sweetheart
  CMS 531 Ballin' the Jack/I Ain't Gonna Give Nobody None of My Jelly Roll
RAY BAUDUC
  Cap 919 Susie/Down in Honky Tonky Town
  Cap 15131 Li'l Liza Jane/When My Sugar Walks Down the Street
NAPPY LAMARE
  Cap 1047 This Is the Life/It Ain't Gonna Rain No Mo'
EDDIE EDWARDS
  CMS 610 Tiger Rag/Barnyard Blues
  CMS 612 Ostrich Walk/Lazy Daddy
BRAD GOWANS
  Vi 20-3230 Singin' the Blues/Jazz Me Blues

LPs
BRAD GOWANS
  Vi(10")LJM-3000
BOBBY HACKETT
  Epic LN-3106 The Hackett Horn (Vo RIs)
EDDIE CONDON
  CMS(10")20017 (RIs)
BUD FREEMAN
  Br(10")BL-58037 (RIs)
  De(10")DL-5213 (RIs)

696. GOZZO, CONRAD t

Born February 6, 1922, New Britain, Conn.
Died October 8, 1964, Los Angeles, Calif.

Noted for powerful lead trumpet and ability to spark brass section in big bands. In late 30s with Isham Jones and Tommy Reynolds. With Red Norvo early 1940, later in year with Scat Davis. Late 1940-1 with Bob Chester. With Claude Thornhill 1941-2 and Benny Goodman briefly late

1942. Military service, World War II, with Artie Shaw's navy band. With Goodman again late 1945, with Woody Herman most of 1946. In 1947 with Boyd Raeburn and Tex Beneke. Settled on west coast to freelance, with Bob Crosby on radio several years. In 1950 with Jerry Gray on radio and on tour. With Sonny Burke 1951 and Billy May 1952. Powerful horn in demand for studio and record work. Career terminated by fatal heart attack.

RECORDS
(all LPs)

CONRAD GOZZO
  Vi LPM-1124 The Great Goz
GLEN GRAY
  Cap W-1022 Sounds of the Great Bands, Vol. 1
TOOTS CAMARATA
  Vista 4047 (S) Tutti's Trumpets
GUS BIVONA
  Mer MG-20304 Plays the Music of Steve Allen
HARRY ZIMMERMAN
  HiFi Record R-602 Band with a Beat
VAN ALEXANDER
  Cap T-1243 The Home of Happy Feet (The Savoy)
RAY ANTHONY
  Cap T-678 Big Band Dixieland
(movie soundtrack)
  De DL-8252 THE BENNY GOODMAN STORY
WOODY HERMAN
  MGM E-3043 Carnegie Hall Concert
DAN TERRY
  Co CL-6288

697. GRAAS, JOHN   Fr-h ar cm
Born October 14, 1924, Dubuque, Iowa
Died April 13, 1962, Van Nuys, Calif.

A foremost performer in jazz on French horn, also talented classical musician with excellent tone and technique. Won national honors on this difficult instrument in high school. Played first French horn in Indianapolis Symphony Orchestra early 40s. With Claude Thornhill's band 1942 when use of French horn in dance band an innovation. Military service, World War II. After discharge played in Cleveland Symphony Orchestra late 1945-6. Later 1946 joined Tex Beneke, to 1948. With Stan Kenton 1949-50. Settled

on west coast to freelance, worked with leading modern jazzmen; won notice with Shorty Rogers groups. Arranging and composing, including *Jazz Symphony No. 1* and *Jazz Chaconne No. 1*. Freelance and studio work on west coast until death from heart attack.

RECORDS
(all LPs)

JOHN GRAAS
  DeDL-8343 Jazz Lab, Vol. 1
  De DL-8478 Jazz Lab, Vol. 2
  Trend(10″)TL-1005 The French Horn
  EmArcy MG-36117 Coup de Graas
WESTLAKE COLLEGE QUINTET (as supervisor-composer)
  De DL-8393
SHORTY ROGERS
  Cap(10″)H-294 Modern Sounds
BOB COOPER
  Cap T-6513 Shifting Winds
PETE RUGOLO
  Co CL-689
(miscellaneous artists)
  De DL-8079 Jazz Studio 2
  De DL-8103 Jazz Studio 3
  BN(10″)5059 Best from the West
LOUIS BELLSON
  Cap(10″)H-348
STAN KENTON
  Cap(10″)P-189

698. GRABLE, BETTY   vo
(RUTH ELIZABETH GRABLE)
Born December 18, 1916, St. Louis, Mo.
Died July 2, 1973, Santa Monica, Calif.
of lung cancer

Singing and dancing star of movie musicals from 30s into 50s. Capable musical performer and actress; career enhanced by her beauty, personality, and especially by much-publicized legs. Received early musical training in St. Louis. Settled in Hollywood 1929 with mother, who pointed Betty toward movie career. Chorine bits in 1930 movies LET'S GO PLACES, NEW MOVIETONE FOLLIES OF 1930 and WHOOPEE. Bit part in THE KID FROM SPAIN (1932), later in year first sizable role in Wheeler & Woolsey movie HOLD 'EM JAIL!. Specialty dance number with Ted Fio Rito band in SWEETHEART OF SIGMA CHI (1933), later with Fio Rito on dance jobs as singer-dancer. Several shorts under name of Frances Dean. Bits in movies STUDENT TOUR and THE GAY DIVORCEE (1934). Sang with Jay Whidden band awhile on west coast. Another sizable role with Wheeler & Woolsey in THE NITWITS (1935). Secondary roles in several movie musicals later 30s, sometimes performed feature number. In 1937 sang with John Payne on radio show Song Time on the West Coast. Much publicity from marriage to former child star Jackie Coogan December 1937; divorced 1940. Starred in low-budget films 1938-9, still not star. Good role in Broadway musical DUBARRY WAS A LADY (1939), won acclaim.

Returned to Hollywood 1940; true star in big movie musical DOWN ARGENTINE WAY. Got break in this and several other 20th Century-Fox movies when star Alice Faye ill. Thereafter Betty in top films, mostly musicals, quickly became a leading star. Married bandleader Harry James July 1943. During World War II top pin-up girl of armed forces; almost two million copies of famous pose in white bathing suit sent to GIs. In movies mostly with Don Ameche, John Payne, Dan Dailey, Dick Haymes, Victor Mature. Among best: MOON OVER MIAMI (1941), SPRINGTIME IN THE ROCKIES (1942), THE DOLLY SISTERS (with June Haver) and DIAMOND HORSESHOE (1945), WHEN MY BABY SMILES AT ME (1948), WABASH AVENUE (1950). During 50s less active in movies. Some TV and night club work, also toured with husband Harry James's band. Divorced James 1964. In 1965 starred in long-running version of stage musical HELLO, DOLLY! in Las Vegas and on tour. In 1967 played same role on Broadway, one of several replacements for original star Carol Channing. Unsuccessful show in London 1969. On TV and in stock companies occasionally in 60s and early 70s; still capable musical performer. Despite extensive musical activities, odd absence of Grable records. Her movie musicals antedated vogue of movie soundtracks on LP. One record with Harry James band under name of Ruth Haag.

MOVIES
(excluding bit roles)

1932—HOLD 'EM JAIL!

1935—THE NITWITS; OLD MAN RHYTHM
1936—COLLEGIATE; FOLLOW THE FLEET; DON'T TURN 'EM LOOSE; PIGSKIN PARADE
1937—THIS WAY PLEASE
1938—COLLEGE SWING; GIVE ME A SAILOR; THRILL OF A LIFETIME; CAMPUS CONFESSIONS
1939—MAN ABOUT TOWN; MILLION DOLLAR LEGS; THE DAY THE BOOKIES WEPT
1940—DOWN ARGENTINE WAY; TIN PAN ALLEY
1941—MOON OVER MIAMI; A YANK IN THE R.A.F.; I WAKE UP SCREAMING
1942—FOOTLIGHT SERENADE; SONG OF THE ISLANDS; SPRINGTIME IN THE ROCKIES
1943—CONEY ISLAND; SWEET ROSIE O'GRADY
1944—FOUR JILLS IN A JEEP; PIN-UP GIRL
1945—THE DOLLY SISTERS; DIAMOND HORSESHOE
1947—MOTHER WORE TIGHTS; THE SHOCKING MISS PILGRIM
1948—THAT LADY IN ERMINE; WHEN MY BABY SMILES AT ME
1949—THE BEAUTIFUL BLONDE FROM BASHFUL BEND
1950—WABASH AVENUE; MY BLUE HEAVEN
1951—CALL ME MISTER; MEET ME AFTER THE SHOW
1953—THE FARMER TAKES A WIFE; HOW TO MARRY A MILLIONAIRE
1955—THREE FOR THE SHOW; HOW TO BE VERY, VERY POPULAR

RECORDS
(as vocalist)

HARRY JAMES
   Co 36867 I Can't Begin to Tell You (pseudonym: RUTH HAAG)

LP
Curtain Calls 100-5 (soundtracks)

699. GRACE, TEDDY   VO
Husky-voiced singer with jazz-influenced phrasing and style, most active in 30s. With Mal Hallett band 1937. Freelanced and recorded under own name with jazz combos. Outstanding with Bob Crosby mid-1939 to end of year. Unfortunately, fine singing failed to click nationally. Active into 40s.

RECORDS

MAL HALLETT

De 1167 The Trouble with Me Is You/I've Got Rain in My Eyes
De 1190 Rockin' Chair Swing
De 1270 Turn Off the Moon
De 1281 The You and Me That Used to Be
De 1282 Alibi Baby
De 1384 Turn on That Red Hot Heat
De 1403 Life of the Party
De 1532 I Want a New Romance
De 1533 You're Out of This World to Me

BOB CROSBY

De 2657 Over the Rainbow/You and Your Love
De 2734 Blue Orchids
De 2776 The Little Man Who Wasn't There
De 2812 I Thought About You
De 2824 Happy Birthday to Love
De 2839 Angry/It's a Whole New Thing
De 2924 The Little Red Fox
De 2935 I Wanna Wrap You Up

MILT HERTH TRIO

De 3284 Down South

TEDDY GRACE

De 1398 Rock It for Me/I'm Losing My Mind Over You
De 1524 Goodbye Jonah/Tears in My Heart
De 1602 I've Taken a Fancy to You/I'll Never Let You Cry
De 2050 Love Me or Leave Me/Crazy Blues
De 2128 Monday Morning/Down-hearted Blues
De 2602-3-4-5-6 (blues songs)
De 3202 Let There Be Love/Left All Alone with the Blues
De 3203 Thunder in My Heart/I Love You Much Too Much
De 3428 I'm the Lonesomest Gal in Town/See What the Boys in the Back Room Will Have
De 3463 Sing (It's Good for Ya)/Gee, But I Hate to Go Home Alone

700. GRAPPELLY, STEPHANE
v p cm B
Born January 26, 1908, Paris, France
Outstanding jazz violinist, noted for 30s work with great guitarist Django Reinhardt in Quintet of the Hot Club of France. Swinging, sweet-toned style, great technique and finesse, very tasteful. Studied and worked as classical violinist early in career, turned to jazz about 1927. Played with and led groups before teaming with Reinhardt 1934. They remained together through 1939; Quintet popular, famous hot combo with substantial record output on foreign labels (later issued in U.S.). Grappelly's violin one of two features of group's sound; Grappelly also chief arranger and organizer. Grappelly settled in England 1940-8, led combos, sometimes played piano. Worked with pianist George Shearing at times. Returned to Paris 1948, worked mostly there, at times in other countries. Active through 50s and 60s. Played in England in 70s. Able to absorb progressive jazz into later playing.
(See DJANGO REINHARDT biography herein for list of Grappelly co-compositions.)

RECORDS

QUINTET OF THE HOT CLUB OF FRANCE

Roy 1753 Dinah/Tiger Rag
Roy 1780 Avalon/Sweet Sue
Roy 1788 Smoke Rings/Confessin'
Roy 1798 Chasing Shadows/I've Had My Moments
Vs 8380 Tiger Rag/Your Sweet Smile
Vi 25511 Limehouse Blues/After You've Gone
Vi 25558 Nagasaki/Shine
Vi 25601 Swing Guitars
Vi 26506 Oriental Shuffle/Are You in the Mood?
Vi 26578 Georgia on My Mind/In the Still of the Night
Vi 26733 Exactly Like You/You're Driving Me Crazy
Vi 40-0123 Ain't Misbehavin'/When Day Is Done
Vi 40-0124 Solitude/Runnin' Wild
Vi 40-0125 Miss Annabelle Lee/Mystery Pacific
De 23021 Limehouse Blues / I've Found a New Baby
De 23262 Them There Eyes/Swing 39
Sw(Fr) 23 Minor Swing / Viper's Dream
Sw(Fr) 40 Paramount Stomp/Swinging with Django

HMV(E) 8669 Solitude/When Day Is
    Done
HMV(E) 8718 Rose Room/Tears
De(E) 6616 Night and Day/Stompin'
    at Decca
De(E) 6639 Honeysuckle Rose/Souve-
    nirs
De(E) 7027 Jeepers Creepers/Swing 39
BILL COLEMAN
Sw(Fr) 9 Rose Room/The Merry-Go-
    Round Broke Down
Sw(Fr) 22 Bill Street Blues/After
    You've Gone
Sw(Fr) 42 Indiana
STEPHANE GRAPPELLY
De(E) 5780 Limehouse Blues/I Got
    Rhythm
De(E) 5824 China Boy/St. Louis Blues
De(E) 7570 Stephane's Tune/After
    You've Gone
De(E) 8204 The Folks Who Live on
    the Hill/Liza
De(E) 8375 Star Eyes/Heavenly Music
De(E) 8451 Star Dust/Au Revoir
Lon(E) 101 Don't You Know I
    Care?/No One Else Will Do
Lon(E) 154 Star Eyes/That Old Black
    Magic
Lon(E) 155 Confessin'/Heavenly Music

LPs

STEPHANE GRAPPELLY
Atl 1391 Finesse Plus Feeling Equals
    Jazz
EmArcy MG-36120 (modern jazz
    style)
QUINTET OF HOT CLUB OF FRANCE
Ace of Clubs(E) ACL-1158 Django
    Reinhardt-Stephane Grappelly
Pres 7614 First Recordings!
Pres 7633 With American Jazz Greats
DeE ECM-2051 Swing '35-'39
GNP Crescendo(E) 9001
GNP Crescendo(E) 9002 Parisian
    Swing
DJANGO REINHARDT
Period 2204 Best of Django
Reprise 96075 The Immortal Django
    Reinhardt
Cap T-10457 The Best of Django Rein-
    hardt, Vol. 1
GARY BURTON-STEPHANE GRAPPELLY
Atl SD-1597 (S) Paris Encounter

701. GRASS, CLIFF   vo as cl

Featured vocalist with Gray Gordon
band late 30s. Military service, World
War II. After discharge joined Guy Lombardo 1945 as sideman-vocalist, continued into 50s.

RECORDS

GRAY GORDON
Bb 7775 When a Prince of a Fella
    Meets a Cinderella
Bb 7784 For the First Time
Bb 7838 There's Something About an
    Old Love/Blue in the Black of the
    Night
Bb 7854 Sixty Seconds Got Together
Bb 10020 After Looking at You/I
    Kissed You in a Dream Last Night
Bb 10142 It's All So New to Me/The
    Moon Is a Silver Dream
Bb 10575 Gone with the Wind/'Way
    Back in 1939 A.D.
Vi 26193 Sing a Song of Sunbeams/
    Hang Your Heart on a Hickory
    Limb
Vi 26200 You're So Desirable/I Can't
    Get You Out of My Mind
Vi 26253 If I Didn't Care
Vi 26270 Stay in My Arms, Cinder-
    ella/You Are My Dream
Vi 26282 An Old Fashioned Tune Al-
    ways Is New/Song of the Metro-
    nome
Vi 26350 It's Funny to Everyone but
    Me/Lingering on Your Doorstep
Vi 26404 Bless You/I Like to Recog-
    nize the Tune

LP

GUY LOMBARDO
De DL-74430 (S) Golden Folk Songs
    for Dancing

702. GRAY, ALEXANDER   vo

Singing star of Broadway shows in 20s
and early movie musicals. Started at odd
jobs, studied singing. In ZIEGFELD FOLLIES
OF 1922. Starring roles in Broadway
shows ANNIE DEAR (1924), TELL ME MORE
(1925), THE MERRY WORLD and NAUGHTY
RIQUETTE (1926). In vaudeville and various concert productions. In star-studded
movie revue SHOW OF SHOWS (1929).
Starred in SALLY, SONG OF THE FLAME,
VIENNESE NIGHTS and NO, NO, NANETTE

(1930). Movie career faded when Hollywood downplayed musicals 1931-2. Supporting role in movie MOONLIGHT AND PRETZELS (1933). Active on 30s radio: Chesterfield show 1932, Voice of America 1934, Chrysler show with Mark Warnow Orchestra 1936, others.

RECORDS

ALEXANDER GRAY
  Co 368-D Tell Me More/Three Times a Day
  Co 427-D What a World This Would Be/Remembering You

703. GRAY, DOLORES   VO

Born June 7, 1924, Chicago, Ill.

Good singer, excellent showman, talented dancer of stage-movies-radio-TV. Grew up on west coast, studied voice. Early in career sang on Rudy Vallee radio show awhile, worked clubs. Small roles in Broadway shows of mid-40s SEVEN LIVELY ARTS and ARE YOU WITH IT?. Sang on Wayne King radio show 1945. Lead role in show ANNIE GET YOUR GUN several seasons in London. Starred in Broadway musicals TWO ON THE AISLE (1951), CARNIVAL IN FLANDERS (1953), DESTRY RIDES AGAIN (1959). Active in early 50s TV, own show. In movies IT'S ALWAYS FAIR WEATHER and KISMET (1955), THE OPPOSITE SEX (1956), DESIGNING WOMAN (1957).

RECORDS

DOLORES GRAY
  De 27832 Shrimp Boats/More, More, More!
  De 27942 I've Got a Feelin' You're Foolin'/Did Anyone Call?
  De 28032 Beware/Frankie
  De 28051 To Be Loved by You/If Someone Had Told Me
  De 28109 Lost in Loveliness/In Paris and in Love
  De 28178 The World Has a Promise/Tattered and Torn
  De 28469 I Don't Care/Two Other People
  De 28676 Big Mamou/Say You're Mine Again
  De 28755 Call of the Far-Away Hills/Darling, the Moon Is Bright Tonight

  De 28783 L-O-V-E/That's Love, I Guess
  De 29031 Sweet Cheat/Flowers for the Lady

LPs

DOLORES GRAY
  Cap T-897 Warm Brandy
(original Broadway casts)
  De DL-8040 TWO ON THE AISLE
  De DL-9075 DESTRY RIDES AGAIN
(movie soundtrack)
  MGM E-3281 KISMET

704. GRAY, GILDA
(MARIANNE MICHAELSKA)

Born c. 1898
Died 1959

Stage performer, including Broadway musicals. Famed as leading exponent of shimmy, dance originating on San Francisco's Barbary Coast. Introduced in New York 1918, considered risque. Miss Gray famous for her version, built career on it. Featured in Broadway shows HELLO, ALEXANDER (1919), SHUBERT'S GAIETIES OF 1919, SNAPSHOTS OF 1921, ZIEGFELD FOLLIES OF 1922—sensation in latter. Top performer in 20s vaudeville. In silent movies. Supporting role in 1936 movie musical ROSE-MARIE.

705. GRAY, GLEN   as B
(GLEN GRAY "SPIKE" KNOBLAUGH)

Born June 7, 1906, Roanoke or Metamora, Ill.
Died August 23, 1963, Plymouth, Mass.

Leader of popular Casa Loma Orchestra in 30s and 40s, a riff-styled swing band that also emphasized ballads—increasingly in later years. Attended Illinois Wesleyan College awhile. Early in musical career with Jean Goldkette unit called the Orange Blossom Band. In 1928 group played the Casa Loma, palace-type building in Toronto originally built to accommodate King and Queen on visit from England, then converted into hotel. Band well received but hotel folded. Band later adopted name Casa Loma Orchestra for jobs in Detroit and environs. Early band members Pee Wee Hunt (tb), Billy Rauch (tb), Joe Hall (p), Gene Gifford (g ar), Pat Davis (ts). Henry Biagini fronted band. In 1929 band reorganized as corporation with Gray president and leader. But for years Gray sat in sax section as violinist Mel Jenssen fronted band. Vocalist-saxman Kenny Sargent joined in 1931, became a top romantic vocalist through 30s into early 40s. Pee Wee Hunt handled novelty and rhythm vocals, jazz trombone. Key jazzmen Clarence Hutchenrider (cl), Grady Watts (t) and Sonny Dunham (t) joined 1931. Pat Davis (ts) hot soloist, Billy Rauch (tb) featured on lead and sweet solos.

Band played New York late 1929, recorded hot numbers for Okeh, began to attract attention. In early 30s began prolific, popular recordings for Brunswick. Gene Gifford was chief arranger 1930-5, responsible for band's style: riff arrangements on swing numbers, intimate moods and danceable arrangements on ballads. Gifford's jazz compositions important to band, helped usher in swing era. Included *Casa Loma Stomp*, *Black Jazz*, *White Jazz*, *Dance of the Lame Duck*, *Maniac's Ball*. Needed much rehearsing because of intricate writing and fast tempos. Gifford wrote band's beautiful theme *Smoke Rings*, featuring Rauch's smooth trombone and Hutchenrider's nervous, reedy clarinet. In late 1934-1936 band on Camel Caravan radio show with comedian Walter O'Keefe, greatly expanded its following. In 1938 band on Burns & Allen radio show.

Gray began fronting band early 1937. Later star Murray McEachern (tb as). Later arrangers Larry Clinton, Dick Jones and Larry Wagner. Eugenie Baird vocalist in early 40s. Red Nichols and Bobby Hackett joined during wartime for short periods. Big record hits *Sunrise Serenade* 1939 and *No Name Jive* 1940 (Larry Wagner cm-ar). Recordings flowed through the years; band switched to Decca late 1934. In movies TIME OUT FOR RHYTHM (1941) and GALS, INC. (1943). Gray retired 1950, came back in 1956 to launch a series of LPs using all-star sidemen recreating sounds of big bands. Musicianship magnificent; records acclaimed by fans and critics.

RECORDS

GLEN GRAY & THE CASA LOMA ORCHESTRA
OK 41403 China Girl/San Sue Strut
OK 41476 Alexander's Ragtime Band/ Put on Your Old Grey Bonnet
OK 41477 Little Did I Know/Overnight
OK 41492 Casa Loma Stomp
Vi 24256 Casa Loma Stomp/Dardanella
Vi 24338 Lazybones / Sophisticated Lady
Br 6242 Black Jazz/Maniac's Ball
Br 6252 Rain on the Roof/Starlight
Br 6289 (theme) Smoke Rings/In the Still of the Night
Br 6486 The Lady from St. Paul/New Orleans
Br 6513 Blue Prelude/Dance of the Lame Duck
Br 6584 Love Is the Thing/Under a Blanket of Blue
Br 6588 Wild Goose Chase/Buji
Br 6611 Blue Jazz/White Jazz
Br 6626 It's the Talk of the Town/ That's How Rhythm Was Born
Br 6775 Carolina/A Hundred Years from Today
Br 6870 Moon Country / Ridin' Around in the Rain
Br 6937 Moonglow/You Ain't Been Living Right
Br 7521 Narcissus/Nocturne
De 200 Nagasaki/P.S., I Love You
De 312 Blue Moon/Where There's Smoke There's Fire
De 986 Shades of Hades/Royal Garden Blues
De 1412 For You/Casa Loma Stomp
De 1473 (theme) Smoke Rings/Always
De 1672 Memories of You/Nutty Nursery Rhymes
De 2292 I Won't Believe It/Could Be
De 2321 Sunrise Serenade/Heaven Can Wait
De 2394-5-6-7-8-9 (Hoagy Carmichael Songs)
De 2777 Tumbling Tumbleweeds/ Through
De 3089 No Name Jive (1 & 2)
De 3261 When Buddha Smiles/Coral Sea
De 4048 City Called Heaven/I Found You in the Rain

De 18479 Don't Do It, Darling/Don't Get Around Much Anymore
De 18596 Sure Thing/Suddenly It's Spring

LPs

GLEN GRAY & THE CASA LOMA ORCHESTRA
Ha HL-7045 The Great Recordings of Glen Gray (Br RIs)
De DL-8570 (De RIs)
De(10″)DL-5089 Musical Smoke Rings (De RIs)
Cor(10″)CRL-56006 Hoagy Carmichael Songs (De RIs)

GLEN GRAY
Cap W-747 Casa Loma in Hi-Fi!
Cap T-1022 Sounds of the Great Bands, Vol. 1
Cap T-1067 Sounds of the Great Bands, Vol. 2
Cap T-1234 Solo Spotlight
Cap T-1506 Please, Mr. Gray
Cap T-1588 Sounds of the Great Casa Loma Band

706. GRAY, JERRY   v acc ar cm B
(real name GRAZIANO)

Born July 3, 1915, Boston, Mass.

Talented arranger especially noted for work with 1938-39 Artie Shaw band and Glenn Miller band 1939-42, also with Miller AAF band. Later prominent as leader of band featuring Miller style. Led local band as youngster, studied arranging. First important job in Artie Shaw's 1936 string band, rejoined 1938 as chief arranger. Wrote famous arrangement *Begin the Beguine*, Shaw's breakthrough 1938-39 hit. Arranged for Andre Kostelanetz. Joined Glenn Miller late 1939 as arranger, scored and composed some of band's hits: *A String of Pearls, Sun Valley Jump, The Spirit Is Willing, Here We Go Again, I Dreamt I Dwelt in Harlem, Pennsylvania 6-5000, Caribbean Clipper*. After Miller disbanded late 1942, Gray freelanced, arranged for Jerry Wald 1943. With Miller arranging for AAF band, went overseas. After Miller's death late 1945, band led by Gray and drummer Ray McKinley. In post-war 40s resumed arranging work in U.S., served as musical director on Philip Morris, Bob Crosby,

Patti Clayton radio shows. In 1950 led band on radio and toured. Big year in 1951, played Club 15 radio show with top personnel 1951-2. Upon revival of Miller style in early 50s, sparked by success of Ralph Flanagan, Gray climbed on bandwagon. Hired Wilbur Schwartz, Miller's star lead clarinetist. Gray's arrangements captured true Miller sound. Recorded frequently in 50s, occasionally backed singers on records. Band continued into mid-60s. Gray settled in California for studio work as arranger-composer, occasionally fronted band. In recent years led band in Dallas. Other Gray compositions *Crew Cut, V Hop, Jeep Jockey Jump, Flag Waver, Introduction to a Waltz*.

ARRANGEMENTS

ARTIE SHAW
Begin the Beguine; What Is This Thing Called Love?; Softly, as in a Morning Sunrise; most others 1938-9

GLENN MILLER
Wonderful One; Make Believe Ballroom Time; The Gaucho Serenade; Beautiful Ohio; Tuxedo Junction; I'll Never Smile Again; Starlight and Music; My! My!; Sierra Sue; Polka Dots and Moonbeams; Boog-It; Anvil Chorus; The One I Love; I Dreamt I Dwelt in Harlem; The Spirit Is Willing; The Air-Minded Executive; The Booglie Wooglie Piggy; Chattanooga Choo Choo; I Know Why (with BILL FINEGAN); Adios; Elmer's Tune; Dreamsville, Ohio; Blue Evening; A String of Pearls; American Patrol; Moonlight Cocktail; Happy in Love; Sweet Eloise; The White Cliffs of Dover; I've Got a Gal in Kalamazoo; Juke Box Saturday Night; Here We Go Again; A Pink Cocktail for a Blue Lady; Caribbean Clipper

RECORDS

JERRY GRAY
De 24956 Star Dust/All the Things You Are
De 24980 Blue Skies/This Can't Be Love

De 24995 Night and Day/What Is This Thing Called Love?

De 27177 In the Mood/A String of Pearls

De 27402 Would I Love You/Say It with Your Kisses

De 27570 Johnson Rag/Farewell Blues

De 27621 Re-stringing the Pearls/Tell Me

De 27866 Jeep Jockey Jump/St. Louis Blues

De 27868 Flag Waver/Shine On Harvest Moon

De 27869 Introduction to a Waltz/V Hop

De 27976 Unforgettable/A Garden in the Rain

De 28782 A Pair of Trumpets/One-Stop Boogie

De 29038 Coronado Cruise/Stop That Dancing

(as conductor)

VIC DAMONE
Mer 5053 I Have but One Heart/Ivy

ROBERTA LEE
De 28520 Do You Know Why?/Hold Me, Thrill Me, Kiss Me

JANE FROMAN
Maj 1048 You, So It's You/Linger in My Arms a Little Longer, Baby
Maj 1049 I Got Lost in His Arms/Millionaires Don't Whistle

LPs

JERRY GRAY
De(10″)DL-5266 Dance to the Music of Jerry Gray & His Orchestra
De(10″)DL-5312 In the Mood
De(10″)DL-5375 A Tribute to Glenn Miller
Vo 3602 A Tribute to Glenn Miller
Golden Tone C-4005 Plays Glenn Miller Favorites
WB 1446 (with PIED PIPERS)

ARTIE SHAW
Epic LN-3112 With Strings (Br, Vo RIs)
Vi VPM-6039 This Is Artie Shaw

GLENN MILLER
Vi LSP-3377 The Best of Glenn Miller
Vi LSP-3564 The Best of Glenn Miller, Vol. 2
Vi LSP-4125 The Best of Glenn Miller, Vol. 3

707. GRAY, WARDELL   ts cl B

Born 1921, Oklahoma City, Okla.
Died May 25, 1955, Las Vegas, Nev.

Outstanding bop tenor sax star in 40s and 50s. Clean tone, cool, driving style, fertile ideas, good taste. Grew up in Detroit; first jobs there. With Earl Hines 1943-5. Settled in Los Angeles; with Benny Carter, Billy Eckstine, Al Killian and Gene Norman's "Just Jazz" concerts. To New York 1948 with Benny Goodman Septet. Later in year with Tadd Dameron and Count Basie. With Goodman's big band about a year, late 1948-9. With Count Basie combo and big band 1950-1. In late 1951 again settled on west coast, led groups, freelanced. Last job with Benny Carter in Las Vegas. Body found with neck broken in field outside of town. Mystery surrounding death never cleared up, but drugs suspected.

RECORDS

EARL HINES
JS(Fr) 617 Blue Keys/Let's Get Started

COUNT BASIE
Co 39406 Little Pony

BENNY GOODMAN SEXTET
Cap 57-621 Oo-Bla-Dee/Bedlam
Cap 10173 Stealin' Apples (SEPTET)
Cap 60009 Blue Lou/There's a Small Hotel (QUARTET)

TEDDY CHARLES
Pres 889 So Long, Broadway

CHARLIE PARKER
Dial 1012 Relaxin' at Camarillo
Dial 1013 Cheers/Carving the Bird

AL HAIG
Seeco 10-002 Sugar Hill Bop/Five Star
Seeco 10-003 In a Pinch/It's the Talk of the Town

J. C. HEARD
Apo 783 Ollopa/This Is It
Apo 790 Sugar Hips/Coastin' with J.C.

TADD DAMERON
BN 559 Lady Bird/Jahbero
BN 1564 Symphonette

GENE NORMAN'S "JUST JAZZ"
Vogue 2022 Hot House (1 & 2)
Mod Holly 641 One O'clock Jump/Two O'clock Jump

DEXTER GORDON-WARDELL GRAY
Bop 102 The Hunt (1 & 2)

WARDELL GRAY
NJ 817 Easy Living/Twisted
Pres 714 Blue Gray/Treadin' with Treadwell
Pres 723 Greyhound/A Sinner Kissed an Angel
Pres 778 Jazz on Sunset (1 & 2)
Pres 840 Bright Boy/April Skies

LPs

WARDELL GRAY
Pres 7343 (2-LP set) Memorial Album (RIs)
Pres(10″)115 Tenor Sax Favorites
Cr 5004 Way Out Wardell
GENE NORMAN'S "JUST JAZZ"
Vogue(E) LDE-101
Vogue(E) LAE-12001
LOUIS BELLSON
Cap(10″)H-348
FATS NAVARRO
BN(10″)5004
(miscellaneous artists)
Mod Rec LMP-1202 Groovin' High

708. GRAYSON, KATHRYN   vo
(ZELMA KATHRYN HEDRICK)

Born February 9, 1922, Winston Salem, N.C.

Singing star of 40s and 50s movies. Clear soprano, capable on classical and pop numbers. Grew up in St. Louis and Hollywood. In late 30s sang on Eddie Cantor radio show. In ANDY HARDY'S PRIVATE SECRETARY in 1941. Beauty and singing quickly established her as star. In quality movie musicals for MGM, several with Frank Sinatra. Mario Lanza began career in her 1949 movie THAT MIDNIGHT KISS; they co-starred in TOAST OF NEW ORLEANS in 1950. Best work in important movie musicals of 50s. Portrayed opera star Grace Moore in SO THIS IS LOVE in 1953. After movie career ended 1956, at intervals played night clubs, concerts and on stage. In 1963 toured in musical CAMELOT.

MOVIES

1941—ANDY HARDY'S PRIVATE SECRETARY; THE VANISHING VIRGINIAN
1942—RIO RITA; SEVEN SWEETHEARTS
1943—THOUSANDS CHEER
1945—ANCHORS AWEIGH
1946—TWO SISTERS FROM BOSTON; ZIEGFELD FOLLIES

1947—TILL THE CLOUDS ROLL BY; IT HAPPENED IN BROOKLYN
1948—THE KISSING BANDIT
1949—THAT MIDNIGHT KISS
1950—GROUNDS FOR MARRIAGE; TOAST OF NEW ORLEANS
1951—SHOW BOAT
1952—LOVELY TO LOOK AT
1953—THE DESERT SONG; SO THIS IS LOVE; KISS ME, KATE
1956—THE VAGABOND KING

RECORDS

KATHRYN GRAYSON
MGM 30073 My Heart Sings/Jealousy
MGM 30133 Love Is Where You Find It/Why Didn't He Kiss Me?
MGM 30232 Lover, Come Back to Me/You Are Love

LPs

KATHRYN GRAYSON
Lion L-70055 Kathryn Grayson
KATHRYN GRAYSON-TONY MARTIN
Vi(10″)LPM-3105 THE DESERT SONG
(movie soundtracks)
MGM E-3077 KISS ME, KATE
MGM(10″)E-150 LOVELY TO LOOK AT
MGM E-559 SHOW BOAT

709. GRECO, BUDDY   p vo ar B
(ARMANDO GRECO)

Born August 14, 1926, Philadelphia, Pa.

Jazz-styled singer of 50s and 60s. Could have had career as good modern jazz pianist but turned to singing as single. As teenager led trio locally from middle to late 40s. Joined Benny Goodman late 1948 as pianist-vocalist, remained a year, did some arranging for band. He and Goodman to England in summer 1949 to perform with English musicians at London's Palladium. In early 50s led combo, then concentrated on career as singer. Played clubs and recorded. Many appearances on TV in later 50s and 60s, own summer series. Popular into 70s, turned mostly to contemporary music.

RECORDS

BENNY GOODMAN
Cap 57-568 Having a Wonderful Wish/Shishkabop
Cap 57-621 Oo-Bla-Dee/Bedlam (both SEXTET)

Cap 828 Little Girl, Don't Cry/Spin a Record
Cap 860 It Isn't Fair/You're Always There
Cap 15409 Ma Belle Marguerite/Undercurrent Blues
Cap 60009 Blue Lou (SEXTET)/There's a Small Hotel (QUARTET)

BUDDY GRECO

Lon 558 Dear Hearts and Gentle People/Fiesta in Old Mexico
Lon 855 I Can't Give You Anything but Love/You Meet the Nicest People in Your Dreams
Lon 894 Honey Hush/Keepin' Out of Mischief Now
Lon 950 Stella by Starlight/Jitterbug Waltz
Mus 569 Baby I'm True to You
Cor 60573 I Ran All the Way Home/The Glory of Love
Cor 61038 Don't Say Goodbye

LPs

BUDDY GRECO

Kapp KL-1033 Broadway Melodies: Songs from the Hit Shows
Epic LN-3771 Buddy's Back in Town
Epic LN-3793 I Like It Swinging
Epic LN-24043 Buddy's Greatest Hits
Epic LN-24057 Sings for Intimate Moments
Ha HL-11248 You're Something Else
Reprise S-6220 (S) With Big Bands and Ballads
Reprise S-6230 (S) In a Brand New Bag
Reprise S-6256 (S) Away We Go

710. GREEN, ADOLPH   lyr vo

Born December 2, 1915, New York, N.Y.

Important lyricist beginning mid-40s. Teamed with Betty Comden to write lyrics and book for major Broadway musicals. Duo joined composers Jule Styne and Leonard Bernstein for several successful scores. Green attended CCNY. Role in road show of HAVING WONDERFUL TIME. Teamed with Miss Comden and young actress Judy Holliday to perform at Village Vanguard in New York late 30s. Later performed at Rainbow Room and Blue Angel, both in New York.

Lyricist for 1974 revival of Broadway musical LORELEI.

(See biography herein on BETTY COMDEN for details on Comden-Green career, show and song listings.)

711. GREEN, BENNY   tb B

Born April 16, 1923, Chicago, Ill.

Good modern jazz trombonist with ability to play any style. Swinging, tasteful, interesting soloist. Joined Earl Hines late 1942 for first big job, remained a year until military service. Rejoined Hines mid-1946 to early 1948. With Gene Ammons awhile later in year. With Charlie Ventura late 1948-50, gained first real attention. Periods again with Hines in early 50s. 1952 in Illinois Jacquet big band. Again with Ventura 1953. Since late 1953 mostly led combo and freelanced. Semi-active in music in later 50s and 60s.

RECORDS

EARL HINES

JS(Fr) 611 Spooks Ball
JS(Fr) 614 Trick a Track
JS(Fr) 618 Throwin' the Switch

J. C. HEARD

Apo 783 Ollopa/This Is It
Apo 790 Sugar Hips/Coastin' with J.C.

CHARLIE VENTURA

Nat 7015 How High the Moon
Nat 9055 Euphoria
Nat 9066 Pina Colada
Vi 20-3552 Boptura/Yankee Clipper

FLIP PHILLIPS

Mer 8908 This Can't Be Love/Cookie

BENNY GREEN

Pres 773 Flowing River/Green Junction
Pres 790 Serenade to Love/There's a Small Hotel
Pres 847 Star Dust/Embraceable You
Pres 908 Bennie's Pennies/Whirl-a-Licks
Pres 920 Tenor Sax Shuffle/Sugar Syrup
De 29152 I Wanna Blow/People Will Say We're in Love

LPs

BENNY GREEN

VJ 1005 The Swingin'est
Jazzland 943 (S) Glidin' Along

Pres 7052 Blows His Horn
Pres 7776 The Best of Benny Green
Pres(10″)123 (one side) Modern Jazz
 Trombones, Vol. 2
Time 52021
Enrica 2002 Swings the Blues

CHARLIE VENTURA
 Vi LPM-1135 It's All Bop to Me
 EmArcy MG-36015 Jumping with
  Ventura (Nat RIs)

JO JONES
 Jazztone J-1242 The Jo Jones Special

BUCK CLAYTON
 Co CL-701 Jumpin' at the Woodside

EARL HINES
 Vogue(E) EPV-1059
(miscellaneous artists)
 VJ 3024 Juggin' Around

712. GREEN, BUD   lyr

Born November 19, 1897, Austria

Lyricist of 20s and 30s. Best-known songs
*Alabamy Bound, That's My Weakness
Now, I'll Always Be in Love with You,
Once in Awhile, The Flat Foot Floogie,
Sentimental Journey.* Brought to U.S. as
infant, grew up in New York. Staff writer
for publishing companies 1920-8, then
formed own company. Wrote special ma-
terial for vaudeville performers including
singers Cecil Lean, Winnie Lightner, Cleo
Mayfield, Sophie Tucker. Collaborators
Ray Henderson, Sam H. Stept, Harry
Warren. Author of book *Writing Songs for
Fame and Fortune.*

SONGS
(with related shows)

1923—Whose Izzy Is He?
1924—Alabamy Bound
1925—I Love My Baby
1926—Ya Gotta Know How to Love
1927—Away Down South in Heaven
1928—That's My Weakness Now
1929—SYNCOPATION movie (I'll Always
 Be in Love with You; Do Something); Good Little Bad Little You
1930—Congratulations
1931—Why Did It Have to Be Me?
1933—SHADY LADY stage show (Swingy
 Little Thingy; Isn't It Swell to
 Dream?; Live, Laugh and Love)
1935—You Fit into the Picture
1936—You're Too Good to Be True

1937—Once in Awhile; You Showed Me
 the Way
1938—Day After Day; The Flat Foot
 Floogie; More Than Ever
1939—After All; If You Ever Change
 Your Mind
1940—Honestly; The Man Who Comes
 Around
1942—On the Old Assembly Line
1944—Sentimental Journey

Other songs: *Oh Boy, What a Girl; In My
Gondola; My Mother's Evening Prayer;
Dream Sweetheart; Blue Fedora; Moon-
light on the River; Speed Limit; Who Can
Tell?; Tia Juana; All the Days of Our
Years; My Number One Dream Came
True*

713. GREEN, CHARLIE   tb

Born c. 1900, Omaha, Neb.
Died February 1936, New York, N.Y.;
 froze to death

Early jazz trombonist with big tone,
broad glissandi, gutty blues style. Worked
locally early 20s, toured with carnivals.
Joined Fletcher Henderson in New York
mid-1924, remained two years. Based in
New York most of career. Recorded with
many blues singers in 20s. With June
Clark band awhile in 1927. With Fats
Waller briefly, jobs with Henderson at
intervals. In 1929 with Zutty Singleton
and Benny Carter. In early 30s periods
with Henderson, Elmer Snowden, Chick
Webb, Jimmie Noone, McKinney's Cotton Pickers, Carter. In 1935 with Louis
Metcalf and Kaiser Marshall. Unable to
get in to his home, spent night outside on
doorstep, died tragically from freezing.

RECORDS

FLETCHER HENDERSON
 Co 395-D Sugar Foot Stomp/What-
  Cha-Call-'Em Blues
 Co 509-D T.N.T./Carolina Stomp
 Vo 14880 A New Kind of Man/The
  Meanest Kind o' Blues
 Vo 14926 Words/Copenhagen
 Vo 14935 Shanghai Shuffle/Naughty
  Man
 Para 20367 Prince of Wails/Mandy,
  Make Up Your Mind
PERRY BRADFORD
 Vo 15165 Lucy Long/I Ain't Gonna

Play No Second Fiddle

DIXIE STOMPERS

Ha 70 Spanish Shawl/Clap Hands! Here Comes Charley

Ha 88 Florida Stomp/Get It Fixed

Ha 153 Nervous Charlie Stomp/Black Horse Stomp

DIXIE WASHBOARD BAND

Co 14171-D King of the Zulus/The Zulu Blues

SEVEN BROWN BABIES

Ajax 17009 Do Doodle Oom/West Indies Blues

Ajax 17011 Dicty Blues/Charleston Crazy

CLARENCE WILLIAMS

OK 8254 Squeeze Me

BESSIE SMITH

Co 14032-D Workhouse Blues/House Rent Blues

Co 14037-D Rainy Weather Blues/Salt Water Blues

Co 14051-D Dying Gambler Blues

Co 14075-D Yellow Dog Blues/Soft Pedal Blues

Co 14232-D Trombone Cholly

CLARA SMITH

Co 14077-D My John Blues

Co 14398-D It's Tight Like That/Daddy Don't Put That Thing on Me Blues

TRIXIE SMITH

Para 12256 Mining Camp Blues/You've Got to Beat Me to Keep Me

Para 12262 Railroad Blues/The World's Jazz Crazy and So Am I

LPs

BESSIE SMITH

Co G-30450 (2-LP set) Empty Bed Blues (Co RIs)

Co CL-855-8 (4-LP set) The Bessie Smith Story (Co RIs)

FLETCHER HENDERSON

Co C4L19 (4-LP set) A Study in Frustration (RIs)

714. GREEN, FREDDIE   g cm

Born March 31, 1911, Charleston, S.C.

Famed as consummate rhythm guitarist. Good chord structures and blend, crisp beat. Long with Count Basie band. Played without amplification, seldom soloed. As youngster he took a few les-sons on guitar, worked way to New York. Jazz buff-critic John Hammond heard Green in New York club, recommended him to Basie. Hired early 1937, final link in forging of Basie's great rhythm section. Other members Walter Page (b), Jo Jones (d) and Basie (p). Save for rare intervals, with Basie into 1973—remarkable tenure in field where frequent personnel changes are the rule. Prolific recording career with Basie and freelance. Composed jazz numbers including *Down for Double*, *Right On*, *Corner Pocket*.

RECORDS

COUNT BASIE

De 1363 One O'clock Jump/John's Idea

De 1880 Swinging the Blues/Sent for You Yesterday

De 2355 Boogie Woogie/How Long Blues (piano solos with rhythm acc.)

De 2498 The Dirty Dozens/When the Sun Goes Down (piano solos with rhythm acc.)

De 2631 You Can Depend on Me/Oh, Lady Be Good

De 2780 Oh! Red/Fare Thee Honey, Fare Thee Well (piano solos with rhythm acc.)

Vo 5169 Nobody Knows/Song of the Islands

Vo 5732 Moten Swing/Evenin'

OK 5987 Who Am I?/Stampede in G Minor

OK 6071 Tuesday at Ten/Undecided Blues

OK 6584 Down for Double/More Than You Know

Co 36709 Bugle Blues/Sugar Blues (both combos)

Co 36710 How Long Blues (piano solo with rhythm acc.)/Royal Garden Blues (combo)

Co 36990 High Tide/Lazy Lady Blues

Co 38888 The Golden Bullet/Bluebeard Blues

Vi 20-2693 My Buddy/Backstage at Stuff's

Vi 20-2695 I Never Knew/Basie's Basement

Clef 89120 Right On/Cherry Point

Clef 89162 April in Paris

MILDRED BAILEY
Vo 3615 If You Ever Should Leave/ Heaven Help This Heart of Mine
Vo 3626 The Moon Got in My Eyes/ It's the Natural Thing to Do

LIONEL HAMPTON
Vi 26557 Dinah/Singin' the Blues
Vi 26608 My Buddy

GLENN HARDMAN
Co 35341 China Boy/On the Sunny Side of the Street

BILLIE HOLIDAY
Vo 3593 Me, Myself and I/Without Your Love
Vo 3605 Born to Love/A Sailboat in the Moonlight
Vo 5302 You're a Lucky Guy/You're Just a No Account

KANSAS CITY FIVE/SIX
CMS 510 I Know That You Know/ Laughing at Life
CMS 512 Pagin' the Devil/'Way Down Yonder in New Orleans

PEE WEE RUSSELL
HRS 1002 I've Found a New Baby/ Everybody Loves My Baby

JOE SULLIVAN
Vo 5531 Solitude/Low Down Dirty Shame

TEDDY WILSON
Br 7824 He Ain't Got Rhythm/This Year's Kisses
Br 7911 Easy Living/Foolin' Myself
Br 8070 When You're Smiling/I Can't Believe That You're in Love with Me

LPs

FREDDIE GREEN
Vi LPM-1210 Mr. Rhythm

COUNT BASIE
Cam CAL-497 Basie's Basement (Vi RIs)
Epic LN-3169 Basie's Back in Town (Vo, OK RIs)
De DL-8049 Count Basie & His Orchestra (De RIs)
Co CL-754 Count Basie Classics (Co RIs)
Verve V-8687 Basie's Beat
Roul R-52024 Basie One More Time

BROTHER JOHN SELLERS
Vang(10")VRS-8005 Songs, Blues and Folk Songs

JOE NEWMAN
Vi LPM-1118 All I Wanna Do Is Swing

SELDON POWELL
Roost 2220 The Seldon Powell Sextet

LESTER YOUNG
Sav MG-12068 The Immortal Lester Young (Sav RIs)

JO JONES
Jazztone J-1242 The Jo Jones Special

715. GREEN, JOHNNY   cm ar p B
Born October 10, 1908, New York, N.Y.

Composer noted for great song *Body and Soul*. Other quality songs though not many. Capable pianist with good touch, style, chord structure. Important figure in movies as composer-arranger-conductor-musical director. Attended Harvard; some arranging-composing there. Summer arranging for Guy Lombardo. Took job awhile on Wall Street but soon concentrated on composing. First song hit *Coquette* 1928. Made name late 1930 when song *Body and Soul* featured by Libby Holman in Broadway show THREE'S A CROWD. Continued composing during 30s with excellent though modest output. In early 30s accompanist for singers Ethel Merman, Gertrude Lawrence, James Melton. Pianist for Leo Reisman early 30s. Some work for Paramount Pictures eastern branch as arranger-composer-conductor. In 1932 pianist and assistant director in Buddy Rogers band. Own band most of 1933-41. Theme *Body and Soul*. In 1934 own radio show, musical advisor for CBS. Led band on radio shows of Ruth Etting 1934, Ethel Merman 1935, Jack Benny 1935-6, Fred Astaire 1936-7, Philip Morris show 1939-40. Settled in movie studios 1942 as arranger-composer-conductor. Radio shows from Hollywood in 40s. Musical director of MGM 1949 into 60s. Figured in important movies in various capacities: BATHING BEAUTY (1944), WEEKEND AT THE WALDORF (1945), EASY TO WED (1946), FIESTA and SOMETHING IN THE WIND (1947), EASTER PARADE (1948), SUMMER STOCK (1950), AM AMERICAN IN PARIS, THE GREAT CARUSO, MR. IMPERIUM and ROYAL

WEDDING (1951), RHAPSODY and BRIG-
ADOON (1954), HIGH SOCIETY and MEET ME
IN LAS VEGAS (1956), RAINTREE COUNTY
(1957), PEPE (1960), WEST SIDE STORY
(1961), BYE BYE BIRDIE (1963). 1970 movie
THEY SHOOT HORSES, DON'T THEY?, story
of dance marathons of Depression era,
featured Green's beautiful 1934 song *Easy
Come, Easy Go* throughout. Sometimes on
TV as conductor of orchestra for Academy Awards. Background music for TV
series Empire. Guest conductor of symphony orchestras in various cities. Chief
collaborators lyricists Ed Heyman, Paul
Francis Webster, Mack David, Billy
Rose, Johnny Mercer.

SONGS
(with related shows)

1928—Coquette
1930—THREE'S A CROWD stage show
(Body and Soul); I'm Yours
1931—Out of Nowhere; I Don't Want
Love
1932—Living in Dreams; Rain, Rain, Go
Away
1933—MURDER AT THE VANITIES stage
show (Weep No More, My Baby);
I Wanna Be Loved; I Cover the
Waterfront; You're Mine, You
1934—THE COUNT OF MONTE CRISTO mov-
ie (The World Is Mine); Not Bad;
Repeal the Blues; Easy Come,
Easy Go; Oceans of Time
1936—I've Got a Heavy Date
1939—You and Your Love
1942—BEAT THE BAND unsuccessful stage
show (The Steam Is on the Beam;
Proud of You; Keep It Casual;
The Four Freedoms); Music for
Elizabeth (serious works for piano
and orchestra)
1947—SOMETHING IN THE WIND movie
(Something in the Wind; The
Turntable Song; You Wanna
Keep Your Baby Lookin' Right)
1957—RAINTREE COUNTY movie (The
Song of Raintree County; Never
Till Now)

RECORDS
JOHNNY GREEN ORCHESTRA
Br 6797 Cocktails for Two/Live and
Love Tonight

Br 6855 Easy Come, Easy Go/Repeal
the Blues
Br 7497 I Never Saw a Better Night/
Fruitas
Br 7521 Picture of Me without You/
Me and Marie
Br 7522 Why Shouldn't I?/When Love
Comes Your Way
Br 7661 I've Got a Heavy Date/
Pixilated Over You
Br 7892 SHALL WE DANCE? Medley (1
& 2)
Co 2940-D A New Moon Is Over My
Shoulder/By the Taj Mahal
Co 2943-D Two Cigarettes in the
Dark/The Fortune Teller
Co 2959-D Were You Foolin'?/The
World Is Mine
Co 2999-D Because of Once Upon a
Time/Tiny Little Fingerprints
Co 3022-D I Won't Dance/Lovely to
Look At
Co 3028-D Go into Your Dance/The
Little Things You Used to Do
Co 3029-D She's a Latin from Man-
hattan/About a Quarter to Nine
Roy 1839 Too Romantic/Sweet Potato
Piper
De 23531 I Cover the Waterfront/Co-
quette
MGM 11069 Easy Come, Easy Go
FRED ASTAIRE WITH JOHNNY GREEN OR-
CHESTRA
Br 7717 Pick Yourself Up/The Way
You Look Tonight
ETHEL MERMAN WITH JOHNNY GREEN OR-
CHESTRA
Br 6995 An Earful of Music/You're a
Builder Upper
Br 7342 You're the Top/I Get a Kick
Out of You
EZIO PINZA WITH JOHNNY GREEN ORCHES-
TRA
Vi 10-3391 Andiamo/Let Me Look at
You

LPs
JOHNNY GREEN
Vi LSP-6005 (2-LP set) An Evening
with Lerner & Loewe
Regent MG-6028 Out of Nowhere
De(10")DL-5203 Piano and Orchestra
(as conductor)

DANNY KAYE
Co(10″)CL-6023
FRED ASTAIRE
Epic LN-3137 The Best of Fred
Astaire (Br RIs)
(movie soundtracks)
MGM(10″)E-93 AN AMERICAN IN PARIS
MGM(10″)E-543 ROYAL WEDDING

716. GREEN, URBIE   tb B
Born August 8, 1926, Mobile, Ala.

Top modern trombonist, one of busiest of
freelance artists with prolific recording
career. Sometimes called modern Jack
Jenney because of similar warm, beautiful
tone and high register. Tasteful modern
style, astonishing virtuosity. Began in early 40s with Tommy Reynolds, Bob Strong
and Jan Savitt. With Frankie Carle 1945-
6 and Gene Krupa 1947-50. First prominent 1951-3 with Woody Herman. Left
Herman early 1953, freelanced in New
York. In 1954 with Lester Lanin, later in
year studio work. Joined Benny Goodman early 1955, remained a year. Special
jobs with Goodman in later 50s, 60s and
70s, including TV and foreign tours. Seen
and heard in 1956 movie THE BENNY
GOODMAN STORY. In 60s freelanced in
New York, led combo at intervals, sometimes played jazz-rock. Busy into 70s, a
trombone giant.

RECORDS
(all LPs)

URBIE GREEN
"X"(10″)LXA-3026 A Cool Yuletide
Vang(10″)VRS-8010
ABC-Para 137 All About Urbie Green
and His Big Band
Vi LPM-1667 Let's Face the Music
and Dance
Vi LPM-1741 Jimmy McHugh in Hi-
Fi
Comm RS-33815 The Persuasive
Trombone of Urbie Green
Beth 14 Urbie
Beth(10″)1015
BN(10″)5036
Project S-5014 21 Trombones
BUCK CLAYTON
Co CL-701 Jumpin' at the Woodside
JOE NEWMAN
Vi LPM-1198 I'm Still Swinging

BILLY BUTTERFIELD
Vi LPM-1590 Thank You for a Lovely
Evening
PHIL SILVERS & SWINGING BRASS
Co CL-1011
ELLIOT LAWRENCE
Fan 3-226 Dream
STEVE ALLEN
Cor 57018 Jazz for Tonight
(movie soundtrack)
De DL-8252 THE BENNY GOODMAN
STORY (Vol. 1)
De DL-8253 THE BENNY GOODMAN
STORY (Vol. 2)
AARON SACHS
Beth(10″)1008
JONAH JONES
Beth(10″)1014

717. GREENBANK, PERCY   lyr
Lyricist who wrote for Broadway shows
beginning early 1900s.

BROADWAY MUSICALS
(as lyricist)

1900—SAN TOY
1901—THE MESSENGER BOY
1902—THE TOREADOR
1904—THE CINGALEE
1905—THE EARL AND THE GIRL
1906—THE BLUE MOON; MY LADY'S MAID
1907—THE LITTLE MICHUS; THE ORCHID
1909—THE BELLE OF BRITTANY
1911—THE QUAKER GIRL
1916—BETTY
1919—GOOD MORNING, JUDGE

718. GREENWOOD, CHARLOTTE
vo
Born June 25, 1893, Philadelphia, Pa.

Long-limbed comedienne and "eccentric"
dancer with long stage-movie-radio career. Featured loose-jointed high kick in
comedy fashion. Chorus girl in early teens
at The White Cat club in New York.
Teamed with Eunice Burnham for vaudeville act. Supporting role in Broadway
show ROGERS BROTHERS IN PANAMA
(1907), won first real attention in THE
PASSING SHOW OF 1912. Performed in
same revue of 1913 and THE MAN WITH
THREE WIVES (1913). First big role in
PRETTY MRS. SMITH (1914). Became known

for "Letty" character in SO LONG LETTY (1916), LINGER LONGER LETTY (1919), LETTY PEPPER (1922). Other Broadway shows MUSIC BOX REVUE OF 1922, HASSARD SHORT'S RITZ REVUE (1924), RUFUS LEMAIRE'S AFFAIRS (1927), and years later OUT OF THIS WORLD (1950-1). Silent movie work, active in early sound movies 1929-32. Top movies in 40s, usually in role of mother or friend of heroine. In over 30 movies including SO LONG LETTY (1929), LET HER GO, LETTY (1930), STEPPING OUT, PALMY DAYS, FLYING HIGH, and PARLOR, BEDROOM AND BATH (1931), DOWN ARGENTINE WAY and YOUNG PEOPLE (1940), MOON OVER MIAMI (1941), SPRINGTIME IN THE ROCKIES (1942), THE GANG'S ALL HERE (1943), OH YOU BEAUTIFUL DOLL (1949), OKLAHOMA! (1955). Own radio show in mid-40s.

719. GREER, JESSE   cm p

Born August 26, 1896, New York, N.Y.

Composer of 20s and 30s. Best-known songs *I'm Gonna Meet My Sweetie Now*; *Just You, Just Me*; *Cheer Up*; *Did You Mean It?*. Early in career worked as pianist in theatre and in music publishing house. Military service, World War I. Began composing in mid-20s. Collaborators lyricists Walter Hirsch, Raymond Klages, Stanley Adams, Harold Adamson.

SONGS
(with related shows)

1925—Freshie
1926—Climbing Up the Ladder of Love; Flapperette; Sleepy Head
1927—I'm Gonna Meet My Sweetie Now; I'll Always Remember You
1928—EARL CARROLL'S VANITIES OF 1928 stage show (Once in a Lifetime); SAY WHEN stage show (One Step to Heaven; How About It?)
1929—HOLLYWOOD REVUE OF 1929 movie (Low Down Rhythm); MARIANNE movie (Marianne; Just You, Just Me; Hang On to Me); Building a Nest for Mary
1930—Cheer Up; Song of the Fool; Kitty from Kansas City
1931—Little Mary Brown; On the Beach

with You; Poor Kid; I Lost My Gal Again
1933—SHADY LADY stage show (Isn't It Swell to Dream?; You're Not the One; I'll Betcha That I'll Getcha; Isn't It Remarkable; Hi Ya, Sucker); Sittin' in the Dark
1934—HARLEQUIN movie (I Couldn't Be Mean to You); Extra! (All About That Gal of Mine); Spellbound
1935—You Fit into the Picture
1936—Did You Mean It?; You're Too Good to Be True
1937—I Can't Lose That Longing for You
1939—All in Favor of Swing Say "Aye"

Other songs: *Baby Blue Eyes*; *I Fell and Broke My Heart*; *Old Mill Wheel*; *What Do I Care?*; *The Hills of My Connecticut*; *You Can't Tell a Lie to Your Heart*; *Two Broken Hearts*; *Wrong*; *Two Timer*

720. GREER, SONNY   d B
(WILLLAM ALEXANDER GREER)

Born December 13, 1903, Long Branch, N.J.

Big-band drummer noted for long service with Duke Ellington. Style fit neatly varied colors and shadings of great Ellington band. First played locally and elsewhere in New Jersey. In pit band at Howard Theatre, Washington, D.C., met Ellington, jobbed with him 1919. Charter member of group that evolved into great Ellington band after modest beginnings in early 20s. Went with Ellington and three others to New York 1922 to join Wilbur Sweatman awhile. Returned to New York 1923, with Elmer Snowden group at Hollywood Club (later Kentucky Club). Ellington later became leader, group named The Washingtonians. Toured New England often 1924-7, returned to Kentucky Club, played New York clubs and theatres. In December 1927 enlarged band opened at New York's Cotton Club under Ellington's name, clicked, went on to fabulous career. Greer with band through all its great years to early 1951, except for brief illness. Six months with Johnny Hodges. Freelanced for rest of 50s; periods with Louis Metcalf, Red Allen, Tyree Glenn, some TV. Freelanced in 60s, led band at intervals, mostly in New York. By late 60s activities slowed; worked occasional jobs only.

RECORDS

DUKE ELLINGTON

  Vi 38008 Diga Diga Doo/I Can't Give You Anything but Love

  Vi 38035 Doin' the Voom Voom/ Flaming Youth

  Vi 38058 Saratoga Swing / Misty Mornin'

  Vi 21490 Blue Bubbles/The Blues I Love to Sing

  Vi 22528 Three Little Words/Ring Dem Bells

  Vi 24617 Cocktails for Two/Live and Love Tonight

  Vi 26598 Me and You/Concerto for Cootie

  Vi 26719 At a Dixie Roadside Diner/My Greatest Mistake

  Vi 26731 Harlem Air-Shaft/Sepia Panorama

  Vi 27356 Jumpin' Punkins/Blue Serge

  Vi 20-1556 Johnny Come Lately/Main Stem

  Br 6510 Tiger Rag (1 & 2)

  Br 6638 Jive Stomp/I'm Satisfied

  Br 7546 Reminiscing in Tempo (1 & 2)

  Br 7547 Reminiscing in Tempo (3 & 4)

  Br 8099 Carnival in Caroline/Braggin' in Brass

  Br 8293 Jazz Potpourri/Battle of Swing

  Br 8297 Slap Happy/Blue Light

  Br 8306 Boy Meets Horn/Old King Dooji

  Mus 463 Overture to a Jam Session (1 & 2)

  Mus 484 Trumpet No End (Blue Skies)/It Shouldn't Happen to a Dream

  Co 38165 Air Conditioned Jungle/It's Monday Every Day

  Co 38950 How High the Moon/Cowboy Rhumba

SIX JOLLY JESTERS

  Vo 15843 Six or Seven Times/Goin' Nuts

  Vo 1449 Oklahoma Stomp

BARNEY BIGARD

  Bb 10981 Charlie the Chulo/A Lull at Dawn

  Bb 11098 Ready Eddy/Lament for Javanette

JOHNNY HODGES

  Vo 4115 Jeep's Blues/Rendezvous with Rhythm

  Vo 4386 The Jeep Is Jumpin'/Prelude to a Kiss

  Bb 11117 Good Queen Bess/That's the Blues, Old Man

  Bb 30-0817 Goin' Out the Back Way/ Passion Flower

WINGY MANONE

  SE 5011 Never Had No Lovin'/I'm Alone Without You

REX STEWART

  Va 517 Rexatious/Lazy Man's Shuffle

COOTIE WILLIAMS

  Va 555 Diga Diga Doo/I Can't Believe That You're in Love with Me

SONNY GREER

  Apo 354 Sleepy Baboon/Kansas City Caboose

  Apo 355 Ration Stomp/Helena's Dream

  Cap 10028 Mood Indigo/The Mooche

  Cap 48013 Bug in a Rug

LPs

DUKE ELLINGTON

  Co C3L27 (3-LP set) The Ellington Era, Vol. 1 (1927-40 RIs)

  Co CL-825 Masterpieces by Ellington

  Vi LPV-517 Jumpin' Punkins (Vi RIs)

  Vi LPV-541 Johnny Come Lately (1942-5 Vi RIs)

  Vi LPT-1004 Duke Ellington's Greatest (Vi RIs)

  Vi LPM-1364 In a Mellotone (Vi RIs)

  Br BL-54007 Early Ellington (Br RIs)

  Cam CAL-459 At the Cotton Club (RIs)

JOHNNY HODGES

  Epic LN-3105 Hodge Podge (Vo RIs)

  Mer(10″)MGC-111 Johnny Hodges Collates

JOHNNY HODGES-REX STEWART

  Vi LPV-533 Things Ain't What They Used to Be (RIs)

REX STEWART

  "X"(10″)LX-3001 (Bb RIs)

721. GREY, CAROLYN   VO

Born May 6, 1922, Los Angeles, Calif.

Good band vocalist of late 30s and 40s.

As teenager some singing in Los Angeles clubs, stint with Carl Ravazza band. Gained first recognition with Woody Herman late 1941-2. In mid-40s with Jack Riley trio in Los Angeles, Sonny Dunham, Shorty Rogers, Tommy Dorsey, Anson Weeks. Joined Gene Krupa mid-1946, remained year, gained more recognition. Began career as single in later 40s, faded from music scene.

RECORDS

WOODY HERMAN
     De 4113 Rose O'Day
     De 18315 She'll Always Remember
     De 18506 Be Not Disencouraged
     De 18512 Jingle Bells
GENE KRUPA
     Co 37067 It's Just a Matter of Opinion
     Co 37078 Just the Other Day
     Co 37158 There Is No Breeze/Aren't You Kind of Glad We Did?
     Co 37209 It's a Good Day
     Co 37270 Old Devil Moon/Same Old Blues
     Co 37354 Yes, Yes, Honey/Dreams Are a Dime a Dozen
     Co 37589 Gene's Boogie

722. GREY, CLIFFORD   lyr

Born January 5, 1887, Birmingham, England
Died September 25, 1941, Ipswich, England

Prominent lyricist-librettist for Broadway stage during 20s. Associated with important musicals. Collaborated on independent songs, wrote songs for movie musicals 1929-30. Most famous songs *If You Were the Only Girl in the World* (1916), *Sally* and *Wild Rose* (1921), *Valencia* and *Sunday* (1926), *Hallelujah* (1927), *March of the Musketeers* (1928), *Got a Date with an Angel* (1931). Most other songs effective within context of shows but attained little popularity. Educated at King Edward VI School in Birmingham, England. Began as actor, turned to writing. After successful work for London stage, came to U.S., began career here 1920. Collaborators Rudolf Friml, Sigmund Romberg, Vincent Youmans, Herbert Stothart, Al Goodman, Oscar Levant, Werner Janssen, Jean Schwartz, Jerome Kern, J.

Fred Coots, Jay Gorney, Lewis Gensler, Johnny Green, Victor Schertzinger, Richard Myers.

BROADWAY MUSICALS
(as lyricist)

1920—KISSING TIME
1921—SALLY
1922—THE HOTEL MOUSE
1923—LADY BUTTERFLY (also wrote book)
1924—ANNIE DEAR; ARTISTS AND MODELS OF 1924; VOGUES OF 1924; MARJORIE (book only)
1925—ARTISTS AND MODELS OF 1925; GAY PAREE; JUNE DAYS; MAYFLOWERS (also wrote book); ZIEGFELD FOLLIES OF 1925; LOUIS THE 14TH; A NIGHT OUT (revue with English cast)
1926—BUBBLING OVER (book only); GREAT TEMPTATIONS; KATJA, THE DANCER; THE MERRY WORLD; A NIGHT IN PARIS
1927—HIT THE DECK
1928—THE MADCAP; THE OPTIMISTS (also wrote book); SUNNY DAYS (also wrote book); THE THREE MUSKETEERS; UPS-A-DAISY (also wrote book)
1930—SMILES

SONGS FOR MOVIES

1929—THE LOVE PARADE (Dream Lover; My Love Parade)
1930—DEVIL MAY CARE (Charming; Shepherd's Serenade; If He Cared); THE ROGUE SONG (The Rogue Song; When I'm Looking at You; The White Dove); IN GAY MADRID (Dark Night); HIT THE DECK (original stage score); THE FLORODORA GIRLS
1931—THE SMILING LIEUTENANT (While Hearts Are Singing; others)

723. GRIER, JIMMIE

       v cl g bn as ts ar cm lyr B

Born March 17, 1902, Pittsburgh, Pa.
Died June 4, 1959, in Calif.

Well-known leader of good sweet-styled band in 30s on west coast. Grew up in California. Studied many instruments, played in various bands late 20s. Sideman-arranger for Gus Arnheim about 1930-1, arranged hit *Sweet and Lovely*. Formed band late 1931, later followed Arnheim into Cocoanut Grove in Los Angeles. Nationwide attention when band on Lucky Strike radio show, which featured "magic carpet" concept of band remotes from various spots across country. Opening theme *Music in the Moonlight*, closing theme *Bon Voyage to Your Ship of Dreams*; composed both. Later theme *Let's Dance and Dream*. At various times used singers Larry Cotton, Harry Barris, Donald Novis, Dick Webster, Pinky Tomlin. Co-composer with Tomlin of popular songs *The Object of My Affection* (1934), *What's the Reason?* and *Don't Be Afraid to Tell Your Mother* (1935). In 30s band heard often on remote broadcasts from west coast, also on shows of Jack Benny 1934, Burns & Allen 1936, Joe Penner late 1936-8. In 1934 movie TRANSATLANTIC MERRY-GO-ROUND, musical shorts. Grier arranged for movies. Military service, World War II; assisted Rudy Vallee in arranging and conducting for coast guard band, organizing big show which toured nation. After discharge organized another band late 1945, played west coast in 40s, cut down to combo 1950. Later in 50s disbanded, worked in real estate.

RECORDS

JIMMIE GRIER

Vi 22970 (theme) Bon Voyage to Your Ship of Dreams/I've Paid for Love
Vi 22971 (theme) Music in the Moonlight/One Hour with You
Vi 24174 Here Lies Love/I Cannot Tell You Why
Vi 24175 I Can Depend on You/Second-Hand Heart for Sale
Br 6597 Learn to Croon/Moonstruck
Br 7306 College Rhythm/Let's Give Three Cheers for Love
Br 7307 Stay as Sweet as You Are/Take a Number from One to Ten
Br 7308 The Object of My Affection/Somebody's Birthday
Br 7381 If the Moon Turns Green/I'm Keeping Those Keepsakes You Gave Me
Br 7760 Sitting on the Moon/I-O-U My Heart
Br 7901 In Your Own Little Way/

You're Looking for Romance
De 1475 Everything You Said Came True/If It's the Last Thing I Do
De 1486 You're My Dish/More Power to You
De 1497 Bob White/Yankee Doodle
De 1797 Says My Heart/You Leave Me Breathless
De 1813 Daydreaming/I Wanna Go Back to Bali
PINKY TOMLIN with JIMMIE GRIER ORCHESTRA
Br 7355 What's the Reason?/Don't Be Afraid to Tell Your Mother
BING CROSBY with JIMMIE GRIER ORCHESTRA
Br 6643 Black Moonlight/Thanks
Br 6644 The Day You Came Along/I Guess It Had to Be That Way
Br 6663 The Last Round-Up/Home on the Range
Br 6694 After Sundown/Beautiful Girl

724. GRIFFIN, CHRIS   t
(GORDON GRIFFIN)

Born October 31, 1915, Binghamton, N.Y.

Trumpeter of 30s and 40s, good soloist and section man. Began professionally at 15 on dance hall job in New York. With Scott Fisher early 30s. With Charlie Barnet 1933-4, later 1934 with Rudy Vallee. Rejoined Barnet awhile 1935, then with Joe Haymes late 1935 to May 1936. On radio with Leith Stevens band 1936. Joined Benny Goodman May 1936, remained till September 1939. Teamed with Ziggy Elman and Harry James 1937-8 to form great trumpet section for Goodman. Late 1939 began as studio musician, including work with Raymond Scott's big band on radio. In 40s, 50s and 60s active mostly in studio work. Brief periods with Goodman again in 40s and 50s. In late 60s formed Griffin-Erwin School of Music in Teaneck, N.J., with veteran trumpet star Pee Wee Erwin. Toured England early 1974 with Warren Covington-Tommy Dorsey band.

RECORDS

JOE HAYMES

Me 60207 Rhythm in My Nursery Rhymes
Me 60211 Polly Wolly Doodle

BENNY GOODMAN
Vi 25445 Riffin' at the Ritz
Co 35301 Boy Meets Horn
Co 35362 Stealin' Apples
Co 39564 King Porter Stomp (lst trumpet solo)

RAYMOND SCOTT ORCHESTRA
Co 35363 Just a Gigolo/Huckleberry Duck
Co 35364 The Peanut Vendor/Business Men's Bounce

LITTLE RAMBLERS
Bb 6043 Streamlined Greta Green/Loveless Love
Bb 6045 Truckin'/Cotton

TEDDY WILSON
Br 7612 Life Begins When You're in Love/Rhythm in My Nursery Rhymes
Br 7736 You Turned the Tables on Me/Sing, Baby, Sing
Br 7739 You Came to My Rescue/Here's Love in Your Eyes

MILDRED BAILEY
Vo 3056 I'd Love to Take Orders from You/I'd Rather Listen to Your Eyes
Vo 3057 Someday Sweetheart/When Day Is Done

TED WALLACE
Br 6251 Mama Don't Allow It/I'm Gonna Sit Right Down and Write Myself a Letter
Br 6252 Goody Goody/Alone at a Table for Two
Br 6253 It's Been So Long/Life Begins When You're in Love
Br 6254 Sing an Old Fashioned Song/Gotta Go to Work Again

BILLY BUTTERFIELD
Cap Album BD-10 (78s) Gershwin Album

JACK LEONARD
OK 5777 I'll Get By/I Could Make You Care

DOLORES HAWKINS
Cor 60832 I'm in the Mood for Love/Sing You Sinners

CHRIS GRIFFIN
VD(12″)845 I Cover the Waterfront/Cowbell Serenade

LPs

BENNY GOODMAN
Vi LPT-6703 (5-LP set) The Golden Age of Swing (Vi RIs)

SAMMY SPEAR
Lon LA-380001 Plays a Little Traveling Music

BOBBY SHORT
Atl 1302 The Mad Twenties

GEORGE SIRAVO
Co(10″)CL-6146 Your Dance Date with George Siravo

725. GRIFFIN, KEN o v

Popular organist of late 40s and 50s. Rose to fame 1948 with hit record *You Can't Be True, Dear*. Organ style simple, always close to melody. Material predominately waltzes, old nostalgic songs, sentimental ballads. Recorded organ music often played at skating rinks. Violinist in early years, self-taught on organ later. Organ for silent movies in Rocky Mountains in 20s. In 30s used portable organ, played hotels and lounges in midwest. Military service, World War II. Resumed career, worked in east and midwest. In 1948 big-selling hit brought better bookings, substantial recording output several years following.

RECORDS

KEN GRIFFIN
Rondo 128 You Can't Be True, Dear/Cuckoo Waltz
Rondo 183 Yes, Sir, That's My Baby/Love Was the Cause of It All
Rondo 197 Skater's Waltz/Take Me Out to the Ball Game
Bcst 460 You Can't Be True, Dear/Barcarolle
Co 38827 When I Lost You/Are You Lonesome Tonight?
Co 38889 Harbor Lights/Josephine
Co 39085 Somebody Loves You/San Antonio Rose
Co 39137 Rememb'ring/Moonlight and Roses
Co 39775 Rosary Lane/In a Chapel by the Side of the Road
Co 39952 Have You Heard?/Till I Waltz Again with You
Co 40062 "O"/Crying in the Chapel
Co 40184 Our Heartbreaking Waltz/Till We Two Are One
Co 40221 I Get So Lonely/Little Old Mill

LPs

KEN GRIFFIN
Rondo-lette A-1 Ken Griffin
Rondo-lette A-30 At the Great Organ
Co CL-662 Lost in a Cloud
Co CL-907 You Can't Be True, Dear
Co CL-1039 Love Letters in the Sand
Co CL-1127 Let's Have a Party
Co CL-1289 Remembering
Co CL-1411 Sweet and Lovely
Co CL-1518 On the Happy Side

726. GRIFFIN, MERV   p vo

Born July 6, 1925, San Mateo, Calif.

Vocalist with Freddy Martin band who later rose to fame as host of TV talk shows. Well controlled high baritone, also played piano capably. Attended universities of Stanford and San Francisco. Early in career sang on San Francisco radio. With Freddy Martin 1948-52; most popular record *I've Got a Lovely Bunch of Cocoanuts* in 1948. After leaving Martin, began recording on his own for Victor. In 1952 began brief movie career, mostly small roles. Best role in 1953 movie so THIS IS LOVE (story of Grace Moore) with Kathryn Grayson. Bit roles in CATTLE TOWN (1952), BY THE LIGHT OF THE SILVERY MOON and THREE SAILORS AND A GIRL (1953). Better roles in THE BOY FROM OKLAHOMA and PHANTOM OF THE RUE MORGUE (1954). Cameo role in HELLO DOWN THERE (1969). In mid-50s singer on TV shows, including regular spot on Robert Q. Lewis show. Fill-ins as host on Jack Paar's late-night TV show displayed Griffin's amiable personality, humor, ad-lib ability. Own daytime TV show 1962-3. Success in later 60s and early 70s as host of late-night show. Admirable feature in 70s: often featured composers, former star singers and bandleaders. Network show dropped in early 1972, but immediately began syndicated show on Metromedia and other stations.

RECORDS

FREDDY MARTIN
Vi 20-3350 So Tired
Vi 20-3384 The Little Old Church in Leicester Square/1400 Dream Street
Vi 20-3554 I've Got a Lovely Bunch of Cocoanuts
Vi 20-3576 Your Kiss/Merry Christmas Polka
Vi 20-4099 Jo-Ann/Never Been Kissed
Vi 20-4223 The Gang That Sang Heart of My Heart

MERV GRIFFIN
Vi 20-4217 Belle, Belle, My Liberty Belle/I Fall in Love with You Ev'ry Day
Vi 20-4270 The Lord's Ridin' with Me Tonight/Twenty-three Starlets
Vi 20-4360 Eternally/If I Forget You
Vi 20-4511 They Say You Cry/Neither Am I
Vi 20-4644 If I Had the Heart of a Clown/With No One to Love Tonight
Co 40026 I Kiss Your Hand, Madame/I'll Be There

LPs

MERV GRIFFIN
MGM E-4326 A Tinkling Piano in the Next Apartment
Carlton 12/134 Merv Griffin's Dance Party!

727. GRIMES, TINY   g d p B
(LLOYD GRIMES)

Born July 7, 1917, Newport News, Va.

Good rhythm guitarist and soloist with ability to fit in with different styles. First played drums and piano locally in mid-30s, also in Washington, D.C. Played in New York late 30s, switched to amplified guitar. Worked with The Cats and the Fiddle, vocal-instrumental group, late 1938-41. Freelanced on west coast, then with Art Tatum combo 1941-4. Led combo in New York, Cleveland and Philadelphia in later 40s and 50s, also toured. Backed Billie Holiday on 52nd Street mid-40s. Considerable playing in rock and roll style late 50s and 60s. Much freelance recording. To Europe with Teddy Buckner 1968, Jay McShann 1970. Active in early 70s.

RECORDS

THE CATS AND THE FIDDLE
Bb 8216 Nuts to You/Killin' Jive

Bb 8248 Gangbusters/Please Don't Leave Me Now

Bb 8402 Chant of the Rain/I'd Rather Drink Muddy Water

ART TATUM

Comet(12″)1 Dark Eyes/The Man I Love

Comet(12″)2 I Know That You Know/Body and Soul

Comet(12″)3 Flyin' Home/On the Sunny Side of the Street

BUCK CLAYTON

HRS 1024 Dawn Dance/It's Dizzy

HRS 1026 On the Sunny Side of the Street

COZY COLE

Cont 6000 Look Here/A Ghost of a Chance

Cont 6001 Willow Weep for Me/Take It on Back

LEONARD FEATHER-DAN BURLEY

Cont 6006-7 Suite in Four Comfortable Quarters (1-2-3-4)

JOHN HARDEE

BN 513 Tired/Blue Skies

BN 514 Hardee's Partee/Idaho

CLYDE HART

Regis 7002 Riding on 52nd Street/All the Things You Are

COLEMAN HAWKINS

Manor 1036 Step On It/Memories of You

BILLIE HOLIDAY

De 23565 Don't Explain/What Is This Thing Called Love?

Alad 3094 Detour Ahead/Be Fair to Me

CHARLIE PARKER

Sav 541 Red Cross/Tiny's Tempo

IKE QUEBEC

BN(12″)37 Blue Harlem/Tiny's Exercise

BN(12″)38 She's Funny That Way/Indiana

BN 515 Topsy/Cup-Mute Clayton

TINY GRIMES

Sav 526 Tiny's Tempo/I'll Always Love You Just the Same

BN 524 Flying Home (1 & 2)

BN 525 Tiny's Boogie Woogie/"C" Jam Blues

Atl 854 Blue Harlem/Boogie Woogie Barbecue

Atl 869 Hot in Harlem/Nightmare Blues

Atl 886 Jealousy/Sidewalks of New York

Atl 990 Begin the Beguine/The Man I Love

LPs

TINY GRIMES

Pres 7144 Callin' the Blues

Br(10″)BL-58013

Dial(10″)206

ART TATUM

Stin(10″)40

728. GRISSOM, DAN   vo as

Leading vocalist with Jimmie Lunceford 1935-43, also played sax. Smooth vocals featured mostly on ballads, rarely on rhythm numbers. After leaving Lunceford, freelanced, worked as single awhile in later 40s. After that, largely disappeared from music scene.

RECORDS

JIMMIE LUNCEFORD

De 628 Charmaine

De 788 The Best Things in Life Are Free

De 960 Living from Day to Day

De 980 I Can't Escape from You

De 1035 My Last Affair

De 1229 Honest and Truly

De 1340 Coquette

De 1364 The First Time I Saw You

De 1617 Like a Ship at Sea

De 1734 The Love Nest

De 1808 By the River Sainte Marie/My Melancholy Baby

De 1927 Down by the Old Mill Stream

De 3718 I Had a Premonition

De 3931 Flamingo

De 4083 Gone

De 18534 You're Always in My Dreams

De 18618 I Dream a Lot About You

Vo 4712 You Set Me on Fire

Vo 4754 You're Just a Dream/I've Only Myself to Blame

Vo 4979 I Love You/Oh Why, Oh Why?

Vo 5033 You Let Me Down

Vo 5116 Who Did You Meet Last Night?

Co 35725 Let's Try Again
Co 35919 Blue Afterglow
GERALD WILSON
UA 509 My Last Affair
RED CALLENDER
Excl 202 I Wonder/Skyline
DAN GRISSOM
Je 2007 Dinah/You Don't Know What Love Is
Je 2008 So You've Fallen in Love/ Wonderful Christmas Night
Je 2009 If You Were Only Mine/Such Is My Love
Je 2011 Living My Life for You/You Can't Kiss a Dream Goodnight

LPs

BILLY MAY
Cap TAO-924 Jimmie Lunceford in Hi-Fi (recreations)

729. GROFE, FERDE　　p viola cm ar B
(FERDINAND RUDOLPH VON GROFE)
Born March 27, 1892, New York, N.Y.
Died April 3, 1972, Santa Monica, Calif.

Talented musician known for his work with Paul Whiteman band as pianist-arranger and for descriptive compositions, notably *On the Trail* from *Grand Canyon Suite*. Grew up in Los Angeles area. Studied piano and viola, became accomplished musician. In Los Angeles Symphony Orchestra 1909-19. Played in and arranged for dance bands. Joined Whiteman around 1920, became important member of band but soon used mostly as arranger. Arrangement of *Rhapsody in Blue* performed by Whiteman in famous concert at New York's Aeolian Hall 1924. Success encouraged composers to try "symphonic jazz" during next few years. Grofe continued with Whiteman into early 30s. Some scoring for 1930 movie KING OF JAZZ starring Whiteman band and singers. Formed dance band 1932, by mid-30s attracted attention through radio work. At dance spots and on remote broadcasts band used theme *On the Trail*, unique piece for dance band. Band on Fred Allen radio show 1934, Burns & Allen show 1935-6, Saturday Night Party late 1936-7. Grofe continued band through 30s, played New York

World's Fair 1939. In later years conducted on radio and in concert. Guest conductor with symphony orchestras in various cities. Also did arranging-composing; descriptive pieces performed by orchestras everywhere. 1942 hit song *Daybreak* based on Grofe's *Mardi Gras* theme from *Mississippi Suite*, lyrics by Harold Adamson. Arranged score of 1945 movie RHAPSODY IN BLUE, story of composer George Gershwin. Composed popular songs *Suez* and *Wonderful One* (1922) and *Count Your Blessings* (1933). Other serious compositions include *Death Valley Suite*; *Piano Concerto in d*; *Hollywood Suite*; *Wheels Suite*; *Symphony in Steel*; *World's Fair Suite* (1964 official theme); *Knute Rockne; 3 Shades of Blue; Killarney; Valley of Enchantment; New England Suite; Atlantic Crossing; A Day at the Farm; Tabloid Suite; Broadway at Night; An American Biography; Metropolis; Americana.*

RECORDS

PAUL WHITEMAN
Vi 18694 Wang Wang Blues
Vi 18826 Everybody Step
Vi 18920 Hot Lips
Vi(12″)35822 Rhapsody in Blue (1 & 2; arrangement)
FERDE GROFE ORCHESTRA
Co 2851-D Temptation / Cinderella's Fella
Co 2858-D Count Your Blessings/Inka Dinka Doo

LPs

FERDE GROFE and NEW SYMPHONY, MITCHELL CHOIR
Everest 3139 Atlantic Crossing
FERDE GROFE and CAPITOL SYMPHONY
Cap DT-272 Grand Canyon Suite/ /Death Valley Suite
FERDE GROFE and ROCHESTER PHILHARMONIC
Everest 3044 Grand Canyon Suite//Piano Concerto in d

729A. GROODY, LOUISE　　vo
Born March 26, 1897, Waco, Texas
Died September 16, 1961, Canadensis, Pa.

Attractive singer-dancer-actress in important Broadway musicals. Biggest hit shows THE NIGHT BOAT; NO, NO, NANETTE; HIT THE DECK.

BROADWAY MUSICALS

1915—AROUND THE MAP
1918—FIDDLERS THREE; TOOT-TOOT!
1920—THE NIGHT BOAT
1921—GOOD MORNING, DEARIE
1923—ONE KISS
1925—NO, NO, NANETTE
1927—HIT THE DECK

RECORDS

CHARLES KING-LOUISE GROODY
  Vi 20609 Sometimes I'm Happy

730. GROSS, WALTER   p hp ar cm B

Born July 14, 1909, New York, N.Y.
Excellent all-around pianist with long musical career; noted for composition *Tenderly*. In early and mid-30s in various minor bands, also with Ted Black and Rudy Vallee. With George Hall 1937-8. Staff pianist for CBS radio. Own show 1938. Briefly with Paul Whiteman. In 1938-9 often on Saturday Night Swing Session show; conductor during final months until show's demise early 1939. Regular staff conductor for CBS early 1941. Military service, World War II; conducted radio programs. Executive with Musicraft Records 1946-7, conductor-arranger-pianist on many record sessions. Composed famous *Tenderly* 1947; popularized in early 50s. Other compositions: *Your Love, To Be Worthy of You, A Slight Case of Ivory, I'm in a Fog About You, Just a Moon Ago, Creepy Weepy, Please Remember, How Will I Remember You?, Mexican Moon, Improvisation in Several Keys, It's Somebody Else That You Love.* Chief collaborators Jack Lawrence, Carl Sigman, Ned Washington, Raymond Klages, Bobby Troup. Settled in California in 50s, played clubs as soloist or led combo.

RECORDS

PAUL WHITEMAN
  De 2073 I Used to Be Color Blind/ Peelin' the Peach
  De 2074 Jamboree Jones/Sing a Song of Sixpence

  De 2145 I'm Comin' Virginia/Aunt Hagar's Blues
JOHNNY WILLIAMS
  Vo 5077 Milenberg Joys/Ma Curly-Headed Baby
  Vo 5213 Memory Lane/Clarinet Marmalade
MAXINE SULLIVAN
  Vi 26344 Ill Wind/Turtle Dove
  Vi 26372 Sing Something Simple/ Jackie Boy
LEITH STEVENS
  Vo 4350 12th Street Rag/Love's Old Sweet Song
ALEC WILDER (harpsichord)
  Br 8294 A Debutante's Diary/Neurotic Goldfish
  Br 8307 Concerning Etchings/Little Girl Grows Up
  Co 35648 The Children Met the Train/Seldom the Sun
  Co 35988 Blue Room/Sweet Sue
RAYMOND SCOTT ORCHESTRA
  Co 35363 Just a Gigolo/Huckleberry Duck
  Co 35364 The Peanut Vendor/Business Men's Bounce
CLARK DENNIS
  Cap 15307 Tenderly/I'm So Lonesome I Could Cry
WALTER GROSS
  Bb 10795 A Slight Case of Ivory/I'm Always Chasing Rainbows
  Bb 10937 Creepy Weepy/Improvisation in Several Keys
  Mus 358-359-360-361 Jerome Kern songs
(as conductor)
PHIL BRITO
  Mus 15080 And Then It's Heaven/ Whatta Ya Gonna Do?
  Mus 15105 Sweet Lorraine/Between the Devil and the Deep Blue Sea
  MGM 10550 Vieni Su/Mattinata
BEA WAIN
  Vi 26311 Stormy Weather/Oh, You Crazy Moon
GORDON MACRAE
  Mus 15084 I'm So Lonesome I Could Cry/The Way the Wind Blows

LPs

WALTER GROSS
  Ha HL-7138

Co(10″)CL-6141
MGM(10″)E-114
MGM(10″)E-214
ALEC WILDER
Co(10″)CL-6181 (Br, Co RIs)

731. GUARNIERI, JOHNNY

p hp ar cm B

Born March 23, 1917, New York, N.Y.

Pianist in swing style, an eclectic mix of
Fats Waller, Earl Hines and Teddy Wilson. Active with many bands and jazz
groups, also worked as soloist and combo
leader. Learned piano early, as youngster
accompanied violinist father. Attended
CCNY. With George Hall 1937-9. Periods
with Mike Riley. With Benny Goodman
December 1939 to summer 1940. Joined
Artie Shaw latter half 1940. Featured with
Shaw's Gramercy Five on harpsichord,
innovation for jazz. Joined Goodman
again early 1941, remained several
months. Rejoined Artie Shaw later 1941
for several months. With Jimmy Dorsey
1942-3. Later 1943 with Raymond Scott
band on radio, also had trio jobs at night
and played with Cozy Cole. In later 40s
freelanced. Much in demand for record
sessions: versatile, could fit with mainstream or bop groups. Led trio in New
York jazz clubs late 40s. In 1949 featured
on many radio broadcasts with quintet
(including trumpet and alto sax), for
which he wrote over a hundred swinging,
clean-cut arrangements. During 1954-62
active mostly as radio staff musician; own
show at times. In 1962 settled in Hollywood, played jobs in comparative obscurity. Introduced new musical style by
playing standards in 5/4 time. Jazz compositions include *Whistle Stop*; *A Gliss to
Remember*; *Looky Here, Here's Me!*; *Gliss
Me Again*.

RECORDS

COOTIE WILLIAMS
OK 6224 Blues in My Condition/Ain't
Misbehavin'
OK 6370 West End Blues/G-Men
ARTIE SHAW GRAMERCY FIVE
Vi 26762 Special Delivery Stomp/
Keepin' Myself for You
Vi 26763 Cross Your Heart/Summit
Ridge Drive

Vi 27335 Smoke Gets in Your Eyes
Vi 27432 My Blue Heaven
ARTIE SHAW ORCHESTRA
Vi 27411 The Blues (1 & 2)
Vi(12″)36383 Concerto for Clarinet (1
& 2)
BENNY GOODMAN SEXTET
Co 35466 Poor Butterfly/The Sheik of
Araby
Co 35482 I Surrender Dear/Grand
Slam
Co 36099 A Smo-o-o-oth One/Air
Mail Special
BENNY GOODMAN ORCHESTRA
Co 35497 Crazy Rhythm
JIMMY DORSEY
De 4356 Murderistic
COZY COLE
Sav 502 Jericho/Nice and Cozy
REX STEWART
Key(12″)1306 Swamp Mist/I'm True
to You
Key(12″)1307 Zaza/The Little Goose
DON BYAS
Jamb 902 Little White Lies/Out of
Nowhere
Jamb 903 Deep Purple/Them There
Eyes
HANK D'AMICO
Nat 9006 Over the Rainbow/Cole
Heat, Warm Feet
BEN WEBSTER
Sav 553 Blue Skies/Honeysuckle Rose
LESTER YOUNG
Key 603 I Never Knew/Just You, Just
Me
Key 604 Sometimes I'm Happy/After-
noon of a BasiE-ite
JOHNNY GUARNIERI
Sav 509 Basie English/Exercise in
Swing
Sav 511 These Foolish Things/Salute
to Fats
Sav 530 Gliss Me Again/Bowing, Sing-
ing Slam
Sav 557 Deuces Wild/Deuces Mild
Maj 1094 Beyond the Moon/My Gal
Sal
Maj 1095 Believe It, Beloved/Flying
Home
Maj 1096 Temptation/Stars Fell on
Alabama
Mer 1119 All My Life/Groovin' with
J.G.

Mer 1120 Why Do I Love You?/ What's the Use?

LPs
JOHNNY GUARNIERI
Cam CAL-345 Cheerful Little Earful
Cam CAL-391 Side by Side
Cor CRL-57085 Songs of Hudson & DeLange
Cor CRL-57086 The Duke Again
Golden Crest 3020 Plays Johnny Guarnieri
Roy(10″)VLP-6047 Johnnie Guarnieri
WILL BRADLEY-JOHNNY GUARNIERI BAND
Vi LSP-2098 (S) Big Band Boogie
LESTER YOUNG
Sav MG-12068 The Immortal Lester Young (Sav RIs)
BENNY GOODMAN
Co GL-500 Benny Goodman Combos (Co RIs)
ARTIE SHAW & HIS GRAMERCY FIVE
Vi LPM-1241 (Vi RIs)

732. GUINAN, TEXAS   vo
(MARY LOUISE CECELIA GUINAN)

Born c. 1888-90, Waco, Texas
Died November 5, 1933, Vancouver, B.C., Canada, of amoebic dysentery

Flamboyant figure of Roaring Twenties, hostess known as queen of the night clubs in New York. First attracted attention in 1908 with act called The Gibson Girl in which she sang and displayed her figure. Played vaudeville and night clubs several years. Minor role on Broadway in THE PASSING SHOW OF 1913. Built name as performer, by 1917 in silent movies. During 20s became much-publicized hostess of Texas Guinan Club and other speakeasies in New York. Many brushes with law during Prohibition, played up in newspapers. Favorite greeting as hostess to incoming customers—"Hello, sucker!"—became trademark. Favorite admonition introducing act was "Give the little girl a great big hand!": another trademark. Starred in Broadway show PADLOCKS OF 1927. Starred in 1929 sound movie QUEEN OF THE NIGHT CLUBS. Small role in movie BROADWAY THROUGH A KEYHOLE in 1933. 1945 movie INCENDIARY

BLONDE based on her life, starred Betty Hutton as Guinan.

733. GUIZAR, TITO   vo g
Born April 8, 1912, in Mexico

Mexican tenor, active in U.S. in 30s and 40s. Studied music in Mexico City and Milan, Italy. Uneventful first appearance in U.S. 1929. In 1931 sang with Chicago Opera Company in New York, remained there to sing at clubs and hotels. Broadened style to include popular music, still featured classical and native music. In 1932 on radio show To the Ladies with Leon Belasco orchestra, also on other shows. Later own show Tito Guizar and His Guitar. In 1936 in all-Spanish film in Mexico, established reputation there. In three 1938 movies in U.S.: BIG BROADCAST OF 1938, ST. LOUIS BLUES and TROPIC HOLIDAY. Other movies BRAZIL (1944), THRILL OF BRAZIL (1946), THE GAY RANCHERO (1948). Active in U.S. in 40s, sometimes toured with own Pan-American ensemble. Continued to sing on radio in 40s.

RECORDS
TITO GUIZAR
Vi 27410 Yours/San Antonio Rose
Vi 27513 Time Was/Querida
Vi 27613 Darling Carmelita/Little Princess
Vi 27748 Ev'rything I Love/Madelaine
Vi 27839 Day Dreaming/Ages Ago
Vi 32858 El Rancho Grande/Guadalajaro
Mer 1019 El Rancho Grande/Linda Mujer
Mer 1021 Guadalajaro/I'll Never Love Again
Mer 5006 I'll Never Love Again/He Like It, She Like It
LPs
TITO GUIZAR
Mer(10″)MG-25032

734. GULLIN, LARS   bs cl p ar cm B
Born May 4, 1928, in Sweden

A foremost Swedish modern jazzman in late 40s and 50s, star on baritone sax. Gutty, forceful style, facile on clumsy horn. Rose to prominence in Sweden with Arne Domnerus and other top Swedish jazzmen, and with visiting U.S. stars. Known in U.S. thanks to LPs featuring Swedish stars issued in early 50s. Worked in Sweden with Goesta Theselius, led own combo. Later in Italy awhile, away from jazz. By late 50s U.S. interest in Gullin and other Swedish stars flagged.

RECORDS

ROLF ERICSON
  Dis 1732 Perdido/Miles Away
SWINGIN' SWEDES
  BN 1605 Pick Yourself Up/Summertime
NEW SOUNDS FROM SWEDEN
  Pres 750 A Handful of Stars
LARS GULLIN
  Pres 793 Gull in a Gulch/Coolin' on the S.S. Cool
  Gazell(Sw) 2017 Laura/Blue Lou
  Gazell(Sw) 2018 All God's Chillun/ Danny-O
  Metro(Sw) 646 Late Date/Dedicated to Lee
  Pol(Sw) 48601 The Continental/I Got It Bad
  Selection(Sw) 812 Hershey Bar/North Express

LPs

LARS GULLIN
  EmArcy MG-36059 With the Moretone Singers
  EmArcy(10")MG-26041
  EmArcy(10")MG-26044 Gullin's Garden
  Atl 1246 Baritone Sax: Lars Gullin
  Pres(10")144 New Sounds from Sweden, Vol. 5
  Co(Sw) 1010 Portrait of My Pals
ROLF ERICSON
  Dis(10")DL-2008 Swedish Pastry
ARNE DOMNERUS
  Vi(10")LPT-3032 Around the World in Jazz—Sweden
BENGT HALLBERG
  Pres(10")176
(miscellaneous artists)
  Pres(10")119 Leonard Feather's Swingin' Swedes

734A. GUNNING, LOUISE　　　　vo

Born c. 1878
Died July 24, 1960, Sierre Madre, Calif.
Beautiful singer-actress in early Broad-

way shows; most famous THE BALKAN PRINCESS.

BROADWAY MUSICALS

1899—THE ROGERS BROTHERS IN WALL STREET
1903—MR. PICKWICK; THE OFFICE BOY
1904—LOVE'S LOTTERY
1907—TOM JONES; THE WHITE HEN
1908—MARCELLE
1911—THE BALKAN PRINCESS
1913—THE AMERICAN MAID

735. GUTHRIE, WOODY

vo g har cm lyr

(WOODROW WILSON GUTHRIE)
Born July 4, 1912, Okemah, Okla.
Died October 4, 1967, Creedmore State Hospital, N.Y.

Folk singer of 30s and 40s, best known for compositions. Left home at 14. Played harmonica wherever possible throughout southwest, eked out bare existence. Later learned guitar. Played and sang on 30s radio shows in California, including regular show. In late 30s to New York, on radio there. At various times worked with folk artists Pete Seeger, Leadbelly and Cisco Houston. In late 1940 on radio show Pipe Smoking Time. Toured in early 40s, sometimes with Almanac Singers. In merchant marine awhile during World War II. In postwar years concentrated more on composing. Reworked or adapted old folk melodies for some tunes. Wrote hundreds; regarded by many as best contemporary folk composer. Best-known songs: *This Land Is Your Land; So Long, It's Been Good to Know You; Grand Coulee Dam; Oklahoma Hills* (with cousin Jack Guthrie); *Philadelphia Lawyer; Union Maid; Hard Travelling; The Reuben James.* Wrote many articles, several books on life among country folk. By late 40s afflicted by serious nerve disease which curtailed activities, later put him many years in hospital before death.

RECORDS

WOODY GUTHRIE
  Vi 26619 Blowin' Down This Road/ Talkin' Dust Bowl Blues

Vi 26620 Do Re Mi/Dust Cain't Kill Me

Vi 26621 Tom Joad (1 & 2)

Vi 26622 Dusty Old Dust/The Great Dust Storm

Vi 26623 Dust Pneumonia Blues/Dust Bowl Refugee

Vi 26624 I Ain't Got No Home in This World Anymore/Vigilante Man

LPs

WOODY GUTHRIE

Vi LPV-502 Dust Bowl Ballads (Vi RIs)

Stin 32 Cowboy Songs Sung by Woody Guthrie-Cisco Houston

Folk 2483/4 (2-LP set) Sings with Leadbelly and Others

Elektra 271-2 Library of Congress Recordings

Archive FS-204

H

736. HACKETT, BOBBY   c t g bn B

Born January 31, 1915, Providence, R.I.

Cornet star with impeccable taste; clean, flowing style easily identifiable. Outstanding on slow ballads; on jazz at best in dixieland combos. Capable rhythm guitarist. At 14 played guitar in restaurant band, later banjo in club job. Then concentrated on cornet, in 30s played New York, Boston, Providence, Cape Cod. In 1936 fronted band at Boston's Theatrical Club: good combo with trombonist Brad Gowans, who wrote dixieland arrangements. To New York 1937. Played in society bands of Lester Lanin, Howard Lanin and Meyer Davis. Then with top jazzmen. Joined Joe Marsala late 1937. Reputation enhanced by spot at Benny Goodman's 1938 Carnegie Hall concert: performed a number in Bix Beiderbecke style. Led small band at Nick's in New York 1938-9, big band at Famous Door and on tour. Recorded excellent sides with latter. With Horace Heidt band September 1939 to mid-1940, again late 1940. Recorded soundtrack for trumpet solos seemingly by Fred Astaire in 1940 movie SECOND CHORUS. Led big band in Boston awhile, then with Glenn Miller on guitar-cornet late 1941-2; cornet featured on several famous solos. NBC staff man late 1942-3. Toured with Katherine Dunham revue 1944. With Glen Gray late 1944-6, with intervals away. Remainder of 40s mostly radio staff musician in New York. Led combo late 40s and 50s in New York, Boston and Philadelphia. TV in 50s included leading band backing Martha Wright on 1954 series. Prominent in mid-50s as featured soloist with lush string orchestra on LPs directed by comedian Jackie Gleason. Later 50s more studio work; led combo into early 60s. Concert tour with Benny Goodman late 1962, also with Goodman spring 1963. In 1965-66 with singer Tony Bennett, including trips abroad. In late 60s and early 70s led groups, jobbed with others. Formed record company 1973.

RECORDS

DICK ROBERTSON
    De 1209 Too Marvelous for Words/ Little Old Lady
    De 1335 Gone with the Wind/The Miller's Daughter Marianne
    De 1620 Bob White/You Started Something

EDDIE CONDON
    CMS 500 Ja-da/Love Is Just Around the Corner
    CMS 505 Meet Me Tonight in Dreamland/Diane (JACK TEAGARDEN)
    CMS(12")1500 Carnegie Jump/Carnegie Drag
    De 23431 My One and Only
    Atl 661 Seems Like Old Times/Time Carries On

ADRIAN ROLLINI
    De 1639 You're a Sweetheart/Josephine
    De 1654 True Confession/I've Hitched My Wagon to a Star

JOE MARSALA
    De 18111 Twelve Bar Stampede/ Feather Bed Blues

PETE BROWN
    De 18118 Ocean Motion/Tempo di Jump

BUD FREEMAN
    CMS 507 LIFE Spears a Jitterbug/ What's the Use?
    CMS 508 Memories of You/Tappin' the Commodore Till

FRANK FROEBA
    De 1500 Tears in My Heart/My Swiss Hilly Billy
    De 1525 Miles Apart/Danger, Love at Work

HORACE HEIDT
    Co 35250 Last Night/Can I Help It?
    Co 35412 My! My!/Say It

GLENN MILLER
    Bb 11287 From One Love to Another
    Bb 11382 A String of Pearls
    Vi 27935 Serenade in Blue
    Vi 20-1529 Rhapsody in Blue

FRANKIE CARLE
    Vo 5155 It's a Whole New Thing/ Chico's Love Song

FRANKIE LAINE
    Co 40022 Te Amo

GLEN GRAY
    De 18843 If I Love Again

JACKIE GLEASON
    Cap 2437 Body and Soul/Alone Together
    Cap 2438 My Funny Valentine/Love Is Here to Stay

RED MCKENZIE
    Vo 3875 Farewell, My Love/Sail Along Silv'ry Moon
    Vo 3898 Georgianna/You're Out of This World

TEDDY WILSON
    Br 8112 Moments Like This/I Can't Face the Music
    Br 8116 Don't Be That Way

BOBBY HACKETT
    Vo 4047 If Dreams Come True/At the Jazz Band Ball
    Vo 4565 A Ghost of a Chance/Doin' the New Low Down
    Vo 4877 Embraceable You/Ain't Misbehavin'
    Vo 5620 That Old Gang of Mine/After I Say I'm Sorry

Br 80009 Soon/Soft Lights and Sweet Music
Br 80101 If There Is Someone Lovelier Than You/What Is There to Say?
Co 39019 Struttin' with Some Barbecue/A Room with a View
Co 39020 Fidgety Feet/I've Got the World on a String

LPs

BOBBY HACKETT
    Epic LN-3106 The Hackett Horn (Vo RIs)
    Co CL-1729 The Most Beautiful Horn in the World
    Co(10″)CL-6165 Jazz Session
    Cap ST-1172 Blues with a Kick
    Cap(10″)L-458 Soft Lights and Bobby Hackett
    Verve V-8698 Creole Cookin'
    Chiaroscuro CR-105 Live at the Roosevelt Grill with Vic Dickenson

BOBBY HACKETT-VIC DICKENSON
    Project 3-PR/5034SD This Is Our Bag

LEE WILEY
    Co(10″)CL-6169 Night In Manhattan

EDDIE CONDON
    De(10″)DL-5137 George Gershwin Jazz Concert

LOUIS ARMSTRONG
    Vi LPM-1443 Town Hall Concert Plus

BOBBY BYRNE
    GA 207-SD (S) Great Song Hits of Glenn Miller Orchestra

JACKIE GLEASON
    Cap(10″) Music to Make You Misty

737. HAENSCHEN, GUS   ar cm B
(WALTER GUSTAVE HAENSCHEN)
Born St. Louis, Mo.

Prominent conductor on radio, particularly during 30s. Attended Washington University of St. Louis. Executive for Brunswick Records pre-1920. Suggested Billy Jones and Ernie Hare form team which became popular in 20s. Haenschen on radio mid-20s; by mid-30s conductor-arranger for top shows. Arrangements used strings effectively. Orchestras boasted classical and jazz musicians. Long tenure on American Album of Familiar Music starring Frank Munn: beginning about 1934 into mid-40s. Another popular show: Maxwell House Show Boat late 1934-6. On Lavendar and Old Lace show 1934-5, with Frank Munn on Bayer Musical Review 1935, on Coca Cola's Song Shop late 1937-8. Another long-running series: Saturday Night Serenade, 1937 into early 40s. Active in later 40s. Composer of *Manhattan Merry-Go-Round*, theme of popular program of same name from 1936 to late 40s. Other compositions: *Silver Star, Underneath the Japanese Moon, Lullaby of Love, Rosita, Easy Melody.*

738. HAGAN, CASS   v ar B
Born 1904, Edgewater, N.J.

Leader of good semi-hot dance band in 20s. Attended Manhattan College. Formed combo, including pianist Lennie Hayton, to play eastern clubs and resorts. First important engagement late 1926 at New York's Hotel Manger (later Taft) with augmented band; Hayton pianist-arranger. Band had excellent ensemble sound; big hit. In 1927 band opened Park Central Hotel. Personnel at times included Red Nichols (c), Al Philburn (tb), Pee Wee Russell (cl), Don Murray (cl). Disbanded early 1928. Later 1928 Hagan reorganized with new personnel, toured midwest. Late 1928 he and Nichols formed excellent combo, toured to west coast. Hagan soon left music except for 1937 venture as night club operator.

RECORDS
CASS HAGAN
    Ed 51959 The Kinkajou/It All Depends on You
    Ed 52012 I Adore You/Lily
    Co 966-D Hallelujah!/Sometimes I'm Happy
    Co 1033-D Melancholy Charlie/Variety Stomp
    Co 1089-D Havana/Broken-Hearted
    Co 1114-D The Varsity Drag
    Co 1138-D Broadway/Manhattan Mary
    Co 1176-D My Lady
    Co 1222-D Dear, on a Night Like This
    Co 1301-D My Ohio Home
    Co 1334-D Golden Gate

739. HAGGART, BOB   b ar cm B
Born March 13, 1914, New York, N.Y.

Excellent bassist active mostly with dixieland groups, best known for playing-arranging-composing with Bob Crosby band 1935-42. Grew up in Douglaston, Long Island. Studied many instruments; much musical training. First with dance bands, mainly Bob Sperling 1932-4, then quick fame with Crosby band. Composer or co-composer of numbers featured by band: *I'm Prayin' Humble, South Rampart Street Parade, Dixieland Shuffle, My Inspiration* (later *Gone but Not Forgotten*, with lyrics added), *Dogtown Blues, I'm Free* (later became standard *What's New?*, with lyrics added), *The Big Noise from Winnetka.* Latter a novelty classic performed by Haggart and drummer Ray Bauduc and featuring Haggart whistling through teeth. Studio work in New York after Crosby disbanded 1942. Freelance recording later 40s and 50s; led bands backing singers on records. Frequent arranging through the years for Louis Armstrong, Billie Holiday, Bing Crosby, Andrews Sisters and Ella Fitzgerald. Some composing for show MADISON AVENUE. In early 50s he and trumpet star Yank Lawson co-led dixieland group on Decca LPs. Played in TV bands, including Tonight Show band. In various Crosby groups at intervals. In late 60s co-leader with Yank Lawson of World's Greatest Jazz Band, a group of veteran stars. Scored much of band's book. Active into 70s as WGJB toured four continents.

RECORDS
BOB CROSBY
    De 825 Dixieland Shuffle/Muskrat Ramble
    De 896 Pagan Love Song/Come Back, Sweet Papa
    De 1094 Sugar Foot Strut/Savoy Blues
    De 1552 Little Rock Getaway/Vieni Vieni
    De 1865 March of the Bob Cats/Who's Sorry Now? (both BOB CATS)
    De 2205 I'm Free (What's New?)/Summertime
    De 2206 The Big Bass Viol/Speak to Me of Love (both BOB CATS)
    De 2208 The Big Noise from

Winnetka/Honky Tonk Train Blues

De 2209 My Inspiration/Loopin' the Loop (both BOB CATS)

De 2210 I'm Prayin' Humble/Swingin' at the Sugar Bowl

De 2482 Hindustan/Mournin' Blues (both BOB CATS)

De 2789 Washington & Lee Swing/ Peruna (both BOB CATS)

De 2848 Boogie Woogie Maxixe/High Society

De 3248 Spain/All by Myself (both BOB CATS)

De 4390 Sugar Foot Stomp/King Porter Stomp

De(12″)15038 Dogtown Blues/South Rampart Street Parade

ALL-STAR BAND

Vi 26144 Blue Lou/The Blues

METRONOME ALL-STAR BAND

Co 35389 King Porter Stomp/All-Star Strut

MOUND CITY BLUE BLOWERS

Ch 40059 Thanks a Million/I'm Sittin' High on a Hilltop

Ch 40060 On Treasure Island/Red Sails in the Sunset

BILL STEGMEYER

Si 15006 Bosco and His Doghouse

JERRY JEROME

Asch 501 Third Floor Rear Boogie/ When I Grow Too Old to Dream

MUGGSY SPANIER

CMS 576 Whistlin' the Blues/The Lady's in Love with You

BOBBY HAGGART

MGM 10699 By the Waters of Minnetonka/Baby, Won't You Please Come Home?

(as arranger/conductor)

MARION MANN

Vogue 731 You Took Advantage of Me/Between the Devil and the Deep Blue Sea

BILLIE HOLIDAY

De 23853 Solitude/No Greater Love

De 24138 Deep Song/Easy Living

GEORGIA GIBBS

Cor 60210 I Don't Care If the Sun Don't Shine/I'll Get Myself a Choo Choo Train

ELLA FITZGERALD

De 23956 Oh, Lady Be Good

CARL RAVAZZA

De 24136 Vieni Su/Pedro

LPs

LAWSON-HAGGART JAZZ BAND

De DL-8182 Jelly Roll's Jazz

De DL-8195 King Oliver's Jazz

De DL-8198 Windy City Jazz

De(10″)DL-5529 South of the Mason-Dixon Line

BOB HAGGART

MGM E-3262 Strictly from Dixie

BOB CROSBY

De(10″)DL-8061 Bob Crosby's Bob Cats (De RIs)

Cor CRL-57089 (De RIs)

Mon-Ever 7026 Mardi Gras Parade

LOUIS ARMSTRONG

Vi LPM-1443 Town Hall Concert Plus

BUD FREEMAN

Mon-Ever MES-7022 The Compleat Bud Freeman

THE WORLD'S GREATEST JAZZ BAND

Project PR/5033SD (S)

Project PR/5039SD (S) Extra!

Atl S-1570 Live at the Roosevelt Grill

740. HAIG, AL   p B
Born 1923, Newark, N.J.

A top modern pianist most prominent in early bop years. Excellent accompanist in combos; soloed along simple lines with full chording. Attended Oberlin College 1940-1. In coast guard bands 1942-4. Then played Boston clubs. Brief period with Jerry Wald. To New York 1945; important in early bop. With Dizzy Gillespie, Charlie Parker, other moderns on club dates and records. Work in later 40s included seven months with Jimmy Dorsey. Often with Stan Getz 1949-51. In comparative obscurity early 50s; with Tommy Reynolds and Tex Beneke 1952-3. Back into limelight with Chet Baker 1954-5 and Dizzy Gillespie 1956-7. Freelanced; since 1960 led combos, worked as single. Active into 70s playing clubs in New York and nearby.

RECORDS

RED RODNEY

Mer 1065 Fine and Dandy/Elevation

EDDIE DAVIS

Sav 904 Hollerin' and Screaming/Maternity

Sav 907 Calling Dr. Jazz/Stealin' Trash

DIZZY GILLESPIE

Vi 40-0130 Night in Tunisia/52nd Street Theme

Vi 40-0132 Anthropology/Ol' Man Rebop

Mus 383 Oop Bop Sh' Bam/A Hand Fulla Gimme

Mus 485 That's Earl, Brother

TEMPO JAZZMEN

Dial 1001 Dynamo A & B

Dial 1003 'Round About Midnight

Dial 1008 Confirmation

MILES DAVIS

Cap 57-60005 Godchild/Jeru

WARDELL GRAY

NJ 817 Easy Living/Twisted

J. C. HEARD

Apo 783 Ollopa/This Is It

Apo 790 Sugar Hips/Coastin' with J.C.

BEN WEBSTER

Br 80177 I Got It Bad

STAN GETZ

Birdland 6001 I've Got You Under My Skin/There's a Small Hotel

Roost 522 On the Alamo/For Stompers Only

AL HAIG

Jade 701 Haig 'n' Haig/Bow Tie

Seeco 10002 Sugar Hill Bop/Five Star

Seeco 10003 In a Pinch/It's the Talk of the Town

Seeco 10006 Poop Deck/Pennies from Heaven

NJ 822 Liza/Stars Fell on Alabama

PJ 626 The Moon Was Yellow/Yardbird Suite

LPs

AL HAIG

Eso(10″)7

Pres 7841 Trio and Quintet (RIs)

Pres(10″)175

Period(10″)1104

DIZZY GILLESPIE

Sav MG-12020 Groovin' High (Mus RIs)

Vi LPM-2398 The Greatest of Dizzy Gillespie (Vi RIs)

MILES DAVIS

Cap T-1974 Birth of the Cool (Cap RIs)

STAN GETZ

Pres(10″)102 Stan Getz, Vol. 1

Pres(10″)104 Stan Getz, Vol. 2

Roost(10″)420 Jazz at Storyville, Vol. 3

WARDELL GRAY

Pres 7343 (2-LP set) Memorial Album (RIs)

741. HAINES, CONNIE   VO
(YVONNE MARIE JAMAIS)

Born January 20, 1922, Savannah, Ga.

Good band singer, best known for work with Tommy Dorsey. Petite; vivacious personality, good showman. Sang as child on radio; own show at 10 in Jacksonville. At 14 played Roxy Theatre in New York. Sang with bands in Miami area late 30s as Yvonne Marie. With Harry James several months mid-1939, changed name to Connie Haines. Joined Dorsey April 1940, remained almost two years. Dorsey work won acclaim, especially on hit *Will You Still Be Mine?*. Left Dorsey early 1942 for career as single. Sang on radio shows 1942-5: Abbott & Costello, Edgar Bergen, Fibber McGee & Molly, Andy Russell. In several movies including TWILIGHT ON THE PRAIRIE and A WAVE, A WAC AND A MARINE (1944), DUCHESS OF IDAHO (1950). Recorded occasionally late 40s and early 50s. With Jane Russell, Beryl Davis and Della Russell formed female quartet specializing in gospel. Their record *Do Lord* 1954 hit. By late 50s Connie less active. Occasional club dates and nostalgic TV into 70s.

RECORDS

HARRY JAMES

Br 8395 Comes Love/I Can't Afford to Dream

TOMMY DORSEY

Vi 26609 I'm Nobody's Baby/Buds Won't Bud

Vi 26636 You Think of Ev'rything

Vi 26660 And So Do I

Vi 26736 That's for Me

Vi 26738 I Wouldn't Take a Million

Vi 26764 Two Dreams Met

Vi 26786 When I Saw You

Vi 26798 Isn't That Just Like Love?

Vi 27219 You Say the Sweetest Things, Baby

Vi 27345 Birds of a Feather

Vi 27350 You're Dangerous

Vi 27392 You Betcha My Life

Vi 27421 Will You Still Be Mine?

Vi 27461 Kiss the Boys Goodbye

Vi 27617 Fifty Million Sweethearts Can't Be Wrong/That Solid Old Man

Vi 27876 Snootie Little Cutie

GORDON JENKINS

Cap 106 He Wears a Pair of Silver Wings

CONNIE HAINES

Si 15168 Will You Still Be Mine?/You Made Me Love You

Si 15235 Stormy Weather/My Man

Cor 60309 Guys and Dolls/A Bushel and a Peck

Cor 60318 Lover Man/The Man I Love

Cor 60799 Mississippi Mud/You Nearly Lose your Mind

CONNIE HAINES-JANE RUSSELL-BERYL DAVIS-DELLA RUSSELL

Cor 61113 Do Lord/Make a Joyful Noise unto the Lord

LPs

CONNIE HAINES

Tops L-1606 A Tribute to Helen Morgan

TOMMY DORSEY

Cam CAL-800 Dedicated to You (Vi RIs)

742. HAJOS, MITZI   vo
(MARISHKA HAJOS)

Born April 27, 1891, Budapest, Hungary

Petite, vivacious beauty, star of Broadway musicals 1911-28. Ordinary singing voice but great personality and vigor. Performed as child in Budapest theatres singing, dancing and doing imitations; billed as The Wonder Child—Mitzi Hajos. Popular in several European countries. To U.S. at 12. In play THE BARNYARD ROMEO (1910). Began Broadway musical career in LA BELLE PAREE (1911). Toured in THE SPRING MAID (1912), then back on Broadway in HER LITTLE HIGHNESS (1913). Beginning 1913 billed simply as Mitzi. Biggest hit SARI (1914). Other Broadway shows POM-POM (1916), HEAD OVER HEELS (1918), LADY BILLY (1921), THE MAGIC RING (1923; non-musical), NAUGHTY RIQUETTE (1926), THE MADCAP (1928). In 1930 quit acting, worked over

20 years in Shubert theatrical offices, retired in early 50s.

RECORDS

MITZI HAJOS

Vi 45091 Evelyn/In the Dark

743. HALEY, JACK   vo

Born c. 1901-2, Boston, Mass.

Star of stage, movies and radio. Adept at light comedy, playing bewildered, inept, reluctant hero. Early career as singer and dancer in vaudeville. Supporting roles in Broadway shows ROUND THE TOWN (1924; unsuccessful) and GAY PAREE (1925). Starred in hit show FOLLOW THROUGH (1929); same role in 1930 movie version led to successful film career. In more than 30 movie musicals and comedies. Returned to Broadway in FREE FOR ALL (1931; unsuccessful), TAKE A CHANCE (1932), HIGHER AND HIGHER (1940), INSIDE U.S.A. (1948). In 1942 vaudeville production SHOW TIME. Important on radio through the years. On popular Show Boat show 1937; late that year Jack Haley's Variety Show. Continued own show in various formats into late 40s. TV show around 1950-1, occasional appearances in later years. Excellent guest and story-teller on late-night talk shows of 60s.

MOVIES

1930—FOLLOW THROUGH

1933—MR. BROADWAY

1934—HERE COMES THE GROOM; SITTING PRETTY

1935—SPRING TONIC; THE GIRL FRIEND; REDHEADS ON PARADE; CORONADO; POOR LITTLE RICH GIRL; PIGSKIN PARADE; MR. CINDERELLA

1936—F-MAN

1937—PICK A STAR; WAKE UP AND LIVE; SHE HAD TO EAT; DANGER: LOVE AT WORK'

1938—ALEXANDER'S RAGTIME BAND; REBECCA OF SUNNYBROOK FARM; THANKS FOR EVERYTHING; HOLD THAT COED!

1939—THE WIZARD OF OZ

1941—MOON OVER MIAMI; NAVY BLUES

1942—BEYOND THE BLUE HORIZON

1944—HIGHER AND HIGHER; TAKE IT BIG; ONE BODY TOO MANY

1945—GEORGE WHITE'S SCANDALS OF 1945; SING YOUR WAY HOME; SCARED STIFF; TREASURE OF FEAR
1946—PEOPLE ARE FUNNY; VACATION IN RENO
1949—MAKE MINE LAUGHS
1969—NORWOOD

RECORDS

JACK HALEY
  Vi 20-2940 Rhode Island Is Famous for You/First Prize at the Fair

LPs
(movie soundtrack)
MGM E-3464 THE WIZARD OF OZ

744. HALL, ADELAIDE   vo
Born c. 1909, Brooklyn, N.Y.

Jazz vocalist of 20s and 30s. Unusual style combined fine soprano with gutty attack. Attended Pratt Institute. Starred in CHOCOLATE KIDDIES show on European tour 1925. In various Negro stage revues including SHUFFLE ALONG and DESIRES OF 1927. Star of BLACKBIRDS OF 1928, later toured Europe with show. In BROWN BUDDIES in 1930. Sang in clubs and theatres; Art Tatum accompanist 1932-3. Toured U.S. at times, worked with leading jazzmen. Returned to Europe 1936, eventually settled in England. Active there on stage-radio-records, played clubs, occasionally toured. Active into 60s. Important role in Broadway musical JAMAICA in 1957.

RECORDS

DUKE ELLINGTON
  Vi 21137 Creole Love Call
  Vi 21490 The Blues I Love to Sing
WILLIE LEWIS
  Pat(Fr) 914 I'm Shooting High
  Pat(Fr) 915 Say You're Mine
FATS WALLER
  HMV(E) 8849 That Old Feeling/I Can't Give You Anything but Love
ADELAIDE HALL with LEW LESLIE'S BLACKBIRDS ORCHESTRA
  Br 4031 Baby/I Must Have That Man
ADELAIDE HALL WITH DUKE ELLINGTON ORCHESTRA
  Br 6518 Baby/I Must Have That Man

ADELAIDE HALL
  Br 6362 This Time It's Love/I'll Never Be the Same
  Br 6376 Strange as It Seems/You Gave Me Everything but Love
  Tono(Den) 6001 There's a Lull in My Life (medley)
  Tono(Den) 6002 Stormy Weather/Where or When
  De(E) 7049 I Have Eyes/I Promise You
  De(E) 7083 Deep Purple/Solitude
  De(E) 7305 My Heart Belongs to Daddy/Have You Met Miss Jones?
  De(E) 7345 The Lady Is a Tramp/Where or When
  De(E) 7501 This Can't Be Love/No Souvenirs
  De(E) 7522 Who Told You I Cared?/Shake Down the Stars
  De(E) 7918 I Hear a Rhapsody/Mississippi Mama
  De(E) 8092 A Sinner Kissed an Angel/Why Don't We Do This More Often?
  De(E) 8202 As Time Goes By/Let's Get Lost
  De(E) 8362 I Heard You Cried Last Night/I Don't Want Anybody at All

LPs
(miscellaneous artists)
Sutton 270 BLACKBIRDS OF 1928 (RIs)

745. HALL, AL   b
Born March 18, 1915, Jacksonville, Fla.

Bassist with swing bands and jazz combos. Grew up in Philadelphia. In local bands 1933-5. With Billy Hicks in New York 1936-7, Skeets Tolbert 1937-8. With Teddy Wilson's big band and combo 1939-41. With Ellis Larkins trio 1942-3. Studio work 1943-4, then pit bands for Broadway shows in later 40s. Owned Wax record company. Freelanced with top jazzmen. In early 70s with Larkins in New York.

RECORDS

REDD EVANS
  Vo 5173 Milenberg Joys/In the Baggage Coach Ahead

BILLIE HOLIDAY
OK 5806 The Same Old Story/Practice Makes Perfect
OK 5831 I Hear Music/I'm All for You
TEDDY WILSON
Br 8112 Moments Like This/I Can't Face the Music
Br 8116 Don't Be That Way
Br 8438 Jumpin' for Joy/The Man I Love
Br 8455 This Is the Moment/Love Grows on the White Oak Tree
Co 35207 Early Session Hop/Lady of Mystery
Co 35220 Exactly Like You/Booly-Ja-Ja
Co 35737 Cocoanut Grove/71
Co 35905 I Never Knew/Embraceable You
Co 36632 Rosetta
Co 36634 China Boy
Mus 332 I Can't Get Started/Stompin' at the Savoy
BON BON
De 3980 I Don't Want to Set the World on Fire/Sweet Mama, Papa's Getting Mad
De 8567 Blow, Gabriel, Blow/All That Meat and No Potatoes
V-DISC ALL-STARS
VD(12″)384 Jack Armstrong Blues
VD(12″)491 Confessin'
THE BE-BOP BOYS
Sav 900 Webb City (1 & 2)
Sav 901 Fat Boy (1 & 2)
CLYDE HART
Cont 6013 What's the Matter Now?/That's the Blues
PETE JOHNSON
Nat 4007 Mutiny in the Doghouse
JOE TURNER
Nat 9011 Watch That Jive/Johnson & Turner Blues
BEN WEBSTER
Wax 104 All Alone/As Long as I Live
DICKY WELLS
Si 28115 Linger Awhile/Hello Babe
Si(12″)90002 I Got Rhythm/I'm Fer It Too
DON BYAS
Super Disc 1010 Melody in Swing/Super Session
Super Disc 1011 Embraceable You/

The Sheik of Araby
OTTO HARDWICK
Wax 105 I Remember Your Eyes/Blue Belles of Harlem
AL HALL
Wax 101 Blues in My Heart/Rose of the Rio Grande
Wax 102 Lazy River/Come Sunday (OTTO HARDWICK)
Wax 103 Emaline/Am I Blue

LPs

BILLY TAYLOR (one side)
Sav MG-12008 Back to Back
DICK CARY
Stereocraft RTN-106 Hot and Cool
TEDDY WILSON
MGM(10″)E-129 Runnin' Wild (Mus RIs)
FATS NAVARRO
Sav(10″)9005
SONNY STITT
Sav(10″)9006
PAUL QUINICHETTE
EmArcy MG-36006 Moods
(miscellaneous artists)
Vi LPV-519 The Be-Bop Era (Vi RIs)
Blue Angel 504 (S) The Night They Raided Sunnie's

746. HALL, ED   cl bs B
(EDMOND HALL)
Born May 15, 1901, New Orleans, La.
Died February 11, 1967, Boston, Mass.

Jazz clarinetist with dixieland and other combos. Strong, liquid tone, buoyant phrasing, driving style. From musical family. Played locally 1919-20. With Buddy Petit early 20s, including tours. After working various cities, to New York early 1928 with Alonzo Ross. Later with Arthur Ford, Billy Fowler and Charlie Skeets. At Savoy Ballroom with Claude Hopkins early 1930; with Hopkins off and on till 1935. Periods with Lucky Millinder 1936 and 1937; with Billy Hicks 1937-8. With Zutty Singleton and Joe Sullivan 1939. Freelanced, joined Red Allen late 1940 for about a year. With Teddy Wilson 1941-4. Beginning later in 1944 led group, mostly at New York's Cafe Society Uptown and Downtown in mid-40s. Considerable freelance recording in 40s, also led group in Boston.

During 1950-5 Eddie Condon's New York club. With Louis Armstrong All-Stars 1955-8. Again with Condon in 60s; also made European tours and played in TV bands. Active until 1967 death from heart attack while shoveling snow.

RECORDS

ROSS DELUXE SYNCOPATORS
Vi 20952 Lady Mine/Mary Belle
Vi 20961 Florida Rhythm/Skad-O-Lee

W. C. HANDY
Vs 8163 Beale Street Blues/St. Louis Blues

CLAUDE HOPKINS
De 184 King Porter Stomp/In the Shade of the Old Apple Tree
De 441 Chasing All the Blues Away

RED ALLEN
OK 6281 Ol' Man River/K.K. Boogie

WILD BILL DAVISON
CMS 549 Clarinet Marmalade/Original Dixieland One Step
CMS 575 At the Jazz Band Ball/Baby, Won't You Please Come Home?

DEPARIS BROTHERS
CMS 552 Black and Blue/I've Found a New Baby

ART HODES
BN 34 Sugar Foot Stomp/Sweet Georgia Brown
BN 35 Squeeze Me/Bugle Call Rag

BILLIE HOLIDAY
Vo 3593 Me, Myself and I/Without Your Love
Vo 3605 Born to Love/A Sailboat in the Moonlight

JOE SULLIVAN
Vo 5496 Oh, Lady Be Good/I Can't Give You Anything but Love
OK 5647 Coquette/I've Got a Crush on You

EDDIE CONDON
De 23433 I'll Build a Stairway to Paradise/My One and Only

ZUTTY SINGLETON
De 18093 Shim-Me-Sha-Wabble/King Porter Stomp

FRANK NEWTON
Va 518 You Showed Me the Way
Va 616 Easy Living/Where or When

GEORGE WETTLING
Co 39497 Collier's Clambake/Collier's Climb

RALPH SUTTON
De 29081 Up Jumped You with Love/Sweet and Lovely

ED HALL
BN(12")17 Celestial Express/Profoundly Blue
BN(12")28 High Society/Blues at Blue Note
BN(12")30 Rompin' in 44/Smooth Sailing
CMS(12")1512 Downtown Cafe Boogie/Uptown Cafe Boogie
CMS 557 Caravan/It's Only a Shanty in Old Shanty Town
CMS 580 Show Piece/I Want to Be Happy
Delta 10 Blues in Room 920/Sweet Georgia Brown
Br 80125 Opus 15/Besame Mucho

LPs

ED HALL
BN 6505 Celestial Express (BN RIs)
(one side) BN 6504 Original Blue Note Jazz, Vol. 1 (BN RIs)
RaeCox 1120 (S) Rumpus on Rampart Street

JAMES P. JOHNSON
BN(10")7012 Jazz Band Ball

WILD BILL DAVISON
CMS(10")FL-20004
CMS(10")FL-20011

VIC DICKENSON
Vang 8520 The Vic Dickenson Septet, Vol. 1
Vang 8521 The Vic Dickenson Septet, Vol. 2

MUTT CAREY (and Punch Miller)
Sav MG-12038 New Orleans Jazz, Vol. 1
Sav MG-12050 New Orleans Jazz, Vol. 2

EDDIE CONDON
Co CL-547 Jam Session Coast-to-Coast (one side)
Co CL-616 Jammin' at Condon's
Co CL-719 Bixieland

747. HALL, FRED   vo p cm B

Born April 10, 1898, New York, N.Y.
Died October 8, 1964, New York, N.Y.

Comedian - singer - bandleader - composer active in 20s. Early in career worked as pianist for publishing companies. Jobs as pianist-singer. Co-composer of popular songs including *I Got a Code Id By Dose, That Old Family Album, There's a Blue Sky 'Way Out Yonder, Eleven More Months and Ten More Days, If You See My Little Mountain Girl, The Man with the Little White Cane;* some in collaboration with Arthur Fields, with whom associated at various times. Hall formed band mid-20s; billed as Fred "Sugar" Hall's Sugar Babies. Band played raucously in hot and novelty style, arrangements providing for solos by sidemen. Recorded 1925-30. Arthur Fields with band as vocalist late 20s. Later Hall and Fields worked as comedy and singing team; on morning radio show 1937. Hall later producer on Voice of America radio.

RECORDS

THE SIZZLERS
    Ed 52463 Diga Diga Doo/Somebody Stole My Gal
THE WHOOPEE MAKERS
    Co 14367-D Sister Kate/Somebody Stole My Gal
FRED "SUGAR" HALL'S SUGAR BABIES
    OK 40410 Look Who's Here!/My Sugar
    OK 40482 Melancholy Lou/Charleston Baby o' Mine
    OK 40891 Is It Possible?/Someday You'll Say "O.K."
    OK 40986 Plenty of Sunshine/Look in the Mirror
    OK 41055 C-O-N-S-T-A-N-T-I-N-O-P-L-E/Chilly-Pom-Pom-Pee
    OK 41112 On the Night We Did the Boom-Boom by the Sea/Butternut
    OK 41123 It Goes Like This/Everything We Like We Like Alike
    OK 41152 I'm Wild About Horns on Automobiles/Come On, Baby
    OK 41183 I Faw Down and Go "Boom"/She Only Laughs at Me
    OK 41239 I Got a Code Id By Dose/Here's That Party Now in Person
    OK 41310 I Lift Up My Finger and Say "Tweet Tweet"/Sophomore Prom
    OK 41317 Piccolo Pete/Sergeant Flagg and Sergeant Quirt
    OK 41369 Harmonica Harry/'Tain't No Sin

FRED HALL'S JAZZ BAND
    Re 8648 Louder and Funnier
    Re 8655 West End Blues/Missouri Squabble

748. HALL, GEORGE   v B

Popular bandleader in 30s, for years a fixture at New York's Hotel Taft. First band in mid-20s called George Hall & His Arcadians; relatively unknown. In 1931 helped popularize *Love Letters in the Sand*, adopted it as theme through 30s. Band gradually became known via Bluebird recordings starting early 1933. Maintained Taft spot during 30s, with good radio coverage. Band had full, beautiful ensemble sound, featured good vocalists; ideal for hotels. Loretta Lee excellent vocalist 1933-5. Johnny McKeever and Sonny Schuyler also sang capably. Dolly Dawn became star vocalist and key factor in band's popularity 1935-41: personable, good showman, effective on ballads and belting out rhythm numbers and novelties. Her ties to Hall so close she became his adopted daughter. In late 30s Hall had excellent rhythm section: Johnny Guarnieri (p), Nick Fatool (d), Tony Mottola (g), Doc Goldberg (b). Hall retired 1941, turned band over to Dolly, who folded band 1942 and became a single.

RECORDS

GEORGE HALL
    Bb 5021 Have You Ever Been Lonely?/In the Valley of the Moon
    Bb 5023 Down a Carolina Lane/In My Dixie Hideaway
    Bb 5112 Blue Prelude/Under a Blanket of Blue
    Bb 5314 Let's Fall in Love/Tired of It All
    Bb 5648 What About Me?/How Can You Face Me?
    Bb 5662 Okay, Toots/When My Ship Comes In
    Bb 5663 An Earful of Music/Your Head on My Shoulder
    Bb 5709 Flirtation Walk/Mr. and Mrs. Is the Name
    Bb 5863 Lovely to Look At/I Won't Dance
    Bb 6015 My Very Good Friend, the Milkman/Young Ideas

Bb 6099 Accent on Youth/Every Now and Then

Bb 6101 Will Love Find a Way?/It Never Dawned on Me

Bb 6127 A Picture of Me without You/Got a Bran' New Suit

Bb 6172 Alone/Santy, Bring My Mommy Back to Me

Bb 6173 You Took My Breath Away

Bb 6214 Moon Over Miami/One Night in Monte Carlo

Bb 6379 Love Came Out of the Night/There's Always a Happy Ending

Bb 6509 South Sea Island Magic/Please Keep Me in Your Dreams

Va 569 Our Penthouse on Third Avenue/Love Is Never Out of Season

Vo 3775 My Cabin of Dreams/Lovely One

Vo 3781 Am I in Love?/Remember Me?

Vo 3943 Always and Always/I Simply Adore You

Vo 4297 My Own/You're as Pretty as a Picture

Vo 5343 Faithful to You/At Sundown

749. HALL, JUANITA   VO

Born c. 1907
Died February 28, 1968, Bay Shore, N.Y.

Singer on Broadway stage, best known for role as Bloody Mary in hit musical SOUTH PACIFIC. Began as member of chorus in SHOW BOAT (1928). Minor roles in shows THE GREEN PASTURES, THE PIRATE, SING OUT SWEET LAND, DEEP ARE THE ROOTS, STREET SCENE. Solo singing tours; also led choral group The Juanita Hall Choir. Good role in Broadway show ST. LOUIS WOMAN (1946), then scored in SOUTH PACIFIC (1949). Night clubs in early 50s; sang pop and show songs. Important roles in Broadway shows HOUSE OF FLOWERS (1955) and FLOWER DRUM SONG (1958). In movie versions of SOUTH PACIFIC (1958) and FLOWER DRUM SONG (1961). Active in 60s.

RECORDS

JUANITA HALL CHOIR
De 8652 Run Li'l Chillun!/We Men Are Free Men

JUANITA HALL
Co 4559-M Happy Talk
Vi 20-3603 Scarlet Ribbons/Blow the Blues Away

LPs

JUANITA HALL
Vs(10")VLP-6012 Stephen Foster Songs
Mon-Ever MES-7020 Juanita Hall
Counterpoint 556 Sings the Blues
(original Broadway casts)
Co OL-4180 SOUTH PACIFIC
Co ML-4969 HOUSE OF FLOWERS
Co OL-5350 FLOWER DRUM SONG

750. HALL, SLEEPY   bn B

Leader of band on and off, late 20s and 30s. Often billed Sleepy Hall & His Collegians. Good hotel-style band. Theme *Sleepy Time Gal*. Played banjo on Rudy Vallee and Shell radio programs c. 1937. Though at times in obscurity, kept active into early 40s. At New York World's Fair 1939. Military service 1943. Early 30s records on Melotone displayed good sweet band with occasional hot soloists; may be studio band using Hall's name as leader.

RECORDS

SLEEPY HALL
Me 12006 Ukulele Moon/On a Little Balcony in Spain
Me 12022 Song of the Fool/Sing Song Girl
Me 12058 Tears/Under the Spell of Your Kiss
Me 12066 It Must Be True/Just a Gigolo
Me 12089 I Hate Myself/Say Hello to the Folks Back Home
Me 12121 Elizabeth/Oh, Donna Clara
Me 12155 Bubbling Over with Love/Fiesta
Me 12190 Soldier on the Shelf/Honeymoon Parade
Me 12204 At Your Command/How the Time Can Fly
Me 12211 A Little Hunka Love/Parkin' in the Moonlight
Me 12236 I Don't Know Why/I'm with You
Me 12256 This Is the Missus/Life Is Just a Bowl of Cherries
Me 12299 Of Thee I Sing/Who Cares?

Me 12311 Wooden Soldier and the China Doll/Dancing on the Ceiling
Me 12323 Strangers/Tired
Vo 4287 (theme) Sleepy Time Gal/The Old Oaken Bucket

751. HALL, WENDELL   vo uk cm lyr
Born August 23, 1896, St. George, Kan.

Famed as The Red-Headed Music Maker. Entertainer of 20s, composed novelty hit *It Ain't Gonna Rain No Mo'*. Attended University of Chicago Prep School. Military service, World War I. In early 20s played vaudeville, singing and playing ukulele. *Rain* brought fame 1923. On radio mid-20s. Travelled the nation from station to station working on radio. Vaudeville in late 20s. Director of 1929 radio show Majestic Theatre of the Air. Other network shows: Fitch Band Wagon 1932-5, Gillette's Community Sing with Milton Berle late 1936-7. Later advertising executive. Other compositions *Whispering Trees, Will You Forget Me While I'm Away?, Underneath the Mellow Moon, Land of My Sunset Dreams, My Carolina Rose, Your Shining Eyes, Red-Headed Music Maker, My Dream Sweetheart, Miss American Legion*.

RECORDS
WENDELL HALL
Vi 19171 It Ain't Gonna Rain No Mo'/Red-Headed Music Maker
Vi 19270 It Looks Like Rain/Comfortin' Gal
Vi 19290 Gwine to Run All Night/Oh, Susanna
Vi 19479 Lonely Lane/Swanee River Dreams (with CARSON ROBISON)
Vi 19725 Sunshine/It Struck My Funny Bone
Vi 19792 Hokey Pokey Diddle Dee Rum/I Don't Think So
Vi 19819 Angry/Whisp'ring Trees, Memories and You
Br 3006 Paddlin' Madelin' Home/Hokey Pokey
Br 3330 She's Still My Baby/No One but You Knows How to Love
Br 3331 Just a Bird's-Eye View of My Old Kentucky Home/Meadow-Lark
Br 3387 Take in the Sun, Hang Out the Moon/I'm Tellin' the Birds, Tellin'

the Bees, How I Love You
Br 3903 I Told You/Will You Remember?
Br 3983 Hot Feet/Oh Lucindy
Br 4004 My Dream Sweetheart/Easy Going
Br 4024 Polly Wolly Doodle/If I Only Knew
Br 4879 Mellow Moon/Land of My Sunset Dreams
Ge 5271 It Ain't Gonna Rain No Mo'/Red-Headed Music Maker
Co 942-D Hot Feet/Down Kentucky Way
Co 1028-D Headin' Home/There's a Trick in Pickin' a Chicken
(with THE VIRGINIANS)
Vi 19226 Blue Island Blues/Blue Bird Blues

752. HALLBERG, BENGT   p
Born September 13, 1932, in Sweden

Swedish piano star in modern style, facile and inventive. Began professionally 1948, soon working with leading Swedish jazzmen. By mid-50s a top pianist in Sweden. In later 50s studio work. Became known in U.S. mid-50s via LPs featuring modern Swedish jazzmen. Played New York 1974 with Arne Domnerus septet.

RECORDS
SWINGIN' SWEDES
BN 1605 Pick Yourself Up/Summertime
STAN GETZ
Metronome 554 Ack, Varmeland Du Skona/S'cool Boy
BENGT HALLBERG
Cup(Sw) 4381 Fine and Dandy/My Love Is Yours
LPs
BENGT HALLBERG
Epic LN-3375
Pres(10″)121 (one side)
Pres(10″)145
Pres(10″)176
HARRY ARNOLD
Jazztone J-1270 The Jazztone Mystery Band
Mer MG-36139 Plus Big Band Plus Quincy Jones Equals Jazz!
LARS GULLIN
EmArcy MG-36059 With The Moretone Singers

EmArcy(10″)MG-26044 Gullin's Garden

LEONARD FEATHER'S SWINGIN' SWEDES
Pres(10″)119

753. HALLETT, MAL   v B

Born c. 1893, Roxbury, Mass.
Died November 20, 1952, Boston, Mass.

Bandleader mostly in New England; best period in 30s. Studied at New England Conservatory. During World War I member of band entertaining U.S. troops in France. Afterwards violinist in Boston hotels and theatres. Own band early 20s; opened at American House in Boston. Early personnel included future alto sax star Toots Mondello. In early 30s Gene Krupa (d), Jack Jenney (tb), and briefly Jack Teagarden (tb) in band. Excellent sweet-swing band in mid-30s. Theme *The Boston Tea Party*. Frankie Carle featured pianist in later 30s. Good vocalists at this time: Teddy Grace, Jerry Perkins, Buddy Welcome, Clark Yocum (later with Pied Pipers). Band well received at New York's Arcadia Ballroom and Roseland Ballroom. In late 30s and 40s considerable touring. Band continued into 1952.

RECORDS

MAL HALLETT
Ed 14080 The Boomerang/Where Butterflies Kiss Buttercups
OK 40578 Whose Who Are You?/Lonesome Me
Ha 126 Whose Who Are You?/Everything's Gonna Be All Right
Co 996-D Ya Gonna Be Home Tonight?/Underneath the Weeping Willow
Co 1287-D The Beggar/My New York
Pe 14618 She's a Corn-Fed Indiana Gal
Me 13201 When My Ship Comes In/Your Head on My Shoulder
Me 13202 An Earful of Music/Okay, Toots
Vo 3235 The Glory of Love/Let's Sing Again
Vo 3278 (theme) The Boston Tea Party/Sweet Misery of Love
De 993 There's Something in the Air/Where the Lazy River Goes By
De 1033 In the Chapel in the Moonlight/Echo Valley

De 1047 Goodnight My Love/One Never Knows, Does One?
De 1110 Timber/If My Heart Could Only Talk
De 1116 One in a Million/Who's Afraid of Love?
De 1162 Boo-Hoo/I Adore You
De 1163 Ridin' High/Big Boy Blue
De 1270 Turn Off the Moon/Easy on the Eyes
De 1281 The You and Me That Used to Be/'Cause My Baby Says It's So
De 1282 Alibi Baby/You're Looking for Romance
De 1532 I Want a New Romance/I'd Love to Play a Love Scene
De 1533 True Confession/You're Out of This World
VD(12″)99 (theme) The Boston Tea Party/Exactly Like You
Hit 7007 Be Careful, It's My Heart/Jingle Jangle Jingle
Hit 7008 I Left My Heart at the Stage Door Canteen/He Wears a Pair of Silver Wings
Hit 7013 Let's Get Lost/There Will Never Be Another You

753A. HALLIDAY, ROBERT   vo

Born Loch Lomond, Scotland

Performer in Broadway musicals. Starred in hit shows THE DESERT SONG (1926) and THE NEW MOON (1928). Began with minor roles in THE ROSE GIRL (1921) and other shows.

BROADWAY MUSICALS

1921—THE ROSE GIRL
1923—DEW DROP INN
1925—TOPSY AND EVA
1926—TIP TOES; THE DESERT SONG
1928—THE NEW MOON
1930—PRINCESS CHARMING
1935—MUSIC HATH CHARMS
1936—WHITE HORSE INN

753B. HAMBLEN, STUART

vo g cm lyr

Born October 20, 1908, Kellyville, Texas

Good entertainer and talented composer in western-folk-gospel fields. Best-known songs *This Ole House, It Is No Secret, Texas Plains, These Things Shall Pass, He Bought My Soul at Calvary, Remember Me*

(I'm the One Who Loves You), But I'll Go Chasin' Women, I'll Find You. Good baritone, effective on ballads and up-tempo numbers. Cowboy youth. Attended McMurray College in Abilene, Texas. School teacher awhile. Began music career early 30s. Early work with Beverly Hill Billies group. Around late 30s to mid-40s daily spot with western combo on Los Angeles radio. Late 40s into 60s concentrated on composing. 1952 ran for president of U. S. on Prohibition ticket. Late 50s he and wife on Los Angeles TV show. Other compositions include *Across the Great Divide, So Dear to My Heart, Without a Girl, My Life with You, Old Glory, Don't Fool Around with Calico, This Ole World, The Toy Violin, Ole Pappy Time, Please Tell Me Why, My Brother, Just a Man, Go On By, Beyond the Sun, Just Let Me Love You, You're Always Brand New, Blood on Your Hands.*

RECORDS

STUART HAMBLEN

Vi 23685 My Mary/My Brown Eyed Texas Rose

Vi 20-5739 This Ole House/When My Lord Picks Up the Phone

Co 20625 Let's See You Fix It/But I'll Go Chasin' Women

Co 20650 Pony Express/Blue Bonnets in Her Golden Hair

Co 20674 Condemnation/Sheepskin Corn and a Wrinkle on a Horn

Co 20714 I'll Find You/Remember Me (I'm the One Who Loves You)

Co 20724 It Is No Secret/Blood on Your Hands

Co 20779 Old Glory/My Life with You

Co 20848 These Things Shall Pass

Co 20880 Just Let Me Love You/You're Always Brand New

Co 21014 Oklahoma Bill/Grasshopper MacClain

LPs

STUART HAMBLEN

Co CL-1588 The Spell of the Yukon

Ha HL-7009 Hymns Sung by Stuart Hamblen

Cam CAL-537 Beyond the Sun

Cor CRL-57254 Remember Me

Vi LPM-1253 It Is No Secret

Vi LPM-1436 The Grand Old Hymns

754. HAMILTON, CHICO   d cl vo B
(FORESTSTORN HAMILTON)

Born September 21, 1921, Los Angeles, Calif.

Leader of avant-garde jazz combo since 1955. Played clarinet early in career. With Floyd Ray, Lionel Hampton, Lester Young 1940-1. Military service, World War II; There took up drums. In later 40s with Jimmy Mundy and Count Basie. Worked with Lena Horne in 1948 and at intervals for several years. To west coast as studio musician and freelance. In Gerry Mulligan's original quartet 1952. In 1955 formed quintet featuring unusual arrangements and instrumentation, including cello and flute. Early group featured Buddy Collette on reeds, Jim Hall (g), Carson Smith (b), Fred Katz (cel). Later personnels included Eric Dolphy, Charles Lloyd, Paul Horn, Jimmy Woods, Gabor Szabo, Albert Stinson. Combo in 1957 movie SWEET SMELL OF SUCCESS. Continued active in 60s, including tours abroad.

RECORDS
(all LPs)

GERRY MULLIGAN

Fan(10")3-6

Pac Jazz(10")1

World Pac PJ-1207

TAL FARLOW

Norg MGN-1014 The Artistry of Tal Farlow

LYLE MURPHY

GNP 9 Four Saxophones in Twelve Tones

CHICO HAMILTON

World Pac 1005 Chico Hamilton Quintet

WB 1344(S) The Three Faces of Chico

Co CL-1619 Chico Hamilton Special

Pac Jazz 1209

Pac Jazz 20108 Jazz Milestones Series

Pac Jazz 20143 Spectacular

De DL-8614 Sweet Smell of Success

Impulse S-29 (S) Passin' Thru

Impulse S-59 (S) Man from Two Worlds

Impulse S-9114 (S) Further Adventures

Impulse S-9130 (S) The Dealer

755. HAMILTON, GEORGE   cm lyr B

Born January 13, 1901, Newport, Vt.
Died March 31, 1957, New York, N.Y.

Leader of hotel bands, best in late 30s. Attended Dartmouth. Conducted orchestra for Chicago Opera several years. Led Barbary Coast Orchestra on west coast early 30s. Late 1936 replaced Shep Fields as band backing famous Veloz & Yolanda dance team in Chicago. Hamilton's band somewhat like Fields' (minus the rippling rhythm): same tinkling piano and accordion fill-ins, similar clipped-style final chorus. Differences: introductions by accordionist playing a cascade of notes; use of harp modulating and leading into each vocal. Hamilton band also bigger, with fuller ensemble sound. In January 1937 at Chicago's Palmer House band introduced gimmick of using an imported music box in its theme, called it "Music Box Music." Vocalist Lee Norton excellent, blended nicely with Hamilton style. Unfortunately, band seldom recorded. Theme *That's Because I Love You.* Hamilton led band in 40s; popular in Cleveland during one period. Composer or lyricist of several songs: *Wild Honey, Here Comes Your Pappy, Bye bye Pretty Baby, Lovely While It Lasted, I Feel Sorry for the Poor People, There's Never Been a Love Like Ours, Hat Check Girl, You Can Say That Again, Iowa Corn Song.*

RECORDS

BARBARY COAST ORCHESTRA
De 501 Star Gazing/Sweet and Slow
GEORGE HAMILTON
Vi 25449 Under Your Spell/I Was Saying to the Moon
Vi 25458 Let's Put Our Heads Together/With Plenty of Money and You
Vi 25602 Sun Showers/I'm Feelin' Like a Million
Vi 25611 Born to Love/There Must Be Paint in the Sky
Vi 25617 Gone with the Dawn/Old Man Moon

756. HAMILTON, JIMMY

cl as ts tb t ar B

Born May 15, 1917, Dillon, S.C.

Jazz clarinetist featured with Duke Ellington for 25 years. Thick symphonic tone, little vibrato, driving style, good technique. Grew up in Philadelphia. Worked locally on trumpet and trombone. Played in New York late 30s, concentrated on alto sax and clarinet. In early 40s with Teddy Wilson, Jimmy Mundy, Eddie Heywood, others. Joined Ellington mid-1943 till 1968. Soon featured. Beginning 1968 mostly combo leader.

RECORDS

DUKE ELLINGTON
Mus 465 Flippant Flurry
Co 38165 Air Conditioned Jungle
Co 38234 Hy'a Sue
Co 39670 VIP's Boogie
OK 6911 Smada
ESQUIRE ALL-AMERICANS
Vi(12")40-4001 Long Long Journey/Snafu
Vi(12")40-4002 The One That Got Away
PETE BROWN
De 8613 Mound Bayou/Unlucky Woman
SONNY GREER
Apo 354 Sleepy Baboon/Kansas City Caboose
Apo 355 Ration Stomp/Helena's Dream
TEDDY WILSON
Co 36737 Out of Nowhere
VD(12")317 Prisoner of Love

LPs

JIMMY HAMILTON
Urania 1003 This Is Jimmy Hamilton
Jazztone J-1238 Accent on Clarinet
Everest SDBR-1100 (S) Swing Low, Sweet Clarinet
DUKE ELLINGTON
Co ML-4418 Masterpieces by Ellington
Co CL-1198 The Cosmic Scene
Co CS-8072 (S) Newport 1958
Beth 60 Historically Speaking—The Duke
Vi LPM-3782 Far East Suite
Cap W-521 Ellington '55
DUKE ELLINGTON/COUNT BASIE
Co CL-1715 First Time! The Count Meets the Duke
MERCER ELLINGTON
Cor CRL-57293 Colors in Rhythm
JOHNNY HODGES
Norg MGN-1060 Used to Be Duke
Verve MGV-8271 The Big Sound

OSCAR PETTIFORD
Beth(10″)1019 Basically Duke

757. HAMILTON, NANCY   lyr vo
Born July 27, 1908, Sewickley, Pa.

Singer-actress-lyricist in Broadway shows. Most famous for collaboration with composer Morgan Lewis on all-time-great song *How High the Moon*. Tune attracted little attention in 1940 Broadway show TWO FOR THE SHOW, but in mid and late 40s became "national anthem" of bopsters, who liked to improvise on its chord changes. Nancy educated at Sorbonne, Paris, and at Smith College. Began stage career 1932 as understudy for Katharine Hepburn in THE WARRIOR'S HUSBAND. In musical revue NEW FACES OF 1934; also contributed book and lyrics. In 1935 play PRIDE AND PREJUDICE. Toured abroad with Katherine Cornell's company playing THE BARRETTS OF WIMPOLE STREET. Wrote for *Stage* Magazine, also wrote material for radio and movies. Collaborated with composer Morgan Lewis on scores for Broadway musicals ONE FOR THE MONEY (1939; also played in this), TWO FOR THE SHOW (1940) and THREE TO MAKE READY (1946). Wrote book for all three and for COUNT ME IN (1942).

SONGS
(with related shows)

1934—NEW FACES OF 1934 stage show (New Faces; Something You Lack; Visitors Ashore; People of Taste; So Low; He Loves Me; On the Other Hand)
1939—ONE FOR THE MONEY stage show (Teeter Totter Tessie; Rhapsody; I Only Know)
1940—TWO FOR THE SHOW stage show (How High the Moon; A House with a Little Red Barn; At Last It's Love)
1946—THREE TO MAKE READY stage show (If It's Love; The Old Soft Shoe; A Lovely Lazy Kind of Day; It's a Nice Night for It)

758. HAMMERSTEIN II, OSCAR   lyr
(OSCAR GREELEY CLENDEN-NING HAMMERSTEIN)
Born July 12, 1895, New York, N.Y.
Died August 23, 1960, Doylestown, Pa.

Great lyricist-librettist of many long-running Broadway shows. Except for Irving Berlin, most prolific lyric writer of all time. Best known for collaboration with composer Richard Rodgers 1943-59. Previously collaborated successfully with composers Jerome Kern, Sigmund Romberg, Rudolf Friml, George Gershwin, Herbert Stothart, Vincent Youmans, Arthur Schwartz and lyricist Otto Harbach. In addition to scores, librettist for majority of his shows. Born into show business family; father manager of historic Victoria vaudeville theatre in New York. Named for grandfather, famed opera impresario and theatre builder; adopted "II" after name, dropped middle names Greeley Clendenning. Attended Columbia University and Law School, wrote and acted in college plays. Later stage manager for uncle Arthur Hammerstein. Tried unsuccessfully to write plays.

Teamed with lyricist Otto Harbach to provide songs for Broadway shows during most of 20s. First modest success, then great success with hit shows ROSE-MARIE (1924), SUNNY (1925), THE DESERT SONG (1926), SHOW BOAT and THE NEW MOON (1928), SWEET ADELINE (1929), MUSIC IN THE AIR (1932), CARMEN JONES (1943). Some hit shows converted into popular movies, which Hammerstein wrote for. After top composer Richard Rodgers lost lyricist Lorenz Hart through illness and death, Hammerstein teamed with Rodgers to form most successful composing team in Broadway history. First show OKLAHOMA! (1943) fantastic success; 2248 performances. Made stage history for style innovations that veered from traditional musical comedy. Other hit shows CAROUSEL (1945), SOUTH PACIFIC (1949), THE KING AND I (1951), FLOWER DRUM SONG (1958), THE SOUND OF MUSIC (1959). Lesser but successful shows ALLEGRO (1947), ME AND JULIET (1953), PIPE DREAM (1955). Several shows made into lavish color movies with top stars. Team scored 1957 TV production of CINDERELLA. Received Pulitzer Prize 1944 for OKLAHOMA!, 1950 for SOUTH PACIFIC. Produced most of own shows and some others including I REMEMBER MAMA, ANNIE GET YOUR GUN, HAPPY BIRTHDAY, JOHN LOVES MARY, THE

HAPPY TIME. Hammerstein's best-known songs: *Rose-Marie*; *Indian Love Call*; *Sunny*; *Who?*; *The Desert Song*; *Ol' Man River*; *Can't Help Lovin' Dat Man*; *Make Believe*; *Bill*; *Lover, Come Back to Me*; *Stout-Hearted Men*; *Why Was I Born?*; *Don't Ever Leave Me*; *The Song Is You*; *I've Told Ev'ry Little Star*; *When I Grow Too Old to Dream*; *The Folks Who Live on the Hill*; *I'll Take Romance*; *All the Things You Are*; *The Last Time I Saw Paris*; *People Will Say We're in Love*; *The Surrey with the Fringe on Top*; *Oh, What a Beautiful Mornin'*; *If I Loved You*; *It Might as Well Be Spring*; *Some Enchanted Evening*; *Bali Ha'i*; *Younger Than Springtime*; *A Wonderful Guy*; *Getting to Know You*; *Shall We Dance?*; *No Other Love*; *I Enjoy Being a Girl*; *The Sound of Music*; *My Favorite Things*; *Climb Ev'ry Mountain*. Author of book *Lyrics*. Hammerstein biographies include *Some Enchanted Evenings* by Deems Taylor and *The Rodgers & Hammerstein Story* by Stanley Green.

SONGS
*(with related shows; *also wrote book)*

1920—ALWAYS YOU stage show* (title song; others); JIMMIE stage show* (Jimmie; Baby Dreams; Cute Little Two by Four); TICKLE ME stage show* (Tickle Me; Until You Say Goodbye; If a Wish Could Make It So)

1922—DAFFY DILL stage show* (Daffy Dill; I'll Build a Bungalow; Two Little Ruby Rings; A Coachman's Heart); QUEEN O' HEARTS stage show* (Queen of Hearts; You Need Someone, Someone Needs You)

1923—WILDFLOWER stage show* (Wildflower; Bambalina; April Blossoms)

1924—MARY JANE MCKANE stage show* (Mary Jane McKane; The Ramble of the Subway; You're Never Too Old to Learn; Toodle-oo); ROSE-MARIE stage show* (Rose-Marie; Indian Love Call; Song of the Mounties; Totem Tom-Tom; The Door of My Dreams)

1925—SUNNY stage show* (Sunny; Who?; D'Ya Love Me?; Two Little Bluebirds)

1926—SONG OF THE FLAME stage show* (Song of the Flame; Cossack Love Song); THE DESERT SONG stage show* (The Desert Song; One Alone; The Riff Song; Romance; Then You Will Know; One Flower Grows Alone in Your Garden); THE WILD ROSE stage show* (The Wild Rose; Brown Eyes; One Golden Hour; We'll Have a Kingdom)

1927—GOLDEN DAWN stage show* (We Two; When I Crack My Whip; Africa; Jungle Shadows; Here in the Dark)

1928—SHOW BOAT stage show* (Make Believe; Why Do I Love You?; Ol' Man River; Bill; Can't Help Lovin' Dat Man; Life Upon the Wicked Stage; You Are Love; Till Good Luck Comes My Way); THE NEW MOON stage show* (Lover, Come Back to Me; Marianne; Softly, as in a Morning Sunrise; One Kiss; Wanting You; Stout-Hearted Men); RAINBOW stage show* (The One Girl; I Want a Man; I Like You as You Are); BIG BOY stage show (wrote book only)

1929—SWEET ADELINE stage show* (Why Was I Born?; Don't Ever Leave Me; Here Am I; 'Twas Not So Long Ago); THE DESERT SONG movie (original stage score)

1930—GOLDEN DAWN movie (original stage score); SONG OF THE FLAME movie (original stage score); VIENNESE NIGHTS movie (I Bring a Love Song; You Will Remember Vienna; Here We Are; I'm Lonely; Ja Ja Ja; Regimental March)

1931—BALLYHOO stage show (I'm One of God's Children Who Hasn't Got Wings; No Wonder I'm Blue); EAST WIND stage show* (East Wind; Are You Love?; I'd Be a Fool; You Are My Woman) FREE FOR ALL stage show* (Not That I Care; others); THE GANG'S ALL HERE stage show (wrote book only); NEW MOON movie (original stage score); SUNNY movie (original stage score)

1932—MUSIC IN THE AIR stage show* (I've Told Ev'ry Little Star; The Song Is

You; And Love Was Born; I'm Alone; We Belong Together)

1935—MAY WINE stage show (I Built a Dream One Day; Somebody Ought to Be Told; Just Once Around the Clock; Something New Is in My Heart; Dance, My Darling); RECKLESS movie (title song); THE NIGHT IS YOUNG movie (The Night Is Young; When I Grow Too Old to Dream); SWEET ADELINE movie (original stage score); MUSIC IN THE AIR movie (original stage score)

1936—GIVE US THIS NIGHT movie (Music in the Night); ROSE-MARIE movie (original stage score); SHOW BOAT movie (original stage score)

1937—HIGH, WIDE AND HANDSOME movie (High, Wide and Handsome; The Folks Who Live on the Hill; Can I Forget You?; The Things I Want; Allegheny Al; Will You Marry Me Tomorrow, Maria?); I'LL TAKE RO-MANCE movie (title song)

1938—THE GREAT WALTZ movie (One Day When We Were Young); THE LADY OBJECTS movie (When You're in the Room; That Week in Paris; A Mist Is Over the Moon)

1939—VERY WARM FOR MAY stage show* (All the Things You Are; All in Fun; That Lucky Fellow; Heaven in My Arms; In the Heart of the Dark)

1940—AMERICAN JUBILEE revue (How Can I Ever Be alone?; Tennessee Fish Fry); NEW MOON movie (original stage score)

1941—SUNNY RIVER stage show* (Sunny River; Along the Winding Road; Call It a Dream; My Girl and I; Let Me Live Today); LADY BE GOOD movie (The Last Time I Saw Paris); SUNNY movie (original stage score)

1943—CARMEN JONES stage show* (adapted Bizet music to lyrics: Dat's Love; Dere's a Cafe on de Corner; Dis Flower; Stan' Up and Fight; Beat Out Dat Rhythm on the Drum); OKLAHOMA! stage show* (Oklahoma!; People Will Say We're in Love; The Surrey with the Fringe on Top; Oh, What a Beautiful Mornin'; Kansas City; I Cain't Say No; Out of My Dreams; All or Nothin'; The Farmer and the Cowman; Pore Jud)

1944—THE DESERT SONG movie (part of original stage score)

1945—CAROUSEL stage show* (If I Loved You; June Is Bustin' Out All Over; You'll Never Walk Alone; Soliloquy; What's the Use of Wond'rin'?; This Was a Real Nice Clambake; When the Children Are Asleep; When I Marry Mr. Snow); STATE FAIR movie (It Might as Well Be Spring; That's for Me; It's a Grand Night for Singing; Isn't It Kinda Fun?; All I Owe I Owe I-oway; Our State Fair)

1946—CENTENNIAL SUMMER movie (All Through the Day)

1947—ALLEGRO stage show* (So Far; A Fellow Needs a Girl; You Are Never Away; The Gentleman Is a Dope)

1949—SOUTH PACIFIC stage show* (Some Enchanted Evening; Bali Ha'i; Younger Than Springtime; Honey Bun; A Wonderful Guy; I'm Gonna Wash That Man Right Outa My Hair; This Nearly Was Mine; Happy Talk; There Is Nothin' Like a Dame; A Cock-Eyed Optimist; Bloody Mary Is the Girl I Love)

1951—THE KING AND I stage show* (Getting to Know You; Shall We Dance?; We Kiss in a Shadow; I Whistle a Happy Tune; I Have Dreamed; March of the Siamese Children; Hello, Young Lovers; Something Wonderful); THE STRIP movie, with Harry Ruby-cm and Bert Kalmar-lyr (A Kiss to Build a Dream On)

1953—ME AND JULIET stage show* (No Other Love; Marriage-Type Love; Keep It Gay; I'm Your Girl; We Deserve Each Other; It's Me); MAIN STREET TO BROADWAY movie (There's Music in You); THE DES-ERT SONG movie (original stage score)

1954—ROSE-MARIE movie (original stage

score); CARMEN JONES movie (original stage score)

1955—PIPE DREAM stage show* (Everybody's Got a Home but Me; All at Once You Love Her; The Man I Used to Be; Sweet Thursday; Think; A Lopsided Bus; The Happiest House on the Block); OKLAHOMA! movie (original stage score)

1956—CAROUSEL movie (original stage score); THE KING AND I movie (original stage score)

1957—CINDERELLA TV show* (Do I Love You Because You're Beautiful?; A Lovely Night; In My Own Little Corner; Ten Minutes Ago)

1958—FLOWER DRUM SONG stage show* (Love, Look Away; I Enjoy Being a Girl; Sunday; Grant Avenue; You Are Beautiful; Like a God; The Other Generation; Don't Marry Me); SOUTH PACIFIC movie (original stage score)

1959—THE SOUND OF MUSIC stage show (The Sound of Music; Climb Ev'ry Mountain; My Favorite Things; Maria; Edelweiss; Do-Re-Mi)

1961—FLOWER DRUM SONG movie (original stage score)

1965—THE SOUND OF MUSIC movie (original stage score)

759. HAMP, JOHNNY   B

Bandleader of 20s and 30s, billed in early years as Johnny Hamp & His Kentucky Serenaders. Theme *My Old Kentucky Home*. Career began in mid-20s. Maintained good dance band in late 20s and 30s. Good arrangments, full, pretty ensemble sound, ability to play semi-hot. Played England 1930. In late 30s outstanding vocalists Johnny McAfee and Jayne Whitney. Bandleader into early 40s.

RECORDS

JOHNNY HAMP

Vi 19756 Cecilia/Promenade Walk
Vi 20101 Black Bottom
Vi 20819 Is It Possible?
Vi 21514 Sweet Lorraine/I Can't Give You Anything but Love
Vi 21615 Half-Way to Heaven/Two Lips

Vi 21632 Blue Shadows/What D' Ya Say?
Vi 21829 Avalon Town
Vi 21838 Where Is the Song of Songs for Me?
Vi 22124 Sunny Side Up/If I Had a Talking Picture of You
Vi 22219 Lady Luck
Vi 22462 Nobody Cares If I'm Blue
Vi 22722 Nevertheless/Look in the Looking Glass
Vi 22795 I Can't Write the Words
Vi 22999 By a Rippling Stream/Cabin in the Cotton
Vi 24000 Hummin' to Myself/Whistle and Blow Your Blues Away
Me 51109 Thanks a Million/I'm Sittin' High on a Hilltop
Me 351003 It's All So New to Me/When I Grow Up
Me 351021 Without a Word of Warning/From the Top of Your Head
Bb 6745 Smoke Dreams/Who's That Knockin' at My Heart?
Bb 6746 The Goona Goo/Mr. Ghost Goes to Town
Bb 6748 Trust in Me/Never Should Have Told You
Bb 6848 Was It Rain?/Love Is Good for Anything That Ails You

760. HAMPTON, LIONEL

d vb p vo cm B

(nickname Hamp)

Born April 12, 1909 or 1913, Louisville, Ky.

All-time jazz great. Bandleader for three decades. Main talent as vibist, also plays drums and piano in flashy style. Swinging, happy style on vibes, complete with grunting, grinning, other antics. Grew up in Birmingham and Chicago. Drummed with minor groups in Chicago, toured, ended up in California about 1927. Jobbed; period with Paul Howard 1929. Long run as house musician at Sebastian's Cotton Club in Culver City. Les Hite led band there early 30s. Hampton took up vibes. Brief spots in several movies. Led band in California 1935-6. Jammed with visiting Benny Goodman and Gene Krupa at Paradise Club in Los Angeles, landed spot with Goodman August 1936, augmenting Goodman Trio to Quartet and winning instant fame. Drummed off and on with Goodman's big band, usually when band was between regular drummers.

Hampton recorded extensively 1937-40 with small groups of top jazzmen. Records since classed among best of combo jazz. Hampton vocals on some. Left Goodman mid-1940, formed big band on west coast. Band featured big sound, swinging arrangements and soloists. Specialized in boogie woogie, jump, later bop. Big hit *Flying Home*, often used as theme. In later years cut size of band, appeared solo on many TV shows in 50s and 60s. Exuberant personality enhanced popularity. Excellent goodwill ambassador on foreign tours. In movies HOLLYWOOD HOTEL (1938), A SONG IS BORN (1948) and THE BENNY GOODMAN STORY (1956). Composer credits include *Flying Home, Midnight Sun, Jack the Bellboy, Ribs and Hot Sauce, Central Avenue Breakdown, Punch and Judy, The Blues in My Flat, The Blues in Your Flat, Opus 1/2, Opus 3/4, Till Tom Special, Board Meeting, Vibraphone Blues*. Rejoined original Benny Goodman Quartet for several 1973 concerts.

RECORDS

LOUIS ARMSTRONG
  OK 41463 Memories of You
  De 914 To You, Sweetheart, Aloha/On a Coconut Island
EDDIE CONDON
  CMS 515 Sunday/California, Here I Come
BENNY GOODMAN QUARTET
  Vi 25398 Dinah/Moonglow
  Vi 25521 Vibraphone Blues/Stompin' at the Savoy
  Vi 25529 Tea for Two/Runnin' Wild
  Vi 25644 Avalon/The Man I Love
  Vi 26044 The Blues in Your Flat/The Blues in My Flat
  Vi 26091 Opus 1/2/Sweet Georgia Brown
  Vi 26240 Opus 3/4/Sugar
BENNY GOODMAN SEXTET
  Co 35254 Flying Home/Rose Room

Co 35320 Soft Winds/Memories of You
Co 35404 Till Tom Special/Gone with "What" Wind
TEDDY WILSON
  Br 7736 You Turned the Tables on Me/Sing, Baby, Sing
  Br 7739 You Came to My Rescue/Here's Love in Your Eyes
LIONEL HAMPTON
  Vi 25527 My Last Affair/The Mood That I'm In
  Vi 25592 I Know That You Know/On the Sunny Side of the Street
  Vi 25658 Confessin'/Drum Stomp
  Vi 25666 Piano Stomp/I Surrender Dear
  Vi 25699 The Object of My Affection/Judy
  Vi 26011 I'm in the Mood for Swing/Shoe Shiners Drag
  Vi 26254 It Don't Mean a Thing/Shufflin' at the Hollywood
  Vi 26304 Memories of You/The Jumpin' Jive
  Vi 26557 Dinah/Singin' the Blues
  Vi 26652 Jack the Bellboy/Central Avenue Breakdown
  Vi 27529 Now That You're Mine/Chasin' with Chase
  De 18394 (theme) Flying Home/In the Bag
  De 18880 Air Mail Special (1 & 2)
  De 23792 Robbins in Your Hair/Blow Top Blues
  De 24429 Midnight Sun / Three Minutes on 52nd Street
  De 24652 The Hucklebuck/Lavender Coffin

LPs

LIONEL HAMPTON
  Cam CAL-402 Jivin' the Vibes (Vi RIs)
  Cam CAL-517 Open House (Vi RIs)
  De DL-4296 Hamp's Golden Favorites (De RIs)
  De DL-79244 "Steppin' Out" Vol. 1 (1942-5 De RIs)
  Co CL-1304 Golden Vibes
  Co CL-1486 Silver Vibes
  Lion L-70064 Lionel Hampton & His Orchestra

Jazztone J-1246 Lionel Hampton's All-Star Groups (RIs)
GNP 15 With the Just Jazz All-Stars Vi(10")LPT-18 (Vi RIs)
Verve MGV-8019 Travelin' Band
Impulse S-78(S) You Better Know It
Folk 2871 Jazzman for All Seasons

BENNY GOODMAN
Co CL-500 Benny Goodman Combos (Co RIs)

CHARLIE CHRISTIAN
Co CL-652 With Benny Goodman Sextet and Orchestra (Co RIs)

761. HANDMAN, LOU cm p

Born September 10, 1894, New York, N.Y.
Died December 9, 1956, Flushing, N.Y.

Composer of 20s and 30s. Best-known songs *Blue (and Broken Hearted)*, *Are You Lonesome Tonight?*, *Puddin' Head Jones*. Professional pianist at 17. Toured Australia in two-man vaudeville act. Military service, World War I. Worked in publishing houses. Began composing 1920. Accompanied singers in vaudeville here and abroad. Chief collaborators Roy Turk and Walter Hirsch.

SONGS
(with related shows)

1920—Give Me a Smile and a Kiss
1922—Blue (and Broken Hearted)
1923—Twelve O'clock at Night; Lovey Came Back; My Sweetie Went Away
1924—When I Was the Dandy and You Were the Belle; I Can't Get the One I Want
1925—I'm Gonna Charleston Back to Charleston
1927—Are You Lonesome Tonight?
1933—Puddin' Head Jones
1936—Bye Bye, Baby; Me and the Moon
1937—RHYTHM IN THE CLOUDS movie (Don't Ever Change); THE HIT PARADE movie (Was It Rain?; Love Is Good for Anything That Ails You; Last Night I Dreamed of You)
1938—Let This Be a Warning to You, Baby
1939—Baby Me

1954—I Solemnly Swear
Other songs: *What Good Would It Do?*; *Is My Baby Blue Tonight? No Nothing*; *Fill Up Your Glasses with Kisses.*

762. HANDY, GEORGE p ar cm
(GEORGE JOSEPH HENDLEMAN)

Born January 17, 1920, Brooklyn, N.Y.

Talented arranger-composer, briefly prominent for modern jazz writing with Boyd Raeburn progressive band in mid-40s. Most famous composition-arrangement *Tonsilectomy*. Learned piano early, studied at Juilliard. Pianist with Raymond Scott 1941. Some writing for movies. With Raeburn 1944-6 off and on; also arranged for Ina Ray Hutton and Herbie Fields. In later 40s dropped from limelight; pianist with Buddy Rich, Bob Chester, others. In 50s and 60s freelance arranging. Composed jazz numbers and semi-classical works.

RECORDS
BOYD RAEBURN
(as pianist-arranger-composer)
Je 10000 Tonsilectomy/Forgetful
Je 10001 Yerxa/Rip Van Winkle
(as arranger)
Je D1-2-3 Over the Rainbow/Body and Soul
Je D1-4 Blue Echoes
Je D1-5-1 Temptation/Dalvatore Sally (Handy composition)
Je 10002 I Only Have Eyes for You
VIVIEN GARRY QUARTET
(as pianist-arranger)
Sarco 101 Hopscotch/Where You At?
Sarco 103 Tonsilectomy/These Foolish Things
Sarco 104 I Surrender Dear/I've Got To, That's All
GEORGE HANDY
(from Norman Granz JAZZ SCENE album of 12" 78's)
The Bloos

LPs
GEORGE HANDY
"X" LXA-1004 Handyland U.S.A.
"X" LXA-1032 By George!

BOYD RAEBURN
Sav(10")MG-15010 Innovations, Vol. 1
Sav MG-15011 Innovations, Vol. 2
Sav MG-15012 Innovations, Vol. 3

763. HANDY, W. C. cm c B
(WILLIAM CHRISTOPHER HANDY)

Born November 16, 1873, Florence, Ala. Died March 29, 1958, New York, N.Y.

Composer known as The Father of the Blues because of classic song *St. Louis Blues*, other leading blues compositions. Wrote blues from snatches of melody performed by Negro singers and musicians. Object: to capture the language of folk singers. As youth worked as school teacher, iron mill laborer. Played cornet, led quartet, played Chicago's World Fair 1893. Bandmaster in Henderson, Ky. Then cornetist-director with Mahara's Minstrels, toured extensively. Teacher-bandmaster at Agricultural & Mechanical College, Huntsville, Ala. Taught music at Clarksdale, Miss. First composition *Memphis Blues*; published and popularized 1912-13. Had royalty trouble, formed publishing company 1913. Biggest hit *St. Louis Blues* in 1914: all-time standard. Other important compositions *Yellow Dog Blues* (1914), *Joe Turner Blues* and *Hesitating Blues* (1915), *Ole Miss* (1916), *Beale Street Blues* and *Hooking Cow Blues* (1917), *Aunt Hagar's Blues* and *Long Gone* (1920), *Loveless Love* (also called *Careless Love*) (1921), *Atlanta Blues* (1923), *Chantez Les Bas* (1931). Led band 1917-23, toured south, recorded. After 1923 concentrated on composing and publishing. Other compositions: *Friendless Blues, Aframerica Hymn, John Henry, Harlem Blues, Basement Blues, East St. Louis Blues, Annie Love, Hail to the Spirit of Freedom, Big Stick Blues March, Roosevelt Triumphal March, In the Cotton Fields of Dixie, Blue Destiny* (symphony). Wrote autobiography *Father of the Blues*. 1958 movie ST. LOUIS BLUES based on Handy's life, with Nat Cole in Handy role.

RECORDS

W. C. HANDY ORCHESTRA
Co A-2418 Bunch of Blues/Moonlight Blues

Co A-2419 That Jazz Dance/Livery Stable Blues
Co A-2420 The Hooking Cow Blues/ Ole Miss Rag
Co A-2421 The Snaky Blues/Fuzzy Wuzzy Rag
Lyratone 4211 Beale Street Blues/Joe Turner Blues
Lyratone 4212 Hesitating Blues/Yellow Dog Blues
Para 20098 St. Louis Blues/Yellow Dog Blues
Para 20112 She's a Mean Job/Muscle Shoals Blues
OK 4789 Aunt Hagar's Blues/Louisville Blues
OK 4880 Gulf Coast Blues/Farewell Blues
OK 4896 St. Louis Blues/Memphis Blues
Vs 8162 Loveless Love/'Way Down South Where the Blues Begin
Vs 8163 St. Louis Blues/Beale Street Blues

LPs

W. C. HANDY
Audio Archives A-1200 Father of the Blues

(artist performing his songs)
LOUIS ARMSTRONG
Co CL-591 Plays W. C. Handy

764. HANIGHEN, BERNIE cm lyr
Born April 27, 1908, Omaha, Neb.

Songwriter of 30s and 40s. Scant output but several popular songs. Best known *The Dixieland Band, The Weekend of a Private Secretary, If the Moon Turns Green, Bob White*. Wrote music for 30s songs, collaborating mostly with lyricist Johnny Mercer. Later as lyricist collaborated with composer Raymond Scott on Broadway show LUTE SONG (1946). Revised libretto and lyrics for 1947 Broadway revival of THE CHOCOLATE SOLDIER. Educated at Harvard. During career served as musical director for record companies. Wrote special material for orchestras and radio shows.

SONGS
(with related shows)

1934—Fare-Thee-Well to Harlem; Here

Come the British; When a Woman Loves a Man

1935—The Dixieland Band; If the Moon Turns Green; Yankee Doodle Never Went to Town

1937—Bob White

1938—The Weekend of a Private Secretary

1939—The Little Man Who Wasn't There; Show Your Linen, Miss Richardson

1941—SECOND CHORUS movie (Poor Mr. Chisholm); The Air Minded Executive

1945—House of Joy

1946—LUTE SONG stage show (Lute Song; Mountain High, Valley Low; Where You Are; Vision Song; Bitter Harvest)

765. HANLEY, JAMES F. cm p

Born February 17, 1892, Rensselaer, Ind.

Died February 8, 1942, Douglaston, N.Y.

Composer for quarter century beginning 1917. Best-known songs *Indiana*; *Rose of Washington Square*; *Second Hand Rose*; *Just a Cottage Small*; *Zing! Went the Strings of My Heart*. Scores for Broadway musicals JIM JAM JEMS (1920), SPICE OF 1922 and PINS AND NEEDLES (1922), HONEYMOON LANE and NO FOOLIN' (1926), SIDEWALKS OF NEW YORK (1927). Songs for other stage shows. Chief collaborators lyricists Ballard MacDonald and Eddie Dowling. Educated at Champion College and Chicago Musical College. Military service, World War I; wrote and produced army show TOOT SWEET. Piano accompanist in vaudeville. Wrote for early sound movies and shorts.

SONGS
(with related shows)

1917—Indiana; Never Forget to Write Home; One Day in June

1918—Three Wonderful Letters from Home

1919—ZIEGFELD'S MIDNIGHT FROLICS stage show (Rose of Washington Square)

1920—JIM JAM JEMS stage show(From Your Heart to Mine; The Magic

Kiss; Raggedy Ann); ZIEGFELD MIDNIGHT FROLIC stage show (Rose of Washington Square—again used)

1921—ZIEGFELD FOLLIES OF 1921 stage show (Second Hand Rose); GEORGE WHITE'S SCANDALS OF 1921 stage show (Mother Eve)

1922—PINS AND NEEDLES stage show (Ah, Ah, Ah; All Pull Together; Melancholy Blues; The Syncopated Minuet); SPICE OF 1922 stage show (I'm in Love with You; Old Fashioned Cake Walk); Gee! But I Hate to Go Home Alone

1923—GEORGE WHITE'S SCANDALS OF 1923 stage show (The Gold Digger; Stingo Stungo)

1925—BIG BOY stage show (Hello 'Tucky); GAY PAREE stage show (Bamboo Babies); Just a Cottage Small; At the End of the Road

1926—HONEYMOON LANE stage show (The Little White House at the End of Honeymoon Lane; Half a Moon; Jersey Walk; Dreams for Sale); NO FOOLIN' stage show (No Foolin'; Honey, Be Mine; Poor Little Marie; Every Little Thing You Do; Nize Baby); QUEEN HIGH stage show (Don't Forget; Beautiful Baby)

1927—SIDEWALKS OF NEW YORK stage show (Playground in the Sky; Wherever You Are; Heading for Harlem)

1928—Little Log Cabin of Dreams; In the Evening

1929—THE RAINBOW MAN movie (Sleepy Valley)

1930—BLAZE O' GLORY movie (Dough-Boy's Lullaby; Put a Little Salt on the Bluebird's Tail; Wrapped in a Red Red Rose); HIGH SOCIETY BLUES movie (High Society Blues; Eleanor; Just Like in a Storybook; I'm in the Market for You; I Don't Know You Well Enough for That); THE BIG PARTY movie (Nobody Knows but Rosie)

1931—The Cute Little Things You Do; Sing Song Girl

1935—THUMBS UP stage show (Zing! Went the Strings of My Heart;

Continental Honeymoon); SWEET
SURRENDER movie (Twenty-Four
Hours a Day)
1937—There's Music in My Heart, Cherie
1940—You Forgot About Me

766. HANNON, BOB   vo

Excellent baritone with various bands
and on radio. Vocalist with Harry Sosnik
1933-4 at Chicago's World's Fair and
Edgewater Beach Hotel. Single in clubs
mid-30s, including Chicago's Chez Paree.
With Henry Busse late 1936-7, Buddy
Rogers 1938, Lou Breese and Paul Whiteman 1939. On radio shows, including own
series, in 40s. Strong, disciplined voice led
him into semi-classical field for much of
later radio work. In late 40s on radio
shows The American Melody Hour and
Waltz Time. Played clubs in 40s. Career
waned in 50s.

RECORDS

HARRY SOSNIK
    Vi 24481 One Minute to One/You
    Vi 24488 Count Your Blessings
    Vi 24570 That's Love/Let's Put Two
      and Two Together
    Vi 24623 How Do I Know It's Sunday?
    Vi 24626 No More Heartaches, No
      More Tears/Fool That I Am
    De 4068 I See a Million People
    De 4088 Miss You/Minka
BUDDY ROGERS
    Vo 4058 Lovelight in the Starlight/
      This Time It's Real
    Vo 4227 Meet the Beat of My Heart/
      Figaro
ROY SMECK
    De 2929 On a Little Street in Singa-
      pore/Careless
ABE LYMAN
    Bb 11005 Marie Elena
HARRY HORLICK
    De 3839 Shadow Waltz/Smilin' Thru
BOB HANNON with JESSE CRAWFORD
    De 3976 Long Long Ago/Juanita
    De 3977 Drink to Me Only with Thine
      Eyes/The Old Oaken Bucket
BOB HANNON
    De 3692 Intermezzo/A Little Old
      Church in England
    De 3758 Love Me and the World Is

Mine/Let the Rest of the World Go
By
    De 27425 Dust Off That Old Pianna/
      Sam, the Old Accordion Man
LPs
BOB HANNON
Ha HL-7033 Sings for Children

767. HANSHAW, ANNETTE   vo p
Born October 18, 1910, New York, N.Y.

Vocal star of records and radio in 20s and
30s. Subtle approach to songs, gentle but
sure. On many early records added
"That's all!" tag at end. Recorded under
pseudonyms Gay Ellis, Dot Dare, Patsy
Young. Studied commercial art, sang at
parties, heard by record executive, tested.
Embarked on singing career mid-20s;
early records popular. Accompaniment
mostly combos, sometimes including top
jazzmen. Prolific recording. On radio
1929, including shows with Clicquot Club
Eskimos. Guest spots, own singing series
early 30s. On popular Show Boat program
and with Glen Gray band on Camel
Caravan show 1934-5. Ended radio work
1936 and retired.

RECORDS

ORIGINAL MEMPHIS FIVE
    Pat 36623 Wistful and Blue/What Do
      I Care What Somebody Said?
FRANK FERERA TRIO
    Ve 2121 Lazy Lou'siana Moon/Pale
      Blue Waters
(as DOT DARE)
    Ha 792 I Wanna Be Loved by You/Is
      There Anything Wrong in That?
(as PATSY YOUNG)
    Ha 878 Button Up Your Overcoat/I
      Want to Be Bad
    HA 1047 He's So Unusual/I Think
      You'll Like It
(as GAY ELLIS)
    Ha 706 I Can't Give You Anything but
      Love/I Must Have That Man
    Ha 1012 What Wouldn't I Do for That
      Man?/Tiptoe Through the Tulips
      with Me
ANNETTE HANSHAW
    Pe 12286 Black Bottom
    Pe 12329 Song of the Wanderer/If
      You See Sally

Pe 12372 It Was Only a Sunshower/
Who's That Knocking at My Door?
Pe 12419 I Just Roll Along/There
Must Be a Silver Lining
Pe 12444 Get Out and Get Under the
Moon/We Love It
Co 1769-D Lover, Come Back to Me/
You Wouldn't Fool Me, Would
You?
Co 1812-D That's You, Baby/Big City
Blues
OK 41292 Moanin' Low/Lovable and
Sweet
OK 41327 The Right Kind of Man/If I
Can't Have You
OK 41351 When I'm Housekeeping for
You/I Have to Have You
OK 41370 Cooking Breakfast for the
One I Love/When a Woman Loves
a Man
Ve 2315 Would You Like to Take a
Walk?/You're Just Too Sweet for
Words
Ve 2393 Ho Hum!/Moonlight Saving
Time
Me 12471 We Just Couldn't Say Good-
bye/Love Me Tonight
Me 12846 Say It Isn't So/You'll Al-
ways Be the Same Sweetheart
Pe 12882 Moon Song/Twenty Million
People
Pe 12921 Sweetheart Darlin'/I Cover
the Waterfront
Pe 12959 Give Me Liberty or Give Me
Love/Sing a Little Lowdown Tune
Vo 2635 This Little Piggie/Let's Fall in
Love

LPs

ANNETTE HANSHAW
Halcyon(E) 5 Sweetheart of the 20s
(RIs)
Fountain(E) FV-201 The Early Years
(1926 RIs)

768. HARBACH, OTTO   lyr

*Born August 18, 1873, Salt Lake City,
Utah*
Died January 24, 1963, New York, N.Y.

Important lyricist-librettist of Broadway
stage. Long, prolific career. Associated
with hit shows MADAME SHERRY (1910),
THE FIREFLY (1912), HIGH JINKS (1913),
KATINKA (1916), GOING UP (1918), THE

LITTLE WHOPPER (1919), MARY (1920), KID
BOOTS and ROSE-MARIE (1924), SUNNY and
NO, NO, NANETTE (1925), SONG OF THE
FLAME, THE DESERT SONG and CRISS CROSS
(1926), GOOD BOY (1928), THE CAT AND
THE FIDDLE (1931), ROBERTA (1933). Co-
author of successful farce UP IN MABEL'S
ROOM (1919). Many successful scores and
librettos in collaboration with lyricist-
librettist Oscar Hammerstein II beginning
1920. Most memorable songs included
*Cuddle Up a Little Closer, Every Little
Movement, Sympathy, The Love Nest,
Rose-Marie, Indian Love Call, Who?, The
Desert Song, She Didn't Say "Yes", Smoke
Gets in Your Eyes, Yesterdays.* Educated
at Collegiate Institute in Salt Lake City
and at Knox College, Professor of English
at Whitman College 1895-1901. New
York newspaper writer 1902-3, ad agency
writer 1903-10. In 1908 collaborated with
composer Karl Hoschna on score of successful Broadway show THE THREE TWINS
featuring hit song *Cuddle Up a Little
Closer,* which established career as lyricist. Joined Hoschna on songs for other
shows. Upon Hoschna's death December
1911, Harbach collaborated with composer Rudolf Friml on successful shows.
Later collaborated with Herbert Stothart,
Louis A. Hirsch, Harry Tierney, Vincent
Youmans, George Gershwin, Sigmund
Romberg, Jerome Kern. Many Harbach
shows later converted into sound movies.
Vice president of ASCAP 1936-40, president 1950-3.

SONGS
*(with related shows; *also wrote book)*

1908—THE THREE TWINS stage show (Cud-
dle Up a Little Closer; others)
1910—BRIGHT EYES stage show (For You,
Bright Eyes; Cheer Up, My Hon-
ey; Good Old Days of Yore);
MADAME SHERRY stage show*
(Every Little Movement; We Are
Only Poor Weak Mortals; The
Birth of Passion; The Smile She
Means for Me)
1911—DR. DELUXE stage show* (For
Every Boy That's Lonely There's a
Girl That's Lonely Too; The Ac-
cent Makes No Difference in the
Language of Love); THE FASCINAT-

ING WIDOW stage show* (Don't Take Your Beau to the Seashore; You Built a Fire Down in My Heart; The Ragtime College Girl); THE GIRL OF MY DREAMS stage show* (The Girl of My Dreams; The Girl Who Wouldn't Spoon; Every Girlie Loves Me but the Girlie I Love)

1912—THE FIREFLY stage show* (Giannina Mia; Sympathy; When a Maid Comes Knocking at Your Door; The Dawn of Love; Love Is Like a Firefly)

1913—HIGH JINKS stage show* (High Jinks; The Bubble; Love's Own Kiss; Something Seems Tingle-ingling; Not Now but Later)

1914—CRINOLINE GIRL stage show (book only); SUZI stage show* (songs unimportant)

1916—KATINKA stage show* (Katinka; Allah's Holiday; My Paradise)

1917—YOU'RE IN LOVE stage show* (You're In Love; I'm Only Dreaming; That's the Only Place Where Our Flag Shall Fly)

1918—GOING UP stage show* (Going Up; The Tickle Toe; Kiss Me; If You Look in Her Eyes; Do It for Me)

1919—TUMBLE INN stage show* (I've Told My Love; Snuggle and Dream; The Thoughts I Wrote on the Leaves of My Heart); THE LITTLE WHOPPER stage show* (Oh, What a Little Whopper; You'll Dream and I'll Dream; 'Round the Corner)

1920—JIMMIE stage show* (Jimmie; Baby Dreams; Cute Little Two by Four); MARY stage show* (Mary; The Love Nest; Anything You Want to Do, Dear; Waiting; Everytime I Meet a Lady); TICKLE ME stage show* (Tickle Me; Until You Say Goodbye; If a Wish Could Make It So)

1921—JUNE LOVE stage show (book only); THE O'BRIEN GIRL stage show* (Learn to Smile; That O'Brien Girl; I Wonder How I Ever Passed You By)

1922—THE BLUE KITTEN stage show* (Cutie; I Found a Bud Among the Roses; When I Waltz with You; Blue Kitten Blues); MOLLY DARLING stage show (book only)

1923—WILDFLOWER stage show* (Wildflower; Bambalina; April Blossoms); JACK AND JILL stage show* (Voodoo Man)

1924—KID BOOTS stage show (book only); ROSE-MARIE stage show* (Rose-Marie; Indian Love Call; Song of the Mounties; Totem Tom-Tom; The Door of My Dreams)

1925—NO, NO, NANETTE stage show* (No, No, Nanette; I've Confessed to the Breeze); SUNNY stage show* (Sunny; Who?; D'Ya Love Me?; Two Little Bluebirds); BETTY LEE stage show* (songs unimportant)

1926—SONG OF THE FLAME stage show* (Song of the Flame; Cossack Love Song); THE DESERT SONG stage show* (The Desert Song; One Alone; The Riff Song; Romance; Then You Will Know; One Flower Grows Alone in Your Garden); THE WILD ROSE stage show* (The Wild Rose; Brown Eyes; One Golden Hour; We'll Have a Kingdom); CRISS CROSS stage show* (You Will, Won't You?; Cinderella Girl; In Araby with You); KITTY'S KISSES stage show (book only); OH, PLEASE stage show* (songs unimportant)

1927—GOLDEN DAWN stage show* (We Two; When I Crack My Whip; Africa; Jungle Shadows; Here in the Dark); LUCKY stage show* (Dancing the Devil Away; The Same Old Moon)

1928—GOOD BOY stage show* (You're the One)

1929—THE DESERT SONG movie (original stage score)

1930—NINA ROSA stage show (book only); GOLDEN DAWN movie (original stage score); SONG OF THE FLAME movie (original stage score)

1931—THE CAT AND THE FIDDLE stage show* (The Night Was Made for Love; Try to Forget; She Didn't Say "Yes"; One Moment Alone; A New Love Is Old; I Watch the

Love Parade; Poor Pierrot); SUNNY movie (original stage score)

1933—ROBERTA stage show* (Smoke Gets in Your Eyes; The Touch of Your Hand; Let's Begin; You're Devastating; Something Had to Happen; Yesterdays)

1934—THE CAT AND THE FIDDLE movie (original stage score)

1935—ROBERTA movie (original stage score)

1936—ROSE-MARIE movie (original stage score)

1937—THE FIREFLY movie (original stage score)

1941—NO, NO, NANETTE movie (original stage score); SUNNY movie (original stage score)

1944—THE DESERT SONG movie (part of original stage score)

1953—THE DESERT SONG movie (original stage score)

1954—ROSE-MARIE movie (original stage score)

769. HARBURG, E. Y. "YIP"   lyr

Born April 8, 1898, New York, N.Y.

Top lyricist of 30s and 40s. Collaborated on many hits. Scores for Broadway musicals BALLYHOO OF 1932, AMERICANA and WALK A LITTLE FASTER (1932), LIFE BEGINS AT 8:40 (1934), HOORAY FOR WHAT? (1937), HOLD ON TO YOUR HATS (1940), BLOOMER GIRL (1944), FINIAN'S RAINBOW (1947), JAMAICA (1957), lesser shows. Also wrote songs independently for other Broadway shows. Chief collaborators composers Harold Arlen and Jay Gorney. Others: Johnny Green, Vernon Duke, Burton Lane (great score for FINIAN'S RAINBOW), Jerome Kern. Best-known songs *April in Paris, It's Only a Paper Moon, What Is There to Say?, You're a Builder Upper, Let's Take a Walk Around the Block, Over the Rainbow, Happiness Is Just a Thing Called Joe, How Are Things in Glocca Morra?*. Memorable lyrics for Jay Gorney's moody melody produced great Depression song *Brother, Can You Spare a Dime?*. Attended CCNY. Ran electrical appliance business during 20s. Began songwriting 1929, great success

many years, still active in 60s. Author of book *Rhymes for the Irreverent*.

SONGS
(with related shows)

1929—EARL CARROLL'S SKETCH BOOK stage show (Kinda Cute; Like Me Less, Love Me More); APPLAUSE movie (What Wouldn't I Do for That Man?); RIO RITA movie (Long Before You Came Along)

1930—EARL CARROLL'S VANITIES stage show (Knee Deep in Daisies; I Came to Life); GARRICK GAIETIES stage show (Too, Too Divine; I'm Only Human After All; Ankle Up the Altar with Me); GLORIFYING THE AMERICAN GIRL movie (What Wouldn't I Do for That Man?); I'm Yours

1931—SHOOT THE WORKS stage show (Muchacha; Hot Moonlight; My Heart's a Banjo); If I Didn't Have You

1932—BALLYHOO OF 1932 stage show (Thrill Me; Riddle Me This; Nuts and Noodles; How Do You Do It?); AMERICANA stage show (Brother, Can You Spare a Dime?; Whistling for a Kiss; Satan's Little Lamb; Let Me Match My Private Life with Yours; Five Minutes of Spring; You're Not Pretty but You're Mine); WALK A LITTLE FASTER stage show (April in Paris; Where Have We Met Before?)

1933—MOONLIGHT AND PRETZELS movie (Moonlight and Pretzels; Ah, But Is It Love?); TAKE A CHANCE movie (It's Only a Paper Moon); Isn't It Heavenly?

1934—ZIEGFELD FOLLIES OF 1934 stage show (I Like the Likes of You; Suddenly; Water Under the Bridge; What Is There to Say?); LIFE BEGINS AT 8:40 stage show (You're a Builder Upper; Let's Take a Walk Around the Block; Fun to Be Fooled; What Can You Say in a Love Song?; Shoein' the Mare); THE COUNT OF MONTE CRISTO movie (The World Is Mine)

1936—THE SINGING KID movie (You're the

Cure for What Ails Me; I Love to Sing-a; Keep That Hi-De-Ho in Your Soul; Save Me, Sister); STAGE STRUCK movie (Fancy Meeting You; In Your Own Quiet Way; The Body Beautiful; The Income Tax); Last Night When We Were Very Young

1937—HOORAY FOR WHAT? stage show (Moanin' in the Mornin'; Down with Love; I've Gone Romantic on You; God's Country; In the Shade of the New Apple Tree); GOLD DIGGERS OF 1937 movie (Let's Put Our Heads Together; Speaking of the Weather)

1939—THE WIZARD OF OZ movie (Over the Rainbow; We're Off to See the Wizard; Ding Dong, the Witch Is Dead; The Jitterbug; If I Only Had a Brain; If I Only Had a Heart; Merry Old Land of Oz; If I Were King; Laugh a Day Away; Follow the Yellow Brick Road; Welcome to Munchkinland; Courage); THE MARX BROTHERS AT THE CIRCUS movie (Two Blind Loves; Lydia, the Tattooed Lady)

1940—HOLD ON TO YOUR HATS stage show (The World Is in My Arms; Don't Let It Get You Down; There's a Great Day Coming Mañana); ANDY HARDY MEETS DEBUTANTE movie (Buds Won't Bud)

1941—BABES ON BROADWAY movie (Chin Up, Cheerio, Carry On)

1942—SHIP AHOY movie (Poor You; Last Call for Love; I'll Take Tallulah; Tampico; Moonlight Bay)

1943—CABIN IN THE SKY movie (Happiness Is Just a Thing Called Joe); THOUSANDS CHEER movie (Let There Be Music)

1944—BLOOMER GIRL stage show (I Got a Song; Evelina; Right as the Rain; Pretty as a Picture; When the Boys Come Home; The Eagle and Me); CAN'T HELP SINGING movie (Can't Help Singing; More and More; Any Moment Now; Califor-niay); HOLLYWOOD CANTEEN movie (You Can Always Tell a Yank); KISMET movie (Willow in the Wind; Tell Me, Tell Me, Evening Star)

1945 THE AFFAIRS OF SUSAN movie (Something in My Heart)

1946—CENTENNIAL SUMMER movie (Cinderella Sue); CALIFORNIA movie (California; Said I to My Heart Said I; California or Bust; I Shoulda Stood in Pennsylvania; Lily-I-Lay-De-O)

1947—FINIAN'S RAINBOW stage show (How Are Things in Glocca Morra?; Old Devil Moon; Look to the Rainbow; If This Isn't Love; When I'm Not Near the Girl I Love; That Great Come-and-Get-It Day)

1951—FLAHOOLEY stage show, Sammy Fain-cm (Flahooley; Here's to Your Illusions; He's Only Wonderful; many more)

1957—JAMAICA stage show, Harold Arlen-cm (Cocoanut Sweet; Take It Slow, Joe; Ain't It the Truth?; Push the Button; Leave the Atom Alone; Napoleon; Savannah; Little Biscuit; Incompatibility)

1961—THE HAPPIEST GIRL IN THE WORLD stage show (unsuccessful)

1962—GAY PURR-EE movie cartoon, Harold Arlen-cm (Little Drops of Rain; Mewsette; Paris Is a Lonely Town; Roses Red—Violets Blue)

1963—I COULD GO ON SINGING movie (title song)

1968—DARLING OF THE DAY stage show, Jule Styne-cm (unsuccessful); FINIAN'S RAINBOW movie (original stage score)

770. HARDING, BUSTER   p ar cm B
(LAVERE HARDING)

Born March 19, 1917, Cleveland, Ohio
Died November 14, 1965, New York, N.Y.

Important arranger in 40s, best known for work with Count Basie. Composed jazz numbers. Earlier arrangements in Kansas City style, simple and hard-swinging; later in modern style. Mostly self-taught on piano, arranging. Led band locally and elsewhere, including Canada. To New York 1938. With Teddy Wilson's big band 1939-40 as arranger and second pianist. Arranged for Coleman Hawkins,

Artie Shaw, Cab Calloway, Dizzy Gillespie big band, Benny Goodman, Count Basie, Roy Eldridge, Glenn Miller, Tommy Dorsey, Earl Hines, Billie Holiday, Jonah Jones. Basie's chief arranger in 40s, later arranged for his modern blues-styled band. Musical director and pianist for Billie Holiday at times. Active into 60s till ill health curtailed work.

ARRANGEMENTS
(many also his compositions)

COUNT BASIE
Stampede in G Minor; 9:20 Special; Hobnail Boogie; Wild Bill's Boogie; Rockin' the Blues; Rusty Dusty Blues; House Rent Boogie; Ain't It the Truth; Mad Boogie; Nails; Paradise Squat; Blee Bop Blues; Rails; Tippin' on the Q.T.; Howzit

ARTIE SHAW
Little Jazz; Bedford Drive; The Glider; The Hornet

CAB CALLOWAY
A Smo-o-o-oth One; Tappin' Off; Jonah Joins the Cab

TEDDY WILSON
Hallelujah

BENNY GOODMAN
Scarecrow

771. HARDWICK, OTTO "TOBY"
as ss bs bs-s B

Born May 31, 1904, Washington, D.C.
Died August 5, 1970, Washington, D.C.

Long-time stalwart in Duke Ellington sax section. Capable soloist on alto sax but featured infrequently. Early in career worked locally with Ellington and Elmer Snowden. With them and two others to New York 1922 to join Wilbur Sweatman awhile. They returned to New York 1923, played Hollywood Club (later Kentucky Club) with Snowden as leader. Later Ellington became leader, called group The Washingtonians. During 1924-7 group toured New England often, returned to Kentucky Club, played New York clubs and theatres. In December 1927 enlarged band opened at New York's Cotton Club under Ellington's name; great success, springboard for fabulous career. Hardwick left band spring 1928, worked awhile in Paris with several bands

including brief period with Noble Sissle. Also own group. Back in U. S. 1929-31 with Chick Webb, Fats Waller, Elmer Snowden and others in New York; led band. Rejoined Ellington spring 1932, remained almost continuously until May 1946. Overshadowed by all-time great altoist Johnny Hodges, but Hardwick's lead sax important band asset. Occasionally featured in straightforward ballads. After leaving Ellington freelanced awhile, soon retired from music.

RECORDS

THE WASHINGTONIANS (Duke Ellington)
Blu-Disc 1002 Choo Choo/Rainy Nights
Ge 3342 Animal Crackers/Li'l Farina
Br 3526 Black and Tan Fantasy

DUKE ELLINGTON
Vo 1064 Birmingham Breakdown/East St. Louis Toodle-oo
Vo 1077 The Creeper/Immigration Blues
Vo 1153 Red Hot Band
Co 953-D Hop Head
OK 40955 Black and Tan Fantasy
OK 41013 Jubilee Stomp
Vi 21284 Washington Wobble
Vi 21580 Jubilee Stomp
Vi 21703 Got Everything but You
Br 6600 Sophisticated Lady
Br 7461 In a Sentimental Mood

FATS WALLER
Vi 38086 Lookin' Good but Feelin' Bad/I Need Someone Like You

JOHNNY HODGES
Va 576 Foolin' Myself/You'll Never Go to Heaven
Vo 3948 My Day/Silv'ry Moon and Golden Sands

COOTIE WILLIAMS
Vo 3890 Watchin'/I Can't Give You Anything but Love
Vo 3922 Jubilesta/Pigeons and Peppers

SONNY GREER
Cap 10028 Mood Indigo/The Mooche

JIMMY JONES
HRS 1014 Old Juice on the Loose/ Muddy Miss
HRS 1015 Departure from Dixie/A Woman's Got a Right to Change
Wax 103 Five O'clock Drag

TIMME ROSENKRANTZ
  Cont 6012 Bouncy/Blues at Dawn
OTTO HARDWICK
  Wax 102 Come Sunday
  Wax 105 I Remember Your Eyes
OTTO HARDWICK-BEN WEBSTER
  Wax 104 All Alone/As Long as I Live
  Wax 105 Blue Belles of Harlem

LPs

DUKE ELLINGTON
  Co C3L27 (3-LP set) The Ellington
    Era, Vol. 1 (1927-40 RIs)
  Vi LPV-517 Jumpin' Punkins (Vi RIs)
  Vi LPM-1364 In a Mellotone (Vi RIs)
  Vi LPM-1715 At His Very Best (Vi
    RIs)
REX STEWART (one side)
  Vi LPV-533 Things Ain't What They
    Used to Be (RIs)

772. HARING, BOB   cm lyr ar B

Born August 21, 1896, Montclair, N. J.
Bandleader of 20s and 30s. Good semi-
hot style in 20s, smooth hotel style in 30s.
Haring musical director for Cameo
Records mid-20s, for Brunswick Records
late 20s. Educated at University of Wash-
ington and Seattle Conservatory of
Music. Conductor on 30s radio, including
brief period late 1936 on Lucky Strike Hit
Parade. Bandleading waned by late 30s.
Later musical editor of publishing house.
Composed *Dawn of Tomorrow, Concerto
for Two, Fanny Tinkle, My Midnight Star.*

RECORDS

BOB HARING
  Ca 683 Doing the Town
  Ca 784 Manhattan/Cecilia
  Ca 954 Mary Lou
  Ca 9058 Buy Buy for Baby
  Ca 9105 Audition Blues
  Br 4273 Weary River/Some Sweet Day
  Br 4288 Dream Boat/Fioretta
  Br 4316 My Cairo Love/Bye and Bye,
    Sweetheart
  Br 4359 Louise/Huggable Kissable
    You
  Br 4382 S'posin'
  Br 4458 Ich Liebe Dich/At Close of
    Day
  Br 4472 There Was Nothing Else to
    Do

Br 4493 Song of Siberia/The Moon-
  light March
Br 4495 How Am I to Know?
Br 4545 Revolutionary Rhythm/When
  the Real Thing Comes Your Way
Br 4608 Georgia Pines/Love Made a
  Gypsy Out of Me
Br 4782 Just Like in a Story Book/I'm
  in the Market for You
Br 4851 Swingin' in a Hammock/All
  Through the Night
Br 4852 I Love You So Much/Betty
  Co-ed
Br 4973 Baby's Birthday Party/One
  Love
Br 6009 Tears/Sing Your Way Home
Br 6031 Chimes of Spring/Two Hearts
  in Three-Quarter Time
Pe 15462 Ho Hum/Let's Get Friendly
Pe 15471 Building a Home for You
Pe 15487 Wrap Your Troubles in
  Dreams/June Time Is Love Time
Pe 15501 It's the Girl

773. HARLAN, BYRON G.   vo

Popular tenor-comedian-imitator from
1900 into 20s. Played vaudeville and minstrel shows. Teamed with Arthur Collins
in comic-singing duo. Active recording
1910-16 in infancy of record industry.

RECORDS

BYRON G. HARLAN-CAL STEWART
  Vi 17854 Village Gossips
BYRON G. HARLAN
  OK 1133 How Ya Gonna Keep 'Em
    Down on the Farm?
  Vi 16095 Two Little Baby Shoes/Why
    Don't They Play with Me?
  Vi 16097 When the Morning Glories
    Twine
  Vi 16122 I'm Tying the Leaves So
    They Won't Come Down
  Vi 16526 School Days
  Vi 17065 They Gotta Quit Kickin' My
    Dog
  Vi 17447 Hello Central, Give Me
    Heaven/Can't You Take It Back
    and Change It?
  Vi 18038 The Georgia Skip
  Vi 18364 I'm a Twelve O'clock Fellow
  Vi 18413 Long Boy

COLLINS & HARLAN
(See ARTHUR COLLINS biography herein for duo's records)

774. HARMONICATS, THE

Harmonica group, rose to fame 1947 with record hit *Peg o' My Heart*. Maintained popularity into 50s. Jerry Murad led group. He and Al Fiore left Borrah Minevitch harmonica group 1944 to form trio in Chicago with Don Les. Murad played lead, Fiore provided chording, Les played bass harmonica. Worked mostly in midwest. 1947 hit led to string of recordings and radio appearances. By later 50s popularity waned but group still worked and occasionally recorded. Murad wrote instruction book *Jerry Murad's Harmonica Technique for the Super-Chronomic*.

RECORDS

THE HARMONICATS
Vita 1 Peg o' My Heart/Fantasy Impromptu
Vita 7 Peggy O'Neil/September Song
Mer 5353 Tea for Two/Harmonicat Jingle
Mer 5869 Night Train/Hootin' Blues
Mer 70007 Sissy/La Paloma
Mer 70069 Till I Waltz Again with You/Back Fence Wail
Mer 70164 Malaguena/The Harmonica Player
Mer 70277 Just One More Chance/Heartaches
Mer 70332 Every Little Movement/That Girl
Mer 70362 Catwalk/Hora Staccata
(with JAN AUGUST)
Mer 5399 Bewitched/Blue Prelude
Mer 70056 Finesse/Ti-Pi-Tin
(with JAN AUGUST-ROBERTA QUINLAN)
Mer 5420 I Never Had a Worry in the World/Buffalo Billy
JERRY MURAD of THE HARMONICATS, with RICHARD HAYMAN ORCHESTRA
Mer 70202 Sweet Leilani/The Story of Three Loves

LPs

THE HARMONICATS
Co CL-1556 Cherry Pink and Apple Blossom White
Co CL-1637 Peg o' My Heart
Co CL-1757 Sentimental Serenade
Co CL-1863 Fiesta!
Co CL-1945 Forgotten Dreams
Co CL-2090 Try a Little Tenderness
Co CL-2166 The Love Songs of Tom Jones
Mer(10″)MG-25128
Mer-Wing MGW-12163 South American Nights
Mer-Wing MGW-12242 Dolls, Dolls, Dolls
Design DLP-202 The Harmonicats

775. HARRIS, BILL   tb g B

> *Born October 28, 1916, Philadelphia, Pa.*
> *Died August 19, 1973, Hollandale, Fla., of heart attack*

Prominent in development of modern trombone style. Work with Woody Herman in mid-40s created jazz sensation. Cool, burred tone with inflections; choppy, uneven attack. Inspired imitators. As youngster played other instruments before trombone. Played locally during 30s until with Ray McKinley and Buddy Williams 1942. With Bob Chester for periods 1943-4. With Benny Goodman August 1943 to March 1944. Played soundtrack for Goodman movie SWEET AND LOWDOWN (1944); theme of film a trombonist's career. Briefly with Charlie Barnet and Freddie Slack, led combo. Joined Herman August 1944 till late 1946. In 1947 led combo, worked with Charlie Ventura. Rejoined Herman 1948-50. In early 50s with Jazz at the Philharmonic, Oscar Pettiford, Sauter-Finegan band. In 1953 co-led Jackson-Harris Herd with bassist Chubby Jackson. With Herman again mid-50s. In later 50s mostly in Florida, including jobs with Flip Phillips and Red Norvo. 1959 European tours with Herman and Goodman. In early 60s led groups in Florida. Worked Las Vegas with Charlie Teagarden 1962-4. With Norvo 1965-6 in Las Vegas and other spots. In later 60s based in Miami for club and TV work. Took up guitar in later years. Active into 70s.

RECORDS

WOODY HERMAN
Co 36803 Apple Honey

Co 36835 Northwest Passage
Co 36861 Bijou
Co 36909 Let It Snow
Co 37059 Blowin' Up a Storm
Co 37238 Woodchoppers Ball
Co 38369 Everywhere/The Goof and I
Cap 57-616 Keeper of the Flame
Cap 57-720 Tenderly

SONNY BERMAN
Dial 1006 Curbstone Scuffle

CHUBBY JACKSON
Key 616 Cryin' Sands/Northwest Passage

JOE BUSHKIN
CMS 565 Pickin' At the Pic/Georgia on My Mind

METRONOME ALL-STARS
Cap 15039 Metronome Riff/Leap Here

FLIP PHILLIPS
Mer 8953 Cheek to Cheek/I've Got My Love to Keep Me Warm

CHARLIE VENTURA
Nat 9036 Synthesis/Blue Champagne

JAZZ OFF THE AIR
Vox 16102-3-4 Sweet Georgia Brown (1-2-3)/High on an Open Mike (1-2-3)

JAZZ AT THE PHILHARMONIC
Mer 11000-1-2 Perdido (1-6)
Mer 11013-4-5 Mordido (1-6)

BILL HARRIS
Key 618 Mean to Me/Cross Country
Key 626 Characteristically B.H./She's Funny That Way
Key 634 Frustration/Everything Happens to Me
Dial 1009 Somebody Loves Me/Woodchoppers Holiday
Cap 60004 How High the Moon/The Moon Is Low
Mer 8969 You're Blasé/Bill Not Phil
Mer 8997 Bijou/Poogerini
Mer 89023 Gloomy Sunday/D'Anjou
Clef 89069 Blackstrap/Imagination

LPs

BILL HARRIS
Clef(10")MGC-125 Bill Harris Collates

CHUBBY JACKSON-BILL HARRIS ALL-STARS
Mer(10")MG-25076 Jazz Journey

TERRY GIBBS-BILL HARRIS
Premier PS-2006 Woodchoppers' Ball

WOODY HERMAN
Ha HL-7013 Bijou (Co RIs)
Co(10")CL-6049 Dance Parade (Co RIs)
Cap T-324 (1948-50 RIs)

CHARLIE VENTURA
Verve V-8132

FLIP PHILLIPS
Verve V-8075

NAT PIERCE
Cor CRL-57091 Kansas City Memories

JAZZ AT THE PHILHARMONIC
Verve VSP-16 Perdido/Mordido

776. HARRIS, DAVE   ts

Swinging, gutty-toned tenor sax man, best known for work in Raymond Scott Quintette 1937-9. With Scott on numerous Saturday Night Swing Session radio programs and on recordings. Scott's fast-moving, intricate arrangements demanded superior musicianship. Harris in Scott's big band 1939-40. Later mostly freelanced and did studio work. Brief period with Tommy Dorsey 1945. Featured with Jerry Gray 1951.

RECORDS

RAYMOND SCOTT QUINTETTE
Br 7992 Twilight in Turkey/Minuet in Jazz
Br 7993 The Toy Trumpet/Powerhouse
Br 8000 Reckless Night on Board an Ocean Liner/Dinner Music for a Pack of Hungry Cannibals
Br 8058 War Dance for Wooden Indians/The Penguin
Br 8144 The Happy Farmer/Egyptian Barn Dance
Br 8404 In an 18th Century Drawing Room/Boy Scout in Switzerland
Br 8452 Siberian Sleigh Ride/The Tobacco Auctioneer
Co 35585 Peter Tambourine/Bumpy Weather Over Newark
Co 37359 The Girl at the Typewriter/Get Happy (big band)

RAYMOND SCOTT ORCHESTRA
Co 35363 Just a Gigolo/Huckleberry Duck
Co 35364 The Peanut Vendor/Business Men's Bounce

RED MCKENZIE
Va 520 Sweet Lorraine/Wanted
MIDGE WILLIAMS
Va 519 Walkin' the Dog/In the Shade of the Old Apple Tree
Va 566 Let's Begin Again/I'm Gettin' Sentimental Over You
BILLIE HOLIDAY
De 23391 That Old Devil Called Love

LPs

RAYMOND SCOTT QUINTETTE
Co(10")CL-6083 Raymond Scott's Drawing Room
BING CROSBY with BOB SCOBEY BAND
Vi LPM-1473 Bing with a Beat
MORTY CORB
Tops L-1581 Strictly from Dixie
(miscellaneous bands)
Golden Tone C-4021 Dixieland

777. HARRIS, JOE   tb vo

Born 1908, Sedalia, Mo.
Died September 1952, Fresno, Calif., in auto accident

Talented jazz singer and trombonist in Jack Teagarden vein. Never attained deserved prominence. As teenager played in southwest. Worked oil fields in Texas and Oklahoma. Later to St. Louis, played riverboats. In 1932 first important jobs with Joe Haymes and Frankie Trumbauer (with latter in Chicago, then on tour). Joined Ben Pollack in Chicago May 1933, remained over a year. Freelanced in New York 1934-5. Briefly member of Bob Crosby band at inception early 1935. With Benny Goodman August 1935 till May 1936; classic jazz performance on trombone and vocal on Goodman recording *Basin Street Blues*. Hollywood studios 1936-7. Out of music 1937-8 due to auto accident. In 1939 joined Carl Hoff on Al Pearce radio show. In early 40s with Ben Pollack, Pee Wee Erwin, Bob Chester, Benny Goodman, Eddie Miller. Hollywood studios in mid-40s. Freelanced in later years.

RECORDS

BEN POLLACK
Co 2870 Got the Jitters
Co 2905-D Here Goes/Beat o' My Heart

Co 2929-D Sleepy Head/Night on the Desert
BENNY GOODMAN
Vi 25195 Santa Claus Came in the Spring/Eeny Meeny Miney Mo
Vi 25245 It's Been So Long
Vi 25247 Breakin' in a Pair of Shoes/Stompin' at the Savoy
Vi 25258 Basin Street Blues
Vi 25268 Madhouse
Vi 25279 Get Happy
JIMMY MCPARTLAND
De 3363 Panama/Eccentric
De 18441 Original Dixieland One-Step/I'm All Bound 'Round with the Mason-Dixon Line
BOB CROSBY
De 479 Beale Street Blues/The Dixieland Band
GENE KRUPA
De 18114 Three Little Words/Blues of Israel
De 18115 Jazz Me Blues/The Last Round-up

LPs

BENNY GOODMAN
Sunbeam SB128-32 (5 LPs) From the Congress Hotel (1935-6 airchecks)

777A. HARRIS, MARION   vo

Born 1896
Died April 23, 1944, New York, N.Y., in hotel fire

Record star of 20s and early 30s. Minor role in Broadway show STOP! LOOK! LISTEN! in 1916. Supporting role in YOURS TRULY in 1927; then star in A NIGHT IN SPAIN same year. Joined cast of THE SECOND LITTLE SHOW (1930) after show started. Performed in London at intervals in 30s.

RECORDS

MARION HARRIS
Co A-2968 He Done Me Wrong/Oh Judge
Co A-3328 Never Let No One Man Worry Your Mind/I'm a Jazz Vampire
Co A-3371 I Ain't Got Nobody/Where Is My Daddy Now Blues
Co A-3433 I'm Nobody's Baby/Sweet Daddy's Gone

Vi 18152 My Syncopated Melody Man/Paradise Blues
Vi 18343 Some Sweet Day/They Go Wild, Simply Wild Over Me
Vi 18398 When I Hear That Jazz Band Play
Vi 18482 There's a Lump of Sugar Down in Dixie
Vi 18509 After You've Gone
Vi 18535 A Good Man Is Hard to Find/For Johnny and Me
Br 2309 I'm Just Wild About Harry/Cradle Melody
Br 2345 Hot Lips/Aggravatin' Papa
Br 2361 Mississippi Choo Choo/Who Cares?
Br 2370 Rose of the Rio Grande/I Gave You Up Just Before You Threw Me Down
Br 2443 Who's Sorry Now?/Waitin' for the Evenin' Mail
Br 2458 Dirty Hands, Dirty Face/Somebody Else Walked Right In
Br 2552 St. Louis Gal/I Don't Want You to Cry Over Me
Br 2610 How Come You Do Me Like You Do?/It Had to Be You
Br 4663 Nobody's Using It Now/Funny, Dear, What Love Can Do
Br 4806 You Do Something to Me/Wasn't It Nice?
Br 4812 I Remember You from Somewhere/Nobody Cares If I'm Blue
Br 4873 Little White Lies/If I Could Be with You
Br 6016 Blue Again/He's My Secret Passion

778. HARRIS, PHIL   d vo B

Born January 16, 1904, Linton, Ind.

Famous bandleader, later personality in radio, movies and TV. Excellent showman, performed well on rhythm and novelty tunes in raspy, half-talking manner. Grew up in Nashville, played drums locally with Francis Craig. With Henry Halstead in mid-20s; toured with bands in U.S. and abroad. Co-leader with Carol Lofner of band on west coast early 30s. Formed hotel-style band to play Cocoanut Grove in Los Angeles. A sensation with showmanship and novelty vocals. Made 1933 movie short SO THIS IS HARRIS;

later in year in movie MELODY CRUISE. On own 1934 radio show Let's Listen to Harris. Later did radio series from New York. In mid-30s had good band; could swing, featured vocalist Leah Ray. Played hotels, theatres. *Rose Room* theme. Joined Jack Benny radio show late 1936, became big name. Band played each show and Phil had important comic role as wise-guy hard-drinking musician stereotype. With show until 1946, filled in on Kay Kyser show 1944-5. 1947-54 co-starred with wife Alice Faye on long-running radio show. Harris associated with novelty songs *That's What I Like About the South*, 1950 hit *The Thing*. A natural for TV, often on in 50s and 60s. TV specials by himself and co-starring with wife. In later 60s and 70s concentrated on country and western songs, handled them well. Still active in early 70s. During career in numerous movies as single or leading band.

MOVIES

1933—MELODY CRUISE
1937—TURN OFF THE MOON
1939—MAN ABOUT TOWN
1940—BUCK BENNY RIDES AGAIN; DREAMING OUT LOUD
1945—I LOVE A BANDLEADER
1950—WABASH AVENUE (best role)
1951—STARLIFT; THE WILD BLUE YONDER
1954—THE HIGH AND THE MIGHTY
1956—ANYTHING GOES; GOODBYE LADY
1963—THE WHEELER DEALERS
1964—THE PATSY
1967—THE COOL ONES
1969—KING GUN

RECORDS

HENRY HALSTEAD
Vi 19511 Bull Frog Serenade
Vi 19514 Panama
LOFNER-HARRIS ORCHESTRA
Vi 22830 I'm Sorry Dear/I Got the Ritz
Vi 22831 Was It Wrong?/River, Stay 'Way from My Door
Vi 22832 Big "C" March/Hail to California March
PHIL HARRIS
Vi 22855 Constantly/When It's Sleepy Time Down South
Co 2761-D What Have We Got to

Lose?/You've Got Me Crying Again

Co 2766-D Was My Face Red?/How's About It?

De 564 I'd Rather Listen to Your Eyes/I'd Love to Take Orders from You

De 565 Now You've Got Me Doin' It/As Long as the World Goes 'Round and Around

Vo 3419 You Can Tell She Comes from Dixie/Where the Lazy River Goes By

Vo 3430 Nobody/Jelly Bean

Vo 3447 Goodnight My Love/Swing High, Swing Low

Vo 3488 Too Marvelous for Words/Sentimental and Melancholy

Vo 3533 Jammin'/That's Southern Hospitality

OK 3583 That's What I Like About the South/Constantly

OK 6325 Nobody/Woodman, Spare That Tree

Vs 8197 Careless/Faithful Forever

Vs 8272 Buds Won't Bud/What's the Matter with Dixie?

Vi 20-2089 That's What I Like About the South/If You're Ever Down in Texas, Look Me Up

Vi 20-2143 The Preacher and the Bear/Where Does It Get You in the End?

Vi 20-2401 Fun and Fancy Free

Vi 20-2614 One More Time/Old Time Religion

Vi 20-2684 Minnie the Mermaid/Pappy's Little Jug

Vi 20-3968 The Thing/Goofus

Vi 20-4070 Southern Fried Boogie/Oh, What a Face

Vi 20-4342 Where the Blues Were Born in New Orleans/Rugged but Right

PHIL HARRIS-BELL SISTERS
Vi 20-4993 Hi-Diddle-Diddle

LPs

PHIL HARRIS
Cam CAL-456 That's What I Like About the South (Vi RIs)

Vi LPM-1985 The South Shall Rise Again

Vi(10")LPM-3203 You're Blasé

779. HARRISON, JIMMY   tb vo

Born October 17, 1900, Louisville, Ky.
Died July 23, 1931, New York, N.Y.

Probably best early jazz trombonist. Career cut short by death at 30. Although influenced by New Orleans trumpet stars King Oliver and Louis Armstrong, veered from New Orleans tailgate style. Sure attack and execution, warm tone; still developing at death. Influenced trombonists. Grew up in Detroit, played jobs there, moved to Toledo. As teenager toured with minstrel show as trombonist-singer. Played 1919-21 with Charlie Johnson, Sam Wooding, Hank Duncan, James P. Johnson and others. To New York 1922, worked with Fess Williams, June Clark, also with Clark in mid-20s. In mid-20s with Billy Fowler, Elmer Snowden, Duke Ellington. Most important period with Fletcher Henderson 1927-30 (except for 1928 interval with Charlie Johnson). In 1930 serious stomach operation. Tried comeback with Henderson late 1930-1 but remained in ill health. With Chick Webb awhile in mid-1931, collapsed on job, died a few weeks later.

RECORDS

CHARLIE JOHNSON
Vi 21712 The Boy in the Boat/Walk That Thing

FLETCHER HENDERSON
Co 1059-D I'm Coming Virginia/Whiteman Stomp

Co 1543-D King Porter Stomp

Co 1913-D Wang Wang Blues/Blazin'

Co 2329-D Somebody Loves Me/Chinatown, My Chinatown

Co 14392-D Easy Money/Come On, Baby

Vo 1092 Fidgety Feet

Br 4119 Hop Off

Vi 20944 Variety Stomp

CHICK WEBB
Vo 1607 Soft and Sweet/Heebie Jeebies

CHOCOLATE DANDIES
Co 2543-D Bugle Call Rag/Dee Blues

Co 35679 Goodbye Blues/Cloudy Skies

Co 36009 Got Another Sweetie Now

PERRY BRADFORD
Para 12041 Fade Away Blues/Daybreak Blues

GEORGIA STRUTTERS
Ha 468 Rock, Jenny, Rock/It's Right Here for You

GULF COAST SEVEN
Co 14107-D Keep Your Temper/Santa Claus Blues

THE JUNGLE BAND
Br 4450 Dog Bottom

LOUISIANA STOMPERS
Para 12550 Hop Off/Rough House Blues

CLARENCE WILLIAMS
OK 8443 Wouldja?/Senegalese Stomp
Co 14434-D In Our Cottage of Love/ Them Things Got Me

BESSIE SMITH
Co 14197-D After You've Gone/Muddy Water
Co 14219-D Alexander's Ragtime Band/There'll Be a Hot Time in the Old Town Tonight

LPs

FLETCHER HENDERSON
Co C4L19 (4-LP set) A Study in Frustration (Co, Ha, Vo RIs)

CHICK WEBB
De DL-9222 A Legend, Vol. 1 (1929-36 RIs)

CHARLIE JOHNSON
"X"(10")LVA-3026 (Vi RIs)

BESSIE SMITH
Co CL-855-8 (4-LP set) The Bessie Smith Story (Co RIs)

780. HART, CLYDE   p ar B

Born 1910, Baltimore, Md.
Died March 19, 1945, New York, N.Y.

Mainstream pianist active in early bop. Adapted to new style but career aborted by death from tuberculosis. Pianist-arranger with Jap Allen 1930-1. With Blanche Calloway several years. Freelanced in New York, often recorded. With Stuff Smith late 1936-8, Roy Eldridge 1939. Periods 1940-2 with Lester Young, Frankie Newton, Lucky Millinder. With John Kirby 1942-3. Active 1944-5 with many groups on record sessions; led band at times and worked as soloist. Many jobs with Don Byas till illness struck.

RECORDS

SHARKEY BONANO
Vo 3353 Mudhole Blues/Swing In, Swing Out
Vo 3380 I'm Satisfied with My Gal/ High Society

RED ALLEN
Vo 3305 Out Where the Blue Begins/ Darling, Not without You
Vo 3306 I'll Sing You a Thousand Love Songs/Picture Me without You

PUTNEY DANDRIDGE
Vo 3304 Sing, Baby, Sing/You Turned the Tables on Me

BILLIE HOLIDAY
Vo 3333 A Fine Romance/I Can't Pretend
Vo 3334 One, Two, Button Your Shoe/Let's Call a Heart a Heart

STUFF SMITH
De 1279 Onyx Club Spree/Twilight in Turkey
De 1287 Where Is the Sun?/Upstairs

LIONEL HAMPTON
Vi 25658 Confessin'/Drum Stomp

CHU BERRY
CMS 516 Sittin' In/Forty-Six West Fifty-Two
CMS(12")1502 Star Dust/Body and Soul

TINY GRIMES
Sav 613 Romance without Finance/I'll Always Love You Just the Same

COZY COLE
Cont 6000 A Ghost of a Chance/Look Here
Cont 6001 Willow Weep for Me/Take It On Back

DEPARIS BROTHERS
CMS 552 Black and Blue/I've Found a New Baby
CMS 567 Change o' Key Boogie/The Sheik of Araby

DON BYAS
Sav 524 Free and Easy/Bass-C-Jam
Sav 581 Riffin' and Jivin'/Worried and Blue

CHARLIE PARKER
Sav 541 Red Cross/Tiny's Tempo

DIZZY GILLESPIE
  Mus 488 Dizzy Atmosphere/All the
    Things You Are
  Manor 1042 Good Bait/I Can't Get
    Started
CLYDE HART
  Sav 598 Dee Dee's Dance/Little Benny
  Regis 7002 All the Things You Are/
    Riding on 52nd Street
  Cont 6013 What's the Matter Now?/
    That's the Blues

LPs

LIONEL HAMPTON
  Jazztone J-1246 All-Star Groups (Vi
    RIs)
  Cam CAL-517 Open House (Vi RIs)
COLEMAN HAWKINS
  GA 33-316 Jazz Concert (Apo RIs)
DIZZY GILLESPIE
  Sav MG-12020 Groovin' High (Mus
    RIs)
(miscellaneous artists)
  Vi LPV-578 Swing, Vol. 1 (Vi, Bb RIs)

781. HART, LORENZ   lyr

Born May 2, 1895, New York, N.Y.
Died November 22, 1943, New York,
N.Y.

Great lyricist famed for collaboration
with composer Richard Rodgers. Team
began writing 1919, successful by mid-
20s. Later regarded by many as top
composing team on Broadway. Smart,
elegant lyrics of Hart combined with
brilliant Rodgers tunes to set their work
apart. Team key influence in shaping
style and music of Broadway musicals in
late 20s and 30s. Hit shows included THE
GIRL FRIEND (1926), PEGGY ANN and A
CONNECTICUT YANKEE (1927), JUMBO
(1935), ON YOUR TOES (1936), THE BOYS
FROM SYRACUSE (1938), TOO MANY GIRLS
(1939), PAL JOEY (1941), BY JUPITER
(1942). Librettist Herbert Fields worked
with team on many early shows. Most
notable songs *Manhattan, The Blue Room,
The Girl Friend, Mountain Greenery, Thou
Swell, My Heart Stood Still, You Took
Advantage of Me, With a Song in My
Heart, Ten Cents a Dance, Isn't It Romantic?, Mimi, Lover, Blue Moon, Dancing*

*on the Ceiling, It's Easy to Remember, My
Romance, Little Girl Blue, There's a Small
Hotel, The Lady Is a Tramp, My Funny
Valentine, Have You Met Miss Jones?, I
Married an Angel, Spring Is Here, This
Can't Be Love, I Didn't Know What Time
It Was.* Hart educated at Columbia, wrote
material for shows there. Met Rodgers,
later Columbia student, formed team.
First success with *Any Old Place with You*
in 1919 Broadway show A LONELY ROMEO.
Seven songs for 1920 show POOR LITTLE
RITZ GIRL. For several years little success;
wrote for amateur shows and minor stage
productions, abandoned songwriting
awhile. Clicked with scores for 1925
Broadway shows GARRICK GAIETIES and
DEAREST ENEMY. Many successes
followed. But several Depression shows
short-lived. Team turned to movie writing
in early and mid-30s. Outstanding movie
scores LOVE ME TONIGHT (1932) and MIS-
SISSIPPI (1935). Several stage hits made
into movies early 30s and later. Back to
Broadway 1935 for most successful period. Hart co-librettist on shows ON YOUR
TOES, BABES IN ARMS, I MARRIED AN ANGEL,
BY JUPITER. In November 1943 early hit A
CONNECTICUT YANKEE revived on Broadway. Hart's eccentric, dissipated life led
to weakened health, then pneumonia.
Died soon after YANKEE opened. 1948
movie WORDS AND MUSIC based on team's
lives; roles played by Tom Drake and
Mickey Rooney (portraying Hart).

SONGS
(with related shows)

1919—A LONELY ROMEO stage show (Any
  Old Place with You)
1920—POOR LITTLE RITZ GIRL stage show
  (You Can't Fool Your Dreams;
  What Happened Nobody Knows;
  Mary, Queen of Scots; others)
1925—GARRICK GAIETIES stage show
  (Manhattan; Sentimental Me; Do
  You Love Me?; On with the
  Dance); DEAREST ENEMY stage
  show (Here in My Arms; Cheerio;
  Bye and Bye; Here's a Kiss; Old
  Enough to Love)
1926—THE GIRL FRIEND stage show (The
  Girl Friend; The Blue Room);

GARRICK GAIETIES stage show (Mountain Greenery; What's the Use of Talking?)

1927—PEGGY ANN stage show (Where's That Rainbow?; A Tree in the Park; A Little Birdie Told Me So; Havana; Maybe It's Me); A CONNECTICUT YANKEE stage show (Thou Swell; My Heart Stood Still; On a Desert Island with Thee; I Feel at Home with You); BETSY stage show (Sing; If I Were You)

1928—PRESENT ARMS stage show (You Took Advantage of Me; Do I Hear You Saying "I Love You"?; A Kiss for Cinderella); SHE'S MY BABY stage show (My Lucky Star; You're What I Need; Try Again Tomorrow); CHEE-CHEE stage show (Singing a Love Song; I Must Love You; Moon of My Delight; Dear, Oh Dear)

1929—SPRING IS HERE stage show (Spring Is Here; Yours Sincerely; With a Song in My Heart; Why Can't I?); HEADS UP stage show (Why Do You Suppose?; My Man Is on the Make; A Ship Without a Sail; It Must Be Heaven)

1930—SIMPLE SIMON stage show (Ten Cents a Dance; Send for Me; many more; Dancing on the Ceiling—dropped before show opened); LEATHERNECKING movie (version of 1928 stage show PRESENT ARMS, featured original score); HEADS UP movie (original stage score); SPRING IS HERE movie (Yours Sincerely and With a Song in My Heart from original stage score)

1931—AMERICA'S SWEETHEART stage show (I've Got Five Dollars; We'll Be the Same; How About It?); BILLY ROSE'S CRAZY QUILT stage show (Rest Room Rose); THE HOT HEIRESS movie (Nobody Loves a Riveter; Like Ordinary People Do; You're the Cats)

1932—LOVE ME TONIGHT movie (Love Me Tonight; Isn't It Romantic?; Mimi; Lover; The Song of Paree; How Are You?; A Woman Needs Something Like That; Poor Apache); THE PHANTOM PRESIDENT movie (The Country Needs a Man; Somebody Ought to Wave a Flag; Give Her a Kiss; The Convention); Dancing on the Ceiling (reached popularity this year)

1933—HALLELUJAH, I'M A BUM movie (You Are too Beautiful; I'll Do It Again; I've Gotta Get Back to New York; What Do You Want with Money?); DANCING LADY movie (That's the Rhythm of the Day)

1934—HOLLYWOOD PARTY movie (Hollywood Party; Hello; Reincarnation); EVERGREEN English movie (old song: Dancing on the Ceiling; new songs: Dear, Dear; If I Give in to You); NANA movie (That's Love); MANHATTAN MELODRAMA movie (The Bad in Every Man; later changed to Blue Moon)

1935—MISSISSIPPI movie (Soon; It's Easy to Remember; Down by the River); JUMBO stage show (My Romance; Little Girl Blue; The Most Beautiful Girl in the World; Over and Over Again; The Circus Is on Parade; There's a Small Hotel —dropped before show opened); Blue Moon (reached popularity this year)

1936—ON YOUR TOES stage show (On Your Toes; There's a Small Hotel; It's Got to Be Love; Quiet Night; Glad to Be Unhappy; Slaughter on Tenth Avenue—ballet music); DANCING PIRATE movie (Are You My Love?; When You're Dancing the Waltz)

1937—BABES IN ARMS stage show (Babes in Arms; Where or When; The Lady Is a Tramp; My Funny Valentine; I Wish I Were in Love Again; Johnny One Note; All at Once; 'Way Out West); THE SHOW IS ON stage show (old song: I've Got Five Dollars; new song: Rhythm); I'D RATHER BE RIGHT stage show (I'd Rather Be Right; Have You Met Miss Jones?; many more)

1938—I MARRIED AN ANGEL stage show (I

Married an Angel; Spring Is Here; I'll Tell the Man in the Street; Did You Ever Get Stung?; How to Win Friends and Influence People); THE BOYS FROM SYRACUSE stage show (This Can't Be Love; Sing for Your Supper; Falling in Love with Love; The Shortest Day of the Year; You Have Cast Your Shadow on the Sea; He and She); FOOLS FOR SCANDAL movie (Fools for Scandal; How Can You Forget?; There's a Boy in Harlem)

1939—TOO MANY GIRLS stage show (I Didn't Know What Time It Was; Love Never Went to College; Give It Back to the Indians; I Like to Recognize the Tune; Spic and Spanish); BABES IN ARMS movie (original stage score); ON YOUR TOES movie (original stage score)

1940—HIGHER AND HIGHER stage show (From Another World; Nothing but You; It Never Entered My Mind; Ev'ry Sunday Afternoon); THE BOYS FROM SYRACUSE movie (original stage score); TOO MANY GIRLS movie (original stage score)

1941—PAL JOEY stage show (Bewitched; I Could Write a Book; many others); THEY MET IN ARGENTINA movie (Amarillo; Simpatica; You've Got the Best of Me)

1942—BY JUPITER stage show (Ev'rything I've Got; Wait Till You See Her; Careless Rhapsody; Nobody's Heart Belongs to Me); I MARRIED AN ANGEL movie (original stage score)

1943—STAGE DOOR CANTEEN movie (The Girl I Love to Leave Behind); A CONNECTICUT YANKEE stage show (revival; new song: To Keep My Love Alive)

1957—PAL JOEY movie (original stage score plus The Lady Is a Tramp; My Funny Valentine; I Didn't Know What Time It Was; There's a Small Hotel)

782. HASKELL, JACK   vo

Good baritone with melodious, straightforward style. Mainly active in 40s and 50s. Attended Northwestern's school of music. Sang on Chicago radio. Military service, World War II. With Les Brown 1946. Later 40s sang in Chicago clubs and on radio, including Dave Garroway show. On early TV, including Garroway's TV show; many guest spots. In late 50s and early 60s on TV frequently, especially on Jack Paar and Johnny Carson. Some announcing and commercials besides singing. Good 1962 supporting role in Broadway musical MR. PRESIDENT. In later 60s changed singing style a bit to conform to shouting pop trend, faded from TV.

RECORDS

LES BROWN
  Co 36972 In Love in Vain
  Co 36977 It Couldn't Be True
  Co 37066 I Guess I'll Get the Papers
  Co 37086 My Serenade
  Co 37153 Years and Years Ago
JACK HASKELL
  De 24786 Over the Hillside/I Know, I Know, I Know
  De 24806 You're Diff'rent/Too-Whit! Too-Whoo!
  Cor 60574 A Kiss to Build a Dream On/Wedding Invitations
  Cor 60596 My One and Only Love/ The Pal That I Love Stole the Gal That I Loved
  Cor 60652 Silver and Gold/Goodbye Sweetheart
  Cor 60686 Be Anything/Come Back

LPs

JACK HASKELL
  Jub 1036 Let's Fall in Love
  Strand SL-1020 Swings for Jack Paar (original Broadway cast)
  Co KOL-5870 MR. PRESIDENT

783. HASSELGARD, STAN   cl B
(AKE HASSELGARD)

*Born October 4, 1922, Bollnas, Sweden
Died November 23, 1948, in auto accident near Decatur, Ill.*

Avant-garde Swedish clarinetist of 40s. Likely top star in progressive jazz but for early death. Brilliant tone, marked facility, inventive, swinging style. Earned reputation in Sweden mid-40s; worked and recorded with Bob Laine and Simon Brehm. To U.S. mid-1947 to study at Columbia. Benny Goodman's protege awhile; played with modern-style septet mid-1947. Later freelanced, led combo late 1948 at New York's Hickory House. Died at 26.

RECORDS

SIMON BREHM
Musica(Sw) 9200 Somebody Loves Me/Hallelujah
Musica(Sw) 9201 All the Things You Are/Hit That Jive Jack
Musica(Sw) 9203 Sweet Lorraine/My Melancholy Baby

BOB LAINE
Cup(Sw) 4011 Blues Cupol/Ain't Misbehavin'
Cup(Sw) 4012 Am I Blue?
Cup(Sw) 4017 Jam Session at Cupol/Ba, Ba, Vita Lamm
Cup(Sw) 4018 Always
Cup(Sw) 4020 Someday Sweetheart

SWEDISH ALL-STARS
Musica(Sw) 9204 How High the Moon/Stomping at the Savoy

STAN HASSELGARD
Cap 15062 Swedish Pastry / Who Sleeps?
Cap 15302 Sweet and Hot Mop/I'll Never Be the Same
VD(12″)900 Cottontop

LPs

(miscellaneous artists)
Cap M-11029 Jazz Classics Vol. 4 (Cap RIs)

---

784. HAVER, JUNE vo p
(JUNE STOVENOUR)

Born June 10, 1926, Rock Island, Ill.

Star of movie musicals mid-40s to early 50s. Beauty, talent as singer-dancer-actress brought quick stardom. Talented youngster; at 8 won Cincinnati Conservatory of Music's Post Music Contest, played piano with Cincinnati Symphony Orchestra. Studied for show-business career. In early 40s sang briefly with Freddy Martin, toured with Ted Fio Rito. Ending up in Los Angeles, made movie short with Fio Rito, another with Tommy Dorsey. Went to high school in Beverly Hills, took screen test, signed with 20th Century-Fox. Bit role in movie THE GANG'S ALL HERE in 1943. Studio head Darryl F. Zanuck groomed June as another Betty Grable.

Scored in supporting role in 1944 movie HOME IN INDIANA. Later in year co-starred with Dick Haymes in his first starring movie IRISH EYES ARE SMILING: excellent biopic of composer Ernest R. Ball. Co-starred with Betty Grable in 1945 movie THE DOLLY SISTERS; they portrayed famous sister act, performed several numbers. June in top-budget movies next eight years. Portrayed stage star Marilyn Miller in 1949 movie LOOK FOR THE SILVER LINING. During early 50s became selective, turned down several roles. Disenchanted with movie life, entered Sisters of Charity religious order in Xavier, Kansas, February 1953. Later in year ill health forced her to leave. Returned to Hollywood, in February 1954 did Lux Theatre radio show with Jack Carson, quit acting, married actor Fred MacMurray June 1954.

MOVIES

1943—THE GANG'S ALL HERE (bit role)
1944—HOME IN INDIANA; IRISH EYES ARE SMILING
1945—WHERE DO WE GO FROM HERE?; THE DOLLY SISTERS; WAKE UP AND DREAM
1946—THREE LITTLE GIRLS IN BLUE
1947—I WONDER WHO'S KISSING HER NOW
1948—SCUDDA-HOO! SCUDDA-HAY!
1949—OH YOU BEAUTIFUL DOLL; LOOK FOR THE SILVER LINING
1950—DAUGHTER OF ROSIE O'GRADY; I'LL GET BY
1951—LOVE NEST
1953—THE GIRL NEXT DOOR

---

785. HAVOC, JUNE vo
(JUNE HOVICK)

Born November 8, 1916, Seattle, Wash.

Singer-actress of stage and movies. Sister of stripper Gypsy Rose Lee (Louise Hovick). Successful Broadway musical GYPSY (1959) based on life of two sisters and their mother. June precocious child star; sang and danced in vaudeville, with mother driving force. Deserted show business awhile by eloping at early age, then tried marathon dancing (as detailed in autobiography *Early Havoc*). Late 1936 supporting role in unsuccessful Broadway musical FORBIDDEN MELODY. Secondary role in hit show PAL JOEY (1940) boosted career. Entered movies 1941; good secondary roles through 40s into 50s. In 1944 hit peak as star of hit Broadway musical MEXICAN HAYRIDE. Later in year starred in SADIE THOMPSON; ran only 60 performances. Movie roles improved in late 40s and early 50s. TV appearances in early 50s. One of best movie roles in WHEN MY BABY SMILES AT ME (1948). In 1958 returned to Broadway in A MIDSUMMER NIGHT'S DREAM. In 1966 in DINNER AT EIGHT revival. In many Broadway plays and road shows.

MOVIES

1941—FOUR JACKS AND A JILL
1942—SING YOUR WORRIES AWAY; POWDER TOWN; MY SISTER EILEEN
1943—HELLO, FRISCO, HELLO; NO TIME FOR LOVE; HI DIDDLE DIDDLE
1944—TIMBER QUEEN; CASANOVA IN BURLESQUE; SWEET AND LOWDOWN
1945—BREWSTER'S MILLIONS
1947—INTRIGUE; GENTLEMAN'S AGREEMENT
1948—WHEN MY BABY SMILES AT ME; THE IRON CURTAIN
1949—RED HOT AND BLUE; CHICAGO DEADLINE; THE STORY OF MOLLY X
1950—ONCE A THIEF; MOTHER DIDN'T TELL ME
1951—FOLLOW THE SUN
1952—LADY POSSESSED
1956—THREE FOR JAMIE DAWN

786. HAWES, HAMPTON   p

Born November 13, 1928, Los Angeles, Calif.

Modern pianist with lightly swinging and tasteful style, especially good on blues. At 16 with Big Jay McNeely and Sonny Criss. During 1948-50 clicked on west coast jazz scene. With Dexter Gordon and Wardell Gray. Prominent in early 50s with Shorty Rogers, Art Pepper, Howard Rumsey's Lighthouse All-Stars. Military service, 1953-4. After discharge formed trio. Teamed with bassist Red Mitchell 1955 as duo, sometimes added drums; mostly in Los Angeles area. Later 50s worked eastern engagements. During 1959-63 jailed in Fort Worth on narcotics charge. Rehabilitated, applied to President Kennedy for executive clemency, got sentence cut in half. Plunged into Holly-

wood work, playing as well as ever. Teamed again with Red Mitchell 1965 in Los Angeles spot. During 1967-8 toured world. Active on west coast into 70s. Adopted some contemporary pop styles in later years. Wrote autobiography 1974.

RECORDS

ART PEPPER
Dis 157 Brown Gold/These Foolish Things
Dis 158 Holiday Flight/Surf Ride
HARRY BABASIN
Dis 163 Night and Day/Where or When
WARDELL GRAY
Pres 840 Bright Boy/April Skies
HAMPTON HAWES
Dis 164 Thou Swell/Jumpin' Jacque
Dis 165 Don't Get Around Much Anymore/It's You or No One

LPs

HAMPTON HAWES
Verve V-9010 High in the Sky
Contemp C-3515 Vol. 2: The Trio
Contemp C-3525 Vol. 1: The Trio
Contemp C-3545-6-7 (3 LP's) All Night Session
Contemp C-3553 Four!
Contemp C-3616 Here and Now
Contemp C-7589 For Real
Contemp C-7614 Green Leaves
SHORTY ROGERS
Cap(10″)H-294 Modern Sounds
SONNY ROLLINS
Contemp C-3564 Sonny Rollins and the Contemporary Leaders
SONNY CRISS
Pres 7628 I'll Catch the Sun
CHARLES MINGUS
Jub 1054 Mingus Three
WARDELL GRAY
Pres 7343 (2-LP set) Memorial Album (RIs)
Pres(10″)147

787. HAWKINS, COLEMAN ts cl bs B
(nicknamed Bean and The Hawk)

Born November 21, 1904, St. Joseph, Mo.
Died May 19, 1969, New York, N.Y.

Pioneer and first star on tenor sax. Made instrument important in jazz. All-time giant, far ahead of his time. Big warm

1063

tone, great technique, powerful driving style, keen chord sense. When modern jazz emerged in mid-40s, absorbed much of it into playing, remained star. Learned piano, cello and tenor sax. Studied music at Washburn College. At 16 played in Kansas City area. Toured with blues singer Mamie Smith 1921-3. Freelanced in New York 1923-4. Joined Fletcher Henderson in 1924, remained ten years. Louis Armstrong's 1924-25 stint with band revolutionized Hawkins style. During later 20s and early 30s recognized as king of tenor sax. Left Henderson early 1934, worked 1934-9 in England, France, Holland, Belgium, other countries, recorded. Returned to U.S. mid-1939, led band in New York. Late 1939 record of *Body and Soul* took jazz world by storm, established Hawkins influence anew.

Led big band late 1939 to early 1941, mostly in New York. Thereafter led combos. Toured 1943, worked on west coast. Opened Billy Berg's club in Los Angeles early 1945. In 1946 on first Jazz at the Philharmonic tour. Visited Europe twice in late 40s. In 50s tours with Jazz at the Philharmonic in U.S. and abroad. Extensive freelance recording in 40s and 50s with mainstream and modern groups. Always dominant. Led combos in 50s and 60s, mostly in New York. In late 1967 toured England. Active until shortly before death.

RECORDS

FLETCHER HENDERSON
Br 3460 Stockholm Stomp
Co 509-D T.N.T.
Co 654-D The Stampede
Co 970-D Rocky Mountain Blues/ Tozo
Co 1002-D P.D.Q. Blues
Co 2352-D What Good Am I without You?/Keep a Song in your Soul
Co 2513 Sugarfoot Stomp/Clarinet Marmalade
Co 2565 It's the Darndest Thing/ Singin' the Blues
Co 2586-D My Gal Sal
Co 2732-D Underneath the Harlem Moon/Honeysuckle Rose
Vi 22955 I Wanna Count Sheep/Strangers

De 18253 It's the Talk of the Town/ Nagasaki
De 18254 I've Got to Sing a Torch Song/Night Life
MOUND CITY BLUE BLOWERS
Vi 38100 One Hour/Hello Lola
OK 41526 Darktown Strutters' Ball/ You Rascal You
MCKINNEY'S COTTON PICKERS
Vi 38102 Miss Hannah/The Way I Feel Today
Vi 38133 I'd Love It
Vi 22736 Wherever There's a Will, Baby
CHOCOLATE DANDIES
OK 8728 That's How I Feel Today/Six or Seven Times
Co 2543-D Bugle Call Rag/Dee Blues
CMS(12")1506 I Surrender Dear/I Can't Believe That You're in Love with Me
SPIKE HUGHES
De(E) 3639 Arabesque
De(E) 3717 Firebird
JACK PURVIS
OK 8782 Poor Richard/Down Georgia Way
COUNT BASIE
OK 6180 Feedin' the Bean
OK 6244 9:20 Special
BENNY CARTER
De 18256 Somebody Loves Me/Pardon Me, Pretty Baby
Vo 5399 Sleep/Slow Freight
BENNY GOODMAN
Co 2892-D Junk Man/Ol' Pappy
Co 2907-D Georgia Jubilee/Emaline
VARSITY SEVEN
Vs 8147 It's Tight Like That/Easy Rider
Vs 8173 Pom Pom/How Long, How Long Blues
ESQUIRE WINNERS
Vi 40-0137 Indiana Winter
COZY COLE
Cont 6000 A Ghost of a Chance/Look Here
Sav 519 Jersey Jump-Off/On the Sunny Side of the Street
JAZZ AT THE PHILHARMONIC
Clef 101-2 J.A.T.P. Blues (1 & 2)
Clef 103-4 J.A.T.P. Blues (3 & 4)

GEORGE WETTLING
Key(12″)1311 Home/Too Marvelous for Words

ALLEN-HAWKINS ORCHESTRA (Red Allen-Coleman Hawkins)
Pe 15802 Shadows on the Swanee/Stringin' Along on a Shoestring
Pe 15808 Ain'tcha Got Music?/The River's Takin' Care of Me

COLEMAN HAWKINS
OK 41566 Jamaica Shout/Heart Break Blues
De(H) 42051 I Wish I Were Twins
De(H) 42059 Netcha's Dream/What Harlem Is to Me
De(H) 42127 A Strange Fact/Something Is Gonna Give Me Away
Vi 26219 Crazy Rhythm/Honeysuckle Rose
Bb 10523 Body and Soul/Fine Dinner
Bb 10770 My Blue Heaven/The Sheik of Araby
Key 610 Bean at the Met (How High the Moon)/I'm in the Mood for Love
Apo 751 Rainbow Mist (Body and Soul)/Woodyn' You
Cap 205 Stuffy/It's the Talk of the Town
Cap 10036 Hollywood Stampede/I'm Thru with Love
Vi 40-0131 Say It Isn't So/Spotlite

LPs

COLEMAN HAWKINS
Verve MGV-8261 The Genius of Coleman Hawkins
Vi LJM-1017 The Hawk in Flight (Bb, Vi RIs)
Riv 12-233 The Hawk Flies High
Jazztone J-1201 Timeless Jazz
GA 33-316 Jazz Concert (Apo RIs)
Pres 7156 Hawk Eyes

FLETCHER HENDERSON
Co C4L19 (4-LP set) A Study in Frustration (Co, Ha, Vo RIs)
"X"(10″)LVA-3013 Connie's Inn Orchestra (Vi RIs)

LIONEL HAMPTON
Jazztone J-1246 Lionel Hampton's All-Star Groups (Vi RIs)
(miscellaneous artists)
EmArcy MG-36023 Battle of the Saxes (RIs)

Cor CRL-57035 East Coast Jazz Scene, Vol. 1

788. HAWKINS, DOLORES   vo
Born Brooklyn, N.Y.

Excellent singer with big voice and confident style. Mostly active late 40s to early 60s. As youngster sang on radio kid shows. At 17 sang with society bands in New York area. With Gene Krupa 1947-9—unfortunately when band recorded infrequently. In later 40s a single. In 1951 Perry Como show awhile on early TV. In 50s and early 60s occasionally on TV and records. Continued to play clubs.

RECORDS

GENE KRUPA
Co 38141 Teach Me, Teach Me, Baby/You Turned the Tables on Me
Co 38590 Watch Out!

DOLORES HAWKINS
OK 6857 Love Me Long/Ooo-Wee
OK 6903 Each Time/Risin' Sun
OK 6949 I've Got a Letter/Scrap of Paper
OK 6976 Happy Tears/Come Home
Cor 60832 Sing You Sinners/I'm in the Mood for Love
Epic 9006 Don't Make Me Love You/A Long Time Ago
Epic 9013 Anything Can Happen Mambo/Stars on the Ceiling
Epic 9049 Hey There/Hernando's Hideaway
Epic 9089 George/Silly

LPs

DOLORES HAWKINS
Epic LN-3250 Dolores

789. HAWKINS, ERSKINE   t cm B
Born July 26, 1914, Birmingham, Ala.

Leader of a swinging big band popular in 30s and 40s. Noted for flashy high-note trumpet spots. Attended Alabama State Teachers College mid-30s, led band there called The 'Bama State Collegians. Band began recording in New York mid-1936. Played Harlem spots including Harlem Opera House, Ubangi Club, Savoy Ballroom. By late 30s band and its recordings popular. Chief arranger pianist Avery

Parrish (noted for piano showcase *After Hours*). Later arrangements also by sidemen Sammy Lowe and Bill Johnson. Featured soloists Bascomb brothers, Paul on tenor sax and Dud on trumpet. On band's 1939 hit *Tuxedo Junction* solo by Dud Bascomb though most thought by Hawkins. (Dud's solos fatter in tone, more swinging and authoritative, lower register than Erskine's.) Band's theme *Swing Out*, composed by Hawkins (who wrote many numbers featured by band); later used *Tuxedo Junction* as theme. Hawkins band routine: a round of Harlem clubs and theatres, then tours, then back to New York for a new cycle. Band worked steadily through 40s into 50s. Big 1945 hit *Tippin' In*. Later in 50s Hawkins led combo. Active in 60s. Led combo in 70s. Compositions included *Raid the Joint, Tuxedo Junction, Gabriel Meets the Duke, Hot Platter, Weddin' Blues, Strictly Swing, You Can't Escape from Me, Gin Mill Special*.

RECORDS

ERSKINE HAWKINS
Vo 3318 Coquette/Big John's Special
Vo 3567 Dear Old Southland/'Way Down Upon the Swanee River
Vo 3668 Red Cap/I Found a New Baby
Bb 7810 Miss Hallelujah Brown/I'm Madly in Love with You
Bb 7826 Let This Be a Warning to You, Baby/Rockin' Rollers' Jubilee
Bb 7839 Weary Blues/King Porter Stomp
Bb 10029 Easy Rider/A Study in Blue
Bb 10224 (theme) Swing Out/Raid the Joint
Bb 10364 Hot Platter/Weddin' Blues
Bb 10409 (theme) Tuxedo Junction/ Gin Mill Special
Bb 10504 Uptown Shuffle/More Than You Know
Bb 10540 Cherry/You Can't Escape from Me
Bb 10671 Whispering Grass/Gabriel Meets the Duke
Bb 10854 Sweet Georgia Brown/Five O'clock Whistle
Bb 10879 After Hours/Song of the Wanderer

Bb 10932 Norfolk Ferry/Put Yourself in My Place
Bb 11001 S'posin'/Soft Winds
Bb 11419 Blue Sea/I Love You Truly
Bb 11439 Sometimes/I Don't Want to Walk Without You
Bb 30-0813 Bear Mash Blues/Don't Cry, Baby
Vi 20-1639 Tippin' In/Remember
Vi 20-2963 Feelin' Low
Vi 20-3585 Who Are You?/Miss Eva
Cor 60361 Tuxedo Junction/After Hours (later versions)
King 4522 Down Home Jump/Lost Time

LPs

ERSKINE HAWKINS
Vi 2227 After Hours
Cor CRL-56061 After Hours

790. HAYES, CLANCY   bn d vo
(CLARENCE LEONARD HAYES)

Born November 14, 1908, Caney, Kansas
Died 1972 in San Francisco, Calif.

Featured vocalist-banjoist with dixieland groups. Sang novelty and jazz numbers in somewhat raucous style, ballads straightforwardly. As youngster played in dance bands, sometimes as leader, also toured in vaudeville. In 1926 settled in San Francisco, began on radio late 20s. Popular on west coast in 30s through radio and club work. In 1938 joined Lu Watters dixieland band for several years. Through 40s important figure in dixieland. In 1949 joined Bob Scobey. In 50s sometimes a single, also with Turk Murphy and Firehouse Five Plus Two. Active in 60s mostly as single. Charter member of World's Greatest Jazz Band late 60s; left soon after founding. Co-composer of 1946 novelty song *A-Huggin' and a-Chalkin'*.

RECORDS

LU WATTERS
JM 3 Muskrat Ramble / Smokey Mokes
JM 7 Fidgety Feet/Temptation Rag
JM 13 Daddy Do/Milenberg Joys
JM 14 London Blues/Sunset Cafe Stomp

BOB SCOBEY
GTJ 53 Dippermouth Blues/Some of These Days
GTJ 60 Melancholy/South
GTJ 66 Do You Know What It Means to Miss New Orleans?/Blues My Naughty Sweetie Gave to Me
GTJ 74 All the Wrongs You've Done to Me/Peoria
GTJ 78 Ace in the Hole/Silver Dollar
GTJ 86 Everything Is Peaches Down in Georgia/A-Huggin' and a-Chalkin'
GTJ 94 Beale Street Blues/Sweet Georgia Brown

CLANCY HAYES with LES PAUL TRIO
Mer 5103 My Extraordinary Gal/Now Is the Hour
Mer 5137 On the Street of Regret/Nobody but You

CLANCY HAYES
Down Home 11 Auntie Skinner's Chicken Dinners/Nobody Knows You When You're Down and Out
Down Home 12 Silver Dollar/Sailing Down Chesapeake Bay
Down Home 13 Ballin' the Jack/Alabamy Bound

LPs

CLANCY HAYES
GTJ 12050 Swingin' Minstrel
Verve V-1003 Clancy Hayes Sings
ABC-Para 591 Live at Earthquake McGoon's

BOB SCOBEY
Vi LPM-1889 Something's Always Happening on the River
GTJ 12009 Scobey and Clancy
Verve V-1001 Bob Scobey's Band

BING CROSBY with BOB SCOBEY BAND
Vi LPM-1473 Bing with a Beat

LU WATTERS-BUNK JOHNSON
GTJ 12024

791. HAYES, EDGAR   p cm ar B
Born May 23, 1904, Lexington, Ky.

Pianist-bandleader, most popular in late 30s. Known for 1938 recording of *Star Dust*. Led swing-styled combos and big bands. Attended Fisk University and Wilberforce University. In early and mid-20s with Fess Williams and Lois Deppe. Made piano rolls, led groups in mid-20s. In late 20s led pit band at Harlem's Alhambra Theatre. With Mills Blue Rhythm Band as pianist-arranger late 1930 to late 1936. In early 1937 formed big band till 1941; Scandinavian tour in 1938. In 1942 based in California, worked as soloist or led combo; many years off and on at Somerset House in Riverside. In 1946 co-led combo with Teddy Bunn at Billy Berg's Club in Los Angeles. In 50s soloist in San Bernadino's Diamond Lounge, in 60s at Reuben's restaurants. Active into 70s. Composer of several songs including *Someone Stole Gabriel's Horn*, *Love's Serenade*, *Out of a Dream*, *African Lullaby*, *The Growl*.

RECORDS

MILLS BLUE RHYTHM BAND
Co 2963-D Let's Have a Jubilee/Out of a Dream
Co 3071-D Harlem Heat/There's Rhythm in Harlem
Co 3135-D Red Rhythm/St. Louis Wiggle

BARON LEE & BLUE RHYTHM BAND
Pe 15605 The Scat Song/Cabin in the Cotton
Pe 15621 The Growl/Mighty Sweet

CHUCK RICHARDS
Vo 2867 Love's Serenade/Like a Bolt from the Blue
Vo 2877 Blue Interlude/Rainbow Filled with Music

RED ALLEN
Vo 3097 Red Sails in the Sunset/I Found a Dream
Vo 3098 On Treasure Island/Boots and Saddle

KENNY CLARKE
Od(Sw) 255509 Once in Awhile/I Found a New Baby
Od(Sw) 255510 You're a Sweetheart/Sweet Sue

ORLANDO ROBERSON
Va 513 Sweet Is the Word for You/Just a Quiet Evening

EDGAR HAYES
Va 586 Manhattan Jam
De 1338 Edgar Steps Out/Caravan
De 1382 High, Wide and Handsome/Satan Takes a Holiday
De 1416 Laughing at Life/Stomping at the Renny

De 1444 So Rare/Love Me or Leave Me
De 1509 I Know Now/When You and I Were Young, Maggie
De 1527 Queen Isabella/Old King Cole
De 1665 Let's Love/Swingin' in the Promised Land
De 1882 Star Dust/In the Mood
De 1940 Meet the Band/Barbary Coast Blues
VD(12″)681 Star Dust
Excl 110 Blues at Dawn (1 & 2)

792. HAYES, HARRY   as B

Leader of English combo in 40s. Tight, swinging arrangements produced full sound. Alto saxist along Benny Carter lines, with clear tone and fluent swing. Combo boasted excellent musicianship. From early 30s Hayes with English bands before leading group.

RECORDS

HARRY HAYES
HMV(E) 9397 Sequence/My Love
HMV(E) 9404 Needlenose/Five Flat Flurry
HMV(E) 9409 Drop Me Off at Harlem/First Edition
HMV(E) 9413 Merely a Minor/Two, Three, Four Jump
HMV(E) 9422 Up/No Script
HMV(E) 9430 Cherry Brandy/Three O'clock Jump
HMV(E) 9450 Midnight Prowl/Play Boy
HMV(E) 9452 Homeward Bound/Swingin' on Lennox [sic] Avenue
HMV(E) 9457 0 Keep Going—Don't Stop (1 & 2)
HMV(E) 9467 Out of Space/Miss Magnolia
HMV(E) 9471 I'll Close My Eyes/Can't You Read Between the Lines?
HMV(E) 9512 Blue Charm/Familiar Moe
HMV(E) 9516 A Flat to C/High as a Kite
HMV(E) 9530 Crazy Rhythm/Rockin' in Rhythm
HMV(E) 9538 Alto Reverie/Let's Get Acquainted

HMV(E) 9559 Ol' Man Rebop/Scuttlebutt
HMV(E) 9566 Lucky Number/Dubonnet
HMV(E) 9595 Dinner Jacket/The Be-Bop

LPs

HARRY HAYES (one side)
Vi(10″)LPT-3034 Around the World in Jazz—England (HMV RIs)

793. HAYMAN, RICHARD

har ar cm B

Born March 27, 1920, Cambridge, Mass.

Prominent conductor and harmonica soloist in 50s. At 18 began three years with Borrah Minevitch's Harmonica Rascals. Later with Leo Diamond group in Hollywood. Played vaudeville at intervals. In 40s arranged background music for movies (under Georgie Stoll), including MEET ME IN ST. LOUIS, GIRL CRAZY, STATE FAIR, AS THOUSANDS CHEER. In late 40s arranged for Vaughn Monroe several years; also harmonica soloist with Horace Heidt troupe awhile. Musical director and arranger for singer Bobby Wayne on Mercury label, then conductor-arranger-harmonica soloist for Mercury. Prominent for 50s records, especially hits *Ruby* and *Dansero*. Composed some numbers featured on his records, including *Dansero, Suzanne, No Strings Attached, Skipping Along, Carriage Trade, Serenade to a Lost Love, Valse d'Amour, Tango for Two, Tambourine, Pops Hoe-Down.*

RECORDS

(as conductor)
BOBBY WAYNE
Lon 972 Runnin' Around/Always You
Mer 5897 Because You're Mine/Madonna of the Rosary
JERRY MURAD
Mer 70202 Sweet Leilani/The Story of Three Loves
DICK HAYMAN & THE HARMONICA SPARKLERS
Stellar 1016 Carolina in the Morning/Missouri Waltz
RICHARD HAYMAN
Mer 5790 Blue Tango/For Sentimental Reasons

Mer 5825 It's a Sin to Tell a Lie/It Had to Be You
Mer 70114 April in Portugal/Anna
Mer 70146 Dansero/Ruby
Mer 70168 Terry's Theme/Eyes of Blue
Mer 70196 Hi-Lili Hi-Lo/Something Money Can't Buy
Mer 70387 Hernando's Hideaway/The Cuddle
Mer 70616 Celeste/Gobelues
Mer 70781 Moritat/I'll Be with You in Apple Blossom Time

LPs

RICHARD HAYMAN
Mer MG-20113 Reminiscing
Mer MG-20123 Love Is a Many-Splendored Thing
Mer MG-20192 MY FAIR LADY
Mer MG-20248 Only Memories
Mer MG-20369 Great Motion Picture Themes of Victor Young
Mer-Wing SRW-16239 (S) Serenade for Love
Comm S-941(S) Cinematic

(as conductor-arranger)
JULIAN "CANNONBALL" ADDERLEY
EmArcy MG-36063 (with strings)

794. HAYMER, HERBIE   ts

Born July 24, 1915, Jersey City, N.J. Died April 11, 1949, Santa Monica, Calif., in auto crash

Tenor sax star of 30s and 40s. Witty, intelligent player. Began in early 30s locally, then in New York. In mid-30s brief periods with Rudy Vallee and Charlie Barnet. Joined Red Norvo combo late 1935, remained when Norvo expanded to big band later in year. Featured with Norvo; subtle style fit perfectly with Eddie Sauter's sophisticated arrangements and band's intimacy. Left Norvo summer 1937. Joined Jimmy Dorsey, again fit with somewhat impish style of band in those years. Joined Woody Herman spring 1941 for about a year. With Kay Kyser 1942-3 about a year, helped transform band into modern outfit that could swing. With Benny Goodman mid-1943. With Dave Hudkins on west coast awhile. Brief period in military service in 1944. With Red Nichols combo late

1944-5. Active in west coast studio work. On Lucky Strike Hit Parade and Chesterfield Supper Club radio shows. With Goodman mid-1947. Much freelancing on records; many with Paul Weston. Top studio and recording sideman when killed in car crash on way home from record session.

RECORDS

LOUIS "KING" GARCIA
Bb 6303 Christopher Columbus
STEW PLETCHER
Bb 6345 I Hope Gabriel Likes My Music/The Touch of Your Lips
FRANK FROEBA
Co 3110-D The Music Goes 'Round and Around/There'll Be a Great Day
RED NORVO
De 691 Gramercy Square/Decca Stomp
De 779 I Got Rhythm/Oh, Lady Be Good
Br 7744 I Know That You Know
Br 7761 When Is a Kiss Not a Kiss?
Br 7896 Jivin' the Jeep/Remember
JIMMY DORSEY
De 2363 You're So Desirable
De 2553 An Old Fashioned Tune Always Is New
De 2918 Rigamarole
De 3711 La Rosita
WOODY HERMAN
De 4076 Three Ways to Smoke a Pipe
De 18526 Hot Chestnuts
KAY KYSER
Co 36526 How Do I Know It's Real?
Co 36676 Pushin' Sand
BOBBY SHERWOOD
Cap 231 Cotton Tail
RED NICHOLS
Cap 15150 Love Is the Sweetest Thing
Cap 40062 When You Wish Upon a Star
Cap 48012 You're My Everything
ANGELS OF MERCY
Gem 3 Sunday
JO STAFFORD
Cap 259 Cindy
HERBIE HAYMER
Sun 7561 Black Market Stuff/Laguna Leap

Sun 10055 I'll Never Be the Same/
Swinging on Central Avenue
Key 640 I Saw Stars/Sweet and Lovely
Key 655 China Boy (also on Mer 1098)

LPs

HERBIE HAYMER
Monarch(10")201 (Sun RIs)
MILDRED BAILEY
Co C3L22 (3-LP set) Her Greatest Per-
formances (1929-46 RIs)
(miscellaneous artists)
Monarch(10")205 All-Star Jazz

795. HAYMES, BOB   p vo ar cm lyr B
Born c. 1922

Younger, less known brother of Dick
Haymes. Early singing with Carl Hoff.
Early 40s in B movies, usually musicals,
sometimes under name of Robert Stan-
ton. Freelance recording, same period.
Military service awhile, World War II. On
Jack Haley radio show 1946 as Bob
Stanton. Clubs in 40s and early 50s. On
TV early 50s; own show on New York TV
late 50s. Disc jockey. Songwriting in 50s
and 60s. Songs include *That's All*; *My
Love, My Love*; *Beyond the Next Hill*; *Her
Tears*.

RECORDS

BOB CHESTER
Bb 11313 The Magic of Magnolias
Bb 11316 Joltin' Joe DiMaggio
Bb 11355 Madelaine
ORRIN TUCKER
Co 36574 Full Moon
FREDDY MARTIN
Vi 20-1515 Can't Get Out of This
Mood
BOB HAYMES-LISA KIRK
Vi 20-4715 Fifty Years Ago/Wait Till
the Sun Shines Nellie Blues
BOB HAYMES
King 15087 I've Never Been in Love
Before/She's Just the Girl I Love
King 15088 Could Be/Don't Ever
Leave Me
Bell(7")1005 With These Hands/No
Other Love
Bell(7")1012 Ebb Tide/That's All

LPs

BOB HAYMES-JIMMY MUNDY ORCHESTRA
20th Fox TFM-3142

796. HAYMES, DICK   VO
*Born September 13, 1916, Buenos Aires,
Argentina*

One of best pop singers, prominent from
early 40s to early 50s. Rich, warm baritone, excellent control and phrasing. Important star in movie musicals of 40s.
Voice training from mother, a concert
singer. Family travelled in many countries, finally settled in New York, later in
California. As youngster Haymes worked
at odd jobs in both locales. At about 16
sang during summer with Johnny Johnson band in east. In Hollywood 1933-8
tried songwriting, sang on radio; extra in
movies, occasional bits in vaudeville or
stock companies. Bit part in 1938 movie
DRAMATIC SCHOOL. Tried to plug his songs
before Harry James; hired by James as
vocalist instead. With James early 1940 to
late 1941, attained first prominence. With
Benny Goodman March-July 1942. Record coupling with Goodman, *Idaho/
Take Me*, popular. Toured with Tommy
Dorsey 1943 (during recording ban, hence
no records). Ended up in Hollywood,
played in movie DUBARRY WAS A LADY.

Single in mid-1943, played clubs in east.
Replaced Buddy Clark on radio network
show Here's to Romance: springboard to
success as Haymes became rival to Bing
Crosby and Frank Sinatra. In 1944 effective secondary role in movie FOUR JILLS IN
A JEEP; featured numbers became popular
record coupling *How Blue the Night/How
Many Times Do I Have to Tell You?*.
Another popular record *In My Arms*.
Real stardom in 1944 movie IRISH EYES
ARE SMILING portraying composer Ernest
R. Ball; sang Ball's great songs excellently. During next several years starred
in good movie musicals. Mid-40s radio
show with Helen Forrest, Everything for
the Boys, then popular show for Autolite
into late 40s. Starred on Lucky Strike Hit
Parade awhile. Big-selling record *Little
White Lies*. During 1949-50 nightly song
series on radio. Hollywood career faded
early 50s. TV in mid-50s. Financial woes,
a succession of wives, even deportation
troubles wore Haymes down. During 60s
worked in foreign countries; mostly in
London and Dublin, later in Madrid.

Returned to U.S. late 1971 for TV specials, commercials, club work.

MOVIES

1944—FOUR JILLS IN A JEEP; IRISH EYES ARE SMILING

1945—STATE FAIR; DIAMOND HORSESHOE

1946—DO YOU LOVE ME?

1947—THE SHOCKING MISS PILGRIM; CARNIVAL IN COSTA RICA

1948—ONE TOUCH OF VENUS; UP IN CENTRAL PARK

1951—ST. BENNY THE DIP

1953—ALL ASHORE; CRUISIN' DOWN THE RIVER

RECORDS

HARRY JAMES

Vs 8221 How High the Moon/You've Got Me Out on a Limb

Vs 8264 Fools Rush In/Secrets in the Moonlight

Vs 8349 Orchids for Remembrance/It's the Last Time I'll Fall in Love

Co 36023 Ol' Man River

Co 36069 Walkin' by the River/Dolores

Co 36246 Yes Indeed/It's So Peaceful in the Country

Co 36255 I'll Never Let a Day Pass By/I Guess I'll Have to Dream the Rest

Co 36412 You've Changed

Co 36698 I'll Get By

BENNY GOODMAN

Co 36613 Idaho/Take Me

Co 36622 Serenade in Blue/I've Got a Gal in Kalamazoo

DICK HAYMES

De 18557 In My Arms/It Can't Be Wrong

De 18558 I Heard You Cried Last Night/I Never Mention Your Name

De 18604 How Blue the Night/How Many Times Do I Have to Tell You?

De 18662 I Wish I Knew/The More I See You

De 18740 It's a Grand Night for Singing/All I Owe I Owe I-oway

De 18747 Slowly/I Wish I Could Tell You

De 18781 You Are Too Beautiful/How Deep Is the Ocean?

De 18878 This Is Always/Willow Road

De 18914 You Make Me Feel So Young/On the Boardwalk in Atlantic City

De 24280 Little White Lies/The Treasure of Sierra Madre

De 24893 When the Wind Was Green/Marta

De 27008 Roses/I Still Get a Thrill

De 27565 Too Late Now/My Prayer

De 28636 Gone with the Wind/Your Home Is in My Arms

VD(12")238 You Send Me

DICK HAYMES-ETHEL MERMAN

De 27317 You're Just in Love

DICK HAYMES WITH ARTIE SHAW ORCHESTRA

De 27042 Count Every Star/If You Were Only Mine

DICK HAYMES-JUDY GARLAND

De 23687 Aren't You Kind of Glad We Did?/For You, for Me, for Evermore

DICK HAYMES-HELEN FORREST

De 23434 I'll Buy That Dream/Some Sunday Morning

De 23472 I'm Always Chasing Rainbows/Tomorrow Is Forever

LPs

DICK HAYMES

De(10")DL-5012 Souvenir Album

De(10")DL-5243 Songs with Helen Forrest

De(10")DL-5335 Sweethearts

De(10")DL-5341 Serenade

Vo VL-3616 (De RIs)

Cap T-787 Moondreams

Warwick 2023 Richard the Lion-Hearted

Ace of Hearts(E) AH-108 (De RIs)

797. HAYMES, JOE   p vo ar cm B

Born 1908, Marshfield, Mo.

Good arranger and leader of little-known but excellent band with good jazzmen during 30s. Band used Haymes arrangements mostly, maintained high level of musicianship equally on ballads, swing and novelty numbers. Late 20s into 1930 arranger for Ted Weems; scored 1929 Weems hit *Piccolo Pete*. Formed band early 30s, played New York's Roseland

and Empire ballrooms. Composed and featured *Let's Have a Party*, featured swinging novelties like *When I Put on My Long White Robe* and *Pray for the Lights to Go Out*. Good recordings steadily through most of 30s. Mid-1935 Tommy Dorsey formed first orchestra with nucleus of Haymes band (having left Dorsey Brothers shortly before). Haymes soon back with another good band, resumed recording. Early 1937 vocalist Barry McKinley led band awhile, with Haymes arranging. Disbanded. In early 40s concentrated on arranging especially for Weems. In mid-40s reorganized band awhile. Movie work, also New York radio work. Finally settled in Dallas, for years continued arranging for various bands.

RECORDS

JOE HAYMES

Vi 24007 Old Fashioned Love
Vi 24040 Pray for the Lights to Go Out/When I Put on My Long White Robe
Vi 24055 Let's Have a Party/Why Little Boy Blue Was Blue
Vi 24123 Hot Jazz Pie
Vi 24152 He's a Curbstone Cutie/He's the Life of the Party
Co 2704-D Let's Have a Party/The Old Man of the Mountain
Co 2716-D When I Put on My Long White Robe/Ain't Gonna Pay No Toll
Co 2739-D Jazz Pie/One-Note Trumpet Player
Co 2781-D I Cover the Waterfront/Uncle Joe's Music Store
Me 12740 Lazybones/Happy as the Day Is Long
Me 12744 Gotta Go/Louisville Lady
Me 13067 Dames/Rolling in Love
Me 13078 Dilly Dally/And the Big Bad Wolf Was Dead
Me 13109 I Saw Stars/I Couldn't Be Mean to You
Me 13189 Mandy/If I Had a Million Dollars
Me 13225 Wild Honey/Singing Between Kisses
Me 13286 In My Country That Means Love/Throwin' Stones at the Sun
Me 13451 Lost Motion/Swinging for the King

Elec 2072 I Never Knew (I Could Love Anybody)
Bb 5918 The Lady in Red/My Melancholy Baby
Bb 5920 Honeysuckle Rose/Now I'm a Lady
Pe 16121 The Lady in Red/To Call You My Own
Pe 351025 I'm on a See-Saw/The Gentleman Obviously Doesn't Believe
Pe 351026 Truckin'/Nothing Lives Longer Than Love
Pe 60404 Wah-Hoo/I'm Gonna Clap My Hands
Pe 60508 No Greater Love/I'll Stand By
Pe 60806 No Regrets/River Man
Pe 61105 Organ Grinder's Swing/Papa Tree-Top Tall
Pe 70207 One, Two, Button Your Shoe/Right or Wrong
Pe 70514 Slap That Bass/Let's Call the Whole Thing Off

798. HAYNES, ROY   d B

Born March 13, 1926, Roxbury, Mass.

Versatile drummer adept at backing jazzmen of all schools. Top drummer during bop period of late 40s. In early 40s with Sabby Lewis and others in Boston. To New York mid-40s; periods with Luis Russell 1945-7, Lester Young 1947-9, Charlie Parker 1949-50. Freelanced with leading jazzmen. Worked with singer Sarah Vaughan several years mid-50s. Led trio awhile. Late 50s included periods with Thelonious Monk and Lennie Tristano. In 60s led quartet with Phineas Newborn. Many jobs with Stan Getz. In 1968 joined Gary Burton combo. In 1970 led combo Roy Haynes & His Hip Ensemble, made Japanese tour. In early 70s some work with Roland Kirk.

RECORDS
(all LPs)

ROY HAYNES

EmArcy(10")MG-26048 Busman's Holiday
PacJazz S-82 (S) People
Impulse S-23 (S) Out of the Afternoon
STAN GETZ
Pres(10")104 Stan Getz Vol. 2
Vi LM-2925 At Tanglewood

LESTER YOUNG
Sav MG-12068 The Immortal Lester Young (Sav RIs)

RED RODNEY
Fan 3-208 Modern Music from Chicago

EDDIE SHU
Beth(10")BCP-1013 Eddie Shu

FATS NAVARRO
BN 1531 The Fabulous Fats Navarro, Vol. 1 (RIs)

WARDELL GRAY
Pres(10")115 Tenor Sax Favorites

BUD POWELL
BN(10")5003

AL HAIG
Pres(10")175

SARAH VAUGHAN
EmArcy(10")MG-26005

GARY BURTON
Vi LSP-3835 (S) Duster

799. HAYTON, LENNIE   p ar cm B

Born February 13, 1908, New York, N.Y.
Died April 24, 1971, Palm Springs, Cal.

Excellent musician with long and varied career mid-20s through 60s. Capable pianist at early age, schooled in concert music. Turned to dance bands, joined Cass Hagan, played eastern clubs and resorts. Remained as pianist-arranger late 1926 when augmented Hagan band landed important engagement at New York's Hotel Manger (later Taft). Pianist-arranger with Paul Whiteman 1928-30; in 1930 Whiteman movie KING OF JAZZ. During late 20s freelance recording with leading jazzmen. Pianist, arranger and musical director on Bing Crosby radio shows in early 30s; also led band on radio shows of Fred Allen, Grace Moore, Ruth Etting, Tom Howard, Lou Holtz. Led band on first Lucky Strike Hit Parade April 1935; singers included Kay Thompson, Johnny Hauser, Gogo Delys. In 1936 played Flying Red Horse Tavern and Ed Wynn shows. During 1937-40 led excellent dance band, toured and recorded, spotlighting own tasteful full-chord piano and good arrangements. Musical director for MGM 1940-53; involved in many movies as arranger, conductor or musical director. Top movies included THE HAR-

VEY GIRLS, ZIEGFELD FOLLIES, THE HUCKSTERS, TILL THE CLOUDS ROLL BY, THE PIRATE, BATTLEGROUND, ON THE TOWN, THE BARKLEYS OF BROADWAY, SINGIN' IN THE RAIN. Later worked on important movies STAR! (1968) and HELLO, DOLLY! (1969). Married singer Lena Horne late 1947, at intervals worked with her as manager-pianist-arranger-musical director, sometimes on tour.

RECORDS

CASS HAGAN
Co 966-D Hallelujah/Sometimes I'm Happy
Co 1033-D Melancholy Charlie/Variety Stomp
Co 1089-D Havana/Broken Hearted

BIX BEIDERBECKE
OK 41088 Ol' Man River/Wa-Da-Da
OK 41173 Rhythm King/Louisiana

MASON-DIXON ORCHESTRA
Co 1861-D What a Day!/Alabamy Snow

MIFF MOLE
OK 41371 Navy Blues/Lucky Little Devil

RED NICHOLS
Br 3626 Ida/Feelin' No Pain
Br 3627 Riverboat Shuffle/Eccentric
Br 3854 Avalon/Nobody's Sweetheart

JACK PETTIS
Vi 38105 Bugle Call Blues

FRANKIE TRUMBAUER
OK 41100 Bless You, Sister/Dusky Stevedore
OK 41145 Take Your Tomorrow/Love Affairs
OK 41268 Shivery Stomp/Reaching for Someone

JOE VENUTI
OK 41361 Apple Blossoms/Runnin' Ragged
Co 2535-D There's No Other Girl/Now That I Need You, You're Gone

DON VOORHEES
Co 1129-D Soliloquy/My Blue Heaven

BING CROSBY with LENNIE HAYTON ORCHESTRA
Br 6329 Cabin in the Cotton
Br 6351 Love Me Tonight/Some of These Days

LENNIE HAYTON
De 1267 I Know Now/You Can't Run Away from Love Tonight
De 1341 Gone with the Wind/What a Beautiful Beginning
De 1348 The Folks Who Live on the Hill/Can I Forget You?
De 1443 Once in Awhile/The Morning After
VS 8125 The Starlit Hour/At the Balalaika
Vs 8134 Peg o' My Heart/As Long as I Live
Vo 5421 One Cigarette for Two/I Love You Much Too Much
Vo 5471 AC-DC Current / Times Square Scuttle (*sic*)

LPs

(as pianist)
RED NICHOLS
Br(10")BL-58009 (Br RIs)
JOE VENUTI
Tom 7 (1929-30 RIs)
(as conductor)
LENA HORNE
Vi LPM-1148 It's Love
Vi LPM-1879 Give the Lady What She Wants
Lion L-70050 I Feel So Smoochie
LENA HORNE-HARRY BELAFONTE
Vi LOP-1507 PORGY AND BESS
(movie soundtracks)
MGM(10")E-113 SINGIN' IN THE RAIN
MGM(10")E-501 TILL THE CLOUDS ROLL BY
20th Fox DTCS-5102 (S) STAR!

800. HAZEL, MONK d c mel v-tb B
(ARTHUR HAZEL)
Born August 15, 1903, Harvey, La.
Died April 1968, New Orleans, La.

Early jazz musician in New Orleans. Worked mostly as drummer but doubled on brass instruments. Began professionally around 1920, played parades and dance jobs in New Orleans. During 20s worked there with Emmett Hardy, Abbie Brunies, Jules Bauduc, Tony Parenti, Johnny Wiggs and others. In late 20s and early 30s led band in New Orleans. With Jack Pettis in New York, with Gene Austin in California and on tour. Several years in Arkansas. Returned to New Orleans 1937

to join Joe Capraro. Later with Lloyd Danton several years. Military service, 1942-3. After discharge in music only as sideline for years. In late 40s and early 50s mostly with Sharkey Bonano. Less active in later years.

RECORDS

CANDY & COCO
Vo 2833 Kingfish Blues/New Orleans
Vo 2849 China Boy/Bugle Call Rag
JOHN HYMAN'S BAYOU STOMPERS
Vi 20593 Ain't Love Grand?/Alligator Blues
TONY PARENTI
Co 1548-D In the Dungeon/When You and I Were Pals
Br 4184 Gumbo/You Made Me Like It, Baby
SHARKEY BONANO
Dixieland 1000 When the Saints Go Marching In/Dippermouth Blues
Dixieland 1002 Milenberg Joys/I Like Bananas
Kappa 115 Farewell Blues/Tin Roof Blues
Kappa 116 Muskrat Ramble/Tailgate Ramble
Kappa 120 That's a-Plenty/Bucket's Got a Hole in It
Kappa 121 Shine/High Society
Cap 795 Bourbon Street Bounce/Pizza Pie Boogie
Cap 846 Over the Waves/I'm Satisfied with My Gal
Cap 951 Sole Mio Stomp/In the Mood
SHARKEY BONANO with MONK HAZEL ORCHESTRA
Dec 513 Sizzling the Blues/High Society (Br RIs)
Dec 514 Ideas/Git Wit It (Br RIs)
MONK HAZEL
Br 4181 Sizzling the Blues/High Society
Br 4182 Ideas/Git Wit It

LPs

MONK HAZEL
Southland 202
Southland 217 New Orleans Jazz Kings
SHARKEY BONANO
Cap T-266 Sharkey's Southern Comfort

Cap T-367 Midnight on Bourbon Street

NICK LAROCCA
Southland 230 Dixieland Jazz Band
JACK DELANEY
Southland 214
BOB HAVENS
Southland 243 And His New Orleans All-Stars

801. HAZZARD, JOHN E.   vo lyr

Born February 22, 1888, New York, N.Y.
Died December 2, 1935, Great Neck, N.Y.

Actor-singer in Broadway musicals and plays 1901-33. Stage debut in minor role in 1901 play THE MAN FROM MEXICO. In revival of play THE TWO ORPHANS early in career. Began in musicals with THE YANKEE CONSUL (1904). Supporting roles several years, then lead roles. Most successful shows VERY GOOD, EDDIE and MISS SPRINGTIME (1916) and THE NIGHT BOAT (1920). Co-author of play TURN TO THE RIGHT, musicals GO TO IT and THE HOUSEBOAT ON THE STYX. Author of books *Poetry and Rot; The Four Flusher; Verse and Worse.* Wrote special material for vaudeville. Compositions *Ain't It Awful, Mabel?; Put on Your Slippers; Queenie Was There with Her Hair in a Braid; Beautiful Lady; Travel along.*

BROADWAY MUSICALS

1904—THE YANKEE CONSUL
1907—THE HURDY-GURDY GIRL
1908—THE GIRLS OF GOTTENBURG
1909—THE CANDY SHOP
1910—THE ECHO
1911—THE DUCHESS; THE RED ROSE
1912—THE GYPSY (unsuccessful)
1914—THE LILAC DOMINO
1916—VERY GOOD, EDDIE; MISS SPRING-TIME; GO TO IT (book only, with Anne Caldwell)
1918—THE GIRL BEHIND THE GUN
1919—LA, LA, LUCILLE
1920—THE NIGHT BOAT
1922—FOR GOODNESS SAKE; GREENWICH VILLAGE FOLLIES OF 1922
1923—ONE KISS
1924—BYE BYE BARBARA (unsuccessful)
1931—SHOOT THE WORKS

1933—CHAMPAGNE SEC

802. HEALY, DAN   vo

Dancer-singer-comic star many years in vaudeville. In Broadway shows A WORLD OF PLEASURE (1915), THE SWEETHEART SHOP (1920), PLAIN JANE (1924), BETSY (1927), ZIEGFELD FOLLIES OF 1927, GOOD BOY (1928). In early sound movie extravaganza GLORIFYING THE AMERICAN GIRL (1930). In 1926 began producing Cotton Club revues in Harlem, continued into 30s. Active night club performer in mid-30s. Husband of novelty singer Helen Kane; with her in Broadway show GOOD BOY.

803. HEARD, J. C.   d vo B
(JAMES CHARLES HEARD)
Born August 8, 1917, Dayton, Ohio

Swing drummer with prolific recording career in 40s. Grew up in Detroit, worked locally in middle to late 30s. Jobs with Sam Price. First important job with Teddy Wilson big band mid-1939. Left 1940 because of illness. With Louis Jordan and Benny Carter later 1940. Rejoined Wilson combo 1941-2. With Cab Calloway 1942-5 with brief intervals away. Led group 1946-7 in New York and Detroit. Toured with Jazz at the Philharmonic, freelanced, led group at intervals. Lived in Japan 1953-7, played there and toured Pacific. Led group in U. S. late 1957-8. Late 1958 toured Europe with Sam Price. Based mostly in New York until mid-60s; periods with Coleman Hawkins, Teddy Wilson, Dorothy Donegan, Red Norvo; also led combo. In later 60s led combo in Detroit.

RECORDS

TEDDY WILSON
Co 35207 Early Session Hop/Lady of Mystery
Co 35711 Sweet Lorraine/Liza
Co 36631 Them There Eyes
Co 36633 I Know That You Know
SIDNEY BECHET
Vi 27337 Egyptian Fantasy/Slippin' and Slidin'
COLEMAN HAWKINS
OK 6284 Rocky Comfort/Passin' It Around

OK 6347 Forgive a Fool/Serenade to a Sleeping Beauty

BILLIE HOLIDAY

OK 5719 Laughing at Life/Tell Me More

OK 6369 Jim/Love Me or Leave Me

SAM PRICE

De 8609 Harlem Gin Blues/Why Don't You Love Me Anymore?

HAZEL SCOTT

De 18129 Minute Waltz/Hungarian Rhapsody No. 2

DIZZY GILLESPIE

Vi 40-0130 Night in Tunisia/52nd Street Theme

Vi 40-0132 Anthropology/Ol' Man Re-bop

EMMETT BERRY

Nat 9001 Sweet and Lovely/White Rose Kick

Nat 9002 Deep Blue Dreams/Byas'd Opinions

PETE BROWN

Key(12")1312 It All Depends on You/I May Be Wrong

CAB CALLOWAY

Co 36786 Let's Take the Long Way Home/Foo a Little Ballyhoo

Co 36816 All at Once/Dawn Time

JONAH JONES

Key 614 Just Like a Butterfly/Lust for Licks

CMS 602 Rose of the Rio Grande/Stompin' at the Savoy

IKE QUEBEC

BN 510 If I Had You/Hard Tack

BN(12")37 Blue Harlem/Tiny's Exercise

J. C. HEARD

Key 623 Groovin' with J. C./All My Life

Cont 6022 The Walk/Heard but Not Seen

Cont 6027 Azure/Bouncing for Barney

Apo 783 Ollopa/This Is It

Apo 790 Sugar Hips/Coastin' with J. C.

LPs

J. C. HEARD

Argo 633 This Is Me, J. C.

Epic LN-3348 Calypso for Dancing

DIZZY GILLESPIE-STUFF SMITH

Verve MGV-8214

TEDDY WILSON

MGM(10")E-129 Runnin' Wild (Mus RIs)

BEN WEBSTER

Norg MGN-1001 The Consummate Artistry of Ben Webster

REX STEWART-WINGY MANONE (one side)

Pres 7812 Trumpet Jive!

(miscellaneous artists)

EmArcy MG-36018 Alto Altitude

RED NORVO

Dial(10")903

ROY ELDRIDGE

Clef(10")150

804. HEATH, PERCY   b

Born April 30, 1923, Wilmington, N.C.

Famed bassist with Modern Jazz Quartet. Grew up in Philadelphia. Military service, World War II. Began professional playing locally 1946. To New York with Howard McGhee combo late 1947; played Paris 1948. In late 40s with Miles Davis, Fats Navarro, J. J. Johnson, other modern jazzmen. With Dizzy Gillespie 1950-2. In demand for recording, often teaming with pianist Horace Silver to provide solid backing for soloists. Replaced Ray Brown in Modern Jazz Quartet in 1954 soon after its debut, remains two decades later.

RECORDS

MILT JACKSON

Hi-Lo 1405 Heart and Soul/Love Me Pretty Baby

Hi-Lo 1412 True Blues/Softly, as in a Morning Sunrise

MILES DAVIS

Pres 777 Dig? (1 & 2)

DIZZY GILLESPIE

DeeGee 3604 The Champ (1 & 2)

LOU DONALDSON

BN 1609 The Best Things in Life Are Free/Sweet Juice

KENNY CLARKE

Sw(Fr) 281 Maggie's Draw

Sw(Fr) 289 Annel/I'm in the Mood for Love

STAN GETZ

NJ 829 My Old Flame/The Lady in Red

Pres 724 Wrap Your Troubles in Dreams

COLEMAN HAWKINS
   Roost 517 Can Anyone Explain?/I Cross My Fingers
   Roost 519 I'll Know/You've Got Me Crying Again

LPs

MILT JACKSON
   Pres(10")183 Milt Jackson Quintet
   BN 1509
   Atl 1294 Bags and Flutes
THELONIOUS MONK
   Pres(10")166
BOBBY BYRNE-KAI WINDING
   MGM(10")E-231 Dixieland vs. Birdland
CLIFFORD BROWN
   BN(10")5032
KENNY DORHAM
   BN 1535
MODERN JAZZ QUARTET
   Atl 1231 Fontessa
   Atl 1265 The Modern Jazz Quartet
   Atl 1299 At Music Inn/Vol. 2
MODERN JAZZ SEXTET
   Norg MGN-1076

805. HEATH, TED   tb ar B
   (EDWARD HEATH)

Born March 30, 1900, Wandsworth, S.W., London, England
Died November 18, 1969, Surrey, England

Long-time English musician and bandleader. Rose to prominence in 50s and 60s leading great band of impeccable musicianship with capable jazz soloists. Outstanding arrangements in modern vein; ensemble sound full and crisp. Band's intonation amazing in view of difficult arrangements and high register brass. Heath began as trombonist in early 20s. With Jack Hylton, Bert Firman, Al Starita; long period with Ambrose 1927-35. With various bands later 30s; with Geraldo 1940-5. Formed band mid-1945, toured England, played on radio. Won recognition 1945 for work with Toots Camarata on musical background for movie LONDON TOWN. Band played many engagements at Hammersmith Palais de Danse. Concerts at London's Palladium important in establishing band. Recordings popular. By mid-50s band well known in U.S. Arrangements in early years simpler than later; sometimes used Glenn Miller reed sound. Topflight jazzmen featured by band: Kenny Baker (t), Jack Parnell (d), Ronnie Scott (ts), Les Gilbert (as), Bobby Pratt (t), Ronnie Verrall (d), Johnny Hawksworth (b), John Keating (tb), Don Lusher (tb). Vocalists included Beryl Davis and Lita Roza. Successful tour in U.S. 1956 and other years. Active in England in 60s.

RECORDS

TED HEATH
   Lon(E) 147 Chelsea/Whitechapel
   Lon(E) 149 Soho/Piccadilly
   Lon(E) 259 Dark Eyes/You Go to My Head
   Lon(E) 471 Song of the Vagabonds
   Lon(E) 638 Narcissus/Harlem Nocturne
   Lon(E) 719 Sidewalks of Cuba/Blue Skies March
   Lon(E) 902 Colonel Bogey/My Very Good Friend the Milkman
   Lon(E) 1256 Vanessa/Early Autumn
   Lon(E) 1421 Pick Yourself Up/The Champ
   Lon(E) 1675 Have You Met Miss Jones?/Faithful Hussar
   De(E) 8661 My Heart Goes Crazy/So Would I
   De(E) 8756 Experiment/Mountain Greenery
   De(E) 9605 Sweet and Lovely/Avalon
   De(E) 10123 The Hawk Talks/Night Train
   De(E) 10145 The Champ/Blues for Moderns
   De(E) 10273 Lush Slide/Fascinating Rhythm

LPs

TED HEATH
   Lon(E) LL-978 The Music of Fats Waller
   Lon(E) LL-1000 100th London Palladium Sunday Concert
   Lon(E) LL-1500 Rodgers for Moderns
   Lon(E) LL-1566 At Carnegie Hall
   Lon(E) LL-1716 All-Time Top Twelve
   Lon(E) LL-1721 Spotlight on Sidemen
   Lon(E) LL-1776 Plays Al Jolson Classics
   Lon(E) LL-3106 The Great Film Hits

Lon(E) PS-138 (S) Swing Session
Lon(E) 44104 (S) Swing Is King
Lon(E) 44113 (S) Swing Is King, Vol. 2

806. HEATHERTON, RAY vo p v B
Born c. 1909-12

Radio singer in 30s, also star of 1937 Broadway musical BABES IN ARMS. Earlier supporting role in GARRICK GAIETIES OF 1930. Sang on sustaining radio shows in middle and late 30s. On radio shows of Harry Reser 1935, Andre Kostelanetz 1936, Leo Reisman 1937, Schaefer Revue late 1937-8. In 1937 own Song Time series. With Paul Whiteman, Frank Black, Victor Young, Lennie Hayton and other bands at intervals. Led dance combo early and mid-40s, mostly in New York. Popular children's show on TV in early 50s as The Merry Mailman. Daughter Joey prominent in movies and TV in 60s and 70s as singer-dancer-actress.

RECORDS
RUBY NEWMAN
  Vi 25543 Sweet Leilani/Swing High, Swing Low

LPs
RAY HEATHERTON
  Ha HL-7034 Songs and Stories for Children

807. HECKSHER, ERNIE bn g p B
Leader of good hotel band beginning early 40s; popular in San Francisco. Born in England to American parents, grew up in U.S. At 16 played banjo on RKO theatre circuit. Attended Stanford, led dance band there. Played first hotel engagement summer 1939. Concentrated on piano, used two pianos in band. Built popularity on west coast with engagements in San Francisco and in 1942 touring. Military service, World War II. After discharge led band in Chicago late 1945-6, then other large cities. Later 40s again various west coast locations including Los Angeles, but San Francisco still scene of greatest popularity. Over ten years at Fairmont Hotel there. Band also played special social events in area. Active during 60s.

1078

RECORDS
(all LPs)
ERNIE HECKSHER
  Verve MGV-4007 Dance Atop Nob Hill
  Verve MGV-4020 At the Fabulous Fairmont
  Verve MGV-4045 Dancing on Broadway
  Verve MGV-4047 Hollywood Hits for Dancing
  MGM E-4024 Dancing Under Paris Skies
  Co CL-2086 That San Francisco Beat

808. HEFTI, NEAL t p ar cm B
Born October 29, 1922, Hastings, Neb.

Capable modern trumpet player early in career. Rose to prominence as leading composer-arranger in modern jazz (with ability to arrange in any style). Began career early 40s. With Bobby Byrne late 1942, Charlie Barnet and Charlie Spivak 1943. 1944-6 with Woody Herman's pioneer progressive band, First Herd. Won acclaim for arrangements like *Wild Root*, *Apple Honey*, *The Good Earth*. Married Herman vocalist Frances Wayne. In 1946 freelance arranging for Buddy Rich and George Auld; *Mo-Mo* outstanding for latter. Later 1946 with Charlie Ventura as sideman-arranger. In late 40s arranged for Harry James, began arranging and conducting for radio-records-TV, continuing in 50s. In 1950 arranged for Art Mooney and Count Basie, furnishing many compositions and arrangements featured and recorded by Basie that helped establish modern sound of band.

Formed own band in 1951 featuring wife Frances Wayne on vocals. Recorded and toured off and on during early 50s. Later in 50s practically abandoned trumpet to concentrate on scoring and conducting. Active on record sessions backing singers and on TV shows of Arthur Godfrey, Kate Smith and others. In 60s based mostly on west coast. Wrote background music for movies, including SEX AND THE SINGLE GIRL, HOW TO MURDER YOUR WIFE, SYNANON, BOEING BOEING, HARLOW, LORD LOVE A DUCK, DUEL AT DIABLO, BAREFOOT IN THE PARK. Wrote music for TV, including Batman and Green Hornet shows. Active into 70s. Compositions include *Li'l Darlin'*; *Cute*; *Coral Reef*; *Plymouth Rock*; *Buttercup*; *Two for the Blues*; *Cherry Point*; *Oh What a Night for Love*; *The Kid from Red Bank*; *Repetition*; *Splanky*; *Sunday Morning*; *Hot Pink*; *Little Pony*; *Blowin' Up a Storm*; *Eee Dee*; *Lake Placid*; *Why Not?*; *The Long Night*; *I'm Shoutin' Again*; *Jump for Johnny*; *The Good Earth*; *Wild Root*; *Late Date*; *It's Always Nice to Be with You*; *Girl Talk*; *I Must Know*; *Batman Theme*; *Uncle Jim*; *Duet*; *Fawncy Meeting You*; *Sure Thing*; *Falling in Love All Over Again*; *Softly with Feeling*; *Time for the Blues*; *You for Me*; *Has Anyone Here Seen Basie?*; *Pensive Miss*; *Scoot*; *Sloo Foot*; *It's Awfully Nice to Be with You*; *Count Down*; *A Little Tempo, Please*; *Pony Tail*; *Bag-a' Bones* —many written especially for Basie band. *Cute* now widely used to showcase drummer or dancer.

RECORDS
(as sideman)
ESQUIRE ALL-AMERICANS
  Vi(12″)40-4001 Snafu
BENNY CARTER
  DeL 1009 Who's Sorry Now/Looking for a Boy
  DeL 1012 Some of These Days/I'm Not the Caring Kind
  DeL 1028 Diga Diga Doo/Rose Room
CHUBBY JACKSON
  Queen 4101 I Gotcha Covered/Popsie
  Queen 4103 Bass Face/Don't Get Too Wild, Child
  VD(12″)665 Meshuga
FLIP PHILLIPS
  Si 28106 Pappiloma/Skyscraper
  Si(12″)90003 Sweet and Lovely/Bob's Belief
CHARLIE VENTURA
  Nat 7013 Either It's Love or It Isn't/Misirlou
  Nat 7015 Please Be Kind/How High the Moon
  Nat 9029 Moon Nocturne (1 & 2)
LUCKY THOMPSON
  Vi 20-2504 Boppin' the Blues/Just One More Chance
NEAL HEFTI (Frances Wayne vocals on some)
  Key 669 I Woke Up Dizzy/Sloppy Joe's

Cor 60562 Coral Reef/If You Hadn't Gone Away
Cor 60599 Charmaine/Cabin in the Cotton
Cor 60727 Sure Thing/Ev'rytime
Cor 60728 Why Not?/Lonesome and Blue
Cor 60840 Mean to Me/Somebody Loves Me
Cor 60914 Uncle Jim/Falling in Love All Over Again

LPs
NEAL HEFTI
  Cor CRL-57241 The Hollywood Song Book
  "X"(10″)LXA-3021 Music of Rudolf Friml
  Vik LX-1039 Presenting Neal Hefti and His Orchestra
  Epic LN-3187 Hearty, Hot 'n' Hefti
  Epic(10″)LG-1013 Neal Hefti's Singing Instrumentals
  UA 6573 (S) Definitely
  Movietone 72006 (S) Leisurely Loveliness
WOODY HERMAN
  Ha HL-7013 Bijou
CHARLIE VENTURA
  EmArcy MG-36015 Jumping with Ventura (Nat RIs)

(as conductor and/or arranger or composer)
FRANCES WAYNE
  Br BL-54022 Frances Wayne
  Epic LN-3222 Songs for My Man
FRANK SINATRA
  Reprise 1005 Sinatra and Swingin' Brass
COUNT BASIE
  Roul 52011 Basie Plays Hefti
STEVE ALLEN
  Cor CRL-57211 Plays Neal Hefti
(movie soundtracks)
  Lib LRP-3413 SYANON
  UA 5137 LORD LOVE A DUCK

809. HEGAMIN, LUCILLE   vo B
(LUCILLE NELSON)

Born November 29, 1894, Macon, Ga.
Died March 1, 1970, New York, N.Y.

Early blues singer. Enjoyed successful career, fruitful record output. As teenager sang locally in church choir and theatre. Joined stock company. Married pianist

William Hegamin, who served as accompanist through the years. To Chicago 1914, sang with leading entertainers and musicians. On west coast 1918-19 with great success. In late 1919 played cabarets in New York. Recording from early 20s into mid-20s. Husband formed band to accompany her on records and tours, called group Lucille Hegamin & Her Blue Flame Syncopators. Two of Lucille's best: *He May Be Your Man but He Comes to See Me Sometimes* and *Arkansas Blues*. In 1922 toured with second SHUFFLE ALONG company. Many theatre appearances next several years. Played Cotton Club in Harlem 1925 and Club Alabam in Philadelphia 1927. Retired late 20s, played some club jobs 1933-4. In early 60s came out of retirement briefly to record.

RECORDS

LUCILLE HEGAMIN
Ba 1014 Arkansas Blues
Ba 1048 He May Be Your Man but He Comes to See Me Sometimes/I've Got the Wonder Where He Went Blues
Bell 58 He's My Man/Mama Whip—Mama Spank
Bell 68 Wang Wang Blues/I Like You Because You Have Such Loving Ways
Bell 69 Strut, Miss Lizzie/Sweet Mama, Papa's Getting Mad
Bell 105 Mississippi Blues/Wabash Blues
Bell 129 He May Be Your Man but He Comes to See Me Sometimes/You've Had Your Day
Para 20127 State Street Blues/High Brown Blues
Para 20151 I've Got to Cool My Puppies Now/Send Back My Honey Man
Ca 254 I've Got What It Takes/Can't Get Lovin' Blues
Ca 317 Syncopatin' Mama/Your Man —My Man
Ca 354 Two-Time Dan/Wet Yo' Thumb
Ca 397 Sweet Papa Joe/Bleeding-Hearted Blues
Ca 494 Chattanooga Man/Rampart Street Blues

Ca 624 Hard-Hearted Hannah/Easy Goin' Mama
Ca 877 No Man's Mama/Dinah
Co 14164-D Nobody but My Baby Is Getting My Love/Senorita Mine
OK 8941 Shake Your Cans/Totem Pole

810. HEIDT, HORACE   p B
Born May 21, 1901, Alameda, Calif.

Leader of band popular in 30s and 40s. Featured commercial style, showmanship, usually cast of singers. Attended Culver Military Academy and University of California at Berkeley. Learned piano as youngster, began playing professionally 1923, for several years in Oakland. In later 20s toured in vaudeville. Formed band, in late 20s and early 30s played primarily in vaudeville. Excellent entertainment group billed as Horace Heidt & His Californians. Booked 1930 into New York's Palace Theatre: a sensation, stayed for long run. Played Monte Carlo, then less successful second run in New York. Theatre and radio work early 30s in San Francisco. To Chicago's Drake Hotel for long run 1935. Became prominent 1936 via radio and records, played good hotels. Fashioned band into high-powered commercial unit. Lightweight arrangements featured triple-tongueing trumpets, glissing sounds, sometimes several singers. Band billed as Horace Heidt & His Musical Knights (or Brigadiers). Regular radio show for Alemite late 1935-8; used catchphrase "Horace Heidt for Alemite." Philip Morris radio show 1937.

Frank DeVol played lead sax and wrote arrangements for band. Featured in later 30s: Alvino Rey on electric guitar (an innovation then) and Frankie Carle on piano. Larry Cotton best vocalist, King Sisters good vocal quartet, Art Carney singing comedian. Blind whistler Fred Lowery also featured. Gordon MacRae singer in early 40s, Bobby Hackett cornetist. Theme song beautiful *I'll Love You in My Dreams*; Heidt co-composer; published 1931. Band hit peak 1938-41 with radio show Pot o' Gold. Show built public interest by giving away big money. (Heidt had worked various giveaway shows on west coast in early 30s.) Heidt troupe featured in 1941 movie POT O' GOLD as result of radio show's popularity. In 1942 started show Treasure Chest; ran several years. 1944-5 Heidt band at best musically, with smart arrangements, rich big band sound, occasional swing. Heidt out of band business most of 1946. Returned, hit another peak of popularity in late 40s with Youth Opportunity Program: radio talent contest with contestants selected from auditions in various cities (from which week's show originated). Series built up interest and suspense. One of show winners accordionist Dick Contino. Show ran 1948-53, switched to TV mid-50s. By late 50s Heidt retired from music.

RECORDS

HORACE HEIDT
Vi 20608 Hello Cutie/Mine
Vi 21957 I'm Ka-razy for You/The Wedding of the Painted Doll
Br 7913 Gone with the Wind/The Miller's Daughter Marianne
Br 7916 The Bells of St. Mary's/Hot Lips
Br 7977 Once in Awhile/Sweet Varsity Sue
Br 7981 (theme) I'll Love You in My Dreams/Bugle Call Rag
Br 8021 Shenanigans/There's a Gold Mine in the Sky
Br 8028 Rosalie/Sail Along, Silv'ry Moon
Br 8048 History of Sweet Swing/The Toy Trumpet
Br 8309 Little Sir Echo/Let's Stop the Clock
Br 8329 How Strange/The Masquerade Is Over
Br 8334 Don't Worry 'Bout Me/What Goes Up Must Come Down
Br 8382 Wishing/This Is No Dream
Br 8414 Moon Love/Let's Make Memories Tonight
Br 8430 If I Were Sure of You/The Man with the Mandolin
Br 8441 Over the Rainbow/Address Unknown
Co 35250 Can I Help It?/Last Night
Co 35412 My! My!/Say It
Co 35709 Falling Leaves/Crosstown

Co 35904 Because of You/A Pretty Girl Milking Her Cow
Co 36610 I Need Vitamin "U"/Heavenly Hideaway
Co 36776 More and More/Lucky to Be Me
Co 36798 Anywhere/My Baby Said Yes
Co 38061 Now Is the Hour/I'll Never Say I Love You

811. HEILBRON, FRITZ   t vo

Trumpet player with Jan Garber from mid-30s to early 40s. Featured on light and novelty vocals with band, also comedy routines. With Don Reid band mid-1943 and 1944.

RECORDS

JAN GARBER
Vi 24880 Here Comes Cookie
Vi 25112 You're an Eyeful of Heaven
Bb 6338 Twenty-Four Hours a Day
Vo 4644 The Funny Old Hills
Vo 4687 It's an Old Fashioned Locket
Vo 4832 Quote and Unquote/Roller Skating on a Rainbow
Vo 4861 That's Right—I'm Wrong/Boom
Vo 5038 Runnin' Down
Vo 5114 Seventeen/Bonnie with the Big Blue Eyes
OK 6039 I Can't Remember to Forget

812. HEIN, SILVIO   cm

Born March 15, 1879, New York, N.Y.
Died December 19, 1928, Saranac Lake, N.Y.

Composer for Broadway musicals 1905-22. Songs attained little popularity; mostly effective only within context of shows. Chief collaborators lyricists George V. Hobart, E. Ray Goetz, A. Seymour Brown, Harry B. Smith. Leading songs *He's a Cousin of Mine, When You're All Dressed Up and No Place to Go, Arab Love Song, Don't Be What You Ain't, Some Little Bug, Old Man Noah, Hottentot Love Song, 'Twas in September, My Queen Bee, Heart of My Heart, I Love the Last One the Best of All, I Adore the American Girl, Maurice Tango.*

BROADWAY MUSICALS
(wrote music)

1905—MOONSHINE
1908—THE BOYS AND BETTY
1910—JUDY FORGOT; A MATINEE IDOL; THE YANKEE GIRL
1913—WHEN DREAMS COME TRUE
1914—MISS DAISY
1915—ALL OVER TOWN
1917—FURS AND FRILLS
1918—FLO FLO; HE DIDN'T WANT TO DO IT
1920—THE GIRL FROM HOME; LOOK WHO'S HERE
1922—SOME PARTY

813. HEINDORF, RAY   cm ar p B

Born August 25, 1908, Haverstraw, N.Y.

Composer-arranger-conductor-musical director in movies late 30s into 60s. Educated at Troy Conservatory of Music. Composed *Pete Kelly's Blues*, title song of 1955 movie. Other compositions included *Some Sunday Morning, I'm in a Jam, Some Sunny Day, Sugarfoot, Melancholy Rhapsody, Ballad in Jive, Hollywood Canteen, Would You Believe Me?*. Most writing film background music.

MOVIES
(partial listing)

(as composer, arranger, conductor and/or musical director)
1939—THE ROARING TWENTIES
1942—YANKEE DOODLE DANDY
1944—HOLLYWOOD CANTEEN; UP IN ARMS
1945—WONDER MAN; RHAPSODY IN BLUE
1946—NIGHT AND DAY; THE TIME, THE PLACE AND THE GIRL; SAN ANTONIO
1947—MY WILD IRISH ROSE; LOVE AND LEARN
1948—ROMANCE ON THE HIGH SEAS
1949—LOOK FOR THE SILVER LINING; FLAMINGO ROAD
1950—THE WEST POINT STORY; YOUNG MAN WITH A HORN
1951—STRANGERS ON A TRAIN; A STREETCAR NAMED DESIRE
1953—CALAMITY JANE; THE JAZZ SINGER
1954—A STAR IS BORN
1955—PETE KELLY'S BLUES
1957—THE HELEN MORGAN STORY
1958—DAMN YANKEES; NO TIME FOR SERGEANTS
1962—THE MUSIC MAN

RECORDS

RAY HEINDORF
Cap DDN-289 Four Deuces/Streetcar
Co 40533 Pete Kelly's Blues/I Never Knew

LPs

RAY HEINDORF
WB 1535 Top Film Themes '64
(movie soundtracks, as musical director)
Cap(10")L-289 A STREETCAR NAMED DESIRE
Vi LOC-1030 THE HELEN MORGAN STORY
WB 1459 (S) THE MUSIC MAN

814. HELD, ANNA   vo

Born March 8, 1873, Paris, France
Died August 12, 1918, New York, N.Y.

Beautiful French actress-singer who became star of U.S. stage and vaudeville. Popularized song *I Can't Make My Eyes Behave* which aptly described her beautiful, expressive eyes. Milk baths part of her publicity. Orphan young, joined touring company, played Holland, Germany and Denmark. At 16 returned to Paris, began singing in musical comedies. Several years later attained popularity, sang in London. American show producer Florenz Ziegfeld brought her to U.S. 1896 for stage debut in A PARLOR MATCH. Ziegfeld served as manager most of her career, married her 1897; divorced 1913. In 1897 starred in operetta LA POUPEE, 1899 in show PAPA'S WIFE. Other Broadway shows THE LITTLE DUCHESS (1901), MAM'SELLE NAPOLEON (1903), HIGGLEDY-PIGGLEDY (1904), A PARISIAN MODEL (1906), MISS INNOCENCE (1908). Featured song *It's Delightful to Be Married*, for which she wrote lyrics, in A PARISIAN MODEL. Retired awhile, then played vaudeville and toured. Returned to Broadway in FOLLOW ME (1916). Died 1918 from rare disease multiple myeloma.

815. HELLER, LITTLE JACKIE
                                        bn vo B

Born May 1, 1908, Pittsburgh, Pa.

Singer most prominent with Ben Bernie band 1932-3. Small (about 115 pounds) but good athlete as youngster; brief boxing career. Eddie Cantor heard Heller's melodious tenor, helped him get job in Texas Guinan's night club in New York. Later toured in vaudeville several years with Benny Davis. In 1932 Ben Bernie heard Heller in Atlantic City night club, hired him as band vocalist. Heller became well known 1932-3 via Bernie's broadcasts. Left Bernie to resume career as single. On 30s radio shows including own singing series. In 1936-7 London hit on stage and radio. Led band in U.S. 1938-9; unit went co-op mid-1939. Role in 1939 Broadway musical YOKEL BOY. Worked clubs 40s into 50s.

816.HENDERSON-DeSYLVA-BROWN

cm lyr

Famous songwriting team of Ray Henderson (cm), Buddy DeSylva (lyr), Lew Brown (lyr). During 1926-30 team had no peer in capturing mood of Roaring Twenties. Contributed host of hits, many for stage or movies. Henderson pianist-composer, DeSylva and Brown lyricists and idea men; worked wonderfully together. All worked with others earlier. Brown and Henderson began collaborating 1922; DeSylva joined 1925 for score of GEORGE WHITE'S SCANDALS. Score music adequate, but outstanding score for 1926 SCANDALS established team. Then scores for Broadway shows GOOD NEWS and MANHATTAN MARY (1927), HOLD EVERYTHING (1928), GEORGE WHITE'S SCANDALS OF 1928, FOLLOW THROUGH (1929), FLYING HIGH (1930). Team wrote songs for early Al Jolson sound movies (e.g. *Sonny Boy, Little Pal, It All Depends on You*), also songs independent of shows. Had own publishing company awhile. In 1929 to Hollywood; great score for popular movie SUNNY SIDE UP starring Janet Gaynor and Charles Farrell. 1930 stage score for FLYING HIGH and several hit songs 1931. Then team broke up as De Sylva moved into movie producing. Henderson and Brown continued together several years, scored for Broadway shows GEORGE WHITE'S SCANDALS OF 1931, HOT-CHA (1932), STRIKE ME PINK (1933). Three men continued in music several years. 1956 movie THE BEST THINGS IN LIFE ARE FREE

based on team's career; roles played by Dan Dailey, Gordon MacRae, Ernest Borgnine. Film well done, featured team's great song hits.

SONGS
(with related shows)

1925—GEORGE WHITE'S SCANDALS OF 1925 stage show (Fly Butterfly; Give Us the Charleston; I Want a Lovable Baby)

1926—GEORGE WHITE'S SCANDALS OF 1926 stage show (Birth of the Blues; Black Bottom; Lucky Day; The Girl Is You and the Boy Is Me)

1927—GOOD NEWS stage show (Good News; The Best Things in Life Are Free; The Varsity Drag; Lucky in Love; Just Imagine); MANHATTAN MARY stage show (Manhattan Mary; Broadway; It Won't Be Long Now; The Five-Step; I'd Like You to Love Me; Nothing but Love); So Blue; Broken Hearted; It All Depends on You; Just a Memory; Magnolia; South Wind; Without You, Sweetheart

1928—HOLD EVERYTHING stage show (Don't Hold Everything; You're the Cream in My Coffee; To Know You Is to Love You; Too Good to Be True); GEORGE WHITE'S SCANDALS OF 1928 stage show (Pickin' Cotton; I'm on the Crest of a Wave; What D'Ya Say?; American Tune); THREE CHEERS stage show (Pompanola; Maybe This Is Love); THE SINGING FOOL movie (Sonny Boy; It All Depends on You); For Old Times' Sake; Sorry for Me; The Song I Love (with Con Conrad); That's Just My Way of Forgetting You; Together

1929—FOLLOW THROUGH stage show (Follow Through; Button Up Your Overcoat; My Lucky Star; I Want to Be Bad; You Wouldn't Fool Me, Would You?); SUNNY SIDE UP movie (Sunny Side Up; If I Had a Talking Picture of You; Turn on the Heat; Aren't We All?; You've Got Me Pickin' Petals Off of Daisies); SAY IT WITH SONGS movie, with Al Jolson-lyr (Little Pal; I'm in Seventh Heaven; One Sweet Kiss; Why Can't You?; Used to You); IN OLD ARIZONA movie (My Tonia); My Sin

1930—FLYING HIGH stage show (Flying High; Thank Your Father; Bad for Me; Red Hot Chicago; Without Love; Wasn't It Beautiful While It Lasted?); FOLLOW THROUGH movie (original stage score); GOOD NEWS movie (original stage score); JUST IMAGINE movie (You Are the Melody; Old Fashioned Girl); SHOW GIRL IN HOLLYWOOD movie (My Sin); Don't Tell Her What Happened to Me

1931—INDISCREET movie (Come to Me; If You Haven't Got Love); One More Time; You Try Somebody Else

1947—GOOD NEWS movie (original stage score)

817. HENDERSON, FLETCHER

p ar cm B

(nickname Smack)

Born December 18, 1898, Cuthbert, Ga. Died December 29, 1952, New York, N.Y.

Most influential swing arranger. Leader of outstanding big bands for two decades, none of which attained deserved success. Pioneer among big bands. Trailblazing arrangements adapted improvisations and beat of jazz giants like Louis Armstrong to big band sections, established voicing, harmonics, style for big band swing. Arrangements key ingredient in Benny Goodman's rise as King of Swing in mid-30s. Older brother of bandleader Horace Henderson. Attended Morehouse College in Atlanta, earned degree in chemistry. To New York 1920 for further study, instead took job as song demonstrator in publishing house. In 1921 house pianist for new Black Swan record company. Recorded and toured with Ethel Waters. In early 20s accompanist on record sessions for leading blues singers Bessie Smith, Clara Smith, Trixie Smith, Ida Cox, Alberta Hunter, Ma Rainey,

Rosa Henderson, Viola McCoy and others. Led first band 1923 with men used on records as nucleus. Band won job at Club Alabam in New York. Altoist Don Redman arrangements influential in developing band's style. Band recorded immediately; total output tremendous. Played Roseland Ballroom later in 1924, its main base for years. At times Sam Lanin band with good early white jazzmen shared dance hall. Young trumpet star Louis Armstrong joined September 1924, stayed till November 1925, fired and transformed band. Outstanding jazz personnel of Henderson band in 20s and early 30s included Joe Smith (t), Buster Bailey (cl), Jimmy Harrison (tb), Bobby Stark (t), Coleman Hawkins (ts), Claude Jones (tb), Benny Morton (tb), Charlie Green (tb), Tommy Ladnier (t), Rex Stewart (t), Benny Carter (as). During 1933-8 stars included Red Allen (t), Hilton Jefferson (as), Chu Berry (ts), Roy Eldridge (t), Jerry Blake (cl), Ben Webster (ts), Keg Johnson (tb), Emmett Berry (t), Sandy Williams (tb), Dick Vance (t), Joe Thomas (t), J. C. Higginbotham (tb), with Hawkins, Jones and Bailey holdovers for a time.

In late 20s Henderson seemed to lose interest somewhat, perhaps because of auto accident that left him scarred. Recordings dropped 1929-30 and bookings in Depression less frequent. Then band landed good spot at Connie's Inn in Harlem and recordings increased. Benny Carter important arranger at this time. Henderson began arranging early 30s, soon developed talents of giant. Arrangements simple but swung mightily, featured great sax section work, with spots for jazz solos enhanced by section work in background. Scores set general swing style from early 30s to mid-40s. Famed for key Benny Goodman arrangements such as *Blue Skies, King Porter, Sometimes I'm Happy, Jingle Bells, Sandman, When Buddha Smiles, Christopher Columbus, Down South Camp Meeting, Star Dust, Somebody Loves Me, Honeysuckle Rose, I Want to Be Happy*, dozens more.

Henderson band attracted first national attention when swing burst upon scene

1936. Good radio coverage helped launch sensational theme *Christopher Columbus*. Many of band's best recordings made in 1936. Began long run at Chicago's Grand Terrace. In late 30s name faded. Henderson disbanded 1939 to concentrate on arranging for Goodman, played piano in band latter half of 1939. Arrangements for Goodman in this period included *Stealin' Apples*, *Spring Song*, *Opus Local 802*, *Night and Day*, *Beyond the Moon*, *Henderson Stomp*, *Taking a Chance on Love*. In early 40s led band again awhile, worked in New York and toured. Worked mostly in Chicago 1945-7, disbanded. Toured with Ethel Waters 1948-9. In late 40s and early 50s furnished Goodman several arrangements including *Sweet and Lovely*, *Back in Your Own Backyard*, *On a Slow Boat to China*, *South of the Border*. Led band and combo 1950. In December 1950 stroke caused partial paralysis, ended active career.

Henderson composed many jazz numbers including *Stampede*; *Down South Camp Meeting*; *Wrappin' It Up*; *Bumble Bee Stomp*; *No, Baby, No*; *It's Wearing Me Down*; *Hotter Than 'Ell*. Besides arrangements for Goodman, Henderson arranged for Isham Jones, Glen Gray, Teddy Hill, Will Bradley, Jack Hylton, Dorsey Brothers. Neither outstanding pianist nor bandleader with showmanship. Main contributions to jazz: organizing first important swing band, later writing arrangements for it and Goodman that gave big band swing its distinctive voice.

RECORDS

ALBERTA HUNTER
Para 12017 Chirping the Blues/Someone Else Will Take Your Place
Para 12021 You Shall Reap Just What You Sow

VIOLA MCCOY
Ajax 17010 Lonesome Daddy Blues/Don't Mean You No Good Blues
Br 2591 If Your Good Man Quits You, Don't Wear No Black/I Ain't Gonna Marry, Ain't Gonna Settle Down

BESSIE SMITH
Co 14133-D Jazzbo Brown from Memphis Town

Co 14137-D Money Blues/Hard Driving Papa

TRIXIE SMITH
Para 12336 He Likes It Slow/Black Bottom Hop

ETHEL WATERS
Co 14125-D Make Me a Pallet on the Floor/Bring Your Greenbacks

SEVEN BROWN BABIES
Ajax 17009 Doo Doodle Oom/West Indies Blues
Ajax 17011 Dicty Blues/Charleston Crazy

BENNY GOODMAN SEXTET
Co 35254 Rose Room/Flying Home
Co 35320 Soft Winds/Memories of You

BENNY GOODMAN ORCHESTRA
Co 35362 Stealin' Apples

SOUTHERN SERENADERS (Fletcher Henderson)
Ha 4 I Miss My Swiss
Ha 5 Alone at Last

DIXIE STOMPERS (Fletcher Henderson)
Ha 70 Spanish Shawl/Clap Hands! Here Comes Charley
Ha 153 Black Horse Stomp/Nervous Charlie Stomp
Ha 166 Tampeekoe/Jackass Blues
Ha 353 Snag It/Ain't She Sweet?

CONNIE'S INN ORCHESTRA (Fletcher Henderson)
Me 12239 Just Blues/Sugar Foot Stomp
Vi 22698 Moan You Moaners/Roll On, Mississippi, Roll On
Cr 3180 You Rascal You/Blue Rhythm
Cr 3212 Milenberg Joys/12th Street Rag

FLETCHER HENDERSON
Vo 14636 Gulf Coast Blues/Down-Hearted Blues
Vo 14654 Dicty Blues/Doo Doodle Oom
Ajax 17022 Mistreatin' Daddy/Old Black Joe's Blues
Br 2592 Sud Bustin' Blues/War Horse Mama
Br 3460 Stockholm Stomp/Have It Ready
Br 4119 Hop Off
Ba 1383 Charley, My Boy

Ba 1490 Prince of Wails
Ge 3286 Honey Bunch
Co 249-D The Meanest Kind of Blues/Naughty Man
Co 395-D Sugar Foot Stomp/What-Cha-Call-'Em Blues
Co 509-D T.N.T./Carolina Stomp
Co 654-D The Stampede/Jackass Blues
Co 970-D Tozo/Rocky Mountain Blues
Co 1543-D King Porter Stomp/D Natural Blues
Co 1913-D Blazin'/The Wang-Wang Blues
Co 2329-D Chinatown, My Chinatown/Somebody Loves Me
Co 2559-D Blues in My Heart/Sugar
Co 2565-D Singin' the Blues/It's the Darndest Thing
Vi 20944 Variety Stomp/St. Louis Shuffle
Vi 22955 Strangers/I Wanna Count Sheep
Vi 25297 I'm a Fool for Loving You/Moonrise on the Lowlands
Vi 25317 Jangled Nerves/I'll Always Be in Love with You
Vi 25379 Jimtown Blues/You Can Depend on Me
De 157 Wrappin' It Up/Limehouse Blues
De 213 Down South Camp Meeting/Tidal Wave
De 555 Hotter Than 'Ell/Liza
Vo 3211 (theme) Christopher Columbus/Blue Lou
Vo 3213 Grand Terrace Swing/Stealin' Apples
Vo 3511 Rose Room/Back in Your Own Backyard
Vo 3534 Stampede/Great Caesar's Ghost

LPs

FLETCHER HENDERSON
Co C4L19 (4-LP set) A Study in Frustration (Co, Ha, Vo RIs)
"X"(10")LVA-3013 Connie's Inn Orchestra (Vi RIs)
De DL-9228 (De RIs)
BESSIE SMITH
Co G-30450 (2-LP set) Empty Bed (Co RIs)

Co CL-855-8 (4-LP set) The Bessie Smith Story (Co RIs)
BENNY GOODMAN
Co CL-524 Presents Fletcher Henderson Arrangements (Co RIs)

818. HENDERSON, HORACE
p ar cm B

Born 1904, Cuthbert, Ga.

Younger brother of jazz great Fletcher Henderson. Though in brother's shadow, talented pianist-arranger-composer and bandleader. Studied piano, attended Wilberforce University, led band there. 1924-8 continued band on jobs and tours. Disbanded after losing key men. 1929 formed new band, toured, played Connie's Inn in New York. In 1931 Don Redman fronted, with Horace pianist-arranger. With brother Fletcher 1933-4, again in 1936; own band in between. 1937-42 led band, mostly in Chicago. Theme *Chris and His Gang*. Military service, late 1942-3. Joined brother's band 1943-4. 1944-5 pianist-arranger-road manager for singer Lena Horne. Led groups mostly in Los Angeles 1945-9, various-sized bands in different locales in 50s and 60s. In later 60s mostly in Denver. Through career arranged for Benny Goodman, Tommy Dorsey, Fletcher Henderson, Don Redman, Coleman Hawkins, Glen Gray, Charlie Barnet, Earl Hines, Jimmie Lunceford. Style similar to Fletcher's. Composed good jazz numbers including *Rug Cutter's Swing, Jeep Rhythm, Big John Special, Hot and Anxious, Comin' and Goin', Jamaica Shout, Riffin', Kitty on Toast, Love for Scale.*

ARRANGEMENTS

BENNY GOODMAN
Walk, Jenny, Walk; I Found a New Baby; Always; Japanese Sandman; Dear Old Southland; Big John Special
FLETCHER HENDERSON
Blue Lou; Big John Special; Moonrise on the Lowlands; Riffin'; Yeah Man; Grand Terrace Rhythm; Queer Notions; Hot and Anxious; Comin' and Goin'; Christopher Columbus

CHARLIE BARNET
Little Dip; Ponce De Leon; Charleston Alley; Little John Ordinary
DON REDMAN
I Heard; It's a Great World After All; Hot and Anxious

RECORDS

CHOCOLATE DANDIES
Co 2543-D Dee Blues/Bugle Call Rag
Co 35679 Goodbye Blues/Cloudy Skies
Co 36009 Got Another Sweetie Now
FLETCHER HENDERSON
Co 2449-D Hot and Anxious/Comin' and Goin'
Vo 3211 Christopher Columbus/Blue Lou
ALLEN-HAWKINS ORCHESTRA
Pe 15802 Stringin' Along on a Shoe String/Shadows on the Swanee
Pe 15808 The River's Takin' Care of Me/Ain'tcha Got Music?
CHU BERRY
Va 532 Too Marvelous for Words/Now You're Talking My Language
Va 587 Limehouse Blues/Indiana
COLEMAN HAWKINS
OK 41566 Jamaica Shout/Heart Break Blues
BALTIMORE BELL HOPS
Co 2449-D Hot and Anxious/Comin' and Goin'
EMMA GOVER
Pat 21060 Oh Daddy Blues
HARLAN LATTIMORE
Co 2675-D Chant of the Weed/Got the South in My Soul
Co 2678-D I Heard/Reefer Man
AL CASEY
Cap 10034 Sometimes I'm Happy/How High the Moon
SID CATLETT
Cap 10032 I Never Knew/Love for Scale
LENA HORNE
Vi 20-1616 One for My Baby/I Didn't Know About You
BUDDY CHARLES
Mer 5766 Au Revoir/Sleepy Time Down South
HORACE HENDERSON
Vo 5433 Kitty on Toast/Oh Boy, I'm in the Groove
Vo 5579 Honeysuckle Rose/They Jittered All the Time
Vo 5606 You're Mine, You/Swingin' and Jumpin'
OK 5632 Chlo-e
OK 5748 When Dreams Come True/Flinging a Whing Ding
OK 5841 Coquette/I Still Have My Dreams
OK 5900 Smooth Sailin'/Ain't Misbehavin'
OK 6026 Turkey Special
Jamb 908 'Deed I Do/Smack's Rhythm
Jamb 909 Make Love to Me/Bunch of Rhythm

819. HENDERSON, LUTHER

p ar cm B

Born March 14, 1919, Kansas City, Mo.

Prominent arranger and conductor in 50s and 60s. Attended Juilliard. Pianist with Leonard Ware 1939-44. Military service, 1944-6. Pianist with Mercer Ellington awhile, then pianist and musical director for singer Lena Horne 1947-50. Active teaching and arranging. In 50s and 60s conductor on TV shows and record sessions with singers; based in New York. Wrote additional music for 1970-3 Broadway revival of NO, NO, NANETTE. Arranged for Broadway shows, including FUNNY GIRL and DO RE MI. Compositions include *Hold On, Solitaire, Ten Good Years.*

RECORDS
(all LPs)

LUTHER HENDERSON
Co CS-8149 (S) Clap Hands
Co CS-8217 (S) The Greatest Sound Around
(as conductor; arranger on some)
EILEEN FARRELL
Co CL-1465 I've Got a Right to Sing the Blues!
Co CL-1653 Here I Go Again
ANNA MARIA ALBERGHETTI
MGM E-4001 Love Makes the World Go Round
POLLY BERGEN
Co CS-8018 (S) My Heart Sings
Co CS-8100 (S) All Alone by the Telephone
JOYA SHERRILL
Co CS-8207 (S) Sugar and Spice

820. HENDERSON, RAY   cm p

Born December 1, 1896, Buffalo, N.Y.
Died New Year's Eve, 1970, Greenwich, Conn.

Composer in famed 20s-30s songwriting team of Henderson-DeSylva-Brown. Collaborated with other lyricists before and after on long list of hit songs. Educated at Chicago Conservatory. Pianist in dance bands and vaudeville. Arranger and song plugger for New York publishing houses. Began working with lyricist Lew Brown and others in 1922. Great early hits: *That Old Gang of Mine*; *Alabamy Bound*; *Five Foot Two, Eyes of Blue*; *Bye Bye Blackbird*; *I'm Sitting on Top of the World*. In 1925 Henderson and Brown joined by lyricist Buddy DeSylva for score of Broadway show GEORGE WHITE'S SCANDALS. Team continued to produce outstanding songs 1925-31.

(See biography herein on HENDERSON-DESYLVA-BROWN for details and song listings of team's career.)

Henderson and Brown continued together several years. Scores for Broadway shows GEORGE WHITE'S SCANDALS OF 1931, HOT-CHA (1932), STRIKE ME PINK (1933). Henderson wrote with other lyricists, mostly for movies. Special material for Ruth Etting's London show 1936. After early 40s music activities ebbed. Some conducting on TV around 1950. Other collaborators lyricists Mort Dixon, Sam M. Lewis, Joe Young, Jack Yellen, Ted Koehler, Billy Rose, Irving Caesar.

SONGS
(with related shows)

(excluding works of HENDERSON-DESYLVA-BROWN)

1922—GREENWICH VILLAGE FOLLIES OF 1922 stage show (Georgette)
1923—That Old Gang of Mine; Annabelle
1924—Follow the Swallow; I Wonder Who's Dancing with You Tonight; Alabamy Bound; Why Did I Kiss That Girl?
1925—Bam Bam Bamy Shore; Don't Bring Lulu; Five Foot Two, Eyes of Blue; If I Had a Girl Like You; I'm Sitting on Top of the World; Too Many Parties and Too Many Pals; If You Hadn't Gone Away

1926—Bye Bye Blackbird; Under the Ukulele Tree; I'm in Love with You, That's Why
1927—Cover Me Up with Sunshine
1925-31—(see HENDERSON-DESYLVA-BROWN)
1931—GEORGE WHITE'S SCANDALS OF 1931 stage show (My Song; The Thrill Is Gone; That's Why Darkies Were Born; Life Is Just a Bowl of Cherries; This Is the Missus)
1932—HOT-CHA stage show (There I Go Dreaming Again; You Can Make My Life a Bed of Roses; Conchita; There's Nothing the Matter with Me)
1933—STRIKE ME PINK stage show (Strike Me Pink; Let's Call It a Day; Love and Rhythm; Restless; It's Great to Be Alive)
1934—SAY WHEN stage show (Say When; When Love Comes Swinging Along); GEORGE WHITE'S SCANDALS movie (Nasty Man; Hold My Hand; My Dog Loves Your Dog; Sweet and Simple; So Nice; Six Women)
1935—CURLY TOP movie (Curly Top; When I Grow Up; Animal Crackers in My Soup; The Simple Things in Life; It's All So New to Me)
1936—GEORGE WHITE'S SCANDALS OF 1936 stage show (Life Begins at Sweet Sixteen; I'm the Fellow Who Loves You; Cigarette; Anything Can Happen; I've Got to Get Hot); Every Once in Awhile
1940—Up the Chimney Go My Dreams
1941—Don't Cry, Cherie
1942—There Are Rivers to Cross; On the Old Assembly Line
1943—ZIEGFELD FOLLIES OF 1943 stage show (Love Songs Are Made in the Night; Hold That Smile; Come Up and Have a Cup of Coffee; Thirty-Five Summers Ago)

821. HENDERSON, ROSA   vo
(ROSA DESCHAMPS)

Born November 24, 1896, Henderson, Ky.
Died April 6, 1968, New York, N.Y.

Leading blues singer; heavy recording

early and mid-20s. Not related to band-leader Fletcher Henderson or blues singer Edmonia Henderson. Began with carnival 1913. Played tent shows for years through south and southwest. Took name Rosa Henderson when married comedian Slim Henderson. Toured with him in Mason-Henderson road show. Began recording 1923, turned out many until 1931. Used record pseudonyms Josephine Thomas, Flora Dale, Mamie Harris, Sally Ritz, Rose Henderson. Accompaniment by good jazzmen including pianists Fletcher Henderson, Cliff Jackson, James P. Johnson. By mid-20s playing good vaudeville theatres and Harlem shows. Husband died 1927. Miss Henderson retired almost completely; occasional appearances in 30s.

RECORDS

ROSA HENDERSON

Vi 19084 Good Woman's Blues/I'm Broke, Fooling with You
Vi 19124 Midnight Blues
Vi 19157 Struttin' Blues/Low-Down Papa
Vo 14682 It Won't Be Long Now/ Every Woman's Blues
Vo 14708 I Want My Sweet Daddy Now/He May Be Your Dog but He's Wearing My Collar
Vo 14795 How Come You Do Me Like You Do?/My Papa Doesn't Two-Time No-Time
Vo 14831 Barrel House Blues/My Right Man
Vo 15011 12th Street Blues/Low-Down Daddy
Vo 1021 Chicago Policeman Blues/ Here Comes My Baby
Vo 1038 Rough House Blues/He Belongs to Me
Co A-3958 Afternoon Blues/I Need You
Co 14130-D Let's Talk About My Sweetie/Mama Is Waitin' for You
Co 14627-D Doggone Blues/Can't Be Bothered with No Sheik
Ajax 17049 I Can't Get the One I Want
Ajax 17069 Memphis Bound/I Don't Want Nobody That Don't Want Me
Pe 119 Git Goin'/Someday You'll

Come Back to Me
Pe 122 Slow Up Papa/Hock Shop Blues
Pe 129 Black Snake Moan/Fortune Teller Blues
(as ROSE HENDERSON)
Pe 12100 He's Never Gonna Throw Me Down/Every Day Blues
(as JOSEPHINE THOMAS)
Pe 12201 Memphis Bound
(as MAMIE HARRIS)
Pe 106 It Takes a Two-Time Papa

822. HENDERSON, SKITCH

p ar cm B

(LYLE HENDERSON)

Born January 27, 1918, Halstad, Minn.

Pianist-bandleader prominent on TV in 50s and 60s. Attended University of California and Juilliard; formal training abroad. Capable classical pianist. Not overpowering at jazz; chief assets deft touch and strong modern chording. Active on west coast late 30s in radio, theatres, dance bands. Accompanist for Judy Garland on tour. Studio work 1939-40. Military service, World War II. In 1946 featured soloist on Frank Sinatra and Bing Crosby radio shows. Led band 1947-9, featured two French horns, good arrangements, Nancy Read vocals. Disbanded early 1950; musical director on Sinatra radio show. Active on early TV on Dave Garroway show plus own show featuring own piano with strings. Late 1954-56 led band on Steve Allen show. Most prominent on TV in 60s. Led band on Tonight summer show with various hosts after Jack Paar left, continued when Johnny Carson took over fall 1962. Capable bandleader-pianist-arranger-humorist. Band brilliant though seldom featured; superb sidemen. Skitch left show in later 60s for freelance arranging and conducting. Guest pianist in concerts; conductor of Tulsa Symphony 1971-2. Compositions include *Skitch's Blues*, *Minuet on the Rocks*, *Skitch's Boogie*, *Skitch in Time*, *Come Thursday*, *Curacao*, and beautiful theme for Tonight summer show of 1962.

RECORDS

SKITCH HENDERSON
Cap 255 Cynthia's in Love/Swan Lake

Cap 287 Five Minutes More/See What a Kiss Can Do

Cap 313 If I'm Lucky/Save Me a Dream

Cap 331 And So to Bed/A Garden in the Rain

Cap 351 Misirlou/Far Away Island

Cap 402 Would You Believe Me?/A Thousand and One Nights

Cap 441 Dancing with a Deb/Dream on a Summer Night

Cap 501 When You're Smiling/Army Air Corps

Cap 619 Pattern in Lace

Cap 881 Mary Lou/Sunday Monday

Cap 10175 Two Cigarettes in the Dark/Jealous

Cap 15092 Beyond the Blue Horizon/A Fella with an Umbrella

Cap 15136 Mine/Somebody Else's Picture

Cap 15234 Maybe/Cornish Rhapsody

Cap 15331 Skitch's Boogie/Crazy Rhythm

LPs

SKITCH HENDERSON

Co CL-2367 Skitch ... Tonight!

Co CS-9475 (S) Eyes of Love

Co CS-9683 (S) A Tribute to Irving Berlin

Vi LPM-1401 Sketches by Skitch

Cap(10")H-110 Keyboard Sketches

(as conductor)

KATE SMITH

Vi LPM-2819 At Carnegie Hall

823. HENDRICKSON, AL   g vo
(ALTON REYNOLDS HENDRICKSON)

Born May 10, 1920, Eastland, Texas

Good solo and rhythm guitarist, capable baritone. Grew up in California. Dance jobs in mid-30s, later studios. With Artie Shaw 1940-1, including spot in Gramercy Five, combo within band. With Freddie Slack and Skinnay Ennis 1942. Military service, World War II. Musical director of Los Angeles radio station early 1946. With Freddie Slack late 1946-7. Joined Benny Goodman March 1947 as guitarist-vocalist, remained till end of year. With Goodman combo in movie A SONG

IS BORN mid-1948. With Ray Noble later 1948, featured on vocals. With Boyd Raeburn and Woody Herman. Early 50s with Sonny Burke, Frank DeVol, Billy May and Jerry Gray, including TV-radio work. Freelance, studios, movie soundtracks in later 50s and 60s.

RECORDS

ARTIE SHAW GRAMERCY FIVE

Vi 26762 Special Delivery Stomp/Keepin' Myself for You

Vi 26763 Cross Your Heart/Summit Ridge Drive

Vi 27289 Dr. Livingstone, I Presume?/When the Quail Come Back to San Quentin

Vi 27335 Smoke Gets in Your Eyes

Vi 27432 My Blue Heaven

BENNY GOODMAN SEXTET

Cap 15008 Nagasaki/Gonna Get a Girl

Cap 15069 Shirley Steps Out

Cap 15166 Cherokee/Love Is Just Around the Corner

Cap 15208 On a Slow Boat to China

(ORCHESTRA)

Cap 15286 The Varsity Drag

RAY NOBLE

Co 38080 Saturday Night in Central Park/I Fell in Love with You

Co 38158 A Little Imagination/What Do I Have to Do?

Co 38206 Judaline

VIC SCHOEN

De 24789 Give Me Your Hand

LPs

BENNY GOODMAN

Cap(10")H-202 Session for Six

ARTIE SHAW

Vi LPM-1241 And His Gramercy Five (Vi RIs)

MATTY MATLOCK

Mayfair 9569 Dixieland

Tops L-1569 And His Dixie-Men

PAUL SMITH

Verve V-2148 Latin Keyboards and Percussion

RAY ANTHONY

Cap T-678 Big Band Dixieland

PAGE CAVANAUGH (6-piece combo)

Cap T-879 Fats Sent Me

SCAT MAN CROTHERS
Tops L-1511 Rock and Roll with "Scat Man"

BARNEY KESSEL
Contemp C-3513 Barney Kessel, Vol. 3

HERBIE HARPER
Noc(10")7

SHORTY ROGERS and ANDRE PREVIN
Vi LJM-1018

824. HENIE, SONJA

Born April 8, 1912, Oslo, Norway
Died October 12, 1969, on ambulance
plane en route from Paris to Oslo

Olympic skating star popular in U.S. movies; staged successful ice shows. Delightful pixie quality, dimpled cheeks, charming accent and personality, flair for light comedy. Not a musical performer but did light song-and-dance numbers occasionally in films (whose scores boasted excellent pop tunes). Began skating early, by 14 won several skating championships in Norway. Won Olympic women's figure skating championship 1928-1932-1936, turned professional. National idol in Norway, popular elsewhere. Staged elaborate ice show 1936 in Hollywood to gain movie career. Signed by 20th Century-Fox. First movie ONE IN A MILLION early 1937 hit, followed by others. Format light comedy, a few good songs performed by entertainers. Always included: Miss Henie's skating. Artist and showman on ice. Between movies toured with own ice shows; financial success. In New York played Madison Square Garden, Roxy Theatre, Center Theatre in Rockefeller Center. Astute business woman. Produced successful 1940 Broadway show IT HAPPENS ON ICE. Final movie 1948 as film popularity waned. Continued ice shows in 50s. 1958 musical travelogue HELLO LONDON. In 1968 she and third husband, shipowner Neils Onstad, gave Norway $3.5 million art museum. (Previous husbands Dan Topping and Winthrop Gardiner Jr.) Died from leukemia.

MOVIES

1937—ONE IN A MILLION; THIN ICE
1938—HAPPY LANDING; MY LUCKY STAR
1939—SECOND FIDDLE; EVERYTHING HAPPENS AT NIGHT

1941—SUN VALLEY SERENADE
1942—ICELAND
1943—WINTERTIME
1945—IT'S A PLEASURE
1948—THE COUNTESS OF MONTE CRISTO
1958—HELLO LONDON (English)

825. HENKE, MEL   p

Born August 4, 1915, Chicago, Ill.

Jazz pianist with unorthodox barrelhouse style. Adept at boogie woogie. Attended Chicago College of Music. Played with Mitch Todd, Frank Snyder and Stephen Leonard groups in Chicago area, also as single. With Horace Heidt awhile after pianist Frankie Carle left late 1943. Work in Chicago middle and late 40s, including radio. Hollywood in early 50s for club and radio-TV, including George Gobel TV show 1954-5. Later composed for TV and movies.

RECORDS

MEL HENKE
CI 100 Henke Stomp/Lady Be Good
CI 102 I Surrender Dear/On a Blues Kick
CI 103 Mrs. Abernathy's Piano/It's Purely Coincidental
Vi 20-1925 Body and Soul/Penthouse Serenade
Vi 20-1926 Goodnight Sweetheart/It's the Talk of the Town
Vita 3 What Is This Thing Called Love?/Alexander's Ragtime Band
Vita 5 In a Mist/Honky Tonk Train
Tempo 442 Dance of the Cavemen/I Surrender Dear
Tempo 444 Shock Treatment/I Can't Believe That You're in Love with Me

LPs

MEL HENKE
Contemp C-5001 Dig Mel Henke
Contemp C-5003 Now Spin This
WB 1472 (S)

GARRY MOORE Presents
Co CL-717 My Kind of Music

826. HENRY, TAL   B

Leader of sweet band mostly in south, late 20s to mid-30s.

RECORDS

TAL HENRY

Vi 21404 Some Little Someone/Song of Songs to You

Vi 21471 Lonesome/I'd Trade My Air Castles

Vi 21573 Louise, I Love You/Why Make Me Lonesome?

Vi 40034 When Shadows Fall/My Little Old Home Down in New Orleans

Vi 40035 Found My Gal/Just You and I

Vi 40133 Shame on You/I Know Why I Think of You

Bb 5364 Don't Say Goodnight/Goin' to Heaven on a Mule

Bb 5365 There Goes My Heart/Dancing in the Moonlight

Bb 5366 I Can't Go On Like This/Carioca

827. HERBECK, RAY   as B

Born c. 1915

Leader of commercial dance band popular in late 30s and early 40s. Lightweight arrangements and "Music with Romance" gimmick. Theme *Romance*. Played Sacramento 1936, then mostly in Chicago and midwest. In middle and late 40s band changed to swing and better arrangements. Played on west coast often, in Las Vegas 1949-50. Left music later 50s, entered real estate in California.

RECORDS

RAY HERBECK

Vo 4436 Sailing at Midnight/Tell Me with Your Kisses

Vo 4551 September Song/It Never Was You

Vo 4611 Simple and Sweet/Gotta Pebble in My Shoe

Vo 4876 A Home in the Clouds/Rose of Washington Square

Vo 4891 Let There Be Love/Stand By for Further Announcements

Vo 4955 Last Trip on the Old Ship/You've Got Me Crying Again

Vo 4983 You're the Moment in My Life/The Little Man Who Wasn't There

Vo 5020 What's New?/You Are My Dream

Vo 5089 Now and Then/Blue Tahitian Moonlight

Vo 5115 Good Morning/My Heart Keeps Crying

Vo 5143 Here Comes the Night/I Just Got a Letter

Vo 5225 We're All Together Now/All's Well

Vo 5250 Oh Johnny, Oh Johnny, Oh!/Chatterbox

Vo 5368 When the Swallows Come Back to Capistrano/The Nearness of You

Vo 5398 My Fantasy/Palms of Paradise

OK 5790 Yesterthoughts/I Just Wanna Play with You

OK 5840 The Moon Fell in the River/Sentimental Me

827A. HERBERT, EVELYN   vo

Born 1898, Philadelphia, Pa.

Beautiful singing star of Broadway musicals. Early career sang with Chicago Opera Company. In 1931 London show WALTZES FROM VIENNA.

BROADWAY MUSICALS

1923—STEPPING STONES

1925—THE LOVE SONG; PRINCESS FLAVIA

1926—THE MERRY WORLD

1927—MY MARYLAND

1928—THE NEW MOON

1930—PRINCESS CHARMING

1933—MELODY

1934—BITTER SWEET (revival)

828. HERBERT, VICTOR   cm cello B

Born February 1, 1859, Dublin, Ireland
Died May 24, 1924, New York, N.Y.

Great composer, most important influence in development of Broadway musicals. Exponent of operetta-style show. Due to paucity of long-running shows in early days, Herbert's shows mostly ran about six months or less. But shows numerous, provided many popular songs that endured. Best productions included BABES IN TOYLAND (1903), IT HAPPENED IN NORDLAND (1904), MLLE. MODISTE and THE RED MILL (1906), NAUGHTY MARIETTA (1910), SWEETHEARTS (1913), PRINCESS PAT (1915). Most famous songs *Gypsy Love Song*; *Toyland*; *Kiss Me Again*; *In Old*

New York; *Every Day Is Ladies' Day with Me*; *Rose of the World*; *Italian Street Song*; *Ah, Sweet Mystery of Life*; *I'm Falling in Love with Someone*; *Sweethearts*; *A Kiss in the Dark*; *Thine Alone*; *Indian Summer* and *Yesterthoughts*; also notable instrumentals *Badinage* and *March of the Toys*. Collaborated with lyricists Henry Blossom, Rida Johnson Young, Glen MacDonough, Harry B. Smith, Robert B. Smith, Buddy DeSylva, Gene Buck.

Formative years in Germany. Became virtuoso on cello. Featured soloist with concert orchestras. First cellist several years with Royal Court Orchestra of Stuttgart. Also composing. Wife Therese Forster, operatic soprano, signed by Metropolitan Opera of New York with Herbert to play in pit orchestra. Couple came to U.S. 1886. Miss Forster sang at Met, soon retired. Victor continued in pit orchestra, performed in concerts as cello soloist. Scores for early musicals. First success in THE SERENADE (1897), first song hit *Gypsy Love Song* in THE FORTUNE TELLER (1898). After several unsuccessful shows, hit in BABES IN TOYLAND (1903). Established as leading Broadway composer.

Early singing star in Herbert shows Alice Nielson, followed by Fritzi Scheff and Emma Trentini. 1894-8 Herbert bandmaster of 22nd Regiment Band, New York National Guard. Conductor of Pittsburgh Symphony Orchestra 1898-1904. Organized own orchestra 1904, at intervals for 20 years played concerts in New York and other cities. In 1914 led group that founded ASCAP. In 1917 began to contribute independent songs to shows as own shows began to fade in popularity. Active until died of heart attack 1924. In later years Herbert hit shows and scores became classics, often revived and performed by amateur and professional groups. Jeanette MacDonald and Nelson Eddy starred in two movies adapted from Herbert shows, NAUGHTY MARIETTA (1935) and SWEETHEARTS (1938). Former launched team, resulted in popular follow-up movies for years. Two early Herbert melodies given lyrics, became song hits: *Indian Summer* (1939) and *Yester-*

thoughts (1940). 1939 movie THE GREAT VICTOR HERBERT featured Allan Jones and Mary Martin performing Herbert songs, Walter Connolly portraying Herbert.

SONGS
(with related shows)

1894—PRINCE ANANIAS stage show (unsuccessful)

1895—THE WIZARD OF THE NILE stage show (Starlight, Star Bright; My Angeline; In Dreamland; Oriental March; There's One Thing a Wizard Can Do)

1896—THE GOLD BUG stage show (The Gold Bug March)

1897—THE SERENADE stage show (I Love Thee, I Adore Thee; In Our Quiet Cloister; Cupid and I; The Singing Lesson); THE IDOL'S EYE stage show (Pretty Isabella; I Just Dropped In; Fairy Tales; Cuban Song; Thou Art Guilty); orchestral piece: Badinage

1898—THE FORTUNE TELLER stage show (Gypsy Love Song; Romany Life; Serenades of All Nations; Here We Are a Gypsy Troupe)

1899—CYRANO DE BERGERAC stage show (Serenade; Waltz Song; Since I'm Not for Thee; Song of the Nose; The King's Musketeers); THE SINGING GIRL stage show (Love Is a Tyrant; The Siren of the Ballet; The Well Beloved; Song of the Danube; Chink, Chink); THE AMEER stage show (Cupid Will Guide Thee; Sweet Clarissa; The Armoured Knight; The Little Poster Maid; Fond Love, True Love)

1900—THE VICEROY stage show (Just for Today; That's My Idea of Love; 'Neath the Blue Neapolitan Skies; The Robin and the Rose; Hear Me)

1903—BABES IN TOYLAND stage show (Toyland; March of the Toys; I Can't Do the Sum; Go to Sleep, Slumber Deep); BABETTE stage show (Letters I Write All the Day; There Once Was an Owl; I'll Bribe the Stars)

1904—IT HAPPENED IN NORDLAND stage show (Absinthe Frappé; Bandan-

1093

na Land; Commandress-in-Chief; A Knot of Blue; Al Fresco)

1905—MISS DOLLY DOLLARS stage show (An American Heiress; A Woman Is Only a Woman but a Good Cigar Is a Smoke); WONDERLAND stage show (Love's Golden Day; The Nature Class; The Only One)

1906—MLLE. MODISTE stage show (Kiss Me Again; I Want What I Want When I Want It; The Time, the Place and the Girl; When the Cat's Away; The Mascot of the Troop); THE RED MILL stage show (Moonbeams; In Old New York; Every Day Is Ladies' Day with Me; Because You're You; I Want You to Marry Me; The Isle of Our Dreams; Whistle It); ABOUT TOWN stage show (A Little Class of One)

1907—DREAM CITY AND THE MAGIC KNIGHT stage show (I Don't Believe I'll Ever Be a Lady; In Vaudeville; Nancy, I Fancy You); THE TATTOOED MAN stage show (Boys Will Be Boys and Girls Will Be Girls; The Land of Dreams; Nobody Loves Me)

1908—ALGERIA stage show (Rose of the World; Love Is Like a Cigarette; Ask Her While the Band Is Playing; Twilight in Barakeesh); LITTLE NEMO stage show (Won't You Be My Valentine?; The Happy Land of Once-Upon-a-Time; In Happy Slumberland); THE PRIMA DONNA stage show (I'll Be Married to the Music of a Military Band; If You Were I and I Were You; A Soldier's Love; Espagnola)

1909—THE ROSE OF ALGERIA stage show (revised version of 1908's ALGERIA; same score plus new song: My Life, I Love Thee); OLD DUTCH stage show (I Want a Man to Love Me; Climb, Climb; You, Dearie)

1910—NAUGHTY MARIETTA stage show (Ah, Sweet Mystery of Life; I'm Falling in Love with Someone; Italian Street Song; Tramp! Tramp! Tramp!; Live for Today; 'Neath the Southern Moon; Naughty Marietta)

1911—THE DUCHESS stage show (Cupid,

Tell Me Why; The Land of Sultans' Dreams); THE ENCHANTRESS stage show (To the Land of My Own Romance; All Your Own Am I; Rose, Lucky Rose; They All Look Good When They're Far Away); WHEN SWEET SIXTEEN stage show (unsuccessful)

1912—THE LADY OF THE SLIPPER stage show (Bagdad; Drums of All Nations; A Little Girl at Home; Princess of Far-Away; Like a Real, Real Man)

1913—SWEETHEARTS stage show (Sweethearts; Pretty as a Picture; Every Lover Must Meet His Fate; The Angelus; The Cricket on the Hearth); THE MADCAP DUCHESS stage show (Love and I Are Playing; Goddess of Mine; The Dance, Young Man; Aurora Blushing Rosily)

1914—THE ONLY GIRL stage show (When You're Away; Tell It All Over Again; You're the Only Girl for Me; When You're Wearing the Ball and Chain); THE DEBUTANTE stage show (The Springtime of Life; All for the Sake of a Girl; The Golden Age; The Love of the Lorelei)

1915—PRINCESS PAT stage show (Neapolitan Love Song; Two Laughing Irish Eyes; All for You; Love is the Best of All)

1916—THE CENTURY GIRL stage show (The Century Girl; You Belong to Me)

1917—EILEEN stage show (Eileen Alanna Asthore; When Shall I Again See Ireland?; When Love Awakes; Thine Alone; The Irish Have a Great Day Tonight); HER REGIMENT stage show (Soldier Men; 'Twixt Love and Duty; Art Song); MISS 1917 stage show (The Society Farmerettes); ZIEGFELD FOLLIES OF 1917 stage show (Can't You Hear Your Country Calling?)

1919—THE VELVET LADY stage show (Spooky Ookum; Life and Love; Fair Honeymoon); Indian Summer (piano piece, revived 1939 as song)

1920—ANGEL FACE stage show (Angel Face; Someone Like You; I Might Be Your Once-in-a-While); ZIEG-FELD FOLLIES OF 1920 stage show (When the Right One Comes Along; The Love Boat); MY GOLD-EN GIRL stage show (My Golden Girl; I Want You; Darby and Joan; Ragtime Terpsichore; A Song without Many Words); THE GIRL IN THE SPOTLIGHT stage show (I Cannot Sleep without Dreaming of You; I Love the Ground You Walk On)

1921—ZIEGFELD FOLLIES OF 1921 stage show (Princess of My Dreams; The Legend of the Golden Tree)

1922—ORANGE BLOSSOMS stage show (A Kiss in the Dark; This Time It's Love; The Lonely Nest; A Dream of Orange Blossoms); ZIEGFELD FOLLIES OF 1922 stage show (Weaving My Dream)

1923—ZIEGFELD FOLLIES OF 1923 stage show (That Old Fashioned Garden of Mine; I'd Love to Waltz Through Life with You; Legend of the Drums)

1924—THE DREAM GIRL stage show (My Dream Girl; If Somebody Only Would Find Me; Bubble Song)

1930—MLLE. MODISTE movie (original stage score)

1934—BABES IN TOYLAND movie (original stage score)

1935—NAUGHTY MARIETTA movie (original stage score)

1938—SWEETHEARTS movie (original stage score)

1939—Indian Summer (old melody, lyrics added)

1940—Yesterthoughts (old melody, lyrics added)

1945—THE RED MILL stage show (revival of note; 531 performances)

RECORDS

VICTOR HERBERT (cello solos)
　Vi 64240 Angel's Whisper
　Vi 64297 Petite Valse
　Vi 64298 Scherzo (Op. 12, No. 2)

VICTOR HERBERT ORCHESTRA
　Vi 45052 Narcissus/Melody in F
　Vi 45054 Venetian Love Song/Minuet

Vi 45165 Humoresque/Kiss Me Again
Vi 45170 At Dawning/Waltzing Doll
Vi 60046 Spring Song
Vi 60050 The Rosary
Vi 60054 Yesterthoughts
Vi 60056 Venetian Love Song
Vi 60080 Babes in Toyland
Vi 60086 Al Fresco
Vi(12")55039 "Sweethearts" Selections/"Lady of the Slipper" Selections
Vi(12")55054 Babes in Toyland/March of the Toys//Naughty Marietta/Intermezzo
Vi(12")70048 March of the Toys
Vi(12")70056 Rose of Algeria

829. HERFURT, SKEETS　as ts cl vo (ARTHUR HERFURT)

Born May 28, 1911, Denver, Colo.

Capable saxman-vocalist with top bands in 30s and 40s, later in studios. Grew up in Denver, attended Colorado University. Dance jobs locally with Vic Schilling early 30s. With Smith Ballew 1934. Joined newly formed Dorsey Brothers band August 1934. Remained after break-up when Jimmy took over band fall 1935, remained about a year. Worked on west coast with George Stoll, Dave Rubinoff and Ray Noble. Joined Tommy Dorsey mid-1937, remained two years. With Alvino Rey late 1939 and early 40s. Military service, 1944-5. Active in studios on west coast late 40s into 70s. Four months with Benny Goodman late 1946-7. In early 50s with Frank DeVol on TV, also with Billy May. With Al Donahue on 1954 TV show, featured as comic. With Guy Lombardo as saxman-vocalist early 70s. Toured England 1974 with Warren Covington-Tommy Dorsey band.

RECORDS

DORSEY BROTHERS ORCHESTRA
　De 117 Annie's Cousin Fannie/Dr. Heckle and Mr. Jibe
　De 119 St. Louis Blues
　De 318 Anything Goes
　De 376 Dinah
　De 480 I'll Never Say "Never Again" Again
　De 515 I've Got Your Number
　De 516 Top Hat

De 519 My Very Good Friend the Milkman

TOMMY DORSEY
Vi 25832 Cowboy from Brooklyn
Vi 26012 Stop Beating Around the Mulberry Bush
Vi 26016 Copenhagen
Vi 26023 Chinatown, My Chinatown/ The Sheik of Araby (both CLAMBAKE SEVEN)
Vi 26030 Ya Got Me/There's No Place Like Your Arms
Vi 26062 Stompin' at the Stadium
Vi 26085 Washboard Blues
Vi 26163 Symphony in Riffs
Vi 26636 Hong Kong Blues

RAY MCKINLEY
De 1019 Love in the First Degree/New Orleans Parade
De 1020 Fingerwave/Shack in the Back

ALVINO REY
Bb 11331 Idaho
Bb 11573 The Major and the Minor

SKEETS HERFURT
Cap 1154 Saxophobia/Sax-O-Phun

LPs

DORSEY BROTHERS ORCHESTRA
Cor CP-27 The Fabulous Dorseys Play Dixieland Jazz (De RIs)

GLEN GRAY
Cap W-1022 Sounds of the Great Bands, Vol. 1

RAY MCKINLEY (one side)
De(10″)DL-5262 Dixieland Jazz Battle, Vol. 2 (De RIs)

BOB EBERLY and HELEN O'CONNELL
WB 1403 Recapturing the Excitement of the Jimmy Dorsey Era (recreations)

830. HERMAN, WOODY

cl as ss vo cm B

(WOODROW CHARLES HERMAN)

Born May 16, 1913, Milwaukee, Wis.

Top bandleader from 1936 into 70s. Capable musician and vocalist, excellent front man and organizer. Clarinetist in blues and swing; warm ballad style on alto sax. Early band featured blues, later straight swing. 1944 "Herman Herd" pioneered big band progressive jazz. Despite decline of big bands in later years Herman continued band almost constantly, featured jazz, held commercialism to minimum. Personnel changed but bands maintained standards, kept in step with trends in jazz and popular music. Debuted in vaudeville at early age, billed as The Boy Wonder of the Clarinet; also song-and-dance routine. Local dance bands, joined Tom Gerun band late 1929, remained over two years, mostly on west coast. With Harry Sosnik and Gus Arnheim 1932-3. With great Isham Jones band 1934-6 as sideman-vocalist. When Jones retired briefly in 1936, Herman formed co-op band with several Jones sidemen, opened in New York October 1936. Joe Bishop of Jones band chief arranger, also played flugelhorn. Other arrangers Gordon Jenkins, Jiggs Noble, Deane Kincaide. Early key sidemen Saxie Mansfield (ts), Neal Reid (tb), Frank Carlson (d), Tommy Linehan (p). Blues-styled numbers featured; orchestra billed The Band That Plays the Blues. Rough early years, but 1939 hit *Woodchopper's Ball* established band, became all-time jazz standard associated with Herman. Another 1939 jazz hit *Blues on Parade*. Band's first theme *Blue Prelude*, later *Blue Evening*, then *Blue Flame*. Dixieland combo within band called Woodchoppers. In early years Herman handled most vocals. Female singers 1939-42 Mary Ann McCall, Carol Kay, Muriel Lane. In early 40s band changed to more swing, featured more ballads and jazz tenor saxists Herbie Haymer and Vido Musso. Dave Matthews important arranger. Herman used female jazz stars Billie Rogers (t vo) and Marge Hyams (vb).

World War II caused personnel changes. By 1944 band leading exponent of emerging progressive jazz style, caused sensation. Dubbed The Herman Herd, later The First Herd, featured exciting new soloists Bill Harris (tb), Flip Phillips (ts), Pete and Conte Candoli (t), Chubby Jackson (b), with veteran Dave Tough (d) great asset. Modern arrangements mostly by pianist Ralph Burns and trumpeter Neal Hefti, later by trumpeter Shorty

Rogers. Band famous for jazz numbers like *Bijou, Apple Honey, Northwest Passage, Wild Root*. 1945 record hit *Happiness Is a Just Thing Called Joe* sung by Frances Wayne, coupled with jazz novelty *Caldonia* sung by Herman. Band played Carnegie Hall concert March 1946 performing Stravinsky's *Ebony Concerto*, written especially for band. Group broke up late 1946. Herman formed another band late 1947-9 known as The Second Herd. 1948 jazz hit *Four Brothers* featured new reed section sound, great saxmen Stan Getz, Zoot Sims, Herbie Steward, Serge Chaloff. Late 1949-early 50 Herman led combo. Mid-1950 led another big band known as The Third Herd. European tour 1954. During 1955-9 personnel and size changed frequently; some bands organized for special engagements. Often used young but capable musicians. In late 50s and 60s Nat Pierce frequently Herman pianist, arranger and aide. Tenor sax star Sal Nistico featured. In 60s band played here and abroad, recorded regularly. Kept pace with new 60s and early 70s style with young mod musicians and jazz-rock-soul-folk style, contemporary tunes. Herman still sang jazz and novelty numbers, played soprano sax frequently. Theme song still *Blue Flame*.

Band in movies WHAT'S COOKIN'? (1942), WINTERTIME (1943), SENSATIONS OF 1945 (1944), EARL CARROLL'S VANITIES (1945), HIT PARADE OF 1947 and NEW ORLEANS (1947). Herman composer or co-composer of jazz numbers *Jukin', Herman at the Sherman, Big Morning, Celestial Express, Wild Root, Blues on Parade, Bessie's Blues, Music by the Moon, Apple Honey, Buck Dance, Early Autumn, Cousin to Chris, Blue Ink, Choppin' Wood, River Bed Blues, Your Father's Mustache, Northwest Passage, Goosey Gander, Blowin' Up a Storm* and pop song *A Kiss Goodnight*. Herman and Joe Bishop composed famous *Woodchopper's Ball*. Herman solos always integral part of bands. Though no progressive, fit with progressive bands because of Herman's rapport with advanced musicians. Long popular with sidemen as well as music lovers. Active playing colleges in 70s.

RECORDS

TOM GERUN (as vocalist)
  Br 6364 Lonesome Me
ISHAM JONES (as vocalist)
  De 605 Thunder Over Paradise/If I Should Lose You
  De 704 No Greater Love/Life Begins When You're in Love
  De 713 The Day I Let You Get Away
ISHAM JONES' JUNIORS
  De 834 Fan It/Nola
SWANEE SWINGERS
  De 1002 Take It Easy/Slappin' the Bass
WOODY HERMAN
  De 1064 Old-Fashioned Swing/Now That Summer Is Gone
  De 1535 You're a Sweetheart/My Fine-Feathered Friend
  De 1801 Twin City Blues/Laughing Boy Blues
  De 1900 Lullaby in Rhythm/Don't Wake Up My Heart
  De 2250 Indian Boogie Woogie/(theme) Blue Evening
  De 2440 Woodchopper's Ball/Big-Wig in the Wigwam
  De 2582 Casbah Blues/Farewell Blues
  De 2933 Blues on Parade/Love's Got Me Down Again
  De 2993 East Side Kick/On the Isle of May
  De 3017 (theme) Blue Prelude/The Sky Fell Down
  De 3140 Cousin to Chris/Fine and Dandy
  De 3272 Jukin'/Herman at the Sherman
  De 3436 The Golden Wedding/Five O'clock Whistle
  De 3643 (theme) Blue Flame/Fur Trappers' Ball
  De 3761 South/Fan It (both WOODCHOPPERS)
  De 3972 Bishop's Blues/Woodsheddin' with Woody
  De 4030 Blues in the Night/This Time the Dream's on Me
  De 4113 Someone's Rocking My Dream Boat/Rose O'Day
  De 4353 Elise/Yardbird Shuffle (both FOUR CHIPS quartet)
  De 18346 Amen/Deliver Me to Tennessee

De 18544 Down Under/Ten Day Fur-
lough
De 18577 The Music Stopped/I
Couldn't Sleep a Wink Last Night
Co 36789 Happiness Is Just a Thing
Called Joe/Caldonia
Co 36803 Apple Honey/Out of This
World
Co 36835 Northwest Passage/June
Comes Around Every Year
Co 36861 Bijou/Put That Ring on My
Finger
Co 36949 Wild Root/Atlanta, G.A.
Co 38213 Keen and Peachy/I've Got
News for You
Co 38304 Four Brothers/No Time
Co 38369 Everywhere/The Goof and I
Cap 57-616 Early Autumn/Keeper of
the Flame
Cap 837 Not Really the Blues/Detour
Ahead
Mars 200 Stompin' at the Savoy
Mars 600 Buck Dance/A Fool in Love
Mars 900 Moten Stomp/Beau Jazz

LPs

WOODY HERMAN
Black Jack LP-3002 (1937-44 tran-
scriptions, airchecks, V-Discs)
De DL-8133 Woodchopper's Ball (De
RIs)
De DL-9229 The Turning Point
(1943-4 De RIs)
Ha HL-7013 Bijou (Co RIs)
Co C3L25(3-LP set) Thundering Herds
(Co RIs)
Co(10″)CL-6049 Dance Parade (1944-
5 Co RIs)
MGM(10″)E-159 At Carnegie Hall,
1946, Vol. II
MGM(10″)E-192 And the Third Herd
Cap T-324 (1948-50 RIs)
Cap T-748 Jackpot! (small combo)
Mars(10″)1 (Mars RIs)
Everest SDBR-1003 The Herd Rides
Again ... In Stereo
Cadet 819 Light My Fire

830A. HERRMANN, BERNARD
cm ar p B

Born 1911, New York, N.Y.

Composer-arranger of movie background
music 1941 into 70s. Studied at NYU,
Juilliard. Led chamber music group as
youth. Joined CBS 1933 as composer-
conductor for dramatic and documentary
radio shows. Worked on many Orson
Welles shows late 30s. Hollywood career
began with scoring of important Welles
films CITIZEN KANE (1941), THE MAGNIF-
ICENT AMBERSONS (1942). In 40s wrote
sparingly for movies, returned often to
New York to conduct for radio and
concerts. Mostly in Hollywood 50s and
60s, scored many important movies. Excellent scores for Alfred Hitchcock thrill-
ers, notably VERTIGO (1958) and PSYCHO
(1960). Several movie themes lengthened
or combined to form suites *Welles Raises
Kane, The Devil and Daniel Webster.*
Other notable works WUTHERING HEIGHTS
(opera), *Piano Concerto* (from movie
HANGOVER SQUARE).

MOVIES
*(as composer and probable arranger-con-
ductor of background music; partial listing)*

1941—CITIZEN KANE; ALL THAT MONEY
CAN BUY
1942—THE MAGNIFICENT AMBERSONS
1944—JANE EYRE
1945—HANGOVER SQUARE
1946—ANNA AND THE KING OF SIAM
1947—THE GHOST AND MRS. MUIR
1951—ON DANGEROUS GROUND; THE DAY
THE EARTH STOOD STILL
1952—THE SNOWS OF KILIMANJARO
1953—BENEATH THE 12-MILE REEF; KING
OF THE KHYBER RIFLES
1954—GARDEN OF EVIL; THE EGYPTIAN
1955—THE KENTUCKIAN; THE TROUBLE
WITH HARRY
1956—THE MAN WHO KNEW TOO MUCH;
THE MAN IN THE GRAY FLANNEL
SUIT; THE WRONG MAN
1957—A HATFUL OF RAIN
1958—VERTIGO; THE NAKED AND THE
DEAD
1959—NORTH BY NORTHWEST; JOURNEY
TO THE CENTER OF THE EARTH
1960—PSYCHO; THE THREE WORLDS OF
GULLIVER
1962—TENDER IS THE NIGHT; CAPE FEAR
1963—JASON AND THE ARGONAUTS
1964—MARNIE
1965—JOY IN THE MORNING
1966—FAHRENHEIT 451
1968—THE BRIDE WORE BLACK

1969—OBSESSIONS; TWISTED NERVE
1970—THE BATTLE OF NERETVA
1971—THE NIGHT DIGGER

RECORDS
(all LPs)

(movie soundtracks; as composer and probable arranger-conductor)

Lon SP-44126 (themes from various movies)

Lon SP-44144 (themes from various movies)

De DL-9014 THE EGYPTIAN (partial score, with composer Alfred Newman; conducted by Newman)

Colpix 414 THE THREE WORLDS OF GULLIVER

Mer MG-20384 VERTIGO

831. HERTH, MILT   o p B
Died June 18, 1969

Organist popular in 30s and 40s; lightly swinging style with commercial appeal. As teenager toured with medicine show as pianist. Learned organ, at 19 theatre job in home town Kenosha, Wis. Later played theatre chain through midwest. Musical director awhile on radio station in Gary, Ind. In 1937 played Hollywood Observer radio show, joined Al Pearce show. Own NBC show and other radio shows beginning 1938. Added pianist Willie "The Lion" Smith and drummer O'Neill Spencer to form Milt Herth Trio. Group's recordings well received. Guitarist Teddy Bunn added for a period; other personnel changes after 1938. Theme *Churchmouse on a Spree.* Occasional vocals by Spencer. Herth's most popular record probably *The Dipsy Doodle.* Active in 40s and 50s, recorded occasionally.

RECORDS
MILT HERTH

De 911 Stompin' at the Savoy/The Madam Swings It

De 1344 Basin Street Blues/12th Street Rag

De 1445 Satan Takes a Holiday/Somebody Loves Me

De 1478 Josephine/After I Say I'm Sorry

De 1533 The Dipsy Doodle/That's a-Plenty

De 1612 Bei Mir Bist du Schon/The Big Dipper

De 1727 Sissy/Jazz Me Blues

De 1736 The Campbells Are Swinging/Popcorn Man

De 1816 The Toy Trumpet/Three Blind Mice

De 2046 The Lambeth Walk/Rockin' in Rhythm

De 2227 Jump Jump's Here/Goblins in the Steeple

De 2336 Annabelle/The Whistler and His Dog

De 2572 In an 18th Century Drawing Room/The Shoemaker's Holiday

De 2818 Scatter-brain/(theme) Churchmouse on a Spree

De 3158 Honky Tonk Train Blues/The Girl with the Light Blue Hair

De 3284 Down South/Dardanella

De 3561 Huckleberry Duck/Worried Mind

De 3664 Down Home Rag/Hoity Hoity

De 4285 Pennsylvania Polka/Jersey Bounce

Cor 60079 Ain't She Sweet/Ting-a-Ling

Cor 60096 The Last Mile Home/Pretty Girl

Cor 60118 Loch Lomond / Down Where the Wurzburger Flows

MILT HERTH with RUSS MORGAN ORCHESTRA

De 24319 Bye Bye Blackbird/I'm Looking Over a Four-Leaf Clover

831A. HERZ, RALPH   VO
Born March 25, 1878, Paris, France
Died July 12, 1921, Atlantic City, N.J.

Comedian-singer of many Broadway musicals. Co-starred with wife Lulu Glaser in early shows MISS DOLLY DOLLARS (1905), LOLA FROM BERLIN (1907).

BROADWAY MUSICALS

1905—MISS DOLLY DOLLARS
1907—LOLA FROM BERLIN; THE WHITE HEN
1908—THE SOUL KISS
1910—MADAME SHERRY
1911—DR. DELUXE
1912—THE CHARITY GIRL
1914—MADAME MOSELLE (unsuccessful); THE WHIRL OF THE WORLD

1915—HANDS UP
1916—RUGGLES OF RED GAP
1917—GOOD NIGHT, PAUL
1919—MONTE CRISTO, JR.
1920—ALWAYS YOU

832. HEYMAN, ED   lyr
Born March 14, 1907, New York, N.Y.

Important lyricist of 30s and 40s. Scores for Broadway shows THROUGH THE YEARS (1932) and PARDON OUR FRENCH (1950), songs for other shows and movies. Best-known songs *Body and Soul*; *Out of Nowhere*; *My Silent Love*; *I Cover the Waterfront*; *You're Mine, You*; *I Wanna Be Loved*; *You Oughta Be in Pictures*; *Blame It on My Youth*; *Easy Come, Easy Go*; *Boo-Hoo*; *Love and Learn*; *They Say*; *Love Letters*; *Bluebird of Happiness*; *When I Fall in Love*. Collaborators included composers Johnny Green, Vincent Youmans, Oscar Levant, Victor Young, Dana Suesse, Nacio Herb Brown, Morton Gould, Rudolf Friml, Sigmund Romberg, Ray Henderson, Jimmy Van Heusen, Arthur Schwartz. Grew up in Chicago. Attended University of Michigan, wrote college musicals. First hit *Body and Soul* (1930) in collaboration with other lyricists and composer Johnny Green. Numerous hits during 30s. Wrote for productions at Radio City Music Hall in New York. Military service, World War II; wrote production AT YOUR SERVICE. Produced shows in Mexico City 1954-61 starring The Players, English-speaking theatre group.

SONGS
(with related shows)

1929—THE VAGABOND LOVER movie (I'll Be Reminded of You)
1930—THREE'S A CROWD stage show (Body and Soul)
1931—Ho Hum; I Don't Want Love; Out of Nowhere
1932—THROUGH THE YEARS stage show (Through the Years; Drums in My Heart; Kinda Like You; You're Everywhere); EARL CARROLL'S VANITIES OF 1932 stage show (My Darling; Forsaken Again); My Silent Love; Rain, Rain, Go Away

1933—MURDER AT THE VANITIES stage show (Me for You Forever; Weep No More My Baby); I Cover the Waterfront; I Wanna Be Loved; You're Mine, You; Two Buck Tim from Timbuctoo; This Is Romance; A Moonlight Memory
1934—CAVIAR stage show (unsuccessful); ZIEGFELD FOLLIES OF 1934 stage show (The House Is Haunted; You Oughta Be in Pictures); SHE LOVES ME NOT movie (After All You're All I'm After); Blame It on My Youth; Easy Come, Easy Go
1935—CURLY TOP movie (When I Grow Up); SWEET SURRENDER movie (see 1935 movie listings)
1936—ANYTHING GOES movie (Moonburn); Darling, Not Without You; Mutiny in the Parlor; For Sentimental Reasons; The State of My Heart
1937—THAT GIRL FROM PARIS movie (Love and Learn; Seal It with a Kiss; The Call to Arms; Moon Face; My Nephew from Nice); Boo-Hoo; Alibi Baby; To Love You and to Lose You; It's High Time I Got the Lowdown on You
1938—They Say; Have You Forgotten So Soon?
1939—Melancholy Lullaby; Heart of Mine; My Love for You
1940—The Sky Fell Down
1942—Fun to Be Free
1943—SO PROUDLY WE HAIL movie (Loved One)
1945—DELIGHTFULLY DANGEROUS movie I'm Only Teasin', In a Shower of Stars; Through Your Eyes to Your Heart
1946—LOVE LETTERS movie (title song); STRANGE LOVE OF MARTHA IVERS movie (Strange Love); THE SEARCHING WIND movie (title song)
1947—NORTHWEST OUTPOST movie (Nearer and Dearer; others)
1948—THE KISSING BANDIT movie (Senorita; If I Steal a Kiss; What's Wrong with Me?); ON AN ISLAND WITH YOU movie (On an Island with You; Takin' Miss Mary to the Ball); Bluebird of Happiness

1950—PARDON OUR FRENCH stage show (I'm Gonna Make a Fool Out of April; A Face in the Crowd; There's No Man Like a Snowman; I Oughta Know More About You)

1952—ONE-MINUTE TO ZERO movie (When I Fall in Love)

1955—Blue Star (theme of TV show Medic)

833. HEYWOOD, EDDIE, JR.

p ar cm B

Born December 4, 1915, Atlanta, Ga.

Jazz pianist who rose to fame mid-40s with record *Begin the Beguine*. Also known for popular composition *Canadian Sunset* 1956. Simple jazz style; unusual and easily identifiable rhythmic approach interpolated bass notes unexpectedly. Pianist father worked with blues singers in 20s and 30s. Piano lessons from father; at 14 theatre job in Atlanta. With father's band and others locally. Toured with bands 1932-5. With Clarence Love band mid-30s in Kansas City. Led Dallas combo c. 1937-9. With Benny Carter 1939-40. Later 1940 with Zutty Singleton, accompanied Judy Holliday and others early 40s at New York's Village Vanguard. Formed sextet 1943, later switched to trio. Clicked with *Begin the Beguine* 1944, followed with well-received records. Led combo in New York clubs, moved to California. In movies THE DARK CORNER and HIGH SCHOOL KIDS in 1946. Retired from music late 40s because of partial paralysis of hands. Exercised, practiced, finally able to resume work 1950. Played clubs 50s and 60s, recorded occasionally. Compositions include *Soft Summer Breeze, Land of Dreams* and *I'm Saving Myself for You*, big 1956 hit *Canadian Sunset*, serious work *Martha's Vineyard Suite*. Played New York 1972.

RECORDS

BARNEY BIGARD
Si 28114 Step Steps Up/Step Steps Down
Si 28116 Tea for Two/Moonglow

SID CATLETT
Delta D-10-3-4 Blue Skies/Thermo Dynamics
Regis 500 Blues in Room 920/Sweet Georgia Brown

ED HALL
CMS 550 The Man I Love/Coquette
CMS(12″)1512 Downtown Cafe Boogie/Uptown Cafe Boogie

COLEMAN HAWKINS
Si 28104 Crazy Rhythm/Get Happy
Si(12″)90001 Sweet Lorraine/The Man I Love

BILLIE HOLIDAY
OK 6134 Let's Do It/Georgia on My Mind
OK 6214 Romance in the Dark/All of Me
OK 6270 God Bless the Child/Solitude
CMS 585 My Old Flame/I'm Yours

REX STEWART
Cap 10035 Dutch Treat/Rexercise

ELLA FITZGERALD with EDDIE HEYWOOD ORCHESTRA
De 23844 Guilty/Sentimental Journey

EDDIE HEYWOOD
CMS(12″)1514 Begin the Beguine/I Cover the Waterfront
CMS 554 'Tain't Me/Save Your Sorrow
CMS 578 Just You, Just Me/'Deed I Do
Si(12″)40001 Them There Eyes/Penthouse Serenade
Si(12″)40002 How High the Moon/Sarcastic Lady
De 23398 Begin the Beguine/Lover Man
De 23427 Blue Lou/Please Don't Talk About Me When I'm Gone
De 23534 The Man I Love/On the Sunny Side of the Street
De 23811 On the Alamo/Temptation
De 23812 Laura/It's Only a Paper Moon
Vi 20-2664 The Continental / Heywood's Boogie
Vi 20-2981 The Moon Was Yellow/The Way You Look Tonight
VD(12″)324 Begin the Beguine
Co 39316 Without a Song/A Pretty Girl Is Like a Melody
Co 39319 Try a Little Tenderness/The Birth of the Blues

LPs

EDDIE HEYWOOD
De DL-8270 Swing Low Sweet Heywood (De RIs)
Cor CRL-57095 Featuring Eddie Heywood
EmArcy MG-36042 Eddie Heywood
Epic LN-3327 Eddie Heywood at Twilight
Lib LRP-3279 Manhattan Beat
Mer MG-20445 Breezin' Along with the Breeze
CMS(10″)FL-20007 His Piano and Orchestra (CMS RIs)
MGM(10″)E-135 It's Easy to Remember

834. HIBBLER, AL   vo

Born August 16, 1915, Little Rock, Ark.

Baritone popular in 40s and 50s; rose to fame with Duke Ellington band. Deep tone, phrasing and inflections distinctive, readily identifiable. Born blind, studied voice at Conservatory for the Blind in Little Rock. Sang with local bands, also in Texas. Late 1942 with Jay McShann band. Developed with Ellington 1943-51. Left Ellington late 1951 for career as single. Record hit *Unchained Melody* 1955. On TV occasionally in 50s. Active into 60s. Returned for occasional festivals and TV shows in 70s.

RECORDS

JAY MCSHANN
De 4418 Get Me on Your Mind
DUKE ELLINGTON
Mus 484 It Shouldn't Happen to a Dream
Vi 20-1618 Don't You Know I Care?
Vi 20-1799 I'm Just a Lucky So and So
Co 38363 Do Nothin' Till You Hear from Me
Co 38464 Don't Get Around Much Anymore
Co 38702 Good Woman Blues
Co 38789 The World Is Waiting for the Sunrise
BILLY STRAYHORN
Sunrise 2002 Solitude
AL HIBBLER with COUNT BASIE ORCHESTRA
Mer 89028 Goin' to Chicago/Sent for You Yesterday

AL HIBBLER with JOHNNY HODGES ORCHESTRA
Mer 89011 Believe It, Beloved/Please
AL HIBBLER
Alad 155 S'posin'
Atl 911 Song of the Wanderer/Danny Boy
Sunrise 503 Poor Butterfly/Tonight I Shall Sleep
De 29441 Unchained Melody/Daybreak
De 29660 He/Breeze
De 29789 Let's Try Again/11th Hour Melody
Mer 89046 It Must Be True/No Greater Love

LPs

AL HIBBLER
De DL-8328 Starring Al Hibbler
De DL-8420 Here's Hibbler
De DL-8697 Torchy and Blue
De DL-78862 Remembers Big Songs
Atl 1251 After the Lights Go Down Low
Norg(10″)4 Al Hibbler Favorites
Reprise R-2005 Sings the Blues
Argo 601 Melodies by Al Hibbler
Grand Prix K-407 (one side) Big Boy Blues

835. HICKMAN, ART   d cm B

Born June 13, 1886, Oakland, Calif.
Died January 16, 1930, San Francisco, Calif.

Early bandleader, pioneer in dance music. Helped establish instrumentation, voicing, style and rhythm of early dance bands. Formed combo 1915. Early engagement at San Francisco's St. Francis Hotel: base off and on for years. Enlarged band; to New York 1919. Composed theme *Rose Room*; became a standard. Band in Broadway musical ZIEGFELD FOLLIES OF 1920. In late 1920 and early 1921 Hickman worked and recorded in England with jazz combo. In 20s big band recorded and toured. In mid-20s on California radio. Ill health late 20s ended career. Other compositions included *Hold Me*; *Dry Your Tears*; *Without You*; *Come Back to Georgia*; *Love Moon*; *June, I Love No One but You*; *Dream of Me*; *My Midnight Frolic Girl.*

RECORDS

ART HICKMAN'S NEW YORK LONDON FIVE
HMV(E) 1200 Jicky/When My Baby Smiles at Me
HMV(E) 1201 Gyptia/Thoughts
HMV(E) 1217 Now and Then/On the Streets of Cairo

ART HICKMAN ORCHESTRA
Co A-2812 Peggy/Tell Me Why
Co A-2858 (theme) Rose Room/Cairo
Co A-2899 Dance It Again with Me/ Hold Me
Co A-2955 Song of the Orient/The Love Nest
Co A-2972 Tell Me, Little Gypsy
Co A-2982 In Old Manila/Cuban Moon
Co A-3322 Avalon/The Japanese Sandman
A-3391 Nestle in Your Daddy's Arms/I Spoiled You
Co A-3409 Dream of Me/Near Me
Co A-3440 Honey Lou/Honeymoon Home
Vi 19379 Mandalay
Vi 19399 Patsy/G'wan with It
Vi 19732 Little Devil/Ships That Pass in the Night
Vi 20633 Roses of Remembrance/The Winding Trail
Vi 20687 Hold Me in Your Arms Again/Down the Lane with You Again
Vi 20688 I'll Just Go Along
Vi 21392 Dream House/Maybe You'll Be the One Who'll Be the One to Care

836. HIGGINBOTHAM, J. C.   tb B

Born May 11, 1906, Atlanta, Ga.
Died May 26, 1973, New York, N.Y.

Jazz trombonist. Enjoyed greatest popularity late 30s and early 40s. Bold gut-bucket style, strong tone; influenced Bill Harris, Eddie Bert. To Cincinnati as teenager, worked there mid-20s. Late 1925-28 toured, played in Buffalo and New York. Late 1928 joined Luis Russell for first big job, remained over two years except for two intervals with Chick Webb. Joined Fletcher Henderson mid-1931, remained over two years. With Benny Carter late 1933. With Mills Blue Rhythm Band 1934-6. With Fletcher Henderson early 1937. Joined Louis Armstrong mid-1937 (in reality old Luis Russell band), remained till late 1940. Joined Red Allen sextet late 1940 until 1947, worked mostly in New York. In late 40s and early 50s mostly in Boston with groups; led band. In mid-50s to New York. Many jobs at Metropole jazz spot; periods again with Allen. In 60s mostly led band, toured abroad several times. Active into 70s. During career much recording with many jazz greats.

RECORDS

FLETCHER HENDERSON
OK 41565 New King Porter Stomp
Co 2732-D Underneath the Harlem Moon/Honeysuckle Rose

HENRY ALLEN, JR. (LUIS RUSSELL)
Vi 38073 It Should Be You/Biff'ly Blues
Vi 38080 Feeling Drowsy/Swing Out

BENNY CARTER
OK 41567 Blue Lou
Co 2898-D Symphony in Riffs

METRONOME ALL-STAR BAND
Vi 27314 Bugle Call Rag/One O'clock Jump
Co 36499 Royal Flush/I Got Rhythm
(ALL-STAR LEADERS)

JACK PURVIS
OK 8782 Poor Richard/Down Georgia Way

COLEMAN HAWKINS
OK 41566 Jamaica Shout/Heart Break Blues

CHOCOLATE DANDIES
OK 8728 That's How I Feel Today/Six or Seven Times

JAMES P. JOHNSON
Vo 4768 Harlem Woogie/After To-night

JELLY ROLL MORTON
Vi 23402 Sweet Peter/Jersey Joe
Vi 23424 Mississippi Mildred

LUIS RUSSELL
Br 80038 Saratoga Drag/Case on Dawn (*sic*; correct title: Ease on Down)

LOUIS ARMSTRONG
De 1560 On the Sunny Side of the Street/Once in Awhile
De 1636 I Double Dare You/Satchel Mouth Swing

De 1842 Something Tells Me
De 2615 Confessin'
De 2934 You're a Lucky Guy

SIDNEY BECHET
Vi 27386 Baby, Won't You Please Come Home?/Coal Black Shine

RED ALLEN
OK 6281 Ol' Man River/K. K. Boogie
OK 6357 Indiana / A Sheridan "Square"
Vi 20-1808 Get the Mop/Buzz Me
Vi 20-1813 Drink Hearty/The Crawl

J. C. HIGGINBOTHAM
OK 8772 Give Me Your Telephone Number/Higginbotham Blues
BN 501 Weary Land Blues
HRS 1013 Dutch Treat/A Penny for Your Thoughts

LPs

J. C. HIGGINBOTHAM
Cable KL-126601 Higgy Comes Home (1966)
Jazzology 28 (1968)

LUIS RUSSELL
Pa(E) PMC-7025 (OK RIs)

TINY GRIMES
Pres 7144 Callin' the Blues

COLEMAN HAWKINS
Vi LJM-1017 The Hawk in Flight (Bb, Vi RIs)

MEZZ MEZZROW
"X"(10")LVA-3015 Swing Session (Vi RIs)

FLETCHER HENDERSON
"X"(10")LVA-3013 Connie's Inn Orchestra (Vi RIs)

FLETCHER HENDERSON ALL-STARS
Jazztone J-1285 The Big Reunion

RED ALLEN
Vi LPM-1509 Ride, Red, Ride in Hi-Fi

837. HILDEGARDE vo p
(HILDEGARDE LORETTA SELL)

Born c. 1906, Adell, Wis.

Singer-pianist, night club and radio entertainer popular in 40s. Grew up in Milwaukee. Pianist in silent movie theatre. Toured in vaudeville in large male orchestra, then in Grand Quartette (or Jerry & Her Baby Grands). Toured as accompanist for various acts; with stock company awhile. Brief period in Gus Edwards

troupe, sang Dutch songs and dressed as immigrant. About 1933-6 worked in London cabarets and clubs, on radio. Late 1936 guest appearances on U.S. radio. On Ripley's Believe It or Not show 1939. Club and hotel work; known for smart evening gowns, arm-length gloves, dainty handkerchiefs. Mid-1943 own radio show Beat the Band, 1944-6 Raleigh Room supper club radio show. Many engagements at New York's Plaza, Savoy-Plaza, Pierre hotels. Top clubs in other cities. Peak popularity mid-40s. Theme *Darling, Je Vous Aime Beaucoup* written by manager Anna Sosenko 1935. Successful 1948 European tour. Continued performing in U.S. and abroad during 50s but less prominent.

RECORDS

HILDEGARDE with CARROLL GIBBONS ORCHESTRA
Co 258-M (theme) Darling, Je Vous Aime Beaucoup/For Me, For You

HILDEGARDE with GUY LOMBARDO ORCHESTRA
De 23550 Sweet Rosie O'Grady/Sidewalks of New York

HILDEGARDE
Co 270-M Goodnight My Love/I Wanna Go to the Zoo
De 23099 Dance, Little Lady/Someday I'll Find You
De 23100 Zigeuner/I'll Follow My Secret Heart
De 23101 A Room with a View/I'll See You Again
De 23133 Thou Swell/My Heart Stood Still
De 23135 Isn't It Romantic/With a Song in My Heart
De 23183 Why Do I Love You?/The Last Time I Saw Paris
De 23219 You Will Remember Vienna/A Little Cafe Down the Street
De 23297 Suddenly It's Spring/Leave Us Face It
De 23348 Lili Marlene/My Heart Sings
De 23378 Who Are We to Say?/Ev'ry Time We Say Goodbye
De 23544 I'll Be Yours/I'm in the Mood for Love

De 23756 I'll Close My Eyes/There's No Holding Me
De 23760 And So to Bed/I Haven't Got a Worry in the World
De 24628 It's a Big Wide Wonderful World/Oh, My Darling
De album 149 (78s) Vernon Duke Songs

LPs
HILDEGARDE
De DL-8656
Seeco CELP-400 Hildegarde

838. HILL, BERTHA "CHIPPIE" vo
Born c. 1900-5, Charleston, S.C.
Died May 7, 1950, New York, N.Y., struck by auto

One of best early blues singers, but only modest success. Grew up in New York. At 14 began singing in clubs there, later worked in Chicago. Travelled south with singer Ma Rainey's shows, later toured as single. Began recording 1925; output modest. Pianist Richard M. Jones frequent accompanist on records. In later 20s played Chicago. During 30s out of show business at intervals. Sang at Chicago's Club DeLisa many years, left there 1942. Career revived 1946 on radio show This Is Jazz; records and clubs in New York. At Paris Jazz Festival 1948. 1949-50 worked clubs in Chicago and, mostly at Ryan's, in New York. Active till tragic accident.

RECORDS
ALL-STAR STOMPERS
Ci 1024 Baby, Won't You Please Come Home?
SCRAPPER BLACKWELL
Vo 1276 Non-Skid Tread
BERTHA "CHIPPIE" HILL
OK 8273 Low Land Blues/Kid Man Blues
OK 8312 Georgia Man/Trouble in Mind
OK 8339 Lonesome, All Alone and Blue
OK 8367 Leavenworth Blues/Panama Limited Blues
OK 8420 Pleadin' for the Blues/Pratt City Blues
OK 8437 Street Walker Blues/Mess, Katie, Mess
OK 8453 Lovesick Blues/Lonesome Weary Blues
OK 8473 Do Dirty Blues/Sport Model Mama
Vo 1224 Weary Money Blues/Christmas Man Blues
Vo 1248 Trouble in Mind/Hangman Blues
Vo 1264 Some Cold Rainy Day/Hard Time Blues
Vo 1406 Pratt City Blues/I Ain't Gonna Do It No More
Ci 1003 Trouble in Mind/How Long Blues
Ci 1004 Careless Love/Charleston Blues
Ci 1013 Around the Clock Blues/Black Market Blues
Ci 1067 Jailhouse Blues/Mistreatin' Mr. Dupree

839. HILL, BILLY   cm lyr p v B
Born July 14, 1899, Boston, Mass.
Died December 24, 1940, Boston, Mass.

Composer of many popular songs of 30s. First renown from big hit *The Last Round-up* 1933. Many songs western or nostalgic in flavor. Other leading songs *Wagon Wheels, The Old Spinning Wheel, The Oregon Trail, Lights Out, Empty Saddles, The Glory of Love, In the Chapel in the Moonlight*. Wrote music and lyrics for most songs. On others Peter DeRose chief collaborator on music and lyrics. As youth travelled through west, worked as cowboy and assistant to surveyors. Played violin and piano in dance halls in west, supposedly led first dance band in Salt Lake City. Began composing in New York early 30s. Sold rights to some early songs for a few dollars, received no recognition as composer.

SONGS
(with related shows)
1933—The Last Round-up; Cabin in the Pines; Louisville Lady; The Old Spinning Wheel
1934—ZIEGFELD FOLLIES OF 1934 stage show (Wagon Wheels; The Last Round-up); Night on the Desert; Rain
1935—The Oregon Trail; Alone at a Table for Two; Lights Out; Put on an

Old Pair of Shoes; When Love
Knocks at Your Heart
1936—RHYTHM ON THE RANGE movie
(Empty Saddles); The Glory of
Love; The Scene Changes; In the
Chapel in the Moonlight
1937—The Miller's Daughter Marianne;
Timber; On a Little Dream
Ranch; Till the Clock Strikes
Three
1938—All Ashore; So Little Time; When
Twilight Comes
1940—Call of the Canyon; On a Little
Street in Singapore

840. HILL, TEDDY   as ts cl B

*Born December 7, 1906, Birmingham,
Ala.*

Leader of hard-swinging 30s band, produced outstanding recordings. Band had
rough edges but good arrangements, spirited performances. After high school Hill
led band backing vaudeville show on
tour, then disbanded. Began working in
New York 1927. With Luis Russell 1928-
30. 1931-3 in pit band at New York's
Lafayette Theatre. Organized band 1934,
played mostly at Harlem's Savoy Ballroom. Began recording early 1935. Personnel at times included jazzmen Chu
Berry, Roy Eldridge, Bill Coleman, Dicky
Wells, Russell Procope, Frank Newton,
Shad Collins, Dizzy Gillespie. Bill Dillard
on most vocals. Theme *Uptown Rhapsody*.
European tour 1937. New York World's
Fair 1939. Disbanded 1940, began long
period managing Minton's jazz club in
Harlem where bop incubated. Continued
at Minton's well into 50s.

RECORDS
HENRY ALLEN, JR. (LUIS RUSSELL)
  Vi 38080 Swing Out/Feeling Drowsy
TEDDY HILL
  Me 13351 Here Comes Cookie/Got
    Me Doin' Things
  Me 13364 When the Robin Sings His
    Song Again/When Love Knocks at
    Your Heart
  Vo 3247 Blue Rhythm Fantasy/At the
    Rug Cutters' Ball
  Vo 3294 Passionette/(theme) Uptown
    Rhapsody
  Bb 6897 The Love Bug Will Bite You/
    Would You Like to Buy a Dream?

Bb 6898 Marie/Where Is the Sun?
Bb 6908 The Harlem Twister/Big Boy
  Blue
Bb 6941 The You and Me That Used
  to Be/China Boy
Bb 6943 A Study in Brown/Twilight in
  Turkey
Bb 6954 I Know Now/The Lady Who
  Couldn't Be Kissed
Bb 6988 San Anton'/King Porter
  Stomp
Bb 6989 I'm Happy, Darling, Dancing
  with You/Blue Rhythm Fantasy
Bb 7013 Yours and Mine/I'm Feeling
  Like a Million

LPs
TEDDY HILL
"X"(10")LVA-3030 (RIs)
LUIS RUSSELL
Pa(E) PMC-7025 (RIs)

841. HILL, TINY   d vo B

*Born July 19, 1906, Sullivan, Ill.
Died 1972*

Leader of swinging cornball band. Big,
colorful front man over 350 pounds. Handled novelty and rhythm vocals in good
commercial style. Attended Illinois State
Normal College. Formed cornball trio,
played jobs in area. In 1933 led big band
awhile. Worked as drummer, formed
dance band. Good entertaining unit,
maintained lively pace, popular in ballrooms especially in midwest. Capable of
fair swing or dixieland. At times trumpet
jazzmen included Sterling Bose, Jack Alexander, Bob Anderson. Capable Allen
DeWitt on romantic vocals late 30s. Well
known for *Angry*; sometime theme. On
All-Time Hit Parade radio show 1943-4.
Continued to record and tour 50s and 60s.

RECORDS
TINY HILL
  Vo 4919 Ain'tcha Comin' Out?/Doin'
    the Chamberlain
  Vo 4957 (theme) Angry/In Love with
    Love
  Vo 5060 Doodle Doo Doo/Dream Girl
  Vo 5128 Mama's Gone, Goodbye/
    Every Little Movement
  Vo 5275 I'll Keep On Loving You/
    Auld Lang Syne

Vo 5340 I Get the Blues When It Rains/Skirts

Vo 5367 Yes, Sir, That's My Baby/He's a Curbstone Cutie

Vo 5387 My Best Girl/You Gotta See Mama Ev'ry Night

Vo 5445 Mickey/Please Don't Talk About Me When I'm Gone

Vo 5469 I Get a Kick Outa Corn/Let's Have Another One

Vo 5530 Heartaches/On a Dew-Dew-Dewy Day

OK 5635 I'm Knee Deep in Daisies/Five Foot Two

OK 5674 Two Ton Tessie/I'm Alone Because I Love You

OK 5775 You Gotta Quit Cheatin' on Me/The Face on the Barroom Floor

OK 5924 All the World Will Be Jealous of Me/The Guy at the End of the Bar

OK 5999 When You Wore a Tulip/Just Plain Folks

OK 6269 Sweet as Honey/Dance and Stay Young

Mer 2024 Sioux City Sue/I'll Keep On Lovin' You

Mer 5508 Back in Your Own Backyard/I'll Sail My Ship Alone

Mer 6022 I Need Lovin'/Pretty Baby

Mer 6076 San/If You Knew Susie

842. HILLIARD, BOB   lyr

Born January 28, 1918, New York, N.Y. Died February 1, 1971, Hollywood, Calif.

Lyricist from mid-40s into 60s. Scores for Broadway shows ANGEL IN THE WINGS (1947) and HAZEL FLAGG (1953). Collaborated with composers Carl Sigman, Jule Styne, Sammy Mysels, Dick Sanford, Sammy Fain. Best-known songs *Civilization, Careless Hands, Dear Hearts and Gentle People, Dearie, Be My Life's Companion, Bouquet of Roses, Every Street's a Boulevard in Old New York.*

SONGS
(with related shows)

1946—The Coffee Song (They've Got an Awful Lot of Coffee in Brazil)

1947—ANGEL IN THE WINGS stage show (The Big Brass Band from Brazil; Civilization; The Thousand Islands Song; Once Around the Moon); Mention My Name in Sheboygan; Red Silk Stockings and Green Perfume

1948—A Strawberry Moon; Careless Hands; My Fair Lady; If It Were Easy to Do

1949—Dear Hearts and Gentle People; Sarong; These Will Be the Best Years of Our Lives

1950—MICHAEL TODD'S PEEP SHOW stage show (Stay with the Happy People; Francie); River of Smoke; Dearie

1951—Be My Life's Companion; Shanghai; Jealous Eyes

1952—ALICE IN WONDERLAND movie cartoon (I'm Late; Very Good Advice; All in the Golden Afternoon); Bouquet of Roses; Downhearted

1953—HAZEL FLAGG stage show, Jule Styne-cm (Every Street's a Boulevard in Old New York; How Do You Speak to an Angel?) Till They've All Gone Home; Sweet Forgiveness

1954—LIVING IT UP movie, Jule Styne-cm (Money Burns a Hole in My Pocket; Champagne and Wedding Cake; That's What I Like; also, Every Street's a Boulevard in Old New York); Send My Baby Back to Me; Somebody Bad Stole de Wedding Bell

1956—Moonlight Gambler

1961—Tower of Strength; You're Following Me

1963—My Summer Love; Our Day Will Come

Other songs: *Chocolate Whiskey and Vanilla Gin; Boutonniere; Castanets and Lace; The Ghost of Barrel House Joe; A Nickel for a Memory; My Little Corner of the World; Seven Little Girls; Any Day Now; Young Wings Can Fly; Baby, Come Home; Imagination Is a Magic Dream; Au Revoir; Don't You Believe It*

842A. HILLIARD, HARRIET   vo
(PEGGY LOU SNYDER)

Born c. 1912, Des Moines, Iowa

Vocalist with husband Ozzie Nelson's band during 30s. Later co-starred with

Nelson in long-running radio-TV show. Parents theatrical. Ballet dancer in vaudeville at 15. Broadway debut as teenager in THE BLONDE SINNER (1926). While working as single changed name to Harriet Hilliard. Early 30s mistress of ceremonies and singer at New York's Hollywood Restaurant. Joined Nelson band 1932. Solos and duets with Ozzie important band asset. Married Ozzie 1935. Harriet and band on Joe Penner's radio show late 1933-5, own show 1936. Played Ripley's Believe It or Not show mid-30s, Bakers Broadcast 1937, Feg Murray show 1937-8. Harriet impressive secondary lead in important 1936 movie FOLLOW THE FLEET starring Astaire-Rogers, sang *Here I Am but Where Are You?* and *Get Thee Behind Me, Satan*. Featured mostly in minor movies following years. Harriet and band on Red Skelton's first radio show 1941. Harriet big hit as mother of "mean little kid" in sketches which won Skelton fame. Long-running radio show The Adventures of Ozzie and Harriet began 1944. Two young sons performed. Series transferred to early TV, ran to 1968. Road shows with Ozzie: MARRIAGE-GO-ROUND (1962, 1972-3), THE IMPOSSIBLE YEARS (1968), STATE FAIR (1969). Returned to TV with Ozzie 1973-4 in series Ozzie's Girls. Career covered in 1973 Nelson autobiography *Ozzie*.

MOVIES

1936—FOLLOW THE FLEET
1937—LIFE OF THE PARTY NEW FACES OF 1937
1938—COCOANUT GROVE; SHE'S MY EVERYTHING
1941—SWEETHEART OF THE CAMPUS; CONFESSIONS OF BOSTON BLACKIE
1942—JUKE BOX JENNY; CANAL ZONE
1943—GALS, INCORPORATED; HI BUDDY!; THE FALCON STRIKES BACK; HONEYMOON LODGE
1944—HI, GOOD LOOKIN'!; SWINGTIME JOHNNY; TAKE IT BIG
1952—HERE COME THE NELSONS

RECORDS

OZZIE NELSON
  Br 6410 It's Gonna Be You
  Br 6443 In the Dim Dim Dawning
  Br 6551 Baby Boy

  Br 6796 I Hate Myself/Poor Girl
  Br 7340 No, No, a Thousand Times No!
  Br 7375 Dust Off That Old Pianna
  Br 7435 There's a Whistle in the Thistle
  Br 7464 Is It Just a Summer Romance?
  Br 7544 Jingle Bells
  Br 7607 Get Thee Behind Me, Satan
  Bb 6987 Our Penthouse on Third Avenue
  Bb 7034 Roses in December
  Bb 7050 The Folks Who Live on the Hill
  Bb 7256 Once in Awhile
  Bb 7528 Says My Heart
  Bb 7825 Forget If You Can
  Bb 10298 South American Way
  Bb 10311 You and Your Love
  Bb 10469 Who Told You I Cared?

LPs

OZZIE & HARRIET NELSON
  Imperial 9049 (semi-rock backing)

843. HIMBER, RICHARD   v cm lyr B
    Born February 20, 1907, Newark, N.J.
    Died December 11, 1966

Leader of excellent dance band in 30s. Often on own radio shows. Learned violin, at 13 summer band job at Coney Island. Jobs in small New York restaurants. Sophie Tucker heard Himber, hired him for act; they toured in vaudeville. During this period got interested in magic, later good amateur magician. Played in Paramount Theatre band awhile. In early 30s managed Buddy Rogers and Harry Barris bands briefly, then over two years as sideman-manager for Rudy Vallee. Formed band mid-1933. Joey Nash vocalist. Early important booking at Essex House in New York. Later Ritz-Carlton and Hotel Pierre in New York. Lush sweet style, often with semi-swing beat, always impeccable musicianship. Usually used *It Isn't Fair* as theme, sometimes closed with *Was I to Blame?*. In 1934 band on radio show starring Eddie Peabody. Late 1934 own Studebaker Champions Show into 1937. Innovation on these shows: used harp interludes between numbers. Late 1937 band on Hit Parade show, 1938 Melody Puzzles Show for Lucky Strike plus show starring Connie Boswell and Kay Thompson. Own shows late 30s. Tried new, intricate gimmick: brass played cascading notes in pyramid style. Called this Rhythmic Pyramids Orchestra, soon abandoned style. Tried another style 1940: strings played slow tempo, followed by contrasting brass and reeds in swing tempo. Himber also featured medleys imitating well-known bands, superbly done. Disbanded 1944, came back with new band late 1945, continued as bandleader through 40s. Numerous recordings, especially good 1934-6 featuring vocalists Joey Nash, then Stuart Allen. Jazzmen Bunny Berigan and Artie Shaw made a few records with Himber 1936. Composer of standard *It Isn't Fair* revived 1950 with hit record by Don Cornell with Sammy Kaye band. Other compositions included *Day After Day, Moments in the Moonlight, After the Rain, Haunting Memories, Time Will Tell, Am I Asking Too Much?, I'm Getting Nowhere Fast with You, Today, In That Hat.*

RECORDS

RICHARD HIMBER

Vo 2526 Love Is the Sweetest Thing/ Love Is the Thing
Vo 2538 My Love/Life's So Complete
Vo 2572 You're My Past, Present and Future/Doin' the Uptown Lowdown
Vo 25008 (theme) It Isn't Fair/It Might Have Been a Different Story
Bb 5419 May I?/Love Thy Neighbor
Bb 5421 Ending with a Kiss/It's Psychological
Vi 24679 You're a Builder Upper/ What Can You Say in a Love Song?
Vi 24680 Let's Take a Walk Around the Block/Fun to Be Fooled
Vi 24745 Stars Fell on Alabama/If I Had a Million Dollars
Vi 24764 Say When/When Love Comes Swinging Along
Vi 24811 June in January/With Every Breath I Take
Vi 24824 I Woke Up Too Soon/In a Blue and Pensive Mood
Vi 24868 Lullaby of Broadway/Zing!

Went the Strings of My Heart
Vi 25037 Footloose and Fancyfree/ Give a Broken Heart a Break
Vi 25189 You Hit the Spot/I Feel Like a Feather in the Breeze
Vi 25293 Tormented/Every Once in Awhile
Vi 25298 Would You?/I've Got a Heavy Date
Vi 25365 Midnight Blue/Me and the Moon
Vi 25441 In the Chapel in the Moonlight/You're Everything Sweet
Vi 25742 Thrill of a Lifetime/I Live the Life I Love
Vi 25754 Parade of Bands (1 & 2)
Vi 26007 Parade of Bands (3 & 4)
Vi 26142 You Call It Madness/ Pyramiding "The Swan"
Vi 26164 Parade of Bands (5 & 6)
De 3578 Whose Theme Song? (1 & 2)
De 3618 (theme) Was I to Blame?/ Blue Moon

MARY MARTIN with RICHARD HIMBER ORCHESTRA

De 18184 Kiss the Boys Goodbye/Do It Again

844. HINES, EARL   p vo cm B
(nicknamed Father or Fatha)

Born December 28, 1905, Duquesne, Pa.

Trailblazing jazz pianist, bandleader with lengthy career. "Trumpet" piano style inspired by Louis Armstrong. Unorthodox rhythmic patterns with left hand ushered in swing piano, influenced almost every pianist. Led bands most of career, swinging groups with excellent personnel. With bands in Pittsburgh beginning about 1918. In 1922 with singer Lois Deppe, toured with her 1923. Led band in Pittsburgh and Chicago, also played solo. Toured theatres mid-20s with Carroll Dickerson troupe, then worked in Chicago with Dickerson and Erskine Tate. With Louis Armstrong 1927, Jimmie Noone late 1927-8. Near end of 1928 led big band at Chicago's Grand Terrace: main base for ten years. Freelance recording with jazz greats, also with own band. Personnel in 30s included Walter Fuller (t vo), Omer Simeon (cl), Darnell Howard (cl), Jimmy Mundy (ts ar), Trummy Young (tb), Budd Johnson (ts). *Cavernism* theme, later *Deep Forest*. Biggest hit 1940's *Boogie Woogie on the St. Louis Blues*. Billy Eckstine joined mid-1939 as featured vocalist, remained till late 1943, starred on hits *Jelly, Jelly* and *Stormy Monday Blues*. 1943 band proving ground for bop, included Dizzy Gillespie (t), Charlie Parker (as), Benny Green (tb). Unfortunately Petrillo ban prevented records then. Disbanded 1948, joined Louis Armstrong All-Stars, left late 1951 to form combo. Work in 50s included long run at Hangover Club in San Francisco. Co-led combo with Jack Teagarden on European tour 1957. In early 60s made Oakland base, had club there awhile. Toured at times, played San Francisco and New York. Toured Europe several times; 1966 government-sponsored tour of Russia with combo. Occasionally on TV. Happy personality; playing remained enthusiastic throughout career. Excellence maintained in early 70s. Most famous compositions *Rosetta*; *A Monday Date*; *Deep Forest* (with Reginald Foresythe); *You Can Depend on Me*. Others: *Cavernism*; *Everything Depends on You*; *Jelly, Jelly*; *Tantalizing a Cuban*; *Dancing Fingers*; *Madhouse*; *Piano Man*; *Life with Fatha'*.

RECORDS

LOUIS ARMSTRONG
OK 8609 A Monday Date/Sugar Foot Strut
OK 8641 Squeeze Me/Two Deuces
OK 8657 Save It, Pretty Mama/St. James Infirmary
OK 41454 Weather Bird

JIMMIE NOONE
Vo 1184 I Know That You Know/ Sweet Sue
Vo 1185 Every Evening/Four or Five Times
Vo 1207 Sweet Lorraine/Apex Blues

JOHNNY DODDS
Br 3567 Melancholy/Wild Man Blues
Vo 15632 Weary Blues/New Orleans Stomp

CLIFFORD HAYES' LOUISVILLE STOMPERS
Vi 23407 Automobile Blues/Shady Lane Blues
Vi 38514 Frog Hop/Shoe String Stomp

SIDNEY BECHET
Vi 26746 Ain't Misbehavin'/Blue for You, Johnny
Vi 27204 Blues in Thirds
Vi 27240 Stompy Jones/Save It, Pretty Mama

EARL HINES
QRS 7036 Blues in Thirds/Off Time Blues
QRS 7037 Chicago High Life/A Monday Date
OK 8653 Fifty-Seven Varieties/I Ain't Got Nobody
OK 8832 Caution Blues/A Monday Date
Vi 38043 Beau Koo Jack/Good Little, Bad Little You
Vi 38096 Grand Piano Blues/Blue Nights
Br 6403 Love Me Tonight/Down Among the Sheltering Palms
Br 6541 (theme) Cavernism/Rosetta
Br 6710 Bubbling Over/I Want a Lot of Love
Br 6872 Blue/Julia
Vo 3379 Darkness/Madhouse
Vo 3501 Pianology/Flany Doodle Swing
De 218 Fat Babes/Maple Leaf Rag
De 337 Rosetta/Copenhagen
De 577 Wolverine Blues/Rock and Rye
Bb 10351 Grand Terrace Shuffle/ Ridin' and Jivin'
Bb 10377 Father Steps In/Piano Man
Bb 10642 Body and Soul/Child of a Disordered Brain
Bb 10674 Number 19/Boogie Woogie on St. Louis Blues
Bb 10727 (theme) Deep Forest/Lightly and Politely
Bb 10792 You Can Depend on Me/ Tantalizing a Cuban
Bb 11065 Jelly, Jelly/I'm Falling for You
Bb 11126 Jersey Bounce/Sally, Won't You Come Back?
Bb 11308 It Had to Be You/Yellow Fire
Bb 11329 Windy City Jive/Water Boy
Bb 11432 The Earl/Somehow
Bb 11567 Second Balcony Jump/ Stormy Monday Blues
Co 35875-6-7-8 (piano solos)

Si 28109 Squeeze Me/I've Got a Feeling I'm Falling
Si 28110 Honeysuckle Rose/My Fate Is in Your Hands
MGM 10382 Keyboard Kapers/Lazy Mornin'

LPs
EARL HINES
"X"(10″)LVA-3023 (Bb, Vi RIs)
Atl(10″)120 Famous QRS Solos (RIs)
De DL-9221 South Side Swing (1934-5 De RIs)
De DL-2202 Hines Rhythm (1933-8 RIs)
Epic LN-3223 Oh, Father! (1937-8 RIs)
Fan 3217 Fatha Plays Fats
Tops L-1599 (band of 50s)
Halcyon HAL-101 Quintessential Earl Hines
Contact 6 Here Comes Earl "Fatha" Hines
Co CL-2320 The New Earl Hines Trio
Vi LPV-512 The Grand Terrace Band (Vi RIs)
Delmark DS-212 At Home
LOUIS ARMSTRONG ALL-STARS
De DL-8329 New Orleans Nights
De(10″)DL-5280 Jazz Concert, Vol. 2
LOUIS ARMSTRONG
Co CL-853 The Louis Armstrong Story, Vol. 3 (OK RIs)
BENNY CARTER
Contemp M-3561 Swingin' the 20s

844A. HINES, ELIZABETH   vo
Born c. 1894
Died February 19, 1971, Lake Forest, Ill.

Beautiful singer-actress in Broadway musicals. Most important LITTLE NELLIE KELLY (1922). Later played original title role in radio serial The Romance of Helen Trent 1933-44 in Chicago.

BROADWAY MUSICALS
1916—MOLLY O'
1919—SEE-SAW
1921—LOVE BIRDS; THE O'BRIEN GIRL
1922—LITTLE NELLIE KELLY
1924—MARJORIE
1925—JUNE DAYS

845. HINTON, MILT   b
Born June 23, 1910, Vicksburg, Miss.
Superior bassist. Many years with Cab Calloway, later freelance with prolific recording output. From swing school but bridged gap into modern jazz, played with leading jazzmen of all styles. Grew up in Chicago, began professional career there late 20s. With Eddie South combo 1931-6 off and on, mostly in Chicago. Early 30s with Erskine Tate, Fate Marable, 1935 with Zutty Singleton. Joined Calloway mid-1936 till 1951. Briefly with Count Basie and Louis Armstrong early 50s. Much in demand for all types of jobs and record sessions; based in New York. Some studio work, jazz clubs. In 60s and 70s busy with concerts, festivals, TV, recording.

RECORDS
EDDIE SOUTH
Vi 22847 Marcheta/Hejre Kati
Vi 24324 Old Man Harlem/No More Blues
Vi 24343 Gotta Go!/My! Oh My!
Vi 24383 Nagasaki/Mama Mockingbird
CAB CALLOWAY
Va 593 Congo/My Gal Mezzanine
Va 662 Queen Isabella / Savage Rhythm
Vo 3896 Every Day's a Holiday/Jubilee
Vo 3995 Three Swings and Out/I Like My Music Hot
Vo 5005 Trylon Swing/The Jumpin' Jive
Vo 5406 Pluckin' the Bass/Give, Baby, Give
OK 6084 Bye Bye Blues/Run, Little Rabbit
Vo 6109 Jonah Joins the Cab/Willow Weep for Me
Vo 6192 Ebony Silhouette/Hep Cat Love Song
Vo 6547 Tappin' Off/Nain Nain
TEDDY WILSON
Br 7762 Easy to Love/The Way You Look Tonight
Br 7768 With Thee I Swing/Who Loves You?
LIONEL HAMPTON
Vi 26209 High Society

Vi 26254 It Don't Mean a Thing

Vi 26343 I Can Give You Love/ Johnny Get Your Horn

Vi 26393 One Sweet Letter from You/ Early Session Hop

J. C. HEARD

Key 623 All My Life/Groovin' with J. C.

JONAH JONES

Key 614 Just Like a Butterfly/Lust for Licks

THE KEYNOTERS

Key(12")1313 You're Driving Me Crazy/I'm in the Market for You

BUDDY DEFRANCO

Clef 89067 Show Eyes/Autumn in New York

MILT HINTON

Key 639 Everywhere/Beefsteak Charlie

Staff 606 If I Should Lose You/If You Believed in Me

LPs

MILT HINTON

Beth BCP-1020

MILT HINTON-WENDELL MARSHALL-BULL RUTHER

Vi LPM-1107 Basses Loaded!

HAL MCKUSICK

Vi LPM-1164 In a 20th-Century Drawing Room

Vi LPM-1366 Jazz Workshop

Cor CRL-57116 Jazz at the Academy

TONY SCOTT

Vi LJM-1022 Scott's Fling

BOB BROOKMEYER

Vik LX-1071 Brookmeyer

NANCY HARROW

Candid 9008 (S) Wild Women Don't Have the Blues

JOE WILDER

Co CL-1319 Jazz from "Peter Gunn"

JOE NEWMAN

Vi LPM-1118 All I Wanna Do Is Swing

CHU BERRY

Epic LN-3124 "Chu" (Va, Vo RIs)

CAB CALLOWAY

Epic LN-3265 (RIs)

KENNY BURRELL

Kapp KL-1326 Lotsa Bossa Nova

LOU STEIN

Epic LG-3101 House Hop

RUSTY DEDRICK

4 Corners FCL-4207 The Big Band Sound

846. HIRSCH, LOUIS A.   cm ar p

Born November 28, 1887, New York, N.Y.

Died May 13, 1924, New York, N.Y.

Composer for Broadway shows from 1907 until death in 1924. Important shows HE CAME FROM MILWAUKEE (1910), VERA VIOLETTA (1911), THE PASSING SHOW OF 1912, ZIEGFELD FOLLIES OF 1915-1916-1918-1922, GOING UP (1918), OH, MY DEAR! (1918), THE RAINBOW GIRL (1918), MARY (1920), THE O'BRIEN GIRL (1921), GREENWICH VILLAGE FOLLIES OF 1922-1923. Also wrote for lesser shows. Last show BETTY LEE opened December 25, 1924, months after death. Collaborators included lyricists Harold Atteridge, Otto Harbach, Gene Buck, Edward Madden, Irving Caesar and composers Melville Gideon, Con Conrad, Dave Stamper. Best-known songs *The Gaby Glide*; *Hello, Frisco!*; *The Tickle Toe*; *The Love Nest*. Attended CCNY; extensive musical study in Germany. Prepared for concert stage as conductor, studied arranging and composing. Pianist for several publishing companies in New York. Wrote material for Lew Dockstader Minstrels. Staff composer for Shubert Brothers 1912-14. Partner in Victoria Publishing Company.

SONGS

(with related shows)

1907—THE GAY WHITE WAY stage show (Aren't You the Girl I Met at Sherry's?); My Twilight Queen

1908—THE MIMIC WORLD stage show (Ragtime Minstrel Man; When Johnny Comes Marching Home from College); MISS INNOCENCE stage show (My Post Card Girl)

1909—THE GIRL AND THE WIZARD stage show (La Belle Parisienne; Military Mary Ann)

1910—HE CAME FROM MILWAUKEE stage show (Love Is Like a Red Red Rose; In Gypsy Land; Merry Wedding Bells; Sentimental Moon; many others)

1911—VERA VIOLETTA stage show (The Gaby Glide; Come and Dance with Me; I've Heard That Before; When You Hear Love's Hello); REVUE OF REVUES stage show (Boardwalk Crawl; The Minstrel Band; Oriental Eyes)

1912—THE PASSING SHOW OF 1912 stage show (Always Together; The Wedding Glide; many others); THE WHIRL OF SOCIETY stage show (How Do You Do, Miss Ragtime; My Sumuran Girl)

1914—Sweet Kentucky Lady

1915—ZIEGFELD FOLLIES OF 1915 stage show (Hello, Frisco!; Hold Me in Your Loving Arms; many others); AROUND THE MAP stage show (There's Only One Thing a Coon Can Do; Katie Clancy; Billie the Blubber)

1916—ZIEGFELD FOLLIES OF 1916 stage show (Beautiful Island of Girls; I Want That Star; I Left Her on the Beach at Honolulu; Bachelor Days)

1917—THE GRASS WIDOW stage show (The Grass Widow; Somewhere There's Someone for Me; Just You and Me)

1918—GOING UP stage show (Going Up; The Tickle Toe; Kiss Me; If You Look in Her Eyes; Do It for Me); ZIEGFELD FOLLIES OF 1918 stage show (Garden of My Dreams; Syncopated Tune; Any Old Time at All; When I'm Looking at You; I Want to Learn to Jazz Dance); OH, MY DEAR! stage show (City of Dreams; You Never Know; I'll Ask No More; If They Ever Parted Me from You; many others); THE RAINBOW GIRL stage show (My Rainbow Girl; I'll Think of You; Alimony Blues; Mister Drummer)

1919—SEE-SAW stage show (See-Saw; When Two Hearts Discover; A World Full of Jazz; I Just Want Girls; When You Dance)

1920—MARY stage show (Mary; The Love Nest; Anything You Want to Do, Dear; Waiting; Everytime I Meet a Lady)

1921—THE O'BRIEN GIRL stage show (Learn to Smile; That O'Brien Girl; I Wonder How I Ever Passed You By)

1922—GREENWICH VILLAGE FOLLIES OF 1922 stage show (You Are My Rain-beau; Nightingale, Bring Me a Rose; A Kiss from a Red-Headed Miss; Sixty Seconds Every Minute I Dream of You); ZIEGFELD FOLLIES OF 1922 stage show ('Neath the South Sea Moon; My Rambler Rose; Throw Me a Kiss)

1923—GREENWICH VILLAGE FOLLIES OF 1923 stage show (Lovey; Seeing Stars; Just a Bit of Heaven in Your Smile; Golden Trail; Raisin' the Roof; Dancing Step Child); Annabel Lee

1925—BETTY LEE stage show (Monterey; Baby Be Good; Along the Rio Grande; Little Pony of Mine; Sweet Arabian Dreams)

847. HIRSCH, WALTER   lyr

Born March 10, 1891, New York, N.Y.

Lyricist during 30s. Output sparse but included popular and worthwhile songs. Wrote *Out of the Night*, many years theme of Ted Weems band. Collaborators included composers Al Goering, Frank Magine, Fred Rose, Spencer Williams.

SONGS
(with related shows)

1926—'Deed I Do

1930—Truly I Love You

1931—Save the Last Dance for Me; That Little Boy of Mine; Who's Your Little Who-zis?

1932—Strange Interlude; Holding My Honey's Hand

1936—Bye Bye, Baby; Me and the Moon

1937—RHYTHM IN THE CLOUDS movie (Don't Ever Change); THE HIT PARADE movie (Was It Rain?; Love Is Good for Anything That Ails You; Last Night I Dreamed of You)

1938—Lullaby in Rhythm

1939—Baby, What Else Can I Do?

848. HIRT, AL   t vo B
(ALOIS MAXWELL HIRT)
Born November 7, 1922, New Orleans, La.

Huge-sized trumpet virtuoso prominent in late 50s and 60s after name band and radio experience. Excellent tone and technique, great power and facility. Only weaknesses: a penchant for crowding too many notes into solos, and difficulty swinging. Early experience in local brass bands. Extensive training; attended Cincinnati Conservatory. Military service 1943-6. Began professionally 1946. With Jimmy and Tommy Dorsey, Ray McKinley, Horace Heidt. Most of 50s staff musician on New Orleans radio. Late 50s formed dixieland combo (included clarinetist Pete Fountain), played Pier 600 Club. Prowess soon became known. TV appearances as single in early 60s brought prominence. Recorded frequently, on top TV shows, own TV summer show 1965. Continued in New Orleans, also Las Vegas; guest soloist in concerts and clinics throughout U.S. Played mostly dixieland with combo, usually at much faster tempo than normal. Capable vocalist, jazz-phrased. He and band did some clowning; Hirt natural showman. Active into 70s, based in New Orleans but played dates elsewhere.

RECORDS
(all LPs)

AL HIRT
  Cor CRL-757389 (S) Bourbon Street
    (with PETE FOUNTAIN)
  Cor CRL-757402 (S) In New Orleans
  Verve V-1012 Jazz Band Ball
  Verve V-1028 Blockbustin' Dixie (with
    PETE FOUNTAIN)
  Southland 211 New Orleans Jazz Stars
  Aud Fid 5877-8 (2-LP set) At Dan's
    Pier
  Aud Fid 5926-7 (2-LP set) Swingin'
    Dixie
  Vi LSP-2354 (S) He's the King
  Vi LSP-2366 (S) Greatest Horn
  Vi LSP-2446 (S) Horn a-Plenty
  Vi LSP-2497 (S) At Mardi Gras
  Vi LSP-2584 (S) Trumpet and Strings
  Vi LSP-2733 (S) Honey in the Horn
  Vi LSP-2917 (S) Cotton Candy
  Vi LSP-3416 (S) At Carnegie Hall
  Vi LSP-3979 (S) Unforgettable
MONK HAZEL
  Southland 217 New Orleans Jazz Kings

849. HITCHCOCK, RAYMOND   vo
Born October 22, 1865, Auburn, N.Y.
Died November 24, 1929, Beverly Hills, Calif.

Star performer on Broadway stage from its early years into 20s. Comedian with rasping "drunkard's singing voice." Grew up in Philadelphia. Began on Broadway 1891 in chorus of THE BRIGAND; later other chorus jobs. Comedian with Castle Square Opera Company. After starring in several Broadway shows, a hit in KING DODO (1902). Top star after THE YANKEE CONSUL (1904). In several shows with wife, singing star Flora Zabelle. Wrote book for show WORDS AND MUSIC (1917). Vaudeville and clubs at intervals. Last stage appearance in Chicago production 1929.

BROADWAY MUSICALS
1900—THE BELLE OF BRIDGEPORT
1901—THE BURGOMASTER; VIENNA LIFE
1902—KING DODO
1904—THE YANKEE CONSUL
1905—EASY DAWSON (nonmusical)
1906—THE GALLOP (nonmusical)
1907—A YANKEE TOURIST
1909—THE MAN WHO OWNS BROADWAY
1911—THE RED WIDOW
1914—THE BEAUTY SHOP
1916—BETTY
1917—HITCHY-KOO
1918—HITCHY-KOO OF 1918
1919—HITCHY-KOO OF 1919
1920—HITCHY-KOO OF 1920
1921—ZIEGFELD FOLLIES OF 1921
1923—THE OLD SOAK (nonmusical)
1924—HASSARD SHORT'S RITZ REVUE
1927—JUST FANCY

RECORDS
RAYMOND HITCHCOCK
  Vi 45137 Six Times Six Is Thirty-Six
  Vi 45201 Old Fashioned Garden
  Vi(12")55046 Burglar Story and High
    Cost of Living/Hitchcock's Curtain
    Speech

Vi(10″)55080 Here Comes the Groom/
Sometime

850. HITE, LES   as cl ar cm B

Born February 13, 1903, DuQuoin, Ill.
Died February 6, 1962, Santa Monica,
Calif.

Leader of big hot band based on west
coast in 30s and 40s; not an outstanding
musician. Studied at University of Illinois. Early jobs in Illinois. In 1925 toured
with road show, ended up in Los Angeles.
With bands there in middle and late 20s,
including jobs with Paul Howard.
Formed band about 1930; main base
Cotton Club in Culver City. Band on
many movie soundtracks, occasionally on
screen. Boasted competent musicians and
good swing arrangements. Personnel in
early 30s included Lionel Hampton (d
vb), Marshall Royal (as cl), Lawrence
Brown (tb). Dizzy Gillespie (t) briefly
with Hite 1942. Louis Armstrong (t)
fronted band 1930, used it on records.
Hite arranged for own band, sometimes
for Benny Goodman (e.g., *Li'l Boy Love*
and *Board Meeting*—own composition).
Featured guitarist-singer T-Bone Walker
1939-40; biggest hit *T-Bone Blues*. Occasionally toured, played engagements in
New York, Chicago, other spots, especially during 1941-2. Theme *It Must Have
Been a Dream*. Left music in 1945.

RECORDS
LOUIS ARMSTRONG & HIS NEW SEBASTIAN
  COTTON CLUB ORCHESTRA (actually Les
  Hite Orchestra)
OK 41442 I'm a Ding Dong Daddy/
  I'm in the Market for You
OK 41448 Confessin'/If I Could Be
  with You
OK 41463 Memories of You/You're
  Lucky to Me
OK 41468 Body and Soul
OK 41478 The Peanut Vendor/You're
  Driving Me Crazy
OK 41486 Just a Gigolo/Shine
Co 2688-D Sweethearts on Parade
LES HITE
Vs 8373 Board Meeting/The World Is
  Waiting for the Sunrise
Vs 8391 T-Bone Blues/(theme) It Must
  Have Been a Dream

Vs 8396 That's the Lick/Waiting for
  You
Hit 7001 Jersey Bounce/I Remember
  You
Hit 7002 Idaho/One Dozen Roses
Bb 11109 Board Meeting/The World
  Is Waiting for the Sunrise
Bb 11210 That's the Lick/T-Bone
  Blues

851. HOBART, GEORGE V.   lyr

Born January 16, 1867, Port Hawks-
bury, N.S., Canada
Died February 1, 1926, Cumberland,
Md.

Important lyricist-librettist on Broadway;
prolific career 1900-22. Songs attained
little popularity but effective within context of shows. Collaborated with composers Reginald DeKoven, Victor Herbert,
A. Baldwin Sloane, Silvio Hein, Raymond Hubbell. Came to U.S. at 17.
Managing editor of newspaper *Sunday
Scimitar* in Cumberland, Md. Later wrote
for *Baltimore American and News*, notably
feature "Dinkelspiel Papers" 14 years.
Wrote plays WILDFIRE, EXPERIENCE, OUR
MRS. MCCHESNEY. Author of 15 books in
John Henry series.

BROADWAY MUSICALS
(book and lyrics unless designated other-
wise)

1900—BROADWAY TO TOKIO; THE MILI-
  TARY MAID (unsuccessful); A MIL-
  LION DOLLARS; MISS PRINNT (book
  only)
1901—THE KING'S CARNIVAL; THE NEW
  YORKERS (lyrics only)
1902—THE BELLE OF BROADWAY (lyrics
  only); THE HALL OF FAME (lyrics
  only); SALLY IN OUR ALLEY
1903—THE DARLING OF THE GALLERY
  GODS (book only); THE JERSEY
  LILY; ROGERS BROTHERS IN LON-
  DON (lyrics only)
1904—ROGERS BROTHERS IN PARIS (lyrics
  only)
1905—THE HAM TREE (book only); MOON-
  SHINE (lyrics only); ROGERS
  BROTHERS IN IRELAND (lyrics only);
  A YANKEE CIRCUS ON MARS (book
  only)

1906—COMING THRU THE RYE; MARRYING MARY (lyrics only)
1908—THE BOYS AND BETTY
1909—THE CANDY SHOP (book only); OLD DUTCH (lyrics only)
1910—ALMA, WHERE DO YOU LIVE?; GIRLIES (book only); THE YANKEE GIRL
1911—WHEN SWEET SIXTEEN (unsuccessful); ZIEGFELD FOLLIES OF 1911
1912—OVER THE RIVER (book only); THE WOMAN HATERS
1913—ZIEGFELD FOLLIES OF 1913
1914—ZIEGFELD FOLLIES OF 1914 (book only)
1916—ZIEGFELD FOLLIES OF 1916
1917—ZIEGFELD FOLLIES OF 1917
1919—BUDDIES (book only); HITCHY-KOO OF 1919 (book only)
1920—KISSING TIME (book only); ZIEGFELD FOLLIES OF 1920 (book only)
1921—MUSIC BOX REVUE (book only)
1922—GREENWICH VILLAGE FOLLIES OF 1922 (book only); LETTY PEPPER (book only); MUSIC BOX REVUE OF 1922 (book only)

852. HODES, ART   p cm lyr B
Born November 14, 1904, Nikoliev, Russia

Blues-based jazz pianist with simple style. Born in Russia, brought to U.S. before first birthday. Grew up in Chicago, began there professionally early 20s. Toured with Wolverines band 1926. In Chicago with Wingy Manone 1928. Freelanced with leading Chicago jazzmen late 20s and 30s. Led groups at intervals, also worked solo. To New York 1938, worked at Hickory House. In next several years periods with Joe Marsala, Mezz Mezzrow, own groups. Led combo regularly 1941-2, also jazz disc jockey on New York radio. Edited magazine *Jazz Record* 1943-7. New York clubs remainder of 40s. In 1950 back to Chicago, joined Park Forest Conservatory as piano teacher. In 50s and 60s worked clubs mostly in Chicago. In 60s presented concert-lecture program "Sound of Jazz" at colleges. Columnist for music magazines. In 1970 first tour abroad. Composer of jazz numbers *Liberty Inn Drag, Porter in Blue, Blues 'n'*

Booze, Stuff and Nonsense, When Jimmy Yancey Was a Young Man, Randolph Street Rag, Meet Me in Chicago, Paging Mr. Jelly.

RECORDS
JOE MANNONE
Vo 15797 Isn't There a Little Love?/Trying to Stop My Crying
SIDNEY BECHET
BN(12")43 Blue Horizon/Muskrat Ramble
BN(12")44 St. Louis Blues/Jazz Me Blues
BN 517 Quincy Street Stomp/Weary Way Blues
BABY DODDS
BN 518 Careless Love/Winin' Boy Blues
BN 519 High Society/Feelin' at Ease
MEZZ MEZZROW
Sess 10-008 Really the Blues/Milk for Mezz
CHICAGO RHYTHM KINGS
Si 104 Song of the Wanderer/There'll Be Some Changes Made
Si 105 Sugar/Randolph Street Rag
ALL-STAR TRIO
JR 1010 Buddy Bolden's Blues/Too Busy
JR 1011 Swanee/Droppin' Shucks
ART HODES
JR 1004 Washboard Blues/Eccentric
JR 1005 No Pay Blues/The Mooche
JR 1006 Chimes Blues/Organ Grinder Blues
Si 101 I Found a New Baby/Four or Five Times
Si 102 Diga Diga Doo/Tin Roof Blues
De 18437 Liberty Inn Drag/Georgia Cake Walk
De 18438 Indiana/Get Happy
B&W 1 Snowy Morning Blues/Four or Five Times
B&W 2 Art's Boogie/St. Louis Blues
BN 505 Maple Leaf Rag/Yellow Dog Blues
BN 506 Slow 'Em Down Blues/She's Crying for Me
BN 507 Doctor Jazz/Shoe Shiner's Drag
BN 532 Memphis Blues/Shine
BN(12")34 Sweet Georgia Brown/Sugar Foot Stomp

BN(12")35 Bugle Call Rag/Squeeze Me

BN(12")45 Shake That Thing/Apex Blues

LPs

ART HODES
Riv(10")RLP-1012 (Si RIs)
BN 6502 The Funky Piano of Art Hodes
BN 6508 Sittin' In, Vol. 1
BN(10")7004 Art Hodes & His Chicagoans
Audiophile AP-54 Mostly Blues
Delmark 209 Albert Nicholas with Art Hodes' All-Star Stompers
Verve VLP-9015 Mama Yancey Sings, Art Hodes Plays Blues

JIMMY MCPARTLAND (one side)
Mer MG-20460 Meet Me in Chicago

BARNEY BIGARD
Delmark 211 Bucket's Got a Hole in It

853. HODGES, JOHNNY

as ss cl cm B

Born July 25, 1906, Cambridge, Mass. Died May 11, 1970, New York, N.Y.

All-time alto sax giant, especially popular in 30s and 40s. Featured soloist almost four decades with Duke Ellington. Sweet-toned lyrical sax on ballads, buoyant, imaginative style on jazz. In mid-20s with Willie "The Lion" Smith, Sidney Bechet, Bobby Sawyer, Lloyd Scott. With Chick Webb late 1926-7. Joined Ellington mid-1928, remained until early 1951. Rose to stardom as Duke's ace soloist. Wealth of recordings with Ellington, many solos. Also recorded under own name and with other jazz stars. Hodges and Charlie Parker two most widely admired altoists in jazz history. Led small group 1951-5; boasted excellent arrangements, good records. At times used Ellington's men. Rejoined Ellington later in 1955, remained almost constantly in late 50s and 60s. Composer or co-composer of *Hodge Podge, Jeep's Blues, Jitterbug's Lullaby, Wanderlust, Mood to Be Wooed, The Wonder of You, Squatty Roo, It Shouldn't Happen to a Dream, Harmony in Harlem, What's It All About?, Shady Side, Latino, Jappa, Krum Elbow Blues,* *Good Queen Bess,* and 1944 hit *I'm Beginning to See the Light.*

RECORDS

DUKE ELLINGTON
Br 4122 The Mooche
Br 4238 Tiger Rag (1 & 2)
Vi 38058 Saratoga Swing
Vi 38065 Hot Feet
Vi 38079 Cotton Club Stomp
Vi 38092 The Duke Steps Out
Vi 38129 Double Check Stomp
Vi 22528 Ring Dem Bells
Vi 24617 Live and Love Tonight
Vi 26610 Never No Lament
Vi 26788 In a Mellotone
Vi 26796 Warm Valley
De 880 Chicago/Harlem Speaks
Br 8044 Harmony in Harlem
Br 8108 I Let a Song Go Out of My Heart
Mus 466 Sultry Sunset
Co 38234 Hy'a Sue
Co 38702 On the Sunny Side of the Street

HARLEM FOOTWARMERS (Duke Ellington)
OK 8746 Syncopated Shuffle

TEDDY WILSON
Br 7867 Carelessly/How Could You?
Br 7884 It's Swell of You/There's a Lull in My Life

LIONEL HAMPTON
Vi 25592 On the Sunny Side of the Street

COOTIE WILLIAMS
Va 527 Blue Reverie/Downtown Uproar
Va 555 I Can't Believe That You're in Love with Me/Diga Diga Doo

REX STEWART
Va 517 Lazy Man's Shuffle/Rexatious
Va 664 Love in My Heart/Sugar Hill Shim-Sham

SANDY WILLIAMS
HRS 1007 Mountain Air

TYREE GLENN
Abbey 5001 Sultry Serenade/Dusty Serenade

AL HIBBLER with JOHNNY HODGES ORCHESTRA
Mer 89011 Believe It, Beloved/Please
Mer 89046 It Must Be True/No Greater Love

1117

JOHNNY HODGES
Va 576 Foolin' Myself/You'll Never Go to Heaven
Vo 4115 Jeep's Blues/Rendezvous with Rhythm
Vo 4242 Pyramid/Lost in Meditation
Vo 4309 A Blues Serenade/Jitterbug's Lullaby
Vo 4386 Prelude to a Kiss/The Jeep Is Jumpin'
Vo 4573 Hodge Podge/Wanderlust
Vo 5100 Rent Party Blues/The Rabbit's Jump
Bb 11117 Good Queen Bess/That's the Blues, Old Man
Bb 11447 Squatty Roo/Things Ain't What They Used to Be
Bb 30-0817 Passion Flower/Goin' Out the Back Way
Norg 101 Good Queen Bess/The Jeep Is Jumping
Clef 8944 Castle Rock/Jeep's Blues
Clef 89086 Jappa/Sheik of Araby
Mer 89035 Latino/Through for the Night

LPs

JOHNNY HODGES
Epic LN-3105 Hodge Podge (Vo RIs)
Mer(10″)MGC-111 Johnny Hodges Collates
Norg MGN-104 Memories of Ellington
Verve V-8150 Used to be Duke
Verve V-8271 The Big Sound
Verve V-8452 With Billy Strayhorn & THE Orchestra
(one side) Vi LPV-533 Things Ain't What They Used to Be (RIs)
ARS G-421 Johnny Hodges & the Ellington All-Stars
JOHNNY HODGES-WILD BILL DAVIS
Verve V-8570 Mess of Blues
Vi LSP-3706 (S) In Atlantic City
JOHNNY HODGES-GERRY MULLIGAN
Verve MGVS-68367 (S) Gerry Mulligan Meets Johnny Hodges
DUKE ELLINGTON
Co C3L27 (3-LP set) The Ellington Era, Vol. 1 (1927-40 RIs)
Vi LPV-517 Jumpin' Punkins (Vi RIs)
Vi LPM-1715 At His Very Best—Duke Ellington (Vi RIs)
EDDIE HEYWOOD
Cor CRL-57095 Featuring Eddie Heywood

854. HODGES, JOY   VO

Born January 29, 1916, Des Moines, Iowa

Good singer of middle and late 30s on radio and stage and in movies. With Ozzie Nelson band middle to late 1936 subbing for Harriet Hilliard. Joined Jimmie Grier band, with him late 1936-7 on Joe Penner radio show. On Fibber McGee & Molly show 1937. Important role with George M. Cohan in 1937 Broadway musical I'D RATHER BE RIGHT. Supporting roles in two unsuccessful shows DREAM WITH MUSIC (1944) and NELLIE BLY (1946). Small roles in movie musicals OLD MAN RHYTHM and TO BEAT THE BAND (1935), FOLLOW THE FLEET (1936). Better role in MERRY-GO-ROUND OF 1938 (1937). Graduated to female lead roles in low-budget movies SERVICE DELUXE and PERSONAL SECRETARY (1938), THE FAMILY NEXT DOOR, THEY ASKED FOR IT, UNEXPECTED FATHER and LITTLE ACCIDENT (1939), LAUGHING AT DANGER (1940). In 40s toured in stage productions. During World War II entertained troops with U.S.O. In mid-40s on New York radio. Returned to Broadway late 1972-3 to join already successful run of musical revival NO, NO, NANETTE.

RECORDS

JIMMIE GRIER
Br 7901 In Your Own Little Way/You're Looking for Romance

855. HOFF, CARL   reeds ar B
(CARL HOFFMAYR)

Born c. 1905, Oxnard, Calif.

Bandleader known for radio work late 30s and 40s. Formed first band 1934, played in Chicago. Sideman-arranger earlier for Paul Ash, arranged for Paul Whiteman and Vincent Lopez. Entered network radio mid-30s, active later 30s. On Lucky Strike Hit Parade show off and on 1936-41, on Al Pearce show 1937-40. Led dance band 1941-3, wrote most arrangements; good band, attained no popularity. Career waned in later years. Co-composer of 1953 hit *Vaya Con Dios*.

RECORDS

CARL HOFF
OK 6404 B-I-Bi/Hoya

OK 6450 Swing Low Sweet Chariot/ When Johnny Comes Marching Home

OK 6478 I Know Why/Kentucky Babe

OK 6538 Pale Moon/The Marriage Broker's Daughter

OK 6556 You're a Sap, Mr. Jap/We Did It Before

OK 6609 Miss You/The Son of a Gun Who Picks on Uncle Sam

855A. HOFFMAN, AL   cm lyr d B

Born September 25, 1902, Minsk, Russia
Died July 21, 1960, New York, N.Y.

Composer of excellent songs in 30s, novelties in 40s and 50s. Usually collaborated with lyricists and composers including Al Goodhart, Maurice Sigler, Ed Nelson, Sammy Lerner, Dick Manning, Jerry Livingston, Milton Drake, Mack David, Mann Curtis, Leo Corday, Leon Carr, Bob Merrill, Walter Kent. Best-known songs *Heartaches; I Apologize; Auf Wiedersehen, My Dear; Fit as a Fiddle; I Saw Stars; Little Man, You've Had a Busy Day; I'm in a Dancing Mood; She Shall Have Music; Mairzy Doats; Chi-Baba, Chi-Baba; There's No Tomorrow; Papa Loves Mambo; If I Knew You Were Comin' I'd've Baked a Cake; Allegheny Moon; The Hawaiian Wedding Song; Takes Two to Tango.* To U.S. 1908. Grew up in Seattle, led band. To New York 1928; drummer in night clubs. Began composing 1930. Scored for stage shows and movies in England 1934-7 with Al Goodhart and Maurice Sigler.

SONGS
(with related shows)

1930—I Don't Mind Walkin' in the Rain

1931—Heartaches; I Apologize; If You Haven't Got a Girl; Makin' Faces at the Man in the Moon; Oh, What a Thrill

1932—Auf Wiedersehen, My Dear; Fit as a Fiddle; Happy-Go-Lucky You; It's Winter Again

1933—Roll Up the Carpet; Meet Me in the Gloaming; Two Buck Tim from Timbuctoo; Black-Eyed Susan Brown

1934—I Saw Stars; Little Man, You've Had a Busy Day; Jimmy Had a Nickel; Who Walks In When I Walk Out?; Why Don't You Practice What You Preach?; Your Guess Is Just as Good as Mine; You're in My Power

1935—Black Coffee

1936—THIS'LL MAKE YOU WHISTLE English stage show (Crazy with Love; I'm in a Dancing Mood; There Isn't Any Limit to My Love; My Red Letter Day); SHE SHALL HAVE MUSIC English movie (She Shall Have Music; My First Thrill); FIRST A GIRL English movie (Everything's in Rhythm with My Heart; Say the Word and It's Yours; I Can Wiggle My Ears); JACK OF ALL TRADES English movie (Where There's You There's Me); COME OUT OF THE PANTRY English movie (Everything Stops for Tea); There's Always a Happy Ending

1937—GANGWAY English movie (Gangway; Lord and Lady Whoozis)

1938—LISTEN, DARLING movie (On the Bumpy Road to Love)

1939—Romance Runs in the Family

1940—Apple Blossoms and Chapel Bells

1942—The Story of a Starry Night

1943—That Wonderful Worrisome Feeling; What's the Good Word, Mr. Bluebird?; Close to You

1944—Mairzy Doats; Goodnight, Wherever You Are

1946—I'm Gonna Lasso a Dream

1947—Chi-Baba, Chi-Baba

1948—Don't You Love Me Anymore?

1949—CINDERELLA movie cartoon (Cinderella; A Dream Is a Wish Your Heart Makes; The Cinderella Work Song; So This Is Love; Bibbidi Bobbidi Boo); There's No Tomorrow

1950—If I Knew You Were Comin' I'd've Baked a Cake; I'm Gonna Live Till I Die

1951—One-Finger Melody

1952—Hold Me in Your Heart; 'Til Now; Fifty Years Ago (I Wish We Were Sweethearts)

1953—Takes Two to Tango; For Me; A Whale of a Tale; He Who Has

Love; Do You Know What It Means to Be Lonely?

1954—Papa Loves Mambo; Boulevard of Nightingales

1956—Hot Diggity; Allegheny Moon

1957—When You Kiss Me

1958—The Hawaiian Wedding Song; Secretly; Oh Oh, I'm Falling in Love Again

1959—La Plume De Ma Tante

Other songs: *O Dio Mio*; *I Must Have One More Kiss Kiss Kiss*; *I Ups to Her and She Ups to Me*; *Fuzzy Wuzzy*; *I'm a Big Girl Now*; *I Had Too Much to Dream Last Night*; *Don't Stay Away Too Long*; *Mama, Teach Me to Dance*; *Ivy Rose*; *Are You Really Mine?*; *You're Cheatin' Yourself*; *If You Smile at the Sun*; *Ashby de La Zooch*

856. HOFFMAN, MAX   cm p v ar
(sometimes spelled HOFF-MANN)

Born December 8, 1873, Gnesen, Poland
Died May 21, 1963, Hollywood, Calif.

Composer for early Broadway musicals. Songs attained little popularity but effective within context of shows. Leading songs *By the Sycamore Tree*, *A Bunch of Rags*, *San Francisco Bay*, *Dixie Queen*, *Rag Medley*, *In Panama*, *If You Want to Learn to Kiss Me*, *The Gertrude Hoffman Glide*, *Bomba-Shay*, *In Washington*, *Ching-a-Ling-a-Loo*, *The Honolulu Dance*, *Artists and Models*, *The American Girl in Paris*. Chief collaborator lyricist George V. Hobart. Brought to U.S. as child 1875, grew up in St. Paul. At 15 violinist with Minneapolis Symphony. Conductor in Chicago vaudeville. Music publishing executive in Chicago. Pioneer in ragtime arranging; orchestrations played throughout U.S. Pianist at Keith's Theatre in Boston. Scores for Broadway shows 1903-12. Directed tours of shows featuring wife, ballerina Gertrude Hoffman. In 1939 musical director for New York theatres, continued in 40s.

BROADWAY MUSICALS
(wrote score)

1903—ROGERS BROTHERS IN LONDON

1904—GLITTERING GLORIA; ROGERS BROTHERS IN PARIS

1905—ROGERS BROTHERS IN IRELAND

1906—A PARISIAN MODEL

1907—ROGERS BROTHERS IN PANAMA

1910—THE YOUNG TURK

1912—BROADWAY TO PARIS

857. HOLIDAY, BILLIE   vo
(ELEANOR GOUGH; nick-named Lady Day)

Born April 7, 1915, Baltimore, Md.
Died July 17, 1959, New York, N.Y.

All-time great jazz vocalist. Though voice small, sang with warmth and emotion. Lagged behind beat, gave distinctive musicianly interpretation to lyrics. Top jazz personnel accompanied her on records and appearances. Illegitimate daughter of guitarist Clarence Holiday. To New York in late 20s; hard years including prostitution. First good singing job at Log Cabin Club. Gained experience at other New York clubs. Jazz critic John Hammond heard her, arranged 1933 recording debut with Benny Goodman. Attracted attention via classic records with Teddy Wilson all-star combos 1935-9. Began recording under own name 1936. With Count Basie 1937-8. With Artie Shaw much of 1938, featured on his radio spots from Boston. Good 1939 runs at New York's Cafe Society. In early and mid-40s worked clubs mainly in New York and Chicago. In 1947 movie NEW ORLEANS. In late 40s singing deteriorated: more commercial style, and voice failing. Drug problem led to jail sentence. Worked her way back early 50s, voice deeper and coarser but approached former jazz style. Toured Europe 1954 with show Jazz Club U. S. A. Appeared solo in Europe 1958. Health deteriorated late 50s; periods of inactivity. 1972 hit movie LADY SINGS THE BLUES based vaguely on Billie Holiday life, starred Diana Ross in Holiday role.

RECORDS

BENNY GOODMAN
Co 2856-D Your Mother's Son-in-Law
Co 2867-D Riffin' the Scotch

TEDDY WILSON
Br 7498 What a Little Moonlight Can Do/A Sunbonnet Blue

Br 7501 I Wished on the Moon/Miss Brown to You

Br 7554 If You Were Mine/Eeny Meeny Miney Mo

Br 7824 He Ain't Got Rhythm/This Year's Kisses

Br 7859 Why Was I Born?/I Must Have That Man

Br 7867 Carelessly/How Could You?

Br 7911 Easy Living/Foolin' Myself

Br 8265 I'll Never Fail You/April in My Heart

ARTIE SHAW

Bb 7759 Any Old Time

PAUL WHITEMAN

Cap 116 Travelin' Light

BILLIE HOLIDAY

Vo 3276 Did I Remember?/No Regrets

Vo 3288 Summertime/Billie's Blues

Vo 3431 One Never Knows, Does One?/I've Got My Love to Keep Me Warm

Vo 3593 Me, Myself and I/Without Your Love

Vo 3605 Born to Love/A Sailboat in the Moonlight

Vo 3947 Now They Call It Swing/On the Sentimental Side

Vo 4208 Says My Heart/Having Myself a Time

Vo 4457 I Can't Get Started/The Very Thought of You

Vo 5021 Some Other Spring/Them There Eyes

Vo 5481 Body and Soul/What Is This Going to Get Us?

OK 6134 Let's Do It/Georgia on My Mind

OK 6270 God Bless the Child/Solitude

OK 6369 Jim/Love Me or Leave Me

OK 6451 Gloomy Sunday/I'm in a Low-down Groove

CMS 526 Strange Fruit/Fine and Mellow

CMS 585 My Old Flame/I'm Yours

De 23391 Lover Man/That Ole Devil Called Love

De 24138 Deep Song/Easy Living

De 24796 You're My Thrill/Crazy He Calls Me

Alad 3094 Detour Ahead

Clef 89108 If the Moon Turns Green/Autumn in New York

LPs

BILLIE HOLIDAY

Co CL-637 Lady Day (mostly TEDDY WILSON Br RIs)

Co CL-2666 Billie Holiday's Greatest Hits (RIs)

Co C3L21(3-LP set) The Golden Years (RIs)

De DL-8702 Lover Man (De RIs)

Verve V-8026 Songs for Torching

Verve V-8257 Songs for Distingue Lovers

Clef MGC-686 Recital by Billie Holiday

Clef MGC-721 Lady Sings the Blues

MGM E-3764 Billie Holiday

Mainstream 6022 Once Upon a Time

ARS G-409

Mer(10″)MGC-118 Billie Holiday Sings

858. HOLLAND, PEANUTS   t vo B
(HERBERT LEE HOLLAND)

Born February 9, 1910, Norfolk, Virginia

Swing-styled trumpet star and rhythm singer, best known for work with Charlie Barnet in 40s. In southwest with Alphonso Trent 1929-33. With Jeter-Pillars, Willie Bryant, Jimmie Lunceford; 1935-6 with Lil Armstrong big band. Led band in Buffalo 1936-8. Freelanced in New York 1939 into early 40s. Periods with Coleman Hawkins and Fletcher Henderson. Led band at intervals. With Charlie Barnet 1942-6. Led band awhile 1946; in September to Europe with Don Redman. Remained abroad playing many countries as leader or sideman from 40s into 60s.

RECORDS

CHARLIE BARNET

De 18378 I Like to Riff/Shady Lady

De 18547 Oh! Miss Jaxson/Washington Whirligig

ANGELS OF MERCY

Gem 3 Sunday

DON BYAS

Blue Star(Fr) 27 Laura/Cement Mixer

Blue Star(Fr) 28 Red Cross/Walking Around

Blue Star(Fr) 29 How High the Moon/Dynamo A

LPs

CHARLIE BARNET
De DL-8098 Hop on the Skyliner (De RIs)

859. HOLLANDER, FRED   cm lyr
Born October 18, 1896, London, England

Composer mostly for movies in 30s and 40s. Best-known songs *Falling in Love Again, Moonlight and Shadows, Whispers in the Dark, True Confession, See What the Boys in the Back Room Will Have.* Chief collaborators lyricists Leo Robin, Sam Coslow, Ralph Freed, Frank Loesser. Educated in German primary schools, Berlin Conservatory of Music. At 18 associate conductor at Prague Opera House. During World War I organized operetta troupe to entertain wounded soldiers. Worked with Max Reinhardt in Berlin. Scored early German sound film THE BLUE ANGEL (1930); well received in U.S. early 1931, since regarded as classic. Film's haunting hit *Falling in Love Again* sung by sensational Marlene Dietrich, became forever associated with her. Scored movies in various European locales, began similar work in U.S. mid-30s.

SONGS
(with related shows)

1931—THE BLUE ANGEL German movie (Falling in Love Again; Naughty Lola)
1936—ANYTHING GOES movie (My Heart and I); RHYTHM ON THE RANGE movie (The House Jack Built for Jill)
1937—THE JUNGLE PRINCESS movie (Moonlight and Shadows); ARTISTS AND MODELS movie (Whispers in the Dark); A HUNDRED MEN AND A GIRL movie (It's Raining Sunbeams); THIS WAY PLEASE movie (Love or Infatuation); TRUE CONFESSION movie (title song)
1938—COCOANUT GROVE movie (You Leave Me Breathless); THRILL OF A LIFETIME movie (title song); YOU AND ME movie (title song); HER JUNGLE LOVE movie (Lovelight in the Starlight); Beside a Moonlit Stream; Stolen Heaven

1939—MAN ABOUT TOWN movie (Strange Enchantment; That Sentimental Sandwich; Man About Town; Fidgety Joe); DESTRY RIDES AGAIN movie (See What the Boys in the Backroom Will Have; Little Joe, the Wrangler; You've Got That Look That Leaves Me Weak)
1940—TYPHOON movie (Palms of Paradise); SEVEN SINNERS movie (I've Been in Love Before); A NIGHT AT EARL CARROLL'S movie (Li'l Boy Love)
1941-6—Musical backgrounds for many movies including THE MAN WHO CAME TO DINNER (1941), THE TALK OF THE TOWN (1942), THE AFFAIRS OF SUSAN (1945), THE GREEN YEARS (1946)
1948—A FOREIGN AFFAIR movie (Black Market; Illusions; Ruins of Berlin); THAT LADY IN ERMINE movie (This Is the Moment; The Melody Has to Be Right; others)

860. HOLM, CELESTE   vo
Born April 29, 1919, New York, N.Y.

Attractive singer-actress of stage, movies and TV. Adept in roles requiring sophistication and witty dialogue. First Broadway experience around 1936; worked up to leading roles over next several years. Featured in plays THE TIME OF YOUR LIFE (1940), PAPA IS ALL and THE DAMASK CHEEK (1942). Gained fame with lusty performance as Ado Annie in hit musical OKLAHOMA! (1943). Starred in musical BLOOMER GIRL (1944). Stage success led to movie career beginning 1946; usually played second lead. Occasionally singer in movie musicals. Academy Award for Best Supporting Actress in GENTLEMAN'S AGREEMENT (1947). Late 40s and 50s on radio. In plays AFFAIRS OF STATE (1950), ANNA CHRISTIE (1952), INVITATION TO A MARCH (1960), A MONTH IN THE COUNTRY (1963). Regular series on TV, occasional other appearances.

MOVIES
1946—THREE LITTLE GIRLS IN BLUE
1947—GENTLEMAN'S AGREEMENT; CARNIVAL IN COSTA RICA

1948—THE SNAKE PIT; ROAD HOUSE; CHICKEN EVERY SUNDAY
1949—COME TO THE STABLE; EVERYBODY DOES IT
1950—CHAMPAGNE FOR CAESAR; ALL ABOUT EVE
1955—THE TENDER TRAP
1956—HIGH SOCIETY
1961—BACHELOR FLAT
1967—DOCTOR, YOU'VE GOT TO BE KIDDING!

RECORDS

CELESTE HOLM
  De 23286 I Cain't Say No
  De 23369 Evelina/Never Was Born
CELESTE HOLM-DAVID BROOKS
  De 23374 Right as the Rain/Sunday in Cicero Falls

LPs

(original Broadway cast)
  De DL-8000 OKLAHOMA!
(movie soundtrack)
  Cap W-750 HIGH SOCIETY

861. HOLMAN, LIBBY   vo

Born May 23, 1906, Cincinnati, Ohio
Died June 18, 1971, Stamford, Conn.

Performer who rose to brief stardom in Broadway musicals as epitome of torch singer. Associated with songs *Moanin' Low, Body and Soul, Something to Remember You By*. Minor role in Broadway show GARRICK GAIETIES (1925), featured in MERRY-GO-ROUND (1927) and RAINBOW (1928). In short-run show NED WAYBURN'S GAMBOLS early 1929. Shortly thereafter star in THE LITTLE SHOW, first real success. Sensation in THREE'S A CROWD (1930) with sultry rendition of *Body and Soul*. Promising career interrupted by 1931 marriage to Zachary Smith Reynolds, tobacco scion shot to death a year later. Libby questioned, cleared. Resumed Broadway career, starring in REVENGE WITH MUSIC (1934) and YOU NEVER KNOW (1938). But Holman magic had dimmed. Summer stock 1939-45. Appeared with Negro folk singer Josh White early 40s in clubs and concerts. During 50s concert tours; program titled "Blues, Ballads and Sin Songs." Mostly inactive in later years.

RECORDS

COTTON PICKERS
  Br 4446 Moanin' Low
  Br 4447 He's a Good Man to Have Around
ROGER WOLFE KAHN
  Br 4699 Cooking Breakfast for the One I Love/When a Woman Loves a Man
LIBBY HOLMAN
  Br 3667 Carefree/Who's Knockin'?
  Br 3798 The Way He Loves Is Just Too Bad/There Ain't No Sweet Man
  Br 4445 Moanin' Low/Am I Blue?
  Br 4506 Can't We Be Friends?/I May Be Wrong
  Br 4570 Here Am I/Why Was I Born?
  Br 4613 More Than You Know/Happy Because I'm in Love
  Br 4666 Find Me a Primitive Man/You've Got That Thing
  Br 4700 What Is This Thing Called Love?/A Ship without a Sail
  Br 4910 Body and Soul/Something to Remember You By
  Br 6044 Love for Sale/I'm One of God's Children
  De 11060 Love for Sale/Moanin' Low (RIs)
  Mer 5071 Body and Soul/Something to Remember You By
LIBBY HOLMAN with JOSH WHITE (g)
  De 18304 Baby Baby/Fare Thee Well
  De 18305 Good Mornin' Blues/When the Sun Goes Down
  De 18306 House of the Risin' Sun/ /Old Smoky/Han'som' Winsome Johnny

LPs

LIBBY HOLMAN
  Mon-Ever MRS-6501 The Legendary Libby Holman
(miscellaneous artists)
  De DEA-7-2 (2-LP set) Those Wonderful Thirties (RIs)
  De(10")DL-7021 Curtain Call (RIs)

862. HOLMES, CHARLIE

                    as ss cl f oboe

Born January 27, 1910, Boston, Mass.

Ebullient saxman with important bands late 20s and 30s. Formal training, played oboe with Boston Civic Symphony 1926. To New York 1927, briefly with Chick Webb and other bands. With Luis Russell part of 1928, off and on in later years. With Mills Blue Rhythm Band 1931-2. Luis Russell again in 1934, remained 1935-40 with Louis Armstrong leader. Briefly with Bobby Burnett group. With Cootie Williams 1942-5. On U.S.O. tour abroad 1945-6. With Jesse Stone 1946. With John Kirby and Billy Kyle 1947. Freelanced in late 40s. In 50s and 60s mostly out of music, played occasional jobs.

RECORDS

HENRY ALLEN, JR. (LUIS RUSSELL)
  Vi 23006 Patrol Wagon Blues
  Vi 23338 Singing Pretty Songs
  Vi 38073 It Should Be You
  Vi 38080 Feeling Drowsy/Swing Out
J. C. HIGGINBOTHAM
  OK 8772 Give Me Your Telephone Number/Higginbotham Blues
LOUIS ARMSTRONG
  OK 8669 I Can't Give You Anything but Love
  OK 8680 Mahogany Hall Stomp
  De 1636 Satchel Mouth Swing
  De 1661 Struttin' with Some Barbecue
  De 1822 So Little Time
  De 2405 Save It, Pretty Mama
  De 2615 Confessin'/Our Monday Date

LPs

LUIS RUSSELL
  Pa(E) PMC-7025 (OK RIs)
LOUIS ARMSTRONG
  De DL-9225 Rare Items 1935-44 (De RIs)
RED ALLEN
  "X"(10")LVA-3033 Ridin' with Red Allen (Vi RIs)

863. HOLMES, LEROY

p b g ar cm lyr B

Born September 22, 1913, Pittsburgh, Pa.

Important arranger-conductor of 50s, active in recording. Attended Northwestern College of Music and Juilliard. Own band 1934, then arranged for Vincent Lopez six years. Arranger for Harry James early 40s. Composed numbers featured by James including *B-19, The Mole, Prince Charming.* Military service, 1943-5. Resumed with James briefly, then scoring in Hollywood for movies and radio. Arranger-conductor for MGM Records; substantial output in 50s with own orchestra playing instrumentals or backing singers. In 1955 led band on college tour. More movie work in 60s, occasional records. Other compositions *The New Dixieland Parade, Sahara, Pennsylvania Turnpike, One Stop Boogie.*

RECORDS

LEROY HOLMES
  MGM 10706 The Sheik of Araby/Dixieland Parade
  MGM 10892 Lying in the Hay/In Your Arms
  MGM 11169 Would You?/If I Forget You
  MGM 11198 You're My Thrill/I'll Walk Alone
  MGM 11247 Isn't This a Night for Love?/Ooh! That Kiss
  MGM 11474 Caravan/Three on a Match
  MGM 11569 Julie/So This Is Love
  MGM 11631 Brazil/The Lately Song
  MGM 11673 Breezin' Along with the Breeze

(as conductor; probably arranger on most)

ART LUND
  MGM 10011 Mam'selle/Sleepy Time Gal
  MGM 10648 Sugarfoot Rag / Wilhelmina
  MGM 11106 I Can't Get Started/Blue Skies
DANNY DAVIS
  MGM 11286 Love Came Out of the Night/Forget
SHIRLEY HARMER
  MGM 11667 If You Love Me/Won'tcha Love Me
TOMMY EDWARDS
  MGM 10884 Once There Lived a Fool/A Friend of Johnny's
  MGM 11395 A Fool Such as I/I Can't Love Another
  MGM 11604 That's All/Secret Love
MARION MORGAN
  MGM 11219 There's a Cloud in My

Valley of Sunshine/The Little Train a-Chuggin' in My Heart

ALAN DEAN

MGM 11187 All My Life/Be Anything

BILL FARRELL

MGM 11193 Sincere/Heaven Knows Why

THE STUARTS

MGM 11782 How About Me?/Get Out and Get Under the Moon

LPs

LEROY HOLMES

UA 3633 The Good, the Bad and the Ugly

UA 6669 (S) Cinema '69

Sun 5247 Sound

MGM E-3172 Lush Themes from Motion Pictures

MGM E-3325 A Hi Fi Salute to the Great Ones

MGM E-3554 A Hi Fi Salute to the Great Ones, Vol. 2

MGM(10")E-215 Songs of Arthur Schwartz-Howard Dietz

(as conductor; probably arranger on most)

TOMMY EDWARDS

MGM E-3805 You Started Me Dreaming

GLORIA LYNNE

Everest LPBR-5090 Try a Little Tenderness

864. HOMER, BEN   ar cm

Born June 27, 1917, Meriden, Conn.

Talented arranger for dance bands, composer of all-time hit *Sentimental Journey*. Attended New England Conservatory of Music. To New York late 30s. Arrangements for Bob Chester, Jimmy and Tommy Dorsey, Raymond Scott, Teddy Powell, Jack Teagarden, Artie Shaw, Nat Shilkret, Benny Goodman. Arranged for Les Brown early and mid-40s; two popular numbers *Mexican Hat Dance* and *Bizet Has His Day*. Composer of two Brown hits *Joltin' Joe DiMaggio* and *Sentimental Journey*. Also movie work. Other compositions included *Shoot the Sherbet to Me, Herbert*; *The Sphinx*; *Flea on a Spree*. In early 50s left music for religious work.

865. HOOKER, BRIAN   lyr

Born November 2, 1880, New York, N.Y.

Died December 28, 1946, New London, Conn.

Lyricist-librettist for Broadway shows; most important THE VAGABOND KING (1925). Wrote book for OUR NELL (1922), WHITE EAGLE (1928), THROUGH THE YEARS (1932). Collaborated with composers Rudolf Friml, Hugo Felix, George Gershwin. Author of plays THE RIGHT MAN, THE PROFESSOR'S MYSTERY, MORVEN AND THE GRAIL. Wrote for operas MONA and FAIRYLAND, Metropolitan Opera award winners in 1911 and 1915. Educated at Yale. Taught at Columbia 1903-5, Yale 1905-9; later lectured at Columbia.

SONGS

(with related shows)

1921—JUNE LOVE stage show (June Love; Don't Keep Calling Me Dearie; Dear Love, My Love; The Flapper and the Vamp)

1922—MARJOLAINE stage show (Marjolaine; River of Dreams; Oh, Love of Mine!; Cuddle Up Together); OUR NELL stage show (Innocent Ingenue Baby; Walking Home with Angeline; Bye and Bye; My Old New England Home)

1925—THE VAGABOND KING stage show (Song of the Vagabonds; Only a Rose; Some Day; Huguette Waltz)

1928—WHITE EAGLE stage show (Give Me One Hour; Regimental Song; Gather the Rose; Silver Wing)

1930—THE VAGABOND KING movie (original stage score)

1956—THE VAGABOND KING movie (original stage score; Johnny Burke wrote some new lyrics)

866. HOOSIER HOT SHOTS

novelty instrumental quartet

PAUL (HEZZIE) TRIETSCH *(song whistle, washboard, drums, alto horn)*

KEN (RUDY) TRIETSCH *(banjo, guitar, bass horn)*

OTTO (GABE) WARD *(clarinet, sax, fife)*

FRANK KETTERING *(banjo, guitar, flute, piccolo, bass, piano)*

Entertaining cornball quartet especially popular in 30s and early 40s. Group performed in high school for plays and dances. Appeared on radio in Fort Wayne. Formed act, toured in vaudeville. Attired in "hick" clothes, used cornball dialogue and antics, topped off act with novelty playing and singing. Favorite line: "Are you ready, Hezzie?" Began on National Barn Dance radio show 1935, appeared regularly through 30s and early 40s. Numerous records. In many low-budget western movies. Dominant group sound: Ward's clarinet. Though exaggerated cornball style, fine tone and technique. Group continued into 50s.

RECORDS

HOOSIER HOT SHOTS
Pe 13117 Oakville Twister/Hoosier Stomp
Me 60262 San/Them Hill-Billies Are Mountain-Williams Now
Me 60557 Wah-Hoo/Bow Wow Blues
Me 60753 Darktown Strutters' Ball/Nobody's Sweetheart
Me 61272 Shake Your Dogs/That's What I Learned in College
Me 70363 Margie/Alexander's Ragtime Band
Vo 03644 Breezin' Along with the Breeze/Sister Kate
Vo 03683 Goofus/Runnin' Wild
Vo 03727 Yes She Do—No She Don't/I'm Looking for a Girl
Vo 03739 Toot Toot Tootsie/You're Driving Me Crazy
Vo 03949 I Ain't Got Nobody/Virginia Blues
Vo 04024 Farewell Blues/Etiquette Blues
Vo 04215 You Said Something When You Said Dixie/After You've Gone
Vo 04352 Milenberg Joys/How Ya Gonna Keep 'Em Down on the Farm?
Vo 04426 Flat Foot Floogie/A Hot Dog, a Blanket and You
Vo 04823 Three Little Fishies/Avalon
Vo 05145 Are You Havin' Any Fun?/Start the Day Right
Vo 05295 Careless/In an Old Dutch Garden

Vo 05390 Ma/I'm Just Wild About Harry

LPs

HOOSIER HOT SHOTS
Tops L-1541

867. HOPE, BOB　　　　vo
(LESLIE TOWNES HOPE)
Born May 26, 1903, London, England
All-time giant of show business; top star 35 years in films, on radio, later on TV. Famous as wisecracking comedian, also sang adeptly with limited vocal talent, performed simple dance steps. Radio and TV monologues often kidded celebrities, current events, politics. Grew up in Cleveland. Tried boxing awhile as youth under name of Packy East. Song and dance man in act Hope & Byrne; played Cleveland, toured in vaudeville and road shows. After team split up Hope worked alone, featured comedy predominately. Bit roles in Broadway musicals UPS-A-DAISY (1928) and SMILES (1930). Featured in BALLYHOO OF 1932, ROBERTA (1933), SAY WHEN (1934). Early 1936 Hope and girl stooge "Honey Chile" (Margaret Johnson) joined radio show Atlantic Family on Tour starring Frank Parker. Later in year Hope prominent in Broadway musical RED HOT AND BLUE. In May 1937 he and Honey Chile joined radio show Rippling Rhythm Revue with Shep Fields band. Late 1937 Hope scored as monologist on Dick Powell's Hollywood Hotel radio show. Own show fall 1938 for Pepsodent.

Movie career began 1938. Adopted *Thanks for the Memory* as radio theme after he and Shirley Ross clicked with song in movie BIG BROADCAST OF 1938. In years following Hope added "thank you" lyrics to fit different guests and occasions. He and Bing Crosby carried on good-natured feud in films and on radio and TV. They co-starred with Dorothy Lamour in 1940 movie ROAD TO SINGAPORE, first of popular Road movies. Hope continued radio show through 40s. Early show featured Skinnay Ennis and band, Frances Langford, Jerry Colonna. Les Brown band began with Hope 1947, continued into 70s on radio, TV and overseas tours to entertain troops. Hope noted for Christmas tours overseas, accompanied by singers, celebrities and Brown band. Announced 1972 tour his last. On TV regularly in 50s and 60s, several times a year with specials and guest appearances in 70s.

MOVIES

1938—BIG BROADCAST OF 1938; COLLEGE SWING; GIVE ME A SAILOR; THANKS FOR THE MEMORY
1939—SOME LIKE IT HOT; NEVER SAY DIE; THE CAT AND THE CANARY; THE MAGNIFICENT FRAUD
1940—ROAD TO SINGAPORE; GHOST BREAKERS
1941—LOUISIANA PURCHASE; ROAD TO ZANZIBAR; CAUGHT IN THE DRAFT; NOTHING BUT THE TRUTH
1942—ROAD TO MOROCCO; STAR SPANGLED RHYTHM; MY FAVORITE BLONDE
1943—LET'S FACE IT; THEY GOT ME COVERED
1944—THE PRINCESS AND THE PIRATE
1946—ROAD TO UTOPIA; MONSIEUR BEAUCAIRE
1947—ROAD TO RIO; VARIETY GIRL; MY FAVORITE BRUNETTE; WHERE THERE'S LIFE
1948—PALEFACE
1949—SORROWFUL JONES; THE GREAT LOVER
1950—FANCY PANTS
1951—THE LEMON DROP KID; MY FAVORITE SPY
1952—SON OF PALEFACE; ROAD TO BALI
1953—OFF LIMITS; HERE COME THE GIRLS
1954—CASANOVA'S BIG NIGHT
1955—THE SEVEN LITTLE FOYS
1956—THAT CERTAIN FEELING; THE IRON PETTICOAT
1957—BEAU JAMES
1958—PARIS HOLIDAY
1959—ALIAS JESSE JAMES
1960—THE FACTS OF LIFE
1961—BACHELOR IN PARADISE
1962—ROAD TO HONG KONG
1963—CALL ME BWANA; CRITIC'S CHOICE
1964—A GLOBAL AFFAIR
1965—I'LL TAKE SWEDEN

1966—BOY, DID I GET A WRONG NUMBER!
1967—EIGHT ON THE LAM
1968—THE PRIVATE NAVY OF SERGEANT O'FARRELL

RECORDS

BOB HOPE-SHIRLEY ROSS
De 2219 Two Sleepy People/Thanks for the Memory
De 2568 The Lady's in Love with You/When We're Alone (Penthouse Serenade)
De 23545 Two Sleepy People/When We're Alone (Penthouse Serenade) (RIs)
BOB HOPE-DOROTHY LAMOUR
Cap 381 Beside You/My Favorite Brunette
BOB HOPE-BING CROSBY
De 28514 Hoot Mon/Merry-Go-Run-Around (also with PEGGY LEE)
De 40000 Road to Morocco/Put It There, Pal
BOB HOPE-JANE RUSSELL
Cap 2109 Wing Ding/Am I in Love?
BOB HOPE
Cap Album CD-26 (78s) I Never Left Home
Cap 15292 Buttons and Bows/That's Not the Knot

LPs

BOB HOPE
Cadet 4046 On the Road to Vietnam (1964)
(movie soundtracks)
De(10")A-926 THE ROAD TO BALI
Lib LOM-16002 THE ROAD TO HONG KONG

868. HOPKINS, CLAUDE   p ar cm B

Born August 24, 1903, Alexandria, Va.

Pianist and leader of swing band most popular during 30s. Excellent arranger. Grew up in Washington, D. C. Attended Howard University. In early 20s co-led combo with banjoist Bernard Addison for a time. Mid-20s with Wilbur Sweatman, also led band accompanying entertainer Josephine Baker on European tour. In 1926 formed band, played at Asbury Park, N. J. Continued as bandleader mostly in New York and Washington, D.

C. In early and mid 30s engagements at New York's Savoy Ballroom, Roseland Ballroom and Cotton Club. Band in films WAYWARD (1932) and DANCE TEAM. Band featured clarinetist Ed Hall and high-voiced singer Orlando Roberson. Hopkins did most arrangements, composed band's theme *(I Would Do) Anything for You*. Later jazzmen included trombonist Vic Dickenson and trumpet star Jabbo Smith. Good radio coverage for band from New York locations. Popular record of *Trees* featuring Roberson vocal. In later 30s band toured. Disbanded 1940. Hopkins led another band 1941-5 on west coast and in New York. Concentrated on arranging awhile for Tommy Tucker, Phil Spitalny, Abe Lyman and others. In late 40s and early 50s led band in New York and Boston. In mid-50s pianist with Red Allen and Herman Autrey. In 60s with Sol Yaged and Wild Bill Davison; led groups at intervals. Active into 70s. Other compositions include *Crying My Heart Out for You, Blame It on a Dream, Washington Squabble, Vamping a Co-ed, Count Off, Low Gravy, Dancing to the Hop, Deep Dawn, Sand Fiddler, Is It So?, That Particular Friend of Mine, Thru with Love Affairs.*

RECORDS

MA RAINEY
  Para 12508 Dead Drunk Blues/Misery Blues
  Para 12526 Slow Driving Moan/Gone Daddy Blues
OVIE ALSTON
  Vo 4448 Junk Man's Serenade/Ja-da
  Vo 4462 How Much Do You Mean to Me?/I Let a Tear Fall in the River
  Vo 4520 Walking the Dog/Home Cookin' Mama
  Vo 4577 Spareribs and Spaghetti/Twinkle Dinkle
CLAUDE HOPKINS
  Co 2665-D (theme) Anything for You/Mad Moments
  Co 2747-D He's a Son of the South/Canadian Capers
  Co 2880-D Ain't Misbehavin'/Harlem Rhythm Dance

Co 2904-D Marie/Minor Mania
Br 6750 Washington Squabble/Mystic Moan
Br 6864 My Gal Sal/Three Little Words
Br 6916 Everybody Shuffle/Margie
De 185 Who?/Just You, Just Me
De 374 Trees/Love in Bloom
De 674 Monkey Business/Zozoi
De 1153 Sunday/Swingin' Down the Lane
De 1316 Honey/My Kinda Love
Ammor 115 Out to Lunch/What's the Matter with Me?
Rbw 10035 Low Gravy/Too Big Papa

LPs

CLAUDE HOPKINS
  Jazz Archives JA-4 (1932-3/1940 RIs)
HERB HALL
  Biog BLP-3003 (S) Herb Hall Quartet
  Sackville 3003 Old Tyme Modern
JOHN HANDY
  Vi LSP-3762(S) Introducing Cap'n John Handy
RED ALLEN-CHARLIE SHAVERS Combos
  Beth BCP-21 Jazz at the Metropole
JIMMY RUSHING
  Co CL-1605 The Smith Girls
(miscellaneous artists)
  Design DLP-38 The Golden Era of Dixieland Jazz

869. HOPPER, DeWOLF   VO
  (WILLIAM D'WOLF)
  Born March 30, 1858, New York, N.Y.
  Died September 23, 1935, Kansas City, Mo.

Star of Broadway musicals and plays from 1880s into 20s. Big man with booming bass voice. Best known for recitations immortalizing Ernest L. Thayer poem "Casey at the Bat." As teenager began in stock companies. Sang in Gilbert & Sullivan productions. Early Broadway roles in DESIREE (1884), THE MIKADO and THE BLACK HUSSAR (1885), THE BEGUM (1887), YEOMEN OF THE GUARD (1888), CASTLES IN THE AIR (1890), THE CHARLATAN (1898). Most famous role in WANG (1891), later in 1904 revival. With wife Edna Wallace Hopper in DR. SYNTAX (1894) and EL CAPITAN (1896). In many

Broadway musicals 1900-28. Later married Hedda Hopper, Hollywood actress who became famous gossip columnist.

BROADWAY MUSICALS

1900—FIDDLE DEE DEE
1901—HOITY TOITY
1903—MR. PICKWICK
1905—HAPPYLAND
1906—THE MAN FROM NOW
1908—THE PIED PIPER
1910—A MATINEE IDOL
1913—HOP O' MY THUMB; LIEBER AUGUST-IN
1917—THE PASSING SHOW OF 1917
1918—EVERYTHING
1921—SNAPSHOTS OF 1921
1922—SOME PARTY
1928—WHITE LILACS

Other productions included Gilbert & Sullivan revivals 1911-12, play THE BEGGAR (1912). Joined comedy-musical THE BETTER 'OLE after Broadway opening; top war comedy 1918-19.

RECORDS

DEWOLF HOPPER
   Vi(12″)35290 Casey at the Bat/The Man Who Fanned Casey

LPs

(miscellaneous artists; one number: Casey at the Bat)
   Vi LCT-1112 Old Curiosity Shop (RIs)

870. HOPPER, EDNA WALLACE . vo

Star of early Broadway plays and musicals. Husband top star DeWolf Hopper; couple appeared in plays DR. SYNTAX (1894) and EL CAPITAN (1896). Edna in plays THE GIRL I LEFT BEHIND ME (1893) and YANKEE DOODLE DANDY (1898). Starred in long-running musical FLORODORA (1900) and other musicals in years following. Performed on stage in various locales; active during 20s.

BROADWAY MUSICALS

1900—CHRIS AND THE WONDERFUL LAMP; FLORODORA
1902—THE SILVER SLIPPER
1908—FIFTY MILES FROM BOSTON
1911—JUMPING JUPITER
1913—THE THINGS THAT COUNT (non-musical)

1918—GIRL O' MINE

871. HORLICK, HARRY   v cm ar B
Born in Kiev, Russia

Known mostly as leader of A & P Gypsies orchestra, string ensemble active on radio in 20s and 30s. When family left for U.S. at start of World War I, Harry remained in Russia, served in army, was prisoner of war. Family and American consul helped get him to U.S. A & P Gypsies a sextet, all Russian-born. Played cafes early 20s. On radio for A & P food stores, whence name. Later a seventh musician joined. Instrumentation: strings, piano, organ. Theme *Two Guitars*, gypsy air arranged by Horlick 1925 as popular song. Group on long-running radio series from late 20s to mid-30s. In later 30s Horlick worked with orchestra under own name, occasionally recorded.

RECORDS

A & P GYPSIES
   Br 3024 (theme) Two Guitars/Shadow of the Past
   Br 3140 Marigny/Fleurs d'Amour
   Br 3188 Gypsy Moon/Farewell, Farewell, My Village
   Br 3745 Lolita/Yesterday
   Br 3882 Fleur de Lis/The Beggar
   Br 3982 Chiquita/Rosette
   Br 4287 Herbertina/White Acacia
   Br 4442 Simple Confession/Faraway Bells
   Br 4903 Bohemian Romance/My Memories
HARRY HORLICK
   De 1776 Wine, Women and Song/Viennese Bonbons
   De 1944 Gypsy Princess/The Merry Widow
   De 2854 Toyland/Gypsy Love Song
   De 3838 Memories/Your Eyes Have Told Me So
   De 3839 Shadow Waltz/Smilin' Thru

LPs

HARRY HORLICK
   Lion 70066 The Greatest Strauss Waltzes
   Vo VL-3608 Strauss Waltzes for Dancing

872. HORNE, LENA   VO

Born June 30, 1917, Brooklyn, N.Y.

Beautiful singing star with distinctive style and elegant manner, popular from 40s into 70s. Top night club, film and TV entertainer. First job at 16 as singer in chorus at Harlem's Cotton Club. Vocalist with Noble Sissle band 1935-6. Single at many New York clubs, including popular runs at Cafe Society; worked other cities also. Early stage experience in Lew Leslie's BLACKBIRDS OF 1939 and 1940. With Charlie Barnet band several months late 1940-1. Effective small role in first movie PANAMA HATTIE (1942) led to other movie musicals in 40s. Married pianist-bandleader Lennie Hayton late 1947. He performed with her many years as pianist-arranger-conductor-manager until death in 1971. Miss Horne active in 40s and 50s. Several European tours; great success at London's Palladium. Starred in Broadway musical JAMAICA (1957). Many TV appearances 50s and 60s. Singing style so well-known that comic-mimics often imitated her. By mid-60s less active; TV and club dates infrequent.

MOVIES

1942—PANAMA HATTIE
1943—CABIN IN THE SKY; STORMY WEATHER; I DOOD IT; THOUSANDS CHEER; SWING FEVER
1944—BROADWAY RHYTHM; TWO GIRLS AND A SAILOR
1946—ZIEGFELD FOLLIES
1947—TILL THE CLOUDS ROLL BY
1948—WORDS AND MUSIC
1950—DUCHESS OF IDAHO
1956—MEET ME IN LAS VEGAS
1969—DEATH OF A GUNFIGHTER

RECORDS

NOBLE SISSLE
  De 778 That's What Love Did to Me
  De 847 I Take to You
CHARLIE BARNET
  Bb 11037 Good for Nothin' Joe
  Bb 11081 The Captain and His Men
  Bb 11093 Haunted Town
  Bb 11141 You're My Thrill
ARTIE SHAW
  Vi 27509 Love Me a Little Little/Don't Take Your Love from Me

TEDDY WILSON
  Co 36737 Out of Nowhere
  VD(12")317 Prisoner of Love
LENA HORNE with CAB CALLOWAY ORCHESTRA
  VD(12")126 Diga Diga Doo/There's No Two Ways About Love//Good for Nothin' Joe
LENA HORNE
  Vi 27817 Moanin' Low/I Gotta Right to Sing the Blues
  Vi 27818 The Man I Love/Where or When
  Vi 27819 Ill Wind/Stormy Weather
  Vi 27820 Mad About the Boy/What Is This Thing Called Love?
  Vi 20-1616 I Didn't Know About You/One for My Baby
  Vi 20-1626 As Long as I Live/I Ain't Got Nothing but the Blues
  B&W 817 Glad to Be Unhappy/At Long Last Love
  B&W 818 More Than You Know/Blue Prelude
  B&W 819 Squeeze Me/You Go to My Head
  MGM 10165 Love of My Life/'Deed I Do
  MGM 30003 Can't Help Lovin' Dat Man

LPs

LENA HORNE
  Vi LOC-1028 At the Waldorf-Astoria
  Vi LPM-1148 It's Love
  Vi LPM-1879 Give the Lady What She Wants
  MGM(10")E-545
  Tops L-1502 Lena Horne
  Lion L-70050 I Feel So Smoochie
  20th Fox TFS-4115 (S) Here's Lena Now!
LENA HORNE-HARRY BELAFONTE
  Vi LOP-1507 PORGY AND BESS
(miscellaneous artists)
  Cam CAL-321 NBC's Chamber Music Society of Lower Basin Street (Vi RIs)

873. HOSCHNA, KARL   cm ar oboe

Born August 16, 1877, Kuschwarda, Bohemia
Died December 22, 1911, New York, N.Y.

Composer of scores for Broadway musicals 1908-12. Promising career cut short by death. Best-known songs *Cuddle Up a Little Closer* and *Every Little Movement.* Chief collaborators lyricists Otto Harbach and Benjamin H. Burt. Studied at Vienna Conservatory. Oboist in Austrian army band. To U.S. 1896. Two years in Victor Herbert orchestra. Arranging for Witmark Music. Last compositions in show WALL STREET GIRL (1912) after death.

SONGS
(with related shows)

1908—THREE TWINS stage show (Cuddle Up a Little Closer; Yama-Yama Man)

1910—BRIGHT EYES stage show (For You, Bright Eyes; Cheer Up, My Honey; Good Old Days of Yore; The Mood You're In); MADAME SHERRY stage show (Every Little Movement; We Are Only Poor Weak Mortals; The Birth of Passion; The Smile She Means for Me)

1911—DR. DELUXE stage show (For Every Boy That's Lonely There's a Girl That's Lonely Too; The Accent Makes No Difference in the Language of Love); THE FASCINATING WIDOW stage show (Don't Take Your Beau to the Seashore; You Built a Fire Down in My Heart; The Ragtime College Girl; The Fascinating Widow); THE GIRL OF MY DREAMS stage show (The Girl Who Wouldn't Spoon; Every Girlie Loves Me but the Girlie I Love; The Girl of My Dreams); JUMPING JUPITER stage show (It All Goes Up in Smoke; I'm Awfully Afraid of Girls; Meet Me Tonight at Nine; Pet of the Family; Thank You, Kind Sir; many others)

1912—WALL STREET GIRL stage show (The Deedle Dum Dee; I Want a Regular Man; On the Quiet)

874. HOUGH, WILL M.   lyr

Born August 23, 1882, Chicago, Ill.
Died November 20, 1962, Carmel, Calif.

Lyricist-librettist of Chicago and New York musicals. Most famous song *I Wonder Who's Kissing Her Now.* Other songs included *I Don't Like Your Family*; *Blow the Smoke Away*; *What's the Use of*

Dreaming?; *When You First Kiss the Last Girl You Love*; *Honeymoon*; *Goodbye, Everybody*; *Be Sweet to Me, Kid*; *Tonight Will Never Come Again.* Chief collaborators Joe Howard, Frank Adams, Harold Orlob. Educated at University of Chicago. Wrote material for vaudeville acts. Wrote book for musicals A MODERN EVE (1915), PITTER PATTER (1920). Wrote book and lyrics for musicals THE LAND OF NOD and THE TIME, THE PLACE AND THE GIRL (1907), THE FLOWER OF THE RANCH and THE GIRL QUESTION (1908), THE GODDESS OF LIBERTY, THE PRINCE OF TONIGHT and A STUBBORN CINDERELLA (1909).

875. HOWARD, BOB   p vo B
(HOWARD JOYNER)

Born June 20, 1906, Newton, Mass.

Pianist-vocalist on swinging records in 30s. Injected humor and showmanship a la Fats Waller into singing and playing, produced lively, happy music. Solo in New York night clubs mid-20s. Began recording 1931. Played New York's Park Central Hotel, Famous Door, Hickory House and other clubs as well as theatres. Recorded frequently in mid-30s with combos at times including Benny Carter, Buster Bailey, Rex Stewart, Ben Webster, Teddy Wilson, Russell Procope, Cecil Scott, Cozy Cole, Bunny Berigan, Artie Shaw, Babe Russin, Al Philburn, Paul Ricci, Marty Marsala, Dave Barbour, Frank Froeba, Slats Long, Billy Kyle. Howard did not play piano on combo records, only sang. European tours as solo entertainer. Own radio series in New York middle and late 30s. Active in 40s and 50s in clubs; many TV shows in early 50s. Based in New York for years, later played other locales such as Las Vegas and Los Angeles.

RECORDS
HOWARD JOYNER
    Co 14623-D I Wanna Sing About You/I'm Thru with Love
    Co 14650-D You Rascal You
    Co 14678-D Underneath the Harlem Moon
BOB HOWARD
    De 343 Throwin' Stones at the Sun/You Fit into the Picture
    De 484 I Can't Dance/Corrine Corrina

De 504 Lulu's Back in Town/If the Moon Turns Green
De 524 I'm Painting the Town Red/I Never Saw a Better Night
De 598 Sugar Plum/It's Written in the Stars
De 689 Whose Big Baby Are You?/You Hit the Spot
De 720 Wake Up and Sing/Spreadin' Rhythm Around
De 722 Garbo Green/Much Too Much
De 839 The Best Things Happen at Night/Let's Not Fall in Love
De 917 Bojangles of Harlem/Sing, Baby, Sing
De 990 Copper Colored Gal/That's What You Mean to Me
De 1205 Me, Myself and I/You Can't Take It with You
De 1306 Formal Night in Harlem/He's a Gypsy from Poughkeepsie
De 1357 Easy Living/Sing and Be Happy
De 1721 Baby, It Must Be Love/There Ain't Gonna Be No Doggone Afterwhile
De 1869 In My Mizz/Toodle-oo
De 2263 On Revival Day/Sweet Emalina, My Gal
Atl 852 Button Up Your Overcoat/Mo'lasses

876. HOWARD, DARNELL   cl as v B

Born c. 1895, Chicago, Ill.
Died September 2, 1966, San Francisco, Calif.

Jazzman from early 20s into 60s; played with jazz greats. Early in career violinist with Chicago groups beginning 1912. Worked also in Milwaukee and Minneapolis. Period with W. C. Handy orchestra. Switched to clarinet as main instrument, still doubled on violin at times. Toured with Charlie Elgar 1921. Tours in Europe 1923-6 with several units, first one led by James P. Johnson. In China awhile with Teddy Weatherford. In U.S. middle and late 20s with King Oliver, Erskine Tate, Carroll Dickerson, Charlie Elgar, Dave Peyton. Led group 1930-1. With Earl Hines 1931-7, then mostly led groups in Chicago until late 40s. Occasionally

with dixieland groups. Usually with Muggsy Spanier late 1948-53, mostly on west coast. Periods with Bob Scobey and Jimmy Archey. With Earl Hines combo 1955-62. Then activities slowed. European tour 1966 with Original New Orleans All-Stars. Upon return to U.S. entered hospital, suffered stroke, died from brain tumor.

RECORDS

LOUIS ARMSTRONG
OK 8482 Alligator Crawl
OK 8496 Melancholy Blues/Keyhole Blues
Co 36376 Chicago Breakdown

JIMMY BERTRAND
Vo 1280 Isabella/I Won't Give You None

RICHARD M. JONES
Sess 12006 New Orleans Hop Scop Blues/29th & Dearborn
Sess 12007 Jazzin' Babies Blues/Canal Street Blues

KING OLIVER
Vo 1049 Tack Annie

TINY PARHAM
De 7780 Frogtown Blues/Spo-De-O-Dee
De 7801 Moving Day

LUIS RUSSELL
OK 8424 Plantation Joys/Please Don't Turn Me Down
OK 8454 Sweet Mumtaz/Dolly Mine

MEMPHIS NIGHT HAWKS
Pe 0205 Georgia Grind
Vo 1736 Jockey Stomp/Sweet Feet
Vo 1744 Biscuit Roller/Come On In, Baby
Vo 2593 Shanghai Honeymoon/Wild Man Stomp

EARL HINES
Br 6541 Cavernism (violin)
De 182 Sweet Georgia Brown
De 183 Cavernism (violin)
De 337 Copenhagen
De 577 Wolverine Blues

KID ORY
GTJ 70 Down Home Rag/1919 Rag
JM 26 Original Dixieland One-Step/Ory's Creole Trombone

DARNELL HOWARD
JM 33 St. Louis Blues/Pretty Baby

JM 34 Some of These Days/Dipper-
mouth Blues
HJCA 73 Sweet Feet/Wild Man
Stomp (MEMPHIS NIGHT HAWKS RIs)

LPs

EARL HINES
De DL-9221 South Side Swing (1934-5
De RIs)
BOB SCOBEY
GTJ 12032 Vol. 1, The Scobey Story
AL WYNN
Riv RLP-426 And His Gutbucket
Seven
RICHARD M. JONES
Pax(10")6010 Jazz Wizards (Sess RIs)
LIL HARDIN ARMSTRONG
Riv RLP-401
ALBERTA HUNTER with LOVIE AUSTIN &
HER BLUES SERENADERS
Riv RLP-418 (recorded in 1961)

877. HOWARD, EDDY   vo g cm lyr B

*Born September 12, 1914, Woodland,
Calif.*
Died May 23, 1963, Palm Desert, Calif.

Vocalist who rose to fame with Dick
Jurgens band in late 30s, then became
successful bandleader in 40s and 50s. Soft
melodic voice and intimate style. Attended San Jose State College and Stanford University Medical School. Began
singing on Los Angeles radio. In early 30s
with Eddie Fitzpatrick, Tom Gerun, Ben
Bernie. With Dick Jurgens 1934-1940.
Popularity with Jurgens peaked with hits
My Last Goodbye and *Careless*, both
Howard compositions. In 1940 began as
single in clubs and on records. Formed
band 1941, through the years maintained
competent hotel-styled group. Theme
Careless. Hit *To Each His Own* 1946.
Howard featured as solo vocalist with
band, also led vocal trio. Popular into 50s,
though ill health forced disbanding a year
1951-2 and again most of 1954. Reor-
ganized band late 1954, active into 60s.
Other compositions included *If I Knew
Then, Now I Lay Me Down to Dream, A
Million Dreams Ago, Soft Summer Breeze,
Something Old—Something New, So Long
for Now, For Sale, Lynn, With Love,
Lonesome Tonight.*

RECORDS

DICK JURGENS
De 269 Wild Honey
Me 61204 Easy to Love/I've Got You
Under My Skin
Vo 4211 I Wish I Was the Willow
Vo 4677 Little Sir Echo/Red Skies in
the Night
Vo 4678 Penny Serenade/Rainbow
Valley
Vo 4874 My Last Goodbye/Rumpel-
Stilts-Kin
Vo 4901 All I Remember Is You/Rag-
time Cowboy Joe
Vo 5074 If I Knew Then/Lilacs in the
Rain
Vo 5233 Careless/I Only Want a
Buddy, Not a Sweetheart
Vo 5338 You Can Depend on Me
Vo 5442 I Concentrate on You/Be-
tween You and Me

GEORGE OLSEN
De 1786 Sixty Seconds Got Togeth-
er/Little Lady Make-Believe
De 1824 Somewhere with Somebody
Else/Why'd Ya Make Me Fall in
Love?

EDDY HOWARD
Co 35455 The Singing Hills/Where
Was I?
Co 35511 Fools Fall in Love/The
Nearness of You
Co 35868 Mean to Me/Or Have I?
Co 35915 Exactly Like You/Wrap
Your Troubles in Dreams
Co 36074 Do I Worry?/My Sister and
I
Co 36432 Two in Love/Miss You
Co 37578 Not Mine/Happy in Love
Maj 1070 To Each His Own/Careless
(theme)
Maj 1073 My Last Goodbye/Lynn
Maj 1089 There Is No Breeze/Bless
You
Maj 1110 Paradise/Once in Awhile
Maj 1111 Don't Tell Her What Hap-
pened to Me
Mer 5630 What Will I Tell My
Heart?/The Strange Little Girl
Mer 5832 All I Do Is Dream of You/
Singin' in the Rain
Mer 5898 Mademoiselle/I Don't
Know Any Better

LPs

EDDY HOWARD
   Mer MG-20082 Shall We Dance?
   Mer MG-20112 Singing in the Rain
   Mer(10″)MG-25011 Eddy Howard &
      His Orchestra
   Mer(10″)MG-25030
   Mer(10″)MG-25031
   Ha HL-7042 Yours (Co RIs)
   Co(10″)CL-6067 (Co RIs)

877A. HOWARD, JOE   cm lyr vo

   *Born February 12, 1878, New York,
   N.Y.*
   Died May 19, 1961, Chicago, Ill.

Composer-singer of early Broadway musicals. Active on Chicago stage. Most famous songs *I Wonder Who's Kissing Her Now*; *Goodbye, My Lady Love*; *Honeymoon*; *Hello, My Baby*. Other songs included *On a Saturday Night*; *There's Nothing Like a Good Old Song*; *Somewhere in France Is the Lily*; *Can't Get You Out of My Mind*; *Love Me Little, Love Me Long*; *Montana*; *Silver in Your Hair*; *Whistle a Song*; *On the Boulevard*; *An Echo of Her Smile*; *I Don't Like Your Family*; *What's the Use of Dreaming?*; *Blow the Smoke Away*; *Be Sweet to Me, Kid*; *When You First Kiss the Last Girl You Love*; *Tonight Will Never Come Again*; *A Boy's Best Friend Is His Mother*. Chief collaborators Will M. Hough, Frank Adams, Harold Orlob. Scored Broadway musicals THE TIME, THE PLACE AND THE GIRL (1907); THE LAND OF NOD (1907); THE FLOWER OF THE RANCH (1908; unsuccessful); THE GIRL QUESTION (1908); THE GODDESS OF LIBERTY (1909); THE PRINCE OF TONIGHT (1909); A STUBBORN CINDERELLA (1909). Scored Chicago shows ISLE OF BONG BONG (1905); THE UMPIRE (1905); HONEYMOON TRAIL (1908); THE GOLDEN GIRL (1909); MISS NOBODY FROM STARLAND (1910); SWEETEST GIRL IN PARIS (1910); THE FLIRTING PRINCESS (1911); A BROADWAY HONEYMOON (1911); LOVE AND POLITICS (1911); LOWER BERTH THIRTEEN (1912); IN AND OUT (1915). Most Chicago shows also played other cities. Vaudeville debut at 11 as boy soprano. Toured with stock company, played vaudeville and night clubs as song and dance man. On radio, including popular Gay Nineties Revue with Beatrice Kay 1939 into mid-40s. 1947 movie I WONDER WHO'S KISSING HER NOW based on life story; actor Mark Stevens in Howard role, Buddy Clark's singing dubbed.

RECORDS

JOE HOWARD
   Br 4340 Honeymoon/Blow the Smoke
      Away
   Vo 3357 I Wonder Who's Kissing Her
      Now/Honeymoon//Hello, My
      Baby/Goodbye, My Lady Love
   DeL 1036 I Wonder Who's Kissing
      Her Now/On a Saturday Night
   DeL 1037 Honeymoon/Goodbye, My
      Lady Love

878. HOWARD, JOE   tb
   (FRANCIS L. HOWARD)

   Born November 3, 1919, Batesville, Ind.

Trombonist, gained recognition in 50s and 60s on mood music LPs. Superb soloist with warm, beautiful tone, smooth style, good high register. Capable jazz soloist. Attended Los Angeles City College late 30s. In early 40s worked mostly on west coast, including stints with Will Osborne, Ben Pollack, Stan Kenton. Later with Woody Herman, Ray Noble, Artie Shaw. In late 40s and 50s freelanced on west coast, worked as studio musician. Despite more than a decade with name bands, up to this point virtually unknown. Then mid-50s and 60s LPs brought belated recognition.

RECORDS
(all LPs)

NORMAN LUBOFF CHOIR
   Co CL-1296 But Beautiful
VAN ALEXANDER
   Cap T-1243 The Home of Happy Feet
      (The Savoy)
TUTTI CAMARATA
   Vista 4048 (S) Tutti's Trombones
GLEN GRAY
   Cap W-1022 Sounds of the Great
      Bands, Vol. 1
   Cap T-1234 Solo Spotlight
   Cap T-1739 They All Swung the Blues!
JERRY FIELDING
   Kapp KL-1026 Plays a Dance Concert

De(12″)DL-8100
De(12″)DL-8450 Fielding's Formula
PAUL WESTON
Co CL-693 Mood for 12
JOE HOWARD
King 661 Golden Sound

879. HOWARD, WILLIE and EUGENE
(real name Levkowitz; both deceased)

Star vaudeville and stage team many years. Willie born in Germany April 13, 1886, Eugene earlier. Willie got the laughs in their act; Eugene straight man. Brothers brought to U.S. from Germany as youngsters; family settled in New York. Duo won amateur contests, then worked separately as professionals in early years. In 1899 Eugene sang in chorus of Broadway show THE BELLE OF NEW YORK; in 1900 small role in A MILLION DOLLARS. In 1901 small singing role for Willie in THE LITTLE DUCHESS. Teamed in 1905 to play vaudeville with comedy, song and dance act. Gradually worked up to top bookings. Beginning 1912 team featured in many Broadway musicals, last in 1939, after which Willie appeared as single in several shows. Performed as team on radio in 30s. Willie died January 12, 1949 in New York.

BROADWAY MUSICALS

1912—THE PASSING SHOW OF 1912
1914—THE WHIRL OF THE WORLD
1915—THE PASSING SHOW OF 1915
1916—THE SHOW OF WONDERS
1918—THE PASSING SHOW OF 1918
1921—THE PASSING SHOW OF 1921
1922—THE PASSING SHOW OF 1922
1925—SKY HIGH (Willie only)
1926—GEORGE WHITE'S SCANDALS OF 1926
1928—GEORGE WHITE'S SCANDALS OF 1928
1929—GEORGE WHITES SCANDALS OF 1929
1930—GIRL CRAZY (Willie only)
1931—GEORGE WHITE'S SCANDALS OF 1931
1932—BALLYHOO OF 1932
1934—ZIEGFELD FOLLIES OF 1934
1936—GEORGE WHITE'S SCANDALS OF 1936

1939—GEORGE WHITE'S SCANDALS OF 1939
1941—CRAZY WITH THE HEAT (Willie only)
1942—PRIORITIES OF 1942 (Willie only)
1943—MY DEAR PUBLIC (Willie only)
1948—SALLY (revival; Willie only)

879A. HOWLAND, JOBYNA   vo
Born March 31, 1880, Indianapolis, Ind.
Died June 7, 1936, Los Angeles, Calif.

Beautiful star of Broadway musicals and plays. Supporting roles in musicals MISS PRINNT (1900), THE MESSENGER BOY (1901), WINSOME WINNIE (1903), THE HAM TREE (1905). Leading roles in THE PASSING SHOW OF 1912, RUGGLES OF RED GAP (1916), FOLLOW THE GIRL (1918). Co-starred with Eddie Cantor in hit KID BOOTS (1924). In plays THE THIRD PARTY (1914), A LITTLE JOURNEY (1918), THE TEXAS NIGHTINGALE (1922).

880. HUBBELL, RAYMOND   cm
Born June 1, 1879, Urbana, Ohio
Died December 13, 1954, Miami, Fla.

Composer for many Broadway musicals, including ZIEGFELD FOLLIES. Wrote all-time hit *Poor Butterfly* for THE BIG SHOW (1916). Other compositions included *The Little Place That I Call Home*; *Somebody Else*; *If I Were a Bright Little Star*; *A Kiss for Each Day in the Week*; *Hello, Honey*; *The Ladder of Roses*; *Look at the World and Smile*; *Hello, I've Been Looking for You*; *Jealous Moon*; *Chu Chin Chow*; *Melodyland*; *Just My Style*; *Life Is a See-Saw*; *Little Girl in Blue*; *Yours Truly*; *What Am I Going to Do to Make You Love Me?*; *Tonight's the Night*. Many songs effective only within context of shows, attained little popularity. Chief collaborators lyricists Robert B. Smith, Harry B. Smith, Glen MacDonough, E. Ray Goetz, George V. Hobart, John Golden, Anne Caldwell. Early in career staff composer in Chicago publishing house. Then to New York for successful career writing for Broadway shows. Also wrote scores for successful circus-style extravaganzas staged at Hippodrome Theatre, GOOD TIMES (1920) and BETTER TIMES (1922).

BROADWAY MUSICALS
(wrote music)

1903—THE RUNAWAYS
1905—FANTANA
1906—MAM'SELLE SALLIE; MEXICANA; ABOUT TOWN
1908—A KNIGHT FOR A DAY; THE GIRL AT THE HELM
1909—THE AIR KING; THE MIDNIGHT SONS
1910—THE BACHELOR BELLES; THE JOLLY BACHELORS
1911—THE NEVER HOMES; THE THREE ROMEOS; ZIEGFELD FOLLIES OF 1911
1912—THE MAN FROM COOK'S; A WINSOME WIDOW; ZIEGFELD FOLLIES OF 1912
1913—ZIEGFELD FOLLIES OF 1913
1914—ZIEGFELD FOLLIES OF 1914
1915—FADS AND FANCIES; HIP-HIP-HOO-RAY
1916—THE BIG SHOW; GO TO IT; COME TO BOHEMIA
1917—CHEER UP; ZIEGFELD FOLLIES OF 1917
1918—HITCHY-KOO OF 1918; THE KISS BURGLAR
1919—HAPPY DAYS; MISS MILLIONS
1924—ZIEGFELD FOLLIES OF 1924
1925—ZIEGFELD FOLLIES OF 1925
1927—YOURS TRULY
1928—THREE CHEERS

881. HUCKO, PEANUTS   cl ts as B
(MICHAEL ANDREW HUCKO)
Born April 7, 1918, Syracuse, N.Y.

Versatile clarinet and tenor sax star with ability to fit with dixieland, swing or semi-modern group. Tone and clarinet style owed much to Benny Goodman. Tenor sax style in Eddie Miller vein. After early local experience moved to New York 1939. Briefly with Jack Jenney, then with Will Bradley fall 1939 to April 1940; rejoined 1941. Early 40s also with Tommy Reynolds, Joe Marsala, Dick Rogers, Charlie Spivak, Bob Chester. Attained stardom with Glenn Miller's AAF orchestra 1943-5. Joined Benny Goodman late 1945 for two months. With Ray McKinley early 1946-7; later 1947 with Jack Teagarden and Eddie Condon. In late 40s freelanced; active in dixieland combos including those of Condon and Wild Bill Davison. 1950-1 with Joe Bush-kin and Bernie Leighton. Mostly in radio-TV 1951-5; active in freelance recording. Toured Japan-Thailand-Burma with Goodman band late 1956 to early 1957, played lead alto. European tour 1957 with Jack Teagarden-Earl Hines combo. With Louis Armstrong's All-Stars 1958-60. More studio work early 60s. Mostly led combo from mid-60s into 1970. In 1967 opened club in Denver, led combo featuring vocalist-wife Louise Tobin. With Lawrence Welk late 1970 to mid-1972 on weekly TV show, often featured on clarinet. Starred with Big Band Cavalcade on tour 1972-4. Replaced Buddy DeFranco as leader of Glenn Miller band early 1974.

RECORDS

WILL BRADLEY
   Co 35376 Jimtown Blues
   Co 35422 Flying Home/So Far, So Good
   Co 35566 As Long as I Live
   Co 36014 It's Square but It Rocks
RAY MCKINLEY QUARTET
   Co 36101 Tea for Two
RAY MCKINLEY TRIO
   Jazz Club(Fr) 131 China Boy/Shoemaker's Apron
BERNIE LEIGHTON
   Mello-Roll 5004 Whispering/Smooth Sailing
TOMMY DORSEY
   Vi 20-3791 'Way Down Yonder in New Orleans/Tiger Rag
EMPERORS OF JAZZ
   Swan 7506 Nobody's Sweetheart/Royal Garden Blues
   Swan 7508 Fidgety Feet
EDDIE CONDON
   Atl 661 Time Carries On/Seems Like Old Times
   De 24217 Nobody Knows/We Called It Music
   De 24218 My Melancholy Baby/Tulip Time in Holland
   De 27035 Jazz Me Blues
   De 27095 Charleston/Black Bottom
JACK TEAGARDEN
   Vi 40-0138 A Jam Session at Victor/Say It Simple
V-DISC JUMPERS
   VD(12")588 Love Is Just Around the Corner

MUGGSY SPANIER
    VD(12″)588 Tin Roof Blues/Cherry//
RED MCKENZIE
    Nat 9027 Ace in the Hole/Peg o' My
    Heart
PEANUTS HUCKO
    VD(12″)792 Someday Sweetheart/Sto-
    len Peanuts//
    VD(12″)799 I Must Have That Man
    VD(12″)859 Ain't We Got Fun

LPs

PEANUTS HUCKO
    GA 33-331 A Tribute to Benny Good-
    man
    (one side) Jazztone J-1250 Dedicated
    Jazz
    (one side) Waldorf 33-L A Tribute to
    Benny Goodman
HELEN WARD with PEANUTS HUCKO OR-
    CHESTRA
    Vi LPM-1464 With a Little Bit of
    Swing
RAY MCKINLEY-PEANUTS HUCKO
    Ga 33-333 The Swinging Thirties
PHIL NAPOLEON
    EmArcy(10)MG-26008 Dixieland
    Classics, Vol. 1 (Swan RIs)
LOUIS ARMSTRONG ALL-STARS
    Vi LPM-1443 Town Hall Concert Plus
DAVE GARROWAY
    Vi LPM-1325 Wide, Wide World of
    Jazz
EDDIE CONDON
    Co CL-881 Treasury of Jazz
LOU STEIN
    Jub 1019 Eight for Kicks, Four for
    Laughs
BOB ALEXANDER (one side)
    GA 33-325 Progressive Jazz
MOREY FELD
    Kapp KL-1007 Jazz Goes to Broad-
    way
GLENN MILLER
    Vi LPT-6702 (AAF Orchestra, 3rd
    Limited Edition Set)

882. HUDSON, DEAN   t B
   Born c. 1906

Leader of good dance band in 40s and
50s. Attended University of Florida in
30s, led band there. Sideman with Ray
Teal, Blue Steele. Organized band as
Dean Hudson & His Florida Clubmen.

Band competent, with round ensemble
sound and smooth style. Sometimes featured band members singing glee club
style. Military service awhile, early 40s.
Discharged late 1943, took over former
Bobby Byrne band after it was fronted
briefly by Jack Jenney when Byrne left
for military service. Band could swing;
arrangements by Sy Oliver. Les and Larry
Elgart, later famous leaders, joined. In 40s
and 50s Hudson busy, especially popular
in south. In early 50s featured trombone
choir and vocal choir. Pianist Lennie
Love wrote arrangements. Early theme
Miami Dreams, later *Moon Over Miami*.
Active into 70s.

RECORDS
DEAN HUDSON
    Bb 7422 (theme) Miami Dreams/An-
    nie Laurie
    Bb 7433 Stormy Weather/Liebestraum
    Bb 7458 Washington & Lee Swing/
    Alma Mater
    OK 6148 Can't You Tell?/Red River
    Valley
    OK 6171 Let's Try Again/I'll Take
    You Home Again, Kathleen
    OK 6355 Holly Hop/Ma, I Miss Your
    Apple Pie
    OK 6460 Blitzkrieg/You're Gone
    Mus 15026 Caravan/Paradise
    Mus 15033 The More I See You/I
    Wuv a Wabbit
    Bullet 1049 (theme) Moon Over Miami
    Bullet 1082 Waiting for the Robert E.
    Lee/Snap Your Fingers

883. HUDSON, WILL   p cm ar B
   Born March 8, 1908, Barstow, Calif.

Bandleader of 30s but more important as
arranger and composer. Attended high
school in Detroit, studied arranging. Early arrangements for McKinney's Cotton
Pickers, Erskine Tate, Cab Calloway. Latter brought Hudson to New York, where
he joined with Irving Mills for arranging
and composing. Arrangements also for
Ina Ray Hutton, Benny Goodman, Andy
Kirk, Earl Hines, Fletcher Henderson,
Don Redman, Louis Armstrong, Jimmie
Lunceford. Writing simple, lean, swinging, in Casa Loma mode. Beginning mid-
30s important jazz and pop composing.
1934 hit *Moonglow* all-time standard.

Composed and arranged two early Lunceford classics *White Heat* and *Jazznocracy*. Arranged all-time jazz classic *Cherokee* for Ray Noble 1938. Instrumental hit *Organ Grinder's Swing* in fall 1936. In late 1935 formed excellent big band with Eddie DeLange as co-leader; called Hudson-DeLange Orchestra. Band featured Hudson ballad and swing arrangements. Ruth Gaylor vocalist. Theme Hudson's popular jazz tune *Sophisticated Swing*. DeLange partnership until spring 1938, when Hudson assumed full leadership till 1941. In early 40s again concentrated on arranging. Some scores for Glenn Miller AAF orchestra. Freelance stock arranging for publishing companies on and off in 30s and 40s. Military service 1943-5. Later 40s studied composition at Juilliard, tried serious works. Music activities decreased. Other compositions included jazz numbers *Cowboy in Manhattan, Yankee in Havana, Eight Bars in Search of a Melody, Monopoly Swing, Hobo on Park Avenue, Mr. Ghost Goes to Town, Devil's Kitchen, Witch Doctor, Hocus Pocus, Black Magic* and *Peakin' at the Deacon*. Popular songs included *Moonlight Rhapsody* and *Remember When* (1934), *With All My Heart and Soul* (1935), *The Moon Is Grinning at Me, You're Not the Kind, Tormented* and *I'll Never Tell You I Love You* (1936), *Popcorn Man* and *You're My Desire* (1937), *There's Something About an Old Love* and *Why Pretend?* (1938), *The World without You* (1940).

RECORDS

HUDSON-DELANGE ORCHESTRA

Br 7598 Tormented/It's a Lot of Idle Gossip

Br 7618 Hobo on Park Avenue/Eight Bars in Search of a Melody

Br 7656 Organ Grinder's Swing/You're Not the Kind

Br 7667 Monopoly Swing

Br 7700 The Moon Is Grinning at Me/It Seems I've Done Something Wrong Again

Br 7708 I Never Knew/When It's Sleepy Time Down South

Br 7715 Mint Julep/Mr. Ghost Goes to Town

Br 7991 (theme) Sophisticated Swing/The Maid's Night Off

Br 8040 Error in the News/College Widow

Ma 112 Never in a Million Years/Wake Up and Live

Ma 125 Star Dust/Bugle Call Rag

Ma 132 You're My Desire/Back in Your Arms

WILL HUDSON

Br 8147 China Clipper/Why Pretend?

Br 8156 On the Alamo/The One I Love

Br 8164 There's Something About an Old Love/Flat Foot Floogie

Br 8177 Hangover in Hong Kong/Lady of the Night

Br 8195 The Corrigan Hop/Miracle at Midnight

Br 8222 Break It Up/Break It Down

De 3429 Peekin' at the Deacon/The World without You

De 3473 On the Verge/Hi Ya, Mr. Chips

De 3579 Three at a Table for Two/Start Jumpin'

De 3702 Black Velvet/Easy Rider

LPs

HUDSON-DELANGE

Bandstand BSR-7105 Hudson-DeLange 1936-1939

---

884. HUG, ARMAND   p cm B

Born December 6, 1910, New Orleans, La.

Ragtime pianist active mostly in New Orleans. Professional at 14, worked locally. In late 20s and 30s worked with leading jazzmen including Sharkey Bonano and Louis Prima. Maritime service, World War II. Resumed career in New Orleans with combos, as single or as combo leader. Own shows on New Orleans TV. Active in 60s and into 70s as single. Compositions include *Huggin' the Keys; Fascinatin' Rag; Dixie Jam Session; Dustin' Off the Ivories; A Summer Holiday; You Cooked Your Goose; Sweet Lovin' Gal; Basin Street Parade; Smokey Mary; Float Me Down the River; Oh! That Band from Dixieland; Vieux Carre Parade.*

RECORDS

JOHNNY WIGGS

New Orleans Record Shop 1 Ultra Canal/Two Wing Temple in the Sky

New Orleans Record Shop 3 Congo Square/Bourbon Street Bounce

SHARKEY BONANO

De 1014 Everybody Loves My Baby/ Yes She Do, No She Don't

Kappa 115 Farewell Blues

Kappa 116 Muskrat Ramble

Kappa 120 Bucket's Got a Hole in It

Kappa 121 High Society

ARMAND HUG-RAY BAUDUC

OK 6802 Little Rock Getaway/ Breezin' Along

OK 6950 Tea for Two/Fascinatin' Rag

ARMAND HUG

NOB 501 You've Cooked Your Goose with Me/Reminiscin'

NOB 502 Edna

NOB 503 That's How Much You Mean to Me

Cap 863 Huggin' the Keys/Dixie Rag

Cap 987 Girl of My Dreams/Wild Flower Rag

GTJ 19 Kansas City Stomps/Good Gravy Rag

GTJ 20 Frog-I-More Rag/The Cosey Rag

LPs

ARMAND HUG

Ci(10″)L-411

Para(10″)114 Plays Armand Piron

Southland 228 Dixieland

Southland 244 Piano in New Orleans

Golden Crest 3045 New Orleans Piano

Golden Crest 3064 (S) Rags and Blues

JOHNNY WIGGS

Southland(10″)204 And His New Orleans Kings

BOB HAVENS

Southland 243 And His New Orleans All-Stars

NICK LAROCCA

Southland 230 Dixieland Jazz Band

885. HUGHES, MARJORIE   vo

Good vocalist, daughter of pianist-bandleader Frankie Carle. Sang with bands in Los Angeles at 19. Attained some prominence 1946-50 as featured vocalist with father's band. Sang on two of band's most popular records *Oh! What It Seemed to Be* and *Rumors Are Flying*. Brief career as single.

RECORDS

FRANKIE CARLE

Co 36892 Oh! What It Seemed to Be

Co 36994 Cynthia's in Love/I'd Be Lost without You

Co 37069 Rumors Are Flying/Without You

Co 37146 Either It's Love or It Isn't/ It's All Over Now

Co 37222 We Could Make Such Beautiful Music/Too Many Times

Co 37337 Midnight Masquerade/ Rockin' Horse Cowboy

Co 37930 I'll Hate Myself in the Morning

Co 38036 Beg Your Pardon

Co 38354 Little Jack Frost Get Lost

Co 38573 I'm Gonna Let You Cry for a Change

Co 38594 Vieni Su/I Want You to Want Me

MARJORIE HUGHES

Co 38524 You're Heartless/I Never Knew (I Could Love Anybody)

Co 38643 A Dream Is a Wish Your Heart Makes/Crazy He Calls Me

886. HUGHES, SPIKE   b ar cm B
(PATRICK C. HUGHES)

Born October 19, 1908, London, England

English arranger and bandleader of early 30s. Sideman-arranger for English bands late 20s and early 30s. In 1930 led combo along lines of Red Nichols U.S. groups. Later formed big band, mostly to record. Joined Jack Hylton 1931. Came to U.S. 1933, recorded own arrangements with Benny Carter band augmented by top jazzmen. Records modern, ahead of their time. Hughes returned to England, soon retired from music. Might have become major arranger. Composed jazz numbers including *Sirocco, Six Bells Stampede, Nocturne, Elegy, A Harlem Symphony*.

RECORDS
*(*recorded in U. S.)*

SPIKE HUGHES

De(E) 1703 Body and Soul/A Miss Is as Good as a Mile

De(E) 1787 The Mooche/St. James Infirmary

1139

De(E) 1861 Harlem Madness/Blue, Turning Grey Over You
De(E) 2114 They Didn't Believe Me/ The Sheik of Araby
De(E) 2166 Misty Morning/Everybody Loves My Baby
De(E) 2217 Button Up Your Overcoat/Moanin' Low
De(E) 2323 Tap Your Feet/High Life
De(E) 2611 Blues in My Heart/Darktown Strutters' Ball
De(E) 2711 A Harlem Symphony (1 & 2)
De(E) 3004 Limehouse Blues/Elegy
De(E) 3311 Tiger Rag/Siesta
De(E) 3563* Nocturne/Someone Stole Gabriel's Horn
De(E) 3606* Pastoral/Bugle Call Rag
De(E) 3639* Arabesque/Fanfare
De(E) 3717* Firebird/Donegal Cradle Song
De(E) 3836* Music at Sunrise/Music at Midnight
De(E) 5101 Air in D Flat/Sweet Sorrow Blues
De 191 Six Bells Stampede/Sirocco

ROOF GARDEN ORCHESTRA (Spike Hughes)
Pa(E) 1175 Blues in My Heart/I Can't Believe She's Mine

BUDDY'S BRIGADE (Spike Hughes)
Pa(E) 1172 Kiss by Kiss/Buddy's Wednesday Outing

LPs

SPIKE HUGHES
De(E) LK-4173 (RIs)
Lon(E) LL-1387 And His All-American Orchestra (RIs)

887. HUMES, HELEN   VO

Born 1913, Louisville, Ky.

Vocalist with Count Basie 1938-41. Sang ballads and rhythm tunes well, with some jazz feeling. Moved to New York as teenager. Early 30s theatre and club work. Worked in Chicago, Cincinnati, other locales. High spot of career with Basie. Then worked as single; some recording. Based mostly on west coast beginning mid-40s. In later 40s switched to rhythm and blues. Appeared at jazz concerts and festivals; some TV. With Red Norvo at intervals in 50s. Toured Australia several times. Career waned in 60s.

RECORDS

COUNT BASIE
De 2212 Dark Rapture
De 2249 My Heart Belongs to Daddy/Sing for Your Supper
De 2284 Blame It on My Last Affair
De 2325 Thursday
Vo 4734 Don't Worry 'Bout Me/What Goes Up Must Come Down
Vo 4748 If I Could Be with You
Vo 4784 And the Angels Sing/If I Didn't Care
Vo 4967 You Can Count on Me/You and Your Love
Vo 5036 Moonlight Serenade
OK 5773 It's Torture
OK 5987 Who Am I?
Co 35338 Someday Sweetheart
Co 35357 Between the Devil and the Deep Blue Sea

HARRY JAMES
Br 8038 Jubilee/I Can Dream, Can't I?
Br 8055 It's the Dreamer in Me
Br 8067 Song of the Wanderer

PETE BROWN
De 48059 Unlucky Blues/Gonna Buy Me a Telephone

HELEN HUMES
B&W 109 Married Man Blues/Boogie
Sav 5513 Fortune Tellin' Man/I Would If I Could
Sav 5514 Suspicious Blues/Keep Your Mind on Me
Dis 519 Rock Me to Sleep/Sad Feeling
De 28113 Loud Talkin' Woman/They Raided the Joint
De 28802 I Cried for You/Mean Way of Lovin'
Philo 105 Blue Prelude/He May Be Your Man
Philo 106 Every Now and Then/Be-Baba-Leba
Philo 122 Central Avenue Boogie/ Please Let Me Forget
Mer 8047 Jet Propelled Papa/Blue and Sentimental
Mer 8056 I Just Refuse to Sing the Blues/They Raided the Joint
Mer 8077 Jumpin' on Sugar Hill/Today I Sing the Blues

LPs

HELEN HUMES
Contemp 7571 Helen Humes Sings
Contemp 7582 Songs I Like to Sing

Contemp 7598 Swingin' with Humes
RED NORVO
Vi LPM-1711 Red Norvo in Hi-Fi
Vi LPM-1729 Red Plays the Blues

888. HUNT, PEE WEE   tb bn vo B
(WALTER HUNT)
Born May 10, 1907, Mt. Healthy, Ohio

Featured vocalist and jazz trombonist with Glen Gray band 1929-43. Later leader of successful dixieland-novelty combo. Played competent trombone but best known for novelty and rhythm vocals. Attended Ohio State and Cincinnati Conservatory. After earlier dance band experience on banjo and trombone joined Jean Goldkette briefly late 1927. Jobs in Detroit 1928-9. Original member and officer of Casa Loma, cooperative orchestra led by Glen Gray. Band evolved from Jean Goldkette unit called Orange Blossoms Band. By mid-30s band one of most popular in nation. Hunt well-known as featured vocalist, heard widely on records and radio. Left band mid-1943, worked awhile as disc jockey in Los Angeles. In 1944 worked on west coast with Lew Gray and Freddie Fisher. In merchant marine 1945, led jazz band. Early 1946 formed combo on west coast, popular during dixieland revival of late 40s. Continued as bandleader in 50s and 60s. Sometimes played cornball style purposely, sometimes good dixieland. Record hits *12th Street Rag* (1948) and *Oh!* (1953).

RECORDS
GLEN GRAY
Vi 24338 Lazybones
Br 6085 When I Take My Sugar to Tea
Br 6602 The River's Takin' Care of Me
Br 6618 Mississippi Basin/Louisiana Lullaby
Br 6626 That's How Rhythm Was Born
Br 6647 Savage Serenade
Br 6708 You're Gonna Lose Your Gal
Br 6870 Moon Country / Ridin' Around in the Rain
Br 6932 I Never Slept a Wink Last Night
Br 6945 Pardon My Southern Accent
Br 6954 Here Come the British
De 193 Judy/You're a Builder Upper

De 339 In My Country That Means Love
De 386 Here Comes Cookie
De 603 Yankee Doodle Never Went To Town
De 696 I'd Rather Lead a Band
De 1541 Mama, That Moon Is Here Again
De 1575 Bei Mir Bist du Schon
De 1679 You Better Change Your Tune/The Old Apple Tree
De 2292 Could Be
De 2395 Lazybones
De 3068 Save Your Sorrow
De 3572 You Say the Sweetest Things, Baby
De 4156 The Bottom Man on the Totem Pole
PEE WEE HUNT
Regent 133 Muskrat Ramble/Basin Street Blues
Regent 139 After You've Gone/On the Sunny Side of the Street
Sav 1141 Royal Garden Blues/Muskrat Ramble
Cap 57-569 Clarinet Marmalade/Bessie Couldn't Help It
Cap 57-773 Dill Pickles/Tiger Rag
Cap 1091 Yes, We Have No Bananas/Fourth Man Rag
Cap 2442 Oh!/San
Cap 2750 Three's a Crowd
Cap 2828 So Blue/The Vamp
Cap 15105 12th Street Rag/Somebody Else, Not Me
Cap 15299 Wabash Blues/High Society

LPs
PEE WEE HUNT
Cap T-573 Dixieland Classics
Cap T-1144 Blues a la Dixie
Cap T-1523 A-Hunting We Will Go
Cap T-1690 Saturday Night Dancing Party
Cap(10″)H-203 Straight from Dixie
Cap(10″)H-492 Swingin' Around with Pee Wee Hunt
PEE WEE HUNT and JOE "FINGERS" CARR
Cap T-783 "Pee Wee" and "Fingers"

889. HUNTER, ALBERTA   vo
Born April 1, 1897, Memphis, Tenn.

Leading early blues singer; extensive recording beginning 1921. Several recordings under pseudonym Josephine Beatty. Helped introduce blues to Europe, working there early 30s. To Chicago, began singing at early age; worked mostly in Chicago about 1912-20. In act awhile with drummer Ollie Powers and pianist Tony Jackson. To New York, began recording, worked clubs and theatres during 20s. Toured at intervals. Busiest recording 1921-6. Accompanists on records: groups led by Fletcher Henderson, Eubie Blake, Perry Bradford, jazz group Red Onion Jazz Babies, other top jazzmen. To Europe in early 30s, again in 1935 and 1936. In late 30s active in New York clubs and on radio. During World War II toured camps for USO, including overseas. Active in later 40s and early 50s; considerable work in Chicago early 50s. Left music mid-50s for nursing.

RECORDS

ALBERTA HUNTER
BS 2008 Bring Back the Joys/How Long, Sweet Daddy, How Long?
BS 2019 Someday, Sweetheart/He's a Darned Good Man
Para 12001 Daddy Blues/Don't Pan Me
Para 12006 Jazzin' Baby Blues/I'm Going Away Just to Wear You Off My Mind
Para 12013 Come On Home/Aggravatin' Papa
Para 12016 'Tain't Nobody's Bizness/If You Want to Keep Your Daddy Home
Para 12017 Chirping the Blues/Someone Else Will Take Your Place
Para 12021 You Shall Reap Just What You Sow/Bleeding Hearted Blues
Para 12049 Stingaree Blues
Para 12065 Experience Blues/Sad 'n' Lonely Blues
Para 12093 Old-Fashioned Love/If the Rest of the World Don't Want You
OK 8286 Your Jelly Roll Is Good/Take That Thing Away
OK 8294 Double Crossin' Papa/I'm Hard to Satisfy
OK 8383 Everybody Mess Around/Heebie Jeebies
Vi 20497 I'll Forgive You 'Cause I

Love You/I'm Gonna Lose Myself 'Way Down in Louisville
Vi 20771 Sugar/Beale Street Blues
De 7644 Chirpin' the Blues/I'll See You Go
De 7727 Downhearted Blues/Someday, Sweetheart
Juke Box 510 Take Your Big Hands Off/He's Got a Punch Like Joe Louis
Juke Box 511 Your Bread May Be Good/Don't Want No Man That's Lazy
(with JACK JACKSON ORCHESTRA in England)
HMV(E) 6542 Stars Fell on Alabama/Long May We Love
Vi 24835 I Travel Alone
JOSEPHINE BEATTY (Alberta Hunter)
Ge 5594 Everybody Loves My Baby/Texas Moaner Blues
Ge 5626 Early Every Morn/Nobody Knows the Way I Feel Dis' Mornin'

LPs

ALBERTA HUNTER with LOVIE AUSTIN & HER BLUES SERENADERS
Riv RLP-418 (recorded in 1961)
LOUIS ARMSTRONG
Riv RLP-101 Young Louis Armstrong (RIs)
(miscellaneous artists)
Vi 534 Women of the Blues (RIs)

890. HUPFIELD, HERMAN
cm lyr vo p v

Born February 1, 1894, Montclair, N.J.
Died June 8, 1951, Montclair, N.J.

Composer of good popular songs, though output scant. Wrote music and lyrics, independent songs for stage shows and movies. Best-known *Sing Something Simple, As Time Goes By, When Yuba Plays the Rumba on the Tuba, Night Owl, Let's Put Out the Lights*. Studied violin in Germany at 9; high school in Montclair, N.J. Military service, World War I. Entertained as pianist-singer in U.S. and Europe. During World War II entertained in camps and hospitals. 1931 song *As Time Goes By* featured in movie CASABLANCA

(1943), enjoyed revival, became all-time standard.

SONGS
(with related shows)

1921—ZIEGFELD'S 9 O'CLOCK FROLIC stage show (Two Quack Quakers)

1927—A LA CARTE stage show (Baby's Blue; The Calinda; Sort of Lonesome; Boo Joom Boo Joom)

1930—Sing Something Simple

1931—EVERYBODY'S WELCOME stage show (As Time Goes By; revived in 1943 movie CASABLANCA); THE THIRD LITTLE SHOW stage show (When Yuba Plays the Rumba on the Tuba)

1932—GEORGE WHITE'S MUSIC HALL VARIETIES stage show (Let's Put Out the Lights); HEY NONNY NONNY stage show (Be a Little Lackadaisical; Wouldn't That Be Wonderful; Let's Go Lovin')

1933—MURDER AT THE VANITIES stage show (Savage Serenade; You Love Me); TAKE A CHANCE movie (Night Owl); MOONLIGHT AND PRETZELS movie (Are You Makin' Any Money?)

1937—THE SHOW IS ON stage show (Buy Yourself a Balloon)

1950—DANCE ME A SONG stage show (unsuccessful)

Other songs: *Goofy Geer*; *Down the Old Back Road*; *My Little Dog Has Ego*; *A Hut in Hoboken*; *Honey Ma Love*

891. HURLEY, CLYDE   t

Born September 3, 1916, Fort Worth, Texas

Trumpet man active with swing and dixieland groups. Attended Texas Christian University. Played in Buster Welch band early in career. Joined Ben Pollack late 1937 in Texas; to California with band. Left after a year; freelance and studio work in California. Joined Glenn Miller in May 1939, remained a year. With Tommy Dorsey June-September 1940. Period with Artie Shaw 1941. Remainder of 40s studio musician in Hollywood. TV 1950-5. With Irvin Verret group in clubs 1950; led own group. With Ted Vesely 1951. Then freelanced on west coast. Featured on LPs by Rampart Street Paraders. Active in 60s.

RECORDS

BEN POLLACK
    De 1851 Morocco/Nobody's Gonna Take You from Me

GLENN MILLER
    Bb 10299 I'm Sorry for Myself/Back to Back
    Bb 10309 We Can Live on Love
    Bb 10317 Slip Horn Jive
    Bb 10352 Pagan Love Song/Sold American
    Bb 10372 Baby Me
    Bb 10399 Wham
    Bb 10416 In the Mood/I Want to Be Happy
    Bb 10498 Johnson Rag

HERBIE HAYMER
    Key 640 I Saw Stars/Sweet and Lovely

JO STAFFORD
    Cap 1039 Pagan Love Song/Simple Melody

BUDDY BAKER
    Excl 10 Baker's Dozen/Be Fair with Me
    Excl 11 I'm Stuck with a Sticker/Sleepy Time Down South
    Excl 218 Gloria/Memories of Home
    Excl 227 She's Funny That Way/It's the Gal from Cal for Me

CLYDE HURLEY
    Key 633 Out of Nowhere/On the Trail

LPs

CLYDE HURLEY ALL-STARS
    Crown CLP-5045

RAMPART STREET PARADERS
    Co CL-648 Rampart & Vine
    Co CL-785 Dixieland, My Dixieland
    Co CL-1061 Texas: U. S. A.

MAXWELL DAVIS
    Cr CLP-5050 A Tribute to Glenn Miller

892. HUTCHENRIDER, CLARENCE
                  cl as bs f B

Born June 13, 1908, Waco, Texas

Underrated clarinet soloist with Glen Gray in 30s and early 40s. Raspy tone, nervous phrasing, fertile ideas. Jobs in Texas middle and late 20s; period with Jack Gardner in Dallas. In Miami 1928 with Larry Duncan; joined Ross Gorman later in year. 1929-31 with Tommy Tucker, Paul Jacobs, Austin Wylie. Joined Glen Gray 1931. A principal jazz soloist with band. Featured regularly on Gray theme *Smoke Rings*. Left Gray late 1943 due to ill health. Radio in later 40s, often in Jimmy Lytell band. Illness forced retirement early 50s. Returned in mid-50s with Glen Moore and Walter Davidson. In late 50s and 60s led combo in New York spots, playing music of 20s. Long run at Bill's Gay Nineties club from 1966 through most of 1972.

RECORDS

GLEN GRAY

    Br 6242 Maniac's Ball/Black Jazz
    Br 6289 Smoke Rings
    Br 6318 Happy-Go-Lucky You
    Br 6486 The Lady from St. Paul
    Br 6513 Blue Prelude
    Br 6588 Wild Goose Chase
    Br 6800 I Got Rhythm
    Br 7325 Panama
    Vi 24256 Casa Loma Stomp
    De 286 Stomping Around
    De 986 Royal Garden Blues/Shades of Hades
    De 1048 Copenhagen/Jungle Jitters
    De 1412 Casa Loma Stomp
    De 1473 Smoke Rings
    De 1755 Malady in F Minor/My Bonnie Lies Over the Ocean
    De 3068 The Fable of the Rose
    De 3261 When Buddha Smiles
    De 3348 Come and Get It

LPs

GLEN GRAY & THE CASA LOMA ORCHESTRA

    Ha HL-7045 The Great Recordings of Glen Gray (Br RIs)
    De DL-8570 (De RIs)
    De(10″)DL-5089 Musical Smoke Rings (De RIs)
    Cor(10″)CRL-56006 Hoagy Carmichael Songs (De RIs)

893. HUTTON, BETTY   vo
(ELIZABETH JUNE THORNBURG)

Born February 26, 1921, Battle Creek, Mich.

Blonde bombshell of 40s movies; noted for uninhibited singing and body gyrations. Performed novelty numbers predominately. Younger sister of singer Marion Hutton. Sisters worked briefly with Vincent Lopez band 1938, changed last name to Hutton. Marion left September to join Glenn Miller; Betty remained as star Lopez attraction late 1938-9. In 1940 Betty landed starring role in Broadway musical TWO FOR THE SHOW which featured newcomers. Later in year supporting role in hit show PANAMA HATTIE. Burst into spotlight with featured role in first movie THE FLEET'S IN (1942); antics and singing stood out. Starred in top-budget films INCENDIARY BLONDE (1945; portrayed entertainer-speakeasy owner Texas Guinan), ANNIE GET YOUR GUN (1950; scintillating performance) and THE GREATEST SHOW ON EARTH (1952). Through movies associated with songs *Arthur Murray Taught Me Dancing in a Hurry*; *"Murder" He Says*; *It Had to Be You*; *Doctor, Lawyer and Indian Chief*. Teamed with Eddie Bracken in several movies. Later on TV in own series, specials, guest spots during 50s. Special stage engagements in New York and London. Career waned late 50s.

MOVIES

1942—THE FLEET'S IN; STAR SPANGLED RHYTHM
1943—HAPPY-GO-LUCKY; LET'S FACE IT
1944—HERE COME THE WAVES; AND THE ANGELS SING; THE MIRACLE OF MORGAN'S CREEK
1945—INCENDIARY BLONDE; DUFFY'S TAVERN
1946—THE STORK CLUB; CROSS MY HEART
1947—PERILS OF PAULINE
1948—DREAM GIRL
1949—RED HOT AND BLUE
1950—ANNIE GET YOUR GUN; LET'S DANCE
1952—SOMEBODY LOVES ME; THE GREATEST SHOW ON EARTH
1957—SPRING REUNION

RECORDS

VINCENT LOPEZ

    Bb 10300 Concert in the Park/Igloo
    Bb 10367 The Jitterbug

BETTY HUTTON

    Cap 155 It Had to Be You/His Rocking Horse Ran Away

Cap 188 Blue Skies/Stuff Like That There

Cap 211 Doin' It the Hard Way/What Do You Want to Make Those Eyes at Me For?

Cap 380 Poppa, Don't Preach to Me/ Rumble, Rumble, Rumble

Cap 409 I Wish I Didn't Love You So/The Sewing Machine

Cap 620 Now That I Need You/I Wake Up in the Morning Feeling Fine

Cap 2522 No Matter How You Say Goodbye/Goin' Steady

Cap 2608 I'm Nobody's Baby/Hot Dog! That Made Him Mad

Cap 2688 I Took the Long Way Home/Broke, Barefoot and Starry-Eyed

Cap 2776 My Cutey's Due at Two to Two Today/Banana Boat

Vi 20-1950 Walkin' Away with My Heart/What Did You Put in That Kiss?

Vi 20-4179 "Murder" He Says/It's Oh So Quiet

LPs

BETTY HUTTON

Cap(10″)H-256 Square in the Social Circle

(movie soundtrack)

MGM(10″)E-509 ANNIE GET YOUR GUN

894. HUTTON, INA RAY   p vo B
(ODESSA COWAN)

Born March 13, c. 1914-16, Chicago, Ill.

Sexy leader of all-girl band early in career, later led all-male bands. Sometimes called Blonde Bombshell of Rhythm. Mother professional pianist Marvel Ray. Singer June Hutton Ina Ray's half sister. As youngster tap dancer in a Gus Edwards revue. In Lew Leslie's CLOWNS IN CLOVER stage show. On Broadway in GEORGE WHITE'S MELODY (1933) and ZIEGFELD FOLLIES OF 1934. Formed all-girl band mid-1934, billed as Ina Ray Hutton & Her Melodears. Featured hot numbers; Ina Ray a sensation with sexy baton-waving, gyrations and dancing. Band made movie shorts mid-30s, played theatres, toured Europe 1935. 1937-9 Ina Ray formed good new all-girl band. Sister June sang with band. Changed to all-male

band late 1939. Excellent band with full ensemble sound; could swing. George Paxton played tenor sax and arranged. Vocalist Stuart Foster. Guitarist Jack Purcell and later pianist Hal Schaefer outstanding sidemen. In mid-40s disbanded, married trumpet star Randy Brooks, faded from music. New band 1946 featuring George Handy arrangements. A natural for TV; in early 50s popular shows on west coast with all-girl band. Summer network show 1956. Active through 50s. Career waned early 60s. In several movies including BIG BROADCAST OF 1936 (1935) and EVER SINCE VENUS (1944).

RECORDS

INA RAY HUTTON

Vo 2801 Georgia's Gorgeous Gal/ Twenty-Four Hours in Georgia

Vo 2816 Wild Party/Witch Doctor

Vi 24692 And I Still Do/How's About Tomorrow Night?

OK 5830 A Handful of Stars/Gotta Have Your Love

OK 5852 Five O'clock Whistle/Make Me Know It

OK 6335 At Last/What's the Good of Moonlight?

OK 6380 Back in Your Own Backyard/Nobody's Sweetheart

El 5007 A Sinner Kissed an Angel/ Madelaine

El 5008 Ev'rything I Love/You Made Me Love You

895. HUTTON, JUNE   vo

Born August 11, c. 1918-21, Chicago, Ill.

Died May 2, 1973, Encino, Calif.

Half sister of bandleader Ina Ray Hutton, sang with her all-girl band late 30s. First used professional name Elaine Merritt briefly. Joined Charlie Spivak with Stardusters vocal group 1941, left September 1943. With Spivak in 1943 movie PIN-UP GIRL. Replaced Jo Stafford with Pied Pipers singing group mid-1944. Group worked as act after leaving Tommy Dorsey band late 1942. Left group 1950 for career as single. Recorded for Capitol early 50s, husband Axel Stordahl providing orchestral backing on some sessions. Career waned by late 50s.

RECORDS

CHARLIE SPIVAK (with THE STARDUSTERS)
OK 6546 I Surrender Dear
OK 6593 I Remember You/Arthur Murray Taught Me Dancing in a Hurry

THE PIED PIPERS
Cap 185 Dream/Tabby the Cat
Cap 207 We'll Be Together Again/Lily Belle
Cap 225 Aren't You Glad You're You?/In the Middle of May
Cap 306 Either It's Love or It Isn't/ Walkin' Away with My Heart
Cap 396 Mam'selle/It's the Same Old Dream
Cap 495 I'll See You in My Dreams/- Ok'l Baby Dok'l

JUNE HUTTON with PAUL WESTON ORCHESTRA
Cap 177 Sleigh Ride in July/Don't You Know I Care?

JUNE HUTTON with ARTIE SHAW ORCHESTRA
De 27580 Dancing on the Ceiling/My Kinda Love

JOHNNY MERCER and THE PIED PIPERS
Cap album CD-36 (78s)

JUNE HUTTON-GORDON MACRAE
Cap 2784 Coney Island Boat

JUNE HUTTON
Cap 2268 Keep It a Secret/I Miss You So
Cap 2369 The Lights of Home/You Are My Love
Cap 2429 Song from Moulin Rouge/ Say You're Mine Again
Cap 2512 I'll Forget You/Oh, These Lonely Nights
Cap 2667 If It's the Last Thing I Do/ For the First Time
Cap 2727 Gee/Too Little Time
Cap 2811 You Say You're Sorry/We Don't Wanna Go Home
De 24918 Be Mine/Tenderly
De 27064 My Sweetie Went Away/ More Than I Should
De 27833 Nothing/Bye, Honey, Bye Bye
De 27870 Thanks/Walkin'

LPs

(miscellaneous artists)
Tops L-1607 PAL JOEY

1146

896. HUTTON, MARION   VO
(MARION THORNBURG)

Born March 10, 1919, Little Rock, Ark.

Older sister of movie star Betty Hutton. Prominent vocalist with Glenn Miller band 1938-42. Good voice and personality; at best on novelty and rhythm tunes. Attended high school in Detroit, began singing in clubs there 1937. She and sister Betty briefly with Vincent Lopez band 1938, changed last name to Hutton. Marion left September 1938 to join Miller. Away from band January-August 1941 awaiting birth of child. In band's second movie ORCHESTRA WIVES (1942). With band till disbanded fall 1942. Marion and featured stars Tex Beneke and Modernaires remained together awhile for theatre tour. In later 40s worked as single in theatres, clubs, movies and radio. In films CRAZY HOUSE (1943), BABES ON SWING STREET (1944), IN SOCIETY (1945), LOVE HAPPY (1949). Semi-active in music by 50s. Married arranger-leader Vic Schoen, settled in California.

RECORDS

GLENN MILLER
Bb 10139 Gotta Get Some Shut-Eye
Bb 10145 Cuckoo in the Clock/Romance Runs in the Family
Bb 10269 But It Didn't Mean a Thing
Bb 10309 We Can Live on Love
Bb 10358 The Man with the Mandolin
Bb 10448 I Just Got a Letter
Bb 10465 Bluebirds in the Moonlight
Bb 10507 Oh Johnny, Oh Johnny, Oh!
Bb 10561 Ooh, What You Said
Bb 10598 The Woodpecker Song/Let's All Sing Together
Bb 10622 Say "Si Si"
Bb 10631 My! My!
Bb 10657 What's the Matter with Me?
Bb 10689 Boog-It
Bb 10900 Five O'clock Whistle
Bb 10906 You've Got Me This Way
Bb 11401 Happy in Love
Vi 27935 That's Sabotage

MARION HUTTON with RANDY BROOKS ORCHESTRA
De 18703 I'm Gonna Love That Guy/ No More Toujours L'Amour

MARION HUTTON
MGM 10252 Borscht/He Sez, She Says

LPs

GLENN MILLER
Vi LPM-2080 (Bb RIs)
Vi LPM-3657 Blue Moonlight (Bb RIs)

897. HYAMS, MARGE   vb B

Born 1923, New York, N.Y.

Able vibist with Woody Herman mid-40s. One of top female jazz players. Heard by Herman in Atlantic City club September 1944, joined band, remained a year. Led combo 1945-6. Later 1946 with Charlie Ventura, 1947 with Phil D'Arcy. Led combo 1948-9. Joined George Shearing combo mid-1949, remained about a year. Retired early 50s.

RECORDS

WOODY HERMAN
Co 36803 Apple Honey
Co 36835 Northwest Passage
FLIP PHILLIPS
Si 28106 Papilloma
Si 28119 A Melody from the Sky
MARY LOU WILLIAMS
Vi 20-2174 It Must Be True/Harmony Grits
GEORGE SHEARING
Dis 105 Midnight on Cloud 69/Be-bop's Fables
Dis 106 Cotton Top/Sorry Wrong Rhumba
Dis 107 Cherokee/Four Bars Short
MGM 10530 East of the Sun/Conception
MGM 10596 The Continental/Nothing but D. Best
MGM 10687 I'll Remember April/Jumping with Symphony Sid
MGM 10763 When Your Lover Has Gone/Carnegie Horizons
MGM 10859 Roses of Picardy/Pick Yourself Up

LPs

GEORGE SHEARING
MGM E-3265 Touch of Genius
Dis(10″)DL-3002

898. HYLTON, JACK   o p B

Born 1892, Lancashire, England
Died January 29, 1965

Leader of top English dance band. Performed ballads and novelties with danceable beat; played hot occasionally. Early in career Hylton played theatre organ. Military service, World War I. In band 1919 at the Queens, Langham Place. Became leader after a year. Began recording and playing top spots in London and through England. Recording star in England. In 1926 band on radio, became broadcast favorite. Ted Heath (tb) joined band 1925, Ella Logan (vo) 1930. Band toured France and Belgium late 20s, Germany 30s. Appeared in Paris with Maurice Chevalier 1930. In late 1931-2 several Hylton recordings issued in U. S. on Victor. One of the best: *Dancing on the Ceiling.* Featured U. S. tenor sax star Coleman Hawkins around 1934-5, again in 1939. Hylton to U. S. late 1935, led band of U. S. musicians including George Wettling, Murray McEachern and Dave Rose about eight months. On radio with Alec Templeton 1935, helped popularize song *She Shall Have Music.* Returned to England mid-1936, resumed career. In later years theatrical producer.

RECORDS

JACK HYLTON
HMV(E) B-5506 Good News/The Varsity Drag
HMV(E) B-5658 Breakaway / That's You, Baby
HMV(E) B-5693 Through/I'm Doing What I'm Doing for Love
HMV(E) B-5759 Just You, Just Me/Hang on to Me
HMV(E) B-5789 Tiger Rag/Limehouse Blues
HMV(E) B-5926 Talkie Hits Medleys (1 & 2)
De(E) 2796 Home/My Heart Is Bluer Than Your Eyes
De(E) 2823 You Try Somebody Else/Now's the Time to Fall in Love
De(E) 3239 St. Louis Blues/Hylton Stomp
De(E) 3395 Just a Little Home for the Old Folks/I'll Never Have to Dream Again
De(E) 3658 Sweetheart Darlin'/In the Valley of the Moon
De(E) 3687 The Last Round-up/It's the Talk of the Town
De(E) 3767 Some of These Days/Black and Blue Rhythm

Br 6295 Close Your Eyes/Tom Thumb's Drum
Br 6328 You're Blasé
Vi 22067 I Lift Up My Finger and Say "Tweet Tweet"/Laughing Marionette
Vi 22434 Give Yourself a Pat on the Back/When the Organ Played at Twilight
Vi 22619 The King's Horses
Vi 22697 Soldier on the Shelf/The Alpine Milkman
Vi 22912 Dancing on the Ceiling
Vi 25275 She Shall Have Music/When the Rain Comes Rolling Down
Vi 25555 Rose Room/Solitude
Vi(12")36027 Body and Soul/With a Song in My Heart
Vi(12")36031 Just a Gigolo/Yours Is My Heart Alone
De 189 Ellingtonia/Dinah
HMV(E) BD-5216 September in the Rain/Melody for Two
HMV(E) BD-5518 White Sails/Moon Love
HMV(E) BD-5550 My Melancholy Baby/Darktown Strutters' Ball

LPs

JACK HYLTON
Vi LPT-1013 Memories of Jack Hylton (Vi RIs)
Mon-Ever 7033 (1929-31 RIs)
World Sound(E) SH-127 (RIs)

899. HYMAN, DICK   p o hp ar cm B
Born March 8, 1927, New York, N.Y.

Talented pianist-organist, good modern jazzman but adept at any style. Early classical training. Military service 1945-6. Attended Columbia University awhile. Began professionally 1948, played club jobs, worked with Victor Lombardo band. In 1949 with Tony Scott and Eddie Shu combos. With Red Norvo early 1950, Benny Goodman spring 1950 for European tour. In 1951 with Alvy West, Flip Phillips, Lee Castle, own combo. Next several years studio musician. Sometimes recorded on harpsichord. Best-known records *Moritat* and *Unforgettable*. Excellent LPs of standard song medleys for MGM. Led combo at intervals. Musical director for Arthur Godfrey TV and radio shows late 50s into early 60s. Worked with Leonard Feather late 50s writing-directing for concert dates and record sessions. With Percy Faith and Mitch Miller on latter's TV series early 60s. Pianist-conductor for Johnny Desmond 1962. Arranged for singers and jazz groups in 60s; active in freelance recording. With Toots Thielemans combo in New York 1970. Active in early 70s. Composer of descriptive pieces including *The Old Professor, Bardolino, Blue Whistler, Down Home Melody, Counterpoint for 6 Valves, Turvy Part 2* and "Shakespeare's Greatest Hits" music for LP.

RECORDS

FLIP PHILLIPS
Mer 8953 Cheek to Cheek/I've Got My Love to Keep Me Warm
DICK HYMAN
MGM 11743 Unforgettable/Out of Nowhere
MGM 11811 Cecilia/East of the Sun
MGM 11889 I've Got My Love to Keep Me Warm/Jealous
MGM 12125 Rockin' the Boogie/Honky Tonk Train
MGM 12149 Moritat/Baubles, Bangles and Beads

LPs

DICK HYMAN
MGM E-3329 The "Unforgettable" Sound of the Dick Hyman Trio
MGM E-3535, 3536, 3537, 3586, 3587, 3588 60 Great All-Time Songs, Vol. 1 to 6
Comm RS862SD (S) Fabulous Dick Hyman & His Orchestra
Proscenium 1 Plays Kurt Weill
LEONARD FEATHER-DICK HYMAN ALL-STARS
MGM E-3650 Oh, Captain
LEONARD FEATHER'S STARS
MGM E-3390 West Coast vs. East Coast
TERRY SNYDER
Comm RS800SD (S) Persuasive Percussion
LEE WILEY
Mon-Ever MES-7041 (S) Back Home Again

RUSTY DEDRICK
  4 Corners FCL-4207 The Big Band
    Sound

MARIAN MONTGOMERY
  Cap T-1884 Swings for Winners and
    Losers

PHIL BODNER
  Cam CAL-985 A Lover's Concerto
  Cam CAL-2196 An Ode to Young
    Lovers

MAXINE SULLIVAN
  Mon-Ever MES-7038 (S) Shakespeare

900. INGLE, RED   ts v vo B

Deceased

Excellent showman, long a vocalist with
Ted Weems. Most noted for zany vocals
and antics with Spike Jones in 40s, later
leading own similar band starting 1947.
With Weems fall 1931 till early 40s; tenor
sax and violin with band. Featured vocalist occasionally on ballads, especially
on novelties. Joined Spike Jones; important in band's rise in comic-cornball field.
Record hit *Tim-Tayshun (Temptation)* on
which Jo Stafford guest-starred in corny
vocal. Ingle band specialized in turning
pops into hillbilly tunes and changing
titles as well. Made hilarious records.
Active in 50s.

RECORDS

TED WEEMS

Vi 22829 Nobody's Baby Is Some-
    body's Baby Now
Vi 24265 Juggling a Jigsaw
Vi 24266 She Changed Her Hi-De-Hi-
    De
Bb 5289 'Tain't So
Bb 5292 I Guess It Had to Be That
    Way
Co 2976-D I'll Keep Warm All Winter
De 822 Celebratin'
De 885 When a Lady Meets a Gen-
    tleman Down South/Knock Knock
De 1705 Swingin' in the Corn/A Shack
    in the Back of the Hills

SPIKE JONES

Vi 20-1654 Chlo-e

Vi 20-1762 You Always Hurt the One
    You Love/The Blue Danube

RED INGLE

Cap 412 Tim-Tayshun (Temptation)/
    For Seventy Mental Reasons
Cap 451 Song of Indians/Them Durn
    Fool Things
Cap 476 Nowhere/Pagan Ninny's
    Keep 'Er Goin' Stomp
Cap 57-713 "A" You're a-Dopey-
    Gal/Two Dollar Pistol
Cap 1076 You Can't Be Fit as a Fid-
    dle/Turn Your Head, Little Darlin'
Cap 1431 Chew Tobacco Rag/Let Me
    In
Cap 15045 Cigareetes, Whiskey and
    Wild Wild Women/Pearly Maude
Cap 15123 Moe Zart's Turkey Trot/
    Get Off the Floor, Hannah
Cap 15210 Serutan Yob/Oh! Nick-O-
    Deemo
Cap 15312 Prisoner of Love's Song
VD(12")905 Prisoner of Love's Song
Mer 70085 Don't Let the Stars Get in
    Your Eyes/Why Don't You Believe
    Me?

901. INK SPOTS   vo

Vocal quartet most popular 1939-40; continuing success in 40s. Sound featured
high tenor lead. Early in career group
performed hot and jive numbers without
much success. Played England mid-30s;
with Jack Hylton band. Changed to slow
tempos, scored with *If I Didn't Care* 1939.
Bill Kenny's sugary high tenor dominant

feature of group, along with talking cho-
ruses by deep-voiced Orville "Hoppy"
Jones. Other singers Charlie Fuqua (also
guitarist) and Ivory "Deek" Watson.
Jones died November 1944, replaced by
Herb Kenny, Bill's brother. Watson replaced later by Billy Bowen. Often on
radio late 30s and 40s, played theatres,
recorded steadily. In movies GREAT AMER-
ICAN BROADCAST (1941) and PARDON MY
SARONG (1942). Other top records *Maybe,
My Prayer, Whispering Grass, We Three,
Do I Worry?, Java Jive*. Active through
40s into 50s. Some confusion 1952 when
two groups used Ink Spots name. Bill
Kenny and Charlie Fuqua each held 50%
title to name, according to court ruling,
and each led own group. Kenny star of
his group. Fuqua's personnel: "Deek"
Watson, Harold Jackson and high tenor
Jimmy Holmes. Later members Leon
Antoine and Isaac Royal. In later 50s Ink
Spots faded but still worked into 70s.

RECORDS

INK SPOTS
De 1036 Stompin' at the Savoy/Keep
    Away from My Doorstep
De 1236 Swing High, Swing Low/
    Whoa Babe
De 1251 Let's Call the Whole Thing
    Off/Slap That Bass
De 2286 If I Didn't Care/Knock
    Kneed Sal
De 2507 Just for a Thrill/It's Funny to
    Everyone but Me
De 2707 Address Unknown/You
    Bring Me Down
De 2790 My Prayer/Give Her My
    Love
De 2966 Memories of You/I'm
    Through
De 3195 When the Swallows Come
    Back To Capistrano/What Can I
    Do
De 3258 Maybe/Whispering Grass
De 3346 I'll Never Smile Again/I
    Could Make You Care
De 3379 We Three/My Greatest Mis-
    take
De 3432 Do I Worry?/Java Jive
De 3626 Ring, Telephone, Ring/Please
    Take a Letter, Miss Brown

De 3987 I Don't Want to Set the
    World on Fire/Hey Doc
De 4045 Someone's Rocking My
    Dream Boat/Nothin'
De 18503 Don't Get Around Much
    Anymore/Street of Dreams
De 18579 I'll Get By/Someday I'll
    Meet You Again
De 18711 I'd Climb the Highest
    Mountain/Thoughtless
De 18817 The Gypsy/Everyone Is Say-
    ing "Hello" Again
De 18864 Prisoner of Love/I Cover the
    Waterfront
De 23615 To Each His Own/I Never
    Had a Dream Come True
(CHARLIE FUQUA GROUP)
King 1297 Ebb Tide/If You Should
    Say Goodbye
King 1304 Changing Partners/Stran-
    ger in Paradise
BILL KENNY
De 27256 Our Lady of Fatima/
    Stranger in the City
De 27326 It Is No Secret/I Hear a Choir

LPs

INK SPOTS
De DL-8154 The Best of the Ink Spots
    (De RIs)
De(10")DL-5056 Ink Spots Vol. 1 (De
    RIs)
De(10")DL-5541 Street of Dreams (De
    RIs)
Waldorf 33-W-2 The World Famous
    Ink Spots
Golden Tone C-4024 The Fabulous
    Ink Spots
Audition 33-5905 The Ink Spots

902. IVES, BURL   bn g vo lyr ar
Born June 14, 1909, Hunt Township, Ill.
Leading folk singer, considerable commercial appeal. After prominence in this
field, became distinguished character actor in movies-stage-TV. Attended Eastern
Illinois State Teachers. Interested in folk
songs at early age. Quit college to travel
two years over the U. S. Lived hand to
mouth, performing where he could, including riverboat jobs. Huge, played some
semi-pro football. In wanderings picked
up folk songs from all sections of country.

Vocal lessons at Indiana State Teachers. To New York; some success in Greenwich Village clubs and summer stock. Studied at NYU School of Music. In late 30s small roles on Broadway stage in I MARRIED AN ANGEL, THE BOYS FROM SYRACUSE, HEAVENLY EXPRESS. Sang at New York's Village Vanguard. Military service awhile, World War II; in THIS IS THE ARMY show. After discharge 1944 club work. Began on radio, soon starred on The Wayfaring Stranger. Good role in 1944 Broadway show SING OUT SWEET LAND. By postwar 40s well known. Began movie career. Small roles initially, soon important roles in major films. In 1954 Broadway revival of SHOW BOAT. Greatest role 1955 in CAT ON A HOT TIN ROOF; repeated role as Big Daddy in movie version 1958. In 50s and 60s frequent guest spots on TV, own series, occasional specials. In early 70s star of The Bold Ones, TV dramatic series. Folk singing relaxed and soothing; talented at projecting lyrics. Often adapted and arranged own unusual material. His guitar accompaniment fit material perfectly. Author of books *Sailing on a Very Fine Day, Tales of America, The Burl Ives Song Book, America's Musical Heritage—Song in America.* Arranged and popularized such songs as *Blue Tail Fly, Foggy Foggy Dew, Wayfarin' Stranger, Ten Thousand Miles, Woolie Boogie Bee, Turtle Dove.*

MOVIES

1946—SMOKY
1948—STATION WEST; GREEN GRASS OF WYOMING; SO DEAR TO MY HEART
1950—SIERRA
1955—EAST OF EDEN
1956—THE POWER AND THE PRIZE
1958—CAT ON A HOT TIN ROOF; THE BIG COUNTRY; DESIRE UNDER THE ELMS; WIND ACROSS THE EVERGLADES; ROBIN AND THE SEVEN HOODS
1959—DAY OF THE OUTLAW
1960—OUR MAN IN HAVANA; LET NO MAN WRITE MY EPITAPH
1962—THE SPIRAL ROAD
1963—SUMMER MAGIC

1964—THE BRASS BOTTLE; ENSIGN PULVER; MEDITERRANEAN HOLIDAY (songs)
1966—THE DAYDREAMER
1967—BLAST-OFF; ROCKET TO THE MOON; THOSE FANTASTIC FLYING FOOLS
1969—THE MCMASTERS

RECORDS

BURL IVES
Co 36733-4-5-6 (folk songs)
Co 38445 Riders in the Sky/Wayfaring Stranger—Medley
Co 38484 Roving Gambler/Bonnie Wee Lassie
Co 38644 Mule Train/Grier County Bacheler
Co 38745 River of Smoke/The Bachelor's Life
Co 38778 Blessed Assurance/When the Roll Is Called Up Yonder
Co 38817 Got the World by the Tail/My Mamma Told Me
Co 38936 Animal Fair/Ballanderie
Co 38937 Robin, He Married/I've Got No Use for Women
De 23405 Foggy Foggy Dew/Rodger Young
De 23439 Big Rock Candy Mountain/Blue Tail Fly//I'm Goin' Down the Road
De 23591 Down in the Valley/Cowboy's Lament
De 23958 It Makes No Difference Now/I'm Thinking Tonight of My Blue Eyes
De 28161 Diesel Smoke, Dangerous Curves/The Little Green Valley
BURL IVES-ANDREWS SISTERS
De 24463 Blue Tail Fly/I'm Goin' Down the Road
BURL IVES with GORDON JENKINS ORCHESTRA
De 29088 Brave Man/True Love Goes On and On

LPs

BURL IVES
Co CL-628 The Wayfaring Stranger
Co CS-9675 (S) Times They Are A-Changin'
De DXB-167 The Best of Burl Ives
De DL-4279 It's Just My Funny Way of Laughin'

De DL-4361 Burl
De DL-4433 Singin' Easy
De DL-4578 Pearly Shells and Other
    Favorites
De DL-8080 Coronation Concert

De DL-8247 In the Quiet of the Night
Ha HL-11275 Got the World by the
    Tail
UA 3117 Sings Irving Berlin

903. JACKSON, CHUBBY b cm B
(GREIG STEWART JACKSON)
Born October 25, 1918, New York, N.Y.

Bassist who rose to fame with Woody Herman band in mid-40s. Important in development of progressive jazz. Good showman and organizer in addition to musical talent. Grew up in Freeport, L.I. Began professionally mid-30s. With Mike Riley 1937-8, Johnny Messner 1938-9, Raymond Scott big band 1939-40, Jan Savitt 1940, Henry Busse 1940-1. Led combo 1942; some work with Charlie Barnet. Joined Woody Herman fall 1943, remained till mid-1946, returned for periods in 1948 and 1952. With Charlie Ventura awhile in 1947. Later in year led avant-garde combo, toured Sweden. Led big band 1949. With Ventura again 1951 in combo called Big Four (other members: Buddy Rich, Marty Napoleon). Formed all-star group with Bill Harris 1953. Settled in Chicago for studio work, led combo there 1957. From 1958 into 60s studios and freelance in New York; led trio in clubs there mid-60s. Late 60s mostly led combo in Florida. Composed jazz numbers, notably *Northwest Passage*.

RECORDS

WOODY HERMAN
VD (12")369 Apple Honey
VD (12")382 Red Top
Co 36789 Caldonia/Happiness Is Just a Thing Called Joe
Co 36803 Apple Honey/Out of This World
Co 36835 Northwest Passage/June Comes Around Every Year
Co 36861 Bijou/Put That Ring on My Finger
Co 36949 Wild Root/Atlanta, G.A.
Co 37059 Fan It/Blowin' Up a Storm
Co 37227 Four Men on a Horse/Lost Weekend
Co 37228 Igor/Nero's Conception
Cap 57-616 Early Autumn/Keeper of the Flame
Cap 15365 Lemon Drop/I Ain't Gonna Wait Too Long

CHARLIE VENTURA
Nat 9036 Synthesis/Blue Champagne

LEONARD FEATHER'S ESQUIRE ALL-AMERICANS
Vi (12")40-4001 Snafu/Long Long Journey

ESQUIRE ALL-AMERICAN AWARD WINNERS
Vi 40-0134 Blow Me Down
Vi 40-0135 Buckin' the Blues
Vi 40-0136 Indian Summer
Vi 40-0137 Indiana Winter

GEORGE AULD
Guild 113 Georgie Porgie/Sweetheart of All My Dreams

CHARLIE BARNET
Apo 1065 Bunny/Atlantic Jump

BILL HARRIS
Key 618 Mean to Me/Cross Country

FLIP PHILLIPS
Si 28106 Pappiloma/Skyscraper

Si (12″)90003 Sweet and Lovely/Bob's Belief

RED RODNEY
Key 670 Elevation/Fine and Dandy

CHUBBY JACKSON
Queen 4101 I Gotcha Covered/Popsie
Queen 4103 Bass Face/Don't Get Too Wild Child
Key 616 Northwest Passage/Cryin' Sands
Key 625 Head Quarters/Sam's Caravan
VD (12″)665 Meshuga
MGM 10228 The Happy Monster/L'Ana
MGM 10354 Follow the Leader/"Mom" Jackson
Rbw 111 Lemon Drop/Crown Pilots
Rbw 112 Boomsie/Dee Dee's Dance
Co 38451 Father Knickerbopper/Godchild
NJ 825 Flying the Coop/I May Be Wrong
NJ 836 New York/Why Not?

LPs

CHUBBY JACKSON
Pres 7641 Sextet and Big Band (RIs)
Pres (10″)105 All-Star Band
Argo 614 Chubby's Back!
Argo 625 I'm Entitled to You
Rbw (10″)708

CHUBBY JACKSON-BILL HARRIS ALL-STARS
Mer (10″)MG-25076 Jazz Journey

CHARLIE VENTURA
Mer (10″)MGC-117 Charlie Ventura Collates

WOODY HERMAN
Ha HL-7013 Bijou (Co RIs)
MGM (10″)E-158 At Carnegie Hall, 1946, Vol. 1
MGM (10″)E-159 At Carnegie Hall, 1946, Vol. 2

ELLIOT LAWRENCE
Vik LX-1113 Jazz Goes Broadway

904. JACKSON, CLIFF   p B
(CLIFTON LUTHER JACKSON)

*Born July 19, 1902, Washington, D.C.
Died May 24, 1970, New York, N.Y.*

Pianist in Harlem stride tradition. First jobs local; to New York 1923. Freelanced there several years, formed Krazy Kats Orchestra early 1927. In middle and late 20s accompanist on records with blues singers. During 30s in New York clubs as soloist or leading combo. In 40s recorded under own name and with other groups. Many jobs at Cafe Society. Toured with Eddie Condon 1946. In 50s more clubs. With Garvin Bushell 1959, J. C. Higginbotham 1960, Joe Thomas 1962. Beginning 1963 often with Tony Parenti until death.

RECORDS

ROSA HENDERSON
Co 14152-D He's My Man/In That Apartment Upstairs
Pe 135 You Can't Have It Unless I Give It to You/Dyin' Crap-Shooter's Blues
Pe 138 Police Blues/Never Let Your Left Hand Know

MAGGIE JONES
Co 14114-D Dallas Blues/South Street Blues
Co 14127-D I'm a Back-Bitin' Mama/Never Drive a Beggar from Your Door

VIOLA MCCOY
Ca 1066 I'm Savin' It All for You/Papa, If You Can't Do Better

JOSIE MILES
Ajax 17066 Believe Me, Hot Mama

MUSICAL STEVEDORES
Co 14406-D Happy Rhythm/Honeycomb Harmony

SIDNEY BECHET
Bb 8509 Make Me a Pallet on the Floor
Vi 26640 Shake It and Break It/Wild Man Blues
Vi 27574 Swing Parade/I Know That You Know

BUNNY BERIGAN
De 18116 I'm Coming Virginia/Blues
De 18117 Chicken and Waffles/You Took Advantage of Me

TOMMY LADNIER
Bb 10086 Ja-da/Weary Blues
Bb 10089 Really the Blues/When You and I Were Young, Maggie

SEPIA SERENADERS
Bb 5770 Nameless Blues/Ridiculous Blues
Bb 5803 Dallas Blues/Alligator Crawl

MARTHA COPELAND
Co 14189-D On Decoration Day/Fortune Teller Blues
IDA COX
OK 6405 Last Mile Blues/I Can't Quit That Man
JOE MARSALA
B&W 18 Cherokee/My Melancholy Baby
PEE WEE RUSSELL
Disc 5053 Since My Best Gal Turned Me Down/Muskogee Blues
CLIFF JACKSON
Globe 1839 Horse Feathers
Rad 951 Torrid Rhythm
B&W 3 Quiet Please/Squeeze Me
B&W 4 Weary/If I Could Be with You
B&W (12")1205 Jeepers Creepers/Cliff's Boogie Blues
Disc 6008 You Took Advantage of Me
Disc 6009 Tea for Two
Disc 6010 Memphis Blues
Cen 4000 Hock Shop Blues

LPs

CLIFF JACKSON
Fat Cat's Jazz 107 Parlor Social Piano
SIDNEY BECHET
"X" (10")LVA-3024 (Bb, Vi RIs)
(miscellaneous artists)
Tops L-1508 Jazz Greats
Vi 542 The Panassie Sessions (Vi RIs)

905. JACKSON, FRANZ

cl ts bas vo ar cm B

Born November 1, 1912, Rock Island, Ill.

Versatile jazzman with jazz and swing bands in 30s and 40s; later successful bandleader. Developed into competent arranger and composer. Attended Chicago Musical College. Began professionally in Chicago about 1930. Periods with Carroll Dickerson, Frankie Jaxon, Reuben Reeves and others. With Jimmie Noone about a year mid-30s. With Roy Eldridge in New York 1939-40. In early 40s with Earl Hines, Fats Waller, Cootie Williams, Pete Brown, Frankie Newton. Toured with Eldridge 1944. With Wilbur DeParis 1945. In later 40s and early 50s toured with U.S.O. units. In Chicago starting early 50s. Formed band 1956 called The Original Jass All-Stars. In late

50s and 60s long stays at Red Arrow and Jazz Ltd. clubs. Bassoon with Community Symphony of Chicago. Acquired Pinnacle Records, recorded on that label. In later 60s based in New York; good traditional swing group well received there. Active into 70s. Composer of jazz numbers including *Red Arrow Blues, Blues to the Dole, Yellow Fire, You're the Maker of Rain in My Heart, Boogie Woogie Camp Meetin', Rompin' and Stompin', Comin' in Home, Lonely Blues, Elephant Swing, Morning Blues, Arcadia Shuffle, Gate Swing Out, Southside, For Bass Only, Escapade, Hip-Hop, No Use Now, That Glorious Feelin', Keep This in Mind, Frivolity, Little Flirt, Roustabout, There's Another World, Incidental Thing, Longing Blues, Pretty Thing, Out of Place, Take Off, Mazie.*

RECORDS

REUBEN "RIVER" REEVES
Vo 2636 Yellow Five/Screws, Nuts and Bolts
Vo 2723 Zuddan/Mazie
DUD BASCOMB
Son 103 Not Bad, Bascomb/Just One More Chance
Son 105 That's My Home/Late Hour Rock
FRANZ JACKSON
De 7330 Summer Rhapsody/Boogie Woogie Camp Meetin'
De 7779 Elephant Swing/You're the Maker of Rain in My Heart

LPs

FRANZ JACKSON
Philips(E) 200113 Jass, Jass, Jass
Riv 406 Original Jass All-Stars
Replica 1006 No Saints
Pinnacle 102 No Saints
Pinnacle 104 A Night at the Red Arrow
Pinnacle 109 Good Old Days
LIL HARDIN ARMSTRONG
Riv 401

906. JACKSON, MAHALIA

vo cm

Born October 26, 1911, New Orleans, La.
Died January 27, 1972, Chicago, Ill., suburban hospital

Considered by most as world's greatest gospel singer. True artist. As youngster in

New Orleans listened to blues singers but shaped vocal style to gospel music. Refused to sing jazz, blues or pops yet could have been star in any. To Chicago 1927, ran beauty shop. Active singing in all types of churches, large or small. Some concerts. Mid-40s began recording for Apollo. Successful, particularly own composition *Move On Up a Little Higher*. Other popular records *I Can Put My Trust in Jesus* and *Silent Night, Holy Night*. In early 50s concert tours in U.S. and abroad. In 1954 began on Columbia LPs. Big hit at Newport Jazz Festival 1957 and 1958. In late 50s and 60s TV advanced career. Sincerity, artistry won army of admirers. In 1958 movie ST. LOUIS BLUES. Active in 60s. Sang abroad, received by royalty. Late in career veered slightly from gospel singing, sometimes worked with large orchestras and sang popular material in good taste. Illness 1964-5 forced her from music; resumed later. On European tour several months before death; tour cut short by illness.

RECORDS

MAHALIA JACKSON
De 7321 Oh, My Lord/God Shall Wipe All Tears Away
De 7341 Keep Me Every Day/God's Gonna Separate the Wheat from the Tares
Apo 145 I Want to Rest/He Knows My Heart
Apo 164 Move On Up a Little Higher (1 & 2)
Apo 181 Dig a Little Deeper/If You See My Saviour
Apo 194 Amazing Grace/Tired
Apo 213 I Can Put My Trust in Jesus/ Let the Power of the Holy Ghost Fall on Me
Apo 217 Walk with Me/Prayer Changes Things
Apo 221 Just Over the Hill (1 & 2)
Apo 235 Silent Night, Holy Night/Go Tell It on the Mountain
Apo 245 The Lord's Prayer/Bless This House
Apo 262 In the Upper Room (1 & 2)

LPs

MAHALIA JACKSON
Apo 482 No Matter How You Pray

Co CL-644 The World's Greatest Gospel Singer
Co CL-1244 Newport 1958, Mahalia Jackson
Co CL-2004 Greatest Hits
Co CS-9405(S) My Faith
Co CS-9490(S) In Concert
Co CS-9659(S) Mighty Fortress
Co CS-9686(S) Best-Loved Hymns of Dr. King
Co CS-9813(S) Right Out of the Church
Ha HL-11279 You'll Never Walk Alone

907. JACKSON, MILT "BAGS"
vb p g B

Born January 1, 1923, Detroit, Mich.

Talented jazzman, pioneer bop vibist. Tasteful, inventive, subtly swinging. Attended Michigan State. With Detroit bands early 40s. To New York 1945; with Dizzy Gillespie. Active in development of progressive jazz. With Tadd Dameron, Thelonious Monk, Howard McGhee. With Woody Herman late 1949-50 and Dizzy Gillespie 1950-2. Original member of Modern Jazz Quartet, which began working steadily 1954 after forming in 1953. Vibes work became more subdued to conform to gentle style of Quartet. Remained with group into 1973. Quartet enormously popular, respected. During occasional Quartet inactivity, Jackson played with own combo.

RECORDS

DIZZY GILLESPIE
Vi 40-0130 Night in Tunisia/52nd Street Theme
Vi 40-0132 Anthropology/Ol' Man Rebop
Mus 447 Emanon/Things to Come
DeeGee 3604 The Champ (1 & 2)
KENNY CLARKE
Cen 1501 You Go to My Head
THE BE-BOP BOYS
Sav 902 Moody Speaks/Smokey Hollow Jump
DINAH WASHINGTON
Apo 368 Wise Woman Blues/No Voot, No Boot
Apo 374 Rich Man's Blues/Walking Blues

COLEMAN HAWKINS
Son 3024 Bean and the Boys/Cocktails for Two
Son 3027 I Mean You/You Go to My Head

TEMPO JAZZ MEN
Dial 1001 Dynamo (A & B)
Dial 1003 'Round About Midnight
Dial 1004 When I Grow Too Old To
Dial 1005 Diggin' for Diz
Dial 1008 Confirmation

MODERN JAZZ QUARTET
Pres 873 Autumn in New York/The Queen's Fancy

MILT JACKSON
Sav 946 Junior/Bubu
DeeGee 3700 Milt Meets Sid/Between the Devil and the Deep Blue Sea
DeeGee 3702 Autumn Breeze/Bluesology
Hi-Lo 1405 Heart and Soul/Love Me Pretty Baby
Hi-Lo 1412 True Blues/Softly, as in a Morning Sunrise
BN 1592 Tahiti/What's New?
BN 1593 Lillie/Bags' Groove
Pres 828 All the Things You Are/La Ronde
Pres 851 Vendome/Rose of the Rio Grande
Pres 882 Autumn in New York/Delaunay's Dilemma

LPs

MILT JACKSON
Atl 1242 Ballads and Blues
Atl 1294 Bags and Flutes
Atl 1417 Vibrations
Sav MG-12061
Sav MG-12070 The Jazz Skyline
Pres (10″)183 Milt Jackson Quintet
Apple ST-3353(S) Under the Jasmin Tree
UA 4022 Bags' Opus
Riv 9429(S) Big Bags: Milt Jackson Orchestra
Impulse 9189 That's the Way It Is

MODERN JAZZ QUARTET
Atl 1231 Fontessa
Atl 1265 The Modern Jazz Quartet
Atl 1299 At Music Inn/Vol. 2

DIZZY GILLESPIE
Sav MG-12020 Groovin' High (Mus RIs)

HOWARD MCGHEE
Vogue(E) (10″)LDE-008 Howard McGhee Sextet

KENNY CLARKE
Sav MG-12006

908. JACKSON, QUENTIN "BUTTER"
tb vo

Born January 13, 1909, Springfield, Ohio

Jazz trombonist best known for work with Duke Ellington using plunger mute a la predecessor Tricky Sam Nanton. Early training on piano, violin and organ, soon concentrated on trombone. Began professionally late 20s. In 1930 with Zach Whyte, then with McKinney's Cotton Pickers late 1930-2. With Don Redman 1932-40, with Cab Calloway 1940-8. With Ellington late 1948 to late 1959. In 60s with Quincy Jones (European tour), Count Basie, others. Freelanced and studio work. Active into 70s.

RECORDS

DON REDMAN
Vi 26266 Baby, Won't You Please Come Home?

MCKINNEY'S COTTON PICKERS
Vi 22811 Wrap Your Troubles in Dreams/Do You Believe in Love at Sight?
Vi 23035 Come a Little Closer

DUKE ELLINGTON
Co 39428 Fancy Dan
Co 39670 Jam with Sam

LPs

DUKE ELLINGTON
Co CL-1198 The Cosmic Scene
Cap T-637
Cap (10″)H-440

JOHNNY HODGES & THE ELLINGTON MEN
Verve MGV-8271 The Big Sound

909. JACOBS, AL
cm lyr p vo

Born January 22, 1903, San Francisco, Calif.

Composer of 30s and 40s. Best-known songs *I'm Just an Ordinary Human* (1935), *Please Believe Me* (1936), *I'm a Lucky Devil* (1939), *This Is My Country* (1940), *But I Did* (1944), *If I Give My Heart to You* (1954). Other songs *I Need You Now*,

'Tain't No Good, Just One More Time, Anybody's Love Song, All I Want Is a Chance, The Last Polka, There'll Never Be Another You, Make a Wish, Scalawag, Will o' the Wisp, Fortune for a Penny, Kon Tiki, My Believing Heart, Time Stands Still, I've Got a Heart Filled with Love, No More Rivers to Cross, Rosie the Redskin, Crime and Punishment, Surprise, My Sailor Boy. Collaborators Jimmie Crane, Joseph Meyer, Larry Yoell, Peter Tinturin, Don Raye. Early in career taught piano, worked as piano salesman. Managed publishing companies. Assistant musical director on Al Pearce radio show; other radio work. Several years in brokerage business. Wrote for several movies including DANCING DAUGHTERS, SEVEN WONDERS OF THE WORLD, KON TIKI.

910. JACQUET, ILLINOIS
ts as ss bas cm B

Born October 31, 1922, Broussard, La.

Underrated tenor sax star; jazz image tarnished by early frantic style, squealing high notes and honking. Later displayed inventive, tasteful modern style, beautiful tone. Great facility on swing, sensitive on ballads. Younger brother of trumpeter Russell Jacquet. Grew up in Houston, played locally late 30s. On west coast 1941 with Floyd Ray, played alto and soprano sax. With Lionel Hampton 1941-2, switched to tenor sax. Won fame with frenzied solos on band's hit *Flying Home*. With Cab Calloway 1943-4. In 1944 led brother Russell's group awhile. Late 1944 recorded frantic sides with Jazz at the Philharmonic group, fueled reputation as wild exhibitionist. With Count Basie 1945-6, settled down to more conventional swing style. Toured with Jazz at the Philharmonic shows at intervals in later 40s and early 50s. Mostly led combos from late 40s into 70s. Led big band on tour 1952. European tour 1954. Based mostly in New York. Took up bassoon mid-60s. Among jazz compositions: *Robbins Nest* and *Black Velvet*. Former became 1951 pop *Just When We're Falling in Love*. Latter became 1950 tune *Don'cha Go 'Way Mad* featured by Harry James.

RECORDS

LIONEL HAMPTON
De 18394 Flying Home
JAZZ AT THE PHILHARMONIC
Asch 453-1 How High the Moon (1 & 2)
Asch 453-2 How High the Moon (3)/Lady Be Good (1)
Asch 453-3 Lady Be Good (2 & 3)
Disc 6024 Blues (1 & 2)
Disc 6025 Blues (3)/Lester Leaps In (1)
Disc 6026 Lester Leaps In (2 & 3)
COUNT BASIE
Co 37070 The King
Co 37093 Mutton Leg
Pa(E) 3014 Rambo
AL CASEY
Cap 10034 Sometimes I'm Happy/How High the Moon
BIG SID CATLETT
Cap 10032 Love for Scale/I Never Knew
Cap 15177 Henderson Romp/Just You, Just Me
EMMETT BERRY
Sav 594 Berry's Blues/Minor Romp
KING COLE QUINTET
Disc 2010 Heads/It Had to Be You
Disc 2011 Pro-Sky/I Can't Give You Anything but Love
ILLINOIS JACQUET
Alad 101 Flying Home (1 & 2)
Alad 179 Jivin' with Jack the Bellboy/You Left Me All Alone
Apo 756 A Ghost of a Chance/Bottoms Up
Apo 758 What's This?/Wondering and Thinking of You
Apo 760 Memories of You/Merle's Mood
Apo 769 Robbins Nest/Jacquet Mood
Apo 777 Jumpin' at the Woodside/Music Hall Beat
Sav 593 Jumpin' Jacquet/Blue Mood
Vi 22-0027 Black Velvet/Adams' Alley
Vi 22-0087 My Old Gal/You Gotta Change
Vi 20-2702 Riffin' at 24th Street/King Jacquet
Mer 8941 All of Me/Pastel
Mer 89036 What's the Riff?/Blues in the Night

Clef 89084 Mean to Me/Sittin' and Rockin'
Clef 89121 Little Jeff/Heads
Clef 89164 Learnin' the Blues/Honeysuckle Rose

LPs

ILLINOIS JACQUET
Alad 803 (RIs)
Mer (10″)MGG-112 Illinois Jacquet Collates
(one side) GA 33-315 (Apo RIs)
Verve V-8065 Kid and The Brute
Roul R-52035 Illinois Jacquet Flies Again
Argo 746 Bosses of the Ballad
Argo 754 Spectrum
Pres 7575 Bottoms Up
Cadet S-773(S) Go Power
JAZZ AT THE PHILHARMONIC
Stin (10″)23

911. JAFFE, NAT   p
Born 1918, New York, N.Y.
Died August 5, 1945, New York, N.Y.

Talented pianist; promising career cut short by early death. Strong piano style, somewhat modern with traditional roots. Most of childhood lived in Berlin. Back to U. S. 1932. Played in New York later 30s. With Joe Marsala and Jan Savitt 1938, Charlie Barnet 1938-9, Jack Teagarden late 1939-40. Freelanced, worked clubs as soloist or led combo.

RECORDS
(entire known output)

CHARLIE BARNET
Bb 10131 Tin Roof Blues/Knockin' at the Famous Door
Bb 10172 Jump Session/Swing Street Strut
JACK TEAGARDEN
Vs 8202 Wham
DICK ROBERTSON
De 1914 Hi Yo, Silver/When Mother Nature Sings Her Lullaby
De 1979 El Rancho Grande
NAT JAFFE
B&W (12″)1208 Blues in Nat's Flat/These Foolish Things
B&W (12″)1209 A Hundred Years from Today/If I Had You
Si 28111 Black and Blue/Zonky

Si 28112 How Can You Face Me?/Keepin' Out of Mischief Now
VD (12″)764 The Jeep's Jumpin'

LPs

CHARLIE BARNET
IAJ RC-8 (one side)
First Time Records 1504 (1938 ETs)

912. JAMES, HARRY   t cm ar B
Born March 15, 1916, Albany, Ga.

Trumpet star who rose to fame with Benny Goodman, then became top bandleader for over three decades. Vigorous style influenced by Louis Armstrong. Great technique; rich, brassy tone. Warm style on ballads produced many 40s hits. Father circus bandmaster, taught Harry trumpet. After travelling, family settled in Beaumont, Texas. Harry played in Texas early 30s, including jobs with Herman Waldman. Toured to New Orleans with Joe Gill around 1934; band included pianist Peck Kelley. First important job with Ben Pollack 1935-6; featured. Joined Benny Goodman January 1937; soon famous for fiery solos. Audiences at Goodman's radio and stage shows usually greeted James solos with applause. Goodman's top soloist 1937-8. Also recorded with pickup groups and small bands under own name. In band's 1938 movie HOLLYWOOD HOTEL. Left Goodman late 1938 to form own big band. Theme showcase *Ciribiribin*. Band modestly popular 1939-40. Future great vocalists Frank Sinatra, then Dick Haymes. Established singer Helen Forrest joined late 1941; featured on James record hits. Popular 1939 record, often reissued: *Two O'clock Jump*.

In early 1941 James broke through with flashy trumpeting on record coupling *The Flight of the Bumble Bee/Carnival of Venice*. Also popular: instrumental *Music Makers*. *I Don't Want to Walk without You* popular early 1942. Other hits of early 40s: *You Made Me Love You, I Had the Craziest Dream, Sleepy Lagoon, Trumpet Blues, I've Heard That Song Before, I'll Get By*. Popular instrumentals: *The Mole, Flatbush Flanagan, Strictly Instrumental, Prince Charming, James Session, Trumpet*

Rhapsody, Jump Town, Velvet Moon, Concerto for Trumpet. James married movie star Betty Grable 1943 (previous wife vocalist Louise Tobin). In early 40s band often on radio on such shows as Jack Benny, Coca Cola, Danny Kaye, own Chesterfield series. Peak popularity these years. James added strings early 40s, achieved lush backgrounds, maintained large orchestra most of 40s. Tenor saxman Corky Corcoran star soloist; with band off and on into 1973.

Arrangers in early 40s: Leroy Holmes, Jack Mathias and Johnny Thompson. Vocalist Kitty Kallen followed Helen Forrest. In later 40s Ray Conniff important arranger-composer for band. Altoist Willie Smith and trombonist Juan Tizol joined mid-40s; important sidemen until 1951, rejoined 1954. Band active despite lean postwar years. Later 50s based in Los Angeles and Las Vegas, toured occasionally. Top drummer Buddy Rich featured off and on in 50s and 60s. Other star soloists of later years Sam Firmature (ts), Jack Percival (p), Ray Sims (tb). Late 50s band featured hard-swinging style with minimum commercialism. Even more jazz-oriented in 60s; sound and style along Count Basie lines. Basie arrangers Ernie Wilkins and Neal Hefti important writers for James. Band played classic swingers, modern jazz, some current well-arranged pops. James adopted trace of progressive style in solos. Always impressive front man, warm and expressive but dignified. Band in movies PRIVATE BUCKAROO and SPRINGTIME IN THE ROCKIES (1942), BEST FOOT FORWARD (1943), BATHING BEAUTY and TWO GIRLS AND A SAILOR (1944), DO YOU LOVE ME? and IF I'M LUCKY (1946), CARNEGIE HALL (1947), I'LL GET BY (1950). James in SYNCOPATION (1942) and THE BENNY GOODMAN STORY (1956). Trumpet on soundtrack of YOUNG MAN WITH A HORN (1950). 1952 band had TV show; later years occasional TV. James composer or co-composer of jazz numbers including *Peckin', Two O'clock Jump, The Mole, Music Makers, LIFE Goes to a Party, Tango Blues, Jughead, Ultra, James Session, Easy, Keb-lah, Friar Rock, Feet*

Draggin' Blues, Trumpet Rhapsody, Concerto for Trumpet, Night Special, Flatbush Flanagan, The Beaumont Ride, Back Beat Boogie, Jump Town, Let Me Up, pops *I'm Beginning to See the Light, Eleven Sixty P.M., Every Day of My Life, From the Bottom of My Heart.*

RECORDS

BEN POLLACK
    Br 7764 Jimtown Blues
    Va 504 Deep Elm/The Moon Is Grinning at Me
    Va 556 In a Sentimental Mood/ Peckin'

THE DEAN AND HIS KIDS
    Vo 3342 Zoom Zoom Zoom/Spreadin' Knowledge Around

TEDDY WILSON
    Br 7940 You're My Desire/Remember Me?
    Br 7943 The Hour of Parting/Coquette
    Br 7964 Ain't Misbehavin'/Honeysuckle Rose
    Br 7973 Just a Mood (1 & 2)

BENNY GOODMAN
    Vi (12")36205 Sing, Sing, Sing, Pt. 2
    Vi 25510 I Want to Be Happy
    Vi 25531 Chloe
    Vi 25621 Peckin' (arranged by James)
    Vi 25627 Roll 'Em
    Vi 25678 I Can't Give You Anything but Love/Sugarfoot Stomp
    Vi 25726 LIFE Goes to a Party (arranged by James)
    Vi 25792 Don't Be That Way/One O'clock Jump
    Vi 25827 Lullaby in Rhythm
    Vi 25871 Big John Special
    Vi 25880 Wrappin' It Up
    Vi 26060 Margie
    Vi 26087 Bumble Bee Stomp
    Vi 26095 Farewell Blues

LIONEL HAMPTON
    Vi 26011 Shoe Shiners Drag/I'm in the Mood for Swing

METRONOME ALL STAR BAND
    Vi 26144 The Blues
    Vi 27314 One O'clock Jump/Bugle Call Rag
    Co 35389 King Porter Stomp/All Star Strut (METRONOME ALL STAR NINE)
    Co 36499 Royal Flush

HARRY JAMES

Br 8035 LIFE Goes to a Party/When We're Alone

Br 8136 Lullaby in Rhythm/Out of Nowhere

Br 8327 (theme) Ciribiribin/Sweet Georgia Brown

Vs 8201 Headin' for Hallelujah/Alice Blue Gown

Vs 8231 Hodge Podge/Carnival of Venice

Co 35242 Willow Weep for Me/My Buddy

Co 35316 (theme) Ciribiribin/Avalon

Co 35340 Concerto for Trumpet/I'm in the Market for You

Co 35932 Music Makers/Montevideo

Co 35947 Flatbush Flanagan/I Never Purposely Hurt You

Co 36004 The Flight of the Bumble Bee/Carnival of Venice

Co 36160 Trumpet Rhapsody (1 & 2)

Co 36232 Two O'clock Jump/One O'clock Jump

Co 36285 I'll Get By/Lost in Love

Co 36296 You Made Me Love You/A Sinner Kissed an Angel

Co 36478 I Don't Want to Walk without You/B-19

Co 36549 Sleepy Lagoon/Trumpet Blues

Co 36579 Strictly Instrumental/When You're a Long, Long Way from Home

Co 36599 The Mole/But Not for Me

Co 36659 I Had the Craziest Dream/A Poem Set to Music

Co 36668 I've Heard That Song Before/Moonlight Becomes You

Co 36672 Velvet Moon/Prince Charming

Co 36677 James Session/I Heard You Cried Last Night

Co 36683 Jump Town/Cherry

Co 36867 (Betty Grable vo: pseudonym Ruth Haag) I Can't Begin to Tell You

Co 37351 Moten Swing (1 & 2)

Co 38557 Ultra/Someone Loves Someone

Co 38902 In a Mist/Brazilian Sleigh Bells

Co 39419 Tango Blues/When the Sun Comes Out

LPs

HARRY JAMES

Co CL-522 One Night Stand

Co CL-581 Soft Lights, Sweet Trumpet

Co CL-655 All Time Favorites (Co RIs)

Co CL-668 At the Hollywood Palladium

Cap T-1093 Harry's Choice!

MGM E-3778 And His New Swingin' Band

MGM E-3848 Harry James Today

MGM E-4265 New Version of Down Beat Favorites

Ha HL-7159 And His Great Vocalists (Co RIs)

Ha HL-7162 Plays Trumpet Rhapsody (Co RIs)

BENNY GOODMAN

Vi LPT-6703 (5-LP set) The Golden Age of Swing (Vi RIs)

Co ML-4590-1 (2-LP set) Concert No. 2 1937-1938 (airchecks)

Co SL-160 (2-LP set) Carnegie Hall Concert

MGM E3788-89-90 (3-LP set) Treasure Chest (1937-1938 airchecks)

LIONEL HAMPTON

Cam CAL-402 Jivin' the Vibes (Vi RIs)

913. JAMES, JONI   vo
(JOAN CARMELLO BABBO)
Born September 22, 1930, Chicago, Ill.

Good pop singer, reached peak early 50s. As youngster danced with troupe playing fairs in Canada. In chorus line at Chicago hotel. Switched to singing, worked up to top midwest spots. Chicago engagement led to 1952 contract with MGM Records. Soon top star. Big hits: *Why Don't You Believe Me?*; *Your Cheatin' Heart*; *Is It Any Wonder?*; *Have You Heard?*; *My Love, My Love*. Busy in early and mid-50s, occasional TV. Faded by late 50s.

RECORDS

JONI JAMES

MGM 11223 My Baby Just Cares for Me/Let There Be Love

MGM 11295 You Belong to Me/Yes, Yes, Yes

MGM 11333 Why Don't You Believe Me?/Purple Shades

MGM 11390 Have You Heard?/ Wishing Ring
MGM 11426 Your Cheatin' Heart/I'll Be Waiting for You
MGM 11470 Is It Any Wonder/Almost Always
MGM 11543 My Love, My Love/ You're Fooling Someone
MGM 11606 Why Can't I?/I'll Never Stand in Your Way
MGM 11637 Christmas and You/ Nina-Non
MGM 11696 Maybe Next Time/Am I in Love?
MGM 11753 In a Garden of Roses/ Every Day
MGM 30829 You're My Everything/ You're Nearer

LPs

JONI JAMES
MGM E-3240 When I Fall in Love
MGM E-3328 In the Still of the Night
MGM E-3346 Award Winning Album
MGM E-3347 Little Girl Blue
MGM E-3348 Let There Be Love
MGM E-3449 Sings Songs by Victor Young and Frank Loesser
MGM E-3739 Sings Songs of Hank Williams
MGM E-4008 After Hours
MGM E-4200 My Favorite Things
MGM (10")E-234 Joni James

914. JAMES, LEWIS   vo

Popular tenor of 20s. Began recording about 1918. Church singer early in career, also concerts. Prolific recording. Second tenor in Revelers vocal quartet active on radio and records late 20s to mid-30s.

RECORDS

IPANA TROUBADOURS
Co 662-D Roses Remind Me of You
NAT SHILKRET
Vi 20474 Rio Rita
Vi 20659 Rainbow of Love
JACQUES RENARD
Vi 20728 Just Call on Me
CHARLES FRY
Vi 21496 Look What You've Done/ Sorry for Me
JEAN GOLDKETTE
Vi 20981 Blue River

THE REVELERS
Vi 19796 Oh, Miss Hannah/Dinah
Vi 20111 Lucky Day/Birth of the Blues
Vi 20457 In a Little Spanish Town
Vi 20678 I'm Looking Over a Four-Leaf Clover/I'm in Love Again
Vi 22270 Chant of the Jungle/Waiting at the End of the Road
LEWIS JAMES with JESSE CRAWFORD-organ
Vi 20463 I'm Looking for a Girl Named Mary
LEWIS JAMES-FRANKLYN BAUR
Co 68-D Sleep
LEWIS JAMES
Co A-2691 I'm Glad I Can Make You Cry
Co 25-D Marcheta/I Love You
Co 250-D You're Just a Flower from an Old Bouquet
Co 564-D Always/Venetian Isles
Co 1327-D Little Log Cabin of Dreams
Ed 50894 Show Me the Way To Your Heart
OK 40056 Mr. Radio Man/Until Tomorrow (with HELEN CLARK)
Vi 19214 The West, a Nest and You
Vi 20490 Let's Forgive and Forget
Vi 21700 Roses of Yesterday/Just a Sweetheart
Vi 22239 A Bundle of Old Love Letters
Vi 22422 Looking at You
Vi 22458 Singing a Song to the Stars/ With My Guitar and You
Vi 22594 The Little Things in Life/ Under the Spell of Your Kiss
Vi 22686 Beautiful Love/By the River Sainte Marie

915. JANIS, CONRAD   tb g B

Born February 11, 1928, New York, N.Y.

Actor of stage, screen and TV; barrelhouse trombonist-leader of dixieland combo in 50s and 60s. Began acting 1941 in show JUNIOR MISS. Youthful roles several years on stage and in movies; good role in 1947 movie MARGIE. Self-taught on guitar, took up trombone 1949. Made record following year with Hollywood jazz enthusiasts, entered it in *Record Changer* Magazine's amateur band contest, won. To New York, active leading jazz groups in 50s. Personnel of first regular band included veterans Danny Barker (g), Pops Foster (b), Freddie Moore (d), young players Dick Smith (c), Tom Sharpsteen (cl), Bob Greene (p). Still active acting; roles in many TV 50s shows, sometimes with band. Broadway roles in THE BRASS RING and TIME OUT FOR GINGER (1952), THE TERRIBLE SWIFT SWORD (1955), VISIT TO A SMALL PLANET (1957), MAKE A MILLION and LET'S ROCK (1958), SUNDAY IN NEW YORK (1961), MARATHON '33 (1963), THE FRONT PAGE (1969). Continued with jazz band into 60s, including trips abroad. Played occasionally in 70s, mostly worked as actor.

RECORDS
TAILGATE JAZZ BAND
Record Changer 101 Chattanooga Stomp/Snag It
CONRAD JANIS
Ci 1076 Kansas City Stomps/Oriental Moon
Ci 3006 Eh, La Bas/Willie the Weeper
Ci 3007 Down by the Riverside/When You and I Were Young, Maggie
Ci 3015 When the Saints Go Marching In (1 & 2)

LPs
CONRAD JANIS
Ci (10″)L-404 Conrad Janis' Tailgate Jazz Band
Riv 12-215 Dixieland Jam Session
Jub (10″)7
(miscellaneous artists)
Ci (10″)L-407 Jamming at Rudi's No. 1

916. JANIS, ELSIE   vo cm lyr
(ELSIE BIERBOWER)
Born March 16, 1889, Columbus, Ohio
Died February 26, 1956, Los Angeles, Calif.

Beautiful and versatile performer of early vaudeville and Broadway stage. As child played in stock companies and vaudeville as Little Elsie. First Broadway musical THE VANDERBILT CUP (1906), later THE HOYDEN (1907), THE FAIR CO-ED (1909), THE SLIM PRINCESS (1911), THE LADY OF THE SLIPPER (1912), MISS INFORMATION (1915; also wrote lyrics for score), THE CENTURY GIRL (1916). Headliner in vaudeville imitating great theatre artists.

Stage appearance in London 1914, recorded there in 20s. Entertained overseas World War I, known as The Sweetheart of the A.E.F. In 1919 she presented stage show ELSIE JANIS AND HER GANG, used all-soldier cast. In 1922 presented another show, same title. Performed on Paris stage 1921, in U.S. concerts 1923-5. Starred on Broadway in PUZZLES OF 1925 wrote book and part of music and lyrics. Retired from stage 1929. Became writer, supervisor and producer of movies. Scenario for early sound movie CLOSE HARMONY. Author of books *Love Letters of an Actress, A Star for a Night, The Big Show, So Far So Good* (autobiography). Late in career performed in stage presentation FRANK FAY VAUDEVILLE. As songwriter wrote mostly lyrics; credits include *Love, Your Magic Spell Is Everywhere* (1929), *Live and Love Today* (1930 movie MADAME SATAN), *Any Time's the Time to Fall in Love, I'm True to the Navy Now* and *What Did Cleopatra Say?* (1930 movie PARAMOUNT ON PARADE), *Oh Give Me Time for Tenderness* (1939 movie DARK VICTORY).

RECORDS
ELSIE JANIS
Vi 60091 Fo' de Lawd's Sake Play a Waltz
Vi 60093 When Antelo Plays the 'Cello
HMV(E) B-488 Florrie Was a Flapper/You're Here and I'm Here (with BASIL HALLAM)
HMV(E) B-489 When We Tango to "The Wearing of the Green"/I Want a Dancing Man
HMV(E) C-566 Prudence/The Same Old Song (with BASIL HALLAM)
HMV(E) C-569 The Fortune Teller

LPs
(miscellaneous artists; one number)
Audio Rarities LPA-2290 They Stopped the Show (RIs)

917. JANSSEN, WERNER   cm p B
Born June 1, 1900, New York, N.Y.
Composer-conductor for stage, radio and movies. Scores for Broadway musicals LOVE DREAMS (1921), LETTY PEPPER (1922), LADY BUTTERFLY (1923), BOOM! BOOM! (1929); contributed songs to ZIEGFELD

FOLLIES OF 1925. After 1929 show studied classical music at American Academy in Rome (Prix de Rome) 1930-3. Conducted symphony orchestras in Berlin, Budapest, Helsingfors, Riga, Rome, Turin. In mid-30s at times conducted New York Philharmonic. Conducted Baltimore Symphony 1937-9. In 1940 founded Janssen Symphony of Los Angeles. Conducted symphony orchestras of Salt Lake City 1946-7, Portland 1947-9, San Diego 1952-4, Toronto 1956-7. Conducted Symphony of the Air 1956, Vienna State Opera Orchestra 1959-61. Concerts at Hollywood Bowl. From mid-30s into 40s scored movies THE GENERAL DIED AT DAWN, BLOCK-ADE, ETERNALLY YOURS, THE SOUTHERNER, CAPTAIN KIDD, GUEST IN THE HOUSE, others. Active on radio; conducted on Chase & Sanborn Hours 1937, own series during 30s and 40s. Popular compositions include *Lady Butterfly*, *Wonderful You*, *Sway with Me*, *Toddle Along*, *Settle Down in a One-Horse Town*, *Everyone Knows What Jazz Is*, *Wisdom Tooth*, *Without the One You Love*, *At the Fireplace*. Serious works *New Year's Eve in New York*, *Obsequies of a Saxaphone*, *American Kaleidoscope*, *Foster Suite*, *Louisiana Suite*.

918. JARRETT, ART   vo tb g B
Born 1909, New York, N.Y.

Good singer of 30s and early 40s. Beautiful tenor voice, smooth and well controlled; romantic appeal. Vocalist-guitarist with Earl Burtnett around 1926-7. Joined Ted Weems late 1927 as vocalist-trombonist-guitarist; featured on records. With Weems until early 1931. Radio in Chicago and New York; several recordings under own name. In 1932 succeeded Buddy Rogers in Broadway musical HOT-CHA. Sang in movies DANCING LADY (1933), SITTING PRETTY and LET'S FALL IN LOVE (1934). Led dance band early 1935-6 mostly in Chicago. Future composing great Jule Styne pianist-arranger for band. Jarrett married swimming star Eleanor Holm, who sang with band 1936. In later 30s mostly a single. Starred in several B Westerns. In movie MY LUCKY STAR (1938) and Broadway musical WALK WITH MUSIC (1940). Took over Hal Kemp

band early 1941 after leader killed late 1940; continued Kemp style. Jarrett vocals featured, along with Smoothies and Gale Robbins (later movie actress). Band played top spots, recorded often. Good run at Chicago's Blackhawk 1942, later faded. Navy service in South Pacific, World War II. Formed another band mid-1946, attained little success. Comparative obscurity in later years. Disc jockey on Cincinnati's WCPO 1948; briefly on WCPO-TV. Led band in Kentucky 1949. To Chicago radio on WGN around 1950-1. Became salesman in New York and Los Angeles, settled in Beverly Hills.

RECORDS
TED WEEMS
Vi 21339 Dream River
Vi 21767 Anything Your Heart Desires
Vi 21809 Me and the Man in the Moon
Vi 22037 Here We Are
Vi 22038 Am I a Passing Fancy?
Vi 22236 All That I'm Asking Is Sympathy
Vi 22499 My Baby Just Cares for Me
Vi 22515 I Still Get a Thrill
Vi 22646 Little Joe/You Gave Me Everything but Love
FRANKIE TRUMBAUER
Br 6159 Honeysuckle Rose/Georgia on My Mind
JIMMIE NOONE
Br 6174 I Need Lovin'/When It's Sleepy Time Down South
Br 6192 It's You/River, Stay 'Way from My Door
RED NICHOLS
Br (12")20107 California Medley (1 & 2)
Br (12")20110 New Orleans Medley (1)
ART JARRETT
Co 2672-D Goodbye Blues/This Time It's Love
Co 2691-D Music, Music, Everywhere/Love Me Tonight
Br 6235 Cuban Love Song/Honest, Really, Truly
Br 6260 Oh, What a Thrill/Just Friends
Vi 24393 Dinner at Eight
Vi 27474 Loveliness and Love/You Started Something
Vi 27527 Foolish/Shepherd Serenade

Vi 27534 The Cowboy Serenade/Call It Anything, It's Love
Vi 27571 Delilah/The Nickel Serenade
Vi 27580 Jim/You Can Depend on Me
Vi 27590 Everything's Been Done Before/It Must Be True
Vi 27612 The Bells of San Raquel/Ma-Ma-Maria
Vi 27620 Magic of Magnolias/Rose O'Day
Vi 27693 Humpty Dumpty Heart/How Long Did I Dream?

918A. JARVIS, AL

Important west coast disc jockey in 30s and 40s. Originator of "Make Believe Ballroom" radio format playing recordings of dance bands and singers. Martin Block later used format with great success. Early Jarvis show 1932 called The World's Largest Make Believe Ballroom on station KFWB in Los Angeles. One-hour show grew to three hours per day. Established successful record shop in Los Angeles. Plugging of Benny Goodman 1935 recordings believed factor in band's great reception August 1935 in trend-setting engagement at Palomar Ballroom in Los Angeles. Potent figure in west coast musical radio. Left KFWB for station KLAC in Los Angeles 1946 to mid-50s, then returned to KFWB. Retired 1959 after rock music invasion.

919. JASON, WILL   cm lyr

Born June 23, 1910, New York, N.Y.
Songwriter who teamed with Val Burton. Several excellent songs though output scant. Most famous song *When We're Alone (Penthouse Serenade).*

SONGS
(with related movies)

1932—When We're Alone (Penthouse Serenade); If It Ain't Love
1933—MELODY CRUISE movie (Isn't This a Night for Love?); Roof Top Serenade
1934—COCK-EYED CAVALIERS movie (The Big Bad Wolf Was Dead; Dilly Dally)

Other songs: *Rhythm in My Heart*; *It Can Happen to You*; *Buy a Kiss*; *Romantic*;

You Alone; *Sincerely Yours*; *Out of the Blue*; *Always You*

920. JASPAR, BOBBY   ts cl f p B

Born February 20, 1926, Liege, Belgium
Died February 28, 1963, New York, N.Y.

Versatile Belgian jazzman with successful later career in U.S. Modern-styled musician on several instruments, particularly good on tenor sax and flute. Musical heritage, studied diligently. In late 40s worked for U.S. Special Services in Germany. With Henri Renaud in Paris 1950; with other groups early 50s. Led combo in Paris 1954-6. Recorded with U.S. jazzmen abroad. With Jimmy Raney, Chet Baker, Bernard Peiffer, Andre Hodeir, David Abram. To U.S. 1956; with J. J. Johnson, Miles Davis, others. Played abroad, returned to U.S. 1959. Married singer-pianist Blossom Dearie; active in U.S. until illness 1962. Died 1963 after heart surgery.

RECORDS
(all LPs)

BOBBY JASPAR QUARTET/QUINTET
  Co(F) FPX-123
  Riv RLP 12-240
JIMMY RANEY
  Dawn 1120 Visits Paris
MORT HERBERT
  Sav MG-12073 Night People
HANK JONES
  Sav MG-12087 Hank Jones Quartet
HERBIE MANN-BOBBY JASPAR QUINTET
  Pres LP-7101 Interplay
J. J. JOHNSON
  Co CL-935 J. J. Johnson Quintet
BARRY GALBRAITH
  De DL-9200
BERNARD PEIFFER
  EmArcy (10")MG-26036
(miscellaneous artists)
  Angel (10")60009 French Toast

921. JAXON, FRANKIE "HALF PINT"
                   vo cm B

Born February 3, 1895, Montgomery, Ala.

Blues-styled singer with long career. Nicknamed because of 5' 2" height. Orphaned in Kansas City. At 15 sang in local clubs and theatres, toured with shows several years. Sang in Atlantic City clubs 1916, returned often to Paradise Cafe there. Worked Chicago clubs, mostly based there 1927-36. Led band in 30s. Left music 1941 for government job. Composed numerous jazz and blues numbers; best-known *Fan It*.

RECORDS
FRANKIE "HALF PINT" JAXON
- Ge 6244 She's Got "It"/I'm Gonna Dance Wit De Guy Wot Brung Me
- Vo 1257 Fan It/How Can I Get It?
- Vo 1285 Let's Knock a Jug/Can't You Wait Till I Get You Home?
- Vo 1424 Corrine Blues/Take It Easy
- Vo 1539 It's Heated/Jive Man Blues
- Vo 1583 Scuddlin'/Chocolate to the Bone
- Vo 2553 Fan It/My Baby's Hot
- Vo 2603 Mama Don't Allow It/Fifteen Cents
- De 7286 She Brings Me Down/Wet It
- De 7304 The Dirty Dozens/Take It Easy Greasy
- De 7345 She Sends Me/You Certainly Look Good to Me
- De 7548 Some Sweet Day/I'm Gonna Steal You
- De 7619 Callin' Corrine/You Can't Put That Monkey on My Back
- De 7638 Fan It Boogie Woogie/Don't Pan Me
- De 7742 When They Play Them Blues/Somethin' Goin' On Wrong
- De 7786 Let Me Ride Your Train/Be Your Natural Self

922. JEAN, GLORIA   vo
(GLORIA JEAN SCHOONOVER)
Born 1928

Pretty teenage singing star in 40s movies. Soprano somewhat like Deanna Durbin. Movie debut as star of THE UNDERPUP (1939). Co-starred with Bing Crosby in IF I HAD MY WAY (1940). Starred in low-budget movies, mostly musicals. By maturity career waned. After 40s mostly inactive.

MOVIES
1939—THE UNDERPUP
1940—IF I HAD MY WAY; A LITTLE BIT OF HEAVEN

1941—NEVER GIVE A SUCKER AN EVEN BREAK
1942—GET HEP TO LOVE; WHAT'S COOKIN'?; WHEN JOHNNY COMES MARCHING HOME
1943—MISTER BIG; IT COMES UP LOVE; MOONLIGHT IN VERMONT
1944—FOLLOW THE BOYS; PARDON MY RHYTHM; THE GHOST CATCHERS; THE RECKLESS AGE; DESTINY
1945—EASY TO LOOK AT; I'LL REMEMBER APRIL; RIVER GANG
1947—COPACABANA
1948—I SURRENDER DEAR; OLD-FASHIONED GIRL; MANHATTAN ANGEL
1949—THERE'S A GIRL IN MY HEART
1955—AIR STRIKE
1961—LADIES' MAN

923. JEFFERSON, BLIND LEMON
vo g cm

Born c. 1889-97 in Texas
Died 1930, Chicago, Ill.

One of better male blues singers. Born blind, as youngster sang and begged on streets, performed at picnics and parties. To Dallas 1917, became wrestler for awhile. Teamed with blues singer Huddie Ledbetter ("Leadbelly") at times. Shouting style suited street singing; guitar playing complemented lyrics. Most songs own compositions, many drawn from experience. To Chicago, began recording late 1925 or early 1926. On most records only accompaniment own guitar. Continued recording until fall 1929. Died in snowstorm 1930.

RECORDS
BLIND LEMON JEFFERSON
- Para 12347 Booster Blues/Dry Southern Blues
- Para 12354 Got the Blues/Long Lonesome Blues
- Para 12367 Black Horse Blues/Corinna Blues
- Para 12394 Beggin' Back / Old Rounders Blues
- Para 12407 That Black Snake Moan/Stocking Feet Blues
- Para 12425 Wartime Blues/Booger Rooger Blues
- Para 12454 Rabbit Foot Blues/Shuckin' Sugar Blues

Para 12487 Teddy Bear Blues/Rising High Water Blues

Para 12493 Hot Dogs/Weary Dog Blues

Para 12608 'Lectric Chair Blues/See That My Grave Is Kept Clean

Para 12622 Prison Cell Blues/Lemon's Worried Blues

Para 12692 Christmas Eve Blues/Happy New Year Blues

Para 12756 That Black Snake Moan No. 2/Tin Cup Blues

Para 12771 Saturday Night Spender Blues/Oil Well Blues

Para 12872 Yo Yo Blues/Bed Springs Blues

Para 12946 Empty House Blues/Bootin' Me 'Bout

OK 8455 Black Snake Moan/Match Box Blues

LPs

BLIND LEMON JEFFERSON

Riv 12-125 Classic Folk Blues (Para RIs)

Riv (10")1014 Folk Blues of Blind Lemon Jefferson (Para RIs)

Riv (10")1053 Penitentiary Blues (Para RIs)

(miscellaneous artists)

Folk FP-253 American Folk Music, Vol. 3 (RIs)

Heritage(E) 1007 The Country Blues —Texas (RIs)

924. JEFFERSON, HILTON   as cl

Born July 30, 1903, Danbury, Conn.
Died November 14, 1968, New York, N.Y.

Star sideman with top swing bands of 30s and 40s. Good lead alto sax, clean lyrical style along Benny Carter lines, impeccable taste. Adept at ballads, light-swinging style on jazz. Slight overtones of progressive jazz later. Attended high school in Boston and Providence. In 1925 played banjo in Philadelphia, switched to alto sax. Late 20s in New York mostly with Claude Hopkins. With Chick Webb off and on 1929-31, with King Oliver and McKinney's Cotton Pickers at intervals. Rejoined Hopkins 1932, then with Fletcher Henderson about two years late 1932-4. Freelanced in mid-30s, periods again with Webb and Hopkins. With Henderson again late 1936-8, then Webb again 1938-9. After Webb's death remained latter half 1939 under leadership of Ella Fitzgerald. With Cab Calloway through 40s, again in 1951. With Duke Ellington eight months from mid-1952. Freelanced awhile, then semi-active. Occasional jobs in later 50s and 60s including stints with Harry Dial and Noble Sissle.

RECORDS

FLETCHER HENDERSON

De 157 Wrappin' It Up

De 158 Shanghai Shuffle/Memphis Blues

De 213 Down South Camp Meeting

De 214 Big John Special/Happy as the Day Is Long

De 342 Wild Party/Rug Cutter's Swing

RED ALLEN

Pe 15970 Pardon My Southern Accent/How's About Tomorrow Night?

Pe 15994 Rug Cutter's Swing/There's a House in Harlem

CAB CALLOWAY

OK 6109 Willow Weep for Me

JONAH JONES

Key 614 Just Like a Butterfly/Lust for Licks

CMS 602 Rose of the Rio Grande/Stomping at the Savoy

CMS (12")1520 You Brought a New Kind of Love to Me/Hubba Hubba Hub

JOE THOMAS

Key 642 You Can Depend on Me/Black Butterfly

TEDDY WILSON

Br 7514 I'm Painting the Town Red/Sweet Lorraine

JOHN KIRBY

Cr 108 Ripples

Cr 118 Schubert's Serenade

Disc 5041 Move Over/Slowly

Apo 762 Natchez Ball/Sampson and De-Lie-Lah

MILT HINTON

Staff 606 If I Should Lose You/If You Believed in Me

LPs

FLETCHER HENDERSON ALL-STARS

Jazztone J-1285 The Big Reunion

REX STEWART
   Felsted FAJ-7001 Rendezvous with Rex
   (one side) GA 33-315 Plays Duke Ellington
   (one side) Jazztone J-1250 Dedicated Jazz
STEWART-WILLIAMS & CO.
   WB 1260 PORGY AND BESS Revisited
JIM TIMMENS
   WB 1324 SHOW BOAT Revisited
(miscellaneous artists)
   EmArcy MG-36018 Alto Altitude
HILTON JEFFERSON-TAFT JORDAN-AL SEARS
   Pres 2010 The Swingsville All-Stars

925. JEFFRIES, HERB   vo cm lyr
Born September 24, c. 1912-16, Detroit, Mich.

Deep-voiced ballad singer noted for work with Earl Hines and Duke Ellington. Sang *Flamingo* with latter, made it feature through the years. In early 30s sang in Detroit, New York, Chicago. With Erskine Tate band among others. Signed by Earl Hines in Chicago for Grand Terrace revue; vocalist with Hines band 1934. Brief period with Blanche Calloway band. Cowboy roles in all-Negro westerns. Joined Duke Ellington early 1940 for over two years. Then career as single, based in Los Angeles. Many recordings late 40s and early 50s, biggest *Basin Street Blues*. Occasional acting in movies and TV in 50s and 60s. Wrote material for theatre and night clubs. Composer or lyricist of songs *The Singing Prophet (Adam and Evil Blues)*; *Which Way Does the Wind Blow?*; *Deep Down in the Middle of Your Heart*; *Don't You Weep, Little Children*.

RECORDS
EARL HINES
   Br 6872 Blue
   Br 6960 Just to Be in Caroline
DUKE ELLINGTON
   Vi 26537 You, You Darlin'
   Vi 26748 There Shall Be No Night
   Vi 27326 Flamingo/The Girl in My Dreams Tries to Look Like You
   Vi 27517 Jump for Joy/Brown Skin Gal
   Vi 27740 What Good Would It Do?

Vi 27804 I Don't Know What Kind of Blues I Got
Vi 20-1584 My Little Brown Book
HERB JEFFRIES
   Excl 23 Palomino/The Things You Left in My Heart
   Excl 29 Jungle Rose/I Wonder What's Become of Sally
   Excl 222 I'm Just a Lucky So and So/I Left My Heart in Mississippi
   Excl 700 Flamingo/Solitude
   Excl 702 Basin Street Blues/These Foolish Things
   Trend 67 One Night in Acapulco/Wicked Woman
   Cor 60425 Love Me/I'm Yours to Command
   Mer 5539 Solitude/These Foolish Things
   Co 38412 Bewildered/Girls Were Made to Take Care of Boys
   Co 38414 It's Easy to Remember/A Dreamer with a Penny
   Co 38511 The Four Winds and the Seven Seas/Never Be It Said
   Co 38732 Our Love Story/Count Every Star
   Co 38738 Baby, Won't You Say You Love Me?/The Flying Dutchman
   Co 38769 There Goes My Heart/Swamp Girl
   Co 38835 Pagan Love Song/Call Her Savage
HERB JEFFRIES with LES BROWN ORCHESTRA
   Cor 60717 Flamingo/Basin Street Blues

LPs
HERB JEFFRIES
   Ha HL-7048 (Co RIs)
   Beth 72 Say It Isn't So
   Cor (10″)CRL-56044 Time on My Hands
   Mer (10″)MG-25089
   Mer (10″)MG-25091

926. JENKINS, GORDON
           cm lyr ar p bn B
Born May 12, 1910, Webster Groves, Mo.

Noted composer-arranger-conductor. Leading songs *Blue Prelude* (1933); *P.S., I Love You*; *You Have Taken My Heart* and

When a Woman Loves a Man (1934); *Blue Evening* (1939); *San Fernando Valley* (1943). Collaborators Joe Bishop, Johnny Mercer. Composed Benny Goodman's moody closing theme *Goodbye* (1935). Early work as banjoist in St. Louis dance band, then staff pianist on radio. Pianist-arranger early 30s with great Isham Jones band; scores vital asset. Later arranged for Paul Whiteman, Benny Goodman, Vincent Lopez, Andre Kostelanetz. Arranger-conductor for Broadway musical THE SHOW IS ON (1937). Musical director for NBC radio on west coast 1938. Wrote music for radio, movies and night clubs. In middle and late 40s conducted on Dick Haymes radio show. In 1945 with Decca Records, first as conductor, later as musical director. Accompanied many singers. Notable records with Louis Armstrong (*It's All in the Game*, etc.) and Artie Shaw (*You're Mine, You*). Known for one-finger piano style. His favorite *Lonesome Town* recorded by Frank Sinatra. Score with lyricist Tom Adair for 1949 Broadway show ALONG FIFTH AVENUE. Busy recording and writing during 50s. Beautiful hit *This Is All I Ask* in early 60s: "singer's song," became standard. Activities ebbed in 60s. Conductor/arranger on Frank Sinatra's comeback TV special 1973. Other compositions include *Homesick, That's All*; *Tomorrow*; *Sally Doesn't Care; Saddest Man in Town;* MANHATTAN TOWER SUITE *(Married I Can Always Get*; *Once Upon a Dream*; *Never Leave Me*);* ALONG FIFTH AVENUE stage score *(Skyscraper Blues; Fifth Avenue; The Best Time of the Day; I Love Love in New York*; *Weep No More*);* Maybe She'll Remember; When You Climb Those Golden Stairs, Goin' Back to Brooklyn; Daylight Savings Blues*; *Once to Every Heart*; The Man Who Loves Manhattan*; *How Old Am I?*; *Indian Giver*; *I Thought About Marie.*

RECORDS

GORDON JENKINS ORCHESTRA
De 24523 My Funny Valentine/Temptation
De 24983 Bewitched/Where in the World?

De 27169 You Have Taken My Heart/Blue Prelude
De27490 Would I Love You?/I Love You Much Too Much
De 28364 My Love and Devotion/Just Say the Word
De 28450 I'll Know My Love/Leave Me Just a Little Bit of You
De 28750 P.S., I Love You/I Thought About Marie

(as conductor)
DOROTHY COLLINS
De 28251 From the Time You Say Goodbye/So Madly in Love
ARTIE SHAW
De 27186 You're Mine, You/I'm Forever Blowing Bubbles
LOUIS ARMSTRONG
De 27899 It's All in the Game/When It's Sleepy Time Down South
De 28076 Indian Love Call/Jeannine, I Dream of Lilac Time
MARTHA TILTON
De 4029 If I Could Be Where I Wanna Be/The Wedding Cake-Walk
PEGGY LEE
De 28395 River, River/Sans Souci

LPs

GORDON JENKINS ORCHESTRA
De DL-8116 Heartbeats
De (10″)DL-5275 Playing His Own Compositions
De (10″)DL-5276 Plays Music of Jerome Kern
De (10″)DL-5307 For You
Cap T-766 Manhattan Tower Suite
Cap (10″)H-264 Time to Dance with Gordon Jenkins
Vo VL-3615 Dreamer's Holiday
Co CSRP-8682 (S) The Magic World of Gordon Jenkins

(as conductor; arranger on some)
LOUIS ARMSTRONG
De DL-8840 Satchmo in Style
JUDY GARLAND
Cap T-835 Alone
ETHEL MERMAN
De (10″)DL-5304 CALL ME MADAME
NAT "KING" COLE
Cap W-824 Love Is the Thing
Cap W-1084 The Very Thought of You
FRANK SINATRA
Cap W-1221 No One Cares

(arranger on some)

ISHAM JONES

Vi LPV-504 The Great Isham Jones and His Orchestra (1932-34 RIs)

927. JENNEY, JACK   tb cm B (TRUMAN ELLIOTT JENNEY)

Born May 12, 1910, Mason City, Iowa
Died December 16, 1945, Los Angeles, Calif.

Trombone star of 30s and 40s with thoughtful, advanced ideas. Much admired by fellow trombonists. Effective in upper register, great lead trombone, beautiful tone, smooth delivery. Shone on ballads but could swing too. Attended school in Cedar Rapids. As youngster played in father's band. Attended Culver Military Academy. Began professionally with Austin Wylie 1928. With great Isham Jones band 1934 after playing 1933 with Mal Hallett. In later 30s radio in New York with Lennie Hayton, Victor Young, Fred Rich, others. Directed 1937 recording session for wife, singer Kay Thompson. Led big band 1938-40. Notable recording *Star Dust* arranged by saxman Hugo Winterhalter. Wrote theme *City Night*. Band died 1940. Jenney joined Artie Shaw several months late 1940-1. Unusual solo on Shaw recording of *Star Dust* parallelled his solo on Jenney band recording. Led trio awhile 1942. In jam session sequence of 1942 movie SYNCO-PATION. Briefly with Benny Goodman late 1942-3, appeared with band in 1943 movie STAGE DOOR CANTEEN. In 1943 fronted Bobby Byrne band awhile after leader entered air corps. Jobbed on west coast later in year. Military service briefly late 1943-4. After discharge on west coast radio until kidney trouble intervened. After appendectomy and complications, Jenney died at 35, tragic loss to music. Co-composer of *Man with a Horn*; popular 1946 after death, later a jazz standard. Co-composer with Kay Thompson of beautiful, little-known *What More Can I Give You?* 1939.

RECORDS

RED NORVO

Co 2977-D Tomboy/I Surrender Dear

Co 3026-D The Night Is Blue/With All My Heart and Soul

Co 3059-D Old-Fashioned Love/Honeysuckle Rose

Co 3079-D Bughouse/Blues in E Flat

JOHNNY WILLIAMS

Va 594 Little Old Lady/Where's My Sweetie Hiding?

Va 638 I'll Build a Stairway to Paradise

ARTIE SHAW

Vi 27230 Star Dust

Vi 27405 Moonglow

RAFAEL MENDEZ

Pan-Am 111 Tea for Two/I Know That You Know

Pan-Am 112 In a Little Spanish Town/Kitten on the Keys

JACK JENNEY

Vo 3972 I've Gone Romantic on You/In the Shade of the New Apple Tree

Vo 4130 Swingin' the Apach'/The Night Is Blue

Vo 4803 Got No Time/What More Can I Give You?

Vo 5223 Moon Ray/High Society

Vo 5304 Star Dust/Cuban Boogie Woogie

Vo 5407 What Is There to Say?/The World Is Waiting for the Sunrise

Vo 5535 (theme) City Night/I Walk Alone

Vo 5494 I'll Get By/After I Say I'm Sorry

Vo 5545 If You Knew Susie/Since You Came into My Dreams

LPs

JACK JENNEY

Co ML-4803 (Vo RIs)

BILL DODGE (Benny Goodman)

Melodeon MLP-7328-9 (2 LPs) Swingin' '34 (1934 ETs by Benny Goodman and all-star pickup groups)

RED NORVO

Epic LN-3128 And His All-Stars (Co, Br RIs)

ISHAM JONES

Vi LPV-504 The Great Isham Jones and His Orchestra (Vi RIs)

ARTIE SHAW

Vi LPM-1244 Moonglow (Vi, Bb RIs)

928. JEROME, HENRY   t cm lyr B

Born November 12, 1917, New York, N.Y.

Bandleader many years, attracted most attention with band of late 40s and 50s in Hal Kemp style. Formed first band in high school early 30s, continued through 30s with much of same personnel. Jobs on steamship lines among others. In 1939 dubbed music "Stepping Tones Style." By early 40s some success in New York spots with sweet style. Three years at Child's Restaurant, later toured occasionally. Kemp style late 40s never equalled Kemp band's. Later in 50s formed modern band with talented young New York musicians. At times used theme *Nice People*, own composition. Later entered record producing business. Issued LPs with some success as Henry Jerome and His Brazen Brass. A&R director for Coral Records 1959. Composer or lyricist of songs including *Oh, How I Need You, Joe*; *I Love You So*; *Tipica Serenade*; *Until Six*; *I Love My Mama*; *Homing Pigeon*; *Dream Talk*; *Night Is Gone*; *Cafe Paree*; *Diamond Heels*; *Be Satisfied*; *Let My People Go* (theme of movie EXODUS); *The Soupy Shuffle*; *Soupy's Theme*; *You're the Only Love I've Ever Known*; *Theme from "Brazen Brass"*.

RECORDS

HENRY JEROME
Davis 2107 They Say It's Wonderful/It Couldn't Be True
Lon 859 A Foggy Day/To Think You've Chosen Me
Lon 979 Orange Blossoms/If It Hadn't Been for You
MGM 11284 I Love You So/I'll Si-Si Ya in Bahia
MGM 11385 Keep It a Secret/Don't Let the Stars Get in Your Eyes
MGM 11526 Here's to the Ladies/Pie Wock a-Jilly Wock

LPs

HENRY JEROME
Lion (10″)L-70004 Designed for Dancing (Kemp style)
De DL-4106 Brazen Brass Plays Songs Everybody Knows
De DL-4125 Brazen Brass Brings Back the Bands
De DL-4127 Brazen Brass Features Saxes
De DL-4187 Brazen Brass Zings the Strings
De DL-4307 Strings in Dixieland
De DL-4440 Vocal Velvet
UA 6620 Henry's Trumpets
Forum SF-9053 (S) Memories of Hal Kemp

929. JEROME, JERRY   ts cl f ar B

Born June 19, 1912, Brooklyn, N.Y.

Tenor sax jazzman, good swing style. Came into prominence with Benny Goodman late 30s. Years of medical study; turned to music. Early experience with Harry Reser 1935. With Glenn Miller's early band 1937. With Red Norvo until spring 1938. New York studios, then Goodman late 1938. Some of best records with Ziggy Elman sessions 1939, small groups using Goodman personnel. When Goodman disbanded July 1940 due to illness, Jerome joined Artie Shaw till March 1941. Radio staff musician 1942-6, at times led band on radio. Two years recording director in later 40s for Apollo, led combos backing singers on records and played local dates. Active in New York radio and TV in 50s and 60s. Led combo at New York Athletic Club 1971-73, featured good musicians and vocalist Lynn Roberts, played clarinet in Goodman-Shaw vein as often as tenor sax.

RECORDS

GLENN MILLER
Br 8034 My Fine Feathered Friend
Br 8041 Every Day's a Holiday
Br 8062 Doin' the Jive
RED NORVO
Br 8088 Please Be Kind
BENNY GOODMAN
Vi 26134 Undecided
Vi 26170 Sent for You Yesterday
Vi 26175 A Home in the Clouds/Cuckoo in the Clock
Vi 26187 I'll Always Be in Love with You/Estrellita
Vi 26211 The Lady's in Love with You

Vi 26230 The Siren's Song
Co 35410 Night and Day
ZIGGY ELMAN
Bb 10316 Zaggin' with Zig/You're
Mine, You
Bb 10342 Let's Fall in Love/I'll Never
Be the Same
Bb 10663 I'm Through with Love
Bb 10855 Bye 'n' Bye
ARTIE SHAW
Vi 27256 Whispers in the Night
Vi 27362 I Cover the Waterfront
Vi 27411 The Blues (pt. 2)
Vi 27432 Prelude in C Major
Vi 27499 Why Shouldn't I?
Vi (12")36383 Concerto for Clarinet
(pt. 1)
LIONEL HAMPTON
Vi 26423 Gin for Christmas
Vi 26453 Munson Street Breakdown
Vi 26595 Flying Home
JOE THOMAS
Key 642 You Can Depend on Me
DEAN MARTIN
Apo 1088 Walkin' My Baby Back
Home/Oh Marie
DICK TODD
De 28506 Till I Waltz Again with
You/Oh, Happy Day
JERRY JEROME
Asch 500 Rainbow Blues/Girl of My
Dreams
Asch 501 When I Grow Too Old to
Dream/Arsenic and Old Face
Asch 502 Misty Blues
Asch 503 Jamming with Jerry/Walking
with Jerry
Asch 504 People Will Say We're in
Love/Rose of Washington Heights
Apo 765 We're Living It/Vamp Till
Ready
Stin album S-359 (78s) Jerry Jerome
Trio

LPs

JERRY JEROME
MGM E-3324 Cole Porter Medleys
Cam CAL-332 Country Club Saturday
Night
Stin 59 (including Asch RIs)
ABC-Para 132 On the Wild Side
BENNY GOODMAN
Co GL-524 Presents Fletcher Henderson Arrangements (Co RIs)

LIONEL HAMPTON
Vi (10")LPT-18 (Vi RIs)

930. JEROME, M. K.   cm p
Born July 18, 1893, New York, N.Y.
Composer with lengthy career, many songs for movies. Best-known songs *Just a Baby's Prayer at Twilight* (famed World War I ballad); *I Idolize My Baby's Eyes*; *My Little Buckaroo*; *You, You Darlin'*; *The Wish That I Wish Tonight*. Collaborators included lyricists Jack Scholl, Ted Koehler, Joe Young, Sam M. Lewis. In high school worked as pianist in movie and vaudeville houses. Staff pianist for publishing firm Waterson, Berlin & Snyder. Founded publishing firm in New York. To Hollywood 1929. With Warner Brothers 18 years.

SONGS
(with related movies)
1918—Just a Baby's Prayer at Twilight
1920—Bright Eyes; Old Pal, Why Don't You Answer Me?
1922—Mary Dear
1927—Dream Kisses
1929—SHOW OF SHOWS movie (If I Could Learn to Love; Motion Picture Pirates)
1931—I Idolize My Baby's Eyes
1936—HERE COMES CARTER movie (Thru the Courtesy of Love)
1937—CHEROKEE STRIP movie (My Little Buckaroo); MELODY FOR TWO movie (Dangerous Rhythm; An Excuse for Dancing; A Flat in Manhattan; Jose O'Neill, the Cuban Heel); Little Heaven of the Seven Seas
1938—SWING YOUR LADY movie (The Old Apple Tree)
1940—You, You Darlin'
1942—THE HARD WAY movie (Youth Must Have Its Fling; Goodnight Oh My Darling)
1943—CASABLANCA movie (Knock on Wood; That's What Noah Done; Muse's Call)
1944—HOLLYWOOD CANTEEN movie (Hollywood Canteen; Sweet Dreams, Sweetheart); SHINE ON HARVEST MOON movie (additional new material)

1945—CHRISTMAS IN CONNECTICUT movie (The Wish That I Wish Tonight)
1946—SAN ANTONIO movie (Some Sunday Morning)
1947—LOVE AND LEARN movie (Would You Believe Me?); MY WILD IRISH ROSE movie (Miss Lindy Lou; Wee Rose of Killarney; The Natchez and the Robert E. Lee; There's Room in My Heart for Them All)
1950—Don't Throw Cold Water on the Flame of Love

931. JEROME, WILLIAM   lyr vo

Born September 30, 1865, Cornwall-on-the-Hudson, N.Y.
Died June 25, 1932, New York, N.Y.

Lyricist for Broadway musicals 1901-12, collaborated mostly with composer Jean Schwartz. Continued writing through 20s. Later collaborators Walter Donaldson, Harry Von Tilzer, Andrew B. Sterling, Louis Hirsch, Harry Tierney. Most famous songs *Bedelia*; *Chinatown, My Chinatown*; *Row, Row, Row*; *Get Out and Get Under the Moon*. Early in career performed in minstrel shows. Later active in music publishing, brought out great World War I song *Over There*.

SONGS
(with related shows)

1901—THE STROLLERS stage show (I'm Tired); THE SLEEPING BEAUTY AND THE BEAST stage show (Rip Van Winkle Was a Lucky Man); HOITY TOITY stage show (When Mr. Shakespeare Comes to Town); Any Old Place I Can Hang My Hat Is Home Sweet Home to Me; It's All Right, Mayme
1902—A CHINESE HONEYMOON stage show (Mister Dooley); THE WILD ROSE stage show (I'm Unlucky); Back to the Woods; Just Kiss Yourself Goodbye
1903—THE JERSEY LILY stage show (Bedelia); MOTHER GOOSE stage show (The Story Adam Told to Eve); MR. BLUEBEARD stage show (I'm a Poor Unhappy Maid; Hamlet Was a Melancholy Dane; Julie; The Yankee Tourist Girl); My Hula Lula Girl

1904—PIFF! PAFF!! POUF!!! stage show (The Ghost That Never Walked; Love, Love, Love; Goodnight, My Own True Love); When You're Broke
1905—FRITZ IN TAMMANY HALL stage show (In Tammany Hall; My Irish Daisy; East Side Lil; When You're in Love; many others); THE HAM TREE stage show (The Merry Minstrel Band; Desdemona; Sweethearts in Every Town); THE WHITE CAT stage show (My Lady of Japan; Highland Mary; Meet Me on the Fence); LIFTING THE LID stage show (Oh, Marie; others); My Irish Molly-O
1906—THE RICH MR. HOGGENHEIMER stage show (Any Old Time at All); THE LITTLE CHERUB stage show (My Irish Rosie)
1907—LOLA FROM BERLIN stage show (songs unimportant); ZIEGFELD FOLLIES OF 1907 stage show (Handle Me with Care)
1908—ZIEGFELD FOLLIES OF 1908 stage show (When the Girl You Love Is Loving); Goodbye, Mr. Ragtime; Kiss Your Minstrel Boy Goodbye; Love Days; Over the Hills and Far Away
1909—IN HAYTI stage show (My Haytian Queen; The Revolutionary Man; Come Toddle Along; Everybody's Ragtime Crazy); THE SILVER STAR stage show (The Cooney-Spooney Dance; Franco-American Ragtime); The Hat My Father Wore on St. Patrick's Day; Honey on Our Honeymoon
1910—UP AND DOWN BROADWAY stage show (Chinatown, My Chinatown; The Military Glide; I'm the Lily; Dreamy Fandango Tune); I'll Make a Ring Around Rosie
1911—VERA VIOLETTA stage show (Rum Tum Tiddle); Come, Love, and Play Peek-a-Boo; I'm Going Back to Reno
1912—ZIEGFELD FOLLIES OF 1912 stage show (Row, Row, Row); HOKEY-POKEY stage show (If It Wasn't for the Irish and the Jews); MY BEST

GIRL stage show (Daphne); WALL STREET GIRL stage show (Whistle It); A WINSOME WIDOW stage show (String a Ring of Roses); And the Green Grass Grew All Around
1913—THE HONEYMOON EXPRESS stage show (Goodbye Boys); A Little Bunch of Shamrocks; On the Old Fall River Line; Sit Down, You're Rocking the Boat!
1914—Sweet Kentucky Lady
1915—HANDS UP stage show (I'm Simply Crazy Over You); Just Try to Picture Me Down Home in Tennessee; Back Home in Tennessee
1916—BETTY stage show (Sometime)
1920—That Old Irish Mother of Mine
1928—Get Out and Get Under the Moon

932. JESSEL, GEORGE   vo lyr

Born April 3, 1898, New York, N.Y.
Entertainer of stage and radio; long career began at nine. Successful movie producer in later years. Extensive traveller much in demand as speaker at banquets and special functions, became known as The Toastmaster General. At nine joined Gus Edwards children's troupe in vaudeville; Eddie Cantor in same act awhile. Toured British Isles 1915 as single. By 1917 known in vaudeville as The Boy Monologist. Top bookings included New York's Palace Theatre. Speaking and singing voice had nasal sound often mimicked in later years. In Broadway shows SHUBERT'S GAIETIES OF 1919 and THE PASSING SHOW OF 1923. Produced and starred in own show GEORGE JESSEL'S TROUBLES OF 1922. Starred in dramatic play THE JAZZ SINGER (1925), which later made history as first sound movie. In 1930 Broadway musical SWEET AND LOW and play JOSEPH. Continued vaudeville late 20s and early 30s; favorite routine talking to mother over telephone. In silent movies GINSBERG THE GREAT (1928) and GEORGE WASHINGTON COHEN (1929); in part-sound LUCKY BOY (1929). Sang *My Mother's Eyes* in latter, became forever associated with it. One of many entertainers in sound movie HAPPY DAYS (1930). Years later brief appearances in several movies. Active in radio middle

and late 30s, hosted shows including 30 Minutes in Hollywood and George Jessel's Celebrity Program. Continued as radio host early 40s; guest spots in later 40s. In Broadway musical THE HIGH KICKERS (1941), contributed to book and lyrics. In 1942 in vaudeville revue SHOW TIME with several stars. Important movie producer in 40s, mostly gaudy musicals like THE DOLLY SISTERS, WHEN MY BABY SMILES AT ME, OH YOU BEAUTIFUL DOLL, DANCING IN THE DARK, I WONDER WHO'S KISSING HER NOW, THE BAND WAGON, THE "I DON'T CARE" GIRL, also drama NIGHTMARE ALLEY. In early 50s own radio and TV shows. In later years frequent TV appearances on talk shows; humorous guest. Active speaking in 70s. Wrote lyrics to songs *And He'd Say "Oo-La-La Wee-Wee"* and *Oh How I Laugh When I Think How I Cried About You* (1919); *Where Do They Go When They Row, Row, Row?* (1920); *Roses in December* (1937); *You'll Be Reminded of Me* (1938); *Stop Kicking My Heart Around* (1939); *Dixieland Rendezvous* (1946); *As Long as You Care* (1953; in movie THE "I DON'T CARE" GIRL). Collaborated with Harry Ruby, Bert Kalmar, Ben Oakland, Herb Magidson, Milton Drake, Roy Turk, William White. Author of books *So Help Me; Hello, Mama; This Way, Miss; Elegy in Manhattan; Sunless Summer; I Had to Open My Mouth.*

RECORDS

GEORGE JESSEL
Vi 21852 My Mother's Eyes/When the Curtain Comes Down
Pat 22418 Dolls/Marcelle
ARA 4513 Oh, How I Miss You Tonight/I Used to Love You
ARA 4514 I Wonder Who's Kissing Her Now/I Wonder What's Become of Sally

LPs

GEORGE JESSEL
Audio Fid AFSP-1708 Songs My Pals Sang
Treasure 408 Sings Tear Jerkers of the Not-So-Gay Nineties
(miscellaneous artists)
De DEA-7-2 (2-LP set) Those Wonderful Thirties (RIs)

933. JOHNSON, ARNOLD   p cm ar B

Born March 23, 1893, Chicago, Ill.

Bandleader of 20s; some success as composer. Studied piano, at 14 played in Chinese restaurant in Chicago. Studied at Chicago Musical College and American Conservatory of Music. Played vaudeville as accompanist and soloist. With sax soloist Rudy Wiedoeft organized Frisco Jazz Band in New York. Later Johnson worked cafe jobs in New York and Chicago. Tried real estate in Florida mid-20s, booked bands and vaudeville acts. Mediocre success turned him back to music. Led good dance band late 20s. Band in Broadway musicals GEORGE WHITE'S SCANDALS OF 1928 and GREENWICH VILLAGE FOLLIES OF 1928. In 30s Johnson musical director and producer on radio, including 1935-6 National Amateur Night on New York radio. Film shorts in 30s. Entertained U.S. troops in Europe, World War II. Composed popular songs *"O" (or Oh)* (1919), *Don't Hang Your Dreams on a Rainbow* (1929), *Goodbye Blues* (1932), *Does Your Heart Beat for Me?* (1936). Other songs *Sweetheart, The Lovelight in Your Eyes, Lilliokalani, Tear Drops, All for You.*

RECORDS

ARNOLD JOHNSON

Br 2339 When the Leaves Come Tumbling Down/You Remind Me of My Mother
Br 2377 Crinoline Days/Away Down East in Maine
Br 3840 I'm Riding to Glory/After My Laughter Came Tears
Br 3980 Georgie Porgie
Br 3986 I'm on the Crest of a Wave/What D'Ya Say?
Br 4037 Pickin' Cotton
Br 4080 Memories of France/That's How I Feel About You
Br 4084 Was It Love?/You're in Love and I'm in Love
Br 4125 Me and the Man in the Moon/Ev'rybody Loves You
Br 4158 My Inspiration Is You/My Tonia
Br 4203 When the World Is at Rest/I'll Never Ask for More
Br 4251 Tear Drops

Br 4348 Breakaway/Big City Blues
Br 4452 Don't Hang Your Dreams on a Rainbow
Vo 3832 Second Hungarian Rhapsody/Anitra's Dance

934. JOHNSON, BUDD

ts as bs cl ss ar B
(ALBERT J. JOHNSON)

Born December 14, 1910, Dallas, Texas

Tenor sax star with gutty, swinging style. Talented arranger. Underrated. Younger brother of trombonist Keg Johnson. Some influence on bop; arranged for early progressive bands. Began locally mid-20s. Played in Texas with Holloway & His Merrymakers, Ben Smith, Eugene Coy. Toured with Jesse Stone (later composer of pop hit *Idaho*). In 1929 with George E. Lee in Kansas City mostly. To Chicago 1932, freelanced. In 1933 with Eddie Mallory, Louis Armstrong. With Earl Hines 1934, with Stone again early 1935. With Hines mid-1935 into 1936. Most of 1936 arranger with Gus Arnheim; helped band switch to swing. With Hines 1937, Fletcher Henderson early 1938, Horace Henderson later 1938. Rejoined Hines late 1938, remained four years except for brief interval in 1940. Occasional freelance arranging for such as Benny Goodman. Toured army camps with Al Sears band USO tour 1943. Began mid-40s to write arrangements for leading progressive bands including George Auld, Earl Hines, Boyd Raeburn, Billy Eckstine, Woody Herman, Dizzy Gillespie. In 1944 helped Eckstine form band, proving ground for progressive jazzmen. Played in early bop combos and on bop recordings. In 1946 musical director for Eckstine. Arrangements in late 40s included some for Auld, Tony Pastor. With Sy Oliver band 1947. In early 50s with Benny Green, Cab Calloway, Dizzy Gillespie. 1952 European tour with Snub Mosley USO unit. Musical director for Atlantic Records. Early 1956-7 with Benny Goodman, including Japan-Thailand-Burma tour. With Quincy Jones 1960, Count Basie 1961-2. Led band at intervals. In mid-60s with Gerald Wilson, Earl Hines. In late 60s two trips abroad with Hines, one as solo performer. Took up soprano and baritone sax in later years, played both well. Played in JPJ Quartet with Bill Pemberton (b), Oliver Jackson (d), Dill Jones (p). European tour with Charlie Shavers early 1970. Active in 70s. Despite long career, Johnson abreast of changes, adapted playing yet retained mainstream thrust.

RECORDS

LOUIS ARMSTRONG
Vi 24257 Some Sweet Day
EARL HINES
Vo 3467 I Can't Believe That You're in Love with Me
Bb 10351 Grand Terrace Shuffle
Bb 10377 Father Steps In
Bb 10792 Tantalizing a Cuban
Bb 10835 Call Me Happy
LIONEL HAMPTON
Vi 26595 Flying Home
Vi 26604 Till Tom Special
GEORGE E. LEE
Br 4684 Ruff Scufflin'/St. James Infirmary
Br 7132 If I Could Be with You/Paseo Strut
UNA MAE CARLISLE
Bea 7170 'Tain't Yours/Without Your Baby
Bea 7171 You Gotta Take Your Time/I Like It 'Cause I Love You
CLYDE HART
Sav 598 Dee Dee's Dance/Little Benny
J. C. HEARD
Cont 6022 The Walk/Heard but Not Seen
Cont 6027 Azure/Bouncing for Barney
PETE JOHNSON
Nat 4001 I May Be Wonderful/1946 Stomp
Nat 4003 Atomic Boogie/Back Room Blues
THE KEYNOTERS
Key (12″)1313 You're Driving Me Crazy/I'm in the Market for You
JOHN KIRBY
Asch 357-1 9:20 Special/Maxixe Dengoza
Asch 357-3 K.C. Caboose/J.K. Special
DICKY WELLS
HRS 1018 Opera in Blue/Drag Nasty

DIZZY GILLESPIE
DeeGee 3604 The Champ (1 & 2)
JOHNNY KING
MGM 11255 Way Downtown at the Bottom of the Hill/Where Were You?
BUDD JOHNSON
Atl 1013 Off Shore/Don't Take Your Love from Me
Faith 315 Groovin' in Birdland/Sometimes I Feel Like Leaving Home

LPs

BUDD JOHNSON
Felsted FAJ-7007 Blues a la Mode
Argo 748 Off the Wall
THE JPJ QUARTET
MJR 8111 Montreaux '71
COUNT BASIE
Roul R-52065 Basie at Birdland
EARL HINES-JIMMY RUSHING
MJR 101 Blues and Things
MAYNARD FERGUSON
Vik LX-1070 Birdland Dream Band
Vik LX-1077 Birdland Dream Band, Vol. 2
CAT ANDERSON
LaBrea L-8026 In the Elegant Ellington Manner
GIL EVANS
WP 1270 Great Jazz Standards
DUKE ELLINGTON-COUNT BASIE
Co CL-1715 First Time! The Count Meets the Duke
(miscellaneous artists)
Cadet 784 Mood to Be Wooed
JIMMY RUSHING
Vi LSP-4566 (S) The You and Me That Used to Be

935. JOHNSON, BUDD p vo ar cm B (WOODROW WILSON JOHNSON)

Born January 10, 1915, Darlington, S.C.
Leader of hard-swinging blues band from 40s to 60s. After experience as pianist, to New York 1938 to play clubs. To Europe 1939 with Cotton Club revue. Later in year formed band, began recording. Hit: *Please Mr. Johnson*. Small combo in early years, later enlarged. Arranged and composed. Long stints at New York's Savoy Ballroom, toured, popular in south. Big band stressed clear melodic lines, strong

beat, volume. Arthur Prysock vocalist late 40s and early 50s; band provided rich vocal backgrounds. Same period Buddy's sister Ella sang with band. In 50s band successful in rhythm and blues. In 60s Johnson led combo. Among compositions excellent jazz numbers *Troyon Swing* and *Southern Exposure*.

RECORDS

BUDDY JOHNSON

De 7684 Stop Pretending/Jammin' in Georgia
De 7700 Reese's Idea/When You're Out with Me
De 8507 Please Mr. Johnson/Swing Along with Me
De 8518 Southern Echoes/You Won't Let Me Go
De 8555 New Please Mr. Johnson/In There
De 8562 Troyon Swing/Southern Exposure
De 8599 I'm Stepping Out/Toodle-Oodle-Oo
De 8632 Baby Don't You Care/Stand Back and Smile
De 8647 I Done Found Out/Let's Beat Out Some Love
De 8671 That's the Stuff You Gotta Watch/One of Them Good Ones
De 11000 Fine Brown Frame/They All Say I'm the Biggest Fool
De 24716 As I Love You/Lovely in Her Evening Gown
De 27416 Jet/No More Love
De 27711 Stormy Weather/I'm in Your Power
De 27998 At Last/Root Man Blues
De 28293 Shufflin' and Rollin'/Baby You're Always on My Mind
De 28530 Just to Be Yours/Somehow, Somewhere
De 48076 Li'l Dog/Far Cry
De 48088 You Better Change Your Ways/I Don't Care Who Knows
Mer 70123 Jit-Jit/That's How I Feel About You
Mer 70321 One More Time/Mush Mouth

LPs

BUDDY JOHNSON

De DL-4628 Arthur Prysock—Songs That Made Him Famous, Featured

with Buddy Johnson Orchestra (De RIs)
Mer-Wing MGW-12111 Rock 'n' Roll Stage Show
Mer-Wing MG-20209 Rock and Roll with Buddy Johnson
Forum F-9022 Go Ahead and Rock

936. JOHNSON, BUNK   c B
(WILLIAM GEARY JOHNSON)
Born December 27, 1879, New Orleans, La.
Died July 7, 1949, New Iberia, La.

Jazz cornetist in traditional New Orleans style. Resurrected from oblivion in New Iberia, La., by jazz buffs early 40s for concerts, club dates, recordings. Cornet style led ensembles firmly, though not overpowering soloist. Career began in 1890s, included jobs with legendary Buddy Bolden. Early 1900s travelled with circus and jazz bands along Gulf coast. With leading jazzmen in New Orleans area beginning 1910. Years later toured again with circus bands, played theatre tours. Played in Texas early 30s. Settled in New Iberia, by 1933 in music part-time. Other jobs included work in rice fields. In late 30s discovered via research by writers William Russell and Frederic Ramsey Jr. Publicity sparked Johnson to get back into playing shape locally. Cut first records 1942 in New Orleans. Worked mostly on west coast late 1942-4, including jobs with Lu Watters. Returned to New Orleans early 1944, recorded, worked there a year. Brief flings at New York and Boston spring 1945, latter one month with Sidney Bechet. Resumed work in Louisiana later in 1945. Led group in New York from fall 1945 to early 1946, then back to Louisiana. Two Chicago concerts later 1946. To New York fall 1947, led band awhile, recorded. Last days in New Iberia; stroke barred further playing. Substantial recording in 40s. Worked with important jazzmen George Lewis (cl), Jim Robinson (tb), Baby Dodds (d). Controversy about Johnson's musical ability. Some critics proclaimed him outdated and not forceful; others considered him overall equal to most cornetists in New Orleans style.

RECORDS

BUNK JOHNSON
JM 8 Down by the Riverside/Panama
JM 9 Weary Blues/Pallet on the Floor
JM 10 Bunk's Blues/Storyville Blues
JI 12 Franklin Street Blues/Weary Blues
JI 14 Sobbin' Blues/Dusty Rag
AM (12")251 Tiger Rag/See See Rider
AM (12")253 Lowdown Blues/Yes Yes in Your Eyes
AM (12")255 Panama/When You Wore a Tulip
AM 101 Just a Little While to Stay Here/In Gloryland
De 25131 Tishomingo Blues/You Always Hurt the One You Love
De 25132 My Maryland/Alexander's Ragtime Band
Vi 40-0126 Snag It/When the Saints Go Marching In
Vi 40-0127 High Society/A Closer Walk with Thee
VD (12")630 I Can't Escape from You
VD (12")658 Snag It
BUNK JOHNSON & THE YERBA BUENA JAZZ BAND
GTJ 34 Ace in the Hole/2:19 Blues
GTJ 37 Nobody's Fault but When I Move to the Sky
GTJ 38 The Girls Go Crazy/Ory's Creole Trombone
GTJ 63 Careless Love/Down by the Riverside
SISTER ERNESTINE WASHINGTON with BUNK JOHNSON'S JAZZ BAND
Disc 6038 Does Jesus Care/The Lord Will Make a Way Somehow
Disc 6039 Where Could I Go but to the Lord?/God's Amazing Grace

LPs

BUNK JOHNSON
GTJ 12048
GTJ (10")17
Co CL-829
Riv (10")1047 Bunk Johnson and Kid Ory
Mainstream 6039 Legend
BUNK JOHNSON & GEORGE LEWIS
Jazztone J-1212
LU WATTERS-BUNK JOHNSON
GTJ 12024 Bunk and Lu

937. JOHNSON, CHARLIE   p cm B

Born November 21, 1891, Philadelphia, Pa.
Died December 13, 1959, New York, N.Y.

Leader of excellent hot band based years at Small's Paradise club in Harlem in 20s and 30s. Sound similar to that of better-known Fletcher Henderson. Grew up in Lowell, Mass. Before opening at Small's in fall 1925, worked mostly in Atlantic City previous decade. At Small's into late 30s, with intervals at Atlantic City or touring. Disbanded 1938. Jobbed in New York late 30s and 40s till illness curtailed career. Recordings unfortunately sparse. Outstanding band at times included Jabbo Smith (t), Sidney DeParis (t), Jimmy Harrison (tb), Edgar Sampson (as), Benny Carter (as), Dickie Wells (tb), Roy Eldridge (t), Frankie Newton (t). Composed jazz numbers *Viper's Dream*, *Fat and Greasy*, others.

RECORDS

CHARLIE JOHNSON
Em 10854 Don't Forget You'll Regret Day by Day
Em 10856 Meddlin' with the Blues
Vi 20551 Paradise Wobble/Birmingham Black Bottom
Vi 20653 Don't You Leave Me Here
Vi 21247 Hot Tempered Blues/You Ain't the One
Vi 21491 Charleston's the Best Dance After All
Vi 21712 The Boy in the Boat/Walk That Thing
Vi 38059 Harlem Drag/Hot Bones and Rice
Bb 10248 The Boy in the Boat/Walk That Thing (RIs)

LPs

CHARLIE JOHNSON
"X" (10")LVA-3026 Charlie Johnson's Paradise Band (Vi RIs)

938. JOHNSON, GUS, JR.   d

Born November 15, 1913, Tyler, Texas

Swing drummer with ability to drive big band. Child prodigy on piano, bass and drums. Worked in Texas and Nebraska mid-20s, in southwest and midwest next decade. With Lloyd Hunter. Joined Jay McShann in Kansas City 1938, later to New York with him. Left 1943 for military service. After discharge, with Jesse Miller in Chicago 1945-7. Periods with Eddie Vinson, Tab Smith, Earl Hines, Cootie Williams. Joined Count Basie 1947, remained till late 1954, including 1950 period with Basie combo. Freelance and studios. Late 50s with singers Lena Horne and Ella Fitzgerald, bands of Eddie Heywood, Duke Ellington (including European tour), Neal Hefti, Woody Herman. Often with Ella in 60s, including tours abroad. Frequently with Gerry Mulligan. In demand for records due to ability to fit with any type of group. In late 60s joined veteran jazzmen in World's Greatest Jazz Band, featured with band into 1973.

RECORDS
(all LPs)

ZOOT SIMS
  Dawn 1102
  Seeco 452 The Art of Jazz
  Argo 608 Zoot
MAXINE SULLIVAN-BOB WILBER
  Mon-Ever MES-6919 Close as Pages in a Book
BUD FREEMAN
  Mon-Ever MES-7022 The Compleat Bud Freeman
SELDON POWELL
  Roost 2220 The Seldon Powell Sextet
COUNT BASIE
  Clef MGC-636
ZOOT SIMS-BOB BROOKMEYER
  Story 907
THE WORLD'S GREATEST JAZZ BAND
  Project 3 Stereo PR5033SD
  Project 3 Stereo PR5039SD Extra!
  Atl S-1570 Live at the Roosevelt Grill
(miscellaneous drummers)
  Vi LSP-2312 (S) Son of Drum Suite, Jr.

939. JOHNSON, HOWARD   lyr p
Born June 2, 1887, Waterbury, Conn.
Died May 1, 1941, New York, N.Y.

Lyricist best known for *On a Dew-Dew-Dewy Day*; *M-O-T-H-E-R, a Word That Means the World to Me*; *I Scream, You Scream (We All Scream for Ice Cream)*; and Kate Smith theme *When the Moon Comes Over the Mountain*. Collaborators included composers Milton Ager, Walter Donaldson, Fred Fisher, George Meyer, Harry Archer, Joseph Meyer, James V. Monaco, Percy Wenrich, Harry Warren, Harry Woods, David Brockman, James Kendis, Archie Gottler. Early in career pianist in Boston theatres. Staff writer for New York publishing house. Military service, World War I. Wrote for Broadway musicals TANGERINE (1921) and PARADISE ALLEY (1924).

SONGS
(with related shows)

1915—M-O-T-H-E-R, a Word That Means the World to Me; Siam; There's a Broken Heart for Every Light on Broadway; You'd Never Know the Old Home Town of Mine
1916—Ireland Must Be Heaven, for My Mother Came from There; What Do You Want to Make Those Eyes at Me For?
1917—I Don't Want to Get Well; Rockaway; Where Do We Go from Here?; Bring Back My Daddy to Me
1919—Freckles
1920—At the Moving Picture Ball
1921—TANGERINE stage show (Sweet Lady; others)
1922—Georgia
1924—PARADISE ALLEY stage show (title song; others)
1926—Am I Wasting My Time on You?
1927—Everything's Made for Love; Lindbergh, the Eagle of the U.S.A.; On a Dew-Dew-Dewy Day; Gid-ap, Garibaldi; I Scream, You Scream (We All Scream for Ice Cream)
1928—Don't Wait Till the Lights Are Low
1930—Just a Little Closer; Singing a Song to the Stars
1931—Think a Little Kindly of Me; When the Moon Comes Over the Mountain

940. JOHNSON, J. C. "JIMMY"
cm lyr p B

Born September 14, 1896, Chicago, Ill.

Versatile musician and composer. Best-known songs *Louisiana*; *I Need Lovin'*; *Don't Let Your Love Go Wrong*; *Believe It, Beloved*. Chief collaborators Fats Waller, Andy Razaf, George Whiting, Nat Burton. Worked in Chicago as pianist and bandleader. Began recording early 20s accompanying blues singers, sometimes used own tunes. Wrote for Negro revues and night club revues for Texas Guinan. Founder of Crescendo Club and Good Hearts Welfare Association in New York. Military service, World War II. After retirement from music, civic leader in Harlem.

SONGS
1923—You Can't Do What My Last Man Did
1926—I Need Lovin'; Alabama Stomp
1928—Dusky Stevedore; Louisiana; When; Take Your Tomorrow; Guess Who's in Town; Do What You Did Last Night; Empty Bed Blues
1930—Trav'lin' All Alone
1931—Dip Your Brush in the Sunshine
1932—Somebody Loses, Somebody Wins
1934—Believe It, Beloved; Don't Let Your Love Go Wrong
1935—Rhythm and Romance
1936—Crying My Heart Out for You
1937—The Joint Is Jumpin'
1939—That Was My Heart; Patty Cake, Patty Cake; The Spider and the Fly

Other songs: *My Particular Man*; *Yankee Doodle Tan*; *How Long Is the Journey?*; *Inside This Heart of Mine*; *Dancin' 'Way Your Sins*; *Without a Shadow of a Doubt*; *Little Black Boy*; *Lord Whatcha Gonna Do with Me?*; *It's Wearin' Me Down*

RECORDS
ETHEL WATERS
  BS 14151 You Can't Do What My Last Man Did
  BS 14155 All the Time/Who'll Get It When I'm Gone?
CLARA SMITH
  Co 14580-D Low Land Moan/Woman to Woman

ALICE CLINTON
  Ge 6501 Do What You Did Last Night/There's Been Some Changes Made
MARTHA COPELAND
  Co 14377-D Mama's Well Has Done Gone Dry/I Ain't Your Hen, Mr. Fly-Rooster
MARY DIXON
  Vo 1199 Dusky Stevedore/I Can't Give You Anything but Love
  Co 14415-D You Can't Sleep in My Bed/Daddy You Got Ev'rything
LONNIE JOHNSON-SPENCER WILLIAMS
  OK 8664 It Feels So Good (1 & 2)
BENNETT'S SWAMPLANDERS
  CO 14557-D Big Ben/You Can't Be Mine and Someone Else's Too
  Co 14662-D Jet Black Blues
BLIND WILLIE DUNN
  OK 8689 Jet Black Blues/Blue Blood Blues
WABASH TRIO
  GG 1711 Hoppin' 'Round
  Rad 7039 Lone Western Blues/Coal Black Blues
J. C. JOHNSON
  OK 8577 G. Burns Is Gonna Rise Again/In the Mornin'
  OK 8838 J. C. Johnson's Blues
  Co 14361-D Explaining/Good Things Come to Those Who Wait

941. JOHNSON, J. J. ("Jay Jay")
tb ar cm B
(JAMES LOUIS JOHNSON)

Born January 22, 1924, Indianapolis, Ind.

Outstanding jazz trombonist. Modern style with mainstream roots, dazzling technique. Pioneer of bop trombone with Benny Carter 1942-5. Earlier experience 1941-2 before joining Carter. With Count Basie 1945-6, further developed technique and solo style. Freelanced; 1947-9 with Illinois Jacquet. Later 1949 with Woody Herman and Dizzy Gillespie. USO tour abroad with Oscar Pettiford late 1951. Out of music two years except for occasional jobs beginning mid-1952. August 1954 teamed with trombonist Kai Winding to co-lead combo. Unique instrumentation and arrangements scored, brought Johnson to jazz trombone heights. Remained with Winding till 1956, rejoined late 1958 awhile. Led combo late 50s and at intervals in 60s. Began to devote time to arranging and composing. With Miles Davis late 1961-2. In 1964 led combo on Japanese tour. In late 60s semi-active; played special jobs and workshop projects, continued with writing. Jazz compositions mostly lengthy works performed in concert. Despite comparative inactivity, retained standing among many as top trombonist.

RECORDS

SAVANNAH CHURCHILL
Manor 1004 All Alone
ESQUIRE ALL-AMERICAN AWARD WINNERS
Vi 40-0137 Indiana Winter
DIZZY GILLESPIE
DeeGee 3604 The Champ (1 & 2)
HOWARD MCGHEE
BN 1572 I'll Remember April/Fuguetta
SONNY STITT
NJ 820 Tea Pot/Afternoon in Paris
COLEMAN HAWKINS
Vi 20-3057 April in Paris/How Strange
Vi 20-3143 Half Step Down Please/ Jumpin' for Jane
KARL GEORGE
Melodisc 111 Grand Slam/Baby It's Up to You
Melodisc 112 Peek-A-Boo/How Am I to Know?
J. J. JOHNSON
Sav 615 Jay Jay/Coppin' the Bop
Sav 930 Mad Be-Bop
Sav 975 Jay Bird/Mr. Dues
NJ 803 Elysses
NJ 806 Opus V/Hilo
NJ 814 Blue Mode/Elora

LPs

J. J. JOHNSON
Co CL-935 J Is for Jazz
Co CL-1030 First Place
Co CL-1383 Really Livin'
Co CS-8109 (S) Blue Trombone
BN (10")5028
Vi LPM-3350 J.J.!
Verve 68530 J.J.'s Broadway
Pres 7253 Looking Back
Impulse S-68 (S) Proof Positive
J. J. JOHNSON-KAI WINDING
Co CL-742 Trombone for Two

"X" LXA-1040 An Afternoon at Birdland
Sav 12010 Jay and Kai
COLEMAN HAWKINS
Riv RS-3049 (S) Think Deep
MILES DAVIS
Cap T-1974 Birth of the Cool (Cap RIs)
(miscellaneous artists)
Vi LSP-3783 (S) Tribute to Charlie Parker
Verve V-8540 Jazz at the Philharmonic in Europe

942. JOHNSON, J. ROSAMOND
cm lyr vo p B

*Born August 11, 1873, Jacksonville, Fla.
Died November 11, 1954, New York, N.Y.*

Early Negro composer. Teamed mostly with lyricist Bob Cole, sometimes with brother James Weldon Johnson. Biggest hit *Under the Bamboo Tree* in show SALLY IN OUR ALLEY (1902). Studied at New England Conservatory of Music; extensive musical training. Toured in vaudeville U.S. and Europe 1896-8. Teamed with Cole 1899 to write songs and play vaudeville. Team in short-run Broadway shows THE SHOO-FLY REGIMENT (1907) and THE RED MOON (1909). Johnson in show CABIN IN THE SKY (1940). Team wrote scores for Broadway shows, additional material for others. Johnson supervisor of music in Jacksonville public schools, musical director of Harlem's Music School Settlement. Military service, World War I. Author of books *Shout Songs, Rolling Along in Song*, others on Negro spirituals, folk and work songs.

SONGS
(with related shows)

1899—Chicken
1900—THE BELLE OF BRIDGEPORT stage show (songs unimportant); Lift Every Voice and Sing
1901—THE LITTLE DUCHESS stage show (Maiden with the Dreamy Eyes); THE SLEEPING BEAUTY AND THE BEAST stage show (The Owl and the Moon; Tell Me, Dusky Maiden); My Castle on the Nile
1902—SALLY IN OUR ALLEY stage show (Under the Bamboo Tree); Oh,

Didn't He Ramble (under Will Handy pseudonym)

1903—A GIRL FROM DIXIE stage show (songs unimportant); MR. BLUE-BEARD stage show (songs unimportant); NANCY BROWN stage show (Congo Love Song; Under the Bamboo Tree—interpolated); Lazy Moon; Magdaline, My Southern Queen; My Mississippi Belle

1904—HUMPTY DUMPTY stage show (songs unimportant); IN NEWPORT stage show (songs unimportant); AN ENGLISH DAISY stage show (songs unimportant)

1907—THE SHOO-FLY REGIMENT stage show (unsuccessful; songs unimportant)

1909—THE RED MOON stage show (songs unimportant); MR. LODE OF KOAL stage show (songs unimportant)

1911—HELLO PARIS stage show (Hello Paris; That Aeroplane Rag; Loving Moon; Look Me Over; others)

1914—Roll Them Cotton Bales

943. JOHNSON, JAMES P.   p cm B

Born February 1, 1891, New Brunswick, N.J.
Died November 17, 1955, New York, N.Y.

Early ragtime pianist, later pioneered Harlem stride style. Early influence on great Fats Waller. As youngster played Harlem rent parties. Professional career began 1912 in New York clubs. Played Atlantic City, toured in shows and vaudeville. Toured England with show PLANTATION DAYS. Important accompanist of blues singer Bessie Smith. Began recording early 20s, often accompanying blues singers. Wrote music for all-Negro Broadway shows RUNNING WILD (1923; long run) and MESSIN' AROUND (1929). Composed standards *Charleston* and *Old Fashioned Love* (1923), *If I Could Be with You* (1930). Busy until Depression, then concentrated on composing, including serious works. Led band at intervals, freelanced. Little recording in 30s. Resumed full-time music 1939 in New York clubs (especially Cafe Society) and recording. Early and mid-40s with Wild Bill Davison, Eddie

Condon, others; led groups. Late 1946 stroke interrupted career; worked in later 40s. In California 1949 writing music for Los Angeles show SUGAR HILL. Severe stroke 1951 ended career, left him invalid. Serious compositions included *African Dreams, Symphonie Harlem, Symphony in Brown, Piano Concerto in A Flat, Yamacraw, Mississippi Moon, Symphonic Suite on St. Louis Blues, City of Steel, Fantasia in C Minor, Sonata in F Major, Improvisations on Deep River, Manhattan Street Scene* (ballet), *Sefronia's Dream* (ballet), *Kitchen Opera* (operetta), *The Husband* (operetta). Lesser jazz and pop numbers *Ivy, Cling to Me; Hey, Hey; Snowy Morning Blues; Stop It, Joe; Don't Cry, Baby; Mama and Papa Blues; Keep Off the Grass; Carolina Shout; A Porter's Love Song to a Chambermaid; Eccentricity Waltz.*

RECORDS

KING OLIVER
Vi 38090 What You Want Me to Do/ Too Late
Vi 38101 Sweet Like This/I Want You Just Myself

BESSIE SMITH
Co 14195-D Preachin' the Blues/Back Water Blues
Co 14232-D Lock and Key
Co 14260-D Sweet Mistreater
Co 14464-D He's Got Me Goin'/It Makes My Love Come Down

MCKINNEY'S COTTON PICKERS
Vi 22511 Baby, Won't You Please Come Home?/Hullabaloo
Vi 23000 Okay Baby/I Want a Little Girl

ETHEL WATERS
Co 14353-D Guess Who's in Town/ My Handy Man

MEZZ MEZZROW
Bb 10085 Comin' On with the Come On (1 & 2)
Bb 10088 Revolutionary Blues

ROD CLESS
B&W 29 Froggy Moore/Have You Ever Felt That Way?
B&W 30 Make Me a Pallet on the Floor/I Know That You Know

EDDIE CONDON
De 23720 Atlanta Blues/Just You, Just Me

SIDNEY DEPARIS
BN (12")40 Everybody Loves My Baby/The Call of the Blues
BN (12")41 Who's Sorry Now?/Ballin' the Jack

ED HALL
BN (12")28 High Society/Blues at Blue Note
BN (12")29 Royal Garden Blues/Night Shift Blues

IDA COX
Vo 05336 Deep Sea Blues/Death Letter Blues

MAX KAMINSKY
CMS 561 Eccentric/Guess Who's in Town
CMS 595 Love Nest/Everybody Loves My Baby

FRANKIE NEWTON
Bb 10176 Rosetta/The World Is Waiting for the Sunrise
Bb 10186 Minor Jive/Rompin'

SIDNEY BECHET
Ci 1057 Who?/September Song

JAMES P. JOHNSON
OK 4495 Carolina Shout/Keep Off the Grass
Vi 19123 Bleeding Hearted Blues/You Can't Do What My Last Man Did
Co 14204-D Snowy Morning Blues/All That I Had Is Gone
Co 2448-D Go Harlem/Just a Crazy Song
Br 4762 Jingles/You've Got to Be Modernistic
Vo 4768 Harlem Woogie/After Tonight
BN (12")24 Gut Stomp/J.P. Boogie
BN (12")25 Back Water Blues/Carolina Balmoral
Asch (12")1001 Impressions/Boogie Woogie Stride
De 23593 Honeysuckle Rose/I've Got a Feeling I'm Falling
De 23594 Ain't Misbehavin'/Keepin' Out of Mischief Now

LPs

JAMES P. JOHNSON
BN (10")7011 Rent Party Piano
BN (10")7012 Jazz Band Ball
Co CL-1780 Father of the Stride Piano
Sounds 1204 Father of the Stride Piano
Riv 12-105 Rare Solos (RIs of 1921-6 piano rolls)

De (10")DL-5228 Plays Fats Waller Favorites

BESSIE SMITH
Co CL-858 The Bessie Smith Story, Vol. IV (Co RIs)

TOMMY LADNIER with MEZZ MEZZROW
"X" (10")LVA-3027 (Bb RIs)

ED HALL
BN (10")7007

(miscellaneous artists)
Vi LPV-578 Swing, Vol. 1 (Vi, Bb RIs)

944. JOHNSON, JOHNNY   p o cm B
(MALCOLM JOHNSON)
Born c. 1902, Washington, Ind.

Bandleader of 20s and 30s; groups always competent and entertaining. Earlier bands semi-hot in style, by 30s sweet. Attended Indiana University, at same time worked as pianist or organist. Later played vaudeville, worked with Harry Yerkes band. Formed band 1922. First active in New Jersey, later played Pelham Heath Inn in Bronx. Jazz cornetist Red Nichols with band several months beginning fall 1923. In 1926 Johnson pianist with Ben Bernie band. Organized band again following year, played New York's Hotel Pennsylvania, later toured. Trombonist Jack Teagarden with band late 1927. Good recordings late 20s. Played Post Lodge, Larchmont, N.Y., early 30s. Co-composer of 1930 novelty *I'd Like to Find the Guy That Wrote the Stein Song* (following popularity of *The Stein Song*). Few records early 30s, recorded often 1935-7. On Tasty-Yeast radio program 1936. Early 40s disbanded, settled in New Jersey. Taught piano, occasionally worked in area as pianist or bandleader.

RECORDS

JOHNNY JOHNSON
Ca 451 Raggedy Ann
Ca 477 Wop Blues
Vi 21016 Together, We Two/Give Me a Night in June
Vi 21113 My One and Only/Thou Swell
Vi 21165 Four Walls
Vi 21224 Say So/Oh Gee, Oh Joy
Vi 21366 Happy - Go - Lucky Lane/Across the Street from Heaven
Vi 22085 Just You, Just Me/Marianne

Vi 22468 On Revival Day/There's a Wah-Wah Girl in Agua Caliente
Vi 22493 I'd like to find the Guy That Wrote the Stein Song/What'll I Do?
Vi 22525 Sittin' on a Rainbow/In My Heart It's You
Bb 6451 On the Parkway/Moonstone (piano solos)
Me 13332 According to the Moonlight/It's an Old Southern Custom
Me 13438 In a Little Gypsy Tea Room/Every Little Moment
Me 13444 Love and a Dime/Shut the Door
Me 60202 I'm Shooting High/I Feel Like a Feather in the Breeze
Me 60301 A Beautiful Lady in Blue/The Broken Record
Me 60303 Lights Out/Too Much Imagination
Me 60501 Goody Goody/The Wheel of the Wagon Is Broken
Me 350906 A Sweet Beginning Like This/Whenever I Think of You
Me 350907 My Very Good Friend the Milkman/You're So Darn Charming
Me 70410 Too Marvelous for Words/Just a Quiet Evening
Me 70411 September in the Rain/How Could You?
Me 70813 Without Your Love/Will You Remember?

945. JOHNSON, KEG   tb g
(FREDERIC H. JOHNSON)

Born November 19, 1908, Dallas, Texas
Died November 8, 1967, Chicago, Ill.

Jazz trombonist, older brother of tenor sax star Budd Johnson. Began with local bands. With Terrence Holder, Jesse Stone, George E. Lee. Played Chicago early 30s. With Louis Armstrong 1933. Later 1933 with Benny Carter in New York. With Fletcher Henderson most of 1934. Joined Cab Calloway early 1935, stayed till 1948. With Lucky Millinder, Gene Ammons, Eddie Vinson. Early 50s settled on west coast, freelanced. Periods with Benny Carter, Duke Ellington. In music part-time several years, full-time late 50s and 60s in east. Joined band

backing singer Ray Charles 1961, stayed till death on tour 1967.

RECORDS
FLETCHER HENDERSON
De 157 Limehouse Blues
De 158 Memphis Blues
De 342 Rug Cutter's Swing/Wild Party
De 555 Liza
RED ALLEN
Pe 15970 Pardon My Southern Accent
Pe 15994 Rug Cutter's Swing/There's a House in Harlem
CHU BERRY
Va 657 My Secret Love Affair/Ebb Tide
Co 37571 Chuberry Jam/Maelstrom
IKE QUEBEC
BN 515 Topsy/Cup-Mute Clayton
BN 539 Basically Blue/The Masquerade Is Over

LPs
FLETCHER HENDERSON
De (10″)DL-6025 (De RIs)
CHU BERRY
Epic LN-3124 "Chu" (Va, Vo RIs)
CAB CALLOWAY
Epic LN-3265 (RIs)

946. JOHNSON, LONNIE vo g v p cm
(ALONZO JOHNSON)

Born February 8, 1889, New Orleans, La.
Died June 16, 1970, Toronto, Canada

Good blues singer, probably best blues guitarist. Sang in simple, moving style. More commercial field in later years, sometimes sang pops. Began professionally 1912. Local jobs with brother, pianist James "Steady Roll" Johnson. Theatre tour in Europe 1917-18. Personal tragedy when many members of large family died in influenza epidemic. To St. Louis early 20s, worked with Charlie Creath and Fate Marable. Began recording 1925. Composed. Worked on guitar, violin or piano on records with other artists. In late 20s based in New York. In Cleveland 1932-7; jobs with Putney Dandridge, others. To Chicago 1937; house musician at Three Deuces club late 30s. In Chicago most of 40s as single; also worked in Detroit and Kansas City. 1948 hit record *Tomorrow*

Night, earlier pop tune. Popular 50s records on King. Concerts in England 1952. Later 50s lived in Cincinnati and Philadelphia, part-time in music. Toured Europe 1963 with other blues performers. Settled in Toronto 1965, attained some popularity running own club. Ill health late 60s checked career.

RECORDS

(as guitarist only)

LONNIE JOHNSON

OK 8558 Playing with the Strings/ Stompin' 'Em Along Slow
OK 8575 Blues in G/Away Down in the Alley Blues
De 7427 Swing Out Rhythm
De 7445 Got the Blues for the West End

LONNIE JOHNSON AND BLIND WILLIE DUNN
(duets with guitarist Eddie Lang)

OK 8637 Two Tone Stomp/Have to Change Keys to Play These Blues
OK 8695 Bull Frog Moan/A Handful of Riffs
OK 8711 Guitar Blues/Blue Guitars
OK 8743 Hot Fingers/Deep Minor Rhythm

LOUIS ARMSTRONG

OK 8535 Hotter Than That/Savoy Blues
OK 8551 I'm Not Rough
OK 8680 Mahogany Hall Stomp

DUKE ELLINGTON

OK 8623 The Mooche/Hot and Bothered
OK 8638 Move Over

CHOCOLATE DANDIES

OK 8627 Paducah/Four or Five Times
OK 8668 Star Dust/Birmingham Breakdown

CHARLES CREATH

OK 8280 Market Street Stomp/Won't Don't Blues (vocal 2nd side)

JOHNNY DODDS

De 18094 Red Onion Blues/Gravier Street Blues

JIMMIE NOONE

De 18095 Keystone Blues/New Orleans Hop Scop Blues

CLARENCE WILLIAMS

OK 8826 Sitting on Top of the World/Kansas City Man Blues

ALMA HENDERSON

OK 8489 Mine's as Good as Yours/ Soul and Body
OK 40823 Red Lips, Kiss My Blues Away/Where the Wild Wild Flowers Grow

TEXAS ALEXANDER

OK 8751 Peaceful Blues/Rocking Mill Blues
OK 8764 Broken Yo Yo/When You Get to Thinking

(as vocalist)

LONNIE JOHNSON

OK 8253 Mr. Johnson's Blues/Falling Rain Blues
OK 8282 Love Story Blues/Very Lonesome Blues
OK 8358 Good Ole Wagon/A Woman Changed My Life
OK 8466 Backwater Blues/Southbound Water
OK 8537 Kansas City Blues (1 & 2)
OK 8822 Deep Sea Blues/Long Black Train Blues
Co 14674-D Unselfish Love/My Love Don't Belong to You
De 7397 Flood Water Blues/I'm Nuts Over You
De 7427 Swing Out Rhythm/It Ain't What It Usta Be
De 7487 Friendless and Blue/Devil's Got the Blues
Bb 8530 Don't Be No Fool/Get Yourself Together
Bb 8779 Chicago Blues/I Did All I Could
Bb 9022 Heart of Iron/Devil's Woman
Bb 34-0714 Lonesome Road/Baby, Remember Me
Disc Album 710 (78s) Blues
Alad 3029 Blues for Lonnie/Don't Blame Her
King 4201 Tomorrow Night/What a Woman
King 4278 You're Mine, You/My My Baby
King 4317 She's So Sweet/Don't Play Bad with My Love
King 4388 Drunk Again/Jelly Roll Baker
Rama 14 Will You Remember (Answer to Tomorrow Night)/Stick with It, Baby

LONNIE JOHNSON-VICTORIA SPIVEY
  OK 8626 The New Black Snake Blues
  (1 & 2)
  OK 8652 Furniture Man Blues (1 & 2)
LONNIE JOHNSON-SPENCER WILLIAMS
  OK 8762 The Monkey and the Baboon/Wipe It Off

LPs

LONNIE JOHNSON
  King KS-1083 (S) Tomorrow Night
  Pres 1007 Blues by Lonnie Johnson
  Pres 1011 Blues and Ballads
  Swaggie 1225 The Blues of Lonnie
    Johnson (1937-8 RIs)
  (one side) Jazzum 2 (1927 RIs)

947. JOHNSON, OSIE   d vo ar cm B

*Born January 11, 1923, Washington,
D.C.*
*Died February 10, 1966, New York,
N.Y.*

Freelance drummer active in 50s and 60s
on record sessions. Mostly with modern
groups. Began about 1941. With Sabby
Lewis 1942-3. Military service, World
War II. Late 40s in Chicago. Early 50s
with Earl Hines, Tony Scott, Dorothy
Donegan, mostly in New York. With
Illinois Jacquet on European tour 1954.
Based in New York mid-50s as busy
freelance. Later active in studios. Illness
curtailed activities; death from kidney
ailment.

RECORDS
(all LPs)

OSIE JOHNSON
  Beth BCP-66 The Happy Jazz of Osie
    Johnson
  Jazztone J-1234 Swingin' Sounds
JOE HOLIDAY
  De DL-8487 Holiday for Jazz
LEONARD FEATHER'S STARS
  MGM E-3390 West Coast vs. East
    Coast
JOE NEWMAN
  Vik LX-1060 The Midgets
KENNY BURRELL
  Kapp KL-1326 Lotsa Bossa Nova
MARY LOU WILLIAMS
  Concert Hall Swing (10″)CHJ-1007
    The Art of Mary Lou Williams

RALPH BURNS
  Jazztone (10″)J-1036 Bijou
SELDON POWELL
  Roost 2220 The Seldon Powell Sextet
JIMMY HAMILTON
  Urania (10″)1003 This Is Jimmy Hamilton
HAL MCKUSICK
  Vi LPM-1366 Jazz Workshop
BILLY BYERS
  Vi LPM-1269 The RCA Victor Jazz
    Workshop
TONY SCOTT
  Vi LJM-1022 Scott's Fling
AL COHN
  Vi LPM-1161 The Jazz Workshop
BOB BROOKMEYER
  Vik LX-1071 Brookmeyer
FRANK WESS
  CMS (10″)FL-20031 Quintet
  CMS (10″)FL-20032 Sextet
SIR CHARLES THOMPSON
  Vang (10″)8009

948. JOHNSON, PETE   p d cm

Born March 24, 1904, Kansas City, Mo.
Died March 23, 1967, Buffalo, N.Y.

Powerhouse boogie-woogie pianist, important in popularizing style late 30s and
40s. Competent in other styles. Early
played drums in Kansas City. Worked
clubs there as pianist 1926-38, mostly
solo. Worked often with vocalist Joe
Turner from early 30s; with him December 1938 in John Hammond's Spirituals
to Swing concert at Carnegie Hall. Guest
on Benny Goodman radio show January
1939. Long runs at Cafe Society in New
York 1939 and later. Began recording,
often played clubs with boogie-woogie
pianists Albert Ammons and Meade Lux
Lewis. During 40s continued to team
frequently with Ammons, occasionally
with Lewis. In California 1947-8, in Buffalo beginning 1949, occasionally played
other locales in 50s. In 1952 toured with
Piano Parade show. Toured Europe 1958
with Jazz at the Philharmonic, singer Joe
Turner included. Inactive often during
50s. Heart attack late 1958 curtailed activities. Composer of boogie-woogie num-

bers including *Roll 'Em Pete, Wee Baby Blues, Kansas City Farewell, Death Ray Boogie.*

RECORDS

HARRY JAMES
  Br 8318 Boo-Woo
JOE TURNER
  De 48042 Little Bittie Gal's Blues/I Got a Gal for Every Day in the Week
CAPITOL JAZZMEN
  Cap 10011 Sugar/Ain't Goin' No Place
MEADE LUX LEWIS-PETE JOHNSON-ALBERT AMMONS
  Vo 4606 Boogie Woogie Prayer (1 & 2)
  Vo 5186 Cafe Society Rag
ALBERT AMMONS-PETE JOHNSON
  Vi 27504-5-6-7 (boogie-woogie numbers)
PETE JOHNSON
  Vo 4607 Roll 'Em Pete/Goin' Away Blues
  Vo 4997 Cherry Red/Baby, Look at You
  Vo 5186 Lovin' Mama Blues
  BN(12") 10 Barrelhouse Breakdown/ Kansas City Farewell
  BN (12")11 Vine Street Bustle/Some Day Blues
  BN (12")12 Holler Stomp/You Don't Know My Mind
  De 3384 Blues on the Down Beat/ Kaycee on My Mind
  De 3830 Basement Boogie/Death Ray Boogie
  De 18121 627 Stomp
  Nat 4001 I May Be Wonderful/1946 Stomp
  Nat 4003 Atomic Boogie/Back Room Blues
  Nat 4005 Pete's Lonesome Blues/ Pete's Housewarmin'
  Apo 768 Minuet Boogie/66 Stomp
  Down Beat 168 Skidrow Boogie/Half Tight Boogie
  JS 659 Yancey Special/J.J. Boogie

LPs

PETE JOHNSON
  BN (10")7019 Boogie Woogie, Blues and Skiffle

  Riv 12-114 (Solo Art RIs)
JOE TURNER-PETE JOHNSON
  EmArcy MG-36014
ALBERT AMMONS-PETE JOHNSON
  Vi (10")LPT-9 (Vi RIs)
JOE TURNER
  Atl 1234 Boss of the Blues
JIMMY RUSHING
  Vang VRS-8508 Listen to the Blues
(miscellaneous artists)
  Riv 12-106 Giants of Boogie Woogie

949. JOHNSON, VAN   VO V
(CHARLES VAN JOHNSON)
Born August 25, 1916, Newport, R.I.
Popular movie star of over 60 movies, mostly in 40s and 50s. Occasionally sang and danced. Played violin as youngster. Minor role in Broadway musical NEW FACES OF 1936. Summer in Catskills as M.C.-singer-dancer-violinist. Baritone in vocal group Eight Men of Manhattan about 1938-9. Minor roles in Broadway musicals TOO MANY GIRLS (1939) and PAL JOEY (1941). Small roles in movies early 40s, stardom in A GUY NAMED JOE (1943) led to important MGM films. Surprised public with song and dance number in star-studded movie musical TILL THE CLOUDS ROLL BY (1947). Other movie musicals TWO GIRLS AND A SAILOR (1944), THRILL OF A ROMANCE (1945), EASY TO WED and NO LEAVE NO LOVE (1946), IN THE GOOD OLD SUMMERTIME (1949), DUCHESS OF IDAHO (1950), EASY TO LOVE (1953), BRIGADOON (1954)—but seldom performed musically in these. Outstanding non-musical movies included THIRTY SECONDS OVER TOKYO and THE WHITE CLIFFS OF DOVER (1944), STATE OF THE UNION and COMMAND DECISION (1948), BATTLEGROUND (1949), REMAINS TO BE SEEN (1953), THE CAINE MUTINY and THE LAST TIME I SAW PARIS (1954). As movies declined, Johnson played night clubs and stock as song and dance man. On TV during 60s; excellent entertainer.

RECORDS

VAN JOHNSON
  MGM 10018 Goodnight Sweetheart/I Wonder, I Wonder

MGM 10727 Let's Choo Choo to Idaho

950. JOHNSTON, ARTHUR cm ar p B
*Born January 10, 1898, New York, N.Y.
Died May 1, 1954, Corona del Mar,
Calif.*

Composer of 30s; best-known songs *Just
One More Chance, Learn to Croon, Down
the Old Ox Road, Thanks, The Day You
Came Along, Cocktails for Two, My Old
Flame, Thanks a Million, Pennies from
Heaven*. Excellent scores with Sam Coslow for two important 1933 Bing Crosby
movies COLLEGE HUMOR and TOO MUCH
HARMONY. Other collaborators lyricists
Johnny Burke and Gus Kahn. At 15
pianist in New York movie houses. At 17
pianist-arranger for publishing firm; chief
arranger several years later. Personal pianist for Irving Berlin, musical director of
his stage productions. To Hollywood
1929. During 30s four trips to England to
write for movies and revues. Military
service, World War II; wrote army show
HUT-TWO-THREE-FOUR.

SONGS
(with related shows)

1924—DIXIE TO BROADWAY stage show
(Mandy, Make Up Your Mind;
I'm a Little Blackbird Looking for
a Bluebird)
1931—Just One More Chance
1933—COLLEGE HUMOR movie (Learn to
Croon; Moonstruck; Down the
Old Ox Road); TOO MUCH HAR-
MONY movie (Thanks; The Day
You Came Along; Black Moon-
light; Bucking the Wind); HELLO,
EVERYBODY movie (Moon Song;
Twenty Million People)
1934—BELLE OF THE NINETIES movie (My
Old Flame; When a St. Louis
Woman Comes Down to New
Orleans; Troubled Waters; My
American Beauty); MURDER AT
THE VANITIES movie (Cocktails for
Two; Live and Love Tonight)
1935—THE GIRL FRIEND movie (Two To-
gether; What Is This Power?; Wel-
come to Napoleon; Napoleon's
Exile); THANKS A MILLION movie
(Thanks a Million; I'm Sittin'

High on a Hill-top; Sugar Plum;
New Orleans; Sing, Brother, Sing;
A Pocketful of Sunshine)
1936—PENNIES FROM HEAVEN movie (Pennies from Heaven; Let's Call a
Heart a Heart; One, Two, Button
Your Shoe; So Do I; The Skeleton
in the Closet)
1937—DOUBLE OR NOTHING movie (The
Moon Got in My Eyes; It's the
Natural Thing to Do; All You
Want to Do Is Dance); GO WEST,
YOUNG MAN movie (I Was Saying
to the Moon; On a Typical Tropical Night)
1938—Between a Kiss and a Sigh
1939—Let There Be Love

951. JOHNSTON, JOHNNIE vo g
Born December 1, 1914, St. Louis, Mo.

Singing star of radio, movies and records.
Pleasant baritone voice, smooth delivery.
Most popular during 40s. Grew up in
Kansas City, taught singing by mother.
Worked at non-musical jobs in California
1932. To Chicago; singing jobs in small
clubs. Brief periods 1936 singing with Art
Kassel and Roger Pryor. In 1937 on
Chicago radio: Club Matinee, Breakfast
Club and sustaining shows. On Holly-
wood radio 1940. In 1942 movies SWEAT-
ER GIRL, PRIORITIES ON PARADE, STAR
SPANGLED RHTYHM, 1944 movie YOU
CAN'T RATION LOVE. To New York for
radio, clubs, theatres. Replaced Perry Co-
mo on Chesterfield radio show, mid-1945
to later 40s. Small role in star-studded
movie TILL THE CLOUDS ROLL BY (1947).
Best role in Esther Williams movie THIS
TIME FOR KEEPS (1947). Later movies MAN
FROM TEXAS (1948), UNCHAINED (1955),
ROCK AROUND THE CLOCK (1956). Impor-
tant role in Broadway musical A TREE
GROWS IN BROOKLYN (1951). Occasional
TV in 50s, for awhile panel show per-
sonality.

RECORDS
RICHARD HIMBER
De 4036 Day Dreaming/Je Vous Aime
Beaucoup
JOHNNIE JOHNSTON
Cap 109 Windmill Under the Stars/
Conchita Lopez

Cap 118 Light a Candle in the Chapel/The Singing Sands of Alamosa

Cap 120 Dearly Beloved/Easy to Love

Cap 130 That Old Black Magic/Can't You Hear Me Calling Caroline?

Cap 152 Irresistible You/Spring Will Be a Little Late

Cap 186 My Heart Sings/What a Sweet Surprise

Cap 196 Laura/There Must Be a Way

Cap 212 Autumn Serenade/Wait and See

Cap 228 As Long as I Live/One More Dream

MGM 10036 You're Not So Easy to Forget/Ain'tcha Ever Comin' Back?

MGM 10089 How Lucky You Are/Why Should I Cry Over You?

MGM 10104 I Love to Dance/Un Poquito De Amor

MGM 10191 Steppin' Out with My Baby/I Bring You Spring

MGM 10222 I Don't Care If It Rains All Night/A Boy from Texas—a Girl from Tennessee

LPs

.(original Broadway cast)

Co OL-4405 A TREE GROWS IN BROOKLYN

952. JOLSON, AL   vo cm lyr
(ASA YOELSON)

Born March 26, 1886, St. Petersburg, Russia
Died October 23, 1950, San Francisco, Calif.

Sometimes rated greatest entertainer of all time. Dynamic personality with great projection on stage. Sang in forceful, dramatic style. Favorite expression "Folks, you ain't heard nothin' yet!" often uttered after well-received number. Starred in important Broadway musicals, also on radio and in movies. Most-famous featured songs *Swanee*; *April Showers*; *Rock-a-bye Your Baby with a Dixie Melody*; *My Mammy*; *Sonny Boy*; *California, Here I Come*; *Toot Toot Tootsie*; *I'm Sitting on Top of the World*; *There's a Rainbow 'Round My Shoulder*. Educated in Washington, D.C. Father, Rabbi M. R. Yoelson, wanted Al to become cantor in

his synagogue. But Al joined travelling burlesque troupe as stooge, later became singer. In vaudeville and minstrel shows, including famous Dockstader's Minstrels. Often worked blackface on stage; white gloves trademark. On Broadway in 1911 musicals LA BELLE PAREE and VERA VIOLETTA. Top star in shows THE WHIRL OF SOCIETY (1912), THE HONEYMOON EXPRESS (1913), DANCING AROUND (1914), ROBINSON CRUSOE, JR. (1916), SINBAD (1918). Collaborated in writing several songs in his shows.

Next show BOMBO (1921); toured in it 1922-4. Then BIG BOY (1925), THE WONDER BAR (1931) and years later HOLD ON TO YOUR HATS (1940). Made entertainment history late 1927 starring in first part-sound movie THE JAZZ SINGER. Starred in other movies 1928-30. Popularity waned somewhat in early 30s; 1933 movie HALLELUJAH, I'M A BUM not well received. Co-starred with Paul Whiteman orchestra on good radio show 1933-4. Early 1933 movie musical 42ND STREET starred fresh young personality Ruby Keeler, Jolson's wife since 1928. Good Jolson role in movie WONDER BAR (1934). He and wife co-starred in big movie musical GO INTO YOUR DANCE (1935). Jolson starred on radio show the Shell Chateau 1935-6, other shows through 30s. He and Ruby divorced 1939. Entertained at army camps, World War II. Another radio series early 40s. Career waned, revived with release of important movie THE JOLSON STORY (1946). Larry Parks portrayed Jolson, with Al's singing dubbed. Great old songs featured; Jolson voice never better. Popularity of movie prompted sequel JOLSON SINGS AGAIN (1949), again with Jolson's singing dubbed for Parks. Jolson bounced back, hosted popular Kraft Music Hall on radio 1947-9 co-starring pianist Oscar Levant.

Recorded often. Led strenuous life capped by grueling 1950 tour entertaining U.S. troops in Far East Command during Korean War. Health deteriorated; died about a month after tour. During career Jolson credited as composer or lyricist of important songs, most featured in his shows and movies, including *'n Everything* (1917); *I'll Say She Does* (1918); *You Ain't*

Heard Nothin' Yet (1919); *Avalon* (1920); *Yoo Hoo* (1921); *Stella* (1923); *California, Here I Come* (1924); *Miami* and *Keep Smiling at Trouble* (1925); *Me and My Shadow* and *Four Walls* (1927); *Back in Your Own Backyard, Golden Gate, Sonny Boy* and *There's a Rainbow 'Round My Shoulder* (1928); *Little Pal, I'm in Seventh Heaven, Used to You, Why Can't You?, Evangeline* and *A Year from Today* (1929); *The Anniversary Song* (1946); *The Egg and I* and *All My Love* (1947). Collaborators included Harry Akst, Dave Dreyer, Billy Rose, Jean Schwartz, Joseph Meyer, Henderson-DeSylva-Brown team.

MOVIES

1927—THE JAZZ SINGER
1928—THE SINGING FOOL
1929—SAY IT WITH SONGS
1930—MAMMY; BIG BOY
1933—HALLELUJAH, I'M A BUM
1934—WONDER BAR
1935—GO INTO YOUR DANCE
1936—THE SINGING KID
1939—ROSE OF WASHINGTON SQUARE; HOLLYWOOD CAVALCADE
1940—SWANEE RIVER
1945—RHAPSODY IN BLUE
1946—THE JOLSON STORY (singing voice only)
1949—JOLSON SINGS AGAIN (singing voice only)

RECORDS

AL JOLSON
Vi 17037 That Haunting Melody/Rum Tum Tiddle
Vi 17075 Snap Your Fingers
Co A-1956 Yaaka Hula Hickey Dula
Co A-2478 I'm All Bound 'Round with the Mason-Dixon Line
Co A-2519 'n Everything
Co A-2560 Rock-a-bye Your Baby with a Dixie Melody
Co A-2836 You Ain't Heard Nothin' Yet
Co A-2995 Avalon
Co A-3500 April Showers
Co A-3705 Toot Toot Tootsie
Co 43-D Arcady
Co 79-D Twelve O'clock at Night
Br 2569 California, Here I Come/I'm Goin' South
Br 2671 Follow the Swallow/I Wonder What's Become of Sally?

Br 3041 I'm Sitting on Top of the World/You Flew Away from the Nest
Br 3775 Golden Gate/Four Walls
Br 3912 My Mammy/Dirty Hands, Dirty Face
Br 4033 Sonny Boy/There's a Rainbow 'Round My Shoulder
Br 4400 Little Pal/I'm in Seventh Heaven
Br 4721 Let Me Sing and I'm Happy/Looking at You
Br 6500 Hallelujah, I'm a Bum/You Are Too Beautiful
Br 6502 April Showers/Rock-a-bye Your Baby with a Dixie Melody
De 23470 Swanee/April Showers
De 23614 My Mammy/Sonny Boy
De 23714 Avalon/The Anniversary Song
De 24108 Back in Your Own Backyard/Where the Black-Eyed Susans Grow
De 24296 Let Me Sing and I'm Happy/If I Only Had a Match
De 24905 Let's Go West Again/God's Country

LPs

AL JOLSON
De DL-9036 Rainbow 'Round My Shoulder (De RIs)
De DXA-169 (2-LP set) The Best of Al Jolson (De RIs)
De (10")DL-5006 Jolson Sings Again
De (10")DL-5026 Songs Made Famous
Br(E) LAT-820 Among My Souvenirs (De RIs)
Ace of Hearts(E) AH-33 Let Me Sing and I'm Happy (1924-8 Br RIs)

953. JONES & HARE   VO

> BILLY JONES *(Born March 15, 1889, New York, N.Y.; died November 23, 1940)*
>
> ERNEST HARE *(Born March 16, 1883, Norfolk, Va.; died March 9, 1939, Jamaica, N.Y.)*

Entertaining team with low-key, relaxed comic-patter style specializing in novelty songs. Both worked early as singles in vaudeville and on records. Hare had small roles in Broadway musicals UP AND DOWN BROADWAY (1910), REVUE OF REVUES

(1911), THE PASSING SHOW OF 1912, THE
WHIRL OF SOCIETY (1912), THE PASSING
SHOW OF 1915, THE PEASANT GIRL (1915),
THE SHOW OF WONDERS (1916). Two met
1919, later formed team at suggestion of
Brunswick recording executive Gus
Haenschen. Began as team on Brunswick
Records, later recorded often for other
companies. On radio as The Happiness
Boys, by late 20s popular pair. Reached
peak 1929-30 on network show for Interwoven Sox; called themselves The Interwoven Pair. In 30s continued theatre
and club appearances though no recordings. Also continued on radio; 1934 Tasty
Loafers show over New York's WOR. A
few appearances on Milton Berle's Community Sing radio show late 1936-7, but
spark gone.

RECORDS

BILLY JONES
Co A-3574 You Can Have Every Light
on Broadway
OK 4409 Tuck Me to Sleep in My Old
'Tucky Home
Vo 14579 Yes, We Have No Bananas/
Don't We Carry On!
Vo 14630 Just a Girl That Men Forget
Re 8046 Horses
Re 8158 Mary Lou
Re 9824 Who Takes Care of the Care-
taker's Daughter?/Titina
BILLY JONES with BENNIE KRUEGER OR-
CHESTRA
Br 2667 Charley, My Boy
Br 2859 Don't Bring Lulu
BILLY JONES with TICKLE TOE TEN
OK 40325 I'll Take Her Back If She
Wants to Come Back
ERNEST HARE
Emer 10274 Avalon
Vo 14069 I'm the Good Man That Was
So Hard to Find/The Moon Shines
on the Moonshine
Vo 14192 Get Hot/Oh, Brother, What
a Feeling
Br 2039 Just Like a Gypsy
Br 2057 Old Pal, Why Don't You An-
swer Me?
Br 2154 I'm a Sentimental Dreamer
ERNEST HARE-AL BERNARD
Ed 50558 I Want to Hold You in My
Arms
Med 8203 See Old Man Moon Smile

ERNEST HARE with GOLDEN GATE OR-
CHESTRA
Pe 14485 Fallin' Down
ERNEST HARE with TICKLE TOE TEN
OK 40325 Yearning
JONES & HARE
Br 2187 Eddie Leonard Blues
Br 2270 Mr. Gallagher and Mr.
Shean/In a Little Red School
House
Br 2396 My Mother's Lullaby/Faded
Love Letters (BILLY JONES)
Br 2428 Barney Google/I Love Me
(BILLY JONES)
Br 2781 How Do You Do?/On My
Ukulele
Vo 14644 Oh Gee, I'm in Love/Maggie
Co 410-D I Miss My Swiss/Collegiate
Co 700-D My Cutey's Due at Two to
Two Today/How Many Times?
Co 941-D Crazy Words—Crazy Tune/
I Gotta Get Myself Somebody
to Love
Pat 32129 Collegiate / Happy Go
Lucky Days
Ba 1719 Thanks for the Buggy Ride/
Gimme a Little Kiss (BILLY JONES)
Pe 12378 Since Henry Ford Apolo-
gized to Me/She Don't Wanna
OK 40421 There's One Born Every
Minute/There Ain't No Flies on
Auntie
Vi 20208 She Knows Her Onions/It
Won't Be Long Now
Vi 21332 He Ain't Never Been to Col-
lege/She's the Sweetheart of Six
Other Guys
Ca 0150 Singin' in the Bathtub

954. JONES, ADA　　　VO

Singer and comedienne, specialized in
dialect and novelty songs. Known mostly
for vaudeville and records. Recordings
from earliest days of industry until about
1920. In songs portrayed Irish colleen,
Negro maid, Bowery tough girl, cowgirl,
country damsel, newsboy, grandmother.
At times teamed with Len Spencer and
Billy Murray.

RECORDS

ADA JONES
Vi 16339 Beautiful Eyes
Vi 16356 My Pony Boy
Vi 16429 Oh, You Candy Kid

Vi 16510 Has Anybody Here Seen Kelly?

Vi 16750 He's Me Pal

Vi 17008 They Always Pick on Me/ Knock Wood (with BILLY MURRAY)

Vi 17076 Oh, Mr. Dream Man

Vi 17205 Row, Row, Row/I've Got the Finest Man

Vi 17576 If They'd Only Move Old Ireland Over Here

Vi 18288 Come Over Here, It's a Wonderful Place

Co A-855 Call Me Up Some Rainy Afternoon

Co A-1457 Pussy Cat Rag

Co A-2190 Cross My Heart and Hope to Die

ADA JONES-BILLY MURRY

Vi 16322 I'm Looking for a Sweetheart

Vi 16346 I'm Awfully Glad I Met You

Vi 16662 Smile, Smile, Smile/The Boy Who Stuttered, the Girl Who Lisped

Vi 16910 My Hula Hula Love

Vi 17152 Be My Little Baby Bumble Bee

Vi 17562 I'm Crying Just for You

Vi 18205 If It Wasn't for You/Put On Your Slippers and Fill Up Your Pipe

Vi 18224 What Do You Want to Make Those Eyes at Me For?

ADA JONES-LEN SPENCER

Vi 16100 Mr. and Mrs. Murphy

Vi 16753 Flannigan's St. Patrick's Day

Ed 50398 Put On Your Slippers and Fill Up Your Pipe

Ed 50558 Oh, Lawdy

ADA JONES-M. J. O'CONNELL

Co A-2330 Some Sunday Morning

ADA JONES-WILL C. ROBBINS

Co A-1694 She Used to Be the Slowest Girl in Town

955. JONES, ALLAN   VO

Born October 14, 1908 or 1909, Scranton, Pa.

Tenor star of movies and radio in 30s and 40s. Early in career sang locally, worked at mining jobs. Attended University of Syracuse Music School. Studied voice in Paris; singing jobs there. Back to U.S.; singing parts in operettas and stage productions in many locales. Minor role in Broadway musical ROBERTA (1933). Good role in 1934 revival of BITTER SWEET. Small role in movie RECKLESS (1935); late in year gained first attention singing *Alone* and *Cosi Cosa* in Marx Brothers movie A NIGHT AT THE OPERA. Voice dubbed for Dennis Morgan bit in movie THE GREAT ZIEGFELD (1936). After minor roles in major films, prominence late 1937 with movie THE FIREFLY. Co-starred with popular Jeanette MacDonald; big hit singing new Rudolf Friml adaptation *The Donkey Serenade*. Good singing role in 1939 movie THE GREAT VICTOR HERBERT. Popular radio series late 30s; continued on radio in 40s as star or guest. In low-budget 40s movies, some non-musical. In 1944 Broadway musical JACKPOT; 69 performances. Career waned in 50s but remained active in night clubs, occasional concerts or stage productions. Infrequently on TV in 50s and 60s. Son Jack Jones popular singer in Frank Sinatra style beginning late 50s.

MOVIES

1935—RECKLESS; A NIGHT AT THE OPERA

1936—ROSE-MARIE; SHOW BOAT

1937—A DAY AT THE RACES; THE FIREFLY

1938—EVERYBODY SING

1939—HONEYMOON IN BALI; THE GREAT VICTOR HERBERT

1940—THE BOYS FROM SYRACUSE; ONE NIGHT IN THE TROPICS

1941—THERE'S MAGIC IN MUSIC

1942—TRUE TO THE ARMY; MOONLIGHT IN HAVANA; WHEN JOHNNY COMES MARCHING HOME

1943—LARCENY WITH MUSIC; RHYTHM OF THE ISLANDS; CRAZY HOUSE; YOU'RE A LUCKY FELLOW, MR. SMITH

1944—THE SINGING SHERIFF

1945—HONEYMOON AHEAD; THE SENORITA FROM THE WEST

1964—STAGE TO THUNDER ROCK

RECORDS

ALLAN JONES

Vi 4380 The Donkey Serenade/ Giannina Mia

Vi 4381 Cosi Cosa/The One I Love

Vi 4446 Thine Alone/I'm Falling in Love with Someone

Vi 4447 Someday/Sweethearts
Vi 4555 Why Do I Love You?/Make Believe
Vi 10-1126 When I Grow Too Old to Dream/Who Are We to Say?
Vi 10-1151 I'll Walk Alone/I Dream of You
Vi 10-1455 Great Day/More Than You Know

LPS

ALLAN JONES
Cam CAL-268 Sings Great Show Tunes

956. JONES, CLAUDE   tb v-tb t vo

Born February 11, 1901, Boley, Okla.
Died January 17, 1962, aboard liner
S.S. "United States"

Jazz trombonist best known for work in 20s and 30s. Good soloist with rhythmic, staccato phrasing. Attended Wilberforce University. Joined Synco Septet early 20s; group led by Bill McKinney, by late 20s augmented and known as McKinney's Cotton Pickers. Jones chief trombone soloist. Left spring 1929, soon joined Fletcher Henderson for two years. With Don Redman two years late 1931-3. Henderson again late 1933-4. Brief intervals early 30s with Chick Webb. Joined Cab Calloway late 1934, stayed till early 1940. In 1940 with Coleman Hawkins, Zutty Singleton, Joe Sullivan. With Henderson again briefly 1941. Left music awhile early 40s for own sausage business. Joined Duke Ellington spring 1944, remained till late 1948. Brief period with Ellington early 1951. Another period with Henderson 1950. Left music early 50s to work as mess steward aboard ocean liner. Died on trip.

RECORDS

MCKINNEY'S COTTON PICKERS
Vi 21611 Milenberg Joys
Vi 21730 Cherry
Vi 38025 Stop Kidding/Put It There
Vi 38097 Plain Dirt
Vi 38102 Miss Hannah/The Way I Feel Today
Vi 38133 Peggy/I'd Love It
FLETCHER HENDERSON
De 214 Happy as the Day Is Long

CONNIE'S INN ORCHESTRA (Fletcher Henderson)
Vi 22721 Sugar Foot Stomp/Singin' the Blues
Me 12239 Just Blues (first chorus)
Br 6176 Radio Rhythm
CHICK WEBB
De 483 Don't Be That Way
De 831 Under the Spell of the Blues
HARLAN LATTIMORE
Co 2678-D Reefer Man
LOUIS ARMSTRONG
De 18090 Perdido Street Blues/2:19 Blues
DON REDMAN
Br 6429 Nagasaki
Bb 10765 Shim-Me-Sha-Wabble
JELLY ROLL MORTON
Bb 10429 Oh, Didn't He Ramble/Winin' Boy Blues
Bb 10434 High Society/I Thought I Heard Buddy Bolden Say
BENNY MORTON'S TROMBONE CHOIR
Key (12")1309 Liza/Once in Awhile
Key (12")1315 Sliphorn Outing/Where or When

LPs

MCKINNEY'S COTTON PICKERS
"X" (10")LVA-3031 (Vi RIs)
FLETCHER HENDERSON
"X" (10")LVA-3013 Connie's Inn Orchestra (Vi RIs)
CHICK WEBB
De DL-9222 A Legend, Vol. 1 (1929-36 RIs)
BENNY MORTON
Mer (10")MG-25071 Trombone Time (including Key RIs)
JELLY ROLL MORTON
CMS (10")FL-20018 (Gen RIs)

957. JONES, HANK   p o

Born July 31, 1918, Pontiac, Mich.

Modern jazz pianist; simple style but rich modern harmonic structure, good rhythmic approach. Excellent accompanist for singers and jazz soloists in combos. Older brother of trumpet star Thad Jones and drummer Elvin Jones. Early career in midwest and Buffalo. To New York 1944 with Hot Lips Page, Andy Kirk, Billy Eckstine, John Kirby, Coleman Hawkins, Howard McGhee. Tours with Jazz at the

Philharmonic late 40s and early 50s. With Ella Fitzgerald several years at intervals. Joined Artie Shaw's Gramercy Five late 1953 awhile. From mid-50s freelanced in New York. With Benny Goodman 1956-7 off and on. Active in TV studios and on LPs in 60s and 70s.

RECORDS

FLIP PHILLIPS
    Mer 8920 Feelin' the Blues/Flip's Boogie

JAZZ AT THE PHILHARMONIC
    Mer 11000-1-2 Perdido (1 to 6)
    Mer 11013-14-15 Mordido (1 to 6)

ILLINOIS JACQUET
    Mer 89036 What's the Riff?/Blues in the Night

CAL TJADER
    Sav 1117 Tangerine/Love Me or Leave Me

ARTIE SHAW GRAMERCY FIVE
    Clef 89117 Sunny Side Up/Imagination

COLEMAN HAWKINS
    Vi 20-3057 April in Paris/Strange
    Vi 20-3143 Jumpin' for Jane/Half Step Down Please
    Alad 3006 Bean-A-Re-Bop/The Way You Look Tonight

JOHN KIRBY
    Cr 107 Peanut Vendor
    Cr 108 Ripples

HOT LIPS PAGE
    Cont 6002 The Lady in Bed/Gee, Baby, Ain't I Good to You
    Cont 6003 Big "D" Blues/It Ain't Like That
    Cont 6015 Sunset Blues/The Lady in Debt
    Melrose 1402 Happy Medium/I've Got the World on a String

HANK JONES
    Dial 1037 Night Music
    Clef 112 Tea for Two/The Night We Called It a Day
    Clef 113 You're Blasé/Yesterdays
    Clef 114 Blue Room/Blues for Lady

LPs

HANK JONES
    Sav MG-12084 Have you Met Hank Jones?
    Sav MG-12087 Hank Jones Quartet

    Mer (10″)MGC-100 Hank Jones Be-Bop Piano
    ABC-Para 496 This Is Ragtime Now!
    Golden Crest S-3042 (S) Swings GIGI

JOE NEWMAN
    Vik LX-1060 The Midgets

ARTIE SHAW GRAMERCY FIVE
    Clef MGC-630 Album 3

MILT JACKSON
    Sav MG-12070 The Jazz Skyline

JACK TEAGARDEN
    Verve V-8495

BUCK CLAYTON
    Vang VRS-8514 Buckin' the Blues

THAD JONES
    Debut DLP-12 Thad Jones Quartet

TYREE GLENN
    Forum SF-9068 (S) At The Embers

BOB BROOKMEYER
    Vik LX-1071 Brookmeyer

JIMMY CLEVELAND
    EmArcy SRE-66003 (S) Rhythm Crazy

ZOOT SIMS-BOB BROOKMEYER
    UA 4023 Stretching Out

---

958. JONES, ISHAM   p ts ar cm B
    Born January 31, 1894, Coalton, Ohio
    Died October 19, 1956, Hollywood, Calif.

Leader of outstanding dance band many years, especially notable 1930-35. Band towered above most contemporaries because of arrangements and impeccable musicianship. Full, rich ensemble sound and good beat enhanced by tasteful use of tuba. Jones tough disciplinarian. Equally important as composer; songs enjoyed great popularity, became standards. Jones to Chicago 1915, played tenor sax and led trio. Later led larger group at Green Mill and Rainbow Gardens. Established reputation by early 20s; good runs at Hotel Sherman. Toured, played New York, appeared in London 1924. Prolific recording. During 20s and 30s fame grew; composed hit tune or two almost every year. By late 20s band excellent; reached peak 1932-4. Top arranger Gordon Jenkins, aided by Joe Bishop (tu) and Jiggs Noble (p). Johnny Carlson fine lead trumpet, Milt Yaner first alto sax and hot clarinet. Other hot soloists at times: Saxie

Mansfield (ts), George Thow (t), Pee Wee Erwin (t), Jack Jenney (tb), Sonny Lee (tb), Howard Smith (p). Vocalist Eddie Stone crowd-pleaser, important asset. Other vocalists Joe Martin and Woody Herman (also featured on clarinet). 1931 recording *Star Dust* pushed band higher in popularity, helped establish song. 1931 Jones composition *You're Just a Dream Come True* band's beautiful theme. On radio shows of note: The Big Show with Gertrude Niesen early and mid-1934 and Chevrolet show late 1934-5. Disbanded 1936; nucleus under Woody Herman organized cooperative band. Jones formed new band 1937 again with vocalists Eddie Stone and Joe Martin (into 1938). Disbanded about 1942, thereafter led bands at intervals. In 40s and 50s based mostly on west coast, composing and occasionally recording; some recordings with vocalist Curt Massey noteworthy. Most notable compositions *I'll See You in My Dreams, On the Alamo, Swingin' Down the Lane, It Had to Be You, No Greater Love, I Can't Believe It's True, The One I Love, The Wooden Soldier and the China Doll, Why Can't This Night Go On Forever?*. Chief lyricists Charles Newman and Gus Kahn.

SONGS

1919—Meet Me in Bubble Land
1922—Broken Hearted Melody; On the Alamo; Ivy, Cling to Me
1923—Indiana Moon; Swingin' Down the Lane
1924—I'll See You in My Dreams; Spain; It Had to Be You; The One I Love; Where Is That Old Girl of Mine?; Why Couldn't It Be Poor Little Me?; Gotta Getta Girl; Never Again
1925—I'm Tired of Everything but You
1926—My Castle in Spain
1928—Down Where the Sun Goes Down
1929—Song of the Blues
1930—What's the Use?; Feeling That Way
1931—I Keep Remembering; My Cradle Sweetheart; I Wouldn't Change You for the World; You're Just a Dream Come True

1932—I Can't Believe It's True; Let's Try Again; Let That Be a Lesson to You; If You Were Only Mine; I'll Never Have to Dream Again; The Wooden Soldier and the China Doll; I Only Found You for Somebody Else; One Little Word Led to Another
1933—You've Got Me Crying Again; Why Can't This Night Go On Forever?; Honestly
1934—It's Funny to Everyone but Me; All Mine—Almost
1935—Give a Broken Heart a Break
1936—No Greater Love
1937—Thanks for Everything; Just to Remind You
1938—More Than Ever
1940—Go Way—Can't You See I'm Dreaming?
1948—How Many Tears Must Fall?
1951—Melinda; Sally Doesn't Care

RECORDS

ISHAM JONES

Br 2245 On the Alamo/By the Sapphire Sea
Br 2438 Swingin' Down the Lane/Who's Sorry Now?
Br 2738 I'll See You in My Dreams/Why Couldn't It Be Poor Little Me?
Br 5011 La Veeda/So Long, Oolong
Br 5065 Ma/Wabash Blues
Br 4826 Not a Cloud in the Sky
Br 4856 Star Dust/Trees
Br 6015 (theme) You're Just a Dream Come True/Lonesome Lover
Br 6161 Spain/Swingin' Down the Lane
Br 6270 What a Life/If It Ain't Love
Br 6308 I Can't Believe It's True/My Silent Love
Vi 24099 Sentimental Gentleman from Georgia/One Little Word Led to Another
Vi 24116 I Only Found You for Somebody Else
Vi 24118 Everyone Says "I Love You"/Always in My Heart
Vi 24213 Why Can't This Night Go On Forever?
Vi 24246 Down a Carolina Lane/A Tree Was a Tree

1197

Vi 24409 Doin' the Uptown Lowdown/You're My Past, Present and Future
Vi 24496 Sittin' on a Log/Got the Jitters
Vi 24519 Junk Man/There Goes My Heart
Vi 24628 Ridin' Around in the Rain/ Don't Let Your Love Go Wrong
Vi 24701 Blue Room/Georgia Jubilee
De 493 Blue Room/Black Magic
De 569 Blue Lament/Dallas Blues
De 605 If I Should Lose You/Thunder Over Paradise
De 610 Don't Mention Love to Me/ Darling
De 713 The Day I Let You Get Away/That Never-to-Be-Forgotten Night
Vo 3544 Twilight in Turkey/I've Got a New Lease on Love
Vo 3911 Outside of Paradise/Shenanigans

AL JOLSON with ISHAM JONES ORCHESTRA
Br 2567 The One I Love/Steppin' Out
Br 2582 Mr. Radio Man/Home in Pasadena

LPs

ISHAM JONES
Vi LPV-504 The Great Isham Jones & His Orchestra (Vi RIs)
Ace of Hearts(E) AH-110 Swingin' Down the Lane (Br RIs)
CURT MASSEY with ISHAM JONES ORCHESTRA
Cap (10'')H-230 (Isham Jones songs)
(artist performing Jones songs)
RUSTY DEDRICK
Mon-Ever MRS-6603 Twelve Isham Jones Evergreens

959. JONES, JIMMY   p g ar cm

Born December 30, 1918, Memphis, Tenn.

Modern pianist with mainstream roots. Inventive harmonically, fit in with bop. Grew up in Chicago. Learned guitar, accompanied vocal trio at 1933 World's Fair. Switched to piano, attended Kentucky State College, played in and arranged for band there. With Stuff Smith in Chicago 1943, New York 1944. Played New York clubs, recorded. With J. C.

Heard 1946-7; 1947-52 mostly accompanied singer Sarah Vaughan. Retired two years due to illness, resumed 1954-6 with Sarah Vaughan including tours abroad. In later 50s and 60s freelanced in New York; in demand as accompanist for singers. Arranging-conducting for concerts and TV. Furnished Duke Ellington arrangements in 60s. European tour 1966 as musical director for Ella Fitzgerald (with Ellington band). Active into 70s. Composed jazz numbers including *Shadowy Sands*, *Riff Street*, *A Touch of Blue*.

RECORDS

HARRY CARNEY
HRS 1020 Minor Mirage/Candy Cane
HRS 1021 Jamaica Rumble/Shadowy Sands
J. C. HIGGINBOTHAM
HRS 1013 A Penny for Your Blues/ Dutch Treat
SANDY WILLIAMS
HRS 1008 Sumpin' Jumpin' 'Round Here/After Hours on Dream Street
JOE THOMAS
HRS 1016 Riff Street/A Touch of Blue
STUFF SMITH
Asch 353-1 Look at Me/Midway
Asch 353-2 Skip It/Stop, Look
Asch 353-3 Don't You Think/Desert Sands
DON BYAS
Sav 574 Candy/Byas-A-Drink
Sav 597 How High the Moon
AL HALL
Wax 101 Blues in My Heart/Rose of the Rio Grande
Wax 102 Emaline/Am I Blue?
COLEMAN HAWKINS
Vi 40-0131 Spotlite/Say It Isn't So
Vi 40-0133 Low Flame/Allen's Alley
J. C. HEARD
Cont 6022 Heard but Not Seen/The Walk
TIMME ROSENKRANTZ
Cont 6012 Bouncy/Blues at Dawn
TONY SCOTT
Go 105 All Too Soon/Ten Lessons with Timothy
JIMMY JONES
HRS 1014 Old Juice on the Loose/ Muddy Miss

HRS 1015 Departure from Dixie/A Woman's Got a Right to Change
HRS 1043 Sunny Side Up/Keeping Up with Jones
Wax 103 Five O'clock Drag/New World a-Comin'
Wax 107 Lover Man/Clair De Lune
Wax 113 On a Turquoise Cloud/When I Walk

LPs

SARAH VAUGHAN
EmArcy MG-36109 Swingin' Easy
Roul R-52060 The Divine One
LEE WILEY
Story (10″)312 Sings Rodgers & Hart
NANCY WILSON (arrangements)
Cap T-1828 Broadway—My Way
ANDY GIBSON
Cam CAL-554 Mainstream Jazz
BEN WEBSTER
Verve MGV-8318 Ben Webster and Associates
THAD JONES
Period SPL-1208 Mad Thad
JOHNNY HODGES (arrangements)
Verve MGV-8680 Blue Notes
(miscellaneous combos)
Riv RLP-145 Giants of Small-Band Swing

960. JONES, JO   d B
(JONATHAN JONES)
Born October 7, 1911, Chicago, Ill.

Outstanding swing drummer, member of great Count Basie rhythm section. Ability to play in various styles. Grew up in Alabama. Left school to tour with carnivals over U.S. With Walter Page band Oklahoma City late 20s; led combo at club there. With bands in Nebraska early 30s. To Kansas City 1933; with Tommy Douglas combo. With Bennie Moten 1934-5. With Count Basie combo awhile late 1935-6. With Jeter-Pillars band in St. Louis; rejoined Basie fall 1936. Vital part of band. Military service 1944-5. With Basie again early 1946-8. In late 40s and early 50s with Illinois Jacquet, Lester Young, Joe Bushkin. Toured with Jazz at the Philharmonic shows. Freelanced in later 50s and 60s. With Tyree Glenn 1956-7. Led trio at intervals in 60s. Took

up teaching drums. Several trips abroad with Jazz at the Philharmonic and Milt Buckner. Many jobs with Teddy Wilson and Claude Hopkins. Still active in 70s.

RECORDS

JONES-SMITH, INC.
Vo 3441 Shoe Shine Swing/Evenin'
Vo 3459 Boogie Woogie/Oh, Lady Be Good
COUNT BASIE
De 1363 One O'clock Jump/John's Idea
De 1770 Topsy/Don't You Miss Your Baby?
De 2212 Jumpin' at the Woodside/Dark Rapture
De 2355 Boogie Woogie/How Long How Long Blues (quartet)
De 2631 You Can Depend on Me/Oh, Lady Be Good
De 2780 Oh! Red/Fare Thee Honey Fare Thee Well (quartet)
Vo 4747 Rock-a-Bye Basie/Baby, Don't Tell on Me
Vo 5036 Moonlight Serenade/I Can't Believe That You're in Love with Me
Co 35521 I Never Knew/Tickle Toe
OK 5732 Moten Swing/Evenin'
OK 5987 Stampede in G Minor/Who Am I?
KANSAS CITY SIX
CMS 555 I Got Rhythm/Jo-Jo
MILDRED BAILEY
Vo 3615 If You Ever Should Leave/Heaven Help This Heart of Mine
Vo 3626 The Moon Got in My Eyes/It's the Natural Thing to Do
LIONEL HAMPTON
Vi 26011 Shoe Shiners Drag/I'm in the Mood for Swing
Vi 26017 Muskrat Ramble
HARRY JAMES
Br 8035 LIFE Goes to a Party/When We're Alone
BILLIE HOLIDAY
Vo 3593 Me, Myself and I/Without Your Love
Vo 5302 You're a Lucky Guy/You're Just a No Account
DICKIE WELLS
Si (12″)90002 I Got Rhythm/I'm Fer It Too

BENNY GOODMAN SEXTET
Co 36039 Breakfast Feud/I Found a New Baby
Co 36254 Air Mail Special (ORCHESTRA)

TEDDY WILSON
Br 7824 He Ain't Got Rhythm/This Year's Kisses
Br 8265 April in My Heart/I'll Never Fail You

TIMME ROSENKRANTZ
Vi 25876 A Wee Bit of Swing/Is This to Be My Souvenir?

LPs

JO JONES
Everest 5023 Jo Jones Trio
Vang VRS-8503 The Jo Jones Special
Vang VRS-8525 Jo Jones Plus Two
Jazztone J-1242 The Jo Jones Special

COUNT BASIE
Epic LN-3107 Lester Leaps In (Vo RIs)
Epic LN-3169 Basie's Back in Town (Vo, OK RIs)
De DL-8049 Count Basie & His Orchestra (De RIs)

COLEMAN HAWKINS
Riv RS-3049 (S) Think Deep
Jazztone J-1201 Timeless Jazz

ROY ELDRIDGE
Verve V-1010 Swing Goes Dixie

JAZZ AT THE PHILHARMONIC ALL-STARS
Verve VSP-16 Perdido//Mordido

BLOSSOM DEARIE
Verve MGV-2037

961. JONES, JONAH   t vo B
(ROBERT ELLIOTT JONES)
Born December 31, 1909, Louisville, Ky.

Trumpet star with good tone and intense drive. Fresh, exciting soloist, particularly in 30s; then mostly played open horn. Later led swinging yet commercial jazz combo, playing mostly muted trumpet. Early job late 20s on riverboat Island Queen. With Horace Henderson 1928-30, Hardy Brothers 1930, Wesley Helvey and Jimmie Lunceford 1931. Joined Stuff Smith combo in Buffalo 1932, remained till 1935. Periods with Lil Armstrong and McKinney's Cotton Pickers 1935. Rejoined Smith in Buffalo late 1935; combo to New York early 1936, acclaimed at

Onyx Club for entertaining, free-wheeling jazz. Jones hailed for trumpet work, remained with Smith till 1940. With Fletcher Henderson briefly 1940; with Benny Carter late 1940 to early 1941. Early 1941 began ten-year period with Cab Calloway. Jobbed with Earl Hines, Joe Bushkin 1952. To Europe 1954, solo sensation. Brief period with Lester Lanin society band. In 1955 formed quartet; first success at The Embers in New York. Hit big with *On the Street Where You Live* and *Baubles, Bangles and Beads.* Novel commercialized jazz style led to top bookings and fast-selling LPs. Jones's muted trumpet melodious, straightforward; semblance of head arrangements gave group more identity. Played predominately show tunes, jazz standards, better pops. Jones excellent showman, sang occasionally. Frequently on TV late 50s and 60s. Latterly grew to quintet. Numerous tours abroad in 60s and early 70s.

RECORDS

STUFF SMITH
Vo 3169 I'se a-Muggin' (1 & 2)
Vo 3170 I Hope Gabriel Likes My Music/I'm Putting All My Eggs in One Basket
Vo 3200 I Don't Want to Make History/'Tain't No Use
Vo 3201 After You've Gone/You'se a Viper
Vo 3234 Robins and Roses/I've Got a Heavy Date
De 1279 Onyx Club Spree/Where Is the Sun?
Vs 8081 My Blue Heaven/My Thoughts

CAB CALLOWAY
OK 6109 Jonah Joins the Cab
OK 6147 Special Delivery

LIL ARMSTRONG
De 7739 Sixth Street/My Secret Flame
De 7803 Riffin' the Blues/Why Is a Good Man So Hard to Find?

LIONEL HAMPTON
Vi 25658 Confessin'/Drum Stomp

MILT HINTON
Key 639 Everywhere/Beefsteak Charlie

THE KEYNOTERS
Key (12")1313 You're Driving Me Crazy/I'm in the Market for You

BILLIE HOLIDAY

Vo 3431 One Never Knows, Does One?/I've Got My Love to Keep Me Warm

Vo 3440 If My Heart Could Only Talk/Please Keep Me in Your Dreams

DICK PORTER

Vo 3478 Poor Robinson Crusoe/Swing Boy Swing

TEDDY WILSON

Br 7702 Guess Who/It's Like Reaching for the Moon

IKE QUEBEC

BN (12")42 Mad About You/Facin' the Face

JONAH JONES

CMS 602 Rose Of the Rio Grande/Stomping at the Savoy

CMS (12")1520 You Brought a New Kind of Love to Me/Hubba Hubba Hub

Sw(Fr) 228 That's the Lick/I Can't Give You Anything but Love

Sw(Fr) 243 I'm Headin' for Paris/Jonah's Wail

Key 614 Just Like a Butterfly/Lust for Licks

Cap (45) F3747 On the Street Where You Live/Rose Room

Cap (45) F3893 Baubles, Bangles and Beads/Seventy-Six Trombones

LPs

JONAH JONES

Vi LPM-2004 At the Embers

Beth (10")BCP-1014

Everest 5099 Vamp 'Til Ready

Angel (10")60006 Jonah Wails: 2nd Wind

Baronet 103 Trumpet on Tour

Vik LX-1135 At the Embers

Cap T-839 Muted Jazz

Cap T-1193 I Dig Chicks

De DL-4688 On the Sunny Side of the Street

De DL-4800 Sweet with a Beat

BENNY PAYNE

Kapp KL-1004 Sunny Side Up

SAMMY PRICE

Jazztone J-1207 Barrelhouse and Blues

SIDNEY BECHET

GTJ 12013 King of the Soprano Saxophone

962. JONES, PHILLY JOE d B
(JOSEPH RUDOLPH JONES)

Born July 15, 1923, Philadelphia, Pa.

Jazz drummer adept at combo and big band work. Good section man; solos original. Began with local bands. To New York 1947. With Joe Morris, freelanced. Gained name early 50s with Tony Scott and Tadd Dameron. Fame grew; with Miles Davis off and on during 50s. In 60s based mostly on west coast, freelancing. In later 60s often toured abroad. Active into 70s.

RECORDS
(all LPs)

PHILLY JOE JONES

Atl 1340 Philly Joe's Beat

Riv 12-282 Blues for Dracula

Riv 12-302 Drums Around the World

PHILLY JOE JONES-ELVIN JONES

Atl 1428 Together

ARCHIE SHEPP-PHILLY JOE JONES

Fan 86018

MILES DAVIS

Co CL-949 'Round About Midnight

Co CL-1193 Milestones

ART PEPPER

Contemp C-3532 Meets the Rhythm Section

KENNY DREW

Riv 12-224 The Kenny Drew Trio

CLARK TERRY

Riv 12-237 Serenade to a Bus Seat

WARNE MARSH

Atl 1291

BLUE MITCHELL

Riv 12-273 Big Six

TADD DAMERON

Pres (10")159 A Study in Dameronia

SONNY ROLLINS

Pres 7047 Tenor Madness

SONNY CLARK

BN 1588 Cool Struttin'

TONY SCOTT

Br (10")BL-58040

JOHN COLTRANE

BN 1577 Blue Train

ELMO HOPE

BN (10")5029 Elmo Hope Trio

HOWARD MCGHEE

Beth BCP-42 The Return of Howard McGhee

963. JONES, RICHARD M.

p o c ar cm B

*Born June 13, 1889 (possibly 1892), New
Orleans, La.*
Died December 8, 1945, Chicago, Ill.

Pianist prominent in New Orleans in
early jazz years; later success in Chicago.
Pioneer in barrelhouse piano. Early jobs
on cornet in Eureka Brass Band. At 19
pianist in Storyville sporting houses. With
King Oliver, Joseph Robichaux, Armand
Piron, Papa Celestin; led band at intervals. To Chicago about 1918, freelanced.
Managerial job with Clarence Williams
publishing company 1919-21. Own music
store 1923-8. Led band mid-20s. Recording director for Okeh 1925-8; recorded
under own name, furnished backing for
blues singers. In 30s toured with band
occasionally. Played New Orleans 1931-2,
Chicago 1934. 1935-9 recording executive
for Decca in Chicago; furnished arrangements and played part-time. World War
II defense work in Chicago, continued
music as sideline. Active in music until
death. Composer credits on several jazz
numbers, though authorship disputed on
some. Compositions include *Trouble in
Mind, Lonesome Nobody Cares, Red
Wagon, Jazzin' Babies Blues, Riverside
Blues, Ball o' Fire, 29th & Dearborn, All
Night Blues, Dark Alley, Hollywood Shuffle, Late Hours Blues, Remember Me?,
Sweet Little Mammy, Mush Mouth Blues,
Bring It On Home to Grandma,* numer-
ous others recorded by Jones.

RECORDS

BERTHA "CHIPPIE" HILL
    OK 8273 Low Land Blues/Kid Man
    Blues
    OK 8312 Georgia Man/Trouble in
    Mind
    OK 8420 Pleadin' for the Blues/Pratt
    City Blues
NOLAN WELSH
    OK 8372 The Bridwell Blues/St. Peter
    Blues
    OK 8425 Bouncing   Blues/Nolan
    Welsh's Blues
LILLIE DELK CHRISTIAN
    OK 8475 Ain't She Sweet?/It All De-
    pends on You

BLANCHE CALLOWAY
    OK 8279 Lazy Woman's Blues/Lone-
    some Lovesick
CHICAGO HOTTENTOTS
    Vo 1008 All Night Shags/Put Me in
    the Alley Blues
JOHNNY DODDS
    De 18094 Red Onion Blues/Gravier
    Street Blues
JIMMIE NOONE
    De 18095 Keystone   Blues/New
    Orleans Hop Scop Blues
KING OLIVER
    Vo 1007 Too Bad/Snag It
RUSSELL'S HOT SIX (Luis Russell)
    Vo 1010 29th & Dearborn/Sweet
    Mumtaz
RICHARD M. JONES
    Ge 5174 Jazzin' Babies Blues/12th
    Street Rag
    OK 8260 Spanish Shawl/29th & Dear-
    born
    OK 8349 Mush Mouth Blues/Kin to
    Kant Blues
    OK 8431 Dusty Bottom Blues/Scag-
    more Green
    Vi 20812 Hollywood Shuffle/Dark Al-
    ley
    Vi 21203 Boar Hog Blues/Jazzin' Ba-
    bies Blues
    Vi 38040 Novelty   Blues/Tickle
    Britches Blues
    Para 12705 Hot and Ready/It's a Low
    Down Thing
    Bb 6569 Trouble in Mind/Black Rider
    De 7051 Bring It On Home to
    Grandma/Blue Reefer Blues
    De 7064 Muggin' the Blues/I'm
    Gonna Run You Down
    Sess 12006 New Orleans Hop Scop
    Blues/29th & Dearborn
    Sess 12007 Jazzin' Babies Blues/Canal
    Street Blues

LPs

RICHARD M. JONES
    Pax (10")6010 (Sess RIs)

964. JONES, SPIKE   d cm B
(LINDLEY ARMSTRONG
JONES)

*Born December 14, 1911, Long Beach,
Calif.*
Died May 1, 1964, Los Angeles, Calif.

Bandleader known as King of Corn. Bands beginning early 40s featured zany arrangements, vocals, antics. Billed as Spike Jones & His City Slickers. Grew up in California. At high school in Long Beach led combo on local radio. In early 30s after junior college drummed in bands of Ray West, Everett Hoagland, Earl Burtnett. Mid-30s to early 40s played in studio bands on radio shows of Burns & Allen, Al Jolson, Bob Burns, Fibber McGee & Molly, Bing Crosby. Began rehearsing band with cornball routines lampooning popular songs. Used such unlikely "instruments" as pistols, cowbells, saws, auto pumps, fire bells, toy whistles. Band heard by RCA executive, signed for Bluebird label. Almost instant popularity with 1942 hit *Der Fuehrer's Face*, which Jones composed. On radio shows later 1942, on Bob Burns show 1943-4. Chase & Sanborn show with Frances Langford 1945. Hits of later 40s included *Chlo-e, You Always Hurt the One You Love, Cocktails for Two, The Glow-Worm, All I Want for Christmas Is My Two Front Teeth.* Key sidemen in 40s banjoists Dick Morgan and Freddy Morgan, trumpeter George Rock. "Vocals" by Rock, Doodles Weaver and Red Ingle. Beginning 1947 Jones' beautiful wife Helen Grayco featured vocalist many years. Radio show late 40s, TV shows in 50s. Band a natural for TV with its visual effects. Jones good front man, intelligent, serious when necessary. In 60s played California and Las Vegas. In movies THANK YOUR LUCKY STARS (1943), MEET THE PEOPLE (1944), BRING ON THE GIRLS (1945), BREAKFAST IN HOLLYWOOD (1946), VARIETY GIRL (1947), FIREMAN SAVE MY CHILD (1954).

RECORDS

SPIKE JONES

Bb 11560 Siam/Come, Josephine, in My Flying Machine
Bb 11586 Der Fuehrer's Face/I Wanna Go Back to West Virginia
Bb 30-0812 Oh, By Jingo/The Sheik of Araby
VD (12")540 The Blue Danube/Toot Toot Tootsie
VD 570 Minka/McNamara's Band

Vi 20-1628 Cocktails for Two/Leave the Dishes in the Sink, Ma
Vi 20-1654 Chlo-e/A Serenade to a Jerk
Vi 20-1733 Holiday for Strings/Drip, Drip, Drip
Vi 20-1762 You Always Hurt the One You Love/The Blue Danube
Vi 20-1893 The Glow-Worm/Hawaiian War Chant
Vi 20-1895 That Old Black Magic/Liebestraum
Vi 20-1983 Lassus Trombone/Minka
Vi 20-2375 Pop Corn Sack/Our Hour
Vi 20-2592 My Old Flame/People Are Funnier Than Anybody
Vi 20-2861 The Man on the Flying Trapeze/William Tell Overture
Vi 20-2949 I Kiss Your Hand, Madame/I'm Getting Sentimental Over You
Vi 20-3177 All I Want for Christmas Is My Two Front Teeth/Happy New Year
Vi 20-3516 Dance of the Hours/None but the Lonely Heart
Vi 20-5067 Winter/I Saw Mommy Kissing Santa Claus
Vi 20-5107 I Went to Your Wedding/I'll Never Work There Anymore
Vi 47-5320 Three Little Fishies/A Din Skal, A Min Skal

LPs

SPIKE JONES

Vi (10")LPM-3054 Bottoms Up
Verve MGV-2021 A Christmas Spectacular
Verve MGV-4005 Dinner Music for People That Aren't Very Hungry
Lib 3338 Washington Square (dixieland combo)
Lib 3349 New Band (dixieland combo)

965. JONES, THAD   t c fl-h ar cm B

Born March 28, 1923, Pontiac, Mich.

Creative modern trumpet star, co-leader of important modern big band. Brother of pianist Hank Jones and drummer Elvin Jones. Self-taught on trumpet. As youngster played in Michigan. With Sonny Stitt in Saginaw. In 1941 toured south in band. Military service, World War II. Later played several years with good but little-known bands including Billy Mitchell combo in Detroit. Led bands early 50s. Joined Count Basie mid-1954, quickly rose to stardom, remained till early 1963. Excellent arranger for Basie. Freelance playing and arranging 1963-5. December 1965 formed big jazz band with drummer Mel Lewis, wrote most of arrangements. Band worked part-time in 60s and into 70s; personnel mostly New York studio musicians. For years played Mondays at Village Vanguard. Russian trip 1972. Jones composed jazz numbers featured by band.

RECORDS
(all LPs)

THAD JONES
Debut (10″)DLP-12 Thad Jones Quintet
BN 1513 Detroit-New York Function
BN 1527 The Magnificent Thad Jones
UA 4025 Motor City Scene
Period SPL-1208 Mad Thad
THAD JONES-CHARLES MINGUS
Debut (10″)DLP-17
THAD JONES-MEL LEWIS
Solid State 17003 The Jazz Orchestra
Solid State 18016 Live at the Village Vanguard
Solid State 18041 Featuring Ruth Brown
THAD JONES with PEPPER ADAMS QUINTET
Milestone 9001
COUNT BASIE
Clef MGC-647 Dance Session Album 2
Clef MGC-666 Basie
Clef MGC-685 The Count
DUKE ELLINGTON/COUNT BASIE
Co CL-1715 First Time! The Count Meets the Duke
BILLY MITCHELL
DeeGee (10″)4009
LEONARD FEATHER'S STARS
MGM E-3390 West Coast vs. East Coast
PAUL QUINICHETTE
Dawn DLP-1109 The Kid from Denver
AL COHN (Jones under name of Bart Valve)
Vi LPM-1161 The Jazz Workshop

THELONIOUS MONK
Co CS-8964 (S) Big Band in Concert
Riv 12-305 Five by Monk by Five

966. JONES, WILMORE "SLICK"
d vb

Born April 13, 1907, Roanoke, Va.
Died November 2, 1969, New York, N.Y.

Drummer best known for work in Fats Waller combo. Beginning 1925 local jobs. Studied at Damrosch Conservatory in New York. With Fletcher Henderson one year early 1935-6, no records. Joined Waller spring 1936, remained till early 1942 with some intervals away. Occasionally played vibes with Waller; recorded often. Late 1942-3 with Stuff Smith, Una Mae Carlisle, Eddie South. Periods 1944-6 with Louis Jordan, Claude Hopkins, Hazel Scott, Don Redman. Late 1946 joined Gene Sedric for several years. Mid-50s in Boston with Wilbur DeParis and Doc Cheatham. With Eddie Durham at Long Island club early 60s.

RECORDS

FATS WALLER
Vi 25530 I Can't Break the Habit of You/You're Laughing at Me
Vi 25565 San Anton'/You Showed Me the Way
Vi 25672 Beat It Out/You've Got Me Under Your Thumb
Vi 25681 Our Love Was Meant to Be/I'd Rather Call You Baby
Vi 25689 The Joint Is Jumping/A Hopeless Love Affair
Vi 25891 There's Honey on the Moon Tonight/Fair and Square
Bb 10035 Yacht Club Swing
Bb 10184 Undecided/Step Up and Shake My Hand
Bb 10658 Cheatin' on Me / Oh Frenchy!
Bb 11115 Let's Get Away from It All/I Wanna Hear Swing Songs
Bb 11262 Chant of the Groove/Come and Get It
UNA MAE CARLISLE
Bb 10853 Now I Lay Me Down to Dream/Papa's in Bed with His Britches On

Bb 10898 If I Had You/You Made Me Love You

PUTNEY DANDRIDGE
Vo 3277 These Foolish Things/Cross Patch

LIONEL HAMPTON
Vi 26423 Gin for Christmas
Vi 26447 I've Found a New Baby/Four or Five Times
Vi 26453 Munson Street Breakdown/I Can't Get Started

DON REDMAN
Vi 26258 Igloo/Chew-Chew-Chew
Vi 26266 Baby, Won't You Please Come Home?/Ain't I Good to You?

DON BYAS
Hub 3002 Fruit Salad/Spots

SEDRIC & HIS HONEY BEARS (Gene Sedric)
Vo 4552 Choo-Choo/The Wail of the Scromph
Vo 4576 The Joint Is Jumpin'/Off Time

LOUIS JORDAN
De 8659 G.I. Jive
De 8668 Mop Mop/You Can't Get That No More

LPs

FATS WALLER
Vi LPM-537 Fractious Fingering (Vi RIs)
Vi LPT-1001 Plays and Sings (Vi RIs)
Vi (10")LPT-14
Jazztone J-1247 Plays and Sings (Bb RIs)
Cam CAL-473 The Real Fats Waller (Vi, Bb RIs)

LIONEL HAMPTON
Vi LJM-1000 (Vi RIs)

SIDNEY BECHET
BN 7014

967. JOPLIN, SCOTT   cm p c B

Born November 24, 1868, Texarkana, Texas
Died April 11, 1917, New York, N.Y.

Leading pioneer and composer of ragtime music. Most famous composition *Maple Leaf Rag* written 1899 near start of career. Early piano instruction from Louis Chauvin. Played in St. Louis cafes, led orchestra in Chicago, played World's Fair 1893. Based awhile in Sedalia, Mo., home of George R. Smith Negro Musical College and hub of Negro musical activity. Cornet in Queen City Negro Band in Sedalia 1894-5, first ragtime band. Sold first composition 1895. After many works became successes, toured U.S. performing own compositions. Played vaudeville. Settled in New York 1905, continued composing until death. Music enjoyed great revival 1973-4 thanks to hit film THE STING, which featured Joplin compositions on Academy Award-winning soundtrack.

COMPOSITIONS
(publishing dates approximate)

1895—Please Say You Will; Picture of Her Face
1896—Crush Collision March; Harmony Club Waltzes; Combination March
1899—Original Rags; Maple Leaf Rag
1900—Swipesy Cake Walk
1901—Pickaninny Rag; The Easy Winners; Pickaninny Days; Sunflower Slow Drag
1902—A Breeze from Alabama; The Entertainer; The Strenuous Life; Elite Syncopations; The Ragtime Dance
1903—Weeping Willow; Palm Leaf Rag; Something Doing; Little Black Baby
1904—The Cascades; The Chrysanthemum; The Sycamore; The Favorite
1905—Eugenia; Sarah Dear
1907—Gladiolus Rag; The Nonpareil; Rose Leaf Rag; Searchlight Rag; Heliotrope Bouquet; When Your Hair Is Like the Snow; Snoring Sampson; Lily Queen
1908—Fig Leaf Rag; Pineapple Rag; Sugar Cane; Sensation Rag
1909—Paragon Rag; Wall Street Rag; Solace; Euphonic Sounds
1910—Stoptime Rag
1911—Felicity Rag
1912—Scott Joplin's New Rag
1913—Kismet Rag
1914—Magnetic Rag
1917—Reflection Rag

Other compositions: *Peacherine*; *Augustan Club Waltzes*; *Cleopha Two-Step*; *Bink's Waltz*; *Bethena*; *Leola*; *March Ma-*

jestic; *Eugenia*; *Rose Bud March*; *Country Club Rag*; *Pleasant Moments*; *Frolic of the Bears*; and operas: *Tremonisha*; *A Guest of Honor*

RECORDS
(all LPs)

SCOTT JOPLIN
    Riv (10″)1006 (ragtime rolls; RIs)
    Riv 1025 (ragtime rolls; RIs)
    Biograph BLP-1006Q Scott Joplin Played by Scott Joplin (RIs)
(artist performing Joplin's compositions)
PROF. JOHN W. (KNOCKY) PARKER
    Audiophile AP-71-72 (2-LP set) The Complete Piano Works of Scott Joplin

968. JORDAN, DUKE   p
(IRVING SYDNEY JORDAN)
Born April 1, 1922, Brooklyn, N.Y.

Early bop pianist with advanced chording and good taste. Capable soloist, adept at accompaniment. Began in New York 1939 with various groups; one year with Al Cooper. Middle and late 40s jobs with Charlie Parker off and on, tours with Jazz at the Philharmonic. Freelanced; periods with Stan Getz, Roy Eldridge, Oscar Pettiford. 1956 European tour with Rolf Ericson. Worked in Paris 1959 as pianist-composer. Co-composer of soundtrack for movie LES LIAISONS DANGEREUSES. Active in U.S. in 60s; mostly New York clubs and freelance recording. Semi-active in later years.

RECORDS

JOE HOLIDAY
    De 29707 Love Is a Many-Splendored Thing/Opening Night
STAN GETZ
    Sav 947 Fast
    Sav 966 Stan Getz Along/Stan's Mood
    Sav 967 Slow
    Mer 89025 Stars Fell on Alabama/The Way You Look Tonight
CHARLIE PARKER
    Dial 1021 Little Bo-Peep/Don't Blame Me
ROY ELDRIDGE
    De 23697 Rockin' Chair
    De 23783 It's the Talk of the Town
    De 24119 Lover, Come Back to Me

ALLEN EAGER
    Sav 908 Donald Jay/Meeskite
LPs

DUKE JORDAN
    Pres 7849 Jordu
    (one side) CP 805 (S) East and West of Jazz
    CP 813 (S) Les Liaisons Dangereuses
ALLEN EAGER
    Sav (10″)MG-9015 New Trends of Jazz
    Sav MG-15044 Vol. 2
CHARLIE PARKER
    Sav MG-12014 The Genius of Charlie Parker (1944-8 RIs)
    Baronet 107 The Early Bird (Dial RIs)
    Jazztone J-1214 The Fabulous Bird (Dial RIs)
JOE HOLIDAY
    De DL-8487 Holiday for Jazz
ROLF ERICSON
    EmArcy MG-36106 And His American All-Stars
EDDIE BERT
    Dis (10″)DL-3020
CECIL PAYNE
    Signal S-1203
GENE AMMONS
    Pres 7039 The Happy Blues
STAN GETZ
    Clef (10″)MGC-137
    Clef MGC-143
SONNY STITT
    Pres (10″)126
OSCAR PETTIFORD
    Beth (10″)BCP-1003

969. JORDAN, LOUIS
                              as cl bs vo cm B
Born July 8, 1908, Brinkley, Ark.

Good showman and leader of entertaining combo especially popular in 40s. Played excellent alto sax, clean-cut and swinging; good vocalist on all types of numbers. Attended Arkansas Baptist College. Early work in Arkansas 1929-30. To Philadelphia early 30s; jobs with Charlie Gaines. To New York 1935, first big job two years with Chick Webb beginning mid-1936. August 1938 formed own Tympany Five, began novelty and blues recording. Combo played tight arrangements in shuffle boogie rhythm. Jordan dominant on vocals and alto sax. Although combo stressed novelties, solid rhythm and blues band with good jazz approach. Hits *Knock Me a Kiss, Is You Is or Is You Ain't My Baby?, G.I. Jive, Beware, Choo Choo Ch' Boogie* (biggest seller), *I'm Gonna Move to the Outskirts of Town, Five Guys Named Moe.* Jordan composed many novelties. Band in movies FOLLOW THE BOYS and MEET MISS BOBBY SOCKS (1944), SWING PARADE OF 1946. Starred 1946 in all-Negro movie musical BEWARE, followed by similar movies. At times in 50s Jordan led big band. Good ballad records early 50s. Single in early 60s. Later reorganized combo; tours abroad in 60s. Less active in later 60s and 70s.

RECORDS

CHICK WEBB
De 1115 Gee, But You're Swell
De 1213 It's Swell of You
De 1273 Rusty Hinge
LOUIS JORDAN
De 7675 Honeysuckle Rose/But I'll Be Back
De 8500 Pompton Turnpike/Do You Call That a Buddy?
De 8525 Pinetop's Boogie Woogie/T-Bone Blues
De 8593 Knock Me a Kiss/I'm Gonna Move to the Outskirts of Town
De 8645 The Chicks I Pick Are Slender, Tender and Tall/What's the Use of Getting Sober?
De 8653 Five Guys Named Moe/That'll Just About Knock Me Out
De 8659 Is You Is or Is You Ain't My Baby?/G.I. Jive
De 8670 Caldonia Boogie/Somebody Done Changed the Lock
De 18818 Beware/Don't Let the Sun Catch You Cryin'
De 23610 Choo Choo Ch' Boogie/That Chick's Too Young to Fry
De 23741 Ain't Nobody Here but Us Chickens/Let the Good Times Roll
De 23810 Texas and Pacific/I Like 'Em Fat Like That
De 27806 May Every Day Be Christmas/Bone Dry
De 28335 All of Me/There Goes My Heart

De 28664 Just Like a Butterfly/It's Better to Wait for Love
De 28820 There Must Be a Way/Time Marches On
LOUIS JORDAN-LOUIS ARMSTRONG
De 27212 You Rascal You/Life Is So Peculiar

LPs

LOUIS JORDAN
De DL-75035 Greatest Hits (De RIs)
Mer MG-20242 Somebody Up There Digs Me
Ace of Hearts(E) AH-85 Let the Good Times Roll (De RIs)
Cor CP-50 Let the Good Times Roll (De RIs)

970. JORDAN, STEVE　　　　g vo
Born January 15, 1919, New York, N.Y.

Able, underrated rhythm and solo guitarist, rhythmic singer. Plays only acoustic guitar, never electric. Raised on Long Island. Pupil of guitarist Allan Reuss. First big job with new Will Bradley band 1939 to early 1942. With Artie Shaw briefly. Military service with Saxie Dowell navy band 1942 to early 1945. With Bob Chester, Freddie Slack, Glen Gray. With Stan Kenton 1947, Boyd Raeburn 1948. New York studios early 50s. With Benny Goodman off and on 1953-7. Left music to become clothing, later advertising salesman late 50s and early 60s. Began at Blues Alley, Washington, D. C., with Tommy Gwaltney combo 1965. Gradually came to be featured on musicianly vocals accompanied by own unamplified guitar in Reuss-George Van Eps style. Performed as single at Blues Alley early 70s.

RECORDS

WILL BRADLEY
Co 35443 O Sole Mio (vocal)/What Can I Say After I Say I'm Sorry?
LPs
WILL BRADLEY
Ep LG-1005
WILD BILL DAVISON
Fat Cat FCJ-106 I'll Be a Friend with Pleasure
Fat Cat MM-238 (EP) And the Washingtonians

1207

STEVE JORDAN
  Fat Cat Jazz 119

971. JORDAN, TAFT   t vo B
(JAMES TAFT JORDAN)

Born February 15, 1915, Florence, S.C.

Trumpet star with inventive hot style; good jazz vocalist. Grew up in Norfolk. Began professionally in Philadelphia early 30s with Jimmy Gorham and Doc Hyder. Joined Chick Webb late 1933, remained until Webb's death 1939 except for mid-1936 with Willie Bryant. Continued in band under Ella Fitzgerald until 1942 disbanding. Led band at New York's Savoy Ballroom 1942-3. Joined Duke Ellington mid-1943 for four years. Freelanced in New York 1947-9. With Lucille Dixon band at Savannah Club 1949-53. With Don Redman backing Pearl Bailey. New York studios in 50s. Co-led band with Dick Vance awhile. With Benny Goodman two months mid-1958, including foreign tour and Brussels World's Fair. Freelanced, led groups at intervals late 50s and 60s. Middle and late 60s in pit band for long-running Broadway musical HELLO, DOLLY!, later FOLLIES. Active into 70s.

RECORDS

CHICK WEBB
  Co 2875-D On the Sunny Side of the Street
  Co 2920-D I Can't Dance
  Vo 3101 True/Lonesome Moments
  De 172 On the Sunny Side of the Street/Blue Minor
  De 173 Rhythm Man
  De 483 Don't Be That Way/It's Over Because We're Through
  De 494 Love and Kisses
  De 995 Devoting My Time to You
  De 1220 You Showed Me the Way
  De 1840 Liza (the 8-bar solo)
  De (12″)15039 Hallelujah

WASHBOARD RHYTHM BAND
  Vi 23348 Just Another Dream of You/My Silent Love
  Vi 23357 Depression Stomp
  Vi 24059 Tiger Rag

DUKE ELLINGTON
  Vi 20-2324 Royal Garden Blues

  Vi 20-3135 Suddenly It Jumped/My Honey's Lovin' Arms
  Mus 466 Jam-a-Ditty
  Mus 484 Trumpet No End (Blue Skies)

WILLIE BRYANT
  Bb 6361 All My Life/The Right Somebody to Love

SONNY GREER
  Cap 10028 Mood Indigo/The Mooche

JACK RICHARDS
  Cor 61063 I've Heard That Song Before

TAFT JORDAN & THE MOB
  Me 13352 Night Wind/If the Moon Turns Green
  Me 13365 Devil in the Moon/Louisiana Fairy Tale

LPs

TAFT JORDAN
  Mer MG-20429 The Mood of Taft Jordan
  Pres-Moodsville MVLP-21 Mood Indigo

TAFT JORDAN-AL SEARS-HILTON JEFFERSON
  Pres SVLP-2010 The Swingsville All-Stars

CHICK WEBB
  De DL-9222 A Legend, Vol. 1 (De RIs)
  De DL-9223 King of the Savoy, Vol. 2 (De RIs)
  Co CL-2639 The Immortal Chick Webb: Stompin' at the Savoy (Co, Vo RIs; also four Taft Jordan Me RIs)

FLETCHER HENDERSON ALL-STARS
  Jazztone J-1285 The Big Reunion

DON REDMAN
  Roul R-25070 Dixieland in High Society

972. JOY, JIMMY   cl B
(JAMES MONTE MALONEY)

Bandleader of 20s to 40s known best for hot band mid-20s. Attended University of Texas, led band there. Early hot band played southwest. Later 20s subdued style for hotels. In 30s and 40s good hotel band popular in midwest, particularly Chicago. Theme *Shine On Harvest Moon*. Early 1947 on Chicago radio gave boost to singer Patti Page.

RECORDS

JIMMY JOY

OK 40251 Mama Will Be Gone/ Milenberg Joys
OK 40329 Clarinet Marmalade
OK 40381 China Girl/Indian Dawn
OK 40388 Riverboat Shuffle/Memphis Bound
OK 40420 Wild Jazz/Be Yourself
OK 40494 Red-Hot Henry Brown/ Fallin' Down
OK 40504 Hay Foot, Straw Foot/Everybody Stomp
OK 40539 My Sweet Gal/St. Louis Blues
OK 40627 Stomp It, Mr. Kelly
Br 3960 Today Is Today/Chilly Pom Pom Pee
Br 4640 Harmonica Harry/Can't You Understand?
Vs 8187 Thank Your Stars/Last Night's Gardenias

973. JURGENS, DICK   t cm B

Born January 9, 1910, Sacramento, Calif.

Leader of good hotel and ballroom band especially popular late 30s and 40s. Full ensemble sound; sweet music in excellent taste. First band 1928. Early 30s hit at San Francisco's St. Francis Hotel. Greatest popularity late 30s in Chicago, particularly at Aragon Ballroom. Numerous radio wires. Popular vocalist Eddy Howard; Ronnie Kemper on novelty vocals. Later singers Harry Cool and Buddy Moreno. Beautiful theme *Day Dreams Come True at Night*; Jurgens co-composer. Theme opened with band by-line "Here's that band again!" Arrangements by pianist Lew Quadling, Carl Brandt and Kemper. Biggest hits *My Last Goodbye*, *Cecilia* and *Careless*. Military service, World War II. After discharge organized band, continued into 70s, never regained former popularity. Co-composer of popular songs *Careless*, *If I Knew Then* and *It's a Hundred to One* (1939), *A Million Dreams Ago* (1940), *Elmer's Tune* and *I Guess I'll Be on My Way* (1941), *One Dozen Roses* and *Knit One Purl Two* (1942), *I Won't Be Home Anymore When You Call* (1947).

RECORDS

WINIFRED SHAW with DICK JURGENS ORCHESTRA

De 408 Lullaby of Broadway/I'm Goin' Shoppin' with You

DICK JURGENS

De 269 Wild Honey/Just Once Too Often
Me 61204 Easy to Love/I've Got You Under My Skin
Vo 4196 A Little Kiss at Twilight/ What Goes On Here in My Heart?
Vo 4211 I Wish I Was the Willow/Silver on the Sage
Vo 4677 Little Sir Echo/Red Skies in the Night
Vo 4678 Penny Serenade/Rainbow Valley
Vo 4874 My Last Goodbye/Rumpel-Stilts-Kin
Vo 5181 Faithful Forever/Bluebirds in the Moonlight
Vo 5235 Careless/I Only Want a Buddy
Vo 5288 Do I Love You?/Katie Went to Haiti
Vo 5313 (theme) Day Dreams Come True at Night/Missouri Waltz
Vo 5405 Cecilia/Love Song of Renaldo
Vo 5442 I Concentrate on You/Between You and Me
OK 5628 A Million Dreams Ago/Avalon
OK 5825 There Shall Be No Night/I Want to Live
OK 5962 Melody/The Last Time I Saw Paris
OK 6022 My Silent Love/Night and Day
OK 6094 My Sister and I/Pardon Me for Falling in Love
OK 6456 The Bells of San Raquel/ Cuddle Up a Little Closer
Co 36643 Why Don't You Fall in Love with Me?/Hip Hip Hooray
Co 37342 Cecilia/I Won't Be Home Anymore When You Call
Co 37541 (theme) Day Dreams Come True at Night
Co 38027 On Green Dolphin Street
Mer 5908 Jingle Jangle Jingle/A Faded Summer Love

LPs

DICK JURGENS
Co (10")CL-6072 Dance Parade
Ha HL-7004 Dance Date with Dick
Jurgens (Co RIs)

974. JURMANN, WALTER   cm

Born October 12, 1903, Austria
Died June 24, 1971, Hollywood, Calif.

Vienna composer; to U.S. 1935 to write
for movies. Most work collaborating with
composer Bronislaw Kaper and lyricist
Gus Kahn. Best-known songs *Cosi Cosa,
San Francisco, All God's Chillun Got
Rhythm.*

SONGS
(with related movies)

1935—A NIGHT AT THE OPERA movie (Cosi
Cosa); MUTINY ON THE BOUNTY
movie (Love Song of Tahiti); ES-
CAPADE movie (You're All I Need)

1936—SAN FRANCISCO movie (title song;
The One Love)

1937—A DAY AT THE RACES movie (All
God's Chillun Got Rhythm; A
Message from the Man in the
Moon; Tomorrow Is Another
Day; On Blue Venetian Waters);
THREE SMART GIRLS movie (Some-
one to Care for Me; My Heart Is
Singing)

1938—EVERYBODY SING movie (The One I
Love; others)

1941—NICE GIRL? movie (Thank You,
America)

1942—SEVEN SWEETHEARTS movie (You
and the Waltz and I)

1943—PRESENTING LILY MARS movie
(When I Look at You; Is It Really
Love?); THOUSANDS CHEER movie
(Three Letters in the Mailbox)

974A. KABIBBLE, ISH　　vo t B
(MERWYN BOGUE)

Comic with Kay Kyser band mid-30s to mid-40s. Capable trumpet section man. Featured on novelty vocals, handled comedy lines on Kyser radio shows. Known for cornball delivery, bang-styled haircut. In Kyser movies including THAT'S RIGHT — YOU'RE WRONG (1939), YOU'LL FIND OUT (1940), PLAYMATES (1942), AROUND THE WORLD (1944). Later 40s worked as single, led big band 1949 in Los Angeles. Early and mid-50s led entertaining combo The Shy Guys. Left show business. Early 70s vice president of World Marketing-Hawaii Ltd., sold lots in Desert Carmel area in Arizona, settled in Hawaii.

RECORDS

KAY KYSER
Br 7453 Ish Kabibble
Br 7555 He's a Devil in His Own Home Town
Br 7701 You'd Be Surprised
Br 7826 A Horse Ain't Got Much Sense
Br 8149 So You Left Me for the Leader of a Swing Band
Br 8165 Hi-Yo, Silver!
Br 8201 When the Circus Came to Town
Br 8358 Three Little Fishies
Co 35248 Hello, Mr. Kringle
Co 35368 Friendship
Co 35411 Tie Me to Your Apron Strings Again

Co 35761 The Bad Humor Man

975. KAHAL, IRVING　　yr vo
Born March 5, 1903, Houtzdale, Pa.
Died February 7, 1942, New York, N.Y.

Successful lyricist of 20s and 30s; songs for stage and movies. Best-known songs *Let a Smile Be Your Umbrella; Wedding Bells (Are Breaking Up That Old Gang of Mine); You Brought a New Kind of Love to Me; Moonlight Saving Time; When I Take My Sugar to Tea; By a Waterfall; I Can Dream, Can't I?; The Night Is Young and You're So Beautiful; I'll Be Seeing You.* Chief collaborator composer Sammy Fain. At early age sang in vaudeville; period with Gus Edwards troupe. Settled in Hollywood early 30s.

SONGS
(with related shows)

1927—I Ain't That Kind of a Baby; I Left My Sugar Standing in the Rain; It Was Only a Sun Shower
1928—Let a Smile Be Your Umbrella; There's Something About a Rose
1929—EARL CARROLL'S SKETCH BOOK stage show (Don't Hang Your Dreams on a Rainbow); Wedding Bells (Are Breaking Up That Old Gang of Mine)
1930—THE BIG POND movie (You Brought a New Kind of Love to Me; Mia Cara)
1931—EVERYBODY'S WELCOME stage show (Even as You and I; Is Rhythm

Necessary?); Moonlight Saving Time; A Little Less of Moonlight; When I Take My Sugar to Tea

1932—THE CROONER movie (Three's a Crowd)

1933—FOOTLIGHT PARADE movie (By a Waterfall; Sittin' on a Backyard Fence; Ah, the Moon Is Here); COLLEGE COACH movie (Lonely Lane)

1934—HAROLD TEEN movie (How Do I Know It's Sunday?; Simple and Sweet; Two Little Flies on a Lump of Sugar); FASHIONS OF 1934 movie (Spin a Little Web of Dreams); MANDALAY movie (When Tomorrow Comes); HAPPINESS AHEAD movie (Beauty Must Be Loved)

1935—SWEET MUSIC movie (Ev'ry Day; There's a Different "You" in Your Heart); GOIN' TO TOWN movie (Now I'm a Lady); Ballad in Blue

1936—Lazy Weather; The Night Is Young and You're So Beautiful

1937—Don't You Know or Don't You Care?; Bluebonnet; You're Here, You're There

1938—RIGHT THIS WAY stage show (I Can Dream, Can't I?; I'll Be Seeing You)

1940—BOYS AND GIRLS TOGETHER stage show (Such Stuff as Dreams Are Made Of; I Want to Live)

1941—SONS O' FUN stage show (songs unimportant); Love Song of Renaldo

1946—NO LEAVE, NO LOVE movie (Old Sad Eyes)

976. KAHN, ART   p B

Pianist-bandleader, early 20s to early 40s. Semi-hot groups in 20s, based mostly in Chicago. 30s bands hotel-styled; good ensemble sound with occasional swing. Good recordings early 30s; Benny Goodman, Bunny Berigan, other good jazzmen on some. Kahn's name used as pseudonym on some records. By mid-40s quit as bandleader, opened Hollywood studio for arranging and vocal coaching.

RECORDS

ART KAHN
Co 16-D Sobbin' Blues/Bit by Bit,

You're Breaking My Heart
Co 109-D There's Yes Yes in Your Eyes/Don't Mind the Rain
Co 310-D Some of These Days/Lucky Kentucky
Co 408-D The Co-ed/Back Home in Illinois
Co 624-D The Hobo's Prayer/What a Man
Co 1097-D Worryin'/Swanee Shore (piano solos)
OK 40857 When Day Is Done/Sometimes I'm Happy (piano, with EDDIE LANG-guitar)
Me 12090 I'm Happy When You're Happy/You Didn't Have to Tell Me
Me 12207 Dancing in the Dark/High and Low
Me 12219 Many Happy Returns of the Day/There's No Other Girl
Me 12284 An Evening in Caroline/By the Sycamore Tree
Me 12309 When We're Alone/All of Me
Me 12322 Love, You Funny Thing/Somebody Loves You
Me 12377 Tell Me Why You Smile, Mona Lisa/With Summer Coming On
Me 12463 Sweethearts Forever/Three's a Crowd
Me 12926 Night on the Water/If I Didn't Care
Pe 15709 Baby/Look Who's Here
Pe 15730 42nd Street/Shuffle Off to Buffalo
Pe 15768 Pettin' in the Park/Gold Diggers' Song
Pe 15841 I'd Be Telling a Lie/Annie Doesn't Live Here Anymore

977. KAHN, GUS   lyr

Born November 6, 1886, Coblenz, Germany
Died October 8, 1941, Beverly Hills, Calif.

Leading lyricist. Prolific career included songs for stage and movies. Most famous hits *Memories*; *Pretty Baby*; *Ain't We Got Fun*; *Carolina in the Morning*; *My Buddy*; *Toot Toot Tootsie*; *Charley, My Boy*; *Coquette*; *I'll See You in My Dreams*; *It Had* to Be You; Chlo-e; Nobody's Sweetheart; The One I Love; I Never Knew; Love Me or Leave Me; Yes, Sir, That's My Baby; Makin' Whoopee; Liza; The Waltz You Saved for Me; Dream a Little Dream of Me; One Night of Love; Thanks a Million; San Francisco; Josephine; You Stepped Out of a Dream. Brought to U.S. by parents 1891, grew up in Chicago. Began composing after high school; little success at first. First break teaming with composer Egbert Van Alstyne. Early 20s in New York wrote hits with top composer Walter Donaldson. Team wrote notable score for WHOOPEE stage show 1928. Kahn also collaborated with composer Isham Jones on several 20s hits. Composer Grace LeBoy married Kahn, collaborated with him on several songs. Other collaborators Richard Whiting, Al Jolson, Buddy DeSylva, Raymond Egan, Ted Fio Rito, Ernie Erdman, Neil Moret, Vincent Youmans, George and Ira Gershwin, Harry Akst, Harry Woods, Edward Eliscu, Victor Schertzinger, Harry Warren, Sigmund Romberg, Bronislaw Kaper, Walter Jurmann, Arthur Johnston. 1951 movie I'LL SEE YOU IN MY DREAMS based on life and songs of Kahn, portrayed by Danny Thomas.

SONGS
(with related shows)

1906—My Dreamy China Lady
1908—I Wish I Had a Girl; It Looks Like a Big Night Tonight
1913—Moonlight on the Mississippi; Sunshine and Roses
1914—Everybody Rag with Me; On the Good Ship Mary Ann
1915—Memories
1916—Pretty Baby; Just a Word of Sympathy
1917—Sailin' Away on the Henry Clay; 'n Everything; Some Sunday Morning; Where the Morning Glories Grow
1918—SINBAD stage show (I'll Say She Does)
1919—ZIEGFELD'S MIDNIGHT FROLICS stage show (Baby); My Isle of Golden Dreams; You Ain't Heard Nothin' Yet; Moonlight on the Nile; Your Eyes Have Told Me So

1921—Ain't We Got Fun; Biminy Bay; Sunset Land
1922—THE PASSING SHOW OF 1922 stage show (Carolina in the Morning); Broken Hearted Melody; Dixie Highway; My Buddy; On the Alamo; Toot Toot Tootsie
1923—Beside a Babbling Brook; Mindin' My Business; No, No, Nora; Sittin' in a Corner; Swingin' Down the Lane; When Lights Are Low
1924—Charley, My Boy; Gotta Getta Girl; I'll See You in My Dreams; Spain; It Had to Be You; The Little Old Clock on the Mantel; Nobody's Sweetheart; The One I Love; Where Is That Old Girl of Mine?; Why Couldn't It Be Poor Little Me?; Worried
1925—HOLKA POLKA stage show (unsuccessful); Alone at Last; Dreamer of Dreams; Got No Time; I Never Knew; I Wonder Where My Baby Is Tonight; Isn't She the Sweetest Thing?; Kentucky's Way of Sayin' Good Mornin'; Old Pal; The Midnight Waltz; My Sweetie Turned Me Down; Sometime; That Certain Party; Ukulele Lady; When I Dream of the Last Waltz with You; When You and I Were Seventeen; Yes, Sir, That's My Baby
1926—KITTY'S KISSES stage show (Kitty's Kisses; I Love to Dance; I'm in Love; Early in the Morning; many others); Barcelona; For My Sweetheart; But I Do—You Know I Do; Just a Bird's-Eye View of My Old Kentucky Home; Let's Talk About My Sweetie; Oh, If I Only Had You; There Ain't No Maybe in My Baby's Eyes
1927—Baby Feet Go Pitter Patter; He's the Last Word; Collette; Dixie Vagabond; Chlo-e; Persian Rug; Sing Me a Baby Song; If You See Sally; My Ohio Home; There's One Little Girl Who Loves Me
1928—WHOOPEE stage show (Makin' Whoopee; I'm Bringing a Red Red Rose; Love Me or Leave Me; My Baby Just Cares for Me; Come West, Little Girl, Come West); Beloved; Coquette; I'm Sorry, Sal-

ly; Indian Cradle Song; Ready for the River; Last Night I Dreamed You Kissed Me; Ten Little Miles from Town; Where the Shy Little Violets Grow

1929—SHOW GIRL stage show (Liza; others); Here We Are

1930—WHOOPEE movie (original stage score); Hangin' on the Garden Gate; Sweetheart of My Student Days; Around the Corner; Where the Golden Daffodils Grow; The One I Love Can't Be Bothered with Me

1931—Dream a Little Dream of Me; Guilty; The Hour of Parting; I'm Through with Love; Now That You're Gone; Old Playmate; The Waltz You Saved for Me; You Gave Me Everything but Love

1932—Goofus; I'll Never Be the Same; Tango Americano; A Little Street Where Old Friends Meet; Lovable; A Million Dreams; Was I to Blame?; So at Last It's Come to This; You're Telling Me; The Voice in the Old Village Choir

1933—FLYING DOWN TO RIO movie (Flying Down to Rio; Carioca; Orchids in the Moonlight; Music Makes Me); Sweetheart Darlin'; What Have We Got to Lose?; You've Got Everything

1934—BOTTOMS UP movie (Waitin' at the Gate for Katy); CARAVAN movie (Ha-Cha-Cha; Wine Song; Happy, I Am Happy); HOLLYWOOD PARTY (I've Had My Moments); KID MILLIONS movie (An Earful of Music; Okay, Toots; When My Ship Comes In; Your Head on My Shoulder); ONE NIGHT OF LOVE movie (title song); STINGAREE movie (Tonight Is Mine); Dancing in the Moonlight; Riptide; How Can It Be a Beautiful Day?; Sleepy Head

1935—THE GIRL FRIEND movie (Two Together; What Is This Power?; Welcome to Napoleon; Napoleon's Exile); LOVE ME FOREVER movie (title song); THANKS A MILLION movie (Thanks a Million; I'm Sittin' High on a Hill-top; Sugar

Plum; New Orleans; Sing, Brother, Sing; A Pocketful of Sunshine); MUTINY ON THE BOUNTY movie (Love Song of Tahiti) ESCAPADE movie (You're All I Need); Clouds; Footloose and Fancy Free

1936—LET'S SING AGAIN movie (title song); HER MASTER'S VOICE movie (With All My Heart); SAN FRANCISCO movie (San Francisco; The One Love); ROSE-MARIE movie (Just for You; Pardon Me, Madame); Gone

1937—A DAY AT THE RACES movie (All God's Chillun Got Rhythm; A Message from the Man in the Moon; Tomorrow Is Another Day; On Blue Italian Waters); THREE SMART GIRLS movie (Someone to Care for Me; My Heart Is Singing); THEY GAVE HIM A GUN movie (A Love Song of Long Ago); CAPTAINS COURAGEOUS movie (Don't Cry, Little Fish; Ooh, What a Terrible Man!); Josephine

1938—EVERYBODY SING movie (The One I Love; others); GIRL OF THE GOLDEN WEST movie (There's a Brand New Song in Town; Shadows on the Moon; Who Are We to Say?; The Golden West; others)

1939—HONOLULU movie (Honolulu; This Night; The Leader Don't Like Music); How Strange

1940—LILLIAN RUSSELL movie (Blue Lovebird); SPRING PARADE movie (Waltzing in the Clouds)

1941—ZIEGFELD GIRL movie (You Stepped Out of a Dream); Day Dreaming

978. KAHN, ROGER WOLFE

as cm B

Born October 19, 1907, Morristown, N.J.
Died July 12, 1962, New York, N.Y.

Leader of good semi-hot bands of late 20s and early 30s; never attained deserved prominence. Son of millionaire Otto Kahn, received financial aid at times from father. Hence orchestra sometimes dubbed The Million Dollar Band. Began as bandleader early 20s. Sometimes played alto sax, could play many instruments. Band based mostly in New York; good runs at Biltmore Hotel in 20s. In mid-20s also owned booking office and night club. Some success as composer; wrote *Crazy Rhythm* and *Imagination* for 1928 Broadway musical HERE'S HOWE. Other songs *All by My Ownsome, Following You Around, Good Time Charlie, I Love You Sincerely, Gentlemen Prefer Blues, Nobody Loves Me, Life as a Twosome, He's Mine, No Place Like Home.* Extensive recording beginning mid-20s. Good personnel at times included Joe Venuti (v), Eddie Lang (g), Arthur Schutt (p), Miff Mole (tb), Manny Klein (t), Alfie Evans (as), Arnold Brilhart (as), Babe Russin (ts). Early Jack Teagarden solo on Kahn record *She's a Great Great Girl.* Band on radio, sometimes on regular shows. Excellent 1932 sweet-swing band included great clarinetist Artie Shaw, other good jazzmen, produced six outstanding records. Continued as bandleader into late 30s, at times inactive. Pilot long interested in aviation, became aviation consultant in New York; test and research flying. World War II test pilot and other aeronautical activities.

RECORDS

ROGER WOLFE KAHN
Vi 19616 Hot-Hot-Hottentot/Yearning
Vi 19935 Song of the Flame/A Cup of Coffee, a Sandwich and You
Vi 19942 Baby/Lantern of Love
Vi 20071 Cross Your Heart/Mountain Greenery
Vi 20327 Clap Yo' Hands
Vi 20573 Following You Around/I Can't Believe That You're in Love with Me
Vi 20599 Sometimes I'm Happy
Vi 20634 Just the Same
Vi 20717 Calling/Where the Wild Wild Flowers Grow
Vi 21326 She's a Great Great Girl
Vi 21368 Crazy Rhythm/Imagination
Vi 21801 A Room with a View/Dance, Little Lady
Br 4479 Liza/Do What You Do
Br 4571 Through/Then You've Never Been Blue
Br 4600 Great Day/Without a Song

Br 4614 Don't Ever Leave Me/'Twas Not So Long Ago
Br 4742 Exactly Like You/On the Sunny Side of the Street
Co 2653-D Lazy Day/My Silent Love
Co 2662-D Tell Me Why You Smile, Mona Lisa/There I Go Dreaming Again
Co 2695-D I Can't Believe It's True/You've Got Me in the Palm of Your Hand
Co 2697-D Another Night Alone/Sheltered by the Stars, Cradled by the Moon
Co 2722-D A Shine on Your Shoes/It Don't Mean a Thing
Co 2726-D Fit as a Fiddle/Just a Little Home for the Old Folks

979. KAHN, TINY   d vb ar cm
(NORMAN KAHN)
Born 1924, New York, N.Y.
Died August 9, 1953, Martha's Vineyard, Mass.

Outstanding modern drummer-arranger; career cut short by fatal heart attack. With Kai Winding combo 1948, Chubby Jackson big band 1949. In 1950 with Herbie Fields and George Auld, 1951 Stan Getz. With Elliot Lawrence 1952-3 including daily CBS radio show. Arranged for many bands, including *Over the Rainbow* for Charlie Barnet, *Leo the Lion* for Woody Herman, *Tiny's Blues* and *Father Knickerbopper* for Jackson, many for Lawrence. Composed jazz numbers for leading bands.

RECORDS

RED RODNEY
Key 670 Elevation/Fine and Dandy
GEORGE AULD
Roost 523 New Air Mail Special/Out of Nowhere
CHUBBY JACKSON
Co 38451 Godchild/Father Knickerbopper
Co 38623 Tiny's Blues/All Wrong
JOHN HARDEE
SIW 503 Boppin' in B Flat/Prelude to a Kiss
THE FOUR BOPS
SIW 507 Cobblestones/Man with a Horn

SERGE CHALOFF
Sav 978 Gabardine and Serge
LPs
STAN GETZ
Roost (10″)407
Roost (10″)411
Roost (10″)420 Jazz at Storyville, vol. 3
GEORGE AULD
Roost (10″)403
(miscellaneous artists)
EmArcy MG-36016 Advance Guard of the 40s
EmArcy (10″)MG-26001 The Young at Bop
(as arranger)
ELLIOT LAWRENCE
Fan 3-219 Plays Tiny Kahn and Johnny Mandel Arrangements

980. KALLEN, KITTY   vo
Born 1922, Philadelphia, Pa.

Good vocalist with big bands and as single; active in 40s and 50s. As youngster on local Children's Hour radio show six years. At 14 sang with Jan Savitt on local radio, worked with bands of Bob Golden and Clem Williams. Joined Jack Teagarden August 1939 till early 1940. On west coast radio early 40s. With Jimmy Dorsey 1943-4, later 1944 joined Harry James about a year. Middle and late 40s on radio shows of Danny Kaye, David Rose, Alec Templeton, others. On early TV. Career waned early 50s, lost singing voice awhile. Came back with 1954 hit record *Little Things Mean a Lot*, revived career for several years.

RECORDS
JACK TEAGARDEN
Co 35215 I'll Remember
Co 35224 I'm Takin' My Time with You/I Wanna Hat with Cherries
Co 35233 Two Blind Loves/Hawaii Sang Me to Sleep
Co 35245 At Least You Could Say Hello/Stop Kicking My Heart Around
Co 35252 A Table in a Corner/So Many Times
Vs 8196 You, You Darlin'/The Moon and the Willow Tree
Vs 8202 Love for Sale/Wham

JIMMY DORSEY
De 18582 When They Ask About You
De 18900 That Wonderful Worrisome Feeling
BOBBY SHERWOOD
Cap 123 Moonlight Becomes You
HARRY JAMES
Co 36758 I'm Beginning to See the Light
Co 36778 I Don't Care Who Knows It/Guess I'll Hang My Tears Out to Dry
Co 36794 I Wish I Knew
Co 36833 I'll Buy That Dream
Co 36838 It's Been a Long Long Time
Co 36867 Waitin' for the Train to Come In
Co 39715 To Be Loved by You/When I Dream
Co 39765 Like the Moon Above You
KITTY KALLEN
Mus 15068 Just the Other Day/Should I Tell You?
Si 15074 Just My Luck/Why Does It Get So Late So Early?
Mer 5291 Happy Talk/I'm Gonna Wash That Man Right Outa My Hair
Mer 5700 The Old Soft Shoe
De 28813 Heartless Love/Lonely
De 29037 Little Things Mean a Lot/I Don't Think You Love Me Anymore
KITTY KALLEN-RICHARD HAYES
Mer 5586 I Don't Want to Love You/ Aba Daba Honeymoon
LPs
KITTY KALLEN
Co CL-1409 If I Give My Heart to You
Vi LPM-2640 My Coloring Book
De DL-8397 It's a Lonesome Old Town
Movietone S-72026 (S) Delightfully Kitty Kallen
Mer (10″)MGW-12241 Sings Hits

981. KALMAN, EMMERICH   cm B
Born October 24, 1882, Siofok, Hungary
Died October 30, 1953, Paris, France

Composer for Broadway musicals of scores first written for productions in other countries. Best-known song *Play*

Gypsies, Dance Gypsies in hit show COUNT-ESS MARITZA (1926). Educated at Musical Academy of Budapest. Composed symphonic works, conducted orchestras performing them. First operetta HERBST-MANOEVER in 1908; performed in U.S. 1909 as THE GAY HUSSARS. Scores for other shows first performed abroad. Collaborators in adapting scores for U.S. included Otto Harbach, Oscar Hammerstein II, Buddy DeSylva, P. G. Wodehouse, Harry B. Smith. Kalman conducted concerts in Amsterdam, London, Vienna, Budapest, Copenhagen and at Kalman festival in Italy. First U.S. trip 1940, conducted concert of own works with Toscanini NBC Orchestra. Many honors and awards including Great Golden Austrian Cross of Merit, Swedish Nordstar Decoration, Danish Dannebrog Order, French Order of Legion of Honor, Hungarian Distinguished Service Cross. Lived many years in Vienna, later in Paris.

SONGS
(with related shows)

1909—THE GAY HUSSARS stage show (The Gay Hussars; Dreaming of Love; Heart to Heart; many others)

1914—SARI stage show (Love's Own Sweet Song; My Faithful Stradivari; Love Has Wings; Softly Thro' the Summer Night; Ha-Za-Za)

1916—HER SOLDIER BOY stage show (Amsterdam; He's Coming Home; Golden Sunshine; many others); MISS SPRINGTIME stage show (Throw Me a Rose; This Is the Existence; Life Is a Game; A Little Bid for Sympathy; The Garden of Romance; Sunrise)

1917—THE RIVIERA GIRL stage show (The Lilt of a Gypsy Strain; Life's a Tale; Just a Voice to Call Me Dear; many others)

1922—THE YANKEE PRINCESS stage show (Roses, Lovely Roses; In the Starlight; I Still Can Dream; many others)

1926—COUNTESS MARITZA stage show (Play Gypsies, Dance Gypsies; Come at the Call of Love; I'll Keep On Dreaming; The One I'm Looking For; many others)

1927—THE CIRCUS PRINCESS stage show (Dear Eyes That Haunt Me; Joy Bells; The Hussars' Song; many others); GOLDEN DAWN stage show (We Two; When I Crack My Whip; Africa; Jungle Shadows; Here in the Dark; Consolation)

1930—GOLDEN DAWN movie (original stage score)

1945—MARINKA stage show (The Cab Song; Treat a Woman Like a Drum; Sigh by Night; One Touch of Vienna; One Last Love Song; If I Never Waltz Again)

982. KALMAR, BERT   lyr

Born February 16, 1884, New York, N.Y.
Died September 18, 1947, Los Angeles, Calif.

Successful lyricist, collaborated mostly with composer Harry Ruby. Songs for stage and movies. Best-known songs *Oh! What a Pal Was Mary*; *Who's Sorry Now?*; *Thinking of You*; *Nevertheless*; *I Wanna Be Loved by You*; *I Love You So Much*; *Three Little Words*. Scores for Broadway musicals, notably HELEN OF TROY, NEW YORK (1923), THE RAMBLERS (1926), FIVE O'CLOCK GIRL (1927), GOOD BOY and ANIMAL CRACKERS (1928), THE HIGH KICKERS (1941). Other collaborators composers Ted Snyder, Oscar Hammerstein II, Herbert Stothart, Harry Tierney, Harry Akst, Con Conrad, Edgar Leslie, Fred Ahlert, Pete Wendling. Ran away from home at ten, worked with tent show as magician. Comedian many years in vaudeville, wrote material for his and other vaudeville acts. Little success at composing until teamed with Harry Ruby. After writing for Broadway 1918-28, team to Hollywood for early sound movies. Biggest hit *Three Little Words* in heralded movie CHECK AND DOUBLE CHECK starring popular Amos 'n' Andy. Kalmar and Ruby became friends with Marx Brothers writing stage score for ANIMAL CRACKERS (1928), later wrote songs for several early Marx movies. Groucho later used team's *Hooray for*

Captain Spaulding as theme for radio and TV shows. Kalmar wrote scenarios for movies LOOK FOR THE SILVER LINING, BRIGHT LIGHTS, DUCK SOUP, others. Last song *A Kiss to Build a Dream On* popularized in 1951 movie THE STRIP four years after death. Important 1950 movie THREE LITTLE WORDS based on life and songs of Kalmar and Ruby; roles played by Fred Astaire and Red Skelton. Movie revived team's songs.

SONGS
(with related shows)

1911—In the Land of Harmony
1912—The Ghost of the Violin
1913—Where Did You Get That Girl?
1915—Hello, Hawaii, How Are You?; I've Been Floating Down the Old Green River
1918—LADIES FIRST stage show (What a Girl Can Do)
1919—Oh! What a Pal Was Mary; Take Your Girlie to the Movies; You Said It; All the Quakers Are Shoulder Shakers
1920—BROADWAY BREVITIES OF 1920 stage show (We've Got the Stage Door Blues); ZIEGFELD FOLLIES OF 1920 stage show (I'm a Vamp from East Broadway); Timbuctoo; So Long, Oo-long; Where Do They Go When They Row, Row, Row?
1921—MIDNIGHT ROUNDERS OF 1921 stage show (My Sunny Tennessee); She's Mine, All Mine!; Mandy 'n' Me; Snoops the Lawyer
1922—GREENWICH VILLAGE FOLLIES OF 1922 stage show (Beautiful Girls); I Gave You Up Just Before You Threw Me Down
1923—HELEN OF TROY, NEW YORK stage show (Helen of Troy, New York; I Like a Big Town; Happy Ending; It Was Meant to Be); Who's Sorry Now?
1924—NO OTHER GIRL stage show (songs unimportant)
1925—PUZZLES OF 1925 stage show (The Doo Dab)
1926—THE RAMBLERS stage show (All Alone Monday; Alma Mater; Just One Kiss; Any Little Tune; You Smiled at Me) TWINKLE, TWINKLE stage show (Sweeter Than You; Whistle)
1927—FIVE O'CLOCK GIRL stage show (Thinking of You; Up in the Clouds; Happy Go Lucky); LUCKY stage show (The Same Old Moon; Dancing the Devil Away)
1928—GOOD BOY stage show (Good Boy; I Wanna Be Loved by You; Some Sweet Someone); ANIMAL CRACKERS stage show (Watching the Clouds Roll By; Who's Been Listening to My Heart?; Hooray for Captain Spaulding)
1930—CHECK AND DOUBLE CHECK movie (Three Little Words); THE CUCKOOS movie (I Love You So Much; Dancing the Devil Away; Wherever You Are); ANIMAL CRACKERS movie (new song: Why Am I So Romantic?; plus songs from original stage score: Watching the Clouds Roll By; Hooray for Captain Spaulding); TOP SPEED stage show and movie (Keep Your Undershirt On; What Would I Care?)
1931—I'm So Afraid of You; Nevertheless
1932—HORSE FEATHERS movie (Everyone Says "I Love You"); THE KID FROM SPAIN movie (Look What You've Done; What a Perfect Combination; In the Moonlight)
1933—DUCK SOUP movie (songs unimportant)
1934—HIPS HIPS HOORAY movie (Keep On Doin' What You're Doin'; Tired of It All; Keep Romance Alive)
1935—KENTUCKY KERNELS movie (One Little Kiss); THANKS A MILLION movie (What a Beautiful Night)
1937—When You Dream About Hawaii; Goodnight Kisses; Who Put the Moon in the Sky?
1939—STORY OF VERNON AND IRENE CASTLE movie (Only When You're in My Arms); Ain'tcha Comin' Out?
1941—THE HIGH KICKERS stage show (You're on My Mind; A Panic in Panama; Time to Sing; Waltzing in the Moonlight)
1947—The Egg and I

1951—THE STRIP movie (A Kiss to Build a Dream On)

Other songs: *He Sits Around*; *Take Me to the Land of Jazz*; *Come On and Play Wiz Me*; *The Sheik of Avenue B*; *Show Me a Rose* (silly song often featured by Groucho Marx through the years); *Omaha, Nebraska*

983. KAMINSKY, MAX   t B

Born September 7, 1908, Brockton, Mass.

Trumpet star with driving style. Played in swing bands, hit peak in 40s with dixieland groups. Began with bands in Boston around 1924. With George Wettling in Chicago 1928. With Bud Freeman and Red Nichols in New York 1929, toured with latter. In early 30s with Leo Reisman and Jack Marshard's society band in Boston. In New York 1934-6 jobbed with Joe Venuti, Eddie Elkins, Jacques Renard, Reisman. With Tommy Dorsey most of 1936. In 1937 brief periods with Pee Wee Russell, Ray Noble, Mezz Mezzrow. With Artie Shaw first half 1938, later in year with Pee Wee Russell and Dorsey. With Bud Freeman combo 1939-40. With Tony Pastor 1940-1, Artie Shaw 1941, Alvino Rey and Joe Marsala 1942. 1942-3 in Artie Shaw's navy band. After discharge led combo in New York most of 1944, in Boston late 1945-6. With Art Hodes, Eddie Condon, other leading dixieland groups. In demand for jobs and records. More freelancing in 50s. European tour 1957 with Jack Teagarden-Earl Hines group, 1958 Asian tour with Teagarden. Based in New York in 60s, freelanced and led groups at intervals. In late 60s and early 70s many jobs at Jimmy Ryan's. Led combo at Gaslight Club 1972, Occasional TV spots on jazz shows like 1973 Timex special. Wrote autobiography *My Life in Jazz*.

RECORDS

ADRIAN'S RAMBLERS (Adrian Rollini)
    Br 6877 I've Got a Warm Spot in My Heart for You/Why Don't You Practice What You Preach?
    Br 6889 I Wish I Were Twins/The Better to Love You

CHOCOLATE DANDIES
    OK 41568 Krazy Kapers
    Co 2875-D I Never Knew
    De 18255 Blue Interlude
TOMMY DORSEY
    Vi 25314 Rhythm Saved the World/At the Codfish Ball (both CLAMBAKE SEVEN)
    Vi 25352 San Francisco
    Vi 25363 That's a Plenty
    Vi 25482 Keepin' Out of Mischief Now
    Vi 25487 Head Over Heels in Love
    Vi 25496 Maple Leaf Rag
LEE WILEY
    LMS 281 My One and Only
    LMS 283 'S Wonderful/Sam and Delilah
BUD FREEMAN
    Bb 10386 China Boy/The Eel
    De 2781 Satanic Blues/The Sail Fish
    Co Album C-40 (78s) Comes Jazz
ART HODES
    BN (12")34 Sweet Georgia Brown/Sugar Foot Stomp
    BN (12")35 Squeeze Me/Bugle Call Rag
    BN (12")45 Apex Blues/Shake That Thing
EDDIE EDWARDS
    CMS 610 Tiger Rag/Barnyard Blues
    CMS 612 Ostrich Walk/Lazy Daddy
JACK TEAGARDEN
    CMS (12")1521 Rockin' Chair/Pitchin' a Bit Short
EDDIE CONDON
    Co 35680 The Eel/Home Cooking
    Co 36009 Tennessee Twilight
    De 18040 Nobody's Sweetheart/Friar's Point Shuffle
    CMS 542 Don't Leave Me Daddy/Fidgety Feet
WILLIE "THE LION" SMITH
    B&W 24 Muskrat Ramble/Bugle Call Rag
GEORG BRUNIS
    CMS 606 I Used to Love You/I'm Gonna Sit Right Down and Write Myself a Letter
    CMS 607 In the Shade of the Old Apple Tree/D.D.T. Blues
MAX KAMINSKY
    CMS 561 Eccentric/Guess Who's in Town

CMS 595 Love Nest/Everybody Loves
My Baby
Br 80124 Dippermouth Blues/Old
Fashioned Love
Br 80137 Someday Sweetheart/Wrap
Your Troubles in Dreams
Cen 4003 Black and Blue/Havin' a
Ball

LPs

MAX KAMINSKY
Jazztone J-1208 Chicago Style
CMS FL-30013 Dixieland Horn
CMS (10″)FL-20019 (Condon and
Kaminsky)
Westminster 6125 Ambassador of Jazz
UA 3174
Vi (10″)LJM-3003
BUD FREEMAN
Ha HL-7046 All Star Jazz (Co RIs)
MEZZ MEZZROW
"X" (10″)LVA-3015 Swing Session (Vi
RIs)
TONY PARENTI
Jazzology 31 A Night at Jimmy Ryan's
BENNY CARTER
Pres 7643 (early RIs)
ART HODES
BN 7004 And His Chicagoans (BN
RIs)

984. KANE, HELEN   vo
(HELEN SCHRODER)

Born c. 1904
Died September 1966

Baby-voiced singer of late 20s and early
30s famed for "Boop-boop-a-doop"
phrase. Adept at inflections and phrasing.
Distinctive style widely imitated, as in
Betty Boop film cartoons. Early career in
vaudeville and night clubs. Virtually unknown when appeared with Paul Ash
band at New York's Paramount Theatre;
big hit. In successful Broadway shows A
NIGHT IN SPAIN (1927), GOOD BOY (1928).
In short-run show SHADY LADY (1933). To
Hollywood 1929 at height of fame. Featured in NOTHING BUT THE TRUTH (1929),
SWEETIE (1929), POINTED HEELS (1930),
DANGEROUS NAN MCGREW (1930), HEADS
UP (1930); one number in all-star extravaganza PARAMOUNT ON PARADE
(1930). Voice on soundtrack of early
movie cartoons; made shorts. Career de-

clined when Hollywood cut back on movie musicals 1931-2. In clubs and theatres
at intervals during 30s. Husband entertainer Dan Healy; couple in show GOOD
BOY. Helen portrayed by Debbie Reynolds in important 1950 movie THREE
LITTLE WORDS; Helen's singing dubbed.
Helen's career revived briefly.

RECORDS

HELEN KANE
Vi 21557 Get Out and Get Under the
Moon/That's My Weakness Now
Vi 21830 Don't Be Like That/Me and
the Man in the Moon
Vi 21863 I Want to Be Bad/Button Up
Your Overcoat
Vi 21917 Do Something/That's Why
I'm Happy
Vi 22080 He's So Unusual / I'd Do
Anything for You
Vi 22192 Ain'tcha?/I Have to Have
You
Vi 22397 Thank Your Father/I'd Go
Barefoot All Winter
Vi 22407 Dangerous Nan McGrew/I
Owe You
Vi 22475 My Man Is on the Make/I've
Got "It"
Vi 22520 If I Knew You Better/
Readin' Ritin' Rhythm
Co 39154 I Taut I Taw a Puddy-Tat/
Beanbag Song
MGM 30241 I Wanna Be Loved by
You

LPs

(miscellaneous artists; one song)
Vi LCT-1112 Old Curiosity Shop (RIs)
(movie soundtrack; one song)
Metro M-615 THREE LITTLE WORDS

985. KAPER, BRONISLAW   cm ar p B
Born February 5, 1902, Warsaw, Poland

Important composer for movies beginning mid-30s. Best-known songs *Cosi
Cosa*; *San Francisco*; *All God's Chillun
Got Rhythm*; *On Green Dolphin Street*;
Hi-Lili, Hi-Lo. Educated at Warsaw Conservatory of Music. Active composing
and conducting in Warsaw, Berlin, Vienna, London, Paris. Wrote concert pieces,
music for movies abroad. Successful in
U.S. writing songs and background music

for movies; also arranging. Conductor or musical director of some movies. Wrote score, adapting Chopin's music, for 1945 Broadway show POLONAISE. Wrote music for TV, including theme for The F.B.I. show. Collaborators included Walter Jurmann, Gus Kahn, Paul Francis Webster.

SONGS
(with related shows)

1935—A NIGHT AT THE OPERA movie (Cosi Cosa); MUTINY ON THE BOUNTY movie (Love Song of Tahiti); ESCAPADE movie (You're All I Need)

1936—SAN FRANCISCO movie (San Francisco; The One Love)

1937—A DAY AT THE RACES movie (All God's Chillun Got Rhythm; A Message from the Man in the Moon; Tomorrow Is Another Day; On Blue Venetian Waters); THREE SMART GIRLS movie (Someone to Care for Me; My Heart Is Singing)

1938—EVERYBODY SING movie (The One I Love; others)

1940—LILLIAN RUSSELL movie (Blue Lovebird)

1942-5—Musical work in movies including KEEPER OF THE FLAME and SOMEWHERE I'LL FIND YOU (1942), BATAAN (1943), GASLIGHT and MRS. PARKINGTON (1944), WITHOUT LOVE (1945)

1945—POLONAISE stage show (adapted Chopin's music)

1947—GREEN DOLPHIN STREET movie (On Green Dolphin Street)

1949—THAT MIDNIGHT KISS movie (I Know, I Know, I Know)

1953—LILI movie (Hi-Lili, Hi-Lo)

1955—THE GLASS SLIPPER movie (Take My Love)

1956—SOMEBODY UP THERE LIKES ME movie (title song)

1957—GREEN MANSIONS movie (Song of Green Mansions); DON'T GO NEAR THE WATER movie (title song)

1962—MUTINY ON THE BOUNTY movie (Follow Me)

1968—A FLEA IN HER EAR movie (title song)

Musical work in other movies including THE RED BADGE OF COURAGE (1951), THE NAKED SPUR (1953), AUNTIE MAME and THE BROTHERS KARAMAZOV (1958), BUTTERFIELD 8 and HOME FROM THE HILL (1960), KISSES FOR MY PRESIDENT (1964), LORD JIM (1965)

986. KARDOS, GENE   as v vo B

Leader of good 30s band. In early 30s played riff style along Casa Loma lines. Good jazz soloists; tuba led strong rhythm section. Assembled good jazzmen to record, including Mike Doty (as cl), Sam Weiss (d), Joe Hostetter (t), Gabe Gelinas (as). In middle and late 30s featured hotel style, played top spots in Catskills and New York. Bea Wain vocalist 1936-7. Vocalist Dick Robertson frequently used band on early 30s records. Some Kardos records under names of pianist Joel Shaw, Gene's Merrymakers or Bob Causer.

RECORDS

GENE KARDOS

Vi 22790 Mean Music/China Boy
Vi 22865 Freddy the Freshman/Now's the Time to Fall in Love
Vi 22897 Tell Tales/You're Foolin' Yourself
Vi 22899 Business in F/Corn-Fed Gal
Vi 22920 Alexander's Ragtime Band/ Glory
Vi 22986 My Extraordinary Gal/When Nobody Else Is Around
Vi 23377 Jam Man/Jazz Rondo
Vi 24009 Crazy People/Who Beside Me?
Vi 24081 Sing/Sheltered by the Stars, Cradled by the Moon
Vi 24122 San/Toll
Vo 2717 Moon Country/Don't Let Your Love Go Wrong
Vo 2722 All I Do Is Dream of You/ With My Eyes Wide Open, I'm Dreaming
Vo 2757 Moonglow / The Very Thought of You
Vo 2794 Learning/Stars Fell on Alabama
Pe 15848 You're Such a Comfort to Me/Did You Ever See a Dream Walking?
Pe 15849 Many Moons Ago/Good Morning Glory

Pe 15882 Love Locked Out/In Other Words—We're Through

Me 60408 Saddle Your Blues to a Wild Mustang/I Like That Face You're Wearing

Me 60513 Yours Truly Is Truly Yours/Breakin' in a Pair of Shoes

Me 70503 You Showed Me the Way/ Lady from Mayfair

Me 70710 Love Is Never Out of Season/Our Penthouse on Third Avenue

Me 71006 Old Man Moon/The Lady from Fifth Avenue

Me 80111 Blue Fantasy/I Knew You When

Me 80305 Love Walked In/Love Is Here to Stay

LPs

GENE KARDOS
TOM 21 (Vi RIs)

987. KASSEL, ART   ts vo cm B

Born January 18, 1896, Chicago, Ill.
Died February 3, 1965, Van Nuys, Calif.

Leader of sweet band billed as Art Kassel & His Kassels in the Air. Attended Chicago Art Institute. Military service, World War I. Later formed first group The Overseas Four. Early 20s in Chicago bands. Formed large band 1924; young Benny Goodman sideman 1924-5. Based mostly in Chicago; long runs at Bismarck Hotel, toured midwest. Composed *Doodle Doo Doo* 1924, theme many years. Later theme own 1932 composition *Hell's Bells*. Band active on early radio. Most recording middle and late 30s. 1935 radio show with Mills Brothers. Long runs at Chicago's Aragon Ballroom early 40s. Later 40s and 50s mostly on west coast. On early TV. Active into early 60s. Other compositions: *Sobbin' Blues* (1922), *Around the Corner* (1930), *Don't Let Julia Fool Ya* (1941). Lesser songs: *You Never Say Yes, Oh What I Know About You, Pennsylvania Dutch, Silvery Moonlight, Chant of the Swamp, Beautiful One, Golden Wedding Day, Bundle of Blue, The Guy Needs a Gal, In 1933* (official song of Chicago World's Fair), *I'm Thinking of My Darling, I've Got a Locket for My Pocket, Little Leaguer, Ship That Never Sailed, Are Yeh Spoken Fer?, And So Goodnight, Just an Old Rag Rug, All I Do Is Wantcha.*

RECORDS

ART KASSEL
Vi 21884 Old Timer/The Waltz I Can't Forget

Vi 21885 I Wish I Knew/He, She and Me

Co 2636-D Sing a New Song/ Goodnight My Love

Co 2643-D What a Life/Strangers

Co 2682-D (theme) Hell's Bells/O.K. America

Co 2687-D Rain, Rain, Go Away/My Heart's at Ease

Bb 5683 Stay as Sweet as You Are/ Take a Number from One to Ten

Bb 5727 June in January/With Every Breath I Take

Bb 5799 A Little White Gardenia/Be Careful, Young Lady

Bb 5800 Clouds/I'm Keeping Those Keepsakes You Gave Me

Bb 5801 If the Moon Turns Green/I Threw a Bean Bag at the Moon

Bb 5968 I'm Just an Ordinary Human/Simply Grand

Bb 7184 (theme) Doodle Doo Doo/ The One I Love

Bb 7255 Rosalie/Thrill of a Lifetime

Bb 7619 Cabin in the Carolines/Music, Maestro, Please

Bb 7696 Silver on the Sage/I'll Still Be Loving You

Bb 10508 (theme) Hell's Bells/Down in the Alley

Bb 10617 Up the Chimney Go My Dreams/Table Truckin'

Bb 30-0803 Where the Mountains Meet the Sky/Pennsylvania Polka

Hit 7090 I'm in Love with Someone/ What a Difference a Day Made

Hit 7110 Magic Is the Moonlight/I Dream of You

Vogue 714 (theme) Doodle Doo Doo/ All I Do Is Wantcha

Vogue 781 Sooner or Later/For Sentimental Reasons

Mer 5088 In a Little Book Shop/I've Got a Feeling I'm Falling

Mer 5200 If I Could Be with You/ Queen for a Day

LPs
ART KASSEL
  Mer (10″)MG-25038

988. KAUFMAN, IRVING   vo
Freelance singer, recorded heavily 20s and early 30s with many bands on many labels, also under own name. Strong theatrical voice somewhat along lines of Al Jolson and Harry Richman. Had perfect pitch, could sing without special arrangements, hence much in demand for records. Sang with Avon Comedy Four pre-1920 and in early 20s. Worked occasionally with singer-brother Jack Kaufman. Radio shows included Broadway Vanities 1934, Lazy Dan 1935, own series. Less active by late 30s. Radio transcriptions in 1946, probably last recordings.

RECORDS
SAM LANIN
  Re 8719 Who Wouldn't Be Jealous of You?
  Re 8871 I May Be Wrong
  Do 3991 Broken-Hearted
  Ha 1168 I Remember You from Somewhere/You for Me
THE ROUNDERS
  Re 8815 Where the Sweet Forget-Me-Nots Remember
LOU GOLD
  Pe 15182 Big City Blues
  Pe 15330 Bye Bye Blues
WILLIAM F. WIRGES
  Br 3910 Laugh, Clown, Laugh
THE CLEVELANDERS
  Ba 0848 I'm Yours
COLONIAL CLUB ORCHESTRA
  Br 3906 Dixie Dawn
  Br 4858 Hittin' the Bottle
THE AMBASSADORS
  Vo 14933 Oh! How I Love My Darling
BEN BERNIE
  Vo 14940 How I Love That Girl
CALIFORNIA RAMBLERS
  Pat 36496 While the Years Go Drifting By
  Pat 36510 Me Too
JOE CANDULLO
  Ha 397 Go Wash an Elephant
GOOFUS FIVE
  OK 41138 Sonny Boy/My Blackbirds Are Bluebirds Now

OK 41141 Blue Shadows
IRVING KAUFMAN-JACK KAUFMAN
  Co A-2780 I'll Be Happy
  Co A-2795 Nobody Knows
IRVING KAUFMAN
  Co A-2091 In Florida Among the Palms/There's a Little Bit of Bad in Every Good Little Girl
  Co A-2815 You'd Be Surprised
  Co 1737-D If I Had You/That's the Good Old Sunny South
  Co 2108-D Singing a Vagabond Song/Danger in Your Eyes, Cherie
  Ha 82 I'm Sitting on Top of the World/Don't Be Afraid to Come Home
  Ha 514 Our American Girl/White Wings, Carry Me Home
  Vi 17942 Don't Bite the Hand That's Feeding You/Are You from Dixie? (with BILLY MURRAY)
  Vi 18202 My Waikiki Ukulele Girl
  Ba 1757 Bye Bye Blackbird/Lonesome and Sorry
  Ba 32054 Fortune Is Smiling
  Di 2771 There's a Rainbow 'Round My Shoulder/Old Man Sunshine
  Vo 15092 Yes, Sir, That's My Baby/New York Ain't New York Anymore
  Pe 12586 That Wonderful Something
  OK 41230 You Were Meant for Me/Broadway Melody
  OK 41265 Used to You/Why Can't You?
  Cr 3261 Home/Now's the Time to Fall in Love

989. KAVELIN, AL   v cm B
Bandleader of 30s and 40s, best known for "Cascading Chords" band of late 30s. Led combo early 30s, enlarged by mid-30s. Big band danceable and commercial but could swing. Pianist Carmen Cavallaro stalwart 1933-7, billed simply as Carmen. Bill Darnell good vocalist 1940. Theme *Love Has Gone*. Co-composer of 1940 song *I Give You My Word*. Continued as bandleader till later 40s, became music publisher in California.

RECORDS
AL KAVELIN
  Vo 2824 (theme) Love Has Gone/Way

Down South in North Carolina
Vo 2845 June in January/With Every Breath I Take
Vo 2868 Blue Moon/I Thrill When They Mention Your Name
De 1113 Tango Oriental/It's You
De 1191 Underneath a Palm Beach Moon/Renita Bonita
Vo 4634 Love, I'd Give My Life for You/Some Rainy Day
Vo 4651 Blue Italian Waters/I Long to Belong to You
Vo 4789 Little Genius/If I Were Sure of You
Vo 4835 Nothing Is Too Perfect for You/Diary of Dreams
Vo 4930 Nola/Grateful
Vo 5367 Romance/Una Furtiva Lagrima
OK 5746 Practice Makes Perfect/The Swiss Bellringer
OK 5829 Who Dreamed You Up?/Whatever Happened to You?
OK 5851 Do You Hear What I Hear?/Goodnight Again

990. KAY, BEATRICE   vo

Singer of raucous novelty songs, mostly Gay Nineties vintage. Stock companies at early age, did imitations in vaudeville. Throat trouble while playing in The Provincetown Follies in New York 1935 caused permanent slight rasp in voice, prompted change to brash beer-garden singing style. Featured over-dramatized ballads of yesteryear, earned special niche late 30s and 40s. Active on radio beginning late 30s on Town Hall Tonight 1937, Earaches of 1938 late 1937-8, Gay Nineties Revue with Joe Howard middle 1939-42, own variety show mid-40s. In movies GAY NINETIES GIRL (1944), DIAMOND HORSESHOE (1945). Recorded in 40s and early 50s. Some early TV. Career waned in 50s.

RECORDS
BEATRICE KAY
Co 35457 Oceana Roll/Here Comes a Sailor
Co 35458 Don't Go in the Lion's Cage Tonight/The Nightingale
Co 35459 I Don't Care/Smarty

Co 35460 Waiting at the Church/My Mother Was a Lady
Co 35806 Heaven Will Protect the Working Girl/Put Your Arms Around Me, Honey
Co 35807 A Bird in a Gilded Cage/What You Gonna Do When the Rent Comes 'Round?
Co 35808 Italian Street Song/Teasing
Co 35809 Honey Boy/Waiting for the Robert E. Lee
Co 36939 The Curse of an Aching Heart/Golden Links Are Broken
Co 36940 If I Was a Millionaire/Saloon
Co 36941 I'm the Lonesomest Gal in Town/Steamboat Bill
Co 36942 Tatters/And Yet I Don't Know
Co 37922 Mention My Name in Sheboygan/Hooray, Hooray, I'm Goin' Away
Co 38232 At the Rodeo/I Wanna Be a Cowboy in the Movies
Co 38493 Put Your Shoes On, Lucy/I'm the Girl Who Married the Man on the Flying Trapeze
Co 38772 Spaghetti Rag/Red Hot Mama
Co 38773 Why Do They Always Say "No"?/The Old Piano Roll Blues

LPs
BEATRICE KAY
Co (10″)CL-6025 Naughty Nineties

991. KAY, HERBIE   B

Born c. 1904
Died May 11, 1944, Dallas, Texas

Leader of good hotel band popular in Chicago and midwest in 30s. Attended Northwestern, led dance band. Theme *Violets and Friends*. Future star Dorothy Lamour sang with band around 1934-6. She and Kay married 1935, divorced 1939. Kay active bandleader into early 40s. Few recordings.

RECORDS
HERBIE KAY
Co 3100-D A Little Bit Independent /Remember Last Night
Co 3109-D Precious Little One/Rhythm Steps

Co 3125-D Swing, Mr. Charlie/Chop Sticks

Co 3126-D Sunday on the Swanee/Za Zooza

Co 36135 (theme) Violets and Friends/Peter, Peter, Pumpkin Eater

Vo 4752 Glorianna/It's All So New to Me

Vo 4820 By Candle Light/Y' Had It Comin' to You

DOROTHY LAMOUR with HERBIE KAY ORCHESTRA

Br 8132 Lovelight in the Starlight/Little Lady Make-Believe

Br 8154 Tonight Will Live/On a Tropic Night

992. KAYE, BUDDY   lyr sax

Born January 3, 1918, New York, N.Y.

Lyricist of 40s and 50s. Big 1945 hit *Till the End of Time* when he and Ted Mossman adapted Chopin melody for movie A SONG TO REMEMBER. Early played saxophone on cruises and at resorts. Wrote special material for Mills Brothers, Ted Lewis, McGuire Sisters, various acts. Wrote theme for movie cartoon series LITTLE LULU. Wrote for POPEYE cartoons and BOUNCING BALL series. Collaborators on pop songs included composers Jimmy McHugh, Jule Styne, Jimmy Van Heusen, Philip Springer, Jerry Ross, Hugo Montenegro, Billy Reid. Later became record producer.

SONGS
(with related movies)

1945—A SONG TO REMEMBER movie (Till the End of Time); I'll Be Walkin' with My Honey

1946—I'll Close My Eyes; Full Moon and Empty Arms; Don't Be a Baby, Baby

1947—THE TREASURE OF SIERRA MADRE movie (title song)

1948—Donna Bella; A Carnival in Venice

1949—"A" You're Adorable

1950—Where Do I Go from You?; Where in the World?; Open Door—Open Arms

1951—And So I Waited Around

1952—My Thrill; I Am a Heart

1953—I'll Know My Love

1954—When I Plunk on My Guitar

1955—NOT AS A STRANGER movie (title song)

1956—Give Me This Day

Other songs: *It's Gonna Be a Long Long Winter; Banjo Boy; A Penny a Kiss, a Penny a Hug; Christmas Alphabet; Speedy Gonzales; Quiet Nights; Little Boat; This Is My Prayer; Never Ending; The Next Time; Sweet William; Welcome Welcome Home; Her Little Heart Went to Loveland; All Cried Out; One More Dream (and She's Mine); Thoughtless; The Things You Left in My Heart; Do You Miss Your Sweetheart?; Help Yourself to My Heart; Warm Kisses in the Cool of the Night; The Dixieland Ball; Over and Over; The Bicycle Song; The Golden Locket; Choir Boy; Once Upon a Nickel; I Love You More Than You Love Me*

993. KAYE, DANNY   vo
(DAVID KUMINSKY)

Born January 18, 1913, Brooklyn, N.Y.

Star of stage-movies-radio-TV. Featured screwball comedy, novelty songs and dances. Adept at tongue-twisters, at best entertaining children. Much special material by wife Sylvia Fine. Capable on ballads. Camp counselor and performer in Catskills. Toured abroad in cast of musical. Played La Martinique club in New York. 1939 in newcomers Broadway show STRAW HAT REVUE; ran two months. Stardom 1941 with successful Broadway shows LADY IN THE DARK and LET'S FACE IT. 1944 starred in first movie UP IN ARMS, followed by comedy-musical movies with novelty material and occasionally good pops. Excellent score by Frank Loesser for movie HANS CHRISTIAN ANDERSEN (1952). Portrayed jazz cornetist in movie THE FIVE PENNIES (1959), life story of Red Nichols. At intervals played vaudeville concerts at New York's Palace Theatre, in London and throughout Europe, always a smash. First radio show early 1945, various series in later years. Own TV show mid-60s, then activities slowed. Starred in Broadway musical TWO BY TWO; no great success.

MOVIES

1944—UP IN ARMS
1945—WONDER MAN
1946—KID FROM BROOKLYN
1947—THE SECRET LIFE OF WALTER MITTY
1948—A SONG IS BORN
1949—THE INSPECTOR GENERAL; IT'S A GREAT FEELING
1951—ON THE RIVIERA
1952—HANS CHRISTIAN ANDERSEN
1954—KNOCK ON WOOD; WHITE CHRISTMAS
1956—THE COURT JESTER
1958—MERRY ANDREW; ME AND THE COLONEL
1959—THE FIVE PENNIES
1961—ON THE DOUBLE
1963—THE MAN FROM THE DINERS' CLUB; THE AMBASSADOR AT LARGE
1964—THAT'S LIFE
1967—THE BIGGEST BUNDLE OF THEM ALL
1969—THE MAD WOMAN OF CHAILLOT

RECORDS

DANNY KAYE
Co 36025 Jenny/Tschaikovsky
Co 36042 My Ship/Princess of Pure Delight
Co 36163 One Life to Live/It's Never Too Late to Mendelssohn
Co 36194 Dinah/Molly Malone
Co 36582 Let's Not Talk About Love/Minnie the Moocher
Co 36584 The Fairy Pipers/The Babbitt and the Bromide
De 24263 Candy Kisses/Thank You
De 24401 Ballin' the Jack/St. Louis Blues
De 24475 The Moon and I/Nightmare Song
De 24637 Nothin' Like a Dame/Honey Bun
De 24745 Mad Dogs and Englishmen/Triplets
De 24784 I've Got a Lovely Bunch of Cocoanuts/The Peony Bush
De 27116 Pigalle/Ladies, Ladies
De 27596 Happy Ending/Rhythm of a New Romance
De 28953 Not Since Nineveh/Night of My Nights
DANNY KAYE-ANDREWS SISTERS
De 23940 Bread and Butter Woman/Civilization

DANNY KAYE-JIMMY DURANTE-JANE WYMAN-GROUCHO MARX
De 27748 Black Strap Molasses/How Di Ye Do

LPs

DANNY KAYE
Co (10″)CL-6023 Danny Kaye
Co (10″)CL-6249 Danny Kaye Entertains
Ha HL-7012 Pure Delight with Danny Kaye (Co RIs)
Ha HL-7314 The Best of Danny Kaye (Co RIs)
De DL-8461 Danny at the Palace
De (10″)DL-5527 Knock on Wood (movie soundtrack)
Dot DLP-9500 THE FIVE PENNIES

994. KAYE, SAMMY   as cl cm B

Born March 13, 1910, Rocky River, Ohio

Leader of dance band with exaggerated sweet style in 30s and 40s, one of most successful bands ever. Featured mellow, syrupy saxes, glissing trombones, lilting rhythmic style. Commercial success throughout long career, even during demise of big bands in 50s and 60s. Attended Ohio University, led band for proms, opened own dance spot Varsity Inn. After graduation 1932, continued with band in Cleveland area, toured. Later played Cincinnati to good radio coverage, became known in midwest. Long run in Pittsburgh helped band. Mid-30s style similar to fast-rising Kay Kyser's. Both employed sweet sound and singing song title gimmick. Themes also similar. Kaye's theme own composition *Kaye's Melody*. Adopted slogan "Swing and Sway with Sammy Kaye." Excellent front man; band put on good stage show with "So you want to lead a band" feature in which fans volunteered.

Band 1938 hit at New York's Hotel Commodore and Paramount Theatre. Featured vocalists Tommy Ryan and Jimmy Brown; later Nancy Norman, Don Cornell, Tony Alamo. Big hit *Daddy* 1941, *There Will Never Be Another You* 1942. Two 1950 hits *It Isn't Fair* and *Harbor Lights*. In movies ICELAND (1942) and SONG OF THE OPEN ROAD (1944). Several radio series, notably Sunday Serenade in late 40s and early 50s. Several entertaining TV shows in 50s. During late 50s and 60s band improved, got big ensemble sound with crisp, swinging style, good brass, mellow saxes, smart arrangements. Singing song titles dropped years earlier. Charlie Albertine late 60s arranger, fused some of Les Elgart sound (his creation) with Kaye sound. Band active into 70s, kept recording. Composed *Until Tomorrow* (1940), *Remember Pearl Harbor* (1942), *Wanderin'* (1950), *Del Rio* and *Tell Me You Love Me* (1951), *The Midnight Ride* and *The Dance of Mexico* (1953).

RECORDS

SAMMY KAYE

Vo 3669 Swing and Sway/My Buddy
Vo 3681 Josephine/Avalon
Vo 3849 The Dipsy Doodle/Swing Is Here to Sway
Vo 4140 I Married an Angel/Whispering
Vi 25874 I Wish I Was the Willow/Beside a Moonlit Stream
Vi 26059 All Ashore/Indiana Moonlight
Vi 26067 Two Sleepy People/Have You Forgotten So Soon?
Vi 26075 They Say/While a Cigarette Was Burning
Vi 26084 Hurry Home/Tell Me with Your Kisses
Vi 26150 Could Be/Penny Serenade
Vi 26267 White Sails/Stairway to the Stars
Vi 26515 A Lover's Lullaby/With the Wind and the Rain in Your Hair
Vi 26594 Where Was I?/Make-Believe Island
Vi 26643 Maybe/Blueberry Hill
Vi 27262 Until Tomorrow/Sidewalk Serenade
Vi 27391 Daddy/Two Hearts That Pass in the Night
Vi 27738 Dear Mom/Remember Pearl Harbor
Vi 27949 There Will Never Be Another You/Let's Bring New Glory to Old Glory
Vi 20-2935 (theme) Kaye's Melody
Vi 20-3609 It Isn't Fair/My Lily and My Rose

Vi 20-3680 Wanderin'
Co 38963 Harbor Lights/Sugar Sweet
Co 39015 Music, Maestro, Please/You've Got Me Crying Again
Co 39769 Walkin' to Missouri/One for the Wonder

LPs

SAMMY KAYE

Co CL-561 Swing and Sway with Sammy Kaye
Co CL-668 Music, Maestro, Please!
Co CL-1107 Midnight Serenade
Ha HL-7187 Dancing with Sammy Kaye in Hi-Fi
Ha HL-7321 MY FAIR LADY
De DL-4121 Dance to My Golden Favorites
De DL-4306 Swing and Sway
De DL-4357 Come Dance with Me

995. KAZEBIER, NATE   t

Born August 13, 1912, Lawrence, Kansas
Died October 22, 1969, Reno, Nev.

Swing trumpeter with top bands in 30s and early 40s. With Austin Wylie 1930, later with Jan Garber, Slatz Randall, others. With Benny Goodman 1935-6. Later 1936-7 in west coast studios and with Ray Noble. With Seger Ellis 1937, Spud Murphy and Noble 1938, Gene Krupa 1939-40, Jimmy Dorsey 1940-3. Military service awhile, World War II. With Benny Goodman 1946-7. Settled in California, active in studios late 40s into 60s. Later 60s played in Reno and Lake Tahoe, also worked as golf instructor.

RECORDS

GENE KRUPA

De 18114 Blues of Israel/Three Little Words
De 18115 The Last Round-up/Jazz Me Blues
Co 35218 Sweetheart, Honey, Darlin', Dear

BENNY GOODMAN

Vi 25215 Sandman
Vi 25279 Christopher Columbus
Vi 25350 Anything for You

JIMMY DORSEY

De 3312 Dolimite/Hep-Tee Hootie
De 3859 Isle of Pines

SEGER ELLIS
De 1350 Bees Knees
RAY BAUDUC
Cap 919 Susie/Down in Honky Tonky Town
Cap 15131 Li'l Liza Jane/When My Sugar Walks Down the Street

LPs

BENNY GOODMAN
Sunbeam 128-132 (5 LPs) From the Congress Hotel (1935-6 airchecks)

996. KEEL, HOWARD vo
(HAROLD CLIFFORD KEEL)
Born April 13, 1919, Gillespie, Ill.

Singing star of 50s movies. Stage experience in long-running Broadway musical OKLAHOMA!, one of several in lead after Alfred Drake left. Well-trained, strong baritone with sure manner, big, handsome, a natural for movies. Began impressively in important musical ANNIE GET YOUR GUN (1950), co-starring with Betty Hutton. Co-starred in top movies with Esther Williams, Jane Powell, Kathryn Grayson, Doris Day, others. Important musicals SHOW BOAT; LOVELY TO LOOK AT; KISS ME, KATE!; CALAMITY JANE; ROSE-MARIE; SEVEN BRIDES FOR SEVEN BROTHERS; KISMET. In addition to musical talent, capable in light comedy and dramatic roles. Late 1959 in Broadway musical SARATOGA; short run of 80 performances. 1963 toured with NO STRINGS show. Occasional TV. Career declined during 60s.

MOVIES

1950—ANNIE GET YOUR GUN; PAGAN LOVE SONG
1951—THREE GUYS NAMED MIKE; SHOW BOAT; TEXAS CARNIVAL; CALLAWAY WENT THATAWAY
1952—LOVELY TO LOOK AT; DESPERATE SEARCH
1953—RIDE, VAQUERO!; FAST COMPANY; KISS ME, KATE!; CALAMITY JANE
1954—ROSE-MARIE; SEVEN BRIDES FOR SEVEN BROTHERS; DEEP IN MY HEART
1955—JUPITER'S DARLING; KISMET
1959—FLOODS OF FEAR; THE BIG FISHERMAN

1961—ARMORED COMMAND
1963—THE DAY OF THE TRIFFIDS
1965—THE MAN FROM BUTTON WILLOW (voice only)
1966—WACO
1967—THE WAR WAGON; RED TOMAHAWK
1968—ARIZONA BUSHWHACKERS

RECORDS

HOWARD KEEL
MGM 30378 The World Is Mine Tonight/My Magic Heart
MGM 30415 Whoa Emma/Young Folks Should Get Married
MGM 30840 Rose-Marie/The Right Place for a Girl

LPs
(movie soundtracks)

MGM E-3077 KISS ME, KATE!
MGM E-3281 KISMET
MGM E-3769ST (2-LP set) ROSE MARIE/SEVEN BRIDES FOR SEVEN BROTHERS
MGM (10″)E-150 LOVELY TO LOOK AT
MGM (10″)E-509 ANNIE GET YOUR GUN
MGM (10″)E-534 PAGAN LOVE SONG
MGM (10″)E-559 SHOW BOAT
Co (10″)CL-6273 CALAMITY JANE
HOWARD KEEL (with GOGI GRANT, ANN JEFFREYS)
Vi LOP-1505 SHOW BOAT

997. KEELER, RUBY vo
Born August 25, 1910, Halifax, Nova Scotia

Dancer-singer popular in movies 1933-7 period, co-starring mostly with Dick Powell in top musicals. Grew up in New York; first chorus job at 13. Won dance contest leading to big job in Texas Guinan's night club. Entertainer Al Jolson saw, wooed, married her 1928. In 1927 supporting roles in Broadway musicals LUCKY and SIDEWALKS OF NEW YORK. Starred in SHOW GIRL (1929). Burst upon movie screen in classic 1933 musical 42ND STREET; overnight sensation with fresh young personality and tap dancing. Public at first unaware of Keeler-Jolson marriage. Keeler and Powell co-starred in popular musicals GOLD DIGGERS OF 1933, FOOTLIGHT PARADE (1933), DAMES and

FLIRTATION WALK (1934), SHIPMATES FOR-EVER (1935), COLLEEN (1936). Co-starred with Jolson in important 1935 movie musical GO INTO YOUR DANCE. Later movies READY, WILLING AND ABLE (1937), MOTHER CAREY'S CHICKENS (1938), SWEETHEART OF THE CAMPUS (1941). Divorced Jolson 1939, remarried, settled in California, raised family. After three decades of retirement, starred 1970-72 on Broadway in sensational revival of NO, NO, NANETTE. Occasionally on 70s TV, mostly talk shows.

998. KEENE, LINDA   vo
(FLORENCE MCCRORY)
Born 1917, Hattiesburg, Miss.

Good jazz-influenced singer with bands of 30s and 40s. With Nye Mayhew 1938, briefly with Glenn Miller summer 1938. In 1939 with Bobby Hackett, Jack Teagarden, Willie Farmer, Lennie Hayton. With Red Norvo mid-1940 to early 1941, with Tony Pastor briefly, then rejoined Norvo briefly. Also with Red Nichols 1941. Radio and clubs as single. On 1944 radio show Dixieland House Party. Continued clubs into 50s.

RECORDS

BOBBY HACKETT
    Vo 4499 Blue and Disillusioned
JACK TEAGARDEN
    Br 8388 White Sails
    Br 8431 Especially for You/You're the Moment in My Life
LENNIE HAYTON
    Vo 5421 One Cigarette for Two/I Love You Much Too Much
    Vs 8125 At the Balalaika/The Starlit Hour
TONY PASTOR
    Bb 11067 Number Ten Lullaby Lane
JOE MARSALA
    B&W (12")1203 Blues in the Storm/Unlucky Woman
LINDA KEENE
    B&W 20 I Must Have That Man/A Ghost of a Chance
    Vi 27829 Embraceable You
    Vi 27830 Georgia on My Mind/'Way Down Yonder in New Orleans
    Vi 27831 Somebody Loves Me

    Vi 27832 Mound Bayou/Someone to Watch Over Me

999. KELLEY, PECK   p B
(JOHN DICKSON KELLEY)
Born c. 1900, Houston, Texas

Jazz pianist based in Texas, never heard by general public but a legend in late 30s and 40s among musicians. Strong, individualistic style, harmonically advanced. Led band Peck's Bad Boys locally early 20s. Personnel at times included Jack Teagarden, Leon Rappolo, Pee Wee Russell. Through the years led big bands and combos. Travelling musicians visited Kelley, spread reports of talent. Heard and praised by critic John Hammond. Music magazines of late 30s featured flattering articles. Kelley steadfastly turned down offers to record or travel. Played mostly in Houston, occasionally in other Texas cities. About 1925 to St. Louis to join Frankie Trumbauer at Arcadia Ballroom, but union forbade. About 1934 to New Orleans with Joe Gill band (which included Harry James). Military service awhile, World War II. Mostly Houston in 40s and 50s leading combos or working solo. Later in 60s inactive.

1000. KELLY, GENE   vo
Born August 23, 1912, Pittsburgh, Pa.

Dancer-singer of stage and screen, important in 40s and 50s movies. Performed strenuous and artistic dances, talented in all styles. Distinctive soft singing and speaking voice. Early experience on Broadway stage with supporting roles in LEAVE IT TO ME (1938) and ONE FOR THE MONEY (1939). Hit as star of popular musical PAL JOEY (1941). Began movies 1942 co-starring with Judy Garland in FOR ME AND MY GAL; acclaimed by critics and fans. Top movie musicals followed. Outstanding: COVER GIRL, ANCHORS AWEIGH, ON THE TOWN, SUMMER STOCK, AN AMERICAN IN PARIS, SINGIN' IN THE RAIN, BRIGADOON, LES GIRLS. Capable dramatic actor, as in CHRISTMAS HOLIDAY and MARJORIE MORNINGSTAR. Occasionally on TV; own short-lived shows. Later movie director of TUNNEL OF LOVE (1958);

GIGOT (1962); HELLO, DOLLY! and THE CHEYENNE SOCIAL CLUB (1969). Occasional recording included narrations on children's records.

MOVIES

1942—FOR ME AND MY GAL
1943—DUBARRY WAS A LADY; THOUSANDS CHEER; THE CROSS OF LORRAINE; PILOT NO. 5
1944—COVER GIRL; CHRISTMAS HOLIDAY
1945—ANCHORS AWEIGH
1946—ZIEGFELD FOLLIES
1947—LIVING IN A BIG WAY
1948—THE PIRATE; WORDS AND MUSIC; THE THREE MUSKETEERS
1949—ON THE TOWN; TAKE ME OUT TO THE BALL GAME
1950—SUMMER STOCK; BLACK HAND
1951—AN AMERICAN IN PARIS; IT'S A BIG COUNTRY
1952—SINGIN' IN THE RAIN; THE DEVIL MAKES THREE
1954—BRIGADOON; CREST OF THE WAVE; DEEP IN MY HEART
1955—IT'S ALWAYS FAIR WEATHER
1956—INVITATION TO THE DANCE
1957—THE HAPPY ROAD; LES GIRLS
1958—MARJORIE MORNINGSTAR
1960—INHERIT THE WIND; LET'S MAKE LOVE
1964—WHAT A WAY TO GO!
1967—YOUNG GIRLS OF ROCHEFORT

RECORDS

JUDY GARLAND-GENE KELLY
  De 18480 For Me and My Gal/When You Wore a Tulip
  MGM 30097 Be a Clown
GENE KELLY-DONALD O'CONNOR
  MGM 30559 Moses/Good Morning (also with DEBBIE REYNOLDS)
GENE KELLY-GEORGES GUETARY
  MGM 30401 'S Wonderful
GENE KELLY
  MGM 30252 You Wonderful You
  MGM 30253 Heavenly Music/Dig-Dig-Dig for Your Dinner (with PHIL SILVERS)
  MGM 30399 I Got Rhythm
  MGM 30402 Love Is Here to Stay

LPs

GENE KELLY
  Co (10")JL-8008 Peter Rabbit (for children)
(movie soundtracks)
  MGM E-3590 LES GIRLS
  MGM (10")E-21 THE PIRATE
  MGM (10")E-93 AN AMERICAN IN PARIS
  MGM (10")E-113 SINGIN' IN THE RAIN
  MGM (10")E-519 SUMMER STOCK
  Vi LSO-1001 BRIGADOON

1001. KELLY, PAULA   vo

Good band singer, later member of Modernaires vocal group many years. Pert and vivacious, good showmanship. With Dick Stabile late 1937-8. Joined Al Donahue spring 1938, remained about two years. Joined Glenn Miller March 1941, featured with Modernaires. Husband Hal Dickinson founder-leader of Modernaires, excellent vocal group. Paula with band in movie SUN VALLEY SERENADE 1941, left August 1941 when former vocalist Marion Hutton rejoined. With Artie Shaw late 1941. In 1943 sang with Bob Allen band on tour. Permanent member of Modernaires mid-40s as group grew to five. Male personnel changed except for Dickinson. Group recorded and played radio, clubs and theatres. Toured with Bob Crosby 1951; on Club 15 radio show 1952. Featured on Bob Crosby daytime TV show mid-50s. In movies CRAZY HOUSE (1943), WHEN YOU'RE SMILING (1950), THE GLENN MILLER STORY (1954). Continued working in later 50s and 60s, inactive at intervals and less prominent. Dickinson died November 18, 1970. Group continued with Paula, featured with Tex Beneke band and Ray Eberle as Miller revival waxed in nostalgic 70s.

RECORDS

DICK STABILE
  Bb 7390 My First Impression of You
  Bb 7476 Lost and Found/My Heart Is Taking Lessons
AL DONAHUE
  Vo 4178 I'm Gonna Lock My Heart
  Vo 4195 Naturally
  Vo 4513 Jeepers Creepers/Hurry Home
  Vo 4550 I Won't Believe It/Between a Kiss and a Sigh

Vo 4621 I'm Always Chasing Rainbows
Vo 4722 East Side of Heaven/That Sly Old Gentleman
Vo 4956 White Sails
Vo 5351 Pinch Me
Vo 5454 Imagination
Vo 5479 This Is the Beginning of the End

GLENN MILLER
Bb 11163 The Booglie Wooglie Piggy
Bb 11203 Peekaboo to You
Bb 11230 Chattanooga Choo Choo/I Know Why
Bb 11263 It Happened in Sun Valley/The Kiss Polka

ARTIE SHAW
Vi 27705 Make Love to Me
Vi 27746 I Don't Want to Walk without You/Someone's Rocking My Dreamboat

PAULA KELLY & THE MODERNAIRES
Co 36800 You Belong to My Heart/There, I've Said It Again
Co 36992 Salute to Glenn Miller/Juke Box Saturday Night
Co 37147 Zip-a-Dee-Doo-Dah/Too Many Irons in the Fire
Co 37220 Connecticut/My Heart Goes Crazy
Co 37569 Something in the Wind/The Turntable Song
Co 37980 The Whistler/The Jingle Bell Polka
Co 8403 Margie/Ain't Misbehavin'
Cor 60726 Goody Goody/Bugle Call Rag

LPs

GLENN MILLER
Vi LPT-1016 Juke Box Saturday Night (Bb, Vi RIs)
Vi LPM-2080 (Bb RIs)

BOB CROSBY
Co CL-766 The Bob Crosby Show (TV cast)

(miscellaneous artists)
WB 1505 Something Old, Something New

THE MODERNAIRES
Cor (10")CRL-56084 Stop, Look and Listen
Co (10")CL-6043 Tributes in Tempo

Mer MG-20546 Like Swing

1002. KELLY, WYNTON   p
Born December 2, 1931, Jamaica, British West Indies

Modern jazz pianist with traditional roots, ability in various styles. Parents brought him to U.S. at about four. Began professionally 1943, played rhythm and blues early in career. Later 40s with Lockjaw Davis and as accompanist for singer Dinah Washington. Freelanced with modern jazzmen including Dizzy Gillespie. Military service 1952-4, later rejoined Gillespie. Own trio 1958. With Miles Davis 1959-63. Formed trio, active into 70s.

RECORDS
(all LPs)

WYNTON KELLY
BN (10")5025
Riv 12-254
Verve V-8576 Comin' in the Back Door
Verve V-8588 It's All Right
Verve V-8622 Undiluted
Verve V-8633 Smoking at the Half Note
Milestone 9004 Full View

ERNIE HENRY
Riv 12-248 Seven Standards and a Blues

BLUE MITCHELL
Riv 12-273 Big Six

CLARK TERRY
Riv 12-237 Serenade to a Bus Seat

NAT ADDERLEY
Riv RLP-330 That's Right

DINAH WASHINGTON
EmArcy MG-36011

ART FARMER
Pres (10")193

J. J. JOHNSON
BN (10")5057

DIZZY GILLESPIE
Verve V-8222
Verve V-8242

MILES DAVIS
Co CS-8456 (S)
Co CS-8469 (S)
Co CS-8470 (S)

1231

1003. KEMP, HAL   as ts cl cm B
(JAMES HAROLD KEMP)
Born March 27, 1905, Marion, Ala.
Died December 21, 1940, near Madera,
Calif., from injuries in auto accident

Leader of popular 30s dance band featuring subdued, sophisticated sweet style. As teenager played local theatre, moved to Charlotte. Attended University of North Carolina, led dance band. In summer 1924 band played ocean liner and residency in England thanks to band-leader-booker Paul Specht. Kemp continued leading band at college late 1924-6. Key members pianist John Scott Trotter, saxmen Saxie Dowell and Ben Williams; Skinnay Ennis on drums and vocals. All remained when band began professionally early 1927. Early engagement in New York, toured south, long run in Miami. Recorded 1929-30 as Carolina Club Orchestra. Played Europe 1930; jazz trumpeter Bunny Berigan on trip. Band played good semi-hot style, changed to sweet early 30s but could still swing. After touring, first prominence via good radio coverage 1933-4 at Chicago's Black Hawk, followed by engagement at New York's Hotel Pennsylvania.

Under John Scott Trotter's arranging, band developed distinctive style featuring muted clip-noted trumpets (often playing triplets), flowing sax section playing intricate passages, lower register clarinets (sometimes blown through megaphones for special effect). Kemp composed beautiful theme *When Summer Is Gone*. Trotter left late 1935; Hal Mooney later important arranger. Personable Skinnay Ennis popular with breathless vocal style. Strong-voiced Bob Allen sang most ballads. Biggest Kemp hits *Got a Date with an Angel* and *Lamplight* featuring Ennis. Female vocalists Maxine Gray and Deane Janis, followed by Nan Wynn and Janet Blair (later in movies). Smoothies vocal trio joined late 30s. Ennis left 1938 to lead own band. Kemp band on radio with Phil Baker late 1935 to end of 1936; early 1937 show with Kay Thompson. Later 1937 on show Music from Hollywood starring Alice Faye. Own show Time to Shine 1938-9. In 1938 movie RADIO CITY REVELS. Rough year 1940 with personnel changes,

some loss of popularity. But good bookings in California for early 1941 made future look brighter. Kemp driving to open at San Francisco's Mark Hopkins Hotel, had fatal accident. Band continued engagement with several men fronting, disbanded after date. Early 1941 reassembled under singer Art Jarrett. Some success 1941-2, then faded.

RECORDS
CAROLINA CLUB ORCHESTRA (Hal Kemp)
OK 41199 The Eyes of Texas/Shine On Harvest Moon
OK 41237 Walking with Susie/That's You, Baby
OK 41309 Miss Wonderful/Somebody Mighty Like You

HAL KEMP
Br 3937 Lovable/I Don't Care
Br 4078 Washington & Lee Swing/ High Up on a Hill-top
Br 4151 Gypsy/My Troubles Are Over
Br 4388 When My Dreams Come True/To Be in Love
Br 4805 Washin' the Blues from My Soul/I Remember You from Somewhere
Br 6943 Love in Bloom/Straight from the Shoulder
Br 6974 Strange/It's All Forgotten Now
Br 7317 Hands Across the Table/Flirtation Walk
Br 7369 Lullaby of Broadway/The Words Are in My Heart
Br 7600 I Can't Get Started/That Moment of Moments
Br 7626 Lost/The Touch of Your Lips
Br 7780 Got a Date with an Angel/ You Don't Love Right
Vi 25598 Whispers in the Dark/Stop! You're Breaking My Heart
Vi 25651 Got a Date with an Angel/ Lamplight
Vi 25722 Goodnight, Angel/Swingin' in the Corn
Vi 25896 I've Got a Pocketful of Dreams/Don't Let That Moon Get Away
Vi 26165 Heart of Stone/You've Got Me Crying Again
Vi 26449 'Way Back in 1939 A.D./ Ooh! What You Said

Vi 26615 The Breeze and I/I Can't Resist You

Vi 26655 Can't Get Indiana Off My Mind/I Just Couldn't Take It, Baby

Vi 27222 Walkin' by the River/So You're the One

Vi 27255 It All Comes Back to Me Now/Talkin' to My Heart

LPs

HAL KEMP

Vi (10″)LPT-3016 This Is Hal Kemp (Vi RIs)

TOM 24 And His Orchestra 1927-1931 (early Br RIs)

1004. KEMPER, RONNIE   p ar cm vo B

Born August 1, 1912, Missoula, Montana

Band singer known for novelty hit *Cecilia* with Dick Jurgens 1940. Joined Jurgens 1934 as pianist, also sang and wrote arrangements 30s into 40s. With Horace Heidt 1941; in 1942 own band. Military service, World War II. Early 1946 began as single. On early TV; own show Kemper's Kapers seven years. Own radio show. Active into 70s. Composed several songs including *It's a Hundred to One, Knit One Purl Two, In a Blue Canoe, Doodle Bug Song, Dine and Dance.*

RECORDS

DICK JURGENS

Vo 5405 Cecilia

Vo 5540 The Kitten with the Big Green Eyes

HORACE HEIDT

Co 36026 G'Bye Now

Co 36148 Goodbye, Dear, I'll Be Back in a Year

1005. KENIN, HERMAN   B

Born c. 1901
Died July 21, 1970, New York, N.Y.

Bandleader of late 20s and early 30s; sweet band with high level of musicianship. Best known to musicians and public 1958: succeeded famed James C. Petrillo as president of American Federation of Musicians.

RECORDS

HERMAN KENIN

Vi 20725 All I Want Is You/Pretty Little Thing

Vi 20782 Some Other Day/Sad 'n' Blue

Vi 21313 Persian Rug

Vi 21314 Rose Room′/Rose of Monterey

Vi 21336 When Love Comes Stealing/ A Canoe with You

Vi 21568 There's Somebody New

Vi 21980 Walkin' Around in a Dream/After Thinking It Over

Vi 21991 Kids Again/Building a Nest for Mary

Vi 22005 I'm the Last of the Red Hot Mamas/He's a Good Man to Have Around

Vi 22006 That's What I Call Sweet Music/Place in the Sun

Vi 22016 I'm Doin' What I'm Doin' for Love

Vi 22058 If I Had My Way

1006. KENNEDY, JIMMY   lyr cm

English songwriter with many popular songs in U.S. beginning mid-30s. Best-known: *Isle of Capri, Red Sails in the Sunset, Harbor Lights, South of the Border, My Prayer, April in Portugal.* Collaborators included Michael Carr, Nat Simon, Will Grosz (last also as Hugh Williams).

SONGS
(with related show)

1934—Play to Me, Gypsy

1935—PROVINCETOWN FOLLIES stage show (Red Sails in the Sunset); Isle of Capri; Roll Along Covered Wagon

1936—Did Your Mother Come from Ireland?; Cafe Continental; The Sunset Trail

1937—Harbor Lights; The Miller's Daughter Marianne

1938—Two Bouquets

1939—Cinderella, Stay in My Arms; South of the Border

1940—My Prayer; The Mem'ry of a Rose

1944—An Hour Never Passes

1947—And Mimi

1948—An Apple Blossom Wedding; On the Painted Desert

1949—Merry-Go-Round Waltz; My Bolero
1950—The Phantom Stage-Coach
1951—Who Knows Love?
1952—Poor Whip-Poor-Will
1953—April in Portugal; An Angel Made
of Ice
1954—Istanbul
1956—Sweet Heartaches

1007. KENNY, CHARLES   cm lyr v
Born June 23, 1898, Astoria, N.Y.
Songwriter of 30s and 40s, collaborated
with brother columnist Nick Kenny.
Best-known songs *Love Letters in the
Sand, There's a Gold Mine in the Sky,
While a Cigarette Was Burning.*

SONGS
(all in collaboration with Nick Kenny)
1931—Love Letters in the Sand
1936—Every Minute of the Hour
1937—Carelessly
1938—Cathedral in the Pines; There's a
Gold Mine in the Sky; While a
Cigarette Was Burning; It's a
Lonely Trail
1939—White Sails; Little Skipper; Last
Night; Running Through My
Mind; Take a Tip from the Whippoorwill
1940—Dream Valley; Leanin' on the Ole
Top Rail; Make-Believe Island
1943—Little Did I Know
1944—Violins Were Playing; Green,
Green Hills of Home
1948—Beyond the Purple Hills
1950—Scattered Toys; Gone Fishin'

1008. KENNY, NICK   lyr
Born February 3, 1895, Astoria, N.Y.
Lyricist of 30s and 40s, collaborated
mostly with brother Charles Kenny.
Well-known as pop poet and radio columnist for newspapers. In 1930 began
long career as radio editor of New York
Daily Mirror. Pioneer in radio; established early amateur show.

(See biography herein on CHARLES KENNY
for listing of songs on which brothers
collaborated.)

Nick collaborated with other writers on a
few songs including *When the Sun Goes*

Down (1934), *I'll Keep the Lovelight Burning* (1942), *And So Little Time* (1943), *Save
Me a Dream* (1946). Retired to Florida.

1009. KENT, WALTER   cm v B
*Born November 29, 1911, New York,
N.Y.*
Composer of 30s and 40s. Best-known
songs *Love Is Like a Cigarette, The White
Cliffs of Dover, I'll Be Home for Christmas.*
Score for 1951 Broadway show SEVEN-
TEEN; songs for movies. Collaborators
included lyricists Kim Gannon, Nat Bur-
ton. Educated at CCNY and Juilliard.
Architect several years with music as
sideline. Led orchestra in radio and the-
atre work.

SONGS
(with related shows)
1932—Pu-leeze, Mr. Hemingway!
1936—Love Is Like a Cigarette
1937—MANHATTAN MERRY-GO-ROUND
movie (Mama, I Wanna Make
Rhythm)
1940—Apple Blossoms and Chapel Bells
1941—The White Cliffs of Dover; Isle of
Pines; Once and for All
1942—When the Roses Bloom Again
1943—FOR WHOM THE BELL TOLLS movie
(title song); I'll Be Home for
Christmas
1944—SONG OF THE OPEN ROAD movie
(Too Much in Love)
1945—EARL CARROLL'S VANITIES movie
(Endlessly)
1948—Ah, But It Happens
1949—The Last Mile Home
1950—I'm Gonna Live Till I Die; I Cross
My Fingers
1951—SEVENTEEN stage show, Kim
Gannon-lyr (This Was Just Another Day; Summertime Is Summertime; Reciprocity; Ode to Lola;
After All, It's Spring; Headache
and Heartache; others)

1010. KENTON, STAN   p ar cm B
*Born February 19, 1912, Wichita, Kan-
sas*
Pioneer in progressive big band jazz,
leader of many outstanding bands beginning 1941. Developed numerous jazz-

men and arrangers who went on to important careers. Capable pianist with simple, virile style rich in harmonic structure. Talented arranger-composer, excellent leader and organizer. Grew up in Los Angeles, played in local bands early 30s. With Everett Hoagland 1934, Gus Arnheim 1936-8, Vido Musso 1939. Some work for Scat Davis, also radio and movie studios. Mid-1941 formed big band, created interest in debut at Balboa Beach with different sound, powerful and exciting. Later in year played New York's Roseland but not a hit. Built popularity on west coast, played Bob Hope radio show 1943. Early hits Kenton's own *Artistry in Rhythm* (theme) and *Eager Beaver*. Early scores featured staccato reed section, driving brass. 1944-6 band attempted commercial style with many vocals and novelties. Hits: *And Her Tears Flowed Like Wine* and *Tampico*. Early vocalists Anita O'Day, Gene Howard, June Christy. Late 1945 band a hit at New York's Hotel Pennsylvania. Middle and later 40s a favorite with musicians and fans, especially college students. Pete Rugolo joined late 1945, relieved Kenton of much arranging, became important asset. Kenton disbanded April 1947 due to illness.

Reorganized, led bands of varying sizes and personnel for next quarter-century, always coming up with new jazz talent. Helped bring to public attention talented vocal group The Four Freshmen. Inactive 1949 due to ill health. Toured 1950 with large orchestra using many strings; show titled Innovations in Modern Music. Early 50s featured vocalist Chris Connor, later 50s Ann Richards. Popular 1952 summer radio show emanating from various cities across country. Summer TV show Music '55. Long 1956 European tour. Many concerts and campus clinics through the years. Steady recording. Quit Capitol 1970 after 27 years, formed own company Creative World Records. Active in sessions and concerts with large group called Los Angeles Neophonic Orchestra. Many tours abroad, latest 1972.

Leading Kenton jazzmen through the years included Vido Musso (ts), Boots Mussulli (as), Kai Winding (tb), Eddie Safranski (b), Milt Bernhart (tb), Eddie Bert (tb), Bob Cooper (ts), Lennie Niehaus (as), Art Pepper (as), Maynard Ferguson (t), Shorty Rogers (t), Bud Shank (as), Shelly Manne (d), Conte Candoli (t), Bill Holman (ts), Lee Konitz (as). Leading arrangers Rugolo, Rogers, Holman, Bill Russo, Johnny Richards. Kenton composer or co-composer of jazz numbers *Artistry in Rhythm, Eager Beaver, Artistry in Tango, Theme to the West, Intermission Riff, Southern Scandal, Concerto for Doghouse, Opus in Pastels, Painted Rhythm, Artistry Jumps, Concerto to End All Concertos, Jump for Joe, Harlem Folk Dance,* many others, also novelty *And Her Tears Flowed Like Wine.*

RECORDS

HOLLYWOOD HUCKSTERS
  Cap 40022 Happy Blues
METRONOME ALL-STARS
  Cap 15039 Metronome Riff
STAN KENTON
  De 4037 This Love of Mine/The Nango
  De 4319 Reed Rapture/El Choclo
  Cap 145 Do Nothin' Till You Hear from Me/Harlem Folk Dance
  Cap 159 (theme) Artistry in Rhythm/Eager Beaver
  Cap 166 And Her Tears Flowed Like Wine/How Many Hearts Have You Broken?
  Cap 202 Tampico/Southern Scandal
  Cap 219 Don't Let Me Dream/It's Been a Long Long Time
  Cap 250 Painted Rhythm
  Cap 298 Intermission Riff/It's a Pity to Say Goodnight
  Cap 382 Concerto to End All Concertos (1 & 2)
  Cap 408 Collaboration/Machito
  Cap 904 Lover/The Peanut Vendor
  Cap 1043 Jolly Roger/Evening in Pakistan
  Cap 2789 Don't Take Your Love from Me/Alone Too Long
  Cap 10040 Balboa Bash
  Cap 20086 Come Back to Sorrento/Artistry in Bolero
  Cap 20088 Opus in Pastels/Safranski

LPs

STAN KENTON

Cap W-724 Stan Kenton in Hi-Fi

Cap T-1026 The Ballad Style of Stan Kenton

Cap T-1796 Adventures in Jazz

Cap T-1985 Adventures in Blues

Cap T-2327 Stan Kenton's Greatest Hits

Cap ST-2655 (S) Plays for Today

Cap ST-2810 (S) World We Know

Cap STBO-1327 (S) (2-LP set) Road Show

Cap STCL-2989 (S) (3-LP set) Deluxe Set

Cap DT-167 Artistry in Rhythm

Cap (10″)L-383 New Concepts of Artistry in Rhythm

De DL-8259 Formative Years (De RIs)

Creative World ST-1015 (S) Live at Redlands University

STAN KENTON-JUNE CHRISTY

Cap T-656 Duet

1011. KEPPARD, FREDDIE   c B

Born February 15, 1889, New Orleans, La.
Died July 15, 1933, Chicago, Ill.

Cornet star of early jazz. Good technique, tone and drive, despite lack of formal training. At 16 led Olympia Brass Band. Freelanced in Storyville hot spots. In 1912 led Original Creole Band on tour across country; stops included Los Angeles, Chicago and New York. Disbanded briefly 1917, then formed group to tour and play residency in Chicago. Settled there 1918, led bands at intervals through 20s. Early 20s with King Oliver, Jimmie Noone, Erskine Tate, Doc Cook, Ollie Powers. Many jobs with Cook middle and late 20s. Toured midwest with own band late 20s; also with Charlie Elgar. Mostly inactive in 30s due to ill health.

RECORDS

ERSKINE TATE

OK 4907 Cutie Blues/Chinaman Blues

JIMMY BLYTHE

Para 12376 Messin' Around/Adam's Apple

BIRMINGHAM BLUETETTE

Herwin 92019 Old Man Blues

COOK'S DREAMLAND ORCHESTRA (Doc Cook)

Ge 5360 So This Is Venice/The One I Love

Ge 5373 Moanful Man/Lonely Little Wallflower

Ge 5374 Scissor-Grinder Joe/The Memphis Maybe Man

Co 727-D Here Comes the Hot Tamale Man/Spanish Mama

Co 813-D Brown Sugar/High Fever

COOKIE'S GINGERSNAPS (Doc Cook)

OK 8369 High Fever/Here Comes the Hot Tamale Man

OK 8390 Messin' Around (1 & 2)

OK 40675 Love Found You for Me

FREDDIE KEPPARD

Para 12399 Stock Yards Strut/Salty Dog

UHCA 73-74 Stock Yards Strut/Salty Dog (RIs)

LPs

FREDDIE KEPPARD

Herwin 101 (Doc Cook-Erskine Tate RIs)

Jazz Treasury 1002 (Doc Cook-Erskine Tate RIs)

1012. KERKER, GUSTAV (or GUSTAVE A.)   cm cello b

Born February 28, 1857, Herford, West-phalia, Germany
Died June 29, 1923, New York, N.Y.

Leading composer of Broadway musicals during development years. To U.S. 1867, family settled in Louisville. Led local orchestras. To New York, directed theatre orchestras; important tenure at Casino Theatre where many of his shows presented. Conducted orchestra for most Lillian Russell performances in New York, wrote show AN AMERICAN BEAUTY for her. Songs attained little popularity outside context of shows, included *Castles in the Air, In Gay New York, La Belle Parisienne, Is It a Dream?, The Good Old Days, They Call Me the Belle of New York, They All Follow Me, Bonjour Monsieur, Teach Me How to Kiss, Loud Let the Bugles Sound, Old Man Manhattan, It's Nice to Have a Sweetheart, You're Just the Girl I'm Looking For, Cynthia Jane, Golly Charlie, Tally-Ho.* Collaborated with many lyricists.

BROADWAY MUSICALS
(wrote scores)

1888—THE PEARL OF PEKIN
1890—CASTLES IN THE AIR
1895—KISMET
1896—IN GAY NEW YORK; THE LADY SLA-
VEY; AN AMERICAN BEAUTY
1897—THE WHIRL OF THE TOWN; THE
BELLE OF NEW YORK; THE TELE-
PHONE GIRL
1901—THE GIRL FROM UP THERE
1902—A CHINESE HONEYMOON
1903—THE BILLIONAIRE; THE BLONDE IN
BLACK; WINSOME WINNIE
1906—THE SOCIAL WHIRL; THE TOURISTS
1907—FASCINATING FLORA; THE LADY
FROM LANE'S; THE WHITE HEN
1912—TWO LITTLE BRIDES

1013. KERN, JEROME   cm p o

*Born January 27, 1885, New York, N.Y.
Died November 11, 1945, New York,
N.Y.*

All-time great composer, important influence in modernizing musical theatre. Wrote largely for stage and movies. Prolific output, many standards. Ability to adapt music to unlikely books; prime example great score for SHOW BOAT. Most famous songs *They Didn't Believe Me, Look for the Silver Lining, Sunny, Who?, Ol' Man River, Make Believe, Can't Help Lovin' Dat Man, Bill, Why Was I Born?, Don't Ever Leave Me, The Night Was Made for Love, She Didn't Say "Yes", The Song Is You, I've Told Ev'ry Little Star, Smoke Gets in Your Eyes, Yesterdays, Lovely to Look At, I Won't Dance, The Way You Look Tonight, A Fine Romance, The Folks Who Live on the Hill, All the Things You Are, The Last Time I Saw Paris, Dearly Beloved, I'm Old Fashioned, Long Ago and Far Away, In Love in Vain.* Collaborators included lyricists Guy Bolton, P. G. Wodehouse, Anne Caldwell, Clifford Grey, E. Y. Harburg, Oscar Hammerstein II, Dorothy Fields, Ira Gershwin, Johnny Mercer.

Learned piano and organ, taught by mother. Educated at New York College of Music; to Europe 1903 for further study. Early experience writing music for London stage. Collaborator P. G. Wodehouse joined him years later in U.S. successes. Returned to U.S. 1904. Worked as rehearsal pianist, also for publishing house as salesman-pianist-writer. Further composing; attracted attention revising English score for 1904 Broadway show MR. WIX OF WICKHAM. Early popular song *How'd You Like to Spoon with Me?* in 1905 show THE EARL AND THE GIRL. Independent songs for Broadway shows, first complete scores for LA BELLE PAREE (1911) and THE RED PETTICOAT (1912). First big hit *They Didn't Believe Me* in THE GIRL FROM UTAH (1914) established him as important composer. In 1917 Kern music in seven Broadway shows plus one 1916 holdover! But many early songs attained little popularity. Biggest Broadway successes VERY GOOD, EDDIE (1916); OH, BOY! (1917); SALLY and GOOD MORNING, DEARIE (1921); STEPPING STONES (1923); SUNNY (1925); SHOW BOAT (1928); SWEET ADELINE (1929); THE CAT AND THE FIDDLE (1931); MUSIC IN THE AIR (1932); ROBERTA (1933). Several later converted into popular movies. Outstanding score for 1936 movie SWING TIME starring Fred Astaire and Ginger Rogers. Last Broadway show VERY WARM FOR MAY (1939); disappointing 59 performances but excellent score.

Thereafter wrote only for movies. In 1945 scored CENTENNIAL SUMMER (1946). To New York fall 1945 for Broadway revival of SHOW BOAT and to discuss a new show. Collapsed after auditioning session, died several days later. New show with producers Rodgers & Hammerstein was to have been ANNIE GET YOUR GUN—great success for composer Irving Berlin 1946. Despite incredibly prolific career, Kern active till death and still writing well. Standout movie musical late 1946-7 TILL THE CLOUDS ROLL BY based on Kern's life. Robert Walker portrayed Kern impressively, with many great Kern songs performed by all-star cast. Musicologist David Ewen wrote biography *The World of Jerome Kern.*

SONGS
(with related shows)

1903—Mister Chamberlain
1904—MR. WIX OF WICKHAM stage show
(From Saturday Till Monday;

Waiting for You; Angling by the Babbling Brook)

1905—THE EARL AND THE GIRL stage show (How'd You Like to Spoon with Me?); THE CATCH OF THE SEASON stage show (Won't You Kiss Me Once Before I Go?)

1906—THE BABES AND THE BARON stage show (March of the Toys); THE LITTLE CHERUB stage show (Under the Linden Tree; Plain Rustic Ride); MY LADY'S MAID stage show (All I Want Is You); THE RICH MR. HOGGENHEIMER stage show (Bagpipe Serenade; Poker Love; Don't You Want a Paper, Dearie?)

1907—THE GAY WHITE WAY stage show (Without the Girl Inside); THE ORCHID stage show (Come Around on Our Veranda); FASCINATING FLORA stage show (The Subway Express; Ballooning); THE DAIRY MAIDS stage show (I've a Million Reasons Why I Love You; I Would Like to Meet Your Father; others)

1908—FLUFFY RUFFLES stage show (Dining Out; Let Me Carry Your Parasol; others); THE GIRLS OF GOTTENBURG stage show (Frieda; I Can't Say You're the Only One); THE WALTZ DREAM stage show (Vienna; I'd Rather Stay at Home)

1909—THE DOLLAR PRINCESS stage show (Not Here, Not Here; A Boat Sails on Wednesday); THE GIRL AND THE WIZARD stage show (The Blue Lagoon; Franzi Frankenstein)

1910—OUR MISS GIBBS stage show (Eight Little Girls; others); THE KING OF CADONIA stage show (Come Along Pretty Girl; Coo-oo, Coo-oo; Every Girl I Know; others); THE ECHO stage show (Whistle When You're Lonely)

1911—THE SIREN stage show (Follow Me Around; I Want to Sing in Opera; My Heart I Cannot Give You; Maid from Montbijou); LITTLE MISS FIX-IT stage show (Turkey Trot; There Is a Happyland); LA BELLE PAREE stage show (Look Me Over, Dearie; I'm the Human Brush; Sing Trovatore; others);

THE KISS WALTZ stage show (Love's Charming Art; Ta-Ta, Little Girl; others)

1912—THE RED PETTICOAT stage show (Little Golden Maid; The Ragtime Restaurant; Since the Days of Grandmama; others); THE GIRL FROM MONTMARTRE stage show (Bohemia; Don't Turn My Picture to the Wall; I've Taken Such a Fancy to You; others)

1913—THE DOLL GIRL stage show (If We Were on Our Honeymoon; Will It All End in Smoke?); OH, I SAY stage show (Alone at Last; I Can't Forget Your Eyes; Katy-Did; Each Pearl a Thought); LIEBER AUGUSTIN stage show (Look in Her Eyes); THE MARRIAGE MARKET stage show (A Little Bit of Silk; I've Got Money in the Bank; I'm Looking for an Irish Husband)

1914—THE GIRL FROM UTAH stage show (They Didn't Believe Me; Same Sort of Girl; The Land of Let's Pretend; Why Don't They Dance the Polka Anymore?); THE LAUGHING HUSBAND stage show (Bought and Paid For; Love Is Like a Violin; Take a Step with Me; You're Here and I'm Here)

1915—NOBODY HOME stage show (In Arcady; You Know and I Know; The Magic Melody; Any Old Night; Another Little Girl); MISS INFORMATION stage show (Some Sort of Somebody; A Little Love); COUSIN LUCY stage show (Those Come Hither Eyes; Two Heads Are Better Than One; Society; Keep Going); A MODERN EVE stage show (Waiting for You; I'd Love to Dance Through Life with You)

1916—VERY GOOD, EDDIE stage show (Babes in the Wood; I've Got to Dance; Isn't It Great to Be Married?; Nodding Roses; If I Find the Girl); ZIEGFELD FOLLIES OF 1916 stage show (Have a Heart; My Lady of the Nile); MISS SPRINGTIME stage show (My Castle in the Air); GO TO IT stage show (When You're in Love You'll Know)

1917—OH, BOY! stage show (Till the Clouds Roll By; Nesting Time in Flatbush; A Pal Like You; Ain't It a Grand and Glorious Feeling; You Never Know About Me; An Old-Fashioned Wife); HAVE A HEART stage show (I Am All Alone; You Said Something; Honeymoon Inn; Have a Heart); LOVE O' MIKE stage show (It Wasn't My Fault; Drift with Me; Don't Tempt Me; Simple Little Tune); LEAVE IT TO JANE stage show (The Siren's Song; Cleopatterer; What I'm Longing to Say; The Sun Shines Brighter; Leave It to Jane); THE RIVIERA GIRL stage show (Will You Forget; Let's Build a Little Bungalow in Quogue); MISS 1917 stage show (The Land Where the Good Songs Go; Tell Me All Your Troubles, Cutie; I'm the Old Man in the Moon; A Picture I Want to See; Peaches); ZIEGFELD FOLLIES OF 1917 stage show (Because You're Just You)

1918—OH, LADY! LADY! stage show (Oh, Lady! Lady!; Before I Met You; When the Ships Come Home; You Found Me and I Found You; Our Little Nest); TOOT-TOOT! stage show (Toot-Toot; Honeymoon Land; If You Only Care Enough; When You Wake Up Dancing); ROCK-A-BYE BABY stage show (Little Tune Go Away; There's No Better Use for Time Than Kissing; The Kettle Song); HEAD OVER HEELS stage show (Head Over Heels; Let's Build a Little Nest; Funny Little Something; The Big Show); OH, MY DEAR! stage show (Go Little Boat); THE CANARY stage show (Take a Chance, Little Girl, and Learn to Dance; Oh Promise Me You'll Write Him Today)

1919—SHE'S A GOOD FELLOW stage show (I've Been Waiting for You All the Time; First Rose of Summer; The Bullfrog Patrol; Teacher, Teacher); THE LADY IN RED stage show (Where Is the Girl for Me?)

1920—THE NIGHT BOAT stage show (Left All Alone Again Blues; Whose Baby Are You?; A Heart for Sale; I Love the Lassies); HITCHY-KOO OF 1920 stage show (It's Kissing Time; Moon of Love; Buggy Riding; Ding-Dong)

1921—SALLY stage show (Sally; Look for the Silver Lining; Wild Rose; On with the Dance; Whip-Poor-Will; The Lorelei); GOOD MORNING, DEARIE stage show (Ka-lu-a; Easy Pickin's; Blue Danube Blues; Good Morning, Dearie; Every Girl; Look for the Silver Lining —repeated)

1922—THE BUNCH AND JUDY stage show (Pale Venetian Moon; Morning Glory; Every Day in Every Way)

1923—STEPPING STONES stage show (Stepping Stones; Once in a Blue Moon; Raggedy Ann; In Love with Love; Everybody Calls Me Little Red Riding Hood)

1924—DEAR SIR stage show (unsuccessful); SITTING PRETTY stage show (On a Desert Island with You; A Year from Today; The Enchanted Train)

1925—SUNNY stage show (Sunny; Who?; D'Ya Love Me?; Two Little Bluebirds); THE CITY CHAP stage show (The City Chap; Sympathetic; He's the Type; I'm Head Over Heels in Love; Journey's End; No One Knows)

1926—CRISS CROSS stage show (You Will, Won't You?; Cinderella Girl; In Araby with You)

1927—LUCKY stage show (Lucky; That Little Something)

1928—SHOW BOAT stage show (Make Believe; Why Do I Love You?; Ol' Man River; Bill; Can't Help Lovin' Dat Man; Life Upon the Wicked Stage; You Are Love; Till Good Luck Comes My Way)

1929—SWEET ADELINE stage show (Why Was I Born?; Don't Ever Leave Me; Here Am I; 'Twas Not So Long Ago); SHOW BOAT movie (original stage score)

1930—RIPPLES stage show (Anything Can Happen Any Day); MEN IN THE SKY movie score

1931—THE CAT AND THE FIDDLE stage show (The Night Was Made for Love; Try to Forget; She Didn't Say "Yes"; One Moment Alone; A New Love Is Old; I Watch the Love Parade; Poor Pierrot); SUNNY movie (original stage score)

1932—MUSIC IN THE AIR stage show (I've Told Ev'ry Little Star; The Song Is You; And Love Was Born; I'm Alone; We Belong Together)

1933—ROBERTA stage show (Smoke Gets in Your Eyes; Yesterdays; The Touch of Your Hand; Let's Begin; You're Devastating; Something Had to Happen; I'll Be Hard to Handle)

1934—THE CAT AND THE FIDDLE movie (original stage score)

1935—ROBERTA movie (original stage score plus new songs: Lovely to Look At; I Won't Dance); I DREAM TOO MUCH movie (I Dream Too Much; I'm the Echo; I Got Love; The Jockey on the Carousel); SWEET ADELINE movie (original stage score); RECKLESS movie (title song); MUSIC IN THE AIR movie (original stage score)

1936—SWING TIME movie (The Way You Look Tonight; A Fine Romance; Pick Yourself Up; Bojangles of Harlem; Never Gonna Dance; Waltz in Swing Time); SHOW BOAT movie (original stage score)

1937—HIGH, WIDE AND HANDSOME movie (High, Wide and Handsome; The Folks Who Live on the Hill; Can I Forget You?; The Things I Want; Allegheny Al; Will You Marry Me Tomorrow, Maria?); WHEN YOU'RE IN LOVE movie (Our Song; Whistling Boy)

1938—JOY OF LIVING movie (You Couldn't Be Cuter; Just Let Me Look at You; What's Good About Good-Night?; A Heavenly Party)

1939—VERY WARM FOR MAY stage show (All the Things You Are; All in Fun; That Lucky Fellow; Heaven in My Arms; In the Heart of the Dark)

1940—ONE NIGHT IN THE TROPICS movie (Remind Me; You and Your Kiss; Ferendola; Simple Philosophy; Your Dream)

1941—LADY BE GOOD movie (The Last Time I Saw Paris); SUNNY movie (original stage score); Day Dreaming

1942—YOU WERE NEVER LOVELIER movie (You Were Never Lovelier; Dearly Beloved; I'm Old Fashioned; Wedding in the Spring; The Shorty George; On the Beam); Windmill Under the Stars

1943—SONG OF RUSSIA movie (symphonic works)

1944—COVER GIRL movie (Long Ago and Far Away; Sure Thing; Put Me to the Test; Cover Girl; The Show Must Go On; Who's Complaining?; Make Way for Tomorrow); CAN'T HELP SINGING movie (Can't Help Singing; More and More; Any Moment Now; Califor-niay)

1946—CENTENNIAL SUMMER movie (In Love in Vain; Up with the Lark; The Right Romance; Railroad Song; All Through the Day; Cinderella Sue)

1951—SHOW BOAT movie (original stage score)

1952—LOVELY TO LOOK AT movie (remake of ROBERTA with original stage score)

1014. KERSEY, KEN   p cm

Born April 3, 1916, Harrow, Ontario, Canada

Excellent mainstream pianist, absorbed progressive style later in career. Played good boogie-woogie. Grew up in Detroit, attended Detroit Institute of Music. Early local jobs; to New York about 1938. With Lucky Millinder, Billy Hicks, Frankie Newton, Roy Eldridge. With Red Allen most of 1941, with Cootie Williams and Andy Kirk 1942. Military service, World War II. After discharge mostly toured with Jazz at the Philharmonic 1946-9. With Ed Hall in Boston 1949-50. In New York with Red Allen 1951-2, Sol Yaged 1952-4, Charlie Shavers 1955. With Yaged until illness forced retirement late 50s. Composed jazz numbers *Boogie Woogie Cocktail, K. K. Boogie*, others.

RECORDS

ANDY KIRK
De 4381 Boogie Woogie Cocktail
RED ALLEN
OK 6281 K. K. Boogie/Ol' Man River
OK 6357 Indiana / A Sheridan "Square"
PETE BROWN
Key (12")1312 It All Depends on You/I May Be Wrong
FRANKIE NEWTON
Vo 4851 Jitters/Jam Fever
TRUMMY YOUNG
Cos 901 Rattle and Roll/Behind the Eight Bar
JAZZ AT THE PHILHARMONIC
Clef 101 J.A.T.P. Blues (1 & 2)
Clef 102 J.A.T.P. Blues (3 & 4)
Clef 103 Slow Drag (1 & 2)
Clef 107 How High the Moon (1 & 2)
Clef 108 How High the Moon (3 & 4)
Clef 2001 Bell Boy Blues (1 & 2)
KEN KERSEY
Ci 3003 Kersey's Boogie/I've Got the Upper Hand
Mer 8948 Sweet Lorraine/J.A.T.P. Boogie

LPs

JAZZ AT THE PHILHARMONIC
Clef (10")MG-6 J.A.T.P. Blues
Clef (10")MG-14 I Got Rhythm/I Surrender Dear
Verve MG-Vol.1 How High the Moon (and others)
RED ALLEN-CHARLIE SHAVERS
Beth BCP-21 Jazz at The Metropole
ANDY KIRK
Vi LPM-1302 A Mellow Bit of Rhythm
SOL YAGED
Herald HLP-0103 It Might as Well Be Swing
JACK TEAGARDEN
Urania 41205 (S) Accent on Trombone
Urania (10")1001
Urania (10")1002
BUD FREEMAN
Beth BCP-29
CHARLIE SHAVERS
Beth (10")1007
(miscellaneous artists)
EmArcy MG-36018 Alto Altitude
Eso ES-548 The Modern Jazz Scene

—1941 (at Minton's and Uptown House)
Ci (10")L-410 Jamming at Rudi's No. 2

1015. KESSEL, BARNEY   g ar cm B
Born October 17, 1923, Muskogee, Okla.

Leading jazz guitarist; good modern style influenced by Charlie Christian. Self-taught guitarist and arranger. At 14 played with local Negro band. To Hollywood 1942. With new Chico Marx band in Chicago, New York, other spots. Settled in Los Angeles 1943; radio studios and freelance with combos and big bands. Early 1945 with Charlie Barnet and Hal McIntyre, last half with Artie Shaw. With Benny Goodman late 1946. Freelanced, returned to radio early 50s. Late 1952 Jazz at the Philharmonic tour working in Oscar Peterson trio. Later 1953-4 on Bob Crosby TV show as composer-arranger-musical director. Later 50s and 60s west coast studios, freelance, records. Occasionally led combo. Many jobs with TV bands. Toured with Newport All-Stars late 60s. Played England early 70s. Composer of jazz numbers *Swedish Pastry, Latin Dance No. 1, Everytime I Hear This Song, Twilight in Acapulco,* others.

RECORDS

JOE BUSHKIN
Je 5004 Indian Summer/Mean to Me
CHARLIE PARKER
Dial 1012 Relaxin' at Camarillo
Dial 1013 Cheers/Carvin' the Bird
Dial 1022 Stupendous
STAN HASSELGARD
Cap 15062 Swedish Pastry/Who Sleeps
Cap 15302 Sweet and Hot Mop/I'll Never Be the Same
RED NORVO
Cap 15253 Bop!/I'll Follow You
FLIP PHILLIPS
Mer 89022 Cottontail/Blues for the Midgets
OSCAR PETERSON
Mer 8959 Love for Sale/Until the Real Thing Comes Along
Clef 89113 It's Easy to Remember/Pooper
WINGY MANONE

Kem 2704 Japanese Sandman/Dixie Land

ARTIE SHAW GRAMERCY FIVE

Vi 20-1647 The Grabtown Grapple/ The Sad Sack

Vi 20-1800 Mysterioso/Hop Skip and Jump

Vi 20-1929 Scuttlebutt/The Gentle Grifter

LUCKY THOMPSON

Vi 20-2504 Boppin' the Blues/Just One More Chance

CHARLIE VENTURA

Lamp 105 Stompin' at the Savoy (1 & 2)

Lamp 107 The Man I Love (1 & 2)

BARNEY KESSEL

Atomic 209 Atom Buster/What Is This Thing Called Love?

Atomic 210 Slick Chick/The Man I Love

Mer 89054 Heat Wave/East of the Sun

LPs

BARNEY KESSEL

Contemp C-3513 Barney Kessel, Vol. 3

Contemp C-3535 The Poll Winners

Contemp C-3556 The Poll Winners Ride Again

Contemp (10")C-2508 Barney Kessel

Contemp (10")C-2514 Barney Kessel, Vol. 2

Atl SD-8235 (S) HAIR Is Beautiful

BARNEY KESSEL-HAROLD LANG

CP 832 El Tigre

BUDDY DEFRANCO

Verve MGC-8315 Bravura

VAN ALEXANDER

Cap T-1243 The Home of Happy Feet (The Savoy)

LIONEL HAMPTON

De DL-4194 Star Dust ("Just Jazz" Concert)

ARTIE SHAW

Vi LPV-582 Featuring Roy Eldridge (Vi RIs)

Vi LPM-1241 And His Gramercy Five (Vi RIs)

FRED ASTAIRE

Mer 1001-2-3-4 (4-LP set) The Fred Astaire Story

HAMPTON HAWES

Contemp C-3553 Hampton Hawes: Four!

BEN WEBSTER

Norg MGN-1001 The Consummate Artistry of Ben Webster

BARNEY KESSEL-TAL FARLOW-OSCAR MOORE

Norg MGN-1033 Swing Guitars

1016. KILLIAN, AL   t B

Born October 15, 1916, Birmingham, Ala.

Died September 5, 1950, Los Angeles, Calif.; killed by landlord gone berserk

Outstanding lead trumpet man effective in upper register work; good soloist with modern leanings. Began professionally mid-30s. Toured South America with Baron Lee band 1937. With Buck & Bubbles big band 1938. First New York job with Teddy Hill. Brief periods with Don Redman and Claude Hopkins. Joined Count Basie early 1940, remained till early 1945 except for 1943 period with Charlie Barnet. With Lionel Hampton briefly spring 1945, then Barnet 1945-6 about a year. Toured with Jazz at the Philharmonic. Late 1946-7 led combo in Hollywood area. Joined Duke Ellington late 1947, remained till summer 1950 (after European tour earlier 1950). A few days before death worked last job with Barnet.

RECORDS

SLIM GAILLARD

Vo 5220 Early in the Morning

Vo 5301 Matzoh Balls/It's You, Only You

Vo 5341 Chittlin' Switch Blues/Huh! Uh Huh!

Vo 5388 Swingin' in the Key of C/ Boot-Ta-La-Za

Vo 5483 Look Out/Beatin' the Board

JAZZ AT THE PHILHARMONIC

Disc 2001 Blues for Norman (1 & 2)

Disc 2002 I Can't Get Started (1 & 2)

Disc 2004 Sweet Georgia Brown (1 & 2)

Disc 2005 Lady Be Good (1 & 2)

SAVANNAH CHURCHILL with AL KILLIAN ORCHESTRA

Manor 1014 Too Blue to Cry/I Can't Get Enough of You

AL KILLIAN

B&W 117 The Killer's Boogie/The Boogie in My Flat

Manor 1098 You're the One/Goin' Down

Baronet(Sw) 5011 Y' Oughta/Body and Soul

Baronet(Sw) 5012 St. Louis Blues/Big Al

LPs

COUNT BASIE
Epic LN-3169 Basie's Back in Town (Vo, OK RIs)

JAZZ AT THE PHILHARMONIC
Verve MG-Vol.1 How High the Moon (and others)
Clef MG-608

CHARLIE BARNET
De DL-8098 Hop on the Skyliner (De RIs)

1017. KINCAID, BRADLEY   vo g cm lyr

Born July 13, 1895, Point Leavell, Ky.

Pioneer in country and western music. During 20s popularized Kentucky mountain songs on radio. Military service, World War I. On Chicago radio 1925 while at George Williams College. First star on Chicago's National Barn Dance 1926-31. Billed as The Kentucky Mountain Boy with His Houn' Dog Guitar. Other radio work; one of few country stars busy in Depression. In Boston and New England mid-30s. Late 30s and 40s popular on Midwestern Hayride radio show from Cincinnati. On many Grand Ole Opry shows in Nashville during 40s. Beginning 1949 on radio awhile in Springfield, Ohio. Later radio executive there. Active in 50s and 60s. Recorded LPs mid-60s on Blue Bonnet. Composed many songs he performed.

RECORDS

BRADLEY KINCAID
Me 12183 Red River Valley/A Picture of Life's Other Side

Me 12184 Lightning Express/True and Trembling Brakeman

Me 12332 Bury Me Out on the Prairie/After the Ball

Bb 5179 Some Little Bug/Long Long Ago

Bb 5201 My Mother's Beautiful Hand/Old Wooden Bucket

Bb 5321 The Little Shirt Mother Made/Sweet Betsy from Pike

Bb 5377 Death of Jimmie Rodgers/ Jimmie Rodgers' Life

Bb 5569 I'll Take You Home Again, Kathleen/The Ship That Never Returned

Bb 5895 The Letter Edged in Black/ Little Rosewood Casket

Bb 5971 In the Hills of Kentucky/Just Plain Folks

Vo 2683 True and Trembling Brakeman/Lightning Express

Vo 2684 The Fatal Derby Day/The Fatal Wedding

Vo 2685 Barbara Allen/The Blind Girl

Vo 2705 For Sale a Baby/Somewhere Somebody's Waiting for You

Vo 04647 Red River Valley/A Picture of Life's Other Side

LPs

BRADLEY KINCAID
Blue Bonnet 105 Mountain Ballads and Old Time Songs, Vol. 1

Blue Bonnet 107 Mountain Ballads and Old Time Songs, Vol. 2

Blue Bonnet 109 Mountain Ballads and Old Time Songs, Vol. 3

Blue Bonnet 112 Mountain Ballads and Old Time Songs, Vol. 4

(miscellaneous artists; one song)
Cam CAL-898 "Maple on the Hill" and Other Old Time Country Favorites (RIs)

1018. KINCAIDE, DEANE

ts as bs cl f p ar

Born March 18, 1911, Houston, Texas

Versatile musician on reeds, busy sideman in 30s; noted mainly for brilliant arranging. Rarely soloed; solid section man. Pioneer in dixieland big-band arrangements. Grew up in Decatur, Ill., learned several grments. 1932 job with Wingy Manone in Shreveport, La. With Ben Pollack 1933-5 as saxist-arranger. With Lennie Hayton mid-1935, playing and arranging. Original member of Bob Crosby band that emerged later 1935 from break-up of Pollack band. Most important Crosby arranger; set band style. Crosby sideman till spring 1937. Joined Woody Herman as sideman-arranger 1937 about six months, then more arranging for Crosby. With Tommy Dorsey as sideman-arranger spring 1938 to early 1940; arranged all-time hit *Boogie Woogie*, most TD jazz of late 30s. With Joe Marsala and Ray Noble 1940, Muggsy Spanier big band 1941; arranged for last two. Arranged for Glenn Miller one month beginning December 1941; no Miller work on record. Military service, World War II. Arranged for Alvino Rey 1946. With Ray McKinley 1946-8 as sideman-arranger, same with Lee Castle 1951. In mid-50s arranged for Ray McKinley & The Glenn Miller Orchestra, perpetuating Miller sound. Freelance arranging later 50s and 60s; much TV work. Settled in Florida.

ARRANGEMENTS

CLARK RANDALL Troublesome Trumpet; Jitter Bug
BOB CROSBY The Dixieland Band; Royal Garden Blues; Little Rock Getaway
TOMMY DORSEY Boogie Woogie; Hong Kong Blues; Indian Summer; Beale Street Blues; Panama; Washboard Blues; Copenhagen; Tin Roof Blues; Hawaiian War Chant; Peckin' with the Penguins; March of the Toys; Swing Low, Sweet Chariot; Sweet Sue (probable); Davenport Blues (probable)
BENNY GOODMAN (1933-5 period) Bugle Call Rag; Love Me or Leave Me; Why Couldn't It Be Poor Little Me?; Hunkadola; Riffin' the Scotch; The Dixieland Band; Tappin' the Barrel (probable); What's the Reason? (probable)
LIONEL HAMPTON Whoa Babe
RAY MCKINLEY Harlem Nocturne

RECORDS

(all LPs, featuring his arrangements)
TOMMY DORSEY
  RCA(Fr) 731-129 The Best of Tommy Dorsey, Vol. 1, 1937-1940
DAVE GARROWAY
  Vi LPM-1325 Wide, Wide World of Jazz
RAY MCKINLEY
  Vi LSP-1522 The New Glenn Miller Orchestra in Hi-Fi
MUGGSY SPANIER
  Ava 12 Columbia—The Gem of the Ocean
BOB CROSBY
  De DL-8061 Bob Crosby's Bobcats (De RIs)

(miscellaneous artists)
  Br (10")BL-58050 Big Band Jazz

1019. KING SISTERS   vocal quartet
(ALYCE, DONNA, LOUISE, YVONNE; last name DRIGGS)

Vocal quartet known for work with big bands and as single act; combined good singing and showmanship. Father William King Driggs; his middle name their professional name. Grew up in Salt Lake City. Father college voice teacher, gave girls early training. With no band experience group joined Horace Heidt in Chicago 1935. Initially billed Six King Sisters: another sister and friend made sextet. On Heidt's Alemite radio show late 1936-8. Became quartet, sang in clubs 1938-9. On Al Pearce radio show 1939. Featured with Alvino Rey (Louise's husband) band 1939-43 as group, also as individual soloists. Theatre and club jobs 1943-4; late 1944 on Kay Kyser radio show. In movies SING YOUR WORRIES AWAY (1942), FOLLOW THE BAND and LARCENY WITH MUSIC (1943), ON STAGE EVERYBODY (1945). In later years worked at intervals; sometimes with fewer than four. TV in 50s. Great comeback in 60s with The King Family TV series: four original sisters augmented by huge cast of relatives and offspring. Here won greatest fame. Continued on TV with periodic specials into 70s.

RECORDS

(as group unless designated otherwise)
HORACE HEIDT
  Br 8021 Shenanigans (Yvonne)
  Br 8148 When They Played the Polka
ALVINO REY
  Bb 11232 Jealous/Don't Take Your Love from Me (Yvonne on both)
  Bb 11448 Blue Shadows and White Gardenias (Alyce)
  Vi 27936 Keep Smilin', Keep Laughin', Be Happy
KING SISTERS
  Bb 10545 In the Mood/Irish Washerwoman
  Bb 10590 Holy Smoke/Give a Little Whistle
  Bb 10733 Six Lessons from Madame LaZonga/Sadie Hawkins

Bb 10746 A Lover's Lullaby/Java Jive
Bb 10834 Call of the Canyon/Fifteen Minute Intermission
Bb 10856 Ferry-boat Serenade/I'll Get By
Bb 10930 I Used to Love You/Don't Go in the Lion's Cage Tonight
Bb 11055 Miss Otis Regrets/Whatcha Know Joe?
Bb 11122 I Understand/My Sister and I
Bb 11154 Music Makers/The Hut-Sut Song
Bb 11184 Back in Your Own Backyard/I Dreamt I Dwelt in Harlem
Bb 11279 Moonglow/Slap-Slap
Bb 11398 Someone's Rocking My Dreamboat/We're the Couple in the Castle
Bb 11431 'Tis Autumn/Arthur Murray Taught Me Dancing in a Hurry
Bb 11582 Daybreak/Kille Kille
Vi 20-1672 Sweetheart of All My Dreams/A Tender Word Will Mend It All
Vi 20-1719 No Can Do/Poor Lenore
Mer 5431 I'll Get By/Somedays There Just Ain't No Fish

LPs

KING SISTERS
Cap T-919 Imagination
Cap ST-1205 (S) Warm and Wonderful
Cam CAL-929 In the Mood (Bb, Vi RIs)
KING FAMILY
WB 1601 (S) The King Family Show
WB 1613 (S) The King Family Album
Ha HL-11293 Wonderful
Cap DT-2352 Love at Home

1020. KING, CHARLES vo

Born 1894
Died January 11, 1944, London, England

Handsome leading man and singer on Broadway stage 1908-30. In two leading 1929 movie musicals BROADWAY MELODY and HOLLYWOOD REVUE OF 1929. Several other early musicals, then character roles in 30s and 40s films—almost 100, majority low-budget westerns. During 30s sang in clubs at intervals. While performing

abroad with USO during World War II, caught pneumonia and died in London.

BROADWAY MUSICALS

1908—THE MIMIC WORLD
1911—THE SLIM PRINCESS
1912—A WINSOME WIDOW
1913—THE PASSING SHOW OF 1913
1914—WATCH YOUR STEP
1917—MISS 1917
1919—GOOD MORNING, JUDGE
1921—GEORGE WHITE'S SCANDALS OF 1921; IT'S UP TO YOU
1922—LITTLE NELLIE KELLY
1924—KEEP KOOL
1926—NO FOOLIN' (later titled ZIEGFELD'S AMERICAN REVUE OF 1926)
1927—HIT THE DECK
1928—PRESENT ARMS
1930—THE NEW YORKERS
1937—SEA LEGS (unsuccessful)

RECORDS

CHARLES KING-LOUISE GROODY
Vi 20609 Sometimes I'm Happy
CHARLES KING
Br 4615 Love Ain't Nothin' but the Blues/Happy Days Are Here Again
Br 4616 Lucky Me—Lovable You/Everybody Tap
Br 4840 Halfway to Heaven/Love Comes in the Moonlight
Br 4849 Here Comes the Sun/Leave a Little Smile
Vi 21964 The Wedding of the Painted Doll/Broadway Melody
Vi 21965 You Were Meant for Me/Love Boat

1021. KING, DENNIS vo
(DENNIS PRATT)

Born November 2, 1897, Coventry, England
Died May 21, 1971, New York, N.Y.

Handsome leading man of Broadway stage. First fame as singing star in musicals, later starred in plays, became distinguished actor. Debut in AS YOU LIKE IT at England's Birmingham Repertory Theatre 1913. Starred in MONSIEUR BEAUCAIRE in London's Palace Theatre 1919. To U.S. 1921; New York debut in non-musical CLAIR DE LUNE. In non-musicals ROMEO AND JULIET, ANTONY AND CLEOPATRA, BACK TO METHUSELAH. Stardom in three important musicals ROSE-MARIE (1924), THE VAGABOND KING (1925; biggest success) and THE THREE MUSKETEERS (1928). In 1932 revival of SHOW BOAT and in other musicals FREDERIKA (1937), I MARRIED AN ANGEL (1938). Starred in plays RICHARD OF BORDEAUX (1934), PETTICOAT FEVER (1935), A DOLL'S HOUSE (1937), THE THREE SISTERS (1942), THE SEARCHING WIND (1944), HE WHO GETS SLAPPED (1946), MEDEA (1947; replaced John Gielgud), THE DEVIL'S DISCIPLE (1950), BILLY BUDD (1951), LUNATICS AND LOVERS (1954), SHANGRI-LA (1956), PHOTO FINISH (1963). Supporting role in A PATRIOT FOR ME (1969-70), still performed well. Played famous role in THE VAGABOND KING again in 1930 when show converted into early sound movie. Supporting singing role in 1933 Laurel & Hardy movie THE DEVIL'S BROTHER. Sang on radio during 30s; regular spot on 1934-5 Enna Jettick show. Radio in early 50s, also occasional TV dramas and musical specials.

RECORDS

DENNIS KING
   Vi 19897 Song of the Vagabonds
   Vi 22263 If I Were King/Michavoi
LPs

DENNIS KING
   Mon-Ever MES-7050   In   Rudolf Friml's THE THREE MUSKETEERS (vocals with Drury Lane Theatre Orchestra) and THE VAGABOND KING (Vi RI of Song of the Vagabonds)

1022. KING, HENRY   p B

Society-style pianist and leader of popular hotel band in 30s and 40s. Piano prominent in band's arrangements. Started as bandleader late 20s. Popular by early 30s from hotel jobs, radio coverage and recordings. Through band's top years in 30s only featured vocalist Joseph Sudy. Theme *A Blues Serenade*. In late 30s and 40s featured Latin-American tunes. Late 1936-7 band on Burns & Allen radio show. King in 1945 movie OUT OF THIS WORLD with other prominent pianist-bandleaders. Active through 40s into 50s, though not as prominent.

RECORDS

DON WALKER (Henry King)
   Vo 2608 Let's Fall in Love/Love Is Love Anywhere
   Vo 2617 Song of Surrender/Coffee in the Morning, Kisses at Night
HENRY KING
   Vo 2550 Night Owl/It's Only a Paper Moon
   Vo 2579 Easter Parade/Not for All the Rice in China
   Vi 24466 Roof Top Serenade/Buy a Kiss
   Vi 24478 April in Paris/Tu Sais
   Vi 24608 Ending with a Kiss/Call of Love
   Vi 24656 The Breeze/Dancing and Dreaming
   Co 2949-D Don't Let It Bother You/A Needle in a Haystack
   Co 2992-D I Woke Up Too Soon/Dancing with My Shadow
   Co 2998-D The Night Is Young/When I Grow Too Old to Dream
   Co 3042-D Thrilled/Song of Spring
   Co 3048-D Chasing Shadows/Footloose and Fancy Free
   De 743 Gloomy Sunday/A Waltz Was Born in Vienna
   De 745 My Romance/Love Is Like a Cigarette
   De 755 I'll Stand By/A Little Robin Told Me So
   De 763 There's a Small Hotel/It's Got to Be Love
   De 1063 (theme) A Blues Serenade/My Day Begins and Ends with You
   De 1192 September in the Rain/Melody for Two
   De 1319 Where or When/The Image of You
   De 1332 So Rare/When Two Love Each Other
   De 1404 The Lady Is a Tramp/Little Fraternity Pin
   De 1978 My Own/You're as Pretty as a Picture
   De 2198 I Have Eyes/The Funny Old Hills
   De 2981 At the Balalaika/One Look at You

LPs

HENRY KING

Tops L-908 Rhumba Favorites
Tops L-932 Latin Rhythms

1022A. KING, PEE WEE

acc vo cm lyr B
(FRANK KING)

Born February 18, 1914, Milwaukee, Wis.

Entertainer and composer of country and western hits. Best-known *Tennessee Waltz, Slow Poke, Bonaparte's Retreat, You Belong to Me* (last two pop hits). Other compositions *Tennessee Tango, Silver and Gold, Bimbo, Walk Me by the River, River Road Two-Step.* First important job 1933 on local radio. With Log Cabin Boys 1935-6 on Louisville radio. Formed combo The Golden West Cowboys. Often on Nashville's Grand Ole Opry 1937-47. Own show on Knoxville radio. Redd Stewart featured on vocals and fiddle, collaborated with King on compositions. Eddy Arnold in band awhile. First band to use electric guitar (played by Clell Summey) and drums on Grand Ole Opry. Band in several western movies. On Louisville radio-TV 1947-57, TV in Cleveland and Chicago late 50s. Active in 60s.

RECORDS

PEE WEE KING

Vi 20-2366 Ten Gallon Boogie/I Hear You Knockin'
Vi 20-2680 Tennessee Waltz/Rootie Tootie
Vi 20-2841 Juke Box Blues/Oh, Monah
Vi 20-2995 Forty-Nine Women/Quit Honkin' That Horn
Vi 20-3106 New York to New Orleans/Say Good Mornin' Nellie
Vi 20-3232 Bull Fiddle Boogie/Chattanooga Bess
Vi 20-4458 Silver and Gold/Ragtime Annie Lee
Vi 20-4655 Busybody/I Don't Mind
Vi 20-5144 Railroad Boogie
Vi 20-5694 Indian Giver/Backward, Turn Backward

Vi 21-0004 Out of My Mind/The Ghost and Honest Joe
Vi 21-0015 Waltz of the Alamo/The Color Song
Vi 21-0086 The Nashville Waltz/Tennessee Polka
Vi 21-0489 Slow Poke/Whisper Waltz

LPs

PEE WEE KING

Vi (10") LPM-3028 Country Classics
Vi (10") LPM-3109 Country Classics Vol. 2
Cam CAL-876 Country Barn Dance
Starday 284 Pee Wee King and Redd Stewart
Nash 2042 Tennessee Waltz and Slow Poke

1023. KING, TEDDI

vo

Born September 18, 1929, Boston, Mass.

Jazz singer who got effects from tone and phrasing rather than by variations on tunes. Sang with excellent taste. Early experience with USO shows and with bands in Boston area. Recorded with Nat Pierce. With Ray Dorey in Boston 1950. On Boston TV 1951. With George Shearing middle 1952-3: first female singer with group. Continued as single into 70s, often at Boston's Storyville jazz club.

RECORDS

NAT PIERCE

Motif 006 You Don't Know What Love Is

GEORGE SHEARING

MGM 11316 It's Easy to Remember/Love, Your Spell Is Everywhere
MGM 11425 Midnight Belongs to You

TEDDI KING

Vi 20-6392 Mr. Wonderful/Are You Slipping Through My Fingers?
MGM 11621 I Wished on the Moon/Moonlight in Vermont
Story 5009 I Saw Stars/Love Is a Now and Then Thing

LPs

TEDDI KING

Vi LPM-1147 Bidin' My Time
Vi LPM-1313 To You
Vi LPM-1454 A Girl and Her Songs

Story 903 Now in Vogue
Story (10″)302
Story (10″)314

1024. KING, TEMPO   vo B

Born c. 1915
Died June 25, 1939, New York, N.Y.
Leader of free-wheeling swing combo in
mid-30s; excellent records 1936-7. King
sang most numbers in swinging, raucous,
humorous style. Capable pianist Queenie
Ada Rubin featured prominently. On
many records: Marty Marsala (t), Joe
Marsala (cl), Eddie Condon (g). Group
billed as Tempo King and His Kings of
Tempo.

RECORDS

TEMPO KING

Bb 6533 Bojangles of Harlem/Organ
     Grinder's Swing
Bb 6535 Papa Tree-Top Tall/I'll Sing
     You a Thousand Love Songs
Bb 6637 Thru the Courtesy of Love/
     To Mary—with Love
Bb 6684 Keepin' Out of Mischief
     Now/You Turned the Tables on
     Me
Bb 6688 An Apple a Day/Something
     Has Happened to Me
Bb 6721 Pennies from Heaven/Nero
Bb 6725 Timber/Someone to Care for
     Me
Bb 6758 He Ain't Got Rhythm/Slum-
     ming on Park Avenue
Bb 6768 Moonlight on the Prairie,
     Mary/There's a Ranch in the Sky
Bb 6770 My Last Affair/Gee, But
     You're Swell
Vo 3630 The Folks Who Live on the
     Hill/High, Wide and Handsome
Vo 3671 Am I Dreaming?/All Over
     Nothing at All
Vo 3716 Our Love Was Meant to Be/
     Cryin' Mood
Vo 3899 The One Rose/I Can Always
     Dream
Vo 4156 I Got a Notion/That's the
     Way It Goes

1025. KING, WAYNE   as cl vo cm B

Born February 16, 1901, Savannah, Ill.
Leader of prominent 30s and 40s dance
band; featured slow, dreamy style, many
waltzes. Known as The Waltz King. Especially popular in Chicago ballrooms
and throughout midwest. King alto sax
and vocals featured, both with thin,
mournful sound. Attended Valparaiso
University, at same time worked with
Benson Orchestra unit in Chicago's Morrison Hotel, commuted by train. In 1921-2
worked for Chicago insurance company
and as garage and railroad mechanic. In
pit band at Riviera Theatre. With Del
Lampe band 1925-7, mostly at Chicago's
Trianon Ballroom. Aragon Ballroom
opened 1927; Lampe organized another
band to play there, made King leader.
Aragon main King base through the
years. Band popular by early 30s. Theme
The Waltz You Saved for Me. Early featured vocalist Ernie Birchill. Early record
hits *Star Dust, Goofus, Blue Hours*. In fall
1931 band began Lady Esther Serenade
radio show, continued till fall 1938. In
mid-30s band toured for first time. In
1937 biggest record hit *Josephine*. Band at
musical best 1940-1, featured vocalist
Buddy Clark on records and radio show.
Military service in Chicago area, World
War II. Formed another band mid-1945.
Began another radio show 1946, had
several series in ensuing years. TV show
1949-52. In later 50s into 70s active at
intervals on special tours presenting stage
entertainment usually featuring vocalist
Nancy Evans. Composer or co-composer
of popular songs *That Little Boy of Mine*
and *The Waltz You Saved for Me* (1931),
Goofus (1932), *Blue Hours* (1933), *Josephine* (1937). Lesser compositions *Annabelle, Baby Shoes, With You Beside Me, So
Close to Me, Corn Silk, I'd Give My
Kingdom for a Smile*.

RECORDS

WAYNE KING

Br 6474 Moon Song/Twenty Million
     People
Br 6580 From Me to You/Love Songs
     of the Nile
Br 6615 Blue Hours/With You Beside
     Me
Br 6712 After Sundown/Our Big Love
     Scene
Br 6735 Song of Surrender/One Morn-
     ing in May

Vi 22399 On a Blue and Moonless Night/Promises
Vi 22575 (theme) The Waltz You Saved for Me/In a Window, in a House, in Caroline
Vi 22600 Goofus/Swamp Ghosts
Vi 22643 Dream a Little Dream of Me/Wabash Moon
Vi 22656 Star Dust
Vi 22825 Goodnight Sweetheart/So Close to Me
Vi 24018 I Love You Truly
Vi 24115 Sweethearts Forever/Three's a Crowd
Vi 25495 Trust in Me/The Night Is Young and You're So Beautiful
Vi 25506 You're Laughing at Me/The Girl on the Police Gazette
Vi 25518 Josephine
Vi 25528 Sweethearts/Sylvia
Vi 26424 Where Was I?/Corn Silk
Vi 26463 At the Balalaika/Leanin' on the Ole Top Rail
Vi 26767 You Are My Sunshine/Maria Elena
Vi 26785 Falling Leaves/Goodbye, Little Darlin', Goodbye
Vi 27201 I Should Have Known You Years Ago/He's My Uncle
Vi 27358 We Could Make Such Beautiful Music/These Things You Left Me
Vi 27373 A Broken Melody/Worried Mind
Vi 27516 Time and Time Again/Blue Danube Waltz

LPs

WAYNE KING
De DL-8277 Enchanted Evening
De DL-8353 Smooth as Silk
De DL-8663 Dream Time
De DL-8823 The Sound of Wayne King
De DL-8876 Orchids to My Lady
De DL-8951 Lady Esther Serenade
Vi (10″)LPM-3057 The Songs of Irving Berlin
Vi LSP-3742 (S) Best
Vo 73840 Smoke Gets in Your Eyes

1026. KIRBY, JOHN   b tu B

Born December 31, 1908, Baltimore, Md.
Died June 14, 1952, Hollywood, Calif.

Best known as leader of tightly knit jazz sextet in late 30s and early 40s billed as The Biggest Little Band in the Land. Featured talented jazzmen, clever arrangements, light swing. Kirby bass style clean, buoyant. Grew up in orphanage, learned trombone. To New York mid-20s, worked odd jobs including period as Pullman porter. Took up tuba late 20s, soon began working jobs, later changed to string bass. With Fletcher Henderson 1930-3, Chick Webb late 1933-5, Henderson again 1935-6. Joined Mills Blue Rhythm Band briefly late 1936. In 1937 became combo leader, scored at Onyx Club on 52nd Street. Peak popularity 1939-42. Kirby's wife Maxine Sullivan gained fame as featured vocalist with group. Some instrumentals lightly swung classics, most featured staudards. Outstanding personnel Charlie Shavers (t), Buster Bailey (cl), Russell Procope (as), Billy Kyle (p), O'Neill Spencer (d), Kirby (b). Shavers arranged. 1940 radio series Flow Gently Sweet Rhythm; on Duffy's Tavern show 1941-2. After 1942 combo's popularity faded and personnel changed. Kirby continued combo several years. Tried to revive original group in postwar years with indifferent results. In 1950-1 Kirby with Red Allen and Buck Clayton, also led combo. Settled on West coast late 1951-2. Jobs with Benny Carter, mostly inactive.

RECORDS

FLETCHER HENDERSON
Co 2329-D Chinatown, My Chinatown/Somebody Loves Me
Co 2513-D Clarinet Marmalade/Sugarfoot Stomp
Co 2732-D Honeysuckle Rose/Underneath the Harlem Moon
Vo 3211 Christopher Columbus/Blue Lou
COLEMAN HAWKINS
OK 41566 Jamaica Shout/Heart Break Blues
CMS 533 Dedication
CHICK WEBB
Co 2926-D Stomping at the Savoy/Why Should I Beg for Love?
OK 41572 Blue Minor/Lonesome Moments

MILLS BLUE RHYTHM BAND
  Co 3162-D Big John Special/Callin'
    Your Bluff
MEZZ MEZZROW
  Vi 25019 Apologies/Sendin' the Vipers
  Vi 25202 Old Fashioned Love/35th &
    Calumet
MILDRED BAILEY
  Vo 3378 'Long About Midnight/More
    Than You Know
  Vo 4939 Moon Love/It Seems Like
    Old Times
BENNY GOODMAN QUARTET
  Vi 26139 I Know That You Know/I
    Cried for You
JOHNNY DODDS
  De 2111 Wild Man Blues/29th &
    Dearborn
  De 7413 Blues Galore/Shake Your
    Can
LIONEL HAMPTON
  Vi 26011 I'm in the Mood for Swing/
    Shoe Shiners Drag
RED ALLEN
  Vo 2965 Body and Soul/Rosetta
BUSTER BAILEY
  Va 668 Dizzy Debutante/Afternoon in
    Africa
  Vo 4089 Sloe Jam Fizz/Planter's
    Punch
JOHN KIRBY
  De 2216 Undecided/From A Flat to C
  De 2367 Pastel Blue/Rehearsin' for a
    Nervous Breakdown
  Vo 4653 Dawn on the Desert/The Turf
  Vo 4890 Anitra's Dance/Drink to Me
    Only with Thine Eyes
  Vo 5048 I May Be Wrong/Opus 5
  Vo 5187 Blue Skies/Royal Garden
    Blues
  Vo 5605 Humoresque/One Alone
  Vo 5805 Blues Petite/Andiology
  Co 36000 Rose Room/20th Century
    Closet
  Co 36001 Sweet Georgia Brown/Sere-
    nade
  Vi 27598 Fifi's Rhapsody/It's Only a
    Paper Moon
  Apo 762 Natchez Ball/Sampson and
    De-Lie-Lah
  Asch 357-1 Maxixe Dengoza/9:20
    Special

LPs

JOHN KIRBY
  Co GL-502 (RIs)
(original band minus Kirby, with Maxine
Sullivan—1955)
  Period 1113 Flow Gently Sweet
    Rhythm
CHICK WEBB
  Co CL-2639 (Co, Vo RIs)
MEZZ MEZZROW
  "X" (10″)LVA-3015 Swing Session (Vi
    RIs)
FLETCHER HENDERSON
  "X" (10″)LVA-3013 Connie's Inn Or-
    chestra (Vi RIs)
WILLIE "THE LION" SMITH
  Ace of Hearts(E) AH-162 The Swing-
    ing Cub Men (De RIs)
(miscellaneous artists)
  Vi LPV-578 Swing, Vol. 1 (Vi, Bb RIs)

1027. KIRK, ANDY   tu b bs b-s cm B
    Born May 28, 1898, Newport, Ky.
Leader of good swing band called Andy
Kirk & His Clouds of Joy. Moderate
success in 30s and early 40s. Band played
easy swing, featured ballads. Interesting
Kansas City-style arrangements stressed
brass riffs, mellow, flowing sax section.
Themes *Until the Real Thing Comes Along*
and *Cloudy*. Kirk grew up in Denver,
learned several instruments, concentrated
on tuba and bass sax. Worked locally
early and mid-20s; long period with
George Morrison band. In Dallas with
Terrence Holder 1926-8, became leader
when Holder left early 1929. To Kansas
City, rivalled Bennie Moten as city's best
band. Saxman John Williams and wife-
pianist Mary Lou (later Kirk's wife) great
assets. Long run at Pla-Mor Ballroom.
Important jobs in New York 1930, including Roseland and Savoy Ballrooms.
House band awhile 1931 at Philadelphia's
Pearl Theatre, but Kansas City main base
until 1936, then toured. 1936 hit *Until the
Real Thing Comes Along* built band's
popularity. Mary Lou Williams key member as piano soloist, arranger, composer
of many jazz numbers featured by band.
Other important sidemen Dick Wilson

(ts; featured), Paul King (t), John Harrington (cl), Ted Donnelly (tb). Floyd Smith joined early 1939, a pioneer on amplified guitar. Great vocalist Henry Wells (tb) helped set band's ballad style mid-30s; followed by smooth baritone Pha Terrell. June Richmond featured late 30s-early 40s. Howard McGhee featured on trumpet early 40s. Kirk continued band amid personnel changes until 1948. During 40s band faded. In later years Kirk booked bands or combos occasionally for special jobs, worked in New York real estate and as hotel manager. Composed *Sittin' Around and Dreamin'*, pop recorded by band 1938.

RECORDS

ANDY KIRK
Br 4694 Mess-a-Stomp/Blue Clarinet Stomp
Br 4893 Corky Stomp/Froggy Bottom
Br 6129 Dallas Blues
De 729 Froggy Bottom/Christopher Columbus
De 772 Corky/Blue Illusion
De 809 (theme) Until the Real Thing Comes Along/Walkin' and Swingin'
De 853 Moten Swing/Give Her a Pint
De 1046 Lotta Sax Appeal/Bearcat Shuffle
De 1085 The Lady Who Swings the Band/What Will I Tell My Heart?
De 1208 (theme) Cloudy/Puddin' Head Serenade
De 1303 Wednesday Night Hop/Worried Over You
De 1422 I Went to a Gypsy/Better Luck Next Time
De 1477 With Love in My Heart/Why Can't We Do It Again?
De 1579 A Mellow Bit of Rhythm/In My Wildest Dreams
De 1827 It Must Be True/What's Mine Is Yours
De 1916 I'll Get By/I Surrender Dear
De 2127 Toadie Toddle/I Won't Tell a Soul
De 2326 Honey/Mary's Idea
De 2483 Floyd's Guitar Blues/Twinklin'

De 2510 S'posin'/I'll Never Learn
De 2962 Wham/Love Is the Thing
De 3350 Midnight Stroll/No Greater Love
De 4042 Big Time Crip/47th Street Jive
De 4381 Boogie Woogie Cocktail/Worried Life Blues
De 4405 McGhee Special/Hey Lawdy Mama
De 18123 The Count/12th Street Rag

LPs

ANDY KIRK
De DL-9232 Instrumentally Speaking (De RIs)
Cor (10")CRL-56019 Souvenir Album, Vol.1 (De RIs)
Vi LPM-1302 A Mellow Bit of Rhythm (modern versions of old numbers)
Ace of Hearts(E) AH-110 Clouds of Joy (De RIs)
Ace of Hearts(E) AH-160 Twelve Clouds of Joy (De RIs)

1028. KIRK, LISA   vo

Good entertainer of 40s and 50s. Early experience as vocalist with Jimmy Palmer band 1944. Minor role in Broadway musical ALLEGRO (1947), featured role in KISS ME, KATE (1949). Highly professional night club act sometimes used male dancers in song-and-dance routines. Sang in strong voice with confidence; sometimes raucous. Records and TV in 50s.

RECORDS

LISA KIRK-EDDIE CANTOR-SAMMY KAYE ORCHESTRA
Vi 20-3751 The Old Piano Roll Blues/Juke Box Annie
LISA KIRK-FRAN WARREN
Vi 20-3696 Dearie/Just a Girl That Men Forget
LISA KIRK
Vi 20-3591 Shame on You/Charley, My Boy
Vi 20-3989 Ja-da
Vi 20-4030 Don't Blame Me/I Feel a Song Comin' On
Vi 20-4031 I Can't Believe That You're

in Love with Me/I'm in the Mood
for Love
Vi 20-4032 You're a Sweetheart/Exactly Like You
Vi 20-4134 Sad and Lonely/Love Is the Reason
Vi 20-4869 How Come You Do Me Like You Do?/If Your Heart Is Breaking
Vi 20-5187 Ohio/Catch Me if You Can
Vi 20-5334 Do Me a Favor/King Size Kisses

LPs

(original Broadway cast)
Co MO-4140 KISS ME, KATE

1029. KITSIS, BOB　　　　　　p

Born September 5, 1917, Boston, Mass.

Swing pianist of late 30s and 40s. Attended Harvard, played in college bands. After college top job in Artie Shaw band one year beginning late 1938. After Shaw abandoned band Kitsis continued in band under George Auld's brief leadership. With Tommy Dorsey and Leo Reisman 1940, Gene Krupa late 1940-1. Freelanced, worked with Red Norvo 1942. Later 1942 military service.

RECORDS

ARTIE SHAW
Bb 10079 Say It with a Kiss
Bb 10202 One Night Stand/One Foot in the Groove
Bb 10347 Go Fly a Kite
Bb 10430 I Surrender, Dear
GENE KRUPA
OK 6034 Boogie Woogie Bugle Boy
OK 6046 Drum Boogie
GEORGE AULD
Vs 8159 Juke Box Jump

LPs

ARTIE SHAW
Vi LPM-1244 Moonglow (Bb, Vi RIs)
Vi LPT-6000(2-LP set) In the Blue Room/In the Cafe Rouge
Cam CAL-465 The Great Artie Shaw (Bb, Vi RIs)
Cam CAL-515 Swings Show Tunes (Bb RIs)
GENE KRUPA
Co C2L-29(2-LP set) Drummin' Man

1030. KLAGES, RAYMOND　　　lyr

Born June 10, 1888, Baltimore, Md.
Died March 20, 1947, Glendale, Calif.

Lyricist of 20s and 30s. Collaborated on a few songs for Broadway musicals including score of important 1922 show SALLY, IRENE AND MARY. Best-known songs *Doin' the Raccoon*; *Just You, Just Me*; *Pardon Me, Pretty Baby*. Collaborators included composers J. Fred Coots, Louis Alter, Jesse Greer, Harry Carroll, Al Hoffman, Vincent Rose, James V. Monaco. Educated at Baltimore City College. Performed in vaudeville, minstrels, other road shows. Wrote special material for vaudeville. Military service, World War I. Worked for New York publishing company. Began songwriting early 20s.

SONGS
(with related shows)

1922—SALLY, IRENE AND MARY stage show (I Wonder Why; Something in Here; Time Will Tell); Early in the Morning Blues
1926—Climbing Up the Ladder of Love; Hugs and Kisses
1928—EARL CARROLL'S VANITIES OF 1928 stage show (Once in a Lifetime; Blue Shadows); SAY WHEN stage show (One Step to Heaven; How About It?); Doin' the Raccoon
1929—HOLLYWOOD REVUE OF 1929 movie (Low Down Rhythm); MARIANNE movie (Marianne; Just You, Just Me; Hang on to Me)
1930—Cheer Up
1931—EARL CARROLL'S VANITIES OF 1931 stage show (Tonight or Never); Pardon Me, Pretty Baby
1932—Kiss by Kiss
1933—It Might Have Been a Diff'rent Story; Roll Up the Carpet
1936—It All Begins and Ends with You
1941—$21 a Day—Once a Month

1031. KLEIN, MANNY (or MANNIE)　　t B

Born February 4, 1908, New York, N.Y.

Trumpet star with prolific freelance recording career, particularly in 30s. Good jazz soloist with clean swing style, not overpowering. Sometimes mistaken for

Bunny Berigan on records. As youngster played in brass bands. Began professionally late 20s; early work with Louis Katzman. With Al Goodman playing for Broadway show FOLLOW THROUGH beginning late 1928. Much in demand on recordings due to able lead trumpet, consistent jazz. In late 20s with Red Nichols, Joe Venuti, Roger Wolfe Kahn, Dorsey Brothers (also 1932-4). Prominent in New York radio. Recorded frequently with Boswell Sisters early 30s. Occasionally led groups. With early Glenn Miller band briefly in spring 1937. Formed big band late 1937-8 with Frankie Trumbauer, who fronted. Settled on west coast, reportedly best-paid studio musician. With Matty Malneck 1938-9, Ray Noble 1939, Artie Shaw 1940. Became MGM studio musician 1942, later in year entered military. After discharge resumed studio work; active in 50s and 60s. Occasional record sessions in later years.

RECORDS

IRVING MILLS & HIS HOTSY TOTSY GANG
Br 4559 Harvey/March of the Hoodlums
Br 4641 Manhattan Rag/What Kind of Man Is You?
Br 4920 High and Dry/Barbaric
BOSWELL SISTERS
Br 6151 It's You/It's the Girl
Br 6173 Shine On Harvest Moon/Heebie Jeebies
DORSEY BROTHERS ORCHESTRA
Br 6624 By Heck/Old Man Harlem
De 118 By Heck
De 208 Heat Wave/Stop, Look and Listen
BEN SELVIN
Co 2426-D You Said It/Learn to Croon
Co 2554-D Little Mary Brown
Co 2575-D Bend Down, Sister
RUBE BLOOM & HIS BAYOU BOYS
Co 2186-D Mysterious Mose/Bessie Couldn't Help It
Co 2218-D On Revival Day/There's a Wah Wah Girl in Agua Caliente
CLAUDE THORNHILL
Vo 3595 Gone with the Wind/Harbor Lights

Vo 3616 Stop! You're Breaking My Heart/Whispers in the Dark
THE SOPHISTICATES
De 1818 Swing Low Sweet Chariot/Liebestraum
ADRIAN ROLLINI
Me 12630 You've Got Me Crying Again
Co 2785-D Blue Prelude/Happy as the Day Is Long
De 265 Sugar/Riverboat Shuffle
De 359 Davenport Blues/Somebody Loves Me
JERRY COLONNA
Co 36092 Lalita
RONNIE GREY & THE JETS
Cap 3174 Run, Manny, Run
FRANKIE LAINE with MANNY KLEIN ORCHESTRA
Mer 5007 That's My Desire/By the River Sainte Marie
HELEN GRAYCO with MANNY KLEIN ORCHESTRA
Lon 761 Diga Diga Doo/Or No Dice
MANNY KLEIN
Br 7605 I'm in Love/Ringside Table for Two
Br 7606 Hot Spell/Juba
Bb 10505 Rainbows Over Paradise/Kamakaeha
Key 631 At Sundown/Bei Mir Bist du Schon
Cor 60032 San/Weary Weasel

LPs

BEN SELVIN
TOM 16 Vol.1 (Co RIs)
BOSWELL SISTERS
Ace of Hearts(E) AH-116 (Br RIs)
BILL DODGE (Benny Goodman)
Melodeon MLP-7328-9 (2 LPs) Swingin' '34 (1934 ETs by Benny Goodman and all-star pickup groups)
ADRIAN ROLLINI (one side)
Br (10″)BL-58039 Battle of Jazz (1934 De RIs)
VAN ALEXANDER
Cap T-1243 The Home of Happy Feet (The Savoy)
GLEN GRAY
Cap W-1022 Sounds of the Great Bands, Vol.1
Cap T-1938 Today's Best

JACK TEAGARDEN
Cap T-721 This Is Teagarden!
PETE RUGOLO
Mer PPS-2016 Ten Trumpets and Two
Guitars
TUTTI CAMARATA
Vista 4047 (S) Tutti's Trumpets

1032. KLEIN, MANUEL   cm lyr E

*Born December 6, 1876, London, Eng
land*
Died June 1, 1919, London, England

Composer-conductor active in early English and American musical theatre. Edu-
cated in London. Musical scores for
American stage shows 1903-13. Musical
director at New York's Hippodrome The-
atre 1905-14. Returned to London as
musical director of Gaiety and Hippodrome Theatres. Most popular composition *Moon Dear* in Broadway hit musical
A SOCIETY CIRCUS (1906). Other songs
*Meet Me When the Lanterns Glow, Home
Is Where the Heart Is, Lucia, My Old
Town, It's a Long Lane That Has No
Turning, If I Love You, I'm Looking for a
Sweetheart, In Siam, Loving, Temple Bells,
Ho! Every One That Thirsteth* (church
anthem). Collaborators lyricists Grant
Stewart, Vincent Bryan, Sydney Rosen-
feld, James O'Dea, R. H. Burnside, Car-
roll Fleming.

BROADWAY MUSICALS
(wrote scores)

1903—MR. PICKWICK
1906—A SOCIETY CIRCUS; THE MAN FROM
NOW
1907—THE TOP OF THE WORLD
1908—THE PIED PIPER
1910—THE INTERNATIONAL CUP AND THE
BALLET OF NIAGARA
1911—AROUND THE WORLD
1913—HOP O' MY THUMB
1921—IT'S UP TO YOU (part of score)

1033. KLINE, OLIVE   vo

Leading recording artist in early days of
industry beginning around 1911. Began
career several years before. Leading concert soprano into 20s; early records still in
catalogs then. Declined to pursue operatic
career, concentrated on concerts and rec-

ords. Guest singer with many sympho-
nies, sang at music festivals. Performed
popular songs well. Member of quartet at
New York's West End Collegiate Church.
In mid-30s made musical education records for children.

RECORDS

OLIVE KLINE
Vi 17345 Message of the Violet
Vi 17401 I Can Live without You
Vi 17459 My Fairy Prince/Adele
Vi 17509 Isle d'Amour
Vi 17665 Love Moon
Vi 17690 When You're Away/Charme
d'Amour
Vi 17879 I Need Affection
Vi 17922 Ladder of Roses/Waltz En-
trancing
Vi 45115 Lo, Hear the Gentle Lark/
Ma Curly-Headed Baby
Vi 45132 Flow Gently Sweet Afton/
Doan Ye Cry, Ma Honey
Vi 45152 Bring Back My Soldier Boy
to Me
Vi 45153 I'll Pray for You
Vi 45167 Chinese Lullaby
Vi 45201 The Japanese Sandman/Old
Fashioned Garden
Vi 45332 Japanese Moon
Vi 45348 A Kiss in the Dark
Vi 45456 Indian Love Call
Vi (12")35278 When a Maid Comes a-
Knocking
OLIVE KLINE-ELSIE BAKER
Vi 19873 Whispering Hope/Abide
with Me
Vi 45309 Indiana Lullaby/Marcheta

1034. KLINK, AL   ts cl f as bs b-s

*Born December 28, 1915, Danbury,
Conn.*

Capable sideman with big bands, underrated soloist on tenor sax. In later years
absorbed aspects of modern jazz, displayed talent on flute. Began locally 1932.
First important job with Glenn Miller in
January 1939. Some solos, though Tex
Beneke featured more prominently on
tenor sax. With Miller until disbanding
September 1942. Joined Benny Goodman
late 1942, with band in movies THE POW-
ERS GIRL and STAGE DOOR CANTEEN. Free-

lanced awhile, then rejoined Goodman fall 1943 to early 1944; in movie SWEET AND LOWDOWN. With Tommy Dorsey mid-1944 to early 1945. Briefly with Goodman 1946, with him many times in 50s and 60s on jobs and records. Late 40s studio work, later freelanced. NBC studio musician mid-50s into early 70s. Regular sideman on Johnny Carson TV show when taping was done in New York; featured occasionally, better than ever. Could play hot, cool or bossa nova. Jobbed with Goodman 1973-4.

RECORDS

GLENN MILLER
Bb 10388 Glen Island Special
Bb 10416 In the Mood
Bb 10498 Johnson Rag
Bb 10970 Yes, My Darling Daughter
Bb 11063 I Dreamt I Dwelt in Harlem
Bb 11110 Sun Valley Jump
Bb 11183 Sweeter Than the Sweetest
Bb 11382 A String of Pearls
Bb 11450 Chip Off the Old Block
Bb 11480 When Johnny Comes Marching Home
Vi 27935 That's Sabotage
Vi 20-1563 Here We Go Again

LPs

AL KLINK (one side)
GA 33-325 Progressive Jazz
GLENN MILLER
Vi LPT-6700
BOBBY BYRNE
GA 207-SD (S) Great Song Hits of Glenn Miller Orchestra
MUNDELL LOWE
Riv 12-208 Guitar Moods by Mundell Lowe
ENOCH LIGHT
Project 5049 (S) Big Band Hits of the 30s
THE COMMAND ALL-STARS
Comm RS-820-SD (S) Reeds and Percussion
RUSTY DEDRICK
Mon-Ever MES-7035 (S) The Many Friends of Rusty Dedrick
SKITCH HENDERSON
Co CL-2367 ... Tonight!
ARTIE SHAW
Cap ST-2992 (S) Recreates His Great '38 Band

1035. KNAPP, ORVILLE   as ts cl ss B

Born c. 1908, Kansas City, Mo.
Died July 16, 1936, Beverly, Mass.; own plane crashed

Leader of hotel band 1934-6; attracted legion of fans during brief career. Brother of movie actress Evelyn Knapp. Early in career with Coon-Sanders and Paul Specht bands among others. Formed band mid-1934 along Freddy Martin lines, but addition of steel guitar and organ gave deep ensemble sound. Later added French horn and soprano sax. Arrangements, many by pianist Chick Floyd, stressed dynamics. Vocalists Edith Caldwell and Leighton Noble. Theme *Three Shades of Blue.* Played west coast hotels and clubs; key spot Beverly-Wilshire Hotel in Los Angeles. On radio remotes, billed as The Music of Tomorrow. Fall 1935 played in Chicago, Denver, Dallas, New York (a hit at Waldorf-Astoria). Band rising fast 1936 when fatal plane crash occurred. George Olsen later took over nucleus of band. Singer Leighton Noble formed band in Knapp style.

RECORDS

ORVILLE KNAPP
De 224 Talkin' to Myself/Believe Me
De 315 Naturally/If You Love Me, Say So
De 316 A Little Angel Told Me So/Me Without You
De 330 Mississippi Honeymoon/If It Isn't Love
De 331 It's Written All Over Your Face/Let's Be Thankful
De 412 I'm Misunderstood/You Opened My Eyes
De 413 You're a Heavenly Thing/I Was Taken by Storm
De 538 Why Stars Come Out at Night/I Want to Learn to Speak Hawaiian
De 539 Speaking Confidentially/Take It Easy
De 554 Accent on Youth/The Girl I Left Behind Me
Br 7649 Robins and Roses/Everything Stops for Tea
Br 7654 Small Town Girl/You Can't Judge a Book by Its Cover
Br 7671 Tonight's the Night/It's High

Time I Got the Lowdown on You
Br 7675 State of My Heart/I'm Just
Beginning to Care

1036. KOEHLER, TED   lyr p

*Born July 14, 1894, Washington, D.C.
Died January 17, 1973, Santa Monica,
Calif.*

Important lyricist of 30s and 40s; numerous hits. Best-known *Between the Devil and the Deep Blue Sea, Stormy Weather, Wrap Your Troubles in Dreams, Let's Fall in Love, Truckin', I'm Shooting High, Don't Worry 'Bout Me.* Chief collaborator composer Harold Arlen. Others included Rube Bloom, Sammy Fain, Jay Gorney, Ray Henderson, Burton Lane, Jimmy McHugh, James V. Monaco, Harry Warren, Sam H. Stept. Songs for Broadway shows, Cotton Club revues, movies. Educated in New York and Newark. Left photo-engraving to work as theatre pianist. Pioneer in exploitation of song hits in important theatres during silent era. Wrote special material for stars of vaudeville and Broadway stage. Produced floor shows for night clubs. Turned to songwriting full-time late 20s. First collaborated with Arlen on early hits.

SONGS
(with related shows)

1922—Dreamy Melody
1923—When Lights Are Low
1929—Baby—Oh, Where Can You Be?
1930—EARL CARROLL'S VANITIES OF 1930 stage show (Hittin' the Bottle; Out of a Clear Blue Sky; One Love); Get Happy
1931—Between the Devil and the Deep Blue Sea; Kickin' the Gong Around; Wrap Your Troubles in Dreams; Linda; Tell Me with a Love Song
1932—EARL CARROLL'S VANITIES OF 1932 stage show (I Gotta Right to Sing the Blues); GEORGE WHITE'S MUSIC HALL VARIETIES stage show (I Love a Parade); Stepping into Love; Minnie the Moocher's Weddin' Day; Music, Music, Everywhere; That's What I Hate About Love
1933—Stormy Weather; Happy as the Day Is Long; I've Got the World on a String; Stay on the Right Side of the Road
1934—SAY WHEN stage show (Say When; When Love Comes Swinging Along); LET'S FALL IN LOVE movie (Let's Fall in Love; Love Is Love Anywhere); I'll Wind; As Long as I Live; Here Goes; Out in the Cold Again
1935—CURLY TOP movie (Curly Top; Animal Crackers in My Soup; The Simple Things in Life; It's All So New to Me); Truckin'; Cotton
1936—DIMPLES movie (Picture Me without You; Hey, What Did the Bluebird Say?; He Was a Dandy); KING OF BURLESQUE movie (I've Got My Fingers Crossed; I'm Shooting High; Lovely Lady; Spreading Rhythm Around; Too Good to Be True); It's Great to Be in Love Again
1937—ARTISTS AND MODELS movie (Stop! You're Breaking My Heart; Public Melody #1)
1938—Feelin' High and Happy; I Can't Face the Music; Let's Waltz for Old Time's Sake
1939—LOVE AFFAIR movie (Sing, My Heart); Don't Worry 'Bout Me; What Goes Up Must Come Down; We've Come a Long Way Together; If I Were Sure of You
1941—When the Sun Comes Out
1942—Ev'ry Night About This Time
1944—UP IN ARMS movie (Now I Know; Tess's Torch Song); HOLLYWOOD CANTEEN movie (What Are You Doin' the Rest of Your Life?; Sweet Dreams, Sweetheart; Hollywood Canteen)
1945—WEEKEND AT THE WALDORF movie (And There You Are; Guadalajara)
1946—SAN ANTONIO movie (Some Sunday Morning); More Now Than Ever
1947—ESCAPE ME NEVER movie (Love for Love); MY WILD IRISH ROSE movie (Miss Lindy Lou; Wee Rose of Killarney; The Natchez and the Robert E. Lee; There's Room in My Heart for Them All); Me and the Blues

1037. KOLLER, HANS   ts B

Born February 12, 1921, Vienna, Austria

Outstanding tenor sax star in cool style along Stan Getz lines. Native of Austria but considered German star because reached fame there. Began professionally in Vienna 1937, attended music school there. Later toured Germany. Known in U.S. via early 50s records.

RECORDS

HANS KOLLER
Dis 1741 Hans Is Hip/I Cover the Waterfront
Dis 1742 Up from Munich/Beat

LPs

HANS KOLLER
Dis (10")DL-2005
Vang VRS-8509 Hans Across the Sea
De DL-8229 (one side) "Das" Is Jazz!
(miscellaneous artists)
MGM E-3157 Cool Europe

1038. KONITZ, LEE   as ts cm B

Born October 13, 1927, Chicago, Ill.

Alto sax star with individual modern style. Creative, technically agile; strong attack, sophisticated harmonics. Around 1943 played tenor sax with Gay Claridge and Teddy Powell in Chicago. On alto sax with Jerry Wald several months. Attended Roosevelt College awhile, then to New York. With Claude Thornhill 1947-8, featured on progressive arrangements. With Miles Davis 1948 and on trendsetting 1949 Capitol record session "The Birth of the Cool." 1949 with pianist Lennie Tristano; greatly influenced by Tristano's ideas and musicianship. Two enjoyed great rapport. Konitz with Bill Russo combo briefly late 1950. Late 1951 in Scandinavian countries. Joined Stan Kenton fall 1952, remained a year. Later 50s freelanced, led combo. With Tristano 1959, again 1964. Settled on west coast early 60s, taught; less active in jazz. Beginning 1965 played clubs and concerts in New York, made European tours. With Machito band 1968. Active into 70s.

RECORDS

LENNIE TRISTANO
Cap 7-1224 Intuition/Yesterdays

Cap 60003 Crosscurrent/Wow
NJ 80001 Subconscious-Lee/Judy
MILES DAVIS
Cap 15404 Move/Judo
Cap 60005 Godchild/Jeru
MILES DAVIS-LEE KONITZ
Pres 755 Yesterdays/Duet for Sax and Guitar (LEE KONITZ-BILLY BAUER)
CHARLES MINGUS
Debut 101 Precognition/Portrait
Debut 103 Montage/Extrasensory Perception
METRONOME ALL-STARS
Cap 1550 Early Spring/Local 802 Blues
Co 38734 No Figs/Double Date
LEE KONITZ
NJ 807 Marshmallow/Fishin' Around
NJ 813 Tautology/Sound-Lee
NJ 827 Palo Alto/You Go to My Head
NJ 834 Rebecca/Ice Cream Konitz
NJ 843 Hi Beck/Ezz-thetic
Pres 753 Odjenar/Indian Summer
LEE KONITZ with GERRY MULLIGAN QUARTET
PJ 608 Sextet/I Can't Believe That You're in Love with Me
PJ 609 Lover Man/Lady Be Good

LPs

LEE KONITZ
Pres (10")101 Lennie Tristano & Lee Konitz
Pres 116 Lee Konitz—The New Sounds
Atl 1258 Lee Konitz Inside Hi-Fi
Story 901 Jazz at Storyville
Verve MGV-8209 Very Cool
Verve MGV-8281 Tranquility
Verve MGV-8399 Motion
Milestone MSP-9013 The Lee Konitz Duets
LENNIE TRISTANO
Atl 1224
CLAUDE THORNHILL
Co CL-6164 (Co RIs)
Ha HL-7088 (Co RIs)
RALPH BURNS
Clef (10")MG C-115 The Free Forms Album
MILES DAVIS
Cap T-1974 The Birth of the Cool (Cap RIs)

STAN KENTON
Cap (10″)L-383 New Concepts of Artistry in Rhythm
GERRY MULLIGAN (one side)
Jazztone J-1253 Mulligan and Baker!
(miscellaneous artists)
Pres 7689 The Alto Summit

1038A. KORNGOLD, ERICH WOLF-GANG   cm ar p B

Born May 29, 1897, Brunn, Czechoslovakia
Died November 29, 1957, North Hollywood, Calif.

Composer-arranger of movie background music mid-30s into 50s. Child prodigy as pianist in Europe, also composed at early age. As teenager wrote short operas THE RING OF POLYCRATES and VIOLANTA performed throughout Europe. Compositions had strong Viennese flavor; influenced by Richard Strauss, Gustav Mahler, Puccini. Pianist in concert hall recitals. Re-scored operetta classics of early composing greats, helped stage them. Conductor several years at Hamburg opera house; his opera DIE TOTE STADT (THE DEAD CITY) first presented there 1920, still played in European opera houses. Around 1927 wrote opera THE MIRACLE OF HELIANE, his favorite. Great prominence in Europe by early 30s. To U.S. 1934, citizen 1943. Began Hollywood career scoring A MIDSUMMER NIGHT'S DREAM (1935). Work selective, only on important movies of own choosing. Given free rein, devoted more time and care than most movie composers. Most notable score for THE ADVENTURES OF ROBIN HOOD (1938). Especially effective on historical and period films. Turned to classical composing when movie writing became passé. Works included *Violin Concerto in D, Piano Trio, Piano Concerto for the Left Hand, Piano Sonata in E.* Arranged and conducted for New York stage production HELEN GOES TO TROY (1944). Opera DIE KATHRIN a failure in Vienna 1950. Last work on Richard Wagner movie biography THE MAGIC FIRE; pianist on soundtrack, excellent scoring of Wagner music. Movie unsuccessful.

MOVIES
(as composer-arranger-conductor of background music; list complete)

1935—A MIDSUMMER NIGHT'S DREAM; CAPTAIN BLOOD
1936—GIVE US THIS NIGHT; ANTHONY ADVERSE; THE GREEN PASTURES
1937—THE PRINCE AND THE PAUPER; ANOTHER DAWN
1938—THE ADVENTURES OF ROBIN HOOD
1939—JUAREZ; THE PRIVATE LIVES OF ELIZABETH AND ESSEX
1940—SEA HAWK
1941—THE SEA WOLF
1942—KING'S ROW
1943—THE CONSTANT NYMPH
1944—BETWEEN TWO WORLDS
1946—OF HUMAN BONDAGE; DEVOTION; DECEPTION
1947—ESCAPE ME NEVER
1955—THE MAGIC FIRE

RECORDS
(all LPs)

(excerpts from movie soundtracks; as composer-arranger)

WB 1438 (conducted by Lionel Newman)
Vi LM-1782 Violin Concerto in D, Opus 35, based on several movie themes (conducted by Alfred Wallenstein; Jascha Heifetz-v)
Lon(E) SP-44173 SEA HAWK suite (conducted by Stanley Black)
Reader's Digest RD4-26 THE CONSTANT NYMPH suite (conducted by Charles Gerhardt)
Reader's Digest RD3-39 KING'S ROW suite (conducted by Charles Gerhardt)

1038B. KOSTA, TESSA   vo

Beautiful singing star of Broadway musicals from 1914 to mid-20s.

BROADWAY MUSICALS

1914—THE BEAUTY SHOP
1917—CHU CHIN CHOW
1919—THE ROYAL VAGABOND
1920—LASSIE
1921—PRINCESS VIRTUE (unsuccessful)
1922—THE ROSE OF STAMBOUL
1923—CAROLINE

1924—PRINCESS APRIL
1926—A SONG OF THE FLAME

RECORDS

TESSA KOSTA
  Co 618-D Song of the Flame/Cossack
  Love Song

1039. KOSTELANETZ, ANDRE

p cm ar B

*Born December 22, 1901, St. Peters-
burg, Russia*

Noted conductor on radio and records,
particularly popular in 30s and 40s. Attended St. Petersburg Academy of Music.
Pianist-conductor in Russia; to U.S. 1922.
Worked as coach and accompanist for
opera singers, toured with them. Entered
radio; own show by 1932. Late 1934
began Chesterfield radio show featuring
guest singers; series ran into late 30s. In
1939 on Tune Up Time show with Kay
Thompson & Her Rhythm Singers, later
1939 featuring Tony Martin; also on
Walter O'Keefe show. From 1941 to late
40s on Coca Cola show. Used large
orchestra with lush arrangements (many
his), featured semi-classical and pop
music. Sometimes used novelty effects;
swung occasionally. In movies ARTISTS
AND MODELS (1937), MUSIC IN MY HEART
(1940). Sometime theme *Carefree*. Married opera and film star Lily Pons, worked with her often. World War II both
active entertaining troops in U.S. and
abroad. Kostelanetz active in 50s into 70s
with recording, composing. Jazz arranger
Eddie Sauter worked for him in recent
years. Composer of hits *Moon Love* (1939)
and *On the Isle of May* (1940), both
adapted from classical themes.

RECORDS

ANDRE KOSTELANETZ
  Br 7873 Goodnight Ladies/Mary Had
  a Little Lamb
  Br 8214 Bugle Call Rag/Turkey in the
  Straw
  Br 8226 Swamp Fire/The Man on the
  Flying Trapeze
  Br 8233 Tiger Rag/Casey Jones
  Vi (12")36142 REVENGE WITH MUSIC
  Medley (1 & 2)

Vi 36161 Chant of the Weed/Rhumba
  Fantasy
Co (12")7417-M OKLAHOMA Medley (1
  & 2)
Co 4268-M All the Things You Are/I
  Got Rhythm
Co 4293-M Dancing in the Dark/I'll
  See You Again
Co 4338-M One Kiss/Will You Re-
  member?
Co Album M-614 (78s) Music of Fritz
  Kreisler
Co Album MM-622 (78s) Music of Jer-
  ome Kern

LILY PONS with ANDRE KOSTELANETZ OR-
CHESTRA
  Co 72049-D A Cupidon/A Une Fon-
  taine
  Co 72460-D The Blue Danube Waltz/
  Estrellita
  Co 72463-D The Last Rose of
  Summer/Les Filles De Cadiz

LPs

ANDRE KOSTELANETZ
  Co CL-729 Music of Cole Porter
  Co CL-765 Music of Victor Herbert
  Co CL-776 Music of Jerome Kern
  Co CL-886 Tender Is the Night
  Co CL-1921 MR. PRESIDENT score
  Co ML-2026 Music of George
  Gershwin
  Co CL-2039 Wonderland of Golden
  Hits
  Co ML-4382 Music of Vincent You-
  mans
  Co ML-4822 Lure of the Tropics
  Co CS-9556 (S) Today's Movie Hits
  Co CS-9623 (S) Scarborough Fair
  Co CS-9691 (S) For the Young at
  Heart

1040. KRAL, ROY

p vo ar cm

Born October 10, 1921, Chicago, Ill.

Pianist-vocalist, teamed with Jackie Cain
to form bop singing duo prominent in late
40s and 50s. Good piano soloist, modern
chording. Military service, World War II.
Radio awhile in Detroit. Pianist-arranger
with Charlie Ventura 1948-9. Joined with
Jackie Cain for unusual vocal duets with
Ventura, most written by Kral. In 1949

pair married, late in year formed combo. Disbanded, then on Chicago TV. Rejoined Ventura mid-1953. Later 50s into 70s worked as act in jazz and supper clubs, mostly in New York and Las Vegas. Recorded, made TV appearances, did commercials for TV and radio.

(See biography herein on JACKIE CAIN for listing of records by duo.)

1041. KRAMER, ALEX   cm lyr p B

Born May 30, 1903, Montreal, Ontario, Canada

Songwriter of 40s and 50s. Collaborated with wife Joan Whitney (Hy Zaret sometimes making it a threesome). Best-known songs *High on a Windy Hill, It All Comes Back to Me Now, My Sister and I, Candy, You'll Never Get Away*. Educated at McGill Conservatory of Music in Montreal. Led orchestra on Montreal radio. To New York 1938. Piano accompanist in vaudeville, vocal coach, orchestra leader. In 1940 staff composer for New York publishing house. He and wife formed publishing firm Kramer-Whitney 1947.

SONGS
(all with Joan Whitney)

1940—High on a Windy Hill;
1941—It All Comes Back to Me Now; My Sister and I
1944—STARS ON PARADE movie (It's Love, Love, Love); Candy
1946—That's the Beginning of the End; Ain't Nobody Here but Us Chickens
1947—Love Somebody; Curiosity
1948—Far Away Places
1949—Why Is It?; I Never Heard You Say
1950—Not Tonight; I Only Saw Him Once; Some Hearts Sing
1952—You'll Never Get Away; To Be Loved by You
1953—Train of Love; I Woke Up Crying; What More Do You Want?
1959—No Other Arms, No Other Lips

1042. KREISLER, FRITZ   v cm ar

Born February 2, 1875, Vienna, Austria
Died January 29, 1962, New York, N.Y.

Noted violin virtuoso and concert artist. Composer of standard solos for violin requiring considerable technique: *Caprice Viennois, Tambourin Chinois, Serenade Espagnole, Violin Concerto in C, La Precieuse*. Composed semi-classical melodies, mostly around 1910: *Songs My Mother Taught Me, The Old Refrain, Liebesfreud, Liebesleid, Schon Rosmarin*. Popular song *Stars in My Eyes* from his musical score for movie THE KING STEPS OUT (1936). Classical works include *Recitativo and Scherzo, Chanson Louis XIII and Pavane, Study on a Choral, Minuet, Sicilienne and Rigaudon, Praeludium and Allegro, String Quartet in A, Preghiera, Aubade Provencale, Allegretto in G, Tempo de Minuetto, La Chasse*. Score for successful Broadway show APPLE BLOSSOMS (1919). Child prodigy, studied with noted teachers abroad. Ages 7-12 studied at Vienna and Paris Conservatories. Played 1888-9 concerts in U.S., returned to Europe to study medicine and art. Continued worldwide tours many years. Officer in Austrian army, World War I. After war to U.S. Active in concerts and composing. Injuries in auto accident incapacitated him much of 1941. Score for unsuccessful Broadway show RHAPSODY (1944). Author of book *Four Weeks in the Trenches*. Biography *Fritz Kreisler* by L. P. Lochner. Kreisler owned large collection of rare violins.

RECORDS
(violin solos)

FRITZ KREISLER
Vi 64130 Old Folks at Home
Vi 64502 The Rosary
Vi 64503 Serenade Espagnole
Vi 64563 Songs My Mother Taught Me
Vi 64655 Poor Butterfly
Vi 64730 Dream of Youth
Vi 64817 Beautiful Ohio
Vi 64947 On Miami Shore
Vi (12")74180 Humoresque
Vi (12")74196 Liebesfreud
Vi (12")74197 Caprice Viennois
Vi (12")74203 Tambourin Chinois
Vi (12")74330 Chanson—Meditation
Vi (12")74333 Liebesleid
Vi 26573 Larghetto/Rosamunde—Ballet Music

1043. KRESS, CARL   g bn B

Born October 20, 1907, Newark, N.J.
Died June 10, 1965, Reno, Nev.

Guitarist with busy freelance and recording career. Good rhythm guitarist, pioneer in chord-style unamplified solos. Later developed good single-string style. Played in New York, prominent around 1927 from recording with jazz groups. In 30s on many radio shows including Show Boat, Town Hall, Jack Benny. Sometimes teamed with guitarist Dick McDonough on radio. Late 30s accompanist for Merry Macs vocal quartet. In mid-40s conducted bands backing singers on Capitol Records. Musical director in radio late 40s. TV in 50s. In 60s formed guitar duo with George Barnes. Fatal heart attack during duo's booking in Reno.

RECORDS

RED NICHOLS
  Br 3961 Panama/Margie
  Vi 21056 Sugar/Make My Cot Where the Cot-Cot-Cotton Grows
  Vi 21560 Harlem Twist/Five Pennies
RED & HIS BIG TEN (Red Nichols)
  Vi 23026 I'm Tickled Pink with a Blue-Eyed Baby/That's Where the South Begins
FRANKIE TRUMBAUER
  OK 40979 Mississippi Mud
  Br 7687 I'm an Old Cowhand/Diga Diga Doo
PAUL WHITEMAN
  Vi 24078 San
BOSWELL SISTERS
  Br 6442 It Don't Mean a Thing/Minnie the Moocher's Wedding Day
  De 574 Cheek to Cheek/Top Hat, White Tie and Tails
HOAGY CARMICHAEL
  Vi 24627 Judy/Moon Country
TOOTS MONDELLO
  Vs 8110 Sweet Lorraine/Beyond the Moon
  Vs 8118 Louisiana
ADRIAN'S RAMBLERS (Adrian Rollini)
  Br 6786 Get Goin'/Keep On Doin' What You're Doin'
  Br 6877 I've Got a Warm Spot in My Heart for You/Why Don't You Practice What You Preach?

PEG LACENTRA
  Bb 10021 Noodlin'/Alexander's Back in Town
MERRY MACS
  De 3390 Dry Bones/Red Wing
CARL KRESS-DICK MCDONOUGH
  Br 6917 Stage Fright/Danzon
  Br 7885 Heat Wave/Chicken a-la-Swing
CARL KRESS
  De 23136 Afterthoughts (1 & 2)
  De 23137 Peg Leg Shuffle/Love Song
  De 23138 Sutton Mutton/Helena

LPs

CARL KRESS
  Cap (10")T-368
CARL KRESS-GEORGE BARNES
  UA 6335 Town Hall Concert
BOBBY HACKETT
  Co (10")CL-6156 Jam Session
ED HALL
  BN 6505 Celestial Express (BN RIs)
BUD FREEMAN
  UA 15033 (S) Something Tender
JIMMY DORSEY
  Co (10")CL-6095
RED NICHOLS
  Br (10")BL-58009 (Br RIs)

1044. KRUEGER, BENNY   as ts cl B

Born c. 1899
Died April 29, 1967

Leader of sweet band; moderate success in 20s and 30s. Sideman a few years pre-1920. With Original Dixieland Jazz Band 1920-1. With Bailey's Lucky Seven and Carl Fenton among others. Bandleader early 20s, semi-hot style early years. Based mostly in Chicago in 20s, toured at times. 30s recordings in good sweet style, occasional swing. On Pick & Pat radio show 1936-8. Led bands at intervals in 30s and 40s. On Rudy Vallee radio show 1946-7.

RECORDS

ORIGINAL DIXIELAND JAZZ BAND
  Vi 18717 Margie/Palesteena
  Vi 18722 Broadway Rose/Sweet Mama
  Vi 18729 Home Again Blues/Crazy Blues

Vi 18772 Jazz Me Blues/St. Louis Blues

Vi 18798 Royal Garden Blues/Dangerous Blues

Vi 18850 Bow Wow Blues

BAILEY'S LUCKY SEVEN

Ge 3243 After I Say I'm Sorry/Dinah

AL BERNARD with CARL FENTON ORCHESTRA

Br 3547 St. Louis Blues/Beale Street Blues

Br 3553 Memphis Blues/Hesitation Blues

BENNY KRUEGER

Ge 4722 Get Hot/Wang Wang Blues

Ge 4751 St. Louis Blues/Beale Street Blues

Br 2109 Dangerous Blues/Ain't We Got Fun

Br 2453 I Cried for You/Tell Me a Story

Br 2485 That Old Gang of Mine/Wonder If She's Lonely Too

Br 2667 Charley, My Boy/Pleasure Mad

Br 3186 Bye Bye Blackbird/What Was I to Do?

Br 6185 I Don't Know Why/I Idolize My Baby's Eyes

Br 6222 Why Did It Have to Be Me?/She's So Nice

Br 6246 Lies/Was That the Human Thing to Do?

Br 6280 Somebody Loves You/Sing a New Song

Br 6287 Lovable/I'm So in Love

Br 6296 Crazy People/Gosh Darn

Br 6334 You've Got Me in the Palm of Your Hand/Come On and Sit Beside the Sea

Br 6359 Same Old Moon/Goodbye to Love

Br 6386 Moon/Sweetheart Hour

Vi 21903 Down Among the Sugar Cane/Sunny South

Co 2918-D Once in a Blue Moon/Goodnight, Lovely Little Lady

Co 2919-D Riptide/A Thousand Goodnights

1045. KRUPA, GENE d cm B

Born January 15, 1909, Chicago, Ill.
Died October 16, 1973, Yonkers, N.Y.,
of cardiac complications brought on by
leukemia

Leading drummer of swing era. Won fame with Benny Goodman, sparking great rhythm section with beat and showmanship. Good technique and jazz feel, handled big bands and combos well. Leader of good bands late 30s and 40s. With minor groups mid-20s. Met Chicago's top jazzmen. Later 20s with Thelma Terry, Mezz Mezzrow, Benson Orchestra, Seattle Harmony Kings. To New York 1929; freelanced, many jobs with Red Nichols 1929-30. With Irving Aaronson 1931, Russ Columbo 1932, Mal Hallett 1933, Buddy Rogers 1934. Joined Benny Goodman late 1934, played Let's Dance radio show. As band grew in fame and popularity, Krupa became leading sideman, country's best-known drummer. Featured also in Goodman Trio and Quartet. With band in movies BIG BROADCAST OF 1937 (1936) and HOLLYWOOD HOTEL (1938). Starred in Goodman's January 16, 1938 Carnegie Hall concert, quit band six weeks later to launch big band.

Move drew considerable publicity. Formed able band with smart arrangements. Featured drumming on showcase numbers. Leading early sidemen saxists Vido Musso, Sam Musiker (cl), Sam Donahue, trumpeters Corky Cornelius, Shorty Sherock. Jimmy Mundy, Fred Norman, Chappie Willett arrangers. Excellent vocalists Irene Daye and Howard DuLany, later Johnny Desmond and Anita O'Day. Roy Eldridge starred on trumpet and novelty vocals early 40s. Eldridge and O'Day teamed on some, including band's hit *Let Me Off Uptown*. Theme *Apurksody*, later *Star Burst*, later *That Drummer's Band*.

Krupa forced out of music awhile 1943 on marijuana possession charge that was later dropped. Comeback with Benny Goodman fall 1943; tumultuous welcome with Tommy Dorsey at New York's Paramount Theatre. With Dorsey till mid-1944. Formed another band, added strings, never recorded with this band due to Petrillo recording ban. Dropped strings for swinging big band with new star Charlie Ventura on tenor sax and featured with trio within band; Ventura later quit to form combo. Krupa led outstanding band later 40s: progressive, with great ensemble sound and swinging arrangements by George Williams and Gerry Mulligan. Saxmen Charlie Kennedy, Lennie Hambro and Buddy Wise star soloists, along with trumpeter Don Fagerquist.

In 50s Krupa mostly led combos, usually featuring Ventura or versatile saxman Eddie Shu. Pianist Teddy Napoleon stalwart in 40s and 50s combos. Krupa toured with Jazz at the Philharmonic shows as single, often featured in drum duels with Buddy Rich. In 1954 opened drum school in New York with Cozy Cole. With combo on TV occasionally in 50s. Movie THE GENE KRUPA STORY 1959; Sal Mineo in title role synchronized movements to Krupa drumming on soundtrack. Spotty health slowed Krupa in 60s and 70s, but still played. Sometimes rejoined Goodman, Teddy Wilson and Lionel Hampton for revivals of original Goodman Quartet. Krupa and band in movies SOME LIKE IT HOT (1939), BALL OF FIRE (1941), GEORGE WHITE'S SCANDALS (1945), MEET THE BAND (1947), MAKE BELIEVE BALLROOM (1949). Krupa alone in SYNCOPATION (1942; in jam session sequence), THE GLENN MILLER STORY (1954), THE BENNY GOODMAN STORY (1956; also in band for soundtrack). Co-composer of *Take Your Love* and *Sweetheart, Honey, Darlin', Dear*, both recorded by own band 1939.

RECORDS

BIX BEIDERBECKE
  Vi 23018 Deep Down South
HOAGY CARMICHAEL
  Vi 38139 Rockin' Chair/Barnacle Bill the Sailor
CHARLESTON CHASERS
  Co 2415-D Basin Street Blues/Beale Street Blues
CHICAGO RHYTHM KINGS
  Br 4001 I've Found a New Baby/There'll Be Some Changes Made
BUD FREEMAN
  OK 41168 Craze-O-Logy/Can't Help Lovin' Dat Man
IRVING MILLS & HIS HOTSY TOTSY GANG
  Br 4838 Railroad Man/Crazy 'Bout My Gal
  Br 4920 High and Dry/Barbaric
MOUND CITY BLUE BLOWERS
  Co 1946-D Indiana/Fireman Blues
  Vi 38100 Hello, Lola/One Hour

RED NICHOLS
  Br 4373 Indiana/Dinah
  Br 4724 Tea for Two/I Want to Be Happy
  Br 6012 Rockin' Chair/My Honey's Lovin' Arms
BENNY GOODMAN
  Vi 25090 King Porter/Sometimes I'm Happy
  Vi 25136 Blue Skies/Dear Old Southland
  Vi 25247 Stompin' at the Savoy/Breakin' in a Pair of Shoes
  Vi 25333 China Boy/Oh, Lady Be Good (both TRIO)
  Vi 25355 Swingtime in the Rockies/I've Found a New Baby
  Vi 25387 Down South Camp Meeting/Pick Yourself Up
  Vi 25505 He Ain't Got Rhythm/This Year's Kisses
  Vi 25510 I Want to Be Happy/Rosetta
  Vi 25678 Sugar Foot Stomp/I Can't Give You Anything but Love
  Vi (12")36205 Sing, Sing, Sing (1 & 2)
GENE KRUPA
  Vi 25263 Mutiny in the Parlor/I'm Gonna Clap My Hands
  Vi 25276 Swing Is Here/I Hope Gabriel Likes My Music
  Br 8166 Wire Brush Stomp / What Goes On Here in My Heart?
  Br 8253 Walkin' and Swingin'/Since My Best Gal Turned Me Down
  Br 8280 Jeepers Creepers/Say It with a Kiss
  Br 8340 Some Like It Hot/The Lady's in Love with You
  Br 8448 Moonlight Serenade/You and Your Love
  OK 5686 Love Lies/Only Forever
  OK 5802 I Hear Music/A Nightingale Sang in Berkeley Square
  OK 5985 The Sergeant Was Shy/He's Gone
  OK 5997 (theme) Apurksody/Jungle Madness
  OK 6046 Drum Boogie/How 'Bout That Mess?
  OK 6210 Let Me Off Uptown/Flamingo
  OK 6278 After You're Gone/Kick It
  OK 6506 Keep 'Em Flying/Thanks for the Boogie Ride

Co 35205 Old Black Joe/My Old Kentucky Home

Co 35324 Drummin' Man/I'd Love to Call You My Sweetheart

Co 35423 Tuxedo Junction/So Long

Co 35444 Manhattan Transfer/Moments in the Moonlight

Co 35508 No Name Jive/Six Lessons from Madame LaZonga

Co 36591 Knock Me a Kiss/Deliver Me to Tennessee

Co 36802 Leave Us Leap/Dark Eyes (TRIO)

Co 36819 (theme) That Drummer's Band/What's This?

Co 37589 Disc Jockey Jump/Gene's Boogie

Co 38590 By the River Sainte Marie/Watch Out!

Vi 20-4234 Off and On/The Sheik of Araby

Mer 89057 Coronation Hop/Paradise

LPs

GENE KRUPA

Co C2L-29 (2-LP set) Drummin' Man

Clef MGC-500 The Gene Krupa Trio at Jazz at the Philharmonic

Clef MGC-703 Drum Boogie

Verve MGV-2008 Drummin' Man

Verve MGV-8292 Plays Gerry Mulligan Arrangements

Verve MGV-8414 Percussion King

Cam CAL-340 Mutiny in the Parlor (misc. Vi RIS, including 1936 Krupa session)

BENNY GOODMAN

Vi LPM-1099 The Golden Age of Benny Goodman (RIs)

Vi LPT-6703 (5-LP set) The Golden Age of Swing (Vi RIS)

Co CL-821 The Vintage Goodman (1931-4 RIs)

RED NICHOLS

Br (10")BL-58008 (Br RIs) (movie soundtrack)

De DL-8252 THE BENNY GOODMAN STORY, Vol.1

De DL-8253 THE BENNY GOODMAN STORY, Vol.2

1046. KYLE, BILLY   p B

*Born July 14, 1914, Philadelphia, Pa.
Died February 23, 1966, Youngstown, Ohio*

Jazz pianist with rhythmic, bouncing style; very tasteful. Began locally early 30s; 1932-4 also in New York and Syracuse. Accompanied singer Bon Bon on radio in Philadelphia. Briefly with Tiny Bradshaw band. Led band awhile 1936. Late 1936-7 with Mills Blue Rhythm Band. With John Kirby sextet 1938-42, became known as group grew popular. Style perfectly fit jaunty, tight arrangements of group. Military service, World War II. Middle and late 40s intervals with Kirby and with Sy Oliver; led band. Early 50s freelanced; pit bands and studios. Joined Louis Armstrong All-Stars fall 1953, remained rest of career. Toured U.S. and abroad, recorded, appeared on TV and in movies. On Youngstown job had ulcer attack, died in hospital days later.

RECORDS

MILLS BLUE RHYTHM BAND

Co 3156-D Barrelhouse

Co 3162 Callin' Your Bluff/Big John's Special

Vo 3808 Blue Rhythm Fantasy/Jungle Madness

RED ALLEN

Vo 3422 I Adore You

Vo 3524 I Was Born to Swing/After Last Night with You

TIMME ROSENKRANTZ

Vi 25876 A Wee Bit of Swing/Is This to Be My Souvenir?

Vi 25883 The Song Is Ended/When Day Is Done

BUSTER BAILEY

Vs 8333 The Blue Room/Am I Blue?

Vs 8337 Should I?/April in Paris

JOHN KIRBY

De 2216 Undecided/From A Flat to C

Vo 5048 I May Be Wrong/Opus 5

Vo 5187 Blue Skies/Royal Garden Blues

ÓK 5805 Blues Petite/Andiology

TEDDY GRACE

De 2128 Monday Morning/Downhearted Blues

JOE MARSALA

De 18111 Twelve Bar Stampede/Feather Bed Lament

LOUIS ARMSTRONG

De 29102 Basin Street Blues (1 & 2)

BILLY KYLE
Va 531 Big Boy Blues/Margie
Va 574 Sundays Are Reserved/Havin'
a Ball
Va 617 Can I Forget You?/All You
Want to Do Is Dance
Va 659 Handle My Heart with Care/
Girl of My Dreams
De 2740 Between Sets/Finishing Up a
Date
Disc 5001 I Want You—I Need You
Disc 5003 All the Things You Are/I
Gotta Right to Sing the Blues
HRS 1032 Contemporary Blues/
H.R.S. Bounce
HRS 1033 Date for Eight/Ooh, Baby,
You Knock Me Out

LPs

LOUIS ARMSTRONG ALL-STARS
De DL-8168 At The Crescendo
De DL-8330 Satchmo on Stage
BUCK CLAYTON
Co CL-614 Jams Benny Goodman
Co CL-701 Jumpin' at the Woodside
JACK TEAGARDEN-REX STEWART
Atl 1209 Big Jazz
JOHN KIRBY
Co GL-502 (RIs)
(original band minus Kirby, with MAXINE
SULLIVAN—1955)
Period 1113 Flow Gently Sweet Rhy-
thm

1047. KYSER, KAY   B

Born June 18, 1906, Rocky Mount, N.C.
Energetic, personable leader of popular
30s and 40s dance band. Great commer-
cial success. Formed band University of
North Carolina, played no instrument.
Band in late 20s and early 30s semi-hot.
1934 summer job at Miramar Hotel in
Santa Monica. Late 1934-5 at Chicago's
Black Hawk; good radio coverage early
1935 established band. Unusual gimmick:
singing song titles at start of each number.
Band then vamped several bars before
each vocal as Kyser announced singer's
name and gave brief introduction to song.
Band sweet. Leading arranger many years
George Duning. Lush, sentimental theme
Walter Donaldson's *Thinking of You* fea-
tured glissing trombone. Capable singers
Ginny Simms, Harry Babbitt, Bill Stoker,

Sully Mason, comic Ish Kabibble (with
weird haircut). Steady recording.

First radio show fall 1936 Elgin's Football
Review. On Surprise Party show 1937.
Early 1938 debut of Kay Kyser's Kampus
Klass for Lucky Strike; network changed
late March and show became Kollege of
Musical Knowledge. Popular; quiz-music
format. Ran through 40s, later called
Musical Quiz; important in popularizing
band. Band and vocalists featured in
movies (with acting roles): THAT'S RIGHT
—YOU'RE WRONG (1939), YOU'LL FIND
OUT (1940), PLAYMATES and MY FAVORITE
SPY (1942), SWING FEVER, THOUSANDS
CHEER and STAGE DOOR CANTEEN (1943;
briefly in latter two), AROUND THE WORLD
and CAROLINA BLUES (1944). Early 40s
band improved musically; achieved beautiful blend, sometimes swung. Duning still
arranged, aided by Van Alexander. Jazzmen Herbie Haymer on tenor sax and
Moe Purtill on drums 1942-3. Personnel
rather stable. Big hits *Praise the Lord and
Pass the Ammunition, Three Little Fishies,
Who Wouldn't Love You?, Strip Polka,
There Goes That Song Again*. Future TV
host Mike Douglas sang with band later
40s. Band and quiz show on TV 1949-50.
By early 50s Kyser tired of entertainment
grind, retired to North Carolina with wife,
former model-singer Georgia Carroll, became active in Christian Science.

RECORDS

KAY KYSER
Vi 40028 Tell Her/Broken Dreams of
Yesterday
Br 7449 (theme) Thinking of You/If
My Love Could Talk
Br 7453 Ish Kabibble/Take Your Girl-
ie to the Movies
Br 7465 Sunbonnet Blue/Star Gazing
Br 7836 Ma/Who's Sorry Now?
Br 7891 The You and Me That Used
to Be/'Cause My Baby Says It's So
Br 8114 Cry, Baby, Cry/Something
Tells Me
Br 8170 I'm Gonna Lock My Heart/
Simple and Sweet
Br 8185 You Go to My Head/Small
Fry
Br 8225 The Umbrella Man/Sixty Sec-
onds Got Together

Br 8244 Two Sleepy People/Have You Forgotten So Soon?

Br 8317 Heaven Can Wait/I Promise You

Br 8358 Three Little Fishies/Show Your Linen, Miss Richardson

Br 8381 Stairway to the Stars/You Don't Know How Much You Can Suffer

Co 35238 Happy Birthday to Love/The Answer Is Love

Co 35350 'Way Back in 1939 A.D./With the Wind and the Rain in Your Hair

Co 35375 Playmates/On the Isle of May

Co 35627 Call of the Canyon/Ferryboat Serenade

Co 35761 I'd Know You Anywhere/The Bad Humor Man

Co 35946 You Stepped Out of a Dream/Too Beautiful to Last

Co 36244 The Cowboy Serenade/You and I

Co 36433 Humpty Dumpty Heart/Romeo Smith and Juliet Jones

Co 36526 Who Wouldn't Love You?/How Do I Know It's Real?

Co 36604 Jingle, Jangle, Jingle/He Wears a Pair of Silver Wings

Co 36635 Strip Polka/Ev'ry Night About This Time

Co 36640 Praise the Lord and Pass the Ammunition/I Came Here to Talk for Joe

Co 36657 Can't Get Out of This Mood/Moonlight Mood

Co 36676 Pushin' Sand/You're So Good to Me

Co 36757 There Goes That Song Again/Gonna See My Baby

Co 36882 Coffee Time/Angel

Co 37073 Ole Buttermilk Sky

Co 37095 The Old Lamplighter

Co 38301 On a Slow Boat to China/In the Market Place of Old Monterey

LPs

KAY KYSER

Co (10″)CL-6061 Dance Parade (Co RIs)

Ha HL-7041 (Co RIs)

Ha HL-7136 Campus Rally

Cap T-1692 Greatest Hits (new versions)